FUNDAMENTALS OF HUMAN NEUROPSYCHOLOGY

A Series of Books in Psychology

FUNDAMENTALS OF HUMAN NEUROPSYCHOLOGY

Third Edition

BRYAN KOLB and IAN Q. WHISHAW

University of Lethbridge

W. H. FREEMAN AND COMPANY

NEW YORK

Cover image: Human cerebral cortex © Biophoto Associates/Photo Researchers, Inc.

Library of Congress Cataloging-in-Publication Data

Kolb, Bryan, 1947–
Fundamentals of human neuropsychology/Bryan Kolb, Ian Q. Whishaw. — 3rd ed.
p. cm.
Includes bibliographical references.
ISBN 0-7167-1973-8
1. Neuropsychology. 2. Human behavior. I. Whishaw, Ian Q., 1939– . II. Title.
[DNLM: 1. Neuropsychology. WL 102 K814f]
QP360.K64 1989
612.8—dc20
DNLM/DLC 89-23574
for Library of Congress CIP

Printed in the United States of America

3 4 5 6 7 8 9 HL 9 9 8 7 6 5 4 3 2 1

CONTENTS

PREFACE

When we began to write the first edition of this book in 1977, neuropsychology as a unified field was just emerging. Researchers working with human and nonhuman subjects, respectively, worked largely independently of one another, and there were suggestions of significant differences in the organization of human and nonhuman brains, especially with respect to memory processes. The 1980s have seen rapid change, however, as there have been significant changes on two fronts, both of which have led to the development of a more unified discipline. First, studies of nonhumans play an increasingly important role in providing a metaphor for human brain function. In particular, there is much new anatomical information regarding the organization of the cortex of the nonhuman primate, and behavioral studies using both rats and monkeys have led to new insights into the functional organization of the forebrain, and there has been convergence of thought regarding memory processes in humans and nonhumans. Second, cognitive psychologists have become more interested in the brain, and more active in studying brain function, largely in human patients. This interest has led to new approaches to the old problems of memory and language, problems that heretofore were largely the province of neurologists. This third edition reflects these two changes in the field. We have further integrated the human and nonhuman work, particularly the work on nonhuman primates, and we have included more discussion of issues in cognitive psychology. In addition, we have continued to emphasize the comparative approach to human brain function.

The first edition of the book was written for senior undergraduates interested in human brain function. We found that the book had a wider appeal, however, especially to graduate students and those whose area of training was not in behavioral neuroscience. This has led us to an expansion of the scope of the book, which we began in the second edition and continue in this third edition. As in the previous editions, we have omitted the dates of many recent works from the text, instead presenting tables and appropriate references at the end of each chapter. We still do not cite all studies that might be relevant to particular issues, expecting that interested students will find more detailed accounts of the relevant literature in many of the reviews, texts, and papers that we do cite. We still simplify some of the more complex issues. Where facts are absent or unclear in their implications, we have continued to speculate and theorize. To improve the book, we have expanded our discussion of the chemical basis of behavior, separating this into a separate chapter. We have extensively reorganized the chapters on the parietal, temporal, and frontal lobes, as well as those on memory, emotion, and space. We have added a chapter on the effects of head trauma and the nature of degenerative diseases such as Alzheimer's disease and chronic alcoholism — an addition that reflects the growing interest of neuropsychologists in these problems. Finally, we have updated all of the chapters and expanded our coverage where appropriate. In particular, we have added more discussion of various species in the anatomical studies (e.g., Chapters 10, 17 – 19, 21, 24), expanded our consideration of disconnection syndromes (Chapter 20), and tried to simplify the discussions of the sensory and motor systems. Finally, we have included an appendix of CT scans, MRI scans, and schematic drawings of the human brain. In trying to discuss complex issues of brain organization we have found that students find it very difficult to capture the three-dimensional nature of brain structure. We hope that the scans will provide a useful resource that readers will refer to often.

It is a curious paradox that some readers have commented to us that there is not enough in the book for a semester course, whereas others have said that the book has grown too large for a single semester! We do not see this as a problem, however, as the core chapters (parts 3, 4, and 5) provide a basis for a solid undergraduate course, and the remaining chapters will provide useful supplementary reading for the interested student, or in more ambitious courses. We feel that many chapters can be understood at a number of levels, depending upon the reader's sophistication in the neurosciences. We find that our beginning students have little interest in history, for example, but as their interest in certain problems increases they find historical or other theoretical information more relevant. Similarly, the chapters on the parietal, temporal, and frontal cortex can be read at one level that emphasizes symptoms or at another level that emphasizes the organization and theoretical processing that must underlie the symptoms.

Again, we must say that we are deeply indebted to those who have written us with advice and comments about how to improve the book, as well as to those from whom we have solicited advice. Of course, the improvements are due to their help but the errors are attributable solely to us. We are grateful especially to Quentin Pittman, Linda Siegal, and Robert Sutherland for their extensive comments on selected chapters, and to Michael Peters and Robert Zatorre for advice on various topics. We must also thank Brenda Kosaka and David Li for their work in providing us with the CT and MRI scans for the appendix. While these two are responsible for the photographs, we must take responsibility for any errors in the schematic drawings. We must also acknowledge the enthusiasm and faith of Buck Rogers of W. H. Freeman and Company who, in 1978, was one of the few who believed that neuropsychology was going to emerge as a significant field of study. We are sad that he has retired from publishing, for the field has lost an important friend. Finally, we must again express our gratitude to Adria Allen for her heroic achievement of typing the entire second edition into a word processor so that we could begin the revision, and to her continuing help in completing the manuscript on time.

Bryan Kolb and **Ian Q. Whishaw**

FUNDAMENTALS OF HUMAN NEUROPSYCHOLOGY

PART 1

BACKGROUND

In principle, it would seem simple to study human brain function: one need only study the behavior of people with known brain damage, note the behavioral changes, and from them infer the function of the region involved. Unfortunately, it is not quite so simple. There are significant technical and methodological problems that must be understood before any conclusions about brain-behavior relations can be made. Thus, students of human neuropsychology must be familiar with the basic principles of brain function if they are to fully appreciate the nature of the neurological basis of complex cognitive processes.

Chapters 1 through 5 present background information about the anatomy and physiology of the brain, methodological problems in the study of the brain and behavior, and the evolutionary origins of the human brain. Although the beginning student may feel that this material is not relevant to the "real stuff" of neuropsychology, we emphasize that neuropsychological theories regarding human brain function are dependent on the basic data of neuroanatomy, neurophysiology, and neurochemistry. Chapters 1 through 5 are written for the beginning student who has not previously had a course in neuroscience, neuroanatomy, or physiological psychology. Students who have had such courses and feel comfortable in their knowledge of these areas can either review the material or proceed directly to Part Two. We recommend that students make use of the glossary found at the end of the text when they encounter words unfamiliar to them. Throughout the book, words listed in the glossary are printed in boldface type the first time they are used in the text.

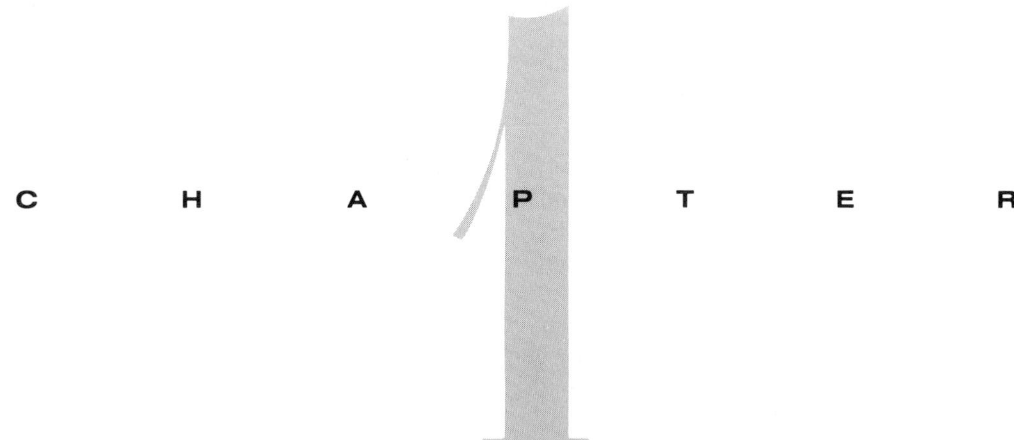

ORGANIZATION OF THE NERVOUS SYSTEM

As Oedipus approached the city of Thebes his way was blocked by the Sphinx, who posed a riddle: "What walks on four legs in the morning, two legs at noon, and three legs in the evening?" The answer given by Oedipus, "A man," was correct for a person crawls as an infant, walks as an adult, and uses a cane when old. The riddle posed by the Sphinx is a riddle of the nature of human beings, and the reply by Oedipus indicates not only that he knew an answer but that he understood the underlying significance of the question. The riddle of human nature is still unanswered, and the object of this book is to pursue the answer in the place where it should most logically be found: the brain.

The simplest and most obvious questions to ask about the brain concern its size. Does size mean anything? Some information suggests that it does. The human brain weighs 400 g (grams) at birth, 850 g at 11 months, 1100 g at 3 years, and 1450 g at maturity. This suggests that the development of adult behavior is related to brain size. Furthermore, at about 30 years of age the brain begins to shrink, until by 75 years it has lost on the average about 100 g. This suggests the suspected decline in human abilities during aging may be related to decreased brain size. The brain has also grown bigger during evolution; for example, the brain of the great apes weighs about 400 g, that of Java man weighed about 850 g, and that of Peking man weighed about 1100 g. This growth suggests that the evolution of modern man's abilities may have been dependent on the evolution of a greater brain size.

Despite these relations, there are facts about brain size suggesting that this conclusion is not unassailable. It is curious that modern man's direct hominid ancestors, Neanderthal and Cro-Magnon, may have had slightly larger brains than modern humans. Perhaps through the process of domestication, which involves specialized roles for individuals and greater dependence on other group members, the brain became smaller. Studies on brain size by Kruska have shown that in animals brain size is reduced in a very short time with domestication and does not return to its former size even when the domesticated animal returns to a feral state. It is also curious that the human brain may have become smaller in the last few thousand years. It is curious that although adult brain size is related to body size (larger people have larger brains than smaller people, and females, who are generally smaller than males, have proportionately smaller brains), the brains of people of extraordinary ability are no different in size from those of people of ordinary ability. It is curious that the brains of both gifted and ordinary people can vary in weight between 1100 and 2000 g. Finally, it is curious that although human beings are apparently unique in their cultural achievements, dolphins may have larger brains, relative to body size, than human. Together, this information suggests that although brain size may be important, size alone does little toward answering the riddle of human nature.

The most obvious questions to ask about the brain concern the relation between its structure and behavior: this is the focus of modern **neuropsychology.** Unfortunately, the complexity of the brain's structure makes it difficult to relate its components to individual capacities. The brain is composed of 180 billion cells, and of these, 50 billion are directly engaged in information processing. Each of these receive up to 15,000 physical connections from other cells. If there were no order in this complexity, it would be incomprehensible. Fortunately, some tentative answers about how this machinery works can be obtained because the cells of the brain seem to be connected in an organized fashion. They are arranged in assemblies, many of which are large enough to be identifiable on superficial examination.

Although the features of the brains of different people vary just as their faces do, the different structures of the brain are common to all human beings. In fact, these structures seem to be common to all mammals. The anatomist Lorente de Nó, after examining the mouse brain through a microscope, remarked that its fine structure was little different from that of the human brain. Since many features of the brain are common to most animals, including human beings, and because many human and animal behaviors are similar, it is possible to learn about the function of the human brain by studying the brains of other animals and vice versa. In the science of neuropsychology both kinds of study are pursued. Perhaps this procedure more than any other has influenced the organization of this book. Consequently, although we are specifically interested in discussing the functions of the human brain, throughout the book we shall frequently do so indirectly, through examination of the brains of other animals. In our view, the answer to the riddle of the nature of human beings lies as much in the study of those other animals as it does in the study of human beings themselves.

ANATOMY OF THE NERVOUS SYSTEM

The nervous system is composed of cells, and these cells and their processes are grouped in an organized fashion. Since brain anatomy is the study of this organization, it is helpful to know how cells give the different parts of the brain their characteristic appearance.

Neurons and Glia

The germinal cells of a developing embryo give rise to two primitive types of nervous system cells: **neuroblasts** and **spongioblasts** (a *blast* is an immature cell). The neuroblasts develop into **neurons** (from the Greek for nerve), or nerve cells, which form the functional units of the nervous system. The spongioblasts develop into **glial cells** (from *glia,* the Greek for glue), which provide various types of support functions to neurons.

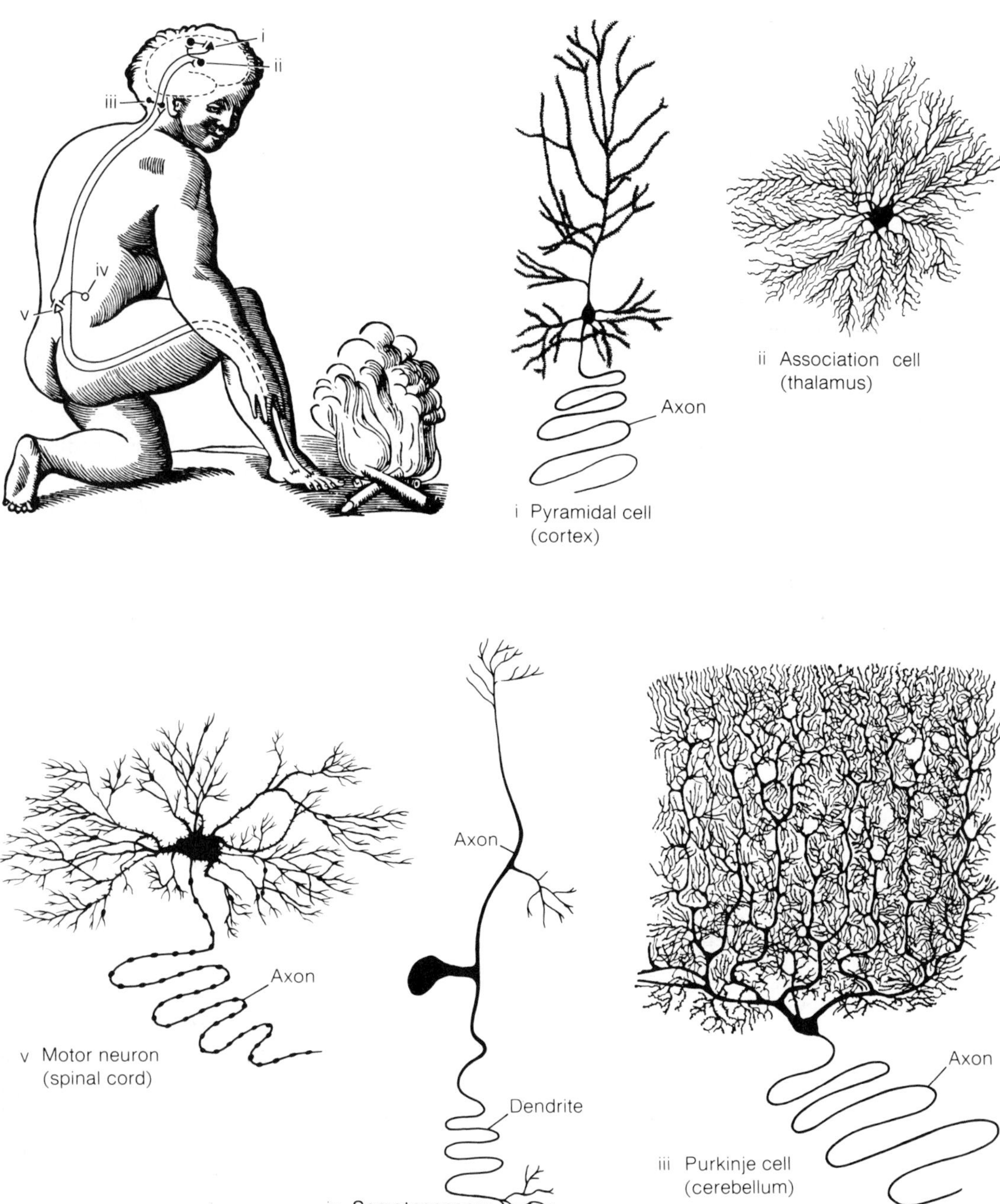

FIGURE 1-1. The nervous system is composed of neurons, or nerve cells, each of which is specialized as to function. The schematic drawings show the relative size, shape, location, and configuration of some neurons.

These two types of cells, neurons and glia, make up the adult brain. Figure 1-1 shows the relative size, shape, and location of some neurons, and Table 1-1 summarizes some functions of glia.

Gray, White, and Reticular Matter. Different parts of the nervous system characteristically appear either gray, white, or mottled and are called gray, white, and reticular matter, respectively. Areas where capillary blood vessels and cell bodies of neurons predominate constitute the **gray matter,** so named for its characteristic gray brown color. From the cell bodies of neurons, long processes, called **axons,** extend to form connections with neurons in other brain areas. These processes are generally covered with an insulating layer of glial cells. The glial cells are composed of a fatty (lipid) substance that gives them a white appearance, much as fat droplets in milk give it a white appearance. As a result, an area of the nervous system rich in axons covered with glial cells looks white and is consequently called **white matter.** An area of the nervous system where cell bodies and axons are mixed together is called **reticular matter** (from the Latin *rete,* meaning net) because of its mottled gray and white, or netlike, appearance.

TABLE 1-1. Glial cells and their function

Type	Function
Astroglia	Give structural support to and repair neurons
Oligodendroglia	Insulate and speed transmission of central nervous system neurons[a]
Schwann cells	Insulate and speed transmission of peripheral nervous system neurons
Microglia	Perform phagocytosis
Ependymal cells	Line the brain's ventricles and produce cerebral spinal fluid

[a] Central nervous system neurons are found within the brain and spinal cord; peripheral nervous system neurons are in the rest of the body.

Nuclei and Tracts. A large number of cell bodies grouped together are collectively called a **nucleus** (from the Latin *nux,* meaning nut); a large collection of axons from neuron cell bodies is called a **tract** (from Old French, meaning path), or sometimes a fiber pathway. Since cell bodies are gray, nuclei are a distinctive gray; since glial cells make axons appear white, tracts are a distinctive white.

Staining. Because of their color, the larger nuclei and tracts of the brain can be seen in fresh brain tissue or brain tissue cut into thin sections, but the appearance of smaller nuclei and tracts must be enhanced to make them visible. The technique of enhancing differences in appearance is called *staining* and consists of placing brain tissue into different colored dyes. Because there are variations in the chemical composition of cells, their various parts selectively take different dyes. Staining techniques aid immensely in differentiating brain tissue, and they are continually being refined. For example, if a nucleus of the brain is destroyed in some way, the axons leading from the cells die. Stains have been found that are selectively taken up by this dying tissue, making it easy to trace axons to their destinations.

A Wonderland of Nomenclature

To the beginning student, the terminology used to label nuclei and tracts of the nervous system might at first seem chaotic. Many structures have several names, often used interchangeably. For example, one structure, the **precentral gyrus,** is variously referred to as the primary motor cortex, area 4, the motor strip, the motor homunculus, Jackson's strip, area pyramidalis, the somatomotor strip, and gyrus precentralis. Clearly such proliferation of terminology is an obstacle to learning, but it is some consolation to know that it reflects the culture and history of the neurosciences. There are many other examples of brain structures that have a number of names, some of which seem quite peculiar. Greek terminology is interchanged with English (e.g., mesencephalon for midbrain), Latin with English (fasciculus opticus for optic tract), and French for English (bouton termineau for synaptic knob). The neuroanatomist's imagination has sometimes strayed to body anatomy (e.g., mammillary bodies), to flora (amygdala, or almond), to fauna (hippocampus, or sea horse), and to mythology (Ammon's horn). Some terminology is a tribute to early pioneers: the fields of Forel, Rolando's fissure, and Deiters' nucleus. Other terms are colorful: substantia nigra (black substance), locus coeruleus (blue area), and red nucleus. Some names seem excessively long: nucleus reticularis tegmenti pontis Bechterewi. Other labels are based on the consistency of the tissue, for example, substantia gelatinosa (gelatinous substance); some seem somewhat mystifying: substantia innominata (nameless substance), zone incerta (uncertain area), nucleus ambiguus (ambiguous nucleus); and finally, some reflect a modern and more technical outlook, as with the nuclei A-1 to A-10.

In this book we have attempted to use consistent and simple terms, but in many cases alternative terms are widely used and so we have included them where necessary.

Approaches to the Study of Anatomy

Neuroanatomists study the structure of the brain using any of four main approaches: (1) comparative, (2) developmental, (3) cytoarchitectonic, and (4) biochemical.

The *comparative* approach consists of describing the brain's evolution from the primitive cord in simple wormlike animals to the large, complex "raveled knot" in the head of human beings. Since new types of behavior have developed as each new layer or protuberance has evolved, clues about the function of new areas can be gained by correlating structure and behavior. However, such analysis is not necessarily simple. The **limbic system,** a middle layer in the mammalian brain, evolved in amphibians and reptiles. Is its function to control new modes of locomotion, the orientation of the animals in a terrestrial world, new types of social behavior, or more advanced learning abilities? The answer is still uncertain. The comparative approach, however, has yielded a key piece of information in neuropsychology: mammals can be distinguished from other animals by their large neocortex (outer covering of brain tissue). Furthermore, this structure is particularly large in humans. It is understandable, then that it is thought to have an important function in conferring abilities unique to mammals, and thus receives proportionately more attention in neuropsychology—particularly human neuropsychology—than do other structures.

In the *developmental,* or ontogenetic, approach the changes in brain structure and size are described during the development of an individual. This approach allows for two useful perspectives. First, the development of new structures can be correlated with emerging behaviors, much as is done in comparative studies. Second, the immature brain can frequently provide the anatomist with a simplified model of the adult brain. The Spanish anatomist, Ramón y Cajal, pioneered this type of analysis to good effect. With the crude equipment and techniques available at the end of the 19th century he was unable to determine whether the adult brain is composed of a net of connected tissue to of individual units. But using embryonic tissue he was able to show that it is composed of units. Furthermore, by examining successively more mature animals he discovered how these units develop into their adult form. Neuropsychologists widely assume that in newborn infants the neocortex is particularly immature in comparison with the rest of the nervous system. As a result, correlating the development of the neocortex with emerging behavior is viewed as a powerful method of uncovering its structural and functional relations.

Cytoarchitectonic analysis consists of describing the architecture of cells: their differences in structure, size, shape, and connections, and their distribution in different parts of the brain. This type of analysis is possible because different parts of the nerve cell have an affinity for different types of dyes, so that when the brain is cut into thin sections and stained, the cells can be examined under a microscope. The cytoarchitectonic approach has been used to particular advantage by neuroanatomists, including Brodmann, who have described regional differences in cell structure and have constructed maps illustrating the topography of those regional differences. These maps have particular value, for they correlate rather well with maps that illustrate functional differences in brain areas. Cytoarchitectonic techniques are being continually refined as new and better microscopes, such as the electron microscope, are developed and new and more ingenious staining procedures are employed. Recently, for example, it was found that all of the processes of a single cell can be stained by injecting a protein, called horseradish peroxidase, into the cell using a very small glass pipette. With this technique not only can one cell's place in the brain be located, but its connections with other cells can be traced.

The most recent analytical technique for studying brain structure is to describe its *biochemical* organization. It is now clear that discrete clusters of cells that send projections to other cell areas contain unique biochemical substances that play a special role in intercellular communication or neurotransmission. This finding illustrates a new dimension of brain organization, and it is of immense practical importance. First, the activity of these systems can be related to different aspects of behavior. Second, abnormalities in the functioning of these systems can be related to some types of abnormal behavior. For example, the chemical dopamine occurs in reduced levels in victims of Parkinson's disease and occurs in heightened levels in victims of certain types of schizophrenia. Third, as these biochemical systems become better understood, the means by which psychoactive drugs work will also be better understood. Various techniques for studying the biochemical organization of the nervous system include performing assays on different regions of the brain to determine their chemical composition, labeling a chemical of interest with a radioactive substance so its course and destination in the brain can be found, and staining the tissue with dyes that produce distinctive colors in areas rich in particular biochemicals. The chemical organization of the brains of a number of animals has been mapped, and studies of the human brain show that its biochemical organization is similar to that of these animals' brains.

ORIGIN AND DEVELOPMENT OF THE BRAIN

The anatomical and functional organization of the adult human brain is difficult to grasp because of the complicated clustering of nuclei and the intricate pathways of their axons. It is easier to understand the nervous system's organization by examining the way it developed phylogenetically. The nervous system developed in four somewhat general steps, as is shown diagrammatically in Figure 1-2.

1. The nervous system was first a simple tube, or *spinal cord,* receiving sensory fibers from the different segments of the body and sending motor fibers to them.

2. One end of the cord then became specialized to respond to special features of the sensory world and so made up the primitive brain, or *brainstem.*

3. The front and the hind ends of the brainstem then sprouted two new, large structures. In front, the cerebral hemispheres developed to become the initiators of movement; at the rear, the cerebellum developed to become the coordinator of movement. These final additions completed the *mammalian brain.*

4. As it continued to evolve, the mammalian brain developed into the *human brain.*

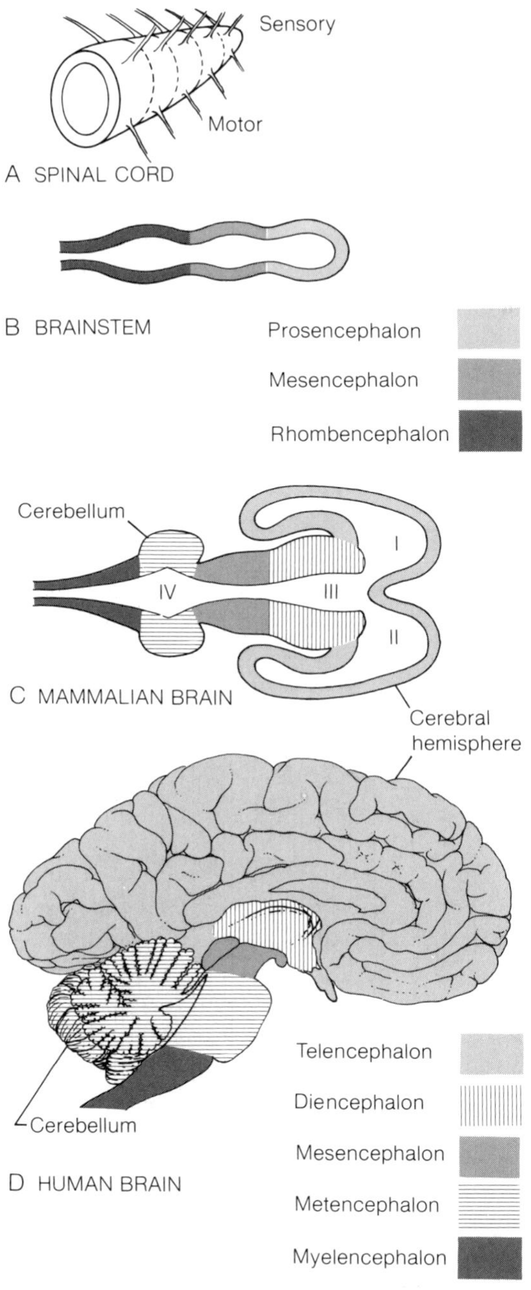

FIGURE 1-2. Steps in the development of the brain. *A.* Spinal cord. *B.* Brainstem. *C.* Mammalian brain, showing ventricles (I–IV). *D.* Side view of the center of a human brain.

The Spinal Cord

In primitive animals (and in the first weeks of mammalian embryonic development), some of the outer, or ectodermal, cells of the dorsal (upper) surface of the body formed a trough running the length of the body; the upper edges of the trough folded to form a tube (the precursor of the adult mammalian spinal cord). At this stage of development the body and the cord were arranged in segments, with sensory receptors on the body sending input to the dorsal part of the cord, while the cord sent axons from its ventral portion (underside, or belly) to control muscles in each of the segments. The primitive system, shown diagrammatically in Figure 1-2*A,* provided the basis for the development of two important mammalian functions: the dorsal portion provided the neural basis of the somatosensory system (skin and muscle senses), and the ventral portion provided the neural basis for movement. In ancestral vertebrates, such as amphioxus, this was the extent of nervous system development.

The Brainstem

During its evolutionary development the front end of the spinal cord increased its neural and functional specialization, forming an *encephalon* (from the Greek, meaning in the head) or brain. The formation of the "brain" probably occurred because the first vertebrates were mobile and found it easier to travel predominantly in one direction; thus, it was adaptive to have special sensory analysis take place at "the end that goes first." The front end then formed three enlargements or vesicles (bladders). The cells surrounding each multiplied to form centers specialized for receiving and responding to particular features of the world. The front enlargement, the **prosencephalon** (forebrain), became specialized mainly for the sense of smell, but possibly also taste. The second enlargement, the **mesencephalon** (midbrain), became specialized for vision and hearing. These parts of the brain made perception of the distant environment possible. The posterior enlargement, the **rhombencephalon** (hindbrain), became specialized for equilibrium and balance, and gave the animal better perception of its place in its immediate environment. The same organization found in the spinal cord continued to be maintained in the brain: the dorsal portion was sensory, the ventral portion motor. This relatively simple brain, similar to the brain of present-day fishes and amphibians, forms the basis of the brainstem of mammals. The general organization of the brainstem is shown in Figure 1-2*B*.

The Mammalian Brain

The brain next developed primarily at its first and third segments. The prosencephalon developed to form two major new divisions: the **telencephalon** (endbrain) and **diencephalon** (betweenbrain). The most important addition in the telencephalon was the cerebral hemispheres, which functionally became the level of highest control for behavior. The rhombencephalon also divided to form two major new divisions: the *metencephalon* (across-brain) and the *myelencephalon* (spinal brain). The feature that distinguishes the development of the metencephalon in mammals was the growth of the cerebellum, which became the coordinating center for all movement. The mammalian brain is diagrammed in Figure 1-2*C*.

The Human Brain

The human brain evolved from the mammalian brain with no change in its basic design (see the sagittal, or side, view of the human brain in Figure 1-2*D*). The only real difference between the two types of brains is that the cerebral hemispheres and the cerebellum of humans have grown considerably larger than those found in other mammals.

The Ventricles

The primitive spinal cord, remember, had the form of a tube with a hollow center. Figure 1-2*B* and *C* show that the central core of the brainstem and of the mammalian brain remain hollow. This cavity is not empty but filled with a substance called **cerebrospinal fluid (CSF),** which is produced by **choroid plexus,** or specialized clusters of glial cells found within the cavity. The cavity is larger in some portions of its length than in others; these enlargements are called **ventricles** (from the Latin, meaning belly). In the mammalian brain there are four ventricles, numbered I to IV, corresponding to the layout in Figure 1-2*C*. It is conventional to call the lateral ventricles the first (I) and second (II) ventricles, the ventricle in the diencephalon the third ventricle (III), and the ventricle in the metencephalon and myelencephalon the fourth ventricle (IV). The ventricle that was in the mesencepahlon of the brainstem has become constricted and is called the cerebral aqueduct. The ventricles are distributed in the human brain exactly as in the mammalian brain.

ANATOMY OF THE HUMAN BRAIN

Table 1-2 summarizes the development of the brain from the stage of having three primary embryonic divisions to one of having five. In addition, the table shows some of the major brain structures found in each division of the fully developed brain. Those who study the development of the brain's structure have divided the nervous system into five major structural divisions. To simplify discussion of its function, however, we will divide it into only three divisions. The lowest division is the **spinal cord,** which includes the brain's connections with the body's organs and muscles. The middle division is the **brainstem,** which is equivalent to the embryologic or primitive premammalian brainstem and includes the diencephalon, the midbrain, and the hindbrain. The highest functional division is the **forebrain,** which includes all the structures

TABLE 1-2. The divisions of the nervous system

Primitive brainstem divisions	Mammalian brain divisions	Portion of fully developed human brain	Functional divisions
Prosencephalon (forebrain)	Telencephalon (endbrain)	Neocortex Basal ganglia Limbic system Olfactory bulb Lateral ventricles	Forebrain
	Diencephalon (between-brain)	Thalamus Epithalamus Hypothalamus Pineal body Third ventricle	
Mesencephalon (midbrain)	Mesencephalon (midbrain)	Tectum Tegmentum Cerebral aqueduct	Brainstem
Rhombencephalon (hindbrain)	Metencephalon (across-brain)	Cerebellum Pons Fourth ventricle	
	Myelencephalon (spinal brain)	Medulla oblongata Fourth ventricle	
			Spinal cord

in the telencephalon, the neocortex, the basal ganglia, the limbic system and olfactory bulbs.

Many structures of the brain are labeled according to their location relative to one another. Six conventional terms are used to indicate anatomical direction: *superior* (top), *lateral* (side), *medial* (middle), *ventral* (bottom), *anterior* (front), and *posterior* (back). Thus one structure can be said to lie superior, lateral, medial, ventral, anterior, or posterior to another. The nervous system is also symmetrically arranged and so consists of left and right sides. If two structures lie on the same side, they are said to be **ipsilateral;** if they lie on opposite sides, they are said to be **contralateral;** if they lie on both sides, they are said to be **bilateral.** Structures that are close to each other are said to be **proximal;** those far from each other are said to be **distal.** Finally, a projection that is approaching the center is said to be **afferent;** one leaving it is said to be **efferent.**

THE SPINAL CORD

The spinal cord, the musculature, and the internal organs of the body have a segmental organization (see Figure 1-3). Each segment of the cord is linked with the organs and musculature of a specific body segment. As Figure 1-3*B* shows, there are 30 spinal cord segments: 8 cervical (C), 12 thoracic (T), 5 lumbar (L), and 5 sacral (S). Figure 1-3*A* shows the segments of the skin and musculature of the body, each labeled to correspond with its cord segment. Each of the body segments, called a **dermatome** (meaning skin cut), encircles the body in a ring formation, a pattern of organization inherited from primitive segmental wormlike animals. Of course, because mammals have limbs and human beings have an upright posture, the ring formation is distorted into the pattern shown in Figure 1-3*A*. It is worth noting that because the cord and body have this segmental structure,

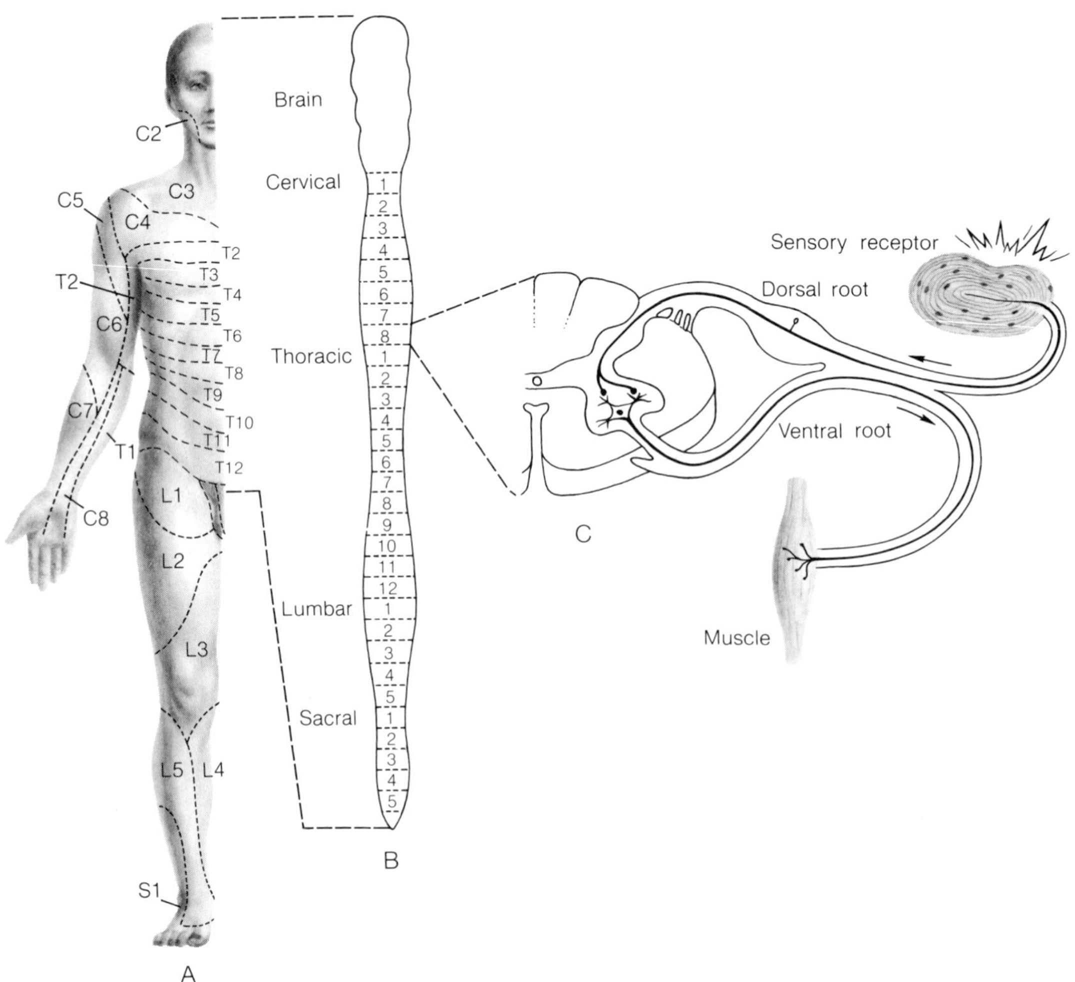

FIGURE 1-3. Relation between the dermatomes of the body and segments of the spinal cord. *A*. Body dermatomes. *B*. Spinal cord segments. *C*. Cross section through one segment of the spinal cord showing that sensory input from a dermatome arrives through the dorsal root, and motor output to the same dermatome goes through the ventral root. (After Truex and Carpenter, 1969.)

rather good inferences can be made about the location of spinal cord damage or disease from changes in sensation or movement in particular body parts.

Figure 1-3*C* shows a cross section of the spinal cord. Its outer portion consists of white matter or tracts, arranged so that with a few exceptions the dorsal tracts (posterior in humans) are sensory and the ventral (anterior in humans) tracts are motor in function. The inner portion of the cord, which has a butterfly shape, is gray matter, that is, it is composed largely of cell bodies. These are arranged so that the cells in the superior portion act as relays for sensory projections from the body, and the cells in the inferior portion send axons to connect with muscles or glands. As can be seen in Figure 1-3*C*, two larger fiber tracts (or roots) of the **peripheral nerves** enter each section of the spinal cord, one on each side. The superior tracts contain projections from the receptors in the body, and the inferior tracts consist of axons from cells in the inferior gray matter that project to muscles or organs. Because of this arrangement, damage to the cord's superior regions will produce changes that are selectively sensory in nature, whereas damage to the inferior portion of the cord will produce changes that are selectively motor in nature.

THE BRAINSTEM

The Diencephalon

The diencephalon consists of the three thalamic structures (thalamus, meaning inner room or chamber, though sometimes translated as couch on which the forebrain rests): the epithalamus (or upper room), the thalamus (described below with the forebrain), and the hypothalamus (or lower room) (see Figure 1-4). The diencephalon has often been called the interbrain and appropriately so, for in addition to having its own nuclei it is also a relay, or thoroughfare, for fibers connecting the forebrain and lower brainstem areas.

The **epithalamus** is of primitive origin, and its function in humans is not known. One of its structures is the **pineal body,** the only nonbilateral structure in the brain. This body has an interesting history, for Descartes, impressed by its solitary nature, suggested that it was the rendezvous between mind and matter and the source of the cerebral spinal fluid that powered movements. Although its function in humans is still not known, the pineal body of some animals plays a role in organizing biological rhythms.

The **hypothalamus** is composed of about 22 small nuclei, fiber systems that pass through it, and the **pituitary gland.** Although composing only about 0.3% of the brain's weight, its small

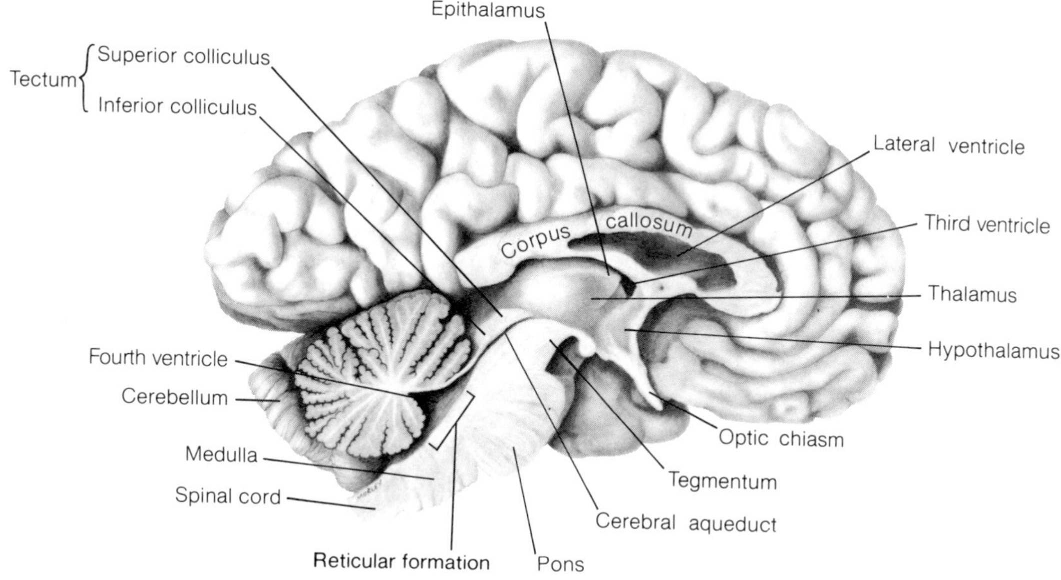

FIGURE 1-4. Medial view through the center of the brain showing structures of the brainstem.

size is deceiving because it is involved in nearly all aspects of behavior, including feeding, sexual behavior, sleeping, temperature regulation, emotional peer behavior, endocrine function, and movement. It has been a favorite area of study in animal neurobiology.

The Midbrain

The **midbrain,** shown in Figure 1-4, consists of two main subdivisions: the **tectum,** or roof, which is the area lying above the cerebral aqueduct, and the **tegmentum,** or floor, which lies below the aqueduct. The tectum consists primarily of two sets of bilaterally symmetrical nuclei: the **superior colliculi** (upper hills) are the anterior pair, and the **inferior colliculi** (lower hills) are the posterior pair. In birds and phylogenetically lower animals these sets of nuclei are their visual and auditory brains, respectively. In mammals, which have neocortical visual and auditory systems, these structures mediate whole body movements to visual and auditory stimuli, respectively. The tegmentum contains four types of structures:

1. Next to the aqueduct are nuclei for some of the cranial nerves.

2. Beneath these are sensory fibers coming from the body senses.

3. Below these are motor fibers coming down from the forebrain.

4. Intermingled among these three structures are a number of motor nuclei such as the **red nucleus** and **substantia nigra,** and some of the nuclei of the reticular system.

The Hindbrain

The **hindbrain** is organized in much the same way as the midbrain. Sensory nuclei of the vestibular system (sensory system governing balance and orientation located in the inner ear) overlie the fourth ventricle; beneath this ventricle are more motor nuclei of the cranial nerves, ascending sensory tracts from the spinal cord, descending fiber tracts to the cord, and more nuclei composing the reticular activating system. Overlying the brainstem is the cerebellum.

The **cerebellum** (see Figure 1-4) is evolutionarily very old and probably initially specialized in sensory-motor coordination. Now, the precise function of the cerebellum varies from one part of the structure to another, depending on the connections with the rest of the nervous system. Parts that receive most of their impulses from the vestibular system help to maintain the body's equilibrium, whereas parts receiving impulses mainly from the body senses are involved with postural reflexes and coordinating functionally related muscles. The major part of the cerebellum receives impulses from the neocortex and primarily effects skilled movements.

The surface of the cerebellum is marked by narrow folds, or *folia,* beneath which lies a thick cortex of gray matter covering a larger central mass of white matter. Within the white matter are several nuclei. The cerebellum is attached to the brainstem by three major fiber pathways in which all afferent fibers pass to its cortex and all efferent fibers originate in the underlying cerebellar nuclei and then pass on to other brain structures.

Damage to the cerebellum results in impairments of equilibrium, postural defects, and impairments of skilled motor activity. Injury to or disease in the cerebellum may therefore break smooth movements into their jerky sequential components; ability to perform rapidly alternating movements may be impaired; and directed movements may overshoot their mark. In addition, muscle tone may be abnormal, so that movements are difficult to initiate.

Some recent research has concentrated on the cerebellum's possible role in learning. According to this line of inquiry, if the cells in the various folia and other divisions of the cerebellum are involved in coordinating movements, they may also be able to modify their connections as a result of motor experience and thus also serve as repositories for motor memory.

The **reticular formation** consists of a complex mixture of nuclei and fiber tracts that stretch from the diencephalon through the hindbrain. These nuclei and fiber tracts have two distinguishing features: first, they do not have clearly defined sensory or motor functions; second, each sends fibers to a number of areas of the forebrain, brainstem, and spinal cord. The reticular formation is more commonly known as the *reticular activating system;* it obtained this distinction in the following way. Until the 1940s it was thought that sleep could be attributed to a lack of sensory stimulation, whereas waking could be attributed to reception of an adequate amount of such stimulation. In 1949, Moruzzi and Magoun stimulated the brainstem of anesthetized cats while brain electrical activity was being recorded from them on an electroencephalogram, or EEG. The EEG of the cats consisted of large-amplitude slow waves, similar to those typically recorded from a sleeping animal, but when electrical brain stimulation was administered, a low-amplitude EEG pattern, similar to that commonly recorded from a waking cat, was recorded. As a result of their experiment, Moruzzi and Magoun proposed that the function of the reticular formation was to control sleeping and waking. Through the influence of these findings, the reticular formation gradually came to be known as the reticular activating system, the function of which was to maintain "general arousal" or "consciousness." However, this notion has subsequently received little experimental support. Recent research has focused on the details of individual nuclear groups within the formation, and as the results from these studies suggest individual functions for individual groups, even the notion that these cells form a functional system has been dropped.

There are 12 sets of **cranial nerves** (summarized in Table 6-1), which convey sensory information from the specialized sensory systems of the head and control the special movements of muscle systems in the head, for example, movements of the eyes and tongue. A knowledge of their organization and function is important for neurological diagnosis; their functions and dysfunctions are discussed in Chapter 6.

THE FOREBRAIN

The forebrain is conventionally divided into five anatomical areas: (1) the neocortex, (2) the limbic system, (3) the basal ganglia, (4) the thalamus, and (5) the olfactory bulbs and tract. The following section will describe the first of these five structures. Since the content of this book is related substantially to the neocortex, it will be described in greatest detail.

The Neocortex

The **neocortex** comprises most of the forebrain by volume. It consists of four to six layers of cells (or gray matter) beneath which their axons form pathways (white matter). The term **cortex** (from the Latin, meaning bark) is used to refer to any outer layer of cells. Frequently the terms *cortex* and *neocortex* are used interchangeably, and so conventionally *cortex* refers to *neocortex* unless otherwise indicated. The neocortex has expanded the most during evolution; it comprises 80% of the human brain. Whereas the brainstems of a human being and a sheep are so similar in size that a novice might confuse them, their neocortexes can easily be distinguished. The human neocortex has an area of up to 2500 cm^2 but a thickness of only 1.5 to 3.0 mm. It is thought to have developed out of two more primitive structures, the **pyriform cortex** and the **hippocampus.** The cortex is wrinkled; this wrinkling is nature's solution to the problem of confining the huge neocortical surface area within a shell that is still small enough to pass through the birth canal. Just as a crumpled sheet of paper can fit into a smaller box than a flat sheet, folding of the neocortex permits the relatively fixed volume of the skull to contain more neocortex.

Fissures, Sulci, and Gyri. The wrinkled surface of the neocortex consists of clefts and ridges. A cleft is called a **fissure** if it extends deeply enough into the brain to indent the ventricles, and a **sulcus** if it is shallower. A ridge is called a **gyrus.** Figure 1-5 shows the location of some of the more important fissures, sulci, and gyri of the brain. There is *some* variation between the location of these features on the two sides of a single individual's brain, and *substantial* variation in both the location and the size and exact structure of the gyri and sulci in the brains of different individuals. The organization of cells in gyri differ, with the change in organization between adjacent gyri usually occurring at the sulci. Since individual gyri can have a characteristic cell organization, they may form units of function and many have been associated roughly with specific functions. Two of the external features of the brain are relatively easy to locate:

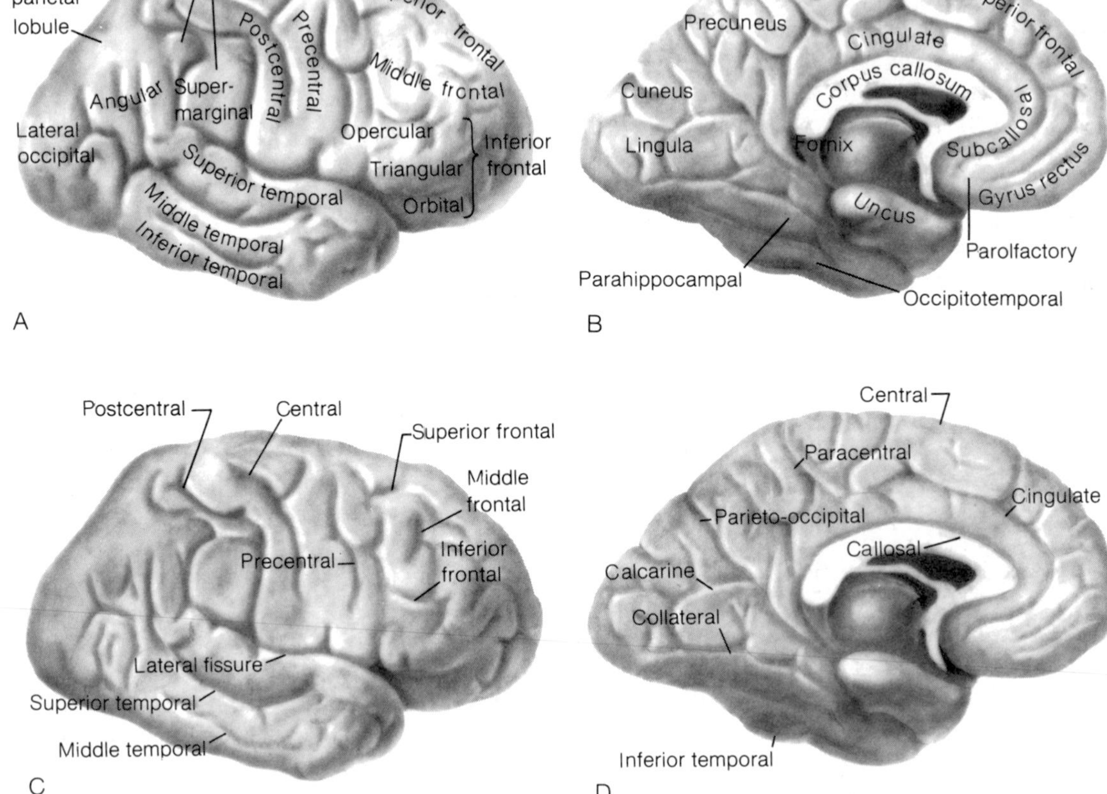

FIGURE 1-5. Gyri and sulci. Lateral *(A)* and medial *(B)* views of the gyri. Lateral *(C)* and medial *(D)* views of the sulci.

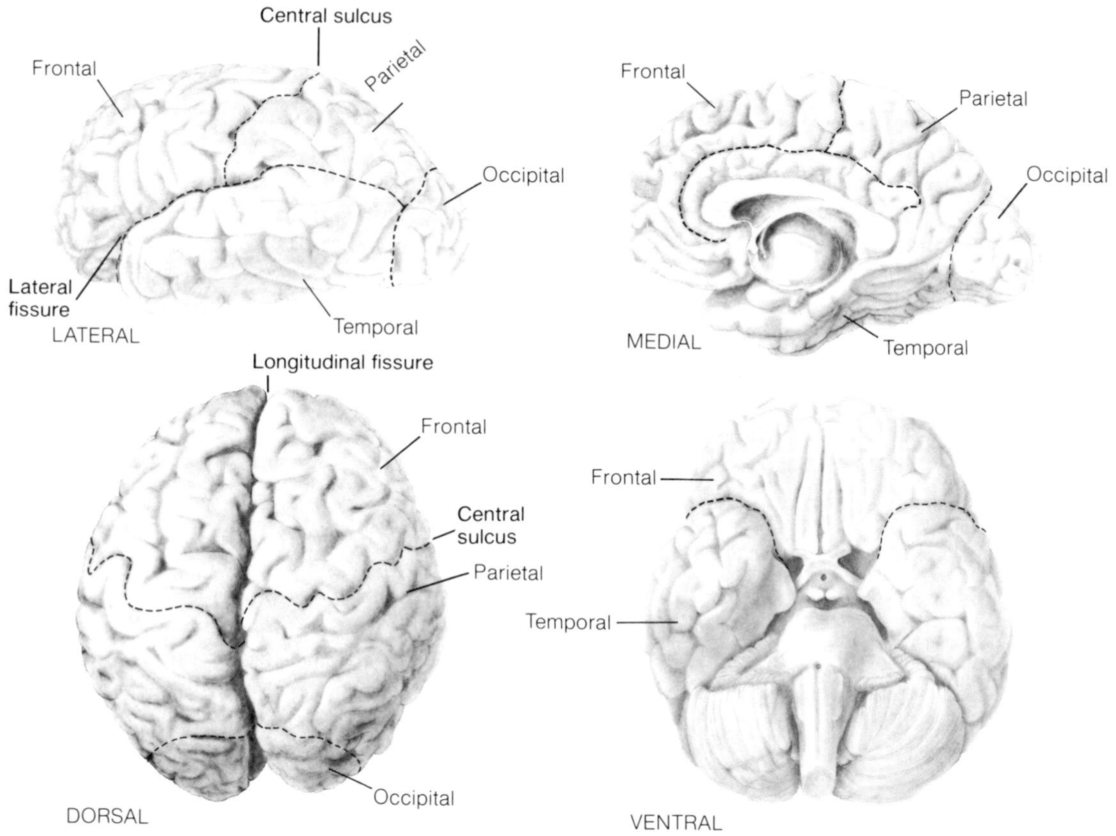

FIGURE 1-6. The location of the frontal, parietal, occipital, and temporal lobes of the human brain

the **lateral fissure,** because it begins in a cleft on the anterior-inferior surface of the cortex, and the **central sulcus,** because it curves toward the posterior part of the brain as it moves medially across the superior surface of the cortex (See Figure 1-5*C*).

The Hemispheres and Lobes. As Figure 1-6 *(dorsal view)* shows, the neocortex consists of two nearly symmetrical hemispheres, the left and the right, separated by the **medial longitudinal fissure.** Each hemisphere is subdivided into four lobes: frontal, parietal, temporal, and occipital. The **frontal lobes** have fixed boundaries: they are bounded posteriorly by the central sulcus, inferiorly by the lateral fissure, and medially by the **cingulate sulcus** just above a large interhemispheric band of fibers called the **corpus callosum.** The anterior boundary of the **parietal lobes** is the central sulcus and their inferior boundary is the lateral fissure. The **temporal lobes** are bounded dorsally by the lateral fissure. The **occipital lobes** are separated from the parietal cortex medially by the **parieto-occipital**

sulcus. On the lateral surface of the brain there are no definite boundaries between the occipital lobes and the parietal and temporal lobes. The areas between the lobes are sometimes referred to as the parietal-occipital area and the temporal-occipital area. It should be noted that the lobes are not functional regions but convenient anatomical regions. They are named after the skull bones under which they are found. Nevertheless, because there are functional differences between them, the terms are used in a rather loose and descriptive way to indicate different functional regions.

As shown in Figure 1-5*A*, in a lateral view there are four major gyri in the frontal lobe: the superior frontal, middle frontal, and inferior frontal, and the precentral (which lies in front of the central sulcus). There are five major gyri in the parietal lobe: the superior and inferior, the postcentral (lying behind the central sulcus), and the supermarginal and angular (on either side of the lateral fissure). There are three major gyri in the temporal lobe: the superior, middle, and inferior gyri. Only the lateral gyrus is obvious in the occipital cortex in this view.

Topography of the Neocortex. The several different kinds of maps that have been made of the neocortex are called **topographic maps.** These maps are constructed from information obtained by the application of specific research techniques:

1. **Projection maps** are constructed by tracing axons from the sensory systems into the brain, and tracing axons from the neocortex to the motor systems of the brainstem and spinal cord.

2. **Functional maps** are constructed by stimulating areas of the brain electrically and noting the elicited behavior, or by recording the electrical activity of the cortex during certain behaviors. Functional maps can also be constructed by relating specific types of brain damage to changes in behavior.

3. **Cytoarchitectonic maps** are constructed from study of the distribution of different types of cells in the neocortex.

Projection Maps. Figure 1-7 shows an example of a projection map constructed by tracing one route that axons take from sensory receptors to the neocortex, and by tracing the motor axons from the neocortex to motor neurons in the spinal cord. This is a projection map of relatively direct projections. As the figure shows, the projections from the eye, the ear, and the body's somatosensory system can each be traced to a specific region of the neocortex; the visual system projects to the posterior occipital lobe, the auditory system projects to the superior temporal gyrus of the temporal lobe, and the somatosensory system projects to the area of the postcentral gyrus in the parietal lobe. The major motor projection appears to originate in the precentral gyrus of the frontal lobe. These areas can be called **primary projection areas,** but it should be noted that the lateral view does not represent their entire extent, because they also project down into the gyri and fissures. The auditory zone, for example, is much larger within the lateral fissure.

Once the primary projection areas are described, their relation to the rest of the neocortex can be considered. The sensory systems send indirect projections into the primary areas as well as into areas adjacent to these primary areas. The motor areas receive fibers from areas adjacent to it. Thus, the entire neocortex can be divided into four fields: visual, auditory, somatic, and motor. Since areas of relatively direct projections can be referred to as primary projection areas, the surrounding areas can be called **secondary projection areas.** According to one tradition of cortical organization, there are areas of association neocortex that receive input from each of the four fields listed. The extent, and even the existence, of these association fields is debated, but they are referred to as **tertiary projection areas.** Speaking speculatively, their function would be to associate or put together the input from the major sensory fields. At this point it

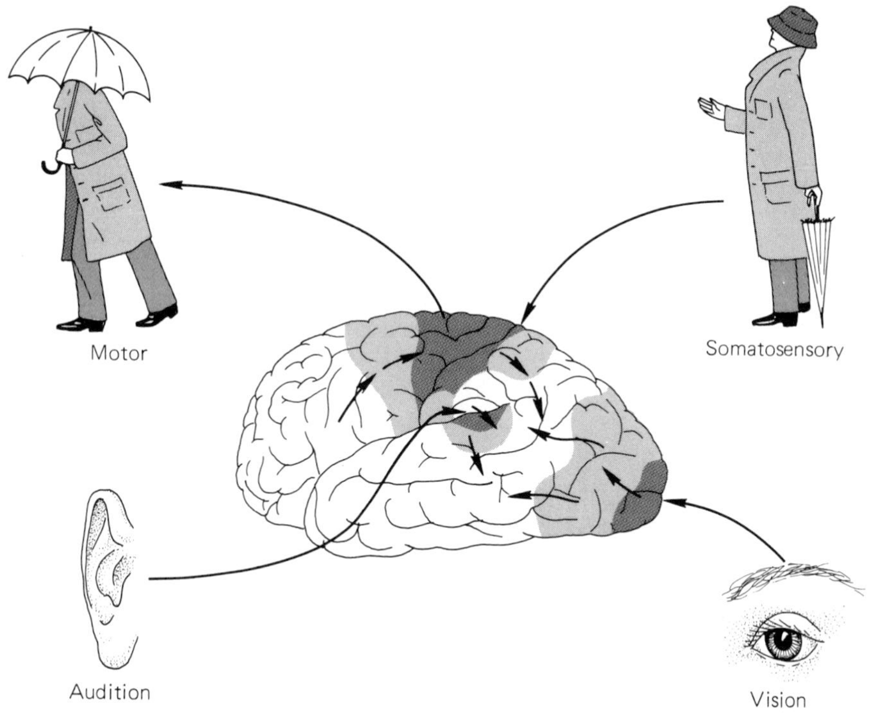

FIGURE 1-7. A projection map. The dots indicate primary zones, which receive input from the sensory systems or project to spinal motor systems. The shaded areas are secondary zones. The unshaded areas are tertiary zones.

would be helpful to produce a simple evolutionary story for the neocortex. One scenario could be that part of the neocortex evolved from the amygdala and part from the hippocampus, and that all of the portions associated with the former are involved in discrete movements of body parts and the identification of objects, whereas all of the portions associated with the latter are involved in controlling whole body movements and the identification of places in space. This sort of speculation must be left for later. For now it is enough to note that some research suggests that the tertiary areas evolved first and the primary areas evolved last, some suggest that the primary areas evolved first and the tertiary areas evolved last, and still others suggest that the tertiary areas have not yet evolved.

It is clear from this topography that the neocortex is highly organized. It is also clear why the posterior neocortex is considered to be largely sensory, and why the anterior neocortex is considered to be largely motor. Finally, it is apparent why each of the lobes is thought to be associated with a particular general function: frontal with motor, parietal with somatosensory, occipital with visual, and temporal with auditory function. We wish to emphasize, however, that this is a simplified description of the neocortex. Each of the major fields of the neocortex has many subdivisions. Furthermore, each area of the neocortex sends fibers to the brainstem motor areas, and so each field can be thought of as having motor functions. Finally, there are many reciprocal connections between the

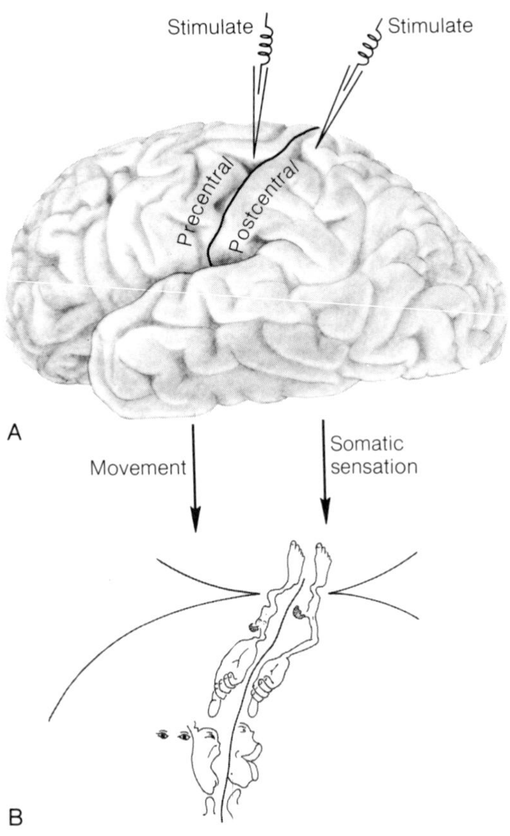

FIGURE 1-8. A functional map. *A*. Electrical stimulation to the precentral or postcentral gyrus through small electrodes. *B*. Movement or sensation is produced at the locations shown by the homunculi, or "little men." (After Penfield and Jasper, 1954.)

sensory relays that project to the cortical fields, between areas within cortical fields, and between the cortical fields themselves.

Functional Maps. Of the many functional maps of the somatosensory and motor areas, the best known is by Penfield and his coworkers. During the course of brain surgery, they stimulated the brains of conscious people through thin wires, or electrodes, with low voltages of electric current. The protocol of such an experiment was to stimulate the cortical tissue briefly, observe whether the person made a movement or reported some sort of body sensation (itch, tickle, etc.), record the location and response, and then move the stimulating electrode to repeat the procedure. The results of several such experiments are shown diagrammatically in Figure 1-8. Areas that produced movement lie in the precentral gyrus in the primary motor-projection area. For both the motor and sensory areas there is a point-to-point relation between parts of the body and parts of the neocortex. Note that in the figure these distributions of the body on the cortex are distorted, the face and hands being far larger proportionately than other parts of the body. This topography is shown schematically by the cartoon men (or *homunculi*), drawn over the motor and sensory areas to indicate the parts of the body represented in different cortical areas.

The face and hands of the homunculi are larger because they are capable of finer perceptions and movements than are other body areas and so require proportionately more neocortex to represent them. The foot area lies in the longitudinal fissure (flexed up in Figure 1-8). The cortical representation of the eyes is actually not in the head region of the motor homunculus; they have their own area just anterior to the head area.

The visual and auditory systems have a neocortical distribution as precise as that for the motor and somatosensory systems (Figure 1-7). The visual field (the area of the world the eyes see) is represented across the visual projection area in the occipital lobe, whereas the sensory area for sound, the basilar membrane, is represented in the primary auditory area of the temporal lobe. The taste area of the brain lies across a tongue-shaped area in the postcentral gyrus in Figure 1-8. Whether or not the olfactory system has any representation in the neocortex is at present uncertain.

Cytoarchitectonic Maps. Cytoarchitectonic maps are constructed by examining the neurons of the neocortex and grouping areas with similar cell

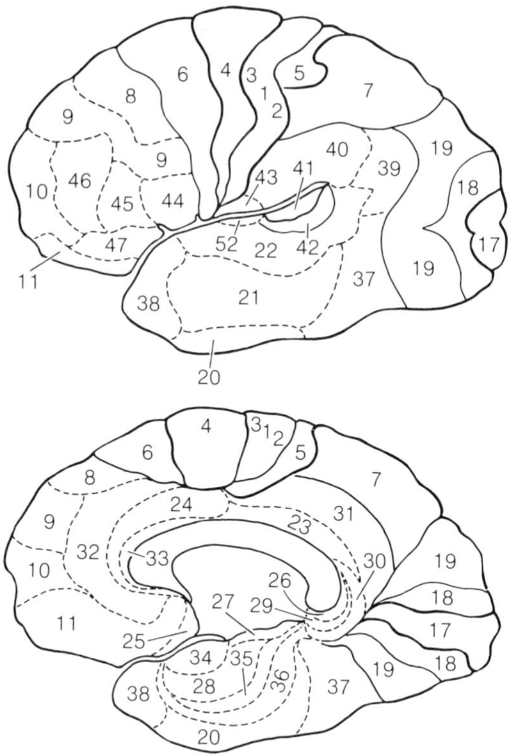

FIGURE 1-9. Brodmann's areas of the cortex. A few numbers are missing from the original sources, including areas 12–16 and 48–51. Some area have histologically distinctive boundaries and are outlined with heavy solid lines; others, such as 6 and 18–19, have less distinct boundaries and are outlined with light solid lines; the remainder have no distinct boundaries but gradually merge into one another and are outlined with dotted lines. (From H. Elliott, *Textbook of Neuroanatomy*. Philadelphia: Lippincott. Copyright © 1969. Reprinted with permission.)

structure together. The many cytoarchitectonic maps of the neocortex differ chiefly in degree of complexity. The map presented in Figure 1-9 is known as **Brodmann's map.** It is by no means the simplest, but it is the most widely used, and it will be used throughout this book.

The neurons of the neocortex are arranged in about six layers, as is shown in Figure 1-10. The number of layers distinguishes the neocortex from other brain areas, such as the limbic system, which has only three layers. The cell layers of the neocortex can be separated into two groups by function: the outer four layers receive axons *from* other brain areas; the inner two layers send axons *to* other brain areas. The cell layers are not distributed uniformly in the neocortex (in fact, it is debatable whether there are really six layers in all neocortical areas). For example, a primary sensory area such as the visual area has a large number of layer-4 cells receiving axons from the eyes but fewer layer-5 cells, whereas the primary motor area has a large number of layer-5 cells sending axons to the subcortical motor system but fewer layer-4 cells. Areas that are neither primarily motor nor primarily sensory have fewer cells in layers 4 and 5 and a greater density of cells in layers 2 and 3. It is on such differences in cell distribution, as well as differ-

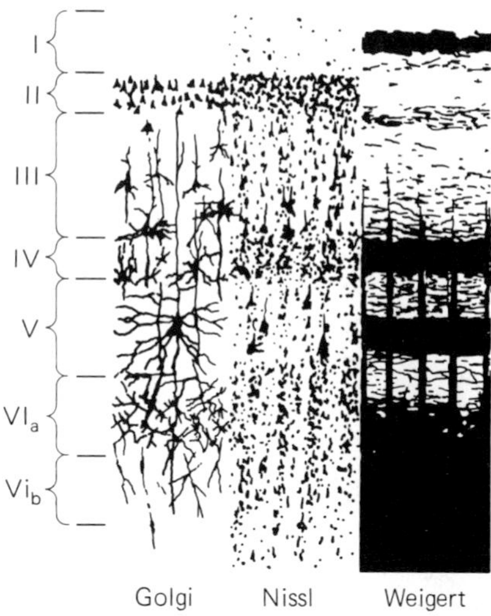

FIGURE 1-10. Structure of he cortex revealed through the use of three different stains. The Golgi stain penetrates only a few neurons but reveals all of their processes, the Nissi stain highlights only cell bodies, and the Weigert myelin stain reveals the location of axons. Note that these staining procedures highlight the different cell types of the cortex and reveal that it is composed of a number of layers, each of which contains typical cell types. (After Brodmann, 1909.)

ences in cell sizes and shapes, that cytoarchitectonic maps are based.

In Brodmann's cytoarchitectonic map, shown in Figure 1-9, each of the areas is numbered, but the numbers themselves have no intrinsic meaning. To do his analysis Brodmann divided the brain at the central sulcus, and then worked through each half in random order, numbering new conformations of cells as he found them. Thus, he found areas 1 and 2 in the posterior section, then switched to the anterior section and found 3 and 4, and thereupon switched back again, and so on in this manner.

Table 1-3 summarizes some of the known relations between each of Brodmann's areas and its functions. As it turns out, the relation between structure and function is stunning. For example, area 17 corresponds to the primary visual projection area, and areas 18 and 19 to the secondary visual projection areas. Similar relations exist for other areas and functions. The boundaries of Brodmann's areas also appear to be related to function because the primary sensory and motor areas have fairly distinct boundaries and functions. The secondary areas have less distinct boundaries and the tertiary areas still less distinct ones. This has been taken to mean that the secondary and tertiary areas have less specified sensory or motor function and more associative or integrative function. At this point the best advice we can give a student with respect to Brodmann's system and its relation to function is to commit the numbers and the location of the primary and secondary areas to memory and then keep in mind that the remaining areas (composing the greater area of the neocortex) are tertiary cortex.

TABLE 1-3. Functional areas and Brodmann cytoarchitectonic areas

Function	Brodmann area
Vision	
primary	17
secondary	18, 19, 20, 21, 37
Auditory	
primary	41
secondary	22, 42
Body senses	
primary	1, 2, 3
secondary	5, 7
Sensory, tertiary	7, 22, 37, 39, 40
Motor	
primary	4
secondary	6
eye movement	8
speech	44
Motor, tertiary	9, 10, 11, 45, 46, 47

A Postscript on Mapping. The maps that we have described and illustrated in this section were chosen for historical and illustrative purposes. There are, however, ongoing improvements in all of the techniques used to generate maps, and our insight into the topographic organization of the cortex changes as a result. It is within this spirit of an evolving science that it is hoped that an understanding of the organization of the cortex will eventually lead to an understanding of its function.

Cortical Connections

The various regions of the neocortex are interrelated by three types of axon projections: (1) relatively short connections between one gyrus and another, (2) longer connections between one lobe and another, and (3) interhemispheric connections, or **commissures,** between one hemisphere and another. Most of the interhemispheric connections link homotopic areas, or corresponding points, in the two hemispheres. Figure 1-11 shows the locations and names of some of these connections. The cortex also makes other types of connections with itself; cells in any area may, for example, send axons to cells in a subcortical area such as the thalamus, and the cells in the area of the thalamus may then send their axons to some other cortical area. These types of relations are more difficult to establish anatomically than those based on direct connections. Yet the connections are of considerable functional interest, because damage to a pathway is often reflected in behavioral deficits as se-

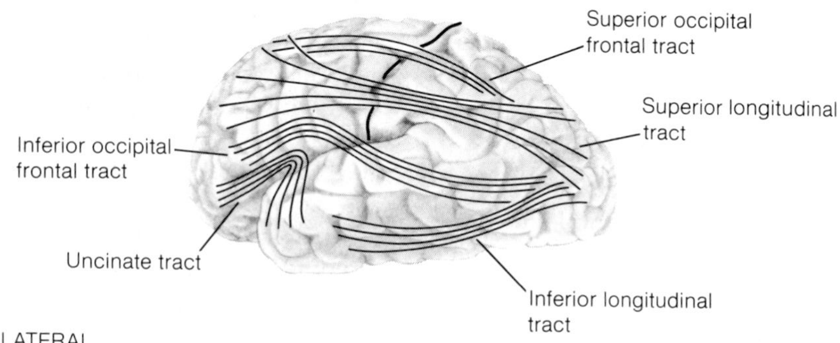

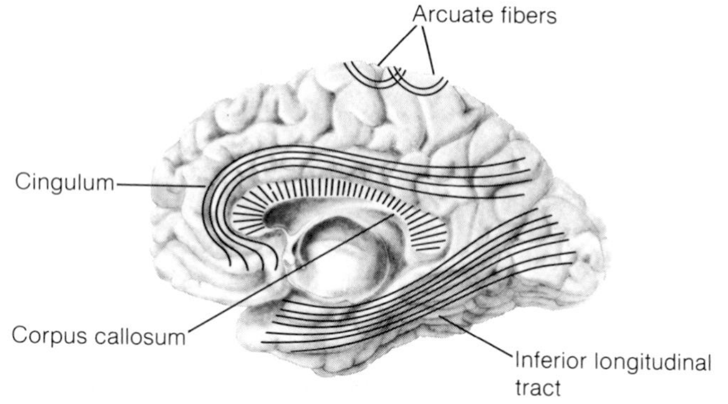

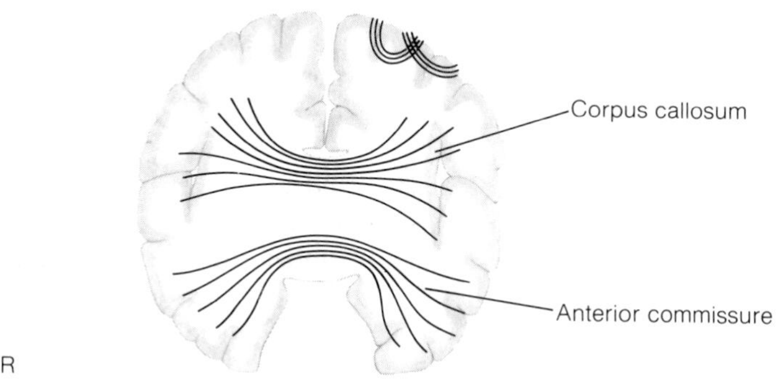

FIGURE 1-11. Connections between various regions of the cortex.

vere as those suffered following damage to the functional areas they connect. A glance at Figure 1-11 will show that it would indeed be difficult to damage any area of the cortex without damaging one or more of its interconnecting pathways.

The Limbic Lobe

During the evolution of the amphibians and reptiles, a number of three-layer cortical structures developed, sheathing the periphery of the brainstem. With the subsequent growth of the neocortex they became sandwiched between the new and the old brain. Because of the evolutionary origin of these structures some anatomists have referred to them as the reptilian brain, but the term *limbic lobe* (from the Latin *limbus,* meaning border or hem), coined by Broca in 1878, is more widely recognized today. The limbic lobe is also referred to as the *limbic system* (which may very well be a misnomer). The limbic lobe consists of a number of structures, including the hippocampus (sea horse), **septum** (partition), and cingulate (girdle) gyrus, or cingulate cortex, which may all have different functions (see Figure 1-12). Nevertheless, the history of how the limbic "lobe" became the limbic "system" is one of the most interesting chapters of the neurosciences.

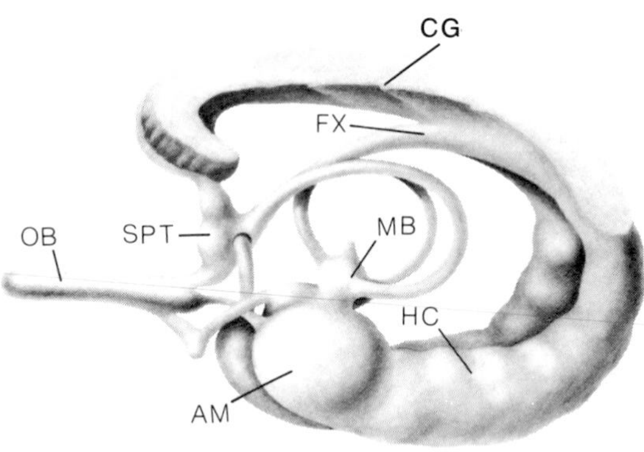

FIGURE 1-12. Model of the human limbic system. Major structures include the hippocampus (HC), amygdala (AM), septum (SPT), mammillary bodies (MB), olfactory bulbs (OB), fornix (FX), and cingulate gyris (CG). (After Hamilton, 1976.)

Initially, anatomists were impressed with the connections between the olfactory system and the limbic lobe. On this evidence it was suggested that the limbic structures were elaborated to deal with olfactory information, and so together they were called the **rhinencephalon,** or smell-brain. Because a number of experiments demonstrated that these limbic structures had little olfactory function, for a time their putative olfactory function lay in a scientific limbo. Then in 1937, Papez, in what was thought at the time to be a scientific tour de force, asked, "Is emotion a magic product, or is it a physiologic process which depends on an anatomic mechanism?" He suggested that emotion, which had no known anatomic substrate, was a product of the limbic lobe, which had no recognized function. He argued that the emotional brain consisted of a circuit in which information flowed from the mammillary bodies in the hypothalamus to the anterior thalamic nucleus to the cingulate cortex to the hippocampus and back to the mammillary bodies. Input could enter this circuit from other structures to be elaborated as emotion. For example, an idea from the neocortex could enter the circuit to be elaborated as "Fear" and ultimately influence the hypothalamus to release hormone that would be an appropriate companion for the idea and its emotional correlary. It is a historical irony that the structures he emphasized as primary, for example, the hippocampus, have subsequently been found to have little emotional function, whereas those he ignored, such as the septum, may indeed have such a function. It would be inappropriate, however, to suggest that the function of the limbic structures is in any way settled. Recently a variety of different functions have been proposed for the different limbic structures. Certainly, to suggest that the limbic system is the emotional brain now seems as much an oversimplification as it is to say that the limbic system has only one function.

The hippocampus, of all the limbic structures,

has received a great deal of attention. It has been successively postulated to play a role in inhibition, learning, memory, organization of movement, and spatial orientation, but its putative role in the formation of memory has caught the imagination of neuropsychology. As noted above, the hippocampus is an evolutionarily old structure, which preceded and probably gave rise to portions of the neocortex. It receives a major portion of its input from the neocortex and sends a major portion of its output back to the neocortex. Unlike most other areas of the brain, its removal results in no obvious sensory or motor deficits; damage in different areas does not produce differential deficits, and its anatomical connections are characterized by enormous overlap and little regional specificity. If it is removed in humans or other animals, new memories (excluding motor skills) cannot be formed, but old memories are retained. Accordingly, it is thought that sensory information is funneled into the hippocampus, where it may be temporarily stored, and then is sent back to the neocortex for permanent storage. For example, visual information may be relayed successively through areas 17, 18, 19, 37, 21, and 38, and then through a number of cell layers of the hippocampus. This information is then returned in a number of stages to subfields of the temporal lobes (see Figure 1-9). Each relay may involve some elaboration of the information, with the elaboration in the hippocampus involving temporary memory storage and the final relay back to the temporal cortex involving permanent memory storage.

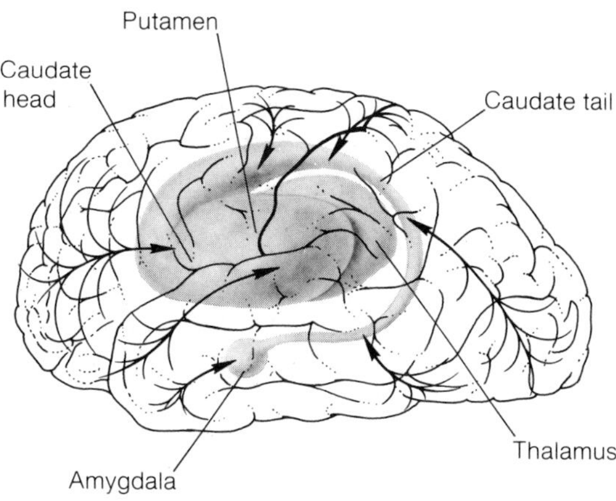

FIGURE 1-13. Relation between the basal ganglia and the cortex. Arrows indicate theoretical projections of various cortical areas into basal ganglia structures.

Basal Ganglia

The **basal ganglia** are a collection of nuclei lying mainly beneath the anterior regions of the neocortex (Figure 1-13). They include the **putamen** (shell), **globus pallidus** (pale globe), the **caudate nucleus** (tailed nucleus), and **amygdala** (almond). These nuclei have extensive connections with the neocortex and thalamus, and they are connected by ascending and descending fibers to midbrain structures such as the red nucleus and substantia nigra. Figure 1-13 shows suggested relations to the neocortex.

A characteristic feature of the basal ganglia is its highly segregated and compartmental architecture. If the caudate nucleus is cut and stained to highlight specific neurotransmitters, the stains highlight *patches* of stained tissue surrounded by a *matrix* of nonstained tissue. The patches are sections of branched three-dimensional labyrinths called *striosomes,* or striped bodies (imagine the underground tunnel system of a ground squirrel). In most mammals that have been studied, the striosomes are rich in opioids and poor in acetylcholine (two neurotransmitters), but other transmitter substances also respect this segregation. The inputs into the caudate are also directed to either the patches or the matrix. The limbic structures (the medial frontal cortex, amygdala, and hippocampus) project to the patches, whereas the sensory and motor cortex project to the surrounding matrix. According to Gerfen, the outputs to the brainstem from these basal ganglial compartments are also different. Thus, one feature of caudate, or basal ganglia, organization is that there are at least two intermixed but parallel systems. A second feature of basal ganglia organization is regional specialization. Damage in one area produces impairments different from those created by damage in other areas. Generally, however, the impairments are similar to those obtained from damaging the region of neocortex that projects to a particular region of the basal ganglia.

The principal function of the basal ganglia has historically been described as motor. Damage to different portions of the basal ganglia can produce changes in posture, increases or decreases in muscle tone, and abnormal movements such as twitches, jerks, and tremors. The basal ganglia may have other functions, such as sequencing a number of complex movements into a smoothly executed response, as occurs during talking.

The Thalamus

The **thalamus** can be divided into two areas, the ventral and dorsal thalami. The ventral thalamus provides a general input into the neocortex that may modulate the activity of the neocortex. The dorsal thalamus, or thalamus proper, is composed of a number of nuclei, each of which projects to a specific area of the neocortex as shown in Figure 1-14. These nuclei receive input from the body's different sensory systems or from other brain areas. The lateral geniculate body (LGB) receives visual projections, the medial geniculate body (MGB) receives auditory projections, and the ventral-posterior lateral nuclei (VPL) receive touch, pressure, pain, and temperature projections from the body. In turn, the lateral geniculate body projects to area 17, the medial geniculate body projects to area 41, and the ventral posterior lateral nuclei project to Brodmann areas 1, 2, and 3. Note that the olfactory system does not project through the thalamus to the neocortex. A large area of the posterior secondary and tertiary cortex sends projections to and receives projections back from the pulvinar (P). Some of the subcortical motor nuclei, such as the globus pallidus, substantia nigra, and dentate nucleus, project to the ventral anterior and ventral lateral nuclei (VA and VL, respectively), and these areas project to primary motor area 4 and secondary motor area 5. The dorsal medial nucleus (DM) receives projections from the amygdaloid complex, temporal neocortex, and caudate nucleus and projects to the remainder of the frontal lobe. The significance of some of these connections will be discussed in subsequent sections of the book.

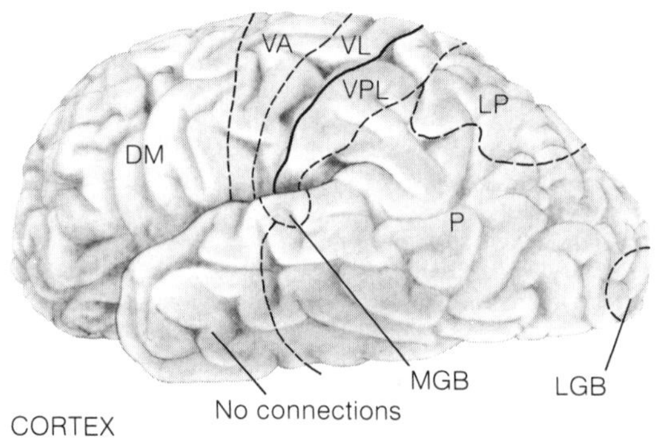

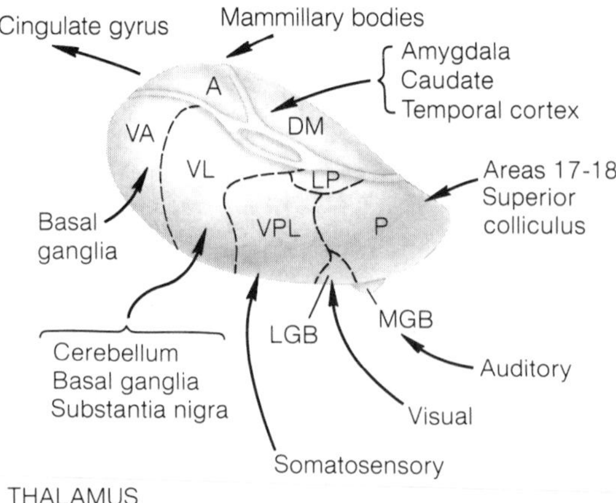

FIGURE 1-14. Relation between thalamic nuclei and various areas of the cortex to which they project. The arrows indicate the sources of input to and output from the thalamus. (A) anterior nucleus, (DM) dorsal medial nucleus, (VA) ventral anterior nucleus, (VL) ventral lateral nucleus, (LP) lateral posterior nucleus, (VPL) ventral lateral posterior nucleus, (P) pulvinar, (LGB) lateral geniculate body, (MGB) medial geniculate body.

THE CROSSED BRAIN

One of the most peculiar features of the organization of the brain is that each of its symmetrical halves responds to sensory stimulation from the contralateral side of the body or sensory world, and controls the musculature on the contralateral side of the body. (See Figure 1-15.) The visual system achieves this effect by crossing half the fibers of the optic tract as well as by reversing the image through the lens of the eye. Nearly all the fibers of the motor and somatosensory system cross. Projections from each ear go to each hemisphere, but there is substantial evidence that auditory excitation from one ear has a preferential route to the opposite hemisphere. As a result of this arrangement, along the center of the nervous system there are numerous crossings, or **decussations,** of sensory and motor fibers. Throughout the book, details of this anatomy will be described where they are relevant to discussions of the function of each of these systems. It is sufficient to say here that because of this arrangement, damage to one side of the brain generally causes sensory and motor impairments not to the same side of the body but to the opposite side.

Anyone reflecting on this crossed arrangement must ask why it occurs and how. There have been a number of imaginative answers to each of these questions.

The Spanish anatomist Santiago Ramón y Cajal was obsessed, as he says, with the following thought: "Everything will have a simple explanation if it is admitted that the correct perception of an object implies the congruence of the cerebral surfaces of projection, that is, those representing each point in space." He suggested that crossing in the visual system is necessary so that a continuous representation of an object is retained in the visual cortex. His explanation of what might happen in an uncrossed system is shown in Figure 1-16. He argued that since the lens reverses the image, and since each eye sees only part of the visual field, an uncrossed system would produce a representation in the cortex in which each half of the image was in one hemisphere but with the peripheries of the image juxtaposed in the center. He suggested that prey taking the path of the external arrow shown in Figure 1-16*A* would be difficult to catch, since its path in the visual cortex would be discontinuous. Crossing the pathway introduces a continuous image (as in Figure 1-16*B*). Cajal thought that reversal of the image's direction was not a problem, because it was compensated for by crossing the motor outflow from the brain.

A second theory advanced to explain crossing is the coil-reflex theory shown in Figure 1-17. Cog-

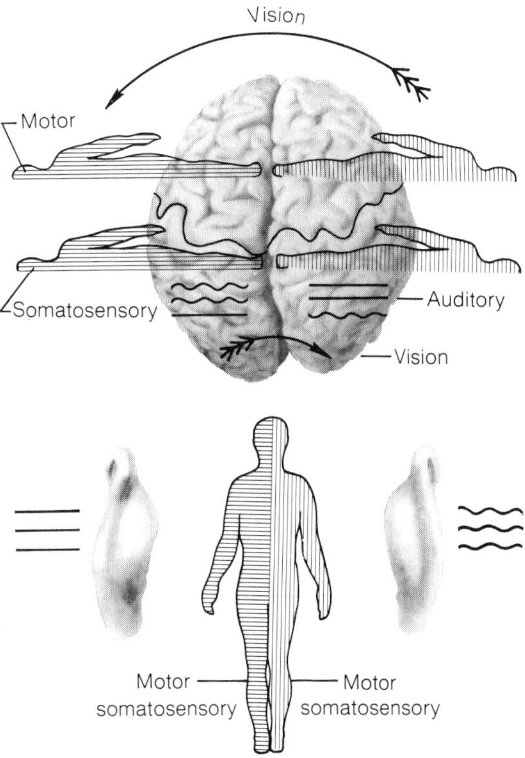

FIGURE 1-15. Schematic of the human brain from a dorsal view showing the projection of visual, auditory, and somatosensory input to contralateral areas of te cortex and the crossed projection of the motor cortex to the contralateral side of the body.

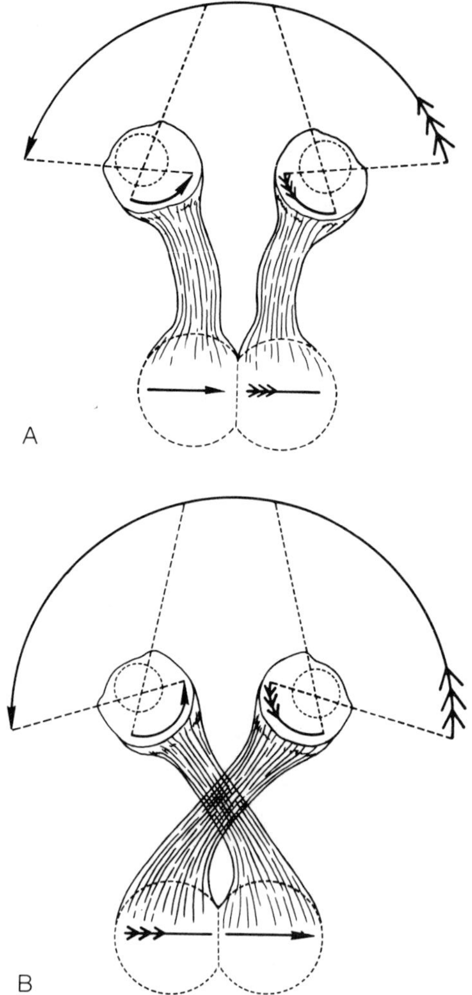

FIGURE 1-16. *A.* Illustration of the incongruous central projection of the images from the two eyes if there were no intercrossing of the optic nerves. *B.* Continuity of the visual image obtained by crossing the optic nerves. (From S. Ramón y Cajal, 1937. Reprinted with permission of the American Philosophical Society.)

hill studied the development of movement in the primitive marine vertebrate *Amblystoma.* He found that its first movement is coiling, which when repeated a number of times forms its basic swimming movement. In this animal, input from sensory receptors goes only to motor cells on the opposite side of the body through an interneuron at the rostral (eating) end. The sensory input is passed to successive motor cells in a rostral-to-caudal, or head-to-tail, sequence, causing contraction of successive myotomes (skeletal muscle segments) that by their action produce the coil. The coil allows the animal to flex away from a predator or a noxious stimulus, and as swimming develops, ensures that stimulation will elicit swimming at the animal's front end. Sarnat and Netsky suggest that this anatomical arrangement forms the basis for the crossed systems in all vertebrates. William Webster has suggested to us that this model explains why the olfactory system is the only sensory system that is uncrossed. The assumption is that the primitive function of the olfactory bulb was to bring an animal to food. A primitive animal would coil toward an olfactory stimulus that signaled food and would, therefore, have to contract muscles on the same side of the body (where the food actually is, not the opposite to where it is). It would, therefore, need an uncrossed projection to the muscles. Furthermore, the Coghill model offers an explanation for why the brain's motor projections to the distal part of the body are also crossed. To be effective, an avoidance response of coiling would require a contralateral limb movement, once the limbs developed.

An imaginative explanation of how the nervous system became crossed has been proposed by Kinsbourne. He notes that invertebrates have an uncrossed and ventrally located nervous system, a dorsally located heart, and a posterior flow of blood in central blood vessels. Vertebrates have a crossed and dorsally located nervous system, a ventrally located heart, and an anterior flow of blood in ventral blood vessels. He proposes that in the transition from invertebrates to vertebrates the body rotated 180° with respect to the head. As a result, blood circulation reversed direction, the heart became located ventrally, the nervous system adopted a dorsal position, and decussations were formed by the rotation.

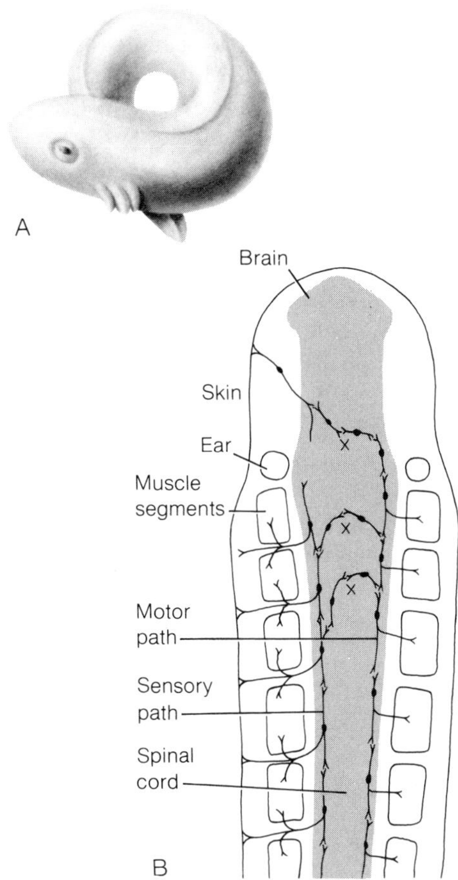

FIGURE 1-17. *A.* Coil reflex in the embryonic *Amblystoma.* *B.* A diagram of the mechanism that accounts for the coil reaction. Sensory neurons are shown on one side of the body, motor neurons on the other. Excitation of a sensory neuron leads to excitation of an interneuron (X) and then to sequential contraction of the contralateral muscles in a head-to-tail direction. (After Coghill, 1929.)

One weakness of Kinsbourne's theory is that it predicts that the sensory and motor pathways of the brainstem should be reversed in a dorso-ventral direction with respect to the spinal cord. This is not the case, for the dorsal portion of the midbrain is sensory, as is the dorsal portion of the spinal cord. A second weakness of the theory is that it does not explain why a 180° rotation would prove adaptive. It may have been a chance occurrence, or it may have occurred to effect the coil reflex. (Alternatively, we could suggest, tongue in cheek, that had the nervous system remained below the esophagus the brain could not have evolved lest it choke off respiration and the route of food to the stomach.)

As our knowledge about brain organization becomes more sophisticated, it becomes increasingly obvious that many functions are *lateralized,* that is, a given region in one hemisphere has a function that is different from the corresponding region of the other hemisphere. A provocative question is, "How did lateralization develop and does it have any relation to the crossed organization of the brain?" Answers to this question are sparse and speculative but there may be a relationship. Imagine a simple animal (like a rat) with eyes on the side of its head such that each hemisphere receives visual input predominantly from the contralateral visual world. If the animal were to watch for an object, such as an edible bug, in one visual field, its perception of the object would be in the contralateral hemisphere. Thus, it would be simplest for it to use that hemisphere to make an orienting response toward the bug to catch it. One could imagine that hemisphere containing the idea of an edible bug as well as a motor score for retrieving the bug. If the animal pursued the bug and a predator suddenly appeared, we could imagine that the hemisphere occupied with bug catching would be unavailable to deal with the predator. The other hemisphere, however, would be free to respond to the predator. In support of this sort of notion, Mittleman and his coworkers have demonstrated that orienting responses can be lateralized in rats. Perhaps song birds that sing with one hemisphere do so for similar reasons, to leave the other hemisphere free to watch for competitors or predators. Thus, at a very primitive evolutionary level we could imagine some adaptive utility for hemispheric specialization that is also related to crossed-brain organization. According to this idea, once lateralization developed for some simple use, it could be subsequently elaborated to the level of specialization found in the human brain where each hemisphere has distinctive functions.

PROTECTION

The brain and spinal cord are supported and protected from injury and infection in four ways. (1) The brain is enclosed in a thick bone, the *skull,* and the spinal cord is encased in a series of interlocking bony *vertebrae.* (2) Within these bony cases are three membranes, the outer **dura mater** (from the Latin, meaning hard mother), a tough double layer of collagenous fiber enclosing the brain in a kind of loose sack; the middle **arachnoid** (from the Greek, meaning resembling a spider's web), a very thin sheet of delicate collagenous connective tissue that follows the contours of the brain; and the inner **pia mater** (from the Latin, meaning soft mother), which is a moderately tough membrane of connective tissue made from reticular, elastic, and collagenous fibers, that clings to the surface of the nervous tissue. (3) The brain is cushioned from shock and sudden changes of pressure by the *cerebrospinal fluid (CSF),* which fills the ventricles inside the brain and circulates around the brain beneath the arachnoid layer, in the subarachnoid space. This fluid is a clear, colorless solution of sodium chloride and other salts and is made by a plexus of cells that protrudes into each ventricle. The CSF is made continually and flows from the ventricles, circulating around the brain, and is then absorbed by the venous sinuses of the dura mater. Although it is unlikely that the CSF nourishes the brain, it may instead play a role in excreting metabolic wastes from the brain. (4) The brain is protected from many chemical substances circulating in the rest of the body by a *blood-brain barrier.* This consists of glial cells that are wrapped around blood vessels in such a way that access from the blood to the brain is prevented for many molecules.

REFERENCES

Brodmann, K. *Vergleichende Lokalisationlehr der Grosshirnrinde in ihren Prinzipien dargestellt auf Grund des Zellenbaues.* Leipzig: J. A. Barth, 1909.

Coghill, G. E. *Anatomy and the Problem of Behavior.* Cambridge: Cambridge University Press, 1929. (Reprinted by Hafner, New York, 1963.)

Curtis, B. A., S. Jacobson, and E. M. Marcus. *An Introduction to the Neurosciences.* Philadelphia: Saunders, 1972.

Elliott, H. *Textbook of Neuroanatomy.* Philadelphia: Lippincott, 1969.

Everett, N. B. *Functional Neuroanatomy.* Philadelphia: Lea and Febiger, 1965.

Gerfen, C. R. The neostriatal mosaic: Compartmentalization of cortistriatal input and striatonigral output systems. *Nature,* 311:461–464, 1984.

Hamilton, L. W. *Basic Limbic System Anatomy of the Rat.* New York and London: Plenum, 1976.

Kinsbourne, M. (ed.). *Asymmetrical Function of the Brain.* Cambridge: Cambridge University Press, 1978.

Kruska, D. How fast can total brain size change in mammals? *Journal Hirnforsch* 28:59–70, 1987.

MacLean, P. D. Psychosomatic disease and the "visceral brain": Recent developments bearing on the Papez theory of emotion. *Psychosomatic Medicine* 11:338–353, 1949.

Mittleman, G., I. Q. Whishaw, and T. W. Robbins, Cortical lateralization of function in rats in a visual reaction time task. *Behavioural Brain Research* 31:29–36, 1988.

Papez, J. W. A proposed mechanism of emotion. *Archives of Neurology and Psychiatry* 38:724–744, 1937.

Passingham, R. E. Brain size and intelligence in man. *Brain Behavior and Evolution* 16:253–270, 1979.

Penfield, W., and E. Boldrey. Somatic motor and sensory representation in the cerebral cortex as studied by electrical stimulation. *Brain* 60:389–443, 1958.

Penfield, W., and H. H. Jasper. *Epilepsy and the Functional Anatomy of the Human Brain.* Boston: Little, Brown, 1954.

Ramón y Cajal, S. *Recollections of My Life,* Memoirs of the American Philosophical Society (vol. 8) 1937.

Ranson, S. W., and S. L. Clark. *The Anatomy of the Nervous System.* Philadelphia: Saunders, 1959.

Sarnat, H. B., and M. G. Netsky. *Evolution of the Nervous System.* New York: Oxford University Press, 1974.

Truex, R. C., and M. B. Carpenter. *Human Neuroanatomy.* Baltimore: Williams and Wilkins, 1969.

Van Valen, L. Brain size and intelligence in man. *American Journal of Physical Anthropology* 40:417–424, 1974.

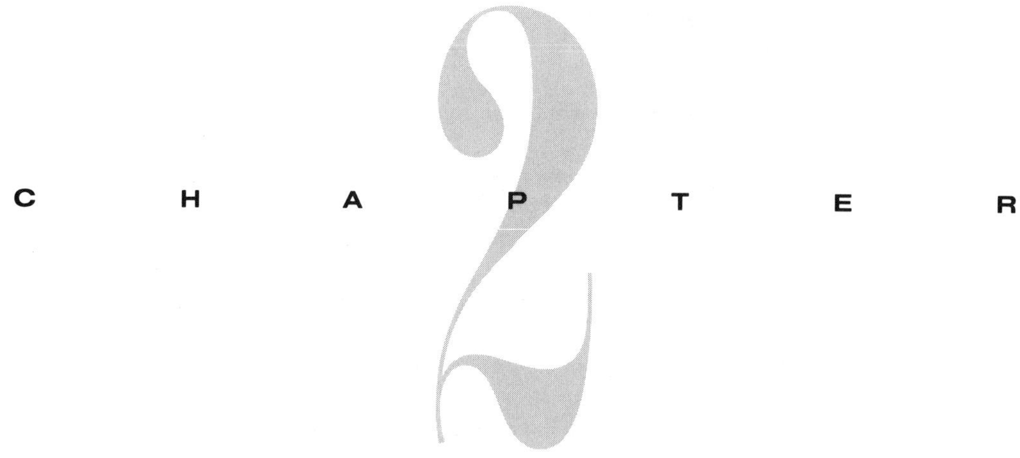

CHAPTER 2

CELLULAR ORGANIZATION OF THE NERVOUS SYSTEM

When male Grayling butterflies are ready to copulate, they fly upward toward females passing overhead. The male's response to females is not unerringly accurate, because sometimes the males fly toward other passing objects. This fact suggested to the ethologist Tinbergen that the most effective stimulus for releasing the male's approach response could be discovered with controlled experiments. Tinbergen made model butterflies, attached them to the line of a fishing rod, and "flew" them to determine which were the most effective in attracting males. Although the females are brightly colored, and the males can see color, it was not an important feature of the stimulus. The males were attracted by dark, large, and irregularly moving stimuli. Furthermore, these characteristics were mutually reinforcing, which suggested to Tinbergen that the nervous system of male butterflies has a "pooling station" that integrates the different features of the stimulating object.

Tinbergen's experiments are an example of excellent behavioral research that, although done with no knowledge or study of the physiology of the butterfly's nervous system, still gives clues about how that system must work. But knowledge of how the process of integration takes place, that is, of how the pooling station works, involves knowing both the anatomical basis of the station and its physiological activity. This story is applicable to neuropsychology. Much can be learned about people's behavior through careful observations and controlled experiments, but detailed knowledge of how the nervous system controls behavior requires study of its cellular physiological organization. This requires knowing the structure of cells and how they work. Although an extensive knowledge of electrophysiology (the study of neuron activity) and neuropharmacology (the study of the biochemical activity of neurons) is not essential for understanding neuropsychology, a general understanding of them is helpful. The following sections give a brief description of (1) the physical features of neurons, including the techniques involved in studying them, and (2) the electrical activity of neurons and the techniques used to record their activity.

THE NEURON'S STRUCTURE

Neurons are cells that act as the integrating units of the nervous system, and although they share many of the characteristics of other cells in the body, they have special characteristics that make them particularly well adapted to their function.

A broad analogy can be drawn between a neuron and a person. Neurons, once formed, do not regenerate, and unless they suffer lethal damage, most live as long as the person in which they are found. Each neuron is separated from physical contact with every other neuron, but it communicates across this separation using a language that is part electrical and part chemical. Neurons vary enormously in size and shape, the differences bearing evidence of each neuron's particular adaptation to its specialized function. Neurons are aggregated into communities, or *nuclei,* each of which makes a special contribution to behavior. Neurons are modifiable: they change their behavior with experience, they learn, they remember, and they forget. At times neurons can malfunction, causing disruptions in normal behavior. There are similarities in the behavior of neurons, but the full significance of their behavior can only be understood within the context of the community in which they function. This anthropomorphic analogy serves to caution us that the function of a neuron within the context of a working brain is not as simple as the neuron's small size might indicate. Having made these generalizations, two exceptions can be noted. First, during development far more neurons develop than will ultimately survive, so cell death is a pronounced developmental stage in sculpting the adult brain. Second, neurons that leave the central nervous system (CNS), such as sensory neurons and motor neurons, retain the capacity to regenerate.

Figure 2-1 is a schematic drawing of a neuron. The neuron is enclosed in a specialized membrane and consists of a **cell body,** or **soma,** branching filaments called **dendrites** (from the Greek, meaning tree), a process called an **axon** (from the Greek, meaning axle), and little end feet, or *terminals,* at the ends of the axon. Associated with each of these parts are other specialized structures that will be described where appropriate in the following sections. The dendrites collect information, which is then integrated at the **axon hillock** close to the cell body; a summary of the input received by the cell is then passed along the axon and through the terminals to other cells. (The word *information* is used here loosely to mean any event or events that the cell actively codifies.)

Although neurons have these basic structures, their configurations differ from one another. For example, a *sensory* cell of the somatosensory system has one very long dendrite coursing from the skin to a point adjacent to its cell body, located near the spinal cord. Here the dendrite connects directly to its axon, which may then travel to the hindbrain. This sensory cell has developed a system of direct information transmission that requires no modification of the signal between receptor and brain. On the other hand, a *motor* cell in the spinal cord has a number of dendrites collecting input and a long axon extending from the cord to muscles. This cell appears to specialize in integrating a variety of inputs for a specific action.

Between these sensory and motor cells are many **interneurons** of various shapes. Some have a densely arborized, or branching, dendritic system, suggesting that their primary function is to collect a great deal of diversified information for integration (for examples of different neuron types see

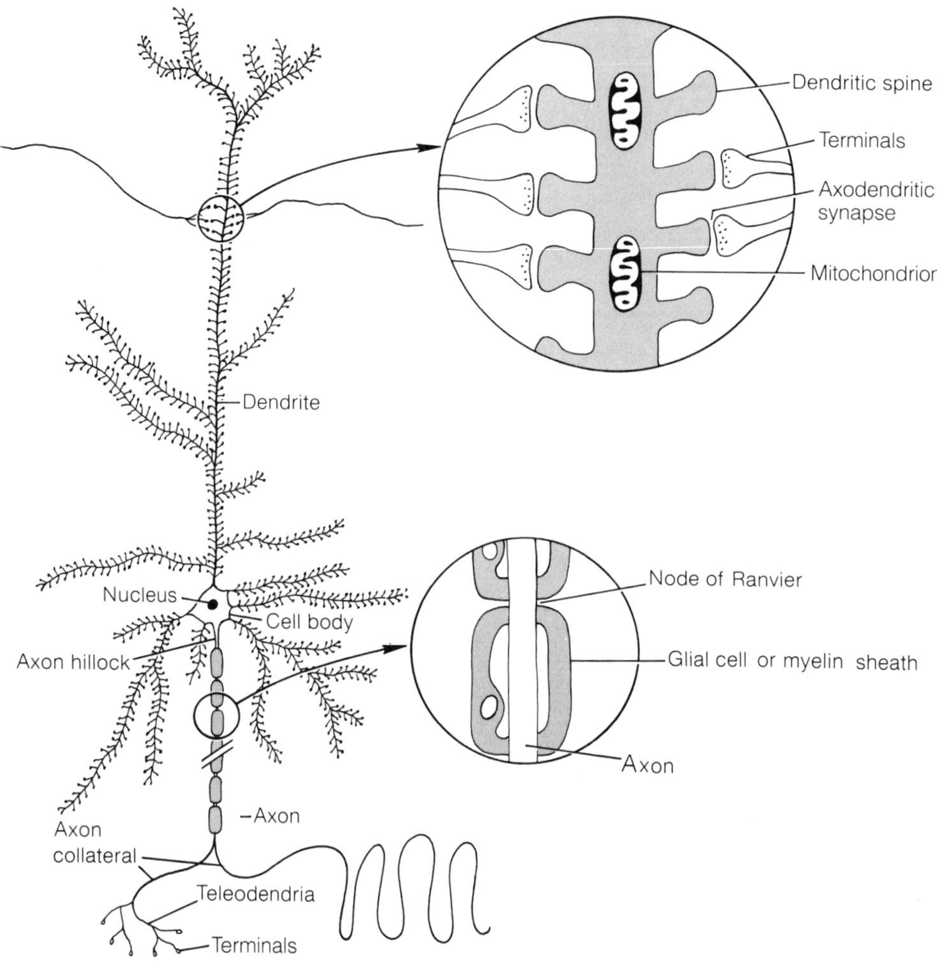

FIGURE 2-1. A typical neuron, showing some of its major physical features.

Figure 1-1). Also, although many neurons communicate chemically—and we stress this feature of their function—some probably communicate electrically.

The Cell Membrane

The cell membrane surrounds the entire cell and consists of a double layer of lipid (fat) molecules. These molecules are polar in structure, meaning that each has a head and two tails; the heads face outward, the tails face inward. The inner portion of the molecule, made up by the tails, is believed to be largely impermeable to many substances, thus providing a barrier to the free movement of electrically charged particles, or ions, through the membrane. The membrane has four general functions. (1) It contains channels—specially designed spaces that allow some ions to penetrate. It actively pumps other ions in and out of the cell. These processes allow the membrane to maintain a charge across its surface with the inside of the cell being negative with respect to the outside. (2) The membrane is the site of the electrical changes that are instrumental in information transmission. (3) The membrane contains receptors to which peptides and hormones attach. These chemicals may be transported into the cell and carried to the cell nucleus. The hormones may act on chromosomes in the nucleus to initiate such processes as sexual differentiation of the cell and its functions. (4) The membrane contains sites for axon terminals as well as receptors. Transmitter substances from the terminals of one neuron attach to the receptors of another, where they induce changes in the electrical charge across the membrane.

The Cell Body (Soma)

The cell body, or soma, is defined as the area of cytoplasm (a semifluid substance filling the space outlined by the membrane) that surrounds the nucleus. The cell body contains a variety of substances that determine its structure and function. The major physical features of the cell body are illustrated in Figure 2-2. An important function of the cell body and its constituents is the manufacture and transportation of proteins and other substances. Some of these proteins may be destined to be secreted as transmitter substances, but most of them are required to maintain the many branching filaments of the neuron. Other substances manufactured in the cell include enzymes for stimulating chemical reactions, proteins that form the receptors on the cell's surface, and structural elements of the cell that maintain the cell's shape or transport substances through its long axons and dendrites.

The Nucleus. Each cell contains a nucleus. Within the nucleus are **chromosomes** and a **nucleolus.** The chromosomes are composed of **deoxyribonucleic acid (DNA),** which combined with some proteins form almost all the genetic material of the cell. The DNA has two func-

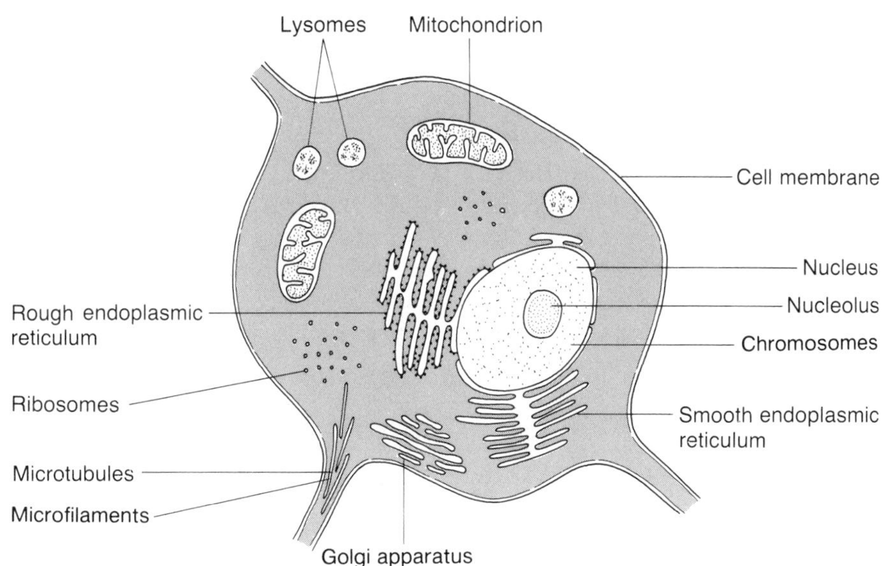

FIGURE 2-2. A typical cell body, showing some of its major physical features.

tions: it controls the growth and development of the cell into its mature form, and once the cell is mature, it continues to produce the protein necessary for maintaining the structure of the cell or for participating in its communication processes. The nucleolus produces material called ribosomal ribonucleic acid (rRNA), a form of **ribonucleic acid (RNA).**

Here is a brief description of how the chromosomes and the nucleolus participate in protein production. Enzymes act on the DNA of the chromosomes to produce *messenger ribonucleic acid (mRNA),* which contains the code for producing a protein such as an enzyme. The mRNA is transported into the cell cytoplasm. Here it joins with the ribosomal RNA, which has been transported from the nucleolus to the cytoplasm, to form a new structure called a *polyribosome.* The polyribosome is the template on which proteins are formed. Finally, once manufactured the proteins are used locally, are transported to other parts of the cell, or are exported from the cell.

The Endoplasmic Reticulum. Extending throughout the cytoplasm is a network of membranelike substance called the *endoplasmic reticulum (ER).* Some ribosomes become attached to the ER, giving it a rough appearance, and so this part is called the *rough ER.* This part of the ER is thought to make protein destined for export from the cell. The remaining part is called the *smooth ER.* When cells were first examined with a light microscope a dense accumulation of material was seen around the nucleus. This was called *Nissl substance.* This substance had a great affinity for certain dyes, and so Nissl stains were, and still are, one of the most commonly used for staining nerve cells for microscopic examination. When the electron microscope was developed, examination of the Nissl substance showed that it was in fact rough ER.

Light-microscopic examination of the cell shows a clump of material named the **Golgi apparatus.** Electron-microscopic examination of the Golgi apparatus shows it to be clusters of smooth ER that are thought to collect proteins from the rough ER and cover them with a membrane so that they form granules. The granules are transported to other parts of the cell or are exported from it.

Lysomes. The cell body contains *organelles* of different sizes that are shaped like sacks. These are called **lysomes** (from the Greek *lyso-*, meaning dissolution). Lysomes contain enzymes that degrade a wide variety of substances coming from within or outside the cell. Lysomes may leave a residue called **lipofuscin granules,** which appear in cells in increasing concentration with aging.

Mitochondria. Most of the processes of the cell require energy which is manufactured by the **mitochondria** (from the Greek *mito,* thread, and *chondrion,* granule). They have a characteristic cigar shape, with a smooth outer membrane and an internal folded one. It is thought that they were originally primitive organisms that were incorporated into cells in a symbiotic relation. Brain cells derive all their energy from glucose, which is extracted from the blood as it is needed (there are no mechanisms for glucose storage in the brain and so deprivation of glucose results in rapid cell death). The mitochondria take up glucose and break it down to form **adenosinetriphosphate (ATP),** which is used by other components of the cell as an energy source. Another function of mitochondria is to store calcium, which is used in regulating the release of transmitter substances from the terminals.

Microtubules and Microfilaments. Cells contain different small fiberlike structures in both the cell body and the cell processes. **Microtubules** of various sizes are thought to be involved in the transport of substances from the cell body to the distal parts of the cell (orthograde transport) or from the distal cell elements to the cell body (retrograde transport). If an amino acid is injected near a cell, it is taken up by the cell, incorporated into protein, and then transported to the terminals. There seem to be two transport systems: in one, some proteins can be seen to travel at 1 mm per day, in the other, different proteins travel at 100 mm or faster per day. The existence of these transport systems has been used to trace connections between neurons. The function of **microfilaments** is uncertain, but they may be involved in controlling the shape, movement, or fluidity of the cytoplasm.

The Dendrites

The *dendrites* are actually extensions of the cell body that allow the neuron to increase the surface area on which it receives information from other cells. The number of dendrites varies from neuron to neuron, some having a few, others more than 20, and each dendrite may branch profusely. Dendrites vary from a few microns to millimeters in length and taper as they branch; some have rough projections called *dendritic spines* on which they receive terminals from other cells.

The Axon

The *axon* originates in the cell body at a transition point called the *axon hillock.* Its function is to transmit information that it receives from the axon hillock to other cells. Each cell has only one axon, which varies in length from a few microns to more than a meter in different cells. Most axons have branches called *collaterals.* At the end of the axon and its collaterals are fine terminations called *teleodendria.* The teleodendria are covered with little knobs, called *terminals,* which make junctions with other cells.

The Terminals

The terminals lie close to other cells. Sherrington coined the term *synapsis* (from the Greek, meaning union) for the "almost" connection between a terminal and another neuron; consequently the terminals became technically known as **synaptic knobs** (abbreviated to **synapses**), when one is speaking of their function or in more general terms. They contain packages of chemical substances that when released influence the activity of other cells. Neurons may make actual contact with each other, but we will limit our description to these commonest almost connections.

The Synapse

There are three features of synapses that give some insight into their function:

First, the shape of the terminals, the appearance of their contents, and the way they connect with other structures show that there are different classes of synapses. For example, there are variations in the size of the granules in the terminals of different cells. The granules contain the transmitter chemical, and the difference in granule size shows that the transmitter substances may vary. There are also variations in the densities of the substances within the terminal and of the substances on the membrane with which they synapse. This diversity in size and density suggest that different synapses have different functions. Although no clear relations are known between the appearance of terminals and their function, it is recognized that some synapses are able to inhibit the activity of the cells across from them *(postsynaptic cells),* whereas other synapses excite these postsynaptic cells.

Second, synapses can make contacts with various portions of a cell. These connections are called *axodendritic, axosomatic, axoaxonic, or axosynaptic,* depending on whether they synapse with dendrites, the cell body, axons, or synapses of other cells, respectively. Examples of these connections are given in Figure 2-3. Neurons may also make other contacts with each other: dendrites make contacts with each other, that is, *dendrodendritic* connections, and the tubular portions of axons may overlie other axons and dendrites, making contact in passing. There are also terminals that do not synapse with other neural elements, but instead secrete their transmitter chemical into the space outside the cell. These are called *axoextracellular* synapses. If the nervous system is thought of as a series of conduits for information, it can be appreciated that the variety of terminal locations provides many opportunities for unique or novel routes of communication. In addition to synapsing with other neural projections, terminals can end on muscles and on capillaries, into which they may secrete hormones (*axosecretory* connections).

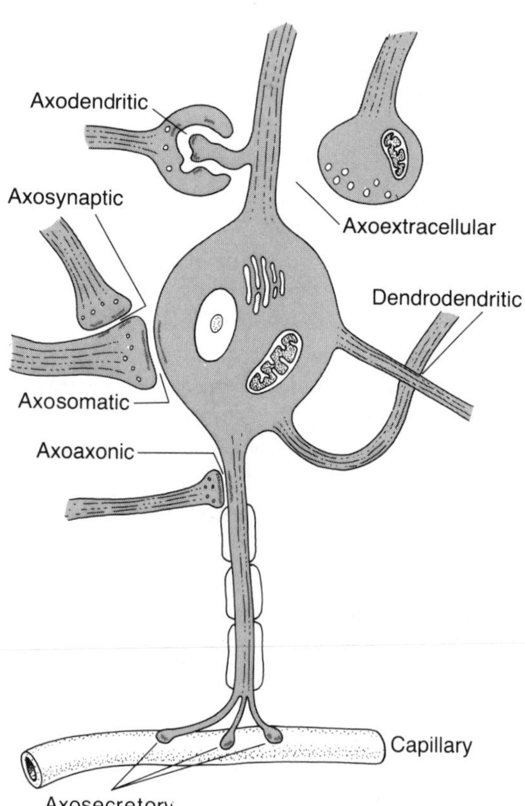

FIGURE 2-3. Types of terminals in the central nervous system.

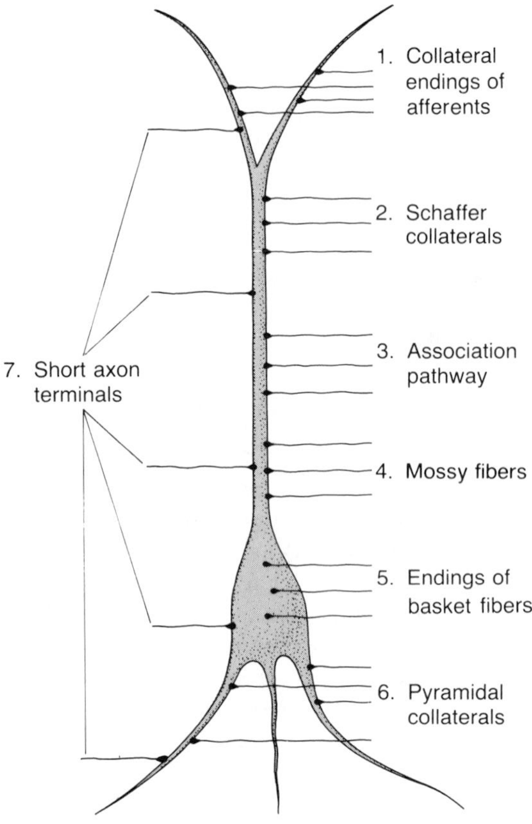

FIGURE 2-4. Segregation of inputs onto a single hippocampal pyramidal cell. (After Kandel and Schwartz, 1981.)

Third, incoming information, or inputs, onto neurons are often highly segregated. This segregation can be seen in the seven inputs onto a pyramidal cell of the hippocampal formation, illustrated in Figure 2-4. Six of these inputs are segregated on segments of the cell; the seventh makes nonsegregated contacts. It is thought that synapses to the cell body are potentially more influential than those on the periphery, as we shall see in the next section. The nonsegregated inputs probably have a general modulatory effect on the cell.

METHODS FOR ANATOMICAL STUDIES

Most of what is known about the anatomical organization of the brain depends upon staining its constituents so they can be visualy examined. Although anatomy is an old science, new techniques are being continually developed, and consequently knowledge about brain structure is continually evolving.

To understand how certain conclusions about brain organization and function are arrived at, it is helpful to understand some commonly used anatomical techniques. Tissue can be examined with the unaided eye but to see more structure in detail, a **light microscope** or an **electron microscope** is needed. A light microscope is the most commonly used microscope in biology laboratories. Tissue is placed on a glass slide and the slide is placed on a stand. Light is directed through the tissue while the observer looks through an eyepiece containing magnifying lenses. The light microscope allows tissue to be effectively magnified up to 1500 times. Light microscopes can be used in a number of versatile ways. Special light sources can be used so that fluorescent tissue can be seen. In addition television cameras can be incorporated into the microscope, allowing images to be taped or to be fed into a computer for quantitative analysis. For electron microscopy, tissue is stained with special substances that provide variable resistance to the passage of electrons. When electrons are beamed at the tissue, the tissue's variable absorption of the electrons can be visualized on a screen or on film. This technique provides detail down to a few Angstrom units (10^{-8} cm (centimeter)). A **scanning electron microscope (SEM)** uses a similar technique except that the beam of electrons is moved back and forth across the tissue. Magnification is somewhat less than that obtained with a conventional electron microscope, but objects can be visualized in three dimensions.

Since methods of staining are central to much of anatomy, a brief description of some of the more commonly used staining techniques is worthwhile. There are four major approaches. (1) Selective stains can be used to highlight features of cells; these include Nissl and myelin stains. (2) Stains can be used to highlight the entire neuron; these include Golgi methods and in vivo dye-injection methods. (3) Stains can be used to label degenerative and reactive processes following injury to tissue; these include the silver-staining methods. (4) Histochemical techniques can be used for mapping pathways or types of cells; these include histofluorescence methods, immunohistochemical techniques, techniques for staining various metals, and autoradiography.

Selective Stains

Franz Nissl, a 19th-century German neurologist, discovered that methylene blue, a dye obtained from distilled coal tar, could stain the cell bodies and glia of brain tissue. The DNA and RNA in the cell body that takes up the dye is known as Nissl substance. There are a number of **Nissl stains,** the most commonly used of which is cresyl violet. Nissl stains provide good definition of cell-rich areas and so highlight cortical cell layers as well as brainstem nuclei. In addition, they provide good identification of cells by body size and shape. Since Nissl stains highlight cell bodies, cell-poor areas, such as fiber tracts, are also highlighted by their absence of staining.

Myelin stains color the myelin sheaths surrounding axons and thus provide a way of highlighting fiber tracts in the brain. Practically speaking, they provide a contrasting view to that provided by Nissl stains. Nissl and myelin stains can be used together, a method called *counter-staining,* so that good definition of both cells and fibers can be obtained in the same tissue sample.

Golgi Stains and Dye Injections

It has been argued that no other technique has been so useful in understanding the geometry and organization of neural cells as the Golgi technique. The technique consists of soaking a small piece of tissue in a solution of potassium dichromate and osmic acid and then transferring it to a weak solution of silver nitrate. When the tissue is subsequently dehydrated and placed on a glass slide, some cells will have become impregnated with a dense precipitate of silver chromate so that they look black against a relatively clear background. The technique accentuates the shape and surface characteristics of an entire neuron, including the cell body and all of its projections. This technique is therefore useful for studying the structural characteristics of a neuron, including its size, shape, development, and dendritic arborization. A drawback of this method is its unpredictability. Only a few neurons are stained, and it is not known why, nor is it known how to predict or control staining.

The dye-injection methods include any method in which a substance is injected into neurons for the purpose of staining nerve cell bodies or projections. One of the most widely used dye procedures requires the injection of **horseradish peroxidase (HRP)** into living tissue. HRP is a **glycoprotein** containing a **heme group** that in the presence of hydrogen peroxide is able to catalyze the oxidation of certain compounds. This yields a visible reaction product within about three days that can vary from black to blue to orange. When injected into tissue, HRP can be incorporated by the cell body by terminals or by axons. It is also subject to **anterograde** (away from) or **retrograde transport** (toward the cell body). As a result, terminals, pathways, or select populations of cells can be labeled depending upon how the procedure is used. HRP can also be selectively injected into a single cell to highlight all of the features of that cell, including its axon, collaterals, and connections with other cells.

Cells send axon collaterals to many different targets, and until recently it was difficult to determine which cells send collaterals to which targets. A simple technique has been developed to double- or triple-label cells by injecting fluorescent dyes into their terminals. The dyes are taken up by the terminals and transported back to the cell body where they remain indefinitely. If different dyes (e.g., true blue, nuclear yellow, propidium iodide) are injected into various brain sites receiving axon collaterals from the same single cell located at some other site, the dyes will all be transported back to that cell's body. Each fluorescent dye requires a particular wavelength of light to be seen and also emits light at characteristic wavelengths. Thus, by using filters on a fluorescent microscope it is possible to identify each of the dyes in a single cell body.

Stains for Degenerative Processes

The reduced-silver methods were developed at the beginning of this century. In the 1930s it was discovered that these methods could be used to stain dying tissue. If a cell-rich area is damaged, its axons and their terminals degenerate. If this degeneration can be detected, then the region to which the damaged cell population projects, including its projection pathway and synaptic terminals, can be identified. There are a number of reduced-silver methods that involve soaking tissue in silver nitrate. These have been derived from the very successful Nauta silver technique. Because we do not understand why this reaction eventually stains the tissue, the choice of the method usually involves both luck and the development of an appropriate recipe. The advantage of the technique is that vast projection and terminal fields of a population of damaged neurons can be determined from the study of a single subject.

Histochemical Techniques

There are a number of **histochemical techniques** that include histofluorescence, immunohistochemistry, heavy-metal staining and autoradiographic 2-deoxyglucose and amino acid methods. The strength of the techniques is that they all identify neuronal populations that have some characteristic in common, including some chemical, metal, or shared activity at certain times.

In mammals, a number of related neurochemical transmitters can be identified by histofluorescence, and so any neurons that contain these transmitters can be localized to identify their distribution. Transmitters that can be identified include dopamine, norepinephrine, epinephrine, and serotonin. The **histofluorescent technique** involves exposing sections of dried tissue to formaldehyde in a gas-phase reaction. The amine transmitters (chemicals with NH_2 attached to them) react with the formaldehyde to produce a fluorescent compound. When the tissue is subsequently examined under a fluorescent microscope, cell bodies, axons, and terminals of the cells containing the transmitter can be seen. From this information, maps of the distribution of these transmitter systems can be constructed. The fluorescent color can be used to identify the compound: generally dopamine appears green, norepinephrine appears green yellow, and serotonin appears yellow.

Many macromolecules, particularly proteins and peptides, can be extracted from tissue and used as antigens, that is, tissue that when introduced into a suitable host will give rise to the formation of antibodies. Techniques have been developed that allow the production of antibodies to a wide variety of molecules and these can be used in **immunohistochemical staining.** If the antibodies are combined with a marker substance that produces a certain wavelength of light, they can be used subsequently to identify certain systems in the brain. For example the enzyme choline acetyltransferase produces the transmitter acetylcholine. If labeled antibodies specific for choline acetyltransferase are washed across brain tissue, they will combine with the enzyme. If the tissue is then examined under ultraviolet light, the parts of the brain and the cells containing the enzyme bound to the antibody can be identified. Since the enzyme is presumably located in neurons containing acetylcholine, these neurons can be selectively highlighted. Presumably, numerous systems in the brain can also be identified in this way. If the antibodies are made by cloning a single antibody, then the technique is referred to as a **monoclonial antibody** technique.

Autoradiography means "writing with one's own radiation." There are a number of autoradiography techniques, all of which involve marking a substance with a radioactive material and introducing the substance into the brain so that it is incorporated in the tissue. When the brain tissue is subsequently cut in sections and placed on a photographic film, the radioactivity exposes the film, giving a picture of the brain drawn by radioactivity intensity. The **2-deoxyglucose (2-DG)** technique involves injecting radioactive 2-DG into the bloodstream of an animal. The animal is then allowed to engage in some activity and the 2-DG is taken up by the brain cells as if it were normal glucose; the cells that are the most active take up the most 2-DG. Since 2-DG is not metabolized quickly, it remains in the cells. The brain can then be sectioned and used to produce pictures that indicate the most metabolically active brain areas. In a similar fashion other labeled substances, such as amino acids, can be introduced into the brain to be incorporated into certain tissue, which in turn can be processed to indicate the sites of incorporation.

THE NEURON'S ELECTRICAL ACTIVITY

Much of the pioneering research done on the neuron's electrical activity, such as the work of Hodgkin and Huxley, used the giant axon of the squid (not the giant squid), on the recommendation of the biologist Young. This axon measures up to a millimeter in diameter and is a hundred times larger than the axons of human nerve cells. The squid's axon is used to contract muscles that squirt water out the end of the squid's body, thereby propelling it through the water. Because effective propulsion requires all the muscles of the body to contract at the same time, the largest axons, which conduct the fastest, connect to the most distant muscles. Because of its size, the giant axon is easily removed from the squid by dissection and is easy to use in experiments on electric conduction in axons.

The Resting Potential

Neurons have a charge across their membrane. If a neuron is undisturbed, the charge remains relatively constant. This charge is called the **resting potential.** The following describes how it is maintained.

From high-school chemistry you know that if a salt is put into a liquid medium, it will dissolve into positive (+) and negative (−) ions, which will eventually become distributed equally throughout the solution. In distributing themselves, the ions respond to two forces, concentration and charge, and the equilibrium they reach represents an equal distribution of both these forces. The membrane of a nerve axon separates two fluid compartments, the intracellular and the extracellular, each of which contains many ions. Of these, negatively charged organic (An^-) and chlorine ions (Cl^-), and positively charged potassium (K^+) and sodium ions (Na^+) are particularly important in electric conduction. These ions would be equally distributed on both sides of the membrane if it did not act as a barrier to their easy passage. It does this in three ways:

1. It provides passive resistance to An^- ions because they are simply too large to pass through it; consequently, they are retained in the intracellular fluid.

2. It is semipermeable to the other ions, allowing some of them to pass through more freely than others. Normally, K^+ passes more freely than Na^+ (Na^+, although smaller than K^+, is bound more strongly to water molecules, which add to its bulk). The permeability of the membrane also changes in certain situations, allowing these ions to pass more freely through it at certain times than at others. In particular, the membrane contains Na^+ channels and K^+ channels, which close or open to control the flow of these ions.

3. The membrane contains a pumping system, or Na^+-K^+ pump, which exchanges intracellular Na^+ for extracellular K^+. Since the membrane is less permeable to Na^+ than to K^+, Na^+ accumulates on the outside of the membrane. Some K^+ flows back out of the cell when pumped, to equalize the K^+ concentration across the membrane. The unlimited outward flow of K^+ is checked, however, by the accumulating extracellular charge carried by the Na^+ (like charges repel each other).

As a result of the action of these three processes, there are 350 times as many An^- ions and 20 times as many K^+ ions on the inside of the cell membrane as on the outside, and 9 times as many Cl^- ions and 20 times as many Na^+ ions on the outside of the cell membrane as on the inside, resulting in a negative charge on the inside of the cell in the range of −75 mV (millivolts).

The Contribution of K^+ Ions. The concentrations of various substances in the intracellular fluid and in the extracellular fluid are known. These values can be used to perform the following imaginary experiment. We erect a nerve membrane and place the stuff of the intracellular fluid on one side of it. This material contains a 385 mmol (millimole) concentration of An^- ions and a 420 mmol concentration of K^+ ions. On the other side of the membrane we place a control fluid composed of large molecules that will not penetrate the membrane. Having done this, we then measure the voltage across the membrane by placing electrodes connected to a voltmeter on each side of it. At first we find that there is no charge across the membrane, but gradually a charge develops until the inside of the membrane is negative by about −75 mV relative to the outside. After this, there is no further change. If the concentrations of the substances on each side of the membrane are then measured, it is found that all of the An^- ions are still on the same side of the membrane; none have escaped. When we measure the K^+ ion concentration, we find that 20 mmol of K^+ ions have crossed the membrane. How and why did they cross? How did such a small change in K^+ ion distribution produce such a large voltage shift? Why did the voltage across the membrane stop changing at precisely this level?

The differential movement of ions across the membrane demonstrates that it is selectively permeable. Since there were no An^- ions placed on the outside portion of the membrane, An^- ions should have crossed to establish equal concentration on each side. Since they did not, the membrane is obviously impermeable to them. Since some K^+ ions did pass through the barrier, it must contain holes large enough to let them pass, but small enough to block the larger An^- ions. These holes have been called *K^+ channels*. The existence of these channels has been confirmed in another way. If tetraethylammonium (TEA) is placed on the membrane, no K^+ ions escape: TEA attaches to and blocks the K^+ ion channels.

To understand how a small change in K^+ ion concentration produces a large voltage, examine Figure 2-5. The cloud of positive (+) charges immediately outside the surface of the membrane represent the K^+ ions that have leaked across the membrane. The negative (—) charges immediately inside represent the An^- ions that could not cross the barrier. Note that the charge difference has accumulated only on the membrane: all other intracellular and extracellular fluid is in equilibrium. Thus, a small movement in K^+ ions creates a large transmembrane charge because the voltage different is focused only on the surface of the membrane. It has been found that a difference of about 1200 charged ions across a square micrometer of membrane will produce a charge difference of 10 mV.

Figure 2-5 also shows why K^+ ions did not continue to leak across the membrane. A point was reached at which the concentration gradient pulling K^+ ions out of the cell was balanced by an electrostatic pressure that pulled them back in.

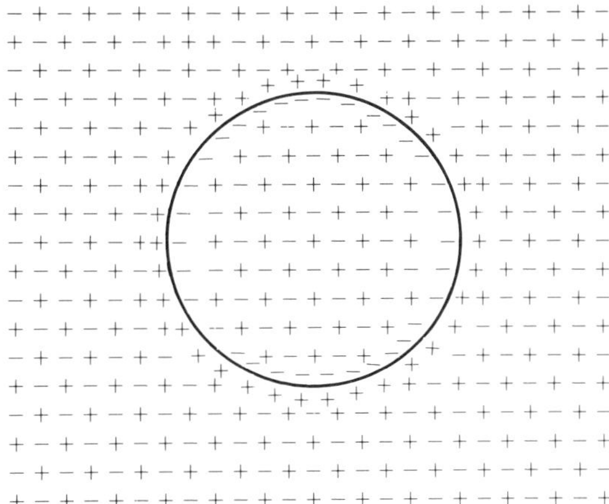

FIGURE 2-5. The net excess of positive charges outside the membrane of a nerve cell at rest represents a small fraction of the total number of ions inside and outside the cell. (After Kandel and Schwartz, 1981.)

When this equilibrium was reached, they stopped their migration. If you like, the negative charges on the An^- ions held back any further escape of the positive charges on the K^+ ions. Actually, in 1902, without performing this experiment, Julius Bernstein used an equation called the Nernst equation to predict the K^+ ion potential across the membrane. In the 1940s, when the experiment became feasible and was performed, it partly confirmed Bernstein's calculation.

The Contribution of Na^+ Ions to the Membrane Potential. The experimental investigations of the 1940s did not quite confirm Bernstein's calculation of the K^+ ion potential. The calculated potential was accurate for glial cells, but apparently something else was contributing to the membrane's charge. The something else turned out to be Na^+ ions. Calculations of extracellular fluid concentrations show that there is a 440 mmol concentration of Na^+ ions in the extracellular fluid and only a 50 mmol concentration in the intracellular fluid. Thus, the membrane was in some way controlling the concentration of Na^+. Experimental work using TEA has demonstrated that the Na^+ ions do not pass through the K^+ ion channels, because TEA does not block their inward flow. This result suggests that Na^+ ions have their own channels, a conclusion confirmed by the finding that *tetrodotoxin* (pufferfish poison) blocks the permeability of the membrane to Na^+ ions. As we have noted above, K^+ ions stop flowing out of the cell because their movement is opposed by the electrostatic pressure created by their outward flow across the membrane. Obviously, the inward flow of Na^+ ions can redress this situation. If there were no other checks, Na^+ ions would continue their inward flow, K^+ ions would continue to flow out, and the charge on the membrane would quickly dissipate. Something must intervene to prevent the unchecked inward flow of Na^+ ions.

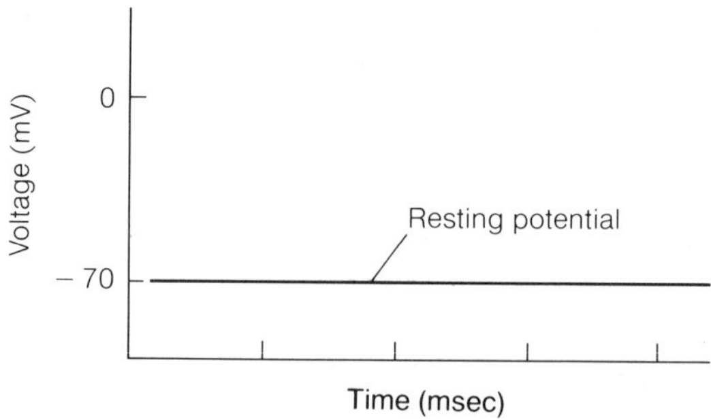

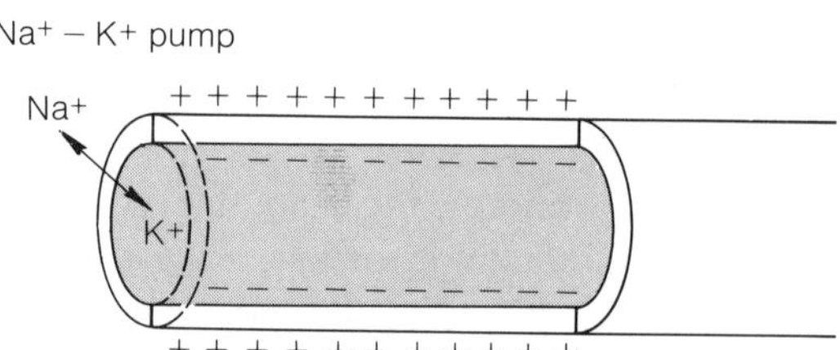

FIGURE 2-6. The nerve membrane, because of its permeability and through the action of the Na^+-K^+ pump, accumulates a charge, the inside of the membrane being negative with respect to the outside. This charge is about −70 mV and is called the resting potential.

The Na^+-K^+ Pump. If Na^+ ions continued to leak into the cell, they would eventually balance the outward flow of K^+ ions and reestablish equilibrium: the charge across the membrane would dissipate. Since this does not occur, it was suggested that the membrane contains "pumps" that pump Na^+ ions back out of the cell. Present theory holds that there is a Na^+-K^+ pump that expels Na^+, exchanging three Na^+ ions for every two K^+ ions. The K^+ ions, of course, quickly leak back out, but the Na^+ ions only slowly leak back in. The important result is that in the squid axon a charge of slightly less than −60 mV is maintained across the membrane. The operation of the Na^+-K^+ pump requires energy. It has been possible to demonstrate that its operation can be arrested with such metabolic poisons as *dinitrophenol* and *ouabain.*

To this point, we have not considered the contribution of Cl^-. Chlorine ions are free to cross the membrane passively. As a result, they respond to chemical and electrical gradients and do not affect the transmembrane potential established by the actively distributed Na^+ and K^+ ions.

Figure 2-6 shows a sketch of the charge across the membrane of an axon and a graph of the transmembrane voltage over time. The voltage across the membrane is about −70 mV in mammalian nerves (the level actually varies between −55 and −90 mV in different animals). Provided that the membrane is undisturbed, the charge across the membrane will remain at that level indefinitely. This stable transmembrane potential is called the **resting potential.**

Stimulation

There are, of course, normal influences on the cell that change the voltage of the membrane in systematic ways. In addition, a wide variety of external (abnormal) agents, such as electric currents and chemicals, and irritation from manual displacement or foreign tissue, can also produce changes in the membrane's voltage. The normal processes provide the mechanisms for the normal functioning of the cell; the other processes more generally lead to various types of pathology. Despite these differences, both the normal and the abnormal influences act in very much the same way; thus, any influence or irritation that leads to a change in the voltage can be called a **stimulus,** and the process, whether normal or abnormal, can be called **stimulation.** In experimental situations stimulation is usually provided by giving brief electric pulses to the axon through small wires called *stimulating electrodes.* The response of the axon is then recorded by measuring its voltage change with a voltmeter or oscilloscope attached to the axon by small wires called *recording electrodes.*

Passive Properties of a Neuron

When an axon or a neuron is electrically stimulated, the voltage across the membrane changes. Depending on the type of stimulation, the transmembrane potential can become larger or smaller. These changes are usually restricted to the area of tissue stimulated; that is, the effect decays over distance (in the same way that a wave decays in size as it moves away from the point where a stone is dropped into the water). The changes are also quite brief. Because they are produced by the action of an external agent and not by the spontaneous actions of the membrane, these changes are called *passive changes.* The rate of decay and the duration of the changes are determined by properties of the axon that are referred to as its *cable properties.* These will not be discussed here. If stimulation produces a change that decreases the transmembrane voltage, the membrane is said to have become depolarized. If stimulation produces a change that increases the transmembrane voltage, the membrane is said to have become hyperpolarized. **Depolarization** is thought to be due to increased inward movement of Na^+ ions, whereas **hyperpolarization** is thought to be due to increased outward movement of K^+ ions or to increased inward Cl^- movement. This suggests that stimulation, whether chemical or electrical, regulates ion flow by opening or closing channels in the membrane to decrease or increase ion movement.

The Action Potential

Although the neuron's membrane responds to weak stimulation by decreasing its permeability to ions in a relatively orderly way, it undergoes a peculiar change of behavior if the stimulation is sufficiently intense to cause the transmembrane voltage to depolarize to about −50 mV. At about this voltage the membrane becomes completely permeable to Na^+; that is, Na^+ rushes into the cell until the voltage across the membrane falls through 0 mV and even reverses to about +50 mV. The sudden permeability of the membrane occurs independently of any further stimulation once the membrane has depolarized to about −50 mV. The change in permeability is quite brief, about half a millisecond, after which the Na^+ channels inactivate. At this time also, the membrane becomes permeable to K^+, which flows out along both a chemical and an electrostatic gradient. The flow of K^+ ions restores and even overshoots the original resting potential. At this point the membrane again becomes resistant to the flow of a Na^+ ions.

Following this sudden change the resting potential of the membrane is restored. In addition, the nerve can undergo many similar successive changes. The voltage at which the membrane undergoes this autonomous change is called its **threshold.** The sudden reversal of polarity and the restoration of the resting potential is called an **action potential.** The process is displayed graphically in Figure 2-7. One can say, therefore, that the threshold for eliciting an action potential is −50 mV.

What triggers the action potential? Hodgkin and Huxley have suggested that the ion conductance channels are controlled by "gates" embedded in the membrane. An example of such a gate is illustrated in Figure 2-8. In Figure 2-8*A,* the charges across the membrane during a resting po-

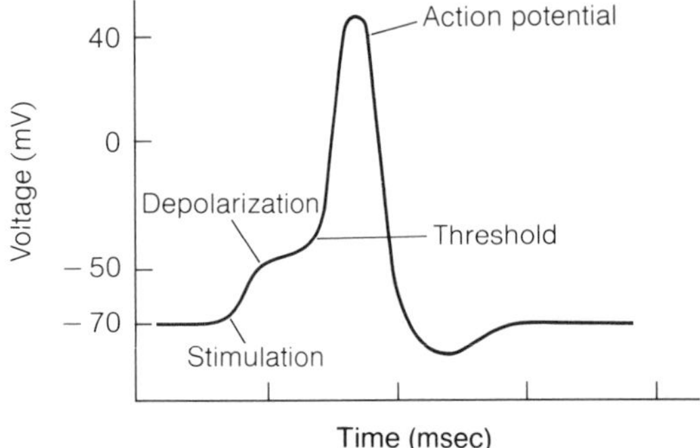

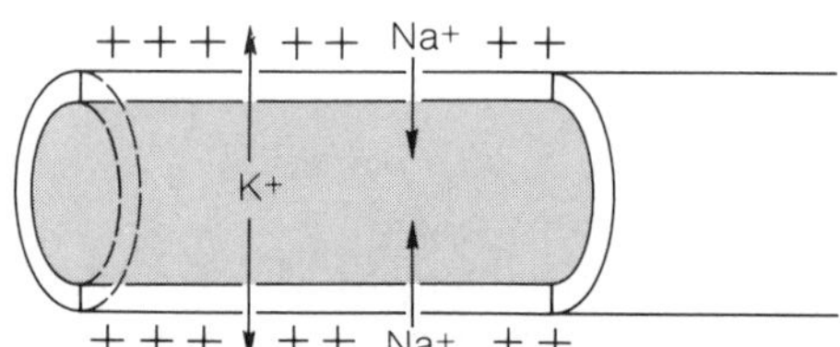

FIGURE 2-7. Stimulation of the membrane causes it to become more permeable to Na^+ ions. As a result the transmembranous potential declines, or depolarizes. At about −50 mV, its threshold, the membrane becomes completely permeable and its charge momentarily reverses. At this point K^+ ions flow out of the cell, restoring the transmembranous potential. This sequence of changes is represented by the peak on the graph called an action potential.

tential attract the charges on the gating molecule, thereby blocking the sodium channel. In Figure 2-8*B,* stimulation reverses the membrane charge. This reversal, in turn repels the charge on the gating molecule, flipping open the Na^+ ion gate to permit the inward flow of sodium ions. According to this model the stimulus required to reverse the membrane voltage, opening a gate, would be an adequate stimulus for producing an action potential. The threshold for the action potential would be the actual voltage at which the gate flipped open.

Conduction of the Nerve Impulse

When an action potential occurs in a region of the nerve membrane, it acts as a stimulus, causing adjacent portions of the membrane to increase their permeability and undergo a similar voltage change. Consequently, an action potential triggered at one end of an axon will be conducted along its length. (Action potentials can travel in either direction, but they normally begin at the cell body and travel away from it.) This movement of the action potential along the length of the axon, shown in Figure 2-9, is called a **nerve impulse** (or, more colorfully and descriptively, *firing* or

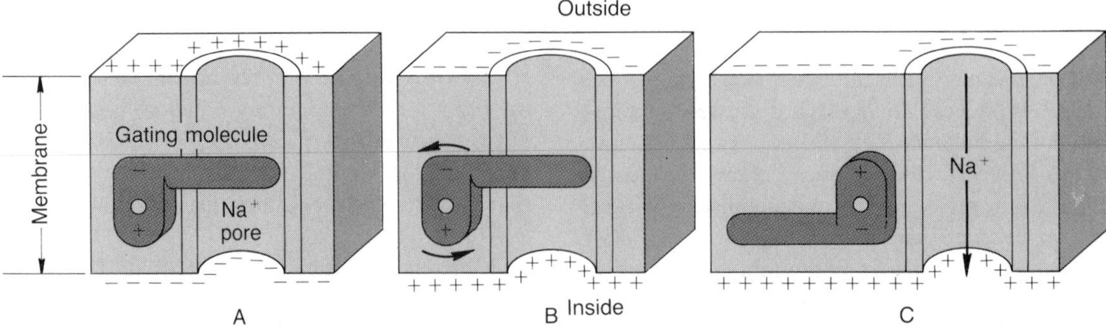

FIGURE 2-8. Hypothetical explanation for molecular events that underlie gating currents. *A.* Active membrane channel of a nerve cell at rest. *B.* Membrane changes during depolarization to open the gate. *C.* Na^+ ions freely cross the membrane. (After Kandel and Schwartz, 1981.)

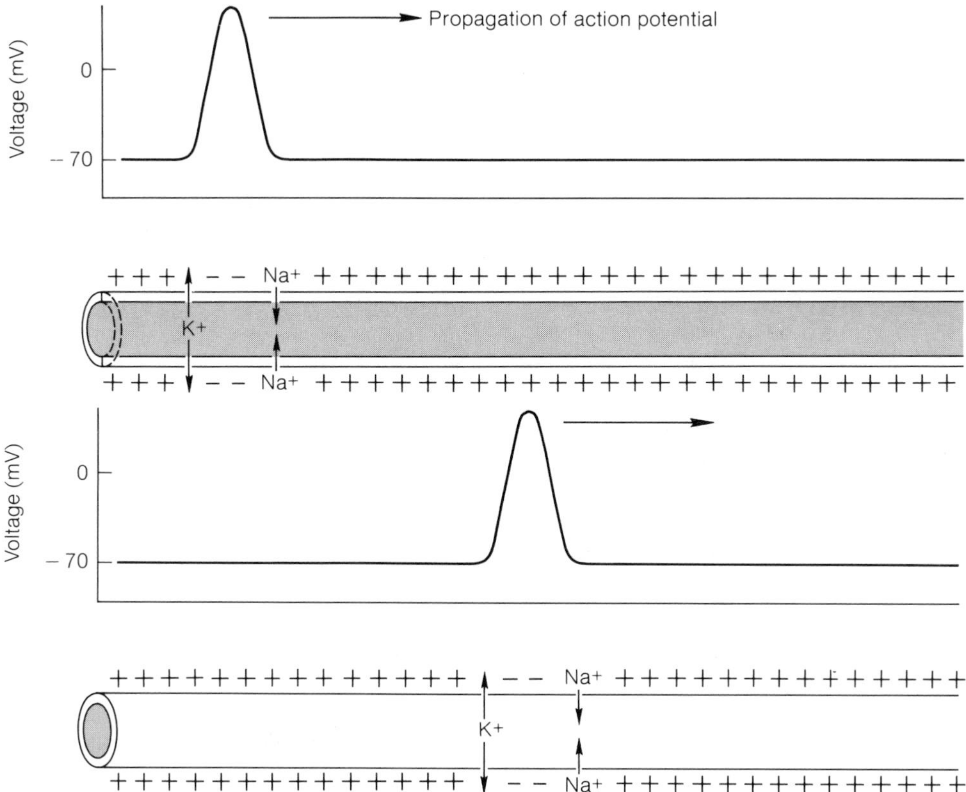

FIGURE 2-9. Because an action potential at one part of the axon stimulates adjacent areas of the axon to produce one, the action potential is propagated along the axon. (After Katz, 1972.)

discharging). The rate at which the impulse travels along the axon, varying from 1 to 100 m/sec (meters per second), is quite slow, but neurons can sustain a wide range of firing rates. Usually they fire fewer than 100 times a second, but they can fire as frequently as 1000 times per second.

The All-or-None Law

A peculiar property of a neuron's behavior is that its threshold is stable, and generally every action potential, and hence every nerve impulse, once triggered has an identical threshold and height. Also, once the nerve impulses are initiated, they require no further stimulus; the neuron provides all the energy required to maintain them. These properties of the neuron's behavior are formulated in the "all-or-none law": action potentials either occur or they do not; there is no in-between condition. Like most laws about the nervous system, there are exceptions to the all-or-none law. Some neurons can produce cascades of action potentials that successively decline in amplitude and so do not obey portions of the law.

Factors Determining Nerve Impulse Speed

The nerve impulse does not travel at exactly the same speed in all neurons. At least two factors affect speed. One is resistance to current along the axon. Impulse speed increases as resistance decreases, and resistance is most effectively decreased by an increase in axon size. Therefore, large axons conduct at a faster rate than small ones. Were the nervous system to rely only on this procedure, axons would have to be cumbersomely large. An alternative procedure has evolved that uses the glial cells to aid in speeding propagation. Schwann cells in the peripheral nervous system and oligodendroglia in the central nervous system wrap around some axons, forming a compact sheath of **myelin** (from the Greek, meaning marrow) against the cell membrane. Between each glial cell the membrane of the axon is exposed by a gap called a *node of Ranvier.* (See Figure 2-10.) In these myelinated axons the nerve impulse jumps along the axon from node to node, a type of conduction called **saltatory conduction** (from the Latin, meaning skip). Saltatory conduction is an extremely effective way of speeding the impulse because a small myelinated axon can conduct an impulse as rapidly as an unmyelinated axon 30 times as large.

The presence of myelin also conserves energy. Since the myelin prevents current flow along most of the length of the axon, the metabolic processes required for maintaining the resting potential need only be maintained at the nodes of Ranvier. Given the role of myelin, the devastating consequences of multiple sclerosis or Guillain-Barré disease, which cause demyelination, can be appreciated.

The Origin of the Nerve Impulse

Graded Potentials. So far we have described the events that occur on an axon when it is stimulated. What happens on dendrites, which are normally the origin of the cell's electrical activity? Dendrites have a membrane similar to the axons' and a similar resting potential; they also undergo changes in potential when they are stimulated. But unlike the axon, the dendrites do not produce action potentials. If a dendrite is stimulated, the voltage changes from the resting potential in proportion to the intensity of the stimulation; the change then spreads along the dendrite away from the point of stimulation, getting smaller with dis-

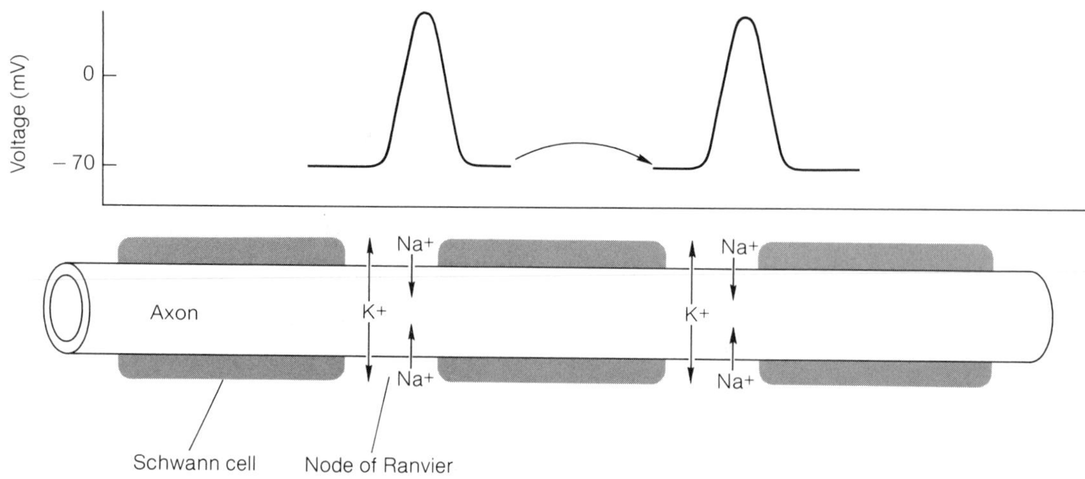

FIGURE 2-10. The nerve impulse jumps from one inter-Schwann cell space, called a node of Ranvier, to the next. This process, saltatory conduction, greatly speeds impulse transmission.

tance. These dendritic voltage changes are called **graded potentials,** and they can occur as a decrease (depolarization) or an increase (hyperpolarization) in transmembrane voltage, depending on the nature of the stimulation. How each of these occurs will be discussed after we have described how graded potentials trigger the nerve impulse on the axon.

Spatial and Temporal Summation. Because dendrites respond to stimulation with graded potentials, they have some interesting properties. If a dendrite is stimulated at two points in close proximity, the graded potentials produced at each point will add. If the two stimuli are identical, the graded potential will be larger than would occur with only one stimulus. If the two stimuli are given at widely different points on the dendrite, the graded potentials will dissipate before they reach each other and will not add. Stimuli given at intermediate distances will produce additive graded potentials, but only at the points that receive the potentials from both sources. Also, the potentials will be smaller because they decay with distance. Similar rules apply when one stimulus hyperpolarizes the membrane and one depolarizes it, with the difference that the graded potentials subtract. This property of adjacent graded potentials to add and subtract is called **spatial summation.**

Another type of change that can occur on dendrites is called **temporal summation.** The graded potential of a stimulated dendrite will decay with time after the stimulus has terminated. A second stimulus given some time later at the same site will produce a similar response. If the second stimulus is given soon after the first, the potentials will add, becoming larger than either is alone. The strength of the graded potential will be determined by the strength of the two stimuli and the interval between them. If one stimulus hyperpolarizes the membrane and the other depolarizes it, then the two stimuli will subtract, and the graded potential will decrease in size accordingly.

If the features of spatial and temporal summation of graded potentials are considered, it is possible to see how the nerve impulse is generated. Recall that the threshold for an action potential is −50 mV. If the dendritic system is influenced so that it is depolarized to −50 mV, and if this graded potential spreads over the cell body to a point adjacent to the axon, then the necessary conditions for eliciting an action potential will be met. In fact, the point of transition between the cell body and the axon, called the axon hillock (Figure 2-1), is the site where the nerve impulse originates. As long as this area is depolarized below −50 mV by the spread of graded potentials, the cell will fire. However, if the graded potentials are not sufficiently strong to depolarize the axon hillock to the threshold, the cell will not fire. Thus, the origin of axonal firing can be traced to the influence of graded potentials from the dendrites of the cell. If the location of the axon hillocks is considered, it can be understood why synapses close to it will be the most influential in producing action potentials.

SYNAPTIC TRANSMISSION

The Origin of Graded Potentials: The Synapse, EPSPs, and IPSPs

It is now widely accepted that neurons communicate chiefly through the agency of the chemicals they release when they fire. These chemicals, known as **neurotransmitters,** are released by the terminals of the neuron.

Figure 2-11 is a diagram of synapse. The terminal is separated from other neurons by a very small space called the **synaptic cleft.** The membrane of the terminal is called the **presynaptic membrane,** and the membrane it synapses with is called the **postsynaptic membrane.** Penetrating the terminal from the axon are microtubules, which may transport precursor chemicals for the manufacture of neurotransmitters into the terminal. There are also *mitochondria* in the terminal which provide energy for metabolic processes. In

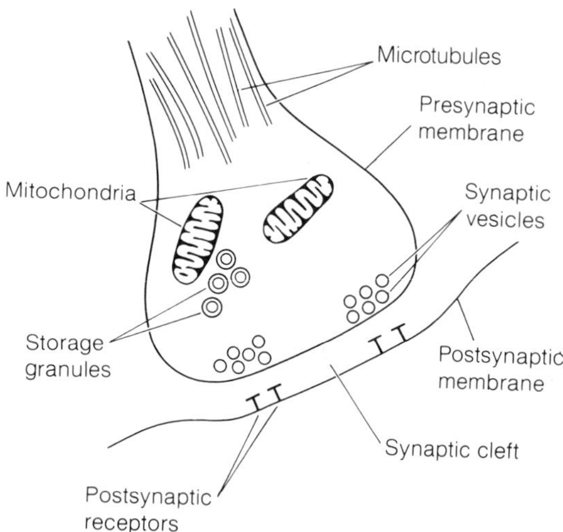

FIGURE 2-11. Diagram of the major features of a synapse.

addition there are two types of vesicles in the terminal: **storage granules,** which are presumed to be long-term storage sites for neurotransmitters, and **synaptic vesicles,** which hold neurotransmitters for immediate use. On the postsynaptic membrane there are specialized proteins that act as **receptors** for the neurotransmitter. The synapse functions in the following way. When a neuron fires, some synaptic vesicles release their neurotransmitter chemical into the synaptic space. The neurotransmitter binds weakly to the receptors on the postsynaptic membrane, after which it is either quickly washed away by extracellular fluid and destroyed or taken back into the presynaptic membrane for reuse.

At this point, we should pause briefly to note that there is quite a long delay, about 0.5 msec (millisecond), in getting a message across a synapse. Only part of this time is taken up by the diffusion of the transmitter across the synaptic space. The greater portion of time is required to release the transmitter from the terminal in the first place. Terminals contain a large number of Ca^{2+} channels. The action potential opens these, so that Ca^{2+} ions enter the terminal. It is their entry that facilitates the release of the neurotransmitter by the synaptic vesicles into the synaptic cleft. There is a close relation between the amount of Ca^{2+} that enters the terminal and the amount of transmitter released.

Eccles stimulated the axons of presynaptic neurons while recording from a postsynaptic cell body in order to clarify how neurotransmitters (released by the firing of a presynaptic neuron) produce graded potentials in a postsynaptic neuron. Postsynaptic graded potentials followed each volley of presynaptic stimulation. These postsynaptic potentials, or PSPs, had a very small amplitude, 1 to 3 mV, but depending on which presynaptic axons were stimulated, they consisted either of depolarization or hyperpolarization of the postsynaptic membrane. Because depolarizing PSPs of course increase the probability of the neuron firing, they are called **excitatory postsynaptic potentials,** or **EPSPs,** and because hyperpolarizing potentials decrease the probability of the neuron firing, they are called **inhibitory postsynaptic potentials,** or **IPSPs.** It is now accepted that the EPSPs and IPSPs are produced by the action of neurotransmitters on the postsynaptic receptors of the cell. Neurotransmitters from certain synapses, called **excitatory neurotransmitters,** are responsible for EPSPs, whereas other neurotransmitters, called **inhibitory neurotransmitters,** are responsible for IPSPs. Eccles suggests that excitatory neurotransmitters produce EPSPs by making the membrane slightly more permeable to Na^+, which enters the cell, lowering the transmembrane voltage. Inhibitory neurotransmitters, on the other hand, make the membrane more permeable to K^+ and Cl^- ions; K^+ flows out and Cl^- flows into the cell, raising the transmembrane voltage.

The origin of the graded potentials of dendrites can be traced to the release and action of neurotransmitters from the terminals of other neurons. There are thousands of terminals synapsing with the dendrites and cell body of any one neuron, and the summed graded potential of the cell is produced by the action of all these inputs. The integration of these inputs by spatial and temporal summation determines whether the neuron will fire or not. If EPSPs predominate, and if there are enough of them to produce depolarization to threshold at the axon hillock, the neuron will fire. If IPSPs predominate, the neuron will not fire.

ANALYZING THE BRAIN THROUGH ITS ELECTRICAL ACTIVITY

The Integration of Neural Activity and Information Processing

The dendritic system of the neuron sums the activity from many other neurons by producing graded potentials that will determine whether or not the neuron fires. The firing of the neuron is an all-or-none response that continues for as long as the firing threshold of the axon hillock is maintained.

Because the activity of nerve cells has an electrochemical basis, it can be recorded with instruments sensitive to small changes in electrical activity. The several techniques for so recording the brain's electrical activity include (1) intracellular and extracellular unit recording, (2) electroencephalographic (EEG) recording, and (3) evoked potential (EP) recording. Relating each of these types of activity to behavior can be used as a way of determining the function and normality of particular brain areas.

Unit Recording. If small wires or pipettes containing an ionized conducting solution are inserted into the brain so that their tips are placed in or near a nerve cell, the changes in a single cell's electrical potentials, that is, its **unit activity,** can be recorded relative to some indifferent electrode or ground. *Intracellular recordings* are made from electrodes with very tiny tips, less than 0.001 mm in diameter, which are placed in the cell; *extracellular recordings,* on the other hand, are made when an electrode tip is placed adjacent to one cell or a number of cells. Both techniques require amplification of the signal and some type of display. The cell's activity is either displayed on an oscilloscope for photographing or recorded on audio tape for computer analysis. In many experiments the signal is played through a loudspeaker so that cell firing is heard as a beep or pop. Both recording techniques require considerable skill because it is difficult to place the electrode in or sufficiently close to the cell without killing it, and once a cell is "captured," it is often difficult to hold it for more than a few minutes or hours before the signal is lost.

Unit recording techniques provide a particularly interesting insight into the brain's function. For example, cell records obtained from the visual cortex of cats and monkeys reveal that each cell has a preferred stimulus and a preferred response pattern. Some cells fire in response to horizontal lines, others to diagonal lines, and still others fire only in response to lines that are oriented in a special way and that also move in a particular direction. In the rat, cells have been found in the hippocampus that only become active when an animal is in a certain spatial location. Unit recoding techniques have also been used to analyze such abnormal cell activity as occurs in epilepsy. In epilepsy, the activity of cells becomes synchronized in an abnormal pattern, and an understanding of epilepsy depends in part on analyzing and controlling this feature of the cell's behavior. Much of the information obtained with unit recordings initially came from experiments performed on anesthetized animals. Contemporary work features the study of freely moving animals and is directed toward describing the relation between cell activity and ongoing behavior.

EEG Recording. A simple technique for recording the electrical activity of the brain was developed in the early 1930s by Hans Berger. He found that it was possible to record "brain waves" from the scalp. These waves, called **electroencepha-**

lograms, or **EEGs,** have proved to be a valuable tool for studying events such as sleep, for monitoring depth of anesthesia, and for diagnosing epilepsy and brain damage.

To record a person's EEG a small metal disk is attached to the scalp to detect the electrical activity of neurons in the underlying brain area. The electrical changes recorded on the scalp are rather small, usually much less than a millivolt, and so they are amplified for display on an oscilloscope or on a paper chart recorder called an *electroencephalograph.*

Although the electrical activity recorded from the scalp represents the sum of all neural activity, action potentials, graded potentials, and so forth it is mostly the measure of the graded potentials of dendrites. As a result, it represents the summed dendritic activity of thousands of nerve cells and can only be considered a rather general measure of the brain's activity. Although it can be used as a crude index of the brain's level of excitation, it tells very little about the activity of single cells as such. During a given EEG pattern any particular single cell may be active or inactive.

Bland and his colleagues have studied the relation between graded potentials and unit activity recorded from the same microelectrode in the dentate gyrus (part of the hippocampus) of freely moving rabbits (see Figure 2-12). In this example the rabbit is walking. The technique of recording both types of activity simultaneously from one electrode is made possible by the fact that they have different frequency ranges. The frequency of the rhythmic waves, or graded potentials, is slow, about 4 to 7 cps (cycles per second). The unit discharge is fast, each lasting about 2 msec. When the line carrying the electric signal is split and the slow waves are filtered out of one of the lines, the unit activity is seen. The top trace of Figure 2-12 displays the rhythmic graded potentials characteristic of the cells in the hippocampus. The bottom trace shows the action potentials, or unit activity, recorded from one of these cells. Even a casual glance at the figure shows that there is an important relation between the EEG activity and the unit activity. The unit activity occurs in bursts when the dendrites depolarize. If the graded potentials increase in amplitude, the cell may fire more frequently with each burst; if the frequency of the EEG rhythm speeds up, the bursts of unit activity will occur more frequently. In this way the graded potentials time, or pace, the unit activity. It is thought that the "information" transmitted by cells such as these is coded in terms of burst frequency, number of unit discharges per burst, the interunit discharge interval, and so forth. (Note: In this figure the electrical activity is recorded from an electrode placed just outside the cell, and so the wave amplitude and polarity are different from those described for squid axons, in which the electrodes were placed across the cell membrane.)

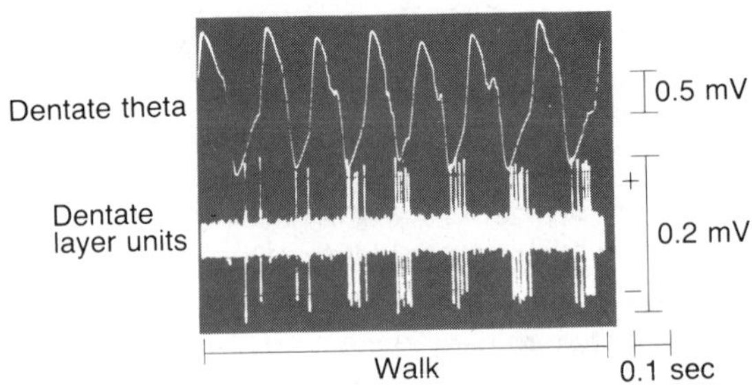

FIGURE 2-12. Dentate layer theta cells and simultaneous slow waves from the same electrode during freely moving behavior of the rabbit. Note the rhythmic slow wave *(theta)* activity and rhythmic cell discharges that occur during walking and that the cells discharge at the negative peak of the theta waves. (Courtesy of B. H. Bland.)

It is now thought that the nervous system works by a combination of analogue (how much) and digital, or binary (yes-no), principles. Analogue functions are a property of the dendritic system and its graded potentials and their unit activity; digital functions are a property of the axons. We can see how these principles determine behavior if we return to the opening description of the male Grayling butterfly's behavior. Recall Tinbergen's suggestion that in the male butterfly's nervous system there is a pooling station that integrates the different features (dark, large, and irregular) of a stimulus object to determine whether or not the male will approach it. Theoretically, all the male butterfly's behavior could be accounted for by the activity of one central neuron. The dendrites of that neuron would serve as the pooling station and the axon would be the system that initiates an approach response. If three channels of input converge on the dendrites (one signaling darkness, one size, and one movement), simultaneous activity in the separate channels signaling dark, large, and irregular would produce EPSPs that when summed would trigger axonal firing and thus approach by the male butterfly. Activity in only one channel might not be sufficient to fire the neuron; activity in two channels might be sufficient to produce a response if input in each were particularly intense. At any rate, it can be seen that the analogue function of the dendrites will integrate the various sources of input, and the digital activity of the axon will determine whether or not approach is to occur. Of course, the analogue feature of dendritic integration can be put to many uses, and the digital properties of the axon can be expressed in many codes (frequency, pattern of firing, etc.).

Many other factors contribute to information processing. Synapses close to the axon hillock may influence cell firing because of their proximity. Inhibition or excitation by more distal axosynaptic connections may allow for more subtle control of intercellular communication. Some synapses may also change structurally with use or disuse, thus becoming increasingly or decreasingly effective in communicating. These factors are beyond the scope of the present discussion, but they are important to the brain's synthesizing and storage abilities.

Human EEG

It was originally thought that each cytoarchitectonic area of the brain had its own pattern of EEG activity, but it is now recognized that variations in activity do not correlate closely with cytoarchitectonic areas. Figure 2-13 shows the characteristic resting rhythms obtained from different parts of the human cortex. These patterns are obtained when the person is awake, resting quietly, with eyes closed. The dominant rhythm of the posterior cortex is an 8 to 12 cps wave form, also called the **alpha rhythm.** The dominant rhythm of the precentral and postcentral sensorimotor area is a 20 to 25 cps **beta rhythm.** The secondary frontal areas have a 17 to 20 cps beta rhythm. And the tertiary frontal area has 8 to 12 cps beta waves. The resting rhythms are replaced by low-voltage fast activity, or **desynchronization,** when the areas of brain are in an active mode. For example, in Figure 2-13 the alpha rhythm of the occipital (visual) cortex desynchronizes when the eyes are open. Penfield and Jasper have recorded from the motor cortex (area 4) while it was exposed during a surgical procedure. They found its EEG activity desynchronized during voluntary movement, such as arm movement. In some cases desynchronization was restricted to the cortical area representing the part of the body that was moved; for example, moving the hand desynchronized only the EEG in the hand area.

Human EEG activity changes in a characteristic way during transitions from sleep to wakefulness (Figure 2-14). Generally, rhythms become slower in frequency and larger in amplitude as a person falls asleep. Large-amplitude slow waves are also present during coma and during anesthesia induced by some drugs; they can also appear in areas of the brain that have been subjected to trauma. A good rule of thumb in interpreting EEG activity is that when the brain is in an active mode, the desynchronized patterns occur, whereas when it is in an inactive mode, the slower, larger-amplitude patterns occur. Sometimes this rule is not easy to apply because it becomes difficult to define *active* (does it mean movement or sensory responsiveness?). Another factor making EEG interpretation difficult is that waveforms that appear visually

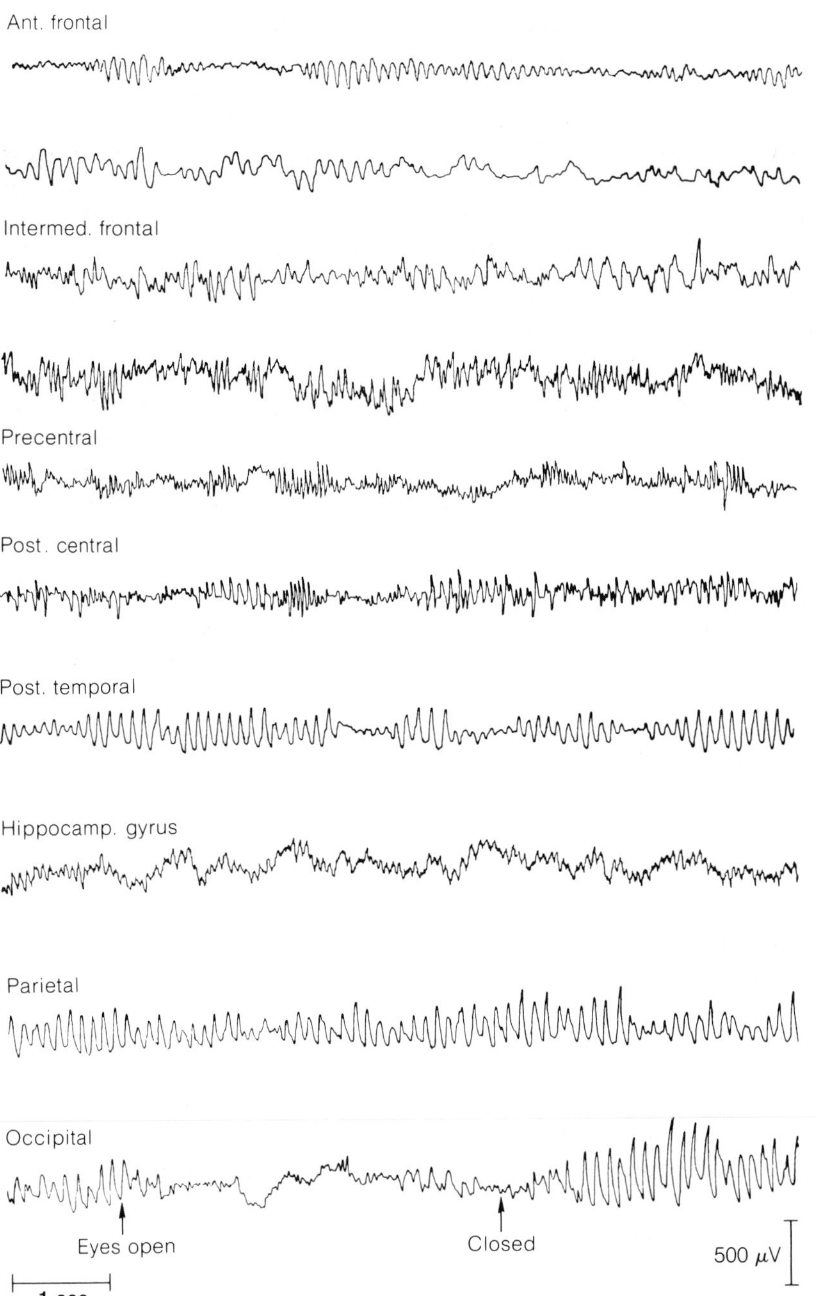

FIGURE 2-13. Spontaneous electrical activity, or resting rhythms, from different human cortical areas. Sample tracings were taken directly from the exposed cortex with bipolar silver chloride cotton-wick electrodes. (From W. Penfield and H. H. Jasper, Copyright © 1954. Reprinted with permission.)

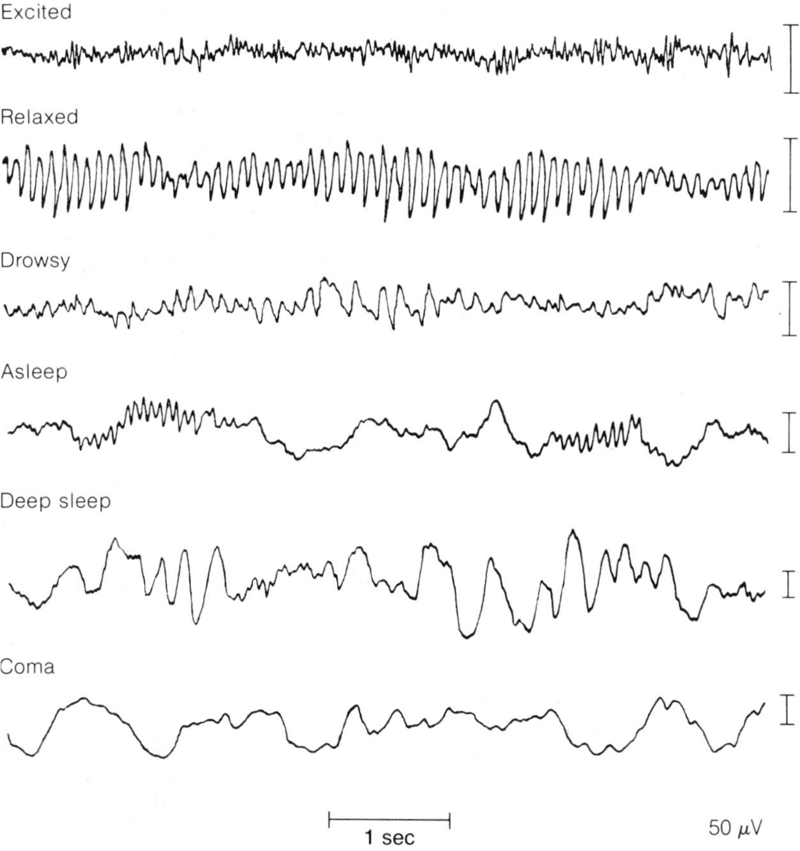

FIGURE 2-14. Characteristic EEG recorded during various behavioral states in humans. (From W. Penfield and H. H. Jasper, Copyright © 1954. Reprinted by permission.)

similar can have quite different pharmacological causes. For example, desynchronized EEG activity can be recorded from people in chronic states of coma. It may look exactly like the EEG activity recorded from an awake, alert, moving individual, yet be biochemically different. For people interested in pursuing the question of the relations between EEG activity and behavior, the classic view is illustrated succinctly by Figure 2-14. Vanderwolf and Robinson, in a very readable review, suggest that EEGs change with behavior and not with "behavioral state," as is illustrated in Figure 2-14. They would, for example, replace "excited" with "talking," "relaxed" with "eyes closed," "drowsy" with "lying still," and so on.

Electroencephalography is used clinically to detect malfunctioning brain areas, and so it is useful for diagnosing epilepsy, or for locating brain lesions or tumors. Large-amplitude spike-and-wave activity may indicate the presence of epilepsy, and slow waves in a behaviorally alert individual may indicate brain damage. (Figure 7-6 shows some abnormal EEG waves recorded from epileptics.) Although the EEG is only a general measure of the brain's activity, rather sophisticated averaging procedures have been developed to localize areas that generate abnormal EEG activity.

Evoked Potentials

Evoked potentials, or **EPs,** consist of a short train of large slow waves and are like the EEG in that they are recorded from the scalp and largely reflect the activity of dendrites. But they occur only under special conditions. If a bright light or noise is presented very briefly, say for 250 msec, electrodes placed on the cortex will record a large slow wave that is clearest and largest over the area of cortex processing the sensory event. For example, in the case of a bright light, the EP will be largest over the visual cortex. Since these potentials vary somewhat in their actual size and shape, it is customary to average several together to obtain an accurate estimate of the "typical" EP. This average is often called an **AEP,** or **average evoked potential.** The evoked potential technique is very tricky because the size of the EP can be influenced by many variables. In animals, the most important variable seems to be movement, for the magnitude of the evoked potential may vary according to what the animal is doing. Movements that affect EP size may be as small and subtle as eye movements or changes in respiration. Nevertheless, the EP is considered by some people to be a useful indicator of the brain's activity in processing information.

Electrical Stimulation

Electrical stimulation of the brain requires some mention at this time because it is an efficient way of activating neurons. Usually a fine, insulated wire with an uninsulated tip is placed in the brain so that the tip lies in a predetermined location.

Low-voltage pulses of current, usually 60 to 100 pulses per second, are then passed through the electrode to stimulate neural tissue adjacent to its tip. Use of this technique on freely moving animals was pioneered by Hess, who developed the procedure of permanently attaching electrodes to the skulls of cats. The electrodes produced little discomfort to the animals and so they could receive brain stimulation while their reactions were observed. Hess found that virtually every behavior that a cat spontaneously performed could be induced by brain stimulation. The elicited behaviors were usually "stimulus bound," meaning they lasted only as long as the stimulation was applied. Every part of the brain of many animals has since been mapped for the effects of electrical stimulation.

Electrical stimulation has also been used in surgery and as a treatment for some neurological disorders. In certain situations requiring brain surgery it is considered important not to damage areas of the brain involved in controlling speech. Under local anesthesia the patient's cortex is exposed and stimulated electrically to identify speech areas. During a stimulation test the patient is asked to speak, electrical stimulation is applied, and if it is found to disrupt speech in particular ways the stimulated area is defined as a speech area.

Therapeutic brain stimulation, although not widespread, has been used. A few seconds of electrical stimulation of the midbrain may arrest otherwise unmanageable pain for periods lasting many hours. Brief periods of stimulation given to the cerebellum have sometimes been found effective in arresting epileptic attacks.

Goddard and McIntyre have found that if certain portions of the limbic system are given from 1 to 2 sec of stimulation each day, the stimulation, which initially has no observable effect on behavior, will begin to produce epileptic attacks. That is, the animals will show convulsions after stimulation. If the treatments are continued for a long enough period, the seizures may begin to occur spontaneously. This procedure has been given the name **kindling,** and it provides a model for studying human epilepsy.

REFERENCES

Bland, B. H., P. Anderson, T. Ganes, and O. Sveen. Automated analysis of rhythmicity of physiologically identified hippocampal formation neurons. *Experimental Brain Research* 38:205–219, 1978.

Eccles, J. The synapse. *Scientific American* 212:56–66, Jan., 1965.

Goddard, G. V., and D. McIntyre. Some properties of a lasting epileptogenic trace kindled by repeated electrical stimulation of the amygdala in mammals. In L. V. Laitinen and K. E. Livingston (eds.) *Surgical Approaches in Psychiatry.* Baltimore: University Park Press, 1973.

Hodgkin, A. L., and A. F. Huxley. Action potentials recorded from inside nerve fiber. *Nature* 144:710–711, 1939.

Kandel, E. R., and J. H. Schwartz. *Principles of Neural Science.* New York: Elsevier North Holland, 1981.

Katz, B. How cells communicate. In J. L. McGaugh, N. M. Weinberger, and R. H. Whalen (eds.) *Psychobiology.* Readings from *Scientific American.* San Francisco: W. H. Freeman, 1972.

Penfield, W., and H. H. Jasper. *Epilepsy and the Functional Anatomy of the Human Brain.* Boston: Little, Brown, 1954.

Shepherd, G. M. *Neurobiology.* New York: Oxford University Press, 1983.

Sinclair, B. R., M. G. Seto, and B. H. Bland. Theta cells in the CA1 and dentate layers of the hippocampal formation: Relations to slow wave activity and motor behavior in the freely moving rabbit. *Journal of Neurophysiology* 48:1214–1225, 1982.

Tinbergen, N. *The Animal in Its World.* London: Allen & Unwin, 1972.

Vanderwolf, C. H., and T. E. Robinson. Reticulo-cortical activity and behavior: a critique of the arousal theory and a new synthesis. *Behavioral and Brain Sciences* 4:459–514, 1981.

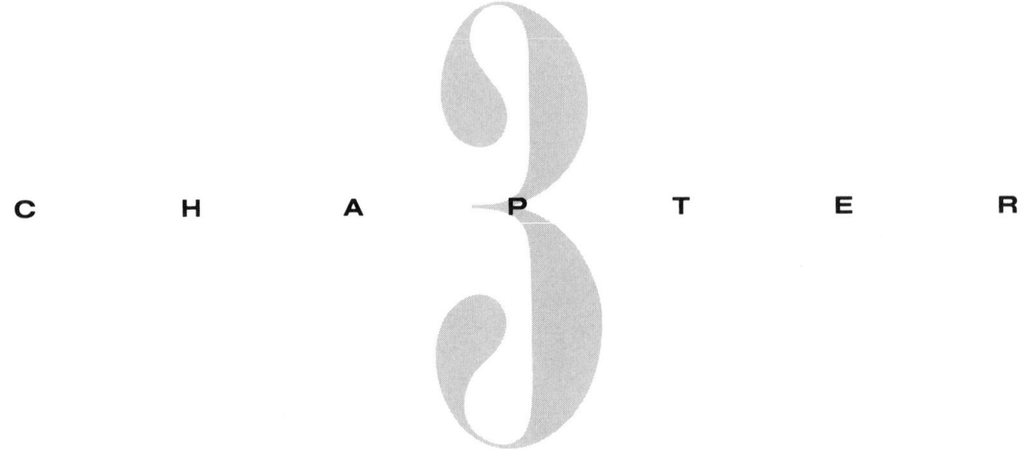

ANALYZING THE BRAIN THROUGH ITS BIOCHEMICAL ACTIVITY

One of the most notable experiments ever performed on the nervous system was that by Otto Loewi in 1921. Loewi stimulated the vagus nerve to a frog's heart, causing the heart's rate of beating to decline. At the same time he washed the heart with a solution that he then collected. When he subsequently poured the solution onto a second heart, its rate of beating also declined. A substance had been liberated from the first heart that slowed the rate of the second. Loewi referred to this substance as *Vagusstoff* (vagus substance) and was able to identify it as acetylcholine within a few years. Loewi was also able to stimulate the vagus to increase heart rate and, by collecting and applying the substance thus produced, to increase the rate of beating of a second heart. This substance turned out to be epinephrine. Although the experiment was initially difficult to replicate — it depends upon the stimulation, the kind of frog, the season, and so forth — the results were eventually reliably obtained and extended to rabbits, cats, and dogs. These pioneering experiments led to modern concepts of how nerves communicate with muscles and glands and eventually to the identification of substances that allow nerves to communicate with each other and the rules that govern this communication. They also led to a scientific basis for *psychopharmacology,* the science of how drugs affect behavior through their action on the nervous system. A particular elegance of the experiments is that they embody most of the procedures that would subsequently be involved in studying neurotransmitters in the brain, including isolating a function, stimulating release of a transmitter, collecting and identifying the transmitter, and verifying its action.

CLASSICAL NEUROTRANSMITTERS AND NEUROPEPTIDES

As we detailed in Chapter 2, neurons communicate with each other and with glands, muscles, and other body organs by releasing small quantities of chemicals called neurotransmitters onto the receptors of the neurons or organs they synapse with or directly into the bloodstream. At the present time many different neurotransmitters are suspected to be active in the nervous system. Still, there are difficulties involved in identifying these substances and their locations within the confined area of the brain, where many thousands of terminals connect with neurons that are only a few microns in size. In order to identify a chemical as a neurotransmitter a set of proofs has been developed, which includes the following:

1. The chemical is shown to be present in the terminals.

2. It is shown to be released when the neuron fires.

3. Placing the chemical on the innervated organ mimics the effect of nerve stimulation.

4. There is a chemical or an uptake mechanism present in the area of the synaptic cleft to inactivate the neurotransmitter.

5. Placing a chemical in the synaptic cleft that destroys or inactivates the neurotransmitter must block the effects of nerve stimulation.

At the present time, technology is simply unable to meet the rigor of all these demands, so chemicals that are strongly suspected of functioning as neurotransmitters can only be labeled putative (or supposed) transmitters.

Although not all of these criteria have been met for any transmitter in the brain, there is agreement that some 10 or so substances are neurotransmitters. Some of these substances are listed in Table 3-1. They are sometimes referred to as the canonical or classical neurotransmitters. In addition, at least 25 short **peptides** (chains of **amino acids**) have been located in neurons and are thought to be involved in neurotransmission. These substances include peptides that are also found in the gut, and

TABLE 3-1. Neurotransmitters and their receptor types, with examples of receptor agonists and antagonists

Transmitter	Receptor type	Agonist	Antagonist
Acetylcholine	Nicotinic	Nicotine	Curare
	Muscarinic	Muscarine	Atropine
Biogenic amines			
Dopamine (DA)	D1, D2	Apomorphine	Haloperidol
Norepinephrine (NE)	$\alpha_1, \alpha_2, \beta_1, \beta_2$	Clonidine	Phenoxybenzamine
Serotonin (5-HT)	5-HT1, 5-HT2	LSD	
Amino acids			
γ-Aminobutyric acid (GABA)	$GABA_A$	Muscimol	Picrotoxin
	$GABA_B$	Baclofen	
Glycine		Taurine	Strychnine
Glutamate	A1	*N*-methyl-D-aspartate[a]	
	A2	Quisqualate	
	A3	Kainate	

[a] All of the agonists to glutamate also act as neurotoxins, destroying cells to which they bind.

TABLE 3-2. Neuroactive peptides

Gut-brain peptides
Vasoactive intestinal polypeptide (VIP)
Cholecystokinin octapeptide
Substance P
Neurotensin
Methionine enkephalin
Leucine enkephalin
Glucagon
Hypothalamic-releasing hormones
Thyrotropin-releasing hormone (TRH)
Somatostatin (growth hormone–release-inhibiting factor)
Luteinizing hormone–releasing hormone (LHRH)
Pituitary peptides
Adrenocorticotropin (ACTH)
β-Endorphin
α-Melanocyte-stimulating hormone (α-MSH)
Others
Angiotensin II, bradykinin, vasopressin, oxytocin, carnosine

Source: After Kandel and Schwartz, 1981.

may play a role in the central control of feeding and drinking; hormones that are released from the hypothalamus; peptides that are released from the pituitary; and others (see Table 3-2). At least two families of peptides act like opiates, that is, they have pain-suppressing properties in addition to producing other opiatelike effects.

There are some general differences between the classical transmitters and the peptides. The classical transmitters generally have lower molecular weight than the peptides and they are synthesized from simpler substances or obtained directly from food. For example, acetylcholine is made in part from choline, which is obtained from the diet. Dopamine and norepinephrine are synthesized from the dietary amino acid tyrosine by minor editing; the sequence of steps is illustrated in Figure 3-1. This sequence is quite notable for the relations between the transmitters produced by it and their involvement in certain mental diseases. Dopamine has been implicated in both Parkinson's disease and schizophrenia, while norepinephrine has been implicated in mania and depression. Serotonin is derived from the dietary amino acid tryptophan, and eating tryptophan-rich foods, such as bananas, has been shown to increase central serotonin activity. The amino acids glutamate, aspartate, and glycine are dietary amino acids obtained directly from protein in an animal's diet. The synthesis of γ-aminobutyric acid (GABA) requires only the removal of a carboxyl group (COOH) from glutamate. These transmitters also generally act in high concentrations and their effects are relatively short lasting.

The neuropeptides, in contrast, consist of two or more amino acids that are made by ribosomes in the cell body according to instructions from chromosomes in the nucleus. They are fractions of larger peptide molecules, are potent in small concentrations, and appear to have long-lasting actions.

It was originally believed that any one neuron would contain the same transmitter in all its terminals. This rule is referred to as *Dale's law.* The law is useful, for if a terminal at one location can be shown to contain a certain transmitter, then collaterals from the same neuron that end in other locations should also contain that transmitter. For example, acetylcholine was known to be the neurotransmitter at the nerve-muscle junction, so when it became apparent that motor neurons had collaterals that remained in the spinal cord it was possible to demonstrate that these terminals were also cholinergic. Similarly, once it was demonstrated that the peptide substance P was located on peripheral nerve endings of sensory neurons, the fact that it was released by sensory neurons in the spinal cord could be established.

More recently, the work of Hokfelt and his coworkers seems to show that the neuroactive peptides may coexist in terminals with the classical neurotransmitters. It is unclear in these situations whether the peptides are acting like transmitters in the full sense or whether they have a modulatory effect on synaptic transmission.

It is also worth noting how views about the

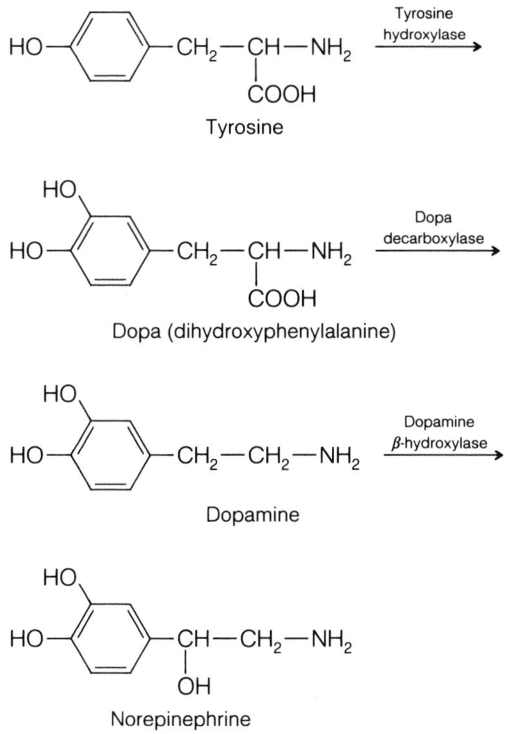

HO—(ring)—CH_2—CH—NH_2 (with COOH on CH) $\xrightarrow{\text{Tyrosine hydroxylase}}$

Tyrosine

HO, HO—(ring)—CH_2—CH—NH_2 (with COOH on CH) $\xrightarrow{\text{Dopa decarboxylase}}$

Dopa (dihydroxyphenylalanine)

HO, HO—(ring)—CH_2—CH_2—NH_2 $\xrightarrow{\text{Dopamine } \beta\text{-hydroxylase}}$

Dopamine

HO, HO—(ring)—CH—CH_2—NH_2 (with OH on CH)

Norepinephrine

FIGURE 3-1. Sequence of steps leading to the synthesis of amine neurotransmitter substances dopamine and norepinephrine. Note that each step in the synthesis requires an enzyme (shown above the arrows). The amines receive their name because of the amine group (NH_2) attached to each. Tyrosine and dopa cross the blood-brain barrier, but dopamine and norepinephrine do not, so generally to increase dopamine centrally, dopa must be administered.

action of neurotransmitters are evolving. For example, crude assays of brain tissue suggest that **amines** make up a small part of neurotransmitter action. There may be as many as a thousand synapses employing an amino acid for every synapse employing a **monoamine.** Thus, the amino acids appear to be the workhorses of the nervous system. Furthermore, although it was once thought that transmitter substances mainly acted by influencing the membrane potential at the postsynaptic receptor, it is now recognized that they can have other actions. Many peptides may act as intercellular messengers, bridging the actions of the classical neurotransmitters and the sensitivity of the postsynaptic membrane. In this role they may help to make the postsynaptic membrane more sensitive to the transmitter, that is, allowing it to learn. Neurons may also release a mixture of a classical neurotransmitter and a peptide. Transmitters, particularly the amines, and also the peptides, can influence cell metabolic activity. Finally, some peptides can act on cells and impede the effects of other transmitters without changing the electrical activity of the cell and without influencing its metabolic activity. Thus, although much of the discussion of this chapter centers on the "transmitting" function of transmitters and emphasizes some substances more than others, the putative interrelationships between nerves is richer and more versatile than our emphasis will indicate.

RECEPTORS

Transmitters act on receptors located on the postsynaptic membrane. The *receptors* are proteins that bind the transmitter substance, and to do so they face outward to catch the transmitter. Receptors are thought to consist of two components: a binder, which grasps the transmitter, and an *ionophore,* which is a channel in the membrane that opens to let ions flow when binding occurs. Some receptors may also stimulate metabolic activity within the cell. This activity consists of a series of biochemical steps that take place within the postsynaptic cell and that in turn may regulate ion flow or may even change the number of receptors or change other structures within the cell. The chemicals involved in this latter postsynaptic activity are sometimes called "second messengers." As noted earlier, such systems seem to contain the potential for modifying cells permanently, perhaps for such activities as learning.

The structure of receptors may determine the actions of a transmitter substance. It is apparent that many transmitter substances interact with more than one type of receptor (Table 3-1). This may allow the transmitter to have an excitatory function through one of its collaterals and an inhibitory function through others. Since pharmacological agents produce some of their actions by binding to receptors (Table 3-1), their choice of a particular receptor may allow them to modulate only part of a transmitter's actions. For example, acetylcholine receptors on nerve-muscle junctions are affected by a different group of drugs than acetylcholine receptors in many parts of the brain or in the autonomic nervous system.

DISTRIBUTION OF TRANSMITTERS

The distribution of neurotransmitters in the brain can be determined in a number of ways. Samples of tissue can be taken from different brain areas and the concentrations of chemicals in the samples compared. This type of analysis gives only a relative measure of neurotransmitter distribution, and most neurotransmitters have been found in all regions of the brain, although in considerably varied concentrations. Generally it is not wise to conclude much about function from concentration differences; for example, a small quantity of neurotransmitter in one region may be just as important for a particular function as a large quantity in some other region. Another technique for determining distribution is to stain the brain tissue with stains that interact with neurotransmitters or with some chemical closely related to the neurotransmitter's function. For example, norepinephrine and dopamine can be stained by exposing sections of tissue to formaldehyde vapor and then illuminating the tissue with ultraviolet light. Both substances fluoresce with a green color, but to distinguishably different shades. The presence of acetylcholine can be identified by staining tissue with a substance called butylthiocholine, which turns acetylcholinesterase, a chemical that breaks down acetylcho-

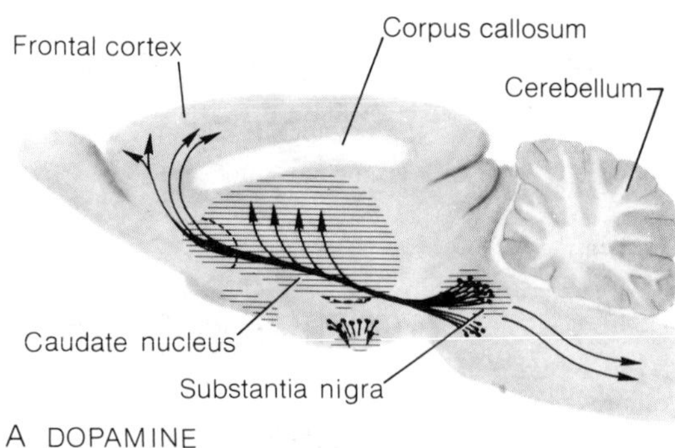

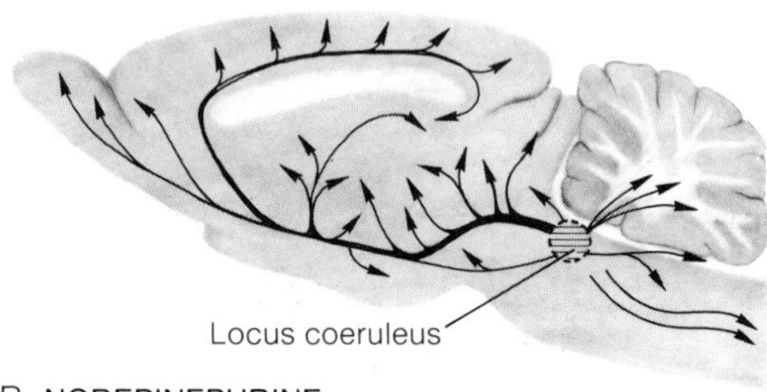

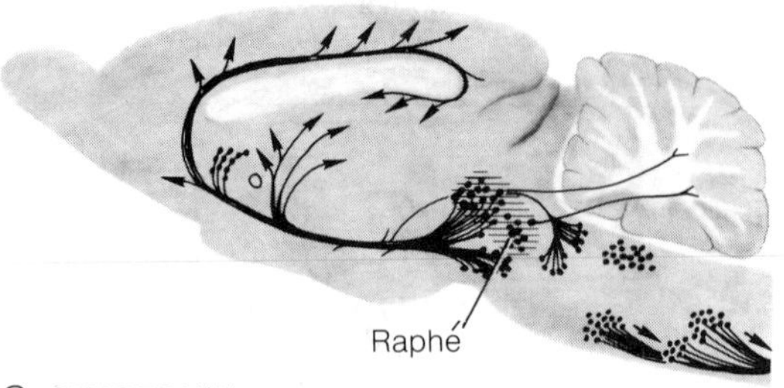

FIGURE 3-2. Location of cell bodies, shown as black dots, and the projections of dopamine, norepinephrine, and serotonin pathways in the rat. (From J. R. Cooper, F. E. Bloom, and R. H. Roth; *The Biochemical Basis of Neuropharmacology.* New York: Oxford University Press. Copyright © 1986 by Oxford University Press, Inc. Reprinted with permission.)

line, black. In most, but not all, brain sites, acetylcholinesterase indicates the presence of acetylcholine. New mapping techniques, particularly immunocytochemical methods, are continually being developed to update maps of transmitter distribution.

Neurochemical mapping procedures have been revealing some extremely interesting insights into the organization of the brain. Some neurochemicals although widely distributed in all regions of the brain, are located in neurons whose cell bodies are found in a number of restricted nuclei. The origin and distribution of the dopamine, norepinephrine, and serotonin systems in the rat are shown diagrammatically in Figure 3-2. These systems resemble hormone systems, except that hormones are carried from their origin throughout the body by the bloodstream rather than by axons. Similar maps have been developed for other transmitter systems, including cholinergic and opioid systems, and generally the organization revealed in the rat (the favorite subject for this type of research) proves to be much the same for other animals, including humans.

BRAIN DYSFUNCTIONS, MENTAL ILLNESS, AND NEUROTRANSMITTERS

Since neurons containing specific neurotransmitters appear to be organized into systems, it seems pertinent to ask whether these different neurochemical systems can be associated with specific functions. Indeed, they seem to be. Quite a long list of behavioral abnormalities have been asso-

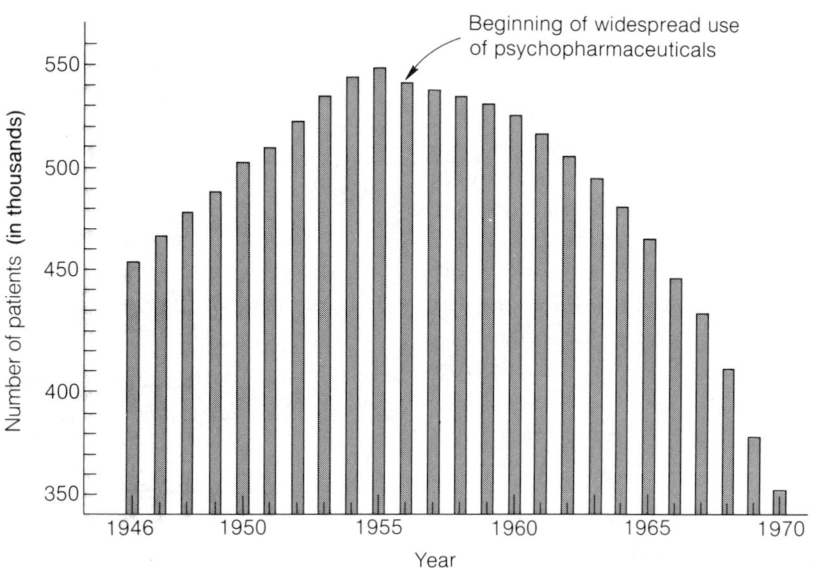

FIGURE 3-3. Numbers of resident patients in state and local government mental hospitals in the United States from 1946 through 1970. Note the dramatic change in the total patient population that began after 1955, when the therapeutic use of psychoactive drugs began (From V. C. Longo, *Neuropharmacology and Behavior.* San Francisco: W. H. Freeman and Company. Copyright © 1972. Modified from D. H. Efron (ed.) *Psychopharmacology: A Review of Progress.* Washington, D.C.: U.S. Department of Health, Education, and Welfare, 1968.)

ciated with metabolic disorders of various kinds (see Cooper, Bloom, and Roth), and a plethora of hypotheses concerning function have been developed. The problem for many systems, however, is not to find a function but to find the *appropriate* function.

Since before the turn of the century it has often been suggested that **psychosis**—an illness such as schizophrenia or manic-depressive behavior—was the result of brain malfunction. It was variously proposed that psychoses were due to actual brain damage, ingestion of toxins that poisoned the brain, or synthesis by the brain itself of a toxin that caused it to malfunction. These ideas were reinforced by the observation that various chemical agents, for example, atropine, when ingested, produced behavior resembling that of psychoses. Then, in 1952, French physicians observed that a preanesthetic agent, chlorpromazine, had a tranquilizing effect on surgical patients. When tried on psychotic patients, it was found to have striking therapeutic action. By 1955 it was in use in North America and was probably instrumental in drastically reducing the patient population of mental hospitals (Figure 3-3). Since then many other antipsychotic drugs have been introduced, and an intense search for the mechanisms of their action has been under way. Because many psychoactive drugs are now thought to produce their effects by modifying synaptic activity, the following sections will describe the synaptic organization and pharmacological influences of some of the better known neurotransmitter systems.

SITES OF DRUG ACTION ON SYNAPSES

Figure 3-4 is a diagram of a generalized synapse showing many of the features typical of most synapses. The following is the sequence of biochemical events outlined in the diagram:

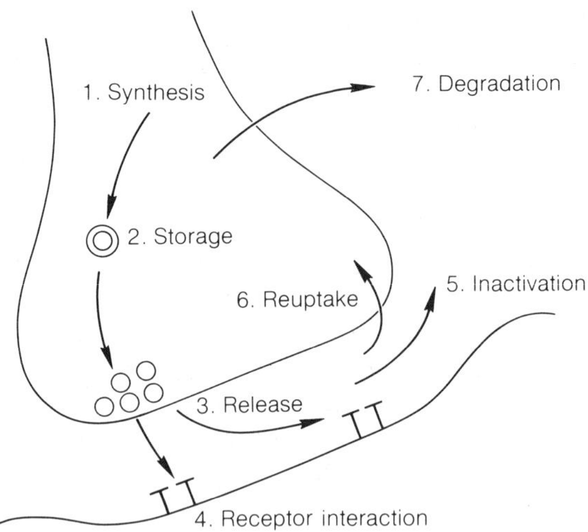

FIGURE 3-4. Steps in synaptic transmission in a generalized synapse.

1. *Synthesis.* Precursor chemicals obtained from food or manufactured in the neuron are transported down the axon into the terminal, where they are synthesized into the neurotransmitter.

2. *Storage.* The transmitter is stored in the terminal in one or more of several ways, at least one of which is in vesicles (shown as circles) available for release.

3. *Release.* When the nerve discharges, some of the vesicles release their content into the synaptic space.

4. *Receptor interaction.* The released neurotransmitter crosses the synaptic space and binds weakly to specialized receptors on the postsynaptic membrane, where it initiates either depolarization or hyperpolarization of the postsynaptic membrane. In many systems more than one type of postsynaptic receptor may be sensitive to the neurotransmitter.

5. *Inactivation.* In some synapses the neurotransmitter is inactivated in the area of the synaptic space.

6. *Reuptake.* In other synapses the neurotransmitter is taken back up into the presynaptic neuron. In some synapses, both inactivation and reuptake may occur.

7. *Degradation.* The free neurotransmitter within the terminal may be degraded to control neurotransmitter concentrations within the neuron.

Many of the chemicals that people ingest by accident, as recreational drugs, or as medicine may influence one or more of these steps in one or more neurochemical systems. This realization has revolutionized modern pharmacology and neuropharmacology and has led to an intense effort to disclose the specific actions of different drugs and to synthesize new drugs with specific actions. This effort also involves a search for a neurological basis for such mental disorders as schizophrenia and depression, on the logic that if a particular drug can ameliorate one of these disorders, and if the neurotransmitter on which the drug acts can be identified, then this may be taken as evidence that some excess or deficiency of that neurotransmitter may be causally related to the disorder. Although this line of reasoning has disclosed some intriguing possibilities, there is as yet no unequivocal evidence proving that any neurotransmitter is causally linked with a particular mental disease.

ADMINISTRATION OF DRUGS AND SYSTEMIC BARRIERS TO THEIR INFLUENCE

If the target of a drug is in the brain, it has a number of barriers to overcome before it gets there. Drugs are most frequently administered orally. As is well known, alcohol administered by this method gets to the brain rather quickly. On the other hand, curare, a neuromuscular blocker that can cause death through respiratory muscle paralysis, has no effect when taken orally. However, if taken through the skin, curare's action is rapid. (For this reason South American Indians could kill animals with curare tipped arrows and then eat the animals with impunity.) Drugs taken by mouth reach the bloodstream by being absorbed through the stomach or small intestine, where absorption may be impaired by food in the system. The nature and form of a drug taken orally will also determine whether it will be absorbed and the rate of that absorption. If the drug is in a solid form it will not be absorbed if it cannot be dissolved by the gastric juices. In general, if a drug is a weak acid it will be absorbed from the stomach but if it is a weak base it will have to pass through the stomach — a process that may destroy it — before it is absorbed from the intestine. The characteristics of drugs that determine their absorption are usually summarized in standard reference sources such as Gilman et al.

The gastrointestinal tract can variously be bypassed by inhaling the drug, allowing the blood to absorb it directly from the lungs; by injecting it into a muscle, allowing to be absorbed by the blood; or by injecting it directly into the bloodstream. Usually, these methods require much smaller drug dosages than those required for oral administration. Once a drug is in the bloodstream, it will be diluted by the person's approximately 6 liters of circulating blood and it is subject to further barriers. If it binds strongly to proteins it may attach itself to blood proteins and stay in the circulatory system. If it is *water-soluble* but not fat-soluble it will pass into the extracellular fluid, and if it is *fat-soluble* it will additionally cross cell membranes and enter cells. The 35 or so liters of water in the extracellular and intracellular fluid will further dilute it.

The brain imposes another barrier, called the

blood-brain barrier. In the body, there are pores present in capillary membranes that allow passage for substances. In the brain, the capillaries are tightly joined together and covered on the outside by a fatty barrier called the **glial sheath,** provided by nearby astrocyte cells. Thus, a drug has to cross the capillary wall and penetrate the glial covering to pass out of the bloodstream into the brain. This acts as a relative obstacle to some drugs, such as penicillin. The blood-brain barrier, therefore, requires that some drugs destined for the brain, if they are to reach their target, be given in special forms or be injected directly into the cerebrospinal fluid or into the brain tissue itself. The latter techniques are widely used on experimental animals but are unlikely to be used with humans because of the danger from possible complications.

Processes that are involved in eliminating drugs will also influence drug action and duration of action. Drugs that are very fat-soluble may be taken up rapidly by fat cells and then only slowly eliminated. Fast-acting anesthetics, for example, are very fat-soluble and their action on the brain is terminated quickly because they are absorbed by fat. Generally, after absorption, drugs are excreted or metabolized by the kidneys, liver, bile, sweat, milk, or through breath exhaled by the lungs. Their persistence in the body will be determined by the route through which they are eliminated and the efficiency of that route. The liver, for example, when challenged by alcohol, increases its metabolic capacity, so that alcohol may be metabolized more quickly in drinkers than in abstainers. Some substances, particularly certain metals, may not be excreted at all and so may, if repeatedly administered, accumulate in the body until they have toxic effects. Drugs are usually manufactured with the routes of administration and elimination in mind so that the rates of absorption and duration of action can be specifically controlled.

Most information concerning drug administration, absorption, elimination, and effects can be found in standard texts, such as Gilman et al. It is a good practice to consult these references before taking a drug or when dealing with patients who are receiving drugs.

CLASSIFICATION OF PSYCHOACTIVE DRUGS

It is possible to classify drugs using a number of systems: by the transmitter they influence, by their structure, or by their action. A widely used drug classification scheme is that developed by the World Health Organization. According to this classification there are five major types of **psychoactive drugs,** grouped according to the effects that they have on behavior. Table 3-3 summarizes the classification. As pointed out above, drugs may intervene in the process of intercellular communication at any of a number of stages, but irrespective of its site of action a drug will have one of two effects: it will either increase or decrease the effectiveness of transmission at the synaptic junction.

Sedative-Hypnotics

Sedative-hypnotics are drugs that at low doses reduce anxiety, at medium doses produce sedation, and at high doses produce anesthesia or coma. Virtually any of these drugs if given in the appropriate dose can produce each of the effects illustrated in Figure 3-5. Sedative-hypnotics are a diverse group of drugs including barbiturates, benzodiazepines (known as minor tranquilizers, of which Valium is an example), and alcohol. They are widely used for their antianxiety actions, are effective in counteracting epilepsy, are used as anesthetics, and can be used to counteract the adverse effects of stimulants. It is thought that these drugs depress the activity of the systems that produce arousal or initiation of behavior. At low doses the sedative-hypnotics may depress the activity of norepinephrine synapses, but their precise mechanism of action is unknown. At higher doses they may block neurotransmission in many systems and thereby produce anesthesia or even coma. The benzodiazepines are thought to act by facilitating γ-aminobutyric acid (GABA) function. They do not stimulate the receptors directly but make the receptor more responsive to GABA. GABA is thought of as an inhibitory transmitter, and since it is widely distributed, facilitating its activity can produce widespread inactivation of brain systems.

Because of the communality of their actions on the nervous system, all of the sedative-hypnotics are additive, or *synergistic,* in effect. When taken together, the effects of two such drugs are often greater than would be predicted from either taken alone. The behavioral depression induced by these drugs is often followed by a period of hyperexcitability. After repeated administrations, the hyperexcitability may be quite severe and can even result in convulsions and death. Prolonged use of sedative-hypnotics generally produces both dependence and tolerance. *Dependence* refers to the desire or necessity of continuing to take the drug. *Tolerance* refers to the decrease in response to the drug after it has been taken repeatedly. Tolerance can occur either because the body improves in its ability to metabolize the drug or because the nervous system becomes less responsive to it. Often with-

TABLE 3-3. Classes of drugs that alter mood or behavior

1. *Sedative-Hypnotics (CNS depressants)*
   - Barbiturates
     - Long-acting: phenobarbital *(Luminal)*
     - Intermediate-acting: amobarbital *(Amytal)*
     - Short-acting: pentobarbital *(Nembutal)*
     - Ultrashort-acting: thiopental *(Pentothal)*
   - Nonbarbiturate hypnotics
     - Methaqualone *(Quaalude)*
   - Antianxiety agents (benzodiazapines)
     - Meprobamate *(Miltown, Equanil)*
     - Chlordiazepoxide *(Librium)*
     - Diazepam *(Valium)*
   - Others
     - Alcohol, bromide, paraldehyde, chloral hydrate, ether, halothane, chloroform
2. *Behavioral Stimulants and Convulsants*
   - Amphetamines: *Benzedrine, Dexedrine, Methedrine*
   - Clinical antidepressants
     - Monoamine oxidase (MAO) inhibitors: *Parnate*
     - Tricyclic compounds: *Tofranil, Elavil*
   - Cocaine
   - Convulsants: strychnine, *Metrazole,* picrotoxin
   - Caffeine
   - Nicotine
3. *Narcotic Analgesics (Opiates)*
   - Opium, heroin, morphine, codeine, Percodan, Demerol
4. *Antipsychotic Agents*
   - Phenothiazines: chlorpromazine *(Thorazine)*
   - Reserpine *(Serpasil)*
   - Butyrophenones: haloperidol *(Haldol)*
   - Lithium
5. *Psychedelics and Hallucinogens*
   - LSD (lysergic acid diethylamide)
   - Mescaline
   - Psilocybin
   - Substituted amphetamines: DOM, MDA, MDMA (Ecstasy), TMA
   - Tryptamine derivatives: DMT, DET, bufotenine
   - Phencyclidine
   - Cannabis: marijuana, hashish, tetrahydrocannabinols

Note: Proprietary drug names in italics.
Source: After Julien, 1985.

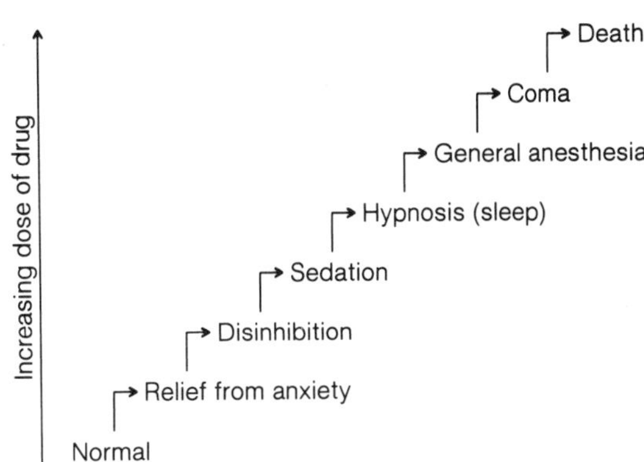

FIGURE 3-5. Continuum of behavioral sedation. How increasing doses of sedative-hypnotic drugs affect behavior. (Adapted from R. M. Julien, 1985.)

drawal from drug abuse (alcoholism is a good example) is complicated by dependence, tolerance, and withdrawal symptoms. Sedative-hypnotics have been widely reported to impair memory, especially for recent events or ongoing events. A final characteristic of sedative-hypnotics is that they display good *cross-dependence;* that is, they can be substituted for each other. Many cases of drug dependence are complicated by multiple drug use in which a person may be taking a benzodiazepine such as Valium for anxiety, using alcohol, and also taking sleeping pills (barbituates). The best treatment for chronic use is gradual withdrawal. For acute intoxication, stimulants may be helpful, but none specifically counteract all depressant actions.

Stimulants

Stimulants are drugs that increase behavioral activity either by increasing motor activity or by counteracting fatigue. Stimulants are diverse drugs, whose synergistic effects differ from those described for the sedative-hypnotics. They can be subdivided into four groups: behavioral stimulants, clinical antidepressants, convulsants, and general stimulants.

Behavioral stimulants include cocaine and the amphetamines, which are thought both to potentiate (augment) release of dopamine from the presynaptic membrane and to block the reuptake mechanism that reabsorbs dopamine back into the synapse after it has acted on the receptor. Both actions would increase not only the amount of dopamine available but also the duration of its availability for action on the receptors. Behavioral stimulants may also act on other amine synapses. The amphetamines have antidepressant properties, but their major clinical use is to counteract narcolepsy, an uncontrollable tendency to fall asleep. Amphetamines are also given to hyperactive children, whom they may help by prolonging their attention span.

Amphetamines produce cognitive arousal and counteract sleepiness when used in low doses. Repeated use creates tolerance and dependence. Tolerance levels can be remarkable: users who start with a 1 mg (milligram) dose may eventually take 1000–2000 mg. If the drug is taken intraveneously, known as "mainlining," tolerance and dependence occur more rapidly, and the user may display a condition of paranoid schizophrenia that is indistinguishable from the naturally occurring condition. Amphetamines also produce *sensitization,* a tendency to show a greater behavioral response as a consequence of intermittent use of the drug (the opposite of tolerance). Hypothetically, sensitization can occur with as little as one experience with a drug and can last indefinitely. A review of some of the effects of amphetamines and the putative changes that underlie sensitization have been summarized by Robinson and Becker.

The *clinical antidepressant* group of stimulants includes cocaine and the tricyclic antidepressants, including desipramine and imipramine. These drugs also act on dopaminergic synapses, but there is good evidence that they more selectively block the reuptake of norepinephrine and serotonin, thereby facilitating transmission by prolonging the time during which the neurotransmitter can act on the receptor. Some tricyclics, such as desipramine, have a more potent effect on norepinephrine reuptake, whereas others, such as imipramine, more selectively block serotonin reuptake. The ability of cocaine to counteract depression was first documented by Sigmund Freud, but today the tricyclics, which are in some ways structurally similar to cocaine, are the treatment of choice for depression. Because different tricyclics are more effective than others in treating quite different depressive populations, van Praag has suggested that there may be at least two types of depression: one attributable to reduced norepinephrine transmission, the other to reduced serotonin transmission.

The *convulsants* include strychnine, picrotoxin, pentylenetetrazole, and bicuculline. Each acts on different transmitter systems and all produce behavioral seizures. Generally, although they have no clinical applications, they are used in experimental research.

General *cellular stimulants* include caffeine and nicotine. Caffeine inhibits an enzyme that ordinarily breaks down cyclic adenosine monophosphate (cyclic AMP). The resulting increase in cyclic AMP leads to an increase in glucose production within cells, thus making available more energy and allowing higher rates of cellular activity. Nicotine is known to stimulate the acetylcholine receptor at nerve-muscle junctions and then to leave a more long-lasting block on the junction. Both compounds are also thought to have a variety of other effects.

Narcotic Analgesics

The *narcotic analgesics,* such as heroin and morphine, although widely abused because of their addictive properties, are nevertheless among the most effective pain-relieving agents available. Their mechanism of action has been clarified recently by the discovery of endogenous opiatelike substances in the brain. It has been suggested that these naturally occurring opiates, such as *endorphins* (a class name meaning that the chemicals act like opiates), are neurotransmitters in the brain, and that opiate drugs produce their effects by mimicking the postsynaptic stimulation of these neurotransmitters. The discovery that there are endogenous opiates has of course provoked tremendous excitement, particularly with respect to their possible use in controlling pain.

Antipsychotic Agents

The *antipsychotic agents* (often referred to as major tranquilizers) are drugs that have been effective in treating schizophrenia; the most widely used of them are chlorpromazine and haloperidol. In fact there are two major classes of antipsychotic drugs, the *phenothiazines,* of which chlorpromazine is an example and which includes many other -zine drugs, and the *butyrophenones,* of which haloperidol is best known. Given the high incidence of schizophrenia, antipsychotic agents are continually being manufactured, and there may be as many as 2000 different drugs available. Although both classes of antipsychotics act on norepinephrine and dopamine systems, their antipsychotic action appears attributable to their action on dopamine. They are thought to reduce dopaminergic transmission by blocking dopamine receptors. The effectiveness of these drugs in treating schizophrenia has led to the "dopamine hypothesis of schizophrenia," which holds that schizophrenia may be related to excessive levels of dopamine. However, this hypothesis should be viewed with caution. Neurotransmitter systems have complex interactions with one another, and it is quite possible that schizophrenia is caused by imbalances in any of a number of known or unknown systems that normally check the level of dopamine transmission.

Psychedelics

The *psychedelic drugs* are a mixed group of agents that alter sensory perception and cognitive processes. There are at least three major groups of psychedelics. (1) Acetylcholine psychedelics either block or facilitate transmission in acetylcholine synapses. Drugs such as atropine block acetylcholine postsynaptic receptors, thus reducing acetylcholine action; others, such as muscarine, stimulate these receptors much as acetylcholine does, thus mimicking acetylcholine activity. (2) Norepinephrine psychedelics include mescaline and possibly cannabis. It is thought that they act by stimulating norepinephrine postsynaptic receptors. (3) Serotonin psychedelics include LSD (lysergic acid diethylamide) and psilocybin, which may mimic serotonin by stimulating postsynaptic receptors of serotonin synapses or which may block the activity of serotonin neurons. In addition, these drugs may stimulate norepinephrine receptors.

Summary

We have seen that many commonly used drugs interact with neurotransmitter systems in the brain. The object of this section was to point out the usefulness of considering drug action and behavior within the context of neurotransmitter function. However, this discussion should not be considered comprehensive on the subject of either neurotransmission or drugs. There are, of course, many more drugs that influence neurotransmission (curare, for example, blocks acetylcholine nerve-muscle junctions), and many other drugs have effects other than at neuron junctions (such as caffeine, which may stimulate metabolic activity within neurons). In addition, the seeming simplicity of neurotransmission is deceptive, because many neurotransmitter systems have a number of types of postsynaptic receptors that are sensitive to the effects of different drugs. For example, the nerve-muscle acetylcholine receptors are blocked by curare, whereas the brain acetylcholine receptors are for the most part blocked by atropine. For a lucid and more detailed review of neuropharmacology we recommend to the reader Cooper, Bloom, and Roth; for a comprehensive source book on drugs and drug action we recommend Gilman et al.

NEUROTOXINS

Neurotoxins are drugs that kill brain cells. In early studies of brain function, brain cells were killed by relatively simple lesion techniques. Tissue was removed by suction, or a wire, insulated except for its tip, was inserted into the brain and an electric current was passed through the wire to damage the tissue around the tip. As information about neurotransmitters developed, it became clear that certain substances that resembled neurotransmitters could be introduced and would be taken up into cells, as if they were an actual transmitter, and once incorporated, could destroy the cell. Such drugs became valuable experimental tools because they could be used to selectively damage certain cell systems in the brain while sparing others.

Among the first such neurotoxins to receive wide use was **6-hydroxydopamine (6-OHDA).** You guessed it. It looks like dopamine and can be used to selectively destroy dopamine cells. In fact, depending upon how it is used, 6-OHDA can destroy either dopamine cells, norepinephrine cells, or both. Its use became so widespread that it has even appeared as a star poison in late night mystery movies. If 6-OHDA is injected into the ventricles of the brain, it usually only destroys norepinephrine cells. If it is given in conjunction with a second compound, pargyline, a monoamine oxidase inhibitor, it also destroys dopamine cells. If desipramine, a norepinephrine uptake blocker, is also given to prevent 6-OHDA uptake into norepinephrine by the cell, then only dopamine cells are destroyed. In selectively being able to remove dopamine cells from the brain, it was possible to produce an animal analogue of human Parkinson's disease, a disease characterized by the selective death of dopamine cells. More recently, it has been found that a synthetic morphine analogue, MPTP, accidently created in an illicit drug factory, can also cause selective loss of dopamine cells in humans. Drug users who took it instantaneously acquired Parkinsonian symptoms. This substance, unlike 6-OHDA, does not have to be injected directly into the brain. The fact that a peripherally administered substance like MPTP can act as a neurotoxin has led to speculation that various chemicals in pollutants might have the capacity to act as neurotoxins. At about the same time that 6-OHDA was developed, it was also found that 5,7-dihydroxytryptamine (5,7-DHT) could be used in much the same way to destroy serotonergic neurons. Thus, it became clear that many substances might be found that could act as neurotoxins on many different systems.

In 1971, Olney and his coworkers reported that

glutamate, a putative excitatory neurotransmitter, and some of its analogues had an excitatory effect on neurons and could kill some of them. The most powerful of these compounds was *kainic acid.* When injected peripherally into mice, it produced behavioral convulsions accompanied by the loss of certain cell populations in the brain. When injected into the brain, it killed cell bodies in the area of injection but did no damage to fibers passing through the area. A number of other glutamate analogues have similar effects with different potencies; the most notable of these include *ibotinic acid.* Not only did the discovery of these neurotoxins provide a tool for selectively lesioning cells in restricted areas of the brain, they provided insight into other possible ways that brain damage could occur. It has been hypothesized, for example, that the brain might produce its own neurotoxins resulting in regional self-destruction. Patients with the disease Huntington's chorea are known to have degeneration of the caudate nucleus, and it has been suggested that the degeneration may be due to an endogenously occurring kainic-acid-type lesion.

The kainic-acid model provides yet another insight into endogenous brain damage. It has been known for a long time that **cerebral hypoxia** (brain oxygen starvation) and **cerebral ischemia** (loss of blood supply to a part of the brain) result in irreparable brain damage. Cerebral ischemia is seen in two common clinical situations, cardiac arrest and arteriosclerosis of the carotid or vertebro-basilar arteries. People who have experienced ischemia often show persistent memory deficits and other neurological symptoms. For a time it was thought that oxygen starvation (anoxia) per se was the cause of much of the damage. There were, however, some inconsistencies in this hypothesis, including the fact that the damage often appeared hours or days after circulation had been restored. More recently, the hypothesis, has been advanced that cells subjected to anoxia release excessive amounts of glutamate. Some cells in the brain appear particularly sensitive to anoxia, such as the CA1 cells of the hippocampus. These cells appear to have high concentrations of *N*-methyl-D-aspartate (NMDA) glutamate receptors. Thus, excessive glutamate release has been hypothetized to be the causative agent in cell death. If this is the case, then blocking glutamate receptors immediately after anoxia or a stroke should prevent cell death. A number of lines of experimental research indicate that glutamate-receptor blockade does retard cell death.

The discovery of a variety of neurotoxins and a clarification of their actions opens many new possibilities for understanding how various kinds of brain damage occur. This broadens our perspective on how brain diseases might progress, how environmental contaminants might affect the brain, and how some injested substances might produce long-lasting behavioral changes. This also suggests new initiatives for preventative and remedial measures.

REFERENCES

Cooper, J. R., F. E. Bloom, and R. H. Roth. *The Biochemical Basis of Neuropharmacology.* New York: Oxford University Press, 1986.

Gilman, A. G., L. S. Goodman, and A. Gilman (eds.). *The Pharmacological Basis of Therapeutics* (6th ed.). New York: Macmillan, 1980.

Hokfelt, T. O., A. Johansson, A. Ljungdahl, J. M. Lundberg, and M. Schultzberg. Peptidergic neurons. *Nature* (Lond.), 284: 515–521, 1980.

Julien, R. M. *A Primer of Drug Action.* New York: W. H. Freeman, 1985.

Kandel, E. R., and J. H. Schwartz. *Principles of Neural Science.* New York: Elsevier North Holland, 1981.

Olney, J. W., O. L. Ho, and V. Rhee. Cytotoxic effects of acidic and sulphur-containing amino acids on the infant mouse central nervous system. *Experimental Brain Research,* 14: 61–67, 1971.

Robinson, T. E. and J. B. Becker. Enduring changes in brain and behavior produced by chronic amphetamine administration: A review and evaluation of animal models of amphetamine psychosis. *Brain Research Reviews,* 11: 157–198, 1986.

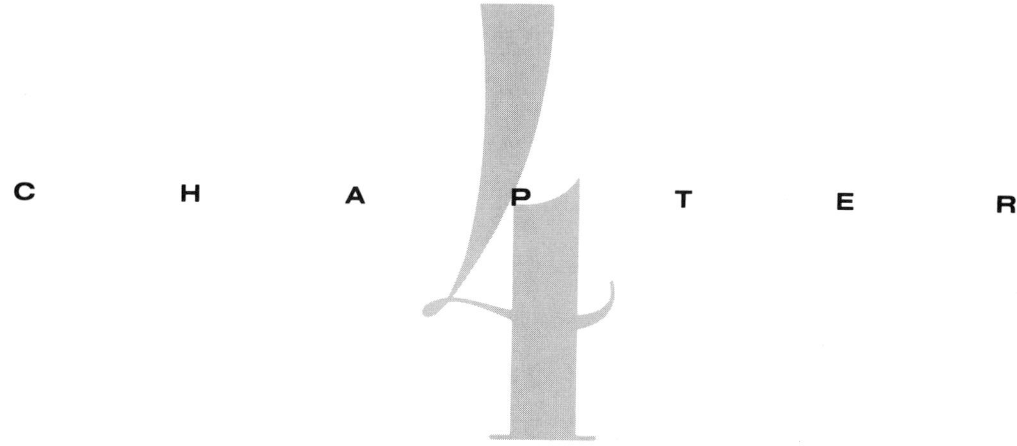

TECHNIQUES, PROBLEMS, AND MODELS

A man was walking from Thistle to Down. The West Wind, resting on the mountains, said to the sun, "Let us amuse ourselves. See the jacket that the man has over his shoulders. Let us have a wager to see who can remove it." With that the wind blew down on the traveler, but the more fiercely he blew, the more tightly the traveler pulled in his jacket and buttoned it. After the wind was exhausted, the sun rose slowly into the center of the sky and shone on the traveler, who shortly unbuttoned the jacket and then removed it. The sun turned to the wind and said, "You see, the technique's the thing."

The problem in using techniques in neuroscience involves knowing not only when to use the appropriate technique, but also how to use it and, more importantly, how to interpret the results obtained with it. A simple example will illustrate the problem.

Imagine four neuroscientists, α, β, δ, and γ, are studying an imaginary brain area called area 101. Area 101 consists of two local circuits, A and B, which generate, respectively, behaviors A and B. Circuit A, however, sends synapses onto circuit B, so that behavior B occurs smoothly and not in jerks. Also in area 101 are fibers of passage C that course through the neighborhood of circuits A and B but have nothing to do with either circuit. These fibers are responsible for the control of behavior C (see Figure 4-1).

Scientists α lesions area 101 and destroys circuits A and B and fibers of passage C. He concludes that area 101 produces a syndrome in which deficits in behaviors, A, B, and C always go together; this becomes known as α's syndrome in neurology texts. When scientists β stimulates area 101 electrically, he obtains either behavior A, behavior B, or behavior C, depending on where his electrode is placed, but he concludes that these behaviors are independent and do not go together.

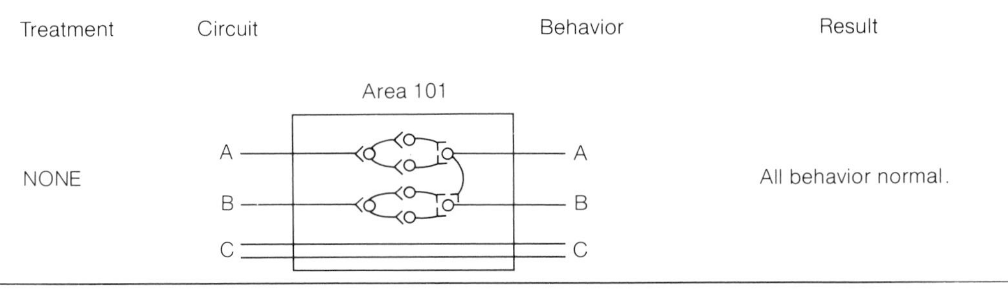

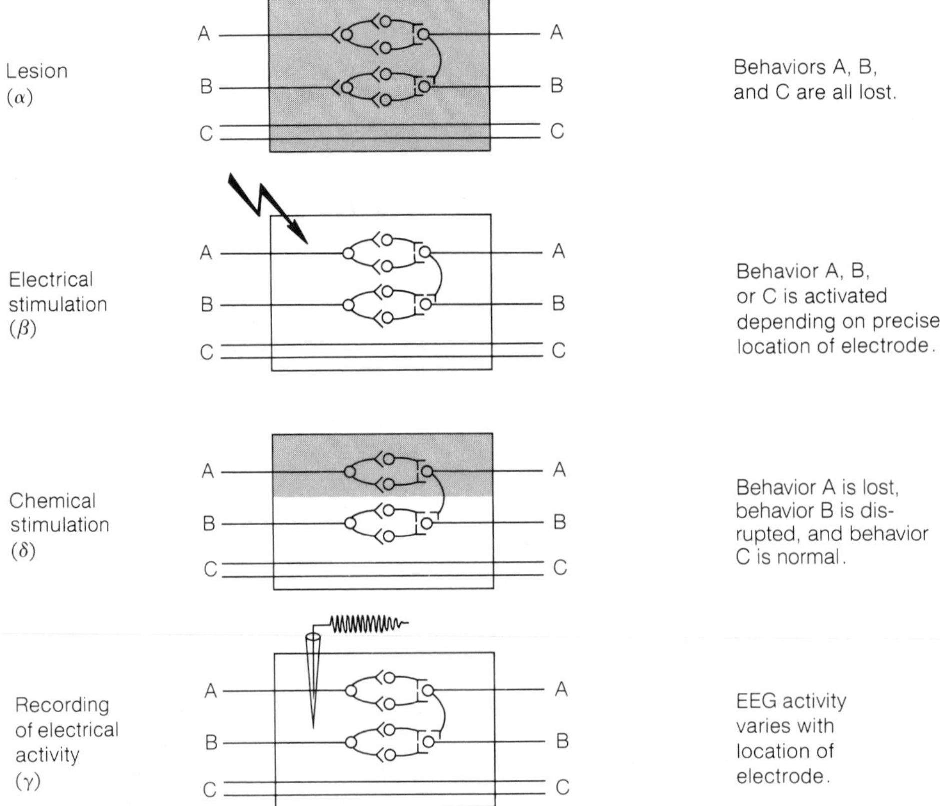

FIGURE 4-1. The different techniques of studying the brain used by scientists α, β, δ, and γ. Each uses a different procedure to study brain-behavior relations, and each arrives at a different conclusion regarding the function of area 101.

In addition, he stimulates other areas of the brain and obtains behaviors A, B, and C (he is in fact stimulating fibers going to and coming from these areas), and he concludes that area 101 really is not all that important for controlling behaviors A, B, and C. Scientist δ chemically stimulates area 101 with a drug that blocks the synaptic activity in the circuit A. She concludes that the area might control behavior A, that the drug also disrupts behavior B because it makes it so jerky, but that area 101 has nothing at all to do with behavior C. Finally, scientist γ records the electrical activity of circuits A and B and the fibers of passage C. He finds two forms of electrical activity: one is related to the details of movement and the other to the amount of sleep the animal had in the previous 24 hours. Scientist γ concludes that circuits A, B, and C all form some sort of functional system involved in sleep and movement.

Clearly, all four scientists are correct, but it is obvious that if they pooled their information they would not be able to construct the circuitry of area 101 without a unifying theory and considerably more experimentation to test that theory.

Something like the problem outlined for area 101 currently exists in the neurosciences, but on an absolutely massive scale. Many clinical disorders such as schizophrenia appear to occur because the brain is behaving abnormally, yet no lesions of the brain produce anything quite like schizophrenia. Many children with no apparent damage to the brain have incapacitating learning disorders, yet others with extensive brain damage are bright and intelligent and show little impairment in learning. These paradoxes have led one neuropsychologist we know to make the cryptic comment: "No brain is better than a bad brain." The beginning student will be mystified by these phenomena unless he or she recognizes that the brain is a large-scale, and considerably more complex, area 101, and that present neuropsychological theory is limited by the experimental techniques available.

There are six major techniques used in neuroscience: anatomy, biochemistry, lesions, stimulation, recording, and behavioral analysis. It is not possible to deal in depth with all the problems posed in using these techniques because they are all multifaceted, but it might be useful to point out some of the more obvious difficulties encountered with each.

ANATOMY

The similarity in the anatomy of the brains of different animals is impressive, as is the similarity of the brains of individuals within any species. Still, there are problems in understanding function from an anatomical approach. First, there is individual variation in the size, topography, and structure of brains. Such differences can clearly be seen in the organization of the gyral patterns of two different individuals illustrated in Figure 4-2. Karl Lashley has noted that even inbred strains of laboratory animals have thalamic nuclei so different that individual animals can be distinguished. Second, some functions do not seem to be fixed to rigid anatomical boundaries. The best example of such flexibility in structure-function relations is the fact that in some people speech is localized in the right rather than in the left hemisphere. It was once thought that deviations from the standard (e.g., speech on the left in right-handed people) were anomalies, but it is now becoming recognized that the anomalies are in fact the norm. When all the factors that influence localization are considered (e.g., sex, handedness, or age), it appears that the conventionally organized brain is in fact the brain of the minority. Third, the relation between brain mass and function has never been adequately explained. This applies both to the apparent diversity in brain size (consider the normal human brain has a range of 1000 to 2000 cm^3 [cubic centimeters]) and to the fact that when parts of a brain area are removed, the remaining tissue has an amazing ability to keep getting the job done. We can illustrate this with an amusing story. During the discussion of a surgical case, the question arose of how

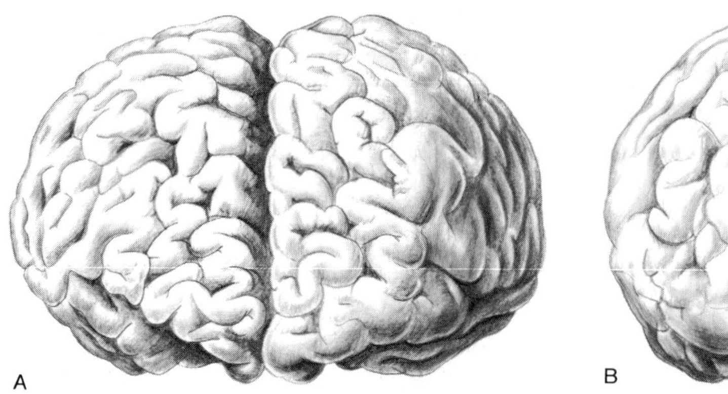

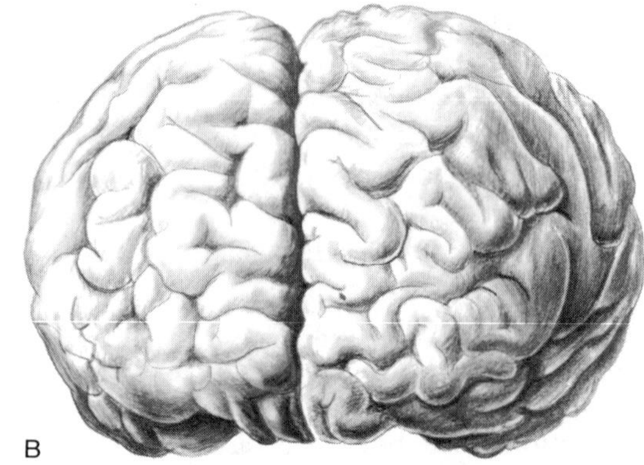

FIGURE 4-2. Reproduced from Wagner (1860), Table 3, showing the frontal lobe of the brain of Gauss (*A*) compared with that of a worker, age 57 (*B*). There is a difference, but part of it is explained by the "stenogyrencephalic" (numerous, narrow gyri) pattern in the former and the "eurygyrencephalic" (fewer but broader gyri) pattern in the latter. Both Retzius' types may occur in well-developed brains. (After Meyer, 1977.)

much temporal lobe could be removed without disrupting speech functions excessively. The professor of surgery, as well as the associate and the assistant professor, all expressed an opinion. It was clear from their estimates that a great deal more of the temporal lobe could be removed, while still sparing speech, if the surgery were done by a professor than if it were done by more junior surgeons!

A final point to note with respect to anatomy is that although our anatomical knowledge continually improves, there are many brain areas whose function is poorly understood. For example, the function of a large brainstem nucleus called the *habenula* is unknown, and the hippocampal formation is thought by different people to be involved in olfaction, emotion, internal inhibition, long-term memory, short-term memory, configural associations, and spatial navigation. The difficulty in making an appropriate correlation exists in part because people have maintained traditional, but unsupported, views, and in part because behavioral theory is still too poorly developed to make adequate structure-function correlations.

BIOCHEMISTRY

Remarkable progress has been made in understanding the biochemical organization of the brain. There are, however, some noticeable gaps in understanding how biochemical organization relates to behavior. These can be illustrated with four examples:

First, one current theory of mental illness proposes that variations in the concentration of neurotransmitters may be the basis of the symptoms of the various diseases. For example, increases in norepinephrine cause mania, whereas decreases cause depression. Studies in rats have shown, however, that all brain norepinephrine can be removed without producing a definite change in the animals' behavior.

Second, another line of research has clearly demonstrated that decreases in the amount of dopamine are related to a motor disease called Parkinson's disease. It is surprising, however, that the symptoms of the disease do not appear until more than 97% of central concentrations of dopamine are depleted. Clearly, the brain has mechanisms that compensate for dopamine insufficiency. The important point conveyed by these two examples is that relating fluctuating levels of neurotransmitters to behavior seems tenuous at best, given some of the evidence currently available from experimental studies.

Third, a great deal can be learned by direct manipulation of the biochemistry of the brains of animals, but these techniques cannot be used with humans. Studies with humans often involve such indirect measures as assays of the urine or cerebrospinal fluid for byproducts of chemical reactions. A high concentration of such a byproduct in a schizophrenic patient may suggest that the precursor of the byproduct is the cause of the schizophrenia. It is equally likely, however, that the behavior of the schizophrenic patient is different from that of a normal person, and the chemical changes are produced by the behavior and are not themselves the cause of the disease. If a schizophrenic patient were very active, for example, it might be expected that biochemical byproducts could be produced by the activity and not the schizophrenia. Such eventualities can be controlled for by having control subjects and experimental subjects engage in identical activities before tests are made, but such procedures are very seldom used.

The fourth problem in biochemical research needs only brief mention, but it is important. Nearly all patients are on some type of drug therapy. The drugs may modify both their brain function and their behavior, with the consequence that any test results obtained from the patient will be confounded by the drug treatments. There is very little that can be done about this problem, except, whenever possible, to collect information from patients before they receive drug therapy.

BRAIN LESIONS

Effects of Brain Lesions on Behavior

The oldest and still most widely used approach to the problem of human brain function is to analyze the effects of lesion, or damage, of circumscribed regions of the central nervous system. In this approach the behavior of humans with restricted lesions resulting from head injury, vascular accidents, tumor, or brain surgery is compared with the behavior of normal control subjects on a variety of standardized behavioral tests. Similar research is done on nonhumans, with the difference that brain lesions can be more precisely located surgically in these species by gently sucking out small portions of tissue with a vacuum pump; by electrolytic lesion, passing strong electric current through a localized area of brain tissue; by heating or cooling tissue; or by placing toxic chemicals in restricted portions of tissue.

The rapid expansion of neuroscience in the past two decades has led to important advances in research methodology that antiquate the lesion technique. For example, with microtechniques a minute quantity of a chemical can be injected into a single neuron of a conscious animal. The effects of the chemical on the behavior of this neuron and others can be recorded, and if special labeling materials are injected into these neurons, the cells and their connections can be located histologically after the death of the animal. Thus, because the larger surgical techniques of neuroscience research have been displaced by the microtechnology of the 1970s and 1980s, the study of the effects of brain lesions on behavior has come under widespread criticism in recent years.

There is a problem in neuropsychology, however: it is not feasible to use most of the modern microtechnology when studying human subjects. Furthermore, because the technology of human neuropsychology is limited, the most direct technique for studying the effects of brain lesions in humans is still to study the effects of analogous lesions in nonhuman animals. In this respect, the lesion technique continues to be an important tool in all of neuropsychology, but its use is fraught with considerable problems. Although brain lesions are relatively simple to produce, correctly interpreting their effects requires a thorough understanding of the problems involved. In the next section we shall consider the effects of brain lesions on brain function, the difficulties associated with the interpretation of lesion studies, and the difficulties in equating lesions with varying neurological disturbances.

Interpreting Brain Lesion Effects

Brain lesions can have three quite different effects on behavior: (1) loss of function, (2) release of function, and (3) disorganization of function.

The most obvious and direct effect of brain lesions is a *loss of function*. For example, if the visual cortex is completely destroyed, pattern vision is permanently lost. Loss of function can also be partial, as when only a portion of the visual cortex is destroyed. It is a general rule that the larger the lesion, the greater the loss of function.

A *release of function* is said to occur if a new behavior appears or the frequency of a particular behavior is drastically increased after a brain lesion occurs. An example of new behavior occurs in victims of Parkinson's disease (the shaking palsy), who develop a tremor in the fingers and hands. Since the loss of some brain area or system could not produce the tremor directly, it is assumed that the lost area normally functioned to prevent tremor, and in its absence tremor is released. An example of increased frequency of a behavior occurs in victims of frontal lobe damage, who often perseverate on, or continue, particular behaviors. For instance, say such a person was required to sort playing cards according to color, and after sorting several cards was then required to sort them by suit; it would be typical of persons with frontal lobe damage to continue sorting by color. Perseverative behaviors imply that one function of the frontal lobe is to inhibit behavior, and damage to that lobe releases behavior from inhibitory control.

Disorganization of function can also follow brain lesion, meaning that bits or pieces of behavior still occur but not in the correct order, or that behaviors occur at the wrong time and place. For example, people with lesions in certain regions of the left hemisphere may be unable to make a cup of tea because they cannot perform the necessary behavioral components (heating water, pouring it over the tea bag into a teapot, pouring the tea into a cup, and adding sugar and milk) in the correct order. Instead, they might place the tea bag in the milk, add sugar to the teakettle, and pour the heated water onto the saucer. It is clear that these people are capable of all the pieces of the behavioral sequence; they simply cannot organize the actions into the correct order.

The inferences drawn from the study of lesion effects depend on whether there is loss, release, or disorganization of function, or, in some cases, a combination of these effects. Behavior must be carefully described, and each of the three principal effects considered, before solid conclusions can be made from the study of brain lesions. A number of factors restrict the inferences one can make about brain function from the study of either humans or nonhumans with brain lesions. These factors include locus of damage, recovery from damage, sparing of function, side effects of damage, disturbances in regions not directly damaged, crowding, and source of damage.

Locus of Damage. It has been recognized for hundreds of years that damage in the brainstem can have more devastating effects on behavior in general than a similar extent of damage in the neocortex. For example, in the winter of 1977 a young skier had a catastrophic spill in a downhill race and landed on his head at a speed in excess of 60 miles per hour. The resulting compression and twisting of the brainstem from the impact of the fall produced a lesion that resulted in permanent coma. Autopsy studies of people with similar traumatic accidents indicate that the lesion in the brainstem responsible for the coma may be very small indeed. This observation stands in stark contrast to the famous case of Phineas Gage. Gage suffered an accidental removal of his frontal lobes when an iron bar was blown through his head, but, remarkably, he was merely stunned for a few seconds and managed to walk to medical assistance. The comparison between the skier and Gage is particularly surprising when one considers that Gage's lesion was 20 to 30 times larger than the skier's.

Recovery from Damage. Following brain injury there are often a number of behavioral changes that are transient and gradually disappear. A middle-aged man, Mr. B., suffered a small stroke in the left hemisphere and was subsequently unable to talk, read, or write. We followed his recovery over a period of 6 weeks, and he gradually began to regain his language skills, although even 3 months after the stroke he was still seriously impaired. When we next saw him, 1 year later, he was much improved and was capable of carrying on a conversation, although his speech was somewhat slower than normal because he had difficulty finding words. Mr. B. illustrates clearly the phenomenon of recovery of function. Although recovery processes such as those observed in Mr. B. are as yet poorly understood, their study is an important part of lesion research because they are a source of inferences regarding function. Had Mr. B. been examined 2 weeks after the stroke, the conclusions about the effect of his lesion would be rather different from those made 1 year later. This issue is further complicated by the variability of recovery in humans: Recovery may take days, weeks, or even years; and in some cases recovery may never occur. Many people with lesions similar to Mr. B.'s never regain the ability to talk, read, and write, even with years of therapy.

Sparing of Function. It has long been known that brain injury sustained in infancy has far less severe effects on behavior than similar damage inflicted in adulthood; if the injury occurs early enough, it may have no effect at all on behaviors that have not yet developed at the time of injury. Thus, just as some functions recover with time, some functions are spared from disruption if the brain lesion occurs early in life. The best example of this phenomenon can be seen in the effects of left hemisphere lesion on speech. Children who suffer left hemisphere cortical damage between about 5 and 10 years of age may initially experience a period in which they are unable to talk, but they usually recover this ability, and they are likely to do so more completely than Mr. B. did. On the other hand, children who suffer such damage before they begin to speak will not experience a period of language disturbance; they begin to speak at the usual time, or they may be retarded by only a few months. These children are said to have a sparing of function, rather than recovery, since the function was never lost. Hence, the conclusions one may draw from brain-behavior relations obviously differ according to whether the brain damage was sustained early in life or in adulthood.

Side Effects of Damage. Brain damage may affect behavior not only directly but also indirectly. A common cause of epilepsy is brain damage in which cells in the region of the lesion are not destroyed but instead act in an abnormal way, thereby producing the characteristic seizures. The appearance of a seizure disorder complicates the study of brain lesions, because change in behavior may be a result of the seizures, not the lesions. Furthermore, certain lesions may produce significant changes in personality that in turn obscure or distort the effects of the lesion on other behaviors. For example, Ms. P. was a 22-year-old undergraduate psychology major who suffered the rupture of a large aneurysm of the middle cerebral artery, resulting in extensive damage to the right temporal and parietal lobes. Prior to the accident she was an excellent student, but subsequent to it she was experiencing difficulties, especially in writing term papers—not because she was unable to read or write, but rather because she had become obsessed with writing the perfect paper, an obsession that resulted in no paper at all. Thus, her lesion indirectly prevented her from writing by producing a change in personality.

Disturbances in Regions Not Directly Damaged. Changes in behavior following brain damage can sometimes be attributed to disturbances in regions not directly affected by the lesion. It is naive to assume that brain lesions affect only the region actually damaged because any lesion initiates changes in those regions that are connected to the damaged area. For example, if lesions occur in the neocortex, cells die in the thalamus, because the axons of thalamic cells, which project to the neocortex, are damaged by the cortical lesion. Furthermore, lesions in some regions of the brain have been shown to produce morphological, biochemical, and physiological changes in areas far removed from the damaged area. To illustrate, lesions of the hypothalamus destroy not only the cells in that region but also fibers passing through it en route from lower centers of the brainstem to the forebrain. Thus, fibers projecting from the substantia nigra to the basal ganglia can be damaged by hypothalamic lesions, resulting in a reduction in the levels of dopamine in the caudate nucleus. It is therefore reasonable to assume that some effects of hypothalamic lesions are actually caused by imbalances in the basal ganglia, which creates difficulties in making inferences about hypothalamic function.

Crowding. There are circumstances when brain lesions can have unexpected effects. Such is the case with *crowding,* which seems to occur with brain lesions in very young children. There is recovery of function, but the recovery seems to be accomplished by the function being mediated by brain areas that would ordinarily not perform it. For the area to take on this new responsibility it gives up control over some or all of the functions it might normally be responsible for. Hence, it is thought that the one function crowds out the other. That crowding can occur enormously complicates the interpretation of the effects of early lesions because the principles used to study these effects are derived from adult cases.

Source of Damage. Although both naturally occurring and surgically induced lesions result in the death of neurons, not all brain lesions in a given zone of tissue produce exactly the same behavioral effects. Tumor patients frequently do not behave like patients with lesions from other causes, because tumors may produce pressure on widespread parts of the brain, resulting in symptoms unrelated to the region where the tumor actually resides. Furthermore, although the primary effects of tumors such as **meningiomas** result from pressure, the primary effects of infiltrating tumors such as **glioblastomas** may result from interference with the normal functioning of neurons in the affected area. An additonal problem in equating lesions of different sources is that the extent of naturally occurring lesions is usually poorly documented, if at all. Various brain scans (see Chapter 6) can provide an estimate of the extent of the damaged region, but visual inspection provides the only certain measure. Since surgically induced lesions of the neocortex can be photographed at the time of surgery, these lesions provide a more precise relation between brain and behavior. However, even here there are other difficulties, because surgical lesions are not purposely introduced into normal human brains. The patient would not be receiving surgery had there not been some prior neurological disorder; thus, there is a potential interaction between disease and surgery. For example, although epileptics are often nearly seizure-free after surgery, it is the usual practice to require continued medication to ensure the absence of seizures. There is another problem associated with epilepsy: years of poorly controlled seizures may have produced significant abnormalities in regions of the brain far removed from the lesion, further complicating any determination of the site of damage.

STIMULATION

Brain stimulation evokes three general types of effects: (1) it produces relatively discrete actions, such as the twitching of a cat's paw when the appropriate portion of the motor cortex is stimulated; (2) it produces an overall energizing effect on behavior, such as when the hypothalamus is stimulated and the animal displays approach or avoidance behavior, eating, or sexual behavior; and (3) it elicits abnormal electrographic effects on brain tissue, which themselves could lead to convulsions or other behaviors. The interpretation of just which type of effect is related to a particular behavior is not always easy, nor are results always wisely interpreted. Let us consider some rather well known results from the human brain stimulation studies of Wilder Penfield. The following is an account from an introductory textbook that summarizes one of Penfield's experiments.

> We are in the operating room of the Montreal Neurological Institute observing brain surgery on Buddy, a young man with uncontrollable epileptic seizures. The surgeon wants to operate to remove a tumor, but first he must discover what the consequences will be of removing various portions of the brain tissue surrounding the tumor. . . . Suddenly, an unexpected response occurs. The patient is grinning; he is smiling; eyes opening when the area is stimulated. "Buddy, what happened, what did you just experience?" "Doc, I heard a song, or rather a part of a song, a melody." "Buddy, have you ever heard it before?" "Yes, I remember having heard it a long time ago, but I can't remember the name of the tune." When another site is stimulated, the patient recalls in vivid detail a thrilling childhood experience.
>
> In a similar operation, a woman patient "relived" the experience she had during the delivery of her baby. As if by pushing an electronic memory button, the surgeon, Dr. Wilder Penfield, has touched memories stored silently for years in the recesses of his patients' brains. (Zimbardo and Ruch, 1975, pp. 48–49)

The interpretation placed on these results is that the brain stimulation was activating actual memory traces that had been placed in the brain many years before. Penfield himself also thought that something like this was occurring, for he remarked, "The astonishing aspect of the phenomenon is that suddenly he is aware of all that was in his mind during an earlier strip of time" (Penfield, 1969, p. 152). This interpretation of Penfield's results has contributed to the belief on the part of many people that information stored in long-term memory is permanent, although not always accessible. Elizabeth and Geoffrey Loftus have arrived at quite a different opinion on the basis of rereading the case reports. First, Penfield only rarely obtained the effect. Of 1132 cases, only 40 showed the phenomena when given brain stimulation. Even considering the fact that only temporal lobe stimulation evoked recall, these 40 cases constituted only 7.7% of the 520 cases that received temporal lobe stimulation. Of the 40 cases, many reported only hearing vague sounds or seeing vague things. When these are excluded, there remain only 22 responses obtained from 12 people seeming to indicate that actual memory traces were being rekindled. Even among these it is not clear that a memory was being activated, because one woman who reported being in a lumberyard stated afterward that in real life she had never been in one. Even if a few cases are examples of what could be memory rekindling, the possibility that something like a dream was being elicited cannot be ruled out.

In a review of these types of elicited response in his own patients and in the patients of others, Halgren makes the following points. First, the effects are uncommon, occurring in less than 8% of patients. Second, in nearly 50% of patients that show the effects stimulation concomitantly produces an epileptiform activity called an **afterdischarge.** Three, there appears to be no relation between the location of stimulation and the category of the experience. Fourth, the same stimulation often evokes different effects. Fifth, after removal of the temporal lobe, some patients may still experience the same phenomena. Sixth, only patients with certain types of personality appear to display the phenomena. Seventh, the phenomena appear to be related often to events of the moment and can be changed by altering the mood of the patient with suggestion. In summary, the evidence suggests that the phenomena may be an artifact of the abnormal electrical activity elicited by the stimulation, that they occur at some site distant from the stimulation electrode, and that they seem more related to the auras that precede epileptic attacks or to hallucinations than to rekindled memory traces.

Of course, the lesson from the stimulation example given here is not that the phenomena are unreal or uninteresting. On the contrary, they are interesting, but they must be critically examined before generalizations about their significance are formed. The same type of critique must be made of other types of stimulation phenomena. It is well documented that animals and humans will press a bar to obtain repeated trains of brain stimulation. Literally hundreds of studies have been carried out to explain this behavior. To date, the explanations include: they like it, it produces an unpleasant aftereffect that can be erased with another stimulation, it produces movements that are reinforcing, it produces sensations that are reinforcing, it produces reinforcement followed by motivation, it produces abnormal brain activity that results in seemingly automatic behavior, and so on. Just to make things a little more complicated, Valenstein has taken a strong theoretical position that the effects of brain stimulation cannot be directly attributed to brain stimulation per se, since a given effect can be obtained from many stimulation sites and can persist even if the stimulated tissue is removed. Of course, any or all of the interpretations may be correct, but the trick lies in establishing the parameters within which any possible interpretation can be considered correct.

RECORDING ELECTRICAL ACTIVITY

Interpreting the electrical activity recorded from the brain has its own special problems. Surprisingly, decisions about whether an electrical event is normal or abnormal are relatively easy to make. This is because a large number of cases can be collected to establish norms. It is interpreting the significance of normal electrical activity that can be difficult. Consider the patterns of EEGs recorded from the neocortex (Figure 2-14). The excited, or activated, pattern (Figure 2-14, topwave) is obtained from a wide range of cortical areas, and in each it appears surprisingly similar, even though there is good evidence to indicate that each area has different functions. Apparently the activated state cannot be used to determine what different areas do. To complicate things further, the activated state looks very similar in different species of animals. The activated EEG obtained from a mammal even looks like recordings obtained from a housefly. Therefore, it is not possible, or at least not easy, to tell species apart by examining EEG activity.

The now-classic interpretation of cortical EEG-behavior relations is shown in Figure 2-14. Stated simply, a fast, desynchronized pattern is thought of as a sign of arousal or consciousness, whereas successively larger and slower waveforms are thought to be correlates of relaxation, sleep, and coma. This interpretation is not without its problems, however. First, the activated pattern occurs during dream sleep. Although one may only hypothesize that the state of dream sleep is different from nondream sleep, it is obvious that dream sleep is not like being awake and conscious. Because the activated EEG occurring during dream sleep so resembles the pattern of the conscious brain, dream sleep was called *paradoxical sleep*. The introduction of this terminology, however, did nothing to change the anomalous relation between EEG and behavior. Second, the EEG-consciousness relation is greatly complicated by the observation that an activated EEG also occurs when people or animals are under certain kinds of anesthetics. It even occurs when they are in a state of coma. Since such observations clearly negated the standard relationship between activated-EEG and consciousness, they were usually ignored. Third, there are times when conscious individuals display a slow-wave EEG. Even having the eyes go out of focus or closing them is sufficient to produce slow waves. It has been suggested, tongue in cheek, that these states should instead be called "paradoxical waking."

In a recent theoretical review, Case Vanderwolf and Terry Robinson suggested that many of the difficulties with current EEG-behavior relations evaporate if the EEG is thought of as a correlate of behavior rather than as a correlate of consciousness, arousal, or attention. The first kind of evidence supporting this view is that there are two types of activated EEGs, virtually indistinguishable to visual inspection but identifiable by pharmacological manipulations. Whenever an activated pattern occurs in an immobile animal, irrespective of whether the animal is awake and alert, immobile in dream (paradoxical) sleep, anesthetized, or in a coma, the activated EEG is the type that can be abolished by anticholinergic drugs such as atropine sulfate. Whenever the activated pattern occurs in a moving animal, irrespective of whether the movement occurs spontaneously or is a twitch or rapid eye movement during paradoxical sleep, the activated EEG is of a type that cannot be abolished by an anticholinergic agent. A second class of evidence for the view of EEG as a correlate of behavior is that whenever slow-wave activity appears, it occurs when animals are immobile, irrespective of whether they are awake and alert, asleep, anesthetized, or in coma. Slow-wave activity does not occur when animals move. This new evidence not only questions the traditional view of EEG-behavior relations, it can be generalized to other kinds of brain events. In short, it suggests that such things as single-unit activity, evoked potentials, and other electrical events are more apt to be related to the behavior of subjects than to such states as consciousness, attention, arousal, motivation, and so forth. This view is, of course, not encouraging to those who believe that the object of neuroscience is to explain these kinds of states, but it is encouraging to those who believe the object is to explain behavior.

BEHAVIORAL ANALYSIS

The rules of good science are usually explicitely taught in laboratory courses. Briefly, proper science requires: (1) stating a theory composed of a set of postulates with all terms operationally defined, (2) making logical deductions or predictions about behavioral outcomes, and (3) comparing the predictions with the results of carefully controlled experiments, leading to a confirmation of the theory. This procedure is called the *hypothetico-deductive method.* There is also another way of doing science, it is the *empirico-inductive method.* It is empirical in the sense that reliance is placed on experience and observation, without regard to systems and theories, and inductive in the same sense that meaningful generalizations or regularities are constructed from the results of the observations. Ideally, both approaches can be used together. The empirico-inductive method can be used to obtain new phenomena and the new insights into behavior and then the hypothetico-deductive method can be used for its more formal strengths. Still, there are difficulties in proceeding in the study of behavior that neither approach can remedy. These include (1) methods of gathering information, (2) the question of the number of subjects required to make an observation significant, (3) decisions about the proper behavior to be studied, and (4) problems of measurement.

Information Gathering

The technique of gathering information in favor of a point has been in use for a long time. Early biological investigations, such as those done by Darwin, used just such a procedure. The most obvious mistake that can be made, and it is one that is often overlooked, is that of *exclusively* gathering information in favor of a position. This was the error made by the phrenologist Gall. He gathered thousands of bits of evidence that purported to support his theory that bumps on people's heads reveal something about their personality. What Gall failed to do was subject his observations to any test. The test that must be used is provided by statistical theory; it is called the null hypothesis. The *null hypothesis* states that there is no difference between two things or groups. Evidence is then collected and the hypothesis is rejected or confirmed on the basis of the evidence. Gall's error was to state that a bump at point *X* indicated personality trait *Y* and then to collect examples. Had he stated his hypothesis correctly—There is no difference between people with bumps at point *X* and people without bumps at point *X*—he would have been forced to examine all people with and without bumps and come to some sort of mathematical decision about whether the hypothesis could be rejected. The error of gathering only information in favor of a point is made surprisingly often. For example, a scientist may state that recovery of function is common and proceed to gather examples of recovery until the reader is overwhelmed by the evidence. The evidence, however, may come from only a small portion of the population of people who incurred brain damage. Much of the early research on patients subjected to psychosurgery contains errors of this sort (see Valenstein); only confirmatory evidence was collected, and that evidence then perpetuated the popularity of the surgery.

Subject Number

There is an unwritten rule in behavioral science that the smaller the subject, the more subjects required to make valid decisions. Generally, a group should consist of 10 mice, 6 rats, 2 monkeys, or 1 elephant. We insist that we are unaware of any reason why an observation on one elephant should be any more valid than an observation on one mouse. Another unwritten rule is that if differences are large, fewer subjects are required. Again, we do not believe that large differences are any more real than small ones. A third unwritten rule is that particularly interesting phenomena do not require the support of a lot of subjects. Here, one could argue that interest is often in the eye of the observer. Apart from these unwritten rules, it is often the case that neuropsychological and neurological journals publish articles based on the study of a single patient. Although these studies are often detailed and competent examinations of the behavior of that particular patient, they are of limited value in constructing a general theory of human neuropsychology because there are serious difficulties in generalizing from the behavior of one person to the behavior of all people. It is commonly recognized that the behavior of individuals varies enormously, but it is also necessary to recognize that brain structure also varies considerably from person to person. A mass of gray matter known as the massa intermedia, which connects the left and right thalami across the midline, is missing in nearly one-quarter of the population; at present there is no known relation between the presence or absence of this structure and behavior. Indeed, even though the convolutions of the human brain are drawn and photographed in every textbook of neurology and neuroanatomy, the pattern of convolutions is not precisely the same in any two brains (Figure 4-2).

To complicate matters, even when there is no gross variation in the structure of two brains, two normal people can vary on neuropsychological tests even to the point that one person appears brain damaged! It is because of such normal variation that most scientific studies of behavior require the use of at least simple statistics to clearly demonstrate the results. The nature of the statistics used generally determines the number of subjects that are used. Studies of individual cases run the risk of making serious errors in inference because of peculiarities in the subject's neuroanatomy or behavior, or an interaction of the two. Although in this book we emphasize studies of more than one patient, we still consider single-case studies, keeping in mind their weaknesses.

Choice of Behavior

There has been a long-standing debate about the behaviors that psychologists should select for examination. Many psychology textbooks reflect their bias in the choice of chapter headings, which include titles such as emotion, attention, arousal, and consciousness. Behaviorists, on the other hand, argue that only observable events can be adequately measured and studied. In part, the problem arose because psychology evolved from philosophy, and problems of mind and mental states were questions that were important to philosophers. Many neuroscientists happened to agree with philosophers. Behaviorists rebelled against this approach. At some point every psychologist involved in research must come to a decision about what to study. We suggest that fewer mistakes are made when observable events are studied than when hypothetical or mental constructs are studied. The following example may serve to illustrate this point. The hippocampus produces a distinctive waveform called the hippocampal *theta* rhythm (see Figure 4-3). In their initial study, Green and Arduini suggested that this waveform is a sign of arousal, because whenever animals were excited, they displayed this rhythm in their brainwaves. Routtenburg observed that the pattern was present in rats before they became habituated to a novel environment, suggesting that it is related to motivation. Adey, however, observed that the frequency of the wave changed as cats mastered a T-maze, suggesting the pattern is related to learning. Finally, Graeff and his coworkers suggested that the pattern is a correlate of fear because it appears when rats receive foot shock. Vanderwolf simply observed animals during spontaneous behavior. He found that the pattern appeared in rats whenever they made a certain class of movements (including running, walking, and turning). As it turns out, the movement hypothesis accounts for the data far more simply and elegantly than other hypotheses. Aroused, motivated, trained, or frightened rats may all have one behavior in common — they move. Just how dramatically an EEG waveform can change with changes in behavior is illustrated in Figure 4-3. Note that both the amplitude and the frequency of the rhythm change; amplitude is large with large movements and frequency is fast with movements that are vigorous or involve rapid acceleration. Once one is adept at reading such records, it almost becomes possible to describe the behavior from the record. Vanderwolf has argued strongly against the study of mental events by stating that the brain is unlikely to be subdivided along the lines of a dictionary. He illustrates his point with the following story:

> Consider the case of Professor Omega, an imaginary researcher who suspected that the somatic [body] muscles had a direct role in mental processes. Omega began his research by recording electromyographic activity (EMG) from m. pectoralis [a muscle] major during behavior in animals. His first finding was that on exposure of an animal to an unfamiliar Skinner box, EMG activity was high initially but declined progressively during continued exposure. Presentation of tones and flashing lights led to temporary increases in EMG activity. These findings suggested a role of the muscle in habituation and attention. When the animal was trained to press a lever in the box, EMG activity rose to a high level. **Extinction** procedures result in a decline to pretraining levels. These facts suggest a role for the muscle in conditioning and learning. Further research showed that EMG activity rose during food deprivation and fell after feeding, suggesting a role in motivational phenomena. Amphetamine increased EMG activity sharply, but anaesthetics abolished it. Tranquilizers had an intermediate effect.

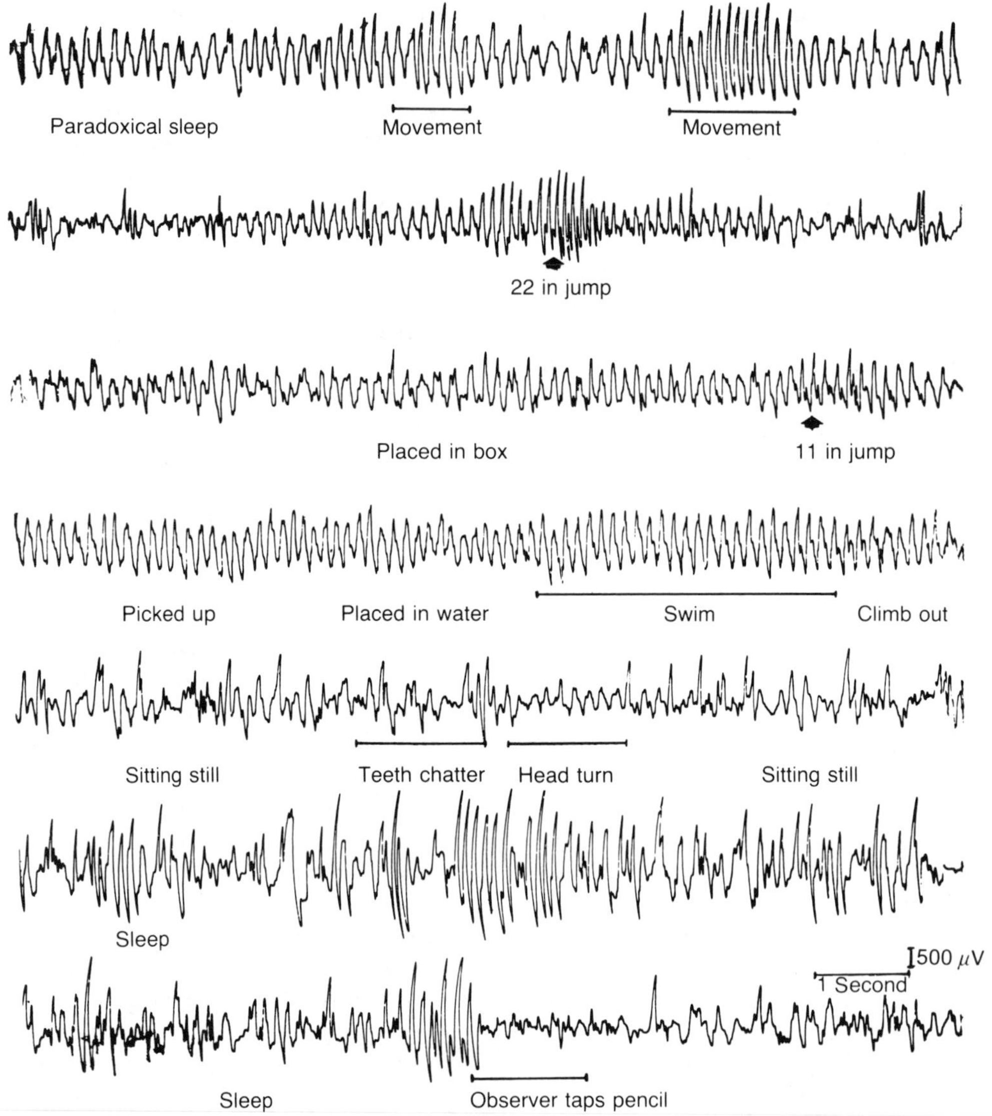

FIGURE 4-3. Electrical activity (*theta* rhythm) at a single hippocampal site during sleep and various behaviors in the rat. Note the following: rhythmical slow activity (RSA) during paradoxical sleep, struggling when held in the hand, swimming, and head movement; large-amplitude irregular activity when sitting still while alert and while chattering the teeth; irregular slow activity and "spindling" during slow-wave sleep; and small-amplitude irregular activity when the rat was awakened but did not move about. Note also the following: increased RSA frequency and amplitude associated with twitching during paradoxical sleep and with jumping in avoidance tasks; different frequencies and amplitudes of RSA associated with head movements, swimming, jumping 11 in and jumping 22 in. Calibration: 1 sec, 500 μV; half-amplitude filters, 0.3 and 75 Hz. Electrode placement: CA1, hippocampus major. (After Whishaw and Vanderwolf, 1973.)

> Omega concluded that the pectoralis muscle was probably the site of action of many drugs.
>
> To his surprise, Omega had great difficulty in publishing his results in scientific journals. In response to criticisms of his work, he pointed out that the methods and experimental design he had used were identical to those adopted by many researchers who had published papers purporting to show that the slow wave or unit activity of the neocortex, the hippocampus and many other parts of the brain is related to attention, learning, motivation, etc.
>
> The error made by Omega seems obvious to everyone because we know that EMG activity is strongly related to movement and posture. Any procedure whatsoever that alters behavior will alter EMG activity. Only recently has it become obvious that similar considerations apply in the brain since brain activity too is likely to be correlated with concurrent movement. (Vanderwolf, 1983, pp. 92–93)

In summary, the reader might consider that mental illnesses are not disorders of the mind but disorders of certain types of behaviors. Septal lesions do not produce emotional disorders, but they do increase the probability that rats will bite in certain unfamiliar situations. Children who write mirror-image letters may not do so because they have a reversed image of the world but because they perseverate in making the movements just used in writing a preceding letter. Hyperactive children do not have a disorder in paying attention, but they make movements incompatible with sitting still. Schizophrenic people do not have a split between cognitive and emotional functions, but they seldom make facial expressions. With practice, it is possible to become quite adept at distinguishing between behavioral and nonbehavioral descriptions.

Measurement. It might be thought that of all the procedures used in neuropsychology, the measurement of things or events might be the easiest to perform and replicate. This is not true. Many measures are made to obtain inferences about some other processes. For example, in the procedure called **dichotic listening,** different words are played through headphones to each ear and the subject is asked to recall as many words as possible. If more words are recalled from the right ear than from the left ear, the inference is made that speech is lateralized to the left hemisphere. The assumptions underlying this inference are relatively simple, yet there are so many variables that affect the result that Bryden has found it necessary to devote an entire book to the problem. Perhaps, one may ask, if a more objective measure of something like brain size were used, would the results be clearer? This, however, seems unlikely. There appear to be so many different ways to measure objects, that almost any result can be obtained. Consider the following.

Probably everyone has had the feeling that their feet are not exactly the same size. Often the difference manifests itself as greater discomfort in one foot when breaking in a new pair of shoes (we have never heard anyone suggest that the shoes might be different sizes). Differences in brain organization may be related to foot size. For example, people in medicine have known for a long time that damage to one hemisphere at an early age leads to smaller limbs in the contralateral side of the body (Figure 4-4). Jere and Jerome Levy attempted to measure differences in foot size in normal people in order to make inferences about cerebral organization. They measured foot size in 150 individuals. They found that significantly more right-handed females had larger left than right feet, whereas significantly more right-handed males had larger right than left feet. Just the opposite result was obtained with left-handed females and males. The Levys' measures were made by converting foot size to shoe size and then converting differences to a 7-point rating scale. A number of studies attempted to repeat the Levys' work. Mascie-Taylor and his coworkers measured foot size using "standard anthropometric technique"

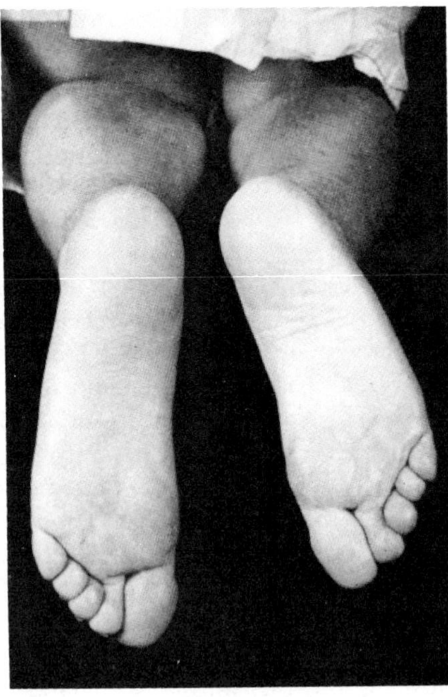

FIGURE 4-4. Growth asymmetry due to destruction of the left frontoparietal region at the time of birth. Such a case demonstrates that growth has a cortical control, quite aside from the effect of disuse, affecting limb size. (From W. Penfield and H. Jasper, Copyright © 1954. Reprinted with permission.)

(described elsewhere as heel to longest toe with the subject seated and with the toenails cut). They found that the left foot was longer than the right in both sexes, confirming seven previous studies. There were no handedness effects. Peters and his coworkers measured the actual foot length from the heel to the longest toe in 365 seated subjects. They found no significant differences between the left and the right foot for any sex or handedness group, and they claimed partial support for their results from three other studies. Yanowitz and his colleagues traced the outline of 105 subjects' feet on a large sheet of paper. They found no differences in foot size with regard to sex or handedness. The final score on this series of studies is: one study for sex and handedness effects, eight studies for a left-foot effect, and two studies for no differences, with three additional studies in partial support for no differences. Of course, this story like all good stories has a sequel, but we refer the interested reader to Peters' recent review.

It might initially have been thought that measuring foot size is a relatively easy matter. This series of studies shows that it is not. Depending on the measuring device, the points across which length is measured, whether subjects are seated or standing, the time of day, and perhaps even shoe type worn before measurement, different measures can be obtained. In many of the studies the importance of these variables was not recognized, and in others the procedure was not described in sufficient detail to permit exact replication. It is interesting that the most objective measure, photography, was not used in any of the studies (see Figure 4-4). A photographic record of the feet would have permitted reevaluation of the results at any time by investigators interested in the question of appropriate measurement.

There are perhaps three lessons that should be derived from this example (one of them is not that it is impossible to make measurements). The first is that if measuring something like feet is difficult, then inferring something about the brain from such measures should be done with caution. The second is, there is nothing wrong with making multiple measures. If they correlate then each is measuring the same thing, but if they do not then the operation of multiple factors is indicated, or else some of the measures are not reliable. The third is that if a measurement is to be made, then it should be the most meaningful one that can be made.

What Should One Measure?

Since earliest times, students of psychology have thought that the central objective of the discipline is to disclose the nature of the mind. Consequently, objectives of research include emotion, motivation, thought, memory, and the like. These sorts of topics are still the major interest of psychology. For example, Skinner has compiled a list of elements of behavior that most people would consider typifies the sorts of things that psychologists should be interested in. These include:

> sensations, habits, intelligence, opinions, dreams, personalities, moods, decisions, fantasies, skills, percepts, thoughts, virtues, intentions, abilities, instincts, daydreams, incentives, acts of will, joy, compassion, perceptual defenses, beliefs, complexes, expectancies, urges, choices, drives, ideas, responsibilities, elation, memories, needs, wisdom, wants, a death instinct, a sense of duty, sublimation, impulses, capacities, purposes, wishes, an id, repressed fears, a sense of shame, extraversion, images, knowledge, interests, information, a superego, propositions, experiences, attitudes, conflicts, meanings, reaction formations, a will to live, consciousness, anxiety, depression, fear, reason, libido, psychic energy, reminiscences, inhibitions, and mental illnesses. (Skinner, 1974, pp. 207–208)

Murdock, a biologist, gives quite a different list that includes none of the preceding items. His behaviors include:

> age-grading, athletic sports, bodily adornment, calendars, cleanliness, training, community organization, cooking, cooperative labor, cosmology, courtship, dancing, decorative art, divination, division of labor, dream interpretation, education, eschatology, ethics, ethnobotany, etiquette, faith healing, family feasting, fire making, folklore, food taboos, funeral rites, games, gestures, gift giving, government, greetings, hair types, hospitality, housing, hygiene, incest taboos, inheritance rules, joking, kin groups, kinship nomenclature, language, law, luck, superstitions, magic, marriage, mealtimes, medicine, obstetrics, penal sanctions, personal names, population policy, postnatal care, pregnancy, usages, property rights, propitiation of supernatural beings, puberty customs, religious ritual, residence rules, sexual restrictions, soul concepts, status differentiation, surgery, tool making, trade, visiting, weaving, and weather control. (G. P. Murdock, 1945, pp. 124–142)

Clearly, all of these things are relevant to people; nevertheless, the sheer extent of these lists demands that some sort of sensible rule be developed about what to study and correlated with brain function. Perhaps **ethology** (from the Greek *ethos,* meaning habit or manner) provides an answer. Ethology emerged from zoology largely through the work of the German biologists Konrad Lorenz and Nikolaas Tinbergen and is based on the idea that there are phylogenetic adaptations in behavior. Zoology, for example, demonstrates that parts of the body are characteristic of a species and are evolved from similar parts in phylogenetic ancestors. In the same way, much of an animal's behavior is just as characteristic of its species as are its body parts, and was probably evolved through similar mechanisms. For example, ducks have a number of physical features that allow them to be identified as ducks. In the same way they have innate behaviors, such as courtship, that although varying between species, are characteristic. Much of the historical background of ethology is found in the many observations of the complex unlearned behaviors of insects, birds, and mammals. The methodology of ethology includes the description of observable behavior, objective recording of behavior, an inventory of all the behavioral patterns of a species, and flexible research procedures. But most important, the essence of ethology is found in its emphasis on observable behavior and its ties to evolutionary theory. An ethological methodology that might be useful to humans is that being evolved by Jane Goodall for the study of chimpanzees. If ethological principles were incorporated into neuropsychology, it is possible that foot size would not be seen as a terribly important subject for measurement.

REFERENCES

Adey, W. R. Neurophysiological correlates of information transaction and storage in brain tissue. In E. Stellar and J. M. Sprague, eds. *Progress in Physiological Psychology,* vol. 1. New York: Academic Press, 1966.

Bryden, M. P. *Laterality: Functional Asymmetry in the Intact Brain.* New York: Academic Press, 1982.

Goodall, J. *The Chimpanzees of Gombe.* Cambridge, MA: The Belknap Press of Harvard University Press, 1986.

Graeff, F. G., S. Quentero, and J. A. Grey. Median raphe stimulation, hippocampal theta rhythm and threat-induced behavioral inhibition. *Physiology and Behavior* 25:253–261, 1980.

Green, J. D., and A. Arduini. Hippocampal electrical activity in arousal. *Journal of Neurophysiology* 17:533–557, 1954.

Halgren, E. Mental phenomena induced by stimulation of the limbic system. *Human Neurobiology* 1:251–260, 1982.

Levy, J., and J. M. Levy. Human lateralization from head to foot: Sex-related factors. *Science* 200:1291–1292, 1978.

Levy, J., and J. M. Levy. Foot-length asymmetry, sex, and handedness. *Science* 212:1418–1419, 1981.

Loftus, E. F., and G. R. Loftus. One the permanence of stored information in the human brain. *American Psychologist* 35:409–420, 1980.

Mascie-Taylor, C. G. N., A. M. MacLarnon, P. M. Lanigan, and I. C. McManus. Foot-length asymmetry, sex, and handedness. *Science* 212:1416–1417, 1981.

Meyer, A. The search for a morphological substrate in the brains of eminent persons including musicians: A historical review. In M. Critchley and R. A. Hanson, eds. *Music and the Brain.* London: Heinemann Medical Books, 1977.

Murdock, G. P. The common denominator of culture. In R. Linton, ed. *The Science of Man in the World Crisis.* New York: Columbia University Press, 1945.

Penfield, W. Consciousness, memory, and man's conditioned reflexes. In K. Pribram, ed. *On the Biology of Learning.* New York: Harcourt, Brace & World, 1969.

Penfield, W., and H. Jasper. *Epilepsy and the Functional Anatomy of the Human Brain.* Boston: Little, Brown, 1954.

Peters, M. Footedness: Asymmetries in foot preference and skill and neuropsychological assessment of foot movement. *Psychological Bulletin* 103:179–192, 1988.

Peters, M., B. Petrie, and D. Oddie. Foot-length asymmetry, sex, and handedness. *Science* 212:1417–1418, 1981.

Routtenburg, A. Hippocampal correlates of consumatory and observed behavior. *Physiology and Behavior* 3:533–535, 1968.

Skinner, B. F. *About Behaviorism.* New York: Knopf, 1974.

Tinbergen, N. *The Study of Instinct.* London: Oxford University Press, 1951.

Valenstein, E. S. The interpretation of behavior evoked by brain stimulation. In A. Wauquier and E. T. Rolls. *Brain-Stimulation Reward.* Amsterdam: North-Holland Publishing Company, 1972.

Valenstein, E. S. *Brain Control.* New York: Wiley, 1973.

Vanderwolf, C. H. The role of the cerebral cortex and ascending activating systems in the control of behavior. In E. Satinoff and P. Teitelbaum, eds. *The Organization of Behavior.* New York: Academic Press, 1983.

Vanderwolf, C. H., and T. E. Robinson. Reticulo-cortical activity and behavior: A critique of the arousal theory and a new synthesis. *The Behavioral and Brain Sciences* 4:459–514, 1981.

Whishaw, I. Q., and C. H. Vanderwolf. Hippocampal EEG and behavior: Changes in amplitude and frequency of RSA (theta rhythm) accompanying spontaneous and learned movement patterns in rats and cats. *Behavioral Biology* 8:461–484, 1973.

Yanowitz, J. S., P. Satz, and K. M. Heilman. Foot-length asymmetry, sex and handedness. *Science* 212:1418, 1981.

Zimbardo, P. G., and F. L. Ruch. *Psychology and Life,* 9th ed. Glenview, IL: Scott Foresman, 1975.

ORIGINS OF THE HUMAN BRAIN AND BEHAVIOR

A badger recounts the story that God created all animals as embryos and called them before his throne, offering them the changes that they desired. They opted for specialized adult features, claws, teeth, hoofs, antlers, and so forth. But the human embryo, trusting God's judgment, accepted the way it was made. The creator was delighted and said that it would therefore remain an embryo until buried but would dominate the other embryos, and feel sorrow and feel joy. (White 1958)

About 5 million years ago this embryo that walked upright diverged from an ancestral ape lineage. It was to become marked by two characteristics that distinguished it from other animals. First, it was bipedal and such a great traveler that its ancestors populated and repopulated every habitable continent. Second, its brain underwent an unmatched evolution, increasing to about five times its original size. Although this book is about the functions of the human brain as it now exists, an important clue to understanding its present function is to consider its origins and the evolutionary forces that sculpted it. In this chapter we shall review the fossil record of the human brain and then examine the similarities and differences between the brains of living humans and nonhumans.

THE EVOLUTIONARY RECORD

There have been three major advances in the study of human evolution. First, the recent and sudden proliferation of **hominid** fossil discoveries has sparked new interest in human evolution, especially in the evolution of the human brain. By careful examination of the structure of bones, it is possible to make a **morphological reconstruction** of a specimen and compare it with other examples in extinct and living species. An example of a morphological reconstruction of Neanderthal man is shown in Figure 5-1. Such reconstructions demonstrate how similar to, rather than how different from, our ancestors we are.

Second, the discovery of this fossil record has been matched by the development of new methods that add biochemical information to morphological descriptions. A problem with strictly morphological methods is that they may not permit a distinction between *homologous structures* of species (structures that have the same origin) and *analogous structures* (structures that look the same and have the same function but have different origins). For example, some Australian and European birds look similar and occupy similar biological niches. **Biochemical techniques** show these birds are distinct species.

There are a number of such biochemical techniques and some of their strengths and weakness have been described by Jorde. Here we mention three of these techniques in the order of their development. Proteins, such as the hemoglobin of blood or albumin that transports nutrients in the blood, are more similar in closely related than in unrelated animals. The differences in protein amino acids between animals can be counted and compared to the known time of divergence of animals. The technique is very similar to the immunochemical techniques used for anatomical studies (Chapter 3). This provides a molecular clock that can then be used to compare species. For example, old- and new-world monkeys diverged from each other 30 million years ago. Their 24 differences in amino acids suggest a rate of one amino acid change every 1.25 million years. This rate of change can be assumed to apply to other species as well. When applied to primates, it indicates that chimpanzees and humans diverged from each other about 5 million years ago. This indicates that the date of divergence was much more recent than initially thought. The fossil record had initially suggested that the date of divergence was 15 million years ago. Relatedness can also be determined by comparing strands of DNA from different species. Using enzymes, DNA can be cut up into short segments. If the segments are placed in a synthetic gel and subjected to an electrical current they line up, longest to shortest, producing a signature of the owner. Signatures of different animals can be compared and calibrated using known time relations (as above) to establish relatedness. Signatures of modern humans and chimpanzees suggest that they are each other's closest relatives. The most recent biochemical technique uses the DNA from mitochondria. **Mitochondria** are found in the cytoplasm of the cell and are passed from females to their offspring through the cytoplasm of the ovum. The DNA of mitochondria are analyzed in the way described above, but the analysis is easier since there are fewer base pairs in mitochondria than in nuclear DNA. Mitochondrial analysis confirms a common ancestor for all modern humans within the last 200,000 years. Future techniques may include analyzing DNA from the Y chromosome, which permits tracking relationships through substances passed only between males.

Third, the development of new methods of behavioral analysis are beginning to disclose the evolutionary forces that sculpted modern humans. The behavioral studies are directed at humans and their proximate relatives (chimpanzees, gorillas, orangutans, and gibbons), as well as their more distant relatives (baboons and monkeys). Goodall's behavioral studies of chimpanzees paint a picture of a relative so close to humans that one has the impression of looking into a mirror. These creatures occupy large territories that the males defend as a group. They also wage war, killing neighbors, to expand their territories. They are great travelers, ambulating along the ground at a rate that humans have difficulty matching for distances of 8 km (kilometers) or more a day. They are omnivores, eating vegetation, fruit, and insects, but they are also capable of hunting cooperatively to catch monkeys, pigs, and other mammals. They

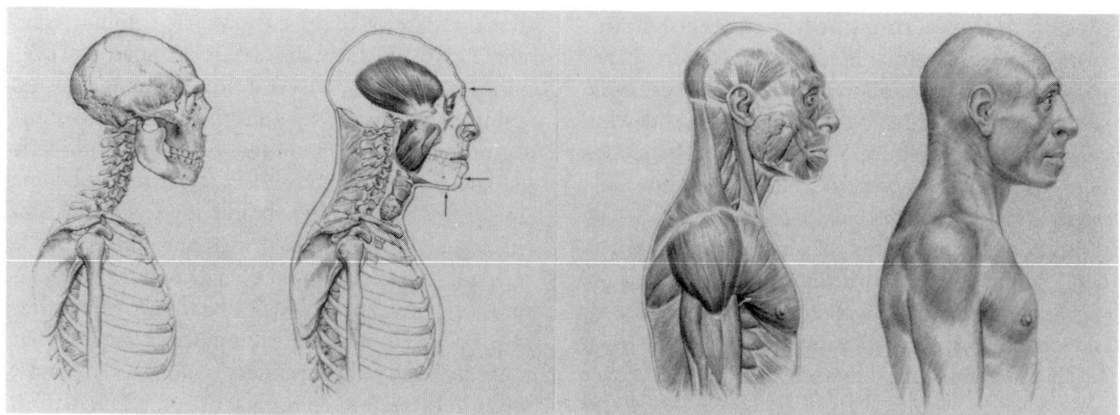

FIGURE 5-1. Reconstruction of the facial features of Neanderthal man. To the bare bones, temporal muscles and an outline of the skin are added. Arrows mark points where thickness is based on needle probes of humans or orangutans. Nose shape is based on projections from bony landmarks. The reconstruction is in striking contrast to previous depictions of Neanderthals as dull-witted and stooped. (Reconstruction by Jay Matternes. From B. Rensberger. Facing the past. *Science 81,* October, 41–81. Copyright © 1981. Reprinted with permission.)

have complex and stable social groups within which family relations are important both for the individual and for group structure. Finally, they have rich manual, facial, and vocal communication capabilities, and they construct and use tools for defense and to obtain food and water.

Human Origins

The story begins in 1859 with Darwin's publication of *Origin of Species.* Darwin carefully avoided the inflammatory subject of human ancestry, preferring to emphasize his studies of barnacles, extinct clams, and exotic animals from the far away Galapagos Islands. In fact, his only reference to human evolution appears at the end of the book, where he states: "Light will be thrown on the origin of man and his history." That was enough! There was an immediate public preoccupation with our alleged ancestral apes, reputedly leading one Victorian lady to have said, "Descended from apes! My dear, we hope it is not true. But if it is, let us pray that it may not become generally known." Our anatomical similarity to apes was difficult to ignore, and soon after *Origin of Species* appeared, T. H. Huxley showed that anatomically we are more similar to apes than apes are to monkeys. (In fact, we now know that more than 99% of our genes are identical with those of chimpanzees.) It was not until 1871 that Darwin concluded in his book *The Descent of Man* that humans descended from a "hairy, tailed quadruped, probably arboreal in its habits." In the following years the public belief emerged that being descended from apes need not be uncomfortable. It was presumed that humans were the pinnacle of a single lineage from extinct apelike animals, which were changed by the perfecting process of natural selection to become the very special product of evolution, *Homo sapiens sapiens.* The only flaws in this view are the facts that have emerged in the past two decades.

Although life may have been on earth for some 650 million years, the fossil record shows that true mammals made their appearance only about 150 million years ago, and monkeylike mammals first appeared only about 25 million years ago. The fossil record of monkeys and apes is very poor, being largely composed of teeth, but it suggested that *Ramapithecus,* the species often claimed to be ancestral to humans and other living apes, lived at least from 8 to 14 million years ago. Biochemical techniques, largely involving the comparison of proteins and DNA in existing humans and apes, suggest a different scenario. Our closest living relatives appear to be the African apes: chimps and gorrilas, and our ancestors diverged from their ancestors about 5 million years ago. The fossil record has not yet revealed exactly who these ancestors were, but about 2 million years ago we see the first appearance of animals that everyone agrees are human. The ancestor is *Australopithecus* (*Australo* meaning southern, and *pithecus* meaning ape). These animals lived in southern Africa and are the first to show a distinctly human characteristic: they walked upright. The conclusion that they walked upright is based on the description of numerous bones and on the discovery of fossilized footprints dated from 3.6 to 3.8 million years ago, footprints that give some indication about how the foot was used. The impressions are hauntingly similar to ours, featuring a well-developed arch and big toe pointing straight ahead, rather than sideways as in apes; they could almost have been made by 20th-century humans.

We have noted that there is a tendency to perceive humans as the end product of a linear process of natural selection, but this view is in error. It is best to think of our recent evolution as being a bush with our species, the only surviving member, sitting alone on one branch. At the base of the bush lie the australopithecines (see Figure 5-2). Fossilized remains of a number of distinct species (*A. afarensis A. africanus,* and *A. robustus)* have been discovered in East Africa and Ethiopia. (For an enjoyable account of the discovery of the Ethiopian fossils we recommend Johanson and Edey's book, *Lucy: The Beginnings of Humankind.*)

The relationship of *Homo* (humans) and australopithecines is controversial. Some people have argued that *A. afarensis* is the common ancestor to *Homo,* to *A. africanus,* and to *A. robustus* (Figure 5-2). *Australopithecus robustus* were apparently more heavily built than *A. africanus* and appear to have had a vegetarian diet; that is, *A. robustus* had massive molars for grinding and developed large ridges around the eyes so that the jaw muscles could be firmly attached to the skull. The development of *A. robustus* is particularly interesting both because it lived side by side with its more slender cousin, *A. africanus,* and because it arose at about the same time and coexisted with the completely new genus, *Homo.* Others have argued that *A. africanus* is the common ancestor or that some other undiscovered creature is the common ancestor.

The oldest fossils to be designated as *Homo* are those found by Louis Leakey in the Olduvai Gorge in Tanzania in 1964, dated at about 1.75 million years old. The specimens are of poor quality and bear a strong resemblance to *Australopithecus,* but Leakey argued that the dental pattern is more similar to modern humans than to australopithecines and, more importantly, that the animal apparently made simple stone tools, which were also found in the Olduvai Gorge. Therefore, Leakey named the species *H. habilis* (i.e., handyman). *Homo habilis* is thought to have given rise to another species of *Homo* (*H. erectus,* upright man, so named because of a mistaken notion that its predecessors were stooped), who first shows up in the fossil record about 1.6 million years ago and lasts until at least 400,000 years ago. *Homo erectus* has a pivotal position in this history because it was a distinct species different from but coexistent with the australopithecines. The brain of this creature was significantly larger than that of any previous animal, and unlike the australopithecines and *H. habilis,* this was a traveler; its remains have been found in East Africa as well as in Java (Java man) and China (Peking man).

According to the fossil record, modern humans, *Homo sapiens sapiens,* appeared in Asia and North Africa about 100,000 years ago and in Europe about 40,000 years ago. The European variety of

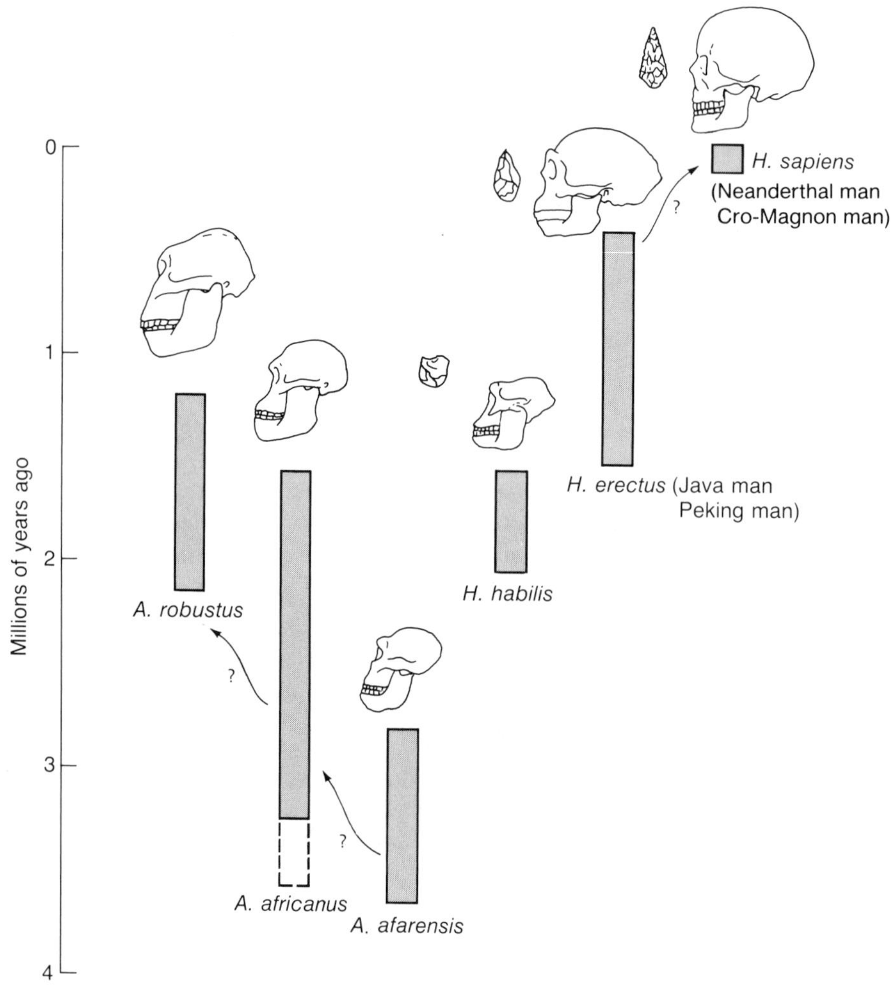

FIGURE 5-2. Summary of the recognized species of the human family. Question marks indicate that the proposed evolutionary relations are uncertain. Notice the development of tools by *Homo* (After Stanley, 1981, and Johanson and Edey, 1981.)

modern man, Cro-Magnon man, displaced Neanderthal man, who then occupied Europe. The designation of this species remains uncertain, some choosing to call it *H. neanderthalensis* and others calling it *H. sapiens neanderthalensis*. It really does not matter a great deal; Neanderthal appeared very much like us, with a brain as large, but was stockier and stronger, apparently being built more for strength than for swiftness. The appearance of Cro-Magnon man was sudden, overlapping with Neanderthal man, although only for a few thousand years.

There has been considerable debate about the relation between Cro-Magnon and Neanderthal man. It has been argued that Neanderthal is ancestral to Cro-Magnon, that Cro-Magnon moved in and mingled with Neanderthal, or that Cro-Magnon simply displaced Neanderthal. If we consider the effects that Europeans have had on other human populations they encountered, the displacement hypothesis is supportable. Within a few years of the Europeans' arriving in the Americas, the numbers of indigenous people were drastically reduced by new diseases and war, and in some places whole populations disappeared. Much the same thing happened in Australia. Thus, it is probable that the early history of *Homo* involved similar interactions.

Mitochondrial analysis of modern people by Cann and her coworkers suggests that all modern people came from an ancestral "Eve" who lived in Africa between 285,000 and 143,000 years ago. This ancestral stock divided into two groups, one of which remained in Africa, the other of which migrated. The analysis further suggests that modern humans did not simply migrate and develop into different races. Rather, there was a great deal of mixing and modern humans migrated around the world intermingling several times before developing into modern races. The kind of migration, intergroup contact, and intermingling that so typifies the last few centuries has apparently been the historical pattern for *Homo sapiens*.

The evolution of modern humans, from the time at which a creature appeared humanlike to the time at which it was morphologically identical to modern man, took nearly 4 million years. Thus, the evolution of the modern human and the modern human brain and its associated cognitive processes must be considered very rapid. Still, most of what has taken place in terms of changed human behavior has taken place recently. *Homo erectus* had discovered the use of fire, but probably did not have the anatomy of the throat needed to be compatible with complex speech as we now know it. Neanderthal man had a brain as large as ours, but may have had a poorly developed vocal apparatus, suggesting that language was still primitive. Nonetheless, Neanderthals apparently buried their dead with flowers, arguably the first evidence of religious belief. By 25,000 years ago Cro-Magnon was producing elaborate paintings on cave walls and carving ivory and stone figurines, providing the first human artistic relics. The tempo of change has quickened in the last 10,000 years. Agriculture and animal husbandry were established in the Middle East by 7000 B.C., followed by ideographic writing in the same region by 3000 B.C. The modern age really began in about A.D. 1500, and it was after this time that most of what we see around us today was invented or discovered. Hence, although most of what we associate with modern humans is of very recent origin, the basic tools for use (i.e., the brain, free hands, and bipedal locomotion) have been with us a very long time. We can only wonder why it took us so long to use our brain as we now do.

In conclusion, modern humans do not represent the final product of a gradual evolution from monkeys, as was envisioned in Victorian times. Several species of hominid creatures have arisen and disappeared, and throughout much of our recent evolutionary history there has been more than one species of hominid alive at a time. None of our ancestors are alive today and, in spite of superficial resemblances to chimpanzees and gorillas, our ancestors diverged from the forerunners of modern apes at least 5 million years ago when they developed an upright stance and bipedal locomotion. The importance of this latter development cannot be underestimated. Bipedalism is not an easy accomplishment. Although all mammals shift their weight forward with their hind limbs, bipedalism required a fundamental reconstruction of the anatomy, particularly of the foot and pelvis. It is presently unknown how bipedalism developed, except that it likely evolved as an adaption to living on open plains instead of in forests. Some people have suggested that bipedalism evolved to allow more efficient pursuit of prey, but a compensation must have been that the hands were simultaneously left free to use tools. By the time

Australopithecus appeared, the change was largely over. We were already different from those animals that became chimpanzees and gorillas, and all subsequent changes in our structure were probably only modifications of the existing structure, rather than a qualitative change such as was required to walk upright.

Episodic Evolution of Humankind

Darwin believed that evolution was gradual, largely being shaped by processes of **natural selection** and **sexual selection.** The fossil record in Darwin's time was poorly documented, but the absence of gradual change in the record was of little concern to Darwin; he simply rejected fossils as a source of evidence for evolution. A hundred years after Darwin the fossil record is well documented, but the data remain the same: there is no evidence for gradual change producing new species. Rather, speciation occurs very rapidly, probably in a few hundred or a few thousand years. Most species exhibit little significant change during their tenure on earth. They appear in the fossil record looking much the same as when they disappeared from it. The view that evolution occurs very rapidly, adopted in the 1980s, marks a major shift in evolutionary biology, and it has two important implications for how we view ourselves and our brain. First, the fact that our ancestors seem to appear suddenly in the fossil record is not an unusual characteristic of hominids; it is a characteristic of most species. Second, the fact that species appear suddenly and then remain static for hundreds of thousands or even millions of years implies that transitional states are unlikely to be discovered. Fossilization of bone only occurs in optimal conditions, and so the bones of animals that lived a static existence for a million years are far more likely to be fossilized than the bones of a transitional stage that may have existed for only a few hundred years. The evolutionary pacemaker was probably climatic change, which required rapid periodic morphological adaptations as our hominoid ancestors were exposed to new climates requiring new survival strategies.

Brain Evolution

Unlike skulls and other bones, soft tissues such as brains do not leave fossil records. Therefore the size and organization of a fossil's brain must be inferred from the shape, size, and other dimensions of the inside of the skull. Two measures are commonly considered: cranial capacity and sulcal pattern.

Cranial Capacity. The cranial capacity of a skull can provide a reasonable estimate of the size of an animal's brain, but we must be wary of assuming that brain size is an index of intelligence. Although it is true that large-brained animals such as chimpanzees appear more intelligent than smaller brained monkeys, we must consider three factors. First, intelligent animals are intelligent in different ways. Animals living in such different ecologies as treetops and water may not require the same size brain to generate their movements. Second, there is considerable variation in the size of brains within a given species. Although human brains average about 1300 g, they range from about 1000 g to nearly 2000 g, with an unreliable correlation between size and apparent intelligence. This range indicates that modern brain size overlaps all but our most ancient predecessors. The organization of the neurons is probably far more important than the mere number. Finally, we must recognize that brain size is based on body size. The larger a body, the more neurons required to convey sensations and move muscles.

Nevertheless, in spite of these difficulties in interpreting brain size, one is still impressed with the dramatic change in cranial capacity between *A. afarensis* and *H. sapiens* (see Figure 5-3). The brain of the early australopithecines was about the same size as that of a modern chimpanzee, about 400 g. None of the australopithecines developed particularly large brains, in spite of the species living for about 3 million years. The first tool-

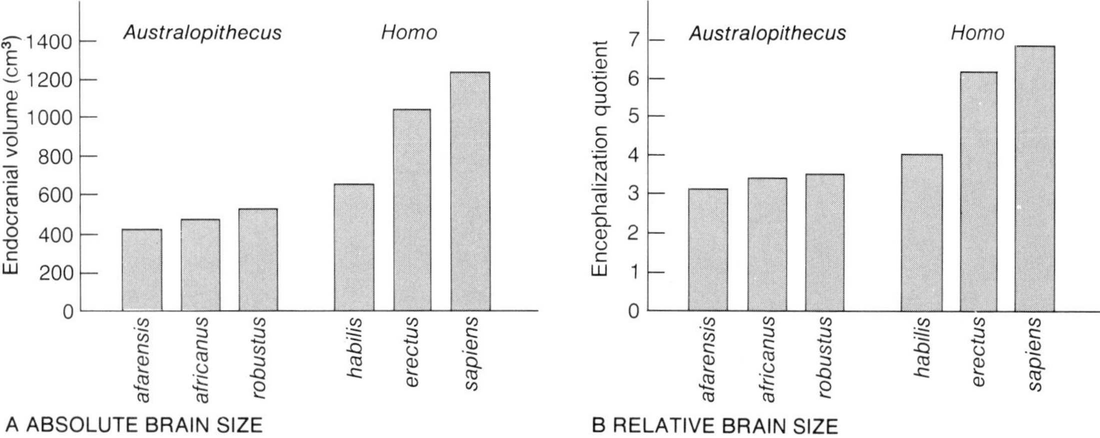

FIGURE 5-3. Endocranial volume (*A*) and encephalization quotients (*B*) for fossil hominids. Notice the sudden increase in brain size in *H. erectus* (Data from McHenry, 1982.)

makers (*H. habilis)* had slightly larger brains, but even theirs were modest, measuring only one-half the size of our brain. The great expansion in brain size obviously occurred in *H. erectus,* because the brain shows an increase in size equal to that of the entire australopithecine brain. The factors that caused the dramatic increase in brain size in *H. erectus* and *H. sapiens* must have acted quickly. The sudden appearance of large-brained *H. erectus* implies that there probably was not a gradual selection of individuals with larger brains, but rather having a larger brain must have conferred a decisive and immediate advantage.

Many explanations have been proposed for this change in brain size — for example, social development, the rigors of an ice age, changes in hunting practices, expansion into more temperature zones — and all may have been contributory. First, humans probably evolved from a chimplike ancestor, who, because it was a highly social creature, required a large brain to maintain effective social relations (see Goodall). Second, humans did get bigger and there is evidence that brain size increase is disproportionately greater than body size increase. Third, humans continuously changed diet, and changes in diet brought with them changes in face and head structure, which may have contributed to increased brain size. Fourth, to the human as a tool user, changes in hand structure and more skillful movements would have been highly advantageous, and these would have contributed to increased brain size, particularly the size of the motor cortex. Fifth, as humans moved into Europe and encountered colder climates there would have been selective advantages for changes in limb and head size for the purposes of heat conservation. Beals and his coworkers argue for the development of a rounder and larger head, because large round objects conserve more heat than smaller oblong ones, thus serendipitously providing more volume. This development would have led to increased brain size. Sixth, throughout this evolutionary period it is apparent that humans were losing strength. Possibly mate selection was being made on the basis of facial features with consequent selection favoring more infantlike features. One such infantile feature is a greater head size relative to body size; this selective preference might have increased brain size and decreased body strength. Whatever the driving factors, any increase in brain size would have produced selective advantages manifest in increased abilities and these in turn would have rapidly reinforced the trend.

As hinted at above, **neoteny** was most likely the mechanism that underlies the evolution of humans. In neoteny, rates of development slow down and juvenile stages of predecessors become the adult features of descendants. Many features of our anatomy link us with juvenile stages of primates including a small face, vaulted cranium, large brain-to-body size, unrotated big toe, upright posture, primary distribution of hair on head, armpits, and pubic areas (Figure 5-4). We also retain behavioral features of infants, including exploration, play, and flexible behavior. An important part of the answer to the Sphinx's riddle about the nature of man is that the man who walks on two legs is sort of an infant chimpanzee.

Is it not likely that the increase in cranial capacity in *Homo* is simply because they are larger animals than the australopithecines? A number of authors, including Jerison and McHenry, have studied this question in detail and have uniformly answered no. Arithmetical correction for differences in body weight can be performed in a number of ways, and in every case the *H. erectus* and *H. sapiens* brains are far larger than would be expected for an australopithecine of the same body size (see Figure 5-3). In summary, there is now little doubt that our brain has undergone a major expansion since we adopted a bipedal style of locomotion. Furthermore, whatever factors caused us to walk upright must have been very different from those that caused our brain to enlarge, because these two major changes are separated by nearly 2 million years.

Sulcal Pattern. The increase in cranial capacity is clearly a hallmark of hominid evolution but, as we have noted, mere size is not the major predictor of intelligence; cerebral organization is at least as important. Attempts to infer the organization of a

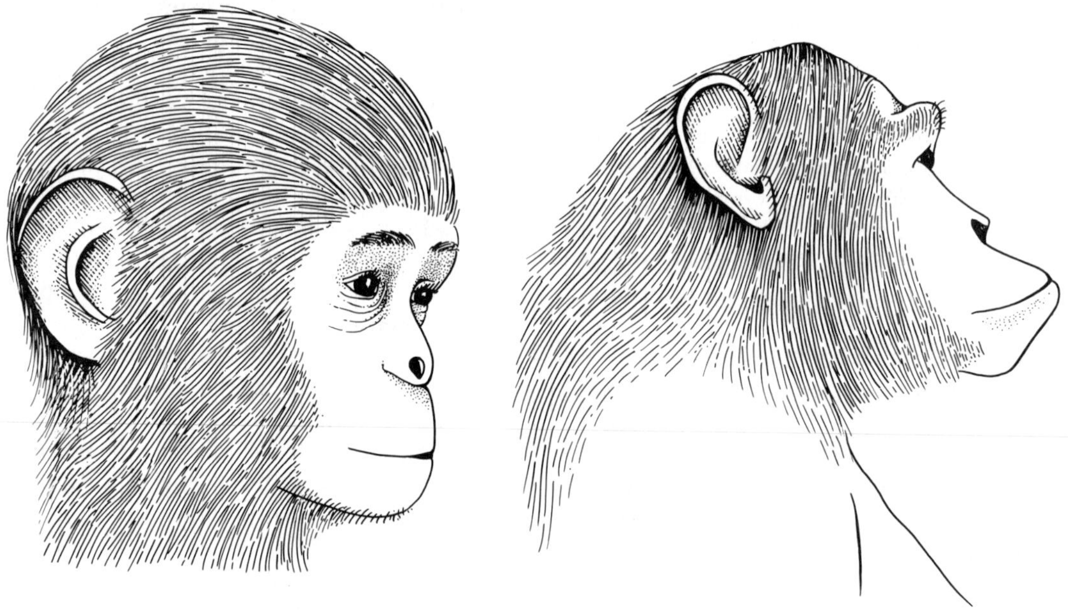

FIGURE 5-4. A juvenile (*A*) and adult (*B*) chimpanzee showing the greater resemblance of humans to the baby chimp and illustrating the principle of neoteny in human evolution. (Adapted from S. J. Gould. *The Mismeasure of Man*. New York: W. W. Norton and Company. Copyright © 1981. Reprinted with permission.)

brain from its size or shape are destined to be controversial, as Gall and his fellow 18th-century phrenologists discovered, but our curiosity about the origin of humankind encourages paleontologists and physical anthropologists to try anyway.

The simplest way to estimate organizational patterns in the brain is to examine the pattern of sulci and gyri on the surface of the cerebral hemispheres. Although this is difficult to infer from the inner wall of the skull, it is possible to determine the position and relative size of the largest sulci, in part because of the indentations on the skull, which correspond to the location of the large cerebral arteries running along these sulci. A number of distinct sulcal patterns can be identified in this manner. Carnivores, ungulates (hooved animals), and primates, for example, have distinctive patterns that differentiate these mammalian orders. Distinctions among families of animals within orders is more difficult, however. Although the brains of chimpanzees and humans have distinctly different sulcal patterns (a pongid [apelike], as opposed to a hominid, pattern), the determination of one pattern or another from the fossilized skulls of australophithecines has proved to be a hazardous preoccupation. Whereas Holloway has argued that these skulls show a definite hominid pattern, Falk and others have been equally convinced that the pattern is either pongid or cannot be categorized at all. In summary, although there is little doubt that consideration of cerebral organization is at least as important as studies of cranial capacity, the organization of the early hominid brain has not yet been demonstrated. Comparative neurology of living mammals, especially apes, is a more likely source of information about the reorganization of the human brain in hominid evolution, and so it is to these brains that we now direct our attention.

WHY STUDY NONHUMAN ANIMALS?

To many people, including many psychologists, human neuropsychology is seen as being wholly independent of the study of animals. It is the study of the *human* brain and *human* behavior. This view largely assumes that both human neuroanatomy and human cognitive processes (i.e., thinking) fundamentally differ from those of other animals. After all, humans talk, read, write, and do all sorts of things that no monkey or rat has ever done. This line of reasoning, however, is shortsighted and wrong. There is no compelling evidence of a qualitative difference in the structure of the human and chimpanzee brains (as we will establish later on in this chapter). One would surely expect there to be such a difference if neuropsychological processes in chimpanzees and humans were fundamentally different. Few psychologists who work with rats or chimps (or any other species) affect a strong interest in rats or chimps for the sake of these animals; their primary interest is in the human brain and in human brain-behavior relations.

Many psychologists agree that comparisons between humans and nonhuman primates such as monkeys and chimpanzees are reasonable, but argue that such comparisons with other species, such as rats or cats, are not. The evolutionary distance between humans and rats is viewed as too great to allow valid generalizations. Indeed, Lockhart and several other authors have argued that the laboratory rat in particular is an indefensible choice for behavioral research. They argue that it has been bred for laboratory work and so for many purposes is a freak, an unnatural animal, and a degenerate compared with its wild cousins. Although domesticated strains of Norway rats no doubt differ in some ways from their wild cousins, Dewsbury has concluded that there is little or no evidence that they are inferior, freaks, unnatural animals or degenerates. Indeed, many aspects of neocortical function in laboratory rats are remarkably similar to those of other mammals, including primates.

We are not suggesting that rats are merely little men in white fur suits. They obviously are not. We are, however, proposing that monkeys, rats, and other animals have an important role in the understanding of human brain-behavior relations, and that to dismiss research on them when discussing human neuropsychology is myopic, unreasonable, and wasteful of valuable information. Furthermore, to insist that nonhuman research be done on primates is morally indefensible at this stage in our knowledge. Many species of nonhuman primates are becoming endangered, and many currently relevant questions would best be studied today using animals that are in no danger of extinction.

What questions can best be addressed through the study of nonhuman species? There are three such primary lines of neuropsychological research: (1) Studies directed toward an understanding of the basic mechanisms of brain functions, (2) Studies designed to produce models of human neurological disorders, and (3) Studies whose aim is to provide a description of the phylogenetic development of the brain. We shall consider each of these separately in the following sections.

The chief purpose of cross-species comparisons in neuropsychology has been to arrive at an understanding of the basic mechanisms of brain function.

> An early example of this method is Harvey's investigation of the function of the heart. In establishing that the blood is transferred by the heart from veins to arteries, Harvey used the fish as a model. In the absence of a secondary circulation to the lungs, the passageway from veins to arteries is apparent. Harvey argued that the pulmonary circulation in mammals had obscured our realization that the function of the heart is the same in all vertebrates. (Diamond and Chow, 1962, p. 174)

In this type of comparative work the species chosen for study depends on the nature of the question under study. For example, neurophysiologists may choose to study the neural activity of giant nerve fibers in the squid because the nerve is so large and accessible. It is assumed that fundamental properties of these nerves are generalizable to mammals and presumably to humans. In addition, sometimes species are merely chosen for convenience. Gerald Schneider chose to study hamsters in his work on subcortical visual mechanisms, not because of an intrinsic interest in hamsters, but because the superior colliculus is more accessible in them than in other mammals.

The second goal of comparative work is to produce models of human neurological disorders. The aim is to produce the disorder, then to manipulate numerous variables in order to understand the cause of the disorder and its course, and ultimately to formulate a treatment. For example, a model of Parkinson's disease has been developed in the rat in order to eventually find the causes of this abnormal behavior in humans and to find treatments to eliminate them. In this type of comparative work animals are really substitutes for humans, because it is assumed that similar principles underlie the cause and treatment of these disorders in humans and nonhumans alike.

The final rationale for using nonhuman species is to provide a neurology of mammalian behavior that emphasizes the phylogenetic development of the human brain. It is assumed that an understanding of the evolutionary development of the human brain is important both for human neuropsychology and, in a broader perspective, for anthropology and related fields. In addressing this question, the choice of species is critical. Experiments with rats, cats, dogs, and rhesus monkeys do not permit inferences regarding evolutionary development because these animals do not form an evolutionary sequence: rats were never ancestral to cats, nor cats to monkeys. All these species evolved independently from some primitive mammalian ancestor, as shown in Figure 5-5. To do comparative work from a phylogenetic perspective, it is necessary to choose closely related species that constitute what Hodos and Campbell have termed a **quasi-evolutionary sequence.** Thus, a series of animals should be used that includes the available living descendants of groups that are believed to be ancestors of more advanced forms (see Figure 5-6). For example, Masterton and Skeen have studied the phylogenetic development of auditory processing by using opossums, hedgehogs, tree

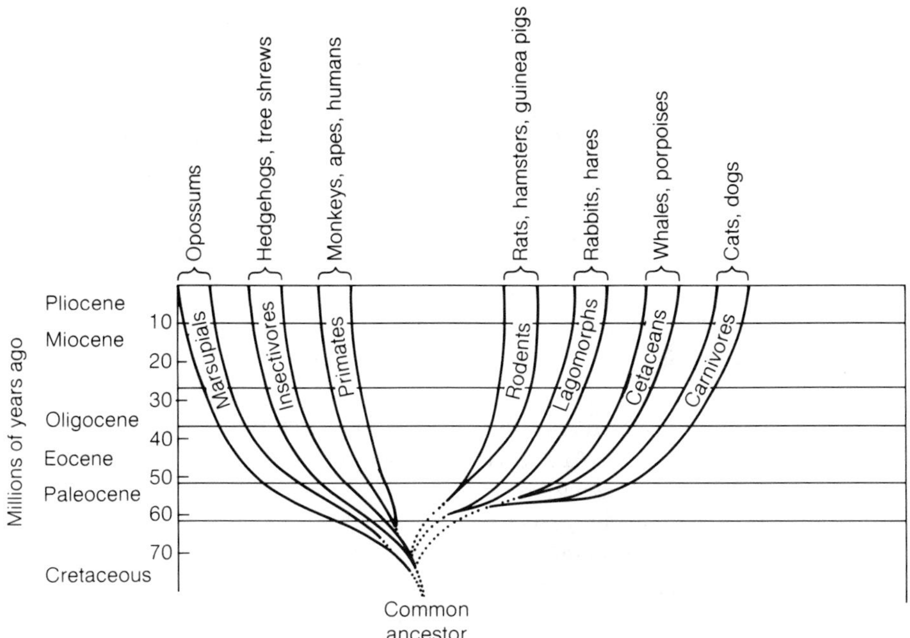

FIGURE 5-5. A phylogenetic tree showing the probable times of origin and affinities of the orders of mammals most commonly studied in comparative psychology and neuropsychology. (After Young, 1962.)

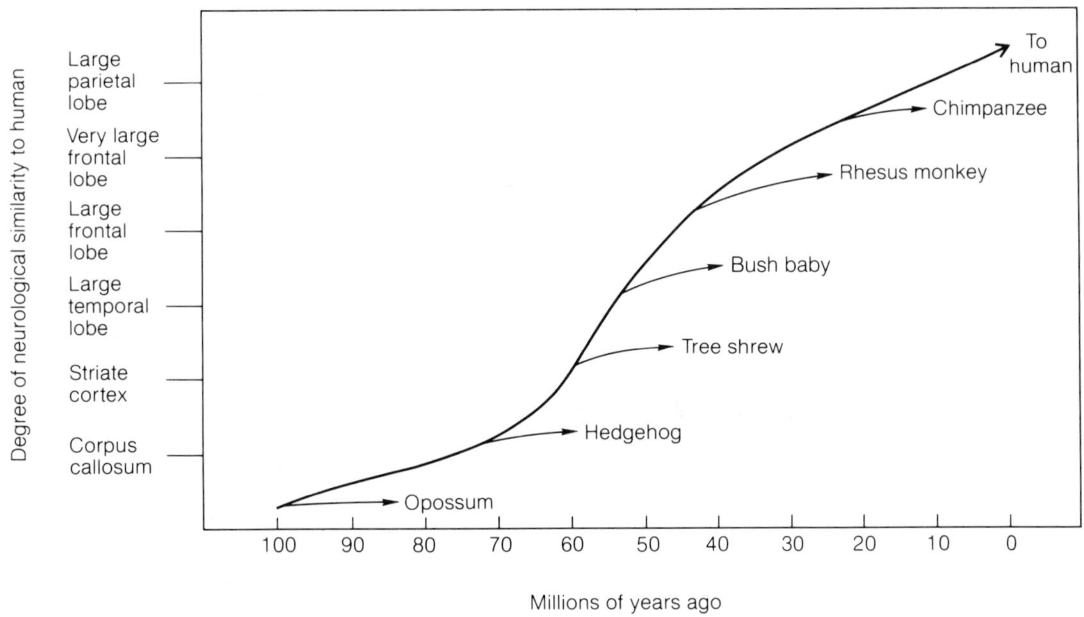

FIGURE 5-6. Phylogenetic relationships among the experimental subjects forming a quasi-evolutionary lineage. Notice that hedghogs, tree shrews, bush babies, monkeys, and apes are living animals taken to be close approximations of the ancestors of humans. (After Masterton and Skeen, 1972.)

shrews, bushbabies, macaques, chimpanzees, and humans. Each succeeding species is believed to have evolved from a species something like the one listed before it.

NEUROANATOMICAL COMPARISONS

The most obvious question to ask is one of the easiest to answer: Is there a significant structural difference between the brains of humans and those of other animals — in particular, other primates? It is not necessary to review the evolution of the brain in detail (see Jerison; Sarnat and Netsky) to answer the question. The answer, quite simply, there are persuasive similarities. Consider the following points.

Brain Size

The most obvious characteristic of the human brain is that it is larger than the brains of most other animals. But what does that imply? After all, one might expect this difference simply because the human body is larger. Likewise, the elephant would be expected to have a larger brain than humans, and indeed it is roughly three times larger. Neuroanatomists long ago realized it was necessary to factor out body size, and Snell in 1891 and Dubois in 1897 compared the relative sizes of brains by taking body weight into account. From these earlier works, Jerison developed what he terms the **encephalization quotient,** or **EQ:** the ratio of actual brain size to expected brain size. The expected brain size is a kind of average for living mammals that takes body size into account. Thus, the average, or typical, mammal (which incidentally is the cat) has an EQ of 1.0. Animals that deviate from 1.0 have brains larger or smaller than would be expected for a mammal of that particular body size. Table 5-1 summarizes the EQs for common laboratory animals and for humans. Notice that the rat's EQ is only 0.4, whereas the human is 6.30. The rat's brain, then, is only 0.4 times as large as expected for the typical mammal of that body size, and the brain of a human is 6.3 times as large as expected. Notice that the chimpanzee brain is much larger than predicted for a typical mammal of that body size (EQ = 2.48), but the EQ is only about one-third as large as that of the human brain. The EQ makes it clear that the human brain is really larger than those of other primates. (This high EQ is not unique to humans, however; the EQ of the dolphin is comparable, having a value of about 6.0.)

Brain Structure

What is the significance of the fact that the human brain is much larger than the brains of other primates? Is the human brain qualitatively different from those other brains, or is it just a larger version of the same basic brain? Stephan and colleagues compared the brains of more than 60 species of mammals and found that although nearly all structures of the brain increase in size as the EQ increases, it is the neocortex that shows the most dramatic increase. It would seem reasonable to suppose that if the human brain is different in some way, the difference would most likely be found in the neocortex. This possibility can be considered by comparing the human brain with

TABLE 5-1. Comparison of brain sizes of species most commonly studied in neuropsychology

Species	Brain volume (ml)	Encephalization quotient
Rat	2.3	0.40
Cat	25.3	1.01
Rhesus Monkey	106.4	2.09
Chimpanzee	440.0	2.48
Human	1350.0	6.30

Note: Values estimated by using Jerison's formula [EQ = Ei/[12 × Pi(2/3)], where Ei = actual brain size of species. "i," Pi = body size of species "i"] and body and brain values.

Source: From Blinkov and Glesner, 1968.

the brain of other primates using a variety of measures of neocortical structure, including volume and distribution of neocortex, and cell density.

Total Neocortex. Stephan and his coworkers have calculated what is called a *progression index:* the ratio of actual neocortex to the expected neocortex of a typical mammal. (This index is an analogue of the encephalization quotient, except that it measures only the neocortex.) The progression index shows that the volume of human neocortex is 3.2 times greater than the predicted volume for nonhuman primates in general and nearly three times greater than that predicted for a chimpanzee of the same body weight. These figures mean that the increase in neocortex from the apes to humans is greater than would have been expected from the trends within the other primates. Where in the neocortex is this increase?

Passingham found that the increase in human neocortex does not appear to occur in the visual, somatosensory, or motor cortex. In fact, there is actually a decrease in the relative extent of area 17. But because there is a trend in primate phylogeny for visual (striate) cortex to decrease relative to total neocortex, this reduction in striate cortex is predictable.

Within primate phylogeny the association cortex surrounding the **primary zones** increases progressively as a proportion of the total neocortex. Nevertheless, although the surrounding cortex makes up a greater proportion of the human neocortex than would be expected from looking at the chimpanzee brain, Passingham concludes that, given the phylogenetic trend, humans do not have more association cortex than would be predicted for a primate with so much neocortex.

There has been some controversy over whether or not nonhuman primates have an association cortex analogous to the human speech zones. Passingham reviews the evidence and concludes that they do have a posterior speech zone, although the existence of an area homologous to Broca's area is still in doubt.

Cell Density. Although the human brain does not differ from other primate brains in gross anatomy, it is reasonable to suppose that it might differ in fine structure. And it does appear to do so in cell size and density: cell size increases and cell density decreases with increasing volume of neocortex. This means that as the volume of neocortex increases, neurons increase in size but are spaced further apart, perhaps reflecting an increase in the number of synaptic connections. Although there is a marked change in cell size and density in the human brain compared with the brains of other primates, Passingham calculates that these changes are predictable given the increase in the volume of neocortex.

Conclusion

The overall conclusion that is forced on us for all the differences between human and other primate brains is the most parsimonious one: the main selection pressure in evolution was for a larger brain with more association neocortex. In other words, although the human brain is larger than would be expected for a primate of our body weight, this increase in brain size is attributable to a general increase in association cortex. There is, therefore, no compelling evidence of a qualitative difference between the brains of humans and those of other mammals.

FUNCTIONAL COMPARISONS

Each mammalian species has a unique behavioral repertory. There has been a tendency to assume that the brain structures necessary to produce unique behaviors must also be unique. This view ignores the fact that mammals share many similar behavioral traits and capacities, although the details of behavior may differ somewhat. For example, all mammalian mothers provide milk and maternal care for their young, although the details of care vary from species to species. Warren and

Kolb have thus suggested that there are behaviors and behavioral capacities that could be designated **class-common behaviors:** behaviors common to all members of the phylogenetic class Mammalia. Hence, it is recognized that many behaviors are not species-specific, and it is in these behaviors that generalizations in neuropsychology should be most meaningful.

If class-common behaviors are considered to be a basis for generalizing in neuropsychology, it is then possible to argue that there is no qualitative difference in the neural control of sensory, associative, and motor functions in mammals. This position is a direct contradiction of the idea that function in mammals has undergone **encephalization** and **encorticalization.**[1] According to the concept of encephalization during evolution there was a shift of function from lower centers, such as the brainstem, to higher centers, such as the neocortex and limbic system. According to the concept of encorticalization, as the neocortex developed, it assumed functions previously controlled by lower structures. This view implies that the functions of the neocortex would be different in highly corticalized species, such as humans and chimpanzees, from the neocortical functions in species with less neocortex, such as rats or cats. This idea, however, is based on inadequate evidence and has been discredited by Weiskrantz, Jerison, and Warren, among others. The best evidence that lesions produce class-common behavioral effects actually comes from the very experiments that disconfirm the encephalization concept. So widely held is this concept of encephalization that it is incumbent on us to at least briefly review the evidence against it. This is most easily done by reviewing the studies demonstrating functional similarities of the sensory, motor, and association cortex among all mammals.

[1] There is some disagreement in the literature as to the use of the term *encephalization.* For example, Ruch, Patten, Woodbury, and Towe use the term to describe the idea that in the course of evolution the forebrain has increased its domination over the lower midbrain and spinal centers. Other authors use the term to describe the course of ontogenetic development of the brain. We are referring here, however, to the idea of a phylogenetic shift of function from lower to higher structures, especially within the neocortex, and we do not take issue with the other uses of the term.

The Visual System

Until recently there was believed to be a steady phyletic progression from rats to monkeys in the severity of the syndrome resulting from damage of the visual cortex. Rats were considered to be less impaired than cats, cats less impaired than monkeys, and monkeys less affected than humans. However, work done in the past 5 to 10 years has shown that this conclusion was in error; the error resulted from differences in experimental procedure with the various species. For example, monkeys are not nearly as impaired as had been believed; earlier studies employed larger lesions that, going beyond the primary visual cortex, included surrounding cortex involved in the visual guidance of behavior. Also, the behavioral assessment techniques used in these studies were crude and misleading, and for one reason or another did not accurately assess visual capacities after the removal of visual cortex. Recently, Humphrey studied a single monkey, with almost no striate cortex, over a period of years. He observed that the monkey could avoid obstacles and find even small objects such as currants with great efficiency. Humphrey was thus able to demonstrate that the effect of removing the visual cortex was really no more severe in the monkey than in the rat. There is no compelling evidence that the effects of visual cortex lesions in humans differ from those observed in monkeys or rats.

The Auditory System

Ravizza and Belmore have shown that the effects of removing the auditory cortex are strikingly similar in many different species of mammals. Monkeys so treated are severely impaired in their ability to approach the site of a brief sound. They can, however, discriminate between sounds presented at different spatial locations, if the required response is pressing a lever rather than walking through space. This result is apparently also true of other species, such as opossums, hedgehogs, bush-babies, and cats. If the functions of the auditory cortex are similar in mammals, those functions should be affected in the same way by the same variations in experimental parameters, as was true in Ravizza and Belmore's study.

The Somatosensory System

The sense of touch is organized in a remarkably similar way in all mammals, although the fine details vary somewhat. Figure 5-7 illustrates the organization of the somatosensory cortex of rats, cats, and monkeys. This organization is comparable to that of the human somatosensory cortex illustrated in Figure 1-8. However, instead of "little men," Figure 5-7 shows a cartoon representation of a rat, cat, and monkey, and the relative importance of the various cortical areas to the animal's functioning. Although the snout of the rat occupies relatively more cortex in the cartoon than that of the monkey, the class-common basic organization is clearly similar.

The Motor System

It was widely held a decade ago that the effects of motor cortex removal on the visual system became progressively more serious as one goes from rats to cats to primates. For example, Lassek contrasted the effects of motor cortex removal in monkeys and carnivores, such as cats and dogs, by stating that removal of Brodmann's area 4 in primates causes "an enduring paralysis of isolated movements especially in the digits. A flaccid type of paralysis occurs in the proximal joints whereas the wrists and fingers pass through a period of moderate spasticity" (Lassek, 1954, pp. 65–66). On the other hand, "the motor cortex appears to be largely dispensable in mammals ranking below primates. **Ablation** of area 4 in the cat or dog is attended by only negligible and transitory deficits" (Lassek, 1954, p. 67).

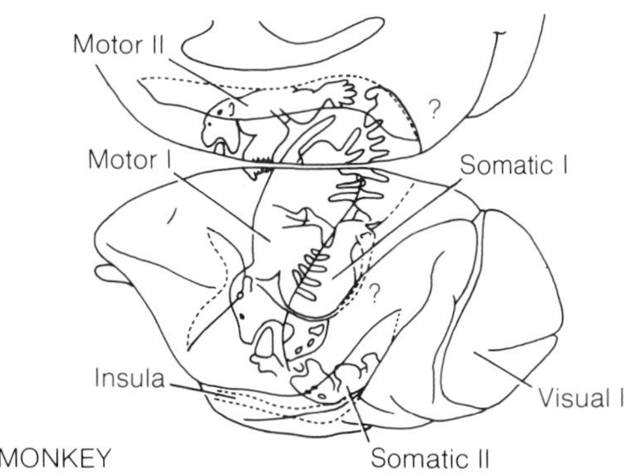

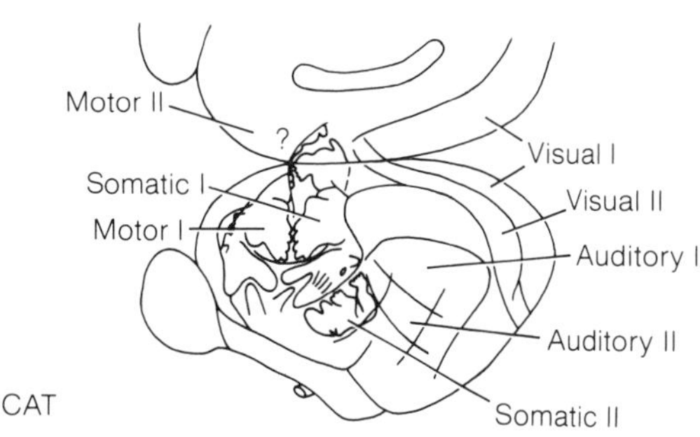

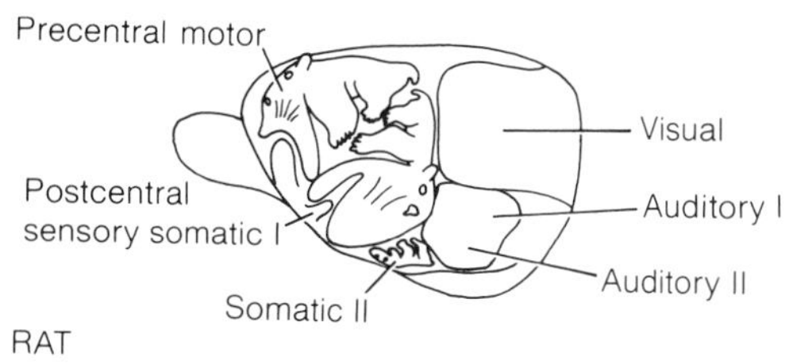

FIGURE 5-7. Functional divisions of the neocortex in three species of mammals as defined by electrical stimulation and recording. The regions not so defined are called association areas. (From C. N. Woolsey, 1958, pp. 63–81. Copyright © 1958. Reprinted with permission.)

However, Lassek's comparison between primates and carnivores is invalid because it is based on different behaviors. The most profound deficits in monkeys were in manual activities, whereas only posture and locomotion were observed to be disturbed in cats and dogs. It is well known that in monkeys posture and locomotion are less severely disturbed by motor cortex lesions than are manual activities. Furthermore, more recent work on the effects of motor cortex removal in cats has shown a permanent impairment in the ability to manipulate objects and to make controlled extension responses with the forepaw. Rats are not capable of very refined movements of the digits of the forepaws, but even they have deficits in manipulation of food and objects following motor cortex removal. This deficit would easily be overlooked, however, if one simply observed rats making gross movements such as walking or swimming—activities that require little fine control of the digits.

To summarize, careful observation shows no difference among mammals in the effects of motor cortex damage. The apparent differences described a decade ago do not reflect a functional difference within the motor cortex of various species, but rather a difference in their most obvious behaviors.

Association Areas

Since the association areas undergo such marked expansion in primates, and in humans in particular, it is reasonable to expect that there might be a qualitative difference in the functions of these regions. But the evidence to date does not support this proposition. Although the higher primates are doubtless capable of more complex associations (i.e., learning) than the lower mammals, lesions of the association cortex have remarkably similar general effects on mammals. This conclusion contradicts much of the prevailing literature. For example, in 1969 Diamond and Hall made a convincing case that the cat had no association cortex in the temporal lobe that could be considered analogous to that found in the primate, suggesting a major difference between carnivores and primates. Recent anatomical and behavioral work indicates that their conclusion was unwarranted. The temporal region had simply not been properly identified in the cat. Also, Campbell has recently shown that lesions of the temporal association cortex produce deficits in visual learning by cats that are strikingly similar to those observed in primates.

PHYLOGENETIC TRENDS

The major difference between the brains of humans and those of other mammals is the increase in the volume of human neocortex; the overall organization of the neocortex, however, is similar in all mammals. This conclusion is no doubt correct with respect to the gross functioning of the neocortex, but a careful examination of the details of cortical organization in mammals discloses two trends in mammalian brain development that must be considered when drawing conclusions from nonhuman species. First, there may be an increase in **lateralization** of function (i.e., a function is restricted to one half of the brain) associated with an increase in EQ. Second, there may be an increase in the number of distinct anatomical and functional subregions within the neocortex as it expands in volume.

Lateralization of Function

One of the most striking characteristics of cerebral organization in humans is that many functions are relatively lateralized to one hemisphere or the other. It has been known for over a century that language functions are localized primarily in the left hemisphere of right-handed people and, although specific functions of the right hemisphere were not discovered until more recently, it has been known for at least 30 years that visuospatial functions are localized primarily in the posterior regions of the right hemisphere. This asymmetry in cerebral organization is a significant feature of human brain organization, and its phylogenetic origins are of particular interest if we are to fully understand its importance in human brain function. Although once believed to be a uniquely human trait, cerebral asymmetry is now thought to represent the result of a phylogenetic trend in the development of the mammalian brain. There is now evidence of such anatomical asymmetries in present-day rodents, carnivores, and nonhuman primates, as well as in the brain endocasts of australopithecines. Thus, just as the human brain is larger and has more cerebral cortex than expected for a mammal of its body size, it also shows greater lateralization of function than expected. The presence of cerebral asymmetry in humans, however, does not represent a qualitative difference from other mammals.

Regional Specialization

Although functional and cytoarchitectonic subdivisions can be identified in the cortex of all mammalian species, there is a trend toward increasing numbers of *distinct* neocortical regions as the EQ increases. For example, whereas the auditory cortex of rats can be differentiated easily into only two or three subregions, the analogous cortex of monkeys can be differentiated into at least twice as many. A similar trend is found in other sensory regions, as well as in motor and association zones. If we assume that each cytoarchitectonically distinguishable region has a distinct functional correlate, then an increase in the number of subregions provides a basis for potential differences between species as the total volume of neocortex increases. Many neuropsychologists believe that it is far-fetched to suppose that all of the cortical subregions in humans are hidden in some diminutive state in animals; with modest EQs, as if awaiting some future expansion and development in the human brain. New functional regions are unlikely to appear suddenly in the human brain, rather, they presumably result from an elaboration of existing regions, although the processes involved in such an evolution remain a matter of speculation. (See Kaas for an interesting discussion of possible processes.)

Increasing neocortical differentiation into cytoarchitectonic and functional subregions probably provides a basis for increasing sophistication in the processing of sensory information and control of movement in animals with large brains. This differentiation does not imply qualitative differences between species, nor does it suggest that class-common behaviors are unrelated to class-common neural functions. It does imply, however, that the fine details of neocortical processing in humans are best inferred from species with large EQs. Although neuroscience has made real progress in identifying general principles of cerebral organization in the past century, we have a very long way to travel before studies using experimental animals will need to concentrate on species with large brains such as monkeys and apes.

CONCLUSIONS

The divergence of the human brain from that of other living species has a history of at least 5 million years. The human brain has undergone a major expansion in the past 2 million years, but the evidence from the study of fossils as well as of contemporary mammals indicates that the human brain has not undergone a qualitative change. The brains of human and nonhuman primates today differ chiefly in overall size and in the volume of neocortex, rather than qualitatively in cerebral organization. Mammals have to deal with the same basic problems imposed by the environment, and the behavioral capacities to cope with these problems are class-common. The evidence indicates that class-common behaviors are mediated by class-common neural mechanisms sufficiently similar among mammals to permit valid generalizations across species. There is no strong evidence for unique brain-behavior relations in any species within the class Mammalia, including *Homo sapiens.* The possibility of considerable generalization across mammalian species does not imply that neuropsychologists should expend their major energies studying rats or monkeys. It does imply, however, that the results of studies on rats, monkeys and animals of other species are valuable in understanding brain-behavior relations in humans and should not be ignored or dismissed simply because nonhumans do not talk.

REFERENCES

Beals, K. L., C. L. Smith, and S. M. Dodd. Brain size, cranial morphology, climate, and time machines. *Current Anthroplology* 25:301–330, 1984.

Blinkov, S. M., and J. I. Glesner. *The Human Brain in Figures and Tables.* New York: Basic Books, 1968.

Campbell, C. B. G., and W. Hodos. The concept of homology and the evolution of the nervous system. *Brain, Behavior and Evolution* 3:353–367, 1970.

Dewsbury, D. A. Comparative psychologists and their quest for uniformity. *Annals of the New York Academy of Sciences* 223:147–167, 1973.

Diamond, I. T., and K. L. Chow. Biological psychology. In S. Koch, ed. *Psychology: A Study of a Science,* vol. 4. New York: McGraw-Hill, 1962.

Falk, D. A reanalysis of the South African australopithecine natural endocasts. *American Journal of Physical Anthropology* 53:525–539, 1980.

Goodall, J. *The Chimpanzees of Gombe.* Cambridge, MA: The Belknap Press of Harvard University Press, 1986.

Hodos, W., and C. B. G. Campbell. Scale naturae: Why there is no theory in comparative psychology. *Psychological Review* 76:337–350, 1969.

Holloway, R. L. Revisiting the South African Tuang australopithecine endocast: The position of the lunate sulcus as determined by the stereoplotting technique. *American Journal of Physical Anthropology* 56:43–58, 1981.

Humphrey, N. K. Vision in a monkey without striate cortex: A case study. *Perception* 3:241–255, 1974.

Jerison, H. J. *Evolution of the Brain and Intelligence.* New York: Academic Press, 1973.

Jerison, H. J. Fossil evidence of the evolution of the human brain. *Annual Review of Anthropology* 4:27–58, 1975.

Johanson, D., and M. Edey. *Lucy: The Beginnings of Humankind.* New York: Warner Books, 1982.

Jorde, L. B. Human genetic distance studies: Present status and future prospects. *Annual Review of Anthropology* 14:343–373, 1987.

Kaas, J. H. The segregation of function in the nervous system: Why do sensory systems have so many subdivisions? *Contributions to Sensory Physiology* 7:201–240, 1982.

Lassek, A. M. *The Pyramidal Tract.* Springfield, IL: Charles C. Thomas, 1954.

Lockhart, R. B. The albino rat: A defensible choice or bad habit. *American Psychologist* 23:734–742, 1968.

Masterton, B., and L. C. Skeen. Origins of anthropoid intelligence: Prefrontal system and delayed alternation in hedgehog, tree shrew and bushbaby. *Journal of Comparative and Physiological Psychology* 81:423–433, 1972.

McHenry, H. M. Fossils and the mosaic nature of human evolution. *Science* 190:425–431, 1975.

McHenry, H. M. The pattern of human evolution: Studies on bipedialism, mastication, and encephalization. *Annual Review of Anthropology* 11:151–173, 1982.

Passingham, R. E. Anatomical differences between the neocortex of man and other primates. *Brain, Behavior and Evolution* 7:337–359, 1973.

Passingham, R. E. Broca's area and the origins of human vocal skill. *Philosophical Transactions of the Royal Society of London* B292:167–175, 1981.

Passingham, R. E. Primate specializations in brain and intelligence. *Symposium of the Zoological Society of London* 46:361–388, 1981.

Passingham, R. E. *The Human Primate.* San Francisco: W. H. Freeman, 1982.

Passingham, R. E., and G. Ettlinger. A comparison of cortical functions in man and the other primates. *International Review of Neurobiology* 16:233–299, 1974.

Ravizza, R. J., and S. Belmore. Auditory forebrain: Evidence from anatomical and behavioral experiments involving human and animal subjects. In R. B. Masterson, ed. *Handbook of Behavioral Neurobiology.* New York: Plenum, 1978.

Ruch, T. C., H. D. Patten, J. W. Woodbury, and A. L. Towe. *Neurophysiology.* London: W. B. Saunders, 1965.

Sarnat, H. B., and M. G. Netsky. *Evolution of the Nervous System.* New York: Oxford University Press, 1974.

Schneider, G. E. Contrasting visuo-motor functions of tectum and cortex in the golden hamster. *Psychologische Forschung* 31:52–62. 1967.

Stanley, S. M. *The New Evolutionary Timetable.* New York: Basic Books, 1981.

Stephen, H., R. Bauchot, and O. J. Andy. Data on the size of the brain and of various parts in insectivores and primates. In C. R. Noback and W. Montagna, eds. *The Primate Brain.* New York: Appleton, 1970, pp. 289–297.

Warren, J. M. Evolution, behavior and the prefrontal cortex. *Acta Neurobiologiae Experimentalis* 32:581–593, 1972.

Warren, J. M., and B. Kolb. Generalization in neuropsychology. In S. Finger, ed., *Recovery from Brain Damage.* New York: Plenum, 1978.

Weiskrantz, L. The interaction between occipital and temporal cortex in vision. In F. O. Schmitt and F. G. Worden, eds. *The Neurosciences: Third Study Program.* Cambridge, MA: M.I.T. Press, 1974.

White, T. H. *The Once and Future King.* London, Collins, 1958.

Woolsey, C. N. Organization of somatic sensory and motor areas of the cerebral cortex. In H. F. Harlow and C. N. Woolsey, eds., *Biological and Biochemical Bases of Behavior.* Madison, WI: University of Wisconsin Press, 1958.

Young, J. Z. *The Life of Vertebrates.* New York: Oxford University Press, 1962.

PART 2

BASIC NEUROLOGY

There are a number of reasons why it is very important to the student of neuropsychology to have a basic grasp of clinical neurology. Neurology concentrates on the diagnosis and treatment of diseases and disorders of the nervous system. One method by which neuropsychologists understand the normal function of the central nervous system is by studying it when it is behaving abnormally. It is therefore of fundamental importance to understand the ways in which the nervous system can become disordered, as well as the methods of identifying and studying these disorders. This need is particularly acute because different disorders affect the nervous in distinctly different ways, and the inferences that can be drawn about normal function thus differ somewhat according to the exact disorder being studied.

Another reason why an understanding of neurology is valuable is that the principles of neuropsychology can be applied in a variety of ways to the treatment of people suffering from neurological disorders. This application, however, requires that the clinical neuropsychologist understand the nature of the disorders well enough to apply the theory efficiently and appropriately. For example, it is pointless to consider occupational therapy in a person with certain disorders, since the disturbance of cognitive function is profound and irreversible. In other cases, people are able to function fairly normally, working around their sometimes considerable cognitive limitations. The neuropsychologist who fails to fully understand the nature of the disorders afflicting a given patient not only does the patient a disservice but also harms the credibility of the entire field of neuropsychology.

Therefore, the two chapters of Part Two consider the clinical examination and specialized tests used to assess neurological disorders (Chapter 6) and provide a basic survey of such disorders (Chapter 7). These chapters introduce an array of specialized terms that are likely to overwhelm the beginning student, but they appear repeatedly throughout the book and will eventually seem natural and straightforward.

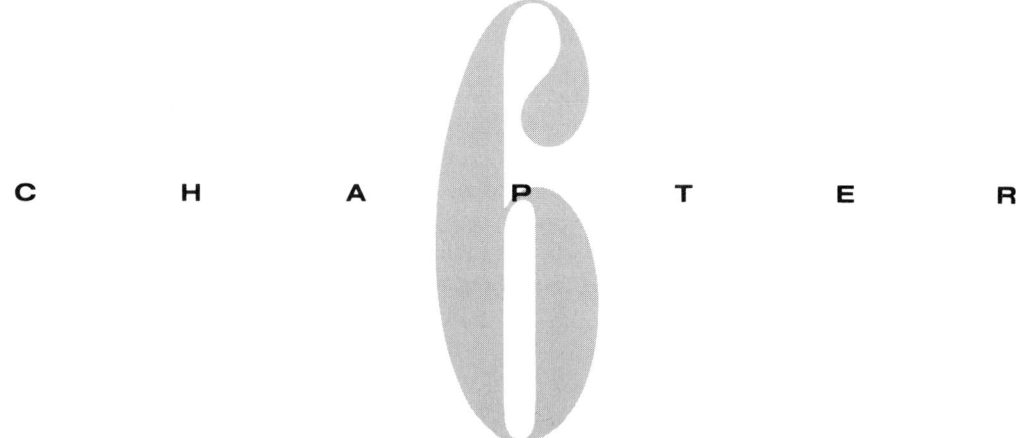

CHAPTER 6

THE NEUROLOGICAL EXAM AND CLINICAL TESTS

People suspected of having some disorder of the nervous system are usually examined by a **neurologist,** a physician specializing in the treatment of such disorders. Although a comprehensive understanding of the neurological exam is not essential to an understanding of the basic principles of neuropsychology, a sense of what this exam entails is useful nevertheless, for a number of reasons. First, since a diagnosis is only as reliable as the procedure used to make it, the neuropsychologist should be aware of the limitations of diagnostic procedures. Second, since neuropsychologists often see clients who should be referred for a neurological exam, they should be aware of the procedures involved and the questions that are asked in this type of examination so they can recognize when to properly refer a client to a neurologist and what information can be gained by the referral. Finally, since neuropsychological tests are extremely effective in spotting certain brain dysfunctions, the psychologist should be able to understand a neurological report in order to compare diagnoses and make recommendations.

The neurological examination is guided by the principle that every function is abnormal until it is examined and found to be normal. The neurologist first takes a history from the patient and makes a general assessment of the patient's appearance; that is, what impression does the person's personality, facial appearance, and body structure make? The neurologist then thoroughly examines the skin and mucous membranes, the orifices, and sensory systems; tests motor functions; listens to the heart, abdomen, head, and blood vessels; and examines every organ system. If what appears to be a deviation is found, it is evaluated with respect to the way and degree to which it differs from the same body part on the opposite side, that body part of family members, and the theoretical norm for a person of like age and sex. The neurologist may recommend additional tests (EEG, brain scans, etc.) as indicated by the persons's history or the initial neurological exam. At the end of an examination the neurologist writes a case summary. This usually consists of a summary of positive and negative historical and physical findings, a provisional diagnosis, a plan for further tests to discriminate between diagnostic possibilities, and suggestions for therapy and therapeutic goals. The following section summarizes the types of tests administered by the neurologist and some aspects of the rationale underlying their use.

THE NEUROLOGICAL EXAM

The Patient's History

The art of diagnosis has been described as coming to a correct answer with too little information. The neurologist's first step is to ask the patient about the problem, and it is a useful rule of thumb that the patient's first descriptive statement about his or her illness is the most important. Information is collected about the person's background, with emphasis placed on previous disease, accidents, and the occurrence of symptoms such as headache, loss of consciousness, and sleep disturbances. Often, incidents that do not seem important to the person can be relevant to the diagnosis of the disorder. Family background is also significant because many diseases, such as epilepsy, may have a high familial incidence.

While the history is being taken, the physician observes other aspects of the patient's behavior. For example, mental status is assessed (Is the person aware of where he or she is, the date, etc.?), facial features are examined for abnormalities or asymmetries, speech is assessed for abnormalities, and posture is observed. The patient's state of awareness is described with adjectives such as *alert, drowsy, stuporous, confused,* and so forth. Facial features and behavior reveal whether the person is agitated, anxious, depressed, apathetic, or restless. Some of the simpler aspects of memory may also be tested by presenting digits and asking for their recall. Delusions and hallucinations are noted when present. The neurologist may also determine whether the person is left- or right-handed and the history of handedness in the family, since this may provide clues about which hemisphere controls speech. A number of simple tests for speech may be given, such as asking the meaning of words, having rhymes or words repeated (e.g., "la-la," "ta-ta"), having objects named, having the patient read and write.

Although the information obtained in a history gives clues about where emphasis should be placed in the subsequent neurological examination, the neuropsychologist should not accept uncritically the neurologist's evaluation of mental state. Many people who appear lucid on cursory examination are found to have severe impairments when thoroughly tested with appropriate neuropsychological tests.

The Physical Examination

To make a physical examination the neurologist uses a number of instruments that then guide the course of the examination. These include (1) a measuring tape for measuring head and body size, the size of skin lesions, and so on; (2) a stethoscope for listening to the sounds of the heart and blood vessels, and an otoscope for examining the auditory canal and drum; (3) a flashlight for eliciting pupillary reflexes; (4) tongue blades for eliciting the gag reflex, and abdominal and plantar reflexes; (5) a vial of coffee for assessing smell, and vials of salt and sugar for taste; (6) a 256-cps tuning fork for testing vibratory sensation and hearing; (7) a cotton wisp for eliciting the corneal reflex and for testing sensitivity to light touch, plastic tubes for testing temperature sensations, and pins for testing pain sensation; (8) a hammer for eliciting muscle stretch reflexes, such as knee jerk; (9) some coins and keys for testing **stereognosis,** the recognition of objects through touch; and (10) a blood pressure cuff for taking blood pressure.

Examination of the Head

One of the most important parts of the neurological exam is the study of the head. Its general features such as size and shape are assessed, and a detailed examination is made of sensory and motor functions. The head is innervated by 12 sets of cranial nerves, many of which have both sensory and motor functions. These nerves have different origins within the brainstem, and their pathways occupy different portions of the brain. The study of their function may reveal malfunctions, providing important clues about the location and nature of nervous system damage. Table 6-1 summarizes the cranial nerves, their function, and some of the commoner symptoms that occur after damage to them. Rather than discuss the function of each nerve in detail, we shall give some examples from the visual system to illustrate the type of information the neurologist can obtain in the examination.

In examining the eye the neurologist first looks at its external covering, the eyelid. If it droops, a condition called **ptosis,** this indicates damage to some portion of the third nerve (oculomotor), which normally elevates it. The visual field can be examined for blind spots or reductions of sensitivity. The occurrence of visual-field defects can reveal quite precisely the existence of damage at nearly any location between the retina and the visual cortex (see Chapter 11). The pupil is controlled by two interocular smooth muscles: the pupilloconstrictor and the pupillodilator muscles of the iris, which act in opposition to each other. There is a relay of the third nerve in the midbrain that coordinates the reactions of both eyes. When the retina of one eye is illuminated with a light, the pupil constricts to block out most of the light, and at the same time the pupil of the unilluminated eye is constricted. Thus, the pupillary constriction and the lack of consensual response of the opposite eye can be used as indicators of possible damage in the retina, optic tract, or midbrain. The pupils also constrict or accommodate a person's looking at a near object. Constriction to accommodation but not to light, the so-called **Argyll Robertson pupil,** has been used to diagnose syphilitic or other damage to midbrain relays of the third nerve. Examination of the *optic fundus,* or central area of the retina, is done with an *ophthalmoscope,* which is a light source with a viewing aperture. This allows the condition of blood vessels (which are visible on the retina) to be examined and a determination to be made of whether there is blurring or swelling in the central retina. A swelling, called **papilledema,** can indicate the presence of such abnormalities as brain tumors; because cerebrospinal fluid extends along the optic nerve, increased pressure in the brain will be reflected as retinal swelling. Finally, symmetrical movements of the eyes are controlled by the third, fourth (trochlear), and sixth (abducens) nerves, and asymmetries may indicate malfunctions of these nerves or of their central relays.

The Motor System

The motor system is examined to assess muscle bulk, tone, and power; to test for the occurrence of involuntary muscle movements, such as shaking and tremors; and to assess the status of reflexes. In addition, coordination is examined by having a patient do such tasks as walking heel to toe in a straight line, touching the neurologist's finger and his or her own nose repeatedly, making rapid alternating movements of the fingers, tapping the foot as rapidly as possible, and so on. Generally, all the muscles of the body are tested in head-to-foot order, and the status of each can be recorded on a standard chart.

A knowledge both of reflex and muscle function and of the central motor pathways can make possible a fairly accurate estimate of the location and nature of possible central motor damage. Various types of motor dysfunction are also characteristic of certain motor diseases. For example, people with Parkinson's disease may show limb tremors when they are resting that are reduced or absent when they move. The analysis of reflexes can give

TABLE 6-1. The cranial nerves

Number	Name	Functions	Method of examination	Typical symptoms of dysfunction
I	Olfactory	(s) Smell[a]	Various odors applied to each nostril	Loss of sense of smell (anosmia)
II	Optic	(s) Vision	Visual acuity, map field of vision	Loss of vision (anopsia)
III	Oculomotor	(m) Eye movement[a]	Reaction to light, lateral movements of eyes, eyelid movement	Double vision (diplopia), large pupil, uneven dilation of pupils, drooping eyelid (ptosis), deviation of eye outward
IV	Trochlear	(m) Eye movement	Upward and downward eye movements	Double vision, defect of downward gaze
V	Trigeminal	(s,m) Masticatory movements	Light touch by cotton baton; pain by pinprick; thermal by hot and cold tubes, corneal reflex by touching cornea; jaw reflex by tapping chin, jaw movements	Decreased sensitivity or numbness of face, brief attacks of severe pain (trigeminal neuraliga); weakness and wasting of facial muscles, asymmetrical chewing
VI	Abducens	(m) Eye movement	Lateral movements	Double vision, inward deviation of the eye
VII	Facial	(s,m) Facial movement	Facial movements, facial expression, test for taste	Facial paralysis, loss of taste over anterior two-thirds of tongue
VIII	Auditory vestibular	(s) Hearing	Audiogram tests hearing; stimulate by rotating patient or by irrigating the ear with hot or cold water (caloric test)	Deafness, sensation of noise in ear (tinnitus); disequilibrium, feeling of disorientation in space
IX	Glossopharyngeal	(s,m) Tongue and pharynx	Test for sweet, salt, bitter, and sour tastes on tongue; pharyngeal or gag reflex by touching walls of pharynx	Partial dry mouth, loss of taste (ageusia) over posterior third of tongue, anesthesia and paralysis of upper pharynx
X	Vagus	(s,m) Heart, blood vessels, viscera, movement of larynx and pharynx	Observe palate in phonation, palatal relfex by touching palate	Hoarseness, lower pharyngeal anesthesia and paralysis, indefinite visceral distubance
XI	Spinal accessory	(m) Neck muscles and viscera	Movement, strength, and bulk of neck and shoulder muscles	Wasting of neck with weakened rotation, inability to shrug
XII	Hypoglossal	(m) Tongue muscles	Tongue movements, tremor, wasting or wrinkling of tongue	Wasting of tongue with deviation to side of lesion on protrusion

[a] s and m refer to sensory or motor function (or both) of the nerve.

important clues about the nature and function of nervous system damage because some reflexes, such as the knee jerk, involve only spinal circuits, whereas others, such as abdominal reflexes, involve circuits that course through the brainstem, midbrain, or cortex. In addition, as we indicated in Chapter 2, different motor pathways cross from one side of the body to another at different levels of the nervous system. This arrangement allows the locations of lesions to be deduced, for when motor deficits occur in a person, a lesion must be located at a point where motor pathways lie adjacent.

The Sensory Systems

A complete sensory examination includes investigation of sensitivity to painful stimulation, touch, and temperature, as well as an analysis of vibration sense, joint position sense, two-point discrimination, tactile localization, stereognosis, and **graphesthesia** (the ability to identify numbers or letters traced on the skin with a blunt object). These sensory tests allow the functions of individual sensory systems to be assessed and also give information about the location of possible dysfunctions. For example, if a person has no tactile sensation in a hand, there could be a problem with the spinal cord or with peripheral nerves. If the person can feel a stimulus but not recognize what it is, the problem is likely to be at a cortical level. Comparing functions of different sensory systems and comparing sensory functions with motor functions also give information about the location of possible dysfunctions. For example, pain and pressure information from a given part of the body, have separate routes through the spinal cord; pain fibers cross to the opposite side of the cord on entering, but the pathways are adjacent through the brainstem, where pressure fibers also cross. Thus, weakness in one type of sensation (e.g., pain) and not the other may indicate a spinal problem, whereas weakness in both may indicate a problem in the brainstem or higher. Similarly, because sensory fibers lie adjacent to particular motor fibers at some levels of the nervous system but are separate at others, sensory and motor deficits that occur together provide diagnostic clues.

CLINICAL TESTS

A variety of clinical tests have been designed to quantify and augment the neurological exam and assist in diagnosis. It would be unusual for all the tests to be done on a single patient, but because all the tests are widely used we shall describe what they are intended to do.

Electroencephalography

Electroencephalography, more commonly called EEG analysis, consists of sampling the electrical activity of the cortex through electrodes posted on specific areas of the skull. There is a standardized system of electrode placement, known as the 10–20 system. It is so named because it divides each of three lines connecting the skull landmarks into segments the length of which are 10% or 20% of the whole line (Figure 6-1). There are a total of 21 electrodes, each of which is named according to its location. The electrical fluctuations recorded by the electrodes are usually amplified and displayed on an ink-writing polygraph. EEG analysis is only a very crude measure of the underlying brain activity, because it gives a measure of only the summed activity of millions of dendrites. Nevertheless, abnormalities in dendritic activity can be indicative of conditions such as epilepsy, and brain tumors. In cases of suspected epilepsy, abnormal discharges may be present in the absence of overt epileptic signs such as convulsions, or the discharges may be elicited by various drugs or by such photic (light) stimuli as a flashing strobe. Differential recordings made with various combinations of electrodes can be used to localize the source of abnormal brain activity quite accurately.

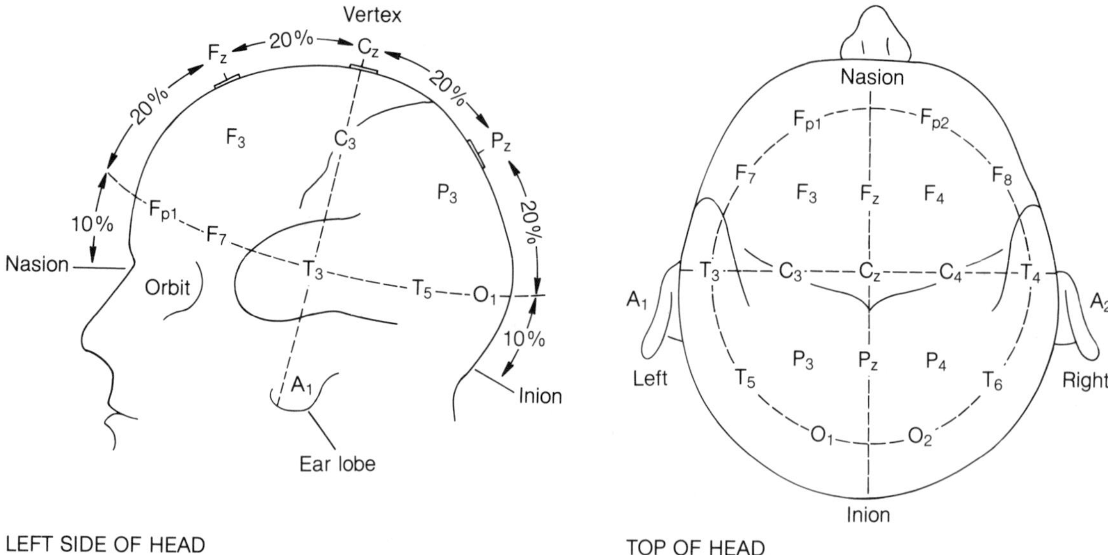

FIGURE 6-1. The international system (10–20) of electrode placement. Odd numbers are to the left and even to the right on the inion-nasion line. Abbreviations: A, aural; C, central; F, frontal, Fp, frontal polar; O, occipital; P, parietal; T, temporal; the subscript z means midline. (Courtesy Grass Instrument Company.)

Evoked Potentials

Evoked potentials (EPs) are slow waves that result from some sensory event (see Chapter 2), such as a click or flash. Most EPs cannot be seen easily on an EEG record because they are generally of low amplitude relative to the normal background brain wave activity. Thus, it is necessary to average the electrical activity over multiple presentations of the same stimulus, as illustrated in Figure 6-2*A*. Since the background EEG activity will be random relative to the sensory event, the EP can be seen clearly after a few trials. A comparison of EPs across normal subjects shows a consistent pattern of electrical activity with predictable peaks in the signal, as illustrated in Figure 6-2*B*. These peaks are labeled as positive (P) or negative (N) and the major peaks described as P_1, N_1, and so forth, or as P_{100}, P_{300}, and so on, the number indicating the typical poststimulus latency. This consistent electrical pattern has allowed the development of several different EPs (visual, auditory, and tactile) as useful clinical and research tools. An abnormal EP may appear either as an increase in the normal latency of a peak or a change in the amplitude of a peak. For example, patients with multiple sclerosis will often show an increased latency of the P_{100} following a visual stimulus, such that the P_{100} peak actually occurs at about P_{135}. By measuring EPs to visual, auditory, and tactile stimuli, it is possible to reach conclusions about the functioning of the different sensory pathways.

Electromyography

Electromyography, or **EMG,** is the analysis of the electrical activity of muscles. The record is made by inserting a needle electrode into the muscle to be tested. When a normal muscle is completely relaxed, no electrical activity can be recorded, but as contraction occurs a characteristic recording, somewhat similar in appearance to an

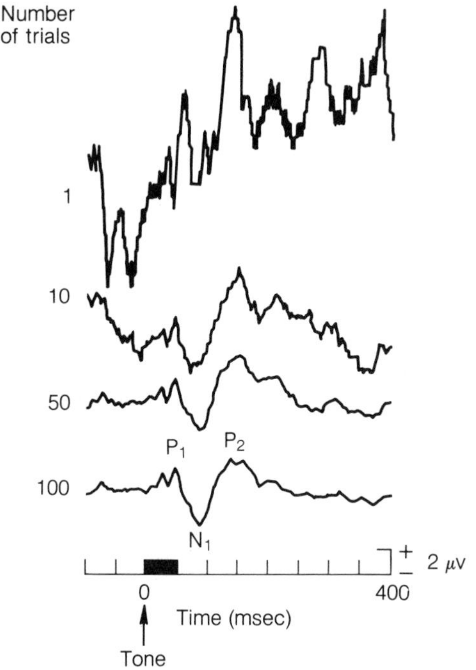

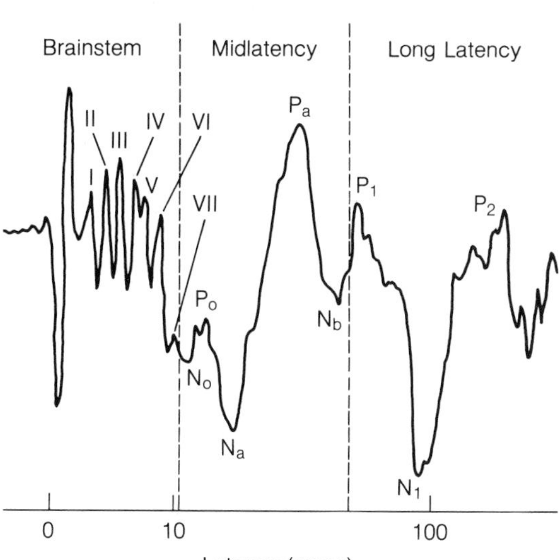

EEG, is produced. EMG recordings are useful for diagnosing damage to or abnormalities in the nerves innervating the muscles from which recordings are being obtained. For example, in disease of the motor neurons of the spinal cord there is a marked reduction in the number of spikes present in the record, because there are fewer normal motor neurons to contract the muscles. By using the EMG the neurologist is able to diagnose the disorder and to evaluate its extent in the spinal cord.

Cerebrospinal Fluid Studies

Analysis of cerebrospinal fluid (CSF) provides the only method of looking at the **subarachnoid space** without opening the skull. CSF is most easily obtained through a puncture made in the lumbar, or lower, portion of the spinal column. It is removed for a variety of purposes: (1) to relieve intracranial pressure and to remove toxic, inflammatory, or other substances in the fluid, as would be found in disorders such as encephalitis or meningitis; (2) to allow an analysis of the CSF for the presence of blood (indicating a vascular accident) or a variety of other substances (such as glucose, white blood cells, or various proteins) that might indicate a variety of central nervous system dysfunctions; (3) to introduce therapeutic substances into the subarachnoid space; and (4) to introduce air or opaque media for radiographic studies (see the next section).

Roentgenography

Roentgenography, or photography using X rays, has been modified in a number of ways to

FIGURE 6-2. *A.* Illustration of the averaging process for auditory-cortex evoked potentials. The number of repeated stimulations (a tone) included in the waveform is indicated on the left. *B.* Schematic auditory evoked potential illustrating the brainstem, midlatency, and long-latency components. (After Squires and Ollo, 1986.)

serve in nervous system diagnosis. Routine X rays are used to scrutinize the skull for evidence of fractures, calcification, or erosion of bone. **Contrast X rays** can be obtained after a special radiopaque dye or air is injected into the ventricles or dye is injected into the arteries. Having a different density from surrounding areas, these substances can be visualized, along with the outline of the arteries or ventricles, on the X-ray negatives. These procedures also make it possible to delineate occlusions or of swellings in the vessels, displacements of vessels or ventricles (indicative of the presence of a tumor), and sometimes it is actually possible to visualize a tumor.

The use of the X-ray technique using a dye injected into the vertebral or carotid artery is called **angiography.** Figure 6-3 shows an example of an angiogram. This technique is particularly valuable in diagnosing and locating vascular abnormalities and some tumors. For example, if an artery appears displaced from its usual position, it can be inferred that something, such as a tumor, has developed, pushing the artery out of place. In **pneumoencephalography,** X rays are taken after the cerebrospinal fluid is replaced with air introduced through a lumbar puncture. By manipulating the posture of the patient, the radiologist is able to force the air to travel through the ventricular sys-

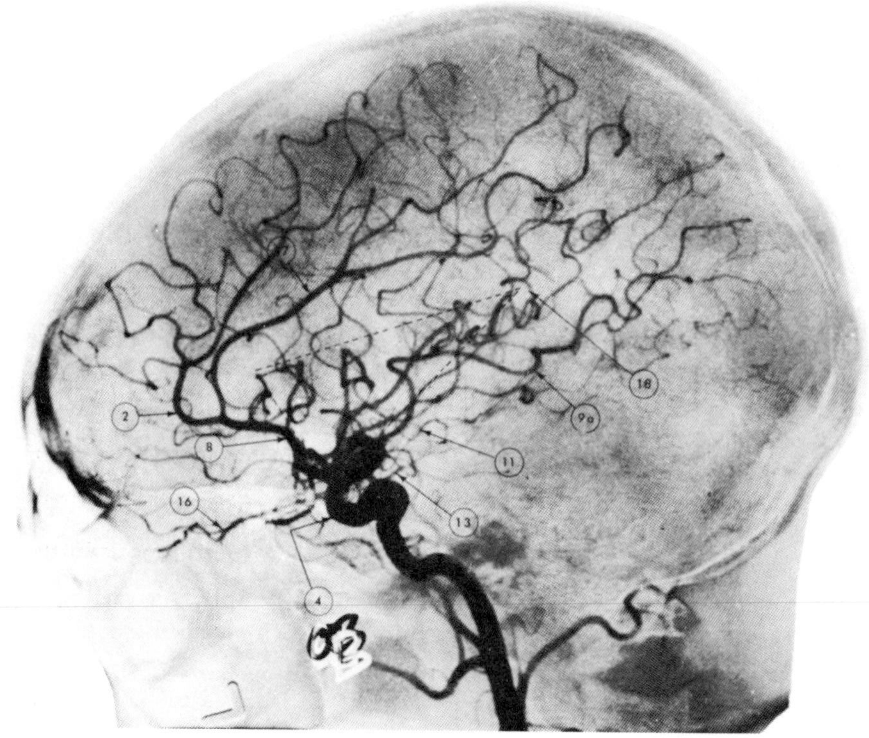

FIGURE 6-3. A normal carotid angiogram. The face is pointed down to the left. Number key: 2, callosomarginal artery; 4, internal carotid artery; 8, anterior cerebral artery; 9a, middle cerebral artery; 11, anterior choroidal artery; 13, posterior communicating artery; 16, ophthalmic artery; 18, approximate end of the Sylvian (lateral) fissure. (From S. J. DeArmond, et al., 1976. Copyright © 1976 by Oxford University Press, Inc. Reprinted with permission.)

tem. Since the air can be seen on an X ray, it is possible to locate blockages in the ventricles, displacements in their position (as might occur with a tumor), or enlargements of them as occurs in **hydrocephalus. Ventriculography** is a similar technique, except that the air or opaque medium is introduced into the ventricle through a cannula, or tube, inserted through the skull. This technique is chiefly used when there is an increase in intracranial pressure and when other procedures have not proved helpful.

Radioisotope Scanning

In the **radioisotope scan** (or **brain scan**) an intravenous injection of a radioisotope is given, and the cranial surface is then scanned with a Geiger counter. Any alteration in blood supply can be detected, including the alterations associated with the growth of a tumor.

Computer-Assisted Imaging

Several new techniques have been devised with which the brain can be imaged by the use of sophisticated computer technology. These include computerized transaxial tomography, positron emission tomography, single-photon emission computed tomography, and magnetic resonance imaging.

Computerized Transaxial Tomography (CT Scan). With conventional X rays the two-dimensional projections of a three-dimensional body appear on the X-ray films as overlapping structures that are difficult to distinguish from one another; the **computerized transaxial tomograph,** or **CT, scan,** on the other hand, provides a three-dimensional representation of the brain. The CT scan works on the mathematical principle that a three-dimensional object can be reconstructed from the infinite set of all its projections. In actuality, a finite set of such projections is used to produce a rough approximation of three-dimensional reality. Briefly, the technique is as follows. A narrow beam of X rays is passed through the brain from one side of the head and the amount of radiation not absorbed by the intervening tissue is absorbed by radiation detectors (Figure 6-4*A*). The X-ray tube is moved laterally across the patient's head and the amount of radiation detected is recorded at 160 equally spaced positions. These data are stored in a computer. The X-ray beam is then rotated 1° and the procedure is repeated. In all, the beam is rotated through 180°. When all the projections are completed, the resulting X-ray sums (160 × 180) are processed by the computer. A reconstruction of the patient's head in cross section is then printed out by the computer (see Figure 6-5). Ordinarily, eight or so cross sections are printed out, each corresponding to a different plane through the head (as illustrated in Appendix Figure A1). The CT scan thus allows a simple, noninvasive examination of the patient's brain in about 25 min.

The CT scanner is an expensive apparatus, but it has become an indispensable tool in neurology because of its greater safety, speed, and accuracy compared with other X-ray techniques. Its greatest potential lies in locating tumors, assessing vascular accidents and head injuries, and in locating a variety of intracranial lesions or brain atrophy. In fact, neurologists have become so dependent on the CT scan that it is nearly impossible to attract neurologists to communities that do not have a CT scanner. As valuable as this machine is, however, it is not perfect and cannot identify many neurological abnormalities, such as epilepsy.

Positron Emission Tomography (PET). Positron emission tomography (PET) is a visual technique in which the subject is given a radioactively labeled form of glucose, which is metabolized by the brain, and the radioactivity is later recorded by a special detector. Unlike the CT scan, a PET scan measures the metabolic activity of different brain regions, the idea being that the most active areas at any given time will use more glucose and hence the radioactivity will be more concentrated there.

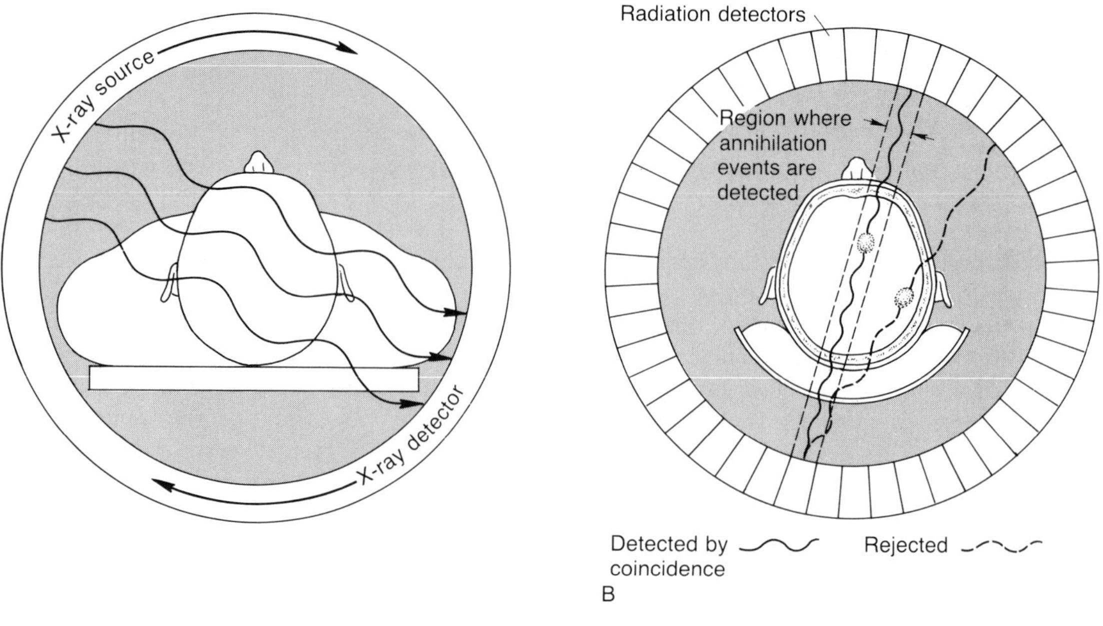

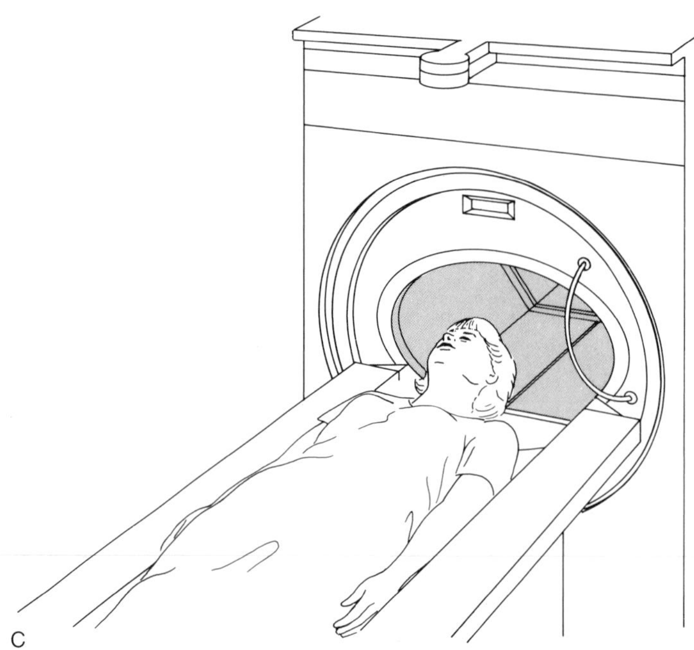

FIGURE 6-4. Schematic illustrations of imaging techniques. *A*. The CT scan makes use of a rapidly rotating X-ray source that takes hundreds of pictures, which are fed into a computer and compiled into one image. *B*. PET measures gamma rays resulting from the collision of a positron and an electron. Only those rays that strike detectors opposite their source are recorded, allowing the computer to determine the line along which the positron was emitted. *C*. Patients must lie down for both imaging procedures, with their heads placed within the machine.

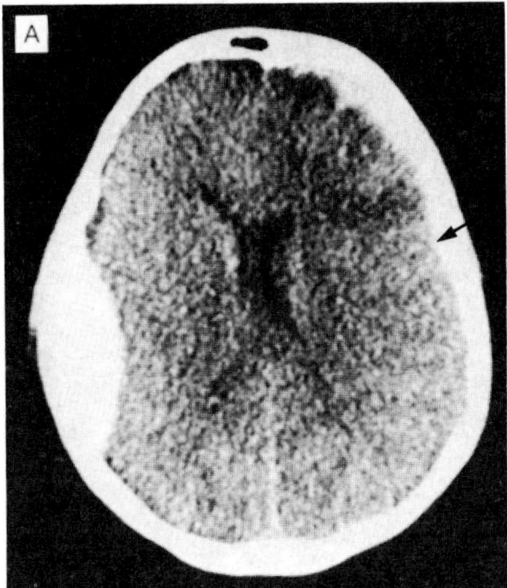

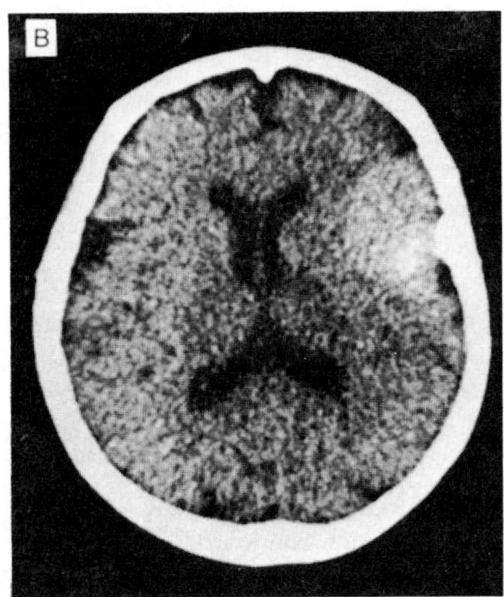

FIGURE 6-5. Examples of CT scans. *A*. The white patch on the left side indicates a blood clot from a hemorrhage caused by a blow to the skull. Diagonally opposite the clot is a shallow pool of blood on the surface of the right hemisphere resulting from a "countercoup" injury (arrow). The ventricles (center) were compressed by the swelling on both sides of the brain. *B*. Scan of a meningioma (white mottled area on right) in the right frontal lobe. The ventricles are quite distinct in this scan. (From S. S. Kety, 1979. Copyright © 1979 by Scientific American, Inc. All rights reserved.)

The detection of radiation in PET is not as straightforward as in traditional brain scans and requires some discussion. Briefly, an element becomes unstable when the number of its electrons is not balanced by an equal number of oppositely charged protons. In the event that a compound has more protons than electrons, the excess protons can be released in the form of neutrons and positrons (positively charge electrons). If the released positrons collide with electrons, they annihilate each other, resulting in the formation of two gamma rays, each moving in opposite directions. Unlike electrons and positrons, which travel only short distances, gamma rays are very energetic and can travel a considerable distance. Thus, in PET it is the gamma rays that are detected since they can escape the brain tissue and pass through the skull to strike detectors (Figure 6-4*B*).

In most current applications of PET, the subject is given a compound such as fluorodeoxyglucose, containing fluorine 18, a very unstable form of fluorine with a half-life of only about 17 min. Since glucose is the only source of energy used by the brain, the fluorine is quickly transported to the brain, with the most active neural areas receiving the largest quantities. Positrons are emitted, gamma rays are formed when the positrons collide with electrons, the gamma rays leave the brain, and the detector monitors the number of them. The origin of the gamma rays can be mapped by a computer, thereby producing an image of the brain. Regions of higher metabolic activity will release more gamma rays, because they take up more glucose to support their neural activity. The computer colorcodes the intensity of gamma radiation, producing a brain map in which different colors represent differences in brain activity. The map is usually presented in horizontal sections, similar to the planes of a CT scan, where the top of the picture is the front of the head. One can, therefore, immediately visualize the relative neural activity in different areas of the brain.

PET has two major groups of applications, namely the assessment of metabolic activity and the measurement of neurotransmitter function. Recently, investigators have begun to use oxygen 15, which has a half-life of only 2 min. Although oxygen 15 is technically difficult to work with, the short life of the isotope is a major advantage because it allows the comparison of metabolic activity in the same subject under a variety of conditions. This allows a significant improvement in the resolution of PET since the scans from two different conditions can be subtracted, leaving the activity that is unique to each condition.

To study neurotransmitter systems a radioactively labeled drug with known pharmacological properties is administered and PET activity is compared with the brain in nondrug conditions. For example, if a subject is given an antipsychotic drug, the dopamine receptors can be labeled. This use of PET has expanded rapidly in recent years, and it is now possible to actually quantify the numbers of receptors in the neuronal membranes under study. The use of PET to image neurotransmitter systems is likely to increase in importance because it allows clinicians and scientists to investigate the brain directly, thus facilitating the study of the effects of different medications on different receptor systems. This will permit better diagnosis as well as the development of better pharmacological agents for treatment.

Single-photon Emission Computed Tomography (SPECT). **Single-photon emission computed tomography (SPECT)** is a scanning technique that uses the technology of CT scan reconstruction, but instead of detecting X rays the machine detects single photons that are emitted from some externally administered tracer. It differs from PET in that the tracer emits a single photon, which is then detected by the machine. The contrast with PET can be seen in Figure 6-4. The PET scan takes advantage of coincident positrons to localize the source. However, if there was only one photon then the machine could not localize by coincidence. Localization can only occur with the detection of numerous particle collisions. This makes the resolution of SPECT much less than PET, but there are several advantages to SPECT. In particular, it is possible to use commercially available tracers so a cyclotron (atomic accelerator) is not required. This makes SPECT much less expensive allowing smaller hospitals to obtain a SPECT machine where the cost of PET would be prohibitive.

Magnetic Resonance Imaging (MRI). **Magnetic resonance imaging (MRI),** which is also known as **nuclear magnetic resonance (NMR),** is based on the principle that certain atoms, such as hydrogen, behave like tiny spinning magnets. Normally, atoms are pointed randomly in different directions, but when they are placed in a magnetic field, they line up in parallel as they orient themselves with respect to the field's lines of force. Atoms spin, and because they are not perfectly symmetrical they wobble; the nuclei of different elements wobble at different frequencies since each element has a different weight. It turns out that if radio waves are beamed across the atoms at right angles to the magnetic field, they will cause the spinning nuclei to wobble synchronously with one another. When the radio waves are turned off, the synchrony induces a voltage in the magnetic field (this is called *magnetic resonance*), which is picked up by a coil of wire around the tissue. As in the previous scanning techniques, the location of different wobbling atoms is analyzed by computer and reconstructed as an image of the brain (see Appendix Figure A2).

MRI images are most easily obtained from the resonance of hydrogen atoms, which is fortunate because the human body is rich in hydrogen and many kinds of hydrogen-rich molecules are known to be altered by many disease states. The images from MRI look very similar to those from CT scans, although the way they are generated is somewhat different (see Appendix Figure A2). MRI shows the makeup and surroundings of cells, whereas CT scans reveal only their density. Like PET, MRI is still largely experimental, but it is thought to be the scanner of the future. Some people believe that since MRI is more sensitive in detecting abnormalities than the CT scan, it will replace the CT scan in the next decade as the imaging technique of choice, although it is more expensive and demands higher overhead costs than the CT scan.

Neuromagnetic Measurement

Neurons maintain an electric potential across their outer membrane, and when the electric potentials of many neurons are summed, it is possible to record them, in the form of an EEG. Under many conditions these same currents generate magnetic fields, which can also be recorded outside the skull, producing a **magnetoencephalogram (MEG).** It is only recently that the technology has become available for the measurement of these minute magnetic fields; but the technique promises to offer a significant advance over conventional EEG. The principal advantages of MEG are that the potentials can be sensed at specific locations, which is very difficult with EEG, and that unlike electric potentials, magnetic potentials are unaffected by the skull. MEG has been used successfully to localize epileptiform activity in the human brain, offering a better indication of the focus of this disorder than standard EEG. Unfortunately, the cost is currently substantially higher than that for EEG.

THE NEUROPSYCHOLOGICAL EXAM

Imaging systems are becoming indispensable in neurology, but they do not replace a careful neurological exam. Much can be learned about disease processes through a careful study of behavioral symptoms, especially in the case of the visual and somatosensory systems. As we shall see in subsequent chapters, the visual system courses directly through the brainstem, so that any abnormality in the brainstem can affect visual processing, including the control of eye movements. However, the precise symptoms of a dysfunction depend on the locus of the pathology. Similarly, in the somatosensory system differences in sensitivity to fine touch and pressure can be compared with changes in sensitivity to pain and temperature to help identify disease processes in the spinal cord or the brainstem. Fancy machinery is an important addition to the neurologist's arsenal, but it does not replace careful observation of behavior, either by the neurologist or, as we shall see throughout this book, the neuropsychologist.

The neurologist carefully examines primarily the sensory and motor functions but leaves other nervous system functions, especially those involved in cognition (i.e., thought), to the neuropsychologist. Indeed, it is not uncommon for patients to exhibit no neurological impairment at all in the neurological exam, only to be found to have clear neuropsychological deficits. This is because many neuropsychological deficits are not obvious without careful assessment of cognitive functions through the use of tests of memory, intelligence, problem solving, and spatial relations, among others. These tests may take 6 to 8 hours to administer, and so it is hardly surprising that a neurologist is unable to assess them in a cursory mental-status exam. Neuropsychology is a relatively new field, but it has become a useful tool, and in many cases a necessary one, in the diagnosis and treatment of neurological disorders. We shall discuss the procedures of neuropsychological assessment in detail at the end of the book because they are best discussed in the context of neuropsychological theory. However, to demonstrate the usefulness of neuropsychological assessment we shall provide an example here.

Mr. R., a 21-year-old left-handed man, struck his head on the dashboard in a car accident 2 years prior to our seeing him. He was unconscious for a few minutes after the accident, but other than a cut on the right side of his forehead and amnesia for the period just before and after the accident, Mr. R. appeared none the worse for his mishap. Prior to his accident Mr.. R. was an honor student at a university, with plans to attend professional or graduate school. However, a year after the accident he had become a mediocre student who had particular trouble completing his term papers on time, and although he claimed to be studying harder than he had before the accident, his marks had fallen drastically in courses requiring memorization. He was referred for a neurological exam by his family physician, but it proved negative and an EEG and a CT scan failed to demonstrate any abnormality. He was referred to us for neuropsychological assessment, which revealed several interesting facts.

First, Mr. R. was one of the one-third of left-handers whose language functions are represented in the right rather than the left hemisphere. This discovery was significant not only in interpreting his difficulties but also in the event that Mr. R. should ever require neurosurgery, since the surgeon would want to respect the speech zones of the neocortex. In addition, although Mr. R. had a superior IQ, his verbal memory and reading speed were only low-average, which is highly unusual for a person of his intelligence and education. These deficits indicated that his right temporal lobe may have been slightly damaged in the car accident, resulting in an impairment of his language skills. On the basis of our neuropsychological investigation we were able to recommend vocations to Mr. R. that did not require superior verbal memory skills, and he is currently studying architecture.

This example illustrates that many effects of brain damage are subtle and difficult to detect without careful neuropsychological assessment. Even the most astute neurologist would have been unable to detect Mr. R.'s deficits without using extensive neuropsychological testing. Indeed, we anticipate that as neuropsychology continues to develop, neurology will place increasing demands on neuropsychological assessment as a tool in the diagnosis of cortical dysfunction.

REFERENCES

Andreasen, N. C. Brain imaging: Applications in psychiatry. *Science* 239:1381–1388, 1988.

Barth, D. S., W. Sutherling, J. Engel, Jr., and J. Beatty. Neuromagnetic localization of epileptiform spike activity in the human brain. *Science* 218:891–894, 1982.

Bannister, R. *Brain's Clinical Neurology,* 5th ed., New York: Oxford University Press, 1978.

Chiappa, K. H. Evoked potentials in clincial medicine. In A. B. Baker and R. J. Joynt, eds. *Clinical Neurology,* vol. 1, Philadelphia: Harper & Row, 1986, Chapter 6.

Curtis, B. A., S. Jacobson, and E. M. Marcus. *An Introduction to the Neurosciences.* Philadelphia: W. B. Saunders, 1972.

DeArmond, S. J., M. M. Fusco, and M. Dewey. *Structure of the Human Brain: A Photographic Atlas,* 2nd ed., New York: Oxford University Press, 1976.

Deecke, L., H. Weinberg, and P. Brickett. Magnetic fields of the human brain accompanying voluntary movement: Bereitschaftsmagnetfeld. *Experimental Brain Research* 48:144–148, 1982.

DeMyer, W. *Technique of the Neurologic Examination.* New York: McGraw-Hill, 1974.

Edelson, E. Scanning the body magnetic. *Science* 83(4):60–65, 1983.

Gordon, R., G. T. Herman, and S. A. Johnson. Image reconstruction from projections. *Scientific American* 233(Oct):56–68, 1975.

Jaffe, C. C. Medical imaging. *American Scientist* 70:576–585, 1982.

Kety, S. S. Disorders of the human brain. *Scientific American* 241:202–214, 1979.

Pykett, I. L. NMR imaging in medicine. *Scientific American* 246:78–88, 1982.

Raichle, M. E. Positron emission tomography. *Annual Review of Neuroscience* 6:249–267, 1983.

Squires, N. K. and C. Ollo. Human evoked potential techniques: Possible applications to neuropsychology. In H. J. Hannay, ed. *Experimental Techniques in Human Neuropsychology.* New York: Oxford University Press, 1986.

CHAPTER 7

NEUROLOGICAL DISORDERS

The normal functioning of the central nervous system can be affected by a number of disorders, the commonest of which are headaches, tumors, vascular problems, infections, epilepsy, trauma from head injury, demyelinating diseases, and metabolic and nutritional diseases. The following is a brief overview of those disorders that a neuropsychologist is most likely to encounter either clinically or in the literature.

VASCULAR DISORDERS

A neuron or glial cell can be damaged by any process that interferes with its energy metabolism, whether it be a reduction in oxygen or glucose, an introduction of some poison or toxic substance, or, more importantly, an interruption in blood supply. Vascular disease can produce serious—even total—reduction in the flow of both oxygen and glucose, resulting in a critical interference with cellular metabolism. If such interference lasts longer than 10 minutes, all cells in the affected region die. Cerebral vascular diseases are among the most frequent causes of death and chronic disability in the Western world. They are of particular concern to the neuropsychologist, because neuropsychology plays an important role in assessing the effect of vascular disorders on cognitive functioning. The neuropsychologist's role is especially important in the planning and assessment of rehabilitation for victims of these diseases.

The brain receives its blood supply from two *internal carotid* and two *vertebral arteries;* one of each is in either side of the body, as shown in Figure 7-1. The internal carotid arteries enter the skull at the base of the brain, branching off into a number of smaller arteries and two major arteries, the *anterior cerebral artery* and the *middle cerebral artery,* which irrigate the anterior and middle portions of the cortex. The vertebral arteries enter at the base of the brain and then join together to form the *basilar artery*. After branching off into several smaller arteries that irrigate the cerebellum, the basilar artery then divides into the *posterior cerebral artery*, which irrigates the medial temporal lobe and the posterior occipital lobe (Figure 7-2*C*).

The middle cerebral and posterior cerebral arteries are actually joined together on each side by the *posterior communicating artery*, and the two cerebral arteries are joined by the *anterior communicating artery*. These interconnections of arteries form the *circle of Willis*, which may compensate when half of the brain has lost flow from one of its carotid or vertebral arteries. In swimming mammals, the circle of Willis may also rapidly equalize arterial pressure in the two hemispheres during diving.

The distribution zones of the anterior, middle, and posterior cerebral arteries are shown in Figure 7-2. Notice, however, that these arteries irrigate not only the cortex but also subcortical structures, as shown in Figure 7-3. Thus, a disruption of blood flow to one of these arteries has serious consequences for subcortical as well as cortical structures. As we shall see in ensuing chapters, the occurrence of both cortical and subcortical damage following vascular accident (stroke) is a major reason why studying stroke victims is such a difficult way to study brain function.

The veins of the brain are classified as external and internal cerebral veins and cerebellar veins.

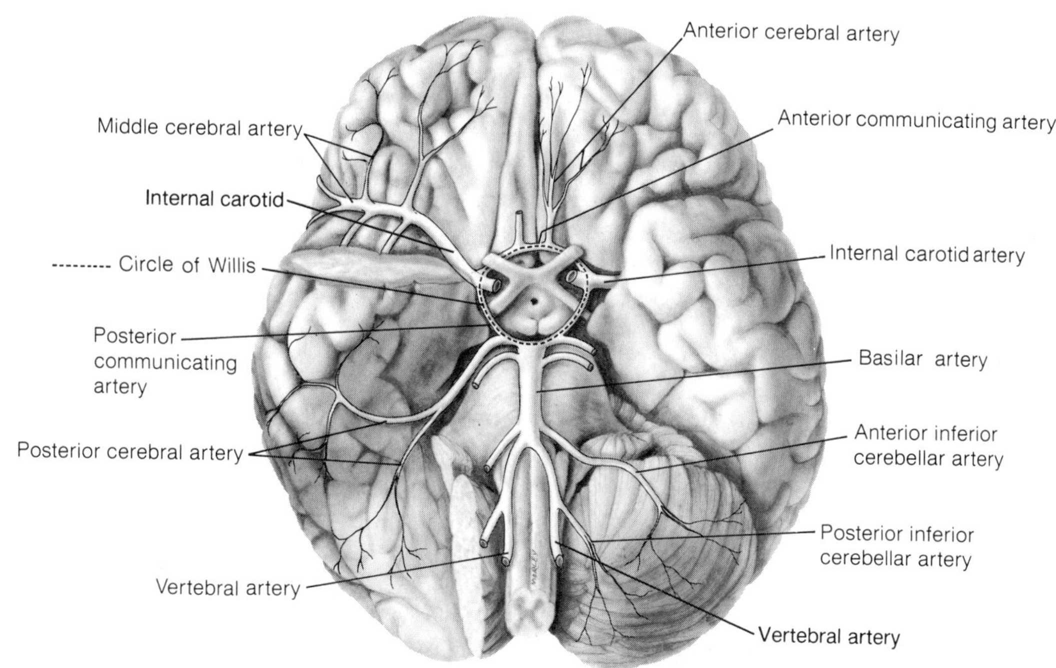

FIGURE 7-1. Major arteries of the brain viewed from below. The cerebellum and temporal lobe on the right hemisphere (left side of figure) have been cut away to reveal the pattern of irrigation, normally hidden from view. The connections formed by the anterior and posterior communicating arteries form the circle of Willis.

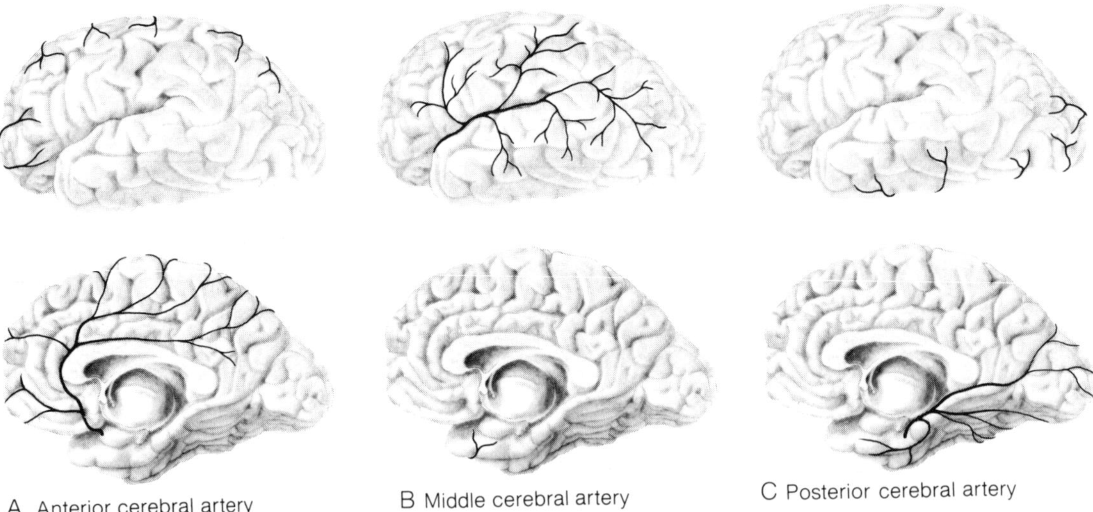

FIGURE 7-2. Distribution of the major cerebral arteries in the hemispheres: *top.* lateral view; *bottom.* medial view.

The venous flow does not follow the course of corresponding arteries but follows a pattern of its own, eventually flowing into a system of venous sinuses, or cavities, that drain the dura mater. Because adequate illustration of the venous-sinal drainage system requires more technical detail than is appropriate for this book, the interested reader is referred to more advanced discussions for more detail.

Symptoms and Diagnosis of Vascular Disorders

A common term used in discussion of cerebral vascular disorder is **stroke,** or **cerebral vascular accident.** A stroke is a sudden appearance of neurological symptoms as a result of severe interruption of blood flow. Stroke can result from a wide variety of different vascular diseases, but not all vascular disorders produce stroke, because the onset of dysfunction can be insidious, spanning months and even years. Stroke often produces an **infarct,** an area of dead or dying tissue resulting from an obstruction of the blood vessels normally supplying the area.

Most disease of the cerebral vascular system affects the arterial system, disease of venous drainage being uncommon in the central nervous system. The type of damage, or **lesion,** its extent, and its symptoms depend on a number of factors, including especially: the size of the blood vessel involved, the health of the remaining vessels, the presence of preexisting vascular lesions, the location of the tissue involved, the type of disorder, the presence of anastomoses, and individual differences.

Size of Blood Vessel. If small blood vessels, such as capillaries, are interrupted, the effects are more limited than the often devastating consequences of damage to such large vessels as the major arteries diagrammed in Figure 7-2. Disturbance of these arteries can result in lesions that include large portions of the brain and produce serious deficits in behavior.

Health of Remaining Vessels. If a stroke or other cerebral vascular disorder occurs in one restricted portion of unusual weakness, the prog-

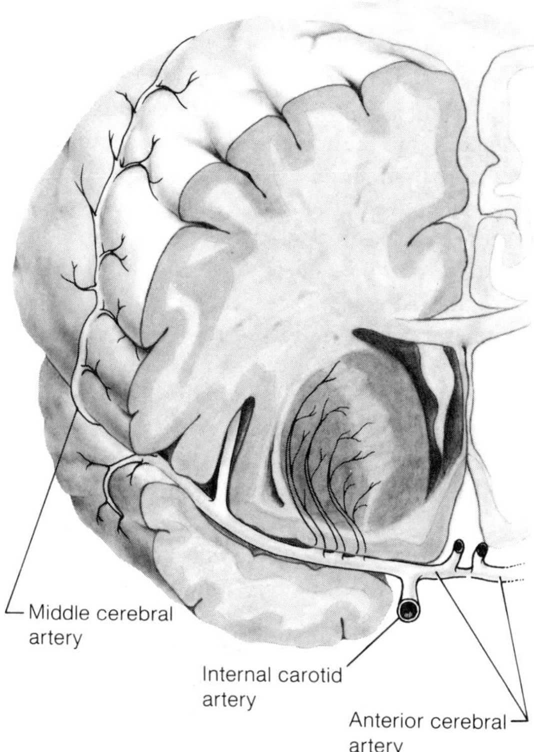

FIGURE 7-3. Irrigation of the deep structures of the brain by the same arteries as irrigate the surface structures. Interruption of the blood supply can thus produce both cortical and subcortical damage. (After Raichle, et al., 1978.)

nosis may be rather good, because vessels in surrounding zones are often able to supply blood to at least some of the deprived area. On the other hand, if a stroke affects a region surrounded by weak or diseased vessels, the effects may be much more serious, because there is no possibility of compensation. In addition, the surrounding weak zones may be at an increased risk of stroke themselves.

Presence of Preexisting Vascular Lesions. A small vascular lesion in a healthy brain will, in the long run, have a good prognosis for substantial recovery of function. However, in the event of preexisting vascular lesions, the effects of the second lesions may be extremely variable. The lesions can be cumulative and obliterate a functional zone of brain tissue, producing serious consequences. Or, less commonly, the lesions can produce what is known as a **serial lesion effect,** in which case there is remarkably little chronic effect from the second lesion. Although the mechanism of the serial lesion effect is unknown (see Chapter 26), the phenomenon is assumed to result from the process of recovery from the first lesion.

Location of Tissue Involved. The behavioral symptoms following vascular lesions depends, as with other lesions, on the exact location of damage. For example, a lesion in the primary visual cortex can produce an area of blindness, a lesion in the hippocampus can produce an impairment in memory, and a lesion in the medulla can produce arrest of breathing, resulting in death. Thus, the behavioral symptoms resulting from vascular disorder are important clues to the neurologist in locating the area of brain damaged and assessing the extent of the damage.

Type of Disorder. Exact symptoms of vascular disorder depend on the precise nature of the disorder. Slowly developing disorders can be expected to produce symptoms that differ from those of disorders of sudden onset. Warning symptoms of many disorders may be similar, however, and can include headache (if there is compression of the brain), as well as dizziness and vomiting.

Presence of Anastomoses. An **anastomosis** is a connection between parallel blood vessels that allows them to mingle their blood flows. The presence of an anastomosis in the brain allows cerebral blood supply to take more than one route to a given region. If one vessel is blocked, a given region might be spared an infarct because the blood has an alternative route to the affected zone. The presence of anastomoses is highly idiosyncratic among individuals, making it very difficult to predict the extent of damage resulting from a stroke to a given vessel. The difficulty is exacerbated by substantial variation in the exact route of even major blood vessels in the brain.

Individual Variation. The precise organization of the blood vessels differs considerably from person to person, as illustrated in Figure 7-4. Thus, damage to the same vessel in different people can produce symptoms that vary considerably although the differences tend to be quantitative rather than qualitative.

Types of Vascular Disorders

Of the numerous vascular disorders that affect the central nervous system, the commonest are ischemia, migraine stroke, cerebral hemorrhage, angiomas, and arteriovenous aneurysms.

Cerebral Ischemia. Ischemia includes a group of disorders in which the symptoms are due to an insufficient supply of blood to the brain. The ischemia may occur suddenly (in which case the term *stroke* is often used) or they may appear gradually. Decreases in blood flow can have any of three causes: (1) a **thrombosis:** a plug or clot in a blood vessel, which has coagulated and remains at the point of its formation; (2) an **embolism:** a clot or other plug brought through the blood from another vessel and forced into a smaller one, where it obstructs circulation (an embolism can be a blood clot, a bubble of air, a deposit of oil or fat, or a small mass of cells detached from a tumor; curiously, embolisms most frequently affect the middle cerebral artery of the left side of the brain); or (3) reduction of blood flow such that not enough oxygen and glucose are supplied (this reduction in blood flow can result from a variety of factors that produce narrowing of the vessels; the commonest example of such narrowing is **cerebral arteriosclerosis,** a condition marked by thickening and hardening of the arteries; other causes of narrowing include inflammation of the vessels (*vasculitis*) or spasm of the vessels).

Aside from embolism, which occurs suddenly, **encephalomalacia** (literally "softening of the brain") usually develops gradually, taking hours or sometimes days. The disease may also be episodic, in which case it may be termed **cerebral vascular insufficiency** or **transient ischemia,** indicating the variable nature of the disorder. The onset of transient attacks is often abrupt, frequently occurring as fleeting sensations of giddiness or impaired consciousness.

Ischemia results in the death of neurons, or an infarct. Neural death from ischemia was once believed to result directly from the loss of blood supply, but it now appears that this is not the case. Rather, when cells are deprived of blood, toxins are produced that act to overstimulate cells, leading to their death. For example, there are NMDA (*N*-methyl-D-aspartate) receptors on cells that are stimulated by the excitatory amino acids produced by the ischemia. The overstimulation of the NMDA receptors is toxic because neurons are literally stimulated to death. There are currently clinical trials of NMDA-receptor blockers that appear to reduce significantly the area of infarction resulting from stroke. It may seem odd that cells would have a "suicide" mechanism, but it appears that the NMDA receptors (and other similar receptors) play a major role in the neural mechanisms of learning. It is an unfortunate accident that when overstimulated they are self-destructive.

Migraine Stroke. People with classic **migraine** experience a transient ischemic attack with a variety of neurological symptoms, including impaired sensory function (especially vision), numbness of the skin (especially in the arms) difficulties in moving, and aphasia. The precise symptoms depend on the vessels involved; however, the posterior cerebral artery is most commonly affected. Although relatively rare, it has been known since the late 1800s that migraine attacks may lead to infarcts and permanent neurological deficits. **Migraine strokes** are believed to account for a significant proportion of strokes in young people

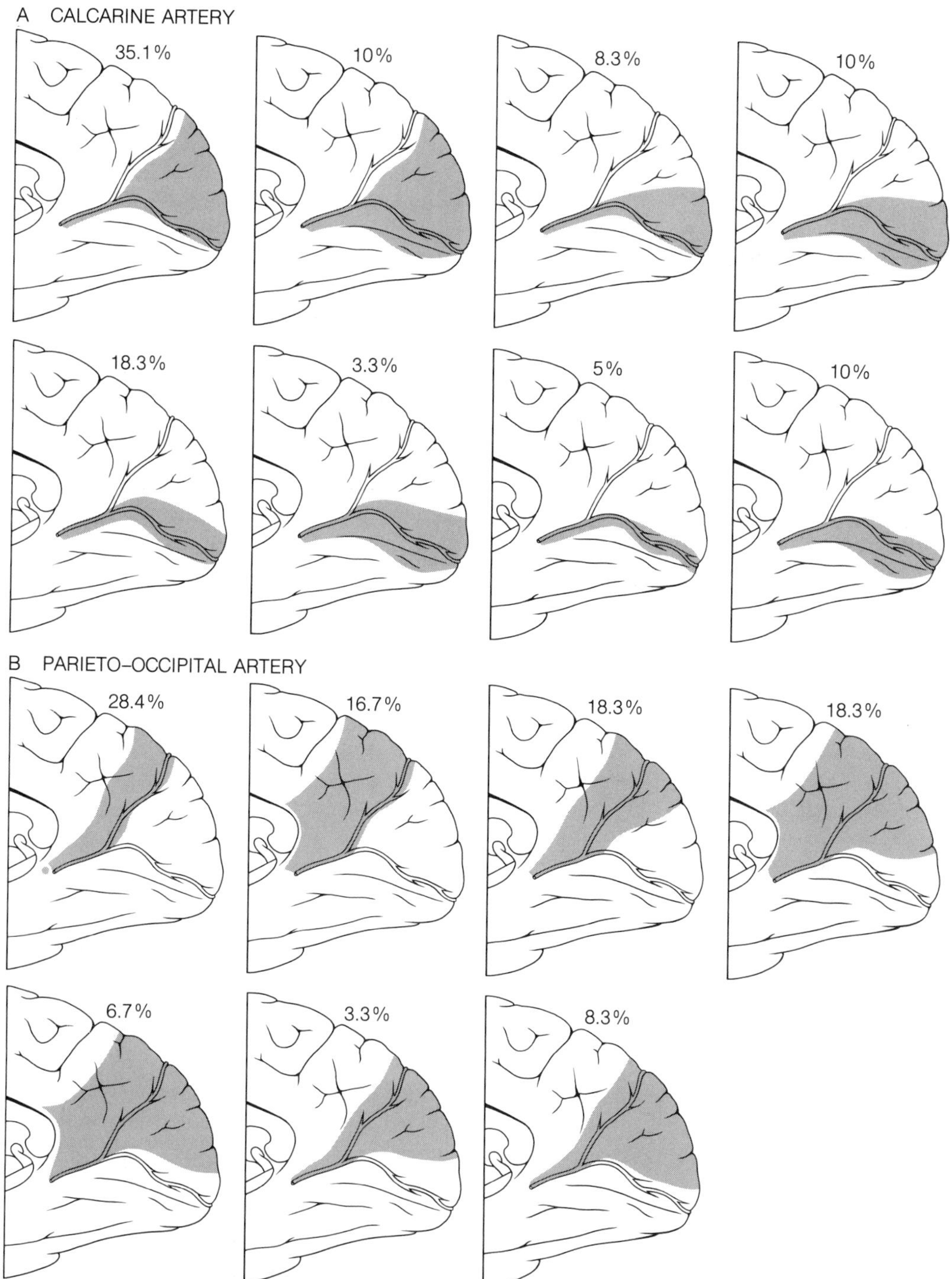

FIGURE 7.4. The gray areas illustrate the variation in the distribution of the calcarine (*A*) and parieto-occipital (*B*) arteries. The numbers indicate the percentage of people with a particular blood distribution pattern. (After Marinkovic et al., 1987.)

(under 40 years of age), especially women. The cause of these strokes is likely some form of vasospasm, but the reason remains a mystery.

Cerebral Hemorrhage. **Cerebral hemorrhage** is a massive bleeding into the substance of the brain. The most frequent cause is high blood pressure *(hypertension)*. Other causes are congenital defects in cerebral arteries, blood disorders such as leukemia, or toxic chemicals. Onset of cerebral hemorrhage is abrupt and may quickly prove fatal. It usually occurs during waking hours, presumably because the person is more active and thus has higher blood pressure. Prognosis is poor in cerebral hemorrhage, especially if the patient is unconscious for more than 48 hours.

Angiomas and Aneurysms. **Angiomas** are congenital collections of abnormal vessels, including capillary, venous, or **arteriovenous (A-V) malformations,** that result in abnormal blood flow. Angiomas are composed of a mass of enlarged and tortuous cortical vessels that are supplied by one or more large arteries and are drained by one or more large veins, most frequently in the field of the middle cerebral artery. By causing abnormal blood flow, angiomas may lead to stroke, because they are inherently weak, or to inadequate distribution of blood in the regions surrounding the vessels. In some cases arterial blood may actually flow directly into veins after only briefly, or sometimes not at all, servicing the surrounding brain tissue.

Aneurysms are vascular dilations resulting from localized defects in the elasticity of the vessel. These can be visualized as balloonlike expansions of vessels, which are usually weak and prone to rupture. Although aneurysms are usually due to congenital defects, they may also develop from hypertension, arteriosclerosis, embolisms, or infections. Symptoms of aneurysm especially include severe headache, which may be present for years because of pressure on the dura from the aneurysm.

Treatment of Vascular Disorders

Most vascular disorders have no specific treatment, although the commonest remedies include drug therapy and surgery. Supportive therapies include such drugs as anticoagulants (to dissolve clots or prevent clotting), vasodilators to dilate the vessels, drugs to reduce blood pressure, and salty solutions or steroids to reduce cerebral edema (swelling). Surgical techniques have been greatly improved in recent years but are practical only for some disorders. For example, the only certain cure for aneurysm is total removal, which is usually not feasible. Aneurysms are sometimes painted with various plastic substances, but the efficacy of this treatment is disputed. In the case of cerebral hemorrhage it may be necessary to operate to relieve the pressure of the blood from the ruptured vessel on the rest of the brain.

TRAUMATIC HEAD INJURIES

Brain injury is an all too common result of automobile and industrial accidents; **cerebral trauma** is the commonest form of brain damage in persons under the age of 40. Cerebral trauma may significantly affect brain function in a number of ways. (1) The trauma may result in direct damage to the brain, such as in a gunshot wound, in which neurons and support cells are damaged directly. (2) Trauma may disrupt blood supply, resulting in ischemia and, if the interruption is prolonged, infarction. (3) Trauma may cause bleeding within the skull, leading to increased intracranial pressure and subsequent additional damage. (4) Like most tissues in the body, the brain swells when traumatized, leading to increased intracranial pressure and the possibility of brain damage. (5) Compound fracture of the skull opens the brain to infection. (6) Head trauma can produce scarring of brain tissue; the scarred tissue becomes a focus for later epileptic seizures. Indeed, the sudden appearance of epileptic seizures in adulthood can frequently be traced to head injury (particularly from automobile accidents) in preceding months or years.

Open-Head Injuries

Open-head injuries include traumatic brain injuries in which the skull is penetrated, as in gunshot or missile wounds, or in which fragments of bone penetrate the brain substance. Open-head injuries show striking differences from closed-head injuries. Many people who have open-head injuries do not lose consciousness, and there is a tendency for them to have distinctive symptoms that may undergo rapid and spontaneous recovery. Neurological signs are often highly specific, with the effects of the injuries often closely resembling those of surgical excision of a small area of cortex, as illustrated in the following case:

> J. S. was injured in November 1944 by a bullet which penetrated the brain in the left parietal region. He did not lose consciousness and walked about two miles to meet the stretcher bearers. For about an hour after the injury he was unable to speak and thereafter his speech was slurred and hesitant [dysphasia]. On examination, during which he was fully conscious and co-operative, he had slight right facial weakness and arm and leg reflexes were brisker on the right. The operation took place in a mobile Neurosurgical Unit 44 hours after wounding. . . . Five days after wounding, he was admitted to the Oxford Head Injuries Centre and was found to be in good general condition but had some numbness of the right hand, chiefly of the third and fourth digits although this had improved since injury. . . . Three months after injury, the hypalgesia [reduced pain sensitivity] of the right side of the face had persisted with slight loss to pin prick over the fingers and palm of the right hand as far as the wrist, and also slight decrease of vibration sense at the fingers and wrist of the right hand. His dysphasia was described as "not very marked" but he was hesitant in spontaneous speech. He read fairly well and retained the content of his reading "very well." (Newcombe, 1969, p. 6)

The specificity of neurological symptoms following open-head injuries makes these patients especially good research subjects. Three thorough investigations of World War II veterans with open-head injuries have been published by Newcombe; Luria; and Teuber and his associates.

Closed-Head Injuries

These injuries result from a blow to the head, which subjects the brain to a variety of mechanical forces. First, there is damage at the site of the blow called a *coup*. The brain is compacted by molding of the bone inward, even if the skull is not fractured. Second, this pressure on the brain at the time of the coup may force the brain against the opposite side of the skull, producing an additional bruise (contusion) known as a *countercoup* (see Figure 7-5 and the CT scan in Figure 6-5). Third, the movement of the brain may cause a twisting or shearing of nerve fibers in the brain, producing microscopic lesions. These may occur throughout the brain but are commonest in the frontal and temporal lobes. In addition, the twisting and shearing may produce damage to the major fiber tracts of the brain, especially those crossing the midline, such as the corpus callosum and anterior commissure. As a result, connection between the two sides of the brain may be disrupted, leading to what is known as a **disconnection** syndrome (see Chapter 20). Fourth, the bruises and strains caused by the impact may produce bleeding (hemorrhage). Since the blood is trapped within the skull it acts as a growing mass (hemotoma), which exerts pressure on surrounding structures. Finally, as with blows to other parts of the body, blows to the brain produce *edema,* which is a collection of fluid in and around damaged tissue, producing another source of pressure on the brain tissue. Closed-head injuries are commonly accompanied by a lack of consciousness resulting from strain on

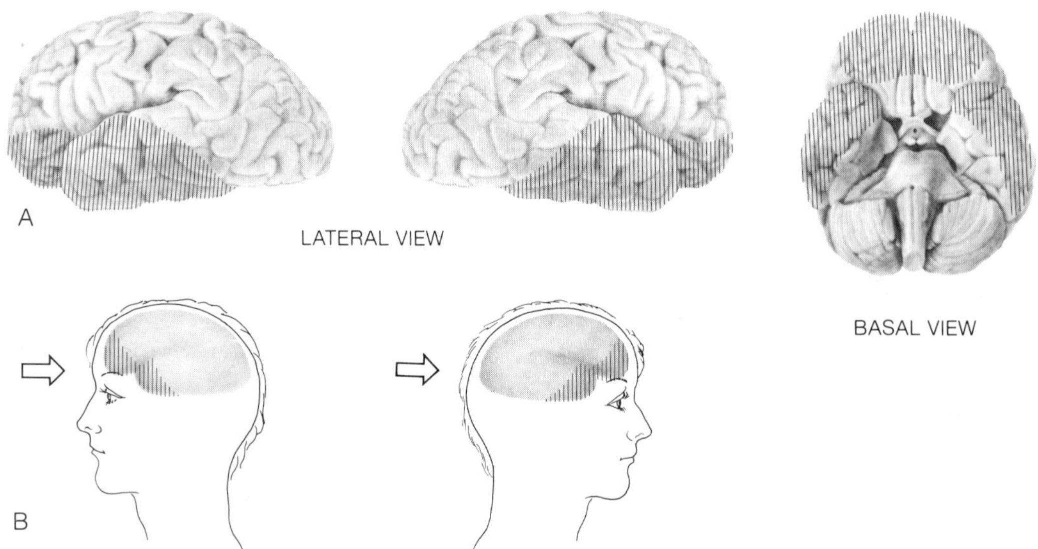

FIGURE 7-5. *A.* Shading represents regions of the cerebral hemispheres most frequently damaged in cerebral contusion. *B.* Demonstration of how a blow (arrow) to the forehead or occiput can produce a cerebral contusion on the frontal and temporal lobes. Left, the blow directly damages the brain. Right, the blow causes the brain to be compressed forward, producing a countercoup injury. (Illustrations after Courville, 1945.)

fibers in the brainstem reticular formation. These fibers often sustain permanent damage, even in cases of simple concussion. According to Lezak, the duration of loss of consciousness — or length of coma — can serve as a measure of the severity of damage, because it correlates directly with mortality, intellectual impairment, and deficits in social skills. The longer lasting the coma the greater the possibility of serious impairment and death.

Closed-head injuries resulting from traffic accidents are particularly severe because the head is moving when the blow is struck, thereby increasing the velocity of the impact and hence multiplying the number and severity of small lesions throughout the brain. CT scans of accident victims suffering prolonged coma show diffuse brain injury and enlarged ventricles — signs associated with poor outcomes.

Two kinds of behavioral effects result from closed-head injuries: discrete impairment of those functions mediated by the cortex at the site of the coup or the countercoup lesion, and more generalized impairments from damage widespread throughout the brain. Discrete impairment is most commonly associated with damage to the frontal and temporal lobes, those areas most susceptible to closed-head injuries (see Figure 7-5). More general impairment, resulting from minute lesions and lacerations scattered throughout the brain, is characterized by a general loss of complex cognitive functions, including reductions in mental speed, ability to concentrate, and overall cognitive efficiency. These difficulties are usually reflected in patients' complaints of inability to concentrate or to do things as well as they could before the accident, even though the intelligence rating may still be well above average. Indeed, in our experience, bright people are the most affected by closed-head injuries because they are acutely aware of a loss of cognitive skill that prevents them from returning to their previous competence level.

Closed-head injuries that damage the frontal and temporal lobes also tend to have significant effects on people's personality and social adjustment. According to Lezak, relatively few victims of traffic accidents who have sustained severe head injuries ever resume their studies or return to gainful employment, or if they do reenter the work force, they do so at a lower level than before.

> Despite residual capacities that are often considerable, one combination or another of impaired initiative and apathy, lack of critical capacity, defective social judgement, childishness and egocentricity, inability to plan or sustain activity, impulsivity, irritability, and low frustration tolerance is likely to render these patients unemployable or only marginally employable. These same qualities also make a person who has sustained moderate to severe head injuries at best a nuisance at home, at worst a terror. By virtue of these qualities, and again despite their residual capacities, these patients are rarely able to form or maintain close relationships, so that those who have not been rendered silly and euphoric or apathetic by their injuries, are often lonely and depressed as well. (Lezak, 1983, p. 170).

The diffuse nature of the chronic effects of closed-head injuries is often not associated with any neurological signs, and patients are often referred for psychiatric evaluation. Psychological assessments are especially useful here, because seriously handicapping cognitive deficits may become immediately apparent in the course of a thorough assessment, even though they are not obvious in casual conversation. Many of these patients appear normal in a psychological examination with standard intelligence tests, or even commercial neuropsychological test batteries, but careful neuropsychological investigation may reveal severe cognitive deficits, a result that underscores the need for a careful and competent neuropsychological assessment (see Chapters 27 through 32).

EPILEPSIES

Epilepsy is a condition characterized by recurrent electrographic seizures of various types that are associated with a disturbance of consciousness. Although epileptic episodes have been termed convulsions, seizures, fits, and attacks, none of these terms is entirely satisfactory, since the episodes can vary greatly in nature. Epileptic seizures are very common; 1 person in 20 will experience at least one seizure during his or her lifetime. Most of these people are not truly epileptic, however, for the seizures do not recur. The prevalance of multiple seizures is much lower, about 1 in 200.

The cause of epileptic seizures was unknown until the development of the EEG by Hans Berger in 1929. The technique made it possible to demonstrate that different varieties of epilepsy are associated with different abnormal electrical rhythms in the brain (see Figure 7-6*B*–*D*). Sometimes epileptic seizures are classifiable as **symptomatic seizures;** that is, they can sometimes be identified with a specific cause, such as infection, trauma, tumor, vascular malformation, toxic chemicals, very high fever, or other neurological disorders. But other seizure disorders, called **idiopathic seizures,** appear to arise spontaneously and in the absence of other diseases of the central nervous system. The cause of the abnormal electric discharge within the cell is poorly understood, although it is likely that it creates some type of abnormality in the neuronal membranes.

Although it has long been known that epilepsy runs in families, it is unlikely that there is a single gene responsible for the seizures, because the incidence is lower than would be predicted from genetic models. It is more likely that certain genotypes have a predisposition to seizure problems given certain environmental circumstances.

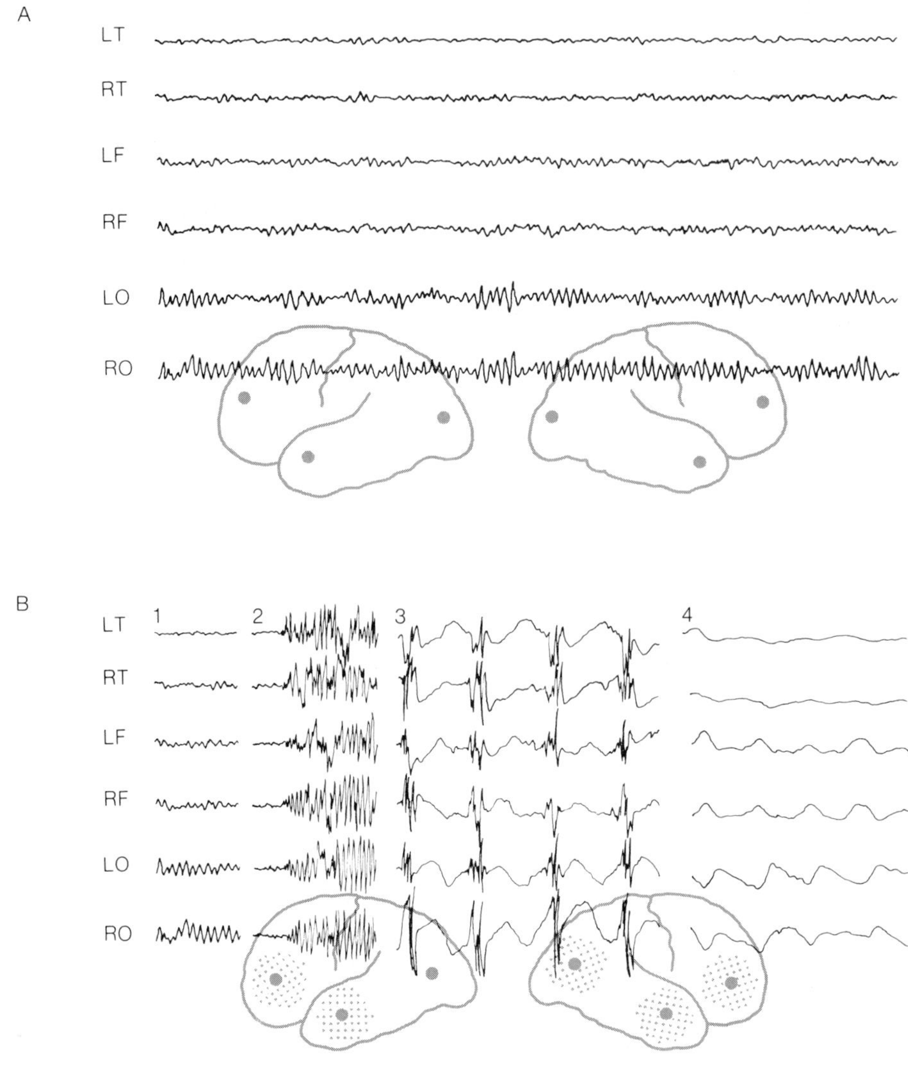

FIGURE 7-6. Examples of EEG recordings from different forms of epilepsy. LT: left temporal. RT: right temporal. LF: left frontal. RF: right frontal. LO: left occipital. RO: right occipital. The black dots on the hemispheres indicate the approximate recording sites. *A*. Normal adult EEG. *B*. Brief excerpts from an EEG taken during a grand mal seizure: (1) Normal recording preceding the attack. (2) Onset of attack. (3) Clonic phase of the attack. (4) Postictal period of coma. Shaded areas represent regions picked up by scalp electrodes. *C*. An episode of a 3/sec spike-and-wave EEG characteristic of petit mal seizures. *D*. Hypsarrhythmia in the EEG of a child. Notice diffuse slow waves with occasional spikes. (From W. B. Hardin, 1978. Copyright © 1978 by Oxford University Press, Inc. Reprinted with permission.)

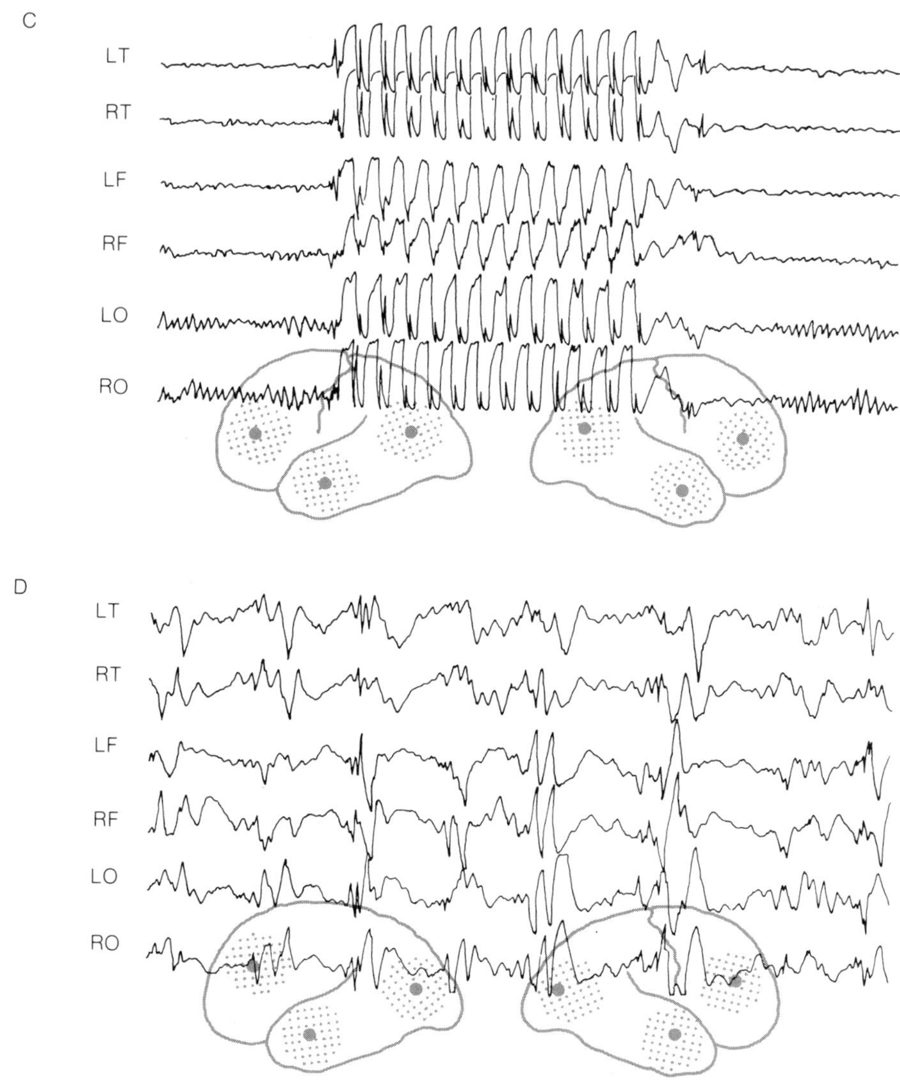

Symptoms and Diagnosis

The most remarkable clinical feature of epileptic disorders is the widely varying intervals between attacks—anywhere from minutes, hours, weeks, or even years. Thus, it is almost impossible to describe a basic set of symptoms to be expected in all, or even most, people with the disease. Three symptoms, however, are found in many types of epilepsy. (1) An aura, or warning, of impending seizure. This may take the form of sensations such as odors, noises, and the like, or may simply be a "feeling" that the seizure is going to occur. (2) Loss of consciousness. This may take the form of complete collapse or simply staring off into space. There is often **amnesia,** the victim forgetting the seizure itself and the period of lost consciousness. (3) Movements. It is common for seizures to have a motor component, although the characteristics vary considerably. In some cases there are shaking movements; in others, automatic movements such as rubbing the hands or chewing.

The diagnosis of epilepsy is usually confirmed by EEG. However, in some epileptics, seizures are difficult to demonstrate except under special circumstances (e.g., an EEG recorded during sleep), and not all persons with an abnormal EEG actually have seizures. In fact, some estimates suggest that 4 people in 20 actually have abnormal EEG patterns! Recently PET has provided a more reliable measure of functional abnormalities, although the cost for this method remains prohibitive. Studies of cerebral blood flow (see Chapter 15) may provide a less expensive alternative (see Engle).

TABLE 7-1. Classification of the epilepsies

Partial seizures (focal)
Simple partial seizures
Motor (Jacksonian)
Sensory (Jacksonian)
Autonomic
Complex partial seizures (temporal lobe, psychomotor)
Absences
Complex hallucinations
Affective symptoms
Automatism
Partial seizures secondarily generalized
Generalized seizures
Bilaterally symmetrical without local onset
Absence attacks (petit mal)
Tonic-clonic (grand mal)
Bilateral myoclonic
Drop attacks (akinetic)
Unclassified seizures
Because of incomplete data, includes many persons with apparently generalized seizures.

Types of Epilepsies

Several classification schemes have been published for epilepsy. Table 7-1 summarizes the ones in common use.

Focal seizures are those that begin locally and then spread. For example, in **Jacksonian seizures** the attack begins with jerks of single parts of the body, such as finger, a toe, or the mouth, and then spreads. If it were the finger, the jerks might spread to other fingers, then the hand, arm and so on, producing the so-called Jacksonian march. Jackson made the prediction in 1870 that such seizures probably originated from the point (focus) in the neocortex representing that region. He was later proved correct.

Complex partial seizures most commonly originate in the temporal lobe, and somewhat less frequently in the frontal lobe. Complex partial seizures are characterized by three common manifestations: (1) subjective feelings, such as forced, repetitive thoughts, alterations in mood, feelings of déjà vu, or hallucinations; (2) **automatisms,** repetitive stereotyped movements such as lip smacking or chewing, or the repetition of acts such as undoing buttons and the like; (3) postural changes, afflicted persons sometimes assuming catatonic, or frozen, postures.

Generalized seizures are bilaterally symmetrical without local onset. The **grand mal attack** is characterized by loss of consciousness and stereotyped motor activity. Typically, patients go through three stages: (1) a tonic stage, in which the body stiffens and breathing stops; (2) a clonic stage, in which there is rhythmic shaking; and (3) a post seizure (also known as postictal) depression, in which the patient is confused. About 50% of these seizures are preceded by an aura.

In the **petit mal,** or **absence attack,** there is loss of awareness during which there is no motor activity except blinking or turning the head or rolling the eyes. These attacks are of brief duration, seldom exceeding about 10 sec. The EEG record of a petit mal seizure has a typical pattern known as 3/sec spike and wave.

Akinetic seizures are ordinarily only seen in children. Usually the child collapses suddenly and without warning. These seizures are often of very short duration, and the child may get up after only a few seconds with no postictal depression. The falls that these children have can be quite dangerous in themselves, and it is not uncommon for the children to wear football helmets until the fits can be controlled by medication.

Myoclonic spasms are massive seizures that basically consist of a sudden flexion or extension of the body and often begin with a cry.

As mentioned earlier, seizures are not continual in any epileptic patients, even though the EEG may be chronically abnormal. Table 7-2 summarizes the great variety of circumstances that appear able to precipitate seizures. Although one is struck by the wide range of factors that may precipitate seizures, a consistent feature is that the brain is most epileptogenic when it is relatively inactive and the patient is sitting still.

TABLE 7-2. Factors that may precipitate seizures in susceptible individuals

Hyperventilation	
Sleep	
Sleep deprivation	
Sensory stimuli:	Flashing lights
	Reading-speaking, coughing
	Laughing
	Sounds: music, bells, etc.
	Reading
Trauma	
Hormonal changes:	Menses
	Puberty
	Adrenal steroids
	Adrenocorticotrophic hormone (ACTH)
Fever	
Emotional stress	
Drugs:	Phenothiazines
	Analeptics
	Tricyclic mood elevators
	Alcohol
	Excessive anticonvulsants

Source: After Pincus and Tucker, 1974.

Treatment of Epilepsy

The treatment of choice for epilepsy is an anticonvulsant drug, such as diphenylhydantoin (DPH, Dilantin), phenobarbital, and several others. Although the mechanism by which these drugs act is uncertain, they presumably inhibit the discharge of abnormal neurons by stabilizing the neuronal membrane. If medication fails to alleviate the seizure problem satisfactorily, surgery can be performed to remove the focus of abnormal functioning in patients with focalized seizures.

The surgical treatment of epilepsy dates back to the late 1800s, when W. Horsley and others removed the cortex in an attempt to alleviate seizures. The modern technique of surgery for epilepsy was pioneered by Otfrid Foerster in the 1920s in Germany. Wilder Penfield, stimulated by his studies with Foerster, began a prolonged scientific study of the surgical treatment of epilepsy in 1928, when he founded the Montreal Neurological Institute for that purpose. Penfield was soon joined by Herbert Jasper, who introduced EEG to the operating room, and by D. O. Hebb and Brenda Milner, who introduced the neuropsychological assessment of Penfield's surgical patients. Together these four and their colleagues developed a technique of cortical removal of the epileptogenic tissue from victims of focal epilepsy. The technique has been remarkably successful for this form of epilepsy. Their team approach to the treatment of a neurological disease provides a model of the marriage of basic and applied disciplines in developing an effective treatment for a neurological disorder.

Today, epilepsy is a particularly important disease for the neuropsychologist, because patients treated surgically for the relief of epilepsy form one of the best populations for neuropsychological study. Because the extent of surgical removal can be carefully charted at surgery and correlated with both preoperative and postoperative behavior, neuropsychologists have an excellent source of information on brain-behavior relations in humans.

TUMORS

A **tumor** (or neoplasm) is a mass of new tissue that persists and grows independently of its surrounding structures and has no physiological use. Brain tumors do not grow from neurons but rather from glia or other support cells. The rate at which tumors grow varies widely, depending on the type of cell that gives rise to the tumor. Tumors account for a relatively high proportion of neurological disease, and next to the uterus, the brain is the commonest site for tumors. It is possible to distinguish between benign (those not likely to recur after removal) and malignant (those likely to recur after removal and that frequently progress, becoming a threat to life) tumors. Although the distinction between benign and malignant tumors is well founded, the benign tumor may be as serious as the malignant one, since many benign tumors in the brain are inaccessible to the surgeon without risk to life. The brain is affected by many types of tumors, and no region of the brain is immune to tumor formation.

Tumors can significantly affect behavior in a number of ways. A tumor may develop as a distinct entity in the brain, a so-called *encapsulated tumor,* and put pressure on the rest of the brain (Figure 7-7). Encapsulated tumors are also sometimes *cystic,* which means they produce a fluid-filled cavity in the brain, usually lined with the tumor cells. Since the skull is of fixed size, any increase in its contents will functionally compress the brain, resulting in dysfunctions. Other tumors, so-called *infiltrating tumors,* are not clearly marked off from the surrounding tissue; they may either destroy normal cells and occupy their place or surround existing cells (both neurons and glia) and interfere with their normal functioning (Figure 7-8).

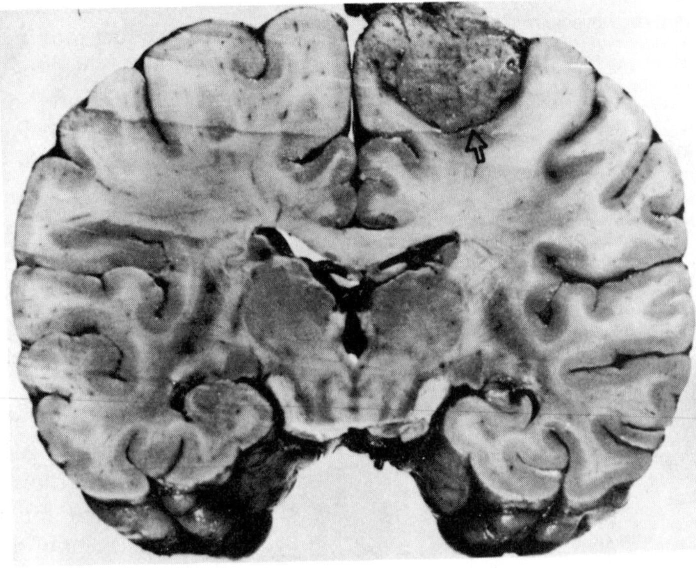

FIGURE 7-7. Frontal section showing a meningioma (arrow) arising in the dura and compressing the right cerebral hemisphere. Notice that the tumor has not infiltrated the brain. (From S. I. Zacks, 1971. Copyright © 1971 by Harper & Row. Reprinted with permission.)

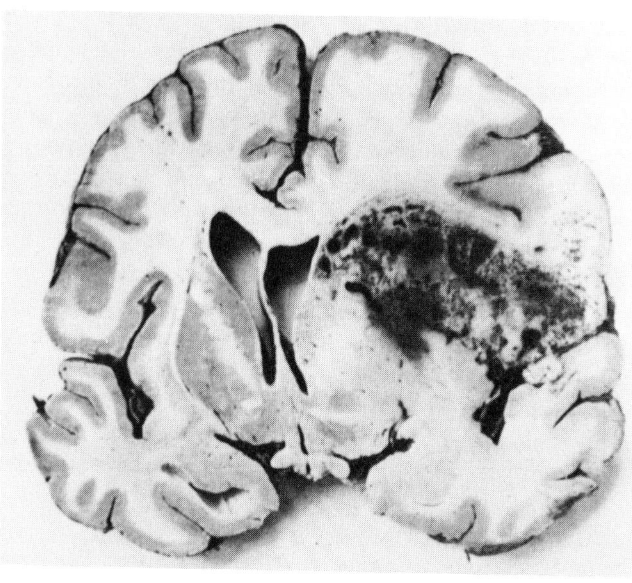

FIGURE 7-8. Frontal section showing a glioblastoma in the right cerebral hemisphere. Note the displacement of the ventricular system and the invasion of brain tissue (dark area). (From R. Bannister, 1978. Copyright © 1978 by Oxford University Press, Inc. Reprinted with permission.)

Symptoms and Diagnosis of Brain Tumors

The recognition of a brain tumor may be divided into three phases: (1) the suspicion that a tumor may be present, (2) the diagnostic confirmation of the tumor, and (3) the precise location of the tumor within the nervous system. The generalized symptoms of brain tumors, which result from increased intracranial pressure, include headache, vomiting, swelling of the optic disk (papilledema), slowing of the heart rate (bradycardia), mental dullness, double vision **(diplopia)**, and, finally, convulsions. It would be rare indeed for a patient to exhibit all these symptoms, most of which result from a marked increase in intracranial pressure. Other signs and symptoms depend on the exact location of the tumor. Thus, a tumor in the speech zones would be more likely to disrupt speech than would a tumor in the visual cortex.

Types of Brain Tumors

There are three major types of brain tumors, distinguished on the basis of where they originate: gliomas, meningiomas, and metastic tumors.

Gliomas. Glioma is a general term for those brain tumors that arise from glial cells and infiltrate the brain substance. Roughly 45% of all brain tumors are gliomas. Gliomas, ranging from the relatively benign to the highly malignant, vary considerably in their response to treatment. Because the detailed description of types of gliomas is more important to the neurologist and neurosurgeon than to the neuropsychologist, we shall briefly describe only the most frequently occurring types of gliomas: astrocytomas, glioblastomas, and medulloblastomas.

Astrocytomas. These tumors result from the growth of astrocytes and are usually slow growing. Astrocytomas account for about 40% of gliomas, being commonest in adults over 30 years of age. Because they are not very malignant, and because of their slow growth rate, they are relatively safe once treated. Thus, the prognosis for patients with this type of tumor is relatively good, with postoperative survivals occasionally being over 20 years.

Glioblastomas. These are highly malignant, rapidly growing tumors commonest in adults, especially men, over 35 years of age. **Glioblastomas** account for roughly 30% of gliomas. This tumor may result from the sudden growth of *spongioblasts,* cells that are ordinarily formed only during development of the brain, although some texts suggest that astrocytes cannot be ruled out as the source of glioblastomas. The tumor may be made up of a variety of cell types (glioblastoma multiforme) or of a single-cell type (glioblastoma unipolare). Because these tumors grow so rapidly, a patient's life expectancy is usually short, seldom extending beyond one year after surgery.

Medulloblastomas. These tumors are highly malignant and found almost exclusively in the cerebellum of children. **Medulloblastomas** account for about 11% of all gliomas. The tumor results from the growth of germinal cells that infiltrate the cerebellum or underlying brainstem. The prognosis for children with these tumors is poor; the postoperative survival period ranges from 1.5 to 2 years.

Meningiomas. **Meningiomas** are growths attached to the **meninges,** or protective outer layer of the brain. They grow entirely outside the brain, are well encapsulated, and are the most benign of all brain tumors. Although meningiomas do not invade the brain, they are often multiple and disturb brain function by producing pressure on the brain, often producing seizures as a symptom. Although most meningiomas lie over the hemispheres, some occur between them. The latter location makes removal more complicated. It is not uncommon for these tumors to erode the overlying bone of the skull. If meningiomas are removed completely, they tend not to recur.

Metastatic Tumors. **Metastasis** is the transfer of disease from one organ or part to another not directly connected with it. Thus, a **metastatic tumor** in the brain is one that has become established by a transfer of tumor cells from some other region of the body, most commonly lung or breast. Indeed, it is not uncommon for the first indication of lung cancer to be evidence of brain tumor. Metastases to the brain are usually multiple, making treatment complicated and prognosis poor.

Other Tumors. We have considered only the major types of primary brain tumors; there are, however, many more less common types. One of these, the *pituitary adenoma,* is a tumor of the pituitary region. Although the pituitary is not really part of the brain, tumors there produce pressure on the brain, and owing to the close relation between the hypothalamus and the pituitary, such tumors can produce significant functional abnormalities in the hypothalamus. For a detailed discussion of other brain tumors, we recommend Baker and Baker's extensive text.

Treatment of Brain Tumors

The most obvious treatment of brain tumors is surgery, which is the only way to make a definite histological diagnosis. If feasible, tumors are removed, but, as with tumors elsewhere in the body, success depends on early diagnosis. Radiation therapy is useful for treating certain types of tumors, such as glioblastomas and medulloblastomas, as well as for some metastatic tumors. Chemotherapy has not yet been very successful in the treatment of brain tumors, owing in part to the difficulty in getting drugs to pass the blood-brain barrier and distribute in the tumor.

HEADACHES

Headache is so common among the general population that rare indeed is the person who has never suffered one. Headache may constitute a neurological disorder in itself, as in migraine; it may be secondary to neurological disease such as tumor or infection; or it may result from psychological factors, especially stress, as in tension headaches. The pain-sensitive structures within the skull that can be responsible for a headache include the dura, the large arteries of the brain, the venous sinuses, and the branches of the 5th, 9th and 10th cranial nerves, and the 1st and 3rd cervical nerves. Pain can be elicited from these structures by pressure, displacement, or inflammation.

Types of Headaches

Migraine. **Migraine** (derived from the Greek *hemi* and *kranion,* meaning half of skull) is perhaps the commonest neurological disorder, afflicting some 5 to 20% of the population at some time in their lives. The World Federation of Neurology defines migraine as a ". . . familial disorder characterized by recurrent attacks of headache widely variable in intensity, frequency and duration. Attacks are commonly unilateral and are usually associated with anorexia, nausea and vomiting. In some cases they are preceded by, or associated with, neurological and mood disturbances." There are several types of migraine including classic migraine, common migraine, cluster headache, and hemiplegic and opthalmoplegic migraine. *Classic migraine* is probably the most interesting form, occuring in about 12% of migraine sufferers, as it includes an **aura,** which usually lasts for 20 to 40 min. Karl Lashley, perhaps the first neuropsychologist, suffered from classic migraine and carefully described his visual aura, which turned out to be common to many migraine sufferers and is shown in Figure 7-9. The aura is presumed to occur because constriction of one or more cerebral arteries has produced ischemia of the occipital cortex. PET studies have shown that during the aura there is a reduction in blood flow in the posterior cortex and this reduction spreads anteriorly at the rate of about 2 mm/min without respecting major vascular distributions. This rate and the distribution of spread is similar to a phenomenon known as **spreading depression.** A puzzle surrounds the question of why the reduced blood flow moves independent of the major vessels, an observation that suggests that the vascular

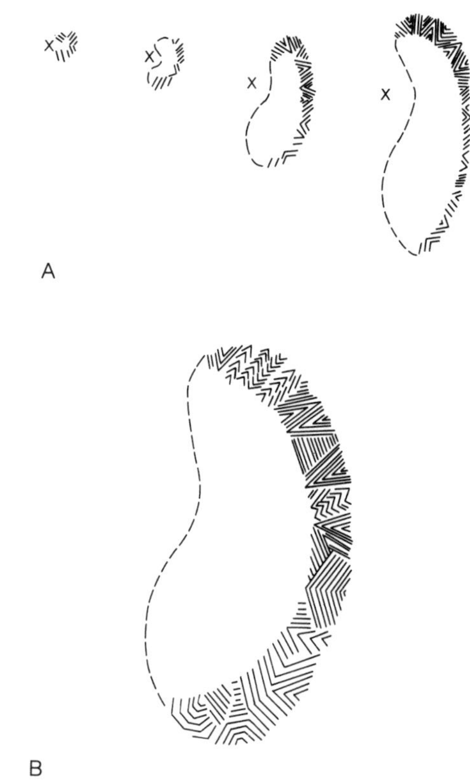

FIGURE 7-9. *A.* Successive maps of a scintillating scotoma (blind spot), showing the characteristic increase in the size of the scotoma and the location of the so-called fortification figures. The *x* in each case indicates the fixation point. The scotoma typically takes about 10 min to fill the visual field. *B.* A sketch to show the fortification figures in detail. (After Lashley, 1941.)

changes are secondary to changes in neural function. The actual headache begins as the vasoconstriction reverses (ending the neurological disturbance) and vasodilation occurs. The headache is manifested as an intense pain localized in one side of the head, although it frequently spreads on the affected side and sometimes to the opposite side as well. A severe headache can be accompanied by nausea and vomiting, and it may last for hours or even days. A significant number of people with classic migraine never suffer the headache but only experience the aura.

Common migraine is the most frequent type of migraine, occurring in more than 80% of migraine sufferers. There is no clear aura as in classic migraine but there may be a gastrointestinal or other "signal" that an attack is pending. *Cluster headache* is a unilateral pain in the head or face that rarely lasts longer than 2 h (hours) but recurs repeatedly for a period of weeks or even months before disappearing, sometimes for long periods, before returning. The final two types of migraine, *hemiplegic* and *ophthalmoplegic migraine* are relatively rare and involve loss of movement of the limbs or eye, respectively.

The frequency of migraine attacks varies from as often as one per week to as seldom as once in a lifetime. In cases where migraine is frequent, the occurrence generally drops with aging and usually ceases in middle age. Migraine was generally believed to be rare prior to adolescence, but in recent years it has been recognized as afflicting children as well, although the actual incidence in this population is uncertain.

A large number of environmental factors appear to trigger migraine attacks, including anxiety, the termination of anxiety (relaxation), fatigue, bright light, and in many persons, specific allergies, particularly to foods and wines.

Headache Associated with Neurological Disease. Headache, a common symptom of many nervous system disorders, usually results from distortion of the pain-sensitive structures. Common disorders producing headache include tumor, head trauma, infection, vascular malformations, and severe hypertension (high blood pressure). The characteristics and location of these headaches vary according to the actual disorder. For example, headache from brain tumor is almost always located on the same side of the head as the tumor, particularly in the early stages of the tumor. However, headaches related to brain tumor have no characteristic severity, for they vary from mild to excruciating. Likewise, hypertension headache, although it is nearly always located in the occipital region, is also highly variable in severity.

Muscle-Contraction Headache. *Muscle-contraction headaches* are the commonest form of headache, also being known as tension, psychogenic, and nervous headaches. These headaches result from sustained contraction of the muscles of the scalp and neck caused by constant stress or tension, especially if poor posture is maintained for any time. Patients describe their symptoms as steady, nonpulsing, tight, squeezing, pressing, or crawling sensations or as the feeling of having the head in a vise. The headaches may be accompanied by anxiety, dizziness, and bright spots in front of the eyes. In some people, caffeine may exacerbate the headaches, presumably because anxiety is increased.

Nonmigrainous Vascular Headaches. A wide variety of diseases and conditions induce headache that is associated with dilation of the cranial arteries. The commonest causes are fever, anoxia (lack of oxygen), anemia, high altitude, physical effort, hypoglycemia (low blood sugar), foods, and chemical agents. In addition, headache may result from congestion and edema of the nasal membranes, often termed *vasomotor rhinitis,* which is assumed to represent a localized vascular reaction to stress.

Treatment of Headache

Migraine is treated by specific drugs at the time of attacks and by preventive measures between attacks. In an acute attack **ergotamine** compounds, often given in conjunction with caffeine, are useful in alleviating the headache, probably because they produce constriction of the cerebral arteries, thus reducing tension in this pain-sensitive structure. In addition, most migraine sufferers find the headache is reduced in a totally dark room. In view of the unpleasantness of migraine, the sufferer should try to avoid those circumstances that experience shows precipitate the attacks.

The most obvious treatment of headache arising from neurological disease is to treat the disease itself. Tension headache can be relieved by muscle-relaxant drugs, minor tranquilizers, application of heat to the affected muscles, and improvement of posture. They can also be prevented by avoiding the life situations that give rise to stress.

INFECTIONS

Infection is the invasion of the body by disease-producing (pathogenic) microorganisms and the reaction of the tissues to their presence and to the toxins generated by them. Because the central nervous system can be invaded by a wide variety of infectious agents, including viruses, bacteria, fungi, and metazoan parasites, the diagnosis and treatment of infection are an important component of clinical neurology. Although infections of the nervous system usually spread from infection elsewhere in the body—especially the ears, nose, and throat—they also may be introduced directly into the brain as a result of head trauma, skull fractures, or surgery. Infections of the nervous system are particularly serious because the affected neurons and glia usually die, resulting in lesions.

There are a number of processes by which infections kill neural cells. First, infections may interfere with the blood supply to neurons, thus producing thrombosis, hemorrhage of capillaries, or even the complete choking off of blood vessels. Second, there may be a disturbance of glucose or oxygen metabolism in the brain cells that is serious enough to kill them. Third, the infection may alter the characteristics of the neural cell membranes, thus altering the electrical properties of the neurons, or alternatively, it may interfere with the basic enzymatic processes of the cell, producing any number of abnormal conditions. Fourth, a byproduct of the body's defense against infection is *pus*—a fluid composed basically of white blood cells, their byproducts, and those of the infectious microorganisms—and a thin fluid called liquor puris. Pus impairs neuronal functioning in at least two ways: it significantly alters the extracellular fluids surrounding a neuron, thus altering neuronal function; and because pus occupies space, its production increases pressure on the brain, disturbing normal functioning. Fifth, and finally, infection often causes edema, which compresses the brain, again resulting in brain dysfunction.

Symptoms and Diagnosis of Infection

Many infections of the nervous system are secondary to infections elsewhere in the body and are accompanied by symptoms associated with those other infections, including lowered blood pressure and other changes in blood circulation, fever, general malaise, headache, and delirium. In addition, symptoms of cerebral infections include both generalized symptoms of increased intracranial pressure, such as headache, vertigo, nausea, convulsions, and mental confusion, as well as focalized symptoms of disturbance of specific brain functions.

Diagnostic tests for infection include CSF studies in addition to conventional methods of infection identification, such as smear and culture studies. CT scans and other brain scans may also be used to diagnose and locate some infectious disorders.

Types of Infections

Unfortunately, there is a good deal of semantic disagreement about the terminology of infections. We shall use the term **encephalitis** to refer to inflammation of the central nervous system caused by infection and the term **encephalopathy** for chemical, physical, allergic, or toxic inflammations. Note that, strictly speaking, encephalitis and encephalopathy do not refer to specific diseases, but rather to the effects of the disease processes.

Four types of infections can affect the central nervous system: viral, bacterial, mycotic (fungal), and parasitic infestations.

Viral Infections. A *virus* is an encapsulated aggregate of nucleic acid that may be made up of either DNA or RNA. Some viruses, such as those causing poliomyelitis and rabies, are called **neurotropic viruses,** because they have a special affinity for cells of the central nervous system. These are different from **pantropic viruses** (such as those causing mumps and herpes simplex), which attack other body tissue in addition to the central nervous system. Most viral infections of the nervous system produce nonspecific lesions affecting widespread regions of the brain, as occur in diseases such as St. Louis encephalitis, rabies, and poliomyelitis.

Bacterial Infections. *Bacterium* is a loose generic name for any microorganism (typically one-celled) that has no chlorophyll and multiplies by simple division. Bacterial infections of the central nervous system result from an infestation of these organisms, usually via the bloodstream. The commonest disorders resulting from bacterial infection are meningitis and brain abcess. In **meningitis,** the meninges are infected by any of a variety of bacteria. **Brain abcesses** are also produced by a variety of bacteria, secondary to infection elsewhere in the body. Abcesses begin as a small focus of purulent (pus-producing) bacteria that cause necrosis (death) of cells in the affected region. As the organisms multiply and destroy more brain cells, the abcess behaves as an expanding mass, frequently hollow in the center; as it expands it produces increasing intracranial pressure.

Mycotic Infections. Invasion of the nervous system by a fungus is known as a **mycotic infection.** A fungus is any member of a large group of lower plants that lack chlorophyll and subsist on living or dead organic matter; the fungi include yeasts, molds, and mushrooms. Ordinarily the central nervous system is highly resistant to mycotic infections, but fungi may invade a brain whose resistance has been reduced by various diseases such as tuberculosis or malignant tumors.

Parasitic Infestations. A *parasite* is an organism that lives on or within another living organism (the host) at the host's expense. Several kinds of parasites invade the central nervous system and produce significant disease, the most important of which are amebiasis and malaria. *Amebiasis* (also known as amebic dysentery), caused by an infestation of the protozoan ameba *(Entamoeba histolytica)*, results in encephalitis and brain abcesses. *Malaria* is caused by protozoa of the genus *Plasmodium,* which are transmitted by the bites of infected mosquitoes. Cerebral malaria occurs when the plasmodia infect the capillaries of the brain, producing local hemorrhages and subsequent degeneration of neurons.

Treatment of Infections

Treatment varies with the type of infection. Viral infections are extremely difficult to treat, for there are no specific antidotes, the only treatment being to let the diseases run their course. Sedatives are sometimes administered to make the patient more comfortable. The important exception to this is the treatment of rabies. Once it is ascertained that a person has had contact with a rabid animal, antirabies vaccine is administered over a period of 2 to 4 weeks in order to produce an immunity before the disease actually develops. Once the disease does develop, rabies is fatal.

Bacterial cerebral infections have become less common with the introduction of antibiotic drugs, the usual treatment for these infections. In some cases it may be necessary to drain abcesses to relieve intracranial pressure, or to do spinal taps to remove

CSF and reduce pressure where there is edema or a build-up of pus.

Neither mycotic nor parasitic infections can be satisfactorily treated, although antibiotics are often used to treat associated disorders.

DEGENERATIVE DISORDERS

Many diseases of the nervous system involve a progressive deterioration of brain tissue and behavior. In most cases there is a specific loss of some region or system in the brain, which produces a distinctive behavioral syndrome. The commonest degenerative disorders and their probable causes are summarized in Table 7-3. We shall consider only the dementias (Alzheimer's, Pick's, and Creutzfeldt-Jakob's diseases) here, as the other disorders are described in detail elsewhere in the book. Parkinson's disease, Huntington's chorea, multiple sclerosis, myasthenia gravis are discussed in Chapter 13; Korsakoff's syndrome is considered in Chapter 21. Alzheimer's disease is further detailed in Chapter 31.

TABLE 7-3. Summary of common degenerative diseases

Disorder	Probable cause
Alzheimer's disease	Loss of cholinergic neurons in nucleus basalis of Meynert leading to development of senile plaques and neurofibrillary tangles
Pick's disease	Atrophy of frontal and temporal lobes from unknown causes
Cruetzfeldt-Jakob's disease	Generalized cortical atrophy from unknown causes
Korsakoff's syndrome	Atrophy of medial thalamus and mamillary bodies from chronic excessive alcohol consumption
Huntington's chorea	Degeneration of basal ganglia, frontal cortex, and corpus callosum due to a genetic abnormality
Parkinson's disease	Loss of striatal dopamine due to degeneration of the substantia nigra
Multiple sclerosis	Abnormal neural activity due to loss of myelin
Myasthenia gravis	Autoimmune disorder causing motor muscle receptors to decrease

Alzheimer's disease accounts for about 65% of the patients diagnosed as demented and has generated a great deal of interest recently because it may provide a good model for the study of senility in general. Although a distinction was once made between the onset of senility prior to age 65 (presenile dementia of the Alzheimer type) and onset over 65 (senile dementia), there are no longer strong grounds for distinguishing between these disorders, since the pathology is similar. The term *Alzheimer's disease* is now commonly used to refer to both presenile and senile dementia. The disease begins insidiously, eventually afflicting about 5% of the population over age 65. Postmortem study of the brains of Alzheimer's patients has recently led to a major breakthrough in our understanding of this and related diseases. It has been known for some time that the brains of these persons are characterized by abnormal **neurofibrils** (neurofibrillatory tangles), **neuritic plaques,** and the loss of nerve cells, but recent neurochemical studies have suggested that there are other changes, including the amount of serotonin, dopamine, and norepinephrine in cells. Careful study of the brains of Alzheimer's patients suggests that the plaque density in the cortex correlates with reductions in these transmitter systems. In addition, cells in the cortex, particularly in the **entorhinal cortex** and hippocampus, degenerate, and cells in tertiary areas of the cortex lose their dendrites.

Behaviorally, Alzheimer's disease is characterized by marked deficits in memory, language, and perception as well as by symptoms of depression. Indeed, it is not uncommon for Alzheimer's patients to be initially treated for depression. It is the loss of memory, however, that has generated the most research interest; research on this is possible because memory can be easily studied in nonhuman species following the administration of drugs that are antagonistic to acetylcholine and appear to interfere with performance in tests of memory.

Pick's and Creutzfeldt-Jakob's diseases are also dementias, although they are less common than Alzheimer's. The cause of the first disease is unknown, and the second is thought to be produced by a virus. *Pick's disease* is characterized by symptoms that are virtually indistinguishable clinically from those of Alzheimer's disease, but at autopsy the diseases can be distinguished. In Pick's disease the cellular degeneration and atrophy are confined to the frontal and temporal cortex, and the plaques and tangles characteristic of Alzheimer's disease are not evident. *Creutzfeldt-Jakob's disease* differs from the other two in that its course is very rapid, leading in just a few months to stupor, coma, and death. Memory loss is prominent from the outset, but deterioration can be measured nearly day to day. At autopsy, there is a generalized thinning of the cortex in addition to generalized abnormalities in subcortical structures.

TABLE 7-4. DSM-III categories of mental disorders

Disorders usually first evident in infancy, adulthood, or adolescence
Organic mental disorders
Substance-use disorders
Schizophrenic disorders
Paranoid disorders
Psychotic disorders not elsewhere classified
Affective disorders
Anxiety disorders
Somatoform disorders
Dissociative disorders
Psychosexual disorders
Factitious disorders
Disorders of impulse control not elsewhere classified
Adjustment disorder
Psychological factors affecting physical condition
Conditions not attributable to a mental disorder that are a focus of attention or treatment

Source: American Psychiatric Association. *Diagnostic and Statistical Manual of Mental Disorders,* 3rd ed. Washington, D.C.: American Psychiatric Associaton, 1980.

MENTAL DISORDERS

The *Diagnostic and Statistical Manual of Mental Disorders* (DSM-III) of the American Psychiatric Association lists 16 different types of behavioral disorders (see Table 7-4); it can be safely assumed that some of these disorders result from abnormal brain function. However, the current limitations in our knowledge about brain function make it impossible to ascertain whether a given behavioral disturbance results directly from abnormal brain functioning or from a response to environmental or social factors.

Two types of disorders likely to result from neurological abnormalities are the schizophrenic and affective disorders, although even in these an environmental influence cannot be ruled out. Both of these disorders have been alleged to result, in part, from abnormalities in the levels of neurotransmitters in the brain (dopamine for schizophrenia and norepinephrine and serotonin for depression); the principal treatment for both disorders is thus pharmacological. We shall consider current neurological theories of schizophrenia and affective disorders in detail in Chapter 23 in the broader context of the neurological control of affective behavior.

REFERENCES

Adams, H. E., M. Feuerstein, and J. L. Fowler. Migraine headache: Review of parameters, etiology, and intervention. *Psychological Bulletin* 87:217–237, 1980.

Alpers, B. J., and E. L. Mancall. *Clinical Neurology,* 6th ed. Philadelphia: Davis, 1971.

Bakal, D. A. Headache: A biopsychological perspective. *Psychological Bulletin* 82:369–382, 1975.

Baker, A. D., and L. H. Baker. *Clinical Neurology,* rev. ed. Philadelphia: Harper & Row, 1982.

Bannister, R. *Brain's Clinical Neurology,* 5th ed. New York: Oxford University Press, 1978.

Corkin, S. Acetylcholine, aging and Alzheimer's disease: Implications for treatment. *Trends in Neurosciences* 4:287–290, 1981.

Courville, C. B. *Pathology of the Nervous System,* 2nd ed. Mountain View, CA: Pacific Press, 1945.

Coyle, J. T., D. L. Price, and M. R. DeLong. Alzheimer's disease: A disorder of cortical cholinergic innervation. *Science* 219:1184–1190, 1983.

Eliasson, S. G., A. L. Prensky, and W. B. Hardin. *Neurological Pathophysiology,* 2nd ed. New York: Oxford University Press, 1978.

Engle, J. Functional localization of epileptogenic lesions. *Trends in Neurosciences* 6:60–65, 1983.

Forster, F. M. *Clinical Neurology,* 3rd ed. St. Louis, MO: Mosby, 1973.

Friedman, A. J. Headache. In A. B. Baker and R. J. Joynt, eds. *Clinical Neurology* vol. 2. Philadelphia, Harper & Row, 1986.

Gloor, P. Contributions of electroencephalography and electrocorticography to the neurosurgical treatment of the epilepsies. *Advances in Neurology* 8:59–105, 1975.

Hardin, W. B. Pathophysiology of clinical epilepsy. In S. G. Eliasson, A. L. Prensky, and W. B. Hardin, eds. *Neurological Pathophysiology,* 2nd ed. New York: Oxford University Press, 1978.

Lashley, K. S. Patterns of cerebral integration indicated by the scotomas of migraine. *Archives of Neurology and Psychiatry* 46:331–339, 1941.

Lezak, M. D. *Neuropsychological Assessment,* 2nd ed. New York: Oxford University Press, 1983.

Lieberman A., and J. Ransohoff. Treatment of primary brain tumors. *Medical Clinics of North America* 63:835–848, 1979.

Luria, A. R. *The Working Brain.* New York: Penguin Books, 1973.

Marinkovic, S. V., M. M. Milisavljevic, M. M., V. Lolic-Draganic, and M. S. Kovacevic. Distribution of the occipital branches of the posterior cerebral artery: Correlation with occipital lobe infarcts. *Stroke* 18:728–732, 1987.

McNeil, E. B. *The Psychoses.* Englewood Cliffs, NJ: Prentice-Hall, 1970.

Newcombe, F. *Missile Wounds of the Brain.* London: Oxford University Press, 1969.

Pincus, J. H., and G. J. Tucker. *Behavioral Neurology.* New York: Oxford University Press, 1974.

Raichle, M. E., C. D. de Vivo, and J. Hanaway. Disorders of cerebral circulation. In S. G. Eliasson, A. L. Prensky, and W. B. Hardin, eds. *Neurological Pathophysiology,* 2nd ed. New York: Oxford University Press, 1978.

Rasmussen, T. Cortical resection in the treatment of focal epilepsy. *Advances in Neurology* 8: 139–154, 1975.

Slager, U. T. *Basic Neuropathology*. Baltimore: Williams and Wilkins, 1970.

Terry, R. D., and P. Davies. Dementia of the Alzheimer type. *Annual Review of Neuroscience* 3: 77–95, 1980.

Teuber, H. -L., W. S. Battersby, and M. B. Bender. *Visual field defects after penetrating wounds of the brain*. Cambridge, MA: Harvard University Press, 1960.

Vinken, P. J., and G. W. Bruyn. *Handbook of Clinical Neurology*. New York: John Wiley, 1969.

Zacks, S. I. *Atlas of Neuropathology*. New York: Harper & Row, 1971.

PART 3

GENERAL PRINCIPLES OF BRAIN FUNCTION

As the simplest level of organization the nervous system consists of a sensory neuron that enters the spinal cord to synapse with a motor neuron. At more complex levels, one or more interneurons intervene between sensory and motor neurons. Chapter 8 presents some general theories about how sensory events are elaborated into motor events by the action of various groups of interneurons. Three important principles underly this discussion.

1. There is a *parallel* organization in the nervous system, in which the sensory systems and their subcomponents have preferential access to one or another motor system that is responsible for executing certain types of movements.

2. There is a *hierarchical* organization in the nervous system that emerges as successive levels of interneurons permit successively more complex or more adaptive behaviors.

3. There is development of *lateralization* of function, such that the very highest levels of function serve somewhat different roles in the two hemispheres.

Chapter 9 is devoted to the anatomical organization of the cortex, since it is the action of interneurons of this structure that are a central focus of the behavior of mammals in general and of humans in particular. Chapter 10 describes the organization and function of the sensory systems, and Chapter 11 describes disorders of sensory function. Chapter 12 describes the organization and function of the motor systems; Chapter 13 describes disorders of motor function.

The process of dividing the nervous system into its sensory, integrative, and motor functions is rather traditional, but it can be argued that it is also artificial. On the one hand, it is a simple matter to argue that the entire nervous system is motor, and that movements begin at the sensory receptor. Indeed, changes in receptor activity can lead to changes in motor activity, whether they are as simple as knee-jerk reflexes or as complex as orienting responses. On the other hand, it can be argued that the nervous system is sensory, because any change in muscle activity brings about changes in the stimulation of sensory receptors. The anatomist Brodal has pointed out, commenting on the symptoms of a stroke he had suffered, that when considering the functions of the damaged brain, practical divisions of function into sensory and motor are difficult:

> The *specificity of the morphological organization of the nervous system* is amazing. The more we know about the structure of the brain, the more we realize how this specificity can be traced to the minutest levels. It is the rule, rather than the exception, that even a small nucleus can be subdivided into parts or territories which differ with regard to cytoarchitecture, glial architecture, vasoarchitecture, fiber connections, synaptic arrangements and by its chemistry. . . . If one focuses attention on the fiber connections of the central nervous system one is struck by another feature of its organization: the *multiplicity of connections*. As a rule each small region receives fibers from a number of others and likewise emits fibers which pass to many other regions. . . . There may, of course, be great quantitative differences among the various contingents of afferent and efferent fibers of a nucleus. Nevertheless, a scrutiny of the fiber connections of the central nervous system as a whole leaves one with the conviction that there are morphological possibilities for an impulse from a certain part of the brain to be transmitted along circumvential routes of varying complexity to virtually every other part of the central nervous system! These multifarious interconnections between structures presumably provide possibilities for cooperation and integration of function between them and make it increasingly difficult and unjustified to describe a certain part of the brain as simply "motor," "visual," etc. (A. Brodal, Self-observations and neuro-anatomical considerations after a stroke." *Brain,* 96: 687–688, 1973)

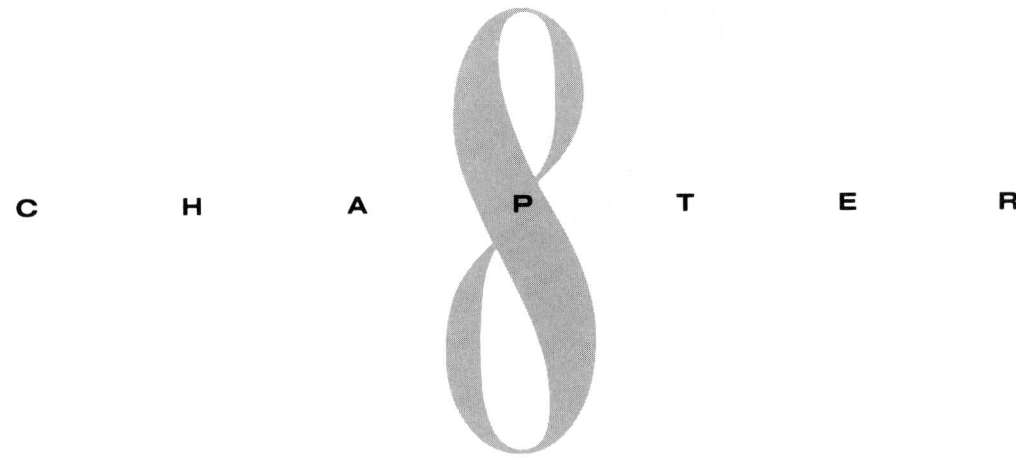

A GENERAL THEORY OF BRAIN ORGANIZATION AND FUNCTION

Once upon a time six blind people from Hindustan examined an elephant to satisfy their curiosity about what it was. Alpha, touching its body, thought it a wall; Beta, touching its tusk, thought it a spear; Delta, touching its trunk, thought it a snake; Gamma, touching its leg, thought it a tree; Terry, touching its ear, thought it a fan; and Tim, examining its tail, thought it a rope.

This popular story illustrates a well-known problem in the neurosciences: How can a concept of brain functions be developed from the disparate descriptions given by the different branches of the neurosciences? The problem is compounded: How can anyone assimilate the staggering amount of data about the brain being generated each year by these different branches of neuroscience?

Fortunately, the answers to both of these questions, although not completely adequate, are at least practical and helpful. First, it is possible to sketch a silhouette of the elephant (i.e., a theoretical framework describing the brain's organization and function) that is agreed on by people in most neuroscience areas. Second, because much of the new information published each year is simply a more refined description of the composition of the "elephant's tusk," it adds little to our knowledge of the elephant as a whole and so it can be temporarily ignored.

In this chapter, which gives an overview of the brain's function, we emphasize the brain's parallel and hierarchical organization. That is, the brain has parallel inputs both from and within different sensory systems, or modalities, and each is organized in a *functional* hierarchy, the higher levels providing more precision.

LEVELS OF FUNCTION FROM SPINAL CORD TO CORTEX

The idea that the brain is organized in functional levels can be dated to Herbert Spencer's mid-19th century speculations that each "step" in evolution added a new level of brain and a new level of behavioral complexity. It then became the basic principle that underlay Hughlings-Jackson's writings. The idea also became a central focus of MacLean's theories of brain function. Figure 8-1 illustrates MacLean's "triune" brain in which levels of function are related to patterns of behavior found in reptiles, early mammals, and late mammals respectively. These general principles are applicable to humans, as attested by evidence from clinical studies.

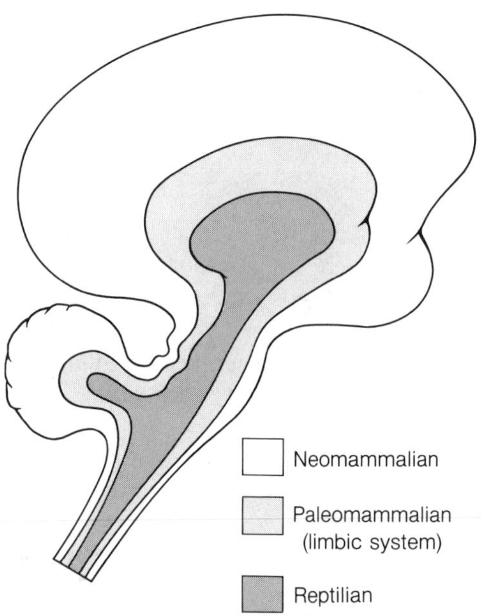

FIGURE 8-1. The triune brain. In its evolution the primate forebrain expands along the lines of three basic formulations that anatomically and biochemically reflect an ancestral relationship to reptiles, to early mammals, and to late mammals. (From MacLean, P. D., 1982, pp. 291–316. Copyright © 1982. New York: Plenum Press.)

The typical question to which an experiment on hierarchical organization is addressed is something like: What can an animal do without a neocortex? The question is answered by surgically removing the animal's neocortex and studying changes in behavior. The question is then rephrased: What can an animal do if the neocortex and the basal ganglia are both removed? By removal of successively more brain tissue, the functions of the spinal cord can eventually be studied in isolation from the rest of the brain. Thus, a brain area can be studied in isolation from some area to which it is normally connected, yielding information about what the removed structure did as well as what the remaining structures do.

Of course, the success of such research depends on the ability of a damaged nervous system to continue functioning after the surgical procedure is complete. As it turns out, the brain has a remarkable ability to survive after parts are destroyed. This resiliency to damage was given popular exposure in 1700 by DuVerney; in a public demonstration he showed that when a nerve and muscle were dissected away from a frog, the nerve continued to function, because when touched it produced muscle contractions. In 1853, Pfluger demonstrated that a frog with only an intact spinal cord could survive and display quite complex responses. If acid was placed on the frog's right side, the right leg would reach up and remove the acid. If the right leg was restrained then after a number of ineffective efforts, the left leg would be used to remove the acid. Other workers, among them Ridi in 1810, demonstrated that if parts of the brainstem were intact, amphibians could walk. In 1884, Fano studied the locomotor patterns of a tortoise with only a lower brainstem; attached to its tail was a brush dipped in aniline, which traced the animal's pathway as it walked. These early experiments were followed by more systematic research into the capacities of different portions of the nervous system, as well as into the details of their structure.

The following section presents that case for levels of function by describing the capacities of spinal animals (animals that have only a spinal cord) and animals with successively more intact nervous systems. Figure 8-2 lists each experimental preparation and the brain tissue that remains intact and summarizes the types of behavior the animal can perform. Parallel conditions that may occur in humans will be noted in the discussion following.

The Spinal Animal: Reflexes

The spinal animal has a comparatively simple nervous system. First, the cord is divided into segments (30 in humans), as is illustrated in Figure 1-3. Second, each segment consists of two symmetrical halves, each of which receives sensory fibers from one unilateral body dermatome and sends motor fibers to the same body dermatome. Third, the dorsal (posterior in the standing human) portion of the cord receives sensory input from fibers that enter the cord as a fiber bundle, or **dorsal root.** The cell bodies of these neurons are just outside the cord, forming the **dorsal root ganglion.** The ventral portion (anterior in humans) contains the cell bodies of the motor neurons and is the origin of the collection of motor fibers that leave each segment in a nerve tract or **ventral root.** The division of the spinal cord into dorsal sensory and ventral motor segments is called the **Bell-Magendie law.**

The story of the discovery of this law includes a long-lasting unpleasant controversy. Francois Magendie, a volatile and committed French experimental physiologist, reported in a three-page paper in 1822 that he had succeeded in cutting the dorsal and ventral roots of puppy dogs, animals in which the roots were sufficiently segregated to allow surgery. He found that sectioning of the dorsal roots was associated with loss of sensibility and that sectioning of the ventral roots was associated with loss of movement. As early as 1811, the Scot, Charles Bell, using anatomical conclusions and the results from somewhat inconclusive experiments on rabbits, suggested somewhat different functions for each of the roots. Following Magendie's paper, priority for the discovery was hotly disputed with at least some success on the part of Bell. Magendie's experiment has been called the most important ever conducted on the nervous system, for it enabled neurologists for the first time to localize nervous system damage from the symptoms displayed by patients.

In its overall function, the spinal cord is thought to be involved in simple behaviors called *reflexes*. In a sense this is true. The spinal animal cannot stand and move spontaneously. Nevertheless, there is internal processing going on at the spinal level that both elaborates and places constraints on behaviors that occur in response to sensory stimulation. An understanding of this function provides an appreciation of the general principles of how the nervous system works. The major thrust toward understanding spinal function came from the work of Sir Charles Sherrington and his coworkers. Sherrington, a British physiologist, published a monumental summary of his research in 1906. Sherrington's work brought forward the idea that complex behavior is formed by the chaining together of a number of simple reflexes. Some schools of psychology exhaustively studied this idea. Although reflexes are thought of as simple in comparison with more complex aspects of behavior, when the nature of receptor, internal spinal cord, and muscle action are each considered in detail, the processes of reflex turn out to be more complicated than can be completely dealt with in the present discussion.

To describe **spinal reflexes,** three aspects of spinal cord organization need to be considered: (1) the somatosensory or afferent nerves from the body, (2) the connections that the afferents make with interneurons and motor neurons in the spinal cord, and (3) the motor, or efferent, nerves that leave the cord for the muscles. Some aspects of the circuitry are illustrated in Figure 8-3.

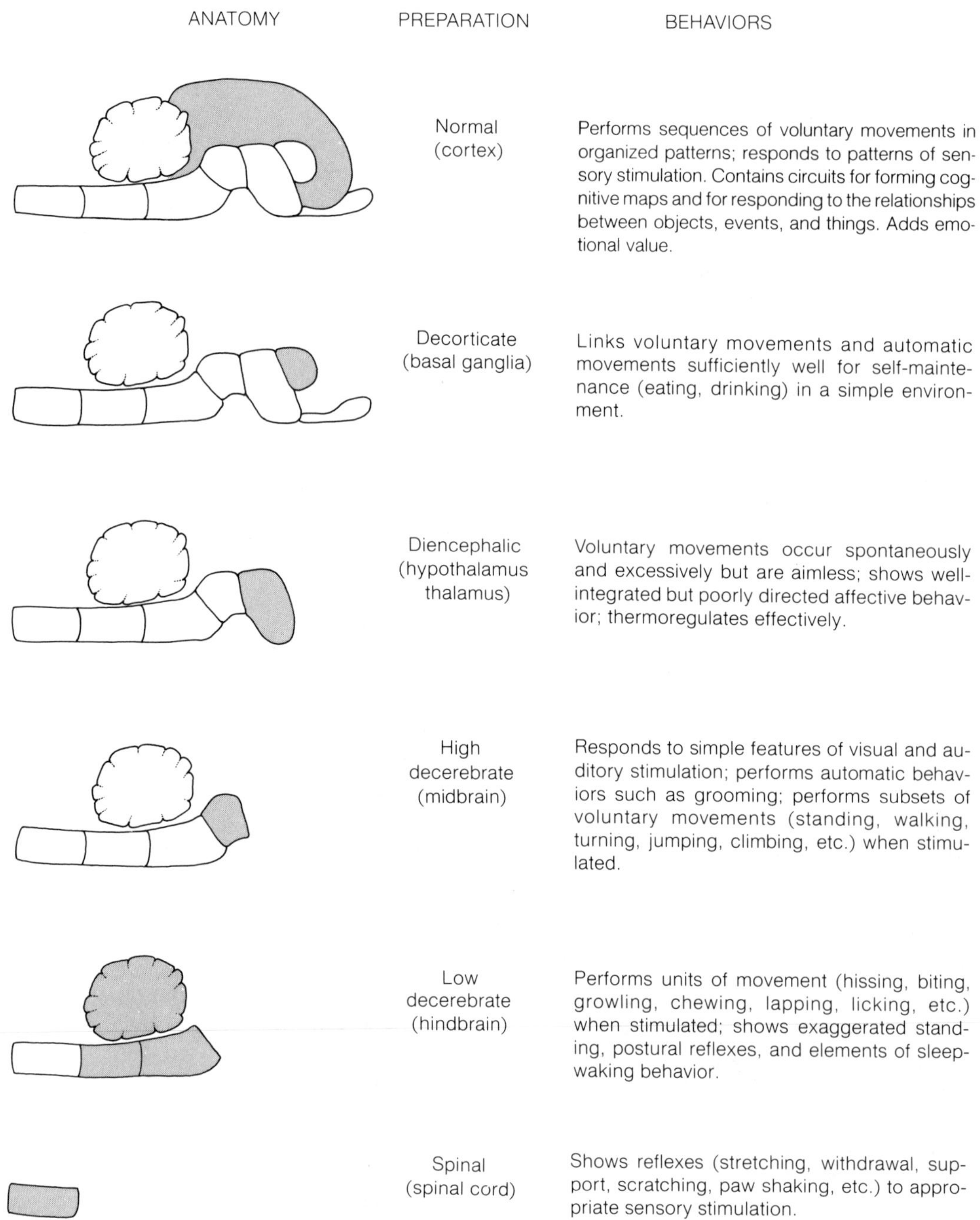

ANATOMY
PREPARATION
BEHAVIORS
Normal (cortex)
Performs sequences of voluntary movements in organized patterns; responds to patterns of sensory stimulation. Contains circuits for forming cognitive maps and for responding to the relationships between objects, events, and things. Adds emotional value.
Decorticate (basal ganglia)
Links voluntary movements and automatic movements sufficiently well for self-maintenance (eating, drinking) in a simple environment.
Diencephalic (hypothalamus thalamus)
Voluntary movements occur spontaneously and excessively but are aimless; shows well-integrated but poorly directed affective behavior; thermoregulates effectively.
High decerebrate (midbrain)
Responds to simple features of visual and auditory stimulation; performs automatic behaviors such as grooming; performs subsets of voluntary movements (standing, walking, turning, jumping, climbing, etc.) when stimulated.
Low decerebrate (hindbrain)
Performs units of movement (hissing, biting, growling, chewing, lapping, licking, etc.) when stimulated; shows exaggerated standing, postural reflexes, and elements of sleep-waking behavior.
Spinal (spinal cord)
Shows reflexes (stretching, withdrawal, support, scratching, paw shaking, etc.) to appropriate sensory stimulation.

FIGURE 8-2. Behavior that can be supported by different levels of the nervous system. Shading indicates the highest remaining functional area.

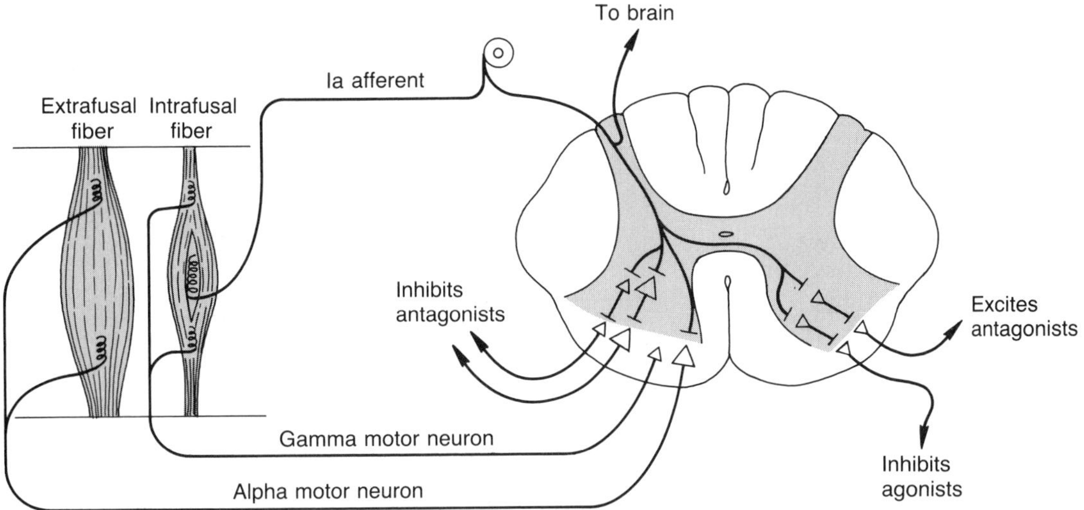

FIGURE 8-3. The stretch reflex. If a load is placed on a muscle, the muscle is stretched. Stretching activates the receptor in the intrafusal muscle fiber (sensory receptor), sending a barrage of excitation to the motor neuron of the extrafusal (working) fiber. It in turn contracts, resisting the stretch and relieving the tension of the intrafusal fiber. Note that input from the same afferent can inhibit antagonist muscles on the ipsilateral side and have the opposite actions on contralateral muscle groups.

Afferents. There are two general kinds of afferents from the body. Their distinguishing features are their size and their degree of myelination (actually, physiologists subdivide them into four or more groups). Large well-myelinated fibers mediate the senses of fine touch, pressure, and position and frequently produce extensor movements. Smaller, less well myelinated fibers mediate the senses of pain and temperature and frequently mediate flexor movements. At a very simple level this is a good example of parallel organization. Most of the fibers come from the skin, muscles, and tendons. Figure 8-3 shows an afferent, called the Ia afferent, that comes from the muscles. It comes from special receptors in the muscle and sends signals to the brain about the position to which a limb has moved. As we shall see, it also signals its own muscle to contract to resist stretch.

Central Connections. In addition to projecting to the brain, somatosensory afferents make two kinds of connections in the spinal cord. They synapse in direct, or monosynaptic, connections with motor neurons, or they synapse with interneurons that in turn synapse with motor neurons. Most afferents have many collaterals, as is shown in Figure 8-3. Note that most synapses are with interneurons.

Efferents. There are two kinds of motor neurons: large motor neurons called *alpha motor neurons* and small ones called *gamma motor neurons.* The first type project to the working, or *extrafusal,* fibers of the muscle, whereas the second type project to the sensory receptors, the *intrafusal* fibers (also called muscle spindles) that are richly distributed throughout muscles.

An Example of a Spinal Reflex. How does the spinal cord produce reflexes? We have a tendency to think of reflexes as events that occur on special occasions, such as when a neurologist taps us on the knee. In fact, they occur continually in order to control the details of many aspects of the movements we make. We can appreciate this action by considering one reflex as an example. This is the **stretch reflex,** the one the neurologist elicits by tapping a patient on the knee.

Consider the reflex circuit illustrated in Figure 8-3. When the muscle is stretched by having a load placed on it, the muscle spindle is stretched and the receptor in its center is activated, sending a barrage of action potentials into the spinal cord. There is only one synapse between the afferent and the motor neuron that sends an axon to the same muscle, and so the discharge is transferred immediately to the muscle. The muscle contracts, counteracting the stretch, with the result that the muscle maintains its length, holding up the load. Contraction of the extrafusal fiber relieves the stretch on the intrafusal fiber and thus reduces the activity of the afferent. This reflex is what makes a person whose hand is held out quickly tense his muscles to hold a heavy book placed in it.

The presence of the stretch reflex is tested for clinically in the following way. If a person, seated on a table with the lower part of his or her leg dangling from the edge of the table, is tapped on the tendon just below the knee (the tap is like a briefly applied load), the leg will swing upward briefly. This is because the tap on the tendon stretches the rectus femoris muscle of the upper leg, exciting its spindles and thereby activating a stretch reflex. Such stretch reflexes exist for all muscles, and many are routinely tested by physicians during neurological examinations in order to check the integrity of different sections of the spinal cord. Obviously, if the stretch reflex is absent or exaggerated, the physician suspects some abnormality in the appropriate section of the spinal cord.

It seems worthwhile to describe two other aspects of the stretch-reflex circuitry. When a group of muscles contract to produce a stretch, what happens to the muscles around the same joint that normally oppose that movement? As is shown in Figure 8-3, collaterals from the afferent connect via interneurons to motor neurons of the antagonist muscles to inhibit their activity.

How does the brain produce movements through the circuit? Available evidence suggests that the brain simultaneously activates both the alpha and the gamma motor neurons, causing parallel contraction in both the extrafusal and intrafusal muscle fiber. During a voluntary movement, the feedback from the muscle spindle, excited by the contraction, can both signal the brain that the limb has moved and signal the spinal cord about the resistance that the limb is meeting when it moves.

A number of other spinal reflexes require a passing mention. The *tendon receptor* (also called the *Golgi tendon organ*) is situated in the tendon and is ideally placed to track the length of a muscle. The more a muscle contracts, the more likely the tendon organ is to be excited. It monitors the length of the muscle and can inhibit the muscle to slow the rate and extent to which it can be stretched. The latter action is called the *inverse stretch reflex.* There is a well-known reflex in people who have muscle rigidity of central origin. If a limb is moved, it will stiffen and resist the movement, but only up to a point. Quite suddenly it will relax and completely give way. This sudden release is called the **clasp-knife reflex** because it resembles the sudden last-minute loss of resistance in the blade of a pocket knife during closure. It was originally thought that this reflex is mediated by the tendon organ, but it is now thought that it is produced by afferents, called Ib afferents, that come from the muscle spindle.

A pinprick of the paw of a spinal cat or dog causes a flexion of the limb. This is a *withdrawal reflex* that removes the limb from danger. If the stimulus is mild, only the distal portion of the limb is withdrawn, but if the stimulus is made successively stronger, the size of the movement increases until the whole limb is withdrawn. The pain afferents produce withdrawal reflexes by exciting flexor muscles and inhibiting extensor muscles. **Tactile** stimulation, such as light pressure on the pads of the foot of a spinal dog, will cause the limb to extend. This *extensor reflex* is the basis of a supporting reaction prerequisite for standing. Afferents from the cutaneous (skin) receptors predominantly excite extensor motor neurons and inhibit flexor motor neurons. As such, the extensor reflex is exactly the opposite of the withdrawal reflex.

So far we have described how a muscle responds to the stimulation of afferents within its own proximity. But muscles do not act in isolation. They are arranged in pairs around joints, such that an *agonist* moves a joint in one direction and an *antagonist* moves it in the other direction. Muscles also work in groups that flex or extend limbs. These groups also act in concert with muscles on the opposite side of the body. For example, during walking, flexors in one limb will be active in raising the limb, while extensors are maintaining support with the other limb. The connections that we have described in the spinal cord (Figure 8-3) are not limited only to single muscles. Collaterals from afferents will distribute themselves to interneurons and motor neurons in the same side of the cord and in the opposite side of the cord such that all muscle groups will act in concert in a coordinated fashion. The inhibition of one group of muscles that permits a second group to move is called **reciprocal inhibition.** Sensory afferents may also send collaterals to many other segments of the spinal cord in order to coordinate movements in other body parts. Again the appropriate connections are made either directly or through interneurons. It can be seen that each motor neuron has many direct and indirect connections, and its activity will reflect the majority influence rather than just the influence of any single synaptic connection.

A Lattice Hierarchy. A model that explains how a limited number of motor neurons can participate in a large number of motor activities is shown in Figure 8-4. It is called a *lattice hierarchy.* The top units in the model represent different types of sensory stimulation, that is from the skin, tendons, or muscles. The middle group of units represent interneurons. The bottom group represents motor neurons. Note that through the connection of the interneurons each type of afferent stimulation can recruit a specific population of motor neurons and thus produce a specific movement. The same motor neurons can be used again and again but in different combinations. The lattice hierarchy explains how a fixed number of motor neurons can produce a wide variety of movements; it also shows that there are certain constraints on how the neurons are used. For example, a motor neuron could not be used to simultaneously produce conflicting movements. The motor neurons have been described as analogous to the keys on a piano: there are a limited number of keys, yet when they are used in combination, a very large number of cords can be played singly, together, or in sequence to produce an almost infinite number of melodies.

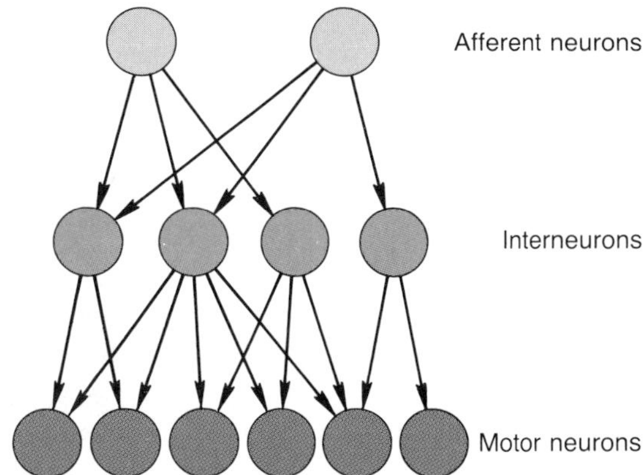

FIGURE 8-4. Lattice hierarchy. Top, afferent neurons; middle, interneurons; bottom, motor neurons. Note that different clusters of motor neurons are activated by different types of sensory stimulation. (After Gallistel, 1980.)

Oscillators

Male spinal cats can make rhythmic movements of pelvic thrusting and female spinal cats can make rhythmic movements of treading. Spinal animals can also scratch with rhythmic movements to remove objects from the body. Grillner has demonstrated that a spinal cat suspended in a sling on a treadmill will display coordinated walking, and after some recovery from surgery to bisect the spine it can use the isolated rear limbs for spontaneous walking. How are these movements produced? It is suggested that the spinal cord contains groups of neurons arranged in such a way that they reciprocally activate and inhibit each other in rhythmic fashion. Such reciprocally acting neuron pools are called *oscillators*. If the activity in an oscillator is self-sustaining, components of its activity could be used to power and time rhythmic movements such as walking, scratching, and pelvic thrusting. It is thought that oscillators are located at many levels of the nervous system and are involved in timing movements such as chewing, licking, grooming, and long-lasting rhythmically occurring behaviors such as sleep, sexual cycles, and migration. Evidence that oscillators do in fact exist is persuasive. Early experiments noted that fish with transected (transversely cut) brains would make continuous movements of the fins in the absence of any sensory stimulation. In frogs and other animals it has been observed that the scratch reflex has an optimal frequency independent of the frequency eliciting it and that scratching may continue long after the stimulus has been removed. In invertebrates, which have relatively simple nervous systems, electrophysiological studies have identified and analyzed the general features of a number of different kinds of oscillators.

Feedback, Feedforward, and Gating

The analysis of spinal reflexes shows that they have a variety of properties not easily accounted for by "straight through" neural circuitry. Increasing intensities of stimulation do not always lead to increasing response amplitudes. Sometimes, a response may have a greater or lesser amplitude than that expected from the intensity of the stimulation. Presentation of two different kinds of stimulation together can produce a response quite different from that found from each stimulus alone. These variations in response can be explained by other properties of spinal cord organization.

Feedback. Anatomists have observed that motor neurons give off collaterals before they leave the spinal cord. These collaterals synapse with an interneuron called the *Renshaw cell* (named after Renshaw, who first observed it). The Renshaw cell in turn synapses with the motor neuron (Figure 8-5*A*). The circuit is an *inhibitory feedback loop*. Each time the motor neuron is excited, it dampens its own activity. This protects it from becoming excessively active. The usefulness of this action can be demonstrated by considering what happens when an animal is given an injection of the stimulant and poison strychnine. The strychnine-poisoned animal displays excessive muscle tone and can frequently be sent into convulsions by sensory stimulation. Strychnine blocks the Renshaw-motor neuron synapse (which is thought to contain glycine). Consequently, the motor neuron, no longer able to inhibit itself, becomes excessively active and produce the violent muscular contractions that characterize a convulsion. Clearly, feedback has a protective influence, preventing excessive activation.

Feedforward. Circuits that can be considered *feedforward* also exist. Stimulation of an afferent may send a message to the motor neuron and also send a message to the brain via a collateral. Should the brain act on the information that it receives, it would find the motor neuron already in a state of readiness for action. A startle response leading to postural adjustments that prepare a person to run can be considered an example of feedforward.

Gating. You know from personal experience that a sensation of pain such as occurs with a burn, an itch, or a tickle can be reduced or stopped altogether by rubbing or scratching. How does rubbing, which activates fine touch and pressure re-

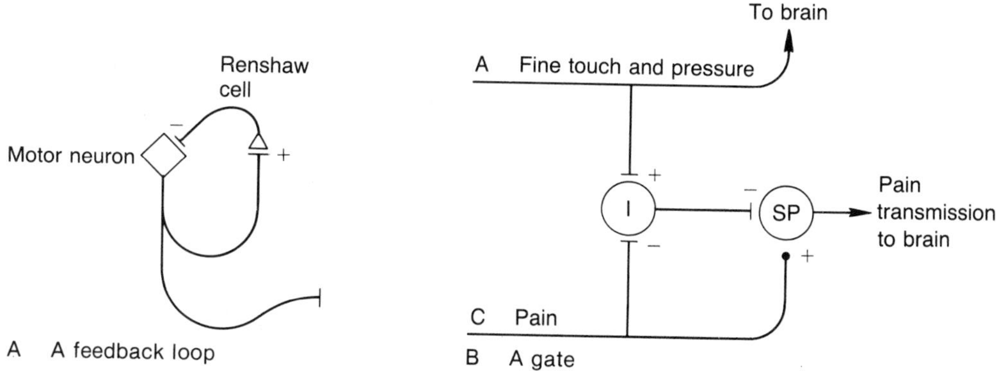

FIGURE 8-5. *A*. Renshaw arc. Note that the motor neuron can decrease its own ability to be reactivated. *B*. A model of the gate proposed by Melzack and Wall. Activation of the fine touch and pressure pathway excites the interneuron (I), but activation of the pain pathway inhibits it. The interneuron inhibits transmission of pain to the secondary pain cell (SP). Thus, fine touch and pressure activity decreased pain transmission. (From R. Melzack and P. D. Wall, 1965.)

ceptors, reduce pain, which is mediated by a different receptor and different-sized nerve fibers? Melzack and Wall suggest that there are gates in the spinal cord that can be opened or closed to regulate the flow of certain kinds of sensory information. Figure 8-5*B* illustrates such a gate. Pathway A represents the fine touch and pressure system. It sends a collateral to an interneuron I. Pathway C represents the pain-conducting system. Note that the pain pathway also synapses with I. When the events in the two pathways vary, it can be seen that if the flow of information in A increases relative to that in C, the A pathway will, through the interneuron, inhibit (or gate) activity in C. By the judicious placement of appropriately connected interneurons, many different kinds of gates serving different purposes can be constructed. There is experimental evidence that there are gates for pain suppression in the spinal cord, and similar gates may also exist in various brain regions. For example, centrally placed gates may explain why, when one is paying attention to an interesting event, an uncomfortable or painful stimulus may go unnoticed. It is thought likely that acupuncture and opioids may both reduce pain by acting through such gates.

Summary

A number of psychological theories popular in the first half of this century attempted to explain behavior in terms of simple stimulus-response (S-R) reflexes that are chained together in various ways. Unfortunately, these theories were popular in the curriculum of psychology courses and became part of many students' understanding of reflexes. Studies by Sherrington and subsequently by other physiologists showed that even the simplest reflexes in the spinal cord provide little support for these theories. Sensory receptors that supply the spinal cord with input act as filters in that they are selective about the features of the stimuli to which they respond. The reflexes that a stimulus elicits are not related in a one-to-one fashion to either the duration or the intensity of the stimulation. In the frog, for example, a stimulus at any intensity or frequency might elicit only a 4 cps (cycles per second) scratch reflex that continues well after the stimulus is removed. Different kinds of stimuli can also add or subtract. Even the same stimulus repeated can elicit quite different responses, as occurs when a toe pinch repeated a number of times elicits first a paw flexion response, then a lower limb flexion response, and finally a withdrawal response from the whole leg. Clearly, the spinal cord is not a passive channel for conducting information but is actively involved in transposing that information through its own internal connections in a way that is consistent with the continually changing state of those connections. Many of the features of brain function are not as well understood as those of the spinal cord, but we may justifiably expect that they will be at least as complex as those of the spinal cord. We may also expect that brain functions will use many of the same principles of transposition found in the spinal cord, for example, oscillators, feedforward, and feedback. It follows, therefore, that explanations of brain function will not be found in S-R-type theories but must be discovered by analyzing the programs that are formed by the multiple connections made by the brain's interneurons.

The Low-Decerebrate Animal: Support

In the *low-decerebrate animal* both the hindbrain and the spinal cord remain. The sensory input into the hindbrain comes predominantly from the head and is carried over cranial nerves IV to XII. Most of these nerves also have motor nuclei in the hindbrain whose efferent fibers control muscles in the head and neck. As relatively few interneurons in the spinal cord are located between sensory projections and motor projections, interneurons in the hindbrain have multiplied to form nuclei as well as more complex coordinating centers such as the cerebellum. Sensory input to the hindbrain is not limited to the cranial nerves, for, as we shall see, the spinal somatosensory system has access to hindbrain motor systems, just as the hindbrain has access to spinal motor systems. Before the function of the hindbrain is discussed, a description of the behavior of low-decerebrate animals might be helpful.

Low-decerebrate cats are described by Bazett and Penfield and by Bard and Macht in experiments in which the animals were kept alive for periods of weeks or months. The animals were generally inactive when undisturbed and showed virtually no effective thermoregulatory ability, but otherwise they were relatively easy to maintain because they swallowed food placed on their tongues and so could be fed. If the animals were stimulated lightly in any of a variety of sensory modalities (e.g., touch, pain, sounds) they moved from their normal reclining position into a crouch. If the stimulation was stronger, they walked, somewhat unsteadily. These stimuli also elicited such affective behaviors of normal cats as biting, hissing, growling, and lashing of the tail.

One of the most characteristic aspects of behavior accorded by the hindbrain is a peculiar kind of stiffness called **decerebrate rigidity.** This is excessive muscle tone, particularly in the antigravity muscles, (those that hold the body up) which are the body's strongest. Because of this rigidity, when an animal is placed in an upright position, its limbs extend and its head flexes upward. Sherrington refers to this rigidity as "exaggerated standing."

How is exaggerated standing produced? An experiment by Sherrington in 1898 showed that if the dorsal roots to a limb were cut, the limb immediately became flaccid. At the time, the observation that severing afferents should abolish motor activity was quite surprising. Later, after muscle spindles had been described, it became clear that decerebrate rigidity was produced in part by brainstem excitation of gamma motor neurons. Note from Figure 8-3 that if these neurons are excited, they cause the intrafusal muscle to contract. This excites the Ia afferents in the same way as if the entire muscle had been stretched. Activation of the Ia afferents then leads to contraction of the muscle. In the decerebrate animal all muscles that sustain posture against gravity are excited through the gamma motor system to produce exaggerated standing. Interestingly, the antigravity muscles in the sloth, which hands upside down, are flexors and the decerebrate sloth displays flexor rather than extensor rigidity.

Against the background of decerebrate rigidity,

a number of *postural reflexes* can be elicited by changes in head position. If the head of a standing animal is pushed down toward the floor, the front limbs flex and the hind limbs extend; if the head is pushed up, the hind legs flex and the front legs extend. The first type of posture would be used by a normal cat looking under a couch, the second by a normal cat looking up onto a shelf. Turning the head to the side elicits extension of the limbs on the same side and flexion of the limbs on the opposite side of the body; this type of response occurs in a normal cat that has turned its head to look at some object and is prepared to pursue it. When the animals are placed on their sides, they extend their lower limbs (those in contact with the floor), and semiflex their upper limbs. This is a static reaction that represents the first stage of the **righting reflex.** The location of the head obviously determines which gamma efferent neurons are activated, thus determining an animal's posture.

There are two types of sleep in normal animals: *quiet sleep,* characterized by muscle tone, and *active sleep,* characterized by an absence of muscle tone (these are commonly referred to as slow-wave and dream sleep). Low-decerebrate animals are described as showing characteristics of both types of sleep at different times. Animals left undisturbed gradually lose their rigidity and subside or droop into a prone posture. Any mild stimulus such as a noise or touch reinstates rigidity. This type of behavioral change seems analogous to quiet sleep. The animals also show a sudden collapse, accompanied by the loss of all body tone, which lasts from 15 sec to 12 min. This type of behavioral change seems analogous to active, or dream, sleep, particularly since some people with an illness called **narcolepsy** similarly collapse in active sleep. Thus, the neural centers producing sleep are located in the hindbrain.

The low-decerebrate animal's behavior, then, differs from the spinal animal's in a number of ways. First, responses such as tail lashing and biting are elicited by several (often cumulative) modes of stimulation. Such responses can be explained in the following way. In its simplest form tail lashing is a withdrawal reflex of the tail from adverse stimulation; it is a spinal reflex. Biting is a jaw reflex elicited by facial stimulation; it is mediated through the hindbrain by the sensory and motor components of the trigeminal (V) nerve. Because the sensory components of the spinal reflexes and hindbrain reflex circuits are linked to each other's motor components, pinching a cat's lip or a cat's tail can produce the same response—tail withdrawal (tail lashing) as well as biting. Spontaneous occurrence of these behaviors may either be elicited by spontaneous activity in the spinal-hindbrain circuits or be triggered by less obvious stimulation carried into the spinal-hindbrain circuits by other nerves such as the vagus (X) nerve. This principle of interlinking sensory and motor components of different levels is an organizational feature of all levels of brain function.

The **vestibular system,** by means of nerve VIII, makes an obvious contribution to the behavior of low-decerebrate animals. There are two vestibular receptors in the middle ear: the **saccule** signals when the head is oriented in the normal position; the **utricle,** which gives off steady signals even when the head is still, signals changes in orientation. It is probable that the upright posture of the head and body is maintained by the saccule or its motor nuclei in the hindbrain. The decerebrate rigidity of the low-decerebrate animal is no doubt the exaggerated product of unchecked activity in this system. When the head is moved, the posture of the animal changes in characteristic ways. These postural changes are probably mediated by the utricle and its motor nuclei.

Since part of the function of the vestibular system is to maintain and adjust posture, it seems logical that a mechanism is built into the hindbrain to check its activity when an upright posture is not needed. Otherwise an animal might remain in a rigid position until its musculature was exhausted. Decerebrate animals do relax, which suggests that there is an inhibitory system in the hindbrain. The inhibition provided by this system is most likely the neurological basis of sleep. The fact that any type of stimulation can restore rigidity after relaxation occurs suggests that spinal and hindbrain sensory systems have input into the nuclei that maintain support and are capable of activating them. Stimulation from these systems probably provides part of the neurological basis for awakening.

The behavioral changes seen in low-decerebrate animals are paralleled in people who have brainstem damage of the type that essentially separates the lower brainstem from the rest of the brain. Barrett and his colleagues have documented a number of such cases. These people may alternate between states of consciousness resembling sleeping and waking, make eye movements to follow moving stimuli, cough, smile, swallow food, display decerebrate rigidity, and display postural adjustments when moved. When cared for, people with such brain damage may live for months or years with little change in their condition.

The High-Decerebrate Animal: Voluntary and Automatic Behavior

The high-decerebrate animal has an intact midbrain containing, in the tectum, the coordinating centers for vision (superior colliculus) and hearing (inferior colliculus) and, in the tegmentum, a number of motor nuclei. Visual and auditory inputs are different from any sensory input received at lower levels because they allow the animal to perceive events at a distance. Correspondingly, it is not surprising to find that the high-decerebrate animal is able to respond to distant objects by moving toward them. However, the assessment of how active high-decerebrate animals are varies from study to study.

Bard and Macht report that high-decerebrate cats can walk, stand, resume upright posture when turned on their backs, and even run and climb when stimulated. Bignall and Schramm found that kittens decerebrated in infancy could orient to visual and auditory stimuli. The animals could even execute and attack response and pounce on objects at the source of a sound. In fact, Bignall and Schramm fed the cats by exploiting this behavior, for they placed food near the source of the sound; attacking the sound source, the cats would then consume the food. Although the cats attacked moving objects, they gave no evidence of "seeing," for they bumped into things when they walked around. Woods has reported that high-decerebrate rats are active and make all the movements of normal rats; Grill and Norgren report that these rats are generally inactive and show normal locomotor abilities only when disturbed. Bignall and Schramm, as well as Woods may have left some hypothalamic tissue intact, which would account for why their animals were more active than animals observed in other studies.

These experiments demonstrate that all the components (or subsets) of **voluntary movements** — movements that take an animal from one place to another, such as turning, walking, climbing, and swimming — are present at the level of the midbrain. Normal intact animals use voluntary movements to provide for a variety of needs, for example, to find food, water, or a new home territory, or to escape a predator. These movements have also been variously called appetitive, instrumental, purposive, or operant. Voluntary movements, being executed through lower level postural support and reflex systems, can also be elicited by lower level sensory input; that is, a pinch or postural displacement can elicit turning, walking, or climbing. Thus, this new functional level is integrated with lower levels by both ascending and descending connections, exactly as the hindbrain and spinal levels are interconnected.

High-decerebrate animals are also able to effectively perform **automatic behaviors:** units of stereotyped behavior linked in a sequence. Grooming, chewing food, lapping water, and rejecting food are representative automatic behaviors of the rat. Generally, automatic behaviors (also variously called reflexive, consummatory, or respondent behaviors) are directed toward completing some sort of consummatory act and are not specifically directed toward moving an animal from one place to another. Grooming is an excellent example of an automatic behavior since it consists of a large number of movements executed sequentially in an organized and quite stereotyped fashion. If a rat's fur is wet, it first shakes its back, then sits on its haunches and shakes its front paws, then licks water from them, wipes its snout rapidly with bilateral symmetrical movements, wipes its face with slight asymmetrical movements, and then turns to lick the fur on its body. Food rejection is similarly complex. If decerebrate rats are satiated and then given food, they perform a series of movements consisting of tongue flicks, chin rubbing, and paw shaking to reject the food. These behaviors are similar to the rejection behaviors made by normal rats in response to food they find noxious. If the animals are not sated, they will lap water and chew food brought to their mouths.

There are a number of accounts of infants born with large portions of the forebrain missing. One child studied by Gamper (Figure 8-6) had no brain present above the diencephalon and only a few traces of the diencephalon intact and was, therefore, anatomically equivalent to a high-decerebrate animal. This child showed many behaviors of newborn infants. It could sit up; it periodically slept and was wakeful; it could suck, yawn, stretch, cry, and follow visual stimuli with its eyes. However, the child showed little spontaneous activity and if left alone remained mostly in a drowsy state. Brackbill studied a similar child and found that in response to stimuli such as 60- to 90-dB (decibel) sounds it oriented in much the same way normal children did. Unlike normal children, however, this child's responses did not change in size and did not **habituate** (gradually decrease in intensity) to repeated presentation. She concluded that the forebrain is not important for producing movements but is important for attenuating and inhibiting them. Generally, children born with such extensive brain abnormalities do not live long, and among those that live for a number of months there is no development of the complex behaviors seen in normal children. They appear to have the same behavioral capacities of high-decerebrate animals.

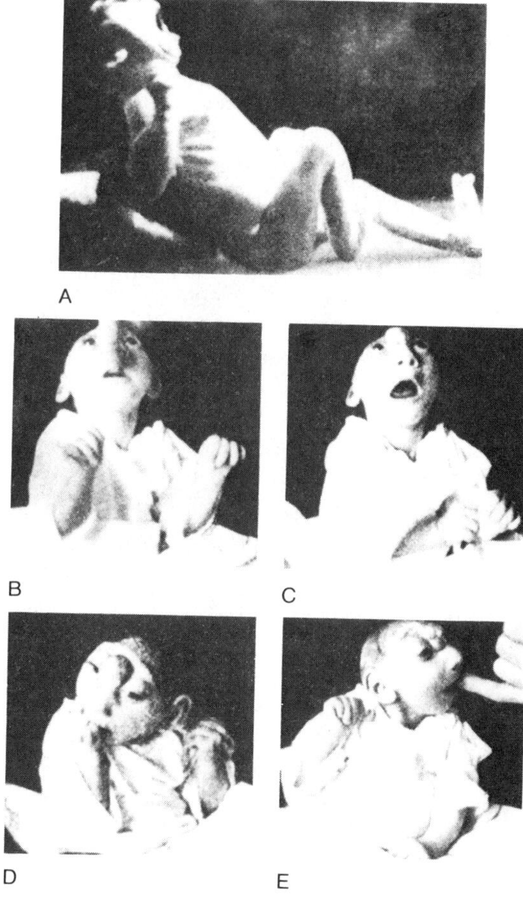

FIGURE 8-6. Instinctive behavior and oral automatisms in Gamper's mesencephalic human. *A.* Yawning with spreading of arms. *B.* Oral adversive movements after the lips are touched, with deviation of the eyes. *C.* Coordinated gaze and snapping movements after finger was removed. *D.* Spontaneous sucking of own hand. *E.* Oral adversion to the left side with deviation of head and eyes and tonic neck reflexes in the arms. (From E. Gamper, *Ztschr. ges. Neurol. Psychiat.* 104:49, 1926.)

In summary, the midbrain adds at least three

new components to behavior. First, the presence of the auditory and optic systems allows the animals to receive sensory input that originates at some distance. Most evidence suggests that these sensory systems respond to only the simpler features of stimuli such as intensity and place. Second, these sensory systems appear to be linked with voluntary motor systems that allow the animals to respond to distant stimuli by moving toward or away from them. Third, the midbrain appears to contain programs that allow the animals to chain together a number of movements to form complex behaviors of the consummatory type, called automatic behaviors.

The Diencephalon: Affect and Motivation

Probably the diencephalon has been studied more than any other brain structure, yet its contribution to the organization of behavior is not well understood. The diencephalic animal has an intact olfactory system, enabling it to smell odors at a distance. The hypothalamus and pituitary are also intact, and their control over body hormonal systems no doubt integrates the body's physiology with the brain's activity. In physiology literature the hypothalamus is thought to be involved in **homeostasis,** that is, maintaining body temperature, chemical balance, energy reserves, and so forth. Diencephalic animals maintain normal body temperature, but they do not eat or drink well enough to sustain themselves. In the traditional literature of physiological psychology, diencephalic functions are often discussed under the headings of affect and motivation. Although these terms have never been defined to everyone's satisfaction, the diencephalon does seem to add a dimension of affect and motivation to behavior if the terms are used in the sense that behavior becomes "energized" and sustained. Some examples of the diencephalic animal behavior will illustrate this point.

As we have mentioned, high-decerebrate animals show many of the component behaviors of rage, but the behaviors are not energetic, well integrated, or sustained. Cannon and Britton studied forebrain-lesioned cats and described what they called "quasi-emotional phenomena" (or sham rage, described below) such as are usually seen in an infuriated animal; the behavior consists of lashing the tail, arching the trunk, making limb movements, displaying claws, snarling, and biting. Sympathetic signs of rage are present, including erection of the tail hair, sweating of the toe pads, dilation of the pupils, micturation, high blood pressure, high heart rate, and increases in epinephrine and blood sugar. These emotional attacks sometimes last for hours. Bard removed various amounts of forebrain and brainstem and found that for this sham rage to occur it was necessary to leave at least the posterior portion of the hypothalamus intact. Clinical reports indicate that similar sham emotional attacks can occur in people who have suffered hypothalamic lesions; that is, there are people who show unchecked rage or who literally laugh until they die.

One of the most pronounced features of the diencephalic animal's behavior is its constant activity; this has been observed by Sorenson and Ellison and by Grill and Norgren in rats and by Goltz in dogs. We have watched diencephalic rats and found that although they attempt to eat, they are unable to remain still long enough to ingest more than a few grams of food over periods lasting for hours. Since normal animals deprived of food and water become active, it is possible to argue that the diencephalic animal's hyperactivity is driven by a deficiency condition; that is, the animal is searching for food or water. Grill and Norgren, however, have found that feeding the animals as much as control rats does not arrest hyperactivity.

These two examples of diencephalic behavior suggest to us that the diencephalon adds an "energizing" dimension to behavior that may justify labeling the behavior affective or motivated. Britton and Cannon, however, were aware of the inappropriateness of the rage behavior of the diencephalic cat (it is overdone and not directed), and so they called it sham rage to distinguish it from the directed rage of the normal cat. Perhaps the hyperactivity of the diencephalic animal should be called sham motivation to distinguish it from the goal-oriented behavior of the normal animal. In this sense the sham affect and sham motivation of the diencephalic animal are something like the exaggerated standing observed in low-decerebrate animals. Under appropriate forebrain control it can be released for functional purposes, but in the absence of that control the behavior of the animal is excessive and seems inappropriate.

The Basal Ganglia: Self-Maintenance

Decortication is removal of the neocortex (either alone or with the limbic system), leaving the basal ganglia and brainstem intact. Decorticate animals have been studied more closely than any others because they are able to maintain themselves without special care in laboratory conditions.

The first careful experiments were done by Goltz with decorticate dogs (Chapter 14), but the most thorough studies have used rats as subjects. Experiments by ourselves and our colleagues show that within a day after surgery rats eat and maintain body weight on a wet mash diet, and eat dry food and drink water brought in contact with the mouth. With a little training at drinking (holding the water spout to the mouth) they find water and become able to maintain themselves on water and laboratory chow within 10 days. They have normal sleeping-waking cycles, run, climb, and swim, and even negotiate simple mazes. The hyperactivity characteristic of diencephalic animals is greatly reduced.

What is observed in the decorticate rat, and what is presumably conferred by the basal ganglia, is the ability to link automatic movements to voluntary movements so that the behaviors are biologically adaptive. A major portion of this linking probably involves inhibition or facilitation of voluntary movements. For example, the animal walks until it finds food or water and then inhibits walking in order to consume the food or water. Thus, the basal ganglia probably provides the circuitry required for the stimulus to inhibit movement so that ingestion can occur.

The most thorough study of animals without a basal ganglia has been done on cats by Villablanca and his coworkers. In this species the basal ganglia can be removed without damaging the motor fibers projecting from the cortex to the brainstem. These cats displayed a compulsive approach syndrome. They followed people, attempting to make contact with them and stick to them. They would return again and again after being repeatedly pushed away. They attempted to grasp any nearby moving object and would approach any sensory stimulus. They were docile, purred continually, and made treading responses in the presence of people. Their movements were abnormal. They lost placing responses (ability to place their limbs on objects) for months after surgery, their reaching movements were poorly controlled, they had difficulty in pressing a bar, and they were hyperactive. Thus, the cats seemed to display all cat-type behaviors, but the acts were often inappropriate and poorly executed, suggesting that the problem was one of "fine-tuning" rather than performance. Some of the features of the behavior of cats with damaged basal ganglia are reminiscent of those of monkeys and cats that have the amygdala removed. These animals display a constellation of abnormalities referred to as **Kluver-Bucy syndrome.** They display "psychic blindness" meaning that they do not seem to recognize familiar objects. They examine every object by placing it in their mouth. They orient to every visual stimulus. They seem to show an absence of the emotional behaviors of anger and fear. They also show increased sexual activity. The constellation of syndromes displayed by animals with both kinds of brain damage suggests not only a deficit in fine-tuning but also an inability to recognize the significance of various objects.

The Cortex

What the cortex *does* can also be ascertained by studying what the decorticate animal (with the neocortex alone removed or with the limbic system also removed) *cannot* do. All the elementary movements that animals might make seem to be part of their behavioral repertory after decortication. They can walk, eat, drink, mate, raise litters of pups, and so forth, in a seemingly adequate fashion. They are also able to sequence series of movements. Copulation involves a number of movements occurring sequentially and lasting for hours, yet the animals can perform the acts almost normally. Grooming also involves sequential use of about 50 discrete movements and it is also performed normally.

There are, however, behaviors that decorticate animals seem unable to perform. They do not build nests, although they engage in some nest-building behaviors. They do not hoard food, although they might carry food around. They also have difficulty making skilled movements with the tongue and limbs for they are unable to reach for food by protruding their tongue or by reaching with one forelimb. They can do pattern discriminations in different sensory modalities, but only if these are relatively simple.

There are a number of models used to study learning in animals. A series of experiments by Oakley have looked at classical conditioning, operant conditioning, approach learning, cue learning, and patter discrimination in decorticate rats and rabbits and have found that the decorticate animals perform all tasks as well or almost as well as normal animals. These experiments confirm that the cortex is not essential for learning per se.

In the first part of this century Edward Tolman suggested that animals have the ability to make maps of their environment and then navigate through that environment using information from the maps. For example, if a rat is trained to travel from the south corner of the room to the north corner and then at some later time is placed in the west corner, it is able to travel to the correct north corner even if it has never experienced taking that route. Classical and operant conditioning theory cannot explain this result. It therefore seems likely that the animal has an ability to form maps of its environment that it can use in novel ways at a later date. Very little is known about the neural circuitry that makes cognitive mapping possible, but available evidence suggests that such maps are formed extremely rapidly, sometimes in one or two trials. This suggests that the maps are formed by specific cognitive processes that are a property of inbuilt neural connections. In other words, they are not formed by some sort of rote trial-by-trial learning procedure. We have recently tested the ability of decorticate rats to navigate using either a cognitive-mapping or a cue-learning strategy. The animals were tested in a task called the Morris water task, designed by Richard Morris. The apparatus consisted of a large circular pool filled with tinted water in which a platform was hidden just below the surface at a fixed location. The animals, placed in the pool at different locations, were required to locate the hidden platform. The only cues they could use for guidance were surrounding room cues. Normal rats mastered this task in a few trials, but the decorticates never learned to navigate to the platform and seemed to find it occasionally only by chance. If the platform was raised above the water so that it was visible, the decorticate rats quickly learned to swim to it. Thus, although decorticate rats can learn, there are certain forms of learning that they obviously cannot do.

CORTICAL FUNCTION

Understanding what the cortex does is not straightforward. Clearly, the findings reviewed above indicate that early theories proposing that the cortex is specialized for simple learning are not supportable, nor are theories that suggest the cortex is necessary for most simple movements or for sequences of movements. Consequently, it has been suggested that the cortex must do something different, presumably something that involves the relationships between things. For example, Phillips and his coworkers suggest that the cortex is the Sherlock Holmes of the brain, sensitive to suspicious coincidence. Passingham makes much the same argument by stating that the cortex is crucial to the ability to relate information that is presented at different times in different places. These kinds of proposals stress a role for the cortex in the synthesis of sensory events. On the motor side of things, Vanderwolf and his coworkers have suggested the cortex instructs voluntary movements so that they occur at the right time and place. If these sensory and motor hypotheses are combined, we have a view of the cortex instructing voluntary movements on the basis of relational properties of sensory events. Luria's theory of cortical function, outlined below, is representative of this view.

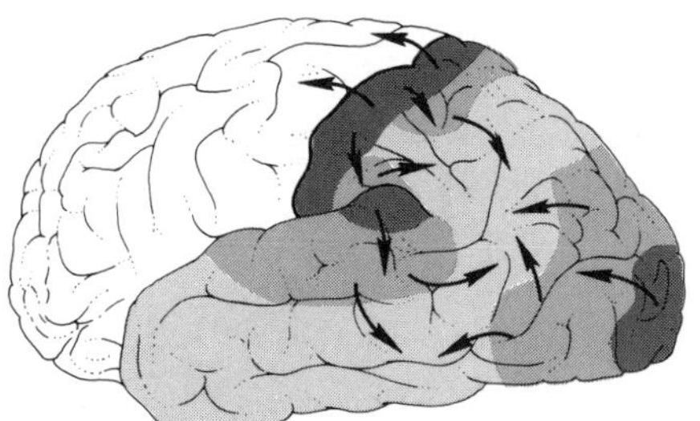

A The sensory unit

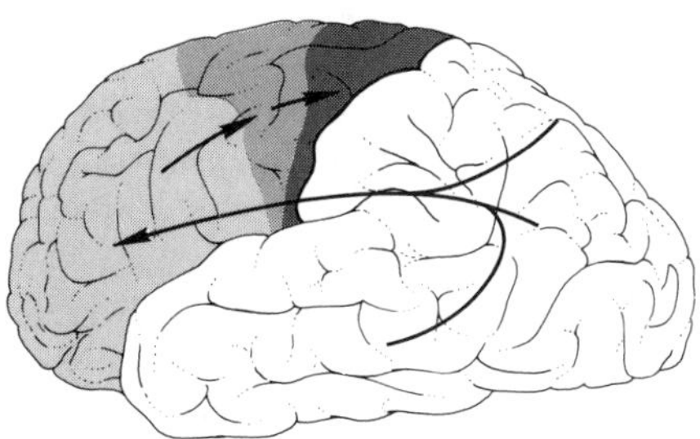

B The motor unit

FIGURE 8-7. *A*. The first functional unit of the cortex — the sensory unit. (Dark-shaded areas are primary zones; medium shaded, secondary zones; light shaded, tertiary zones.) Sensory input travels from primary to secondary to tertiary and is thereby elaborated from sensation into symbolic processes. *B*. The second functional unit of the cortex — the motor unit. Symbolic processes from the sensory unit are translated into intentions in the tertiary motor zones and then into patterns of action in the secondary and primary motor zones (After A. R. Luria, 1973. Copyright © 1973. The Copyright Agency of the USSR. Reprinted with permission.)

Luria's Formulation

Since the mid-19th century it has been recognized that the anterior cortex is more involved than the posterior in motor functions and that the posterior cortex is more involved than the anterior in sensory functions. It has also been recognized that the cortex can be divided into three types of areas: (1) primary sensory and motor areas; (2) secondary sensory and motor areas; and (3) tertiary, or association, areas.

Luria divides the cortex into two functional units (Figure 8-7). The first, the posterior portion of the neocortex (parietal, temporal, and occipital lobes), is the *sensory* unit. It receives sensory impressions, processes them, and stores them as information. The second, the anterior cortex (frontal lobe), is the *motor* unit. It formulates intentions, organizes them into programs of action, and executes the programs. In both cortical units there is a hierarchical structure, with three cortical zones arranged functionally one above the other. These zones are distinguished by their cytoarchitecture and can therefore be described with Brodmann's numbering system.

The Sensory Unit. In the sensory unit the *primary zones* consist of the projection areas of vision (area 17), audition (area 41), and body senses (areas 1, 2). In these zones the general features of sensory stimulation are organized in an array representing the topography, intensity, and pattern of stimulation. The *secondary zones* comprise the projection areas of these primary zones; in the case of vision, for example, the secondary zones are areas 18 and 19. The secondary zones retain the modality (e.g., visual) of sensation but have a less fixed topographic organization (e.g., for vision remapping the retina). The *tertiary zones* lie on the boundary between the occipital, temporal, and parietal cortex and include Brodmann's areas 22, 37, 39, and 40—an area of about one-quarter of the posterior unit's total mass. These zones also include the hippocampus and amygdala—areas into which the cortex projects and from which it receives reciprocal connections. The function of the tertiary zones is to integrate the excitation arriving from the different sensory systems. It is in these tertiary zones, Luria believes, that sensory input is translated into symbolic processes, and concrete perception is translated into abstract thinking.

The Motor Unit. The motor unit, or frontal lobes, also consists of three hierarchically organized zones. The *primary zone* is the motor strip, area 4, which is the final cortical motor-command area. The *secondary zone* is the premotor area, area 6, where motor programs are prepared for execution by the primary area. The most important part of the motor functional unit is the *tertiary zone,* comprising the prefrontal, or granular frontal, cortex: areas 9, 10, 45, 46, and 47. It is here that intentions are formed. Luria describes the tertiary zone of the frontal unit as the most highly integrated area of function: "the superstructure above all other parts of the cerebral cortex."

Sensory-Motor Connections

Some of the connections between the sensory and motor units are shown in Figure 8-7. These include connections from the primary to secondary to tertiary areas. There are, however, other connections that are not shown. Secondary and tertiary areas of the sensory unit project to secondary and tertiary areas of the motor unit, respectively. Tertiary areas of the sensory unit also project to the hippocampus, amygdala, and basal ganglia, which in turn project into the motor unit. The sensory and motor units also have projections to subcortical areas, including the thalamus, brainstem, and spinal cord. Nevertheless, the basic idea behind the model is that information is elaborated sequentially through the sensory unit and then passed to the motor unit so that programs of action can be executed.

Properties of the Cortical Zone

Diminishing Specificity. A cortical area is said to show *specificity* if it analyzes only one mode of sensory input, for example, visual or auditory. According to Luria, the lowest cortical zones are very specific in function (e.g., the primary visual zone analyzes only visual input), whereas the highest zones are very nonspecific (e.g., the tertiary zone analyzes all sensory information—visual, auditory, tactile, etc.). In other words, the primary zones process for a specific sensory modality, recording chiefly its primary features of intensity and spatial distribution, whereas the higher zones process the more abstract features, with the tertiary zone synthesizing the abstract features of a number of modalities.

Progressive Lateralization. A cortical area is said to show *lateralization* if it has a function not shared by the homotopic area (same point) of the contralateral hemisphere. Speech, for example, is lateralized in the left hemisphere of most right-handed people. Luria postulates that there is progressive lateralization at higher levels of the cortical hierarchy. In other words, lateralization should be expected to be absent in primary visual area 17 but should be expected to be most pronounced in the tertiary areas. These expectations appear to be correct, because the most lateralized functions (speech in the left, spatial perception in the right) are functions of the tertiary zones. Lateralization does not appear to be as pronounced in the tertiary zone of the frontal cortex, if available evidence is accepted. Luria, however, predicts that this area, which he describes as the superstructure above all other cortical structures, should show the most pronounced lateralization.

An Example of Cortical Function

Luria conceives of the cortex as working in the following way: sensory input enters the primary sensory zones, is elaborated in the secondary zones, and is integrated in the tertiary zones of the sensory, or posterior, unit. For an action to be executed, activity from the posterior tertiary sensory zones is sent to the tertiary zone of the motor, or frontal unit, to the secondary zone, and then to the primary motor zone, where execution is initiated.

To give a very simplified example of how Luria's model of the cortex might function, say one were walking along and came upon a soccer game. In the primary visual area the actual perception of the movements of people and the ball would occur. In the secondary sensory zone, recognition that those activities constituted a soccer game would occur. In the tertiary zone the sounds and movements of the game would be synthesized into the realization that one team had scored and was ahead and that the game had a certain significance for league standings. This information would be passed on to the hippocampus for processing as a memory and also passed on to the amygdala where its emotional value would be assessed. These cortical events could then lead, in the tertiary zone of the frontal (motor) cortex, to formation of the intentions or plans to play soccer. The programs to execute such a plan would be formulated in the secondary frontal zones. The actual movements to play the game would be initiated in the primary zone of the frontal cortex.

Using the same example of a soccer game, we can describe the effects of brain lesions. A lesion in the primary visual area would produce a blind spot in some part of the visual field, requiring the person to move his or her head backward and forward to see the entire game. A lesion in the secondary area might produce a perceptual deficit making the person unable to recognize the activity as a soccer game. A lesion in the tertiary area might make it impossible for an individual to recognize the significance of the game in its abstract form; that is, that one team wins. Damage to the hippocampus would leave no memory of the event, and damage to the amygdala would leave the person unresponsive to the event's significance. A lesion in the tertiary frontal area might prevent the formation of the intention to become a soccer player and join a club, buy a uniform, or get to practice on time. A lesion in the secondary frontal zone might make it difficult for the individual to execute the sequences of movements required in plays. Finally, a lesion in the primary zone might make it difficult for the individual to execute the discrete movements required in the game, for example, kicking the ball.

Assessment of Luria's Model

Although Luria's model is a useful way to begin thinking about how the cortex works, it contains some pitfalls, at least three of them worthy of mention. First, although it is extremely difficult to make distinctions between sensory and motor functions at any level of nervous system function, it is even more difficult at the level of the cortex. Consider the following points. (1) Any movement we make produces changes in sensation, just as changes in sensation provoke movement. It could be argued, then, that movement is partly a sensory function, since it produces changes in sensation, and that sensation is partly a motor function, since it provokes movement. (2) The perception of the same object in different instances can produce different responses. For example, a dog perceiving a man begins to bark and run away; then, "recognizing" the man as its master, it runs forward wagging its tail. (We can all recall similar experiences of our own in which changes in perception have produced changes in behavior.) Since in Luria's model perception occurs in the posterior (sensory) unit, changes in perception could arguably produce changes in movement; thus, the posterior cortex is partly motor and not entirely sensory. In fact, many neuropsychologists argue just that point. (3) It might be thought that the corticospinal tract from area 4 of the motor cortex is "very motor"; Sherrington in fact called cells of this tract upper motor neurons. The sensory tracts in the dorsal cord carrying fine touch and pressure directly from body sensory receptors might be thought to be "very sensory." Yet Adkins and his colleagues have shown that the two are intertwined functionally: the corticospinal fibers give off collaterals to the ascending sensory fibers presumably to amplify the input on the sensory channel. When a motor tract is found to perform such functions, it is difficult to argue that it is purely motor. We could give many other similar examples of sensory-motor integration, but suffice it to say that the terms *sensory* and *motor* are used relatively: the former means more sensory than motor; the latter, more motor than sensory.

A second difficulty with Luria's model is that it is not clear just how much behavior is elaborated through a circuit that involves sequential processing from primary to tertiary sensory cortex and then from tertiary to primary motor cortex. As we shall see in subsequent chapters, there are ways in which information can bypass the frontal cortex completely, and other ways in which it can bypass the primary motor cortex.

A third problem with Luria's model is that although it seems to account for our perception of how we process information and behave, it is quite possible that our perceptions are in error. In our description of the organization of the cortex (Chapter 9) we point out that there is anatomical evidence that the cortex may be made up of many parallel sensory-motor systems any of which could be selectively removed by appropriate anatomical manipulation. One could, for example, selectively delete pain or color perception abilities, or one could selectively delete short-term memory for auditory-verbal, for auditory-nonverbal, or for visual events. A good example of parallel processing comes from studies on the visual system. The visual systems that mediate **circadian** (daylike) **rhythms,** pupillary constriction to light, and pattern and color vision are quite separate anatomically and they function in a largely independent fashion. It is quite possible that all cortical systems are organized as independent parallel systems in much the same way. The only difficulty in adopting this view is that it does not lend itself easily to an explanation of how perception is integrated.

APPLICATIONS FOR HIERARCHICAL PRINCIPLES

As we stated earlier, it was John Hughlings-Jackson who adopted the idea of a hierarchically organized nervous system and applied its principles to the analysis of the brain's function. Some 50 years later the usefulness of Hughlings-Jackson's approach was reaffirmed by Henry Head, and again by Luria still another 50 years later. The following sections describe some of the ways in which hierarchical principles have been used in the analysis of behavior. It should be noted that when levels of function, or centers, are used in these theoretical approaches to problems, the structures being referred to are *theoretical constructs,* and not necessarily anatomical structures.

Brain Damage

Using the concept of functional levels for clinical diagnosis, Hughlings-Jackson reasoned that two types of symptoms should follow brain damage: loss of function (negative symptoms) and release of function (positive symptoms). The term *negative symptoms* refers to behaviors that disappeared after brain damage and were therefore presumably generated by the damaged area. *Positive symptoms* refers to behaviors that emerged or became commoner after brain damage and were thus presumed to reveal the function of remaining structures. We can illustrate these two types of symptoms with a hypothetical example. Say a person stops eating, becomes excessively active, is unable to sleep and is given to outbursts of rage at the slightest provocation. The negative symptoms are the absence of normal quiet behavior, sleep, and eating; the positive symptoms are hyperactivity and excessive emotional response. These symptoms, reminiscent of the behavior of diencephalic animals, suggest that the diencephalon is released from normal forebrain control — which could occur because of a tumor or an infection in the forebrain. (Symptoms not unlike these have been associated with encephalitis or infections of the forebrain.)

Quite often positive symptoms take bizarre forms, yet if they are thought of as reflecting lower levels of function, situations in which they are, or once were, appropriate can be found. For example, Denny-Brown has described the reappearance of rooting and sucking reflexes in adults who have suffered some forms of frontal-lobe damage. With such damage and loss of normal frontal-lobe function, the normal smooth flow of behavior disappears, and the disappearance is labeled as a negative symptom. The frontal lobe also inhibits lower levels that produce reflexive behavior, so that in its absence reflexive behaviors reemerge, and they are labeled as positive symptoms. Although the positive symptoms appear peculiar in the adult, by the logic of this example they were once appropriate, for they supported feeding in infancy. The disappearance of both the positive and the negative symptoms can be used as a diagnostic indicator to gauge the rate and extent of recovery from brain damage.

Insanity

Hughlings-Jackson's concept of insanity was entirely hypothetical. When he discussed brain damage, he generally had particular anatomical structures in mind — for example, frontal cortex, basal ganglia, spinal cord — but with reference to insanity, he reasoned that the cortex was divided into sublevels that are also arranged hierarchically. Disorders of these levels, he assumed, would produce insanity with positive symptoms that manifest as aberrant behaviors. In face, he concluded that the highest levels of the hierarchy would be the most complex in structure and therefore the most susceptible to dysfunction. In his own words:

> Cases of insanity should, I think, be classified and investigated on the basis supplied by the doctrine of evolution of nervous centers. We shall have enormous help in the work Spencer has done in his *Psychology*. We have already explained that we use the term dissolution as the opposite of evolution. Insanity is dissolution, beginning in the highest nervous system processes. Moreover, of course, what we call the scientific investigation of insanity is really an experimental investigation of mind; and in this regard the slightest departures from a person's standard of mental health are to be studied, and not only the cases of patients who require to be kept in asylums. (Hughlings-Jackson, 1932, p. 4)

Although Hughlings-Jackson's reasoning has been little applied to the study of mental disorders, it may become more relevant since those disorders are increasingly studied as neuropsychological problems. His conceptualizations suggest that at the very least the problem in some types of mental disorders lies in the highest zones of the cortex. For example, the inappropriate chatter symptomatic of **hebephrenic schizophrenia** resembles in some respects **fluent aphasia;** thus, it could be taken as a positive symptom of a dysfunction of the highest language zones.

Dreams and Illusions

Hughlings-Jackson considered both dreams and illusions to be positive symptoms revealing the activity of particular brain structures released from inhibition. He thought that sleep released dreams by inhibiting higher levels of the brain that normally held dreaming in check. **Illusions, hallucinations,** and similar phenomena had an analogous cause, with the difference that higher centers were inactivated by mental disease, drugs, or brain damage. His intriguing suggestion has never been put to a test. It is interesting to contrast Hughlings-Jackson's theory with Freud's wish-fulfillment theory of dreams, which was predicated on the absence of the ego (or rational part of the personality) during sleep. There are similarities in the two theories.

Development

Perhaps no area of psychology makes more use of hierarchical concepts than developmental psychology (for example, see Bronson): many aspects of the development of behavior are believed to reflect the maturation of successively higher levels of the nervous system. From a developmental perspective, negative symptoms (the absence of certain behaviors) can be attributed to the immaturity of higher centers, whereas positive symptoms (e.g., play behavior, hyperactivity) can be considered as reflecting the activity of lower centers. Developmental approaches to brain function analysis have an advantage over studies using surgical techniques insofar as they reveal brain organization in intact individuals.

THE GENERALITY OF LEVELS OF FUNCTION

After summarizing some of the available information on levels of function, it seems appropriate to ask: Are the results from these lesion studies consistent with those obtained from research using other approaches? The answer is yes. For example, Flynn and his coworkers have studied the organization of predatory behavior in the cat by stimulating the brainstem electrically. Stimulation in the midbrain gives responses that are not associated with the autonomic signs of arousal that typically accompany attack behavior elicited by hypothalamic stimulation. Similarly, many other stimulation studies on rats and other animals confirm that the simpler components of motor behavior are organized in the lower brainstem (e.g., Bernston and Micco; Buchholz; and Robinson).

Another source of confirmatory evidence for levels of function is studies on the electrical activity (EEG) of the forebrain. Vanderwolf and his colleagues found that the electrical activity of the neocortex and hippocampus changes with behavior: "activated" patterns of EEG always occur during voluntary movements but not always with more reflexive or automatic behaviors. The hippocampal EEG of the rat shows this relation most clearly (see Figure 8-8): a rhythmical wave pattern called a **theta rhythm,** or **activity** (having a frequency of 4 to 7 Hz) is found to be correlated with voluntary movements (type 1) but is generally absent during automatic movements (type 2). According to the argument that the forebrain's function is to produce patterns of movement by putting together subsets of voluntary movement, it is understandable that the forebrain is in an "active mode" during these behaviors. It is controlling voluntary movements to ensure that they are appropriate in sequence, time, and place. The forebrain need not be active in the same way during automatic movements, since, once the animal is in a position to perform them, they are executed wholly at lower functional levels.

Why Levels?

Why is the brain organized into functional levels that are integrated in such a way that each level controls a large number of behaviors? Satinoff suggests that the answer has three parts. First, selective (evolutionary) pressure encouraged the development of new brain in order to refine the animal's ability to respond to specific features of the world. A good example is **thermoregulation**—any physiological or behavioral response intended to maintain normal body temperature. Response to

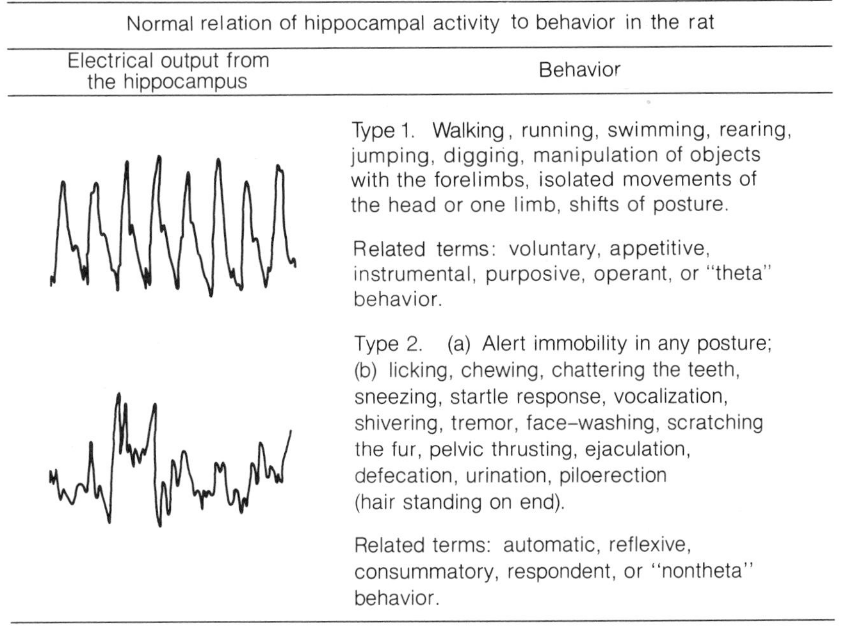

Normal relation of hippocampal activity to behavior in the rat	
Electrical output from the hippocampus	Behavior
	Type 1. Walking, running, swimming, rearing, jumping, digging, manipulation of objects with the forelimbs, isolated movements of the head or one limb, shifts of posture. Related terms: voluntary, appetitive, instrumental, purposive, operant, or "theta" behavior.
	Type 2. (a) Alert immobility in any posture; (b) licking, chewing, chattering the teeth, sneezing, startle response, vocalization, shivering, tremor, face–washing, scratching the fur, pelvic thrusting, ejaculation, defecation, urination, piloerection (hair standing on end). Related terms: automatic, reflexive, consummatory, respondent, or "nontheta" behavior.

FIGURE 8-8. Hippocampal activity in relation to spontaneous behavior in the rat. (After Vanderwolf et al., 1975.)

temperature change in spinal animals begins at temperature extremes of 36° to 41 °C; in decerebrates the range narrows to between 37° and 39 °C; in diencephalics it is around 38 °C; whereas in normal animals thermoregulatory responses are ongoing to maintain a precise body temperature that seldom deviates more than a fraction of a degree. The second part of the answer is that the brain took a great deal of time to evolve, and the development of any new structure conferring a new behavior had to integrate its activity through the systems already present. Third, once a new ability was developed it was frequently co-opted for other purposes in addition to those for which it was initially evolved. For example, upright walking on four legs was evolved to move an animal rapidly from one place to another, but the upright posture, once developed, could then support an animal when shivering. Another example might be that once an animal was able to balance on its hind legs to rear or jump, its front paws were free for manipulating objects. As a consequence of these three developments, we find behaviors integrated at each level in such a way that the entire organization of the brain can be viewed as a hierarchy of functional levels.

There is one additional reason the brain is organized in levels. The process of brain evolution was determined in a very real way by the sequence in which animals evolved into new habitats. In an aquatic environment they first had to develop locomotion. In a terrestrial environment the form of locomotion had to be modified; the animal required supporting musculature to lift it from the ground and legs to enable it to traverse various terrestrial obstacles. Once animals could travel on land, the development of new types of feeding skills and thermoregulatory abilities became advantageous. For those animals that were highly mobile, new types of guidance systems became useful. Finally, once animals were dispersed, the ability to communicate over great distances became advantageous. It can be postulated that had animals evolved in some other way and encountered various environmental obstacles in another sequence, the functional organization of the brain might be quite different from what we now find it to be.

REFERENCES

Adkins, R. J., R. W. Morse, and A. L. Towe. Control of somatosensory input by cerebral cortex. *Science* 153:1020–1022, 1966.

Bandler, R. J., C. C. Chi, and J. P. Flynn. Biting attack elicited by stimulation of the ventral midbrain tegmentum of cats. *Science* 177:361–366, 1972.

Bard, P. A diencephalic mechanism for the expression of rage, with special reference to the sympathetic nervous system. *American Journal of Physiology* 84:490–515, 1928.

Bard, P., and M. B. Macht. The behavior of chronically decerebrate cats. In G. E. W. Wolstenholm, and C. M. O'Connor (eds.) *Ciba Foundation Symposium on Neurological Basis of Behavior.* London: J. and A. Churchill, 1958.

Barrett, R., H. H. Merritt, and A. Wolf. Depression of consciousness as a result of cerebral lesions. *Research Publications of the Association for Research in Nervous and Mental Disease* 45:241–276, 1967.

Bazett, H. C., and W. G. Penfield. A study of the Sherrington decerebrate animal in the chronic as well as the acute condition. *Brain* 45:185–265, 1922.

Bernston, G. G., and D. J. Micco. Organization of brainstem behavioral systems. *Brain Research Bulletin* 1:471–483, 1976.

Bignall, K. E., and L. Schramm. Behavior of chronically decerebrate kittens. *Experimental Neurology* 42:519–531, 1974.

Brackbill, Y. The role of the cortex in orienting: Orienting reflex in an encephalic human infant. *Developmental Psychology* 5:195–201, 1971.

Bronson, G. The hierarchical organization of the central nervous system: Implications for learning processes and critical periods in early development. *Behavioral Science* 10:7–25, 1965.

Brooks, D. M. The role of the cerebral cortex and of various sense organs in the excitation and execution of mating activity in the rabbit. *American Journal of Physiology* 120:544–553, 1973.

Buchholz, D. Spontaneous and centrally induced behaviors in normal and thalamic opossums. *Journal of Comparative and Physiological Psychology* 90:898–908, 1976.

Cannon, W. B., and S. W. Britton. Pseudoaffective medulliadrenal secretion. *American Journal of Physiology* 72:283–294, 1924.

Denny-Brown, D. The nature of apraxia. *Journal of Nervous and Mental Diseases* 126:9–32, 1958.

Flynn, J., H. Venegas, W. Foote, and S. Edwards. Neural mechanisms involved in a cat's attack on a rat. In R. E. Whalen, R. F. Thompson, M. Verzeano, and N. M. Weinberger (eds.) *The Neural Control of Behavior.* New York: Academic, 1970.

Freud, S. D. *The Standard Edition of the Complete Psychological Works of Sigmund Freud.* J. Stachey and A. Freud (eds.) London: Hogarth, 1950.

Gallistel, C. R. *The Organization of Action.* Hillsdale, NJ: Lawrence Erlbaum Associates, 1980.

Gamper, E. In J. Field, H. W. Magoun, and V. E. Hall (eds) *Handbook of Physiology* (vol. 2). Washington, D. C.: American Physiological Society, 1959.

Goltz, F. On the functions of the hemispheres. In G. von Bonin (ed.) *The Cerebral Cortex.* Springfield, IL: Charles C. Thomas, 1960.

Grill, H. J., and R. Norgren. Chronically decerebrate rats demonstrate satiation but not baitshyness. *Science* 201:267–269, 1978.

Grill, H. J., and R. Norgren. Neurological tests and behavioral deficits in chronic thalamic and chronic decerebrate rats. *Brain Research* 143:299–312, 1978.

Grillner, S. Locomotion in the spinal cat. In R. B. Stein (ed.) *Control of Posture and Locomotion.* New York: Plenum, 1973.

Hughlings-Jackson, J. Remarks on dissolution of the nervous system as exemplified by certain post-epileptic conditions. In J. Taylor (ed.) *Selected Writings of John Hughlings-Jackson* (vol. 2.) London: Hodder and Stoughton, 1932.

Kluver, H., and P. C. Bucy. Preliminary analysis of the functions of the temporal lobes in monkeys. *Archives of Neurology and Psychiatry* 42:979–1000, 1939.

Kuhn, R. A. Functional capacity of the isolated human spinal cord. *Brain* 73:1–51, 1950.

Liddell, E. G. T., and C. S. Sherrington. Reflexes in response to stress (mystatic reflexes). *Proceedings of the Royal Society of London* 96:212–249, 1924.

Luciani, L. *Human Physiology.* London: Macmillan, 1915.

Luria, A. R. *The Working Brain.* Harmondsworth, England: Penguin, 1973.

MacLean, P. D. On the origin and progressive evolution of the triune brain. In E. Armstrong and D. Falk (eds.) *Primate Brain Evolution.* New York: Plenum Press, 1982.

Melzack, R., and P. D. Wall. Pain mechanisms: A new theory. *Science* 150:971–979, 1965.

Morris, R. G. M. Spatial localization does not require the presence of local cues. *Learning and Motivation* 12:239–260, 1980.

Oakley, D. A. Cerebral cortex and adaptive behavior. In D. A. Oakley and H. C. Plotkin (eds.) *Brain, Evolution and Behavior.* London: Methuen, 1979.

Passingham, R. E. Cortical mechanisms and cues for action. *Philosophical Transactions of the Royal Society of London* B308:101–111, 1985.

Phillips, C. G., S. Zeki, and H. B. Barlow. Localization of function in the cerebral cortex. *Brain* 107:327–361, 1984.

Robinson, T. E. Electrical stimulation of the brain stem in freely moving rats: I. Effects on behavior. *Physiology and Behavior* 21:223–231, 1978.

Satinoff, E. Neural organization and evolution of thermal regulation in mammals. *Science* 201:16–22, 1978.

Sherrington, C. S. *The Integrative Action of the Nervous System.* New Haven: Yale University Press, 1906.

Sorenson, C. A. and G. D. Ellison. Striatal organization of feeding behavior in the decorticate rat. *Experimental Neurology* 29:162–174, 1970.

Tolman, E. C. *Behavior and Psychological Man.* Berkeley: University of California Press, 1961.

Vanderwolf, C. H., B. Kolb, and R. K. Cooley. Behavior of the rat after removal of the neocortex and hippocampal formation. *Journal of Comparative and Physiological Psychology* 92:156–175, 1978.

Vanderwolf, C. H., R. Kramis, L. A. Gillespie, and B. H. Bland. Hippocampal rhythmical slow activity and neocortical low voltage fast activity: Relations to behavior. In K. H. Pribram and R. L. Isaacson (eds.) *The Hippocampus: A Comprehensive Treatise*. New York: Plenum, 1975.

Villablanca, J. R., C. E. Olmstead, and I. de Andres. Effects of caudate nuclei or frontal cortical ablations in kittens: Responsiveness to auditory stimuli and comparisons with adult-operated littermates. *Experimental Neurology* 61:635–649, 1978.

Whishaw, I. Q. The decorticate rat. In B. Kolb and R. Tees, eds. *The Neocortex of the Rat*. Cambridge, MA: M.I.T. Press, 1989.

Woods, J. W. Behavior of chronic decerebrate rats. *Journal of Neurophysiology* 27:634–644, 1964.

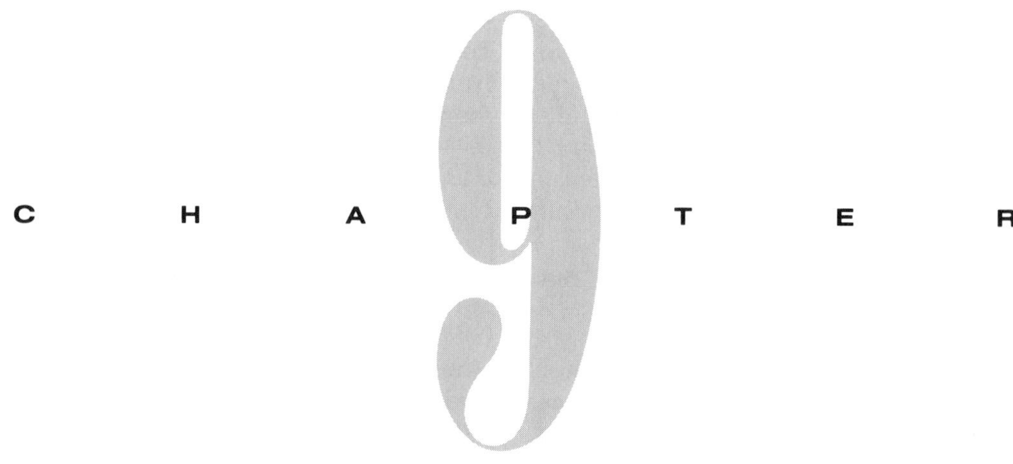

PRINCIPLES OF NEOCORTICAL ORGANIZATION

Mr. Higgins decided that he should learn French so that he could enjoy French literature. After a year's intensive study Higgins was almost fluent in French but it became clear to him that in order to really understand French, he was going to have to study Latin. Higgins had always been interested in Latin and so he plunged into it, only to find after a year's intense study that in order to master Latin, he really must study old Greek. Higgins was determined to learn French, and so he began a serious study of Greek. Alas, after a year's intense study of Greek, Higgins determined that he must now learn Sanskrit if he were to really appreciate Greek. This posed a problem, for there were few scholars of Sanskrit, but with a few months' effort, he managed to locate an old man in India who was a true scholar of Sanskrit. Excited at the possibility of soon learning French, Higgins moved to India to begin his study of Sanskrit. After six months the old man died. Demoralized because he did not yet have a good knowledge of Sanskrit, Higgins returned home and concluded that it was not possible to really learn French.

This story illustrates the difficulty encountered by the psychologist who wishes to study the neurological bases of human behavior. The psychologist obviously must study the basic structure and organization of the brain, especially the neocortex, and must keep abreast of the latest developments in neuroanatomy, neurochemistry, and neurophysiology. The problem for the psychologist, however, is in knowing where to stop. Having a knowledge of the microstructure of mitochondria in the presynaptic ending may be fascinating and necessary for understanding how a neuron functions, but will this knowledge make it any easier to study the neurological control of language? There is, of course, no easy answer to this question; the psychologist must avoid being trapped by Sanskrit but must be aware of where French came from. In this chapter, which is an elaboration of our discussion of the organization of the neocortex in the previous chapter, we outline some of the details of cortical organization that we feel are necessary for the psychologist to know before beginning the study of the functional organization of the cortex. We have simplified much of the material, hoping to avoid a regression to Sanskrit, but the student should be aware that our discussion has been simplified and that a good deal more is known about the details (Greek and Sanskrit) of cortical organization than we have presented.

We shall make six points in this chapter, each of which will be considered separately: (1) the cortex is composed of many types of neurons, which are organized into six layers, (2) the cortex is organized into functional columns, (3) there are multiple representations of sensory and motor functions in the cortex, (4) these representations exhibit plasticity, (5) cortical activity is influenced by feedback loops from several forebrain regions, and (6) the cortex functions using both hierarchical and parallel processing.

CELLS AND LAYERS OF THE CORTEX

We have already described the layered structure of the cerebral cortex in Chapter 1. Here we shall consider the types of cells that make up those layers, the nature of the connections between them, and their functions.

Two main categories of nerve cells can be easily distinguished in the cortex by their general shape. **Pyramidal cells,** which have cell bodies in the general shape of a pyramid, represent the major efferents of the cerebral cortex and are found in layers II, III, and V (Figure 9-1). The pyramidal cells of layer V are the largest, projecting to the brainstem and spinal cord. Those in layers II and III are smaller and project to other cortical regions (Figure 9-2). **Stellate cells** (star-shaped cells) are interneurons and represent a collection of different types of cells, which are named largely on the basis of the configuration of their axons and dendrites. For example, one type of stellate cell is called a basket cell because its axon projects horizontally, forming synapses that envelop the postsynaptic cell like a basket. Stellate cells also include granule cells, double-bouquet cells, chandelier cells, and fusiform (spindle-shaped) cells, among others. Stellate cells are found in all the layers of the cortex, but the heaviest concentration of them is in layer IV, especially in the sensory cortex. Stellate cells receive afferents from subcortical structures, as well as providing interconnections between the cortical afferents and efferents, as summarized in Figure 9-2.

The cells of the middle layers of the cortex (especially in and around layer IV) can be conceived as composing a zone of *sensory analysis,* whereas the cells of layers V and VI can be thought of as composing a zone of *output* from the cortex. It is therefore hardly surprising that the sensory cortex has a relatively large layer IV and a small layer V. Figure 9-2 illustrates this difference and shows that although the different cortical layers can be distinguished through the cortex, the thickness of the layers is far from uniform: the fourth layer may be virtually absent in the motor cortex, and the sensory cortex is far thinner overall than is the motor cortex.

Figure 9-2 also illustrates another feature of cortical organization. Afferents to the cortex are of two general types: specific and nonspecific. *Specific afferents* are those that terminate in relatively discrete regions of the cortex, usually in only one or two layers. These include projections from the thalamus as well as those from the amygdala. Most of these projections terminate in layer IV, although projections from the amygdala and certain thalamic nuclei may terminate in the more superficial layers. Nonspecific afferents are those that terminate diffusely over large regions of the cortex, in some cases over all of the cortex. The norepinephrinergic projections from the brainstem, the cholinergic projections from the basal forebrain, and

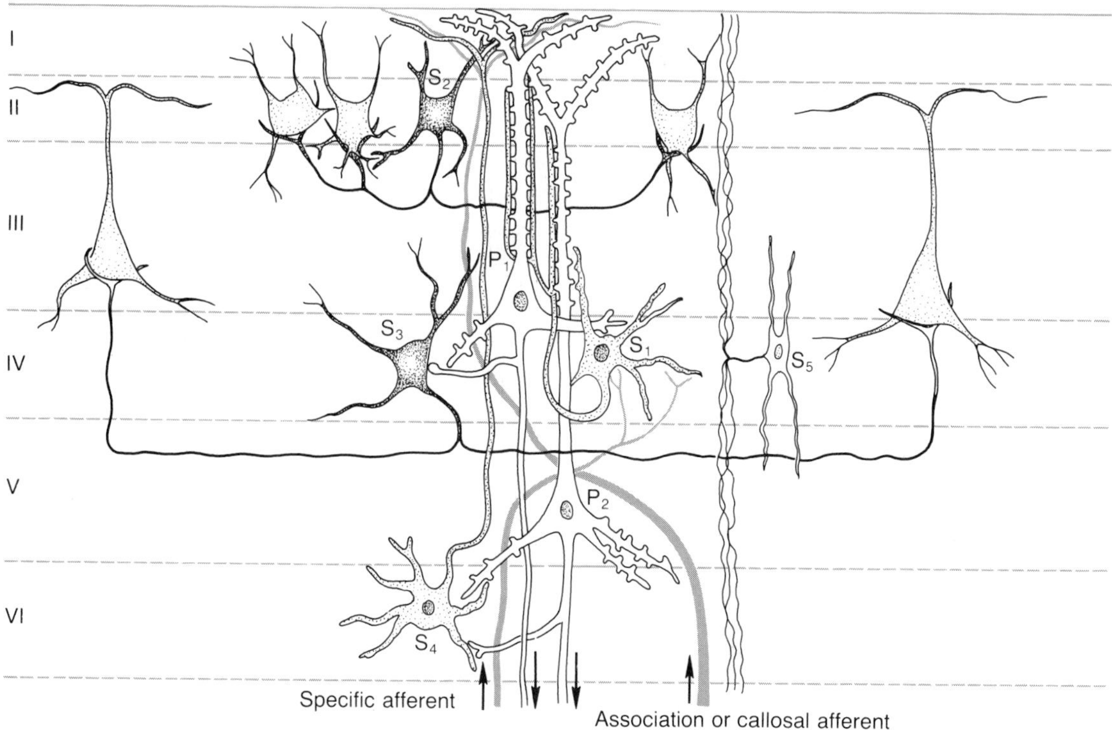

FIGURE 9-1. Illustration of the most important neocortical cell types. Pyramidal cells (P_1 and P_2) are found in layers III and V. The stellate cells are found throughout the cortex and include several types of cells ($S_1 - S_5$). Thalamic afferents arrive in layer IV and synapse on stellate interneuron S_1. Associative or callosal afferents feed into the more superficial layers to synapse on interneurons or on the long apical (vertical) dendrites of pyramidal neurons. Basket-type stellate interneurons (S_2) establish connections within the superficial layers, probably functioning to inhibit the cells to which they project. Larger basket interneurons (S_3) located in the deeper layers may also spread inhibition laterally in the deeper layers. Fusiform (spindle-shaped) stellate cells (S_4) are primarily located in layer VI, sending excitatory axons vertically. Double bouquet-type stellate cells (S_5) may secure the spread of excitation over the entire depth of the cortex when layer IV is stimulated by incoming afferents. (Direction of arrows indicate afferents [up] or efferents [down].) (Adapted from Szentagothai, 1969.)

the projections from certain thalamic nuclei are examples of nonspecific afferents. Nonspecific afferents often terminate in many or all the layers of the cortex and presumably serve some general function such as the enhancement of ongoing cortical activity.

Finally, it should be realized that most of the interactions between the layers of the cortex are with cells directly above or below, and with relatively less interaction with cells more than a couple of millimeters on either side (see Figure 9-1). This vertical bias in cortical organization forms the basis for a second type of neocortical organization: the column.

CORTICAL COLUMNS

If a microelectrode is moved vertically through the sensory cortex from layer I to layer VI, all the

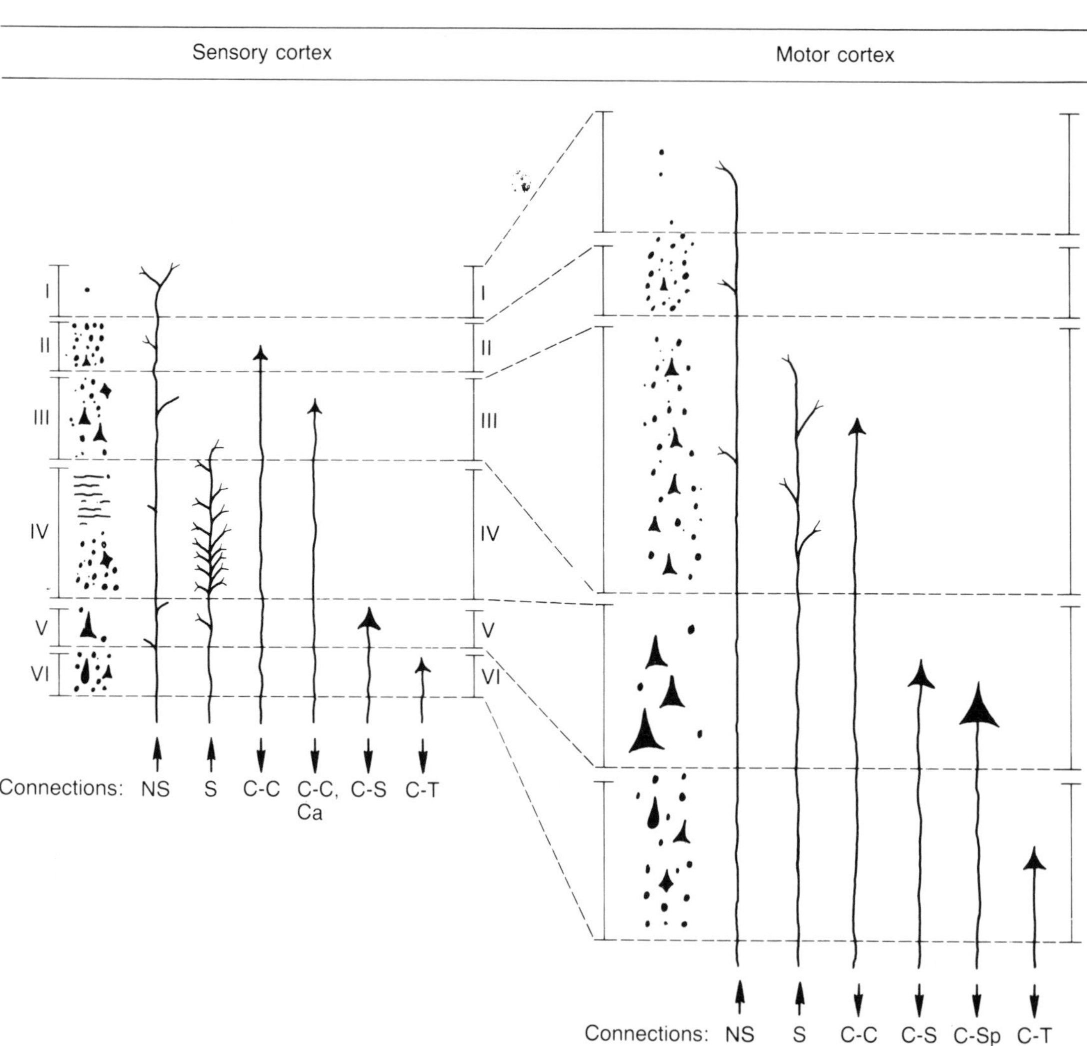

FIGURE 9-2. Schematic illustration of the neuronal elements of the sensory and motor cortex. The sensory cortex is much thinner than the motor cortex, and the size of each layer is markedly different in the sensory and the motor cortex. The specific (S) and nonspecific (NS) inputs to the cortex illustrate the different distribution of these afferents to the different laminae (layers). The outputs from the cortex arise from different layers, depending on the destination. Cortical-cortical (C-C) efferents arise from layers II and III, callosal (Ca) efferents arise from layer III, cortical-subcortical (C-S) and cortical-spinal (C-Sp) efferents arise from layer V, and cortical-thalamic (C-T) efferents arise from layer VI, as illustrated. (Direction of arrows at bottom of figure indicate afferents [up] or efferents [down].) (After Shepherd, 1979.)

neurons encountered appear functionally very similar. For example, if an electrode is placed in the somatosensory cortex and lowered vertically from layer I to VI, neurons in each layer are excited by a particular tactile stimulus (e.g., a light touch) in a particular part of the body (e.g., the left thumb). The cells of layer IV are activated earliest by an afferent input, as would be expected by the direct afferent connections to this layer. Cells of the other layers must necessarily have longer latencies, since they would have at least one more synapse on an interneuron in layer IV before receiving the sensory input. The pyramidal neurons of layer V are the last to be activated, again as would be expected since these are the efferents. The functional similarity of cells across all six layers at any point in the cortex suggests that the simplest functional unit of the cortex is a vertically oriented column of cells that composes a minicircuit. Thus, the cortex is organized into narrow vertical columns from 0.5

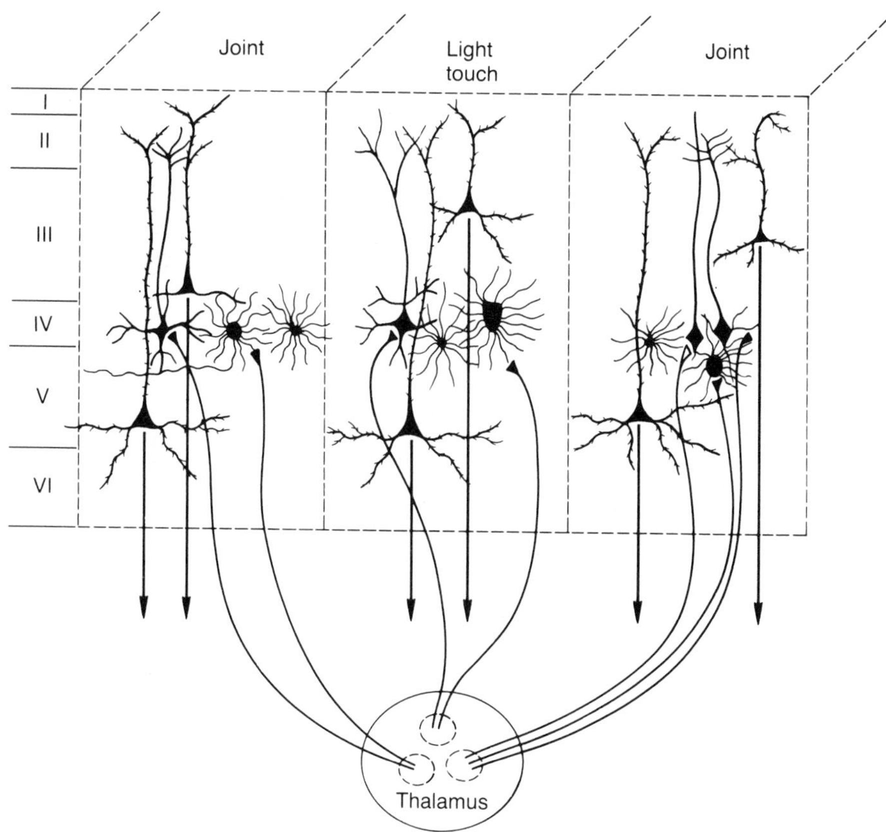

FIGURE 9-3. Highly schematic diagram illustrating the columnar organization of the neocortex. Thalamic input synapses on stellate cells, with interneurons and pyramidal cells transferring information vertically. In this example each column is specific for a subcategory of somatosensation. Interneurons between the columns are not drawn. (Arrows indicate efferents.)

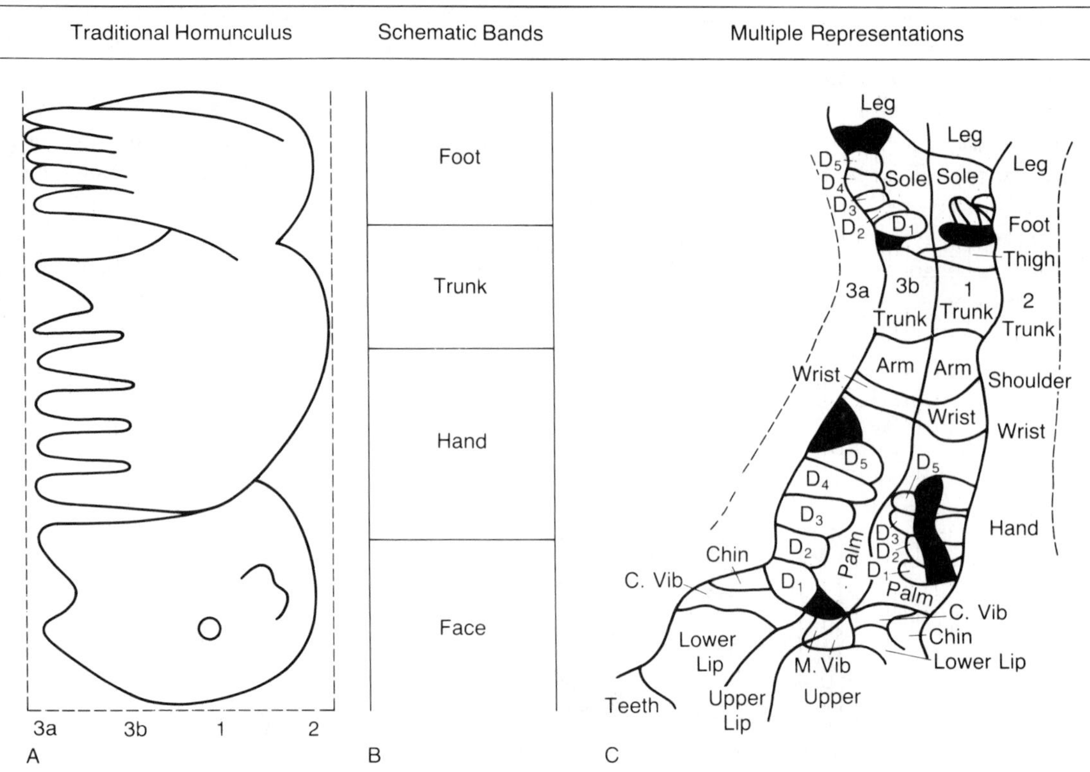

FIGURE 9-4. Three conceptions of the organization of the somatosensory cortex in the postcentral gyrus of the monkey. *A.* Representation of a traditional homunculus. *B.* Major body parts represented as functional bands. *C.* Multiple representations of the body in which each architectonic field contains one representation. The traditional homunculus was mapped using large electrodes, whereas the multiple representations were discovered using microelectrodes. (After Kaas et al., 1979.)

to 1.0 mm wide, running from the cortical surface to the white matter, in which each neuron in such a column is functionally similar to the others (Figure 9-3). Afferents terminate on interneurons in layer IV and these interneurons transmit information vertically to synapse on other interneurons or pyramidal cell dendrites. Little information transfer occurs laterally, the principle direction of information travel being vertical. Physiological studies have shown that adjacent columns are maximally excited by different afferents, providing further evidence that each column functions as a minicircuit.

For example, in the somatosensory system each cell in one column might be responsive to the movement of hairs, whereas cells in an adjacent column might respond to the movement of a joint (Figure 9-3). Each of the columns has a somatosensory function, but for each column the particular feature of somatosensation is different. It is apparent that a single vertical column 1 mm in diameter is hardly sufficient to analyze all the sensations of a particular aspect of touch from the whole body. Thus, there must be multiple columns for this, and indeed there are. Columns for skin touch intermingle in a mosaic pattern within the somatosensory cortex with columns for joint position, hair movement, stretch, and so forth. Although the various columns appear to mingle at random at any point on the cortex, there is a rather highly organized structure inherent in the mosaic. Columns responsive to different sensations in the thumb are grouped together, as are those for the hand, leg, trunk, face, and so on. Therefore, if one were to look at the cortex from above, there would be regions devoted to the hand, face, leg, and so on, as illustrated in Figure 9-4*A*.

We have used the somatosensory system as an example of columnar organization, yet such organization is a feature of the entire neocortex, although little is known about the details of columnar organization outside the somatosensory and motor cortexes. Furthermore, outside the somatosensory and motor cortexes the mosaic of the columns would not form a neat homunculus but would appear more like strips or patches of functionally related columns.

MULTIPLE REPRESENTATIONS

When Penfield and his colleagues stimulated the motor and somatosensory strips of their patients at the Montreal Neurological Hospital, they found that it was possible to identify regions of the pre- and postcentral gyri, respectively, that appeared to represent localized body parts such as the leg, hand, and face (see Figure 1-8). In order to summarize their observations, they constructed a homunculus in which different body parts are represented in discrete regions of the cortex. We must remember, however, that the homunculus that they drew is imaginary and was not actually observed in each patient. By stimulating dozens of points in different patients they were able to determine the boundaries of the motor and sensory fields, but the detailed organization was really just an educated guess. Subsequent studies by Woolsey using nonhuman subjects confirmed Penfield's findings, as there appeared to be analogous representations in other species (see Figure 5-7). Like Penfield, however, Woolsey did not actually observe a detailed map on the cortical surface but rather observed something like illustration Figure 9-4*B*. That is, the stimulation allowed the investigators to identify a series of functional bands corresponding to different parts of the body. The fact that the cortical representation does not relate on a one-to-one basis with the body surface is not a problem because common experience tells us that some body parts are indeed less sensitive to touch than are others (e.g., the back as opposed to the face). Similar representations of the visual and auditory fields, as well as of the motor cortex, were constructed, leading to the consensus that the sensory world is represented directly in a number of regions in the cortex. It is this view that is described in most current introductory psychology, neurology, and biology textbooks, but the actual story appears to be somewhat more complex.

We have seen that the cortex is functionally organized into columns, with adjacent columns devoted to different aspects of sensory input. For example, we saw in Figure 9-3 that within the somatosensory cortex one column might code touch and an adjacent column might code pressure. Are these distinct sensations accounted for within the single representation of the body? Recent experiments using microelectrodes to study somatosensory representation in the monkey brain have shown that they are not. The somatosensory area is actually composed of three, and perhaps four, smaller representations of the body, as illustrated in Figure 9-4*C*. It can be seen that within the area devoted to the leg, for example, there are at least three separate representations, each one coding some different aspect of somatosensation. Each of the subareas has its own pattern of sensory activation and its own distinctive pattern of connections. It is now clear that although Penfield's maps are useful summaries of his observations, his relatively crude procedures led to the erroneous belief that there is a single representation of the body surface in the postcentral gyrus. In fact there are multiple representations of the body surface, each of which appears to function independently of the others.

Evidence of multiple representations of somatosensation leads to the question of whether the visual world and the auditory world are also represented repeatedly in the cortex. Indeed they are, as we shall see in the next chapter. Furthermore, there is good evidence that there are also multiple representations of the body in the motor system. Both Penfield and Woolsey identified a complete motor representation on the medial surface of the cortex, which Woolsey termed the **supplementary motor cortex** (Figure 5-7), and according to Evarts, there is little doubt that significant functional divisions exist within the motor cortex of the precentral gyrus. Similarly, the cortex lying just in front of the primary motor cortex (the *premotor cortex* or Brodmann's areas 6 and 8) may contain one or more additional representations.

STABILITY OF SENSORY REPRESENTATIONS IN THE CORTEX

One of the striking things about the stimulation studies of Penfield and his colleagues is the remarkable variation among patients in the exact organization of the sensory and motor representations. Part of this variation is almost certainly due to slight differences in the testing procedure from patient to patient, but there is reason to believe that much of the variation can be accounted for by genetic and experiential factors. It is generally assumed that sensory representations in the cortex occupy fixed, presumably genetically programmed, locations throughout life. Although it has been recognized that people with pre- or postnatal disorders frequently have unusual sensory or motor representations, such as the remarkable dexterity of toe use in people with no hands, these peculiar phenomena have generally been attributed to the apparent plasticity of the infant nervous system. However, recent evidence questions this assumption, leading us to consider an important change in our conceptions of sensory and motor organization.

In their studies of somatosensory organization in monkeys, Merzenich and Kaas severed the median nerve of the right hand. This nerve normally innervates the palm side (also referred to as the glabrous side) of the thumb and the first two fingers, as well as the right side of the palm. Immediately following nerve section, the cortex in areas 3b and 2 that was previously responsive to stimulation of the skin serviced by the median nerve became unresponsive. However, in most monkeys, small fragments of cortex that were formerly devoted to the glabrous digits became immediately responsive to the dorsal (back-of-the-hand) surface of these digits, which is innervated by other nerves. Over several weeks these small fragments of newly responsive cortex enlarged to represent more of the skin dorsal surface of the digits. Furthermore, cortical representations of skin surfaces bordering the skin field of the median nerve began to expand to occupy the denervated zone. Some of these expansions were truly remarkable, because some skin sites, which were formerly entirely outside the denervated zone, moved to fall completely within it, allowing more distal skin sites to expand into the evacuated "territory." That is, there was a remarkable shift in cortical representation. An area that formerly did one thing now does something else. These results, which have also been found in other mammalian species, have important implications for principles of cortical organization.

First, they imply that cortical and presumably subcortical, representations of sensory surfaces are plastic, even in mature individuals. Second, map changes may involve significant changes in anatomical organization, either in terms of the effectiveness of synapses or in the development of new synaptic contacts or both. Third, the dramatic reorganization observed in the cortex may not be a curious effect of peripheral nerve injury but may actually reflect a normal process of dynamic organization in the cortex. In other words, it may be that there is a normal competition of inputs for neocortical space, a competition that is influenced by peripheral effects, including environmental stimulation. It is well known that environmental stimulation can influence a variety of neocortical characteristics, including cortical weight and thickness, and so it may not be surprising that cortical organization might also be influenced by environmental stimulation. Indeed, the common observation that movements and sensations are changed after prolonged experience in a cast may have its foundation in significant changes in the organization of cortical sensory and motor representation, changes that can be reversed by therapy.

In summary, maps of the cortex apparently change, the apparent stability in them being a consequence of balanced competition. Changing the balance results in an orderly sequence of change that produces a new balance and a new organization. Merzenich and Kaas speculate that it should be possible to change this balance not only by removing an input but also by increasing or decreasing the levels of activity produced by given skin surfaces or by a given set of receptors. Thus, somatosensory cortical fields may be subject to alterations in sensory use. In fact, there is preliminary evidence that learning a sensory-motor skill could actually modify a cortical map, and the modifications could be responsible, at least in part, for the increased skill. The fact that these changes occur in mature individuals also implies that it may be possible to teach old dogs new tricks after all. On the other hand, the apparent difficulty in doing so may imply that there is a relative loss in the plasticity of neocortical fields with age, although this is purely speculation.

FEEDBACK LOOPS

Governments, universities, corporations, and other large institutions are normally run by a relatively small group of people who form a cabinet, council, or board. This group may make the final decisions on behalf of a very large number of people (millions in the case of governments), but it does not normally reach its decisions without significant input from other bodies. The commonest source of such input is the committee, which may include people from the inner group as well as a sample of people from outside. The committee is given a mandate from the upper group, and then later reports back to it with recommendations. An analogous organization is found in the brain in the form of cortical-subcortical feedback loops. If the cortex is thought of as the cabinet or board, various subcortical regions such as the thalamus, striatum, and amygdala can be considered committees. These regions receive input from the cortex and in turn send output back to it. These regions also send other output to the brainstem, but it is the input to the cortex that is especially important in the current context, for it must have a significant effect on cortical functioning. The principal cortical-subcortical feedback loops are illustrated in Figure 9-5.

Cortical-Thalamic Loops

The thalamus plays a central role in the functioning of the neocortex since it provides the major sensory afferents to the cortex (Figure 1-14). In addition, however, the thalamus receives projections back from the cortex, projections that probably function to inhibit or to excite thalamic-cortical connections (Figure 9-5*A* and *B*). For example, if one is startled while walking through a park at night, the cortical-thalamic projection could function to amplify the sensory afferents to the cortex. Since the thalamus plays a key role in providing the cortex with specific afferents, we should not be surprised to discover that disruptions of thalamic functioning have significant consequences for neocortical functioning. In **Korsakoff's syndrome** the medial thalamus is destroyed by chronic alcohol ingestion, leading to severe memory loss and

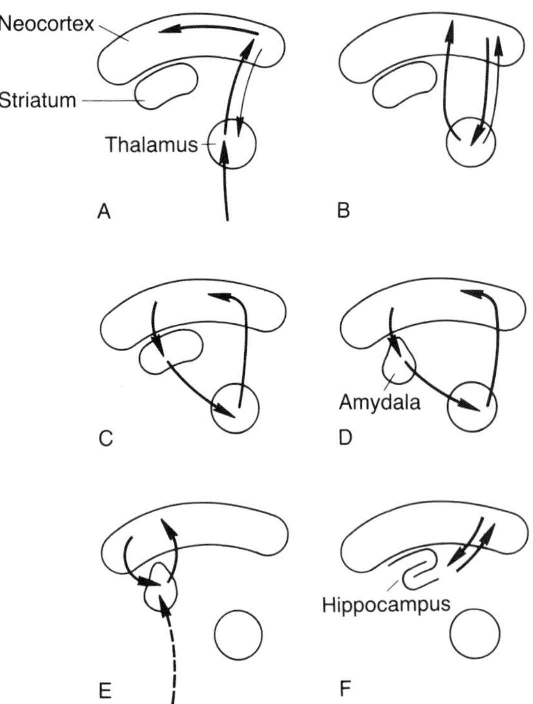

FIGURE 9-5. Schematic diagrams illustrating the cortical-subcortical feedback loops. *A* and *B* show two different thalamic loops. *C* shows the cortical-striatal-thalamic loop, *D* the cortical-amygdala-thalamic loop, *E* the cortical-amygdala loop, and *F* the cortical-hippocampal loop. Each of these feedback loops presumably functions to modify ongoing cortical activity. Thickness of the arrows refers to the relative size of the connections. The dashed lines indicate various subcortical inputs to the amygdala.

various signs suggestive of frontal-lobe damage. Since the medial thalamus provides the principal subcortical afferents to the frontal cortex, the frontal-lobe symptoms presumably result from a disturbance of cortical function secondary to the thalamic damage.

Cortical-Striatal Loops

The striatum is one of the major efferent targets of the cortex. Unlike the cortical projections to the brainstem, however, the striatum does not send many projections in turn to the spinal cord but rather sends its major projections back to the cortex by way of the thalamus (see Figure 9-5*C*). The principal function of the striatum therefore must be to modify cortical activity rather than to control behavior directly, since the only way the striatum can effectively change behavior is by influencing cortical function. The striatum must have an especially important role in the control of movement since striatal damage can produce a wide range of movement disorders. The best known of these disorders is **Parkinson's disease,** in which an absence of dopamine in the striatum produces a bewildering array of motor (as well as cognitive) symptoms, which we shall discuss in detail in Chapter 13.

Cortical-Amygdala Loops

The amygdala has two different feedback loops to the cortex. The first is indirect, via the medial thalamus, and the second is direct, as illustrated in Figure 9-5*D* and *E*. The function of the cortical-amygdala loop is not well understood, but the role of the amygdala in the control of affective behavior suggests that it may play some role in adding affective tone to cortical activity. For example, a ferocious dog may generate a strong affective response in us as it charges up, in part because the amygdala adds affective tone to the visual input of the dog. Indeed, in the absence of the amygdala, laboratory animals appear to have absolutely no fear of threatening objects. We have seen cats whose amygdalas have been removed take leisurely strolls through rooms housing large monkeys, whereas no normal cat would even contemplate doing such a thing.

Cortical-Hippocampal Loops

The hippocampus does not provide the large source of cortical afferents that the thalamus, striatum, or amygdala do, but it does receive cortical input and does influence neocortical activity. The hippocampus is probably one of the most intensely studied and poorly understood structures in the forebrain, as is attested by the numerous theories regarding its function. As we shall see in later chapters, the hippocampus has a crucial role in memory and may have a role in many other functions including movement, affect, language, and spatial behavior. This role is most likely due largely to the major cortical-hippocampal projections, but it is likely that the hippocampus has some influence on cortical function as well, via feedback loops through the thalamus or limbic cortex.

HIERARCHICAL AND PARALLEL PROCESSING

In the previous chapter we emphasized the hierarchical nature of brain organization. Within the cortex, we suggested that Luria's concept of primary, secondary, and tertiary areas provides a useful conceptual model of cortical function. Having considered the cortex in more detail in this chapter, we are now ready to elaborate on Luria's simple model in order to incorporate features such as multiple representations and feedback loops and to consider a second type of cortical processing, namely parallel processing. We shall begin by reconsidering the types of cortex.

Cortical Types

We have seen that the sensory and motor cortex are very different in their structure. The motor cortex is thicker overall and the relative sizes of the layers in the two types of cortex are rather different. We have also seen in Chapter 8 that in addition to both primary sensory and motor cortex there is secondary cortex, which is closely associated with specific primary regions, and tertiary cortex, which is multimodal and not specifically associated with any primary sensory or motor region. Luria's distinction into different levels of cortex was based largely upon clinical observations, but more recent anatomical and behavioral studies, largely on nonhuman primates, have shown that the division of cortex in this manner is an oversimplification. On the basis of cytoarchitectonic and cortical-connection data Pandya and Seltzer have proposed that there are four types of cortex: primary, association, multimodal, and paralimbic.

Primary Cortex. Figure 9-6*A* illustrates the overall organization of the primate cortex and shows a first and second sensory region for somatosensory (S_I, S_{II}), auditory (A_I, A_{II}) and visual senses (V_I, V_{II}), as well as a single region for the gustatory system (G). It is important to emphasize that Pandya's use of first and second (or primary and secondary) does not correspond to Luria's; both the primary and secondary zones of Pandya, which are distinguished on anatomical grounds, are **primary cortex** in Luria's terminology. Thus, S_I and S_{II} each have a sensory, or somato, homunculus (see Figure 5-7). Similarly, both A_I and A_{II} have a tonotopic, or sound-location, map and V_I and V_{II} have complementary maps of the visual world that are mirror images of each other. Figure 9-6*A* also illustrates areas M_I and M_{II}, each of which also has a motor homunculus, much like that for S_I and S_{II}. M_{II} is usually referred to as supplementary motor cortex.

Association Cortex. The cortical areas next to the primary sensory regions are termed first-order parasensory **association cortex,** and those areas beyond whose connections lie further away are termed second- or third-order association areas (Figure 9-6*B*). The first- and second-order association areas probably correspond to Luria's secondary cortex. The first- and second-order association areas can be distinguished as two separate types of cortex on the basis of their connections (Figure

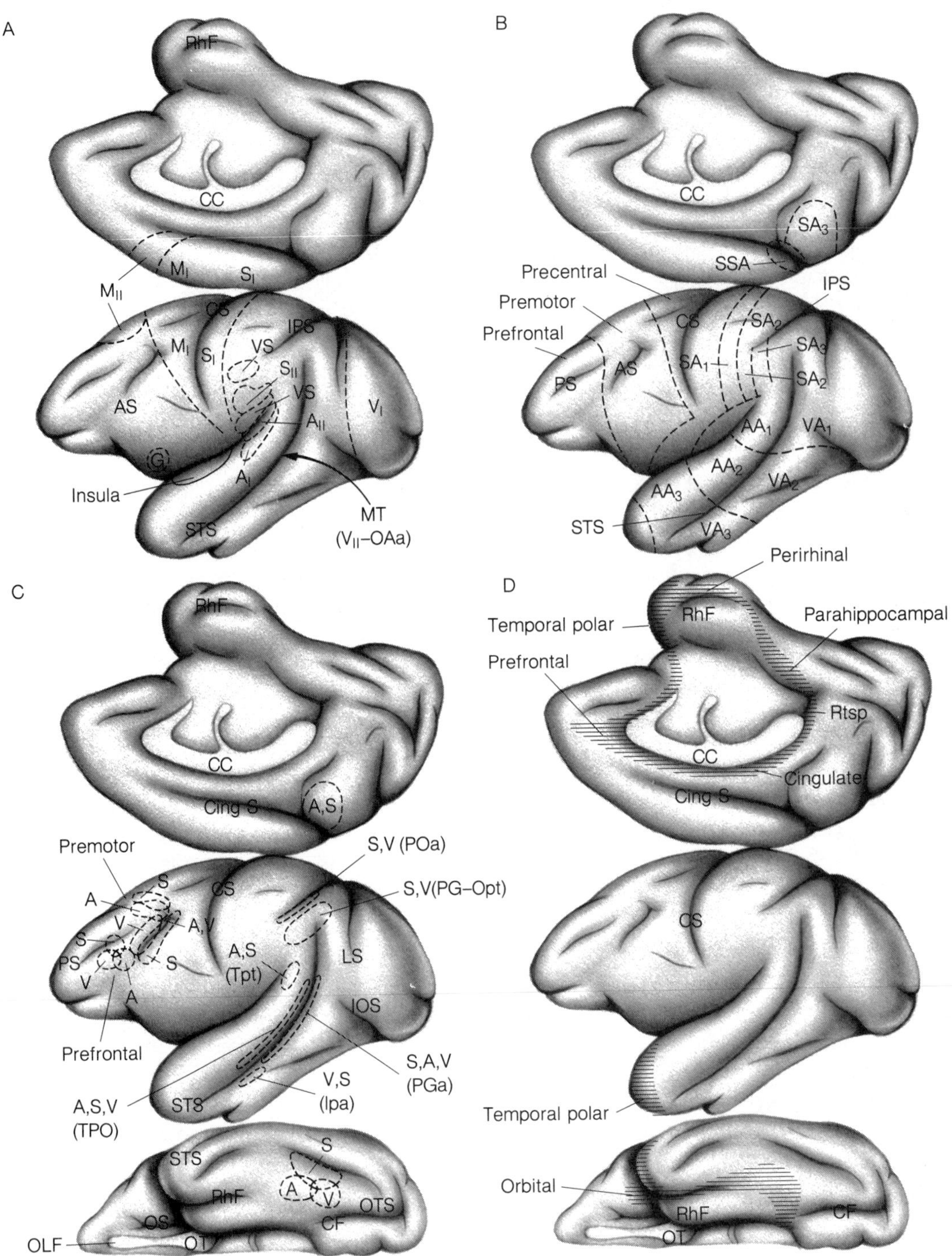

A
RhF
CC
M_{II}
M_I
S_I
CS
IPS
VS
S_{II}
VS
AS
V_I
A_{II}
G
A_I
Insula
STS
MT
(V_{II}–OAa)
B
CC
SA_3
SSA
Precentral
Premotor
Prefrontal
IPS
CS
SA_2
SA_3
SA_1
SA_2
AS
PS
AA_1
VA_1
AA_2
AA_3
VA_2
STS
VA_3
C
RhF
CC
Cing S
A,S
Premotor
S,V (POa)
S
CS
S,V(PG–Opt)
A
A,V
V
S
A,S
(Tpt)
LS
PS
S
V
A
IOS
Prefrontal
S,A,V
(PGa)
V,S
(Ipa)
A,S,V
(TPO)
STS
STS
S
A
V
RhF
OTS
OS
CF
OLF
OT
D
Perirhinal
Temporal polar
RhF
Parahippocampal
Prefrontal
Rtsp
CC
Cingulate
Cing S
CS
Temporal polar
Orbital
RhF
CF
OT

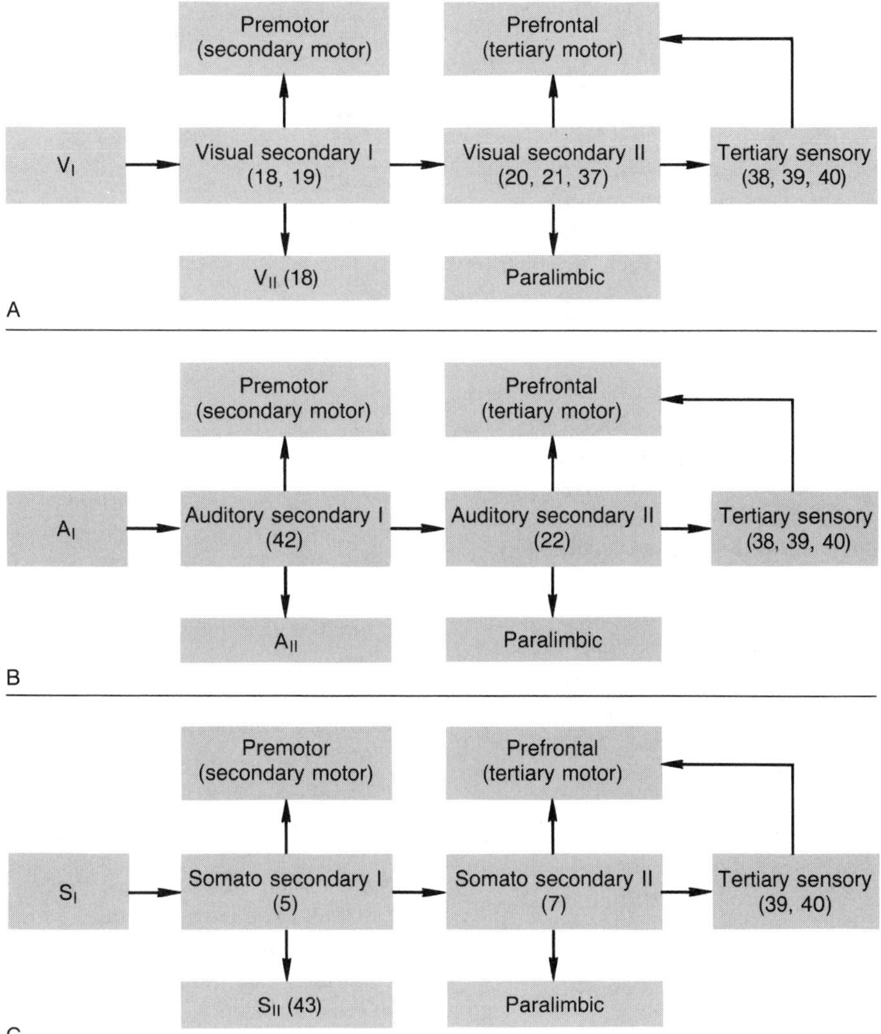

FIGURE 9-7. Schematic diagrams illustrating the principal serial connections between the primary, secondary (I and II), and tertiary zones and the motor zones.

FIGURE 9-6. Diagrams of the lateral, medial, and ventral surfaces of the cerebral hemisphere of the rhesus monkey. *A.* The primary and secondary sensory and motor areas. *B.* The parasensory association areas and frontal lobe association areas. *C.* The locations of the multimodal sensory-convergence areas (dashed circles). *D.* The paralimbic areas. (Abbreviations: A, auditory cortex; AS, arcuate sulcus; CC corpus callosum; CF, calcarine fissure; Cing S, cingulate sulcus; CS, central sulcus; G, gustatory area; IPS, intraparietal sulcus; M, motor cortex; RhF, rhinal fissure; S, somatosensory cortex; V, visual cortex; VS, vestibular cortex.)

9-7). The first area (secondary I in Figure 9-7) receives projections from primary cortex and projects to the premotor cortex as well as to secondary II. This latter region sends its projections to the prefrontal cortex, to the paralimbic system, and to the tertiary cortex. In animals with large brains, such as cats, monkeys, and humans, the association areas are made up of several smaller and distinct cytoarchitectonic regions, each of which has its own connections. We shall return to these regions shortly.

Multimodal Cortex. There are cortical regions, adjacent to the parasensory association areas, that are termed *polymodal* or **multimodal cortex.** It is in these areas that there is a convergence of sensory inputs as illustrated in Figure 9-6*C* (note the dashed circles). For example, in the parietal lobe there is an area in which somatic and visual projections overlap, suggesting that visual and somatic characteristics of sensory events are being combined here. Similarly, in the temporal lobe there is an area of auditory and somatic overlap, and so on. In addition to the multimodal zones in the posterior cortex, there are similar zones in the frontal cortex, which presumably have some function in guiding movements to multimodal stimuli. The multimodal cortex in the parietal and temporal lobes, along with the third-order associational cortex, is probably part of Luria's tertiary cortex.

Paralimbic Cortex. There is a final type of cortex, **paralimbic cortex,** that is not primary, associational, or multimodal cortex, but rather is older cortex and composed of roughly three layers. It can be seen in two places: (1) on the medial surface of the temporal lobe, where it is known as pyriform, entorhinal, and parahippocampal cortex, and (2) just above the corpus callosum (CC) in each hemisphere, where it is referred to as cingulate cortex (Brodmann's areas 23, 24, 25, and 32) (See Fig. 9-6*D*). The paralimbic cortex receives projections from secondary II regions and thus offers an alternative route for sensory information, rather than just from secondary to tertiary cortex.

Cortical Connections: Heirarchical Processing

Our description of the cortical areas suggests a sequential nature to information flow, beginning in the primary zones. There is more to the story, however. First, we can see that as information leaves the primary cortex (V_I, A_I, S_I) it can travel to different places in the association cortex. Thus, we can have several parallel heirarchical routes through the cortex. For example, Mishkin and his colleagues have shown that there is one distinct route beginning in V_I that is concerned with determining the *what* of visual information, and a complementary second route, which also begins in V_I, that is concerned with determining the *where* of visual information (Figure 9-8). The pathway to discern the *what* involves the visual association regions of the temporal lobe, whereas the pathway to determine the *where* involves the parietal association regions. The pattern of connections illustrated in Figure 9-8 is complex but three simple points can be made. (1) There are multiple visual areas that have rich interconnections. (2) The connections flow towards two regions, one to the temporal lobe (area TE) and one to the parietal lobe (area PG). (The terms PG and TE are based upon a different nomenclature and correspond roughly to SA_3 and VA_3, respectively.) (3) The information flow is not one way; there are reciprocal connections that undoubtedly form some sort of feedback loop. As a general rule, the connections that flow away from V_I terminate in layer IV; those that flow toward V_I terminate in other layers, largely II and III. Such a difference in terminal patterns implies that the function of the connections must be different.

Cortical Connections: Parallel Processing

In the traditional view of the thalamic-cortical pathways of the sensory systems, each of the pri-

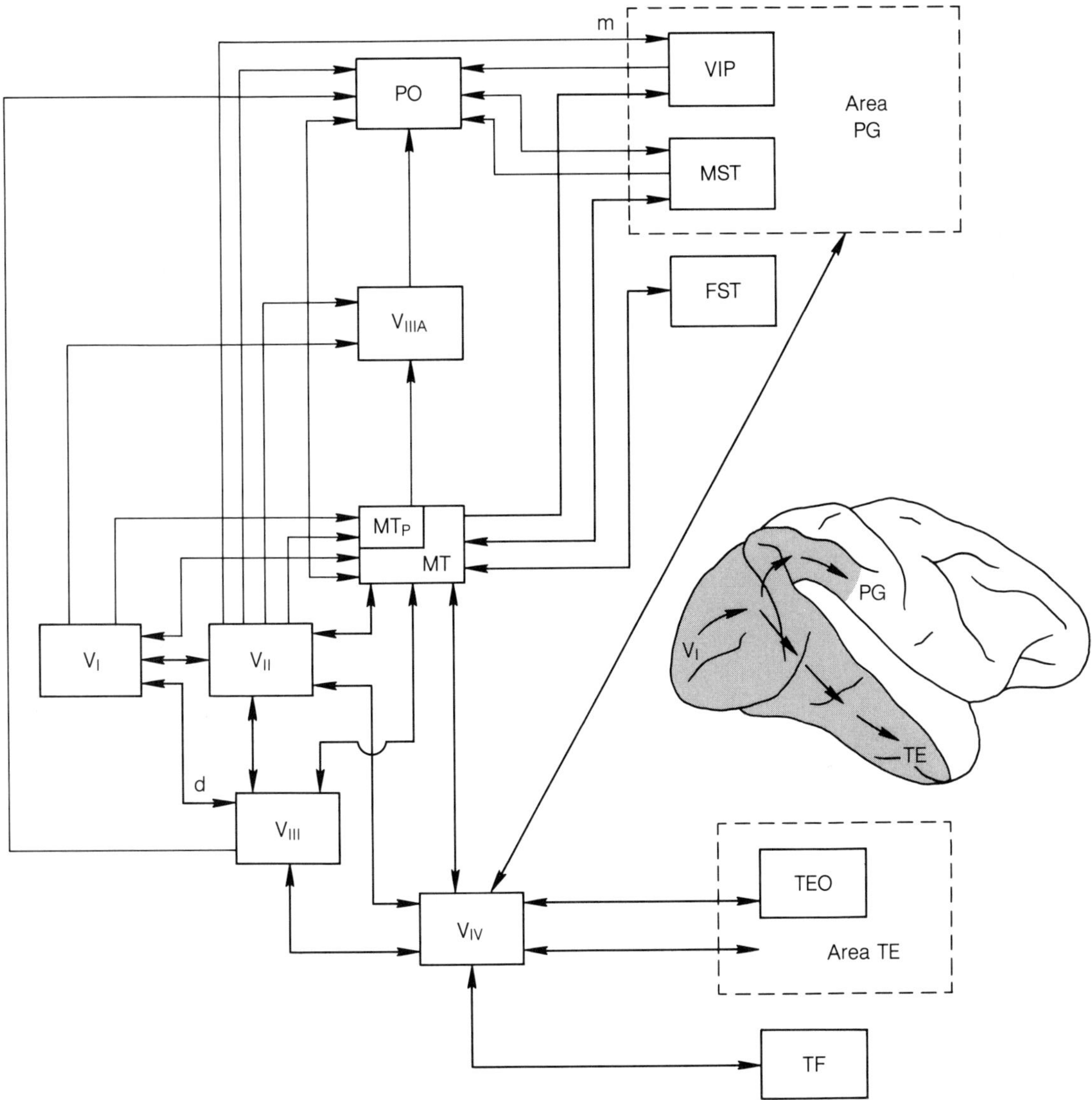

FIGURE 9-8. Summary of visual cortical areas of the rhesus monkey and their known connections. Depending on the point of view, the drawing of the cortex shown on the right can be seen as an oversimplification, or the flowchart to the left as overly complex! The important point is that there are two major pathways of visual information, each of which is made up of smaller, independent pathways. Each of the functional visual areas is denoted by an alphanumeric (V1, V2, V3, V3A, V4) or alphabetic (PO, MT, MTp, VIP, MST, FST, TEO, TF) designation. Areas PG and TE refer to larger neuroanatomic areas. (After Ungerleider and Desimone, 1986.)

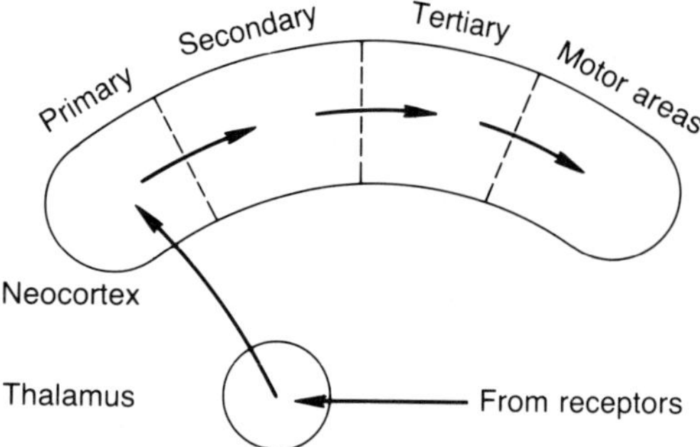

A Traditional hierarchical model

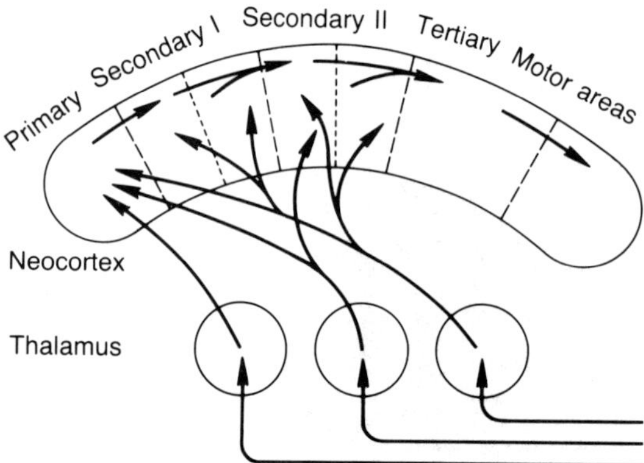

B Hierarchical/parallel model

FIGURE 9-9. Highly schematic diagrams illustrating the traditional hierarchical model and the hierarchical/parallel model of cortical processing. *A*. In the traditional hierarchical model sensory inputs progress serially from the thalamus to the primary, secondary, and tertiary regions, respectively, before going to the motor cortex. *B*. The hierarchical/parallel model recognizes additional cortical regions and multiple thalamic inputs. Sensory input may be processed as in the straight hierarchical model or it may proceed directly to secondary areas via direct thalamic projections that miss the primary zone altogether. Approximately 15 different regions that appear to have visual functions are identified. Most are part of Pandya's secondary visual areas.

mary sensory areas receives input from a single thalamic nucleus, as illustrated in Figure 9-9*A*. The identification of multiple sensory areas has coincided, however, with the discovery that the thalamic-cortical connections are actually made up of parallel pathways with overlapping projections, as illustrated in Figure 9-9*B*.

The organization of these parallel pathways can best be understood by considering several features of thalamic-cortical anatomy, which appear to be common to each of the sensory systems. First, Diamond suggests that the neocortex of a sensory system should be conceptualized as forming a field. A *field* is defined as a constellation of small cortical areas constituting one continuous larger cortical area, functionally unified by the reception of sensory projections in a given modality. Thus, there would be fields for vision, audition, and somatosensation, and possibly also for visceral sensation (taste and olfaction).

Second, there is a *core* area within each field that is characterized by the maximum development of the fourth cortical layer. This is Luria's primary zone. There is one thalamic nucleus that projects principally, if not exclusively, to the core area. In the visual system, the core area would be Brodmann's area 17, and the projections would arise in the lateral geniculate nucleus. For the auditory system, the core area would roughly correspond with area 41, and the pathway would originate in the ventral division of the medial geniculate nucleus. In the somatosensory system the core area is probably area 3b, and the thalamic projections originate in the ventral posterior nucleus.

Third, at least one thalamic nucleus projects to all subdivisions in the field (e.g., the pulvinar in the visual system), and at least one thalamic nucleus projects to more than one subdivision but fewer than all the subdivisions of the field (e.g., the lateral nucleus in the visual system).

The fourth principle is that the laminar (layered) distribution for these thalamic projections differs, with the core projection terminating in cortical layer IV and the other projections terminating in layer I, rather than in layer IV, in regions where the terminations overlap with the core projections. Therefore, although there are indeed parallel pathways to the sensory cortex, the function of the parallel projections is almost certainly different from that of the primary projections to the core area.

OVERVIEW OF CORTICAL ORGANIZATION

Our discussion of cortical organization has emphasized that the neocortex can be considered in terms of its laminar and columnar organization; in a broader view in terms of its relation with subcortical structures, especially the thalamus; and in terms of its cortical-cortical interactions. What is left now is for us to consider the functional implications of this organization. Two general principles can be established. The first is that functions are organized in parallel. The second is that imposed on this parallel organization is an overall hierarchical organization.

Parallel Processing

The fact that the anatomical and electrophysiological evidence clearly indicates a parallel organization of the sensory, and probably the motor, systems in the cortex implies that these parallel areas may have distinct, independent functions. Thus, cortical columns have functions that can be distinguished from one another and so do each of the larger individual representations of the sensory surface. It follows therefore that damage to or disorganization in individual columns or in individual sensory representations could produce a specific behavioral effect. In view of the size and mosaic pattern of the columns, it is improbable that direct cortical damage could selectively destroy one class of columns (although some selective neurotoxin could, theoretically, do it), but direct cortical damage certainly could interfere with the functioning of a single sensory representation within a larger sensory field. The neurological literature confirms this expectation, providing numerous examples of highly specific functional deficits arising from restricted cortical lesions. For example, there are numerous case reports of human patients suffering limited combinations of losses of vibratory, pain, tactile pattern, or joint-position sense following different parietal lobe lesions, and analogous specific symptoms have been reported frequently for visual and auditory modes as well. (We must add a cautionary note that one should be wary of claims of specific deficits consequent to cerebral injury since, in our experience, deficits that appear remarkably specific in the clinic become far less so under careful, systematic examinations in the laboratory!)

Hierarchical Processing

The pattern of cortical-cortical projections both within the sensory fields and beyond implies that a dominant feature of cortical processing must be hierarchical, or serial. Although it is recognized that each of the sensory representations provides a unique contribution to the overall perception, it is certainly the case that the core area of each sensory field is more critical to sensory experience than are any of the other areas. Hence, even though damage to individual sensory representations within the secondary regions might produce specific symptoms, damage within the core area produces a more severe and generalized effect on perception. Furthermore, interruption of pathways from one zone to another (primary to secondary I, secondary I to secondary II, secondary II to tertiary, etc.) produces behavioral symptoms, known as **disconnection syndrome,** that persist in spite of the continuing activity of the individual sensory areas. For example, disconnection of the sensory field from the tertiary cortex will produce what appears to be a loss of "memory" or of "perception," as the individual may be unable to name an object even though the visual system has accurately represented the object in the neocortex. If this sensory representation is not passed on to the appropriate effectors, it will appear as though the sensory representation itself was absent. (We shall proceed with a detailed discussion of this phenomenon in Chapter 20.)

The existence of both serial and parallel systems in the cortex has several implications for cortical processing. First, perception appears to be a product of the nearly simultaneous activation of a number of topographic sensory representations, unified by serial cortical connections. For example, depression of the skin activates neurons in each of the four somatosensory representations at about the same time. We perceive a spatially unified perception of this sensory event, so it is therefore likely that the serial organization within the sensory field has a major role in providing a single experience. Second, differences in the perception of a given stimulus from one person to the next may result from variations in the relative size of each of the parallel sensory representations within a sensory field. Thus, our six blind men from Hindustan (from Chapter 8) could each have examined the same region of the elephant, but owing to individual differences in somatosensory representations, they might still have arrived at different impressions of the animal. Or, put another way, beauty really is in the eye (or sensory field!) of the beholder. Similarly, individual differences in motor skills may be at least partly due to individual differences in the cortical organization of motor circuitry. Third, Merzenich and Kaas propose that differences in the perception of a given stimulus by the same person at different times may be the result of variations in the contributions of individual topographic representations under different conditions of expentancy, set, or other factors. This is a possibility that could probably be extended to include the motor system as well. These variations probably result from some plasticity in the nature of the serial processing as the sensory representation in the cortex proceeds to the paralimbic regions. Recall, for example, that the size of cortical representations can be affected by environmental stimulation, so that changes in perceptions over time may result from real changes in the size and nature of cortical representations.

GENERALIZING ABOUT CORTICAL ORGANIZATION

In Chapter 5 we emphasized the similarities among the general cortical organizations in different mammalian species, but we would be remiss if we left the reader with the belief that there are not any significant differences across different mammalian species. This issue is especially germane here because most of the work that has led to general principles of cortical organization has come from studies of nonhuman primates. It is reasonable to ask if there are species differences and whether our principles can be generalized across mammals. Overall, we can say that all of the principles we have discussed can be validly generalized to all mammals. There are, however, two differences.

Multiple Areas Are Species Variable

We indicated in Chapter 5 that animals with large brains tend to have more areas than animals with smaller brains. According to Kaas, when one looks across all mammals studied to date, it appears that just a few basic areas are found in most or all mammals. These include primary and secondary visual and somatosensory fields (that is, V_I, V_{II}, S_I, S_{II}), a motor field (M_I), a primary auditory (A_I) field, probably taste cortex, prefrontal cortex (defined as the area connected to the dorsal medial nucleus of the thalamus), a small region of temporal cortex that is probably visual, and the paralimbic cortex. We have seen, however, that the rhesus monkey brain has far more areas than this (Figure 9-8) and so do most other mammals, such as cats. The difficulty is that the existing mammalian lines diverged at a time when brain development probably only included the regions common to all mammals. Therefore, different mammals independently developed additional areas, presumably because of different pressures in their environments. Only cats and monkeys have been studied in enough detail to allow a proper comparison between species, but in these species it is clear that both lines have developed additional somatosensory, visual, and auditory areas. Both cats and monkeys have at least 10 visual areas and at least 5 or more auditory and somatosensory areas. The difficulty for comparative neurology is that all of these areas evolved independently, and it is therefore impossible to directly equate them. In other words, they are not homologous. As a general statement it appears that the major development in cortical evolution has been the increase in the number of unimodal sensory-association areas. Thus, mammals with more advanced brains appear to have more areas than animals with simpler brains. Clearly, if we wish to reach valid conclusions about the details of the organization of human sensory-association areas we will need to use species that are more closely related to us than rats and cats. Indeed, it is even difficult to make valid generalizations about the organization of Old World and New World monkeys. The two most studied species, the rhesus and owl monkeys, respectively, appear to have significant differences in the details of their sensory-cortical organization. In contrast, however, if we are interested in making generalizations about the basic principles of cortical function outlined in this chapter, rats, cats, and other species are quite satisfactory.

Multiple Connections Are Species Variable

We have seen the complexity of the connections of cortical areas (Figure 9-8). Furthermore, we have seen that species vary in their number of secondary sensory regions and in the details of these regions. It is therefore not surprising to find that species can differ considerably in their cortical connections. The lateral geniculate nucleus projects only to area 17 in the monkey and rat but to both areas 17 and 18 in the cat. Indeed, even relatively closely related species such as the rhesus and owl monkeys differ in the connections found between their sensory areas. This suggests that although the details may be important for understanding the organization of any given species cortex, it is the general principles that we must try to extract and attend to if we are to understand the riddle of our own brain.

REFERENCES

Diamond, I. T. The subdivisions of neocortex: A proposal to revise the traditional view of sensory, motor, and association areas. *Progress in Psychobiology and Physiological Psychology* 8:1–43, 1979.

Diamond, I. T. The functional significance of architectonic subdivisions of the cortex: Lashley's criticism of the traditional view. In J. Orback, ed. *Neuropsychology after Lashley*. Hillsdale, NJ: Lawrence Erlbaum Associates, 1982.

Evarts, E. V. Motor cortex output in primates. In E. G. Jones and A. Peters, eds. *Cerebral Cortex,* vol. 5. New York: Plenum Press, 1986.

Graybiel, A. M., and D. M. Berson. On the relation between transthalamic and transcortical pathways in the visual system. In F. O. Schmitt, F. G. Worden, G. Adelman, and S. G. Dennis, eds. *The Organization of the Cerebral Cortex.* Cambridge, MA: M.I.T. Press, 1981.

Jones, E. G. Anatomy of cerebral cortex: Columnar input-output organization. In F. O. Schmitt, F. G. Worden, G. Adelman, and S. G. Dennis, eds. *The Organization of the Cerebral Cortex.* Cambridge, MA: M.I.T. Press, 1981.

Kaas, J. H. The organization of neocortex in mammals: Implications for theories of brain function. *Annual Review of Psychology* 38:129–151, 1987.

Kaas, J. H., R. J. Nelson, M. Sur, C. -L. Lin, and M. M. Merzenich. Multiple representations of the body within the primary somatosensory cortex of primates. *Science* 204:521–523, 1979.

Merzenich, M. M. and J. H. Kaas. Principles of organization of sensory-perceptual systems in mammals. *Progress in Psychobiology and Physiological Psychology* 9:1–42, 1980.

Merzenich, M. M. and J. H. Kaas. Reorganization of mammalian somatosensory cortex following peripheral nerve injury. *Trends in Neurosciences* 5:434–436, 1982.

Mishkin, M., B. Malamut and J. Bachevalier. Memories and habits: Two neural systems. In G. Lynch, J. L. McGaugh, N. M. Weinberger, eds. *Neurobiology of Learning and Memory*. New York: Guilford Press, 1984.

Pandya, D. N., and B. Seltzer. Association areas of the cerebral cortex. *Trends in Neurosciences* 5:386–390, 1982.

Penfield, W., and E. Boldrey. Somatic and motor sensory representation in the cerebral cortex of man as studied by electrical stimulation. *Brain* 60:389–443, 1937.

Shepherd, G. M. *The Synaptic Organization of the Brain,* 2nd ed. New York: Oxford University Press, 1979.

Szentagothai, J. Architecture of the cerebral cortex. In H. H. Jasper, A. A. Ward, and A. Pope, eds. *Basic Mechanisms of the Epilepsies*. Boston: Little, Brown, 1969.

Ungerleider, L. G., and R. Desimone. Cortical connections of visual area MT in the macaque. *Journal of Comparative Neurology* 248:190–222, 1986.

Wise, S. P., and E. V. Evarts. The role of the cerebral cortex in movement. *Trends in Neurosciences* 4:297–300, 1981.

Woolsey, C. N. Organization of somatic sensory and motor areas of the cerebral cortex. In H. F. Harlow and C. N. Woolsey, eds. *Biological and Biochemical Bases of Behavior*. Madison: University of Wisconsin Press, 1958.

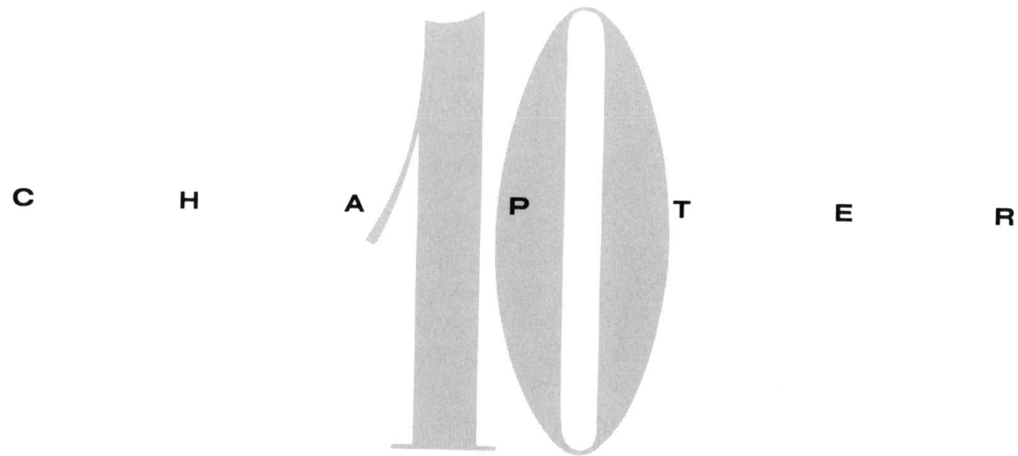

CHAPTER 10

ORGANIZATION OF THE SENSORY SYSTEMS

The human sensory systems present some of the most obvious evidence of brain function to the average person. We are aware of sensations (e.g., sight, hearing, and touch) all our waking hours, and most people accept that the brain is responsible for these sensations. To recognize the role of the brain is one matter, to understand how nerves can turn energy (such as light waves) into meaningful sensations, which in turn lead to thoughts, is another. The operation of the sensory systems is complex, and in spite of intense research in neuropsychology over the past three decades, it is still largely unexplained. In this chapter we shall present the general workings of the five sensory systems (vision, audition, touch, taste, and olfaction), identifying principles that allow us to understand their basic operation and the operation of other sensory systems (vestibular, pain, autonomic). We do not propose to present a detailed description of the physiological mechanisms of sensory processing, as this is beyond the scope of our concern. (The interested reader is directed to Uttal or Masteron or to other standard texts for detailed accounts of each of the sensory systems.) Since naturally occurring lesions seldom respect the boundaries of individual components of the sensory systems, we are forced to rely principally on anatomical, physiological, and functional evidence from nonhuman species, especially cats and monkeys, although data from humans are considered whenever available.

GENERAL PRINCIPLES OF THE SENSORY SYSTEMS

Each of the sensory systems can be understood in terms of a number of principles, some of which will be described here before we discuss specific sensory systems.

Receptors

In each sensory system there are specialized cells called *receptors*. The function of these receptors is to transduce, or convert, sensory energy (e.g., light waves) into neural activity in the form of either graded potentials or action potentials. The receptors in each sensory system are different, and so the sensory energy they can detect is different. For vision, light energy is converted into chemical energy in the receptors of the retina, and this chemical energy is in turn converted into neural activity. In the auditory system, sound waves are converted into mechanical energy in the form of the movement of the little bones in the ear and the movement of the basilar membrane, which contains the actual hair receptors. It is only after the receptor hair cells are activated that a neural discharge occurs. In the somatosensory system, mechanical energy in the form of touch, pressure, vibration, and so on activates mechanoreceptors, which in turn generate neural activity. For taste and olfaction, various molecules carried by the air or contained in food fit themselves into receptors of various shapes to activate relevant neural activity. For pain sensation, a very curious transduction step is thought to occur between the damaged tissue, the cause of the pain, and neural activation. It is thought that tissue damage releases a chemical that is called *neurokinin*. This in turn is thought to act like a neurotransmitter to activate pain fibers. The neurokinin explanation does have the virtue of accounting for why tissue damage can result in pain sensations that last for hours or days.

Receptive Fields

Not only do receptors act as filters, letting only certain forms of energy activate them, they also have what are called **receptive fields.** For some sensory systems the receptive field is fairly straightforward. For example, for vision, if the eyes are fixated, all the visual world that can be seen forms the receptive field for vision. If one eye is closed, the remaining world that can be seen by the open eye forms the receptive field for that eye. Within that eye is a cup-shaped retina, which contains thousands of receptor cells. Because of the shape of the retina, each cell points in a particular direction, like a telescope pointing at a particular part of the sky, and the little part of the world that each receptor receives light from forms its receptive field. The part of the skin on which a skin receptor is located forms its receptive field and generally consists of a few square millimeters of tissue. However, the receptive field for all tactile reception will consist of the entire body surface. The function of receptive fields is of course to allow stimuli to be located in space or on the body surface. Some systems such as olfaction are not very good at location: we do have two nostrils but there is some question about how sensitive they are to the direction of odors. On the other hand, in the auditory system both ears hear most sounds, so that a sound is pinpointed not so much by differences in each ear's detection but by differences in loudness; that is, the ear closest to the sound hears it as loudest. For sensations of taste, there are interesting topographic organizations for the receptors sensitive to different stimuli. Receptors for sweet substances are mainly on the tip of the tongue, receptors for bitter substances are mainly on the back of the tongue, and receptors for saltiness and sourness are along the tongue's margins. Hence, there are different receptive fields for tastes, but the location of the fields may have more to do with deciding questions of ingestion than with pinpointing the food per se. The tip of the tongue is a good place for sweet receptors, because sweet foods are good to eat and can be swept into the mouth. Bitter foods, however, are usually poisonous and so when detected on the back of the tongue they can be coughed out.

Localization and Detection

An important question each sensory system must answer is: Where is it?, that is, where is the stimulus located? The receptive fields of individual receptors overlap, which helps to solve the problems of localizing a stimulus and identifying it. If one receptor is more activated by a stimulus than another, then the object in question must be located more precisely in the receptive field of that receptor. For vision, a light source will shine across the retina, variously activating the different receptors, thus locating the light source. Movement of the light could be tracked by the change in luminance on the receptors. We must note, however, that in many sensory systems there are cells specialized for detecting moving objects; for example, many hair receptors on the body are only activated if the stimulus is moving in a particular direction.

Sensory systems must also answer questions such as: Is it there? and, What is it? Detection of a stimulus is often determined by receptor density and overlap. Tactile receptors on the fingers are numerous as compared with those on the back; the fingers can therefore discriminate remarkably well, unlike the back. In the visual system the organization of receptors has two quite different arrangements to facilitate detection. In the fovea (a small area of the retina that provides acute vision) the receptors (called cones) are small and densely packed to make fine discriminations in bright light. In the periphery of the retina the receptors (called rods) are larger and more scattered, but large numbers of rods give their input to only a few neurons. The discrimination ability of rods is not good, but their ability to detect light (e.g., a lighted match at the distance of 2 miles on a dark night) is quite remarkable.

Neural Relays

Each sensory system requires three to four neurons, connected in sequence, in order to get information from the receptor cells to the cortex (e.g., the visual and somatosensory systems have three, and the auditory system has four). Two important events can occur at the synapses between the neurons in the relays. First, some kind of motor response can be produced. For example, axons from pain receptors first synapse in the spinal cord, where they can produce a withdrawal reflex. They next synapse in the brainstem, where they can produce whole limb or body movements, presumably withdrawal from the painful stimulus. Finally, they synapse in the thalamus, where, in conjunction with their connections in the cortex, they can produce anticipation and hence avoidance of the stimulus. The second thing that can happen at a synapse is that the code carrying the message can be modified in a variety of ways: for example, descending impulses from the cortex can block or amplify it, or the code can simply be made more elaborate or more precise. When one considers the convergence of the sensory systems with each relay and their subsequent divergence when they reach the cortex, it becomes apparent that there must be a change in the code from level to level. This is illustrated in Figure 10-1 for the visual system. Lashley calculated that there are about 9 million rods and cones, 3.5 million bipolar cells, 0.2 million ganglion cells, 0.03 million lateral geniculate cells, and 0.6 million area-17 cells at the different levels in the rat's visual system. (These types of cells are discussed in detail in the following section labeled The Visual System.) It seems quite obvious that there is not a straight-through, point-to-point correspondence between one relay and the next, but rather a recoding of activity in successive relays.

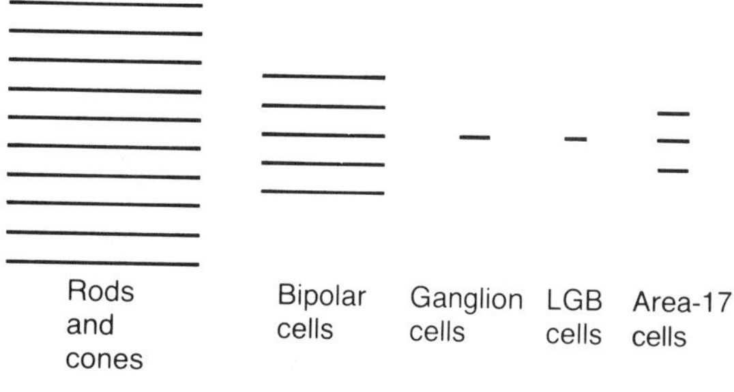

FIGURE 10-1. Diagrammatic representation of the numbers of cells at each level of the visual system. Both the length and the numbers of lines represent relative cell numbers.

Information Transmission

In some of the sensory systems it takes one or more cells to transduce the stimulus energy into neural energy (e.g., for taste, one taste receptor; for vision, a light-sensitive cell and then a bipolar cell), but once transduced, all sensory information from all sensory systems is coded by action potentials. The sensory information is conducted into the brain by bundles of axons, called *nerves* until they enter the brain or spinal cord and *tracts* thereafter, and every nerve carries the same kind of signal. This raises some interesting questions. How do action potentials code the differences in sensations? How do action potentials code the features of particular sensations? The answers to parts of these questions seem easy and the answers to other parts are very difficult. The presence of a stimulus can be coded by an increase or decrease in the discharge rate of a neuron, and the amount of change can code the intensity. Qualitative visual changes, such as a change from red to green, can be coded by activity in different neurons or even by different levels of discharge in the same neuron (i.e., more activity = redder, less activity = greener). What is less clear, however, is how we perceive such sensations as touch, sound, and smell as being different from one another. One explanation is that the neural areas that process these sensations in the cortex are distinct. Another explanation is that we learn through experience to distinguish them. A third explanation is that each sensory system has a preferred link with certain kinds of movements, which ensures that they remain distinct at all levels of neural organization. Of course, the problem of distinguishing between types of sensation requires a great deal more study, but it should be noted that such distinctions are not always clear. There are people who can hear in color or identify smells by the sounds that they make. This ability is called **synesthesia,** or mixed senses. Of course, everyone who has shivered during certain notes of a piece of music (or at the noise that chalk or fingernails can make on a blackboard) has "felt" sound.

Sensory Subsystems

There are multiple pathways in each sensory system, from the sensory receptor to the brain, that form subsystems with specialized functions. We are used to thinking of the visual system as a single entity, but if we refer to the schematic illustration Figure 10-2, we see that the visual system is really made up of a number of subsystems. There is a pathway to the superoptic nucleus (1) of the hypothalamus that controls daily rhythms of such behaviors as feeding and sleeping; a pathway to the pretectum (2) in the midbrain that controls pupillary responses to light; a pathway to the superior colliculus (3) in the midbrain that controls head orienting to objects; a pathway to the pineal body (4) that controls long-term circadian rhythms; a pathway to the accessory optic nucleus (5) that moves the eyes to compensate for head movements; a pathway to the visual cortex (6) that controls pattern perception, depth perception, color vision, and tracking of moving objects; and a pathway to the frontal cortex (7) that controls voluntary eye movements. The pathways to many of these "visual centers" are often more indirect than the figure indicates, and they may involve other brain centers as well. Furthermore, just as there are many visual systems projecting into different brain regions, there are multiple subsystems projecting to the visual cortex. Thus, there are a number of parallel visual systems going through the visual cortex, each of which may have a rather specialized output. For example, the systems for pattern perception, color vision, depth perception, and visual tracking may be as independent from one another as are the systems that code hearing or those that code taste. The fact that they are in close anatomical proximity may not mean that they are functionally identical or interchangeable.

Multiple Representation

The neocortex represents the sensory field not once but a number of times (Figure 10-3). For example, the entire retina (or visual field) is represented

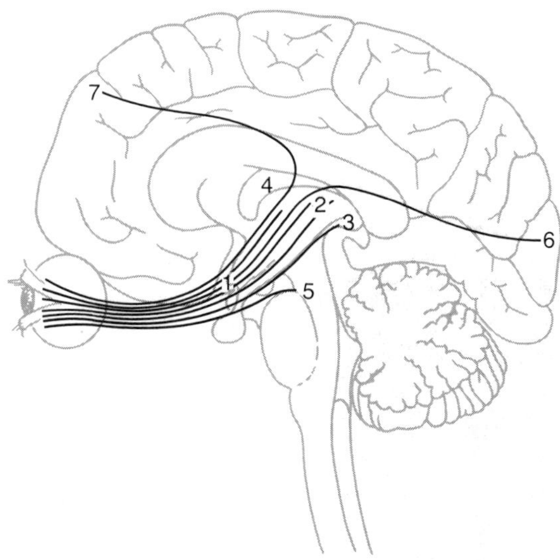

Visual System	Postulated Function
1. Superoptic nucleus	Controls daily rhythms (sleep, feeding, etc.) in response to day-night cycles.
2. Pretectum	Produces changes in pupil size in response to light-intensity changes.
3. Superior colliculus	Head orienting, particularly to objects in peripheral visual fields.
4. Pineal body	Long-term circadian rhythms.
5. Accessory optic nucleus	Moves eyes to compensate for head movements.
6. Visual cortex	Pattern perception, depth perception, color vision, tracking moving objects.
7. Frontal eye fields	Voluntary eye movements.

FIGURE 10-2. Schematic representation of visual subsystems. The numbers stand for brain structures; the lines for the individual visual pathways. Each pathway and each number represents a particular subsystem as detailed in the text.

several times in the visual cortex. Each sensory system has a primary area, which has one representation, and two secondary areas, each of which also has several representations. The same principle of multiple representation applies in each sensory system, but as yet the functional differences in each of the representations are not fully understood. Nevertheless, it is likely that each representation is devoted to coding one specific aspect of a sensory modality.

THE VISUAL SYSTEM

Visual Receptors

A schematic illustration of the eye and its visual receptor surface, the retina, is presented in Figure 10-4. When light enters the eye, it is bent slightly by the cornea and then more profoundly by the lens so that images are focused on the receptors at the back of the eye. An unusual feature of the eye is

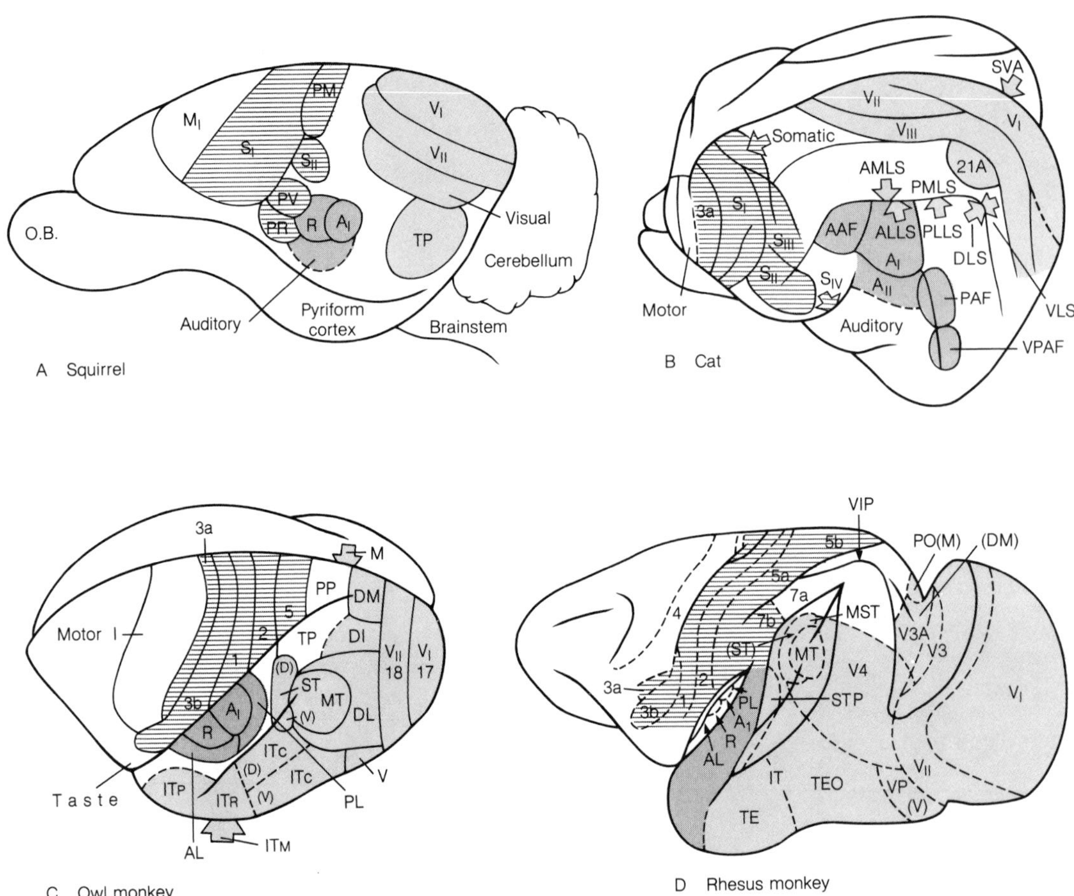

FIGURE 10-3. Subdivisions of sensory cortex in several extensively studied mammals. *A*. Squirrel. There are five somatic regions, two to three auditory regions, and two to four visual regions. *B*. Cat. Twelve visual areas have been defined, four somatic areas, and five auditory areas. *C*. Owl monkey. To date, 14 visual areas have been demonstrated, 4 auditory areas, and 5 somatic areas. *D*. Rhesus monkey. Twelve visual areas, four auditory areas, and eight somatic areas have been defined. The major posterior gyri of the rhesus monkey have been schematically opened to expose the tissue within. Labels have been given to different cortical areas by various authors and are confusing at best. Labels may refer to primary motor (M_I), primary and secondary somatosensory (S_I, S_{II}), or primary and secondary visual (V_I, V_{II}) in all species. Other fields are named either by location, as in IT (inferior temporal) or MT (medial temporal), function and location, as in AAF (anterior auditory field), or related to a traditional architectonic field of Brodmann's, as in 3, 5, 21, etc. For more details and references see Kaas (1987). (After Kaas, 1987.)

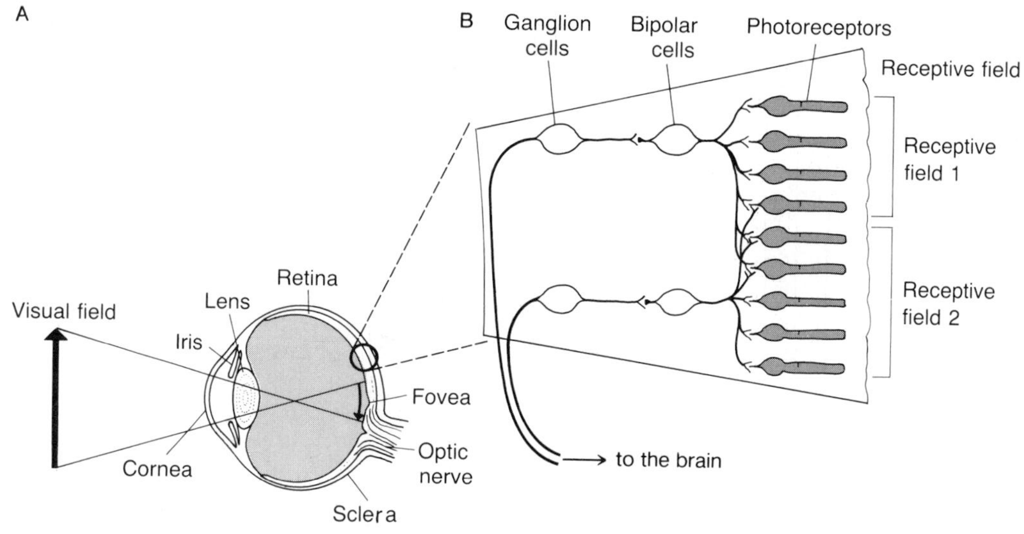

FIGURE 10-4. *A*. Anatomy of the eye. *B*. Anatomy of the retina. (After Bailey, 1981.)

that light must travel through the outer layers of the retina in order to strike the photoreceptive cells that lie on its inner surface. The chemical reactions that light induces in the receptors actually occur at the distal end of the receptor. The barrier provided by the retinal cells has little effect on our visual acuity for two reasons. First, the cells are relatively transparent and the photoreceptors are extremely sensitive; they can be excited by the absorption of a single photon of light. Second, many of the fibers forming the optic nerve skirt the central portion, or fovea, of the retina to facilitate light access to the receptors. This accounts for why the fovea is seen as a depression on the retinal surface.

The human retina contains two types of photoreceptive cells, rods and cones, both of which function to transduce light energy into action potentials. *Rods,* sensitive to dim light, are utilized mainly for night vision. *Cones* are better able to transduce bright light and are used for daytime vision and color vision. There are three types of cones, maximally responsive to wavelengths producing hues of red, blue, or yellow, respectively. Rods and cones differ in their distribution across the retina; cones are packed together densely in the foveal region and rods are more sparsely distributed in the periphery of the retina. The significance of this distribution can be appreciated at night when, to see something, it is best to look slightly away from it.

The photoreceptive cells are connected to very simple cells called *bipolar cells,* in which the receptor cells induce graded potentials. The bipolar cells in turn induce action potentials in ganglion cells. As is illustrated in Figure 10-4, it is the *ganglion cells* that actually send axons into the brain.

Visual Pathways

The axons of ganglion cells leave the retina to form the optic nerve. Just before entering the brain the optic nerves partly cross, forming the **optic chiasm** (from the Greek, meaning a cross-shaped crossing). At this point about half of the fibers

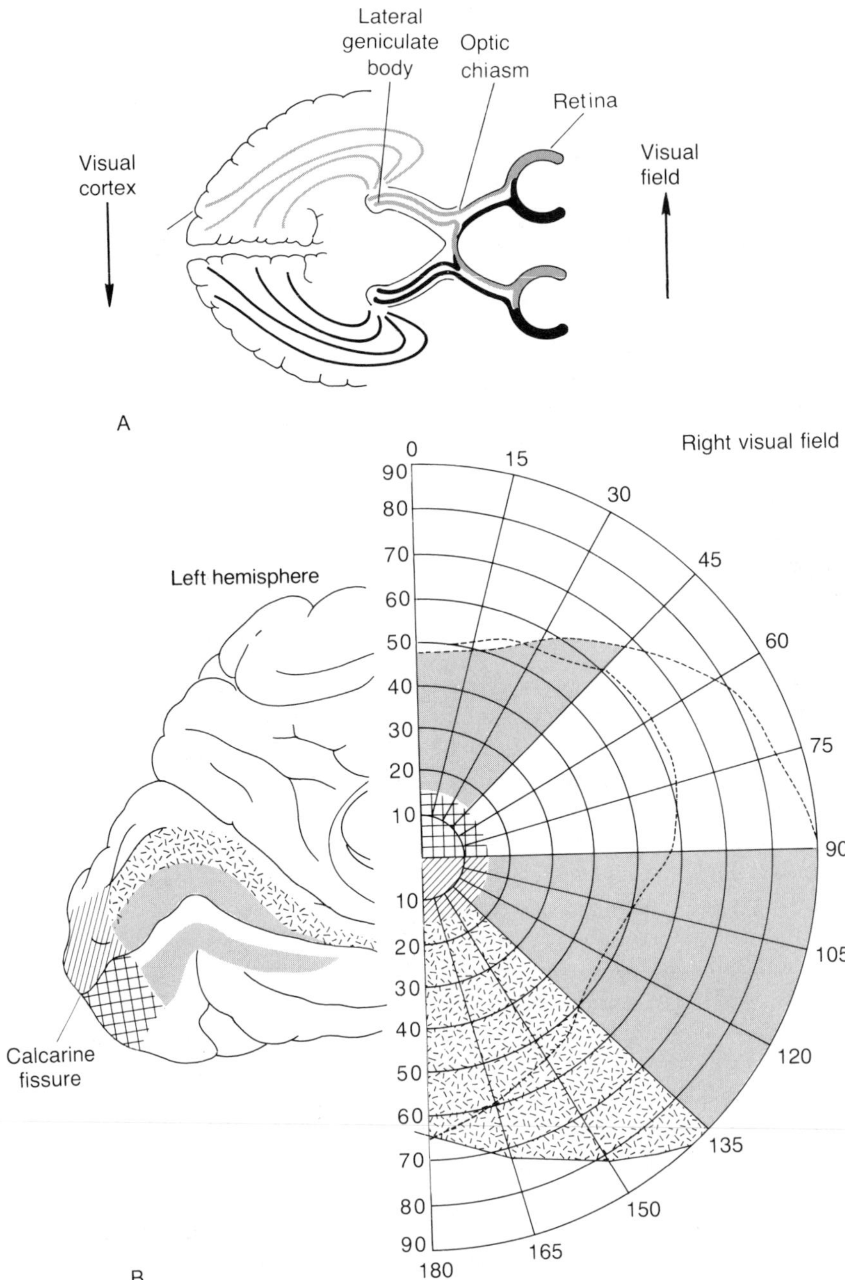

FIGURE 10-5. *A*. Projection of the visual system. Note that the visual fields are projected to the contralateral visual cortex. *B*. Projection of the right visual field on the left hemisphere (medial view). Note the relation between the topography of the visual field and the topography of the cortex. (After Poggio, 1968.)

from each eye cross, as is illustrated in Figure 10-5*A*, in such a way that each visual half-field will be represented in the opposite hemisphere of the brain. Having entered the brain, the ganglion cells divide, forming a number of separate pathways. The largest of these is the **geniculostriate system:** the projection that goes to the lateral geniculate nucleus or body (LGB) of the thalamus and then to the visual cortex. The ganglion cells of the geniculostriate system synapse in the LGB. The LGB has six well-defined layers: layers 2, 3, and 5 receive fibers from the ipsilateral eye and layers 1, 4, and 6 receive fibers from the contralateral eye. The topographic relation of the visual field is also maintained in the LGB, with the central portion representing the central visual field and the peripheral portions representing the peripheral visual field. The LGB cells project to the visual cortex, where they are distributed in such a way that the visual field is again topographically represented. This representation is illustrated in Figure 10-5*B*. The representation is quite easy to remember if it is noted that everything is upside down and backward. The central part of the visual field is represented at the back of the brain and the peripheral part is represented toward the middle of the brain. The upper part of the visual field is represented below the calcarine fissure and the lower part of the visual world is represented above the calcarine fissure. Of course, we have already noted that the left visual field is represented in the right hemisphere and the right visual field is represented in the left hemisphere. Other visual pathways go to the superior colliculus, accessory optic nucleus, pretectum, and superoptic nucleus, as is shown in Figure 10-6. Note also that in Figure 10-6 the projections to the superior colliculus can reach the cortex through relays in the lateral posterior-pulvinar complex of the thalamus.

The six layers of the LGB can be subdivided into two groups on the basis of cell size and the kind of information they signal (see Figure 10-7). Layers 5 and 6, which are known as the *magnocellular layer,* are large cells and code information about luminance contrast. Layers 1–4, which are known as the *parvocellular layer,* are small cells that code information about color. The inputs to these two zones are from distinctly different populations of ganglion cells and the outputs to the visual cortex are segregated as well. Thus, there is a zone in layer IV of the cortex that receives input only from the parvocellular layer, one that receives input from the magnocellular layer, and one that receives input from both. This segregation continues in V_{II} (area 18) as well. It is believed that these distinct pathways form the basis of three distinct cortical-visual systems, specialized for shape, motion and depth (i.e., space), and color, respectively. Thus, it appears that there are at least three independent visual processing systems that are differentiated right from the retina through to the cortex. Livingston and Hubel have suggested that there may be species differences in the elaboration of these different systems, with the shape system being the most elaborated in primates.

Visual Cortex

In addition to their main projections to area 17 of the cortex the thalamocortical pathways terminate in the cortex to produce several independent representations of the retina. The precise number of these retinal representations is not known for humans, but in monkeys there may be as many as 10 independently organized areas, as illustrated in Figure 9-8. The entire visual field is systematically represented in each of these independently organized areas (the details of this representation in the secondary cortex are still uncertain). These visual representations are not mere copies of one another, because the size of each field is different (the core area being the largest), and there are significant differences in organization. For example, careful examination of the regional representation of the retina also shows marked differences between the regions. In area DM of the owl and rhesus monkey (see Figure 10-3*C* and *D*), it is the central retina that is principally represented, with few cells re-

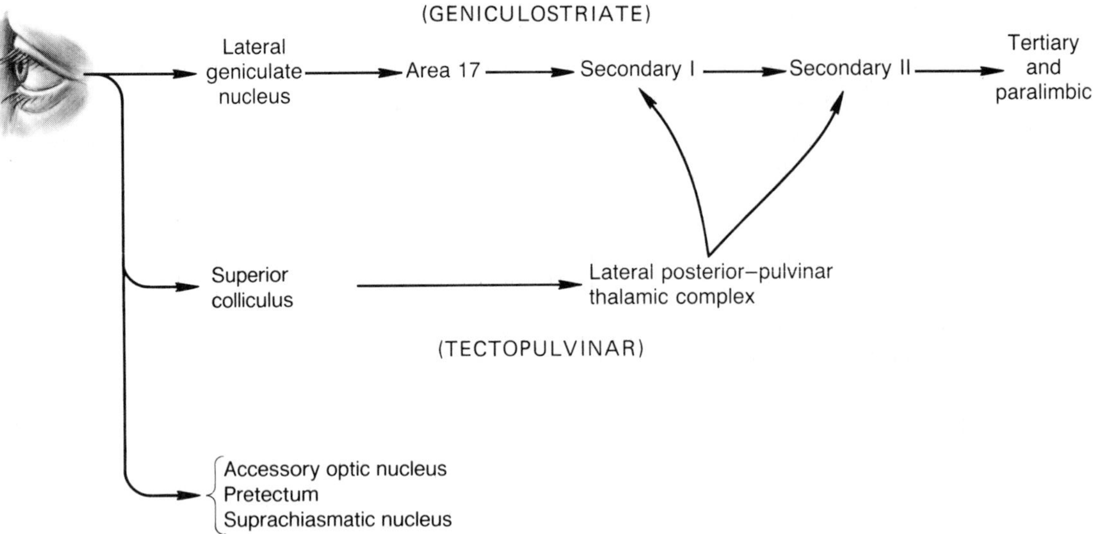

FIGURE 10-6. The connections of the visual system. One subsystem, the geniculostriate system, is specialized for pattern analysis; the other, the tectopulvinar system, is specialized for the detection of and orientation to visual stimuli.

sponding to visual stimuli at the periphery. In contrast, there are many cells in both area 17 and in area V_{II} that respond to stimuli in the periphery and relatively fewer cells that respond to stimuli in the center of the visual field. Similarly, cells in area 17 are unresponsive to color, whereas cells in some temporal areas (e.g., V_4) are maximally excited by certain hues.

Properties of Cells in Visual Areas

By the use of microelectrodes neurophysiologists have recorded the activity of cells in anesthetized cats and monkeys while visual stimuli are presented on a screen placed in the animals' visual field. As we have noted, cells at each level of the visual system are responsive to a specific region of the visual field, known as the receptive field. Cells at each level of the visual system differ in two ways, however. First, the receptive fields tend to be larger at each succeeding level closer to the secondary cortex. Second, cells in different levels of the visual system respond to different properties of visual stimulation. The nature of the visual input that maximally excites cells at each level has been extensively investigated, but there is still disagreement over exactly what the cells are responding to. (For a discussion of this controversy see Held et al.) Nevertheless, some characteristics of the cells have been agreed on.

Generally, the farther along a cell is in the visual system, the more complex the visual stimulus must be to excite it. For example, cells in the retina are most responsive to spots of light falling in the center of their receptive fields. In some retinal cells this light rapidly increases the firing rate of the cell, and in others it inhibits all firing of the cell. In contrast, cells in area 17 are more responsive to bars of light of a particular orientation. Some cells are most responsive to bars of light oriented at 90° from the horizontal, whereas others are most responsive to bars oriented at other angles. Cells in areas 18 and 19 require more complex stimuli, being most responsive to bars of light oriented at a particular angle and moving in a particular direction. Still more complex cells are maximally responsive to more complicated patterns of light, such as corners; in the inferotemporal cortex, cells may require a very specific shape for maximum response (e.g., a hand or face), yet they can tolerate substantial changes in the size of the stimulus, a characteristic that may be a physiological basis for **object constancy.**

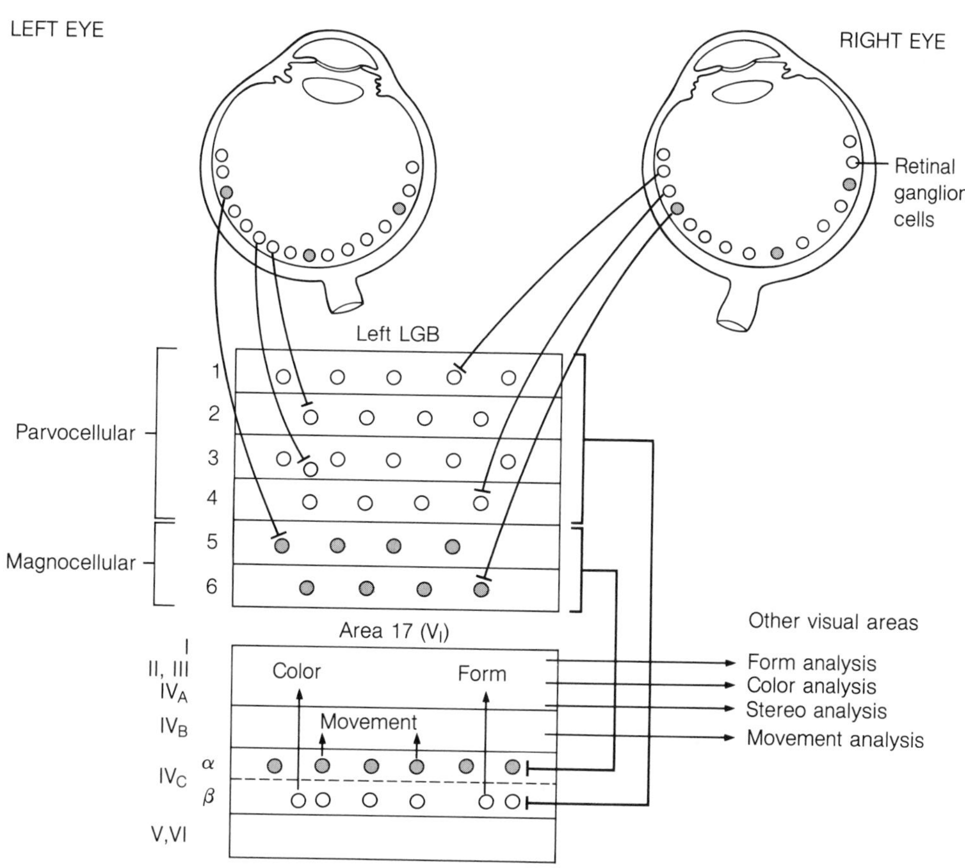

FIGURE 10-7. A highly schematic figure showing that the primate visual system consists of several independent subdivisions that differ in their sensitivity for movement, color, depth (stereopsis), and shape. At the level of the retina there are two types of retinal ganglion cells that project either to the parvocellular or magnocellular divisions of the lateral geniculate body (LGB). (Note that the projections of the two eyes are to different layers of the LGB.) The LGB neurons project to different parts of layer IV of area 17 and, in turn, these two layers have different connections in the cortical columns, leading to a segregation of color, form, and movement systems. These systems project to other cortical visual areas and add another function, namely the ability to detect depth.

THE AUDITORY SYSTEM

Auditory Receptors

To understand how the ear transduces sound waves into action potentials we must take a look at the anatomy of the ear, as illustrated in Figure 10-8. When sound waves strike the eardrum it vibrates. The vibrations are transmitted via three small bones (ossicles) to the fluid of the inner ear. One of the ossicles (the stirrup) acts on the fluid like a tiny piston, driving the fluid back and forth

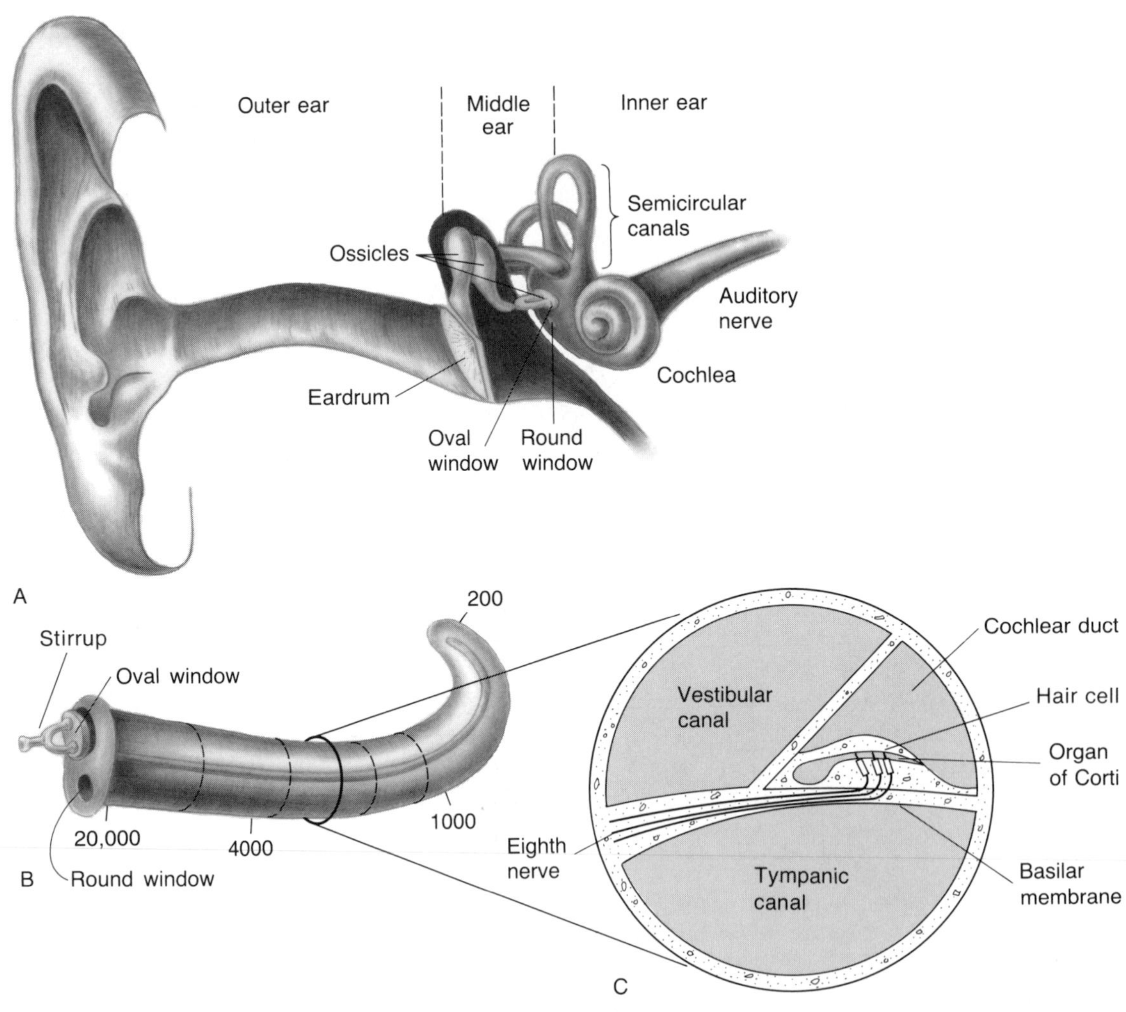

FIGURE 10-8. *A.* Anatomy of the ear. *B.* Anatomy of the cochlea and basilar membrane. The numbers represent frequencies that the basilar membrane is maximally responsive to.

to the rhythm of the sound waves. These movements of the fluid cause a thin membrane (the basilar membrane) to resonate. Finally, the movement of the basilar membrane causes movements of the auditory receptors (hair cells in the organ of Corti), whose membrane potentials are altered, resulting in neural activity. The basilar membrane and the organ of Corti are within a spiral-shaped structure known as the cochlea, and it is the structure of the cochlea and the basilar membrane that allows the hair cells to code different frequencies of sound. The basilar membrane is not a uniform structure; it is narrow (100 μm [microns]) and taut near the ossicles and wider (500 μm) and floppier near the apex of the cochlea. It was Hermann von Helmholtz who in the late 1800s proposed that different portions of the basilar membrane resonate with different frequencies of sound because of this structure. Although von Helmholtz was not precisely correct, it was not until 1960 that Georg von Békésy was able to directly observe the basilar membrane to show that a traveling wave moves along it, starting at the oval window. The peak of the wave on the basilar membrane varies with the frequency of the sound, higher sounds causing maximum peaks near the base of the basilar membrane and lower sounds causing maximum peaks near the apex. As a rough analogy, consider what happens when a garden hose is shaken at one end. If it is shaken very quickly, the waves are very small and the first wave on the hose reaches its peak size very quickly. In contrast, if the hose is shaken very slowly, the first wave reaches its peak farther down the hose. The difference between the basilar membrane and the hose is that the basilar membrane is very short (33 mm) and there is only one peak, whereas on the longer hose the wave travels along the hose, repeating itself. The hair cells in the organ of Corti are maximally disturbed at the point of the peak of the wave, resulting in the maximal neural response of hair cells at that point. A signal composed of many frequencies will cause several different points along the basilar membrane to vibrate and will excite hair cells at all of these points.

As in the visual system, each of the receptor cells in the auditory system has its own receptive field, as do each of the cells in the higher auditory centers. The receptive field of the hair cells is not a point in space, as in the visual system, but rather a particular frequency of sound. Thus, in contrast to the retinotopic maps in the visual system, the auditory system is composed of tonotopic maps.

Auditory Pathways

The axons of the hair cells leave the cochlea to form the major part of the auditory nerve, the eighth cranial nerve. This nerve first projects to the level of the medulla in the lower brainstem, synapsing either in the dorsal or the ventral cochlear nuclei, or in the superior olivary nucleus. The axons of cells in these areas form the lateral lemniscus, which terminates in discrete zones of the inferior colliculus. Two distinct pathways emerge from the colliculus, coursing to the ventral and the dorsal medial geniculate bodies, respectively (Figure 10-9). The ventral region projects to the core auditory cortex, A_I, and the dorsal region projects to the secondary regions, thus corresponding to the general pattern of multiple independent ascending pathways to the cortex. In contrast to the visual system, the projections of the auditory system provide both ipsilateral and contralateral inputs to the cortex, so that there is bilateral representation of each cochlear nucleus in the cortex. The majority of the input is contralateral, however, a fact of importance in understanding the studies of cerebral asymmetry in Chapter 15.

Auditory Cortex

In contrast to studies of the visual and the somatosensory cortex, there has been relatively little re-

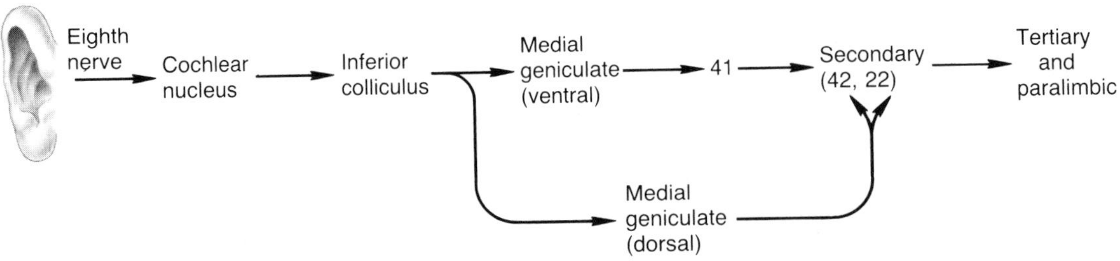

FIGURE 10-9. The major connections of the auditory system.

search on the auditory cortex of primates, most of the research having been done with cats, in which direct homologies to the human auditory cortex are uncertain (see Figure 10-3). Nevertheless, there are sufficient data to provide a basis for general principles of auditory cortical organization in primates. We include the cat in our discussions, however, to aid the interested reader in understanding the animal literature on the auditory cortex, most of which is based on work with cats.

There are several auditory areas in the cortex, because different regions of the medial geniculate nucleus project to independent tonotopically organized cortical zones in both cats and monkeys. These zones include the core auditory cortex (A_I) and at least four other zones surrounding it.

In the human, the core area is within Heschl's gyrus (see Figure 10-10) and is surrounded by seven secondary areas (labeled a–g in the figure). Although the auditory cortex is normally thought of as being in the temporal lobe, it can be seen in Figure 10-10 that it actually extends into the parietal lobe, both into the parietal operculum, which is the parietal tissue on the upper side of the Syl-

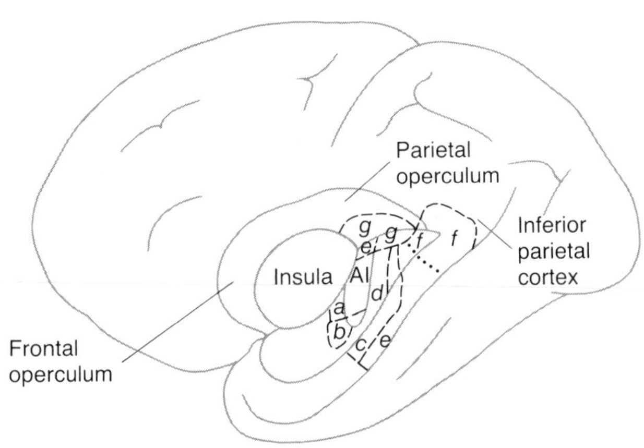

FIGURE 10-10. Representation of the auditory areas of the human. Dashed lines indicate borders between areas; solid lines indicate sulci. The Sylvian fissure has been schematically opened up to illustrate the cortex within. The secondary areas are labeled a–g. (After Galaburda & Sanides, 1980.)

vian fissure, and into the inferior parietal cortex, which is the parietal cortex at the caudal end of the Sylvian fissure. The tonotopic organization of each of the auditory areas remains to be completely mapped, although in general it appears that in each subfield that has been mapped low tones are represented caudally and high tones more rostrally.

There may be a species difference in the organization of the secondary cortex, as there is a marked anatomical asymmetry in humans that has not been described in cats or monkeys (see Figure 15-1). In right-handed people the secondary cortex (known as the **planum temporale**) is larger on the left, whereas the primary cortex (Heschl's gyrus) is larger on the right. There is uncertainty over the posterior boundary of auditory cortex in the monkey since it may include more parietal cortex than previously suspected, so that it is difficult to be certain that there is no asymmetry, although there are no compelling grounds at present for believing there to be any.

Properties of Cells in the Auditory System

Microelectrode studies have shown that single neurons in the auditory system code the frequency (or pitch) of sounds, different neurons being maximally sensitive to different sound frequencies. In general, cells in subcortical nuclei are responsive to a broader band of frequencies than are cells higher in the system. Thus, a neuron in the cochlear nucleus may have a tuning curve with maximum sensitivity at 7000 Hz and partial sensitivity to frequencies between 1000 and 12,000 Hz, as compared with a neuron in A_I, whose tuning curve is also maximally sensitive to 7000 Hz, but which is partially responsive to frequencies between only 5000 and 9000 Hz. In some of the secondary areas the specificity of frequency is reduced slightly, because the cells are also responsive both to very small differences in arrival time in the two ears (as little as 30 μs, or 300 millionths of a second) and to other special characteristics of sound such as harmonics. It is likely that there are cells in the secondary, and possibly tertiary, auditory areas that are maximally sensitive to phonemes (e.g., da, la, ma), although this has not yet been demonstrated.

THE SOMATOSENSORY SYSTEM

The visual and auditory systems are known as *exteroceptive systems* because they are sensitive to stimuli from the external environment. The somatosensory system also has an exteroceptive function. In addition, however, it is *proprioceptive,* meaning that it provides information about the relative position of body segments to one another and the position of the body in space; it is also *interoceptive,* meaning that it records internal bodily events such as blood pressure. The somatosensory system is therefore not a single sensory system but a multiple one composed of several submodalities: (1) touch-pressure, which is sensation elicited by mechanical stimulation of the body surface; (2) position sense, or **kinesthesia,** which results from mechanical disturbances in the muscles and joints; this system has two subcomponents, the sense of static limb position and the sensation of limb movement; (3) heat and cold; and (4) pain, which is elicited by noxious stimulation.

Somatosensory Receptors

The somatosensory system does not have a single type of receptor cell, but at least 20 different types, each transducing a different form of energy. Furthermore, the receptor surface of the somatosensory system is much larger than that of any other sense, because there are receptors in all body tissues except the brain itself. However, the basic organization of the receptors is the same as in the two previously discussed systems because the membrane potential of each is altered by a particular form of energy, and because each has its own receptive field, which is an area of body tissue.

Hair Receptors. Hair receptors are located in hair follicles and are exquisitely sensitive to the bending of a hair. There are a number of types of hair receptors, each with distinctive morphological and physiological properties.

Touch Receptors. Touch receptors are quite varied in the spectrum of stimuli that excite them and in the morphology of their receptor specializations. They respond to stimulus characteristics such as vibration, skin indentation, and certain types of hair movements, with some receptors responding to the velocity of onset of stimulation and others to the duration of stimulation, or to moving stimuli. Touch receptors include Pacinian corpuscles, field receptors, Meissner's corpuscles, Merkel cell-neurite complexes, Ruffini endings, and mechanoreceptors.

Temperature Receptors. Temperature receptors (cold receptors and warm receptors) are sensitive to temperature change, showing a discharge that is related to skin temperature. Cold receptors are excited by decreases in skin temperature when the initial skin temperature ranges from approximately 15° to 40°C. Warm receptors respond maximally to increases in temperature in the approximate range of 30° to 48°C. Other types of receptors (some touch receptors and nociceptors) also respond to rapid temperature changes, but they are not specialized *just* for temperature changes as are the temperature receptors.

Nociceptors. Nociceptors, or pain receptors, are sensitive to mechanical or thermal stimuli that begin near levels that damage the tissue. In addition, some of these fibers respond to chemical stimuli. There are four types of nociceptors: mechanical nociceptors, mechanical and thermal nociceptors, deep pressure-pain receptors, and visceral afferents. The discharge of each of these receptor types is associated with the experience of pain.

Joint Receptors. These receptors are responsive to the movements and positions of limbs. There are at least three types, including Ruffini endings, Paciniform corpuscles, and Golgi receptors.

Muscle and Tendon Receptors. These receptors are located in the muscles and tendons, responding primarily to stretch and contraction of these organs. They include muscle spindle receptors and Golgi tendon organs.

It should be apparent from our brief overview of the somatosensory receptors that the central representation of the information from all these receptors must be very complex indeed if there is to be a representation of all this information in the cortex, and if it is all to be integrated to allow us a perception of touch.

Somatosensory Pathways

The somatosensory system can be seen as two subsystems, one for fine touch, pressure, and kinesthesis, the other for pain and temperature. Fibers that form the first system leave the receptors and ascend via the dorsal columns of the spinal cord to synapse in the cuneate and gracile nuclei of the lower brainstem. The fibers then cross to the opposite side of the brain to form the medial lemniscus, which terminates in the ventroposterior region of the ventrobasal thalamus (see Figure 10-11). This thalamic nucleus then projects primarily to Brodmann's areas 3b and 1, to form independent somatotopic maps, as illustrated in Figure 10-3. In contrast to this pattern, the fibers of the pain and temperature system leave the receptors to synapse in the dorsal horn (the substantia gelatinosa) of the spinal cord. The cells in this area then cross over to the other side of the cord and form the lateral spinothalamic tract, which primarily terminates in the dorsal portions of the ventrobasal thalamus (ventroposterior oral and ventroposterior superior) as well as the posterior thalamus. These nuclei project in turn to areas 3a (ventroposterior oral), 2 (ventroposterior superior), 5 (lateral posterior),

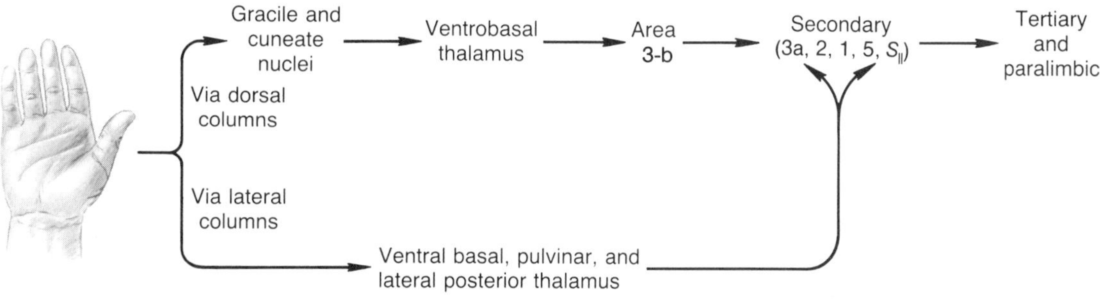

FIGURE 10-11. Major connections of the somatosensory system. It has two major subdivisions that converge on the somatosensory cortex: one for fine touch, pressure, and kinesthesis; the other for pain and temperature.

and S_{II} (posterior). Thus, we see that as was the case in other sensory systems, there are multiple pathways to independent representations of the receptor surface in the somatosensory system.

Somatosensory Cortex

In Chapter 9 we discussed somatosensory cortical organization as an example of sensory neocortical organization, and so we shall not repeat the details here. Like the other sensory systems, the somatosensory system is composed of a primary core area, a secondary cortex, and a tertiary projection area. The core area is not so anatomically distinct in this system, presumably because the somatosensory system is composed of so many subsystems, but Kaas has suggested that there are grounds for considering it to be Brodmann's area 3b. In this case, areas 3a, 2 and 1 are likely candidates for the secondary-I cortex, and areas 5 and part of 7 are probably secondary-II cortex. The tertiary projections fall in parts of areas 7 and 40.

The somatotopic maps are particularly intriguing because they are disproportionate to the surface of the body (Figure 10-12) but proportionate to

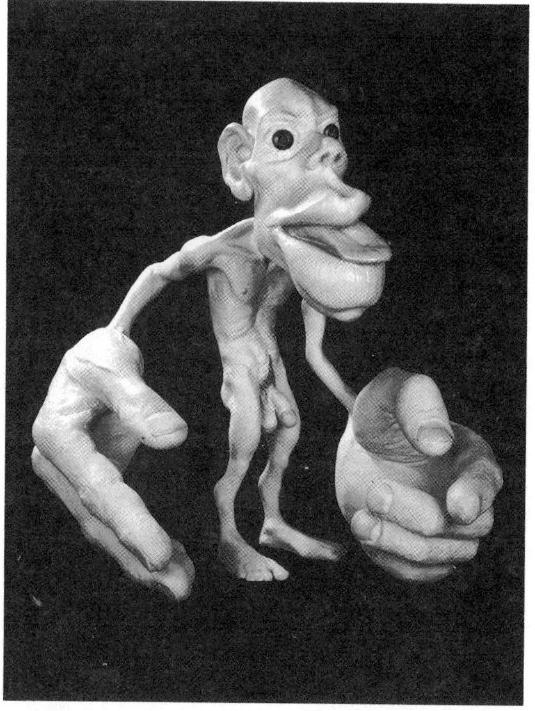

FIGURE 10-12. The misshapen appearance of this little man (or homunculus) reflects the disproportionate areas of the somatic sensory cortex devoted to different parts of the body. (After Bloom and Lazerson, 1988.)

the subjective experience of sensitivity in different parts of the body. Thus, the lips, tongue, hands, and fingers take up much more cortical area than the rest of the body and, of course, they are the most sensitive areas of our body. Species vary considerably in their distribution of body surface in the somatotopic maps. For example, the representation for the face of the rat, including the tactile hairs known as vibrissae, is very large relative to any other body part (see Figure 5-7). The face and vibrissae of the rat are thus extremely sensitive, enabling rats to make tactile discriminations with only a single vibrissa!

Properties of Cells in Somatosensory Areas

Microelectrode studies have suggested that at least five basic sensations are independently coded throughout the somatosensory system: light touch to the skin, deep pressure to the fascia below the skin, joint movement, pain, and temperature. Within the thalamus, cells are highly specific, any given cell being maximally responsive to only one mode of stimulation. Within the next higher level, the cortex, the cells are just as specific to particular stimuli, but a given cell is responsive to a smaller region of skin. Thus, in the cortex there is increased discrimination of spatial location on the receptor surface. In addition some cells, especially in the hand region, have very complex properties, responding to movement of stimuli in one direction or another or to the precise orientation of tactile stimuli on the skin surface. These neurons probably play some special role during movements of the hand designed to explore the shape of an object, and they play a role in **stereognosis,** the ability to perceive a three-dimensional structure tactilely. There may be other properties of these cells in areas 7 and 40 that integrate visual and tactile information in coding the position of the body in extrapersonal space, a problem we shall return to in Chapter 24.

TASTE AND SMELL

The senses of taste and smell (or **olfaction**) do not have the extensive cortical representation that vision, audition, and touch do, and thus do not appear as attractive (or perhaps as glamorous!) to neuroscientists for study. As a result there is far less known about these, even at the level of receptors, than for the other senses. Our discussion of these senses therefore will be limited, especially with respect to cortical contributions to taste and olfaction.

Receptors

In contrast to the other senses in which the stimuli are physical energy, the stimuli for taste and smell are chemical. There are specialized receptors in each system, as one would expect. For taste, the receptors are the tastebuds, which are mistakenly believed by most people to be the bumps on the tongue. In fact, the bumps, called papillae, probably help the tongue grasp food; the taste buds lie buried around them. Saliva coats the tongue and the chemicals in food are held in the saliva to be tasted. If the tongue is dry, the taste buds work poorly and it is difficult to taste. There are four different taste receptor types, each responding to a different chemical component of food, namely sweet, sour, salty, and bitter. The receptors for bitter lie exclusively at the back of the tongue and those for sweet at the front. Those for sour and salty are found on the sides. The taste specificity of a particular receptor is not absolute because single fibers can respond to a variety of chemical stimuli. It appears likely that the perceived taste of any stimulus results from a pattern of firing of the entire population of taste receptors. Curiously, there are significant differences in the taste preferences both within and between species. For example, humans and rats both like sucrose and saccharin solutions but dogs reject saccharin and cats are indifferent to both. Similarly, within the human species there are clear differences in taste thresholds. Older people generally have higher thresholds, largely because there is a dramatic reduction in the number of taste buds during aging. It is little wonder that children tolerate spices poorly: their taste is stronger. Furthermore, Bartoshuk has shown that there are absolute differences between adults: some people perceive certain tastes as strong and offensive, whereas others are indifferent to them.

The receptor surface for olfaction is the olfactory epithelium, which is located in the nasal cavity. The surface is composed of three cell types: receptor cells, supporting cells, and the cells below them, called basal cells. The receptor cells are covered by a layer of mucous in which receptor cilia are embedded. Thus, odors must pass through the mucous to reach the receptors, which means that changes in the properties of the mucous (such as when we have a cold) may influence how easily an odor can get to the receptors. The axons of the receptor cells form the olfactory tract. It is interesting to note in passing that the area of the epithelium varies considerably across species. Estimates of its area are on the order of 2 to 4 cm^2 in humans, 18 cm^2 in dogs, and 21 cm^2 in cats. Such differences imply that there will be interspecies differences in sensitivity to odors, which would seem to be true.

It is not clear how different odors produce different activity in the olfactory receptors. Individual receptors are not specific to single odors so it is likely that different proteins in the receptors are responsive to specific molecules of a given odor. Perhaps different receptors have different distributions of receptor proteins. Presumably it is the summed action of many receptors that leads to a particular pattern of neural activity that the olfactory system identifies as a particular odor.

Pathways

Three cranial nerves carry information from the tongue: the glossopharyngeal nerve (IX), the vagus nerve (X), and the chorda tympani branch of the facial nerve (VII). All three nerves enter the solitary tract, which forms the main gustatory nerve. There are two pathways originating in the solitary tract, as illustrated in Figure 10-13. One route goes to the ventroposterior medial nucleus of the thalamus, which in turn leads to two pathways — one to S_I, and the other to a region just rostral to S_{II}, in the insular cortex (see Figure 9-5*A*). The latter region is probably a pure taste area as it is not responsive to tactile simulation. In

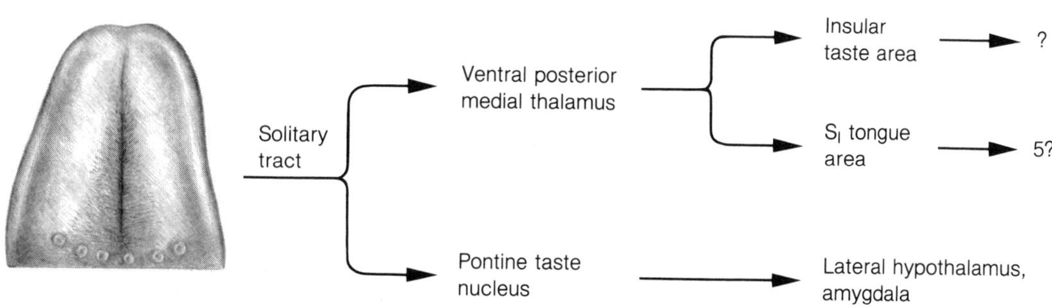

FIGURE 10-13. The major connections of the taste system.

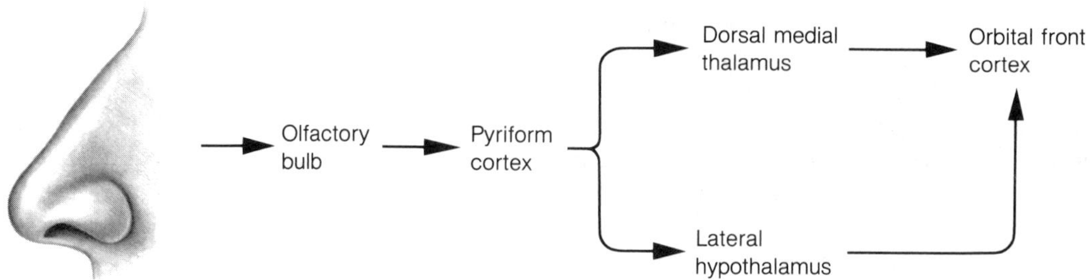

FIGURE 10-14. The major connections of the olfactory system.

contrast, the S_I projection is sensitive to tactile stimuli and is probably responsible for the localization of tastes on the tongue. Those who enjoy wine are familiar with this distinction because wines are described not only by their gustatory qualities but also by their locations. A second pathway of the solitary tract leads to the pontine taste area, which in turn projects to the lateral hypothalamus and amygdala. Both of these areas are involved in feeding, although the precise role of the taste information is uncertain.

The axons of the olfactory receptor cells synapse in the olfactory bulb, which may be seen as an analogue to the retina and is made up of several layers. Unlike the retina, however, little is known of the physiological organization of the olfactory bulb. The major output of the bulb is the lateral olfactory tract, which passes ipsilaterally to the pyriform cortex (Figure 10-14). This cortex, which is old cortex rather than neocortex, is found on the base of the brain as illustrated for the squirrel in Figure 10-3*A*. In the human, this tissue is found medially, just in front of the optic chiasm (see Figure 1-6). The primary projection of the pyriform cortex is to the central portion of the dorsal medial nucleus of the thalamus, which in turn projects to the orbitofrontal cortex (see Figure 1-5*A*). Thus, the orbitofrontal cortex can be seen as the primary olfactory neocortex. There does not appear to be a secondary olfactory cortex. A second pyriform projection goes to the lateral hypothalamus, which in turn projects to the orbitofrontal cortex. Thus, like the other sensory systems, there are two parallel routes for olfactory input to the cortex.

We have seen that both the taste and olfactory systems have access to the orbitofrontal cortex. In the olfactory system the projection is from the pyriform cortex via the dorsal-medial thalamus to the orbitofrontal cortex, whereas in the taste system the projection is from the amygdala to the dorsal-medial thalamus to the orbitofrontal cortex. Unfortunately, the role of this cortex in the chemical senses is largely unexplored, although cells in this cortex are known to be responsive to specific odors. This cortex does play a significant role in social and sexual behavior, however, which suggests that chemical information plays a significant role in these behaviors. We shall return to this issue in our discussion of the frontal lobe in Chapter 19.

PERCEPTION

We have reviewed the basic organization of the sensory systems, illustrating the neural pathways from the receptors to the tertiary cortex, and identifying principles that govern the operation of the sensory systems. We have described a very sterile picture, however, since our experiences of sensory stimuli are far richer than the description of the anatomy and physiology would lead us to believe. Our sensory impressions are obviously affected by our past experience, the contexts in which they occur, our emotional state and so on. There is certainly far more to the sensory systems than the transduction of physical energy into nervous activity. Our subjective experience of the physical energy is perception, and it is perception, rather than sensory transduction, that is of most interest to the psychologist.

Sensation and perception can be distinguished quite simply: **sensation** is the result of activity of receptors and their associated afferent pathways to the corresponding neocortical sensory areas; **perception** is the result of activity of cells in the cortex beyond the first synapse in the sensory cortex. Thus, in the neocortex sensory information is transformed into a percept by such factors as experience and context; the percept may differ in a number of ways from the sensory information sent to the neocortex. For example, if a motorist comes on a road sign that is partially covered with mud and reads "ST," she would most likely stop her vehicle because her perception is of the word "STOP" although her sensation was only of "ST." From her previous experience with road signs, the motorist's sensation is transformed by mediation processes to a perception with considerable meaning.

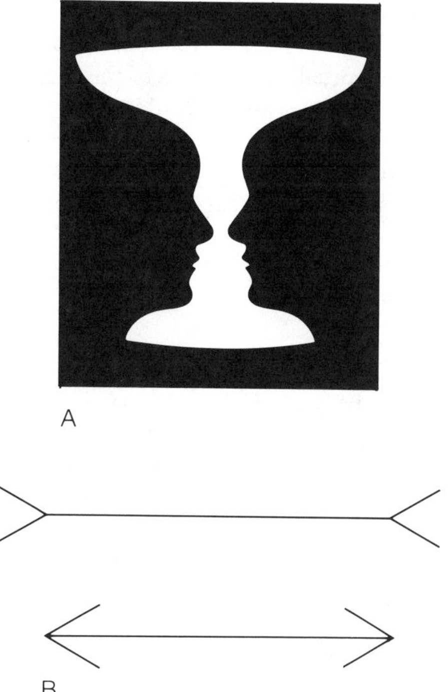

FIGURE 10-15. Demonstration of the distinction between sensation and perception. *A*. An ambiguous or reversible figure first described by Rubin. The figure can be seen as a vase or as two faces. *B*. The Müller-Lyer illusion: the top line appears longer than the bottom line because of contextual cues (the arrowheads).

The clearest proof that perception is more than sensation is the transformation of the same sensory stimulation into totally different perceptions, and the fact that perceptions are affected by the context of the sensory input. The classic demonstration of the former effect is illustrated with such ambiguous figures as Rubin's vases (see Figure 10-15*A*). The figure may be seen either as a vase or as two faces, and if one fixates on the center, the perceptions alternate even though the sensory stimulation remains constant. Similarly, the Müller-Lyer illusion in Figure 10-15*B* demonstrates the influence of context. The top line is perceived as longer than the bottom although both are the same length. The contextual cues (the arrowheads) alter the perception of line length. Ambiguous figures and illusions involve complex perceptual phenomena that are mediated by the neocortex at a functional level beyond the primary sensory cortex. They also illustrate the complexity of perceptual phenomena produced by the secondary and tertiary sensory regions, and allow us some insight into the bases of cognitive processes.

The distinction between sensation and perception is particularly useful to neuropsychology because it allows different predictions to be made about the effects of lesions to lower (sensory) and upper (perceptual) components of the sensory systems. Specifically, damage to the sensory system up to and including the core sensory cortex should produce distortions of the details of the world around us, whereas damage to the higher sensory regions of the neocortex, and the areas receiving projections from these parasensory regions, should result in deficits in understanding or comprehending the meaning of the incoming sensory information. These predictions are indeed confirmed by the evidence, which we shall review in the next chapter.

REFERENCES

Bailey, C. H. Visual system I: The retina. In E. R. Kandel and J. H. Schwartz eds. *Principles of Neural Science.* New York: Elsevier, 1981.

Barlow, H. B. and J. D. Mollon, eds. *The Senses.* Cambridge: Cambridge University Press, 1982.

Bartoshuk, L. M. Gustatory system. In R. B. Masterton, ed. *Handbook of Behavioral Neurobiology,* vol. 1. New York: Plenum, 1978.

Bloom, F. E. and A. Lazerson. *Brain, Mind, and Behavior.* New York: W. H. Freeman and Co., 1988.

Cowey, A. Why are there so many visual areas? In F. O. Schmitt, F. G. Worden, G. Adelman, and S. G. Dennis, eds. *The Organization of the Cerebral Cortex.* Cambridge, MA: M.I.T. Press, 1981.

Galaburda, A., and F. Sanides. Cytoarchitectonic organization of the human auditory cortex. *Journal of Comparative Neurology* 190:597–610, 1980.

Held, R., H. W. Leibowitz, and H. -L. Teuber. *Perception. Handbook of Sensory Physiology,* vol. VIII. New York: Springer-Verlag, 1978.

Imig, T. J., M. A. Ruggero, L. M. Kitzes, E. Javel, and J. F. Brugge. Organization of auditory cortex in the owl monkey *(Aotus trivirgatus). Journal of Comparative Neurology* 171:111–128, 1977.

Imig, T. J., and A. Morel. Organization of the thalamocortical auditory system in the cat. *Annual Review of Neuroscience* 6:95–120, 1983.

Jones, E. G., S. P. Wise, and J. D. Coulter. Differential thalamic relationships of sensory-motor and parietal cortical fields in monkeys. *Journal of Comparative Neurology* 183:833–882, 1979.

Kaas, J. H. What, if anything, is SI? Organization of first somatosensory area of cortex. *Physiological Reviews* 63:206–231, 1983.

Kaas, J. H. The organization and evolution of neocortex. In S. P. Wise, ed. *Higher Brain Functions.* New York: John Wiley, 1987.

Kandel, E. R., and J. H. Schwartz. *Principles of Neural Science.* New York: Elsevier, 1981.

Lashley, K. S. The mechanisms of vision. XVI. The functioning of small remnants of the visual cortex. *Journal of Comparative Neurology* 70:45–67, 1939.

Livingston, M., and D. Hubel. Segregation of form, color, movement and depth: Anatomy, physiology, and perception. *Science* 240:740–749, 1988.

Masterton, R. B., ed. *Handbook of Behavioral Neurobiology,* vol. 1. New York: Plenum, 1978.

Merzenich, M. M., and J. F. Brugge. Representation of the cochlear partition on the superior temporal plane of the macaque monkey. *Brain Research* 50:275–296, 1973.

Poggio, G. F. Central neural mechanisms in vision. In V. B. Mountcastle, ed. *Medical Physiology.* St. Louis: Mosby, 1968.

Uttal, W. R. *The Psychobiology of Sensory Coding.* New York: Harper & Row, 1973.

Van Essen, D. C. Visual areas of the mammalian cerebral cortex. *Annual Review of Neuroscience* 2:227–263, 1979.

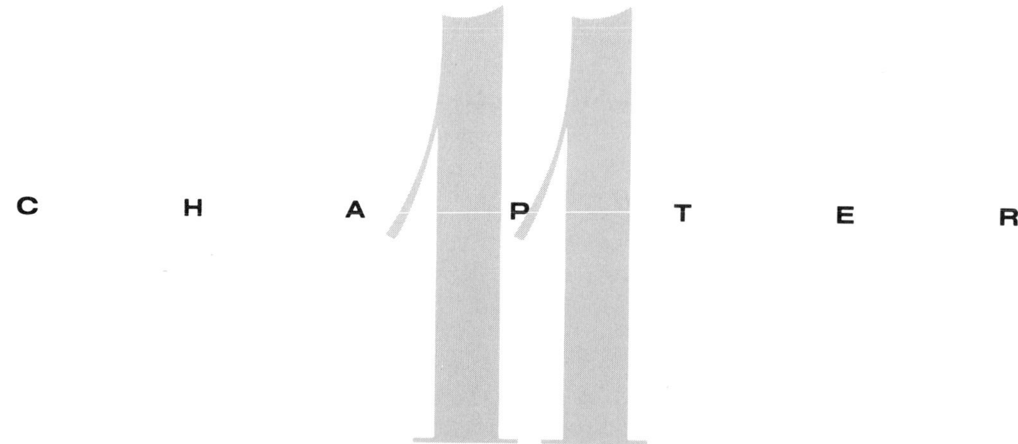

DISORDERS OF SENSATION AND PERCEPTION

The following account by Saletsky, who suffered a bullet wound to the brain in the battle of Smolensk in 1943, gives a vivid illustration of the difference between sensation and perception.

> The instructor gave me a needle, spool of thread, some material with a pattern on it, and asked me to try to stitch the pattern. Then he went off to attend to other patients—people who'd had their arms or legs amputated after being wounded, or half their bodies paralyzed. Meanwhile, I just sat there with the needle, thread and material in my hands wondering why I'd been given these; I sat for a long time and did nothing. Suddenly the instructor came over and asked: "Why are you just sitting there: Go ahead and thread the needle!" I took the thread in one hand, the needle in the other, but couldn't understand what to do with them. How was I to thread the needle? I twisted it back and forth but hadn't the slightest idea what to do with any of these things. When I first looked at those objects, but hadn't yet picked them up, they seemed perfectly familiar—there was no reason to think about them. But as soon as I had them in my hands, I was at a loss to figure out what they were for. I'd lapsed into a kind of stupor and wouldn't be able to associate these two objects in my mind—it was as though I'd forgotten why they existed. (Luria, 1976, pp. 47–48)

Clearly the patient's problem was not simply one of visual sensation or of movement; he was able to pick up the needle and thread without difficulty. The problem was not restricted to the recognition of objects, as demonstrated by two other excerpts:

> I tried to figure out what directions north, south, east, and west were by the sun, but just couldn't. I

> even had trouble understanding where the sun should have been—whether to the right or the left. I confused east with west and couldn't remember what those words meant. When someone passed by, I asked him how to get to Kazanovka. But he just smirked and walked on, since the settlement was right there—you could see it through the hedges. I still couldn't believe it and asked another person. "Look for yourself," he said, "it's right here!" And sure enough, when I looked around, I recognized the houses in Kazanovka. It's so weird—I simply can't orient myself to a place, just have no sense of space. (Luria, 1976, p. 58)

> I went into the hall to look for a bathroom I'd been told was next door. I went up to the room and looked at the sign on the door. But no matter how long I stared at it and examined the letters, I couldn't read a thing. Some peculiar, foreign letters were printed there—what bothered me most was that they weren't Russian. When a patient passed by, I pointed to the sign and asked him what it was. "It's the men's room," he replied. "What's the matter with you, can't you read?" I stood there as though rooted to the spot, simply unable to understand why I couldn't read that sign. After all, I could see, I wasn't blind. But why was it written in a foreign alphabet? Wasn't someone playing a joke on me—a sick man? (Luria, 1976, p. 62)

These disorders vividly demonstrate the complexity of deficits in sensation and perception. In this case there is little doubt that the patient could "see" in the sense that the term is normally used, but there is equally little doubt that he had a severe visual impairment. Alterations of this sort pose a peculiar problem for the neuropsychologist. To the patient these alterations are often quite obvious, whether they are the outright and persistent loss of some sensory ability, or more subtle disabilities, which are only noticed on certain occasions. To the neuropsychologist, these alterations present a challenge, as they must be demonstrated and quantified, a difficult task when the patient is unable, or unwilling, to describe how the sensory world has changed. The psychologist's task is made more complicated by the fact that patients easily misinterpret their condition, making accurate description a real challenge in some cases. Studies of sensory processing in human patients are therefore among the most tedious of all neuropsychological investigations, and many sensory dysfunctions continue to represent large areas of ignorance in neuropsychology. The nature of many sensory disorders has still not been adequately investigated, and conceptions of many disorders are based on clinical description alone. Clinical description cannot take the place of careful quantification, however, and many clinical descriptions in the literature (or in patients' files) are based on cursory observation and do not accurately describe the condition. Furthermore, clinical shorthand expressions such as "agnosia" conceal the diversity of mechanisms that can be disturbed, providing an illusion of understanding because a condition has been named. We must be wary of being trapped into thinking that because a patient is described as having "object agnosia" that this patient's symptoms and neurological condition are similar to those of other patients with the same label. It is only by careful description of the patient's perceptual abilities that the course of particular symptomatology can be identified. The question to keep asking in studies of disorders of sensation and perception is, "Why does a particular symptom appear?"

In this chapter we shall briefly survey the types of functional sensory abnormalities most commonly encountered in the visual, auditory, and somatosensory domains. We shall not be overly concerned with trying to localize the disorders to specific cortical regions, in part because so little is known about this, and in part because we shall return to many of these disorders in our more detailed discussions of clinical syndromes in later chapters.

TYPES OF DISORDERS

At the risk of oversimplifying, we can identify two broad categories of sensory disorders: (1) complete or partial loss of some sensory process, and (2) distortion or loss of some aspect of perception, in spite of apparent awareness of the existence of the sensory stimulus.

Complete Loss

Evidence of complete loss of sensory ability would seem rather simple to demonstrate, but we shall see that the absence of response to sensory input does not necessarily provide evidence of the absence of sensory processing. Consider the following. If the optic nerve is severed before it enters the brain, there can be little doubt that a person will be blind in the visual field served by the nerve. Let us suppose, however, that the nerve enters the brain, making its first synapse in the thalamus or brainstem. If the primary sensory cortex is damaged, sensory input can still get to the secondary cortex, and so we might ask: Are such people completely blind? They claim to be blind, and they act as though they are blind, but testing can show that they do have certain visual capacities, which they are apparently unaware of, and with which they make no, or only poor, motor responses. The difficulty is obvious: At what point do we conclude that there is a complete loss of sensory ability? As a rule of thumb, we can conclude that complete loss of sensory function is only certain after the sensory nerve or nucleus of the first synapse is damaged. Damage in the primary sensory areas has the severest effect on sensation, but even in cases of complete removal, it is normally possible to demonstrate some type of response to sensory input, although in the visual system it is far less than might be expected, given that several other intact representations of the retina are still functional.

Partial Loss or Distortion

It follows from our discussion of cortical organization of the sensory systems that damage beyond the primary area in one of the multiple representations of a given sensory system would be expected to produce some type of relatively specific sensory or perceptual impairment. This is easier to predict than to prove. Damage to restricted regions of the cortex, or to connections between cortical areas, is often claimed to produce relatively specific perceptual abnormalities, but careful neuropsychological examination normally finds a more general impairment in perception than initially believed. Nevertheless, even though the perceptual deficits are less specific than we might have predicted, there is little doubt that people can have disturbances in sensory processing that are quite different from an apparent loss in sensory function. Saletsky did not claim to be blind and did not act blind; he had some disorder in visual processing that occurred even though he was able to perceive that something was in the visual world. This condition is clearly different from a case of complete loss and certainly must have a different anatomical basis. It is likely that partial loss is most commonly a result of damage to secondary regions or to connections between secondary regions, although it is still an unproved hypothesis that damage to a particular sensory representation will produce specific loss of some sensory or perceptual function.

EFFECTS OF LESIONS OF THE VISUAL SYSTEM

The nature of a visual disturbance will depend on the location of the damage (see Figure 11-1). Destruction of the retina or optic nerve of one eye produces **monocular blindness,** the loss of sight in that eye. A lesion of the medial region of the **optic chiasm** severs the crossing fibers, producing **bitemporal hemianopia** — loss of vision of both temporal fields. A lesion of the lateral chiasm results in a loss of vision of one nasal field, or **nasal hemianopia.** Complete cuts of the optic tract, lateral geniculate body, or area 17 will result in **homonomous hemianopia,** blindness of one

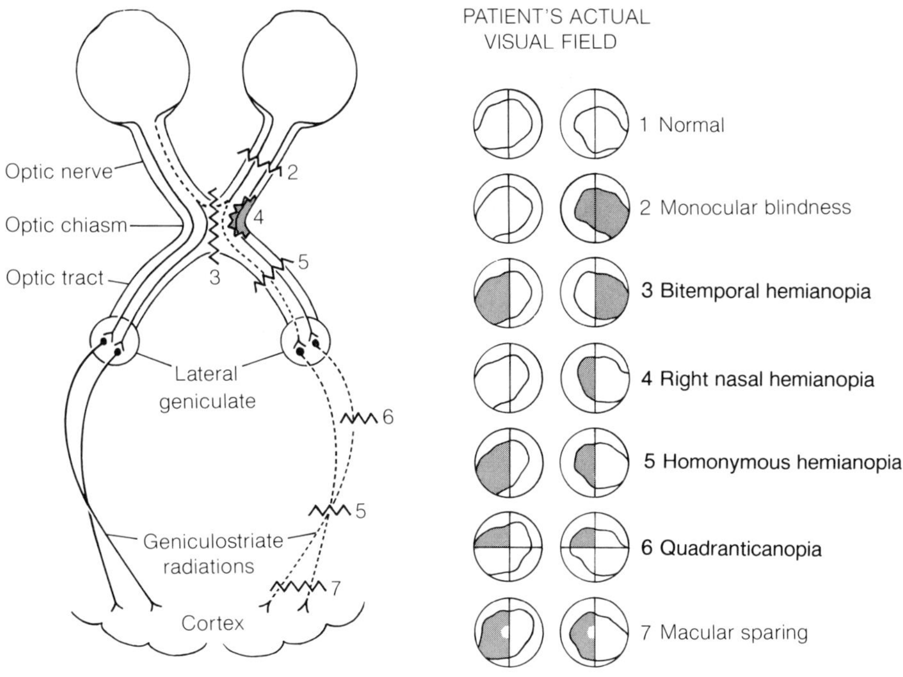

FIGURE 11-1. Visual defects following damage at different levels of the visual system as denoted by numbers. A darkened region in the visual field denotes a blind area. (After Curtis, 1972)

entire visual field. Should this lesion be partial, as is often the case, **quadrantic anopia** occurs: destruction of only a portion of the visual field. Lesions of the occipital lobe frequently spare the central, or macular, region of the visual field, although the reason is uncertain. The most reasonable explanations of this **macular sparing** are: that this region receives a double vascular supply, from both the middle and the posterior cerebral arteries, making it more resilient to large hemispheric lesions; or that the foveal region of the retina projects to both hemispheres, so that even if one occipital lobe is destroyed, the other receives projections from the fovea. The former explanation is more likely. Macular sparing helps to differentiate lesions of the optic tract or thalamus from cortical lesions, since macular sparing occurs only after lesions (usually large) to the visual cortex. Macular sparing does not always occur, however, and many people with visual cortex lesions have a complete loss of vision in one quarter or half of the fovea.

Small lesions of the occipital lobe often produce **scotomas,** small blind spots in the visual field. A curious aspect of these defects is that people are often totally unaware of them, because of **nystagmus,** constant tiny involuntary eye movements, and "spontaneous filling in." Because the eyes are usually in constant motion the scotoma moves about the visual field, allowing the brain to perceive all the information in the field. If the eyes are held still, the visual system actually completes objects, faces, and so on resulting in a normal percept of the stimulus, just as we are unaware of our own blind spot. The visual system may cover up the scotoma so successfully that its presence can only be demonstrated to the patient by "tricking" the visual system. This can be achieved by placing objects entirely within the scotoma and, without allowing the patient to shift gaze, asking what the object is. If no object is reported, the examiner moves the object out of the scotoma so that it suddenly "appears" in the intact region of the patient's visual field, thus demonstrating the existence of a blind region. A similar phenomenon can be demonstrated in one's own "blind spot." Stand beside a table, close one eye, stare at a spot on the table, and move a pencil along the table laterally, from directly below your nose to between 20 and 30 cm towards the periphery. Part of the pencil will vanish when you reach the blind spot. You can move the pencil through the blind spot slowly and it will suddenly reappear on the other side.

More complex effects on visual perception result from lesions in the visual system beyond the primary visual cortex. It is in these higher levels, especially in areas 20 and 21, that cerebral asymmetry becomes apparent, for lesions on the right produce larger deficits in perception of complex visual forms, such as faces and geometric patterns, whereas lesions on the left produce larger deficits in perception of verbally related material. For example, lesions in the region of Brodmann's area 39, particularly in the angular gyrus, produce **dyslexia** (deficits in the ability to read,) because letters no longer form meaningful words. We shall return to these perceptual deficits in our discussion of partial loss of visual functions.

Case B. K.

The nature of different types of visual disturbances and their relation to anatomy can be demonstrated by the experience of one of us (B. K.). One morning in January, 1986, at age 38, B. K. awoke to discover that he was hemianopic in the left visual field. Given a history of classic migraine, in which the aura was nearly always in the left visual field, it is likely that he had a migraine stroke. Within a few hours the lower field began to return but the right upper quadrant was slow to show any change. A CT scan (Figure 11-2*A*) showed a clear infarct in the right occipital area. Reference to Figure 10-5 leads to the prediction that the left upper quadrant field defect would be associated with a lesion of the lower bank of the calcarine fissure in the right hemisphere, and this is the case. The size of a field defect is routinely measured with *perimetry*. This is a standardized method of measuring the size of a visual defect in which the subject fixates on a black dot in the center of a large white hemisphere. A small light is moved around the field and the task is to indicate when it can be seen. The brightness and size of the light can be varied, thus manipulating the difficulty of the task. The performance is mapped by indicating the area of "blindness" on a schematic of the visual fields (see Figure 11-2*B*). Size in the visual field is measured by visual angle, which is indicated in degrees. Thus, for B. K. the area of complete inability to perceive even a very large bright light is 6° up along the vertical midline and about 15° lateral along the horizontal midline. The area beyond this zone in the left upper quadrant does not have normal vision, however, as there is still an inability to perceive less bright lights in this area.

The nature of the visual defects can be illustrated best in the context of their poststroke evolution. For the first 2 to 3 days the field appeared dark, much as though a piece of smoked glass was blocking the view of the world beyond. On the fourth day, this darkness had disappeared and was replaced with "visual noise," called a *scintillating scotoma,* throughout much of the field, especially in the area of the scotoma. This noise is best described as being like colored "snow" in a TV set. About the same time, there was the first perception of movement in the field. This movement was perceived as a traveling "wave," much like ripples on a pond. There was no perception of form or pattern. One curious phenomenon was first observed during perimetry testing four days after the

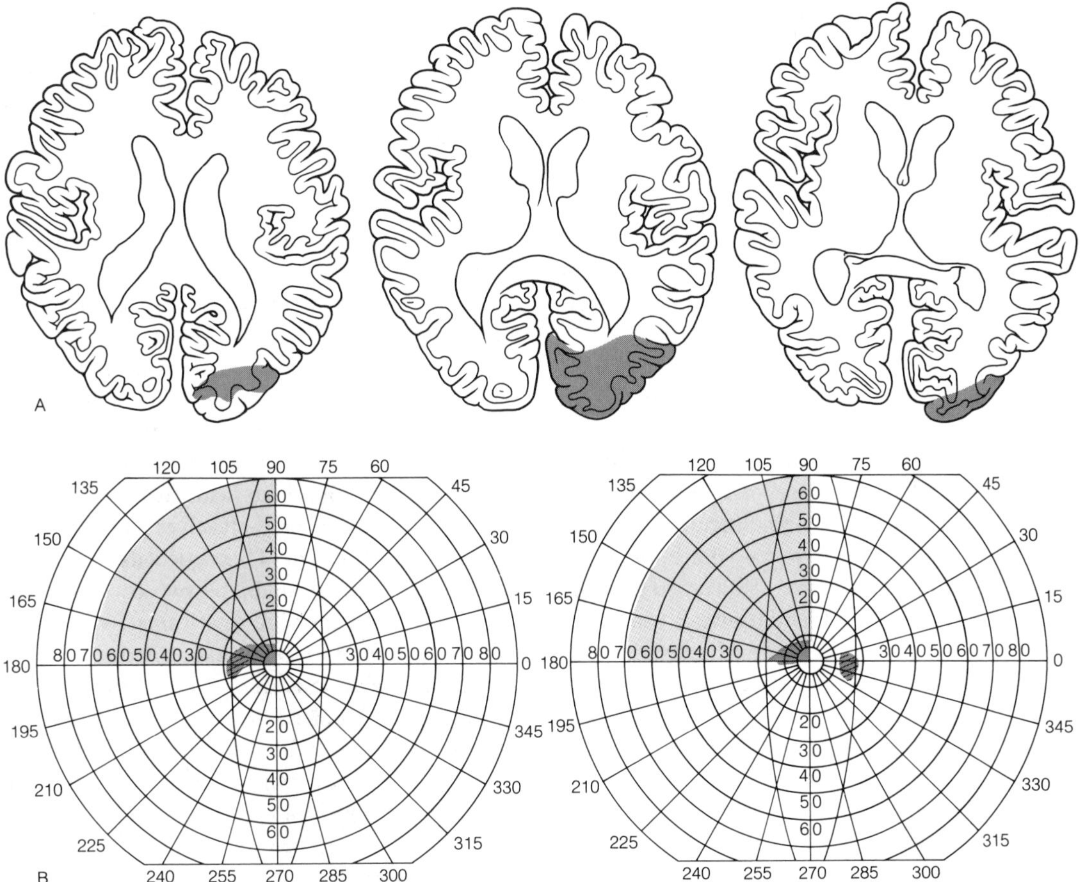

FIGURE 11-2. *A.* Schematic illustration of B. K.'s CT scan, showing the infarct in the right occipital area. *B.* Illustration of the visual fields of B. K. 6 months after the stroke. The black region shows the area of scotoma, the stippled region shows the area of reduced acuity.

stroke. If the stimulus light was moved into the blind field, it was not perceived until it moved into another quadrant. Curiously, however, B. K. immediately became aware (in hindsight) that the light had been present in the blind field and could accurately state where it entered the field. In other words, B. K. perceived location without being able to perceive content. Over the ensuing 4 to 6 months the area of blindness decreased somewhat and acuity in the periphery improved significantly. Nonetheless, form vision remains poor in the left upper quadrant, outside the scotoma. The scintillating color snow is still present, showing little change from the first few days after the stroke.

The visual phenomena observed by B. K. indicate that the primary visual cortex probably has an area of total cell death (the dense scotoma) and another area of partial cell death, possibly due to the loss of some class of cell that is especially sensitive to ischemia. It also shows that the secondary cortex is operative, because there is color perception even though there is no form perception. Thus, B. K. can identify accurately the color of objects that he cannot identify. Those who are myopic (nearsighted) will have experienced a similar phenomenon; the colors of objects or lights can be appreciated, while the form is not recognizable B. K.'s stroke thus indicates the presence of at least four independent visual functions: form (which is absent), and color, movement, and location (which are spared).

The loss of one quarter of the fovea leads B. K. to make a variety of visual errors. Immediately after the stroke he was able to read only with great difficulty. If one looks at a word, the fixation point is in the center of the word, so for B. K. half of the word is absent. Indeed, it was difficult to find the edge of the page since it was in the blind field. Normal reading returned as B. K. learned to direct his gaze slightly to the left and upwards (probably about 2° in each direction), which allowed words to fall in the normal-seeing visual field. This "recovery" took about 6 weeks. Returning to playing squash and tennis was equally challenging, for once a ball entered the scotoma it was lost. Similarly, facial recognition is slower than it was before the stroke, because the information in the left visual field appears to be particularly important for face recognition (see the following section). Finally, B. K. has had to learn to "overscan" a room when looking for someone or something. In one humorous incident about 2 weeks after the stroke, B. K. was looking for I. Q. W. because they were to go to a meeting together. B. K. looked into a large room and saw nobody. Having concluded that I. Q. W. had left without him, he left, feeling annoyed. In fact, I. Q. W. was on the telephone and was seated to the left of B. K. I. Q. W. believed that B. K. had looked directly at him and was waiting for him somewhere. In fact, I. Q W. must have fallen in B. K.'s scotoma and therefore did not exist. Confusion followed as each proceeded on the basis of the obvious information available!

Evidence for Two Visual Systems

Curiously, in neuropsychology, many ideas about brain function that were introduced around the turn of the century were extremely insightful although usually based on inference from only a few patients; most such ideas were ignored until the 1960s and 1970s. The idea that there are two parallel visual systems is a good case in point.

In 1918, Holmes reported a series of patients with unique visual deficits. These patients all had intact vision in the center of the visual field — that is, they could identify objects when asked to — but they often failed to notice objects that were within their range of vision. They had difficulty as well in following moving objects with their eyes, judging depth, and orienting themselves visually in the space around them. These deficits implied to Holmes that there might be two components to the visual system: one to discriminate visual stimuli, and a second to locate and attend to stimuli in the visual field. This theory was supported by a phenomenon reported the previous year: Riddoch described patients who were apparently blind but were able to grasp objects in motion and could indicate the direction of motion, even if they reported not having seen the object! Weiskrantz recently dubbed this phenomenon *blindsight,* implying functional vision in cortically blind people. Recall also, that in B. K.'s case he could identify the location of a light that he could not see. Weiskrantz and others have extended Riddoch's observations and have termed B. K.'s experience "blindsight in hindsight." (For an excellent detailed account of a patient with blindsight, we highly recommend Weiskrantz's recent book, *Blindsight: A Case History and Implications.)*

Riddoch and Holmes, and later others, have supplied evidence supporting the notion of two functional visual systems corresponding to the two anatomical pathways illustrated in Figure 10-6. The detection, location, and following of objects by the eyes are thought to be primarily functions of the tectopulvinar system, whereas form and color analysis are primarily functions of the geniculostriate system. Animal studies support this conclusion; several groups have developed convincing animal models of two anatomical and functional visual systems in species as diverse as hamsters and monkeys. Schneider, for example, demonstrated that ablation (removal) of the superior colliculus has little effect on pattern discrimination but produces deficits in orientation to visual stimuli. Conversely, lesion of the striate cortex severely disrupts pattern vision but does not impair orientation to visual stimuli.

Partial Loss of Visual Functions

Partial loss of sensory function can be described in terms of clearly defined perceptual deficits or clinical syndromes called **agnosias** (from the Greek *a*, meaning not, and *gnosis,* meaning perception). We shall consider psychological studies of visual perceptual deficits in this section and agnosias in the next.

We have summarized the major types of visual disorders in Table 11-1, identifying three types of partial loss of visual functions: visuoperceptual disturbances, visuospatial disturbances, and visuomotor disturbances.

TABLE 11–1. Summary of visual disorders

Visuoperceptual disturbances
Impaired discrimination of complex stimuli
Impaired visual recognition
Impaired color recognition
Impaired figure-ground differentiation
Impaired visual integration
Visuospatial disturbances
Defective localization of points in space
Defective judgment of direction and distance
Defective topographic orientation
Unilateral visual neglect
Visuomotor disturbances
Defective eye movements
Defective assembling performance
Defective graphomotor performance

Source: Modified from Benton, 1979.

Visuoperceptual Disturbances. Individuals with complete, or nearly complete, visual fields may have disturbances in at least five types of *visuoperceptual* skills. First, they may be impaired at the discrimination of complex stimuli. Although it is uncommon for individuals to have difficulty in discriminating single attributes of stimuli such as size, brightness, or length, patients with temporal lobe excisions are impaired at discriminating between complex visual configurations that differ in some subtle characteristic. For example, Meier and French found that temporal lobe patients had great difficulty in picking out one of four drawings of concentric circular patterns, differentiated on the basis of only one cue (see Figure 11-3*A*).

Second, individuals may be unable to recognize stimuli. Thus, when presented with an object or other visual stimulus, the individual is unable to identify it. In its simplest form, this could be attributed to an inability to name things rather than an inability to actually recognize them. Although many cases of apparent inability to recognize are undoubtedly due to difficulties in naming, most workers in the field conclude that this cannot account for all recognition deficits. For example, there are people whose primary complaint is an inability to recognize familiar faces. Recognition deficits may present a form of complex visual-discrimination deficit, because objects (or faces) that normal people perceive as being very different may actually be differentiated on the basis of relatively subtle cues, which only become distinctive with visual experience.

Third, individuals may be unable to name or to use colors correctly, even though they can pass tests of color blindness and can name objects appropriately. There are many different disabilities in color perception that are observed clinically, and we shall consider them in more detail in our discussion of color agnosia.

Fourth, impairment in the ability to separate figure from ground is a common feature of visuo-

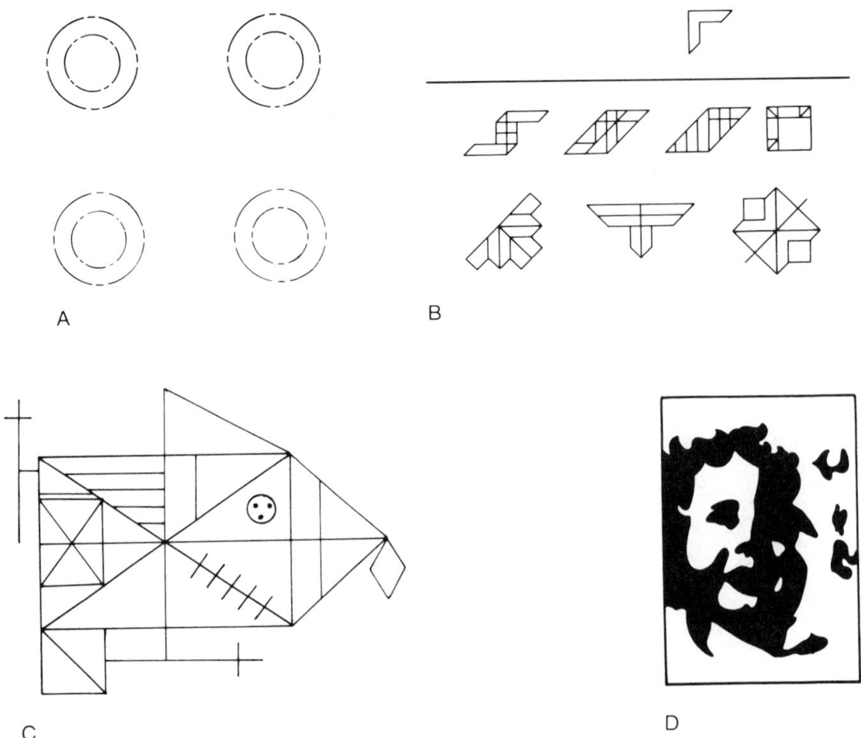

FIGURE 11-3. Examples of tests for visual disorders. *A*. Meier and French's Test, in which the subject must identify the drawing that is different. *B*. Sample of the Gottschaldt Hidden-Figure Test. The task is to detect and trace the sample (upper drawing) in each of the figures below it. *C*. Rey-Osterith figure. The subject is asked to copy it as exactly as he or she can. *D*. Sample of the Mooney Closure Test. The task is to identify the face in the ambiguous shadows.

perceptual deficits. This difficulty is easily shown by tasks such as the Gottschaldt figures, illustrated in Figure 11-3*B*, or by Luria's test of visual recognition, illustrated in Figure 11-4. Although the cause of this disorder is not known, it is common, being observed in a significant proportion of persons with focal brain disease, independent of the locus of their lesions.

Fifth, individuals with posterior lesions, especially in the right posterior-temporal region are impaired at synthesizing the content of a picture. This can be demonstrated in any test in which the visual material is ambiguous and must be interpreted in some manner. In a simple example, the Mooney Visual-Closure Test requires that a person examine a complex pattern of shadows, integrating the information to identify an object, often a face (see Figure 11-3*D*). In a more difficult test, the McGill Picture Anomalies, a person is to identify what is wrong or unusual in a drawing, such as the Mona Lisa hanging in a monkey cage.

It is evident that the disorders of visuoperceptual abilities are often subtle, and that they are very different from **anopias** (i.e., blindness). The anatomical bases of perceptual disabilities are less certain, although they presumably arise from damage

FIGURE 11-4. Luria's test of visual recognition of crossed-out figures is found to be difficult for sufferers of visual agnosias. One response to the crossed-out watch was "chick hatching from an egg and some funny circles."

in secondary or tertiary zones, especially of the right hemisphere.

Visuospatial Disturbances. Faulty perception of spatial aspects of visual experience may lead to a number of disorders grouped under the rubric of *visuospatial.* Although we consider these disorders in detail in Chapter 24, we shall briefly review them in the context of visual disorders.

Benton has grouped these disorders into four basic categories, as summarized in Table 11-1. Defective localization of points in space can be demonstrated easily by asking a person to touch points in space (defined by the investigator's finger) while maintaining a fixed forward gaze. A second class of visuospatial disorders can be observed in persons with difficulties in judging direction and distance of or length of stimuli. Hence, these persons are impaired at estimating the angle of orientation of lines or the length of the lines. Further, they may be impaired at perception of depth, although this has not been as thoroughly studied. A third type of visuospatial disturbance is a deficit in topographical orientation. In this case people have great difficulty in describing how to travel from one place to another, or even in describing the floor plan of their own home. People with these difficulties are frequently lost, apparently being unable to appreciate their spatial location using prominent landmarks as cues. Finally, individuals may exhibit a symptom known as **unilateral visual neglect.** In this disorder they completely fail to respond to stimuli in one or the other lateral visual fields, almost as though they were anopic. It can be shown, however, that they are not anopic but rather fail to respond to stimuli in the visual field. We return to this disorder in our discussion of symptoms of parietal lobe damage in Chapter 17.

Visuomotor Disturbances. We use the term *visuomotor disturbance* to refer to any deficit in making movements directed by visual stimuli, of which there are at least three distinct types. The first disorder is one in moving the eyes to scan visual stimuli. Normal subjects have a very complex but consistent manner of looking at objects, pictures, and the like. This organized pattern is completely disrupted in many subjects with perceptual disorders, who may produce largely random eye movements as illustrated in Figure 11-5. Inability to scan visual material normally may be an important factor in many of the visuoperceptual disorders described above, although this possibility has not been systematically studied. The two other forms of visuomotor disturbances are quite different; although both require the subject to reconstruct something presented visually In the first case, a deficit sometimes described as **acopia** (from the Greek, meaning not copy) or a *graphomotor* dysfunction, the person is asked to draw a geometric figure that is placed in front of him or her. Difficulties in copying the Rey-Osterith figure (Figure 11-3*C*) provide a good example of this difficulty. The drawings are frequently badly

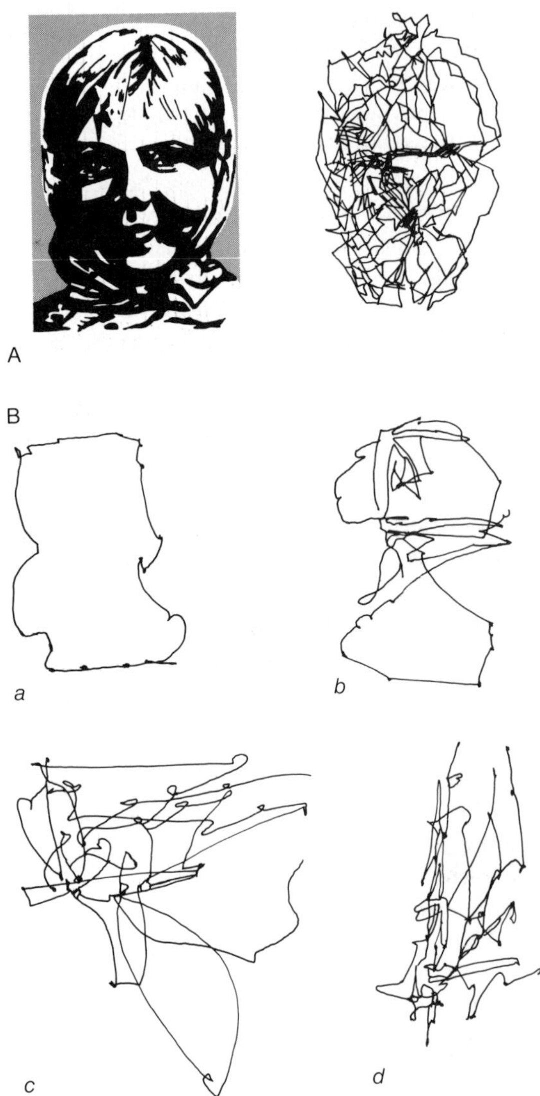

FIGURE 11-5. Eye movements during the examination of a visual stimulus. *A*. The concentration of eye movements (by a normal subject) to distinctive features of the face (eyes, nose, mouth); these movements are directed more at the left side of the photograph. *B*. The eye movements of a normal subject examining a sphere (*a*) and a bust (*b*); *c* and *d* represent the eye movements of an agnosic subject examining the same shapes. Note the random movements of the agnosic subject. (From A. R. Luria, *The Working Brain*. Copyright © 1973, The Copyright Agency of the USSR. Reprinted with permission.)

distorted or have material missing. The final type of visuomotor disturbance is a deficit in visuomotor construction, which is sometimes referred to as a *visuoconstructive disorder*. That is, the subject is asked to construct, often with blocks, some design or structure that is placed in front of him or her. Like the copy of the Rey-Osterith figure, the construction is often drastically altered, frequently with only superficial resemblance to the original. This type of disturbance is often referred to as **constructional apraxia,** a disorder we shall return to in later chapters.

Visual Agnosias

Visual agnosia is the term coined by Sigmund Freud for the inability to combine individual visual impressions into complete patterns—thus, the inability to recognize objects or their pictorial representations, or to draw or to copy them. This definition includes many of the visual deficits that we described above, but we present them here as clinical syndromes, since they are often encountered in this form in the neurological literature. There are several types of commonly observed visual agnosias, summarized in Table 11-2 and described below. (For a particularly interesting case history of visual agnosia in an artist, see Wapner et al.)

Visual Object Agnosia. A person with visual object agnosia, when shown an object, can see it but is unable to name it, demonstrate its use, or remember having seen it before. Hécaen and Albert describe one patient who identified a bicycle as "a pole with two wheels, one in front, one in back." Visual object agnosias are rare, leading to controversy over their existence and the precise location of the lesion leading to this condition. Hécaen and Angelergues found only four instances of object agnosia among 415 patients with cortical lesions. The consensus is that a lesion of the left occipital lobe extending into subcortical white matter is necessary for the condition to occur. It is

TABLE 11–2. Summary of the major agnosias

Type	Deficit	Most probable lesion site
Visual angosias		
Object agnosia	Naming, using, or recognizing objects	Areas 18, 19, 20, 21 on left + corpus callosum
Agnosia for drawings	Recognition of drawn stimuli	Areas 18, 19, 20, 21 on right
Prosopagnosia	Recognition of faces	Areas 18, 19, 20, 21, 37 bilaterally
Color agnosia	Association of colors with objects	Areas 18, 19 on right
Color anomia	Naming colors	Speech zones or connections from areas 18, 19, 37
Achromatopsia	Distinguishing hues	Areas 18, 19, 37
Visual spatial agnosia	Stereoscopic vision, topographical concepts	Areas 18, 19, 37 on right
Auditory agnosias		
Amusia	Tone deafness; melody deafness; disorders of rhythm, measure, or tempo	Areas 42, 22 on right
Agnosia for sounds	Identifying meaning of nonverbal sounds	Areas 42, 22 bilaterally?
Somatosensory agnosias		
Asterognosis	Recognition of objects by touch	Area 5, 7
Anosognosia	Awareness of illness	Areas 7, 40 on right
Anosodiaphoria	Response to illness	Areas 7, 40 on right
Autotopagnosia	Localization and naming of body parts	Areas 7, 40? on left
Asymbolia for pain	Reaction to pain	Area 43?

common for the damage to be bilateral, often including the corpus callosum and the inferior longitudinal fasciculus in the right hemisphere.

Visual Agnosia for Drawings. Visual agnosias affect recognition of a variety of drawn stimuli, including realistic representations of simple objects, complex scenes, schematic reproductions of objects, geometric figures, meaningless forms, incomplete figures, and abstract drawings. The lesion producing this condition is most likely located in secondary and tertiary visual cortex areas 18 through 21 in either hemisphere, although lesions in the right hemisphere seem to be implicated more frequently.

Prosopagnosia: Agnosia for Faces. In 1947, Bodamer (cited in Hécaen and Albert) described the inability of three patients to recognize faces although they were able to recognize objects, forms, and colors. This deficit, although rare, has since been confirmed by many others and is known as **prosopagnosia** (from the Greek *proso,* face; *a,* not; and *gnosis,* perception). People with prosopagnosia cannot identify faces but can identify the voice of people when they speak. They also may be able to identify a person from some salient characteristic such as style of gait or clothing. Although once believed to be a relatively pure agnosia, this visual deficit is not limited to faces. Patients may fail to recognize other familiar visual stimuli such as buildings, certain groups of animals, makes of cars, and so forth. In addition, according to Damasio they invariably have a deficit in color perception. There is little agreement on the best explanation of prosopagnosia, but it appears that the damage must be bilateral and generally includes parts of areas 18 and 19, and sometimes 20, 21, and 37. According to Damasio there have been 12 postmortem studies on prosopagnosics, and the damage in all these people has been bilateral. This result implies that the process of facial recognition must be bilateral, although the contribution of each side is probably not equivalent. Unilateral damage to both the left and right occipital area leads to difficulties in face recognition, although the right hemisphere plays a dominant role. It appears that memory for faces is impaired by lesions of the right temporal lobe, and perception of faces by lesions of the right parietal lobe.

Color Agnosia. Impaired color recognition can take any of three different forms: achromatopsia, color anomia, and color agnosia. **Achromatopsia** is an inability to distinguish different hues although normally pigmented calls are present in the retina. It can be described as cortical color blindness, which differs from congenital color blindness in that achromatopsia affects all parts of the color spectrum. All colors appear less bright, and the environment is "drained of color" or, in severe cases, totally lacking color. **Color anomia** (from the Greek for no meaning), or *color aphasia,* is an inability to name the characteristic colors of familiar objects and is generally associated with other aphasic symptoms. **Color agnosia** is an inability to associate particular colors with objects or particular objects with colors. Hécaen and Albert characterize color agnosia as (1) preservation of color perception as determined by tests of color discrimination, and (2) inability to select all colors of the same hue from a group of colored objects, to pick out or point to colors on command, to name colors in the absence of aphasia, and to evoke the specific colors of color-specific objects such as a tomato or grass.

Anatomical studies have not conclusively indicated which lesions result in the various types of disturbances in color perception and recognition. Meadows presented a theoretical anatomical model, which we have altered somewhat in Figure 11-6. Achromatopsia appears to result from bilateral lesions of the occipital-temporal area, presumably including those areas in which cells are responsive to color. Damasio describes an interesting case of a unilateral lesion in the same territory that produced a hemiachromatopsia in the contralateral hemifield. Achromatopsia usually occurs in combination with other visuoperceptual impairments, but it can apparently occur in remarkably pure form, suggesting that there is a specialized area in the secondary cortex devoted to color perception. Color aphasia or anomia results from a lesion of the speech zones or a disconnection of the speech zones from visual areas specialized for color perception, thus isolating the regions from one another. Color agnosia could result from a variety of lesions that disconnect the color cells from the memory functions. In this case, color could be seen but not recognized. Correlated defects in linguistic ability could result from damage to the connections with the language zones or to the language zones themselves.

Visual Spatial Agnosias. A variety of disorders of spatial perception and orientation have been described. These deficits, caused mainly by right posterior hemispheric lesions (particularly in the right parietal and occipital cortex), include defective stereoscopic vision, loss of topographical concepts, and neglect of one side of the world. We shall return to spatial agnosias in our discussion of the parietal lobes in Chapter 17.

Are Faces Special?

Faces convey a wealth of social and affective information to humans. This importance of faces as visual stimuli has led several authors to postulate a special mode for the analysis of faces that is analogous to the left hemisphere's apparent innate predisposition for the analysis of words. When the visual system encounters words, a special processing mechanism in the tertiary visual region of the left hemisphere is invoked to allow their comprehension. Teuber suggested that when faces are encountered, they are analyzed by a special processing mechanism in the right hemisphere so that

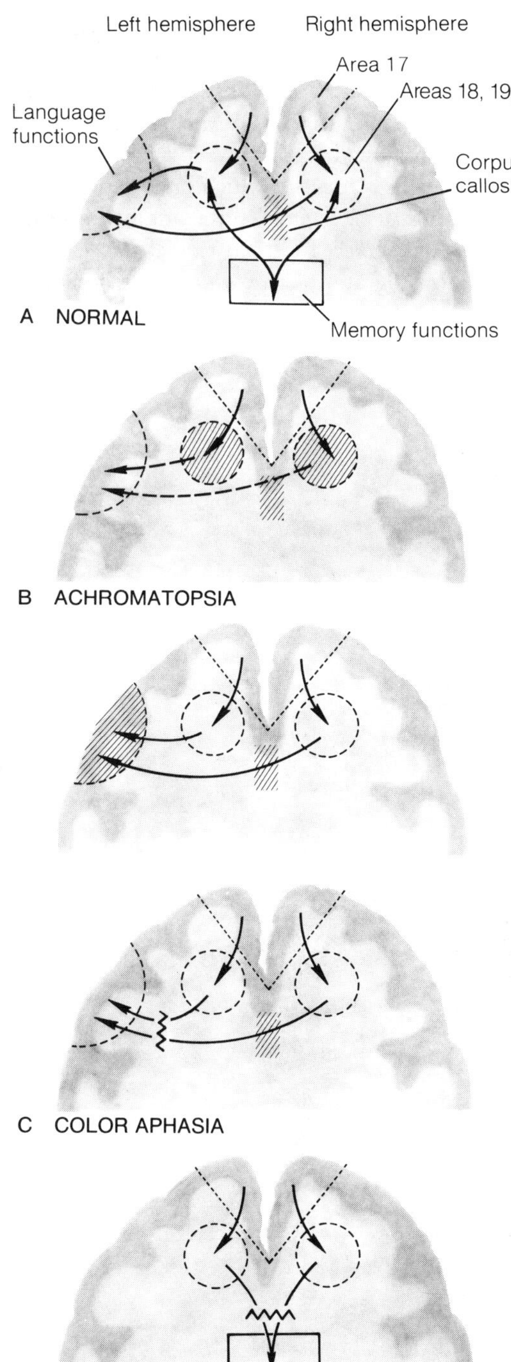

they are recognized in a manner analogous to words. One source of support for this idea comes from the observation that the perception of faces is strongly influenced by their orientation. For example, Yin found that the memory of photographs of faces was impaired in patients with right posterior lesions but that this handicap was reduced when the photographs were presented upside down or when other complex visual stimuli, such as houses, were used instead. Yin concluded that photographs of faces presented upright are processed by a special mechanism in the right hemisphere so that they are recognized in a manner analogous to words. Because faces presented upside down do not stimulate the special mechanism, right posterior lesions do not affect the recognition of these stimuli.

The possibility that faces might be special raises several questions. First, if there is a special processing mechanism for faces, where is it located? The tertiary cortex of the right parietal lobe is a likely candidate but, as we noted earlier, prosopagnosia is not very common, even in the presence of large right parietal lesions that produce many other deficits (see Chapter 17). Second, there is some doubt as to the nature of the special perceptual mechanism. Teuber appears to have assumed it to be a mechanism devoted to combining features of facial stimuli into a whole, or *gestalt,* but it is uncertain how this mechanism would be specific for faces. In fact, a clever study by Diamond and Carey suggests that it is not specific to faces, because they found that dog experts, who could distinguish

FIGURE 11-6. Cerebral function demonstrating possible mechanisms of various abnormalities of color vision. Each diagram represents a schematic section through the brain illustrating visual association cortex (areas 19, 20, 21), language functions, and a theoretical memory function. Memory functions are drawn as a single box, but it is understood that this is schematic and may not represent a brain structure. (After Meadows, J. C. Disturbed perception of colours associated with localized cerebral lesions. *Brain* 97:615–632, 1974.)

individual dog faces of the same breed, were just as sensitive to the inversion of dog photographs. These authors suggest that it is because we are experts at distinguishing faces of humans (or dogs) that we are disturbed differentially when face photographs are rotated. The fact that children are poor at distinguishing faces and are relatively unaffected by inversion is consistent with this idea. Nonetheless, there is little doubt that faces are processed in a special way by the right hemisphere. We presented subjects with photographs of faces as illustrated in Figure 11-7. Each of the two lower photographs is a composite of the left or the right side of the original face shown in the upper photograph. Asked to identify which of the composite photographs most resembled the original, normal subjects consistently matched the left side of the original photograph to its composite, whether or

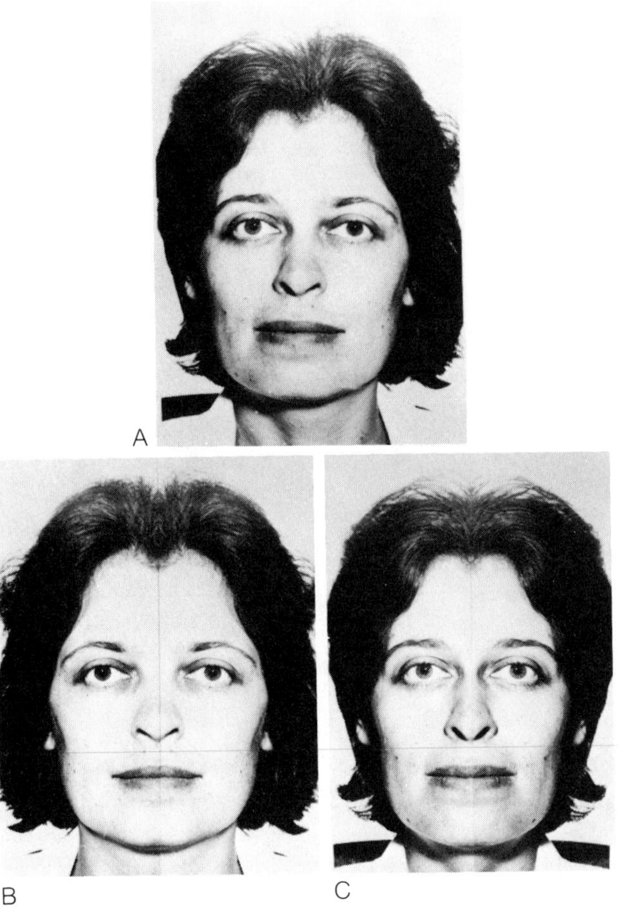

FIGURE 11-7. An example of the split-faces test. Subjects were asked which of the two bottom pictures, *B* or *C*, most closely resembles the top picture, *A*. Picture *C* was chosen by controls significantly more often than *B*. Picture *C* corresponds to that part of *A* falling in the subjects' left visual field. (After Kolb, Milner, and Taylor, 1983.)

not the photographs were presented upright or inverted. Furthermore, patients with either right temporal or right parietal removals failed to match consistently to either side of the face in either the upright or the inverted presentation.

The idea that "faces are special" is intriguing, but we believe that the data on facial perception and memory warrant a more parsimonious interpretation: the posterior part of the right hemisphere is specialized for the processing of complex visual patterns, whether they be faces, geometric patterns, or the like. Perception of faces is particularly sensitive to the effects of right posterior damage because faces are especially complex and because there are so many different faces, many of which appear superficially highly similar. Indeed, the uniqueness of individual human faces is based on very small differences, and mastery of the differentiation of faces requires considerable practice, and possibly includes a genetic predisposition. In this regard, deficits in facial perception might result, in part, from deficits in the identification of the distinctive features used in differentiation, rather than in the flawed formation of an actual gestalt of a particular face. As we noted, if the normal pattern of visual scanning of faces is disrupted, recognition of faces might be impaired in spite of a relatively intact percept of a given face. Indeed, the difficulty that normal adults initially have in differentiating individuals of an unfamiliar race may imply that one must learn to scan the faces of different racial groups in particular ways to identify the cues necessary for accurate identification.

Finally, we consider the perception of our own face. This provides a unique example of visual perception since our own image of our face comes largely from looking in a mirror, thus providing a reversed image, whereas others' image of our face comes from direct view. Inspection of Figure 11-7 illustrates the implications of this difference. The top photograph is the image that other people see of this woman and, since there is a left visual-field bias in our perception, most right-handers choose the bottom right as the picture most resembling the original. Consider the choice of the woman herself, however. Her common view of her face is the reverse of ours and hence she is more likely to choose (and in fact did) the other composite photograph as the most resembling her own face. One intriguing consequence of our biased self-facial image is our opinion of personal photographs. Many people complain about not being photogenic, that their photographs are never taken at the correct angle, that their hair wasn't just right, and so on. The problem may be rather different: we are accustomed to seeing ourselves in a reversed mirror image and hence when we view a photograph, we are biased to look at the side of our face that we do not normally selectively perceive. Indeed, we appear not to see ourselves as others see us!

EFFECTS OF LESIONS OF THE AUDITORY SYSTEM

The classic identification of the neocortex with the capacity for visual sensation led to the prediction by H. Munk in the 1880s that bilateral damage to the auditory cortex would result in "psychic deafness," a term later replaced in the 1930s with *cortical deafness.* Although people with bilateral damage to the auditory cortex are relatively rare, both the available clinical evidence and evidence from animal studies do not support this prediction. There is in fact little disruption of sensitivity to changes in frequency or intensity after either bilateral or unilateral auditory cortex lesions in any mammal studied. Nonetheless, the auditory cortex is involved in certain types of complex auditory analysis, which can be documented both in terms of audioperceptual and audiospatial deficits, as well as by auditory agnosias.

Audioperceptual Deficits

There are at least five relatively independent impairments in audioperception following temporal lobe lesions, which include core, secondary, and tertiary auditory regions (see Table 11-3). First, although the processing of simple acoustic information is accomplished normally after cortical damage, the detection of brief sounds is markedly impaired. For example, Tallal and Piercy found that patients with lesions which include auditory cortex were impaired at discriminating 43-msec sounds of changing frequency but performed normally when the duration of the sounds was increased to 95 msec. A second, related impairment is observed in the judgment of the simultaneity of brief sounds. Cortical lesions appear to increase the time needed *between* sounds in order to discriminate the sounds. This impairment is presumably related to the common complaint among patients with left temporal and parietal lobe damage that people are talking quickly. The problem is not so much the quickness of the speech but the inability of these people to discriminate between sounds quickly presented—a difficulty commonly encountered by normal people during the acquisition of a new language. A third audioperceptual impairment is also related to timing of auditory stimuli, namely the judgment of temporal order in sounds heard. If a normal subject is presented with two sounds, a temporal separation of only 50 to 60 msec is sufficient to identify correctly which of the two sounds was presented first. Subjects with temporal lobe lesions may require as much as 500 msec (a tenfold increase) in order to perform at the same level. Each of these first three audioperceptual impairments appears to be more severe following left rather than right temporal lobe lesions—a result suggesting that these auditory skills are especially important in the discrimination of speech sounds. It is therefore not surprising that left but not right temporal lobe lesions produce a marked deficit in the discrimination of speech sounds, the fourth audioperceptive impairment. For example, persons with such lesions who are asked to repeat pairs of oppositional phonemes, such as da-ta, ba-pa, or sa-za, have difficulty doing so correctly. Instead, they repeat da-da, ba-ba, and so on. In a more difficult test, known as **dichotic listening,** subjects are presented with two words or digits simultaneously, one to each ear. Persons with left temporal lobe lesions have a marked deficit in the recall of dichotically presented digits or words, although they have no difficulty if the words are presented monoaurally. Rather than being specific to the right ear, the deficit appears in both ears, suggesting some sort of deficit in selectively attending to and differentiating between simultaneous speech sounds. One might predict that people afflicted would have a very difficult time listening to a conversation in the midst of much background talking, such as at a party.

TABLE 11-3. Summary of auditory disorders

Audioperceptual
Defective detection of brief sounds
Defective discrimination of simultaneously presented sounds
Defective judgment of temporal order of sounds
Defective discrimination of speech sounds
Defective discrimination of time, loudness, timbre, and tonal memory in music
Audiospatial
Impaired binaural localization of sounds

Finally, there is an audioperceptual symptom that is specific to the right temporal lobe, namely the perception of certain characteristics of music. Milner gave patients the six subtests of the Seashore Measures of Musical Talents Test: pitch discrimination, loudness, rhythm, time, timbre, and tonal memory. Patients with right temporal lobe lesions were impaired at all of the tests, although they were significantly worse than left temporal lobe patients only on the tests of time, loudness, timbre, and tonal memory—the difference being largest on the last two subtests. The timbre test measures the ability to distinguish between complex sounds that differ only in harmonic structure. It consists of 50 pairs of tones; for each pair the subject must judge whether the tone quality of the two is the same or different. On the tonal memory test a sequence of notes is played twice in rapid succession; the sequences are identical except that one note in the sequence is changed in the second playing. The subject must compare the two tonal patterns and identify, by its number in the sequence, the note that was changed at the second playing. Thus, the deficit in the analysis of music observed after right temporal lobe damage is enhanced as the subtests become more difficult, including an element of timing or temporal ordering, a result that is parallel to the deficit in processing speech sounds after left temporal lobe damage.

Audiospatial Impairment

Like the visual system, the auditory system functions to identify the spatial location of sensory information, but unlike the visual system, deficits in spatial localization are difficult to demonstrate reliably. Studies of cats with complete removal of the auditory cortex shows a complete inability to localize sound but smaller, partial lesions leave localization unaffected. If this result can be generalized to humans, it would be expected that partial removal of the temporal lobe would have a limited effect on audiospatial localization, whereas complete removal would be more likely to impair this ability. To date, the data are conflicting, but there is some evidence that large temporal-parietal lesions, especially of the right hemisphere, do impair the ability to localize sound in space. (See de Renzi for a review of the controversial data.)

Auditory Agnosias

An **auditory angnosia** is the impaired capacity to recognize the nature of nonverbal acoustic stimuli. Like visual agnosias, auditory agnosias presumably result from a variety of perceptual disturbances, although these are not as well understood as those in visual agnosias. The commonest auditory agnosias are **amusia** (agnosia for music) and agnosia for other sounds (see Table 11-2).

Amusia. Amusias can be subdivided into various forms, including *tone deafness* (the inability to discriminate various tones in a scale) and *melody deafness* (impaired recall or recognition of a melody) as well as disorders of rhythm, measure, or tempo. To date there are only scattered case reports of these various amusias, and there are no compelling quantitative studies demonstrating **double dissociation** to show they are independent. Lesions resulting in amusias usually have been located in the right middle temporal regions.

Agnosia for Sounds. Agnosia for sounds is characterized by an inability to identify the meaning of nonverbal sounds, such as a bell ringing. Sounds either may sound all alike to the patient or, if they are distinguished, may be confused for one another. In the former case all sounds may be labeled as birdsong, whereas in the latter case birdsong and bell tinkling may be confused. Some individuals remain able to recognize speech and music, but more usually amusia and word deafness (inability to discriminate words) are associated.

To date, the location of the lesions resulting in agnosia for sounds is uncertain, although the evidence favors bilateral temporal damage. We suspect that the syndrome of perceiving all sounds as similar may result from damage, perhaps bilateral, to secondary auditory areas. On the other hand, different sounds may be confused because the auditory percept is disconnected from the verbal or memory components necessary to label the sound, much as is the proposed cause of color agnosia (Figure 11-6).

Is Music Special?

In 1926, Henschen reported 16 patients who had musical agnosia but had no language deficit. Since preservation of musical abilities in aphasic musicians had been documented many times since the 1920s, Henschen concluded that the two functions are in opposite sides of the brain. This argument was not unanimously accepted, and today it is difficult to find a convincing case of amusia in the absence of a language or perceptive disorder.

Nevertheless, there is some evidence that Henschen's idea may be partly correct. For example, left hemisphere lesions can produce **aphasia** while leaving singing ability relatively intact. Thus, we are inclined to agree with Henschen: we think it reasonable to propose that some aspects of music and language are juxtaposed in the brain and to expect right hemisphere lesions to produce a condition of amusia analogous to the aphasia that results from left hemisphere lesions. Further support for this idea comes from the common clinical observation that many severely aphasic patients can carry a tune and an even sing the words to previously learned songs. We saw a middle-aged woman with severe left hemisphere damage and dense aphasia who was able to sing with some coaxing and even managed a recognizable version of the national anthem — much to the surprise of herself, us, and the attending nurses. (See Chapter 22 for a detailed discussion of aphasia.)

Proof of Henschen's proposal requires more than case histories, however, and this proof has been very elusive. In the past two decades there have been many experiments on normal subjects as well as numerous case reports of amusias in musicians, but there is still no clear consensus on the nature of hemispheric processing of music. A major difficulty appears to be that people listen to or perform music differently. In particular, there is good reason to suppose that musical training or practice may change the way in which music is processed. Werner observed in 1948 that "musically experienced listeners have learned to perceive a melody as an articulated set of relations among components rather than as a whole." If Werner is correct, we might predict that musical training causes a shift in processing from the right hemisphere to include processing by both hemispheres, or even predominantly by the left, a prediction that finds some support in studies of normal subjects (e.g., those of Bever and Chiarello). However, there is little supporting evidence for this view in the neurological literature, and so this intriguing idea is still best considered as a hypothesis.

There has been very little study of musical processing in patients, other than musicians, but recent work suggests that right hemisphere lesions lead to a selective deficit in the processing of complex harmonic sounds. Similarly, right hemisphere lesions appear to have a greater influence on the control of vocal pitch in language and song. These results suggest a special role for the right hemisphere in music, although the exact role is not entirely clear.

Overall, we are impressed with a particularly thoughtful review by Brust, who concludes that current conceptions of the cerebral organization of music, including the view that increasing musical sophistication causes a shift in locus of musical processing, are oversimplifications. The door would seem wide open for imaginative studies of cerebral processing of musical perception and production in both brain-damaged and normal people, especially if we are to demonstrate the specialness of music.

EFFECTS OF LESIONS OF THE SOMATOSENSORY SYSTEM

Alterations in somatic sensation and its various submodalities, including touch-pressure, appreciation of limb position and limb motion, and sensitivity to temperature and pain, are powerful indices of posterior cortical damage, although the tedious nature of the assessment discourages most neuropsychologists from doing thorough assessments. Nevertheless, it is now possible to identify a number of sensory and perceptual deficits associated with damage to the postcentral gyrus (areas 3a, 3b, 1, and 2) and the adjacent cortex (areas 5,7, and S_{II}).

Verger in 1902 and Dejerine in 1907 published the first descriptions of somatosensory loss resulting from cortical lesions. Symptoms of this Verger-Dejerine syndrome include loss of tactile localization, loss of sense of a limb's position in space, loss of tactile form discrimination, and impaired recognition of objects by touch (astereognosis). On the basis of thorough clinical studies Henry Head elaborated the Verger-Dejerine syndrome, and he concluded in 1920 that lesions of the somatosensory cortex produce three largely independent effects: (1) the threshold for appreciation of the intensity of tactile, thermal, or painful stimuli is raised; (2) stereognosis is impaired; and (3) spatial recognition is impaired, because information about the spatial position of a limb is lost. This distinction of three types of disorders holds today, and we shall consider them using Head's categorization (See Table 11-4).

Somatosensory Thresholds

Damage to the postcentral gyrus is normally associated with marked changes in somatosensory thresholds. The most thorough studies of these changes were made by Semmes and her colleagues in 1960 on war veterans with missile wounds to the brain and by Corkin and her coworkers, who assessed patients who had undergone cortical surgery for relief of epilepsy. Both groups found that lesions of the postcentral gyrus produced abnormally high sensory thresholds, impaired position sense, and deficits in stereognosis. For example, in the Corkin and coworkers' study, patients performed poorly at detecting light touch to the skin (i.e., pressure sensitivity), at determining if they were touched by one or two sharp points (two-point threshold), and at the localization of points of touch on the skin on the side of the body contralateral to the lesion. If blindfolded, the patients also had difficulty in reporting whether the fingers of the contralateral hand were passively moved or not. Whereas the Semmes and Corkin groups are agreed on the effects of damage within the postcentral gyrus, they fail to agree on the effects of damage beyond it. In their study Semmes and her colleagues found an apparent asymmetry in the somatosensory system: missile wounds in the right hemisphere produced a sensory defect indicating that somatosensory function was diffuse throughout the right hemisphere. In the left hemisphere, by contrast, only lesions that invaded the region of the postcentral gyrus produced deficits. The apparent asymmetry in somatosensory function is remarkable, and surprising, for two reasons: first, lesions to primary areas in the visual and auditory systems do not produce asymmetrical effects, and second, many of the lesions studied must have been outside the primary sensory zone. Corkin and her colleagues failed to find any evidence of asymmetrical organization in their surgical patients, however—a result that leads us to question the nature of cerebral injuries in the two patient populations. Because the cerebral injuries in the war veterans occurred naturally, these lesions would be less restricted than those of the surgical patients, whose injuries would normally be limited to cortical tissue. For this reason, the data from the latter patients must be given more weight, but the issue is not yet resolved.

Lesions of the postcentral gyrus may produce a variety of other deficits not reported by the Semmes and Corkin studies. For example, Luria reported a symptom that he calls **afferent paresis:** movements of the fingers are clumsy because the person has lost the necessary feedback about their exact position. If lesions of the postcentral gyrus cause loss of representation of the face area in the left hemisphere, another defect is often observed: **motor aphasia,** a transient aphasia in

TABLE 11–4. Summary of somatosensory disorders

Somatosensory thresholds
- Raised threshold for the detection of touch, temperature, and painful stimuli
- Impaired sense of limb motion and position

Somatoperceptual
- Impaired tactile appreciation of object qualities (astereognosis)
- Simultaneous extinction

Somatospatial
- Imapired arm or limb placement in the absence of visual guidance

which the person appears unable to figure out how to position the lips and tongue to pronounce the desired sounds. Although motor aphasia is possibly analogous to Luria's afferent paresis, motor aphasia is not observed following lesions to the homologous region in the right hemisphere.

Somatoperceptual Disorders

The presence of normal somatosensory thresholds does not preclude the possibility of other types of somatosensory abnormalities. First, both the Semmes and the Corkin group noted a **stereognosis,** a disturbance that can be demonstrated in tests of tactile appreciation of object qualities, illustrated in Figure 11-8. In these tests subjects are told to handle shapes or they have objects placed on the palm of their hand. The task is to match the original shape or object to one of several alternatives, which are also out of view. According to Teuber, subjects with impaired somatosensory thresholds almost always exhibit astereognosis, although the association is not mandatory. Subjects who demonstrate astereognosis alone are less common, normally having more posterior lesions that also result in "spatial deficiencies." We will consider this condition below.

A second somatoperceptual disorder, **simultaneous extinction,** can only be demonstrated by special testing procedures. The logic in this test is that a person is ordinarily confronted by an environment in which many sensory stimuli impinge on him or her simultaneously, yet the person is able to distinguish and perceive each of these individual sensory impressions. Thus, a neuropsychological test that presents stimuli one at a time represents an unnatural situation that may underestimate, or miss altogether, sensory disturbances. Hence, in order to present more complicated sensory stimulation, two tactile stimuli are presented simultaneously to homologous or heterologous body parts. The objective of such double simultaneous stimulation is to uncover those situations in which each of the two stimuli would be reported if applied singly, and those situations in which only one of the two stimuli would be reported if both were applied together. Bender has described a failure to report one stimulus as **extinction.** Damage to the somatic secondary cortex, especially in the right parietal lobe, is most commonly associated with extinction, although it can occur from damage to other regions as well.

As Teuber has noted, much remains to be done in exploring the role of intensity, place, and timing

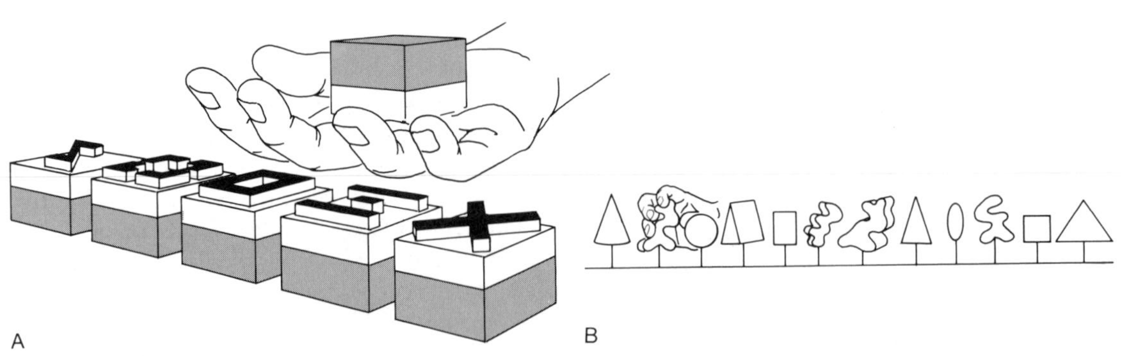

FIGURE 11-8. Examples of tests for tactile appreciation of objects. *A*. A pattern is placed for 5 sec on the subject's palm, and then placed within the array. The task is to identify the original by handling all six patterns. *B*. A duplicate of one of the patterns is handled by the subject. The task is to identify, again by handling, the matching pattern in the array. (After Teuber, 1968).

of the stimuli that tend to produce extinction, not only in the tactile but also in the visual and auditory modes. One intriguing finding is that stimulation of nonhomologous body points (e.g., one side of the face and the contralateral hand) may reveal *rostral dominance.* That is, the subject is more likely to report the touch on the face than that on the hand. Similar results are often found in studies of recovery of sensory orientation in animals, and rostral dominance should probably be studied more extensively in human patients.

Blind Touch

We have seen that in the visual system there is evidence that patients can identify the location of visual stimuli even though they deny "seeing" it. Paillard and his colleagues reported a case of a woman who appears to have a tactile analogue of blindsight. In their case a woman with a large lesion of areas 5, 7, and 39 had a complete anesthesia of the right side of the body that was so severe that she was liable to cut or burn herself without being aware of it. In spite of this, she was able to point with her left hand to points on her right hand where she had been touched, even though she failed to report feeling the touch. Although this is a single case report, the phenomenon is clearly reminiscent of blindsight. The presence of a tactile analogue of blindsight is important for it suggests that there are two tactile systems that are specialized for detection and localization, respectively. This may be a general feature of sensory system organization.

Somatospatial Disorders

People with posterior parietal damage, including the secondary somatosensory regions in areas 5 and 7, frequently have difficulty in accurately placing the limbs to points in space, especially in the absence of visual guidance. One cause of this disorder could be the loss of sensory feedback about limb position (i.e., kinesthesis), thus making limb placement difficult. However, as we shall see in later chapters, this disorder could also result from a loss of the normal marriage of tactile and visual information, presumably due to damage to tertiary cortex.

Somatosensory Agnosias

There are two major types of somatosensory agnosias: *astereognosis* (from Greek *somatos,* meaning body), the loss of knowledge or sense of one's own body and bodily condition. Although astereognosis is essentially a disorder of tactile appreciation, we include it here because it is often described clinically as an agnosia.

Astereognosis. Astereognoses have been recognized since 1844. In 1885, Karl Wernicke divided tactile agnosias into two categories: primary agnosia and secondary agnosia, or asymbolia. Primary agnosia is an inability to recognize tactile qualities of an object, allegedly because of an inability to evoke tactile images. In **asymbolia,** the tactile images are preserved but are disconnected or isolated from other sensory representations; thus, the full significance of the object cannot be appreciated. According to classic neurological doctrine, the principal locus for astereognosis is the posterior parietal cortex, roughly areas 5 and 7. The Corkin study reviewed earlier failed to observe this effect, for tactile agnosias were consistently correlated with defects in sensation, implying that the lesion included primary sensory regions. Clinical cases of tactile agnosia in the absence of any primary sensory defect have been reported, but they are rare.

Asomatognosia. **Asomatognosia,** the loss of knowledge about one's own body and bodily condition, is one of the most curious of all agnosias. It is an almost unbelievable syndrome—until one has actually observed a person neglecting part of his or her body or denying an obvious illness. There are a variety of different asomatognosias, including **anosognosia,** the unawareness or denial of illness; **anosodiaphoria,** indifference to illness; **autotopagnosia,** an inability to localize and name body parts; and **asymbolia for pain,** the absence of normal reactions to pain. A case study of a patient with asomatognosia is described in Chapter 17.

Asomatognosias may be for one or both sides of the body. Unilateral anosognosias and anosodiaphorias, resulting from lesions of the posterior parietal region in the right hemisphere, are most commonly of the left side of the body. Autotopagnosias result from lesions of the left parietal cortex. The lesion location responsible for asymbolia for pain has not yet been established, although it most frequently results from left hemisphere lesions, possibly because S_{II} either has suffered a lesion or has been disconnected from affective regions of the brain.

EFFECTS OF LESIONS ON TASTE AND OLFACTION

As humans, one of our greatest pastimes is eating and drinking (including all of its cultural aspects) both of which are dependent upon the taste and olfactory systems. It is thus remarkable that virtually nothing is known of the effects of brain injury in humans on either of these sensory systems. This is all the more surprising since a common complaint of stroke and closed-head injury patients is that food has lost its taste and smell.

Taste

Behavioral studies of gustatory cortex lesions in nonhumans are not only few in number but also contradictory; some studies find a change in taste threshold and some do not. An extensive series of studies by Braun have shown that bilateral lesions of the gustatory area produce reliable deficits in learning to associate novel tastes with subsequent illness (known as *taste-aversion learning*), and the characteristic reluctance of rats to consume novel flavors (known as *neophobia*). There are no comparable studies of humans, but it is reasonable to predict parallel results. The inability to form taste associations can be conceptualized as a form of taste agnosia, which leads to the prediction that gustatory lesions in humans might produce an agnosia. If this proves true it suggests a different organization than that seen in the visual, auditory, and somatosensory systems, and indeed, the absence of secondary or tertiary cortex for the sense of taste is consistent with this possibility.

Olfaction

John Hughlings-Jackson first recognized in 1899 that temporal lobe seizures were often preceeded by olfactory auras. Similarly, Penfield and Jasper elicited olfactory sensations from stimulation of the medial temporal region, including the amygdala and its hooklike protrusion, or uncus (see Figure 18-2). Several recent studies have shown that patients with temporal lobectomies have a variety of olfactory deficits, including a slight reduction in the sensitivity to odors, deficits in odor identification, and deficits in odor memory. Little is known about the relative contribution of cortical and subcortical regions of the temporal lobe in these effects.

In addition to temporal lobe involvement in olfaction it is reasonable to expect that orbitofrontal lesions might interfere with olfaction since this region receives the major projection from the olfactory system (see Chapter 10). The available data are limited, but there appears to be a decrement in the abilities to differentiate and to identify odors. In particular Jones-Gotman and Zatorre found that orbitofrontal lesions produced bigger deficits than did temporal lobe lesions and that frontal lesions that spared the orbitofrontal area did not produce any deficit at all. It would be interesting to see if orbital lesions interfere with odor associations, as this would parallel the gustatory results discussed earlier.

In summary, although taste and olfaction provide notable sensory experiences, they are little studied in neurological patients. It is curious that there are not even any case histories of individual patients following brain injury. For example, it would be fascinating to hear of the taste and olfactory abilities of experts such as chefs or wine vinters who have experienced brain injuries.

HIGHER LEVEL SENSORY SYSTEM INFLUENCES

As we have seen, the secondary and tertiary sensory zones produce a selective picture of the external world by a process known as perception. Normal perception may be disrupted either directly or indirectly. *Direct disruption* occurs either by an absence of sensory input, in which case there may be no perception at all, as in blindness or deafness, or by a lesion of the secondary and tertiary sensory zones, in which cases there is an agnosia. *Indirect disruption* can also occur if higher level control of the perceptual process is altered. As Figure 11-9 shows, sensory information is relayed to the frontal and anterior temporal lobes in the form of a perception; these higher levels in turn project back on the sensory systems. Thus, a feedback loop is formed whereby perceptions can be influenced by previous experience, cognitive set, ongoing behavior, and so on — influences beyond the scope of the sensory representation of the external world. Consider the following possibilities.

If the sensory input is ambiguous, the perception may be influenced either by cognitive set or by a change in behavior. For example, imagine that you are walking through a park at dusk. Shapes become indistinct in the darkness because the sensory input is inadequate to provide a clear percept of your surroundings. If you are worried that a mugger might be hiding in the bushes (i.e., your set is for muggers), every noise and shape is perceived in that context. On the other hand, if you have no such set, the higher levels may produce behavior necessary to gather more information. Noises and vague shapes are explored to provide a

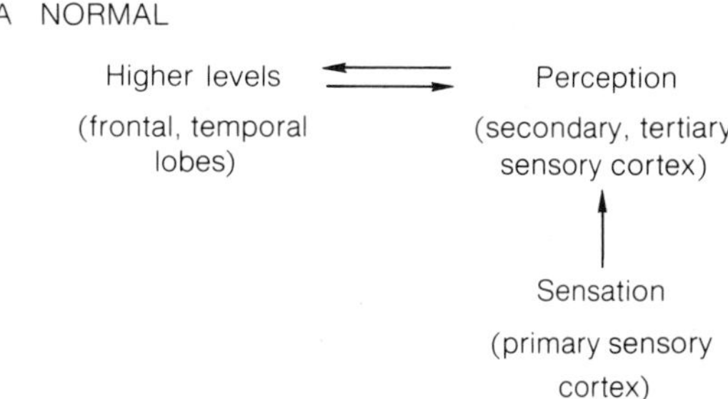

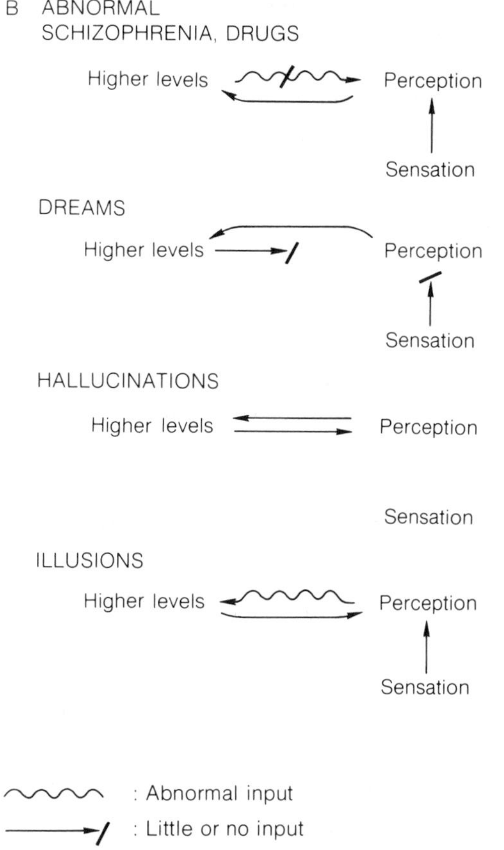

FIGURE 11-9. *A.* The role of higher levels in the activity of the sensory systems. Sensory input travels to the frontal and temporal (anterior and medial) lobes, which can in turn influence the perception via a feedback loop. *B.* Hypothetical disturbances in the higher level control of sensory systems resulting in various perceptual phenomena.

clearer sensory representation and hence modify the perception.

The influence of the higher levels may also sometimes be inhibitory on the sensory systems, preventing perceptions from dominating behavior. For example, one is unlikely to flee suddenly from the park because of one's perceptions concerning muggers. Fleeing is inhibited, and frequently, so-called displacement behaviors such as whistling or humming, are produced instead.

The higher levels also allow sensory input to be interpreted in the context of behavior, If you move your eyes, you do not preceive the world to move because there is **corollary discharge:** input from the frontal lobe informing the perceptual systems of the eye movement. If you gently push down on your eyelid with your finger, the eye moves but there is no corollary discharge, and so the world is perceived as moving when it did not. In the absence of higher level input, the sensory stimulation is perceived literally and possibly erroneously. (The effects of frontal-lobe lesions on corollary discharge are discussed in Chapter 19).

Finally, the higher levels add the influence of experience to sensory input (recall our motorist who perceived "ST" as "STOP"). In the absence of higher level input, sensory input is difficult to interpret, and perhaps can even be meaningless. Nakamura and Mishkin beautifully demonstrated this phenomenon when they surgically removed the frontal cortex, parietal cortex, and portions of the temporal cortex of monkeys, leaving the visual and limbic systems intact. The remarkable result was that although the visual and limbic systems were intact, the monkeys were behaviorally blind. Food could only be found by tactile and auditory cues, fearful objects were ignored, and unfamiliar environments were explored using only tactile cues. Although the visual system was intact, it was unable to influence behavior because the sensory input was disconnected either from the motor output or from the descending influence of higher cortical areas. This conclusion is supported by Nakamura and Mishkin's subsequent observation that the activity of individual cells in the visual areas was similar to the activity in seeing animals.

Higher Level Control Disorders and Perceptual Disorders

Seeing the sensory systems as hierarchical and as being influenced by higher level input makes it possible to understand a number of complex perceptual phenomena such as illusions, hallucinations, and dreaming, in addition to the complex perceptual disturbances found in drug intoxication or schizophrenia.

During the surgical treatment of epilepsy, Penfield, working with Jasper and with Perrot, discovered that stimulating the neocortex produces several remarkable phenomena: **illusions** (perceptual distortions), **hallucinations** (apparent perception of sights, sounds, etc., that are not actually present), and dreamlike states similar to what Hughlings-Jackson had described as dreamy states or psychical seizures in epileptic attacks. These phenomena reported by Penfield are of great interest, because they provide a key to understanding illusions, hallucinations, and dreams under more normal circumstances.

Penfield reported illusions of four basic forms. (1) Auditory illusions (sounds seem louder, fainter, more distant, or nearer) occurred when the superior temporal gyrus (area 22) of either hemisphere was stimulated. (2) Visual illusions (objects seem nearer, farther, larger, or smaller) occurred predominantly when the right temporal lobe was stimulated. (3) Illusions of recognition in which present experience seems either familiar (déjà vu) or strange, unreal, and dreamlike occurred predominantly when the right temporal lobe was stimulated. (4) Emotional illusions such as feelings of fear, loneliness, or sorrow occurred when either temporal lobe was stimulated.

Hallucinations took the form of dreamlike states in which familiar voices, music, scenes, and so on were experienced as being there, even when the patient knew that they could not be. Like illusions, the auditory hallucinations occurred when area 22 of either hemisphere was stimulated, whereas the visual hallucinations occurred primarily when the right temporal lobe was stimulated. An example of the responses of one of Penfield and Jasper's patients follows.

This French Canadian veteran, age 24, had had seizures for 6 years. His attacks were ushered in by a dizziness in which there was a sense of rotation. Then he might hear a voice calling "Sylvere, Sylvere, Sylvere." Sylvere was his own first name. As the years passed the warning changed to a feeling of nausea which he located behind his sternum. The warning gave him time to lie down so that he would not fall. There was a lapse of consciousness which might only last for 30 seconds. At times there was a major convulsive seizure.

Psychical precipitation. He volunteered the information that an attack was sometimes precipitated when he sought to recall the name of a person or to reflect whether or not he had seen a thing before. He illustrated this in a conversation with Dr. Robert Sears as follows, "Now, for example, if I thought I had seen you somewhere, perhaps in a crowd, and if I tried to make certain in my mind whether I had seen you or not, I might have an attack.

The precipitating factor seemed to be the intellectual process involved in comparing the present experience with the memory of past similar experiences. This is the same mechanism which must be interfered with during perceptual illusions. In an *illusion of familiarity* ("déjà vu") there is false activation of the mechanism. When this patient tried to make normal use of that mechanism he evidently precipitated an epileptogenic discharge in the temporal cortex.

The focus of the seizures was shown by preoperative electroencephalograms to be right temporal. Ventricular pneumography showed some enlargement of the right temporal horn of the ventricle.

Right osteoplastic craniotomy [opening of skull to expose the right hemisphere] was carried out.

There was evidently an *arteriovenous anastomosis* within the temporal lobe. The substance of the temporal cortex was of normal consistency on its lateral aspect but the superior surface of the temporal lobe became quite abnormal where it lay in contact with the insula. Here it was yellow and tough. This toughness extended into the uncus and amygdaloid nucleus where it was grayish-yellow in color.

The Rahm stimulator [electrical stimulator] was set at 50 cycles and 1 volt for points 1 to 5. After that it was changed to 2 volts for succeeding stimulations. The following were some of the responses to stimulation.

Numbers 1 to 13 mark the sites of origin of somatic sensory and motor responses. Curiously enough, at point 11 the patient opened his mouth. This was followed by a *sneeze* and chewing movements.

14. "Just like someone whispering, or something, in my left ear. It sounded something like a crowd." Warning was then given but no stimulation. He reported, "Nothing."

15. "Again someone trying to speak to me, a single person." When asked, he added, "Oh a man's voice, I could not understand what he said."

16. (While the electrode was held in place.) The patient said, "Something brings back a memory, I could see Seven-Up Bottling Company—Harrison Bakery."

Warning given again, but no stimulus applied. Again he was not fooled and replied, "Nothing."

17. (While the electrode was held in place.) "Again something I have heard of but I cannot remember it." On questioning he added that it was a word but he could not remember that word.

18. (Stimulus applied without warning the patient.) He said he was a little drowsy, then, "Someone was there in front of me right where the nurse is sitting."

19. (During stimulation.) "I am trying to find

the name of a song. There was a piano there and someone was playing. I could hear the song, you know. It is a song I have sung before but I cannot find out quite what the title of the song is." The electrode was removed. After listening to the above dictation the patient added, "That was what I was trying to do when you finished stimulating!"

19. (Repeated without warning.) After withdrawal of the electrode, he said, "Someone speaking to another and he mentioned a name, but I could not understand it." When asked whether he saw the person, he replied, "It was just like a dream." When asked if the person was there he said, "Yes, sir, about where the nurse with the eyeglasses is sitting over there."

19. (Repeated again without warning the patient and without questioning him.) "Yes, 'Oh Marie, Oh Marie'—someone is singing it." He was then asked who it was and replied, "I don't know, Doctor, I cannot recognize the voice."

19. (Repeated again without warning.) He observed, while the electrode was being held in place, "Again, 'Oh Marie, Oh Marie.'" He explained that he had heard this before. "It is a theme song," he said, "on a radio program. The program is called the 'Life of Luigi.'" The patient then discussed the identity of the song with Dr. Sears and he ended by singing the well-known refrain, "Oh Marie, Oh Marie." All in the operating room recognized the song.

21. "Someone telling me in my left [contralateral] ear 'Sylvere, Sylvere!' It could have been the voice of my brother."

23. "It is a woman calling something but I cannot make out the name."

24. (Deep stimulation with coated needle, the point being directed toward the buried transverse gyrus of Heschl.) "Buzzing sound."

25. (Stimulation without warning.) "There is someone near my left eye."

25. (Repeated without warning.) "Oh my left eye! I see someone." Then he explained that there were men and women. "They seemed to be sitting down and listening to someone. But I do not see who that someone might be.

22. Nausea.

19 was restimulated several times toward the close of exploration. Instead of causing him to hear the song, it produced nothing. The voltage was increased from 2 to 3 and the stimulation was repeated. This made him feel nauseated and he vomited, but it resulted in nothing else. (Penfield and Jasper, 1954, pp. 452–455)

The illusions and hallucinations described by Penfield and Jasper are remarkably similar to those observed in dreams or during epilepsy, sensory deprivation, drug intoxication, and other disorders. It is imperative to emphasize, however, that brain stimulation produces these states only in epileptic patients and not in patients with other neurological disorders, implying that epileptic brains are significantly different from other brains. Nonetheless, the similarity of spontaneous illusions and hallucinations to those observed by Penfield and Jasper is of great interest because it implies that these phenomena can be understood as disturbances in the normal functioning of the sensory systems.

Illusions. A variety of theoretical explanations have been proposed for illusions, but they are difficult to test empirically. Many such theories assume that illusions result from a failure of sensory and higher level input to become synthesized, since normal perception is assumed to rely on the integration of input from these sources. The result is a distorted perception of the world.

Hallucinations. Hallucinations can be thought to result from stimulation of the sensory cortex without stimulation of the receptors. Normally the higher levels (presumably the frontal lobe) exert an influence to resolve this discrepancy. If this frontal influence is absent, a pathological state occurs. An example will illustrate. It is a common occurrence to "see" nonexistent things out of the corner of one's eye, to "hear" nonexistent noises, or to "feel" nonexistent irritations on the skin. Ordinarily this sensory input is confirmed or discarded by the higher levels, which direct orienting behavior to investigate the perceived stimulation. But what if this behavioral response were not produced? Consider what happens if you intentionally inhibit your response to reach for a possible insect on your skin: the stimulation becomes intolerable, both becoming more intense and increasing your uncertainty about the significance of the stimulation—even though there may be absolutely nothing there. Normally behavior is produced to resolve the ambiguity, but schizophrenics or people under the influence of psychogenic drugs may fail to produce this behavior normally, if at all. The result may be perception of stimuli not actually present. Support for this admittedly speculative proposal comes from indirect evidence of frontal-lobe dysfunction in both schizophrenia and drug intoxication. The neurochemistry of the tertiary zones of the frontal lobes is known to differ from that of other neocortical regions, because there are catecholaminergic synapses in the frontal lobe and apparently few, if any, elsewhere in the neocortex. Since schizophrenia and the effects of psychogenic drugs are generally thought to produce major changes in dopaminergic synapses in the neocortex and elsewhere, it is reasonable to suggest that the frontal lobe's higher level influences on perception may be impaired. Although this interpretation is speculative, it provides a reasonable neuropsychological explanation of disordered perception in schizophrenia and drug intoxication.

Dreams

Remember that Penfield and Jasper produced "dreamy states" by electrically stimulating the higher level sensory zones of the temporal lobes, especially of the right temporal lobe. This suggests that dreams may normally result from activation of the temporal lobes (possibly more so of the right than of the left). As electrophysiological work in cats has shown, sensory input from the receptors is blocked during dreaming, correlating with the common observation that people are difficult to arouse during dreaming. As Hughlings-Jackson originally proposed, it seems probable that during dreaming, input from the frontal lobe and sensory systems is at least partially blocked from reaching the sensory zones. As a result the sensory zones are released from the influence of this source of higher control. These zones can still be influenced, however, by the medial temporal regions. Thus, the temporal lobe memory system activates the sensory zones—which may account, in part, for the realism of many dreams. This admittedly speculative proposal obviously fails to explain *why* the temporal lobe (and hence dreaming) should be activated during certain periods of sleep, but it does explain the perceptual component of dream activity. Probably the sensory zones are activated by an ascending input from the brainstem, although the genesis of this input remains uncertain. One testable prediction of this model can be made: patients from whom a temporal lobe, especially the right lobe, has been surgically removed should have significantly different dream activity, both in the content and nature of the sensory experience and, possibly, even in the frequency of dreaming.

SUMMARY AND QUESTIONS

Three fundamental principles describe the functional organization of the sensory systems:

1. The sensory systems are arranged hierarchically from the receptors at the bottom to the neocortex at the top, with coding complexity increasing at each higher level.

2. There are multiple representations of sensory information in at least the visual, auditory, and somatosensory systems.

3. Function is lateralized at the highest levels.

Lesions in the primary visual, somatosensory, and auditory systems produce serious deficits in sensory discrimination by significantly reducing acuity. Often after lesions in the secondary zones acuity is preserved, but although intellectual functioning is not disturbed, there is an inability to recognize objects or patterns. Further, there is tentative evidence of specific neurological substrates of illusions, hallucinations, and dreaming.

A nagging question remains: How much of a specific sensory system must remain intact to allow that sense to be processed? Why, for example, does unilateral removal of area 41, the primary auditory area, have negligible effects on hearing? A second question is: Do specific agnosias in fact consistently occur in the absence of other deficits? This issue has raised heated debate since the concept of agnosia was first proposed, and it is far from settled. The disagreement has its historical roots in the debate over localization of function. If functions are truly localized, it is logical to presume that somewhere there are people who have specific agnosias (e.g., for faces) and who exhibit no other deficits. In principle, this would seen simple to determine. Skepticism develops, however, when there is a consistent question about how thoroughly patients have been examined for other disorders.

REFERENCES

Bender, M. B. Extinction and precipitation of cutaneous sensations. *Archives of Neurology and Psychiatry* 54:1–9, 1945.

Benton, A. Visuoperceptive, visuospatial, and visuoconstructive disorders. In K. M. Heilman and E. Valenstein, eds. *Clinical Neuropsychology,* 2nd ed. New York: Oxford University Press, 1985.

Bever, T. G., and R. J. Chiarello. Cerebral dominance in musicians and nonmusicians. *Science* 185:537–539, 1974.

Braun, J. J., P. S. Lasiter, and S. W. Kiefer. The gustatory neocortex of the rat. *Physiological Psychology* 10:13–45, 1982.

Brust, J. C. M. Music and language: Musical alexia and agraphia. *Brain* 103:367–392, 1980.

Corkin, S., B. Milner, and T. Rasmussen. Somatosensory thresholds. *Archives of Neurology* 23:41–58, 1970.

Critchley, M., and R. A. Henson, eds. *Music and the Brain.* London: Heinemann Medical Books, 1977.

Curtis, B. Visual system. In B. A. Curtis, S. Jacobson, and E. M. Marcus, *An Introduction to the Neurosciences.* Philadelphia and Toronto: W. B. Saunders, 1972.

Damasio, A. R. Mechanisms of face recognition. In A. W. Young and H. D. Ellis, eds. *Handbook of Research on Face Processing.* New York: North Holland 1989.

Damasio, A. R., H. Damasio, and G. W. Van Hoesen. Prosopagnosia: Anatomical basis and behavioral mechanisms. *Neurology* 32:331–341, 1982.

Dejerine, J. A propos de l'agnosie tactile. *Revue de Neurologie* 15:781–784, 1907.

Diamond, R., and S. Carey. Why faces are and are not special: An effect of expertise. *Journal of Experimental Psychology: General* 15:107–117, 1986.

Eskenazi, B., W. S. Cain, R. A. Novelly, and R. Mattson. Odor perception in temporal lobe epilepsy patients with and without temporal lobectomy. *Neuropsychologia* 24:553–562, 1986.

Hebb, D. O. *The Organization of Behavior.* New York: Wiley, 1949.

Hécaen, H., and M. L. Albert. *Human Neuropsychology.* New York: Wiley, 1978.

Hécaen, H., and R. Angelergues. *La Cécité Psychique.* Paris: Masson et Cie, 1963.

Henschen, S. E. On the function of the right hemisphere of the brain in relation to the left hemisphere in speech, music and calculation. *Brain* 49:110–123, 1926.

Holmes, G. Disturbances of vision by cerebral lesions. *British Journal of Ophthalmology* 2:353–384, 1918.

Holmes, G. Disturbances in visual orientation. *British Journal of Ophthalmology* 2:385–407, 1918.

Jones-Gotman, M. and R. Zatorre. Olfactory identification deficits in patients with focal cerebral excision. *Neuropsychologia* 26:387–400, 1988.

Kolb, B., B. Milner, and L. Taylor. Perception of faces by patients with localized cortical excisions. *Canadian Journal of Psychology* 37:8–18, 1983.

Konorski, J. *Integrative Activity of the Brain.* Chicago: The University of Chicago Press, 1967.

Luria, A. R. *The Working Brain.* New York: Penguin, 1973.

Luria, A. R. *The Man with a Shattered World.* Chicago: Regnery, 1976.

Meadows, J. C. The anatomical basis of prosopagnosia. *Journal of Neurology, Neurosurgery and Psychiatry* 37:489–501, 1974.

Meadows, J. C. Disturbed perception of colours associated with localized cerebral lesions. *Brain* 97:615–632, 1974.

Meier, M. S., and L. A. French. Lateralized deficits in complex visual discrimination and bilateral transfer of reminiscence following unilateral temporal lobectomy. *Neuropsychologia* 3:261–272, 1968.

Milner, B. Laterality effects in audition. In V. B. Mountcastle, ed. *Interhemispheric Relations and Cerebral Dominance.* Baltimore: Johns Hopkins University Press, 1962.

Milner, B., and H.-L. Teuber. Alteration of perception and memory in man: Reflections on methods. In L. Weiskrantz, ed. *Analysis of Behavioral Change.* New York: Harper & Row, 1968.

Nakamura, K., and M. Mishkin. Chronic blindness following lesions of nonvisual cortex in the monkey. *Experimental Brain Research* 63:173–184, 1986.

Oscar-Berman, M., S. Blumstein, and D. DeLuca. Iconic recognition of musical symbols in lateral visual fields. Cited in M. A. Wyke. Musical ability: A neuropsychological interpretation. In M. Critchley and R. A. Henson, eds. *Music and the Brain.* London: Heinemann Medical Books, 1977.

Paillard, J., F. Michel, and G. Stelmach. Localization without content: A tactile analogue of 'blind sight.' *Archives of Neurology* 40:548–551, 1983.

Piercy, M., H. Hécaen, and J. de Ajuriaguerra. Constructional apraxia associated with unilateral cerebral lesions—left and right cases compared. *Brain* 83:225–242, 1960.

Penfield W., and H. H. Jasper. *Epilepsy and the Functional Anatomy of the Human Brain.* Boston: Little Brown, 1954.

Penfield, W., and P. Perrot. The brain's record of auditory and visual experience. *Brain* 86:595–696, 1963.

Ravizza, R. J., and S. M. Belmore. Auditory forebrain: Evidence from anatomical and behavioral experiments involving human and animal subjects. In R. B. Masterton, ed. *Sensory Integration. Handbook of Behavioral Neurobiology,* vol. 1. New York: Plenum, 1978.

Renzi, E. de, *Disorders of Space Exploration and Cognition.* New York: Wiley, 1982.

Rhodes, G. Lateralized processes in face recognition. *British Journal of Psychology* 76:249–271, 1985.

Riddoch, G. Dissociation of visual perceptions due to occipital injuries, with special reference to appreciation of movement. *Brain* 40:15–47, 1917.

Schneider, G. E. Two visual systems. *Science* 163:895–902, 1969.

Semmes, J., S. Weinstein, L. Ghent, and H.-L. Teuber. *Somatosensory Changes after Penetrating Brain Wounds in Man.* Cambridge, MA: Harvard University Press, 1960.

Semmes, J., S. Weinstein, L. Ghent, and H.-L. Teuber. Correlates of impaired orientation in personal and extra-personal space. *Brain* 86:747–772, 1963.

Sidtis, J. J. Music, pitch discrimination, and the mechanisms of cortical hearing. In M. S. Gazzaniga, ed. *Handbook of Cognitive Neuroscience.* New York: Plenum, 1984.

Sweet, W. H. Cerebral localization of pain. In R. A. Thompson and J. R. Green eds. *New Perspectives in Cerebral Localization.* New York: Raven Press, 1982.

Tallal, P., and M. Piercy. Developmental aphasia: Rate of auditory processing and selective impairment of consonant perception. *Neuropsychologia* 12:83–93, 1974.

Teuber, H.-L. The brain and human behavior. In R. Held, H. W. Leibowitz, and H.-L. Teuber, eds. *Perception. Handbook of Sensory Physiology* vol. VII. Berlin: Springer-Verlag, 1978.

Teuber, H.-L., and S. Weinstein. Performance on a formboard task after penetrating brain injury. *Journal of Psychology* 38:177–190, 1954.

Wapner, W., T. Judd, and H. Gardner. Visual agnosia in an artist. *Cortex* 14:343–364, 1978.

Warrington, E. K., M. James, and M. Kinsbourne. Drawing disability in relation to laterality of cerebral lesions. *Brain* 89:53–82, 1966.

Warrington, E. K., and P. Rabin. Perceptual matching in patients with cerebral lesions. *Neuropsychologia* 8:475–487, 1970.

Warrington, E. K., and A. M. Taylor. The contribution of the right parietal lobe to object recognition. *Cortex* 9:152–164, 1973.

Warrington, E. K., and L. Weiskrantz. An analysis of short-term and long-term memory defects in man. In J. A. Deutsch, ed. *The Physiological Basis of Memory.* New York: Academic Press, 1973.

Weiskrantz, L. *Blindsight: A case History and Implications.* Oxford: Oxford University Press, 1986.

Werner, H. *Comparative Psychology of Mental Development.* New York: International Universities Press, 1948.

Wyke, M. A. Musical ability: A neuropsychological interpretation. In M. Critchley and R. A. Henson, eds. *Music and the Brain.* London: Heinemann Medical Books, 1977.

Yin, R. K. Face recognition by brain-injured patients: a dissociable ability? *Neuropsychologia* 8:395–402, 1970.

ORGANIZATION OF THE MOTOR SYSTEMS

Animals are able to execute a remarkable number of movements. They can swim, crawl, walk, jump, and fly as well as use parts of their body, such as the limbs and mouth, for more discrete manipulations. The findings we present in this chapter suggest that the motor system can be subdivided into a number of subsystems, organized so that they can differentially control whole-body movements, independent movements of limbs, and independent movements of body parts and fingers. This organization can be seen in the evolution and development of movement and in the anatomical organization of the motor system. Primitive and infant animals are able to move only with whole-body movements, as fish do when they swim. More advanced and older animals move by making coordinated limb movements, as cattle or horses do when they walk. Primates including humans, in addition to being able to make whole-body movements and coordinated limb movements, can make discrete movements of the limbs and fingers. Studies of the neural basis of these successively evolved movement capacities figure prominently in studies of the motor system.

THE DEVELOPMENT OF MOVEMENT

The development of movement can be described from two perspectives: phylogenetic and ontogenetic. From a phylogenetic perspective it is apparent that the movements we refer to as whole-body movements evolved rather early. Primitive vertebrates and fish are restricted largely to whole-body movements, which they use in swimming. Amphibians make whole-body movements similar to those of fish but have also developed limbs with which they can make patterned movements for locomotion. The ability to make coordinated limb movements and independent limb movements developed only later, when mammals evolved; many mammals use one or two limbs independently of the others to engage in such behaviors as eating, nest building and fighting. Relatively independent movements of the arms and fingers, however, are seen only in primates and are most highly developed in humans. Thus, the phylogenetic story suggests the following independent, sequential evolution of movements: whole-body movements, coordinated limb movements, independent limb movements, and relatively independent finger movements. This sequential evolution suggests that there should have been a parallel evolution of brain structures to produce them. As we will show, subcortical motor systems are clearly involved in the production of whole-body movements, such as those used in swimming and walking, whereas the motor systems of the neocortex evolved to produce relatively independent movements of the limbs. Of the cortical motor systems, the cells projecting directly to the spinal motor cells appear to have been the most recent evolutionary development, and they are responsible for producing relatively independent limb and finger movements.

Two developmental studies illustrate the sequences of movement ontogeny: those by Coghill and by Twitchell. Coghill described the **ontogeny** of movement in the newt *Amblystoma*. The animal develops locomotion in a series of stages that permitted Coghill to correlate the anatomical changes in its nervous system with the development of new patterns of locomotion. The first movements made by *Amblystoma* are coiling movements of the whole body. The coiling is gradually modified until repeated alternating coils propel the animal through the water. Since the development of swimming in *Amblystoma* recapitulated that of swimming in vertebrates, Coghill was moved to observe that with the attainment of locomotion *Amblystoma* had passed one of the most significant landmarks in the evolution of animal behavior. The development of *Amblystoma,* however, does not stop with swimming, for the newt grows first front limbs and then hind ones. At first its walking movements are secondary to swimming, its limbs being used only in conjunction with whole-body coiling. As the animal matures the coiling diminishes in amplitude until the body is carried as a fixed trunk by the coordinated movements of the legs. This stage of motor development reached by *Amblystoma* is fairly representative of the locomotion of most amphibians and reptiles on land.

Everyone is aware of the development of locomotion in human infants. Infants are at first unable to walk, but with development they learn first to crawl and then to walk. The way in which infants learn to reach and grasp is less obvious. The ontogeny of relatively independent arm movements and relatively independent finger movements is seen most clearly in Twitchell's 1965 description of the development of the grasping reaction in human infants (Figure 12-1). Before birth the infant's movements are essentially whole-body movements, but after birth the infant gradually develops the grasping reaction, the ability to reach out with one limb and bring objects toward itself. The grasping reaction develops in a number of stages. Shortly after birth the infant can flex all the joints of an arm in such a way that it could scoop something toward its body, but it is not at all clear that this movement is executed independently of other body movements. Between 1 and 4 months of age the infant can grasp objects that come in contact with its hands but can do so only by closing all the fingers of a hand simultaneously. Between 3 and 11 months it orients its hand toward, and gropes for, objects that have contacted it. Between 8 and 11 months it develops the "pincer grasp," using the index finger and thumb in opposition to each other. The development of the pincer grasp is extremely significant, because it allows the infant to make a very precise grasping movement as well as to manipulate small objects or objects located in hard-to-reach places. In summary, then, we see the sequential develop-

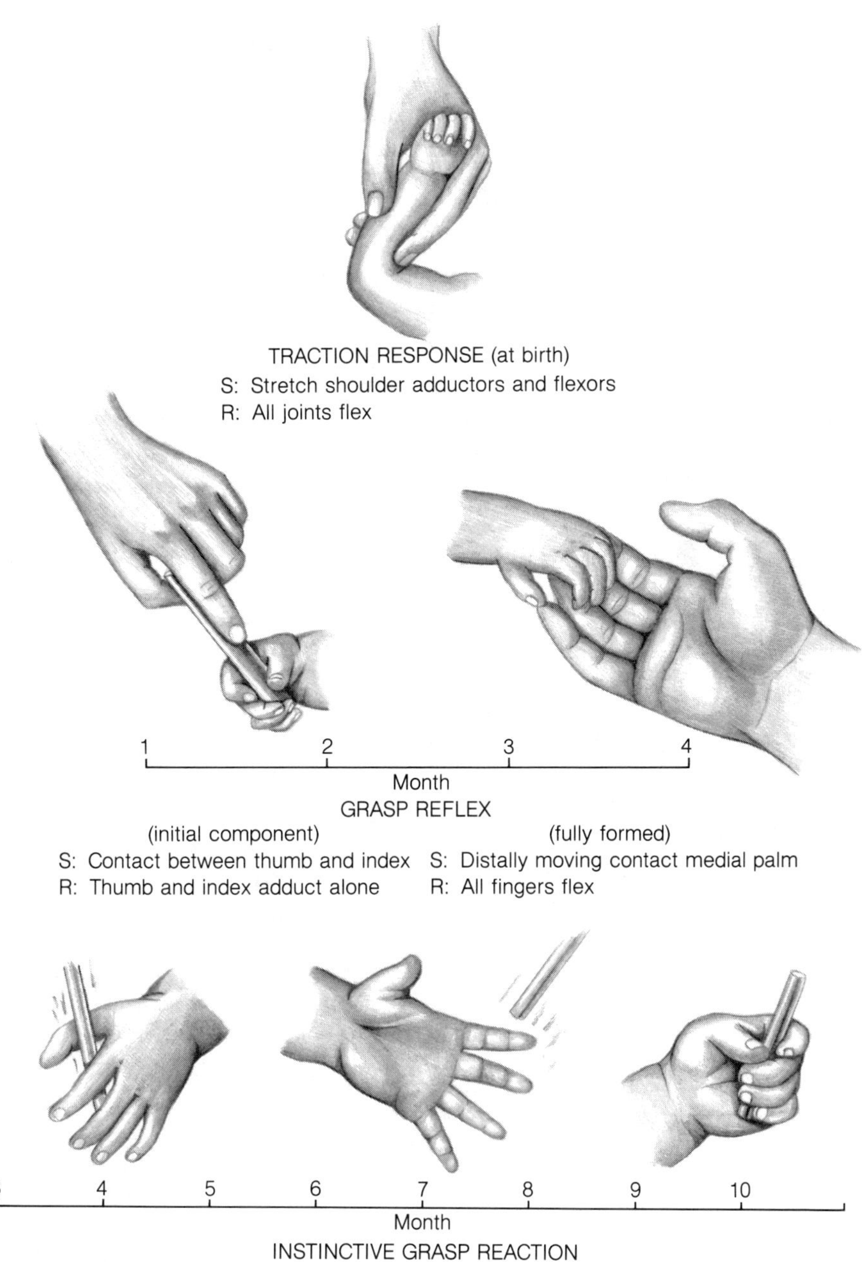

FIGURE 12-1. Evolution of the automatic grasping response of infants (After Twitchell, 1965).

ment of an independent limb movement quite clearly in the development of the infant's grasping reaction: first scooping, then reaching and grasping with all fingers, then independent movements of the fingers, as seen in the pincer grasp. Maturation of the motor cortex, as measured by its degree of **myelination,** parallels the development of the grasping reaction: small motor fibers from the precentral gyrus become myelinated at about the time that reaching and grasping develop; the giant Betz cells of the precentral gyrus become myelinated at about the time the pincer grasp develops. As we shall discuss in more detail later, these different motor fibers are thought to control arm movements and finger movements, respectively.

THE ANATOMY OF THE MOTOR SYSTEM

The motor system can be divided into a number of subsystems. These include the spinal cord, the brainstem, the cerebellum, the basal ganglia, and the neocortex. There are many interconnecting pathways between these structures. They also have a hierarchical organization and a parallel organization, which are illustrated in Figure 12-2. That is, the brainstem and cortex can each independently influence the spinal cord to elicit movements, but they also have interconnections that permit them to mutually influence each other.

Our current understanding of the motor systems leans heavily on work by Lawrence and Kuypers, who used an ingeniously simple procedure to disclose its organization. They traced motor fibers from muscles of the body back to their cells of origin in the spinal cord. They then traced the fibers that connected with these spinal cord cells to their origins in various places in the brain. What they discovered is conceptually quite simple. The muscles of the fingers, arm, and shoulder seem to be controlled by one set of pathways from the brain, and the trunk of the body seems to be controlled by a second set of pathways.

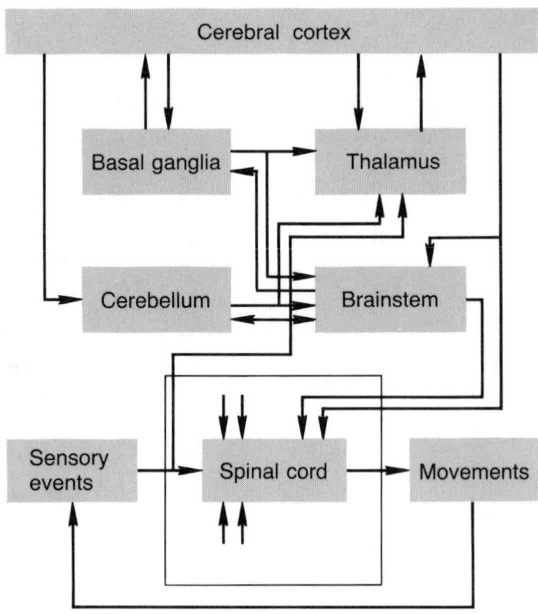

FIGURE 12-2. Diagrammatic representation of the organization of the motor system showing its major structures and connections.

Not only are these two pathways distinguished by their routes and origins, they are distinguished in another way. The pathways that control hand and arm movements are crossed, whereas those that control trunk movements are not. Stated simply, each hemisphere controls the trunk of the body of the same side and the arms and legs of the opposite side. This anatomical organization seems to have a quite obvious relation to the evolution and development of movement described above. Before pursuing this story it may be worthwhile to briefly describe the organization of the spinal cord.

THE SPINAL CORD

General Structure of the Spinal Cord

The spinal cord receives projections from the sensory receptors of the body through its dorsal roots.

Some of these projections synapse with motor neurons and interneurons to produce reflexes, whereas others project to the brain to participate in the production of more complex movements. There are also large projections back from the brain. Finally, there are many connections between segments of the spinal cord. All of these inputs influence muscles via the motor neurons of the spinal cord. For this reason the motor neuron projection to muscles is referred to as the *final common path.* The path, however, is segregated with respect to the muscles it innervates. Simply speaking, muscles are divided into a number of groups partly in relation to their location and partly in relation to their function. *Proximal* will be used to refer to muscles of the trunk and *distal* will refer to muscles of the arms and legs. The assumption is made in this discussion that trunk musculature is under somewhat different motor control than distal musculature. We will also subdivide distal musculature into shoulder, arms, and fingers. The implication is that these muscle groups are also under partly different motor control. For example, during walking, the arms are moved mainly from the shoulder and all limbs are moved together in a coordinated fashion. During a movement such as reaching, a single arm is used, and it is moved in a more complicated way around a number of joints. Finger movements can be made when the limb is otherwise still. We do not mean to imply that these categories of movement are absolutely clear-cut. If it is held in mind how fish swim, how quadrupeds walk, how primates can use a limb for independent movements and how humans can use fingers in a skilled independent fashion, then that is the general idea. What we are going to suggest is that it is helpful to relate these movement categories and muscle groups to different anatomical structures.

The spinal cord can be subdivided functionally and anatomically into two rings, an inner and an outer ring. The inner ring is gray matter, a core of cells with a "butterfly" shape. The dorsal wings are called the *dorsal columns* and the ventral wings are called the *ventral columns* (Figure 12-3*A*). The outer ring is white matter, made up of fiber tracts running to and from the brain. The dorsal and ventral columns of gray matter subdivide the white matter into three *funiculi* (from the Latin for cord): the dorsal, the lateral, and the ventral funiculi.

The spinal cord can also be divided into a dorsal portion, which is mainly sensory, and a ventral portion, which is mainly motor (in upright humans the appropriate terms would be *posterior* and *anterior*). The cells in the dorsal column mainly receive sensory information from the body, whereas the cells in the ventral column are interneurons and motor neurons involved in controlling movement. The *dorsal funiculi* contain *proprioceptive pathways;* that is, fibers from skin and muscle receptors that carry information about skin sensation, muscle position, and movements of the body to the brain. The *lateral* and *ventral funiculi* consist mainly of descending motor pathways from the brain. Thus, damage or cuts to the dorsal portion of the cord mainly impairs sensation, whereas damage or cuts to the ventral portion of the cord mainly impairs movement.

Motor Neurons and Interneurons

Cells that project to muscles are called **motor neurons.** They are located in the nuclei of the cranial nerves and in the ventral columns of the spinal gray matter (Figure 12-3*B*). All movements are produced via these cells. As it turns out, very few other cells connect directly to motor neurons. They instead synapse first with **interneurons,** which in turn synapse with the motor neurons. The motor neurons are located in two zones of the ventral columns of the spinal cord: a lateral cell groups is called the *dorsolateral cell group,* and a medial group is called the *ventromedial cell group* (Figure 12-3*B*). The interneurons are located more dorsally and medially in the *intermediate zone* of the spinal gray matter. Motor neurons and interneurons for the cranial nerves are similarly arranged, but for simplicity we shall describe only the spinal cord.

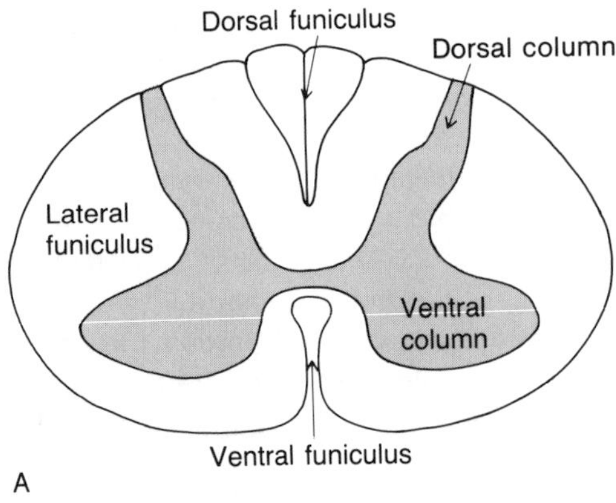

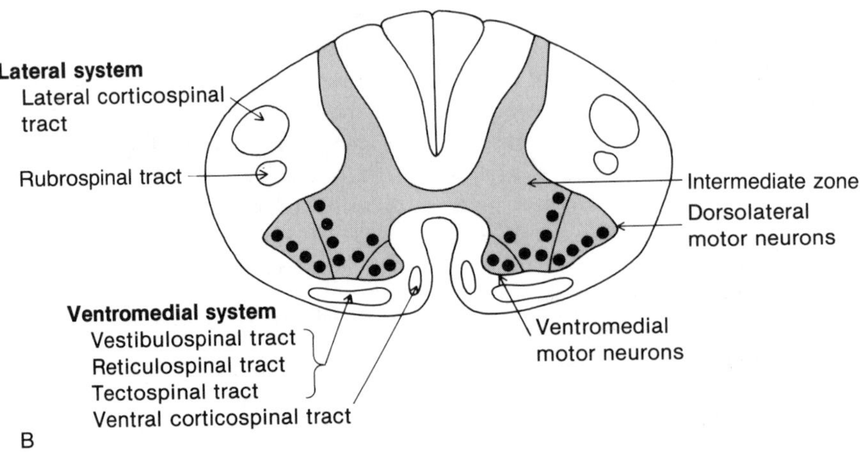

FIGURE 12-3. *A*. Major structures of the spinal cord. *B*. Location of the lateral and ventromedial systems and the interneurons and motor neurons of the ventral columns.

Motor neurons of the dorsolateral cell group innervate distal musculature, including the fingers, hand, and arm muscles. They are arranged in such a way that motor neurons innervating the fingers are more dorsal and those innervating the arm and shoulders are more ventral. Motor neurons in the ventromedial cell group innervate the axial musculature, that is, the musculature of the body midline (Figure 12-4*A*). The interneurons are similarly organized: the interneurons located in the dorsolateral portion of the intermediate zone connect to dorsolateral motor neurons; interneurons located in the ventromedial portion of the intermediate zone connect to ventromedial motor neurons. As a result, the dorsolateral interneurons eventually control distal musculature, and the ventromedial motor neurons eventually control proximal musculature.

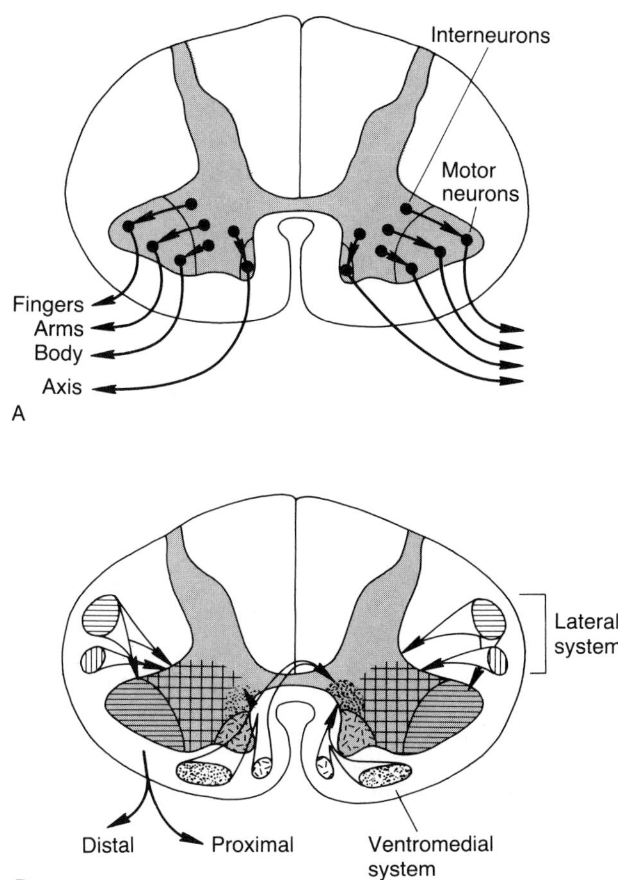

FIGURE 12-4. *A*. Topographic relation between interneurons, motor neurons, and the body locations to which motor neurons project. *B*. Projection of pathways of the lateral system and ventromedial system onto interneurons and motor neurons. Arrows indicate areas to which fiber tracts project. Different areas of crosshatching correspond to area labeled in Figure 12-3.

In addition to the relation between motor neurons and body muscles, there is a lateral-medial organization of the motor neurons. More laterally placed cells tend to produce extensor movements when active, and more medially located cells tend to produce flexor movements. Since extensor and flexor movements are produced by different muscle groups, both the organization with respect to body muscles and the organization with respect to movements suggest that the interneurons and motor neurons are arranged in pools that control specific muscle groups.

Projections to Interneurons and Motor Neurons

Each motor neuron receives thousands of terminals from other neurons, so to contract a muscle, it must ultimately reflect the majority opinion from these various sources. Comparatively very little of the input onto a motor neuron is direct; rather, most comes indirectly through interneurons. There are three major sources of input: from the body, from the brain, and from other spinal cord segments. We will restrict our description to projections from the brain.

There are at least nine fiber projections from the brain, and each is probably involved in producing a different kind of movement. These projections can be divided into two major groups or systems (Figure 12-3*B*). The **lateral system** connects with dorsolateral interneurons and motor neurons. There are two major tracts in the lateral system: the *lateral corticospinal tract* (literally from cortex to spinal cord) and the *rubrospinal tract* (*rubro* for red, so from red nucleus of the midbrain to spinal cord). The **ventromedial system** connects with ventromedial interneurons and motor neurons. Its tracts include the *vestibulospinal tracts,* the *reticulospinal tracts,* and the *tectospinal tracts* from the brainstem and the *ventral corticospinal tract,* which originates in the neocortex (Figure 12-4*B*). As we shall later describe, the division of the motor tracts into two systems has functional implications. The tracts in the lateral system are largely concerned with producing limb movements, whereas those of the ventromedial system are largely concerned with producing body movements.

The Central Origin of Motor Tracts

As noted above, two systems project from the brain to spinal cord. Each of these systems contains at least one projection from the cortex and one from the brainstem. Thus, it seems that the brain exerts a dual control over movement. The cortex can control distal musculature through a lateral system projection and it can control proximal musculature through a ventromedial system projection. The brainstem divides its projections in the same way. We will describe the cortical and brainstem levels of control separately.

The Brainstem

The brainstem has a more complex architecture than the spinal cord, but within the arrangement of its structures can be recognized the basic plan of the spinal cord. The sensory and motor fibers of the spinal cord have their continuation in the sensory and motor fibers of the 12 cranial nerves that enter the brainstem. The spinal motor-neuron cell groups have their counterparts in the motor nuclei of the cranial nerves. The spinal ventromedial cell group differentiates into the hypoglossal (XII) nucleus and then more rostrally into nuclei that control eye movements [the abducens (VI), trochlear (IV), and oculomotor (III) nuclei]. The lateral motor-neuron cell group, which innervates distal musculature of the body, has its counterpart in the nuclei that control facial movements [the facial (VII), hypoglossal (XII), and trigeminal (V) nuclei]. In particular, the medial facial nucleus, which innervates the ear muscles, may be the counterpart of the more medially located dorsolateral motor neurons. On the other hand, the lateral facial nucleus, which innervates muscles of the mouth and muscles around the eyes, may be the counterpart of the more laterally located motor neurons.

Brainstem Origins of the Ventromedial System. The brainstem contains a number of nuclear groups that send fiber tracts to the brainstem motor nuclei and to the motor cells of the spinal cord. Tracts that form the ventromedial system originate in the vestibular nuclei, the reticular formation, and the tectum. The vestibulospinal tract is the origin of information from the vestibular system of the middle ear, and it functions to maintain posture and balance. The tectospinal tract contains fibers that originate in the superior colliculus, the midbrain visual center. Its function is to produce orienting movements to visual stimuli. The reticulospinal tracts come from many cell groups in the reticular formation. In turn, it receives projections from most of the sensory systems

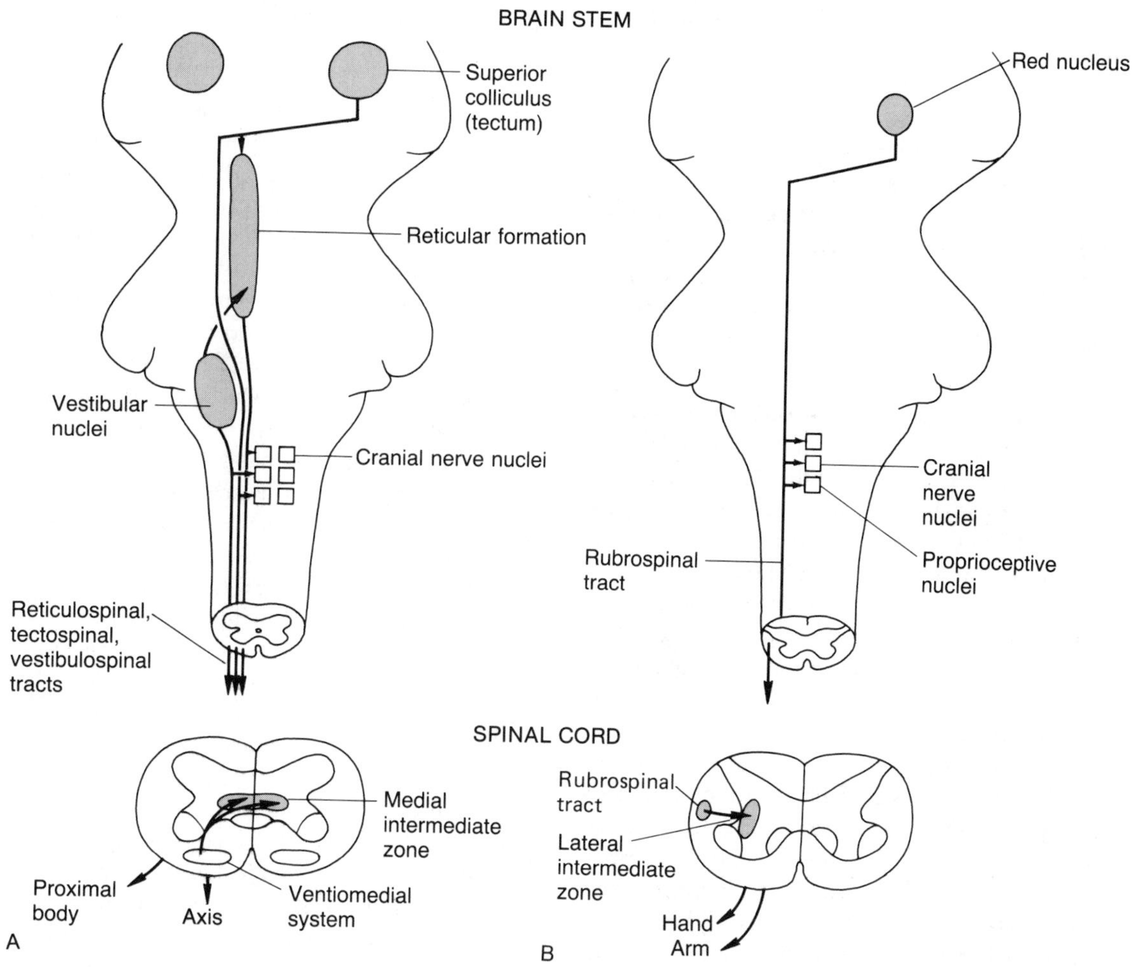

FIGURE 12-5. *A*. Brainstem structures that contribute fibers to the ventromedial system. *B*. Brainstem structures that contribute fibers to the lateral system. (After Ghez, 1981).

of the brainstem and spinal cord. Its descending pathways are probably involved in producing various organized movements including walking, swimming, and running. The pathways of the ventromedial brain system are illustrated in Figure 12-5*A*. Note that, with the exception of the tectum, these pathways do not cross in the brainstem, but do project bilaterally to medially located interneurons in the intermediate zone of the spinal cord. The axons of fibers in the ventromedial system give off a large number of collaterals to many interneurons in many spinal cord segments. This feature of their distribution as well as their termination within the medially located interneurons of the spinal cord suggests that they produce whole-body movements involving many muscle groups of the axial (trunk) and proximal body musculature. The fibers of the ventromedial system also project to the extraocular motor neurons in cranial nerves III, IV, and VI as well as to the vagus (X), glossopharyngeal (IX), and spinal accessory (XI) nuclei. Through these nuclei these cranial nerves control eye and head movements as well as some movements of the oral cavity.

The reticulospinal projection also includes fibers from norepinephrinergic, serotonergic, and dopaminergic neurons. These projections are thought to be involved in the modulation of movement rather than in the production of movement per se.

Brainstem Origins of the Lateral System. The red nucleus of the midbrain sends its projection, the rubrospinal tract, through the lateral system of the spinal cord (Figure 12-5*B*). One of its notable features is that its fiber tract crosses the midline to innervate the contralateral spinal cord. It also sends projections to the cranial nuclei that control facial movements [the facial (VII) and hypoglossal (XII) nuclei]. The rubrospinal fibers terminate on interneurons of the lateral portion of the intermediate zone of the spinal cord. They have fewer collaterals and make connections with fewer spinal cord segments than fibers of the ventromedial system. Their organization and termination suggests that their function is to control independent movements of the distal musculature, such as movements of the hands, feet, arms, and legs. The rubrospinal tract also gives off collaterals to the sensory trigeminal nucleus (the fifth nerve, which receives fibers from the face), which in turn gives off collaterals to the dorsal column nuclei (nuclei that receive and relay proprioceptive input from the body). These connections suggest that it has a modulatory action on sensory input from the body.

The Cortex

The cortex can produce and control movement in two ways. (1) It sends *corticofugal fibers* (*cortico* meaning cortex and *fugal* meaning flight) to brainstem motor nuclei and to dorsal column interneurons and motor neurons of the spinal cord. The fibers that go to the motor nuclei are called *corticobulbar fibers,* and those that go to the spinal cord are called *corticospinal fibers.* The corticobulbar motor fibers control head muscles, and corticospinal motor fibers control body muscles. (2) There are corticofugal fibers that go to the brainstem nuclei, which in turn give rise to the tracts forming the brainstem portions of the lateral and ventromedial systems, described above. These projections allow the cortex to modulate movement through existing subcortical movement systems. An important feature of the cortical motor projections is the way in which they parallel the subcortical motor systems. Remember that the subcortical motor system has two components one of which contributes to the lateral system and one of which contributes to the ventromedial system. The projections from the cortex divide in the same way. Part of the corticofugal fibers cross the midline of the brain and terminate on brainstem nuclei, cranial nuclei, and spinal cord interneurons and motor neurons that control distal musculature. The other part of the corticofugal fibers do not cross and they terminate on brainstem nuclei, cranial nuclei, and spinal cord interneurons and motor neurons that control proximal musculature.

A diagram showing the projections of the corticofugal pathways is given in Figure 12-6. Figure 12-6*A* shows the route of the corticofugal component of the lateral system. Some of these fibers connect to the red nucleus, some connect to the motor nuclei of the cranial nerves, and still others descend into the pyramids (large pyramid-shaped protuberances at the base of the brain), where they cross in the pyramidal decussation to form the lateral corticospinal tract. The fibers of the lateral system end mainly on interneurons in the lateral part of the intermediate zone and on more laterally located motor neurons. Through these connections the projections control distal movements.

The corticofugal fibers of the lateral system come mainly from Brodmann areas 4 and 6, motor areas of the frontal cortex, but accompanying this projection are corticofugal fibers from areas 3, 2,

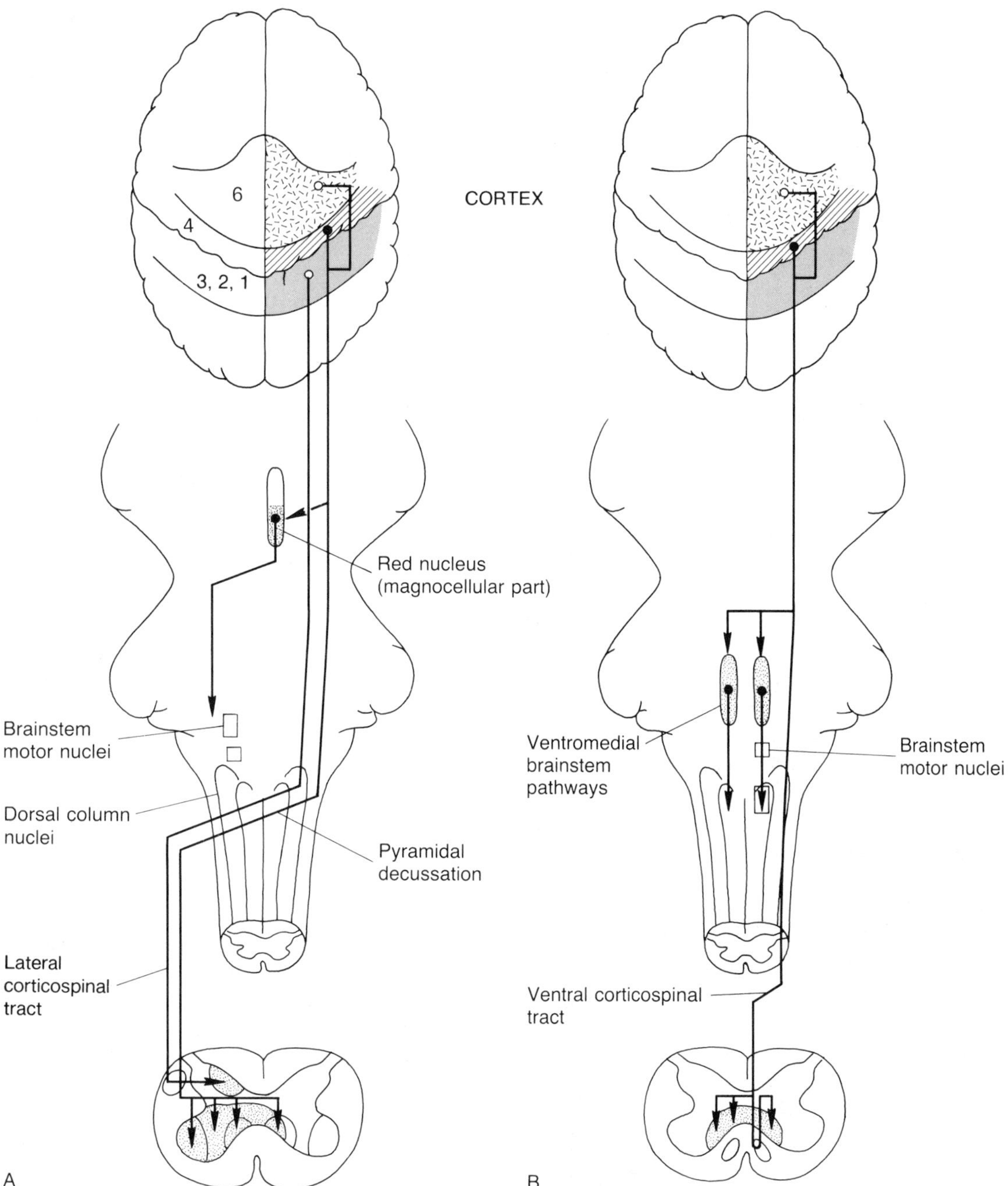

FIGURE 12-6. *A*. Corticospinal projections that contribute to the lateral system. *B*. Corticospinal projections that contribute to the ventromedial system. (After Ghez, 1981.)

and 1 of parietal somatosensory cortex. These fibers terminate on the dorsal column nuclei and on cells in the dorsal columns of the spinal cord. The relationship between sensory and motor cortex is not fully understood, but these two cortical areas are traditionally included together as part of the corticofugal motor projection. The *dorsal column nuclei* are cell groups that relay sensory information from the body to the brain. The projections to the sensory nuclei are thought to be involved in modulating sensory input. For example, Adkins and colleagues have shown that if the pyramidal tract, which contains this projection, is electrically stimulated, the somatosensory field in the cortex expands, presumably to increase the area of skin from which each cortical cell gathers information. This would, presumably, be useful when an insect is detected on the skin and the cortex needs to amplify signals from the skin to precisely localize the insect.

Figure 12-6*B* shows the route of corticofugal fibers in the ventromedial system. Some of the fibers terminate on brainstem nuclei, particularly those involved in controlling eye movements and head movements, whereas others continue along the same side of the brainstem into the spinal cord to form the ventral corticospinal tract. These fibers terminate bilaterally on the most medially located interneurons and motor neurons. Through these connections they control whole-body movements.

The Relation between Motor Cortex and Subcortical Motor Systems

We have described the organization of the motor cortex previously. It is topographically organized so that its different parts control different body movements. This topographical organization is often represented by a homunculus in humans or by a corresponding cartoon in other animals. What relation does the motor cortex have to the lateral and ventromedial systems that we have just described? Kuypers and Brinkman and others have described the corticofugal projections in a number of species of animals, but the projections in the monkey will serve for the purposes of illustration (Figure 12-7). First, the motor cortex sends projections to the subcortical nuclei of the lateral and ventromedial systems. The part of motor cortex representing the limb and distal part of the body sends projections to the red nucleus, whereas the part representing the medial part of the body sends projections to nuclei of the ventromedial system. These projections are not illustrated in Figure 12-7. The projections that are illustrated are those that make up the corticospinal tracts. The different parts of the homunculus have the following relations with these tracts and their terminations in the spinal cord.

1. Projections from the digit (fingers/toes) area of the motor cortex mainly connect directly to motor neurons in the dorsolateral cell group of the spinal gray matter. This pathway decussates (crosses from one side of the brain to the other) at the junction of the medulla and spinal cord, forming protuberances on the ventral aspect of the brainstem that are called the pyramids. Hence, these fibers form a portion of what is known as the *pyramidal tract*. This direct corticomotor-neuron projection is found only in animals capable of independent movements of the digits: primates, including humans, and also hamsters and raccoons, which have good control of the digits. Animals such as cats have no direct connections and no independent digit control.

2. Cells in the digit, hand, and limb area of the motor cortex project to the interneurons in the dorsolateral portion of the intermediate zone in the contralateral half of the spinal cord. They also form part of the pyramidal tract. Because of their origin and termination, these fibers are thought to be responsible for producing relatively independent hand and arm movements. For example, an animal such as a cat that can only flex all digits together, does so using this projection.

3. Cells in the body area of the motor cortex project to the interneurons of the ventromedial portion of the intermediate zone both ipsilaterally and contralaterally. Part of this projection follows

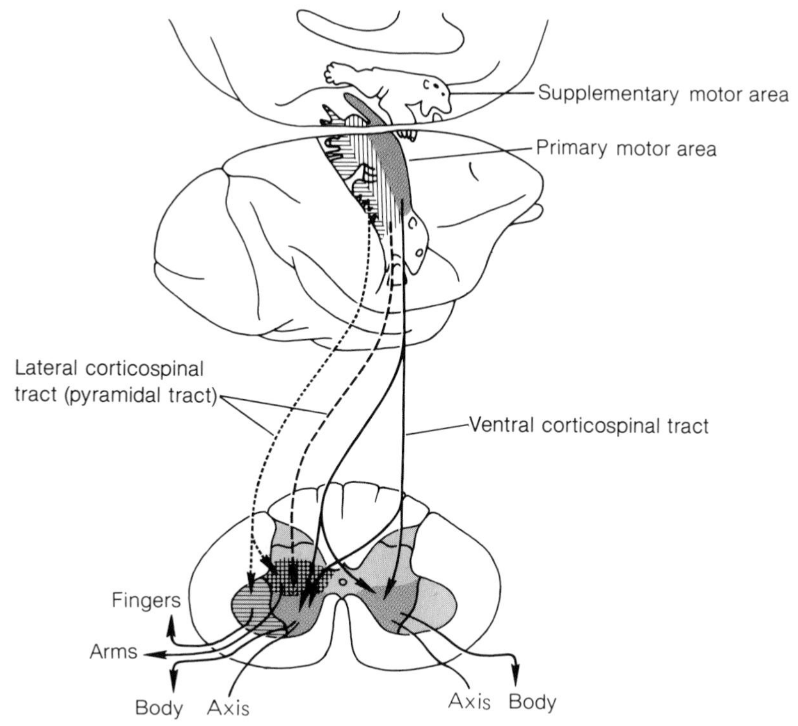

FIGURE 12-7. The relation among primary motor cortex, descending tracts, spinal cord interneurons, motor neurons, and body musculature in the monkey. (After Lawrence and Kuypers, 1968.)

the crossed pyramidal tract and part remains uncrossed to form the ventral corticospinal tract. Because of its origin and termination, this system is thought to control movements of the body and proximal limbs for such activities as walking or turning the body, such as in getting up from a prone position.

Cortical Access to Motor Systems

So that finger, arm, and body movements can be controlled by sensory and cognitive processes, all regions of the cortex must have access to the different motor pathways. Kuypers and Lawrence, and others, have described a number of alternative routes through which movements can be controlled.

Figure 12-8 shows some of these alternatives. Figure 12-8*A* shows the three corticospinal projections (already described) from Brodmann area 4 that control finger, arm, and body movements, respectively. Figure 12-8*B* shows indirect projections from area 4 into the lateral system through the red nucleus, and into the ventromedial system through the other brainstem nuclei. Additional projections may occur indirectly through the basal ganglia. The existence of these additional projections has been shown both anatomically and electrophysiologically. In the electrophysiological experiments, the spinal tracts were sectioned and the motor cortex was then stimulated electrically. Such stimulation no longer produced movements of the fingers, but it still produced movements of the

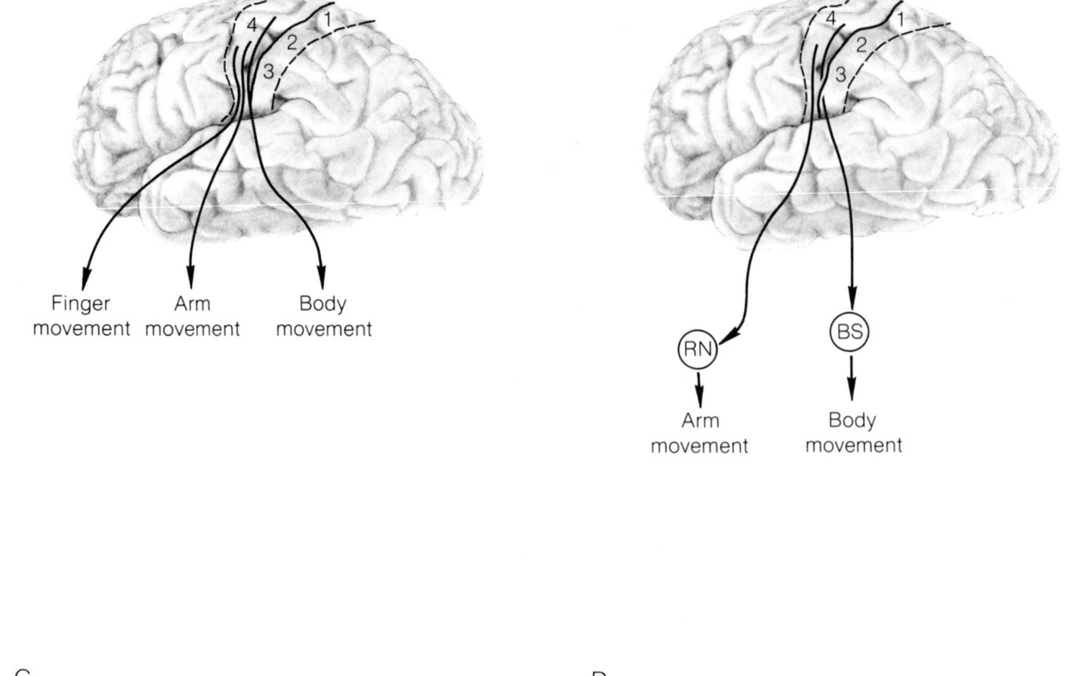

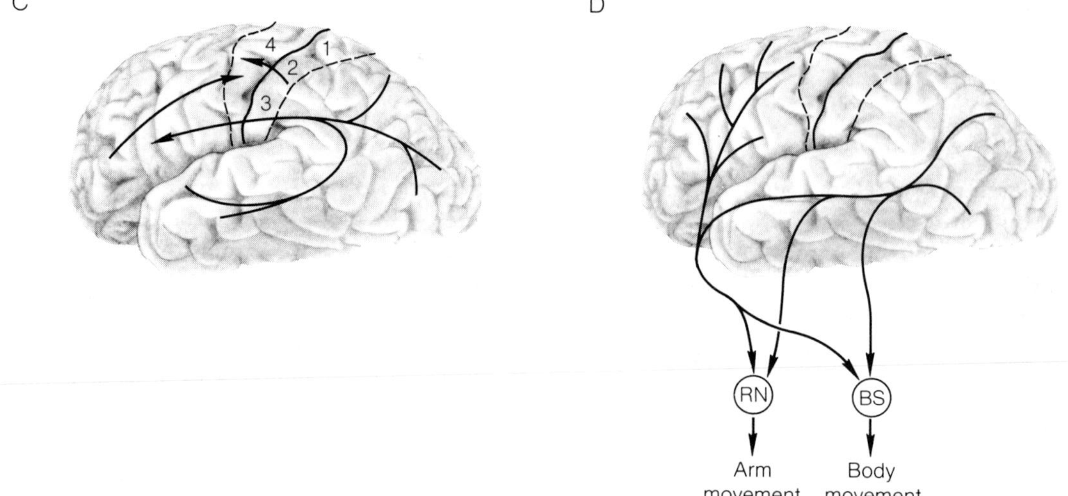

FIGURE 12-8. Motor pathways from the cortex. *A*. The corticospinal tracts. *B*. Indirect projections from Brodmann area 4 to the lateral system via the red nucleus (RN), and to the ventromedial system via other brainstem (BS) nuclei. Additional connections may be made through the basal ganglia. *C*. Connections of different areas of the cortex to area 4. *D*. Connections of frontal and parietal cortex to subcortical nuclei of the lateral and ventromedial systems. The numbers refer to Brodmann areas.

limbs and body. The fact that the finger movements were lost is proof that the corticospinal tract is essential for finger movement, but the fact that stimulation could produce other movements demonstrates that the motor cortex has other routes to the spinal cord, presumably indirectly through subcortical motor systems.

Figure 12-8*C* shows how other areas of the cortex obtain access to the motor pathways from area 4 to the spinal cord. Because only the postcentral gyrus (Brodmann primary sensory areas 3, 1, 2) projects into area 4, other posterior cortical regions must project into frontal cortex and from there into area 4. Among the other cortical areas, it is thought that the supplementary motor cortex (area 6) plays a role in planning movements. Roland and his coworkers asked human subjects to perform three simple tasks: flexing a finger, making a sequence of finger movements, and mentally rehearsing the finger-movement sequence. During task performance the researchers measured blood flow with scalp detectors, after intravenous injection of radioactive xenon. During finger flexion, primary sensory and motor cortex were active. During the finger-movement sequence the supplementary motor area was additionally active, but during mental rehearsal only supplementary motor cortex was active. The results suggest that supplementary motor cortex is involved in movement planning and only involves primary motor cortex to produce a movement.

Figure 12-8*D* shows that there are alternative connections from frontal cortex and parietal cortex that bypass primary motor cortex (between dashed lines) and project into the brainstem motor systems either directly or indirectly via the basal ganglia. Note that although these projections give these areas of the cortex access to control of arm movement via the lateral system and of body movements via the ventromedial system, they have no access to the control of finger movements. Finger movements must be controlled through area 4 of the cortex. In general, these projections most probably control orientation of the head, body, and eyes, since stimulation of this cortex produces these types of movements. In addition to interhemispheric and corticofugal projections, the motor cortex has intrahemispheric connections through the corpus callosum for all body parts except the hand area.

Species and Individual Differences in Corticospinal Projections

It is immediately obvious to anyone who observes the behavior of animals, that there are striking differences in the movements that they make. Some of these differences can be accounted for by differences in connections made by the descending motor pathways to the brainstem cranial nuclei and spinal cord. The corticospinal pathway can be selectively sectioned in the pyramids of the ventral brainstem (the pyramids are composed of the corticospinal fibers and are easy to reach surgically because of their superficial location). When this projection is cut, the terminations of the fibers can be determined by locating the degenerating terminals with the reduced-silver staining technique and the Nauta stain and its modifications. Kuypers and others have studied terminal distribution in different species; an example of some of their results is illustrated in Figure 12-9. Some animals, sometimes described as being primitive, such as the opossum, have no terminals in the ventral column. Terminals are restricted to the dorsal column. Other species, such as the cat, which is unable to make independent digit movements, have no terminals on motor neurons but do have terminals on interneurons. Animals such as the rhesus monkey, which can make independent digit movements, have terminals only on the most laterally located motor neurons. Finally, animals such as the chimpanzee (and humans) have terminals on all motor neurons and interneurons. The parallel between direct connections on motor neurons and the ability to make skilled movements suggests that the direct connections are directly re-

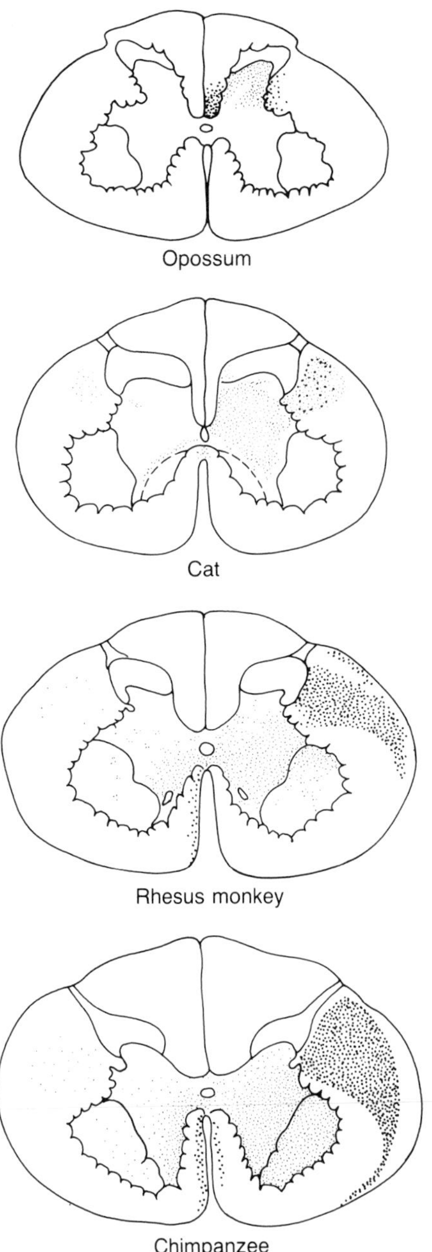

FIGURE 12-9. Distribution of corticospinal fibers (shown as gray areas) from the left hemisphere to low cervical spinal gray matter in the opossum, cat, rhesus monkey, and chimpanzee. (After Kuypers, 1981).

sponsible for them. If we knew nothing of the behavior of an animal but knew its anatomy and understood the significance of the corticospinal connections of Figure 12-9, we could predict its motor abilities. We would be able to say that the opossum should be capable of few independent limb movements, the cat should be able to make such movements, and the rhesus monkey should be able to make independent digit movements. Humans and the chimpanzee, however, should be capable, not only of skilled movements of the digits, but of other parts of the body as well. Of course, we know that this is indeed the case.

Studies that have been done on animals of different ages show that the corticospinal terminations on interneurons and motor neurons are not established at birth. The connections are made gradually, with development, and as they are made, there is a concomitant development of more skilled movements. In addition, studies on fiber diameter show that the thickest fibers, which are capable of the most rapid information conduction, make up only a small fraction of all the corticofugal fibers, but it is they that make the most direction connections with motor neurons. These fibers also tend to mature and become functional last in development. Thus, the largest and fastest fibers are those that have the latest maturation, connect directly with motor neurons, and are those that are responsible for late-maturing skilled movements.

Examination of corticofugal pathways in humans shows that there is considerable variation among individuals. Nyberg-Hansen and Rinvik have described some of these variations; including no uncrossed corticospinal tract, no crossed corticospinal tract, and two crossed or two uncrossed corticospinal tracts. The functional significance of such variation is simply not known. Yakovlev and Rakic have examined the size of the corticospinal pathways, and they note that 80% of individuals have larger tracts on the right side of the spinal cord. In the remaining 20% the pattern is reversed. It might be thought that this asymmetry is related to handedness; that is, most people are right-handed and receive larger corticospinal projections on the right. This study found that there is not a perfect relation between handedness and the size of the corticospinal pathways. Thus, at present this anatomical bias has not been conclusively correlated with function.

Summary

This section has described the anatomical organization of the motor systems. There are two descending systems from the brain. The lateral system projects from one hemisphere to the spinal cord of the opposite side. The corticospinal component of this system connects directly with motor neurons and appears involved in control of musculature of the fingers and hands. The rubrospinal component connects with interneurons, and it eventually controls musculature of the shoulders, arms, and hand. The ventromedial system projects to interneurons of the spinal cord from the cortex and brainstem of the same side. It eventually connects with the musculature of the trunk. Species comparisons and developmental studies suggest that as the corticospinal projections connect, first with interneurons and then directly with motor neurons, skilled movements of the limbs and fingers also develop.

BRAIN LESIONS

As can be seen from its anatomical organization, the motor system can be divided into cortical and subcortical systems. The cortical system controls all body movements, including arm and finger movements. The subcortical system controls distal movements through its lateral spinal cord projection, and proximal movements through its ventromedial spinal cord projection, but it cannot control independent finger movements. To analyze the contributions made by these different systems Lawrence and Kuypers studied rhesus monkeys, which have a motor anatomy quite similar to that of humans. They made three types of lesions in the monkeys. They cut the corticospinal tracts at the level of the pyramidal decussation in the medulla. They then subdivided the animals in this group into two groups, each of which received a second lesion. In one group they lesioned the rubrospinal tracts, either in the brain or in the cord, by cutting their lateral columns. In the other group they lesioned the tracts of the ventromedial column in the brain, or cut the ventromedial columns in the cord. The logic of this protocol was that first the functions of the corticospinal projections could be assessed, and then, since this system overlaps to some extent with the remaining lateral and ventromedial pathways, their function could be assessed independently in the absence of the cortical projections.

The Function of the Corticospinal System

Within 6 to 8 h after surgery animals with corticospinal lesions were able to right themselves from a lateral posture, but their limbs tended to hang loosely or were poorly placed on the floor. Within 24 h they could stand, grip the cage, and take a few climbing steps. They attempted to bite food, but for the first 10 to 15 days they could not swallow and so needed to be specially fed. Once they began to eat they would reach through their cage bars for food. However, they were hesitant to fully extend their arms and frequently caught their fingers on the opening. Once they reached the food their fingers closed in concert, but weakly, and grasping was associated with a hooking movement of the whole arm. Gradually, speed and strength of movements increased, yet the animals continued to display two striking deficits. First, they were unable to grasp food with the pincer grasp of the thumb and index finger opposed. Second, once they had grasped food with a whole-hand grip, they had difficulty in releasing it; to do so they rooted for it with their snouts. During locomotion, however, they had no difficulty in letting go of the bars of the cage.

In summary, following corticospinal lesions, locomotion was minimally disturbed, whereas independent movements of the limbs in the absence of body movement were initially impaired but recovered to near-normal levels. In contrast, the animals never recovered the ability to fully use movements of the hand, as in releasing food, or to use relatively independent movements of the fingers to grasp food or manipulate objects. Beck and Chambers measured the functions of monkey limbs after lesions of the corticospinal tract. Their results are in accord with those given above. The monkeys showed slowed reaction times on two-choice tasks using the affected limb, showed greater loss of strength in flexion than in extension, and showed weaker flexion at the wrist than at the elbow or shoulder. From these and other observations it can be concluded that the corticospinal pathways provide speed, strength, and ability to limb movements and the capacity to make discrete movements of the extremities — in particular the relatively independent movements of the fingers. The recovery from the initial difficulties in moving the limbs presumably can be attributed to actions of the rubrospinal projection of the lateral system.

A more general perspective of the contribution of the cortex via its corticospinal tracts has been revealed by Passingham and coworkers. They unilaterally removed the motor cortex (area 4) and the sensory cortex (areas 3, 2, 1), from which the majority of corticospinal projections originate, in rhesus monkeys. After a period of recovery, the monkeys regained the ability to use the contralateral arm for climbing and moving around the cage and, with some prompting, for reaching for food. But, just as Lawrence and Kuypers had reported, the monkeys were not able to use the pincer grasp to pick pieces of food out of a trough, although they could grasp food with whole-hand movements. Further impairment in reaching was revealed in the following way. The monkeys were required to insert their hand through a hole in a clear plastic wall and dislodge a piece of food attached to the wall on the other side. Thus, when their hand was inserted through the hole they had to turn it to the side, turn it up, or turn it down to reach the food. The monkeys were found to be unable to rotate their wrist or elbow to reach the food in these tests. This experiment demonstrates that not only is the cortex necessary for individual finger movements, it appears to be necessary for most skilled movements around individual joints.

The Function of the Rubrospinal System

Once the corticospinal system had been removed, Lawrence and Kuypers made lesions in the same animals in the rubrospinal system, either in the brain or by lateral cord section. After the lesions, the animals were able to sit unsupported, stand, walk, run, and climb. The most striking changes in movement occurred in the limbs, particularly the forelimbs. When the animals were sitting, the limbs hung loosely from the shoulder with the hand and fingers extended. The arm was not used discretely for reaching for food, but if food was within reach, the arm was carried by a shoulder movement to rake food in toward the mouth with the hand extended. If the hand fell on the food, it was unable to grasp and hold the food. In contrast to these deficits in using the limb for independent movements of reaching and grasping for food, the arm was used well, although somewhat weakly, in locomotor activities such as walking, and climbing. Thus, interruption of the rubrospinal system severely disrupts the relatively independent use of the limbs in reaching and grasping but spares their ability to participate in whole-body movements.

The Function of the Ventromedial System

Lawrence and Kuypers examined animals that had their corticospinal system removed and had also received a second lesion in the brainstem nuclei of the ventromedial system or that had the ventromedial columns of the cord cut. Animals with such lesions showed striking abnormalities in posture but were considerably less impaired in the use of their extremities. They showed a prolonged inability to achieve upright posture and severe difficulty in moving the body or in moving the limbs at the proximal joints. They also showed pronounced flexion of the head, limbs, and trunk, which lessened with recovery but did not disappear. They were not able to sit up for 10 to 40 days and required frequent repositioning and had to be fed by stomach tube. When they were able to sit, they were unsteady and tended to slump forward with the shoulders elevated. Slight movements or sudden sounds made them fall, and when starting to fall, they failed to make corrective movements to support themselves. The animals had great difficulty in walking; they walked with a narrow-based gait, frequently veered off target and bumped into things. In contrast to the severe impairments of body movement, the distal parts of the limbs and hands were less impaired. The animals could cling to cage bars, reach and grasp food, and bring it to their mouths. When reaching for food, they executed movements mainly at the elbows and hands while the rest of the body remained relatively immobile. Thus, interruption of the ventromedial system disrupted body movements relatively selectively, leaving limbs, which are controlled by the rubrospinal system, relatively unimpaired.

Summary

In this section we have described the effects of brain lesions targeted at portions of the motor system. If the cortex is damaged or if the corticospinal tracts are cut, animals are able to locomote reasonably well and they are able to reach for objects with an affected limb and grasp food with a whole-arm movement. They cannot, however, use their fingers independently or make skilled rotary movements around limb joints. Thus, the cortical portion of the lateral system is responsible for skilled movements of the extremeties. If the second portion of the lateral system, the rubrospinal tract, is damaged along with the cortical spinal tract, animals are no longer able to reach at all with an independent limb movement and the affected limb simply hangs limply at the animal's side. If the ventromedial tracts are damaged, however, animals have difficulty making body movements. Nevertheless, although they have trouble making a righting response, they can use a limb to reach for objects. These experiments demonstrate that the lateral system and the ventromedial system can be functionally dissociated, with the former controlling distal musculature and the latter controlling proximal musculature. They show additionally, that the lateral system's rubrospinal projection can control limb movements sufficiently well to allow reaching, but that the cortex projections are necessary for individual movements of the fingers, for the pincer grasp, and for skilled movements around joints.

SENSORY-MOTOR INTEGRATION

There are close anatomical relations between the sensory and motor systems. In the spinal cord, sensory afferents form monosynaptic or disynaptic connections with motor neurons. At the level of the cortex, somatosensory cortex (areas 3, 2, 1) has direct projections to motor cortex (area 4). Furthermore, there is a direct projection from somatosensory receptors to motor cortex: this projection is well developed from the distal portion of the limbs. Given the close anatomical relations between sensory and motor systems, it might be asked: How functionally interdependent are they? Is movement possible in the absence of sensory input?

There is an extensive literature on the effect of **deafferentation** (removing somatosensory input by cutting sensory fibers which convey sensory information from the body to the brain) on animal locomotion. The major result of these studies show that there is a surprisingly wide range of movements that are possible in the absence of sensory information from one or more limbs. Rothwell and colleagues have examined the effects of deafferentation on the movements of the rhesus monkey. If only one forelimb is deafferented, the animal tends to neglect the limb and use its other limbs. If this is prevented by binding the contralateral forelimb, the animal will learn to make very good use of the deafferented limb. If both forelimbs are deafferented, then after a period of recovery lasting a few weeks, very effective use is again possible. The animal can climb, walk, cling to the bars of its cage, and even reach for objects using the pincer grip. The capacity involved in making these movements does not need to be exercised before deafferentation. Rothwell's group deafferented preterm monkeys (removed from the uterus and replaced after surgery) and found that they displayed good postnatal development of movement. Of course, the monkeys do have vision, so that it is possible that their movements are performed under visual guidance. To examine this possibility, Rothwell's group sutured the infants' eyes closed and found that they still displayed effective locomotion. They could even reach and use the pincer grasp, provided that they were trained so that they knew there were objects they could reach for. These experiments demonstrate that there are central nervous system programs for movement that can operate in the absence of sensory stimulation or sensory feedback. Of course, movements are not completely normal and many spinal reflexes are absent, but the unambiguous development of ambulation, climbing, and reaching satisfactorily demonstrates the existence of the central motor programs that can operate in the absence of sensory input.

It would be misleading to leave the topic of deafferentation without describing some features of the disabilities that do follow deafferentation in humans. Walking is disturbed and knowledge about the location of limbs is severely impaired. The importance of sensory information for normal walking in humans is demonstrated by the **ataxia** shown by people who suffer from a genetic disorder called *Friedreich's ataxia*. These people have degeneration of the dorsal funiculi, which contain the afferents conducting fine touch and pressure information from the body. They have little or no position sense and a poor sense of passive movement and vibration. When they walk, they support their body on a broad base, legs apart, and they tend to shuffle, reel, and stagger. Similar difficulties have been observed in a patient who had suffered an accidental severing of the dorsal columns (see Chapter 13). For humans, walking involves a bit of a balancing act; weight must be shifted from one leg to the other, and balancing is required as weight is carried forward on one limb. This balancing obviously requires afferent input, for ataxia does not lessen with time or practice. Thus, locomotion is more severely impaired in people than in monkeys, but the difference is due to the more complex mode of locomotion used by humans (monkeys walk with four feet on the ground) and not to the inability to produce movement.

Rothwell and coworkers have described the motor abilities of G. O., who was deafferented by a severe peripheral sensory disease. His motor power was unaffected and he could produce a range of finger movements with accuracy. He could make individual finger movements and outline figures in the air with his eyes closed. He could move his thumb accurately through different distances and at different speeds, judge weights, and match forces with his thumb. He could also drive his old car but was unable to learn to drive a new car. Nevertheless, his hands were relatively useless to him in daily life. He was unable to write, to fasten shirt buttons, or to hold a cup. His difficulties lay in maintaining force for any length of time. He could begin movements quite normally but as he proceeded, the movement patterns gradually fell apart and became unrecognizable. This was best illustrated when he tried to carry a suitcase.

He would quickly drop it unless he continually looked down at it to confirm that it was there. G. O.'s symptoms support the findings with monkeys in suggesting that sensory feedback is not required to generate a movement. His symptoms do suggest that sensory feedback is necessary to sustain a single movement or series of movements.

It is well known that people who have lost a limb still have a central image of the limb. This phenomenon is referred to as a *phantom limb.* Melzack and Bromage have shown that in normal people who have a limb anesthetized a phantom limb develops very quickly especially when they are prevented from seeing the limb. They are, however, usually unable to accurately report the location of the limb under these circumstances. When they saw their limb in a location in which they had not expected to see it, they were surprised and often thought that it might belong to someone else. These observations demonstrate rather dramatically that afferent input is necessary for knowing about the location and movement of body parts even though images of them may exist in its absence.

THE BASAL GANGLIA

The basal ganglia comprise a collection of nuclei in the forebrain that make connections with the midbrain, diencephalon, thalamus, and cortex. The basal ganglia make no direct connections to the spinal cord, but they have been traditionally considered as part of the motor system. This tradition is in large part based on clinical observations that damage to various parts of the basal ganglia produces such change in movements as **akinesia** (an absence of spontaneous movements) and **hyperkinesia** (excessive slow or rapid involuntary movements). The basal ganglia have at least two functions in movement control. First, they form part of a circuit that links most of the neocortex with the motor cortex. This can be thought of as their public role because they participate in effective cortical function. But they also have a private role because direct damage to them can result in movement abnormalities or deficits that are different from those involving cortical circuitry.

The anatomical relation between structures that make up the basal ganglia, including their afferent and efferent connections, and the cortex is shown in Figure 12-10. The architecture of these structures and their relations to the cortex suggests that they form a loop for modulating motor functions. Projections from all parts of the cortex enter the neostriatum. The neostriatum then projects through the external and internal pallidum (also called the globus pallidus) and from there goes to the ventral-anterior and ventral-lateral thalamus and then terminates in the premotor cortex. Thus, superficially at least, it appears that all parts of the cortex are able to exert a modulating influence of some sort on the motor cortex via supplementary motor cortex. The *neostriatum* is composed of the caudate nucleus and the putamen, and it is phylogenetically the most recent structure in the basal ganglia. The pallidum, in turn, is developmentally related to the diencephalon. The amygdala is often included anatomically as a basal ganglial structure, but it is also often discussed functionally as being part of the limbic system. The basal ganglia receive input from the subthalamic nucleus of the diencephalon and from the substantia nigra of the midbrain. They also receive connections from the cerebellum via a relay in the thalamus. Part of the functional implication of this circuitry is that damage to any part of it should produce a similar impairment. This is one of the reasons that effects of cortical and subcortical damage are sometimes difficult to distinguish.

Understanding basal ganglial function is complicated, not only by the nature of their circuitry, but also by the difficulties involved in interpreting the effects of damage to their components. Motor fibers from the cortex pass through or close to the basal ganglia, making it difficult to determine whether behavioral changes are due to damage to

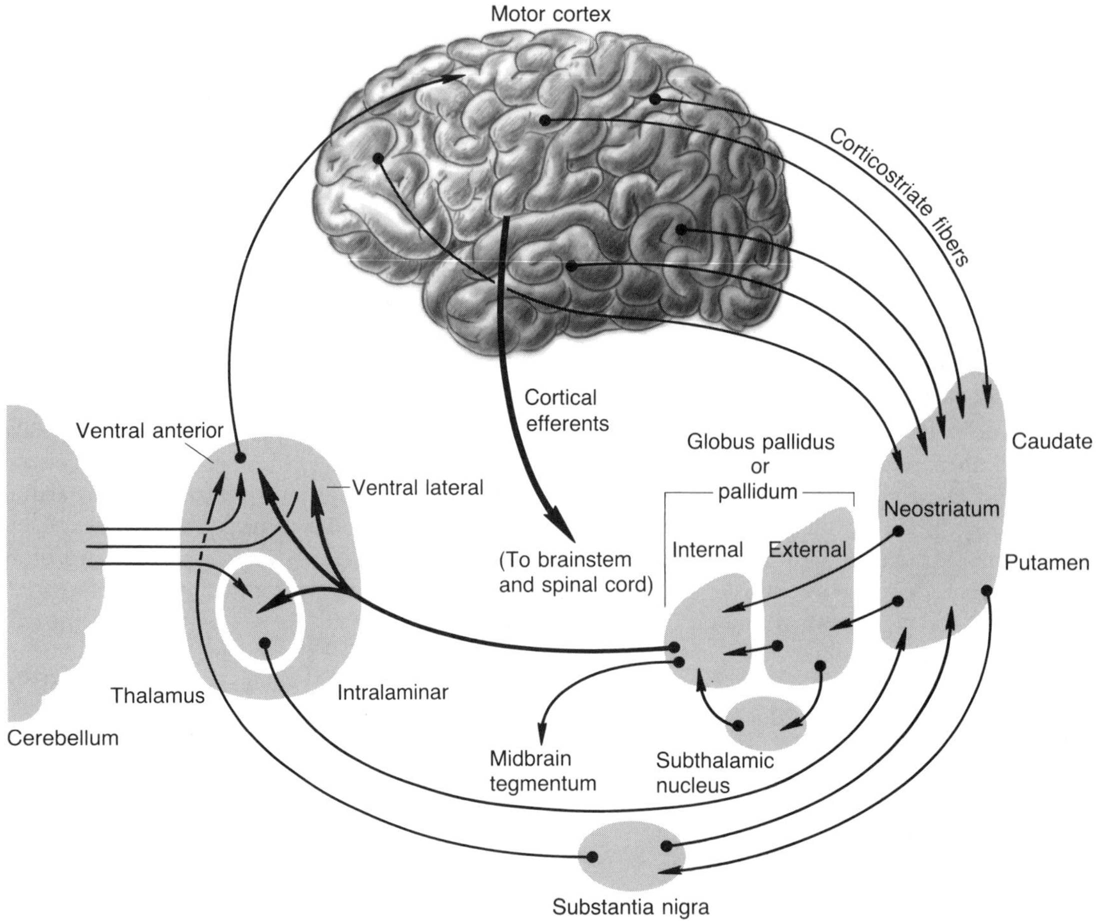

FIGURE 12-10. Circuitry showing the relation between the basal ganglia and cortex. Note that projections from all parts of the cortex enter the basal ganglia but that only premotor cortex receives projections from the basal ganglia via the circuit. (After DeLong, 1974).

the basal ganglia themselves or to damage to these fibers of passage. The symptoms of basal ganglial disorders are also different depending on how they are damaged. If the dopaminergic projection from the substantia nigra is severed, a condition of rigidity and akinesia, called **Parkinson's disease,** ensues (Chapter 13). It is likely that cells that normally function to inhibit movement are released from control by the substantia nigra, thus excessively impeding voluntary movements. If cells within the basal ganglia are damaged, quite different symptoms occur. Involuntary movements become common. Thus, it seems that cells within the basal ganglia are involved in checking these types of movements. If, however, the entire structure is removed a syndrome consisting of a "release of following" or "approach" behavior occurs. Neither the akinetic nor hyperkinetic symptoms are displayed.

Early theories of basal ganglial function suggested that they were involved in making the postural adjustments against which the cortex produced more skilled or precise movements. More recently it has been suggested that they are involved in making slow movements, whereas the corticospinal systems are involved in rapid movements. Evidence cited in favor of this idea is that parkinsonian patients display a poverty of movement, yet preserve normal reaction times. These ideas are of course difficult to reconcile with the type of basal ganglial symptoms that follow complete removal of the basal ganglia. In fact, studies suggest that the persistent following behaviors and exaggerated "positive" behavior of cats is due less to a disorder of motor behavior per se than the cats' inability to modify their behavior in response to the negative consequences of their actions. A still more recent theory of neostriatum function, which is based on cell structure and connections, has been proposed by Groves. He suggests simply that there is an inhibitory circuit and an excitatory circuit in the neostriatum that together are involved in preparing the motor system for the production of voluntary movements.

Many people who have suffered strokes are paralized on one side of the body **(hemiplegia)** and are unable to recover movement of the contralateral arm. This impairment seems more severe than the monkey studies suggest it should be. Recall that monkeys with large cortical lesions lost skilled movements and independent finger movements, but otherwise they were able to reach quite well. The explanation for this difference can be accounted for by the additional damage done by vascular accidents. In addition to damaging the cortex, they usually also damage the basal ganglia. The contributions of the basal ganglia to skilled movements have been neglected in descriptions of motor pathways. This is because it has not been determined precisely how their more indirect connections eventually control motor neurons. Nevertheless, studies using rats (see Whishaw and coworkers for a review of this work) have demonstrated that severe impairments in limb-use follow selective damage to cells in the caudate-putamen or damage to dopamine projections to the caudate-putamen. This suggests that for some movements there is dual control: the basal ganglia can elicit some features of the movement and they additionally participate in the cortical control of the movement. It seems likely, therefore, that the severe impairments that follow vascular accidents are attributable to combined damage to the cortex and basal ganglia. As was long ago recognized by Hughlings-Jackson, many of the severe impairments of movements that follow vascular accidents, including paralysis and speech deficits, may well be caused by damage to the basal ganglia.

CEREBELLAR ACCESS TO MOTOR SYSTEMS

The cerebellum is generally thought of as an important part of the motor system, but rather than sending projections directly to motor neurons or their interneurons, it projects to a number of nuclei that then join, either directly or indirectly, the lateral or ventromedial systems of the spinal cord. (Figure 12-11 gives a simplified representation.)

The archicerebellum composes the entire cerebellum in fishes and is the first cerebellar structure to differentiate in the human fetus. In mammals it makes up the more medial and ventral portion of the cerebellum. Projections from the archicerebellum pass from the fastigial nucleus to the reticular formation and the vestibular nuclei. Tracts from these areas form part of the ventromedial projection of the spinal cord, which, as we have seen, is instrumental in controlling more proximal move-

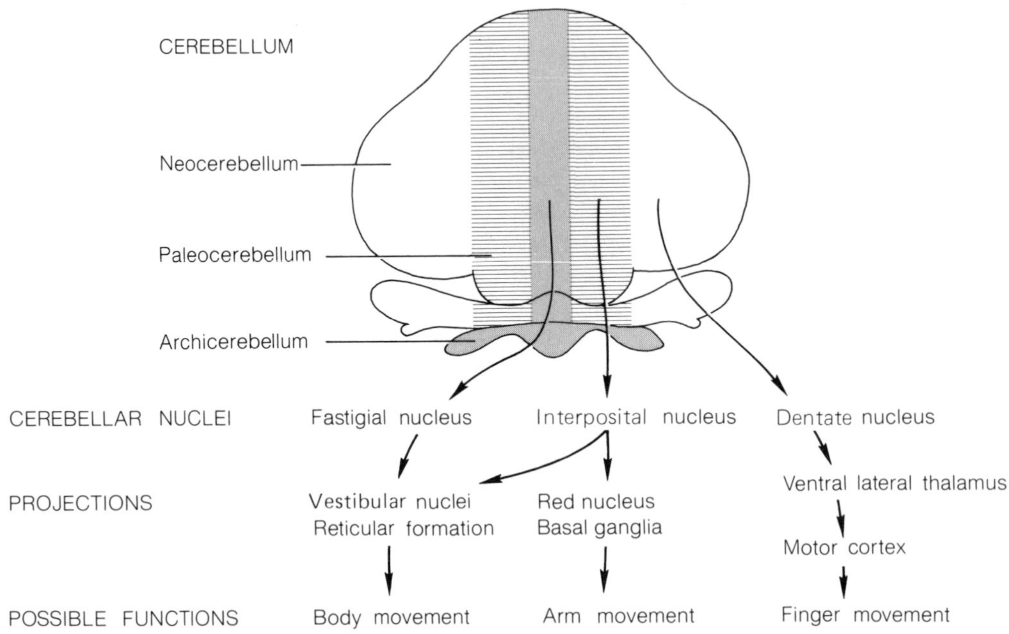

FIGURE 12-11. Projections from different cerebellar areas to spinal cord motor pathways controlling different portions of body musculature.

ments of the body, such as posture and locomotion. Tumors or damage to this area disrupt upright posture and walking but do not substantially disrupt other movements such as reaching, grasping, and finger movements. For example, a person with medial cerebellar damage may, when lying down, show few symptoms of such damage.

The paleocerebellum is the dominant cerebellar structure in quadrupeds from amphibians to mammals and seems closely related to the development and use of the limbs in locomotion. Projections from the nuclei of this area go to the red nucleus, and possibly to the other brainstem nuclei as well. Thus, this system is probably involved in the control of limb movements through the lateral system and body movements through the ventromedial system. The predominant effect of damage to this area, although such damage is rare, is an increase in rigidity of the limbs, which disrupts distal movement more than proximal movement.

The neocerebellum makes up the outermost lateral portion of the cerebellum. Although well developed in animals capable of nonsymmetrical limb movements, it shows its greatest development in primates. Projections from the lateral nuclei that serve this area go to the ventral thalamus and from there to the precentral motor cortex. Thus, this area has access to the corticospinal tract that controls more distal movements of the arms and fingers as well as proximal movements of the body. Damage to the neocerebellum produces weakness and a tendency to fatigue, difficulty in localizing or pointing to body parts correctly, and a variety of deficits in the control of the extremities such as overshooting the mark when pointing, flailing at the joints, staggering, and an inability to carry out repeated rhythmic movements.

In summary, therefore, the development and anatomy of these three cerebellar areas and their relations to other portions of the motor system suggest that they form an integral part of these systems and participate in differentially controlling whole-body movements and relatively independent movements of the limbs and of the fingers.

REFERENCES

Adkins, R. J., R. W. Morse, and A. L. Towe. Control of somatosensory input by cerebral cortex. *Science* 153:1020–1022, 1966.

Beck, C. H., and W. W. Chambers. Speed, accuracy, and strength of forelimb movement after unilateral pyramidotomy in rhesus monkeys. *Journal of Comparative and Physiological Psychology* 70:1–22, 1970.

Coghill, G. E. *Anatomy and the Problem of Behavior.* New York and London: Hafner, 1964.

DeLong, M. R. Motor functions of the basal ganglia: Single-unit activity during movement. In F. O. Schmitt, and F. G. Worden, eds. *The Neurosciences: Third Study Program.* Cambridge, MA: M.I.T. Press, 1974.

Ghez, C. Introduction to the motor systems. In E. R. Kandel and J. H. Schwartz, eds. *Principles of Neural Science.* New York: Elsevier, 1981.

Groves, P. M. A theory of the functional organization of the neostriatum and the neostriatal control of voluntary movement. *Brain Research Reviews* 5:109–132, 1983.

Kuypers, H. G. J. M. The descending pathways to the spinal cord, their anatomy and function. In J. C. Eccles and J. P. Schade, eds. *Organization of the Spinal Cord,* vol. 11. Amsterdam, Elsevier, 1964.

Kuypers, H. G. J. M. Anatomy of descending pathways. In V. B. Brooks, ed. *The Nervous System. Handbook of Physiology,* vol. VII. Bethesda, MD.: American Physiological Society, 1981.

Kuypers, H. G. J. M., and J. Brinkman. Precentral projections to different parts of the spinal intermediate zone in the rhesus monkey. *Brain Research* 24:29–48, 1970.

Kuypers, H. G. J. M., and D. G. Lawrence. Cortical projections to the red nucleus and the brain stem in the rhesus monkey. *Brain Research* 4:151–188, 1967.

Lawrence, D. G., and H. G. J. M. Kuypers. The functional organization of the motor system in the monkey. I. The effects of bilateral pyramidal lesions. *Brain* 91:1–14, 1968.

Lawrence, D. G., and H. G. J. M. Kuypers. The functional organization of the motor system in the monkey. II. The effects of lesions of the descending brain-stem pathways. *Brain* 91:15–36, 1968.

Melzack, R., and P. R. Bromage. Experimental phantom limbs. *Experimental Neurology* 39:261–269, 1973.

Nyberg-Hansen, R., and E. Rinvik. Some comments on the pyramidal tract, with special reference to its individual variations in man. *Acta Neurologica Scandinavia* 39:1–30, 1963.

Passingham, R. E., V. H. Perry, and F. Wilkinson. The long-term effects of removal of sensorimotor cortex in infant and adult rhesus monkeys. *Brain* 106:675–705, 1983.

Roland, P. E., B. Larsen, N. A. Lassen, and E. Skinhøj. Supplementary motor area and other cortical areas in organization of voluntary movements in man. *Journal of Neurophysiology* 43:539–560, 1980.

Rothwell, J. C., M. M. Traub, B. L. Day, J. A. Obeso, P. K. Thomas, and C. D. Marsden. Manual motor performance in a deafferented man. *Brain* 105:515–542, 1982.

Twitchell, T. E. The automatic grasping response of infants. *Neuropsychologia* 3:247–259, 1965.

Yakovlev, P. E., and P. Rakic. Patterns of decussation of bulbar pyramids and distribution of pyramidal tracts to two sides of the spinal cord. *Transactions of the American Neurological Association* 91:366–367, 1966.

Whishaw I. Q., W. T. O'Connor, and S. B. Dunnett. The contributions of motor cortex, nigrostriatal dopamine and caudate-putamen to skilled forelimb use in the rat. *Brain* 109:805–843, 1986.

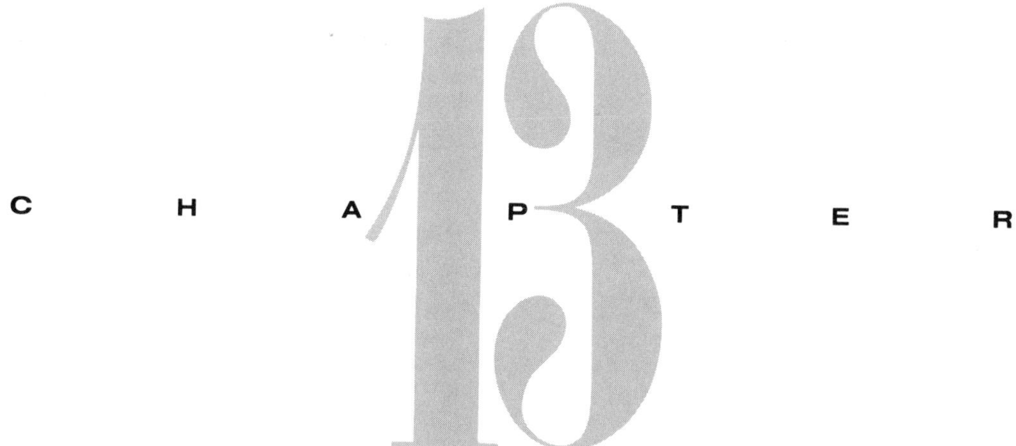

DISORDERS OF THE MOTOR SYSTEMS

There are more disorders of movement caused by malfunctions of various portions of the brain than can be discussed in this chapter. Comprehensive descriptions can be found in texts of clinical neurology such as those by Baker and Baker and by Walton. In addition, many disorders have been dealt with in discussions of special issues in other chapters, and these will be referred to in the appropriate places. This chapter is limited to a description of those disorders that are common or are of interest because of the insights they give into the organization and function of parts of the nervous system. Brain lesions of an experimental nature will not be dealt with in this chapter since we discussed those in Chapter 12. This chapter is so organized that disorders are described in ascending hierarchy: disorders of motor neurons and spinal cord are described first, followed by general disorders of movement, and then by disorders of the basal ganglia and neocortex. A final section describes "higher order" motor disorders, which are disorders of the *control* of movement rather than of movement per se. Table 13-1 defines some commonly used terms for movement disorders.

DISORDERS OF MOTOR NEURONS AND THE SPINAL CORD

This section provides descriptions of a number of spinal cord disorders. These include myasthenia gravis, a disorder of the muscle receptor; poliomyelitis, a disorder of the motor neuron cell body; multiple sclerosis, a disorder of myelinated motor fibers; and paraplegia and Brown-Sequard's syndrome, which are due to complete or hemitransections of the spinal cord, respectively.

TABLE 13-1. Some commonly used terms for movement disorders

Apraxia: Inability to carry out purposeful movements or movements on command in the absence of paralysis or other motor or sensory impairments. Usually follows damage to cortex tertiary areas.

Ataxia: Failure of muscular coordination or an irregularity of muscular action. Commonly follows cerebellar damage.

Athetosis: A condition in which ceaselss slow, sinuous writhing movements occur, especially in the hands. Due to abnormal function of the extrapyramidal system.

Catalepsy: A condition marked by muscular rigidity in which voluntary movements are reduced or absent but posture is maintained. It is a feature of Parkinson's disease due to dopamine loss.

Cataplexy: Complete loss of movement and posture during which muscle tone is absent but consciousness is spared.

Chorea: Literally means *dance* but refers to the ceaseless occurrence of a wide variety of jerky movements that appear to be well coordinated but are performed involuntarily.

Hemiplegia: Complete or partial paralysis to one half of the body. Usually follows damage to the contralateral motor cortex.

Palsy: Means a paralysis of movement and usually refers to persisting movement disorders due to brain damage acquired perinatally.

Paralysis: Complete loss of movement or sensation (but more commonly movement) in a part of the body. Usually permanent after damage to motor neurons; temporary after damage to motor cortex (area 4).

Paraplegia: Paralysis or paresis of the lower torso and legs, as can occur following spinal cord damage.

Spasticity: An increase in the tone of certain muscle groups involved in maintaining posture against the force of gravity. If the limb is moved against the rigidity, resistance will initially increase but then tone will suddenly melt (clasp-knife relfex). Spasticity is thought to be produced by damage to the extrapyramidal motor fibers from the neocortex.

Tardive dyskinesia: The occurrence of slow, persistent movements, particularly of the mouth and tongue. Usually follows long-term treatment with antipsychotic drugs.

Myasthenia Gravis

Myasthenia gravis (severe muscle weakness) is characterized by muscular fatigue after muscles have been exercised a few times. It may be apparent after a short period of exercise or work, toward the end of a long conversation, or sometimes even after a few repetitions of a movement. Recovery follows a period of rest. Its rapid onset after exercise distinguishes it from other disorders such as depression or general fatigue. Examination of muscles shows that there is no obvious muscle pathology. Myasthenia can occur in people of any age, but it is commonest in the third decade of life, and women are more often affected. All the muscles of the body may be affected, but those supplied by the cranial nerves are usually involved first. Here the initial symptoms are diplopia (double vision), ptosis (drooping of the eyelid), weakness of voice, and difficulty in chewing and swallowing or holding up the head. In some people only the limbs are involved. Usually the symptoms are the most apparent at the end of the day and are relieved after sleep. The severity of the disease varies from a mild unilateral ptosis in some people to an incapacitating generalized weakness with a threat of loss of life coming from respiratory paralysis in others.

Muscular weakness is due to a failure of normal neuromuscular transmission. It has long been known that drug treatment that prevents the destruction of acetylcholine (ACh), allowing it to remain in the area of the neuromuscular junction for a longer period, will partially reverse symptoms. The breakdown of acetylcholine in the synaptic space requires the enzyme acetylcholinesterase (AChE). The action of AChE can be blocked by drugs such as physostigmine (eserine), which permits the accumulation of ACh. If, on the other hand, the neuromuscular junction is partially blocked with drugs such as curare, neuromuscular weakness is enhanced. There are at least three possible explanations of myasthenia in terms of transmitter function. The terminal may release an insufficient supply of ACh, the postsynaptic receptors may be reduced in number or function ineffectively, or there may be an excessive supply of AChE in the vicinity of the terminal. Research in the past 15 years or so suggests that the problem is with the receptor.

In 1970, Changeux and colleagues, a group of chemists studying snake venom, isolated the toxin α-bungarotoxin, which causes paralysis by binding irreversibly with the motor end plate. Their discovery led to the chemistry that made possible the isolation of the nicotinic receptor for acetylcholine (AChR). When the receptors were bound with α-bungarotoxin, they could be separated from the muscle. In 1973, Patrick and Lindstrom in the United States injected the receptor, isolated from the electric eel *Torpedo* (the electric organ of the animal is a rich source of receptors), into rabbits in order to induce the formation of antibodies to the receptor. It was intended that these in turn could be labeled and used to locate the receptors. When the antibodies formed, however, the rabbits became "myasthenic," with symptoms similar to those shown by humans. Their weakness was reversed by physostigmine and enhanced by curare. The explanation for their myasthenia was that antibodies formed to attack the foreign receptors also attacked the rabbits' own receptors, which appeared identical. This finding suggests that the disease in humans might be an **autoimmune disease;** that is, humans form antibodies to their own AChR. Subsequently, antibodies to human AChR have been found in a majority of myasthenic patients' serum. Furthermore, drainage of the lymph fluid, which contains antibodies, improved symptoms, whereas replacing it returned symptoms. Finally, Albuquerque and coworkers in 1976 demonstrated that the receptor responsiveness in myasthenic muscle is reduced, and Fambrough and colleagues showed that there is a reduction in the number of receptors of the myasthenic muscle.

Although the receptor model of myasthenia provides a palatable explanation, it does leave some unresolved problems. It is not known how the production of antibodies starts, and it is not completely clear how the antibodies deactivate the receptors. It is also unclear why circulating antibodies are absent in some patients and why all the muscles of the body are not equally affected.

Treatment now has two objectives. First, AChE therapy is used to relieve symptoms. Second, for prolonged relief, attempts are made to arrest the disease with *thymectomy* (surgical removal of the thymus to reduce antibody formation) and with immunosuppressive drug treatment. As a result of treatment, mortality is currently very low.

Poliomyelitis

Poliomyelitis is an acute infectious disease caused by a virus that has a special affinity for the motor neurons of the spinal cord and sometimes also for the motor neurons of the cranial nerves. In extreme infections it causes paralysis and wasting of the muscles. If it attacks the motor neurons of the respiratory centers, death can result from asphyxia. Not all people who are infected by the virus show symptoms of the disease, but they nevertheless can pass on the disease to others. Infections in individuals can be accelerated by exercise, exertion, or minor surgical operations. Even exercise of a limb may hasten the viral attack on the motor neurons that innervate that limb. The disease usually occurred sporadically and occasionally epidemically in the North America until the Salk and Sabin vaccines were developed in the 1960s. Since then, the disease has been well controlled. There are, however, cases reported every year, and the incidence of the illness in tropical third-world countries is still a concern. Many of those infected by the virus after vaccination against it show no symptoms, others show signs of a mild infection, and still others have fever, headache, malaise, and so forth, but only a minority develop paralysis. Paralysis usually reaches its maximum within the first 24 h and improvement occurs after about a week. Of the muscles that are paralyzed, only a portion remain permanently paralyzed, so that after an attack considerable recovery of movement is possible. The process of recovery often lasts for over a year. It is not known why the virus has a special affinity for motor neurons, but this type of predilection of some viruses for certain classes of brain cells is thought to be a possible cause of other brain disorders such as Parkinson's disease and schizophrenia.

Multiple Sclerosis

Multiple sclerosis (MS) (*sclerosis* is from the Greek meaning hardness) is a disease characterized by the loss of myelin largely in motor, but also in sensory, tracts. The loss of myelin is not uniform but occurs in patches. In many cases the early signs of the disease are followed by improvement, so that remissions and relapses are a striking feature of the disease. The course of the disease may run from a few years to as long as 50 years. The eventual condition may be one in which the affected person is confined to bed with the classic feature of ataxic paraplegia.

The first pathological accounts of the disease were given in the early part of the 19th century. The signs of the disease consist of small circumscribed lesions in which the myelin sheath and sometimes the axons are destroyed. Eventually a *sclerotic plaque* may form in these areas. The cause of MS is still not known. It has been thought that it is due to an infection, a virus, environmental factors, or an immune response of the central nervous system. It often occurs a number of times in the same families, but there is not clear evidence that it is inherited or that it is transmitted from one individual to another. MS is most prevalent in Northern Europe and somewhat less common in North America. It is rare in Japan and in more southerly or tropical countries. In regions in which it occurs its incidence of 50 per 100,000 still makes it one of the commonest structural diseases of the nervous system. Only Parkinson's disease is equally common. It occurs in a female-to-male ratio of about 6 to 4, and progress of the disease is often more rapid in females than in males.

The onset of MS is usually rapid; symptoms are fully apparent within a day or two. In one-half of affected persons the first symptoms are weakness or loss of control over the limbs, in 30% the symptoms are blindness or other disorders of vision in one or both eyes, and in 20% the symptoms are sensory sensations, tremors, epilepsy, or vertigo. The motor symptoms usually consist of a loss of power in the lower limbs or arms. Muscular wasting is rare because of the patchy nature of the disease and because muscles receive multiple innervation from many motor neurons. The first symptoms usually appear in adulthood, and after remission symptoms may not occur again for years. In cases in which the disease is fatal, the average age of death is between 65 and 84 years. There are no specific treatments for the disease other than to treat the symptoms and encourage the affected persons to continue working and leading an active life as long as possible. Some people with MS are described as displaying an optimistic euphoria, possibly because the disease has attacked diencephalic structures, which is thought to be helpful in their management. Affected persons, however, may also occasionally show symptoms of apathy and depression.

Paraplegia

Paraplegia (from the Greek *para,* beyond, and *plegia,* stroke) is a condition in which both lower limbs are paralyzed (*quadraplegia* is the paralysis of all four extremities). It is a direct consequence of a complete transection of the spinal cord. Immediately after a complete section, the cord distal to the section is devoid of all activity, and all movement, sensation, and reflexes are absent. Due to loss of reflex activity, thermoregulatory control is absent (leaving the skin cool and dry without sweating) as is bladder control (requiring drainage of the bladder to prevent urinary retention). This condition, called spinal shock, lasts from 4 days to about 6 weeks. Gradually, there is a return of some spinal reflexes until a stabilized condition is reached after a year or so. No sensations, voluntary movements, or thermoregulatory control ever reappears below the lesion. Even though no sensation is felt, certain reflexes can be elicited. A pinprick, for example, may elicit a withdrawal reflex such as the *triple response,* which consists of flexion of the hip, knee, and ankle. Later, extensor activity may become sufficiently strong that weight may be briefly supported, but spinal circuits are too dependent on brain facilitation to permit prolonged standing in its absence. After a year or two a paraplegic person may be in one of a number of conditions: (1) *Paraplegia in extension,* in which tone predominates in extensor muscles, resulting in a predominantly extensor, or rigidly straight, posture. In this condition (about two-thirds of all paraplegics) the withdrawal reflex is difficult to produce. (2) *Paraplegia in flexion,* in which flexor spasms predominate and major flexor activities can occur, including the flexor withdrawal reflexes and excretory and sexual reflexes. (3) *Flaccid paralysis,* in which no tone is present, occurs in fewer than 20% of paraplegics.

Brown-Sequard Syndrome

Brown-Sequard syndrome refers to the consequences of a unilateral section through the spinal cord. Since some of the ascending and descending pathways are uncrossed and some are crossed, symptoms will occur on both sides of the body below the cut. Contralateral to the side of section there will be a loss of pain and temperature sensation, since these pathways cross at the point that they enter the cord. Sensations of fine touch and pressure will be preserved, since their pathways do not cross until they reach the caudal medulla. Ipsilateral to the section there will be a loss of fine touch and pressure, but not in pain and temperature sensation; sensation and voluntary movements of distal musculature will be lost. According to Nathan and Smith, walking recovers well within two to three days because control of this movement is bilateral.

GENERAL DISORDERS OF MOTOR FUNCTION

This section describes three disorders that are due primarily, but not exclusively, to dysfunctions in subcortical areas. In each case the effects of the disorders are widespread and involve most brain or behavioral functions in general. These disorders include cerebral palsy, hydrocephalus, and disorders of sleep.

Cerebral Palsy

Cerebral palsy is usually defined as a disorder primarily of motor function caused by brain trauma during fetal development or birth. Any simple definition is difficult, however, because (1) the motor symptoms take many forms, (2) there can be many different accompanying cognitive impairments, and (3) the disorder has diverse causes. As such, cerebral palsy cannot be called a disease, a syndrome, or even a condition since, depending on the nature of the brain damage, it will take different forms in every individual. Because brain damage is involved, it is not curable, but it often is amenable to therapy and training. *Cerebral palsy* has its most useful meaning in an administrative sense, for it covers individuals who are handicapped in many different ways by motor disorders due to nonprogressive brain abnormalities. A more detailed discussion of the problems of definition, form, incidence, and treatment has been presented by Cruickshank.

Cerebral palsy was first described in the medical literature in 1853 by the London physician

William Little. He recognized that the motor abnormalities of some babies are related to abnormal parturition, difficult labor, premature birth, and asphyxia. He also recognized the permanent nature of the disabilities and their associated intellectual impairments; changes in personality, such as irritability and temper tantrums; and epilepsy. More importantly, he pointed out that the problems could be severely aggravated by subsequent improper training and education.

The incidence of cerebral palsy is not precisely known because many cases are not reported, but it is estimated at about 6 per 1000 births. The number of males and females afflicted is about equal. Estimates on degree of impairment suggest that about 10% of afflicted persons require no special services, 65% need services on an ambulatory basis, and about 25% need special schooling or custodial care. With respect to type of cerebral palsy by motor symptoms, about 50% of persons with the disorder are spastic, about 25% are athetoid, about 10% are afflicted with rigidity, and about 10% are ataxic. As might be expected, cerebral palsy has many causes, the most frequent of which are listed in Table 13-2. Nearly 50% of all cases are due to birth injury or injury suffered during development, 9% are secondary to convulsions, and 8% are due to prematurity. Smaller numbers result from other diverse causes. Incidence is also importantly related to the mother's

TABLE 13-2. Potential causes of cerebral palsy

Hereditary
- Static—familial athetosis, familial paraplegia, familial tremor
- Progressive—demyelinating diseases of viral or undetermined origin (chromosomal breakages are rare in cerebral palsy, as are disorders of metabolism)

Congenital (acquired in utero)
- Infection rubella, toxoplasmosis, cytomegalic inclusions, herpes simplex, and other viral or infectious agents
- Maternal anoxia, carbon monoxide poisoning, strangulation, anemia, hypotension associated with spinal anesthesia, placental infarcts, placenta abruptio
- Prenatal cerebral hemorrhage, maternal toxemia, direct trauma, maternal bleeding diathesis
- Prenatal anoxia, twisting or kinking of the cord
- Miscellaneous toxins, drugs

Perinatal (obstetrical)
- Mechanical anoxia—respiratory obstruction, narcotism due to oversedation with drugs, placenta previa or abruptio, hypotension associated with spinal anesthesia, breech delivery with delay of the after-coming head
- Trauma—hemorrhage associated with dystocia, disproportions and malpositions, of labor, sudden pressure changes, precipitate delivery, caesarean delivery
- Complications of birth—"small for date" babies, prematurity, immaturity, dysmaturity, postmaturity, hyperbilirubinemia and isoimmunization factors (kernicterus due to Rh factor, ABO incompatability), hemolytic disorders, "respiratory distress" disorders, syphilis, meningitis, and other infections, drug addiction reactions, hypoglycemic reactions, hypocalcemic reactions

Postnatal-Infancy
- Trauma (subdural hematoma, skull fracture, cerebral contusion)
- Infections (meningitis, encephalitis, brain abscess)
- Vascular accidents (congenital cerebral aneurism, thrombosis, embolic, hypertensive encephalopathy, sudden pressure changes)
- Toxins (lead, arsenic, coal tar derivatives)
- Anoxia (carbon monoxide poisoning, strangulation, high-altitude and deep-pressure anoxia, hypoglycemia)
- Neoplastic and late neurodevelopmental defects (tumor, cyst, progressive hydrocephalus).

Source: From E. Denhoff, Medical aspects. In W. M. Cruickshank, ed. *Cerebral Palsy*. Syracuse, NY: Syracuse University Press, 1976, p. 33. Reprinted with permission.

ability to carry a baby to term, and to factors such as her body size, health habits, and weight gain during pregnancy.

Denhoff has described the medical features of the movement disorders and the part of the body involved, that is, spastic, ataxic, choreiform, and so forth. In addition to these characteristics, the degree of the impairment (mild, moderate, or severe), with a description of muscle tone (hypertonic, hypotonic) and other associated dysfunctions may also be specified. Lesions involving the corticospinal tracts, basal ganglia, brainstem, and cerebellum are presumed to be responsible for the disorders. Yet in cerebral palsy clear-cut relations between lesion and clinical findings are difficult to make. A conservative classic interpretation would associate corticospinal damage with spasticity, basal ganglial damage with dyskinesia, and cerebellar damage with ataxia. Simply because many of these brain systems traverse the entire brain and make many connections throughout it, localization is difficult.

Hydrocephalus

Hydrocephalus is characterized by an increase in the volume of the cerebrospinal fluid (CSF). This can occur in two ways. In the first, enlarged ventricles are a secondary result of shrinkage or atrophy of surrounding brain tissue. This is more likely to occur in adults. The second, more typical cause of hydrocephalus is the obstruction of the flow of CSF, resulting in a buildup of pressure in one or more ventricles and eventually causing their expansion. This type is more typical in infants. It is not certain that a simple overproduction of CSF is ever a cause of hydrocephalus.

Figure 13-1 is a drawing made from a cast of the lateral ventricles. Normally the ventricles are filled with CSF. In all, there is only about 130 cm^3 of CSF in an adult and about one-third of this is in the spinal cord's great lumbar cistern. The clear, colorless fluid is made by the choroid plexus in the ventricles. Most of the CSF is made in the lateral ventricles. From there it flows through the interventricular foramina (windows) of Monro into the third ventricle, through the cerebral aqueduct, and then into the fourth ventricle. It finally escapes through three little holes in the roof of the fourth ventricle. These are the two laterally located foramina of Luschka and the medial foramina of Magendie. (The mnemonic is: lateral, Luschka; medial, Magendie). The fluid then enters the subarachnoid space — the space beneath the arachnoid covering of the brain and spinal cord. It is absorbed into the veins and is carried away by the bloodstream.

The circulation in the ventricles can be blocked at either of the interventricular foramina, causing an increase in pressure followed by expansion of either lateral ventricle. It can also be blocked at the level of the cerebral aqueduct (causing hydrocephalus of the first three ventricles) or be blocked by closure of the foramina in the roof of the fourth ventricle (producing hydrocephalus of the entire ventricular system). If CSF flow is suddenly obstructed, there is a rapid rise in intracranial pressure, ventricular dilation, and finally coma. If CSF pathways are gradually obstructed, as might be produced by a tumor, increase in pressure and dilation is less rapid and symptoms may include the gradual appearance of visual disturbances, palsies, dementia, and so on.

Infant hydrocephalus is characterized by a conspicuous enlargement of the head. It usually occurs during the first few months of life. As many as 27 of 100,000 newborn babies may suffer from hydrocephalus. In about 14% of cases there is a malformation that impedes CSF circulation; inflammation or trauma produce most other cases. About 4% of cases are due to tumors. As the ventricles distend they push the cerebral hemispheres into a balloon shape. Because the skull bones of an infant are not yet fused, continued pressure causes the expansion of the head in all directions. If expansion damages the cortex, intelligence may be impaired and dementia may result. If the cortex is undamaged, intelligence may be

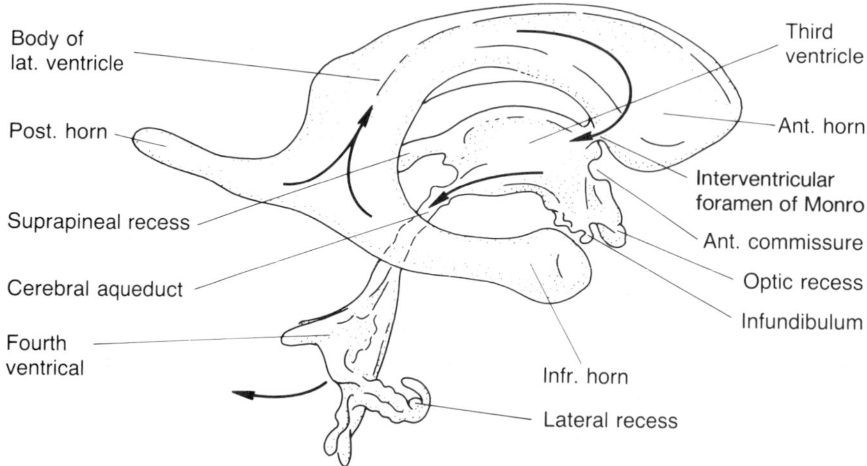

FIGURE 13-1. Drawing of a cast of the ventricular system of the brain as seen from the side. The arrows show the direction of flow of cerebral spinal fluid. (After Everett, 1965.)

unimpaired even after the cortex is stretched into a sheet of tissue less than a centimeter thick. If untreated, hydrocephalus often causes death or severe mental or motor disabilities. It can now be treated with some success by inserting a valve and tube into one lateral ventricle that passes into a jugular vein to drain into the cardiac atrium. Lorber reports that individuals with extreme hydrocephalus and extensive cortical loss develop normally and have normal abilities when adults. We question this conclusion. Perhaps in these cases the cortex is quite thin and has been unfolded and spread out by fluid pressure while still maintaining its integrity and connections. If people were able to develop normally without a cortex, most of the conclusion of this text and neuropsychology in general would be questioned.

Disorders of Sleep

Sleep is a behavior characterized by the absence of obvious responses to most surrounding events and the absence of most kinds of voluntary movements. Originally, sleep was thought to be a passive act that resulted when sensory stimulation was low. This view was seemingly supported by Bremer, who in 1935 transected the brain between colliculi in cats (called the *cerveau isolé* preparation) and observed that large-amplitude slow waves characteristic of sleep were a permanent feature of the cat's EEG as long as it survived. If the transection was made lower down (the *encéphale isolé* preparation), the cat showed normal sleep and waking EEG cycles. Bremer believed that the difference between these two preparations was that the cranial nerves provided stimulation in the latter preparation, whereas in the former they were separated from the forebrain and could not do so.

Bremer's idea, also referred to as the *passive hypothesis of sleep,* has not received much support. Experiments that deprived humans of sensory stimulation showed that deprivation did not induce or prolong sleep. Perhaps the single most influential experiment performed to oppose the passive view was that by Moruzzi and Magoun in 1949. They implanted stimulating electrodes into the reticular formation of cats and recording electrodes into the neocortex. When the reticular formation was stimulated, the slow waves of the cortex were replaced by a pattern of low-voltage fast activity characteristic of a waking cat. The fast activity outlasted the period of stimulation by a considerable duration. A mapping study suggested that a pathway from the reticular system to the forebrain was responsible for producing the "wakinglike" EEG pattern. The consequence of Moruzzi and Magoun's experiment was that the dominant hypothesis of sleep became what is known as the *active hypothesis of sleep.* Stated simply, the hypothesis is that sleep is produced by changes in the activity of certain brain neurons. The hypothesis has led to the search for the brain structure that produces sleep, and in the course of this search, it has been found that sleep as a behavior is very complex. There seem to be at least two different kinds of sleep, which are produced by the interaction of a number of different brain structures. Ironically, "the structure" that produces sleep has not yet been satisfactorily identified. Nevertheless, enough is now known about sleep mechanisms for a beginning explanation to be available for a number of classic disorders of sleep.

Before we give a description of the disorders of sleep, it is important to point out that sleep is a phenomenon that varies considerably for different individuals and for the same individual at different stages of life. We have all been subjected to the idea that 8 h of sleep each night is necessary for good health. In fact, there are both long and short sleepers. Some people have been found to stay healthy on as little as an hour of sleep each day, whereas other people may sleep as much as 10 to 12 h a day. Webb has studied long sleepers (longer than 9.5 h per day) and short sleepers (fewer than 4.4 h per day) and found little difference in their overall health. It does seem that the proper amount of sleep is an individual affair. Short sleepers may not be able to sleep any longer and long sleepers may not function efficiently after only a short period of sleep. The definition of what constitutes adequate sleep must therefore be made within the context of an individual's past sleep history.

Initially, sleep was thought to be one behavioral state. Subsequent studies have shown that it comprises at least two states that periodically alternate with each other during a complete sleep session. Based on their respective EEG activity patterns, one state is called *D-sleep,* for its characteristic desynchronized EEG pattern, and the other is called *S-sleep,* for its characteristic slow-wave EEG pattern. D-sleep is characterized by a desynchronized (low-voltage fast-activity), or wakinglike, EEG, during which rapid eye movements (REMs) and twitches of the fingers, toes, and other body parts occur in short bursts. S-sleep is characterized by a slow-wave (large-amplitude slow-activity) EEG of various degrees. Large movements such as tossing and turning occur. S-sleep is generally divided into four stages: stage 1 has the least amount of slow-wave activity and stage 4 has the most, with stages 2 and 3 between the two. S-sleep and D-sleep occur in an alternating pattern in the "average" individual, as illustrated in Figure 13-2. When sleep begins, stages 1 through 4 of S-sleep appear in succession and then give way to D-sleep. After a period of D-sleep, S-sleep again occurs, and so on throughout the night. As a night's sleep progresses, however, stage 4 sleep becomes less frequent and the periods of D-sleep tend to last longer.

What accounts for the two types of sleep and their alternation? The answer to this question is intimately linked to the question of the function of sleep. A biological explanation of sleep is that it is an adaptive process to conserve energy at night (a time during which food-gathering would be difficult). A problem to be overcome, however, is that the process of evolution has placed a premium on developing rhythms of locomotor activity (thought to occur every two hours or so, during which food gathering and other survival activities would occur). The activity cycles would obviously be incompatible with a full night's sleep. In order to cope with the dual demands of conserving

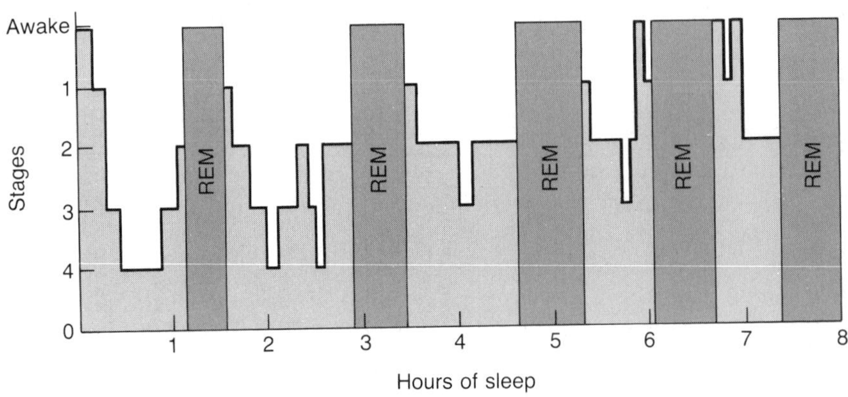

FIGURE 13-2. Course of events during a typical night's sleep for one individual. Stages represent those defined by EEG recordings. The light gray areas represent S-sleep; the dark areas represent D-sleep. Note: Stage 4 S-sleep typically occurs early in the evening; D-sleep increases in duration as the night's sleep progresses. (After Hartmann, 1967.)

energy and of maintaining activity cycles, an innovative adaption occurred. Periodically, when a waking cycle should occur, immobility was maintained by inhibiting the musculature selectively, while only the brain entered the active cycle.

Experimental evidence supports this hypothesis rather well. Pompeiano has recorded electrical activity from the brainstem, spinal cord, motor neurons, and musculature during S- and D-sleep. During D-sleep there is an increase in the activity of certain brainstem and spinal cord pathways while motor neuron and muscle activity are almost completely suppressed. Presumably, some central structure (located just below the cerebellum) is actively suppressing movement. When this area is damaged in cats, they display gross body movements rather than paralysis during D-sleep. The inhibition does not completely extend to the cortex, however, because physiological measures of brain activity show that during paralysis oxygen use, temperature, and metabolic activity increase, supporting the EEG data that the brain is in an active state. (The activity may be so intense that excitement occasionally breaks through the inhibition to produce movements of the eyes, fingers, toes, etc.) Peripherally, however, in the absence of muscle activity, all thermoregulation stops and body temperature falls toward room temperature. In addition, any gross body movements such as rolling around are effectively blocked. It is still not entirely understood why central activity does not manifest itself in consciousness. Part of the explanation may also be that the inhibition blocks some critical part of brain activity that is necessary for consciousness. Nevertheless, although consciousness seems blocked and recall is incomplete, studies by Dement and Kleitman and by others, in which sleeping people are awakened, have shown that D-sleep is a time during which vivid dreaming invariably occurs.

Disorders of sleep are generally classified into two major groups: (1) **narcolepsy,** which is characterized by excessive sleep or brief inappropriate episodes of sleep, often associated with other symptoms; and (2) *insomnia,* which is characterized by an inadequate amount of sleep, an inability to fall asleep, or frequent inconvenient arousals from sleep. Both types of disorders can have a variety of causes, including brain damage, viral infections, drug abuse, and so forth. They may, however, also occur in the absence of obvious precipitating factors. In addition to these two types of disorders, there are many other behaviors that occur during sleep that are disturbing to the afflicted individual. These include night terrors, sleepwalking, teeth grinding, and *myoclonic jerks* (sudden vigorous movements), but they are usually transitory, infrequent, or not sufficiently disruptive to be called sleep disorders, per se.

Narcolepsy. Narcolepsy is defined as an inappropriate attack of sleep. The afflicted individual has an overwhelming impulse to fall asleep or simply collapses into sleep at inconvenient times. The attacks may be infrequent or occur many times a day. The disorder is surprisingly common: estimates suggest that as many as 0.02% of the population may suffer from these attacks. Males and females seem equally affected. Although there is a high incidence of narcolepsy in the families of afflicted individuals, no genetic causality has been demonstrated. Symptoms usually appear in people when they are between the ages of 10 and 20, and once sleep attacks are developed they continue throughout life. Amphetamine-like stimulants and tricyclic antidepressants have been found useful in treatment.

Narcolepsy has four characteristic features: (1) sleep attacks, (2) cataplexy, (3) sleep paralysis, and (4) hypnagogic or hypnopompic hallucinations. All the symptoms do not necessarily occur at once or in the same individual, but they do occur together sufficiently often to be considered interrelated.

Sleep Attacks. Sleep attacks are brief, often irresistible episodes of sleep that last about 15 min and can occur at any time. Their onset is sometimes recognizable but they can also occur without warning. The episodes are most apt to occur during times of boredom or after meals, but they can also occur during such activities as sexual intercourse, scuba diving, or baseball games. After a brief sleep attack the individual may awaken completely alert and be resistent to a second attack for a number of hours.

Cataplexy. *Cataplexy* (from the Greek *cata,* down, and *plexy,* strike) is a complete loss of muscle tone or a sudden paralysis that results in "buckling" of the knees or complete collapse. The attack may be so sudden that the fall results in injury, particularly because the collapse involves a loss of muscle tone and loss of the reflexes necessary to break the fall. During the attack the patient remains conscious, and if the eyelids are open, or are opened, the patient can recall visual events that occur during the attack. In contrast to sleep attacks, cataplectic attacks usually appear at times of emotional excitement, such as when a person is laughing or angry. If emotions are held under tight control, the attacks can be prevented.

Sleep Paralysis. *Sleep paralysis* is an episode of paralysis that occurs at the transition periods between wakefulness and sleep. The period of paralysis is usually brief but can last as long as 20 min. Sleep paralysis has been experienced by half of all people, if classroom surveys are an indication of its frequency. In contrast to cataplexy, the paralyzed individual can easily be aroused by touching or name-calling, and if the individual is experienced with the attacks, he or she can terminate them by using a strategy such as grunting.

Hypnagogic and Hypnopompic Hallucinations. *Hypnagogic* (from the Greek *hypno,* sleep, and *gogic,* enter into) *hallucinations* are episodes of auditory, visual, or tactile hallucination that occur during sleep paralysis as the individual is falling sleep. *Hypnopompic (pompic,* leading away) *hallucinations* are similar experiences that occur during paralysis as the individual is awakening. The hallucinations are generally frightening: the individual may feel a monster or something equally terrifying is lurking nearby. The same kinds of hallucinations can occur during episodes of cataplexy. A curious feature of the hallucinations is that the individual is conscious and often aware of things that are actually happening, so that the hallucinations are even more bizarre, because they can become intermixed with real events.

The symptoms of narcolepsy fit together to form what Rechtschaffen and Dement feel may be a syndrome involving the unwanted sudden onset of D-sleep. Recall from the description of sleep types that D-sleep is characterized by muscular paralysis and vivid dreams. The parallel in narcolepsy is the cataplex and sleep paralysis and the hypnagogic hallucinations that are common in both conditions. Two types of evidence support Rechtschaffen and Dement's view. First, during an attack of cataplexy or sleep paralysis, and even though individuals are conscious, they experience hallucinations that have a dreamlike character. Second, EEG recordings taken from narcoleptics have shown that rather than going through an hour or so of S-sleep, they enter D-sleep almost immediately. Individuals who suffer from narcolepsy display the symptoms described above at different times and in different combinations, but the usual pattern is that the sleep attacks appear first (usually without other symptoms). Cataplexy, which may be a sudden onset of D-sleep, will develop in about 70% of patients. Sleep paralysis with hallucinations occurs in about 30%. It may involve entering a D-sleep stage before losing consciousness, or regaining consciousness during a D-stage of sleep.

There may be other forms of narcolepsy, but they have received less experimental description than the form just described. It is thought that individuals may suffer from a type of narcolepsy in which they are prone to enter S-sleep. Obviously one of the problems with describing this type of narcolepsy is that it is difficult to distinguish it from genuine fatigue. At least one distinguishing feature of S-sleep narcolepsy is that individuals still feel fatigued when they wake up, unlike D-sleep narcoleptics, who feel refreshed.

Insomnia. Studies on people who claim that they do not sleep, do not sleep well, or wake up frequently from sleep show that their insomnia can have many causes. Rechtschaffen and Monroe recorded EEGs before and during sleep from poor sleepers and found that they exaggerated the length of time that it took them to get to sleep. But the individuals did have decreased D-sleep, they made more body movements, and they went through more changes in sleep stages than did normal individuals. When awakened from S-sleep, they also claimed that they were not sleeping. The investigators concluded that even though these poor sleepers did sleep by EEG criteria, they did not seem to benefit completely from the restorative properties of sleep. Surveys suggest that as many as 14% of people claim to suffer from insomnia, but the causes are divergent and include general factors such as anxiety, depression, fear of sleeping, environmental disturbances, and travel into new time zones. Some factors in insomnia seem directly related to the sleep situation. These include (1) nightmares, (2) sleep apnea, (3) restless legs syndrome, (4) myoclonus, (5) drug-induced insomnia, and (6) insomnia due to brain damage.

Nightmares. *Nightmares* are intense, frightening dreams that lead to arousal. They are commoner than night terrors (*parvor nocturnus*). *Night terrors* are attempts to fight or flee accompanied by panic and such utterances as bloodcurdling screams. Nightmares occur during D-sleep, but night terrors occur during stage-4 S-sleep. Night terrors are usually brief (1 or 2 min), and the individual usually cannot remember the episode. Both kinds of events are commoner in children than adults, perhaps because adults are more experienced with disturbing dreams and so are not easily awakened. Both types of events can be sufficiently disturbing to disrupt sleep and lead to insomnia.

Sleep Apnea. *Sleep apnea* (from the Greek for not breathing) is a cessation of respiration that occurs periodically, lasting about 10 or more seconds, and occurs only during sleep. There are two types of sleep apnea. *Obstructive sleep apnea* occurs mainly during D-sleep and seems to be due to a collapse of the oropharynx during the paralysis of D-sleep. Patients with this problem invariably have a history of loud snoring: sounds produced as a consequence of the difficult breathing through the constricted air passage. The obstruction can be reduced through surgical intervention. *Central sleep apnea* stems from a central nervous system disorder. It occurs primarily in males and is characterized by a failure of the diaphragm and accessory muscles to move. Apnea periods may last for up to 3 min. Both types of sleep apnea require all-night recording sessions to detect. Both types interrupt sleep, for the individual is awakened partly or fully by the oxygen deprivation. Although individuals may be unaware of their apnea, they complain of chronic daytime fatigue. Similar apnea in newborn babies may be a causal factor in sudden infant death syndrome.

Restless Legs Syndrome. *Restless legs syndrome* is characterized by a severe, difficult-to-describe, generalized painful sensation felt in the legs, which is relieved by leg movements. The movements produce insomnia in the individual and any partner by delaying sleep onset.

Myoclonus. *Nocturnal myoclonus* is sudden body jerks that occur when an individual is falling asleep. It is sometimes accompanied by dreamlike sensations or images. The movements usually wake up everyone in the bed.

Drug-induced Insomnia. Many drugs, whether stimulants or sedatives, eventually lead to insomnia. Hypnotics and sedatives may at first promote sleep, but habituation occurs. These drugs also deprive the user of D-sleep. Stimulants directly reduce sleep, but they may have their greatest effect on S-sleep. Drug withdrawal is usually an effective treatment.

Insomnia due to Brain Damage. Brain-damage-induced insomnia is relatively rare, but there are descriptions of patients who showed reduced sleep or no sleep following brain damage. Certain viral infections, such as the *encephalitis lethargica* of the 1920s, described by von Economo, can lead to insomnia that is so long-lasting it can prove fatal. One treatment given for this type of insomnia was to anesthetize the patients for 8 to 10 days, with brief respites for feeding, until recovery occurred. It is likely that the virus of encephalitis attacks brain centers responsible for sleep induction. Nauta has described a rat analogue of this condition: he observed that rats with large anterior hypothalamic lesions became excessively active and insomniac until they died.

DISORDERS OF THE EXTRAPYRAMIDAL SYSTEM

Classically, the *extrapyramidal system* consists of motor structures that do not send motor fibers to the spinal cord through the pyramidal tract. Often, however, the term is used in a more restricted sense to refer to the basal ganglia and their major pathways. The lack of clarity of the term *extrapyramidal* is widely recognized and so will not be discussed here. Nevertheless, there is a group of diseases having clinical symptoms marked by abnormalities in movement and posture that are referable to dysfunctions of the basal ganglia and so are traditionally called *extrapyramidal disorders.* The major symptoms of these disorders are an excess of spontaneous, aimless movements, and a persistent increase in motor tone with no essential change in spinal reflexes. Clinically, two groups of symptoms are distinguished: *hyperkinetic-dystonic syndromes,* characterized by an excess of motor activity (including chorea, ballism, athetosis, Wilson's disease, and perhaps Tourette's syndrome), and the *hypokinetic-rigid syndrome* (Parkinson's disease).

Huntington's Chorea

Huntington's chorea (*chorea* is from the Greek for dance) is a genetic disorder that results in intellectual deterioration and abnormal movements as the afflicted reach certain ages in life. George Huntington was 8 years old when he first saw people with "that disorder," as it was then called. He was driving with his father in his native New York when they came upon two women who were tall, thin, and twisting and grimacing. No doubt the disorder was familiar to his father and grandfather, who were both physicians. Nevertheless, the sight of these women left such a profound impression on him that he studied the disease when he later became a physician. In 1872, when he was 22, he wrote the first complete description of the disease. The history of the disease and its origin in the United States have been told by Vessie, who traced it to the village of Bures in England in 1630. At that time whole families in Bures and its vicinity were branded and tried as witches. Some family members, who had or carried the disease, sailed to America among the 700 passengers of the John Winthrop fleet in 1630. In 1653, Ellin Wilkie (name fictitious), who had arrived with Winthrop, apparently had the disorder, for she was tried and hanged for witchcraft. Her granddaughter was later tried and pardoned in 1692. Part of the early history of establishing the genetic basis for the disease involved tracing the family background of afflicted individuals whose ancestors had arrived among the Winthrop passengers and who had moved to other areas of the country. In other countries that were colonized by Europeans, there have been similar family histories constructed that trace the disease back to one or a few immigrants. In actuality, Huntington's chorea is relatively rare, with death rates of 1.6 per million population per year. It is commonest among white Europeans and their descendants; it is very rare in other racial groups such as orientals and blacks. The number of people who will develop the disease is now thought to be on the decline because of advances in genetic counseling.

Huntington's chorea, or hereditary chorea, is a progressive degenerative disease. The first symptom is usually a reduction of activity and restriction of interest. The first restless and involuntary movements may be attributed to hysteria or some other disorder. The first movements usually appear within a year of the onset of the psychiatric symptoms. The involuntary movements are initially slight and consist of little more than continuous fidgeting, but they slowly increase until they are almost incessant. The movements never involve single muscles but include whole limbs or parts of a limb. They are also irregular and follow no set pattern. A reliable sign of the disease is that a sustained muscular contraction is not possible: when an object is held, grip fluctuates; also the tongue cannot be held protruded. Eventually, the movements become uncontrollable and affect the head, face, trunk, and limbs — impeding speech, swallowing, walking, writing, or other voluntary movements. Sometimes individuals may attempt to mask the abnormal movements with purposeful ones. There are emotional and personality changes, impairments of recent memory, defective ability to manipulate acquired knowledge, and slowing of information processing. Apraxia, aphasia, and agnosias, which result from certain cortical diseases such as Alzheimer's disease, however, do not develop. The emotional changes that result include anxiety, depression, mania, and schizophrenialike psychoses. Suicide is not uncommon in younger patients.

The first symptoms of the disorder usually occur in people 30 to 50 years of age. About 5% of cases, sometimes called "juvenile chorea," begin before age 20. In contrast with adult cases, juvenile cases may exhibit muscle rigidity and slow movements, somewhat similar to those in Parkinson's disease, and they may also have muscle spasms, tremor, disturbances of eye movement, and epilepsy. Adult patients live an average of 12 years after disease onset, but the progress of the disease is far more rapid in the juvenile cases.

Huntington's chorea is transmitted genetically as a autosomal dominant with complete penetrance, meaning that half of all offspring of an affected individual will develop the disease. The approximate location of the gene is now known and a marker can be used to determine whether a family member (even in utero) will develop the disease before symptoms appear. Using recombinant DNA procedures and a population in Venezuela, Gusella and his colleagues have been able to narrow the locus of the gene to a portion of the short arm of chromosome 4 and to detect a marker linked with this gene.

At autopsy the brains of Huntington's chorea individuals show shrinkage and thinning of the cerebral cortex. The basal ganglia is also grossly atrophied and shows a marked loss of its intrinsic neurons. One dominant explanation of the disease is that there is an imbalance among the various neurotransmitter systems of the basal ganglia. A simplified model of the transmitter systems involved is shown in Figure 13-3. They include: (1) a glutamate projection from the cortex to the basal ganglia, (2) a γ-aminobutyric acid (GABA) projection from the basal ganglia to the substantia nigra, (3) a dopamine (DA) projection from the substantia nigra to the basal ganglia, (4) and acetylcholine (ACh) neurons in the basal ganglia. It is postulated that the intrinsic neurons of the basal ganglia (GABA and ACh neurons) die during the course of the disease, leaving a largely intact nigrostriatal DA pathway. As a result of the decrease in inhibition of the DA cells by the GABA pathway, there is an increase in DA release in the basal ganglia. The hyperactivity of the dopamine system is thought to produce the characteristic abnormal movements. Exactly how the movements are produced is not clear, but if the basal ganglia have a modulatory function on the corticobulbar and corticospinal systems, then the release of these two systems from modulation could produce the typical abnormal movements. Support for the idea that there is an increase in dopamine activity comes from two sources. First, biochemical analysis of the brain tissue of Huntington patients at autopsy shows a significant increase in dopamine levels. Second, drugs that tend to ameliorate chorea, such as major tranquilizers, are those that block dopamine, whereas those that aggravate chorea, such as amphetamines, are dopamine agonists.

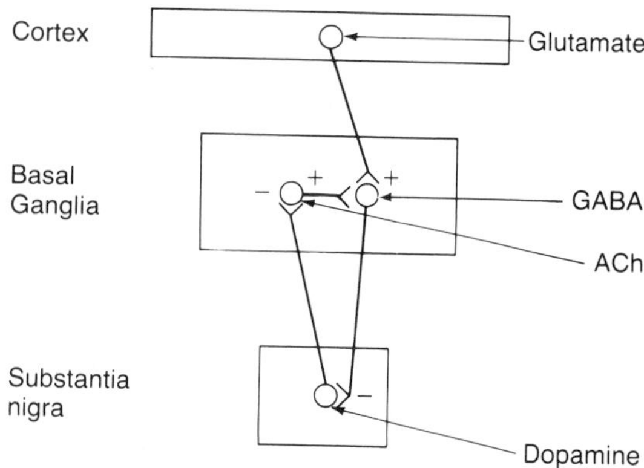

FIGURE 13-3. Model of transmitter systems involved in Huntington's chorea. It is thought that ACh and GABA neurons in the basal ganglia die, and as a result dopamine cells are released from GABA inhibition and become hyperactive, thus producing abnormal movements. The death of GABA cells may be produced by excessive activity of the glutamate pathway.

Over the past 10 years there has been a surge of interest in the mechanisms that produce Huntington's chorea. A volume edited by Chase and colleagues has been devoted to the disease. An animal model has also been developed that offers at least a partial explanation of how the disease progresses. In the animal model it has been found that an analogue of glutamate called kainic acid will attach to glutamate receptors and kill cells by overstimulating them. When kainic acid is injected into the basal ganglia of rats, many neurons containing GABA and ACh, as well as other transmitters, are destroyed. Accordingly, an explanation of the cell loss in humans is that the glutamate pathway from the cortex to the basal ganglia becomes hyperactive and destroys cells in the basal ganglia with which it connects. There is some independent support for this suggestion, but there are also some unanswered questions. For example, the rat models of Huntington's chorea do display some learning impairments, but they do not display abnormal movements. In addition, there is still no explanation of how the disease takes different forms or why it has an age-related onset. These unanswered questions provide fruitful areas for future investigation.

Sydenham's Chorea

Sydenham's chorea is named after the English physician Thomas Sydenham (1624–1689). It also goes by its German name, **St. Vitus' dance,** although it is likely that the group dances of the Middle Ages that received this name were not performed by people with the disorder that Sydenham described. (St. Vitus was a child martyred under the emperor Diocletian and was the patron saint of those afflicted with compulsive dancing: it was to St. Vitus' shrine near Strassburg that the afflicted went for treatment.) Sydenham's chorea is relatively rare, and thus few cases have come to autopsy or have received biochemical examination. Where autopsy has been performed, diffuse changes in the basal ganglia and cortex have been observed.

Sydenham's chorea occurs in children and young people 5 to 20 years of age and is thought to be due to acute childhood rheumatism or other infections. Heredity may play some part in the etiology, since some families appear susceptible to acute rheumatism. People of European ancestry are more susceptible than other races, and the disorder is three times more likely to occur in females than in males.

The onset of the chorea is insidious, and the child may at first be thought to be clumsy. As movements become more obvious the child is described as fidgety, restless, or unable to keep still. The involuntary movements are usually described as quasi-purposive and follow one another in a disordered fashion. They include bilateral facial movements: frowning, raising the eyebrows, smiling, and other movements of the mouth and tongue, and the eyes and head may be rolled from side to side. When severe, the facial movements may interfere with chewing and swallowing, so that special feeding may be required. Movements of the upper limbs involve all joints. For example, the limb may be flexed with the fingers closed and will then be flung out in full extension. Lower limb movements usually are less pronounced. Voluntary movements are generally not impaired, but muscle tone is increased so that voluntary movements become exaggerated. Usually the child is emotionally excitable and suffers from insomnia. The chorea disappears during sleep.

Most affected persons recover in 2 to 3 weeks, but they may have a number of attacks at intervals of about a year. No obvious disabilities have been described after recovery. Treatment consists of confining the individual to bed until the movements cease. Drug therapy with sedatives and major tranquilizers appears to be helpful in reducing the chorea.

Hemiballism

Hemiballism is a term applied to involuntary movements that occur on one side of the body. It consists of violent movements of the limbs, which resemble a forceful throwing movement. These movements exhaust and incapacitate the person and can lead to death unless arrested. The first summary of persons with this disorder was made by Martin in 1927. He reviewed 21 patients in all and called the disorder the "syndrome of the Body of Luys" because of the frequent association of damage to this structure and the contralateral movements in the patients. Descriptions of the disorder are infrequent. The body of Luys is now called the subthalamic nucleus, and as noted in

Chapter 12, it forms part of the basal ganglia. Symptoms can be the result of vascular disease, tumor, or infection involving this structure. Surgery of the thalamus has been found successful in treating the disorder, presumably because the lesion cuts the flow of information between the basal ganglia and the motor cortex.

Athetosis

The term **athetosis** (from the Greek, meaning without fixed position) was coined by the American physician William Alexander Hammond in 1871. The German anatomists Cecil and Oscar Vogt described a number of cases between 1911 and 1924 in which there was bilateral atrophy of the basal ganglia. The symptoms of the disease resemble chorea but the movements are slower, coarser, and more writhing than choreic movements. Athetosis, particularly if it is bilateral, may be congenital or result from damage to the basal ganglia. It may also develop during adolescence as a progressive disorder terminating in rigidity. Sometimes the term *torsion dystonia* is used as a description of athetosis, meaning that movements involve more proximal parts of the body.

Congenital athetosis is first noticed when a child is several months to 2 years old. The child makes peculiar movements and is often hypotonic (having subnormal muscle tone). This is sometimes known as a "floppy infant." Facial movements include frequent grimaces of all kinds associated with involuntary laughing and crying. If athetosis is unilateral, the facial movements may be exaggerations of normal ones. In the limbs, distal movements are commoner than proximal movements. The hand is usually flexed at the wrist, and this position is frequently interrupted by slow writhing movements of flexion and extension. The movements usually completely interfere with the voluntary movements of the limbs, and the person may attempt to restrain the hand by holding it or leaning on it. The movements always become exaggerated when voluntary movements are attempted. Athetosis has proved difficult to treat. A variety of drugs including major and minor tranquilizers have not been consistently effective and the results of attempts to arrest the movements with thalamic surgery have been inconsistent.

Wilson's Disease

Wilson's disease, also known as *hepatolenticular degeneration,* is a progressive disease of early life that is due to an autosomal recessive gene. It was first described by Wilson in 1912, and although one of the rarest disorders of movement, it is one of the first for which a rational treatment became available. It is characterized by a disorder of copper metabolism in which copper concentrations of the brain and liver increase, leading to a degeneration in certain brain regions, particularly the basal ganglia, and to cirrhosis of the liver. A particularly good diagnostic sign of the disease is corneal pigmentation (the Kayser-Fleischer ring), which consists of a 2-mm-diameter zone of golden-brown pigmentation on the cornea. It is due to a deposit of copper and may be present before nervous system symptoms develop. The disorder leads to increasing muscular rigidity, tremor, and progressive dementia. The incidence of the gene is about 1 per 1000 population and it is found in all races. Symptoms of the disease usually become apparent between 10 and 25 years of age. Choreiform movements of the face and hands are the first symptoms and occur when the person is at rest, but they are reduced by relaxation. The rigidity is general and resembles that of Parkinson's disease. Loss of emotional control occurs, with involuntary laughing and crying, and there is always mental deterioration, ending in mild dementia. Individuals may survive from 1 to 6 years or longer when untreated. When treated with D-penicillamine, the disease is arrested, and if treatment occurs early, subjects remain symptom-free. D-penicillamine acts by binding, or chelating, copper, aiding in its excretion.

Gilles de la Tourette's Syndrome

Tourette's syndrome (TS) was described by Gilles de la Tourette in a two-part paper published in 1885. In most important ways this paper is still a remarkably good description of the disorder. Until Tourette's review this syndrome was seen either as an undifferentiated chorea or a symptom of hysteria, and it went by a variety of different names depending on where it had been observed. The symptoms of the syndrome have a tendency to evolve and become more elaborate with age. Tourette described three stages to the syndrome. In the first stage only multiple tics (twitches of the face, limbs, or of the whole body) occur. In the second stage inarticulate cries are added to the multiple tics. In the third stage the emission of articulate words with **echolalia** (repeating what others have said, but also repeating actions) and *coprolalia* (*copro* from the Greek for dung, but now meaning obscene or lewd, and *lalia* meaning speech) are added to the multiple tics and inarticulate cries. The following is a case history reported by Tourette that illustrates most of the major features of the syndrome.

> *Case VIII. Miss X. by Professor Pitres of Bordeaux.* Miss X., fifteen years old, spent several months at the Longchamps hydrotherapy institution at Bordeaux during the winter of 1883, where she was treated for convulsive attacks of chorea and ejaculations of loud vulgar and obscene words. Miss X. was very intelligent, she learned the lessons given her by her teacher with the greatest ease, and she played the piano well. She was tall and largely built. She was not well disciplined.
>
> Her mother had never had a neurological disease. Her father had a convulsive, though not painful, facial tic. She had a strange, almost crazy, aunt, who lived alone. She had fits of hysteria, morbid hunger, and sometimes long periods of melancholy in which she refused to talk to anyone.
>
> When nine, Miss X. began having violent and irregular choreiform tics of the face, arms, and legs. At the same time she occasionally uttered a few vulgar words. After a few months the attacks disappeared. A year later they came back again. The tics first reappeared in the shoulders, then in the arms, and then in the face, where they were accompanied by loud guttural sounds. These indistinct sounds became very clearly articulated when she was thirteen. At that time her most frequent words were "get away, go away, imbecile." A little later her words became more frequent and much clearer, and were rough and lewd. She remained that way until the present.
>
> Miss X. belonged to an upper-class family. Her education was excellent. She never left her mother, who surrounded her in continuous, tender loving care. One had to wonder how and where she picked up the words she continually uttered: e.g., "In God's name, fuck, shit, etc." When she is in her calm normal state such words never pass her lips.
>
> Whenever Miss X. was in the presence of someone she was afraid of, or who intimidated her, she was able to suffocate the sounds by a sheer effort of will. By clenching her teeth convulsively she could prevent the words from being understood. All one heard then was a kind of vague growling. As soon as she was alone the usual words poured out in added abundance.
>
> The words were always pronounced with a series of convulsive tics of the face, the shoulders, the trunk. Often, convulsive attacks happened without any word being spoken. At other times the words could be smothered and rendered incomprehensible by an intense effort of will. During sleep, spasmodic movements and involuntary words ceased altogether.
>
> Professor Pitres sent us some additional observations on October 27: It would seem that "Miss de M.," has not clearly presented the echolalia phenomena. To be sure we have not sought them out by pronouncing the coarse words that are so familiar to her. On the contrary, the patient's mother has tried to substitute the vulgar words with indifferent words and banal exclamations. To this end she ordered the governess to shout out

several times a day in front of her daughter, "Oh my God!" or "Mother!" The governess fulfilled her duty faithfully, but the patient did not repeat the exclamations that she had heard.

One single fact observed by the governess seemed to have some bearing on echolalia. One evening in 1883, while Miss X. was undressing to go to bed, a dog came and barked under the window of her room. She immediately began involuntarily to echo the dog's barking. She was unable to sleep till one in the morning because her body was continually wracked by muscular spasms that accompanied the noisy barking, exactly like the dog's. Here is another bit of curious information: Miss X. had quite a pronounced tendency to imitate actions and to take up queer postures that she had seen and that had struck her. One day she was walking with her governess in a fairground, and she spied a cardboard model of Gargantua whose mouth opened and shut with a regular motion, gobbling up everything that was presented. The child looked at the astonishing sight for a moment, and for the rest of the walk she never stopped opening and shutting her mouth, involuntarily, just as she had seen it done by Gargantua. (*Gilles de la Tourette, 1885,* pp. 41–42; translated by Lorna Whishaw)

Tourette recognized that individuals with the syndrome could be intelligent and productive and that they were not neurotic or psychotic. He also noted that the syndrome, or parts of it, ran in families and thus seemed hereditary. Tourette pointed out that there was no treatment (although the symptoms lessened or disappeared during fevers), so that the symptoms were likely to be with the person for life. Recently there has been renewed interest in TS largely through the work of the Tourette Society in North America. Many TS patients have been misdiagnosed as troublemakers, hysterics, schizophrenics, and so forth no doubt because they seemed intelligent yet displayed bizarre behavior. This is now changing, and there is great interest in trying to understand the cause of the disorder in terms of brain function. Much of the research that has been done to date has been summarized in an edited work by Friedhoff and Chase.

The incidence of TS is less than 1 in 100,000, but the incidence can vary with the degree of professional knowledge about the disorder. In our area, which has a population base of about 100,000, a child psychiatrist interested in the disorder has diagnosed over 10 cases. Thus, the incidence may actually be somewhat higher. From work by Shapiro and Shapiro the following features of TS are known. TS occurs in all racial groups, and the male to female ratio is about 3 to 1. It seems to be hereditary because between 30 and 40% of TS individuals have a family member with the disorder or who displays various types of tics. It also seems commoner for female members to transmit the disorder. Nevertheless, the genetic basis of the disorder is not known, and it has been suggested that there are hereditary and nonhereditary groups of TS individuals. The average age of onset ranges between 2 and 15 years, with a median of 7 years, and by 11 years symptoms have appeared in 97% of cases. The most frequent symptoms are tics involving the eye, head, or face (97%), upper limbs (81%), and lower limbs and body (55%). Complex movements including touching, hitting, and jumping occur in between 30 and 40% of cases. Coprolalia may develop in up to 60% of cases and then disappear in a third of these. As noted above, TS is not associated with neuroses, psychoses, or other disorders. EEG activity is frequently normal although some patients may display some abnormalities. Evoked-potential studies show that the premovement potentials associated with willed, voluntary movements do not occur with the tics in TS patients, which testifies to the involuntary nature of the movements.

It is thought that TS has a subcortical origin, possibly in the basal ganglia. This idea is supported in part by studies that have found Tourette-like symptoms in patients with other basal ganglial disorders that have been induced by other diseases or by long-continued use of major tranquilizers. There have been very few autopsy examinations of the brains of TS patients, and of those that have been done there is one report of an excessive number of small cells in the basal ganglia and other reports that the cells there are normal. A major piece of evidence that implicates the basal ganglia comes from effective drug therapy. To date, the most consistent improvements are obtained with antidopaminergic agents such as haloperidol; thus it is thought that there may be some abnormality in the dopamine system in the basal ganglia. Clonidine, a norepinephrine receptor agonist, also is reported to be effective in some cases. A number of neuropsychological studies have been done, and there is a suggestion from these that there are abnormalities in some cognitive functions usually supported by the right hemisphere. The results of the neuropsychological studies will be considered in Chapter 30.

Tardive Dyskinesia

Tardive dyskinesia (from the French and Greek, meaning later appearing abnormal movements) is a disorder caused mainly by long-term use of antipsychotic agents (phenothiazines and butyrophenones) that act primarily as dopamine-blocking agents. People with tardive dyskinesia display an excess of motor activity, especially of the face and tongue. The movements disfigure the face and become so severe that they interfere with eating. They usually do not appear until individuals have been taking antipsychotic agents for months or years. Once developed, tardive dyskinesia is extremely difficult to treat. Lowering the dosage of drug treatment tends to worsen the symptoms. Stopping drug use may not always lead to lessening of the symptoms. If symptoms do stop with a "drug holiday," they may begin again almost immediately with renewed drug treatment. Not all patients treated with antipsychotics develop tardive dyskinesia, but it is more likely to occur in older patients, those who may have some form of brain damage, and in females. Because tardive dyskinesia is a serious side effect of antipsychotic therapy, the drugs are only administered where this type of treatment is mandatory. Even then it has been suggested that patients or their families be apprised of the possibility of developing tardive dyskinesia and required to sign a consent form before medication is begun.

Parkinson's Disease

The individual symptoms of **Parkinson's disease** have been described by physicians from the time of Galen, but their occurrence as a syndrome was not recognized until 1817. In that year James Parkinson, a London physician, published an essay in which he argued that several different motor symptoms could be considered together as a group forming a distinctive condition. His observations are interesting not only because his conclusion was correct but also because he made his observations in part at a distance by watching the movements of parkinsonian victims in the streets of London. Parkinson's disease has been called at different times the *shaking palsy* or its Latin equivalent, *paralysis agitans,* but received its commoner designation from Jean Charcot, who suggested that the disease be renamed to honor James Parkinson's recognition of its essential nature.

Parkinson's disease is fairly common, estimates of its incidence varying from 0.1 to 1.0% of the population. It is also of considerable interest for a number of other reasons. First, the disease seems related to the degeneration of the **substantia nigra,** and to the loss of the neurotransmitter substance dopamine, which is produced by cells of this nucleus. The disease, therefore, provides an important insight into the role of this brainstem nucleus and its neurotransmitter in the control of movement. Second, because a variety of pharmacological treatments for Parkinson's disease relieve different features of its symptoms to some extent, the disease provides a model for understanding pharmacological treatments of motor disorders in their more general aspects. Third, although Parkinson's disease is described as a disease entity, the symptoms vary enormously among people, thus making manifest the complexity with which the components of movement are organized to produce fluid motion. Fourth, because many of the symptoms of Parkinson's disease strikingly resemble changes in motor activity that occur as a consequence of aging, the disease provides indirect insight into the more general problems of neural changes in aging.

There are four major symptoms of Parkinson's disease: tremor, plastic (cogwheel) rigidity, akinesia, and disturbances of posture, each of which may be manifest in different body parts in different combinations. Since some of the symptoms involve the appearance of abnormal behaviors and others the loss of normal behaviors we shall discuss the symptoms in these two major categories: positive and negative. Positive symptoms are behaviors not seen in normal people or seen only so rarely, and then in such special circumstances, that they can be considered abnormal. Negative symptoms are marked not by any particular behavior but rather by an absence of a behavior or by an inability to engage in an activity.

Positive Parkinsonian Symptoms. Since positive symptoms are common in Parkinson's disease, they are thought to be held in check, or inhibited, in normal people but released from inhibition in the process of the disease. The commonest positive symptoms are the following.

Tremor at Rest. This consists of alternating movements of the limbs when they are at rest, but which stop during voluntary movements or during sleep. The tremors of the hands often have a "pillrolling" quality, as if a pill were being rolled between the thumb and forefinger.

Muscular Rigidity. Muscular rigidity consists of increased muscle tone simultaneously in both extensor and flexor muscles. It is particularly evident when the limbs are moved passively at a joint; movement is resisted but with sufficient force the muscles yield, for a short distance, then resist movement again. Thus, complete passive flexion or extension of a joint occurs in a series of steps, giving rise to the term *cogwheel rigidity*. This should be contrasted with the **clasp-knife rigidity** of hemiplegia, in which initial resistance to flexion or extension gives way suddenly, permitting free movement of the joint. The rigidity may be sufficiently severe to make all movements difficult. One man less severely afflicted by rigidity was moved to comment to us, "The slowness of movement is conscious but not willed. That is, I form a plan in my mind; for instance, I wish to uncork that bottle. Then I deliberately invoke the effort that sets the muscles in motion. I'm aware of the slowness of the process; I'm unable to increase [its speed], but I always get the bottle open."

Involuntary Movements. These may consist of continual changes in posture, sometimes to relieve tremor and sometimes to relieve stiffness, but often for no apparent reason. These small movements or changes in posture, sometimes referred to as **akathesia** or "cruel restlessness," may be concurrent with general inactivity. Other involuntary movements are distortions of posture, such as occur during *oculogyric crisis* (involuntary turns of the head and eyes to one side), which last for periods of minutes to hours. Since the positive symptoms are "actions," they are caused by the activity of some brain area. Before drug therapy became commoner, one of the treatments used to stop them was to localize the source of the symptom and make a lesion there. For example, tremor was treated by lesions made in the ventral thalamus.

Negative Parkinsonian Symptoms. J. P. Martin divided severely parkinsonian patients into five groups, after detailed analysis of negative symptoms.

Disorders of Posture. There are disorders of fixation and equilibrium. A *disorder of fixation* consists of an inability to maintain, or difficulty in maintaining, a part of the body (head, limbs, etc.) in its normal position in relation to other parts. Thus, a person's head may droop forward, or a standing person may gradually bend further forward until he or she ends up on the knees. *Disorders of equilibrium* consist of difficulties in standing or even sitting when unsupported. In less severe cases individuals may have difficulty standing on one leg, or, if pushed lightly on the shoulders, they may fall passively without taking corrective steps or attempting to catch themselves.

Disorders of Righting. These consist of difficulty in achieving a standing position from a supine position.

Disorders of Locomotion. Normal locomotion requires support of the body against gravity, stepping, balancing while the weight of the body is transferred from one limb to another, and pushing forward. Parkinsonian individuals have difficulty initiating stepping, and when they do, they shuffle with short footsteps on a fairly wide base of support because they have trouble maintaining equilibrium when shifting weight from one limb to the other. Often parkinsonian individuals who have begun to walk demonstrate **festination:** they take faster and faster steps and end up running forward.

Disturbances of Speech. These consist mainly of difficulties in the physical production of sound; rigidity may play a prominant role in these disturbances.

Akinesia. **Akinesia** refers to a poverty or slowness of movement, which may also manifest itself in a blankness of facial expression, or a lack of blinking, swinging of the arms when walking, spontaneous speech, or normal movements of fidgeting. It is also reflected in difficulty in making repetitive movements, such as tapping, even in the absence of rigidity. People who sit motionless for hours slow akinesia in its most striking manifestation.

Other negative symptoms include **aphagia**—difficulty in chewing and swallowing—but these symptoms do not fit easily or clearly into any of the above five categories.

The symptoms of Parkinson's disease begin insidiously, often with a tremor in one hand and with slight stiffness in the distal portions of the limbs. Movements may next become slower, the face becoming masklike with loss of eye blinking and poverty of emotional expression. Thereafter the body may become stooped, while the gait becomes a shuffle with the arms hanging motionless at the sides. Speech may become slow and monotonous, and difficulty in swallowing saliva may make drooling a problem. Although the disease is progressive, the rate at which the symptoms worsen is variable, and only rarely is progression so rapid that a person becomes disabled within 5 years; usually 10 to 20 years elapse before symptoms cause incapacity. One of the most curious aspects of Parkinson's disease is its on-again/off-again quality: symptoms may suddenly appear and as suddenly disappear. Partial remission of Parkinson's disease may also occur in response to interesting and activating situations. Sacks recounts an incident in which a parkinsonian patient leaped from his wheelchair at the seaside and rushed into the breakers to save a drowning man, only to fall back into his chair immediately afterward and become inactive again. Although remission of some symptoms in activating situations is common, remission is not usually as dramatic as is recounted in this case.

Causes of Parkinsonism. There are three major types of Parkinson's disease: idiopathic, postencephalitic, and drug-induced. Parkinson's disease may also result from arteriosclerosis, may follow poisoning by carbon monoxide or manganese intoxication, or may result from syphilis or the development of tumors. As is suggested by its name, the *idiopathic* cause of Parkinson's disease is not known. Its origin may be familial, or it may be part of the aging process, but it is also widely thought that it might have a viral origin. It most often occurs in people who are over 50 years of age. The *postencephalitic* form originated in the sleeping sickness *(encephalitis lethargica)* that appeared in the winter of 1916–1917 and vanished by 1927. Although the array of symptoms was bewilderingly varied, such that hardly any two patients seemed alike, Constantin von Economo demonstrated a unique pattern of brain damage associated with a virus infection in the brains of patients who had died from the disease. A third of those affected died in the acute stages of the sleeping sickness, in states either of coma or of sleeplessness. Although many people seemed to completely recover from the sickness, most subsequently developed neurological or psychiatric disorders and parkinsonism. The latency between the initial and subsequent occurrences of the disease has never been adequately explained. Specific searches for viral particles or virus-specific products in Parkinson patients have revealed no evidence of viral cause. The third major cause of Parkinson's disease is more recent, and is associated with ingestion of various drugs, particularly major tranquilizers that include reserpine and several phenothiazine and butyrophenone derivatives. The symptoms are usually reversible, but they are difficult to distinguish from those of the genuine disorder.

Recently it has been found that external agents can cause parkinsonian symptoms quite rapidly. Langston and coworkers have reported that a contaminant of synthetic heroin, MPTP, when taken by drug users is converted into MPP^+, which is extremely toxic to dopamine cells. A number of young drug users were found to display a complete parkinsonian syndrome shortly after using contaminated drugs. This finding has suggested that other substances might cause similar effects. Demographic studies of patient admission in the cities of Vancouver and Helsinki show an increase in the incidence of patients getting the disease at ages younger than 40. This has raised the suggestion that water and air might contain environmental toxins that work in a fashion similar to MPTP.

Although parkinsonian patients can be separated into clinical groups on the basis of cause of the disease, it is nevertheless likely that the mechanisms producing the symptoms have a common origin. Either the substantia nigra is damaged, as occurs in idiopathic and postencephalitic cases, or the activity of its cells is blocked or cells are killed, as occurs in drug-induced parkinsonism. The cells of the substantia nigra contain a dark pigment (hence its name); in Parkinson's disease this area is depigmented by degeneration of the melatonin-containing neurons of the area. Why the relatively selective degeneration occurs is not known, but it is possible that in viral cases the virus disturbs the metabolic pathways related to the formation of the pigment. The cells of the substantia nigra are the point of origin of fibers that go to the basal ganglial frontal cortex and to the spinal cord. The neurotransmitter at the synapses of these projections is dopamine. It has been demonstrated by bioassay of the brains of deceased parkinsonian patients, and by analysis of the major metabolite of dopamine, homovanallic acid, which is excreted in the urine, that the amount of brain dopamine is reduced by over 90% and is often reduced to undetectable amounts. Thus, the cause of Parkinson's disease has been identified with some certainty as a lack of dopamine or, in drug-induced cases, with a lack of dopamine action. However, dopamine depletion may not account for the whole problem in some people, since decreases of norepinephrine have been recorded, and there have been a number of reports that cells in some of the nuclei in the basal ganglia may degenerate as well.

The Nature of the Motor Defect. It is not known precisely how a reduction in brain dopamine produces Parkinson's disease, but J. P. Martin has performed the best analysis of the disease's negative symptoms. He compared the function of mechanisms controlling posture and locomotion in normal people with those controlling locomotion in parkinsonian patients.

In normal people postural reflexes are under the control of vision; the labyrinths, or balance receptors, of the middle ear; and proprioception, or sensation, from muscles and joints. Of these three senses proprioception appears to be the most important, because whereas adequate locomotion can still occur in the absence of vision and labyrinthine function, it is severely impaired if proprioception is absent. Martin described the difficulties of a man whose proprioceptive pathways of the spinal cord had been cut accidentally. His locomotor difficulties appear in some ways surprisingly like those of people with Parkinson's disease.

> This patient, in spite of years of physiotherapy and training, has never regained the ability to walk in any normal manner. His greatest difficulty is in starting to walk and in propelling himself forward. When he first began to walk—about a year after his injury—he held his hands out in front of him, which, of course, had the effect of bringing his center of gravity forward. Now, after several years of practice, he advances his hands less and he bends his head and body forward. He walks on a wide base and rocks his body but he does not bend his legs and so shows no proper stepping. If he loses his balance, he shows no reaction to protect his equilibrium and he has learned to fall with his body forward without help. He is also unable to rise from a chair. He cannot crawl or place himself in the all-fours posture. When standing or walking he is entirely dependent on vision and falls down if he closes his eyes. At first he was unable to maintain his position on an ordinary chair when he closed his eyes but he had gradually acquired the ability to do this. (Martin, 1967, p. 32)

When Martin tested labyrinthine and proprioceptive function in Parkinson patients, he found the receptors and their afferent pathways intact, but still neither seemed to function to aid locomotion. Perhaps the important feature in locomotion for humans is its bipedal nature, which requires balancing as weight is shifted from one limb to the other. Proprioception may be particularly important for this aspect of walking, and it is balance that the person with Parkinson's disease seems intent on preserving with the wide-based, shuffling walking style. The mechanisms for normal locomotion seem intact, for if walking is brought more directly under visual control, it appears quite normal. Martin accomplished increased visual control by having the patients walk over a series of wood blocks: as the patients walked over the blocks, walking suddenly and dramatically became normal, but it ceased to be so when the last of the blocks was reached. Actually, visual stimuli are not essential; parkinsonian individuals may walk briefly with normal stepping motions if asked to do so. The initiation of normal walking in people is usually accomplished by leaning forward and rocking from side to side. These movements, which will unbalance parkinsonian individuals, are resisted, making initiation of walking difficult. But leaning them forward (or having them carry something before them, which accomplishes the same effect) and rocking them from side to side, both of which are automatic reflexes of walking, can reinstate more normal walking. Thus, in Parkinson's disease, when the proprioceptive system is intact and the stepping mechanisms of the motor system are functional, normal walking nevertheless fails to occur. Thus, it can only be concluded that the connection between sensory input and motor output is not being made. Since dopamine is implicated in Parkinson's disease, and since a primary projection of the dopamine systsem is from the substantia nigra to the basal ganglia, it can be concluded that dopamine is required in the basal ganglia to maintain the connection between the proprioceptive sensory system and the movement system.

Treatment of Parkinson's Disease. There is no known cure for Parkinson's disease, and none will be in sight until the factors that produce the progressive deterioration of the substantia nigra are known. As a result, treatment is symptomatic and directed toward support and comfort. The major symptoms of parkinsonism are influenced by psychological factors, a person's outcome being affected by how well he or she can cope with the disability. As a result, individuals should be counseled early regarding the meaning of symptoms, the nature of the disease, and the potential for most of them to lead long and productive lives. Physical therapy should consist of simple measures such as heat and massage to alleviate painful muscle cramps, and training and exercise to cope with the debilitating changes in movement.

The drug treatments for Parkinson's disease are of considerable theoretical as well as practical interest. In recent years understanding of the structure and function of synapses has been greatly advanced. Parkinson's disease provides an excellent model for understanding brain function with respect to synaptic action, because a specific constellation of symptoms has been linked with changes in a known neurotransmitter. Pharmacological treatment has two main objectives: first, increase the activity in whatever dopamine synapses remain; second, suppress the activity in structures that show heightened activity in the absence of adequate dopamine action. Drugs such as L-dopa, which is converted into dopamine in the brain; amantadine; amphetamine; monoamine oxydase inhibitors; and tricyclic mood elevators are used to enhance effective dopamine transmission. Naturally occurring anticholinergic drugs, such as atropine and scopolamine, and synthetic anticholinergics, such as benztropine (Cogentin), and trihexyphenidyl (Artane), are used to block the cholinergic systems of the brain that seem to show heightened activity in the absence of adequate dopamine activity.

The Effectiveness of Drug Therapy. The effectiveness of drug therapy depends on the progression of the disease, as has been described by Hornykiewicz. Unless dopamine is depleted by more than 80%, the disease is clinically silent. Manifestation of symptoms seems prevented in two major ways: the remaining dopamine fibers become overactive, and there is a proliferation of the excitatory D-2 receptors, allowing the remaining excitatory pool of DA to have a greater effect, a phenomenon called **denervation supersensitivity.** Other compensatory actions may also be occurring, including decreases in serotonin and GABA activity (which are thought to inhibit dopamine function), decreases in the number of D-1 receptors (which have inhibitory functions) and increases in the activity of that portion of the norepinephrine system that normally facilitates dopamine action. Once dopamine depletion reaches the point that these compensatory actions are no longer effective, the symptoms of the disease start appearing. L-dopa, the most effective treatment, does not become effective until denervation supersensitivity appears; that is, until the disease is well developed. As denervation supersensitivity becomes more pronounced, L-dopa becomes difficult to administer in a dose that does not produce side effects. In the early stages of the disease, L-dopa therapy may reverse denervation supersensitivity, making treatment ineffective. A "drug holiday" is thought to be useful for restoring the receptor proliferation that is the prerequisite of effective L-dopa therapy. The best description of the effects of drug therapy on the condition of Parkinson's disease is given in a series of case histories described by Sacks. Although drugs such as L-dopa have been called miracle drugs, they are not a cure for the disease. Generally it is necessary to treat each patient as an individual, experimenting with different available drugs and with different dosages. In some cases symptoms are dramatically relieved and patients are immensely helped; in other cases the drug treatments may prove to have side effects as unpleasant and as debilitating to the patient as the disease symptoms. An additional complexity in treatment is the progressive nature of the disease. Drug therapy must be continually reevaluated, and it may become ineffectual in the latter stages of the disease. The following is an example of the "side effects" on a patient, Miss N., described by Sacks.

> In September for the third time I gave her L-dopa and her responses were not quite different from either of the first two times. She complained of rapid breathing and difficulty in catching her breath, and she had the beginnings of respiratory crises. She developed very rapid "saluting" tics in both of her arms, her hand flying from her lap to her face three or four times every minute. She also developed palilalia, repeating her words innumerable times. Her reaction at this time was remarkably similar to that of her room-mate Miss D., so much so that I wondered if either was automatically "imitating" the other. By the middle of September, Miss N. was . . . [producing tics] 60 times to the minute, 60 minutes to the hour, and saying an incessant palilalic repetition of the following verse she had learned years before:
>
> I thought it said in every tic,
> I am so sick, so sick, so sick.
> Oh death, come quick, come quick,
> come quick!
> Come quick, come quick, come quick,
> come quick!
>
> Since she was exhausting herself and maddening her fellow patients, I again found it necessary to stop L-dopa.
>
> Following this excited state Miss N. showed a severe "rebound" when L-dopa was stopped, becoming so rigid, tremulous, akinetic and voiceless, and having so much difficulty in swallowing, that we had to tube-feed her. This "withdrawal reaction" continued for the remainder of September without any lessening in severity whatever. (From Sacks. Copyright © 1973 by Oliver Sacks. Reprinted by permission of Doubleday & Company, Inc., and Gerald Duckworth & Co., Ltd.)

It is unlikely that L-dopa would produce such side effects if given to normal people. It does so in parkinsonian patients because postsynaptic receptors proliferate as dopamine end feet degenerate; there being fewer and fewer synapses, there are concomitantly more and more receptors. Thus, as parkinsonian symptoms develop and as L-dopa becomes more necessary it also unfortunately produces more side effects.

Psychological Aspects of Parkinson's Disease. Although Parkinson's disease patients are often described as manifesting many features of depression, they are also widely thought to show no psychological changes that parallel their motor disabilities. This latter view may be incorrect. On the basis of clinical observations, Sacks suggests that there are cognitive changes parallel to those reflected in motor activity. He emphasizes festination and resistance as positive symptoms of cognitive activity. As mentioned earlier, festination is manifest as an acceleration of walking, but it is also seen as a rushing of speech and even thought. Resistance, however, has the opposite effect: as soon as speech or thought is attempted, it may be blocked by resistance. Thus, the two positive effects are in a sense opposites, and parkinsonian individuals might find themselves embattled, with festination counteracting resistance. Sacks has also emphasized that there are negative components of the disease in cognitive function. There is an impoverishment of feeling, libido, motive, and attention; individuals may sit for hours apparently lacking the will to enter or continue on any course of activity.

Bowen has reported on the performance of parkinsonian patients on a number of more formal neurological and psychological tests. Although verbal IQ was normal, patients performed significantly less well on memory tests than their spouses, who were used as the control group. Parkinsonian patients also showed significant deficits on tests of extrapersonal orientation, personal orientation, the Wisconsin Card-Sorting Test, and Aubert's test of setting an illuminated rod to the vertical. (These tests, which are sensitive to frontal-lobe damage are described in some detail in Chapter 19.) Thus,

Parkinson's disease would seem to be associated with cognitive changes, particularly those changes normally found in patients with frontal-lobe or basal ganglial lesions. In a sense this association is not so surprising, because there are intimate relations between the functions of the basal ganglia and of the frontal cortex, and because there are dopamine projections into the frontal cortex that might be expected to degenerate in the same way that those of the basal ganglia degenerate. Having also tested patients before and after L-dopa treatment, Bowen reports that test performance is not noticeably improved by drug therapy.

Animal Models of Parkinson's Disease. In recent years considerable attention has been given to developing animal models of Parkinson's disease. Although no animal models reliably produce all the symptoms of the human condition, many symptoms resembling those of parkinsonism appear in animals with experimentally reduced dopamine concentrations. Specifically, the injection of the **neurotoxin** 6-hydroxydopamine into the ventricles or into specific brain areas can greatly deplete dopamine by destroying the terminals of DA neurons. Animals so treated show many symptoms resembling those of Parkinson's disease, including akinesia, rigidity, abnormal postures, and compulsive fidgeting. Some of these symptoms can be relieved by administration of anticholinergic drugs or L-dopa, but the threshold for eliciting side effects is nearly the same as the threshold for relief of symptoms. The animal models provide insights into the neurological basis of the disease and will be useful in the development of new pharmacological treatments and assessment of their therapeutic value. Also, in some relatively new developments, a number of people have reported that embryonic brain cells transplanted into adult rats will grow and seemingly make normal connections. This has been demonstrated for dopamine and norepinephrine cells: if the animals are previously depleted of these neurotransmitters, the brain grafts will begin to restore brain concentrations of the neurotransmitters, and to restore as well some features of more normal behavior. Theoretically, these results offer a new approach to the treatment of Parkinson's disease.

DISORDERS OF CORTICAL FUNCTION

The account that we give here of disorders of cortical function is limited to two dysfunctions: **hemiplegia** and **apraxia.** In the first, there is clear impairment of movement, which can also be accompanied by various psychological and intellectual deficits such as **aphasia** and **agraphia.** However, only the movement dysfunctions will be described here. Unlike all the preceding disorders of movement, apraxia is a disorder in which posture and movement are "normal" but skill is lost. Rather than a disorder of movement per se, it is a disorder of the systems that command movement. For a more detailed review of apraxia than that provided here, see the volume edited by Roy.

Hemiplegia

The characteristics of hemiplegia are loss of voluntary movements on one side of the body, changes in postural tone, and changes in the status of various reflexes. Hemiplegia results from cortical damage that occurs contralateral to the motor symptoms. Once referred to as a pyramidal, as opposed to an extrapyramidal, disorder, it is now recognized that the complete range of symptoms is not produced by pyramidal tract damage only, and thus must result from damage to the cortex, its corticospinal fibers, and associated damage in the basal ganglia. In infancy damage may result from birth injury, epilepsy, or fever. Infant hemiplegia is usually discussed under the umbrella of cerebral palsy. In young adults hemiplegia is usually caused by rupture of a congenital aneuryism, an embolism, a tumor, or a head injury. The largest group that suffer from hemiplegia are the middle-aged to elderly, and their hemiplegia is usually due to hemorrhage occurring as a consequence of high blood pressure and a degenerative condition of the blood vessels.

The commonest site of a vascular disease producing a hemiplegia is in the middle cerebral artery, which supplies the greater part of the main motor area (Figures 7-1 and 7-2). The motor pathways from the cortex run through the basal gauglia, and so a small lesion in this area can also cause similar impairments to those that follow cortical damage.

Damage to the motor cortex first produces a loss of all voluntary movement on the contralateral side of the body and a paralysis of movement in which muscles are in an almost flaccid state and reflexes are absent. The course and rate of recovery in individuals is quite variable, as has been described by Twitchell (see also Chapter 26). Within a period of days to weeks the muscles become spastic until they become hypertonic. At the same time there is an increase in tendon reflexes (stretch reflexes such as the knee-jerk reflex) until they are more responsive than normal *(hyperreflexia)*. The spasticity is most pronounced in the antigravity muscles (the antigravity muscles are also called *physiological extensors* even though the action of some of them is to produce flexion; for example, flexors hold the arm up against gravity, and flexion, or curling down, of the toes helps maintain standing against gravity). Once spasticity is developed, it affects posture in a definite, recognizable pattern. The arm is abducted and flexed at the elbow, with the fingers tightly curled into the palm (an exaggeration of the posture of the abducted arm typical of a person running or sitting). The extension of the leg is exaggerated, giving it a pillarlike character that also permits it to be used for walking. Inability to move the joints independently, however, requires that the leg be moved as a whole: steps with the affected leg are initiated by raising the pelvis on that side and bringing the leg through with circumduction from the hip, keeping the knee extended. Spasticity is dependent on posture. When a person takes a quadrupedal position, the arms become spastic in an extended position. It is important to note here that the spasticity is still serving the function of antigravity support: spasticity is not a property of independent muscles, but occurs in groups of muscles in a purposeful way.

The spasticity of hemiplegia has a number of characteristics that distinguish it from the rigidity of extrapyramidal disorders such as Parkinson's disease. It is unidirectional as a result of being greater in antigravity muscles. The resistance of the spastic muscle to passive movement is greater with rapid than with slow movements. Tendon reflexes are hyperactive. Finally, the limbs show a clasp-knife response after initially resisting forced movement. For example, when an attempt is made to extend the forearm, resistance to the forced movement gradually increases and then quite suddenly melts away (as noted in Chapter 12, the name comes from the sudden snap of the blade of a jackknife, which when closed is stiff during the first half of the closure and then suddenly snaps shut). By contrast, the rigidity of Parkinson's disease is bidirectional, independent of the velocity of movement, not accompanied by hyperreflexia, and clasp-knife responses do not occur. Decerebrate rigidity, however, is very much like spasticity and is therefore a good animal analogue of spasticity, except that the clasp-knife response is absent.

The damage that produces hemiplegia also results in changes in a number of reflexes that are diagnostically important. Scratching the sole of the foot of a normal person with a dull object produces a downward flexion of all toes. In hemiplegia there is an upward flexion, especially of the big toe, and outward fanning of the toes (Figure 13-4). This response is caused by activation of physiological flexors and is often accompanied by flexion of the leg at the knee and hip. The response is called the *Babinski sign* or *extensor plantar response*. It has been referred to as the single most important sign in clinical neurology because it reliably indicates damage to cortical motor neurons (or as they are sometimes called, *upper motor neurons*). This sign is

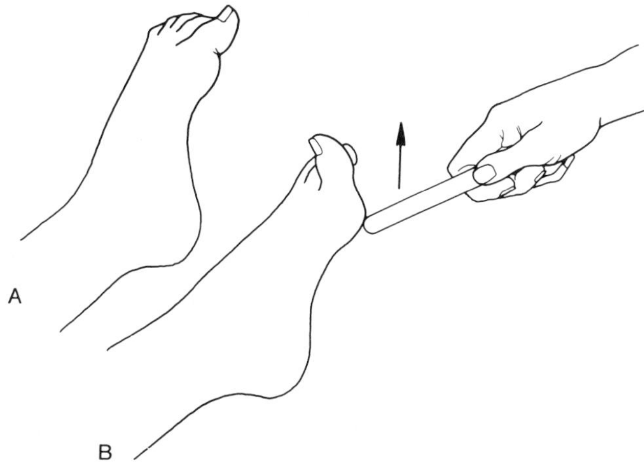

FIGURE 13-4. The Babinski sign. *A.* The normal adult response to stimulation of the lateral planar surface of the left foot. *B.* The normal infant and abnormal adult response. (After Gardner, 1968.)

in fact only one of a family of flexion responses that occur after motor cortex or pyramidal tract damage. Two other reflexes are absent in hemiplegia. In normal people, stroking the abdominal muscles causes their retraction (the *abdominal reflex*) and stroking the inner thigh causes retraction of the testicles *(cremasteric reflex):* these reflexes are absent after cortical lesions.

Since the neocortex is the source of the pyramidal tract, which projects to the spinal cord through the pyramids, as well as being the source of motor fibers that project to other brain areas involved in movement, one could ask: What contribution do each of the different motor projections make to the motor disturbances of hemiplegia? Damage to the pyramidal tract produces loss of fine movements of the limbs, loss of strength, and loss of movement speed. It also produces loss of reflexes: the Babinski sign is present and abdominal and cremasteric reflexes are absent (see Chapter 12 for a description of the contribution of the pyramidal tract to reaching movements made by monkeys). Damage to the nonpyramidal motor efferents is thus responsible for the spasticity and the exaggerated stretch reflexes. The distinction between the contributions of the two efferent systems is important because they are partly separate as they traverse the brain and so damage can be localized to some extent by the degree to which one or the other group of symptoms is present.

Hemiplegia also involves abnormalities in muscles other than those in the limbs. There is difficulty in deviating the eyes and rotating the head opposite to the side of the lesion, weakness of voluntary movements of the lower face (such as in retracting the lips and pursing them), and weakness in the jaw and tongue on the opposite side. Emotional expressions, however, (smiling, crying) are usually not affected. Because muscles of the head are under greater bilateral control than those of the limbs, most affected head movements show relatively rapid recovery.

There is a great deal of variation in the recovery that occurs after hemiplegia, but treatment may have one or a combination of objectives. The person may be trained to use the unaffected side, to use the affected side as much as spasticity and residual abilities allow, or to make movements that lessen spasticity so that voluntary movements can in turn be performed as much as is possible. The last therapeutic procedure is described in detail by Bobath. Briefly, it is based on the fact that the strength of spasticity is related to posture. For example, bending over lessens spasticity, therefore if the arm is extended and the head turned toward the arm, flexion spasticity is lessened. Use of such alternative movements may be sufficiently effective to allow an affected limb to be used. Treatment of hemiplegia is, of course, constrained by accompanying intellectual and behavioral changes, which differ depending on the size of the lesion or the hemisphere in which it is located. Some patients may be willing to work to compensate for their impairments; others may be unwilling to make any effort at all.

Apraxia

Steinthal coined the term *apraxia* in 1871, but the symptoms had first been described some 5 years earlier by Hughlings-Jackson. He noted that some aphasic patients were totally unable to perform voluntary movements, such as protruding the tongue, even though there was no evidence of weakness in the muscles involved and the tongue could be protruded as part of licking the lips after drinking. Although this symptom was subsequently noted by several authors, it was Liepmann who began the first detailed analysis of apraxic symptoms. In 1900, he reported the case of an aphasic man who was unable to carry out hand movements when asked to do so. Curiously, he could follow directions if the required movement was a whole-body movement, such as sitting down, and could make *spontaneous* hand movements. In the ensuing years Liepmann studied many patients with this unusual movement problem, and in 1920 he proposed his now classic theory of apraxia of which two important points are: apraxia results from lesions of the left hemisphere or of the corpus callosum; there are several different types of apraxia, each most likely resulting from damage to a specific locus in the left hemisphere.

Strictly defined, **apraxia** means no action (the Greek *praxis* means action). The term *apraxia,* however, is hardly ever used in this strict sense; today it is used to describe all sorts of missing or inappropriate actions that cannot be clearly attributed to paralysis, **paresis,** or other more primary motor deficits on the one hand, or to lack of comprehension, motivation, and so on, on the other.

Defining Apraxia. Until recently, discussion of apraxia was invariably of specific case histories rather than of carefully designed scientific studies. The result was conflicting interpretations of the behaviors described. Consider the following case as an example.

> A woman with a biparietal lesion had worked for years as a fish-filleter. With the development of her symptoms, she began to experience difficulty in carrying on with her job. She did not seem to know what to do with her knife. She would stick the point in the head of a fish, start the first stroke and then come to a stop. In her own mind she knew how to fillet fish, but yet she could not execute the maneuver. The foreman accused her of being drunk and sent her home for mutilating fish.
>
> This same patient also showed another unusual phenomenon which might possibly be apraxic in nature. She could never finish an undertaking. She would begin a job, drop it, start another, abandon that one, and within a short while would have four or five uncompleted tasks on her hands. This would cause her to do such inappropriate actions as putting the sugar bowl in the refrigerator, and the coffee pot inside the oven. (Critchley, 1965, pp. 158–159)

Although we can agree with Critchley that the filleter had a motor problem that cannot be readily attributed to paralysis or paresis, we could argue that she had forgotten how to fillet fish, that she had an agnosia for fish and knives, that she had attention problems, that she was absentminded, and so on. A more systematic analysis of her behavior is obviously required if we are to understand her deficit.

The several standard clinical tests often used to assess apraxia have similar weaknesses. For example, a patient may be asked to demonstrate the use of a particular object in its absence, for example, to comb the hair or to hammer a nail. An apraxic person's response may be to do nothing or else to use a part of the body as if it were the implement — to stroke a finger through the hair as if it were a comb, or to hit the table with a fist as though it were a hammer. A normal person would pretend to be holding the comb or hammer. Another test of apraxia might be to ask a person to perform such symbolic movements as saluting or waving goodbye; the person might remain still or respond by making an unrecognizable movement. Although these tests are useful for "on the spot" assessments of apraxia, they do not permit objective quantification or more penetrating analysis.

Clinical description presents a further difficulty, namely that classifications of apraxia tend to be somewhat arbitrary. Also, new types of apraxias tend to proliferate, not because actual new symptoms are discovered, but because either new questions are put to the patients or new ways of assessing the responses are developed. As a result there are such terms as **ideational apraxia, ideomotor apraxia, limb kinetic apraxia,** and so on, the definitions of which are often disputed. Finally, slight variations in lesion location might often be used as justification that one apraxia differs from another. Rather than pursue this type of analysis, let us return to a different approach.

Recently a number of laboratories have begun to analyze apraxias under fairly rigorous experimental conditions. The objectives of these experiments are to (1) use a standard test, (2) quantify the response, (3) define the range of motor responses that are impaired, and (4) categorize those responses that are unimpaired. The goal of this research is eventually to specify what function each area of the cortex has in generating particular movements.

In any study of apraxia it is necessary to distinguish between deficits that result from direct damage to the motor system and those that result from damage to other areas that "command" it. Finger, hand, or arm movements can be analyzed to determine whether the deficit is unilateral. (Remember, one hemisphere controls the contralateral limb; thus, a deficit in only the contralateral limb can be confidently attributed to motor system damage.) Because other movements (face, head, body) are controlled bilaterally, a deficit in their control is most likely to be apraxic. Most studies of apraxia also include tests for paralysis and paresis.

Table 13-3 summarizes two groups of tests of motor behaviors. The tests listed in the top half of the table — hand strength, finger-tapping speed, and so on — are ones on which people with cortical damage usually show no impairment or only unilateral impairment. Therefore, these tests are not particularly useful for diagnosing apraxia, although they are good for assessing paralysis or paresis; that is, they are good control tests for assessing the ability to make movements.

Listed in the bottom half of Table 13-3 are tests on which bilateral impairment can be demonstrated. These, then, are tests of apraxia; they are assumed to require higher level control for their execution. Figures 13-5 and 13-6 show examples of three of these tests. In the Kimura Box Test (Figure 13-5) the person is asked to either push the button *(A)*, pull the lever *(B)*, or depress the bar *(C)* as a test of paresis, and then is asked to make the responses in sequence. The devices are connected to timers and counters that record accuracy and speed. In the tests in Figure 13-6, the person first is asked to make any one of the individual arm or facial movements. If the person is able to make the individual movements, he or she is then asked to watch and repeat each of the sequences of movement. The person's response is scored for the accuracy of each movement, for the number of correct movements, and for the sequence of response.

TABLE 13-3. Effects of right- or left-hemisphere lesions on various motor behaviors

Test	Basic reference
Tests in which there is no bilateral impairment[a]	
Hand strength	Kimura, 1977
Finger-tapping speed	Carmon, 1971
Steadiness in static position	Haaland et al., 1977
Unidirectional moving steadiness	Haaland et al., 1977
Repetitive screw rotation	Kimura, 1980
Imitation of single hand posture	Kimura and Archibald, 1974
Imitation of single oral movements	Mateer and Kimura, 1977
Imitation of single facial movements	Kolb and Milner, 1981
Tests in which there is bilateral impairment	
Demonstration of object use	de Renzi et al., 1968
Rapid directed arm movements	Wyke, 1967, 1968
Finger tapping—two keys	Wyke, 1967
Finger tapping—rhythms	Luria, 1973
Stylus maze	Haaland et al., 1977
Pegboard	Haaland et al., 1977
Pursuit rotor	Heilman et al., 1975
Manual sequence box	Kimura, 1977
Imitation of multiple oral movements	Mateer and Kimura, 1977
Imitation of multiple facial movements	Kolb and Milner, 1981
Oral movements on request	Poeck and Kerschensteiner, 1975
Imitation of meaningful single oral movements (e.g., kiss, whistle)	de Renzi et al, 1966

[a] Note that in the absence of damage to the motor cortex, there may be no impairment at all on these tests.

These tests are very objective; the responses can be quantified, and different laboratories can use the test with little difficulty. Furthermore, the tests can be designed to analyze different contributions to motor control, as a comparison of the tasks shown in Figure 13-5 and 13-6 illustrates. The box test primarily requires movement of the distal musculature of the hand and fingers in a fairly discrete spatial locus. The arm-movement test, on the other hand, requires movements of both the distal and proximal musculature over a large spatial area. In view of what is known about the differential input of the frontal and parietal cortex in the control of proximal and distal musculature, it is likely that tests of these kinds will be differentially affected by lesions to different regions of the cortex. This likelihood, however, remains to be studied.

Asymmetry of Movement Control. One of the most important proposals in Liepmann's theory of apraxia was that the left hemisphere plays a special role not shared by the right hemisphere in the control of movement. This feature of apraxia is reflected in all the studies cited in the bottom half of Table 13-3. In each study a bilateral impairment was produced by a left hemisphere lesion.

Another line of evidence supporting Liepmann's left hemisphere proposal comes from a study by Milner and her colleagues. They taught patients a complex series of arm movements prior to injecting the sedative sodium Amytal into the carotid artery. After the injections the patients were required to perform the movements. Only injections into the speaking hemisphere disrupted the movements, even though the movements were to

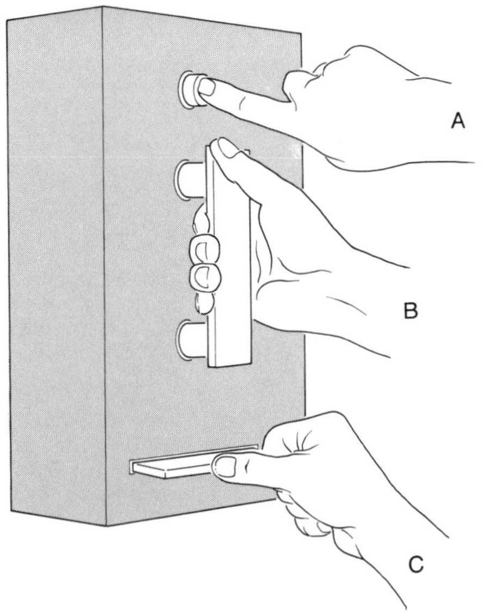

FIGURE 13-5. Kimura Box Test. Subjects are required to learn the movement series of *(A)* pushing the top button with the index finger, *(B)* pulling the handle as shown, and *(C)* pressing down on the bar with the thumb. Apraxic subjects are impaired at this task, and they may be unable to learn it at all, even with extended practice.

be performed with the ipsilateral limb (controlled by the contralateral motor cortex that had not received an injection). Thus, the results of sodium Amytal injections support the results of lesion studies in confirming a special role for the left hemisphere in the control of movement.

Confronted with the left hemisphere's special control of many types of movement, the reader will immediately be moved to ask whether the right hemisphere might not also control certain types of movement. In fact, there is a group of movements that can be selectively disrupted by right hemisphere lesions. These are used in tests in which a variety of components are to be assembled to form an object. Such tasks include (1) assembling pieces of a jigsaw puzzle together to form a picture; (2) drawing a clock face, map, or similar object; (3) copying a design with sticks of various lengths; (4) building bridges or towers with blocks; and (5) copying designs with different colored blocks. Deficits on such tests are sometimes called *constructional apraxias.*

What is special about these constructional tasks? All of them require that objects be ordered in extrapersonal space. Dealing with the spatial relations of objects is believed to be a function of the right hemisphere, especially of the right parietal cortex. Although left parietal lesions can also produce some similar deficits, their occurrence may have a different cause: left hemisphere deficits may result from the person's inability to adjust the parts of his or her own body, rather than the inability to adjust the position of an external object. This theoretically interesting proposition has yet to be clearly tested experimentally.

Are Aphasia and Apraxia Correlated? Since many apraxias stem from left hemisphere lesions, are they secondary to deficits in comprehension? Although aphasia frequently accompanies apraxia, three lines of evidence indicate that the symptoms can be dissociated. First, de Renzi and colleagues gave patients tests for both aphasia and apraxia; the test scores were poorly correlated. Second, patients with surgical excisions outside the speech zones may have no detectable dysphasias but may be dyspraxic, especially when tested on objective tests of movement-copying skills. Third, whereas surgical removal of speech areas may produce severe aphasia, the accompanying apraxia is surprisingly mild; cortical damage does not appear to be sufficient to produce dense apraxia, although it can be enough to produce dense aphasia.

Neuroanatomical Basis of Apraxia. Classical neurological theory concerning the basis of apraxia is derived from a model originally proposed by Liepmann and subsequently popularized by Geschwind. Briefly, Liepmann proposed that the left parietal cortex (specifically around area 40)

FIGURE 13-6. *A.* Examples of items of a serial arm-movement copying test. Subjects are asked to copy each of the series as accurately as they can. *B.* Examples of items from a serial facial-movement copying test.

is the critical region for control of complex movement. This control would be mediated via the left frontal lobe and area 4 in control of the right side of the body. Disruption anywhere along this route in the left hemisphere would produce apraxia of the right limbs. Control over the limbs of the left side was proposed to be mediated through a series of corticocortical connections running from the left parietal cortex to the left frontal cortex and finally to the right frontal cortex via the corpus callosum. This model is often cited in psychology and neurology texts, but it has at least four serious shortcomings.

First, since there are clearly separable "motor systems," each with unique anatomical input, models and studies of apraxia should consider different types of movements separately. Thus, assessment of apraxic syndromes should carefully consider the control of distal (finger, toe, and face) movements, hand and limb movements, and whole-body movements. The Liepmann-Geschwind model does not consider different movement types separately, nor have most studies of apraxic behaviors. It is possible that subtypes of apraxia can be determined on the basis of the system(s) disrupted. For example, Kolb and Milner compared the performance of patients with unilateral cortical excisions at copying both arm- and facial-movement sequences and did indeed find evidence of differential input of the frontal and the parietal cortex to the control of movement. Whereas left parietal lobe lesions significantly disrupted the copying of arm-movement sequences, these lesions had no significant effect on the copying of facial-movement sequences (Figure 13-7). In contrast, left frontal lobe lesions had relatively little effect on the copying of arm-movement sequences but produced larger impairment in the copying of facial-movement sequences. Unfortunately, Kolb and Milner did not try to separate the control of limb, hand, and finger movements in their study. Nonetheless, their results show that it is possible to dissociate the relative contribution of different cortical areas to the control of different types of movements. A similar dissociation has also been made by Kimura in her study of stroke patients. An important additional finding by Kimura, however, was that the complexity of the movement is important. She found that patients with either left anterior or left posterior lesions did not do as well as those with equivalent right hemisphere damage at tasks requiring the reproduction of a series of multiple oral or manual sequences. However, on a test requiring the reproduction of single movements the only group significantly impaired was the left anterior group, whereas on single hand postures the only group impaired was the left posterior group.

Second, since the posterior parietal and prefrontal cortex have no direct projections onto the spinal motor neurons, theories emphasizing the importance of these cortical regions in apraxia must attempt to specify just how it is that they might influence movement. Indeed, although it is widely assumed that the posterior parietal and prefrontal cortexes are the primary cortical regions for the production of apraxia, patients with circumscribed cortical excisions do not typically demonstrate chronic abnormalities on standard clinical tests of apraxia. Also, compared with stroke patients, patients with posterior parietal and prefrontal cortical damage have relatively minor impairments on tests of movement copying; even massive removals of the left hemisphere produce rather small movement-copying deficits when compared with the performance of persons with naturally occurring lesions. The implications of this cannot be underestimated: the direct contribution of the prefrontal and the parietal cortex (and the connections between them) to praxis must be less than is generally implied from clinicoanatomical studies. The failure to demonstrate unequivocal apraxialike disorders in nonhuman species with cortical ablations may therefore not reflect a species difference, as is commonly presumed; rather the severity of movement impairment may actually be equivalent in humans and nonhumans with surgical removals of the cortex.

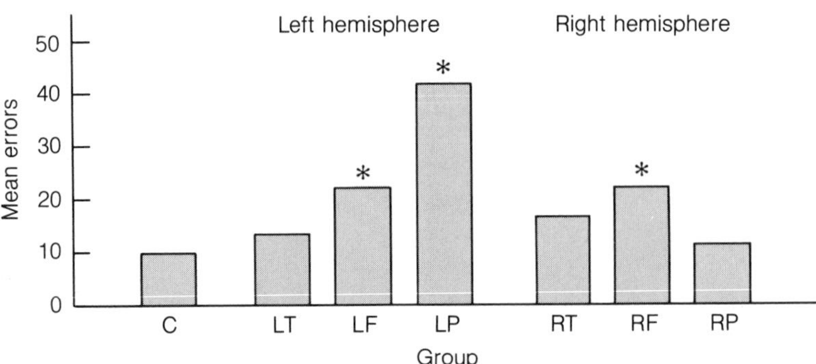

A Arm-movement copying

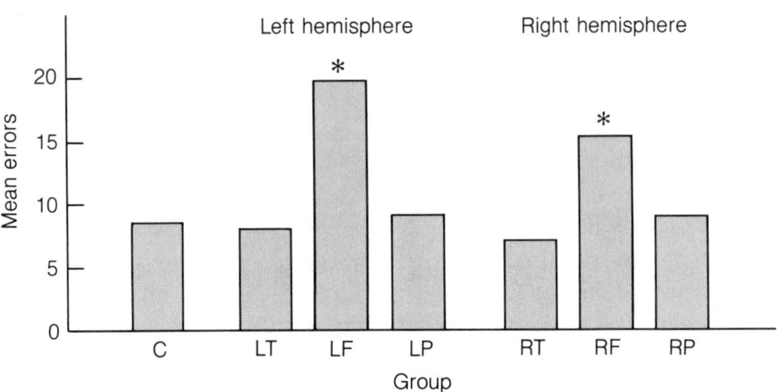

B Face-movement copying

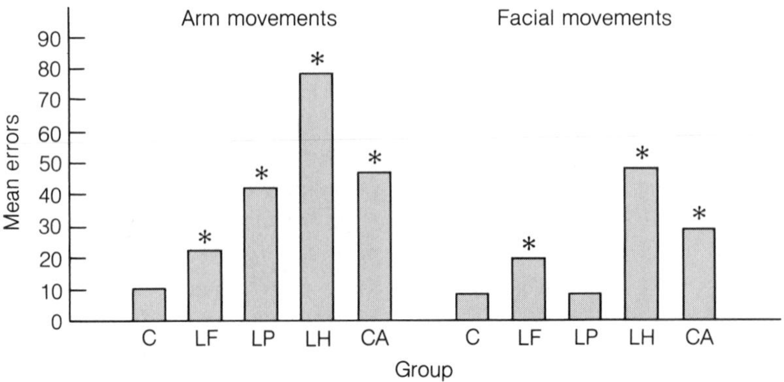

C Comparison of excision, stroke, and callosal patients

Third, the Liepmann-Geschwind model does not recognize the likely role of the basal ganglia and thalamus in apraxic syndromes. These regions provide major access routes for cortical influence on motor output. The fact that cortical excisions have far lesser effects on praxis than do strokes, which presumably affect both the cortex and the basal ganglia and/or the thalamus, implies that damage to subcortical structures may be essential to producing severe clinical apraxia (Figure 13-7).

Fourth, since the limbs and face, but not the hands, are connected via the corpus callosum, it should be determined whether or not the extent of bilateral apraxia is similar in tests of hand, finger, face, and limb movements. Although the importance of transcallosal connections has been emphasized in accounts of apraxic syndromes, emphasis usually has been placed on the inability of the hand ipsilateral to the speaking hemisphere to perform movements to verbal command. Few attempts have been made to carefully describe the abilities of the limbs, fingers, and face to perform particular movements. In one attempt to consider this problem Milner and Kolb studied the ability of four patients, in whom the corpus callosum had been severed as a treatment for epilepsy, to copy meaningless sequences of arm or facial movements with either the left or the right hand. The data showed that the subjects were very badly impaired at copying these movements, even when compared with patients with left parietal lesions (Figure 13-7). Perhaps most surprisingly, the patients were equally impaired with either hand in executing the arm movements, a result that would not be predicted from previous clinicoanatomical studies, and certainly not by the Liepmann-Geschwind model. Unfortunately, the movement sequences in the Kolb and Milner study confounded both limb and finger movements, although most of the errors of movement appeared to be in the positioning of the arms, rather than the fingers. Since the transcallosal connections of the fingers and arms are different, this impression should be followed up with additional studies.

In summary, although the Liepmann model of the neuroanatomical basis of apraxia has been a useful one, it does not account for the data and must be reevaluated in the light of what is now known about the organization of intact and dysfunctioning motor systems.

REFERENCES

Albuquerque, E. X., J. E. Rash, R. F. Mayer, and J. R. Satterfield. An electrophysiological and morphological study of the neuromuscular junction in patients with myasthenia gravis. *Experimental Neurology* 51:536–563, 1976.

Baker, A. D., and L. H. Baker. *Clinical Neurology*. Cambridge: Harper & Row, 1982.

Bobath, B. *Adult Hemiplegia: Evaluation and Treatment*. London: Heinemann Medical Books, 1970.

FIGURE 13-7. *A*. Mean error of cortical excision patients on the arm-movement copying test. Note that left parietal lobe patients (LP) are the most impaired. *B*. Mean errors of cortical excision patients on the face-movement copying test. Note that the frontal lobe patients (LF and RF) are the most impaired. *C*. Comparison of mean errors of callosal patients (CA), left hemisphere stroke patients (LH), large left frontotemporal excision patients (LF) and left parietal excision patients (LP). Note that the stroke patients who have subcortical damage, and the callosal patients are more impaired than the excision patients. C represents the control group. Note: asterisks indicate differences from the control group at $p < .05$. (After Kolb and Milner, 1981; Milner and Kolb, 1985.)

Bowen, F. P. Behavioral alterations in patients with Parkinson's disease. In M. D. Yahr, ed. *The Basal Ganglia.* New York: Raven Press, 1976.

Bremer, F. Cerveau isolé et physiologie du sommeil. *Comptes Rendus de la Societe de Biologie* 118:1235–1242, 1935.

Brinkman, J., and H. G. J. M. Kuypers. Cerebral control of contralateral and ipsilateral arm, hand and finger movements in the split-brain rhesus monkey. *Brain* 96:653–674, 1973.

Carmon, A. Sequenced motor performance in patients with unilateral cerebral lesions. *Neuropsychologia* 9:445–449, 1971.

Changeux, J.-P., M. Kasai, and C.-Y. Lee. The use of a snake venom toxin to characterize the cholinergic receptor protein. *Proceedings of the National Academy of Sciences* 67:1241–1247, 1970.

Chase, T. N., N. S. Wexler, and A. Barbeau, eds. *Huntington's Disease. Advances in Neurology,* vol. 23. New York: Raven Press, 1979.

Critchley, M. *The Parietal Lobes.* New York: Hafner, 1965.

Cruickshank, W. M. *Cerebral Palsy.* Syracuse, NY: Syracuse University Press, 1976.

Dement, W., and N. Kleitman. Cyclic variations in EEG during sleep and their relation to eye movements, body motility and dreaming. *Electroencephalography and Clinical Neurophysiology* 9:673–690, 1957.

Denhoff, E. Medical aspects. In W. M. Cruickshank, ed. *Cerebral Palsy.* Syracuse, NY: Syracuse University Press, 1976.

Economo, C. von. *Encephalitis Lethargica: Its Sequence and Treatment.* Oxford: Oxford University Press, 1931.

Everett, N. B. *Functional Neuroanatomy.* Philadelphia: Lea and Febiger, 1965.

Fambrough, D. M., D. B. Drachman, and S. Satyamurti. Neuromuscular junction in myasthenia gravis: Decreased acetylcholine receptors. *Science* 182:293–295, 1973.

Friedhoff, A. J., and T. N. Chase, eds. *Gilles de la Tourette Syndrome. Advances in Neurology,* vol. 35. New York: Raven Press, 1982.

Gardner, H. *Fundamentals of Neurology.* Philadelphia: Saunders, 1968.

Geschwind, N. The apraxias: Neural mechanisms of disorders of learned movement. *American Scientist* 63:188–195, 1975.

Gilles de la Tourette, G. Étude sur un affection, nerveuse charactérisée par l'incoordination motrice accompanagnée d'écholalie et de copralalie (Jumping, Latah, Myriachit). *Archives of Neurology* 9:19–42, 158–200, 1885.

Gusella, J. F., N. S. Wexler, P. M. Conneally, S. L. Naylor, M. A. Anderson, R. E. Tanzi, P. C. Watkins, K. Ottina, M. R. Wallace, A. Y. Sakaguchi, A. B. Young, I. Shoulson, E. Bonilla, and J. B. Martin. A polymorphic DNA marker genetically linked to Huntingon's disease. *Nature* 306:234–238, 1983.

Haaland, K. Y., C. S. Cleeland, and D. Carr. Motor performance after unilateral damage in patients with tumor. *Archives of Neurology* 34:556–559, 1977.

Haaxma, R., and H. G. J. M. Kuypers. Intrahemispheric cortical connections and visual guidance of hand and finger movements in the rhesus monkey. *Brain* 98:239–260, 1975.

Hammond, W. A. *A Treatise of the Diseases of the Nervous System.* New York: Apple-Century-Crofts, 1871.

Hartmann, E. *The Biology of Dreaming.* Springfield, IL: Charles C. Thomas, 1967.

Heilman, D. M., H. D. Schwartz, and N. Geschwind. Defective motor learning in ideomotor apraxia. *Neurology* 25:1018–1020, 1975.

Hornykiewicz, O. Parkinson's disease. In T. J. Crow, ed. *Disorders of Neurohumoural Transmission.* New York: Academic Press, 1982.

Huntington, D. On chorea. *Medical Surgical Reporter* 26:317–321, 1872.

Kimura, D. The neural basis of language and gesture. In H. Avakina-Whitaker and H. A. Whitaker, eds. *Studies in Neurolinguistics.* New York: Academic Press, 1976.

Kimura, D. Acquisition of a motor skill after left-hemisphere damage. *Brain* 100:527–542, 1977.

Kimura, D. Neuromotor mechanisms in the evolution of human communication. In H. D. Steklis and M. J. Raleigh, eds. *Neurobiology of Social Communication in Primates: An Evolutionary Perspective.* New York: Academic Press, 1980.

Kimura, D. Left-hemisphere control of oral and brachial movements and their relation to communication. *Philosophical Transactions of the Royal Society of London* B298:135–149, 1982.

Kimura, D., and Y. Archibald. Motor functions of the left hemisphere. *Brain* 97:337–350, 1974.

Kolb, B., and B. Milner. Performance of complex arm and facial movements after focal brain lesions. *Neuropsychologia* 19:491–503, 1981.

Langston, J. W., P. Ballard, J. W. Tetrud, and I. Irwin. Chronic parkinsonism in humans due to a product of meperidine-analog synthesis. *Science* 219:979–980, 1983.

Liepmann, H. Die linke Hemisphäre und das Handeln. In *Drei Aufsätze aus dem Apraxiegebiet.* Berlin: Springer, 1908.

Little, W. J. *Deformities of the Human Frame.* London: Longmans, 1853.

Lorber, J. The results of early treatment of extreme hydrocephalus. *Developmental Medicine and Child Neurology Supplement* 16:21–29, 1968.

Luria, A. R. *The Working Brain.* New York: Penguin, 1973.

Martin, J. P. *The Basal Ganglia and Posture.* London: Ritman Medical Publishing, 1967.

Martin, M. P. Hemichorea resulting from a local lesion of the brain (Syndrome of the Body of Luys). *Brain* 50:637, 1927.

Mateer, C., and D. Kimura. Impairment of nonverbal or oral movements in apraxia. *Brain and Language* 4:262–276, 1977.

McLennan, J. E., K. Nakano, H. R. Tyler, and R. S. Schwab. Micrographia in Parkinson's disease. *Journal of Neurological Science* 15:141–152, 1972.

Milner, B. Hemispheric asymmetry in the control of gesture sequences. *Proceedings of XXI International Congress of Psychology.* Paris, 1976, p. 149.

Milner, B., and B. Kolb. Performance of complex arm movements and facial-movement sequences after cerebral commissurotomy. *Neuropsychologia* 23:791–799, 1985.

Moruzzi, G., and H. W. Magoun. Brainstem reticular formation and activation of the EEG. *Electroencephalography and Clinical Neurophysiology* 1:455–473, 1949.

Nathan, P., and M. Smith. Effects of two unilateral cordotomies on the mobility of the lower limbs. *Brain* 96:471–494, 1973.

Nauta, W. J. H. Hypothalamic regulation of sleep in rats: An experimental study. *Journal of Neurophysiology* 9:285–316, 1946.

Parkinson, J. Essay on the shaking palsy. Reprinted in M. Critchley, eds. *James Parkinson.* London: Macmillan, 1955.

Patrick, J., and J. Lindstrom. Autoimmune response to acetylcholine receptor. *Science* 180:871–872, 1973.

Poeck, K., and M. Kerschensteiner. Analysis of the sequential motor events in oral apraxia. In K. J. Zulch, O. Creutzfeldt, and B. C. Galbraith, eds. *Cerebral Localization.* Berlin: Springer-Verlag, 1975.

Pompeiano, O. Mechanisms of sensorimotor integration during sleep. In E. Stellar and L. Sprague, eds. *Progress in Physiological Psychology,* vol. 3. New York: Academic Press, 1970.

Rechtschaffen, A., and W. Dement. Studies on the relation of narcolepsy, cataplexy, and sleep with low voltage random EEG activity. *Research Publications: Association for Research in Nervous and Mental Disease,* XLV:488–498, 1967.

Rechtschaffen, A., and L. J. Monroe. Laboratory studies of insomnia. In A. Kales, ed. *Sleep: Physiology and Pathology.* Philadelphia: Lippincott, 1969.

Renzi, E. de, A. Pieczuro, and L. A. Vignolo. Oral apraxia and aphasia. *Cortex* 2:50–73, 1966.

Renzi, E. de, A. Pieczuro, and L. A. Vignolo. Ideational apraxia: A quantitative study. *Neuropsychologia* 6:41–52, 1968.

Roy, E. A., ed. *Neuropsychological studies of apraxia and related disorders.* New York: North-Holland, 1985.

Sacks. O. *Awakenings.* New York: Doubleday, 1973.

Shapiro, E., A. K. Shapiro, and J. Clarkin. Clinical psychological testing in Tourette's syndrome. *Journal of Personality Assessment* 38:464–478, 1974.

Twitchell, T. E. The restoration of motor function following hemiplegia in man. *Brain* 74:443–480, 1951.

Vessie, P. R. On the transmission of Huntington's chorea for 300 years — the Bures family group. *Journal of Nervous and Mental Disorders* 76:533–565, 1932.

Vogt, C. Sur l'état marlove du striatum. *Journal of Psychiatry and Neurology* 31:256, 1924–25.

Walton, J. N. *Brain's Diseases of the Nervous System.* New York and Toronto: Oxford University Press, 1977.

Webb, W. B. *Sleep the Gentle Tyrant.* Englewood Cliffs, NJ: Prentice-Hall, 1975.

Wilson, S. A. K. Progressive lenticular degeneration: A familial nervous disease associated with cirrhosis of the liver. *Brain* 34:295, 1912.

Wyke, M. Effect of brain lesions on the rapidity of arm movement. *Neurology* 17:1113–1120, 1967.

Wyke, M. The effect of brain lesions in the performance of an arm-hand precision task. *Neuropsychologia* 6:125–134, 1968.

PART 4

GENERAL PRINCIPLES OF HUMAN NEUROPSYCHOLOGY

This section discusses the core of neuropsychology. Chapter 14 gives the history of neuropsychology, describing how the major hypotheses of brain function were developed to shape current thinking and research on its function. Chapters 15 and 16 describe the fascinating division of function, almost unique to humans and certainly most elaborated in them, between the two cerebral hemispheres. This division has not only been an object of study in its own right but has also provided a key that opens new insights into cortical function. Chapters 17, 18, and 19 describe the functions of the lobes. Of course, the lobes do not work in isolation and so Chapter 20 describes their functional interrelation.

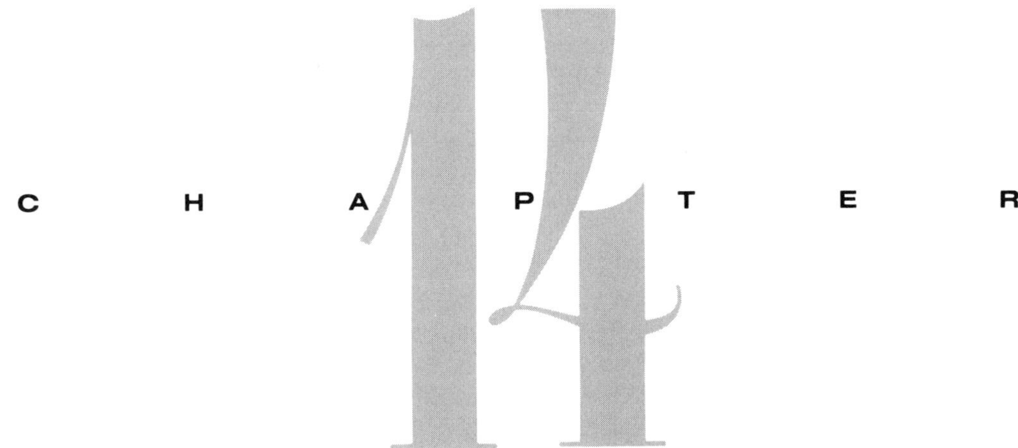

CHAPTER 14

THE DEVELOPMENT OF NEUROPSYCHOLOGY

According to Bruce, the term *neuropsychology* was first used by William Osler. It was then used by D. O. Hebb, in a subtitle in his 1949 book *The Organization of Behavior: A Neuropsychological Theory.* Although neither defined nor used in the text itself, the term was probably intended to represent a study that combined the neurologist's and physiological psychologist's common interests in brain function. By 1957, the term had become a recognized designation for a subfield of the neurosciences, since Heinrich Kluver, in the preface to *Behavior Mechanisms in Monkeys,* suggested that the book would be of interest to neuropsychologists and others. (Kluver had not used the term in the 1933 preface to the same book.) The term was given wide publicity when it appeared in 1960 in the title of a collection of K. S. Lashley's writings —*The Neuropsychology of Lashley*—most of which were rat and monkey studies edited by Beach. But again neuropsychology was not used or defined in the text.

The term, then, is of relatively recent origin. We define neuropsychology as the study of the relation between brain function and behavior. Although the study draws information from many disciplines—for example, anatomy, biology, biophysics, ethology, pharmacology, physiology, physiological psychology, and philosophy—its central focus is the development of a science of human behavior based on the function of the human brain.

Although neuropsychology was developed only recently (as was much of science itself), its contemporary definition is strongly influenced by two traditional foci for experimental and theoretical investigations in brain research: the **brain hypothesis,** the idea that the brain is the source of behavior; and the **neuron hypothesis,** the idea that the unit of brain structure and function is the neuron. In this chapter the development of these two ideas is traced, after which the more recent advances leading to the modern science of neuropsychology are described. It will be seen that although the science is new, its major ideas are not. A consensus that these were important ideas was not easily arrived at, however. For much of our past we humans were groping in the dark for concepts that would help to describe the brain's function. From time to time an idea was serendipitously formulated, was sometimes grasped, sometimes examined, and then was discarded only to be later rediscovered. Today we are still finding, examining, and reexamining ideas. Through this history we hope to encourage the reader to become a participant and to see the science not as a dogma but as a dialogue about some of the ideas that have emerged.

THE BRAIN HYPOTHESIS

The Brain versus the Heart

Since earliest times humans have believed that their behavior is controlled by a soul, a spirit, or a rational system. We have also held a variety of views about the nature and location of the controlling factor; among the earliest hypotheses that survive in record were those of Alcmaeon of Croton (ca. 500 B.C.) and Empedocles (ca. 495–435 B.C.). Alcmaeon located mental processes in the brain, and so subscribed to what is now called the brain hypothesis; Empedocles located mental processes in the heart, and so subscribed to what could be called the cardiac hypothesis.

The relative merits of those two hypotheses were debated for the next 2000 years, evidence and logic being presented in support of each. For example, Plato (427?–347 B.C.) developed the concept of a tripartite soul and placed its rational part in the brain because that was the part of the body closest to the heavens. Aristotle (384–322 B.C.) had a good knowledge of brain structure and realized that, of all animals, humans have the largest brain relative to body size. Nevertheless, he decided that because the heart was warm and active it was the source of mental processes; the brain, because it was cool and inert, served as a radiator to cool the blood. He explained away the large size of the brain as evidence of a relation to intelligence by stating that humans' blood is richer and hotter than other animals' and so requires a larger cooling system. Physicians such as Hippocrates (460–370 B.C.) and Galen (A.D. 130–200) described some aspects of brain anatomy and argued strongly for the brain hypothesis. They were no doubt influenced by their clinical experience. For example, before becoming the leading physician in Rome, Galen had spent 5 years as a surgeon to gladiators and was well aware of the behavioral consequences of brain damage. He went to great pains to refute Aristotle on logical grounds, for example, by pointing out that the nerves from the sense organs go to the brain, not to the heart. He also did experiments to compare the effects of pressure on the heart and brain. He noted that light pressure on the brain caused cessation of movement and even death, whereas pressure on the heart caused pain but did not arrest voluntary behavior.

Although the cardiac hypothesis is no longer a serious scientific position, it left its mark on our language. In literature as in everyday speech, matters of emotion are frequently referred to the heart: love is symbolized by an arrow piercing the heart; a person distressed by unrequited love is said to be heartbroken; and unenthusiastic person is said to be not putting his or her heart into it; an angry person is said to have boiling blood. Thus, it was not initially obvious what organ controlled behavior, and elegant arguments for the brain hypothesis developed only gradually and then only as a result of logical argument, careful observation, and experimentation.

Localization of Function: Early Developments

Of course, simply knowing that the brain controls behavior is not enough: formulation of a complete hypothesis required knowledge of *how* it controls behavior. Much of the research directed to this end has addressed the issue of **localization of function** — the notion that given behaviors are controlled by specific areas of the brain. Theories of localization of function are as old as theories about nervous system involvement in mental processes. Today, localization of function is generally used to mean that functions are distributed among different segments of the neocortex: visual perception in the occipital lobe, auditory perception in the temporal lobe, and so forth. This idea took some time to develop: the first problem to be solved was whether mental processes were the product of the brain or mind; the second problem was locating the control of different aspects of behavior within the brain.

Modern thinking about the mind began with René Descartes (1596 – 1650). Descartes replaced the Platonic concept of the tripartite soul with that of a unitary mind that is the reasoning or rational soul. Being nonmaterial and having no spatial extent, the mind is fundamentally different from the body. The body is a machine that is material and thus clearly has spatial extent; it responds reflexively to sensory changes by action of the brain. Nonhuman animals have only bodies and no rational minds; thus their behavior can be explained, according to Descartes, as purely mechanical action. However, any account of human behavior requires that the functions of both mind and body be considered. In proposing that the mind and body are separate but can interact, Descartes originated the *mind-body problem,* namely: What is the relation between the mind and the body, or, more simply, how do they interact? Some *dualists* (as those holding mind and body to be separate are called) have argued that the two causally interact, but they have never convincingly explained how. Other dualists have avoided this problem by reasoning either that the two function in parallel without interacting or that the body can affect the mind but the mind cannot affect the body. Thus, both dualist positions allow for theorizing about behavior without considering mind. Those philosophers called *monists* avoid the mind-body problem by postulating that the mind and body are both the same and either are both material or both nonmaterial. Clearly, the latter monist position might be an embarrassing one for a neuroscientist.

The belief, widely held through Descartes' influence, that the mind was an indivisible substance forced two conclusions, also widely held. First, since the mind was indivisible, theories that subdivided brain function could not be correct. (Some of the history of this debate will be traced in subsequent pages.) Second, since mind existed apart from the body, the functions of mind would require separate consideration; complete understanding of the body and how it worked would not bring complete understanding of human behavior. During the 19th century, physiologists would often describe the physiology of some newly discovered reflex system and then speculate as to how mind worked through it. (Even today some physiologists devote a portion of their writing to the problem of mind — for example, Eccles, *The Neurophysiological Basis of Mind: The Principles of Neurophysiology,* 1956.) Many modern neuroscientists assert that the body portion of the mind-body polarity is their proper domain of study and ignore the mind or dismiss it by saying that, although it may very well exist, it cannot be studied by using recording or stimulating electrodes. Others, more skeptical, refer to the mind as the bogey in the brain, the ghost in the machine, or, as some psychologists have referred to it, the little green man in the head. They argue, as does the philosopher Gilbert Ryle, that *mind* is simply a term for the brain and its activities and not a separate entity, just as *city* is a term for a collection of buildings and people and not a separate thing. Still others, equating mind with the soul, keep their views on the mind private and make no pretense that once everything about neural system is known the mind-body problem will be solved.

Prior to Descartes there had been a persistent belief, held by Galen and many subsequent writers, that mind was located in the fluid of the ventricles rather than in the matter of the brain. This belief was reinforced in the 10th century when it came to be thought that the muscles were moved by being filled with a fluid that traversed the nerve centers. Ventricular fluid was the prime candidate for being that fluid. In fact, some of the theories of how fluid in different ventricular cavities controlled different aspects of behavior are quite elegant. The cogent arguments of Andreas Vesalius (1514–1564) finally discredited the ventricular theories. Vesalius dissected brains and noted that the relative size of the ventricles in animals and humans is the same. He concluded that since rational man distinguished himself by having the largest brain, it is the brain and not the ventricles that mediate mental processes. Descartes, however, was the first to locate mental processes precisely within brain tissue. He located the mind in the pineal body, on the logic, first, that this body is the only structure in the nervous system not composed of two bilaterally symmetrical halves, and, second, that it is located in proximity to the ventricles. (The rest of the brain was seen not as functioning neural tissue but as the cortex, or bark, that protected the important internal mechanisms.) Thus, by thinking of the mind as unified and located precisely in a single structure, Descartes simultaneously initiated the debate on localization of function and enunciated the negative position.

Localization of Function: The Phrenologists

The argument for localization of function began with the phrenological theory of Franz Josef Gall (1758–1828) and Johann Casper Spurzheim (1776–1832). Their theory, in the broad lines of its arguments, is of such scope and brilliance that it could not be ignored, but its details are so improbable that it was immediately rejected by most of their contemporaries. Their theory of localization of function stunningly resembles modern theories; had their methodology been a little different they could have anticipated much of modern neuropsychology.

Gall and Spurzheim, both anatomists, made a number of important discoveries in neuroanatomy that alone would have given them a place in history. They realized that the cortex is composed of functioning cells that are connected with the subcortical structures. They described the crossing of the pyramids and recognized that the spinal cord is divided into white and gray matter. They also recognized that the two symmetrical halves of the brain are connected by commissures. But as soon as they went beyond anatomy and attempted to ascribe functions to different parts of the brain, everything they did was conceptually brilliant but hopelessly in error.

From observations made in early youth Gall believed that students with good memories had large, protruding eyes. He thought it possible that a well-developed memory area of the brain located behind the eyes could cause them to protrude. From this beginning, Gall and Spurzheim undertook to examine the external features of the skull and to correlate its bumps and depressions with what they thought to be important aspects of behavior. A bump on the skull indicated a well-developed underlying cortical gyrus and therefore a greater faculty for a particular behavior; a depression in the same area indicated an underdeveloped gyrus and a concomitantly reduced capacity. Thus, a person who had a high degree of what they called **amativeness,** or an inclination to love, had a large bump in the area shown in Figure 14-1*B*, whereas a person who had a low score on this trait had a depression in this same area. Their behavioral traits consisted of a long list of faculties such as wit, inquiry, and faith. Each of these faculties, which they had devised or had borrowed from English or Scottish psychology, they assigned to a particular portion of the skull or by inference to the underlying portion of the brain. Figure 14-2 shows the resulting map. Spurzheim called the study of the relation between the skull's surface features and a person's faculties **phrenology.**

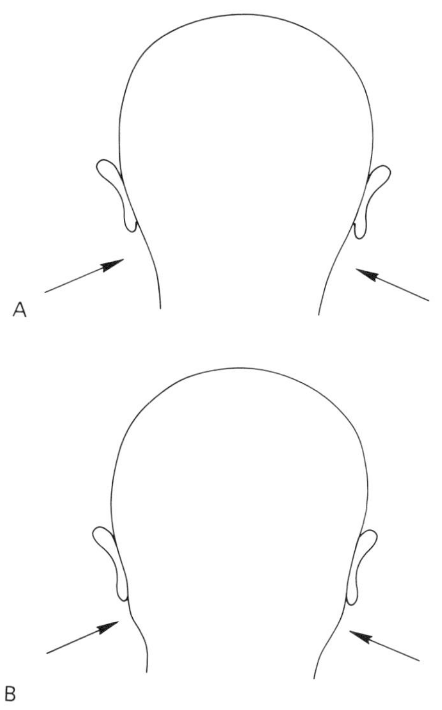

FIGURE 14-1. According to phrenologists, depressions (*A*) and bumps (*B*) on the skull indicate the size of the underlying area of brain, and when correlated with personality traits, indicate the part of the brain controlling the trait. Gall, examining a patient (who because of her behavior became known as "Gall's Passionate Widow"), found a bump at the back of her neck that he thought located the center for "amativeness" in the cerebellum (arrows in *B*). Flourens refuted this hypothesis by removing the cerebellum from a dog to show that the cerebellum was involved in coordinating movement. As phrenology was popularized, bumps and depressions were indicated on the head in places that were no longer adjacent to the brain—as was the case with amativeness. (From C. H. Olin, 1910.)

Gall and Spurzheim went to considerable effort to gather evidence for their theory, and Gall states that he devoted himself to observation and waited patiently for nature to bring her results to him. In developing his idea of the carnivorous instinct, Gall examined the skull of meat- and plant-eating animals and detailed evidence from over 50 species, including anecdotal evidence from his own lapdog. He studied the behavior of men, including an account of a parricide and a murderer and the details on 25 other skulls. He included descriptions about people who delighted in witnessing death or in torturing animals, or who historically were noted for cruelty and sadism, and he even considered evidence from numerous paintings and busts. One might ask why it was that he "made thousands of observations on this subject, and never found an exception." Young makes the telling point that Gall's entire method was geared toward seeking confirmations. He never considered the possibility that his observations should meet certain standards or that they should be tested in any objective way. Even when he made good observations that may have been subjected to more rigorous examination, he gave them little more weight than any anecdote. Gall also placed no emphasis on evidence from cases of brain damage. He has been credited with giving the first complete account of a relation between left frontal brain damage and aphasia (Figure 14-2), yet he felt this type of finding was not evidence per se but rather confirmation of a finding that was already established by phrenological evidence.

Despite the ingenuity behind Gall and Spurzheim's research it failed, for four reasons. First, the psychology of faculties bore little relation to real behavior: faculties such as faith, self-love, and veneration were hopelessly impossible to define and to quantify objectively. The first breakthroughs in localization came only when people chose an objective behavior, such as speech, to correlate with an area of the brain. The second cause of the phrenologists' failure was their belief that the superficial features of the skull, the analysis of which they called *cranioscopy,* could be used to estimate brain size and shape. Incredibly, they failed to realize that the outer skull did not mirror the inner skull or the surface features of the neocortex. Had they instead investigated gyral size, history might have been kinder to them. They might have discovered the asymmetries of structure, such as the

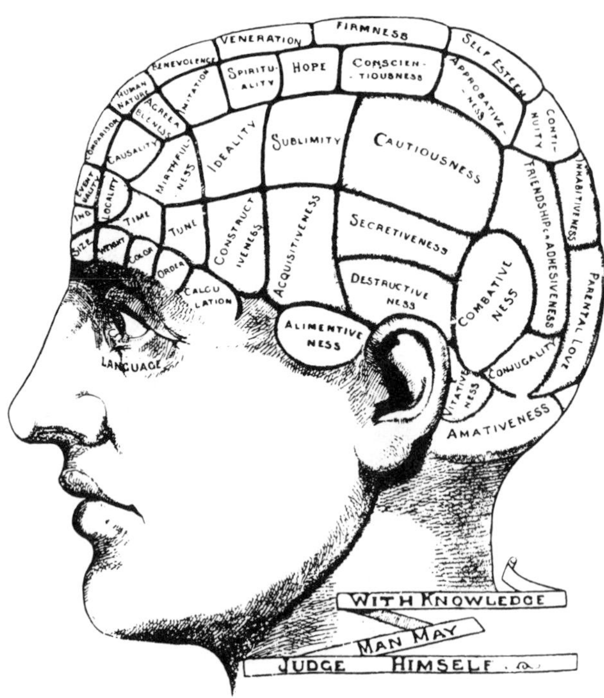

FIGURE 14-2. Originally Gall's system had 27 faculties. As phrenology (Spurzheim's name for the theory) expanded, the number of faculties increased. The figure shows the location of faculties according to Spurzheim. Language, indicated in the front of the brain (below the eye), actually derived from a case study of Gall's: a soldier had received a knife wound that penetrated the frontal lobe of his left hemisphere through the eye. The soldier became aphasic; he was thus the first comprehensive report of aphasia following left frontal damage.

larger planum temporale of the left posterior cortex, which is now thought to reflect lateralization of language to the left hemisphere. But they thought of gyral patterns as random wrinkles, such as those that might be found in a crumpled shirt, and so gave them no attention. The third cause of failure was that phrenology invited quackery and thus, indirectly, ridicule by association. Because its followers devoted themselves to extremely superficial personality analysis, the entire endeavor was quickly brought into disrepute. In the eyes of their contemporaries, however, there was a more damning criticism, which was the fourth cause of their failure. Gall and Spurzheim had postulated that the brain is the organ of the mind, that personality characteristics are innate, and that the brain (or mind) is composed of independent functioning units. The prevailing opinion still reflected Descartes: the mind is nonmaterial and functions as a whole. Since these views are still held by many people today, it is possible to understand the hostility their criticism evoked nearly 200 years ago.

In reflecting on the contributions made by phrenological thought, it should not be believed that phrenology has been entirely abandoned. Hebb has remarked that it takes about 50 to 100 years for scientific ideas to become common sense, and if they are wrong, another 100 years to get rid of them. Perhaps the second figure should be revised upward: phrenological ideas are still widely held. Despite the periodic failure of scientific attempts to correlate appearance and various aspects of behavior, it is not uncommon to hear people accord virtues to others soley on the basis of their physical appearance. Readers may ask themselves how accurate they would be if asked to judge intelligence on the basis of photographs of others. Social psychologists have found that university students are not unwilling to make such judgments; they do so using the rule: beauty equals intelligence. In fairness to Gall, we may note that at least some of his science, inaccurate as it appears to have been, attempted an actual physical measurement.

Localization of Function: The First Experiments

Because of its weaknesses and the hostility it provoked, Gall and Spurzheim's phrenology had little chance of success. Nevertheless, Pierre Flourens (1794–1867) is generally credited with the definitive demolition of their science. Flourens, who accepted the concept of a unified mind, buttressed philosophical arguments against Gall and Spurzheim with experimentation. Nor was he above using ridicule to discount them, as the following story from Flourens' book *Comparative Psychology,* excerpted by Krech, shows:

> The famous physiologist, Magendie, preserved with veneration the brain of Laplace. Spurzheim had the very natural wish to see the brain of a great man.
>
> To test the science of the phrenologist, Mr. Magendie showed him, instead of the brain of Laplace, that of an imbecile.
>
> Spurzheim, who had already worked up his enthusiasm, admired the brain of the imbecile as he would have admired that of Laplace. (Krech, 1962)

In his experimental work, Flourens developed the technique of lesioning the brains of animals to study the changes produced in their behavior. He concluded that the cerebrum is the seat of intelligence, that the cerebellum coordinates locomotion, and that the medulla oblongata, since damage to it arrested respiration and resulted in death, is the seat of the principle of life. He concluded that there is no localization of function in the cerebrum, that all intellectual faculties resided there coextensively. He argued that loss of function is correlated with the extent of ablation of cortical tissue; that if all tissue was gone all intellectual functions were gone, and that if sufficient tissue remained intact there was recovery of all function.

Not only did Flourens make a number of important contributions to experimental psychology, he encumbered it with a number of millstones, some of which it has still not completely removed. He was a strict Cartesian, even to the point of dedicating his book to Descartes. He argued that the cortex had no motor or sensory functions. It would be years before brain stimulation studies showed him to be wrong on this point. Still, the idea that there is uncommitted cortex (now called association cortex) available for all sorts of hypothetical higher functions is still widely believed, although it is no more than a Flourensian notion applied to a more circumscribed portion of the cortex.

Currently, a number of lines of investigation are committed to demonstrating that the idea of uncommitted cortex is a fallacy. Flourens invested the cortex with the properties that Descartes had ascribed to the mind, including the functions of will, reason, and intelligence, and advocated that the only proper approach to their function is through introspection. Even today, Hebb finds it necessary to advocate that neuroscientists should be behaviorists and study observable events rather than directing their studies toward mentalistic constructs. Finally, the idea that the mind is indivisible has had its advocates in this century, including people such as Lashley, who came to doubt that psychological functions could be localized successfully, and Finger and Stein, who imply that the nonspecific potential of the cortex permits extensive possibilities for recovery of function. Perhaps the most commonly applied erroneous Flourensian notion is in pedagogy, where it is expressed as, "Most people never use more than 10% of their brain."

The conclusion that Flourens' experiments devastated Gall and Spurzheim was persuasive at the time, but is difficult to support in retrospect. Most of Flourens' experiments were performed with pigeons and chickens—animals with virtually no neocortex. His behavioral tests were assessments of activities such as eating and wing flapping and bore no relation to the faculties proposed for the cortex by Gall and Spurzheim. Finally, many of the deficits from which his animals appeared to suffer may have been the result of postsurgical shock, brain swelling, or removal of far more tissue than the forebrain. Certainly subsequent workers who removed only the cerebrum did not find that pigeons lost all intellectual faculties as Flourens had defined them.

Localization of Language

Gall and Spurzheim's theory of localization of function was in disrepute for about 50 years while Flouren's concept of holistic function was dominant. Jean Baptiste Bouillaud (1796–1881), however, by supporting Gall's idea that language function is localized in the frontal lobe, provided the impetus for localization theory to take a new direction. On 21 February 1825 he read before the Royal Academy of Medicine in France, a paper in which he argued from clinical studies that function is localized in the neocortex, and specifically that speech is localized in the frontal lobes just as Gall had suggested. (Gall had correlated frontal cortex with language after studying a penetrating brain injury.) Observing that acts such as writing, drawing, painting, and fencing were carried out with the right hand, Bouillaud also suggested that the part of the brain that controlled them might possibly be the left hemisphere. Why, he asked, should people not be left-brained for the movements of speech as well? A few years later, in 1836, Marc Dax read a paper in Montpellier about a series of clinical cases demonstrating that disorders of speech were constantly associated with lesions of the left hemisphere. Dax's manuscript was published by his son in 1865.

Though neither Bouillaud's nor Dax's work had much impact when first presented, Ernest Auburtin, Bouillaud's son-in-law, took up Bouillaud's cause. At a meeting of the Anthropological Society of Paris in 1861 he reported the case of a patient who ceased to speak when pressure was applied to his exposed anterior lobes. He also gave the following description of another patient, with a challenge:

> For a long time during my service with M. Bouillaud I studied a patient, named Bache, who had lost his speech but understood everything said to him and replied with signs in a very intelligent manner to all questions put to him. This man, who spent several years at the Bicetre, is now at the Hospital for Incurables. I saw him again recently and his disease has progressed; slight paralysis has appeared but his intelligence is still unimpaired, and speech is wholly abolished. Without a doubt this man will soon die. Based on the symptoms that he presents, we have diagnosed softening of the anterior lobes. If, at autopsy, these lobes are found to be intact, I shall renounce the ideas that I have just expounded to you. (Stookey, 1954)

Paul Broca (1824–1880), founder of the society, attended the meeting and heard Auburtin's challenge. Five days later he received a patient, Leborgne, who had lost his speech and was able to say only "tan" and utter an oath. He had paralysis on the right side of his body but in other respects he seemed intelligent and normal. Broca invited Auburtin to examine Tan, as he came to be called, and together they agreed that if Auburtin was right, Tan should have a frontal lesion. Tan died on 17 April 1861, and the next day Broca submitted his findings to the Anthropological Society. The left anterior lobe was the focus of Tan's lesion. By 1863, Broca had collected eight more cases similar to Tan's and stated:

> Here are eight instances in which the lesion was in the posterior third of the third frontal convolution. This number seems to me to be sufficient to give strong presumptions. And the most remarkable thing is that in all the patients the lesion was on the left side. I do not dare draw conclusions from this. I await new facts. (Joynt, 1964)

It is usual to credit Broca with four contributions to the study of cortical function: describing a behavioral syndrome that consists of an inability to speak despite the presence of intact vocal mechanisms and normal comprehension (**Broca's aphasia**), coining the word *aphemia* to describe this syndrome, correlating aphemia with an anatomical site now known as Broca's area, and elaborating the concept of *cerebral dominance* of language in the left hemisphere, or, as he phrased it, "nous parlons avec l'hemisphere gauche."

Largely because these contributions marked a change in the approach to analysis of brain function, they have been carefully scrutinized by historians, some of whom have judged them as either not original, not enduring, or not accurate. First, the clinical symptoms that Broca described were already known, as is demonstrated by Auburtin's account of the aphasic Bache—and this Broca acknowledged. Second, the term *aphemia* was criticized by Trousseau, who argued that it meant infamy and was thus inappropriate as a clinical designation. Trousseau suggested the word *aphasia,* which Broca criticized as also inappropriate, since it meant "the state of a man who has run out of arguments"; but it nevertheless became universally accepted, whereas aphemia was discarded. Third, language and the frontal lobes had previously been correlated by Gall, Bouillaud, and Auburtin, whose priority Broca recognized. Fourth, Broca's anatomical analysis was criticized by Pierre Marie, who reexamined the brains of Broca's first two patients, Tan and Lelong, 25 years after Broca's death. Marie pointed out in his article, "The Third Left frontal Convolution Plays No Particular Role in the Function of Language," that Lelong was probably a victim of a senile dementia, with general nonspecific atrophy of the brain common in senility, and was not aphasic, and that Tan had additional extensive damage in his posterior cortex that may have accounted for his aphasia. In fairness, Broca had been aware of Tan's posterior damage but had concluded that, whereas the posterior damage contributed to his death, the anterior damage had occurred earlier, producing his aphasia. A fifth criticism is that Dax was the first to suggest the doctrine of cerebral dominance. This Broca also acknowledged, although, according to Joynt, he was never able to establish to his own satisfaction that Dax had read a paper in Montpellier in 1836 in which he stated that speech was lateralized on the left.

There is substance to the details of all these criticisms, but in a way they miss the mark, for Broca's more enduring contribution was to synthesize the theory of localization of function, the clinical descriptions of brain-damage effects, and neuroanatomy with such clarity that it excited neuroscientists and the lay public alike and so altered the direction neurobehavioral analysis was to take.

Wernicke: Sequential Programming and Disconnection

Broca's description of aphasia as a condition resulting from left frontal lesions (confirmed by findings from a number of other sources) makes two rather simple, but fundamental, points for localization: (1) a behavior is controlled by a specific brain area; and (2) destroying the area selectively destroys the behavior.

People who interpreted Broca in this way have been called strict localizationists. There were, however, those who disagreed with these points on both logical and clinical grounds. Among the most notable to dissent were Hughlings-Jackson, Bastian, and Wernicke. The position of Carl Wernicke (1848–1904) initially gained widest recognition (He, like Broca, had an area of the brain named after him). He also made two findings devastating to strict localization: first, there is more than one language area; second, damage that spared an area could nevertheless produce deficits indistinguishable from those resulting from damage to the area. The first finding suggested that behaviors such as language result from the serial processing of information; that is, they are *sequentially programmed;* the second advanced the concept of disconnection.

Theodore Meynert (1833–1892) was the first to suggest that the cortex behind the central fissure is sensory in function. In addition he described the projection of the auditory nerve to the cortex of the Sylvian fissure of the temporal cortex. He suspected a relation between hearing and speech and even described two cases of aphasic patients with lesions in this auditory projection area. It was his associate Wernicke, however, who subsequently described the details of this temporal lobe aphasia —or, as it has come to be called, **Wernicke's aphasia** or **fluent aphasia**—and placed it within a theoretical framework.

Wernicke described four major features of the aphasia that made it different from what Broca described: (1) there was damage in the first temporal gyrus, in what is now known as Wernicke's area; (2) there was no contralateral hemiplegia or paralysis; (3) the patients could speak fluently, but what they said was confused and made little sense —hence the term *fluent* aphasia, or paraphasia; and (4) although the patients were able to hear, they could not understand or repeat what was said to them.

In addition to describing a new kind of aphasia, Wernicke provided a model for how language is organized in the left hemisphere: it involves sequential programming of activity in two language areas (see Figure 14-3). Wernicke theorized that the sound images of objects are stored in the first temporal gyrus (**Wernicke's area**), whence they are sent over a pathway (later identified as the **arcuate fasciculus**) to **Broca's area,** where the representations of speech movements are retained. If the temporal lobe were damaged, speech movements could occur but the speech would make no sense, because the person would be unable to monitor what he said. However, because damage to Broca's area produces loss of speech movements without the loss of sound images, aphasia is not accompanied by a loss of comprehension.

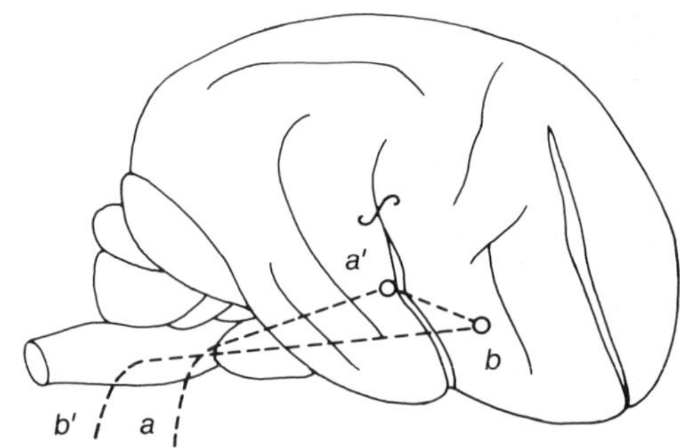

FIGURE 14-3. Wernicke's (1874) model showing how language is organized in the brain. Sounds enter the brain on the auditory pathway (*a*). Sound images are stored in Wernicke's area (*a'*) and are sent to Broca's word area (*b*) for articulation over the motor pathway (*b'*). Lesions on the pathway *a-a'-b-b'* could produce different types of aphasia, depending on lesion location. It is curious that Wernicke drew all his language models on the right hemisphere and not the left, which is the dominant hemisphere for language, as Wernicke believed. It is amazing that his model was that of an ape, which could not speak, as Wernicke knew. (After C. Wernicke, 1874.)

Wernicke suggested that if the fibers connecting the two speech areas were damaged (disconnected), then, without damage to Broca's or Wernicke's area, a speech deficit would occur. Wernicke called such a disconnection **conduction aphasia:** both speech sounds and movements would be retained, as would comprehension, but speech would still be paraphasic because the person would not be able to judge the congruity of what he or she said.

The analysis of brain lesion effects by subsequent neurologists was much influenced by Wernicke's concept of disconnection, because it provided a methodology linking anatomy and behavior, permitting prediction of new brain syndromes and the testing of hypotheses. Using this methodology, Dejerine in 1892 was able to describe a case in which **dyslexia**—loss of the ability to read—resulted from disconnecting the visual area from Wernicke's area. And Wernicke's student Liepmann (1863–1925) was able to show that apraxia, followed disconnection of motor areas from sensory areas. The importance of the idea of disconnection cannot be overemphasized, because the behavioral deficit that follows a disconnection in the absence of a lesion in a given locus can be identical to a deficit that follows damage to that locus. As a result, any concept of strict localization of function becomes unworkable.

Electrophysiological Confirmation of Localization

The work of clinical neurologists such as Broca, Wernicke, and others seemed to indicate that behavior was somehow localized in the neocortex. Although many were excited by the idea, others maintained strong objections; what was needed was a different research approach that would support one or the other position. Almost on cue, this was provided by the development of the technique for electrically stimulating the brain.

In 1870, Gustav Theodor Fritsch (1838–1929) and Eduard Hitzig (1838–1907) published their extraordinary paper "On the Electrical Excitability of the Cerebrum." Hitzig had previously elicited eye movements by stimulating the temporal cortex of a man, and he may have derived the idea of stimulating the cortex from an observation made while dressing a wound, that mechanical irritation of the brain caused twitching in the contralateral limbs. Working in Hitzig's bedroom, the two performed a successful preliminary experiment with a rabbit and then examined the effects of stimulating the exposed neocortex of a dog. At the time, nearly everyone was of the opinion that the neocortex was inexcitable by electrical stimulation. Fritsch and Hitzig demonstrated that not only is the neocortex excitable, it is selectively excitable. Direct application of galvanic current to portions of the anterior neocortex caused movements on the opposite side of the body, whereas stimulation of the posterior neocortex produced no movement. They also found that stimulation of restricted portions of the anterior neocortex elicited movement of particular body parts, which suggested that on the neocortex there are *centers* or topographic representations of the different parts of the motor system. In summary, their findings contributed toward overthrowing three dictums that had been defended by Flourens. They showed that (1) the cortex is excitable, (2) the cortex plays a role in producing movement, and (3) function is localized. Over the next few years David Ferrier (1843–1928) refined the stimulation technique and confirmed Fritsch and Hitzig's results in monkeys, dogs, cats, rabbits, guinea pigs, pigeons, fish, and frogs. Fritsch and Hitzig summarized the interpretation of their findings in the conclusion to their 1870 paper:

> Furthermore, it may be concluded from the sum of all our experiments that, contrary to the opinions of Flourens and most investigators who followed him, the soul in no case represents a sort of total function of the whole cerebrum, the expression of which might be destroyed by mechanical means in toto, but not in its individual parts. Individual psychological functions, and probably all of them, depend for their entrance into matter or for their formation from it, upon circumscribed centers of the cerebral cortex. (Fritsch and Hitzig, 1960)

Although Fritsch and Hitzig may have stimulated the cortex of wounded soldiers, the first experiment in which electrical stimulation on the cortex of a human was formally reported was performed by R. Bartholow (1831–1904) in Cincinnati, in 1874. Mary Rafferty, a patient in his care, had a cranial defect that exposed the posterior part of each cerebral hemisphere. The following is an extract from his report of that experiment:

> Observation 3. *To test faradic reaction of the posterior lobes.* Passed an insulated needle into the left posterior lobe so that the non-insulated portion rested entirely in the substance of the brain. The other insulated needle was placed in contact with the dura mater, within one-fourth of an inch of the first. When the circuit was closed, muscular contraction in the right upper and lower extremities ensued, as in the preceding observations. Faint but visible contraction of the left orbicularis palpebrarum [eyelid], and dilation of the pupils, also ensued. Mary complained of a very strong and unpleasant feeling of tingling in both right extremities, especially in the right arm, which she seized with the opposite hand and rubbed vigorously. Notwithstanding the very evident pain from which she suffered, she smiled as if much amused. (Bartholow, 1874)

Bartholow's work was not met with acclaim. In fact its publication caused such an outcry that he was forced to leave Cincinnati. Also, it is unlikely that he had stimulated the cortex, because in his account his electrodes were inserted about an inch into the brain tissue. Nevertheless, he had demonstrated that the electrical stimulation technique could be used on people; that is, the technique could be used with a conscious person, who could report the subjective sensations produced by stimulation. (The pain that Mary was reported to have suffered was not caused by stimulation of pain receptors in the brain — since there are none — but was probably a genuinely evoked sensation from brain stimulation.) It was not long before electrical stimulation was being used on humans in other experimental situations. And, of course, from there it has evolved into a standard part of many brain surgery procedures.

The Antilocalization Position of Goltz

In his extremely vigorous history of this period, Henry Head labeled Wernicke and others of his school the "diagram makers." This somewhat derogatory term was a reference to their oversimplification of the deficits that followed brain damage, as well as to their selection ("lop and twist," as he phrased it) of symptoms to fit their models. In fact, Head's criticisms were not unreasonable, because in the period preceding and following 1900 there was a proliferation of maps and diagrams showing the supposed location of all types of functions. Furthermore, Head argued, they persisted in concluding that because we have words for behaviors such as speech, eating, walking, and so forth, there must be one place in the brain that controlled each behavior. Head preferred to argue that there were many forms of speech, eating, and walking, each of which was probably controlled by many different parts of the brain. Rather than review the complexities of the work through this period, it is perhaps more instructive to look at the type of evidence brought forward in opposition to localization of function. The most instructive opposition came from Goltz's experiments with dogs.

When Fritsch and Hitzig made their historical discovery that stimulation of a restricted portion of the neocortex resulted in specific movements, they concluded that the cortex was "the place of entry of psychic functions into matter." The electrophysiological localization of Fritsch and Hitzig, Ferrier, and others led quite logically to the view that the cortex produced and controlled specific movements as well as other behaviors. The experiments performed by Friedrich L. Goltz (1834–1902) in 1892 were intended specifically to question this position. Goltz's methodology resembled Flourens' in that he was addressing the question of what would happen if the entire neocortex were removed from an animal. But unlike Flourens, he chose dogs with a well-developed neocortex and a repertory of easily observable mammalian behaviors. He took his animals throughout Europe and displayed them everywhere, and he even made sure that when they were sacrificed to confirm brain lesion extent, many of the important neurologists and physiologists of the day had a chance to examine the brains to ensure that the lesions were complete.

Goltz reasoned that if a portion of the neocortex had a function, then removal of the cortex should lead to a loss of that function. Goltz removed the neocortex, most of the basal ganglia, and parts of the midbrain from three dogs, which he then studied for 57 days, 92 days, and 18 months, respectively. The dog that survived for 18 months was studied in the greatest detail. It was more active than a normal dog, alternated periods of sleep and waking (though these were shorter than normal), and panted when warm and shivered when cold. It walked well on uneven ground and was able to catch its balance when it slipped. If placed in an abnormal posture, it corrected its position. After hurting a hind limb on one occasion it trotted on three legs, holding up the injured limb. It was able to orient to touches or pinches on its body and snap at the object that touched it, although its orientations were not very accurate. If offered two portions of food — the first a piece of meat soaked in milk, the second a piece of meat soaked in bitter quinine — it accepted the first and rejected the second. It responded to light and sounds, although its response thresholds were elevated.

Goltz interpreted his findings as indicating a general lowering of the will and intellect that was proportional to the size of the lesion. He argued that his findings did not support the localization-of-function hypothesis. With reference to experiments of his time, he stated that if stimulation of a particular portion of the brain were found to produce movement, and if the stimulated area were concluded to be a motor center, it followed that removal of this area should abolish movement. Goltz's experiments, however, elegantly demonstrated that cortical removal did not abolish movement. In fact, decortication did not appear to completely eliminate any function, though it seemed to reduce all functions to some extent. This demonstration appeared to be a strong argument against localization of function.

Hughlings-Jackson and Hierarchical Organization

Goltz's experiments should not be ignored, because they reiterated what had been said previously by Flourens and because arguments very much like them were to be made again through the first half of the 20th century, particularly by Lashley. The fundamental difference between Goltz and those whom his experiments were intended to criticize was to be resolved by the hierarchical concept of brain function proposed by the English neurologist John Hughlings-Jackson (1835 – 1911), who has been described as the founder of modern neurology. Hughlings-Jackson was extremely prolific, writing over 300 papers, but his work was often not given the attention it deserved, perhaps because he was more reflective and philosophical than is usually popular.

Hughlings-Jackson thought of the nervous system as being organized in a number of layers arranged in a functional hierarchy. Each successively higher level would control more complex aspects of behavior but do so through the lower levels. Often Hughlings-Jackson described the nervous system as having three levels: the spinal cord, the basal ganglia and motor cortex, and the frontal cortex. But equally often he designated no particular anatomical area for a nervous system level. He had adopted the theory of hierarchy from Herbert Spencer's argument that the brain evolved in a series of steps, each of which brought animals the capacity to engage in a constellation of new behaviors. But what Hughlings-Jackson did with the theory was particularly novel. He suggested that diseases or damage that affected the highest levels would produce **dissolution,** the reverse of evolution: the animals would still have a repertory of behaviors, but those behaviors would be simpler, more typical of an animal that had not yet evolved the missing brain structure.

If the logic of this argument is followed, it becomes apparent how the results from Goltz's experiments can be reconciled with those of his opponents. Goltz's dogs were "low-level" dogs: they were able to walk and to eat, but if food had not been presented to them — had they been required to walk in order to find food — they would have failed and starved. For them walking would not have served a useful biological function. Similarly, all the other behaviors of the dogs were low-level behaviors. For example, they could regulate their body temperature by shivering and panting, but had they been placed in a situation requiring them to perform a complex series of acts to leave a cold or warm area for a neutral thermal zone, they would have failed and so would not have been able to behaviorally thermoregulate as normal dogs do. It can be seen, therefore, that Hughlings-Jackson's concepts allowed the special role of the cortex in organizing purposeful behavior to be distinguished from the role of subcortical areas in supporting the more elementary components of behavior.

Hughlings-Jackson applied his concepts of hierarchical organization to many other areas of behavior, including language and aphasia. It was his view that every part of the brain is involved in language, with each part making some special contribution. The relevant question was not where language is localized but what unique contribution is made by each part of the cortex. Thus if, for example, the nondominant (the nonlanguage hemisphere) hemisphere is not involved in language but in spatial organization, then damage to that hemisphere would be revealed not just in spatial disabilities but also in language impoverishment because spatial concepts cannot be employed. With respect to this logic Hughlings-Jackson was particularly modern — so much so, in fact, that his ideas are receiving more serious consideration today then they did in his own time.

THE NEURON HYPOTHESIS

The second major influence on modern neuropsychology was the development of what has become known as the *neuron hypothesis:* the hypothesis that the nervous system is composed of discrete, autonomous cells, or units, that can interact but are not physically connected. The opposite position, known as the *nerve net hypothesis,* that the nervous system is composed of a continuous network of interconnected fibers, was held at one time. At the cellular level, support for the neuron theory depended on the solutions to three problems: (1) How does the nervous system conduct information? (2) How is it constructed? and (3) How is it itself interconnected and how is it interconnected with muscles? The first problem was solved by advances in physiology and physiological recording techniques, the second by advances in anatomy, and the third by advances in biochemistry and pharmacology.

Information Conduction

Early views of how the nervous system moves muscles involved some type of hydraulic theory requiring gas or liquid to flow through nerves into muscles. Such theories have been called *balloonist theories,* since movement was thought to be caused by the filling and emptying of muscles. Certainly Descartes espoused the balloonist hypothesis, for he argued that a fluid from the ventricles flowed through nerves into muscles to make them move (Figure 14-4). Francis Glisson in 1677 made a direct test of the balloon theory by immersing a man's arm in water and measuring the change in the water level when the muscles of the arm were contracted. Since the water level did not rise, Glisson concluded that no fluid entered the muscle.

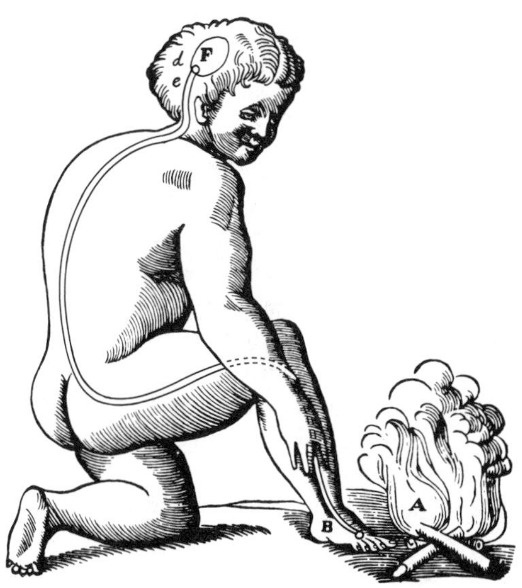

FIGURE 14-4. The concept of reflex originated with Descartes. In this example heat from the flame causes a thread in the nerve to be pulled, releasing ventricular fluid through an opened pore. The fluid flows through the nerve, causing not only the foot to withdraw but also the eyes and head to turn to look at it, the hands to advance, and the whole body to bend to protect it. His concept was stimulated by the mechanical principles of displays used in water gardens fashionable in France in his day. A visitor in the gardens would step on a plate that mechanically caused statues to hide, appear, or squirt water. In fact, his use of the reflex concept was for behaviors that would today be considered more than reflexive, whereas what is held as reflexive today was not conceived of by Descartes. (From R. Descartes, 1664.)

Swammerdam in Holland had reached the same conclusion from similar experiments on frogs, but his manuscript had lain unpublished for 100 years.

Isaac Newton may have been the first person to advance a theory of nerve function that approximates a modern view. In 1717, he suggested that nerves were not hollow tubes but solid. He then postulated that they worked by the vibration of an "elastic aether" that was propagated along their length. Albrech von Haller (1708–1777) seems to have developed the concept of nerve irritability; that is, when irritated by touch or chemicals, the nerves would make muscles move. Haller was aware that electricity was a candidate for the medium of nerve conduction, but he and others of his time, thinking of electrical conduction in a wire, believed that nerves lacked the insulation prerequisite for conduction.

The impetus to adopt a theory of electrical conduction came from Stephen Gray, who in 1731 attracted considerable attention by demonstrating that the human body could be electrified. In an ingenious demonstration he showed that static electricity from a rod could pass through the body: when a charged glass tube was brought close to the feet of a boy suspended by a rope, a grass-leaf electroscope (thin strip of conducting material) was attracted to the boy's nose. It was only much later, however, that Luigi Galvani (1737–1798) demonstrated that electrical stimulation of a frog's nerve could cause muscle contraction, and Friedrich Humboldt (1769–1859) confirmed that nerves contain intrinsic "animal" electricity. In 1859, F. Pfluger suggested that electricity does not flow along the nerve but sets up a wave motion within it. Finally, in 1886 J. Bernstein developed the theory that the membrane of a nerve is polarized, and that the action potential is a propogated depolarization of this membrane. Many of the details of ionic conduction were worked out during the past 30 years, and A. L. Hodgkin and A. F. Huxley received the Nobel Prize in physiology in 1963 for their pioneering efforts in this field.

As successive findings brought hydraulic models of conduction into disfavor and more dynamic electrical models into favor, hydraulic theories of *behavior* were also critically reassessed. For example, Freud's theory of behavior, involving the different levels id, ego, and superego, is very much a hydraulic model (e.g., how much of each is there). Although conceptually useful for a time, it had no impact on concepts of brain function, because almost as soon as the theory was proposed it became clear that the brain does not function as a hydraulic system.

Nervous System Structure

Early views of the nervous system showed little concern for its structure, probably because to superficial examination it resembled little more than jelly. There was a general awareness that nerves led to muscles, and it was widely believed that the nerves were hollow, fluid-containing tubes. One of the first cellular anatomists, Anton van Leeuwenhoek (1632–1723), examined nerves with a primitive microscope but was unable to find hollow tubes. By 1717, he had described what may have been a nerve fiber surrounded by myelin. Van Leeuwenhoek also described what he called "globules," but it is doubtful that these were cell bodies. They may have been either blobs of fat or optical aberrations (artifacts) produced by the crude microscopes of the day. From van Leeuwenhoek's time until the 1830s, when the achromatic microscope was developed to eliminate color distortions, the frequency of artifacts aroused a general distrust of microscope results. However, in 1781, Felice Fontana did succeed in describing the nerve fiber. Then, in 1833, using the achromatic microscope, Christian G. Ehrenberg described nerve cells in the brain; in 1836, Gabriel G. Valentin described the cell body, nucleus, and nucleolus; and in 1838, Robert Remak distinguished myelinated from nonmyelinated fibers and suggested that fibers connect to cell bodies. From these findings and others Theodor Schwann in 1839 enunciated the cell theory; that is, that cells are the basic structural unit of the nervous system. It was not until 1849, however, that Rudolf A. van Koelliker had definitely established that nerve fibers are linked to the cell body.

Understanding of cell structure was advanced chiefly by improvements in technology. The earliest anatomists who tried to examine the substructure of the nervous system were faced with a gelatinous white substance. In 1809, Johann C. Reil developed the technique of fixing and hardening tissue by placing it in alcohol to remove fluid from the plasma. A more effective fixer, chromic acid, was found by Adolph Hannover in 1840. The formaldehyde technique, the preferred modern fixative procedure, was discovered in 1893 by Ferdinand Blum. In the 1830s, Luigi Rolando devised techniques for cutting thin sections of tissue, and in 1842, Benedikt Stilling discovered that the tissue could be cut into extremely thin sections if it was first frozen. The technique of freezing permitted serial reconstruction of fibers and of cellular tissue components and also permitted a more effective use of stains.

The most exciting development in neuroanatomy was the technique of staining, which allows different portions of the nervous system to be visualized. In 1858, Joseph von Gerlach devised the carmine stain, which turns cells and their processes red; in 1882, Carl Weigert developed a technique for staining myelin; and, in 1894, Franz Nissl developed the methylene blue technique (Nissl stain), which stains cells bodies but not fibers, revealing many of their internal structures. The most amazing cell stain was developed by Camillo Golgi in 1875. Impregnating tissue with silver nitrate, Golgi found that a few cells would take up the stain, and that each of these cells in its entirety —cell body, dendrites, and axons—became encrusted with reduced silver. Thus, finally the entire neuron and all its processes could be visualized at one time.

As cells were visualized with microscopes it became clear that, far from resembling a bowl of jelly, the brain has an enormously intricate substructure with components arranged in complex clusters, each of which is interconnected with many others. Psychologists who were separating behavior into parts by faculties could only have been encouraged by the details of the brain revealed by the anatomists. There was a genuine theoreticians' banquet on hand, and for every conceivable behavioral trait there was a newly discovered nucleus or pathway begging to be attached. The feast may have been too rich, for the clear message from anatomists to psychologists was that things were probably more complex than they appeared to be. This may have been why for the first half of this century many psychologists turned away from the brain and not toward it for enlightenment.

Nervous System Connections

Was the brain a net of physically interconnected fibers, or a collection of discrete units? If it were an interconnected net, then it would follow that changes in one part would, by diffusion, produce changes in every other part. Since it would be difficult for a structure thus organized to localize function, a netlike structure would favor a holistic, or gestalt, type of brain function and psychology. Alternatively, a structure of discrete units would favor psychology based on localization of function, since—at least theoretically—each unit could function autonomously.

The concept of a nerve net originated in 1855 with Franz von Leydig, who observed and described numerous interlacing fibrils in the nervous system of a spider. Later J. von Gerlach (1820–1896), while studying dendrites in vertebrates, found what he considered a similar network. In 1883, Golgi dismissed Gerlach's hypothesis of an interlinking network of dendrites, suggesting instead that axons were interconnected, forming an axonic net. A number of anatomists opposed Golgi's idea; the most definitive work in opposition was done by Santiago Ramón y Cajal (1852–1934), using Golgi's own silver staining technique. In 1891, summarizing Cajal's work on nerve cells, Wilhelm Waldeyer coined the term *neuron* (from the Greek for nerve) and popularized the *neuron hypothesis,* which states that neurons are not physically connected through their axons. Golgi and Cajal jointly received the Nobel Prize in 1906; each in his acceptance speech argued his position on the neuron hypothesis, Golgi supporting the nerve net and Cajal supporting the position now considered to be correct, the neuron hypothesis.

Largely because of the development of the electron microscope, more recent work in the early part of the 20th century fully supports the neuron hypothesis. It is accepted that axons have terminal knobs on their ends, and that cells are separated by gaps, which are bridged by chemical messengers. (It is a nice historical irony that something like the idea that a fluid passes from the end of a nerve to activate a muscle turns out to be true.) It has been repeatedly demonstrated that neurons have a certain autonomy of function; thus, localization of function could be argued at the level of the cell. On this principle Hebb, in 1949, brilliantly advanced an associative learning theory by proposing that individual cells could, by being activated at the same time, come to form cell assemblies (a semimininerve net, so to speak) that form the structure in which memory is housed.

In conclusion, many of the constituent concepts of the neuron hypothesis were formulated at roughly the same time as the developments in behavioral theory we reviewed earlier, and they did so almost in parallel, seemingly without influencing how people thought behavior was produced. But the influence was there: knowing that the nervous system is composed of a uniform substance allowed it to be viewed as a single organ, knowing that it is electrically active led to experiments in which it was stimulated, knowing that some parts of the nervous system are composed of cell bodies and other parts of fibers permitted speculation about the relative effects of cell damage versus fiber damage, and being able to see subtle differences in cell structure under a microscope permitted the development of cytoarchitectonic maps that are strikingly similar and that gave support to functional maps constructed from lesion studies. Thus, although it may seem that behavior was effectively studied in ignorance of the brain's fine structure, actually it was not—and it is unlikely that it will be in the future. In fact, the discovery that cells are organized in neurochemical systems may now be the predominant influence on how we think about behavior. In our view, although the influence of cell study on psychological theory has perhaps lagged somewhat, it is likely that the neuron hypothesis is catching up and may soon begin to shape psychological theory.

THE DEVELOPMENT OF MODERN NEUROPSYCHOLOGY

Given the 19th-century developments in knowledge about brain structure and function — the brain and neuron hypotheses, the concept of the special nature of cortical function, the concepts of localization of function and of disconnection — it seems surprising that psychologists did not become more interested in the brain earlier. Why did the science of neuropsychology not develop by 1900 rather than by 1949, when we first dated the use of the term? There are several possible reasons for the latency. One factor was that in the 1920s neurologists, such as Henry Head, rejected the classical approach of Broca, Wernicke, and others, arguing that their attempts to correlate behavior and anatomical site represented approaches little better than those of the phrenologists. This criticism was partly reasonable at the time, since some people, such as K. Kleist, had attempted to correlate every aspect of behavior and language with a particular anatomical location. A second reason for neuropsychology's slow coming of age was the intervention of two world wars, which disrupted the development of science in many countries. A third reason may have been that psychologists, who traced their origins to philosophy rather than to biology, were not interested in physiological and anatomical approaches, directing their attention instead to behaviorism, psychophysics, and the psychoanalytical movement.

A number of modern developments have made a contribution to the growth of neuropsychology as an identifiable discipline in the neurosciences. These deserve some mention and include (1) neurosurgery; (2) **psychometrics** — the method of measuring human abilities — and statistical analysis; and (3) technological advances.

Neurosurgery

Penfield and Jasper have provided a brief but informative history of neurosurgery. Clearly, brain surgery was performed by prehistoric peoples, because skulls that had been subject to surgery (the skulls show postsurgical healing) have been obtained from the Neolithic period in Europe and from the early Incas in Peru. It is likely that these early peoples found surgery to have a beneficial effect for some types of brain problems. Later, Hippocrates gave written directions for trephining (cutting a circular hole in the skull) on the side of the head opposite to the site of a local convulsion as a means of therapeutic intervention. During the period between the 13th and 19th centuries there were a number of attempts, some quite successful, to relieve various symptoms with surgery. The modern era began once antisepsis, anesthesia, and the principle of localization of function were developed. In the 1880s, a number of surgeons reported the success of operations for the treatment of abscesses, tumors, and epilepsy-producing scars. Subsequently, the Horsley-Clarke "stereotaxic device" was developed for holding the head in a fixed position, local anesthetic procedures were developed so that the patient could contribute to the success of surgery by responding to the effects of localized brain stimulation, and devices such as the EEG and pneumoencephalographs were developed to locate the area of brain malfunction more precisely before surgery began. The value of the idea of localization of function cannot be underestimated in this account. The first surgeons used signs of trauma on the skull as a means of localizing brain damage, but once it was realized that a variety of behavioral symptoms could be used to better localize damage, the surgeon had a far clearer idea where to make the surgical penetration.

The development of neurosurgery as a practical solution to some types of brain abnormality has had a profoundly positive influence on neuropsychology. In animal research the ablation technique was developed to the point that it became one of the most important sources of information about brain-behavior relations. Yet in human research, most information came from patients with relatively poorly defined lesions; strokes produced damage that included subcortical structures as well as the cortex, and brain trauma produced lesions that were diffuse, irregular, or incomplete. Furthermore, patients lived for years after injury and histological localization was thus impossible. Neurosurgery provided a serendipitous solution to all these problems. Surgical removal of cortical tissue was often so localized that it equaled that produced in animal experiments. Since the surgeon drew a map of the lesion and sometimes even electrically stimulated the surrounding tissue, the location of the lesion was known in advance. The variation in surgical technique necessary to perform such things as focal lesions, hemispherectomies, and commisurectomies also allowed for refined analysis of the contributions of different brain areas to behavior. Information about behavior was obtained from patients with circumscribed lesions, and in turn became useful for diagnostic purposes in new patient populations.

Psychometrics and Statistical Evaluation

The first experiments on individual differences in psychological function were made by an astronomer, Friedrich Wilhelm Bessel in 1796. Bessel had become curious about the dismissal of an assistant at the Greenwich observatory near London for being one or so seconds slower than his superior in observing stars and setting clocks. Bessel began a study of reaction time and found quite large differences among people. Individual differences were very much a part of Gall and Spurzheim's phrenology, but unlike their idea of localization of function, this feature of their science attracted little interest among neuroscientists. Charles Darwin's English cousin, Francis Galton, maintained a laboratory in London in the 1880s where for three pennies he measured physical features, perceptions, and reaction time with the goal of finding individual differences that could explain why some people were superior to others. Galton's elegant innovation was to apply the statistical methods of Quetlet, a Belgian statistician, to his results and so rank his subjects on a frequency distribution. This innovation was essential for the development of modern psychological tests. It was fitting that Galton's work was directed to describing individual differences, since Darwin's evolutionary theory of natural selection required individual differences with which to work. Yet the measures that Galton selected were not those that permitted him to distinguish the characteristics of people who were eminent from those who were ordinary.

Modern test procedures for intelligence were developed by the French physician, biologist, and psychologist Alfred Binet for the purposes of solving a quite practical problem. Binet (1857–1911) experimented with a wide variety of measurements, including those of head size, facial features, and handwriting style, and found them to be inadequate for distinguishing mental differences. Then in 1904 the Minister of Public Instruction commissioned Binet to develop tests that could identify retarded children and so single them out for special instruction. In 1905, in collaboration with Théodore Simon, Binet produced what is now known as the 1905 Binet-Simon scale. The tests were derived empirically by administering questions to 50 normal 3- to 11-year-old children and some mentally retarded children and adults. The tests were designed to evaluate judgment, comprehension, and reason, which Binet thought were essential features of intelligence. The scale was revised in 1908, unsatisfactory tests were deleted, others were added, and the student population was increased to 300 children aged 3 to 13 years. From the tests a *mental level* was calculated, which was a score that 80 to 90% of normal children of a particular age attained on the test. In 1916, Lewis Terman in the United States produced the Stanford-Binet test, in which IQ—mental age divided by chronological age times 100—was first used. In 1940, D. O. Hebb gave IQ tests to brain-damaged people in Montreal, with the resultant surprising discovery that lesions in the frontal lobes—until then considered the center of highest intelligence—did not decrease IQ scores. This counterintuitive finding identified the utility of using such tests for assessing brain damage and effectively created a bond of common interest between neurology and psychology. Many of the clever innovations used for assessing brain function in various patient populations are strongly influenced by intelligence-testing methodology. Particularly notable is the fact that the tests are brief, easily and objectively scored, and are standardized using statistical procedures. Many neuropsychologists use features of IQ scores to assess regional brain contributions to IQ, whereas others use IQ only as a measure of general psychological function for the purposes of evaluating other test results. Although the concept of "mental testing" as it is used in many applications has been criticized a number of times, even harsh critics, such as Gould, feel that it has an appropriate use in neuropsychology. In fact, it is likely that mental tests will themselves be modified by advances in neuropsychology.

Advances in Technology

Because the advances that have been made in technology are so numerous, and because they are discussed elsewhere, they will not be detailed here. What should be remembered is the frequently echoed statement, "Methods give the results." This was Flourens' exclamation when he advocated the experimental method rather than Gall's anecdotal and confirmatory approach. It was also Fritsch and Hitzig's statement when they overthrew Flourens' dogma on the electrical excitability of the cortex. Progress in science includes advancements in theory and methodology but must also include improvements in technology. In fact, in response to the question of why methods papers are the most cited papers in science, one wag has declared that you cannot conduct an experiment with a theory. It has been only through technological advance that the internal structure of neurons could be visualized, their electrical activity recorded, and their biochemical activity analyzed and modified. It is only through technology that the processes of disease, degeneration, and regeneration in the nervous system can be understood. In fact, it is often the case that the methodology and the results are so intimately linked that they cannot be dissociated. For this reason, technological advances provide new opportunities to review old and well-established ideas, and it is the reason that old and well-established ideas should be thrown into the mill of technological innovation for confirmation.

SUMMARY

This chapter traced the advance of our understanding that the brain is the organ of the mind and that the cell is the material from which the brain is constructed. It was not enough to speculate that it is so, as some of the ancients were correctly able to do, it was necessary to support the hypothesis with fact. The thrust and parry of this endeavor not only provided the history, they give definition to the present science of neuropsychology. To have met Flourens is to have been introduced to issues of recovery of function; to have met Wernicke and Dejerine is to have been introduced to disconnection theory; to have met Liepmann is to have been introduced to an origin of hypotheses on the neural organization of movement; to have met Gall and Dax and Broca is to have been introduced to the puzzle of asymmetry of function; and to have met van Leeuwenhoek is to have received an introduction to advances that will come from the principles underlying modern anatomy. Still, the hypotheses that have flowered in this history are sufficiently broad and vague that they will require generations of careful examination before they can be sketched in colors that reflect their truth. We leave the reader with the advice that to know history is to be able to replicate it, to advance it, and perhaps to confound sphinxes with it.

REFERENCES

Bartholow, R. Experimental investigation into the functions of the human brain. *American Journal of Medical Sciences* 67:305–313, 1874.

Beach, F. A., D. O. Hebb, C. T. Morgan, and H. W. Nissen. *The Neuropsychology of Lashley.* New York, Toronto, and London: McGraw-Hill, 1960.

Benton, A. L. Contributions to aphasia before Broca. *Cortex* 1:314–327, 1964.

Brazier, M. A. B. The historical development of neurophysiology. In J. Field, H. W. Magoun, and V. E. Hall, eds. *Handbook of Physiology,* vol. 1. Washington, D. C.: American Physiological Society, 1959.

Bruce, D. On the origin of the term "Neuropsychology." *Neuropsychologia* 23:813–814, 1985.

Broca, P. Sur le siege de la faculté du langage articule. *Bulletin of the Society of Anthropology* 6:377–396, 1865.

Broca, P. Remarks on the seat of the faculty of articulate language, followed by an observation of aphemia. In G. von Bonin, ed. *The Cerebral Cortex.* Springfield, IL: Charles C. Thomas, 1960.

Clark, E., and C. D. O'Malley. *The Human Brain and Spinal Cord.* Berkeley and Los Angeles: University of California Press, 1968.

Descartes, R. *Traité de l'Homme.* Paris: Angot, 1664.

Eccles, J. C. *The Neurophysiological Basis of Mind: The Principles of Neurophysiology.* Oxford: Clarendon Press, 1956.

Finger, S., and D. G. Stein. *Brain Damage and Recovery.* New York: Academic Press, 1982.

Flourens, P. Investigations of the properties and the functions of the various parts which compose the cerebral mass. In G. von Bonin, ed. *The Cerebral Cortex.* Springfield, IL: Charles C. Thomas, 1960.

Fritsch, G., and E. Hitzig. On the electrical excitability of the cerebrum. In G. von Bonin, ed. *The Cerebral Cortex.* Springfield, IL: Charles C. Thomas, 1960.

Geschwind, N. *Selected Papers on Language and Brain.* Dordrecht, Holland; and Boston: D. Reidel Publishing Co., 1974.

Goltz, F. On the functions of the hemispheres. In G. von Bonin, ed. *The Cerebral Cortex.* Springfield, IL: Charles C. Thomas, 1960.

Gould, S. J. *The Mismeasure of Man.* New York: Norton, 1981.

Head, H. *Aphasia and Kindred Disorders of Speech.* London: Cambridge University Press, 1926.

Hebb, D. O. *The Organization of Behavior: A Neuropsychological Theory.* New York: Wiley, 1949.

Hebb, D. O., and W. Penfield. Human behavior after extensive bilateral removals from the frontal lobes. *Archives of Neurology and Psychiatry.* 44:421–438, 1940.

Hughlings-Jackson, J. *Selected Writings of John Hughlings-Jackson,* Taylor, J., ed. vols. 1 and 2. London: Hodder, 1931.

Joynt, R. Paul Pierre Broca: His contribution to the knowledge of aphasia. *Cortex* 1:206–213, 1964.

Kluver, H. *Behavior Mechanisms in Monkeys.* Chicago: The University of Chicago Press, 1933, 1957.

Krech, D. Cortical localization of function. In L. Postman, ed. *Psychology in the Making.* New York: Knopf, 1962.

Lenneberg, E. H. *Biological Foundations of Language.* New York: Wiley, 1967.

Luciani, L. *Human Physiology.* London: Macmillan, 1915.

Luria, A. R. *The Working Brain.* New York: Penguin, 1973.

Olin, C. H. *Phrenology.* Philadelphia: Penn Publishing Co., 1910.

Penfield, W., and H. Jasper. *Epilepsy and the Functional Anatomy of the Human Brain.* Boston: Little, Brown, 1954.

Pribram, K. H. *Languages of the Brain.* Englewood Cliffs, NJ: Prentice-Hall, 1971.

Rothschuk, K. E. *History of Physiology.* Huntington, NY: Robert E. Krieger, 1973.

Stookey, B. A note on the early history of cerebral localization. *Bulletin of the New York Academy of Medicine* 30:559–578, 1954.

Wernicke, C. *Der Aphasische Symptomenkomplex.* Breslau, Poland: M. Cohn and Weigert, 1874.

Young, R. M. *Mind, Brain and Adaption in the Nineteenth Century.* Oxford: Clarendon Press, 1970.

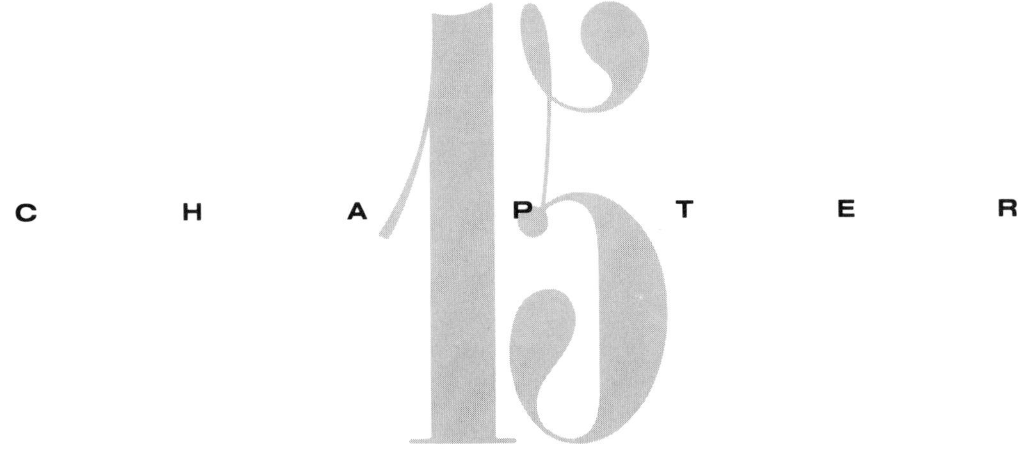

CHAPTER 15

PRINCIPLES OF CEREBRAL ASYMMETRY

It is over 100 years since Marc Dax and Paul Broca discovered that damage to the left hemisphere produced an inability to talk, but that damage to the right hemisphere did not affect speech. Since then it has been generally accepted that the left hemisphere plays a special role in language, not shared by the right hemisphere. But language is not the only special function of the left hemisphere; at the beginning of this century Liepmann compared the movements of patients with lesions of either the left or the right hemisphere and demonstrated that the left hemisphere has a role in controlling movement that is not shared by the right. The special functions of the right hemisphere remained a mystery until comparatively recently, when the work of Zangwill, Hécaen, Milner, and others showed that it is more involved than the left in the analysis of the visuospatial dimensions of the world.

Although these findings superficially appear to simplify the problem of understanding lateralization, the problem is complicated by the following three variables:

1. **Laterality** of function can be affected by environmental factors as well as genetically determined factors, such as gender and handedness; the cerebral organization of some left-handers and females appears to have less functional asymmetry than that in right-handers and males.

2. Laterality is relative, not absolute because both hemispheres play a role in nearly every behavior; thus, although the left hemisphere is especially important for the production of language, the right hemisphere also has some language capabilities.

3. Whereas a functionally asymmetrical brain was once believed to be a uniquely human characteristic — one that suggested a straightfor-

ward relation between asymmetry and language —this idea has proved to be incorrect. There is evidence that certain songbirds, rats, cats, monkeys, and apes have a functionally and anatomically asymmetrical brain.

This chapter addresses the basic principles of cerebral asymmetry; the next chapter examines the factors that produce variations in the "basic pattern" of cerebral asymmetry. The answers to most questions about the nature of cerebral asymmetry are as yet incomplete, but our tentative answers take into account information about the brain's anatomical and functional asymmetry, the relation of hand preference and gender to asymmetry, the influence of culture and education on asymmetry, the nature of lateralized functions, and finally the incidence of asymmetry in nonhumans.

ANATOMICAL ASYMMETRY IN THE HUMAN BRAIN

According to Hughlings-Jackson, Gratiolet first observed in the 1860s that the convolutions on the left hemisphere mature more rapidly than those on the right. Anatomical asymmetry was described again later in the 19th century by a number of authors, but these observations were largely ignored until the 1960s, when von Bonin reviewed the earlier literature and Geschwind and Levitsky described significant anatomical asymmetry in a large series of human brains. The latter authors reported that the **planum temporale,** which is the cortical area just posterior to the auditory cortex (Heschl's gyrus) with the **Sylvian fissure,** was larger on the left in 65% of the brains studied. On the average, the planum temporale in the left hemisphere was nearly 1 cm longer than in the right (see Figure 15-1*B* and Table 15-1). This report generated renewed interest in anatomical asymmetries in humans and other animals, and it put to rest the notion that the two hemispheres are structurally identical.

Many anatomical differences between the two hemispheres of the brain have now been reported. The eight major differences can be summarized as follows:

1. The right hemisphere is slightly larger and heavier than the left, but the specific gravity of the left hemisphere exceeds that of the right. Von Bonin suggested that these differences may indicate that there is actually more gray matter in the left than in the right hemisphere, a proposal that has been confirmed by Gur and his colleagues.

2. There is a marked asymmetry in the structure of the temporal lobes. Geschwind and Levitsky's finding that the planum temporale is larger on the left has now been replicated by numerous other investigators, although the percentage of cases having a larger planum temporale on the left varies from 65 to 90% in different samples. In contrast, the primary auditory cortex of Heschl's gyrus is larger on the right, as there are usually two Heschl's gyri on the right and only one on the left (see Figure 15-1*B*). Thus, there is a complementary asymmetry in the temporal lobes, an asymmetry that may provide an anatomical basis for the functional dissociation of the temporal lobes in language and in musical functions, respectively. This complementary specialization of the hemispheres may be present very early in cerebral development, as the anatomical asymmetries are present as soon as the temporal gyri are recognizable, normally during the last trimester of fetal life.

3. The asymmetry in the cortex of the temporal lobes is correlated with a corresponding asymmetry in the thalamus. Thus, Eidelberg and Galaburda found that the lateral posterior nucleus, which projects to the parietal cortex just caudal to the planum temporale, is larger on the left; whereas the medial geniculate nucleus, which projects to the primary auditory cortex, is larger on the right. This anatomical asymmetry complements an

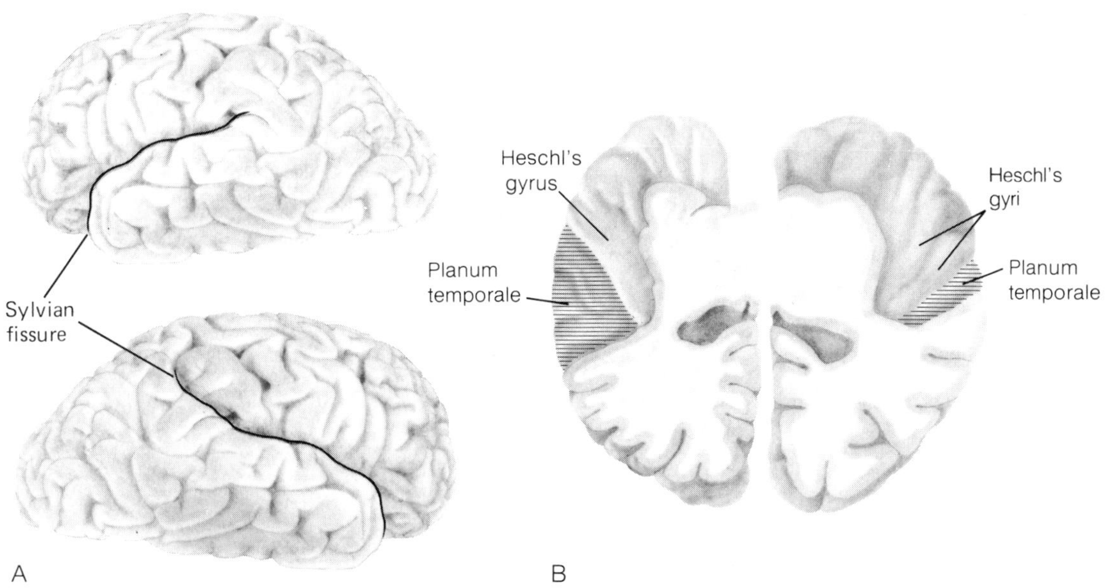

Figure 15-1. Anatomical differences between the two hemispheres are visible in the temporal lobes. *A*. The Sylvian fissure on the left (top) has a gentler slope than the fissure on the right. *B*. A knife has been moved along the Sylvian fissure of each hemisphere and through the brain, cutting away the top portion. The planum temporale (darkened area) is larger on the left than on the right. (*B* after Geschwind, 1972.)

apparent functional asymmetry in the thalamus, the left thalamus being dominant for language functions.

4. The slope of the Sylvian fissure is different in the two sides of the brain, being gentler on the left than on the right (see Figure 15-1*A*). This difference can be seen by gross inspection of the brain as well as from angiograms, since the middle cerebral artery follows the course of the Sylvian fissure. The region of the temporal-parietal cortex lying ventral to the Sylvian fissure therefore appears larger on the right. We shall see that this enlarged region has a specialized role in integrating the spatial characteristics of sensory stimuli.

5. The **frontal operculum** (Broca's area) is organized differently on the left and right. The area visible on the surface of the brain is about one-third larger on the right than on the left, whereas the area of cortex buried in the sulci of the region is greater on the left than the right. This asymmetry probably reflects the functional dissociation of the regions, the left side being involved in producing language and the right one possibly influencing tone of voice (see Chapter 22).

6. The distribution of various neurotransmitters is asymmetrical, in both the cortical and subcortical regions. The particular asymmetries in the distribution of acetylcholine, GABA, norepinephrine, and dopamine are dependent on the structure under consideration. (See Falzi et al., Glick et al., and Oke et al.)

7. The right hemisphere extends farther anteriorly than the left, the left hemisphere extends farther posteriorly than the right, and the **occipital horns** of the lateral ventricles are five times more likely to be longer on the right than on the left.

TABLE 15-1. Summary of studies demonstrating anatomical asymmetry

Measure	Basic reference
Asymmetries favoring the left hemisphere	
Greater specific gravity	Von Bonin, 1962
Longer Sylvian fissure	Eberstaller, 1884; LeMay and Culebras, 1972; Heschl, 1878
Larger insula	Kodama, 1934
Doubling of cingulate gyrus	Eberstaller, 1884
Relatively more gray matter	Von Bonin, 1962; Gur et al., 1980
Larger planum temporale	Geschwind and Levitsky, 1968; Galaburda et al, 1978; Teszner et al., 1972; Witelson and Pallie, 1973; Wada et al., 1975; Rubens et al., 1976; Kopp et al., 1977
Larger lateral posterior nucleus	Eidelberg and Galaburda, 1982
Larger inferior parietal lobule	LeMay and Culebras, 1972
Larger area Tpt of temporoparietal cortex	Galaburda and Sanides, 1980
Wider occipital lobe	LeMay, 1977
Longer occipital horn of lateral ventricles	McRae et al., 1968; Strauss and Fitz, 1980
Larger total area of frontal operculum	Falzi et al., 1982
Asymmetries favoring the right hemisphere	
Heavier	Broca, 1865; Crichton-Browne, 1880
Longer internal skull size	Hoadley and Pearson, 1929
Doubling of Heschl's gyrus	von Economo and Horn, 1930; Chi et al., 1977
Larger medial geniculate nucleus	Eidelberg and Galaburda, 1982
Larger area of convexity of frontal operculum	Wada et al., 1975
Wider frontal lobe	LeMay, 1977

These asymmetries presumably reflect some as yet unspecified gross difference in cerebral organization.

8. The details of anatomical asymmetry are affected both by sex and handedness, as we shall see in the next chapter.

Because these anatomical asymmetries of the left hemisphere center primarily on the language areas, it is tempting to speculate that they evolved to subserve the production of language. Moreover, the presence of these asymmetries in preterm infants might be taken as support for the proposition that humans have an innate predisposition for language. It should be noted, however, that the brains of australopithecines share many of these asymmetries, but they did not have a vocal apparatus that would allow language as we conceive of it. Furthermore, some asymmetries, such as a heavier and larger right hemisphere, as well as a longer Sylvian fissure, can also be seen in many nonhuman species. Finally, we caution that undue emphasis has been placed on finding anatomical asymmetries that can be associated with language. Enlarged areas in the left hemisphere must be balanced by smaller areas elsewhere on the same side or larger areas in other lobes on the contralateral hemisphere.

The emphasis upon the demonstration of gross morphological asymmetries in the human brain is a natural starting point in comparing the two hemispheres but we must remember that the activities of the brain are carried out by neurons. It is reasonable, therefore, to ask if the structure of neurons might differ on the two sides of the brain. Identification of structural differences in the neurons in any two areas of the brain is a formidable

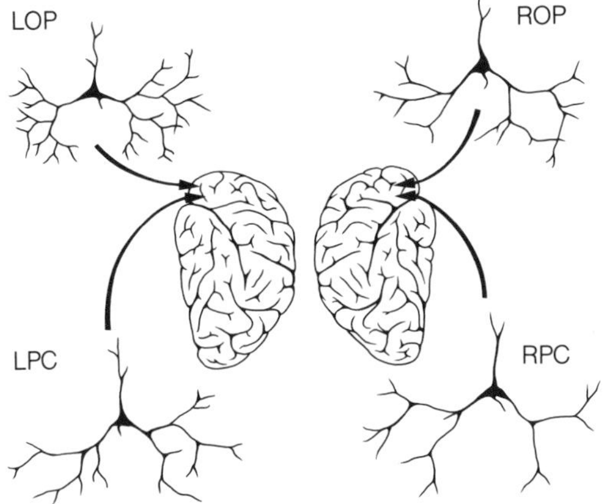

Figure 15-2. Schematic drawing emphasizing differences among the dendritic trees in the four areas: left triangularis-opercularis (LOP), right triangularis-opercularis (ROP), left precentral (LPC), and right precentral (RPC). (From Scheibel et al., 1985.)

task in view of the sheer number of neurons. Nonetheless, Scheibel and his colleagues recently have compared the dendritic fields of pyramidal cells in Broca's area (Figure 15-2:LOP) with those in the facial area of the motor cortex of the left hemisphere (LPC), and with homologous regions in the right hemisphere (ROP and RPC). Their results show that the neurons in each of these regions have a distinct pattern of branching. It can be seen that there are far more branches in cells in Broca's area than in the other areas. The degree or pattern of branching is important because each branch represents a potential location of enhancement or suppression of the graded potentials in the dendritic tree. Thus, more branch points allows more degrees of freedom with respect to the final activity of the cell. We must caution that Scheibel's data are from a small sample of brains ($n = 6$), but it is curious that five of the six brains were similar to the pattern in Figure 15-2. These five brains were from right-handers; the abberant brain was from a non-right-hander!

ASYMMETRY IN NEUROLOGICAL PATIENTS

Cerebral asymmetry was first established by studying patients with neurological disease that was lateralized to one hemisphere. The improvement in neurosurgical treatment for neurological disorders, especially epilepsy, has provided a large source of subsequently healthy subjects who are normally very willing to participate in neuropsychological studies. Thus, a good deal is now known from these patients about both the lateralization and the localization of functions in the cerebral cortex, and it is information from these patients that forms the basis for a large part of the remainder of this book. In this section we consider the evidence demonstrating lateralization of function in these patients, emphasizing the study of patients with lateralized lesions and those undergoing commissurotomy, as well as of those who had one hemisphere anesthetized with intracarotid injections of sodium Amytal.

Patients with Lateralized Lesions

The oldest method of studying hemispheric specialization has been to study the effects of circumscribed unilateral lesions that occur as a result of strokes, surgery, and so forth, and to infer the function of the area from behavioral deficits. However, in order to conclude that the area has a special or lateralized function, it is also necessary to show that lesions in other areas of the brain do not produce a similar deficit. The method that has proved strongest for demonstrating lateralization of function is one that Teuber calls **double dissociation,** an inferential technique premised on the following observations. It has been consistently demonstrated that lesions in the left hemisphere of right-handed patients can produce deficits in language functions (speech, writing, and reading) that do not follow lesions of the right hemisphere. Thus, the functions of the two hemispheres can be said to be dissociated. On the other hand, anecdotal and experimental evidence suggests that performance of spatial tasks, singing, playing musical instruments, and discriminating tonal patterns is more disrupted by right hemisphere than by left hemisphere lesions. Since right hemisphere lesions disturb tasks not disrupted by left hemisphere lesions and vice versa, the two hemispheres can be said to be doubly dissociated. A similar logic is used for localizing functions within a hemisphere. That is, behavioral tests that are especially sensitive to damage to a specific locus and not to others can be used to localize functions within a hemisphere, as illustrated in Table 15-2. Two hypothetical neocortical regions, 102 and 107, are doubly dissociated on tests of reading and writing: damage to area 102 disturbs reading, whereas damage to area 107 impairs writing. In principle, this logic can be extended to functionally dissociate additional areas concurrently by triple dissociation, quadruple dissociation, and so on.

To illustrate the nature of lateralized functions in neurological cases, we contrast two patients from the Montreal Neurological Hospital, neither of whom was aphasic at the time of assessment (see Figure 15-3). The first patient, P. G., was a 31-year-old man who had developed seizures over the course of six years prior to his surgery. At the time of his admission to the hospital his seizures were poorly controlled by medication, and subsequent neurological investigations revealed a large lesion, which turned out to be a glioma, in the anterior part of the left temporal lobe. Preoperative psychological tests showed this man to be of superior intelligence, with the only significant deficits being on tests of verbal memory. Two weeks following surgery, psychological testing showed a general decrease in intelligence ratings and a further decrease in the verbal memory scores. Performance on other tests, including tests of recall of the Rey-Osterith figure (see Figure 11-3*C*) were normal. The second patient, S. K., had an astrocytoma removed from the right temporal lobe. In contrast to the results from P. G., preoperative testing of S. K. showed a low score on the recall of the Rey-Osterith figure (see Figure 15-3*B*). Two weeks after surgery, repeat testing showed a marked decrease of the performance IQ rating and a decline of the nonverbal memory score, both on simple designs and on an alternative form of the Rey-Osterith figure. Comparison of these two patients provides a clear example of double dissociation: the patient with removal of the left temporal lobe was impaired only on verbal tests, whereas the patient with removal of the right temporal lobe was impaired only on nonverbal tests. Furthermore, both patients performed normally on many tests, providing evidence for localization, as well as lateralization, of function.

TABLE 15-2. Hypothetical example of a double-dissociation behavioral test

Neocortical lesion site	Reading	Writing
102	Impaired	Normal
107	Normal	Impaired

Patients with Commissurotomy

Epileptic seizures may begin in a restricted region of one hemisphere and then spread via the fibers of the corpus callosum to the homologous location in the opposite hemisphere. To prevent the spread of the seizure when medication has failed to impose control, the procedure of cutting the 200 million nerve fibers of the corpus callosum was performed in the early 1940s by William Van Wagnen, an American neurosurgeon. The procedure initially appeared to be too variable in its therapeutic outcome and was subsequently abandoned until the 1960s, when research by Myers and by Sperry with nonhuman species led to a reconsideration of the procedure. Two California surgeons, Joe Bogen and Philip Vogel, performed complete sections of the corpus callosum and of a smaller commissure known as the **anterior commissure** in a new series of about two dozen patients suffering from

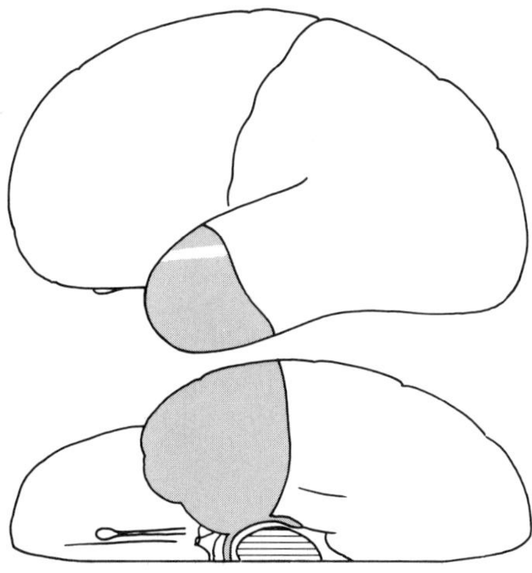

	Preop.	Postop.
Full scale IQ	123	109
Verbal IQ	122	103
Performance IQ	121	114
Memory quotient	96[a]	73[a]
Verbal recall	7.0[a]	2.0[a]
Nonverbal recall	10.5	10.5
Card sorting	6 categories	6 categories
Drawings: Copy	34/36	34/36
Recall	22.5/36	23.5/36

[a]Significantly low score.

A Left temporal lobectomy

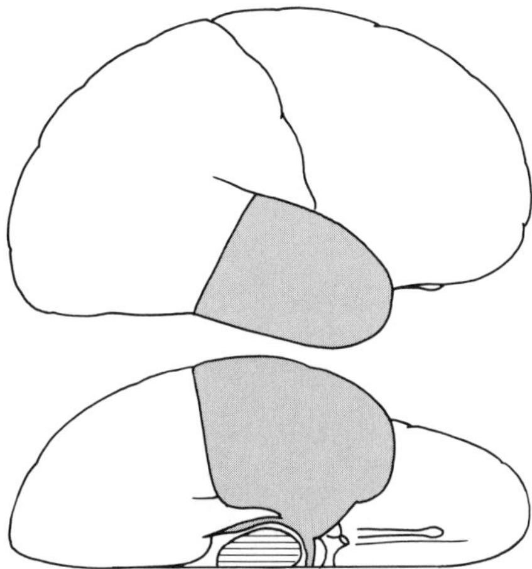

	Preop.	Postop.
Full scale IQ	114	103
Verbal IQ	115	115
Performance IQ	110	89[a]
Memory quotient	121	101
Verbal recall	16.0	12.0
Nonverbal recall	7.5	5.5[a]
Card sorting	3 categories	3 categories
Drawings: Copy	31/36	28/36[a]
Recall	11/36[a]	13/36[a]

[a]Significantly low score.

B Right temporal lobectomy

Figure 15-3. A comparison of psychological test results for a patient with a left temporal lobectomy (*A*) and a patient with a right temporal lobectomy (*B*) at the Montreal Neurological Hospital. The region removed is represented by the darkened zone, estimated by the surgeon at the time of operation. (Modified from Taylor, 1969.)

intractable epilepsy. The procedure was medically beneficial, leaving some patients virtually seizure-free afterward, with only rather minimal effects on their everyday behavior. More extensive psychological testing by Roger Sperry and his colleagues soon demonstrated, however, that these patients have a unique behavioral syndrome: a syndrome that has provided new insights into the nature of cerebral asymmetry.

Figure 15-4 illustrates the effect of commissur-

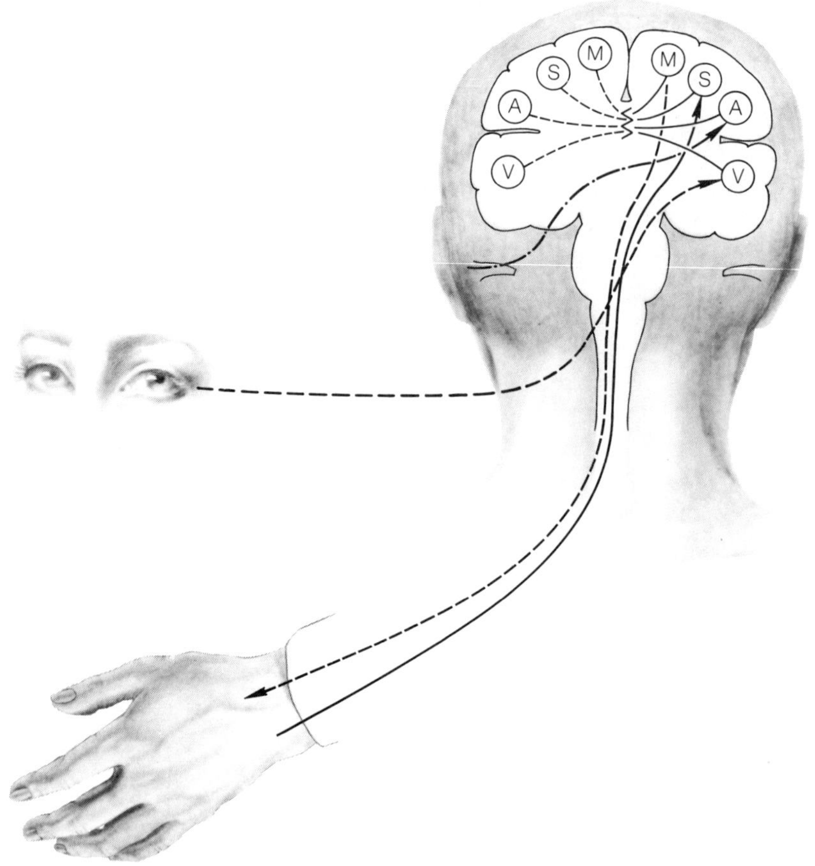

Figure 15-4. The effect of commissurotomy on connections between the hemispheres and to the sensory and motor systems. Note that although the connections between the visual (V), auditory (A), somatosensory (S), and motor (M) cortical regions and the receptors and effectors are unaffected, the connections between homotopic points in the two hemispheres are severed. Each hemisphere therefore functions independently of the other and without access to the other's sensations, thoughts, or actions.

otomy on the normal function of the brain. After sectioning, the two hemispheres are independent; each receives sensory input from all sensory systems, and each can control the muscles of the body, but the two hemispheres can no longer communicate with each other. Because the functions in these separate cortexes or "split brains" are thus isolated, sensory information can be presented to one hemisphere and its function studied without the other hemisphere having access to the information.

From the numerous studies performed on split-brain patients it is now widely recognized that when the left hemisphere has access to information, it can initiate speech and hence communicate about the information. The right hemisphere apparently has reasonably good recognition abilities but is unable to initiate speech because it lacks access to the speech mechanisms of the left hemisphere. The following example helps to illustrate the phenomenon.

> Patient N. G., a California housewife, sits in front of a screen with a small black dot in the center. She is asked to look directly at the dot. When the experimenter is sure she is doing so, a picture of a cup is flashed briefly to the right of the dot. N. G. reports that she has seen a cup. Again she is asked to fix her gaze on the dot. This time, a picture of a spoon is flashed to the left of the dot. She is asked what she saw. She replies, "No, nothing." She is then asked to reach under the screen with her left hand and to select, by touch only, from among several items the one object that is the same as she has just seen. Her left hand manipulates each object and then holds up the spoon. When asked what she is holding, she says "pencil." (Springer and Deutsch, 1981, pp. 29–30)

The behavior of patient N. G. provides a clear demonstration of the behavior of the two hemispheres when they are not interacting. The picture of the cup was presented to the speaking left hemisphere, which could, of course, respond. The picture of the spoon was presented to the right hemisphere and, since the right hemisphere does not speak and the speaking left hemisphere was not connected to the right, N. G. failed to correctly identify the picture (see Figures 15-5 and 15-6). The abilities of the right hemisphere are demonstrated when the left hand, which is controlled by the right hemisphere, is used to identify the object. Finally, when asked what the still-out-of-sight left hand is holding, the left hemisphere does not know and incorrectly guesses "pencil."

The special capacities of the right hemisphere in facial recognition (see Chapter 11) can also be demonstrated in the split-brain patient. Levy devised the chimeric figures test, which consists of faces and other patterns that have been split down the center and recombined (see Figure 15-7). When the recombined faces were presented selectively to each hemisphere, the patients appeared unaware of the gross discordance between the two

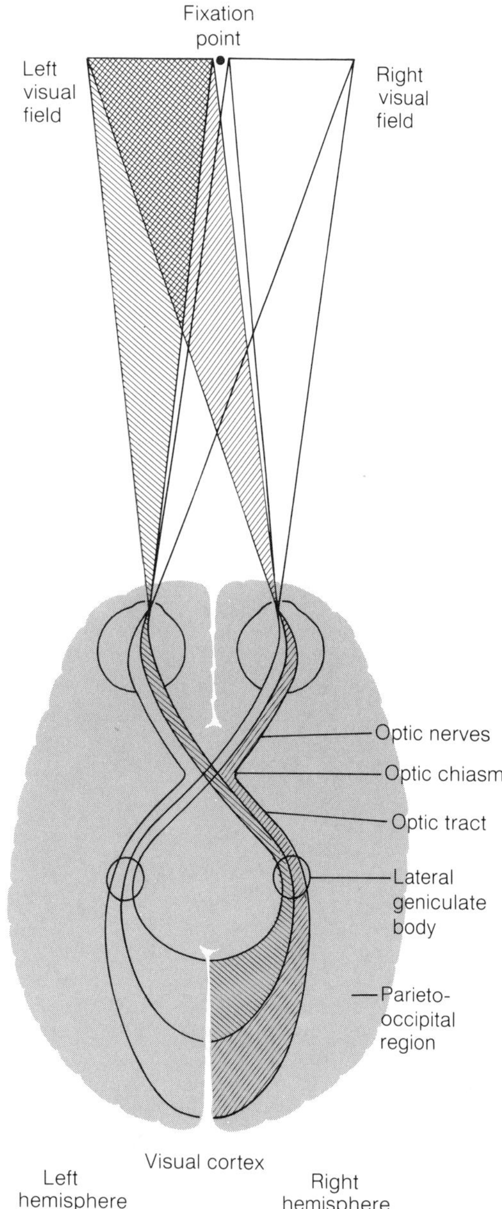

Figure 15-5. Visual pathways are crossed; thus visual fields (and not eyes) are represented in each hemisphere. All the field left of the fixation point (shaded region) is represented in the right visual cortex, and all the field right of the fixation point is represented in the left visual cortex.

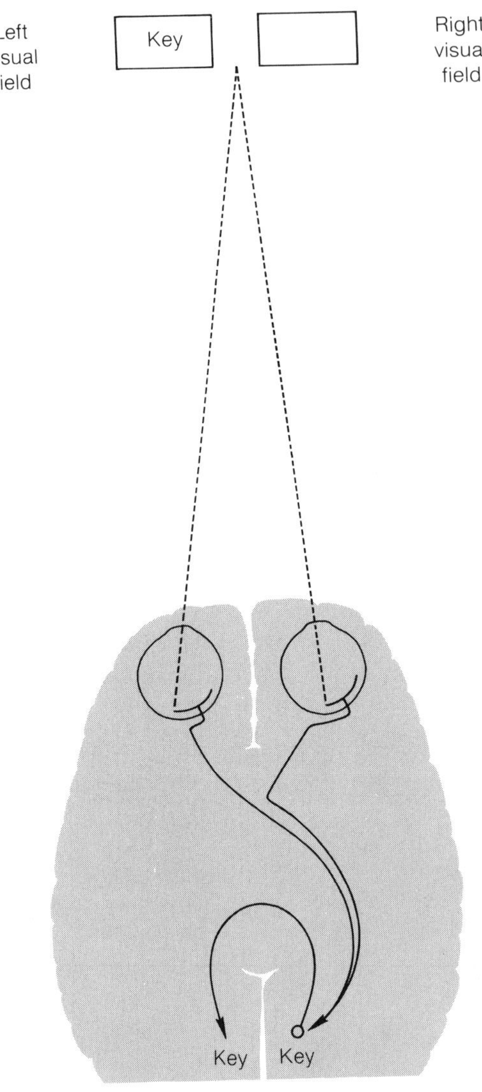

Figure 15-6. Visual input is transferred from the left visual field to the left visual cortex via the corpus callosum. Cutting the callosum would prevent such a transfer.

sides of the pictures. When asked to pick out the picture they had seen, they chose the face seen in the left visual field (i.e., by their right hemisphere), demonstrating that the right hemisphere has a special role in the recognition of faces.

In summary, careful and sometimes ingenious studies of patients with commissurotomies have provided clear evidence of the complementary specialization of the two cerebral hemispheres. It must be recognized, however, that as interesting as these patients are, they represent only a very small population and their two hemispheres are by no means normal. Most of these patients had focal lesions, which caused the initial seizure disorder, and some may have had brain damage early in life, leading to significant reorganization of cerebral function. Thus, generalizations and inferences must be made cautiously from these fascinating patients. We shall return to them in Chapter 20.

Brain Stimulation

In the early 1930s Wilder Penfield and his associates at the Montreal Neurological Institute pioneered the use of surgical treatment for epilepsy in patients whose seizures were poorly controlled by drug therapy. The logic of this procedure is to remove the region of cortex where the abnormal discharge originates. Since this is elective therapeutic surgery it can be planned for, and considerable care can be taken to ensure that areas of the cortex critical for the control of speech and movement are not damaged. To identify speech and movement areas, as well as to localize the extent of the epileptogenic tissue, the surgeon stimulates the exposed cortex and records the responses of the conscious patient. Careful study of hundreds of patients in Montreal by Penfield and his students, especially Theodore Rasmussen, and more recently by George Ojemann and his colleagues at the University of Washington, has provided clear evidence of cerebral asymmetry: stimulation of the left hemisphere can block the ability to speak, whereas stimulation of the right hemisphere seldom does so. The importance of this technique for neuropsychology cannot be underestimated. Following surgery, psychologists often have the opportunity to study patients and to correlate the results of cortical stimulation and psychological assessment; the

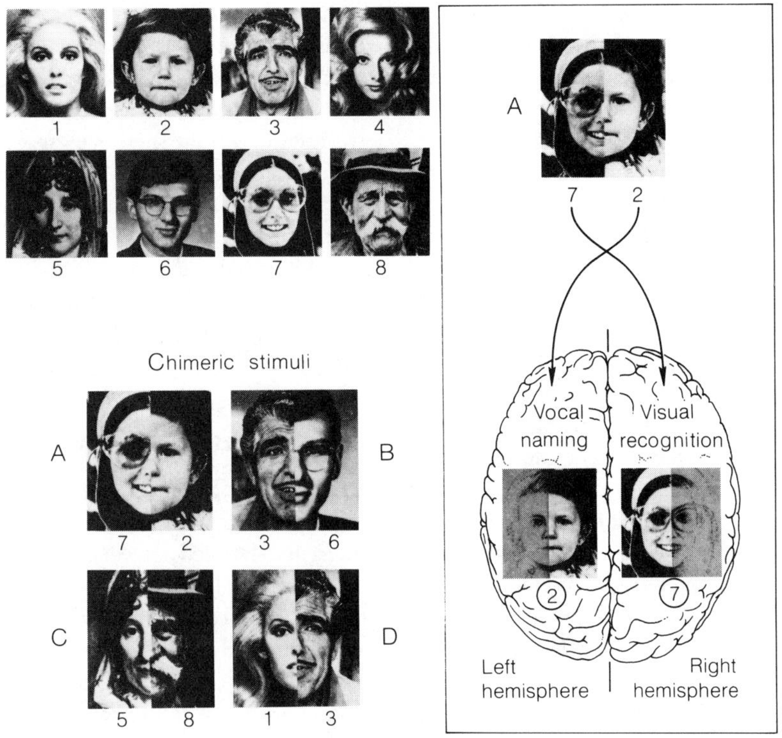

Figure 15-7. Composite faces used by Levy and coworkers to demonstrate the special role of the right hemisphere in facial recognition. Commissurotomy patients were shown the chimeric stimuli (composite pictures) *A* through *D*. When asked to choose the face they had seen from among the array of original pictures, 1 through 8, the patients chose the face that was in the left visual field, as the right-hand side of the figure illustrates. (From J. Levy et al., 1972. Reprinted with permission of Oxford University Press, Oxford.)

work of Rasmussen and Brenda Milner at the Montreal Neurological Institute provides an excellent example of such collaboration.

Application of an electric current to the cortex of a conscious patient has four general effects: three excitatory and one inhibitory. First, stimulation can produce localized movements, localized dysthesias (numbness or tingling in the skin), light flashes, or buzzing sensations. These are normally evoked respectively from primary motor, somatosensory, visual, and auditory areas and pathways and are produced by stimulation of either hemisphere with about the same frequency, a result that illustrates the often overlooked fact that the brain has symmetrical as well as asymmetrical functions. Second, stimulation can produce what Penfield called "interpretive" and "experiential" responses, an example of which was provided in Chapter 11. These uncommon but often highly reliable phenomena include alterations in the interpretation of the patient's surroundings, such as déjà vu, fear and dreaming states, and the reproduction of visual or auditory aspects of specific previous experiences. These phenomena usually occur from tissue showing epileptogenic discharge, but there is an asymmetry in their occurrence:

stimulation of the right temporal lobe produces these phenomena more frequently than stimulation of left temporal lobe, which suggests that the right hemisphere has perceptual functions not shared by the left. Third, stimulation of the left frontal or temporal regions may accelerate the production of speech. Ojemann suggests that this acceleration may result from a type of "alerting response" and may occur in other cognitive processes, especially memory, although this is difficult to demonstrate unequivocally. Finally, stimulation blocks function. This effect is most evident in complex functions such as language and memory and is only apparent when current is applied while the patient is actively engaged in these behaviors. Stimulation to the same site in a quiet patient is without a discernible effect. Disruption of speech is a well-documented effect of stimulation of the left hemisphere (see Chapter 22 for a detailed account of this), but it is only recently that stimulation of the right hemisphere has been shown to disrupt behavior. Ojemann and his colleagues have reported that stimulation of the right hemisphere disrupts judgments of line orientation, labeling of facial expressions, and short-term memory for faces, the effects coming almost exclusively from the temporoparietal cortex: a result consistent with the presumed role of this cortex in visuospatial behavior. Unfortunately the authors fail to report data on the effects on visuospatial behaviors of stimulation of the left hemisphere, although they presumably expect that, like the effect of stimulation of the right hemisphere on language, stimulation of the left hemisphere would have negligible effects on visuospatial functions. Perhaps they will test this assumption in future studies.

In summary, stimulation of the cortex has proved a useful tool in demonstrating both localization and lateralization of function. The effect of disrupting stimulation is frequently quite localized, often changing as the site of stimulation is moved as little as a few millimeters, and it is often very reliable for individual patients. Indeed, this technique probably provides the best degree of localization of function presently available in the study of brain-behavior relations in humans. One additional intriguing aspect of data from cortical stimulation is that there is a great deal of variation from patient to patient in the exact location and extent of sites with particular effects on behavior. One can speculate that this variation forms a basis for individual differences in skills, as people presumably have different amounts of cortex devoted to particular functions. (See Ojemann for preliminary results of this type of analysis.)

Carotid Sodium Amytal Injection

Although language is usually located in the left hemisphere, a small percentage of people, most of them left-handed, have language represented in the right hemisphere. In the event of elective surgery for the treatment of disorders such as epilepsy, avoiding inadvertent damage to the speech zones requires that the surgeon be certain of their location. To achieve certainty in doubtful cases Wada and Rasmussen pioneered the technique of injecting sodium Amytal into the carotid artery to produce a brief period of anesthesia of the ipsilateral hemisphere. This procedure results in an unequivocal localization of speech, because injection into the speech hemisphere results in an arrest of speech lasting up to several minutes, and as speech returns it is characterized by aphasic errors. Injection into the nonspeaking hemisphere may produce no, or only brief, speech arrest. The carotid Amytal procedure has the advantage that each hemisphere can be studied separately in the functional absence of the other, anesthetized one. Since the period of anesthesia lasts several minutes, it is possible to study a variety of functions, including memory and movement, to determine the capabilities of one hemisphere in the absence of the anesthetized one.

The test is always performed bilaterally, with the two cerebral hemispheres being injected on separate days to be sure that there is no residual drug effect from the injection of the first hemisphere at the time of injection of the opposite side. At the Montreal Neurological Hospital, where Wada initially developed the procedure, a small catheter is inserted, under X-ray control, well up into the internal carotid artery, and an angiogram is then carried out. The patient is then moved to the testing room and a dry run is carried out to familiarize the patient with the tests that will be done during and after the drug injection. This establishes a baseline performance level against which to compare the postinjection performance. He or she is then given a series of simple tasks, involving immediate and delayed memory for both verbal (sentences or words) and nonverbal (photographs of faces or objects) material, for the same purpose. Moments before the drug is injected, the patient lies flat on his or her back with both knees drawn up, both hands raised, and the fingers and toes moving. The patient is asked to count backward from 20, and without warning the neurosurgeon injects the drug through the catheter over 2 to 3 sec. Within seconds, there are dramatic changes in behavior.

The contralateral arm and leg fall to the bed with a flaccid paralysis and there is no response whatsoever to a firm pinch of the skin of the affected limbs. If the injected hemisphere is nondominant for speech, the patient may continue to count and carry out the verbal tasks while the temporary hemiparesis is present, although there is often a period of up to 20 to 30 sec during which the patient appears confused and is silent, but typically can resume speech with urging. When the injected hemisphere is dominant for speech, the patient typically stops talking and remains completely aphasic until recovery from the hemiparesis is well along, usually in 4 to 10 min. Speech is tested by asking the patient to name a number of common objects presented in quick succession, to count and recite the days of the week forward and backward, and by simple naming and spelling. In addition to aphasia and paresis, patients with anesthesia of either hemisphere are totally nonresponsive to visual stimulation in the contralateral visual field. For example, there is no reflexive blinking or orientation toward suddenly looming objects. Finally, injection of the speaking hemisphere not only produces contralateral hemiparesis but also renders the ipsilateral side dyspraxic, as we described in our discussion of apraxia in Chapter 13.

The sodium Amytal test, like direct brain stimulation, has been very useful in determining which hemisphere controls speech. Table 15-3 shows the relation between hand preference and the lateralization of cerebral speech processes for a large sample of patients ($n = 262$), who were studied by Rasmussen and Milner. As would be expected from the data from brain stimulation, there is a strong preponderance for left hemisphere speech representation: 96% of the right-handers and 70% of the left-handers show speech disturbance after Amytal injection into the left hemisphere and not after injection into the right. Curiously, 4% of their right-handed sample had their speech functions lateralized to the right cerebral hemisphere. This figure certainly overestimates the proportion of right hemisphere speech in the normal population (remember that all of these patients had epileptogenic lesions), but it does remind us that speech is sometimes found in the right hemisphere of right-handed people. The results for left-handed patients support the view that the pattern of speech representation is less predictable in left-handed and ambidextrous subjects than in right-handers,

TABLE 15-3. Speech lateralization as related to handedness

		Speech representation (%)		
Handedness	Number of cases	Left	Bilateral	Right
Right	140	96	0	4
Left	122	70	15	15

Source: After Rasmussen and Milner, 1977.

but that the majority of left-handers do have speech represented in the left hemisphere. It is interesting, however, that whereas none of the right-handers showed evidence of bilateral speech organization, in 15% of the non-right-handers there was some significant speech disturbance following injection of either side. These patients probably did not have a symmetrical duplication of language functions in the two hemispheres: injection of one hemisphere tended to disrupt naming (e.g., names of the days of the week), whereas injection of the other hemisphere disrupted serial ordering (e.g., ordering the days of the week). Hence, although people may have bilateral representation of speech, this representation is probably asymmetrical and need not imply that the person has "two left hemispheres." Further study of these patients would likely have revealed that visuospatial functions were bilaterally and asymmetrically represented as well, although this is mere conjecture on our part.

ASYMMETRY IN THE INTACT BRAIN

The study of neurological patients demonstrates a clear functional difference between the hemispheres, particularly in the control of language. We have noted earlier, however, that there are many problems in trying to make inferences about the functioning of the normal brain from clinical studies of the dysfunctioning brain. Just because a specific behavioral symptom is associated with damage to a particular brain area does not necessarily mean that the region once controlled the disrupted function. Confirmation is needed from the study of normal brains, especially since the two hemispheres are unlikely to function independently in the intact brain but must play some type of complementary role with each other in nearly all behaviors. The challenge is to devise ways of studying the contribution made by each hemisphere to behavior in the intact brain.

One approach to the study of the normal brain forms the subfield of neuropsychology called **laterality.** Laterality studies take advantage of the anatomical organization of the sensory and motor systems to "trick" the brain into revealing its mode of operation. Laterality research now forms a very large and growing subfield within human neuropsychology, a field that itself now forms the basis for entire textbooks. We shall review the major findings and problems in laterality research and refer the reader interested in details to the recent account by Bryden.

Asymmetry in the Visual System

The organization of the visual system provides an opportunity to selectively present each hemisphere with specific visual information. Figure 15-6 shows the relation between each visual field and its field of projection in the visual cortex: visual stimuli in the left visual field are projected to the right visual cortex, whereas stimuli in the right visual field travel to the left visual cortex. By using a special instrument called a **tachistoscope** visual information can be presented to each visual field independently. Subjects are asked to fixate on a center point marked by a dot or cross (see Figure 15-6). An image is then flashed in one visual field for about 50 msec—a time short enough to allow the image to be processed before the eyes can shift from the fixation point. By comparing the accuracy with which information from the two visual fields is processed, it is possible to infer which hemisphere is best suited to processing different types of information.

In the early 1950s Mishkin and Forgays first used the tachistoscopic procedure to demonstrate that normal right-handed subjects could identify English words presented to the right visual field more accurately than when they were presented to the left visual field. Mishkin and Forgays believed that acquired directional reading habits (i.e., left to right in English) were responsible for this bias, but the studies with the Californian commissurotomy patients a decade later suggested another interpretation: information presented to only one visual field is processed most efficiently by the hemisphere that is specialized to receive it. Words presented to the left hemisphere are therefore processed more efficiently than words presented to the nonverbal right hemisphere. This conclusion was very important not only because it was consistent with the clinical inferences about cerebral specialization but also because it suggested that differences between the processing carried out by the right and left hemispheres could be studied in normal subjects.

The strongest evidence that visual-field differences in tachistoscopic studies are measuring functional asymmetries in the brain is that the asymmetries in tachistoscopic tasks are the same as those demonstrated with neurological patients. Thus, a right visual-field advantage is found with normal subjects in a variety of tasks using verbal material such as words and letters, and a left-visual field advantage is found for stimuli thought to be processed by the right hemisphere, including faces and other visuospatial stimuli (see Table 15-4).

Asymmetry in the Auditory System

The auditory system is not as completely crossed as the visual — both hemispheres receive projections from each ear. However, the crossed connections do appear better developed and may have a preferred access to the cortex. Thus, sounds projected to the right ear are processed primarily by the left hemisphere, and those to the left ear are processed primarily by the right hemisphere, as shown in Figure 15-8.

In the early 1960s Doreen Kimura, working at the Montreal Neurological Institute, studied patients performing **dichotic-listening** tasks. Pairs of spoken digits (e.g., "two" and "six") were presented simultaneously, one of which was heard in each ear through headphones connected to a stereo

TABLE 15-4. Summary of relative asymmetry of function in studies of normal subjects

Function	Task	Left hemisphere dominance[a]	Right hemisphere dominance
Visual (tachistoscope)	Letters	1.2	1.0
	Words	1.5	1.0
	Two-dimensional point localization	1.0	1.2
	Dot and form enumeration	1.0	1.2
	Matching of slanted lines	1.0	1.1
	Stereoscopic depth perception	1.0	1.3
	Faces	1.0	1.2
Auditory (dichotic listening)	Words	1.9	1.0
	Nonsense syllables	1.7	1.0
	Backward speech	1.7	1.0
	Melodic pattern	1.0	1.2
	Nonspeech sounds (cough, laugh, etc.)	1.0	1.1
Manual	Skilled movements	1.0	1.0
	Free movements during speech	3.1	1.0
	Tactile dot (Braille)		Significantly higher

[a] Numbers indicate the ratio of hemisphere dominance for each task.
Source: Adapted from Kimura, 1973.

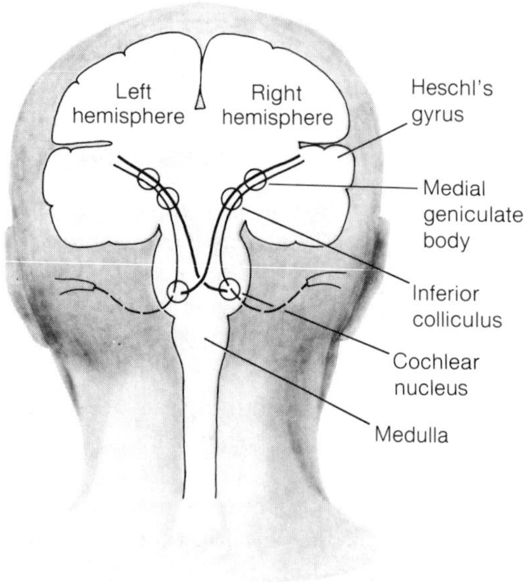

Figure 15-8. Auditory pathways from the ears to the cerebral auditory receiving areas in the right and left hemispheres are partially crossed. Although each hemisphere can receive input from both ears, the neural connections from one ear to the hemisphere on the opposite side are stronger than those to the hemisphere on the same side. When ipsilateral (same side) and contralateral (opposite side) inputs compete in the auditory neural system, it is thought that the stronger contralateral input inhibits or occludes the ipsilateral signals. (After Kimura, 1973.)

tape recorder. Each patient was presented with three pairs of digits and then asked to recall as many of the six digits as possible, in any order. Kimura was interested in the auditory processing capacities of patients with temporal lobe lesions, but she noticed that all subjects, regardless of lesion locus, recalled more digits that had been presented to the right ear than had been presented to the left. The right-ear advantage was also found in normal control subjects. This led Kimura to propose that when different stimuli are presented simultaneously to each ear, the pathway from the right ear to the speaking hemisphere has preferred access, and the ipsilateral pathway from the left ear is relatively suppressed. Thus, during a dichotic task, the stimulus to the left ear must travel to the right hemisphere and then across the cerebral commissures to the left hemisphere. This more difficult route via the left ear puts stimuli into this ear at a disadvantage, and words played to the right ear are recalled more accurately. Having found a right-ear advantage for the perception of dichotically presented speech stimuli, it was an obvious next step to search for tasks that gave a left-ear superiority. In 1964, Kimura reported just such an effect in the perception of melodies. Two excerpts of instrumental chamber music were played simultaneously through headphones, one to each ear. After each pair, four excerpts (including the two that had been played dichotically) were presented binaurally (to both ears), and the subject's task was to identify the two that had been heard previously. Amazingly, Kimura found a left-ear advantage for normal subjects on this task.

It should be noted that not all subjects show the expected ear advantages in dichotic studies, the effects are not large when they occur (seldom exceeding a twofold difference in accuracy in the two ears), and dichotic results are apparently affected by various contextual and practice effects. Nonetheless, the Kimura studies have played a seminal role in laterality studies, since they complemented the results from the neurological literature. As a result, they opened up an entire field of research to anyone with imagination and a stereo tape recorder. More importantly, her experiments provided a noninvasive technique for identifying the hemisphere dominant for language, a question of special clinical importance, particularly in left-handed patients. Furthermore, the test has other clinical uses since patients with left temporal lobe damage are very poor at this task and patients with damage to the corpus callosum exhibit an almost complete inhibition of words presented to the left ear, even though they can recall words presented to this ear if there is no competing stimulus to the right ear. In summary, the dichotic-listening procedure has proved to be an invaluable tool both

TABLE 15-5. Summary of ear advantages for various dichotic signals

Test	Basic reference
Tests showing a right-ear advantage	
Digits	Kimura, 1961
Words	Kimura, 1967
Nonsense syllables	Kimura, 1967
Formant transitions	Lauter, 1982
Backward speech	Kimura and Folb, 1968
Morse Code	Papcun et al., 1974
Difficult rhythms	Natale, 1977
Tone used in linguistic decisions	Zurif, 1974
Tonal sequences with frequency transitions	Halperin et al., 1973
Ordering temporal information	Divenyi and Efron, 1979
Movement-related tonal signals	Sussman, 1979
Tests showing a left-ear advantage	
Melodies	Kimura, 1964
Musical chords	Gelfand et al, 1980
Environmental sounds	Curry, 1967
Emotional sounds and hummed melodies	King and Kimura, 1972
Tones processed independent of linguistic content	Zurif, 1974
Complex pitch perception	Sidtis, 1982
Tests showing no ear advantage	
Vowels	Blumstein et al., 1977
Isolated fricatives	Darwin, 1974
Rhythms	Gordon, 1970
Nonmelodic hums	van Lancker and Fromkin, 1973

Source: After Noffsinger, 1985

clinically and in the field of laterality (see Table 15-5).

Asymmetry in the Somatosensory System

Experiments of laterality in somatosensation have not been as popular as those on vision and audition. Nevertheless, the somatosensory system is almost completely crossed, a feature that allows an easy comparison of the two sides, just as in vision or audition (see Figure 15-9). By blindfolding subjects and requiring them to perform various tasks, such as reading Braille or handling objects separately with each hand, it is possible to identify differences in each hand's efficiency—differences that can be taken to imply functional asymmetry in cerebral organization.

One type of research has compared the performance of the left and right hands in the recognition of various shapes, angles, and patterns by testing each hand separately. The left hand of right-handed subjects is superior at nearly all tasks of this type. For example, Rudel and coworkers found that both blind and sighted subjects read Braille more rapidly with the left hand. Some children are actually fluent readers with the left hand but totally unable to read with the right. Since Braille patterns are spatial configurations of dots, this observation is congruent with the proposal that the right hemisphere has a role in processing spatial information not shared by the left.

A second type of somatosensory test utilizes an analogue of the dichotic procedure, the **dichaptic test,** which was used first by Sandra Witelson. She

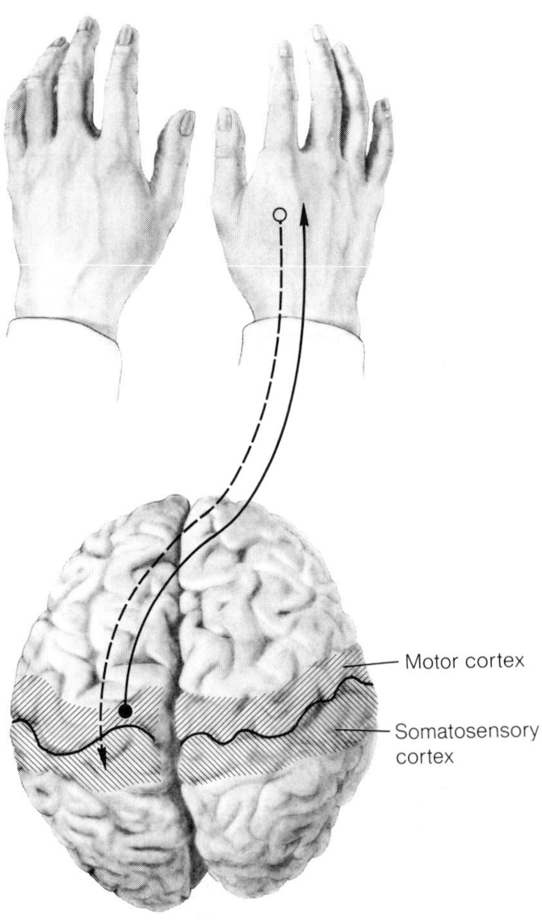

Figure 15-9. Somatosensory and motor pathways are almost wholly crossed; each hand is served primarily by the cerebral hemisphere on the opposite side.

simultaneously presented a different, unfamiliar complex shape that could not be seen to each hand. The subjects felt the objects and then were allowed to look at an array of objects and select those they had previously touched. The results showed a left-hand (right hemisphere) superiority in the recognition of objects. More recently, Gibson and Bryden have been able to dissociate the performance of the left and right hands. In their experiment, subjects were dichaptically presented with cutouts of irregular shapes or letters made of sandpaper, which were moved slowly across the fingertips. Their subjects showed a right-hand advantage for identifying letters and a left-hand advantage for identifying nonsense shapes.

Perhaps the most elegant somatosensory study was carried out by Nachson and Carmon in 1975. They presented subjects with two different tasks —one that they described as "spatial" and another described as "sequential." In these tasks the index, middle, and ring fingers were stimulated by tapered metal rods. Depending on the task, the subjects had to respond by pressing microswitches next to the rods. In the spatial task one finger was stimulated once, another twice, and a third not at all. The subject's task was to indicate the pattern of stimulation by pressing the appropriate microswitches. In the sequential task, the three fingers were stimulated in random order and the subjects had to press the switches in the same sequence as they had been stimulated. With bimanual presentation, subjects made more errors with the left hand on the sequential task and more errors with the right hand on the spatial task. This result is important, for it implies that the left hemisphere has a special role in sequential analysis, a capacity that would presumably be very important in the control of complex movement, a control that we have already seen may be a special function of the left hemisphere (Chapter 12).

Asymmetry in the Motor System

Although the motor system has a significant uncrossed component, clinical studies, first by Wyke and more recently by Kimura and others, have suggested that there is a functional asymmetry in the control of the movement. Following the logic of the study of asymmetry in the intact sensory systems, it would seem reasonable to look for asymmetries in motor control. One difficulty that immediately confronts us, however, is that since there is an asymmetry in the accuracy of response to sensory input, the study of motor asymmetries is potentially confounded by the fact that the two sides do not start off equally. For example, if we found that the right hand reacted to verbal stimuli faster than the left, we would be unable to conclude that this was due to a motor asymmetry per se; it could be due entirely to the perceptual asymmetry. Two different types of experiments have therefore been devised to assess motor asymmetries: (1) direct observation of motor asymmetry, and (2) interference tasks.

Direct Observation. If there is an inherent asymmetry in the control of movement, it is possible that this asymmetry might be observable when people are engaged in other behaviors. For example, perhaps the right hand is more active during the performance of verbal tasks, which do not require a manual response, and the left hand is more active during the performance of nonverbal tasks, which also do not require a manual response. To examine this possibility Kimura and her students have done a number of intriguing experiments. It is a common observation that people often gesture when talking. By videotaping subjects talking or humming, Kimura was able to show that right-handed people tend to gesture with their right hands when talking but are equally likely to scratch, rub their nose, or touch their body with either hand. Kimura interpreted the observed gesturing with the limb contralateral to the speaking hemisphere to indicate a relation between speech and certain manual activities. Since differences in gesturing, which favor the right hand in right-handed subjects, could simply reflect a difference in preferred hand rather than imply a functional asymmetry in motor control, another series of studies compared hand-movement asymmetries during analogous verbal and nonverbal tasks. The procedure involved videotaping right-handed subjects while they assembled blocks in three different types of tests. The first type, a "neutral task," required subjects to combine white blocks to form a 5-by-5 matrix. The second type, a "verbal task," required subjects to combine blocks with letters on them in a series of crossword-puzzle tasks. In the third type, a "nonverbal task," subjects did jigsaw puzzles with the same size blocks as in the preceding two types of tasks. Analysis of the movements showed that in the neutral task, subjects manipulated blocks with the right hand while supporting them with the left. Other movements seldom occurred. On the verbal tasks, most task-directed movements showed a right-hand preference. In contrast, on nonverbal tasks, task-directed movements showed a leftward shift from the neutral condition, subjects now making far more movements with the left hand. These results suggest that the two hemispheres may have complementary roles in the control of movement—an asymmetry that is moderated by a native hand preference.

A second type of observed motor asymmetry has been reported in the performance of complex movements of the mouth. Wolf and Goodale have done single-frame analysis of videotaped mouth movements when people make verbal or nonverbal movements. Figure 15-10 illustrates their principal finding: the right side of the mouth opens wider and more quickly than the left for both verbal and nonverbal tasks. The location of the movement was an important factor in determining the size of the right bias, since movements embedded within a series showed a greater asymmetry than movements at the beginning. Goodale's observations support the idea that the left hemisphere has a special role in the selection, programming, and production of verbal and nonverbal oral movements. In view of claims that the left side of the face shows emotions more strongly than the right side, it would be interesting to use Goodale's technique to analyze the onset time of spontaneous facial expressions. It is reasonable to predict that if the right hemisphere is dominant in the control of facial expression that the onset would be sooner on the left side of the face.

Another fascinating observation of lateralization of movement control is that concentration on a

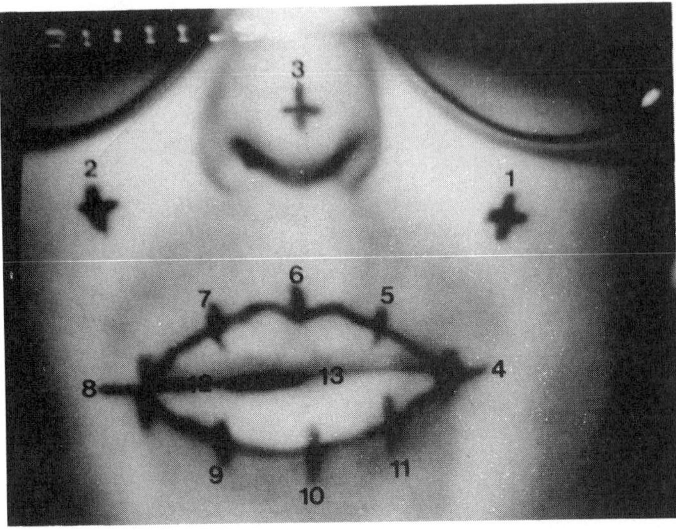

A

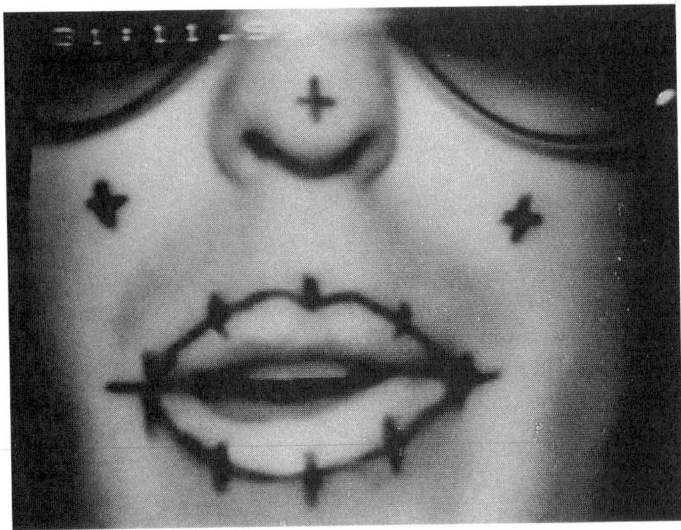

B

Figure 15-10. Successive video frames illustrating the mouth opening during the production of the syllable "ma" in the sequence "mabopi". Frame *B* occurred 67 msec after frame *A*, and frame *C* occurred 50 msec after frame *B*. (Reprinted with permission from *Neuropsychologia* 25, Wolf and Goodale, Oral asymmetries during oral and nonoral movements of the mouth, copyright 1987.)

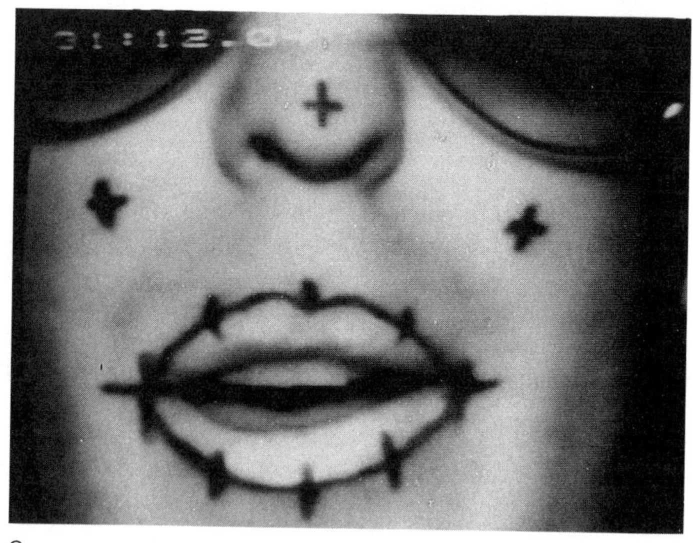

C

different problem frequently causes the eyes, and often the head, to turn laterally to the left or right. Careful study indicates that right-handed people usually turn head and eyes to the right when solving verbal problems, but look up and to the left when solving numerical and spatial problems. This phenomenon, labeled *lateral eye gaze,* has been interpreted as resulting from predominant activation of the hemisphere most vigorously involved in processing the material of the task. In other words, people gaze right while doing a verbal problem because the activation of the left hemisphere "spills over," affecting motor activation toward the right side. The converse is true of spatial or numerical tasks. This phenomenon, although slow in gaining credibility among many neuropsychologists, is nevertheless interesting and provocative.

Interference Tasks. A variety of laboratories have recently examined a well-known phenomenon that most people manifest: the difficulty in doing two complex tasks at the same time. If subjects are asked to balance a dowel on their left or right index fingers while talking, they are able to maintain the balance much longer with the left hand than with the right. Similar results are also reported for other complex tasks such as tapping a sequence of movements with the fingers; speaking interferes only with performance of the left hand. Perhaps the most interesting interference study we know of is an unpublished experiment by Hicks and Kinsbourne. They persuaded several unemployed musicians to come to their laboratory daily to play the piano. The task was to learn a different piece of music with each hand so that the two pieces could be played simultaneously. Once the musicians had mastered this very difficult task, the experimenters then asked them to speak or to hum while playing. Evidently speaking disrupted playing with the right hand, and humming playing with the left.

As interesting as interference studies may be, interference effects are poorly understood and appear to be capricious. It is a common observation that as we become proficient at motor tasks we are less prone to interference effects. Consider the difficulty in talking while learning to play tennis; an interference paradigm of little challenge to a tennis professional. Interference studies provide a useful way to study the roles of the two hemispheres in the control of movement, but much more work will be needed before we can identify the complementary roles of the two hemispheres in movement. It will be necessary to identify which types of movements each hemisphere is especially good at controlling since these movements will likely be resilient to interference effects. Further, there should be studies of the capacities of the hemispheres to produce simultaneous finger versus limb movements. Perhaps finger movements are more sensitive to interference effects when performed by the right than the left hemisphere. Studies of interference effects are important, however, as they may provide fresh insights into the nature of apraxia in clinical populations.

What Do Laterality Studies Tell Us about Brain Function?

Laterality studies provide an important complement to the study of neurological patients and have served as the basis for much of the current theorizing about the nature of cerebral asymmetry. It should be recognized that these studies are a very indirect measure of brain function and are far from being the ideal tools they are often assumed to be. Consider the following problems.

Measures of laterality do not correlate perfectly with invasive measures of cerebral asymmetry. For example, dichotic-listening studies show a right-ear bias for words in about 80% of right-handed subjects, but sodium Amytal testing and brain stimulation show language to be represented in the left hemisphere in over 95% of right-handers. What causes this discrepancy? There are several possibilities, one being that the test is measuring several things, only one of which is relative cerebral dominance. However, the behavioral tests may correlate with anatomical asymmetries more closely than the stimulation and Amytal data do. Thus, it is known that only about 75 to 80% of brains show a left-sided advantage in the posterior Sylvian area of right-handers, yet 99% of these brains show language in the left hemisphere in a sodium Amytal test. Strauss and colleagues have proposed that there may be correlations between anatomy and behavior, and present some preliminary data suggesting this. Unfortunately, we are still left with the question of why both the Amytal test and brain-damage studies show a larger percentage of people with left hemisphere speech.

Measures of laterality do not correlate very highly with one another. We might expect that tachistoscopic and dichotic measures of laterality in the same subjects would be highly concordant, but they are not. Perhaps these tests are not really measuring the same things after all.

There is no simple way to correlate individual differences in the neural pathways to the cortex, or the functional representations in the cortex, with individual performance on laterality tests. Individual differences in the brains of normal subjects almost certainly add a great deal of variance to the results, but there is currently no way of identifying a systematic relation between anatomy and performance.

The strategies that subjects adopt in laterality tasks can significantly alter performance. If subjects are instructed to pay particular attention to words entering the left ear in dichotic tasks, they can do so, abolishing the right-ear effect. Subjects can also enter tests with preconceived biases, which may affect test performance. Finally, laterality effects may simply be a result of experiential, rather than biological factors. Suspicion is reinforced by the observation that repeated testing of the same subjects does not always produce the same results.

Laterality studies are very easy to do and can be done by most undergraduate psychology majors if they have access to a tachistoscope or a stereo tape recorder. Although this is good pedagogically, it has encouraged a proliferation of experiments on small samples of subjects in which the experimenters are not always fully aware of the tenuous nature of the inferences about brain function. We cannot emphasize strongly enough that laterality studies are just one technique for drawing inferences about cerebral functioning. Theories about hemipheric organization must consider data from many sources, only one of which is the study of intact brain.

MEASURES OF CEREBRAL BLOOD FLOW AND METABOLIC RATE

In 1890, Roy and Sherrington first postulated that when regions of the brain are functionally activated, the blood supply will correspondingly increase in these areas. The measurement of moment-to-moment variations of cerebral blood flow is difficult but is thought to be accurate, and measurements have been made since 1890 using some ingenious techniques. The modern development of computerized systems for collecting and synthesizing large amounts of data has made possible the parallel development of highly reliable techniques for measuring both local cerebral blood flow and local cerebral glucose metabolism. In the former procedure, a solution containing a substance such as xenon 133, a radioactive isotope of xenon which accumulates in areas of increased blood flow, is injected into an artery while special detectors on the skull monitor its concentration. (In a new, less accurate variant of this procedure the xenon 133 is inhaled.) If a subject is asked to handle an object with one hand, an increase in xenon 133 concentration is found over the somatosensory zones of the contralateral hemisphere, suggesting their involvement in tactile processing. The measurement of glucose metabolism takes advantage of the PET scanner (see Chapter 6). Since there is a close link between functional activity and local metabolism in the brain, it is possible to infer the relative functional activity of local regions of the brain by measuring the rate of glucose metabolism. In this method a short-lived radioactive tracer ([^{18}F]-2-deoxy-2-fluoro-D-glucose, abbreviated [^{18}F]-FDG), is intravenously injected while a subject is engaged in a task. When this glucose is metabolized, a labeled product of the metabolism ([^{18}F]-FDG phosphate) is essentially trapped in the tissue for a few minutes and can be measured by a PET scanner.

The use of both of these techniques is still in its infancy and a significant increase in resolution is required before effective mapping of active cortex can be carried out. But with improved instrument resolution these procedures will become major techniques in the study of cerebral functioning, in both the study of localization and of lateralization of functions (see the review by Reivich).

Localization of Function

Owing to the low resolution and slow speed of the xenon 133 and the [^{18}F]-FDG procedures, cortical activation lasting only a few seconds will be missed. Therefore, most studies to date have utilized simple tasks, which are repeated over a period of several minutes. Nevertheless, the results are exciting. Regional blood-flow measurements have been used to determine the normal resting pattern of activity of the brain when subjects are sitting still with their eyes closed and ears plugged. A highly reliable resting pattern emerges in which the frontal lobe receives relatively more blood, roughly 15% more than the mean for the entire hemisphere. The pattern of cerebral activation changes markedly during basic auditory, visual, and tactile stimulation or during rhythmic movements. For example, auditory input bilaterally activates both superior temporal gyri, visual input activates the contralateral occipital cortex, and simple tactile object discrimination with the hand, mouth, or foot activates the corresponding part of the contralateral sensorimotor areas. Similarly, rhythmic movements of the hand, fingers, lips, and toes activate the respective contralateral sensorimotor regions as well. Activation is not restricted just to the primary sensory and motor regions, however; it is usually accompanied by activation in at least part of the frontal lobe. For example, rhythmic movements often activate the supplementary motor cortex, and tactile discrimination is associated with an increase in activity in the superior frontal sulcus, observations that are consistent with the proposed role of the frontal cortex in sensory processing and movement (see Chapter 19).

Blood Flow during Thinking

One of the most exciting findings with blood-flow and PET studies has come from the novel work of Roland and his colleagues, who have shown evidence of localization of cortical blood flow and cortical metabolic activity during specific types of thinking. In one study subjects were given three mental tasks to perform while regional blood flow was measured. In the first, the "50 − 3" task, the subjects started with 50 in their minds and then continuously subtracted 3 from the result. In the "jingle" task the subjects mentally jumped every second word in a nine-word jingle. In the "route-finding" task the subjects imagined that they started at their front door and then walked alternatively to the left or right each time they reached a corner. There were three major findings of this study. First, regional blood flow outside the primary sensory and motor areas was increased by thinking. Second, different types of thinking activated different cortical fields. There were changes in the frontal, temporal, and parietal cortex that were unique to each task, and, in addition, there were areas that were activated by one or two tasks. Areas of the prefrontal cortex of both hemispheres were activated by all tasks in all subjects, suggesting a role for the prefrontal cortex in organizing mental activity. Importantly, the primary and secondary auditory and somatosensory regions were never activated, suggesting that the observed changes were not a simple generalized increase in cerebral activity. Third, the results clearly show that thinking requires metabolic activity. What is curious is that the thinking required a *greater increase* in activity than Roland found in previous studies in which subjects made voluntary movements or processed sensory stimulation. (Is it any wonder that thinking is so much more tiring than watching TV!) Finally, there were asymmetries in this cerebral activity, although for most tasks there was a bilateral increase, the difference was in the relative level of activity in the two hemispheres.

Lateralization of Function

Both regional blood-flow and cerebral metabolism tests have been used to identify asymmetries in cerebral functioning. As might be expected, there is an asymmetrical uptake of the tracers when subjects either listen to or engage in conversation (see Figure 15-11). For example, when a subject is listening to speech, both hemispheres show regional changes in cerebral activity especially within the auditory cortex, but the left hemisphere also shows increased activity in Broca's and Wernicke's areas. When speaking, subjects also show activity of the motor areas that represent the face, mouth, and the supplementary motor cortex. Somewhat curiously, repetition of what has been called "automatic" speech, such as naming the days of the week over and over again, fails to produce an increase in activity in Broca's area, a result that would not have been predicted from the idea that this area is involved in producing movement or from the sodium Amytal or stimulation studies discussed earlier. In contrast to the left side increase during speech perception, there is an increase in right side uptake of tracer in the temporal lobe when subjects are played the tonal memory and timbre tests of the Seashore Musical Aptitude Test, a result consistent with Milner's demonstration that right temporal lobe lesions impair performance of these results. Finally, Dabbs and

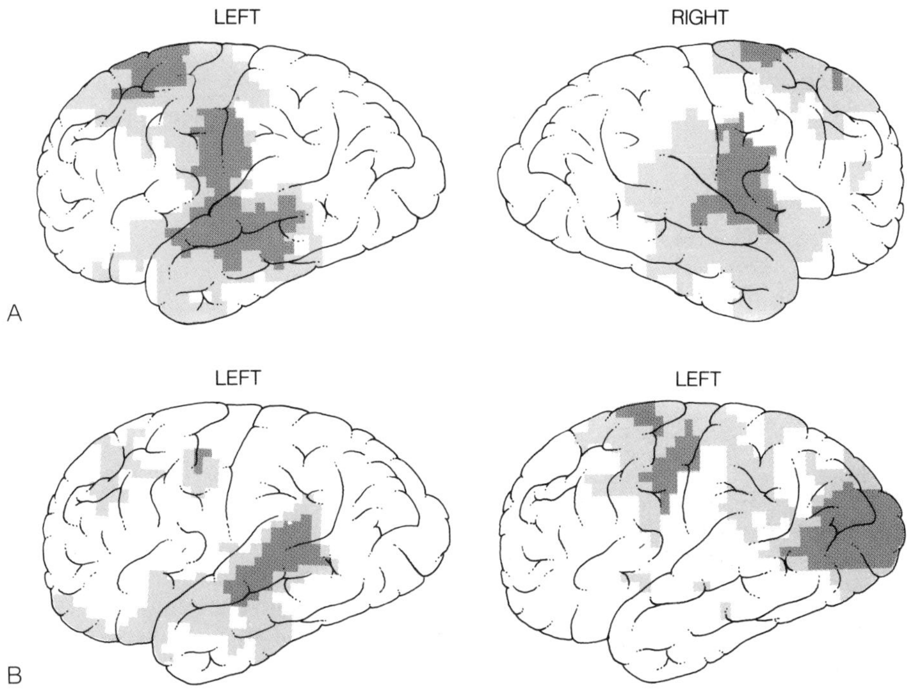

Figure 15-11. Relating brain function to regional blood flow. Because the pattern of blood flow varies with the behavioral task, the relative importance of different areas in different functions can be inferred: light shading indicates the average level of blood flow; dark shading indicates higher-than-average blood flow; the absence of shading indicates lower-than-average blood flow. *A*. Speaking activates the mouth-tongue-larynx of the motor and somatosensory cortex, the supplementary motor area, and the auditory cortex. These images, averaged from nine different subjects, show differences in the activity of the left and right hemispheres; in the left hemisphere the mouth area is more active and the auditory cortex, including part of area 22, is considerably more active. *B*. Sensory perception changes the pattern of blood flow in the cortex, revealing the localization of areas that mediate the processing of sensory information. During the study at the right the subject followed a moving object with his eyes, resulting in high activity in the visual cortex and frontal eye fields. During the study at the left the same subject listened to spoken words, resulting in increased activity localized to the auditory cortex. Note that the position of the Sylvian and central fissures is approximate; the actual position could be determined only by opening the skull. The squared shapes are an artifact of the recording and averaging procedure and thus do not accurately indicate the shapes of areas in the brain. (Simplified from Lassen et al., 1978.)

others have found evidence that there may be an overall difference in blood flow to the two hemispheres: the right hemisphere receives slightly more blood flow than the left. This may be because the right hemisphere is larger or it may occur for other reasons.

In summary, measures of regional blood flow and glucose-uptake hold great promise for the future, once the instrumentation can be improved to make possible faster and finer resolution. The cost of these procedures will remain prohibitive, however, and so it is likely that only a small number of laboratories will be able to perform this type of research. Further, it should be recognized that with the available technology, quickly occurring cognitive events (e.g., less than 45 sec in duration) cannot be measured.

ELECTRICAL RECORDING

The electrical activity of the brain of normal subjects can be recorded (as noted in previous chapters) by the EEG and the average evoked potential (AEP). Both of these recordings can be related to different stimuli over time, and the electrical activity in the immediate pre- and poststimulus periods can be correlated with the stimulus and response. Recently, these components of the waves have been known as event-related potentials (ERPs), which includes many of the components illustrated in Figure 6-2 (e.g., N_{100}, P_{200}). The late-occurring wave (P_{300}) has received much attention since it appears to occur reliably when a person is actively processing ("attending to") incoming stimuli. Since the two hemispheres function differently, and since the EEG, AEP, and ERP reflect the function of neurons, it follows logically that there ought to be asymmetry in the EEGs, AEPs, and ERPs recorded from the two hemispheres. Indeed, over the past 10 years numerous experiments have attempted to demonstrate this asymmetry, and there have been promising results, for on some behavioral tasks EEGs, AEPs, and ERPs do appear to be asymmetrical over the two hemispheres. The results are far from conclusive, however. In a recent review, Donchin and colleagues conclude that the literature is fraught with serious methodological inadequacies related to recording techniques, behavioral tasks, data analysis, and the like. These problems are not unsurmountable, however, and the development of new techniques, such as the one described in 1981 by Gevins and his colleagues, is intriguing and may prove to be more reliable than the more traditional approaches. In summary, although interhemispheric differences in EEG, AEP, and ERP recordings are apt to be minute, the techniques are promising as a means of investigating hemispheric lateralization. For recent reviews of this complex material we recommend Brandies and Lehmann, Kutas and Hillyard, and Squires and Ollo.

WHAT IS LATERALIZED?

It is tempting to conclude that the functional asymmetries described so far represent a larger fundamental difference in the basic cognitive processes of the left and right hemispheres. However, before considering this issue we will summarize the data, since any theoretical statements are best considered in light of the available information.

Table 15-6 summarizes the major data on cerebral lateralization and illustrates the range of functions lateralized principally in the left and right hemispheres, respectively. In right-handed people the left hemisphere has a greater role in language and in the control of complex voluntary movement than does the right hemisphere, and the right hemisphere has a greater role in the control of certain types visuospatial abilities.

Theoretical Arguments

In recent years there have been a truly enormous number of proposals on what is lateralized in the brain (see Allen for a readable summary). In general, there are two types of theories. One type proposes unique functions for each hemisphere; the other proposes some sort of cooperative interaction of the two hemispheres.

Unilateral Specialization Models. In its extreme form, this model states that only one hemisphere facilitates a given psychological process. For example, it has been argued since Broca that the left hemisphere alone performs language functions. Perhaps the most thorough modern version of the "left-for-language" theory is Lenneberg. A

TABLE 15-6. Summary of data on cerebral lateralization

Function	Left hemisphere	Right hemisphere
Visual system	Letters, words	Complex geometric patterns Faces
Auditory system	Language-related sounds	Nonlanguage environmental sounds Music
Somatosensory system	?	Tactile recognition of complex patterns Braille
Movement	Complex voluntary movement	Movements in spatial patterns
Memory	Verbal memory	Nonverbal memory
Language	Speech Reading Writing Arithmetic	Prosody?
Spatial processes		Geometry Sense of direction Mental rotation of shapes

Note: Functions of the respective hemispheres that are predominantly mediated by one hemisphere in right-handed people.

modification of the language theory is one proposed by Liepmann at the turn of the century. He proposed that the left hemisphere was specialized for some form of motor control, which would account for why both aphasia and apraxia are major symptoms of left hemisphere damage. Kimura extended this idea by proposing that although the left hemisphere mediates verbal function, it is specialized not for verbal function per se, but rather for certain kinds of motor function, both verbal and nonverbal. Kimura's argument is based on two premises. First, lesions of the left hemisphere disturb the production of voluntary movement—an impairment correlated with disturbance in speech. Second, Kimura proposes that verbal communication evolved from a stage that was primarily gestural, though with vocal concomitants, to one that is primarily vocal but that retains the capacity for manual communication. Since the neurological control of speech and language thus evolved out of a system of motor control of gesture, the left hemisphere is not specialized for language per se, but rather for motor control. Several authors (e.g., Efron) have made the suggestion that it is not motor control, per se, that is located in the left hemisphere, but rather the capacity for fine resolution of stimuli in time. In other words, since the analysis and production of speech requires fine discrimination and production of speech over very short intervals, the left hemisphere might be specialized for temporal sequencing (organizing behavior and/or information over time). Elaborations of this idea have stressed the capacity of the left hemisphere for making fine discriminations in time, whether the stimuli be verbal or not (e.g., Sergent). Most proposals of left hemisphere specializations have not been matched by similar concrete proposals for right hemisphere functions, although it is often said the right hemisphere is specialized for "visuospatial functions." One exception is the temporal-discrimination hypotheses, which suggest that the right hemisphere specializes in grosser discriminations. For example, Sergent proposed that the right hemisphere is superior at recognizing faces because it is the grosser aspects of face stimuli (the gestalt) that is more important in recognition.

Rather than specifying different processing of specified psychological processes, other specialization models have focused on the idea that the two hemispheres might process information in distinctly different ways. The first clear proposal of this sort was made by Semmes in 1968. On the basis of her previous studies of World War II veterans suffering from penetrating brain injuries she concluded that the left hemisphere functions as a collection of focalized regions, whereas the right hemisphere functions more diffusely, in a manner consistent with Lashley's notions of mass action and equipotentiality (Chapter 8). Her logic was as follows. She had noticed that small lesions of the left hemisphere produced a wide variety of specific deficits (e.g., impaired spelling and reading), the precise deficit depending on the locus of the lesion; similar-sized lesions within the right hemisphere were frequently without obvious effect. In contrast, large lesions of *either* hemisphere produced a large number of deficits. To account for this differential effect Semmes argued that a person with a small lesion of the right hemisphere exhibits no deficits because specific functions are not localized in discrete regions in the right hemisphere, the functions being diffusely represented. A large lesion of the right hemisphere produces many more deficits than would be predicted from the total of smaller lesions because an entire functional field is removed — a proposition that is consistent with Lashley's **mass action hypothesis.** Large lesions of the left hemisphere produce many deficits simply because many small focal regions have been destroyed; in the left hemisphere the total is equal to the sum of the parts.

Semmes proposed that this differential organization of the two hemispheres is advantageous for efficient control of their respective functions. The diffuse organization of the right hemisphere is seen as advantageous for spatial abilities, since spatial analysis requires that different kinds of information (visual, auditory, tactile) be integrated into a single percept. Language functions are not integrated in the same manner, but remain as individual units.

From these basic ideas about distinct functions of the two hemispheres has arisen the idea that the hemispheres represent two distinct modes of cognitive processing (e.g., Levy; Sperry).

> The left hemisphere operates in a more logical, analytical, computer-like fashion, analyzing stimulus information input sequentially, abstracting out the relevant details to which it attaches verbal labels: the right hemisphere is primarily a synthesizer, more concerned with the overall stimulus configuration, and organizes and processes information in terms of gestalts or wholes. (Harris, 1978, p. 463)

Although these ideas have stimulated interest among philosophers and the general public, it is important to remember that they are entirely based upon inference, and have jumped a long way from the data (such as that summarized in Table 15-6).

Interaction Models. All the various forms of interaction models share the common idea that the two hemispheres have the capacity to perform given functions, but they do not. It is the specification of the reasons "why not" that has spawned numerous debates, experiments, and models. Consider some of the versions of the interaction model. First, there is the idea that the two hemispheres function simultaneously, but they work on different aspects of processing. This is a direct analogue to the multiple-channel idea of sensory processing. It is merely taken one step further so that the two hemispheres represent two more classes of sensory channels. Although this type of model is generally appealing, there has yet to be a satisfactory explanation of how the information is combined to provide a single percept or behavior. Second, there is a group of models that propose that although the two hemispheres have the capacity to perform a given function, they inhibit or suppress each other's activity (e.g., Kinsbourne; Moscovitch). Thus, the left hemisphere inhibits language processing in the right hemisphere, and the right hemisphere inhibits musical processing in the left. Developmentally, this type of model has some appeal since it appears that functions, such as language, can develop in the "wrong" hemisphere if the normally dominant hemisphere is damaged. Thus, if the language zones are damaged in infancy, language can develop in the right hemisphere. One difficulty with these models is that the physiological mechanisms of inhibition have not been clearly specified. A third type of model is an information-processing model, and may suggest either that the two hemispheres receive information preferentially and thus perform different analyses, or that there is some mechanism enabling each hemisphere to "pay attention" to specific types of information, thus leading to different analyses (e.g., Moscovitch). The details of these models are complex, based heavily on the information-processing theory of cognitive psychology. An interesting feature of some of these models is that if one hemisphere is busy, it ought to be able to allocate other functions to the remaining hemisphere. A problem with the information-processing models is that they are necessarily vague on what physiological mechanisms might be responsible for selected attention.

In summary, the question of what is lateralized does not have a simple, nor a generally accepted, answer. There is no shortage of ideas and inferences. What is needed is more information about the nature of asymmetry and its origins, both developmentally and phylogenetically.

Preferred Cognitive Mode

From the previous theoretical arguments it is possible to speculate that individual differences in the behavior of normal subjects result, at least in part, from individual differences in how the cerebral hemispheres are organized and how functions are lateralized. Thus, subjects who are very logical, analytical, and verbal could be assumed to be more efficient in using their left hemispheres to solve problems in everyday life, whereas subjects who are predominantly concerned with wholes or general concepts could be assumed to be more efficient in using their right hemispheres. For example (a tongue-in-cheek one), two professors, Alpha and Beta, are both excellent scholars, but they are totally different in how they work and think.

Alpha is meticulous and leaves no detail to chance; when learning new material he masters every detail and has total command of the topic. Alpha is verbal and can easily win debates with his quick thinking and elegant arguments. His writing is clear and concise with flawless grammar and spelling. Alpha is athletic, and a nationally ranked tennis player. Curiously, he is only mediocre at other sports, but with prolonged practice he is able to master their details as well. Finally, Alpha's office is neat and tidy, with every item carefully placed in its correct location. On his desk is the project he is currently working on and nothing else.

Beta, on the other hand, only appears to learn the generalities of new material, and seldom recalls the minute details. He grasps ideas quickly, however, and is often able to tie very diverse concepts into a meaningful picture. His thinking often appears muddled to those around him, for he has difficulty expressing his ideas, but given enough time he often impresses his colleagues with his insight into problems. His writing is poor in comparison with Alpha's, for he expresses himself with tortuous constructions and is plagued by grammatical and spelling errors about which he appears totally unconcerned. Nevertheless, Beta has a remarkable knack for asking the correct questions and tying together seemingly diverse literature. Like Alpha, Beta is athletic, but unlike Alpha, Beta acquires the general motor skills of new sports rapidly, although he has never been able to become a top participant in any event. Beta's office is messy and his desk is a pile of papers and books, because he works on several projects concurrently.

Alpha and Beta represent extremes of what could be described as left hemisphere and right hemisphere individuals, respectively. The fundamental difference between them is that each attacks problems by using what has been described as a different **preferred cognitive mode.** Alpha is analytical, logical, verbal, and meticulous, whereas Beta is a synthesizer, more concerned with organizing concepts into meaningful wholes. Thus, in both the cognitive and the motor skills of Alpha and Beta, there is a basic difference that is assumed to reflect a fundamental difference in either brain organization or the "dominance" of one hemisphere over the other.

As intriguing as this analysis of Alpha and Beta appears to be, we caution that it is pure speculation, without empirical basis. It is probable that factors other than brain organization may contribute to preferred cognitive mode. For example, a study by Webster and Thurber demonstrates that **cognitive set** can affect some tests of lateralization. They repeated Witelson and Pallie's dichaptic test (described earlier) but added an additional variable. One group (the gestalt group) was encouraged to learn the shapes by imagining the overall appearance, or gestalt; a second group (the analytic group) was encouraged to identify distinctive features of each shape and list them to themselves. This manipulation demonstrably influenced the degree of left-hand superiority, because the gestalt group had a significantly larger performance difference between the hands than did the analytic group. Although the basis for this effect is uncertain, it implies that strategies used by subjects can significantly influence tests of lateralization. It thus seems reasonable to assume that differences in preferred cognitive mode may reflect socialization or environmental factors in addition to neuronal, biological, or constitutional factors. Nevertheless, that individual differences in behavior result in part from individual differences in brain organization seems a provocative assumption worthy of serious study.

CONCLUDING REMARKS

We have shown how the two hemispheres of the human brain are both anatomically and functionally asymmetrical. Two important points must be emphasized before we consider variations in the "textbook pattern" of cerebral asymmetry in the next chapter, lest we leave the reader with two common misunderstandings.

First, many functions of the cerebral hemispheres are not asymmetrical. Rather, they are symmetrical. In an examination in our undergraduate course in human neuropsychology we asked: In what ways is the human brain symmetrical? Thinking it to be a trick question, a majority of the students answered: "It isn't symmetrical, it's asymmetrical." This is wrong, of course, since many functions, especially of the primary sensory and motor areas, appear identical on the two sides of the brain. Furthermore, we must realize that the functional differences between the two hemispheres are not absolute, but relative. Just because sodium Amytal renders one hemisphere aphasic does not mean that language functions are only carried out in the aphasic hemisphere.

Second, cerebral site is at least as important in understanding brain function as cerebral side, a fact that is often overlooked when people theorize about cerebral organization. Thus, although the frontal lobes are asymmetrical, the functions of the two frontal lobes are more similar to one another than they are to those of the posterior cortex on the same side. In fact, it is often very difficult to localize lesions in neurological patients to one hemisphere in the absence of neurological data, even though the site (frontal as opposed to temporal or parietal) may be immediately obvious. Perhaps it is best to think of the functions of the cerebral cortex as being localized, and hemispheric side as being only one step in localizing them.

REFERENCES

Allen, M. Models of hemispheric specialization. *Psychological Bulletin* 93:73–104, 1983.

Amaducci, L., S. Sorbi., A. Albanese, and G. Gainotti. Choline acetyltransferase (ChAT) activity differs in right and left human temporal lobes. *Neurology* 31:799–805, 1981.

Blumstein, S., V. Tartter, D. Michel, B. Hirsch, and E. Leiter. The role of distinctive features in the dichotic perception of vowels. *Brain and Language* 4:508–520, 1977.

Bonin, B. von. Anatomical asymmetries of the cerebral hemispheres. In V. B. Mountcastle, ed. *Interhemispheric relations and cerebral dominance.* Baltimore: Johns Hopkins Press, 1962.

Brandeis, D., and D. Lehmann. Event-related potentials of the brain and cognitive processes: Approaches and applications. *Neuropsychologia* 24:151–168, 1986.

Broca, P. Sur la faculté du langage articulé. *Bulletins et Mêmoires de la Sociêté D'Anthropologie de Paris* 6:377–393, 1865.

Bryden, M. P. *Laterality: Functional Asymmetry in the Intact Brain.* New York: Academic Press, 1982.

Cain, D. P., and J. A. Wada. An anatomical asymmetry in the baboon brain. *Brain, Behavior and Evolution* 16:222–226, 1979.

Carmon, A., Y. Harishanu, E. Lowinger, and S. Lavy. Asymmetries in hemispheric blood volume and cerebral dominance. *Behavioral Biology* 7:853–859, 1972.

Chi, J. G., E. C. Dooling, and F. H. Gilles. Left-right asymmetries of the temporal speech areas of the human fetus. *Archives of Neurology* 34:346–348, 1977.

Crichton-Browne, J. On the weight of the brain: Its component parts in the insane. *Brain* 2:42–67, 1880.

Cunningham, D. F. *Contribution to the Surface Anatomy of the Cerebral Hemispheres.* Dublin: Royal Irish Academy, 1892.

Curry, F. A comparison of left-handed and right-handed subjects on verbal and nonverbal dichotic listening tasks. *Cortex* 3:343–352, 1967.

Dabbs, J. M. Left-right differences in cerebral blood flow and cognition. *Psychophysiology* 17:548–551, 1980.

Darwin, C. Ear differences and hemispheric specialization. In F. O. Schlmitt and F. G. Worden, eds. *The Neurosciences: Third Study Program.* Cambridge, MA: M.I.T. Press, 1974.

Deuel, R. K., and C. C. Moran. Cerebral dominance and cerebral asymmetries on computed tomogram in childhood. *Neurology* 30:934–938, 1980.

Divenyi, P., and R. Efron. Spectral versus temporal features in dichotic listening. *Brain and Language* 7:375–386, 1979.

Donchin, E., M. Kutas, and G. McCarthy. Electrocortical indices of hemispheric utilization. In S. Harnad, R. W. Doty, L. Goldstein, J. Jaynes, and G. Krauthamer, eds. *Lateralization in the Nervous System.* New York: Academic Press, 1977.

Eberstaller, O. Zur Oberflächenanatomie der Grosshirnhemisphären. *Wien. Med. Blätter* 7:479–482, 542–582, 644–646, 1884.

Economo, C. V. von, and L. Horn. Über Windungsrelief, Masse and Rindenarchitektonik der Supratemporalfläche, ihre individuellen und ihre Seitenunterschiede. *Zeitschrift für Neurologie and Psychiatrie* 130:678–757, 1930.

Efron, R. Temporal perception, aphasia, and déjà vu. *Brain* 86A:403–424, 1963.

Eidelberg, D., and A. M. Galaburda. Symmetry and asymmetry in the human posterior thalamus. *Archives of Neurology* 39:325–332, 1982.

Falzi, G., P. Perrone, and L. A. Vignolo. Right-left asymmetry in anterior speech region. *Archives of Neurology* 39:239–240, 1982.

Fried, I., C. Mateer, G. Ojemann, R. Wohns, and P. Fedio. Organization of visuospatial functions in human cortex: Evidence from electrical stimulation. *Brain* 105:349–371, 1982.

Galaburda, A. M., M. LeMay, T. L. Kemper, and N. Geschwind. Right-left asymmetries in the brain, *Science* 199:852–856, 1978.

Galaburda, A. M., and F. Sanides. Cytoarchictectonic organization of the human auditory cortex. *Journal of Comparative Neurology* 190:597–610, 1980.

Gelfand, S., S. Hoffmand, S. Waltzman, and N. Piper. Dichotic CV recognition at various interaural temporal onset asynchronies: Effect of age. *Journal of the Acoustical Society of America* 68:1258–1261, 1980.

Geschwind, N. Language and the brain. *Scientific American* 226:340–348, 1972.

Geschwind, N., and W. Levitsky. Left-right asymmetries in temporal speech region. *Science* 161:186–187, 1968.

Gevins, A. S., J. C. Doyle, B. A. Cutillo, R. E. Schaffer, R. S. Tannehill, J. H. Ghannam, V. A. Gilcrease, and C. L. Yeager. Electrical potentials in human brain during cognition: New method reveals dynamic patterns of correlation. *Science* 213:918–921, 1981.

Gevins, A. S., G. M. Zeitlin, J. C. Doyle, C. D. Yingling, R. E. Schaffer, E. Callaway, and C. L. Yeager. Electroencephalogram correlates of higher cortical functions. *Science* 203:665–668, 1979.

Gibson, C., and Bryden, M. P. Dichaptic recognition of shapes and letters in children. *Canadian Journal of Psychology* 37:132–143, 1983.

Glick, S. D., D. A. Ross, and L. B. Hough. Lateral asymmetry of neurotransmitters in human brain. *Brain Research* 234:53–63, 1982.

Gordon, H. Hemispheric asymmetries in the perception of musical chords. *Cortex* 6:387–398, 1970.

Gordon, H. W., and J. E. Bogen. Hemispheric lateralization of singing after intracarotid sodium amylobarbitone. *Journal of Neurology, Neurosurgery, and Psychiatry* 37:727–738, 1974.

Gur, R. C., I. K. Packer, J. P. Hungerbuhler, M. Reivich, W. D. Obrist, W. S. Amarnek, and H. Sackheim. Differences in distribution of gray and white matter in human cerebral hemispheres. *Science* 207:1226–1228, 1980.

Halperin, Y., I. Nachson, and A. Carmon. Shift of ear superiority in dichotic listening to temporally patterned nonverbal stimuli. *Journal of the Acoutistical Society of America* 53:46–50, 1973.

Hampson, E., and D. Kimura. Hand movement asymmetries during verbal and nonverbal tasks. *Canadian Journal of Psychology* 38:102–125, 1984.

Harris, L. J. Sex differences in spatial ability: Possible environmental, genetic, and neurological factors. In M. Kinsbourne, Ed. *Asymmetrical Function of the Brain*. Cambridge, MA: Cambridge University Press, 1978.

Hécaen, H. Clinical symptomology in right and left hemisphere lesions. In V. B. Mountcastle, ed. *Interhemispheric Relations and Cerebral Dominance*. Baltimore, MD: Johns Hopkins University Press, 1962.

Heschl, R. L. *Über die vordere quere Schlafentwindung des Menschlichen Grosshirns.* Wien: Braumüller, 1878.

Hicks, R. E. Intrahemispheric response competition between vocal and unimanual performance in normal adult human males. *Journal of Comparative and Physiological Psychology* 89:50–61, 1975.

Hoadley, M. D., and K. Pearson. Measurement of internal diameter of skull in relation to "pre-eminence" of left hemisphere. *Biometrika* 21:94–123, 1929.

Hughlings-Jackson, J. *Selected Writings of John Hughlings-Jackson,* J. Taylor, ed. New York: Basic Books, 1958.

Kimura, D. Some effects of temporal-lobe damage on auditory perception. *Canadian Journal of Psychology* 15:156–165, 1961.

Kimura, D. Left-right differences in the perception of melodies. *Quarterly Journal of Experimental Psychology* 16:355–358, 1964.

Kimura, D. Functional asymmetry of the brain in dichotic listening. *Cortex* 3:163–178, 1967.

Kimura, D. The asymmetry of the human brain. *Scientific American* 228:70–78, 1973.

Kimura, D., and S. Folb. Neural processing of background sounds. *Science* 161:395–396, 1968.

King, F., and D. Kimura. Left-ear superiority in dichotic perception of vocal, non-verbal sounds. *Canadian Journal of Psychology* 26:111–116, 1972.

Kinsbourne, M. Eye and head turning indicates cerebral lateralization. *Science* 176:539–541, 1971.

Kinsbourne, M., and J. Cook. Generalized and lateralized effects of concurrent verbalization on a unimanual skill. *Quarterly Journal of Experimental Psychology* 23:341–345, 1971.

Kinsbourne, M., and R. E. Hicks. Functional cerebral space: A model for overflow, transfer and interference effects in human performance. In J. Requin, ed. *Attention and Performance,* vol. VII. New York: Academic Press, 1978.

Kodama, K. Beitrage zur Anatomie des Zentralnervensystems der Japaner. VIII. Insula Reil ii. *Folia Anatomica Japan* 12:423–444, 1934.

Kopp, N., F. Michel, H. Carrier, A Biron, and P. Duvillard. Étude de certaines asymmetries hemispheriques du cerveau human. *Journal of the Neurological Sciences* 34:349–363, 1977.

Kutas, M., and S. A. Hillyard. Event-related potentials in cognitive science. In M. S. Gazzaniga, ed. *Handbook of Cognitive Neuroscience.* New York: Plenum Press, 1984.

Lassen, N. A., D. H. Ingvar, and E. Skinhøj. Brain function and blood flow. *Scientific American* 239:62–71, 1978.

Lauter, J. Dichotic identification of complex sounds: Absolute and relative ear advantages. *Journal of the Acoustical Society of America* 71:701–707, 1982.

LeMay, M. Asymmetries of the skull and handedness. *Journal of the Neurological Sciences* 32:243–253, 1977.

LeMay, M. Morphological aspects of human brain asymmetry. *Trends in Neurosciences* 5:273–275, 1982.

LeMay, M., and A. Culebras. Human brain-morphologic differences in the hemispheres demonstrable by carotid arteriography. *New England Journal of Medicine* 287:168–170, 1972.

Lenneberg, E. *Biological Foundations of Language.* New York: John Wiley and Sons, 1967.

Levy, J. The origins of lateral asymmetry. In S. Harnad, R. W. Doty, L. Goldstein, J. Jaynes, and G. Krauthamer, eds. *Lateralization in the Nervous System.* New York: Academic Press, 1977.

Levy, J., C. Trevarthen, and R. W. Sperry. Perception of bilateral chimeric figures following hemispheric deconnection. *Brain* 95:61–78, 1972.

Mazziotta, J. C., M. E. Phelps, R. E. Carson, and D. E. Kuhl. Tomographic mapping of human cerebral metabolism: Auditory stimulation. *Neurology* 32:921–937, 1982.

McRae, D. L., C. L. Branch, and B. Milner. The occipital horns and cerebral dominance. *Neurology* 18:95–98, 1968.

Milner, B. Hemispheric specialization: Scope and limits. In F. O. Schmitt and F. G. Worden, eds. *The Neurosciences: Third Study Program.* Cambridge, MA: M.I.T. Press, 1974.

Mishkin, M., and D. G. Forgays. Word recognition as a function of retinal locus. *Journal of Experimental Psychology* 43:43–48, 1952.

Morrell, L. K., and J. G. Salamy. Hemispheric asymmetry of electrocortical responses to speech stimuli. *Science* 174:165–166, 1971.

Moscovitch, M. Information processing and the cerebral hemispheres. In M. Gazzaniga, ed. *Handbook of Behavioral Neurobiology,* (vol. 2). New York: Plenum Press, 1979.

Myers, R. E. Functions of the corpus callosum in interocular transfer. *Brain* 57:358–363, 1956.

Nachson, I., and A. Carmon. Hand preference in sequential and spatial discrimination tasks. *Cortex* 11:123–131, 1975.

Natale, M. Perception of nonlinguistic auditory rhythms by the speech hemisphere. *Brain and Language* 4:32–44, 1977.

Nishizawa, Y., T. K. Olsen, B. Larsen, and N. A. Lassen. Left-right cortical asymmetries of regional cerebral blood flow during listening to words. *Journal of Neurophysiology* 48:458–466, 1982.

Noffsinger, D. Dichotic-listening techniques in the study of hemispheric asymmetries. In D. F. Benson and E. Zaidel, eds. *The Dual Brain.* New York: Guilford Press, 1985.

Ojemann, G. A. Brain organization for language from the perspective of electrical stimulation mapping. *Behavioral and Brain Sciences* 6:189–230, 1983.

Oke, A., R. Keller, I. Mefford, and R. N. Adams. Lateralization of norepinephrine in human thalamus. *Science* 200:1411–1413, 1978.

Papcun, G., S. Krashen, D. Terbeek, R. Remington, and R. Harshman. Is the left hemisphere organized for speech, language and/or something else? *Journal of the Acoustical Society of America* 55:319–327, 1974.

Rasmussen, T., and B. Milner. The role of early left brain injury in determining lateralization of cerebral speech functions. *Annals of the New York Academy of Sciences* 299:355–369, 1977.

Reivich, M. The use of cerebral blood flow and metabolic studies in cerebral localization. In R. A. Thompson, and J. R. Green, eds. *New Perspectives in Cerebral Localization.* New York: Raven Press, 1982.

Rodney, M. L. *Motor sequencing and hemispheric specialization.* Unpublished doctoral dissertation. University of Waterloo, Canada, 1980.

Roland, P. E., L. Eriksson, S. Stone-Elander, and L. Widen. Does mental activity change the oxidative metabolism of the brain? *Journal of Neuroscience* 7:2372–2389, 1987.

Roland, P. E., and L. Friberg. Localization of cortical areas activated by thinking. *Journal of Neurophysiology* 53:1219–1243, 1985.

Roland, P. E., E. Skinhøj, N. A. Lassen, and B. Larsen. The role of different cortical areas in man in the organization of voluntary movements in extrapersonal space. *Journal of Neurophysiology* 43:137–150, 1980.

Roy, C. S., and M. B. Sherrington. On the regulation of the blood supply of the brain. *Journal of Physiology* 11:85, 1890.

Rubens, A. B. Anatomical asymmetries of human cerebral cortex. In S. Harnad, R. W. Doty, L. Goldstein, J. Jaynes, and G. Krauthamer, eds. *Lateralization in the Nervous System.* New York: Academic Press, 1977.

Rubens, A. B., M. W. Mahowald, and J. T. Hutton. Asymmetry of the lateral (Sylvian) fissures in man. *Neurology* 26:620–624, 1976.

Rudel, R. G., M. B. Denckla, and E. Spalten. The functional asymmetry of Braille letter learning in normal sighted children. *Neurology* 24:733–738, 1974.

Scheibel, A. B., I. Fried, L. Paul, A. Forsythe, U. Tomiyasu, A. Wechsler, A. Kao, and J. Slotnick. Differentiating characteristics of the human speech cortex: A quantitative Golgi study. In D. F. Benson and E. Zaidel, eds. *The Dual Brain.* New York: Guilford Press, 1985.

Seitz, M. R., B. A. Weber, J. T. Jacobson, and R. Morehouse. The use of averaged electroencephalic response techniques in the study of auditory processing related to speech and language. *Brain and Language* 11:261–284, 1980.

Semmes, J. Hemispheric specialization: A possible clue to mechanism. *Neuropsychologia* 6:11–26, 1968.

Sergent, J. Role of the input in visual hemispheric asymmetries. *Psychological Bulletin* 93:481–512, 1983.

Sidtis, J. Predicting brain organization from dichotic listening performance: Cortical and subcortical functional asymmetries contribute to perceptual asymmetries. *Brain and Language* 17:287–300, 1982.

Sperry, R. W. Lateral specialization in the surgically separated hemispheres. In F. O. Schmitt and F. G. Worden, eds. *The Neurosciences: Third Study Program.* Cambridge, MA: M.I.T. Press, 1974.

Springer, S. P., and G. Deutsch. *Left Brain, Right Brain.* San Francisco: W. H. Freeman, 1981.

Squires, N. K., and C. Ollo. Human evoked potential techniques: Possible applications to neuropsychology. In H. J. Hannay, ed. *Experimental Techniques in Human Neuropsychology.* New York: Oxford University Press, 1986.

Strauss, E., and C. Fitz. Occipital horn asymmetry in children. *Annals of Neurology* 18:437–439, 1980.

Strauss, E., B. Kosaka, and J. Wada. The neurological basis of lateralized cerebral function: A review. *Human Neurobiology* 2:115–127, 1983.

Strauss, E., B. Kosaka, and J. Wada. Visual laterality effects and cerebral speech dominance determined by the carotid Amytal test. *Neuropsychologia* 23:567–570, 1985.

Sussman, H. Evidence for left hemisphere superiority in processing movement-related tonal signals. *Journal of Speech and Hearing Disorders 22:224–235, 1979.*

Taylor, L. B. Localisation of cerebral lesions by psychological testing. *Clinical Neurology* 16:269–287, 1969.

Teszner, D., A. Tzavaras, and H. Hécaen. L'asymetries droite-gauche du planum temporale: À-propos de l'etude de 100 cerveaux. *Revue Neurologique* 126:444–449, 1972.

Teuber, H.-L. Physiological psychology. *Annual Review of Psychology* 6:267–296, 1955.

Van Lancker, D., and V. Fromkin. Hemispheric specialization for pitch and "tone": Evidence from Thai. *Journal of Phonetics* 1:101–109, 1973.

Wada, J. A., R. Clarke, and A. Hamm. Cerebral hemispheric asymmetry in humans: Cortical speech zones in 100 adult and 100 infant brains. *Archives of Neurology* 32:239–246, 1975.

Wada, J., and T. Rasmussen. Intracarotid injection of sodium Amytal for the lateralization of cerebral speech dominance. *Journal of Neurosurgery* 17:266–282, 1960.

Webster, W. G., and A. D. Thurber. Problem solving strategies and manifest brain asymmetry. *Cortex* 14:474–484, 1978.

Witelson, S. F., and W. Pallie. Left hemisphere specialization for language in the newborn: Neuroanatomical evidence of asymmetry. *Brain* 96:641–646, 1973.

Wolf, M. E., and M. A. Goodale. Oral asymmetries during verbal and non-verbal movements of the mouth. *Neuropsychologia* 25:375–396, 1987.

Wyke, M. The effect of brain lesions on an arm-hand precision task. *Neuropsychologia* 6:125–134, 1968.

Zangwill, O. L. *Cerebral Dominance and Its Relation to Psychological Function*. Springfield, IL: Charles C. Thomas, 1960.

Zurif, E. Auditory lateralization: Prosodic and syntactic factors. *Brain and Language* 1:391–401, 1974.

VARIATIONS IN CEREBRAL ASYMMETRY

Cerebral asymmetry is one of the most remarkable features of cerebral organization and continues to be a source of much theorizing in both the popular and the scientific literature. An important feature of cerebral asymmetry is the considerable individual variation in the pattern of left-right differences in both anatomical and functional asymmetry. By studying the nature of this variation, we may be able to separate the processes that are lateralized and gain insights into the nature of cerebral asymmetry.

INDIVIDUAL VARIATION IN ANATOMICAL ASYMMETRY

No two brains are alike. Brains differ in their size, gyral patterns, distribution of gray and white matter, cytoarchitectonics, vascular patterns, neurochemistry, and so forth. The question is whether variations in anatomical organization are related in any meaningful way to factors such as handedness or gender, and whether variations are correlated with functional differences.

Handedness

Witelson thoroughly reviewed the evidence for a relation between anatomical asymmetries and handedness, finding evidence in 1985 that hand preference is correlated with right-left asymmetry in the parietal operculum, frontal cortex, occipital region, vascular patterns, and cerebral blood flow (see Table 16-1). The overall conclusion is that in comparison with right handers, a higher proportion of left-handers show no asymmetry or a reversal of the direction of anatomical asymmetry. Is this difference of functional significance? To examine this, Ratcliffe and his colleagues correlated the

TABLE 16–1. Variations in anatomical asymmetry related to handedness

Measure	Handedness	Anatomical differences		
		Left larger (%)	Right larger (%)	No difference (%)
Blood volume	Right	25	62	13
	Left	64	28	8
Parietal operulum	Right	67	8	25
	Left	22	7	71
Frontal width	Right	19	61	20
	Left	27	40	33
Occipital width	Right	66	9	25
	Left	38	27	35
Occipital horns	Right	60	10	30
	Left	38	31	31

Source: Data from Hochberg and LeMay (1975), Lemay (1977), Carman et al. (1972), and McRae et al. (1968).

asymmetry in the course of the Sylvian fissure, as revealed by carotid angiogram, with the results of carotid sodium Amytal speech testing. They found that left- and right-handers with speech in the left hemisphere had a mean right-left difference of 27° in the angle formed by the vessels leaving the posterior end of the Sylvian fissure. Left- and right-handers with speech in the right hemisphere or with bilaterally represented speech had a mean difference of 0°. Thus, the anatomical asymmetry in their population was related to speech representation and not necessarily to handedness. In other words, the location of speech was a better predictor of individual variation in anatomical organization than was handedness.

Handedness may appear more closely related to anatomical anomalies because there is more variance in lateralization of speech in left-handers. A series of studies by Yakovlev and Rakic is germane. In a careful study of over 300 cases, they found that in 80% of the cases the pyramidal tract descending to the right hand contains more fibers than does the same tract going to the left hand. Apparently, there are more fibers descending to the right hand both from the contralateral left hemisphere and from the ipsilateral right hemisphere than there are to the left hand. In addition, the contralateral tract from the left hemisphere crosses at a higher level in the medulla than does the contralateral tract from the right hemisphere. To date, data are only available for 11 left-handers, but the pattern is remarkably similar to that observed in the population at large: 9 of 11 (82%) of these cases had the typical right-side bias. Since two-thirds of these left-handers could have been expected to have speech on the left, there appears to be a closer relation between locus of language and pyramidal tract organization than between handedness and the organization of the pyramidal tract.

A difficulty in accounting for variations in anatomical asymmetries is that there are both left- and right-handers in whom there is a marked dissociation between morphological and functional asymmetry. Thus, carotid Amytal testing may show speech to be in the left hemisphere, but the enlarged temporoparietal speech zone is inferred from other neurological studies to be in the right hemisphere. Consider also that a large percentage of the right-handed cases summarized in Table 16-1 do not show the "expected asymmetries" but have reversed asymmetries or no differences at all. These cases do pose a significant interpretation problem, and they suggest that other, as yet unknown, variables may also account for individual differences in both left- and right-handers.

One of the possible variables is that the connections of the two hemispheres may differ. To test this idea Witelson studied the hand preference of terminally ill subjects on a variety of unimanual tasks. She later did postmortem studies of their brains, paying particular attention to the size of the corpus callosum. She found that the cross-sectional area (see Figure 16-1) was 11% greater in left-handed and ambidextrous people than in right-handed subjects, as summarized in Table 16-2. It remains to be determined whether the larger callosum of non-right-handers contains a greater total number of fibers, thicker axons, or more myelin. If the difference is due to the number of fibers, it would represent some 25 million fibers! If Witelson's result is confirmed by others, it will imply that there is greater interaction between the hemispheres of left-handers, and suggests that the pattern of cerebral organization may be fundamentally different in left- and right-handers.

Gender

Less of the variance in anatomical asymmetry of the cerebral hemispheres can be associated with differences between males and females than with differences related to handedness. Although it is frequently stated that the cerebral hemispheres of females are less symmetrical than those of males, this conclusion is based largely on nonsignificant trends or impressions. We are aware of only three statistically reliable differences related to gender in

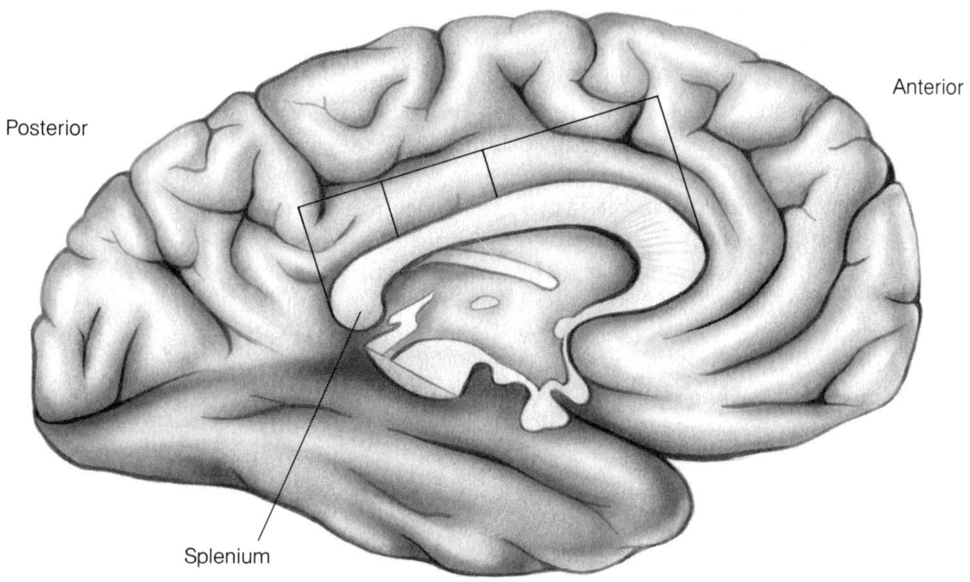

FIGURE 16-1. The human corpus callosum shown in midsagittal section. The subdivisions that are typically measured are indicated: the entire length and cross-sectional area; the anterior and posterior halves; and the splenium.

TABLE 16–2. Summary of brain measures in four hand-sex groups

Group	*n*	Age (yr.)	Brain weight (g)	Callosal area (mm²)
Males				
RH	7	48	1442	672
MH	5	49	1511	801[a]
Females				
RH	20	51	1269	655
MH	10	49	1237	697[a]

Note: RH = consistently right-handed; MH = left-handed or ambidextrous
[a] Differs significantly from other same-sex group.
Source: Simplified from Witelson, 1985.

humans. First, according to Wada there are more females than males exhibiting a reversed asymmetry pattern in the planum temporale, although the predominant pattern is still like that observed in males. Second, Lansdell and Davie studied pneumoencephalograms of neurological patients for the presence of the **massa intermedia** (a band of tissue joining the thalami but absent in about one-third of males and one-quarter of females) and correlated performance on the verbal and nonverbal sections of the Wechsler-Bellevue Intelligence Test. Although males with a massa intermedia had lower nonverbal scores than those without this structure, there was no comparable result in females. One interpretation of this result is that the presence of the massa intermedia in males produces competition and interference between the lateralized functions of the two hemispheres. This hypothesis remains to be proved, however. Third, de Lacoste-Utamsing and Holloway reported that the posterior part of the corpus callosum (the **splenium**) is significantly larger in females than in males (Figure 16-1). These authors also noted a qualitative difference: the female splenium is bulbous and widens markedly with respect to the body of the callosum; the male counterpart is approximately cylindrical and is relatively continuous with the body of the corpus callosum. These callosal data have sparked considerable controversy as they have not been replicated by others doing either postmortem examinations (see Witelson's data in Table 16-2) or using MRI scans. To date, we are aware of five different studies claiming to replicate the result and six failing to do so. A cautious reading of the literature must therefore lead to the conclusion that a sex difference is not yet established for the corpus callosum.

Peters has recently pointed out an interesting fact about the callosal data in the literature, however: although male brains are clearly larger than female brains, the male corpus callosum is not correspondingly larger (e.g., see Table 16-2). We have noted elsewhere (Chapter 5) that bigger bodies come with larger brains, so the larger male brain is hardly surprising. What is surprising, however, is that the corpus callosum is not proportional to brain size in males and females. Regardless of whether the callosum of females is larger or the same size as males, *it should be smaller.* It remains unclear why this is not the case and it is even less clear what it might mean. Like the callosal differences related to handedness, we do not know if the size represents more connections, larger fibers, more myelin, or what. In any event, there seems to be little doubt that there is a sex difference.

The absence of more evidence of sex differences (excepting the corpus callosum) in anatomical organization in humans does not mean that there is not a major difference related to gender. There are now numerous reports of large sex differences in both the neocortex and the hypothalamus of rats, which appear related to hormonal variables. There is no reason to believe that similar differences are not present in humans, although they have not been demonstrated yet.

HANDEDNESS AND FUNCTIONAL ASYMMETRY

As the term *sinister*—usually used to mean wicked or evil, but originally meaning left-hand-side in Latin—implies, left-handedness has historically been viewed as somewhat strange or unusual. The most commonly cited figure for left-handedness is 10%, representing the number of people who write with the left hand, but when other criteria are used, estimates range from 10 to 30%. The problem is that handedness is not absolute; some people are nearly totally left-handed, whereas other are ambidextrous (that is, they use either hand with equal facility). A rather useful distribution of handedness has been described by Annett (Table 16-3), who asked over 2000 adults to indicate the hand they used to perform each of 12 different tasks. It can be seen that the incidence of left-handedness on Annett's tasks varied from a low of about 6% when cutting with scissors to a high of about 17% when dealing cards.

TABLE 16-3. Percentages of "left," "right," or "either" responses to each question

Task	Left (%)	Either (%)	Right (%)
Dealing cards	17.02	3.32	79.66
Unscrewing jar	16.50	17.49	66.01
Shoveling	13.53	11.89	74.58
Sweeping	13.49	16.89	69.62
Threading needle	13.10	9.74	77.16
Writing	10.60	0.34	89.06
Striking match	9.95	8.74	81.31
Throwing ball	9.44	1.29	89.47
Hammering	9.22	2.54	88.24
Using toothbrush	9.18	8.49	82.33
Using racket	8.10	2.59	89.31
Using scissors	6.20	6.81	86.99

Note: Percentages based on 2321 respondents.
Source: Adapted from Annett, 1970.

Theories of Hand Preference

The many theories put forward to account for hand preference can be categorized according to their environmental, anatomical, or genetic emphases.

Environmental Theories. There are three variations on an environmental theory of handedness, and they stress the utility of behavior, reinforcement, or accident, respectively. The first variation, the behavioral (sometimes called the theory of the Peloponnesian Wars, or the sword-and-shield hypothesis) is that a soldier who held his shield in his left hand better protected his heart and improved his chances of survival. Since the left hand was holding the shield, the right hand became more skilled in various movements and eventually was used for most tasks. According to a female variant of this theory, it is adaptive for a mother to hold an infant in her left hand so that it will be soothed by the rhythm of the mother's heart; the mother, like the soldier, then has the right hand free and so uses it for executing skilled movements. Such theories have difficulties, the most obvious being failure to consider the possibility that right-handedness preceded, and thus is responsible for, the behavior.

The second variant on an environmental theory, that of reinforcement, has been elaborated by Collins. It is based on some ingenious experiments on "handedness" in mice: Collins raised mice in a world biased in such a way that the mice were forced to use either their left or right paws to obtain food located in a tube adjacent to the wall of their home cage. He found that the proportion of adult right- or left-pawed mice was directly related to which type of world they were raised in. Thus, he suggested, their preference was established by the contingencies of reinforcement from their environment. This view can be adapted to humans. The child's world is also right-handed in many ways, which reinforces the use of that hand. In addition, children in the United States were once forced to write with their right hands. Although emphasizing the potential importance of environmental factors, Collins' theory does not account for the difference between familial and nonfamilial handedness or the relation of handedness to cerebral dominance. It also seems to be negated by what happened when children were given their choice of which hand to learn to write with in U.S. schools: the incidence of left-handed writing rose only to 10%, which is the norm in most societies that have been studied.

According to the third variant of environmental influences on hand preference, there is a genetically determined bias toward being right-handed, but left-handedness occurs through some cerebral deficit caused by accident. To account for the familial aspect of left-handedness Bakan and his colleagues have argued that there is a high probability of stressful births among left-handers, which increases the risk of brain damage and so maintains the incidence of left-handedness. This theory would predict that some consistent deficit in cognitive functioning in adult left-handers should result from their brain damage, but no such deficit has been shown. It could be argued that since the alleged damage occurs in infancy, the brain compensates in such a way that the only symptom that appears in adulthood is left-handedness, but this argument is hardly compelling support for the theory.

Anatomical Theories. Of the several anatomical theories of handedness, two, which are well documented, explain hand preference by alluding to anatomical asymmetry. In the first theory right-handedness is attributed to enhanced maturation and ultimately greater development of the left hemisphere. Generalizing from this assumption, it is predicted that nonfamilial left-handers should show an asymmetry mirroring that of right-handers, whereas familial left-handers should show no anatomical asymmetry. These predictions are difficult to assess because no studies have specifically considered anatomical asymmetry with respect to handedness or with respect to familial history and handedness. A major problem with this theory is that it simply pushes the question one step backward, asking not "why handedness?" but instead "why anatomical asymmetry?"

The second theory addresses this problem in part. As Morgan has pointed out, many animals have a left-sided developmental advantage that is not genetically coded. For example, there is a left-sided bias for the location of the heart, the size of the ovaries in birds, the control of birdsong, the size of left temporal cortex in humans, the size of the left side of the skull in the great apes, and so on. This predominance of left-favoring asymmetries puts the more celebrated left hemisphere speech dominance in the more general perspective of all anatomical asymmetries. Since neither genetic evidence nor genetic theory accurately predicts these human asymmetries, Morgan assumes that they all result from some fundamental asymmetries in human body chemistry. The problem with Morgan's theory applied to handedness is that it fails to explain left-handedness in the presence of other "normal" asymmetries such as the location of the heart.

Hormonal Theories. Geschwind and Galaburda proposed a novel theory in which they suggested that cerebral asymmetry can be significantly modified during early life, leading to anomolous patterns of hemispheric organization. A central part their theory is that one of the factors acting to alter cerebral organization during development is testosterone, the principal male hormone. Testosterone is known to have an effect on the development of the hypothalamus and cortex of nonhuman species, as well as on nonneural tissues, so it is reasonable to suggest that it has an effect on the brain of humans as well. Geschwind and Galaburda suggest that testosterone's effect is largely inhibitory, meaning that higher than normal levels of testosterone will slow down development, possibly acting directly on the brain, or indirectly through an action on genes. Central to the Geschwind-Galaburda theory is the idea that testosterone's inhibitory action occurs largely in the left hemisphere, thus allowing the right hemisphere to grow more rapidly. This leads to altered cerebral organization and, in some people, to left-handedness. A further feature of the theory is that testosterone also affects the immune system, leading to more diseases related to a malfunctioning immune system. (A parallel theory of the relation between the immune system and male afflictions has been proposed by Gualtieri and Hicks.)

The details and arguments of the Geschwind-Galaburda theory are many, and beyond us here. (See Geschwind and Galaburda for an extensive discussion.) The theory does, however, account for several observations that are relevant to theories of cerebral asymmetry and handedness: (1) Left-handedness is more common in males. This would be predicted if testosterone were involved. (2) Developmental disorders related to left hemisphere function (e.g., learning disabilities) are more common in males and in left-handers. (3) Females are, on average, superior at certain left hemisphere abilities including verbal skills and some fine-motor skills **(praxis).** (4) Males are, on average, superior at certain putative right hemisphere abilities including some spatial skills and visuospatial movements. (5) Immune disorders are more common in non-right-handers.

The absence of direct evidence that testosterone can actually affect cerebral organization in a way that would influence handedness presents a major challenge for the Geschind-Galaburda theory. On the other hand, the theory is appealing because the actions of testosterone on cortical organization can be studied in nonhuman species as a partial test of the theory. Furthermore, the idea that a single mechanism (testosterone) might be related to the two major contributors to variance in cerebral asymmetry is attractive for its simplicity. This theory is likely to generate considerable debate in the coming years.

Genetic Theories. Of the many genetic models for handedness, most postulate a dominant gene or genes for right-handedness and a recessive gene or genes for left-handedness, but none of these models can accurately predict the probability of left-handedness.

The two best attempts to develop genetic models of handedness are those of Annett and of Levy and Nagylaki. Annett has proposed that there may be a gene for right-handedness but not for left-handedness. In the absence of the right-handed gene the displayed handedness will be random. The incidence of right-handedness would be slightly higher in the group without the gene because of environmental factors predisposing the choice of the right hand. The theory proposed by Levy and Nagylaki is somewhat more complex. They propose a two-gene, four-allele model. That is, there is a gene for handedness and a gene for hemispheric representation of speech. The gene for left-handedness is recessive as is the gene for having speech in the right hemisphere.

Genetic theories have been criticized on a number of grounds (see Hardyck and Petrinovich), and none is totally satisfactory. For example, there is no attempt to differentiate between familial and nonfamilial left-handers.

From this brief review of theories of handedness it is clear that we do not know why there is handedness, and we may never know. (To the multiplicity of theories of handedness we add our own: a man named Noah was disliked by his fellow townspeople because he was right-handed and they were southpaws, and because he insisted on building an ark in the desert. A great flood came and everyone was drowned except Noah and his right-handed family. The rest is history.)

Cerebral Organization in Left-Handers

There appears to be a widespread belief in the neurological literature that cognitive functions are more bilaterally organized in left-handers than in right-handers. This conclusion likely arose from the aphasia literature, in which there are reports that aphasia occurs more often in left-handers than in right-handers with comparable damage, but that recovery from aphasia is more rapid and complete in the left-handers. Careful examination of the literature suggests, however, that these conclusions are based largely on compilations of scattered individual cases rather than on systematic studies of unselected cases. Two recent large-scale studies suggest that the well-known difference between cerebral organization in left- and right-handers may be wrong. First, in the previous chapter we discussed the sodium Amytal procedure and reported the data of Rasmussen and Milner. They found that 70% of left-handers appear to have language represented in the left hemisphere, 15% in the right hemisphere, and 15% bilaterally. Second, Kimura reported the incidence of aphasia and apraxia in a consecutive series of 520 patients selected only for unilateral brain damage. The frequency of left-handedness in her population was within the expected range, and these patients did not have a higher incidence of either aphasia or apraxia than right-handers. In fact, the incidence of aphasia was approximately 70% of the incidence in right-handers, exactly what would be predicted from the Amytal studies. Thus, although a small proportion of left-handers may have bilateral speech or right hemisphere speech, the majority of left-handers do not.

It has been suggested that on the basis of family background left-handers can be subdivided into two populations differing in cerebral organization: familial left-handers, who have a family history of left-handedness, and nonfamilial left-handers, who have no such family history. According to Hécaen and Sauguet, nonfamilial left-handed patients with unilateral lesions perform like right-handed patients on neuropsychological tests. In contrast, familial left-handers perform much differently, suggesting to Hécaen and Sauguet that they have a different pattern of cerebral organization. Although this conclusion is interesting, it must be considered cautiously. First, the distinction between familial and nonfamilial left-handers can be criticized on the grounds that the designation to one group or the other is based on loose criteria. Normally, subjects are merely asked if they have any left-handed relatives. In our experience, people are very unreliable at accurately reporting this information. Future studies should actually measure the handedness of the relatives. Second, it is possible that familial left-handers have a different pattern of cerebral organization because they represent the left-handers that do not have speech exclusively located in the left hemisphere. This is an empirical question and could easily be tested.

In summary, we can find little evidence that the cerebral organization of speech or nonspeech functions differs (from those functions in right-handers) in the 70% of left-handers with speech represented in the left hemisphere. One caveat must be issued, however: There is a larger incidence of left-handedness among mentally defective children and children with various neurological disorders than is found in the general population. This is not surprising, however, because if the dominant hemisphere is injured at an early age, handedness and dominance can move under the control of what would normally be the non-dominant hemisphere. Since there are so many more right-handed children, it would be expected by probability alone that more right-handed children with left hemisphere damage would switch to right hemisphere dominance than would switch in the reverse direction. That this can occur, however, cannot be used as grounds for predicting cognitive deficits or differences in cerebral organization in the general population of left-handers.

An additional question concerns the organization of the cerebral hemispheres in left-handers who have right hemisphere speech. It is reasonable to wonder if these people simply have a straight reversal of functions from one hemisphere to the other. Unfortunately, little is known about cerebral organization in people who have right hemisphere speech and otherwise normal brains. It is known, however, that people with left temporal lobe lesions and right hemisphere speech do not appear to have a typical "reversed" pattern of cerebral organization. For example, in studying the ability of people with left temporal lesions and right hemisphere speech to copy series of movements, Milner and Kolb studied a group of 10 patients, finding all of them to be impaired. They found this surprising since neither right nor left temporal lobe lesions in people with left hemisphere speech interfere with performance on this task. Milner and her colleagues have found other parallel examples, suggesting that more is different than the locus of speech in people with right hemisphere speech. Of course, all of her subjects were likely to have had early brain damage, so we still must wonder about people who have right hemisphere speech but no early brain damage.

SEX DIFFERENCES IN CEREBRAL ASYMMETRY

One of the most obvious sources of individual variation in the behavior of humans is gender: males and females behave differently. The question is whether any differences in cognitive behavior between males and females can be attributed to biological differences between the brains of the two sexes. There is substantial anecdotal and experimental evidence of cognitive differences between males and females, and there have been several attempts to relate these to differences in brain organization. If any one principle can be abstracted to distinguish the sexes, it is that females tend to be more fluent than males in the use of language, and males tend to be better than females at spatial analysis. These differences have been attributed to the possibility of a difference in the pattern of cerebral organization between the sexes, but before considering the theories we shall review the data.

Evidence of Sex Differences

Evidence supporting the argument that there are significant sex differences in cerebral organization derive primarily from studies of normal subjects, laterality studies, cerebral blood-flow measurements, and neurological patients.

Normal Subjects. The place to start in the study of cognitive differences between males and females is with *The Psychology of Sex Differences,* a book published by MacCoby and Jacklin in 1974. In their thorough review of the literature to 1974 they found four reliable sex differences. First, girls have greater verbal ability than boys. At about age 11, the sexes begin to diverge, with female superiority increasing through high school and possibly beyond. Girls score higher on tasks involving both receptive and productive language, and on "high-level" verbal tasks (analogies, comprehension of difficult written material, creative writing), as well as on lower level measures (fluency). A simple demonstration of this sex difference can be seen when males and females are asked to fill in the blanks as illustrated in Figure 16-2*D*. In this test the first letter of each of four words is provided. The task is to fill in missing letters to make a meaningful sentence. Females are much better at this task than males. Overall the magnitude of female superiority at verbal skills is small, in the range of one-quarter of a standard deviation.

Second, males excel in visual-spatial ability. This means that on tests of recall and detection of shapes, mental rotation of two- or three-dimensional figures, geometry, maze learning, map

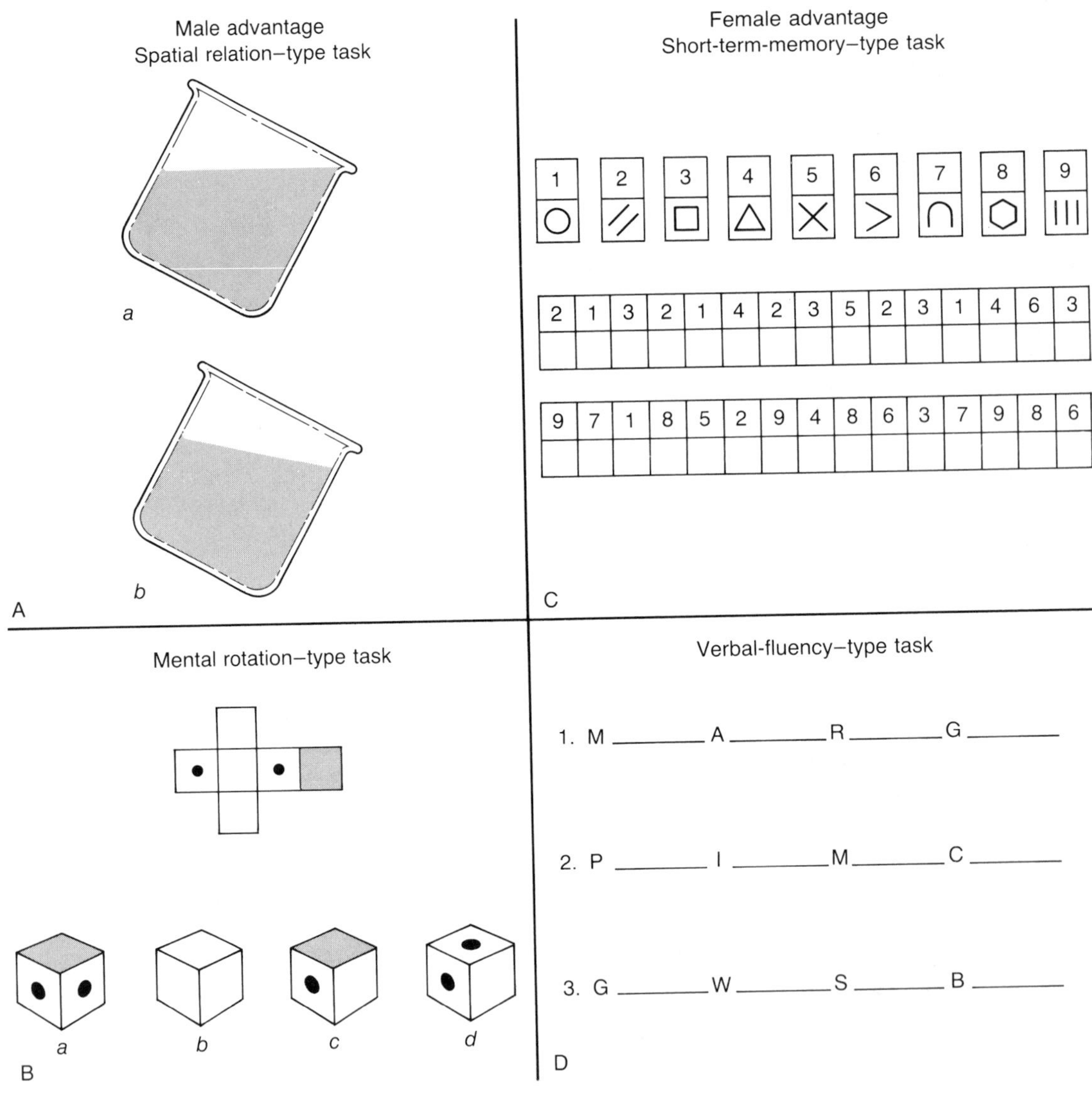

FIGURE 16-2. Examples of four types of tasks that reliably show sex-related differences. *A.* The top drawing shows a line drawn to indicate waterline in which the response indicates comprehension of the concept of horizontality of fluid level. The bottom illustration shows the line drawn incorrectly, indicating no comprehension of the concept. The bottom response is typical of about two-thirds of females. *B.* This task, which is similar to those in the spatial relations test of the Differential Aptitude Test, requires the subject to choose the one box from the bottom four that could be made from the plan above. Males typically find this task much easier than females. *C.* In this test the subject must fill in the empty boxes in the bottom rows with the appropriate symbols from the examples at the top. This is similar to the digit symbol test on the Wechsler Intelligence tests. When given a larger number of boxes to fill and a time limit of 90 sec, females complete 10–20% more items than males. *D.* This test of verbal fluency requires the subject to fill in each blank in order to form words that make a sentence. Females are faster at this type of test than males.

reading, aiming at and tracking objects, and geographical knowledge, males perform better on average than do females. Simple tests, that can be used to demonstrate this sex difference are illustrated in Figure 16-2. For example, in the water level task *(A)* used by Thomas and coworkers, subjects are shown a tipped flask and asked to draw in the waterline. The researchers report that among 62 randomly chosen college men the error in estimating the angle of the water was about 2° off the horizontal. Of 91 women, 28 (31%) showed the same performance as men, whereas the remainder showed an error of 15° to 20°. In other words, although the men in his sample understood that the waterline remained horizontal, 69% of the women did not. In developmental studies Thomas and colleagues report that by 12 years of age most males indicate that the waterline is horizontal, but that females who perform in this way do so at a somewhat later age. Like the verbal advantage of females, the spatial advantage of males is not absolute, the difference being only about 0.4 of a standard deviation.

Third, boys excel in mathematical ability. Although the two sexes are similar in their early acquisition of quantitative concepts and their mastery of arithmetic, beginning at about age 12 to 13 boys' mathematical skills increase faster than girls'. The better mathematical skills of boys is partly a function of the number of mathematics courses taken, since boys do take more courses, but this accounts for only part of the difference. Recently, a controversy has arisen over the basis of this sex difference (see Benbow and Stanley), but there is little argument over the fact that males perform better at math.

Fourth, males are physically more aggressive than females. A sex difference is present as early as social play begins, at age 2 to 3 years, and remains through the college years. Studies with nonhuman primates, largely using rhesus monkeys, show that the increased aggression in males is probably a result of the male hormone androgen both pre- and postnatally. How this influences the brain is unknown.

The appearance of sex differences in the performance of what appears to be simple tests has important implications for neuropsychological assessment, since gender may be important in predicting what normal performance levels should be. Consider the following example. We gave school-age children three tests widely used in neuropsychological assessment and found sex differences on two of the tests (Figure 16-3). On the Draw-a-Bicycle Test (see Chapter 32 for the scoring procedure) males performed better than females; on the Chicago Word-Fluency Test (the test requires the subject to write as many words beginning with "s" as possible in 5 min and as many four-letter words beginning with "c" as possible in 4 min) females performed better — at some ages by as much as 10 words — than males. On the copy and recall of the Rey figure (See Figure 11-3*D*), there was no sex difference. The appearance of reliable sex differences on these clinical tests implies that separate norms are necessary for the clinical assessment of males and females, although to date these separate norms have not been established for very many clinical tests.

The sex differences described by MacCoby and Jacklin have often been described as a "spatial" advantage for males and a "verbal" advantage for females, but more recent research has indicated that this dichotomy is too simple; there is a broader pattern of differences that cannot be labeled easily as verbal and spatial. According to Harshman and his coworkers' recent review, females excel at both perceptual speed (Figure 16-2*D*) and visual memory *(C)*, whereas males are better at perceptual closure (See Figure 11-3*D*) and the disembedding of visual patterns from complex arrays (see Figure 11-3*B*). The fact that females are superior at perceptual speed and visual memory is not predicted from a simple "verbal" description of their superior abilities, although males still appear to perform best at "spatial-type" tests. Finally, some

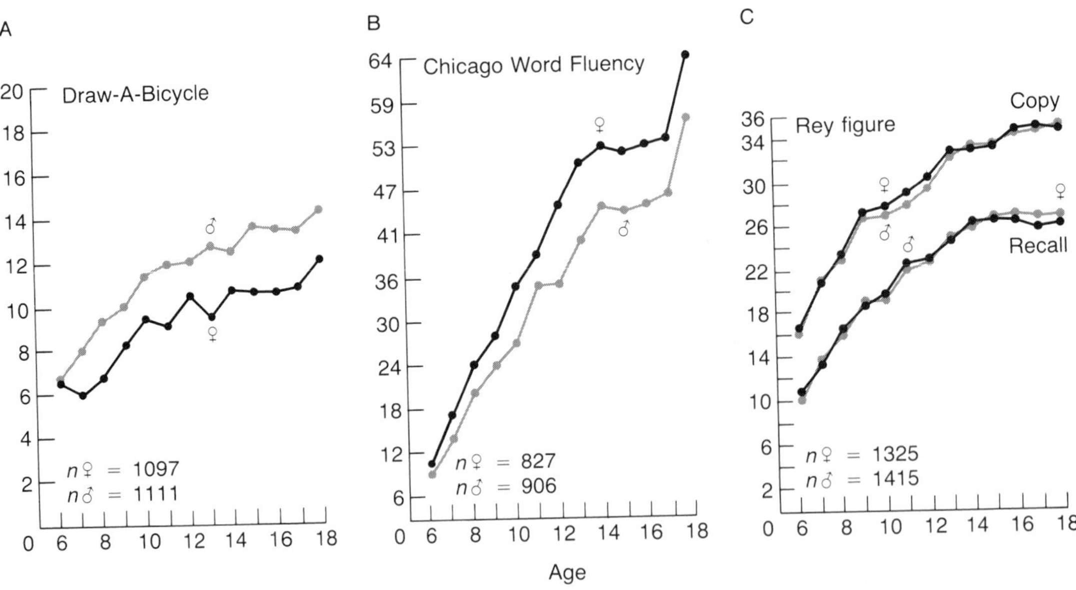

FIGURE 16-3. Performance of males and females of different ages on three neuropsychological tests. *A*. On the Draw-a-Bicycle Test males obtain higher scores than females. *B*. On the Chicago Word-Fluency Test females perform better than males. *C*. On the copy and recall of the Rey figure there is no difference in the performance between males and females. (Whishaw and Kolb, unpublished.)

researchers have been impressed by anecdotal evidence that males appear to excel at chess and musical composition. In the Soviet Union, where chess is a national pastime, no women have achieved grand-master status, and women compete in separate tournaments. In music, women appear to be as competent in performing as men, but fewer excel in composition. It has been suggested that men have an advantage in these fields because both involve spatial ability. Harris described the spatial structure of music as follows:

> For instance, there is the sense in which certain kinds of sounds naturally seem to belong in certain parts of space relative to other sounds. Why are high notes and low notes *called* high notes and low notes? Why does the flute seem to float above the bassoon, and the violin above the cello? Pitch and resonance seem to impart "spatial" qualities to sound in more than a merely metaphorical sense. . . .
>
> There are many other examples of spatial structure in music, including cross-relations (appearance in different voices of two tones of mutually contradictory character that normally are played as a melodic progression in one voice); cross-rhythms (simultaneous use of conflicting rhythmic patterns); bitonality; and polytonality.
>
> Perhaps the ability to recognize and to execute and, above all, to create, a melodic pattern is a spatial ability not unlike the visual detection of an embedded figure or the mental rotation of a geometrical form so as to anticipate how it will look from a different spatial perspective. The recognition of counterpoint or of variations on a theme may depend on similar abilities to [disassemble] a figure from a complex background, to remember

it, and to follow it through a variety of transformations. (Harris, 1978, pp. 424–425)

There may be substance to the argument that sex differences in chess and musical composition can be attributed to spatial factors, but it is also easy to suggest cultural and environmental reasons why women have not excelled in these areas. Similar arguments about the spatial aspects of literature could also be advanced, but it would be somewhat more difficult to demonstrate sex differences in creative writing ability.

Laterality Studies. If the differences described above are physiological rather than cultural, one might expect to find a sex difference in the distribution of verbal and spatial functions between the hemispheres in laterality studies. The literature on sex-related differences in lateralization is characterized by inconsistencies, however. As Bryden emphasizes, procedural differences, small samples, and great variability plague this research, and it is difficult to be certain that observed differences truly reflect differences in laterality in the population. Nonetheless, he concludes that the majority of the verbal dichotic and verbal tachistoscopic studies that show any sex-related effects indicate a greater degree of lateralization in males. Furthermore, although sex-related differences are not as consistent on tests of spatial processing, there is some evidence that males are more lateralized on tests in both the visual and the tactile senses. We must emphasize, however, that sex differences in the degree of perceptual asymmetries can be profoundly influenced by the way in which the subjects approach the task. For example, women may tend to use verbal strategies to solve spatial problems and to encode spatial displays, and this may generate a laterality effect, not because of a difference in cerebral lateralization of function between the sexes, but because of a difference in strategy or preferred cognitive mode used to solve the task. On the basis of the evidence to date, we must concur with Bryden that this alternative explanation seems at least reasonably plausible.

Cerebral Blood Flow. Some of the variance in studies of changes in cerebral blood flow during cognitive activity is apparently related to gender as well as to handedness. In 1982, Gur and his colleagues found that females and left-handers have a high rate of cerebral blood flow and a greater percentage of fast-perfusing tissue (rapid blood exchange) than do right-handed males. All groups showed an increase in blood flow to the left hemisphere during verbal tasks and a complementary increase in blood flow to the right hemisphere during spatial tasks, but females and male left-handers showed reliably greater increases than right-handed males. The authors took these data to suggest possible differences in the distribution of gray and white matter in the two hemispheres of males and females, although confirmation of this hypothesis awaits postmortem studies. The authors failed to find support for a simple difference between verbal and spatial processing in the two sexes, however, because both sexes exhibited an increase in left hemisphere blood flow during the verbal task and in the right hemisphere during the spatial task.

Neurological Patients. Although Lansdell first reported a sex-related difference in the effects of left and right temporal lobectomies in 1962, it was a series of papers by McGlone in the late 1970s and early 1980s that proved to be seminal for the study of sex differences in neurological patients. On the basis of her studies of stroke patients with lateralized lesions she made three clear and testable proposals: (1) There is a sex-related difference in the effects of left and right hemisphere strokes on the performance of the Wechsler Adult Intelligence Scale (WAIS), (2) Aphasia is commoner in males than in females, and (3) There is a greater degree of functional asymmetry in right-handed men than in right-handed women. McGlone's conclusions are important both because they have led many researchers to consider the possibility of sex-related differences in their studies of neurological patients, and because the ideas that have come from her work, as well as from subsequent work by others, provide new insights into the nature and complexity of cerebral asymmetry.

McGlone's initial studies showed a double dissociation of the effects of left and right hemisphere lesions in males on achievement on the verbal and performance subscales of the WAIS (see Chapter 27 for details of the WAIS). Left hemisphere lesions were associated with a decline in verbal IQ, whereas right hemisphere lesions were correlated with a depression of the performance IQ. In contrast, she failed to find a selective verbal or performance deficit after unilateral brain injury in females; females with either left or right hemisphere lesions exhibited a severe depression of verbal intelligence and memory. Furthermore, in McGlone's population, aphasia was three times more likely in males than in females. McGlone interpreted these results as indicating greater functional asymmetry in males than in females. Although there has been some support for her conclusions, there appears to be five reasons to suggest that some revision may be in order.

First, Inglis and Lawson reviewed the literature and found 16 studies that reported the effects of lateralized lesions on the performance and verbal achievement subscales of the WAIS. By using various statistical procedures with these data, they showed that although left and right hemisphere lesions differently affected verbal and performance subscales in males, as McGlone had found in her smaller sample, left hemisphere lesions in females depressed both IQs equally and right hemisphere lesions failed to depress either IQ (see Figure 16-4). Thus, in contrast to McGlone, Inglis and Lawson found an equivalent effect of left hemisphere lesions on verbal IQ in both sexes — a result suggesting that left hemisphere lesions are equally disruptive to verbal behaviors in males and females. Second, several groups have failed to find any evidence of a difference between the sexes in the incidence of aphasia. For example, Hier and Kaplan tabulated the frequency of aphasia in three large samples ($n = 767$) and found the ratio of men to women aphasics to be about 1.2 : 1. Similarly, de Renzi and his colleagues found the ratio, in a sample of 1244 patients, to be 1 : 1 : 1. Third, aside from performance IQ data, there is little compelling evidence that right hemisphere lesions in females are less disruptive to nonverbal behaviors. For example, Hier and his coworkers found no evidence of a sex difference in the incidence of a variety of symptoms commonly associated with right hemisphere damage, including anosognosia, simultaneous extinction, **contralateral neglect,** drawing agnosia, prosopagnosia, constructional apraxia, or dressing apraxia (inability to dress oneself). One might have expected a difference on these symptoms if the female brain were less lateralized. Fourth, our reanalysis of the effects of small left or right hemisphere excisions on the verbal and performance IQs of patients (Kolb and Milner) revealed only a quantitative difference in performance: males tend to show greater effects than females on verbal and performance IQs after left and right hemisphere lesions, respectively. Finally, a 1983 study by Kimura showed that the pattern of cerebral organization *within* each hemisphere may differ between the sexes. Although males and females were nearly as likely to be aphasic following left hemisphere lesions, males were likely to be aphasic and apraxic after damage to either the anterior or the posterior cortex, whereas females were far more likely to experience speech disorders and apraxia after anterior than posterior lesions. Kimura also reported data from a small sample of patients that suggest an analogous sex-related difference following right hemisphere lesions. Anterior, but not posterior, lesions in females impaired performance of the block design and object-assembly subtests of the WAIS, whereas males were equally affected on these tests by either anterior or posterior lesions.

Taken together, the data from neurological patients support the idea that unilateral lesions have different effects in males and females. How the sexes differ in cerebral organization is simply not known at present. McGlone's conclusion that the

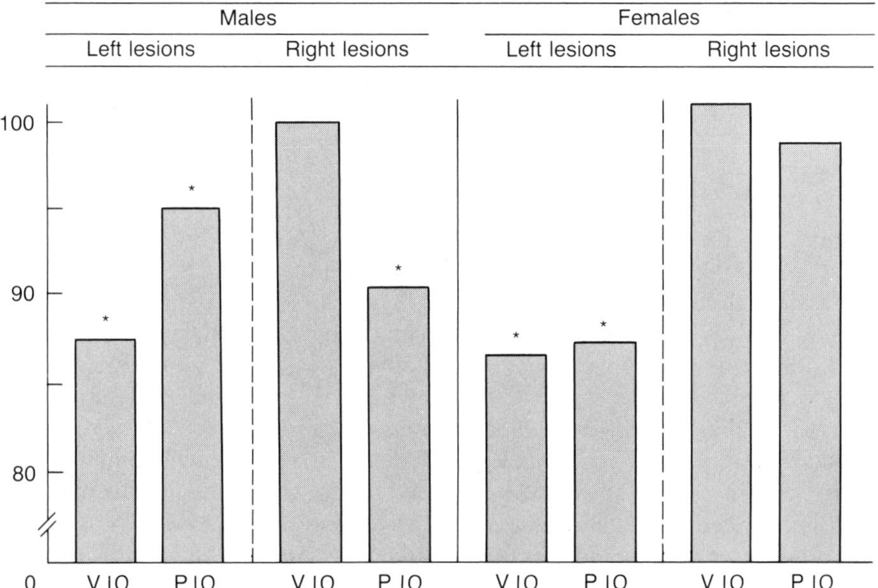

FIGURE 16-4. Summary of Inglis and Lawson's tabulation of studies reporting verbal and performance IQ scores in neurological patients. A clear sex difference emerged in which males with left hemisphere lesions exhibited a depression in verbal IQ (VIQ), whereas males with right hemisphere lesions exhibited a complementary deficit in performance IQ (PIQ). In contrast, females with left hemisphere lesions showed reductions in both verbal and performance IQs, but females with right hemisphere lesions showed no significant depression in either IQ scale. The asterisks indicate scores that differ significantly from 100.

female brain is more symmetrical than the male brain appears to be too simple to account for the data. Kimura's results suggest that there may be intrahemispheric differences in cerebral organization, but her study needs to be replicated by others. Further, there should be an examination of cortical stimulation data to see if speech is affected by posterior stimulation differently in males and females. Finally, we must be aware that apparent differences between the sexes, especially left-right ones, may reflect different strategies of problem solving in the two sexes rather than real neurological differences. For example, if females tend to solve relatively nonverbal problems with verbal strategies, unilateral brain damage would appear to have less specific effects in females than in males; left hemisphere lesions in females would depress performance of both verbal and nonverbal tests, whereas right hemisphere lesions might appear to have little effect on either type of task.

In conclusion, gender appears to account for some of the observed variability in cerebral asymmetry, although more research is needed to determine how much of the variance is accounted for by gender and how gender interacts with handedness. Gender may be important in accounting for the observed behavioral differences between males and females and should be studied systematically, particularly in neurological patients.

Explanation of Sex Differences

We can identify six different explanations commonly advanced to account for sex differences:

(1) differential brain organization, (2) hormonal effects on cerebral function, (3) genetic sex-linkage, (4) maturation rate, (5) environment, and (6) preferred cognitive mode.

Differential Brain Organization. In previous sections we considered sex differences in cerebral organization as inferred from studies of neurological patients, anatomy, and laterality studies. There is now good evidence that lesions affect males and females differently, but it has not been proved that this is due to differences in brain organization.

Hormonal Effects. There are clear sex differences in the neural control of a wide variety of reproductive and nonreproductive behavior patterns in most vertebrate species. In birds and mammals the presence of testosterone at critical times during development has unequivocal effects on the structure of both hypothalamic and forebrain structures, and it is believed that the observed morphological effects are responsible for the behavioral dimorphism. The influence of gonadal hormones on brain and behavior is often referred to as an *inductive* or *organizing effect,* and in the brain this organizing effect is said to lead to *sexual differentiation.* The actions of gonadal hormones (largely androgens) during development are permanent, but the mechanisms of action are still not well understood. It appears that androgens (typically "male" hormones) are converted into estradiol (normally "female" hormones) in the brain and the binding of this estradiol to receptors leads to masculinization of the brain. Estradiol receptors have been found in the developing cortex of rodents and nonhuman primates, but they are not found in the adults. This suggests that the hormones may have an organizing effect on the brain of mammals only during development, although they can still influence neuronal function later in life. One way they have a later influence is by altering the susceptibility of cortical neurons to the influence of environmental stimuli. For example, Juraska has found that the exposure to gonadal hormones perinatally (i.e., around birth) determines the later ability of environmental stimulation to alter dendritic growth. Changes in dendritic growth are important because they provide a mechanism for adaptation and learning (see Chapter 21 for details). Furthermore, we saw in Chapter 15 that even small changes in dendritic structure are correlated with differences in function (see Figure 15-2).

In addition to the organizing effects of hormones on the brain, it is known that **catecholamine** (e.g., epinephrine and dopamine) levels are affected by estrogen and that their levels fluctuate during the estrus cycle in rats. In view of the importance of catecholamines in movement and other behaviors, it is obvious that estrogen could alter behavior through its stimulation of dopamine receptors in particular. Preliminary work by Hampson and Kimura has shown changes during the human menstrual cycle on performance of a variety of timed manual and articulatory (word-making) tests, as well as on some spatial tests. It is still not known, however, whether gonadal hormones can affect the function of the cerebral hemispheres in adulthood. There are dopamine receptors in the prefrontal cortex and medial temporal region, so there is a good possibility that estrogen could alter functioning in these regions.

In summary, there is no question that gonadal hormones have significant effects on brain development and function. Although there is little direct evidence regarding how this might relate to the sex differences in cognitive function, there is good reason to suppose that at least some sex differences are related to gonadal hormones. Perhaps the most interesting possibility is that gonadal hormones alter the brain and make male and female brains more or less plastic in different environments. This would provide a route whereby social factors could influence the brain differently in males and females, leading to sex-related variations.

Genetic Sex-Linkage. A number of authors have proposed that the major factor in determining variation in spatial ability is genetic. It is postulated that a recessive **gene** on the X (female) **chromosome** is responsible. Every normal person has 46 chromosomes arranged in 23 pairs, one set from the father and one from the mother. The 23rd pair is composed of the sex chromosomes; if both are X, the child is female (XX), but if one is X and the other Y, the child is male (XY). If a gene for a particular trait is recessive, the trait will not be expressed in a female child unless the gene is present on both X chromosomes. However, the gene need be present only on one chromosome if the child is male. Thus, if a mother carried the gene on both of her X chromosomes, all of her sons will present the trait, but her daughters will show it only if the father also carries the recessive gene on his X chromosome. Notice that for boys it is irrelevant whether or not the father carries the trait because he will have contributed his Y chromosome to a boy, and sex-linked traits are attached to X chromosomes only. Males, then, have a greater chance of expressing a sex-linked trait than females, because males only require one X chromosome with the trait rather than two. Figure 16-5 illustrates the principle. If this model were correct, there would be a near-zero correlation between the spatial ability if a father provided the Y chromosome, but there would be a significant correlation between mother and son as well as between father and daughter since in the latter cases the parents contribute genetic information. These correlations have indeed been claimed.

From Figure 16-5 the number of males and females who would possess the trait can be predicted: 50% of males and 25% of females. From this we can predict that 25% of females will exceed the average male's score in spatial ability; this percentage is consistently observed.

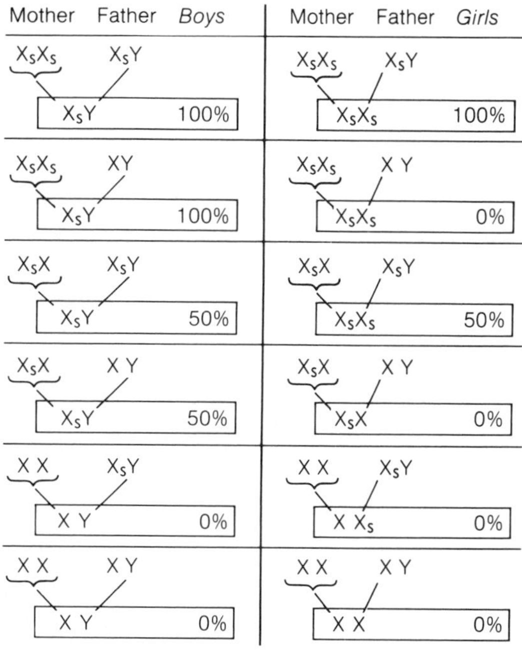

FIGURE 16-5. Model demonstrating sex-linked recessive trait for spatial ability. The percentages represent the number of offspring having the genotype for spatial ability. That genotype in males (X_sY) is more likely than in females (X_sX_s), since males have only a single X chromosome. Since the gene for spatial ability (s) is recessive, females require both X chromosomes to carry the gene before the trait is expressed. (After Harris, 1978.)

Maturation Rate. Developmental studies indicate that a fundamental difference in male and female cerebral maturation may help to account for the sex differences observed in adulthood. It has long been known that girls begin to speak sooner than boys, develop larger vocabularies during childhood, and, as children, use more complex linguistic constructions than do boys. Further, the speech of young girls may be better enunciated than boy's speech, and girls are generally better readers than boys. Although developmental studies of laterality in children have yielded conflicting results, dichotic and tachistoscopic studies frequently indicate an earlier evolution of asymmetry in girls than in boys. Since it is well known that females attain physical maturity at an earlier age than do males, it is reasonable to propose that the male brain matures more slowly than the female brain, and that maturation rate is a critical determinant of brain asymmetry. That is, the more slowly a child matures, the greater the observed cerebral asymmetry. A study by Waber demonstrates just this finding. She reported that, regardless of sex, early-maturing adolescents performed better on tests of verbal than of spatial abilities, whereas the late-maturing ones did the opposite. This study, then, implies that maturation rate may affect the organization of cortical function. Since, on average, females mature faster than males, superior spatial abilities in males may be directly related to their relatively slow development.

The relation between maturation rate and cerebral asymmetry has an intriguing implication for the genetic model of spatial ability. It may be that what is transferred by the recessive gene is slow maturation rate, not spatial ability per se. Thus, superior spatial skills are an indirect effect of slow maturation rate, which is determined by the presence of the recessive gene. To test this prediction it would be necessary to show that females who develop slowly are the same ones who perform as well as the average male on spatial tests and whose spatial ability correlates with their parents as predicted in Figure 16-5. This study has not been done yet.

Environment. Probably the most influential psychological view of sex-related differences is that different environmental factors shape the behavior of males and females. For example, in the case of spatial ability, it is presumed that male children are expected to exhibit greater independence than females, and thus engage in activities such as exploring and manipulating the environment—activities that improve spatial skills. In a recent review, Harris considered all the research support for this argument and concluded that although a few studies can be found to support the view, the bulk of the evidence fails to do so. For example, in a study by Thomas and colleagues on the horizontality of a liquid (Figure 16-2*A*), females who had failed the task were repeatedly shown a bottle half-filled with red water that was tilted at various angles. They were asked to adjust the "pretend waterline" by moving a disk, half red, half white, in a second bottle. Even when the subjects simply had to adjust the pretend waterline to match the visible real waterline, the women failed to show much improvement and were likely to state that "water is level when the bottle is upright but is inclined when the bottle is tilted." Males or females who perform correctly state that "water is always level." A priori, one would have expected females to have had as much experience as males with tilting vessels, and that even if they had not, special instruction would be helpful. This, however, does not seem to be the case. In conclusion, although environmental theories may be appealing, there is no evidence that the observed sex differences in verbal and spatial behaviors can be accounted for solely on the basis of environmental or social factors.

Preferred Cognitive Mode. We have mentioned several times that the strategies that males and females use to solve different tasks may be at least partly responsible for the observed sex differences. It may be that genetic, maturational, and environmental factors predispose males and females to prefer different modes of cognitive analysis. In other words, females develop in such a way that they prefer to solve problems primarily by using a verbal mode. Since this mode is less efficient at solving spatial problems, the female exhibits an apparent deficit. By the same logic, females should do better than males at primarily verbal tasks. This proposition has yet to be thoroughly investigated.

Summary

There is evidence of at least four significant cognitive differences that are sex-related: verbal differences, visuospatial differences, differences in mathematical ability, and differences in aggression. Although the causes of cognitive sex-related differences are unknown, it is likely that they are at least partly biological. Consider the following data. Harshman and his associates recently completed a very ambitious study of the interaction of sex and handedness on cognitive abilities. They found a significant interaction between sex and handedness; that is, sex-related differences in verbal and visuospatial behavior varied as a function of handedness. It is difficult to imagine how social or environmental factors alone could account for this type of result. It is thus very plausible to account for sex-related differences as at least partly due to neurological factors that may be modulated by the environment.

ENVIRONMENTAL EFFECTS ON ASYMMETRY

Environment is known to produce significant effects on brain growth in laboratory animals and so it is reasonable to presume that different environments might affect the human brain differently and produce variance in the pattern of cerebral asymmetry. Two environmental variables would seem to be especially good candidates to consider: culture and literacy.

Cultural Effects on Asymmetry

Most studies of cultural differences have centered on the study of language. It has been proposed that non-European languages such as Japanese or Chinese might have more right hemisphere involvement since there seems to be more **prosody** (or song) to them. It has also been suggested that those who speak two or more languages may have a different pattern of language organization than those who speak only one. Laterality studies have lent some support to the idea that Asian and native-American languages may be more bilaterally represented in the brain. However, as we have seen, laterality studies can be influenced by many factors such as strategy or task requirements, and so one would want to be very cautious about making inferences regarding cultural differences in brain organization from these studies. (See Uyehara and Cooper and Obler and colleagues for good discussions of the difficulties.)

Studies of neurological patients have provided no evidence for culturally or linguistically based differences in cerebral organization. A good example is a study by Rapport and coworkers. They evaluated the language functions of seven Chinese-English polyglots, whose mother tongue was Malay, Cantonese, or Hokkien. Their methods included using carotid sodium Amytal, cortical stimulation, and clinical examination. They found that all of these patients were left hemisphere dominant for both the Chinese and the English languages; there was no consistent evidence for increased participation by the right hemisphere for language functions. Although bilinguals probably have all languages located in the left hemisphere, this does not rule out the possibility that the language zones may be enlarged in the left hemisphere or that they might be slightly different in microorganization. Recall that experience is known to alter somatosensory organization (see Chapter 9), so that an analogous effect on the language zones would seem to be a reasonable expectation. It is likely, however, that the major effects of language and environment on the brain are on the development of particular styles of problem solving (i.e., cognitive mode), which are heavily culture-dependent, rather than on changes in cerebral asymmetry per se.

Literacy, Hearing, and Asymmetry

Both education and congenital deafness have been alleged to alter hemispheric specialization. The evidence that schooling changes cerebral organization is scanty and inconclusive. Laterality studies do not generally support the idea, nor do studies on the frequency and quality of aphasias in illiterate populations, because illiterate aphasics do not appear to differ from educated ones. There is some evidence that congenital deafness may alter cerebral processing, however. Although left hemisphere damage produces aphasia in people who use American Sign Language, possibly because of the praxic requirements, several laterality studies have failed to find the expected right visual-field effects (Figure 15-5) for words in deaf subjects. For example, Kelly and Tomlinson-Keasey found that in contrast to hearing children, deaf children have a left visual-field advantage for most visually presented material. The data suggest that in the absence of verbal auditory input, young deaf children rely heavily on the right hemisphere to process visual stimuli. There is no evidence that the brain itself has been changed by the lack of auditory input, it may simply be the strategy or mode of processing that has changed. Studies of aphasic and apraxic deaf people with left, but not usually right, hemisphere lesions are consistent with this view.

In summary, although environmental experience may affect the way in which stimuli are processed, there is no evidence that the environment actually changes the organization of the cerebral hemispheres. The bulk of the evidence implying environmental influence on cerebral organization derives from laterality studies. But because performance on dichotic or tachistoscopic tasks is susceptible to variability within subjects, we maintain a healthy skepticism. Convincing evidence must come from neurological patients, and to date this evidence has favored a view that the "basic left-for-language and right-for-space" organization of the cerebral hemispheres is unaffected by experience.

ASYMMETRY IN NONHUMANS

Cerebral asymmetry in the human brain is a crucial element in neuropsychology. The precise pressures that led to the development of an asymmetrical brain are unknown, but language and handedness are often considered to be strong candidates. Various factors such as gender, culture, and education are often claimed to influence asymmetry, especially insofar as they relate to language. It is implicitly assumed in many discussions of the nature of asymmetry and its role in behavioral diversity in humans that cerebral asymmetry is linked with specially human intellectual characteristics. However, asymmetry may not be a uniquely human characteristic. If this is the case, then theories regarding the nature of asymmetry and the reasons for variations in it must be reevaluated in light of the evidence from nonhuman species. We will not review all the studies seeking to find asymmetry in the nonhuman brain, but rather will highlight the most stimulating and robust data gathered thus far in birds and mammals, beginning with anatomical asymmetry, then going on to handedness, and finally to cognitive behaviors.

Anatomical Asymmetry in Nonhumans

Anatomical asymmetry in the brains of nonhuman primates was first noticed by Cunningham in 1892. As with human brains, there is a greater upward slope in the Sylvian fissure on the right in the chimpanzee, orangutan, and gorilla brains, and the right frontal pole is longer than the left in baboons. Similarly, the gyral patterns in the two hemispheres of cats are asymmetrical in about 45% of cases, although the asymmetries are not constant from cat to cat. Although most rodents do not have gyrencephalic brains, making the analysis of gyral patterns difficult, the existence in the rat brain of both morphological and neurochemical asymmetries has been established. Like the right hemisphere of the human, that of the rat is larger and heavier than the left, and the right frontal pole extends farther anterior than does the left. The neocortex of the right hemisphere is thicker in the posterior parietal and visual cortex, a difference that Diamond and her colleagues find to be modulated both by age and sex. In addition to those morphological asymmetries, neurochemical asymmetries have been found in norepinephrine concentrations, GABA turnover, and the uptake of serotonin, norepinephrine, and choline. Finally, the right hemisphere of cats, mice, and rabbits is also heavier than the left. The presence of morphological and neurochemical asymmetries in nonhumans is especially intriguing because at least some of them parallel those reported for humans.

Thus, the right hemisphere of both humans and other mammals is apparently heavier and extends farther anterior than the left. Further, the Sylvian fissure of at least the great apes is asymmetrical in a pattern resembling that observed both in humans and in australopithecine endocasts.

Handedness

Consistent preference for the use of one hand in a variety of manipulations is a defining characteristic of handedness in humans. Although some cats, rats, and monkeys have strong hand preferences that are consistent on several different tasks, most do not. Mike Warren began a beautiful series of experiments in the 1960s by looking at the hand preferences in cats and monkeys in a wide range of manipulations including different types of unilateral cortical damage. In a thoughtful review, he was unequivocal in his conclusions: (1) The distribution of hand preferences in nonhuman species in symmetrical, with no disproportionate number of right- and left-handed individuals. (2) The hand preferences of nonhuman mammals are frequently inconsistent in different testing situations and are strongly affected by learning. (3) Hand preferences are not a heritable trait in rats, cats, and mice.

Recently, McNeilage and his colleagues have proposed a novel theory to explain hand preferences in nonhuman primates. They argue that because previous studies concentrated on particular types of movements, a hand preference in monkeys has been overlooked. Their basic premise is that as primates evolved there was a preference for reaching with one limb (the left) while supporting the body with the other (the right). As the prehensile hand developed and primates began to adopt a more upright posture, the need for a hand devoted to postural support diminished, and because it was free, this hand became specialized for manipulating objects. This hypothesis would seem to account for the existing hemispheric asymmetries in motor control in modern-day humans but it is very difficult to evaluate in our nearest primate relatives without designing experiments to test the idea specifically. (See MacNeilage et al., and the accompanying commentaries, for more details of this interesting hypothesis.)

Cognitive Behavior

Fernando Nottebohm reported a startling discovery in 1971. He severed the left hypoglossal nerve in canaries, but not the right, and found severe disruption of the bird's song. Subsequently, he has found similar results from lesions all along the pathway from the hypoglossal nerve to the higher cerebral nuclei on the left but not on the right. If the left nerve is severed in young canaries, the right hypoglossal nerve assumes the control of birdsong — a finding remarkably similar to that for human children with left hemisphere damage in infancy who subsequently develop language centers in the right hemisphere. Although Nottebohm's results are provocative, he has also found that some highly vocal species such as parrots do not have lateralized control of song, whereas some relatively inarticulate birds (e.g., domestic fowl) do. Furthermore, although he has carefully examined the structure of forebrain vocal-control nuclei, he has failed to find any consistent right-left asymmetry.

Subsequent work in many laboratories (e.g., Arnold; Nottebohm) has found that there are large sex-related differences in the size of vocal-control regions of the brain, and that these differences are controlled by sex hormones. Thus, the neurons of male birds exposed to androgens are changed by experience and in some species fluctuate with the seasons (the androgens fluctuate as well). To date there has not been any relationship demonstrated between asymmetry of birdsong control and steroid hormones, however.

Nottebohm's studies lead one to wonder if similar asymmetries might be present in mammals, but few mammals have the rich vocalizations of birds. Most studies of functional asymmetries in mammals have focused, therefore, on other behaviors, especially postural/motor behaviors and cognitive behaviors (but see monkey vocalizations below).

Postural/Motor Behaviors. Studies of postural/motor asymmetries have been conducted largely with rats. For example, Denenberg and his colleagues report that under certain conditions of environmental enrichment in infancy, left and right cortical ablations asymmetrically affect such behaviors as open-field activity and turning preference. Similarly, R. G. Robinson has found that damage to the right frontal cortex produces a postoperative period of hyperactivity not seen after left frontal cortex damage—a result we and our colleagues were able to replicate. Further, there are now dozens of studies of postural asymmetries and rotational (circling) behavior in a variety of species. For example, Glick and his colleagues have found that rats given amphetamine tend to circle consistently to one side or the other. Since amphetamine increases dopamine levels in the brain, particularly in the caudate nucleus, they hypothesized that such circling could be induced by differential amounts of dopamine levels in the two caudate nuclei. Bioassays of rats confirmed this hypothesis: normal rats have a 10–15% asymmetry in dopamine content in the two caudate nuclei, a difference that is potentiated by amphetamine to 25–30%. Furthermore, the biochemistry and behavior are associated, because rats rotate toward the side with the lower level of dopamine. In recent years there has been great interest in the neural correlates of circling behavior because of the ease of using it as an assay of asymmetrical behavior, which can be correlated with neuroanatomy and neurochemistry (see the review by T. E. Robinson et al.). Although studies of postural/motor asymmetries in nonhuman species have an uncertain relation to cognitive asymmetries in humans, they do suggest that one should study postural/motor asymmetries in humans. For example, T. E. Robinson has suggested that the basis of asymmetrical hand preference in humans may be related to neurochemical asymmetries. This is an intriguing idea, since to date there is no obvious neuroanatomical correlate of handedness in humans.

Cognitive Behaviors. If anything akin to cerebral asymmetry in humans is to be demonstrated in other mammals, it seems reasonable to expect that tests of perception, orientation in space, sequencing of movement, and affective behavior would reveal it. To date, the results have been disappointing, since unequivocal evidence of functional asymmetry in monkeys has been elusive. Studies of the visual system have consistently yielded negative results, which is surprising considering the anatomical similarity of the visual system in humans and other primates. For example, one might have predicted an asymmetry in the perception of faces in monkeys, in which facial expression is a significant social cue, but work by Hamilton and by Overman and Doty has yielded no such evidence. Nonetheless, a recent study by Hamilton's group has shown that the two hemispheres may differ in their production of facial expressions. Split-brain monkeys viewed videotapes of people, monkeys, other animals, and scenery, and the amount of time spent watching the recordings, and the number of species-typical facial expressions made were recorded. The number of facial expressions elicited from the right hemisphere was greater than the number made when using the left hemisphere, which is what one would predict from the study of human brains.

Studies of functional asymmetry in the auditory system are somewhat more encouraging. Dewson removed the superior temporal gyrus in rhesus monkeys (roughly area 22), producing a lasting deficit on an auditory-visual task if the lesion was in the left hemisphere but not if it was in the right. The monkeys were required to press a panel that activated one of two acoustic stimuli, either a 1-kHz (kilohertz) tone or white noise. They were then presented with two panels, one green, one red. If the tone was heard, the monkeys pressed the red panel; if the white noise was heard, they pressed the green panel to receive the reward. Superior temporal gyrus lesions on the left impaired performance of this task, but lesions to the analogous area on the right did not.

Prudence dictates a measure of caution in interpreting this exciting result. The number of cases is small and the results of histological examination are not yet available. The possibility of asymmetry in the auditory system is confirmed, however, by the work of Petersen and colleagues. They compared the ability of Japanese macaques to discriminate among communicatively relevant sounds and irrelevant sounds. The animals were able to discriminate relevant sounds presented to the right ear better than those presented to the left. The researchers suggested that the Japanese macaques engage in left hemisphere processing in a way that is analogous to that in humans. A further study by Heffner and Heffner supports this conclusion. They trained monkeys to discriminate between two forms of their "coo" vocalization. They then removed the left or right superior temporal gyrus or the left or right parietal cortex. Removal of the left, but not the right, temporal cortex produced an impairment in performance on this task. Parietal lesions were without effect. Curiously, with training, the animals with left temporal lesions were able to relearn the task. However, when the remaining side was later removed, the animals had a permanent deficit in the task, and were unable to relearn it. The results of the experiments on the auditory system are exciting and may be an important step in demonstrating laterality in the nonhuman primate brain. Indeed, recent evidence from studies of house mice also suggest that the left hemisphere has preferential access to species-typical vocalizations — a result that suggests that there may be basic asymmetry in the analysis of species-typical auditory stimuli in mammals.

Denneberg and his coworkers have reported that under certain conditions ablations of the right hemisphere of rats have different effects on affective behavior, and others have found subtle asymmetrical effects of unilateral forebrain lesions in certain types of learning tasks. In contrast, in an extensive study of praxic, spatial, and social behavior of rats with left or right hemidecortications, we were completely unable to demonstrate any functional asymmetry whatsoever, even though we have consistently observed anatomical asymmetries between the two hemispheres of rats. These results are puzzling and disappointing since it is a general principle of human cerebral organization that the highest cognitive functions are the *most* lateralized behaviors. Nevertheless, the data show that asymmetries in rats are most obvious in relatively simple behaviors such as turning or general activity.

Summary

The brains of nonhuman mammals exhibit clear anatomical asymmetry, which may be analogous to that observed in humans. Evidence of functional asymmetry has been more elusive, however. There is little doubt that nonhumans do not show asymmetrical hand preference, although there is preliminary evidence of other behavioral asymmetries that may have analogues in humans. The demonstration of anatomical asymmetry in nonhuman brains implies that asymmetry in the human brain is not directly related either to handedness or to language. We are inclined to believe that the hemispheres of mammals are more likely to be specialized for praxic, perceptual, spatial, and/or affective behavior, but with the exception of studies of species-typical vocalizations, the behavioral evidence from studies of nonhumans does not yet lend a great deal of credence to this suggestion. It would seem safe to conclude, therefore, that even if evidence of functional asymmetry is eventually forthcoming in nonhuman mammals, lateralization of function is a far less salient feature of the cerebral cortex of rodents than of humans.

CONCLUDING REMARKS

The discovery of systematic relations between normal variations in cerebral organization and individual differences in cognitive abilities represents one of the most challenging goals of neuropsychology. The complexity of the human brain makes the task difficult, but the problems are not intractable. Each of us has unique behavioral capacities, as well as shortcomings (i.e., "Achilles lobes"), which must surely be related to cerebral organization in some manner. Demonstrations of variations related to handedness imply that some variance is innate, although environmental variables must almost certainly modify cerebral organization. Finally, we must point out that although we have emphasized variations in the asymmetrical organization of the cerebrum, the individual variance *within* each hemisphere may be as large as that *between* the hemispheres.

REFERENCES

Annett, M. A classification of hand preference by association analysis. *British Journal of Psychology* 61:303–321, 1970.

Arnold, A. P., S. W. Bottijer, E. J. Nordeen, K. W. Nordeen, and D. R. Sengelaub. Hormones and critical periods in behavioral and neural development. In J. P. Rauschecker and P. Marler, eds. *Imprinting and Cortical Plasticity.* New York: John Wiley, 1987.

Bakan, P., G. Dibb, and P. Reed. Handedness and birth stress. *Neuropsychologia* 11:363–366, 1973.

Benbow, C. P., and J. C. Stanley. Sex differences in mathematical ability: Fact or artifact? *Science* 210:1262–1264, 1980.

Bryden, M. P. *Laterality: Functional Asymmetry in the Intact Brain.* New York: Academic Press, 1981.

Carmon, A., Y. Harishanu, E. Lowinger, and S. Lavy. Asymmetries in hemispheric blood volume and cerebral dominance. *Behavioral Biology* 7:853–859, 1972.

Collins, R. L. Toward an admissible genetic model for the inheritance of the degree and direction of asymmetry. In S. Harnad, R. W. Doty, L. Goldstein, J. Jaynes, and G. Krauthamer, eds. *Lateralization of the Nervous System.* New York: Academic Press, 1977.

Dennenberg, V. H. Hemispheric laterality in animals and the effects of early experience. *The Behavioral and Brain Sciences* 4:1–50, 1981.

Dennenberg, V. H., J. Garbanati, G. Sherman, D. A. Yutzey, and R. Kaplan. Infantile stimulation induces brain lateralization in rats. *Science* 201:1150, 1978.

Dewson, J. H. Preliminary evidence of hemispheric asymmetry of auditory function in monkeys. In S. Harnad, R. W. Doty, L. Goldstein, J. Jaynes, and G. Krauthamer, eds. *Lateralization in the Nervous System.* New York: Academic Press, 1977.

Diamond, M. C., R. E. Johnson, and C. A. Ingham. Morphological changes in the young, adult, and aging cerebral cortex, hippocampus, and diencephalon. *Behavioral Biology* 14:163–174, 1975.

Diamond, M. C., G. M. Murphy, Jr., K. Akiyama, and R. E. Hohnson. Morphologic hippocampal asymmetry in male and female rats. *Experimental Neurology* 76:553–565, 1982.

Ehret, G. Left hemisphere advantage in the mouse brain for recognizing ultrasonic communication calls. *Nature* 325:249–251, 1987.

Geschwind, N., and A. M. Galaburda. *Cerebral Lateralization: Biological Mechanisms, Associations, and Pathology.* Cambridge, MA: M.I.T. Press, 1987.

Glick, S. D., T. P. Jerussi, and B. Zimmerberg. Behavioral and neuropharmacological correlates of nigrostriatal asymmetry in rats. In S. Harnad, R. W. Doty, L. Goldstein, J. Jaynes, and G. Krauthamer, eds. *Lateralization in the Nervous System.* New York: Academic Press, 1977.

Goy, R. W., and B. S. McEwen. *Sexual Differentiation of the Brain.* Cambridge, MA: M.I.T. Press, 1980.

Gualtieri, T., and R. E. Hicks. An immunoreactive theory of selective male affliction. *Behavioral and Brain Sciences* 8:427–477, 1985.

Gur, R. C., R. E. Gur, W. D. Obrist, J. P. Hungerbuhler, D. Younkin, A. D. Rosen, B. E. Skolnick, and M. Reivich. Sex and handedness differences in cerebral blood flow during rest and cognitive activity. *Science* 217:659–660, 1982.

Gur, R. C., I. K. Packer, J. P. Hungerbuhler, M. Reivich, W. D. Obrist, W. S. Amarnek, and H. A. Sackheim. Differences in the distribution of gray and white matter in human cerebral hemispheres. *Science* 207:1226–1228, 1980.

Halpern, D. F., and S. Coren. Do right-handers live longer? *Nature* 333:213, 1988.

Hamilton, C. R. An assessment of hemispheric specialization in monkeys. *Annals of the New York Academy of Sciences* 299:222–232, 1977.

Hampson, E., and D. Kimura. Reciprocal effects of hormonal fluctuations on human motor and perceptual-spatial skills. *Behavioral Neuroscience* 102:456–459, 1988.

Hardyck, C., and L. F. Petrinovich. Left-handedness. *Psychological Bulletin* 84:384–404, 1977.

Harris, L. J. Sex differences in spatial ability: Possible environmental, genetic, and neurological factors. In M. Kinsbourne, eds. *Asymmetrical Function of the Brain.* Cambridge: Cambridge University Press, 1978.

Harshman, R. A., E. Hampson, and S. A. Berenbaum. Individual differences in cognitive abilities and brain organization, part I: Sex and handedness. Differences in ability. *Canadian Journal of Psychology* 37:144–192, 1983.

Hécaen, H., M. DeAgostini, and A. Monzon-Montes. Cerebral organization in left-handers. *Brain and Language* 12:261–284, 1981.

Hécaen, H., and J. Sauguet. Cerebral dominance in left-handed subjects. *Cortex* 7:19–48, 1971.

Heffner, H. E., and R. S. Heffner. Temporal lobe lesions and perception of species-specific vocalizations by macaques. *Science* 226:75–76, 1984.

Herron, J. *Neuropsychology of Left-Handedness.* New York: Academic Press, 1980.

Hier, D. B., and J. Kaplan. Are sex differences in cerebral organization clinically significant? *Behavioral and Brain Sciences* 3:238–239, 1980.

Hier, D. G., J. Mondlock, and L. R. Caplan. Behavioral abnormalities after right hemisphere stroke. *Neurology* 33:337–344, 1983.

Hochberg, F. H., and M. LeMay. Arteriographic correlates of handedness. *Neurology* 25:218–222, 1975.

Holloway, R. L., and M. C. de la Coste-Lareymondie. Brain endocast asymmetry in pongids and hominids: Some preliminary findings on the paleontology of cerebral dominance. *American Journal of Physical Anthropology* 58:101–110, 1982.

Ifune, C. K., B. A. Vermeire, and C. R. Hamilton. Hemispheric differences in split-brain monkeys viewing and responding to videotape recordings. *Behavioral and Neural Biology* 41:231–235, 1984.

Inglis, J., and J. S. Lawson. Sex differences in the effects of unilateral brain damage on intelligence. *Science* 212:693–695, 1981.

Inglis, J., and J. S. Lawson. A meta-analysis of sex differences in the effects of unilateral brain damage on intelligence test results. *Canadian Journal of Psychology* 36:670–683, 1982.

Inglis, R., M. Rickman, J. S. Lawson, A. W. MacLean, and T. N. Monga. Sex differences in the cognitive effects of unilateral brain damage. *Cortex* 18:257–276, 1982.

Juraska, J. Sex differences in developmental plasticity of behavior and the brain. In W. T. Greenough and J. M. Juraska, eds. *Developmental Neuropsychology*. New York: Academic Press, 1986.

Kelly, R. R., and C. Tomlinson-Keasey. The effect of auditory input on cerebral laterality. *Brain and Language* 13:67–77, 1981.

Kertesz, A., and N. Geschwind. Patterns of pyramidal decussation and their relationship to handedness. *Archives of Neurology* 24:326–332, 1971.

Kimura, D. Sex differences in cerebral organization for speech and praxic functions. *Canadian Journal of Psychology* 37:19–35, 1983.

Kimura, D. Speech representation in an unbiased sample of left-handers. *Human Neurobiology* 2:147–154, 1983.

Kolb, B., A. MacKintosh, I. Q. Whishaw, and R. J. Sutherland. Evidence for anatomical but not functional asymmetry in the hemidecorticate rat. *Behavioral Neuroscience* 98:44–58, 1984.

Kolb, B., and B. Milner. Performance of complex arm and facial movements after focal brain lesions. *Neuropsychologia* 19:491–503, 1981.

Kolb, B., R. J. Sutherland, A. J. Nonneman, and I. Q. Whishaw. Asymmetry in the cerebral hemispheres of the rat, mouse, rabbit, and cat: The right hemisphere is larger. *Experimental Neurology* 78:348–359, 1982.

Lacoste-Utamsing, C. de., and R. L. Holloway. Sexual dimorphism in the human corpus callosum. *Science* 216:1431–1432, 1982.

Lake, D. A., and M. P. Bryden. Handedness and sex differences in hemispheric asymmetry. *Brain and Language* 3:266–282, 1976.

Lansdell, H. A sex difference in effect of temporal-lobe neurosurgery on design preference. *Nature* 194:852–854, 1962.

Lansdell, H., and J. Davie. Massa intermedia: Possible relation to intelligence. *Neuropsychologia* 10:207–210, 1972.

LeMay. Asymmetries of the skull and handedness: Phrenology revisited. *Journal of Neurological Sciences* 32:243–253, 1977.

Levy, J. Possible basis for the evolution of lateral specialization of the human brain. *Nature* 224:614–615, 1969.

Levy, J., and T. Nagylaki. A model for the genetics of handedness. *Genetics* 72:117–128, 1972.

MacCoby, E., and C. Jacklin. *The Psychology of Sex Differences.* Stanford, CA: Stanford University Press, 1974.

MacNeilage, P. F., M. G. Studdert-Kennedy, and B. Lindblom. Primate handedness reconsidered. *Behavioral and Brain Sciences* 10:247–303, 1987.

Manning, A. A., W. Gobel, R. Markman, and T. LaBrech. Lateral cerebral differences in the deaf in response to linguistic and nonlinguistic stimuli. *Brain and Language* 4:309–321, 1977.

McGlone, J. Sex differences in the cerebral organization of verbal function to patients with unilateral brain lesions. *Brain* 100:775–793, 1977.

McGlone, J. Sex differences in human brain asymmetry: A critical survey. *Behavioral and Brain Sciences* 3:215–263, 1980.

McGlone, J., and W. Davidson. The relation between cerebral speech laterality and spatial ability with special reference to sex and hand preference. *Neuropsychologia* 11:105–113, 1973.

McGlone, J., and A. Kertesz. Sex differences in cerebral processing of visuospatial tasks. *Cortex* 9:313–320, 1973.

McKeever, W. F., H. W. Hoemann, V. A. Florina, and A. D. Van Deventer. Evidence of minimal cerebral asymmetries in the congenitally deaf. *Neuropsychologia* 14:413–423, 1976.

Miceli, G., C. Caltagirone, G. Gainotti, C. Masullo, M. C. Silveri, and G. Villa. Influence of age, sex, literacy and pathologic lesion on incidence, severity and type of aphasia. *Acta Neurologica Scandinavia* 64:370–382, 1981.

Morgan, M. Embryology and inheritance of asymmetry. In S. Harnad, R. W. Doty, L. Goldstein, J. Jaynes, and G. Krauthamer, eds. *Lateralization in the Nervous System.* New York: Academic Press, 1977.

Nottebohm, F. Asymmetries in neural control of vocalization in the canary. In S. Harnad, R. W. Doty, L. Goldstein, J. Jaynes, and G. Krauthamer, eds. *Lateralization in the Nervous System.* New York: Academic Press, 1977.

Nottebohm, F. Brain pathways for vocal learning in birds: A review of the first 10 years. *Progress in Psychobiology and Physiological Psychology* 9:85–124, 1980.

Obler, L. K., R. J. Zatoree, L. Galloway, Jr., and J. Vaid. Cerebral lateralization in bilinguals: Methodological issues. *Brain and Language* 15:40–54, 1982.

Overman, W. H., Jr., and R. W. Doty. Hemispheric specialization of facial recognition in man but not in macaque. *Society for Neuroscience Abstracts* 4:78, 1978.

Peters, M. Corpus callosum. *Canadian Journal of Psychology* 42:313–324, 1988.

Petersen, M. R., M. D. Beecher, S. R. Zoloth, D. B. Moody, and W. C. Stebbins. Neural lateralization: Evidence from studies of the perception of species-specific vocalizations by Japanese macaques *(Macada puscata). Science* 202:324–326, 1978.

Porac, C., and S. Coren. *Lateral Preferences and Human Behavior.* New York: Springer-Verlag, 1981.

Rapport, R. L., C. T. Tan, and H. A. Whitaker. Language function and dysfunction among Chinese- and English-speaking polyglots: Cortical stimulation, Wada testing, and clinical studies. *Brain and Language* 18:342–366, 1983.

Ratcliffe, G., C. Dila, L. Taylor, and B. Milner. The morphological asymmetry of the hemispheres and cerebral dominance for speech: A possible relationship. *Brain and Language* 11:87–98, 1980.

Renzi, E. de. The influence of sex and age on the incidence and type of aphasia. *Cortex* 16:627–630, 1980.

Robinson, R. G. Differential behavior and biochemical effects of right and left cerebral infarction in the rat. *Science* 205:707–710, 1979.

Robinson, T. E., J. B. Becker, and D. M. Camp. Sex differences in behavioral and brain asymmetries. In M. Myslobodsy, eds. *Hemisyndromes: Psychobiology, Neurology, and Psychiatry.* New York: Academic Press, 1984.

Sherman, G. F., A. M. Galaburda, and N. Geschwind. Neuroanatomical asymmetries in non-human species. *Trends in Neurosciences* 5:429–431, 1982.

Thomas, H., W. Jamison, and D. D. Hummel. Observation is insufficient for discovering that the surface of still water is invariantly horizontal. *Science* 191:173–174, 1973.

Tzavaras, A., G. Kaprinis, and A. Gatzoyas. Literacy and hemispheric specialization for language: Dichotic listening in illiterates. *Neuropsychologia* 19:565–570, 1981.

Uyehara, J. M., and W. C. Cooper, Jr. Hemispheric differences for verbal and nonverbal stimuli in Japanese- and English-speaking subjects assessed by Tsunoda's method. *Brain and Language* 10:405–417, 1980.

Waber, D. P. Sex differences in cognition: A function of maturation rate. *Science* 192:572–573, 1976.

Wada, J. A., R. Clarke, and A. Hamm. Cerebral asymmetry in humans: Cortical speech zones in 100 adult and 100 infant brains. *Archives of Neurology* 32:239–246, 1975.

Walker, S. F. Lateralization of functions in the vertebrate brain: A review. *British Journal of Psychology* 71:329–367, 1980.

Warren, J. M. Functional lateralization in the brain. *Annals of the New York Academy of Sciences* 299:273–280, 1977.

Warren, J. M. Handedness and cerebral dominance in monkeys. In S. Harnad, R. W. Doty, L. Goldstein, J. Jaynes, and G. Krauthamer, eds. *Lateralization in the Nervous System.* New York: Academic Press, 1977.

Webster, W. G. Functional asymmetry between the cerebral hemispheres of the cat. *Neuropsychologia* 10:75–87, 1972.

Webster, W. G., and I. H. Webster. Anatomical asymmetry of the cerebral hemispheres of the cat brain. *Physiology and Behavior* 14:867–868, 1975.

Witelson, S. F. Sex and the single hemisphere: Right hemisphere processing for spatial processing. *Science* 193:425–427, 1976.

Witelson, S. F. Early hemisphere specialization and interhemispheric plasticity: An empirical and theoretical review. In S. J. Segalowitz and F. A. Bruber, eds. *Language Development and Neurological Theory.* New York: Academic Press, 1977.

Witelson, S. F. Neuroanatomical asymmetry in left-handers: A review and implications for functional asymmetry. In J. Herron, ed. *Neuropsychology of Left-Handedness.* New York: Academic Press, 1980.

Witelson, S. F. The brain connection: The corpus callosum is larger in left-handers. *Science* 229:665–668, 1985.

Wittig, M. A., and A. C. Petersen. *Sex-Related Differences in Cognitive Functioning.* New York: Academic Press, 1979.

Yakovlev, P. E. A proposed definition of the limbic system. In C. H. Hockman ed. *Limbic System: Mechanisms and Autonomic Function.* Springfield, IL: Charles C. Thomas, 1972.

Yakovlev, P. I., and P. Rakic. Patterns of decussation of bulbar pyramids and distribution of pyramidal tracts on two sides of the spinal cord. *Transactions of the American Neurological Association* 91:366–367, 1966.

Yeni-Komshian, G., and D. Benson. Anatomical study of cerebral asymmetry in the temporal lobe of humans, chimpanzees and rhesus monkeys. *Science* 192:387–389, 1976.

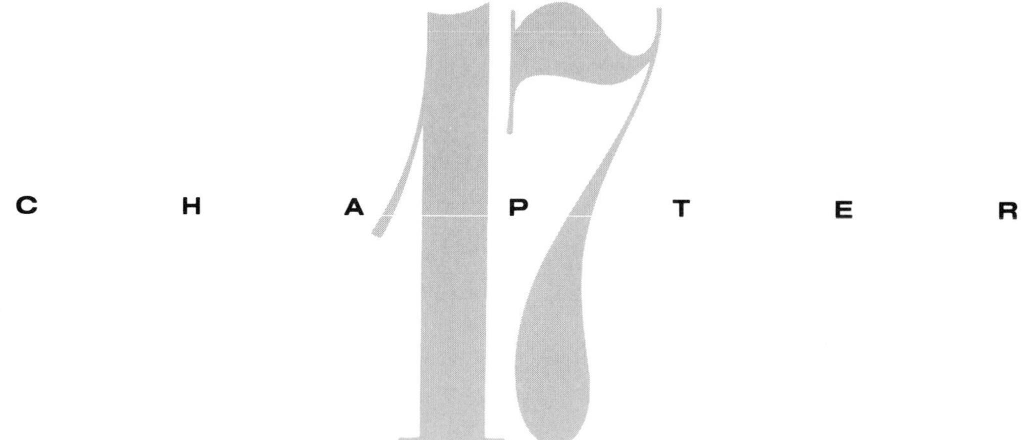

THE PARIETAL LOBES

CEREBRAL REQUIREMENTS FOR HUMAN COGNITION

To understand how the parietal, temporal, and frontal cortexes function, it is useful first to consider what processes are needed to account for our behavior. We have discussed the sensory systems and seen that each sensory modality is composed of multiple pathways, allowing multiple routes for sensory information to access the cortex. There is much more to the analysis of sensory information than we have considered to this point, however, for we have not yet addressed those aspects of cerebral activity often referred to as thought or cognition. One way to approach this topic is to ask what it is that a neural system must be able to do if we are to account for even simple aspects of cognition. We shall consider several such aspects before proposing how or where they might be performed. Our discussion is necessarily brief and can only begin to consider the questions of cognitive neuroscience.

We have seen the inputs of the different sensory systems as being independent, yet we experience a sensory event as a single perceptual experience. For example, when we touch a cat we have several concurrent sensations: the cat has fur that has a particular texture; the cat's fur has color; the cat may be purring, meowing, or growling; and the cat has an odor. These pieces of sensory information are not perceived separately, however, but together as a single sensory experience. Furthermore, we learn that a particular object that has a certain appearance will have a corresponding texture or shape. Say an object is placed in a person's hand and handled but kept out of sight; the person is then asked to choose the object visually from among a group of objects. The person must integrate the tactile and visual input to arrive at the solution; that is, to form a single percept of the object. The ability to recognize concurrent sensory signals as a single percept is known as *cross-modal matching*. Cross-modal matching can occur with any combination of visual, auditory, and somatic stimuli; in each case the matching is assumed to occur in the tertiary cortex where the inputs overlap.

We also have seen that each of our sensory systems produces a point-to-point representation of the receptor surface. On the basis of this representation it should be possible to extract information about where the information is coming from. There are several problems, however, that make it reasonable to have a spatial system independent of the detailed analysis of each of the sensory systems. First, our sensory representations are biased. For example, our hands and face take up more cortex than our back, and our fovea has a greater representation than the periphery. Thus, if spatial location were inferred directly from the sensory maps it would be distorted. Hence, it is necessary that our understanding of where things are, our so-called *spatial map,* is independent of this perceptual bias; we need a spatial coordinate system that gives us a faithful reproduction of space, independent of the proportional representation of the receptor surface. Besides the problem of bias, there is the difficulty with coding both location and content of sensory input in the same neurons. Neurons that are sensitive to color, for example, want to respond to color regardless of where it might be, whereas neurons sensitive to location want to respond to only a small region of the world. If the latter cells also coded pattern information, we would need redundancy throughout the field, which would be very inefficient. Third, we need a spatial coordinate system that guides motor responses independent of sensory content. That is, we need to be able to identify stimulus location without knowing what an object is. For instance, we are able to duck from a low flying missile, such as a snowball, even though we could not have identified what we ducked away from. In this case the details of the stimulus are irrelevent to the necessary motor response.

We have assumed that sensory information arrives, we respond to it, more arrives, we respond to it, and so on. This is obviously too simple since sensory information is continuous and voluminous, both at any given moment and also over time. The volume of information suggests that we need a system that can filter information, responding only to the relevant portion of it. This filtering process, which is often referred to as *selective attention,* functions to select a small amount of information and to ignore most of the rest. For instance, as you read this page you ignore its shape, its color, the TV next door, the feel of your shoes, the taste in your mouth, and so on. If we were unable to ignore irrelevant input, we would find it very difficult to comprehend anything!

Attention is a double-edged sword, however, because once we have directed our attention to a particular configuration of stimuli, we need to be able to direct it elsewhere when it becomes appropriate. Thus, we need a mechanism that will allow shifts of attention and do so at the right times. If we fail to shift we may be said to be *perseverating,* and if we shift attention too easily we may be too distractable.

Although our response to a sensory input is sometimes immediate, it is often delayed, sometimes for quite some time, especially if the response depends upon additional information. Consider the example of listening to a long-winded joke. We make no response until the punch line and often need to store crucial information from the early part of the story in order to appreciate the humor. We encounter similar examples continually as we read a newspaper article, have a discussion, listen to music, compare the tastes of wines, and so on. An interesting characteristic of this storage system is that it only needs to hold most information for a short time and can then discard it. Indeed, it is obvious that we could not possibly store all that we experience, or even all that we filter out for our attention, or we soon would be overwhelmed with information. The fact that we do not expunge all of this information is curious for it implies that we may have some sort of filtering system that chooses the information for longer storage, and perhaps even plays a role in the storage process. And, of course, there is the long-term storage system itself, which must be able to store information and to allow access to it, for an entire lifetime.

Much of our sensory processing appears to be organized innately, and requires little experience to be processed. We can record visual evoked potentials from newborns. Similarly, babies respond to touch, temperature, taste, and so on. Indeed, the decorticate rat responds to these stimuli too, suggesting a minor role of the neocortex in such experiences. Other sensory events, however, are heavily dependent upon experience, and at the extreme there is afferent information that is abstract and has meaning only because of learning. In the absence of experience it is meaningless. For instance, when we read the word *cat* we first recognize the ink scratches on the page as meaningful printing and we then identify the word and its meaning. Other configurations of letters such as *cta* are not processed in the same manner and are without meaning. This suggests that we have some sort of store of words (sometimes called a **lexicon**) that we sift through to compare against the words we hear or read. Furthermore, the word *cat* has all sorts of meanings (both denotations and connotations) that are also stored. There must be parallel stores for other types of visual information too, such as musical scores, international road signs, numbers, mathematical equations, and so on, which obviously are learned and have no intrinsic meaning to the nervous system. Further, such stores of abstract material are not restricted to the visual system. Stores must be present for aurally presented material, such as words or musical notes or phrases. The presence of stores in different modalities is intriguing, because it is obvious that there needs to be a cross-modal match for these abstract stimuli too, just as there is for less complex material.

Next, there need to be mechanisms that register body movements and inform the sensory systems. For instance, if we are playing baseball and must run to catch a fly ball, the ball will appear to have two sources of movement: one is the ball's actual movement and the other is due to our head's movement back and forth as we run. In both cases the image of the ball is moving across the retina but the cause is different. The fact that we can accurately intercept the ball (at least with practice!) implies that the brain can distinguish between the movement generated by the ball's velocity and the movement due to our head bobs. The process whereby this occurs is known as **reafference.** It appears that the motor systems "inform" the sensory systems of the movements that are made, which allows the sensory systems to subtract the movement from that of the object. The system can be fooled if there is no reafference such as occurs when our body is moved by an external force. If you carefully move your eye by pressing your finger against the eyeball the world appears to move. A similar movement of the eye made by the eye muscles results in no perceived movement because of reafference.

At any moment, our behavior is controlled by information about the world. This information may arise directly from events and things currently present in the external world, or it may be "representational" in the sense that it is an internal representation of what was (and perhaps still is) in the external world. The simplest example of a direct response is a reflex. A more complex example would be that of someone walking down a busy street and stopping to buy an ice cream at a streetside stand. In this instance we avoid bumping into people and decide to buy the ice cream in response to sensory cues that are actually present. On the other hand, when behavior is guided by "representational memory" it is guided by a neural record that is independent of concurrent sensory input. This may take several forms. A simple example is observing an object being placed in a drawer and then being able to retrieve it later, even though it is not visible. Our behavior is guided by a "mental representation" of the object in the drawer. In a more complex example, we may travel some distance to a favorite restaurant taking a route that we have not previously taken. In this case the behavior is guided by an internalized representation of the restaurant and its location in some sort of "cognitive map" of the world. Internal representations are not simple because they must include various types of information including both a spatial location of sensory information as well as the nature of the sensory information (color, pitch, odor, etc.). In the absence of representational information, behavior is dependent upon direct information, and people may be unable to plan ahead or to show any imagination.

Finally, if we are to make movements at the right time and place, we need to have a record of what movements have just occurred and a plan, or program, for what is to be done. The principal idea here is that it is only with the knowledge of what is ongoing that new units or series of units can be initiated. If you are sitting and wish to walk to another room, walking cannot be initiated until you have stood up. This requires feedback that standing has occurred and may also require inhibition of leg movements in order to stand. A further requirement may be that there is a plan of the movements that will be made, which can be called a prospective **motor program.** The idea here is that the movements can be organized in the correct order in advance and the motor program can be "read" by the brain to produce the correct movements in the right order.

It should be obvious by now that the complexity of human behavior requires considerably more processing of sensory information than simply recognizing patterns of input in the various sensory channels. It is the tertiary cortex in particular that is responsible for much of the cognitive processing that occurs. It is difficult to assign discrete packets of cognitive activity to different pieces of cortical tissue, both because the complexity of the processes requires continual interaction of the different areas and because there are multiple solutions to different problems and different regions may play greater or lesser roles in particular aspects of the processing involved in different strategies. Nevertheless, we can make some broad generalizations that will provide a basic framework for exploring the parietal, temporal, and frontal association areas.

ANATOMY OF THE PARIETAL LOBES

The parietal lobe is the region of cerebral cortex underlying the parietal skull bone; this area is roughly demarcated anteriorly by the central fissure, ventrally by the Sylvian fissure, dorsally by the cingulate gyrus, and posteriorly by the parietal-occipital sulcus (see Figure 17-1*A*). The principal regions of the parietal lobe include the postcentral gyrus (Brodmann's areas 1, 2, and 3), the superior parietal lobule (areas 5 and 7), the inferior parietal lobule (areas 40 and 43), and the angular gyrus (area 39) (see Figure 17-1*B*). These areas can be divided into three functional zones: an anterior zone including areas 1, 2, 3, and 43 as well as portions of area 5, and two more posterior zones including area 7, and areas 39 and 40. The anterior zone is principally primary and secondary somatosensory cortex; the more posterior zones are tertiary cortex and are referred to as the posterior parietal cortex.

Subdivisions of the Posterior Parietal Cortex

Although the first cytoarchitectonic division of the parietal cortex was Brodmann's, who used the numeral system we have referred to throughout

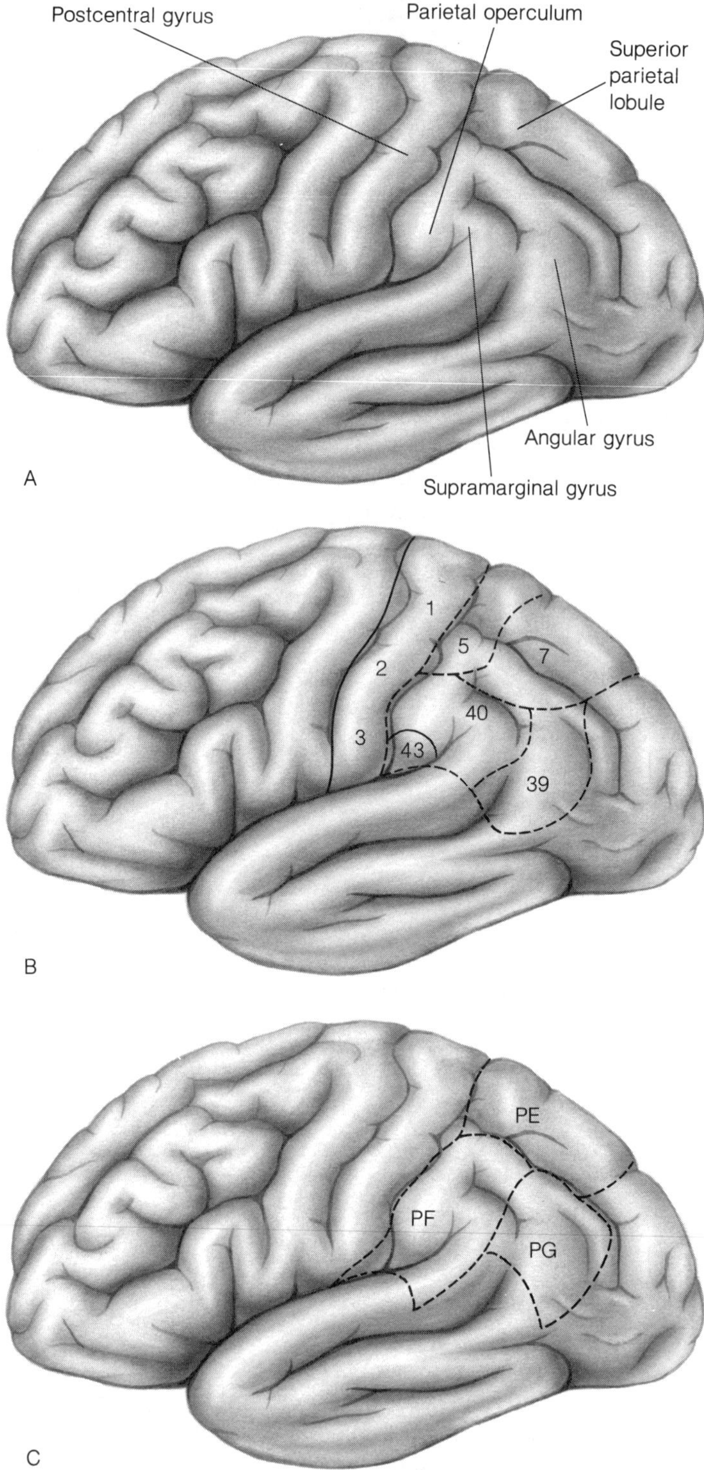
Postcentral gyrus
Parietal operculum
Superior parietal lobule
Angular gyrus
Supramarginal gyrus
A
1
2
3
5
7
40
43
39
B
PE
PF
PG
C

the book to this point, more recent work has used a different system using alphabetic characters. In this system areas of the parietal lobe are demarcated as PA, PB, PC, and so forth, and subdivisions of these larger areas by a third, sometimes lowercase, letter (e.g., PFG, PEc). Similarly, the occipital cortex is described as OA, OB, OC, and so on, and the frontal and temporal cortex by FA, FB, FC, TA, TB, TC, respectively. The alphabetic nomenclature has an advantage in that it is simple to include new parcellations, subdivisions, or of previously described areas by simply adding a third letter. No similar method has been devised for the Brodmann system. Thus, as newer anatomical techniques have allowed more precise identification of cortical areas, Brodmann's system has proven cumbersome. Figure 17-1 illustrates the original parcellation of the parietal cortex by Brodmann *(B)* and von Economo's alphabetic system *(C)*. Notice that in von Economo's map, Brodmann's areas 5 and 7 were described as a single area, PE. Areas 39 and 40 were described as PG and PF, respectively. Since von Economo's parcellation appears to be more consistent with that in other species, we shall adopt it here as well.

Until recently little was known of the subdivisions of the human parietal cortex because most of the modern anatomical work was done on the rhesus monkey (Figure 17-2*A*). Pandya and Yeterian and others have described about nine major subdivisions of the posterior parietal cortex including PE, PEc, PF, PFG, PG, PGm, Opt (a transition zone between occipital and parietal cortex), and the cortex in the intraparietal sulcus, which is labeled PEa and POa (see Figure 17-2*B*). Recently, a strikingly similar description of the human brain was proposed by Eidelberg and Galaburda (see Figure 17-2*C*). Most of the nomenclature is the same, although one difference is area OPE in the human, which is equivalent to Opt in the monkey. The remarkable similarity in the organization of the parietal cortex of the human and monkey is important, because many writers (e.g., Luria, Geschwind) have argued strongly that there were fundamental differences in parietal cortex that are related to language development in humans. This does not appear to be the case, although there are at least three human-monkey differences: (1) the overall size of the parietal cortex is bigger in humans; (2) there are probably more subdivisions of the major areas in humans; and (3) there is evidence of asymmetry in humans, but this is not seen in monkeys. Specifically, it appears that within the angular gyrus there has been a trend toward a larger PEG on the right and a larger PG on the left.

Corticocortical Connections of the Posterior Parietal Cortex

The principal afferents to the posterior parietal cortex project from the pulvinar in the posterior thalamus, and other cortical regions. The parietal lobe in turn sends its major projections to the frontal and temporal association cortex (Figure 17-3) as well as to subcortical structures including the pulvinar and the posterior region of the striatum, midbrain, and spinal cord. The corticocortical projections to the frontal lobe provide sensory input to the frontal lobe, because there are no direct sensory projections to this region. The descending projections to the striatum and spinal cord in particular probably function as a guidance system in the control of movements in space (as described later in the chapter).

Little is known of the details of the connections of the subregions of the posterior parietal cortex in humans, but, in view of the similarity in the cy-

FIGURE 17-1. Gross anatomy of the parietal lobe. *A.* The major gyri and sulci. *B.* Brodmann's cytoarchitectonic regions. *C.* von Economo's cytoarchitectonic regions.

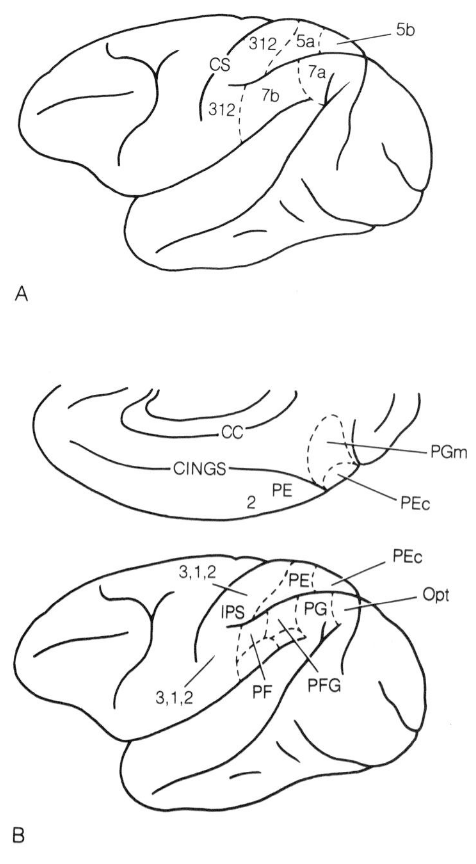

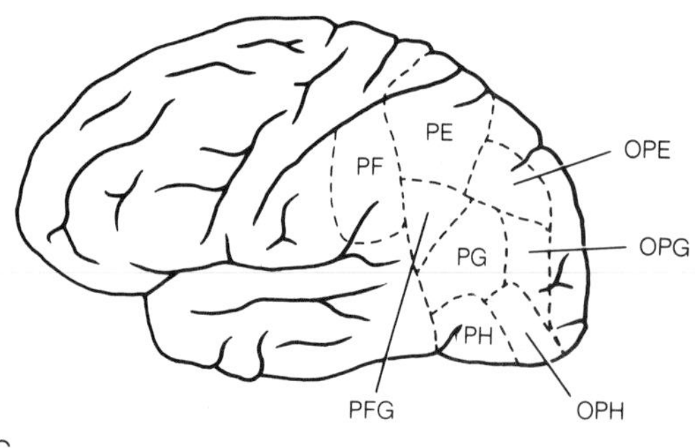

FIGURE 17-2. Cytoarchitectonic organization of the parietal cortex of the rhesus monkey and human. *A.* Brodmann's areas in the rhesus monkey. *B.* Pandya's areas in the rhesus monkey. *C.* Eidelberg and Galaburda's areas in the human.

toarchitecture of humans and monkeys, it is likely that the two species share similarities in connections as well. Figure 17-4 schematically illustrates these connections. Notice that there appear to be five types of connections: (1) those to the secondary motor cortex (areas 6, 8, and M_{II}), which originate largely from PE, PEc, and PGm; (2) those to tertiary frontal cortex (area 46), which originate from PF, PFG, and PG; (3) those to the hippocampal formation from Opt; (4) those connecting PG to the polymodal cortex of the temporal lobe; and, (5) those from PG to the cingulate cortex. It is likely that the projections to secondary motor cortex have a role in the guidance of arm, head, and eye movements (known as *visuomotor guidance*), and it is interesting that PE's cortical input is largely visual whereas PGm's is largely somatosensory. The projections to the hippocampal formation probably have some role in memory, and again there are both somatosensory (PF) and visual (PG, PG-Opt) contributions. The projections to the cingulate and the tertiary frontal cortex may have a role in attention.

A THEORY OF PARIETAL LOBE FUNCTION

If the anterior (somatosensory) and posterior parietal zones are considered as functionally distinct regions, two independent functions of the parietal lobes can be identified. One is primarily concerned with somatic sensations and perceptions; the other is specialized primarily for integrating sensory input from the somatic and visual regions, and to a lesser extent, from other sensory regions. We are primarily concerned here with the function of the posterior parietal zone, the somatosensory functions having already been discussed in Chapter 10.

We saw earlier in this chapter that sensory information needs to be analyzed in various ways, which we called **cognition,** in order to allow the brain to produce behavior. Much of this analysis is carried out by the posterior parietal cortex because

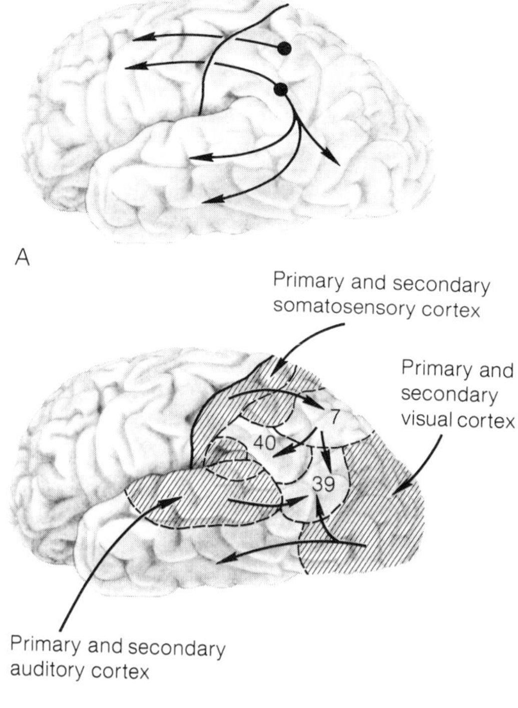

FIGURE 17-3. *A.* Schematic of the long corticocortical projections of the parietal lobe to the frontal and temporal lobes. *B.* Schematic of the short corticocortical projections from the primary and secondary somatosensory, visual, and auditory cortex to the tertiary zone of the parietal lobe.

a convergence of sensory inputs from different modalities occurs here. It is in the integration of this sensory input that we begin to find evidence of processes of "thought" or cognition.

Perhaps the simplest function of this system is cross-modal matching, which we discussed earlier. Sensory information is integrated to form a single percept made up of several modalities. A second function of this system is the construction of a spatial coordinate system to represent the visual and somatic spatial worlds. Thus, sensory events are assigned spatial locations independent of the actual sensory information. We considered such a system when we discussed blindsight in Chapter 11. Thus, we saw that it is possible for people with visual cortex damage to assign spatial location to visual information in the absence of pattern vision, or even the awareness of visual stimulation. Similarly, we saw that there is a somatic equivalence of blindsight, which we called blindtouch, which can result from somatosensory cortex injury. It is the parietal cortex that provides the information about spatial location, and it follows that if parietal cortex is damaged the person should be able to identify objects but not know where the objects are. In addition to locating sensory information in space, the parietal cortex is involved in the guidance of movements to points in space and in relation to

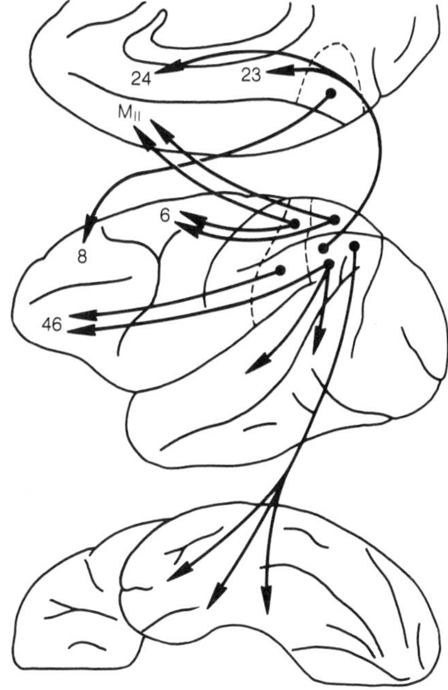

FIGURE 17-4. Schematic drawing of the major corticocortical projections of the subdivisions of the parietal cortex of the monkey. There are four major projections: (1) a motor projection from area PE and PEc; (2) a prefrontal projection from area PF and PG; (3) a medial temporal projection from Opt; and, (4) a projection to the polymodal cortex of the superior temporal sulcus from PG.

objects in space. In both types of movement control there is a need for feedback from the somatic system to inform the brain where the limbs or eyes are at any given moment. Thus, the parietal cortex creates a neural record of the position and movements of the body, head, and eyes in relation to the surrounding space.

The posterior parietal cortex appears to play a major role in recognizing, and possibly producing, abstract stimuli. Thus, lesions in the angular gyrus disturb processes needed for abilities such as reading and arithmetic. This disturbance may be subtle, as illustrated by a patient we studied who had a left posterior parietal astrocytoma. She was able to identify a clock as a clock, but she was totally incapable of telling the time from the position of its hands. Thus, she did not have a visual agnosia, but rather a more complex deficit: she was unable to integrate the visual information necessary to decipher the meaning of the position of the hands.

Finally, we have seen that the parietal cortex is involved in forming unitary percepts from diverse sensory events, it is involved in coding spatial location of sensory information, and it is involved in forming abstract concepts. It therefore seems likely that it is also involved in manipulating the spatial coordinates of abstract (i.e., mental) stimuli. Thus, if one is asked to imagine looking at a bicycle and then to draw it from the perspective of the rider, it is necessary to manipulate the mental representation of the bicycle to draw it. Patients with parietal lesions find such a task extremely difficult.

We have greatly simplified the integrative function of the tertiary cortex of the parietal lobe (we expand on it in the next section). Nevertheless, this integrative function demonstrably represents a complex form of sensory analysis that includes many of the elements commonly referred to as thought or cognition. It should not be surprising, therefore, that a person's performance on an intelligence test is profoundly affected by lesions of the posterior parietal area. Indeed, relative to other cortical regions, the loss of the posterior parietal area probably has the most debilitating effects on a person's intellectual life, especially if he or she loses the ability to understand abstract concepts.

Asymmetry of Tertiary Sensory Function

One of the principles of hierarchical organization is that cerebral asymmetry is far more likely to be found at the highest functional levels. Thus, as would be expected, the greatest asymmetry is found in the cognitive functions of the tertiary zone. From our discussion of cerebral asymmetry in Chapter 15 we would expect the left parietal-temporal cortex to have a special role in language processes and the right parietal-temporal cortex to have a special role in spatial processes, and this is indeed the case.

The left parietal-temporal region is specialized for processing symbolic-analytic information like that found in language and arithmetic, in which the incoming sensory stimulation stands for, or abstractly symbolizes, something else. For example, the word *cat* describes a four-legged furry feline and assumes the characteristics of the animal (a form of cross-modal matching), even though the word itself in no way resembles a cat. Auditory, visual, and somatic input of a real object is therefore integrated and represented by an abstract stimulus that itself has auditory, visual, and somatic properties. One hears or reads the word *cat*—or, if the word is written in raised lettering, one can somatically "read" the word by touch—and in each case the object is understood. Geschwind, Luria, and others have proposed that this ability of cross-modally matching the various attributes of a real stimulus into an abstract, symbolic representation is the necessary foundation for the evolution of language. They hypothesize that the function is performed by the angular and supramarginal gyri, roughly areas 39 and 40.

The right tertiary sensory zone is specialized for processing a different aspect of sensory input from that done by the left. Analysis of visual, auditory, and somatic input requires that the information be integrated, not only about *what* is being perceived but also about *where* it is coming from. In other words, only when the spatial characteristics of sensory inputs are integrated can a complete perception of the world around us be developed. The complexity of this integration can be demonstrated in a number of ways. For instance, a student in a classroom is able to describe the room from the professor's point of view, even if the student has never stood where the professor stands. To do this, the student must construct an integrated spatial representation of the room, primarily visual and auditory, and then rotate the representation so that the professor's position is assumed. The complexity of this cognitive process is underscored by the observation, made by Jean Piaget and others, that this ability does not develop in children until about 10 years of age.

Parietal Lobe Motor Functions

Mountcastle and his colleagues have proposed that the tertiary parietal cortex receives afferent signals not only of the sensory representation of the world but also of the position and movement of the body in space; the region uses this information to function as "a command apparatus for operation of the limbs, hands, and eyes within immediate extrapersonal space." Thus, the parietal lobe not only integrates sensory and spatial information to allow accurate movements in space, but also functions to direct or guide movements in the immediate vicinity of the body. Note, however, that the parietal lobe is not thought to control the details of muscular contraction during execution of movements — a function of the frontal lobe (principally area 4) and subcortical structures. Rather, it directs or aims movements toward behavioral goals. Note also that the parietal lobe is not considered to be the *only* motor command system, but rather one of several, each providing a different control function, as yet unspecified.

This view of parietal lobe function accords with much anatomical and behavioral data. It is known that the parietal lobe has substantial efferents to subcortical motor structures including the basal ganglia and spinal cord. These motor projections contribute to the control of proximal movements (e.g., gross-limb movements), but not to distal movements (e.g., fine-digit control), which are primarily controlled by area 4 of the frontal lobe. Thus, parietal lobe lesions would be expected to disturb gross movements of the arms (in space) but to have little effect on distal movements of the fingers or face. Consistent with this prediction is the observation that parietal lobe lesions produce severe bilateral apraxia when limb movements are required, but only mild apraxia when facial movements are required (see Chapter 13).

Like other functions of the parietal lobe, motor control of the left and right parietal cortex is asymmetrical. Because (as noted earlier) the left hemisphere has a special role in controlling movement, we would expect the theory to apply more to the left parietal lobe than to the right. In 1977, Kimura proposed that the left parietal control function provides a system for accurate internal representation of moving body parts and thus is important for controlling changes in their spatial positions. She argued that apraxia results from a disturbance in this function of controlling accurate positioning of limb and oral musculature. To move a limb from one position to another a person must have an accurate representation of where the limb is currently positioned. Without this information, changes of position are awkward and frequently in error. The right parietal lobe also has a motor function, as observed in constructional apraxia, discussed in Chapter 12. We propose, however, that the two motor functions are totally dissimilar, because the right directs motor movements for reproducing the spatial properties of objects in the world. Right parietal lesions disturb the motor control of drawing or constructional abilities, because the inadequate sensory-spatial representation deprives the frontal motor system of sufficient information to carry out the appropriate movements.

Therefore, drawings are distorted, blocks are

assembled in bizarre designs, maps lack spatial organization, and so forth.

Further Implications of the Theory

This relatively simple model of parietal lobe function allows us to make inferences about the organization of other cognitive functions such as memory and personality.

Memory. For sensory input to be effectively integrated, it must be held long enough to be used. It could therefore be predicted that parietal lobe dysfunction would disturb short-term, or working, memory—that is, the memory for things that have just happened. For example, a person asked to repeat the digits 3292401 must hold them briefly in order to process and to repeat them, and indeed left parietal-temporal lesions seriously impair the ability to recall strings of digits. On the other hand, if there is no primary sensory defect, or agnosia, then a person with this lesion should be able to remember the digits with repeated practice, provided the mechanisms involved in long-term storage (located primarily in the medial temporal lobes) are intact. This prediction appears to be confirmed by observation. Furthermore, there is an asymmetry in this short-term memory function: the left parietal-temporal region is involved primarily in holding verbal material and the right parietal-temporal region primarily in holding nonverbal material, such as the spatial location of particular sensory inputs.

Personality. We have seen that a person's behavior is influenced by the integration of sensory stimuli to produce a unified perception of the world. If a lesion in the left parietal lobe occurs, producing a disturbance of abstract, symbolic integration, then behaviors such as talking, reading, and writing are disturbed. Similarly, a disturbance of spatial integration resulting from a lesion of the right parietal lobe produces a disturbance in behaviors requiring spatial orientation. Thus, since changes in sensory integration alter our behavior, it follows that how the affected person appears to others (that is, the person's personality) will be altered. And indeed, right parietal-temporal lesions commonly produce profound changes in personality. Luria describes a group of such patients with lesions (tumors and aneurysms) of the right parietal-temporal region, who showed a severe loss of direct orientation in space and time.

> They firmly believed that at one and the same time they were in Moscow and also in another town. They suggested that they had left Moscow and gone to the other town, but having done so, they were still in Moscow where an operation had been performed on their brain. Yet they found nothing contradictory about these conclusions. Integrity of the verbal-logical processes in these patients, despite the profound disturbance of their direct self-perception and self-evaluation, led to a characteristic overdevelopment of speech, to verbosity, which bore the character of empty reasoning and which masked their true defects. (Luria, 1973, p. 168)

Even when there are less bizarre changes in cognitive function, there can be changes in personality that may relate directly to other parietal lobe symptoms. For example, parietal lesions produce a variety of alterations in spatial abilities, but may especially affect the ability to see the relationship between objects or things in space (see Chapter 24 for an extended discussion). Thus, the person is reduced to using spatial cues that are essentially ego-centered, meaning that space is perceived in relation to one's own body. Similar egocentric changes may also be observed in cognitive functions so that a person may have difficulty not only in understanding spatial concepts from another's point of view, but there may be difficulties in understanding the relationship between cognitive concepts as well. Such changes could easily be manifest in social interactions, too, rendering the individual unable to understand other points of view. Such people might be described in the more usual sense as egocentric. We caution the reader that our last conclusion is complete speculation, although it is concordant with our clinical experience with several parietal lobe patients.

EFFECTS OF PARIETAL LOBE LESIONS

Although we have described a simple theory of how parietal lobe function is organized, we have not discussed in any detail the bewildering array of symptoms characteristic of patients with parietal lobe lesions. In this section we take a brief historical look at the interpretations of the symptoms of left and right parietal lobe disease. We then describe some of the typical symptoms observed in these patients.

Symptoms of Left Parietal Lobe Lesions

In 1924, Josef Gerstmann described a patient with an unusual symptom following a left parietal stroke—finger agnosia: the patient was unable to name or indicate recognition of the fingers on either hand. This discovery aroused considerable interest, and over the ensuing years other symptoms were reported to accompany finger agnosia, including right-left confusion, **agraphia** (inability to write), and **acalculia** (inability to perform mathematical operations). These four symptoms collectively became known as the **Gerstmann syndrome.** Gerstmann and others argued that these symptoms accompanied a circumscribed lesion in the left parietal lobe, roughly corresponding to the **angular gyrus** (area 39). If these four symptoms occurred as a group, the patient was said to demonstrate the Gerstmann syndrome, and the lesions could be localized in the angular gyrus. The storm of controversy that followed such claims continues to this day. The major issue is whether all these symptoms occur together, and whether these are the only symptoms.

The important question from our point of view is whether these symptoms occur: they do. Do they ever occur as a pure syndrome? They probably do, but not often enough to make them a useful diagnostic tool in routine investigations. Today various other symptoms of left parietal lesions are known; many of these are illustrated in the following case history.

On 24 August 1975, Mr. S., an 11-year-old boy, suddenly had a seizure, which was characterized by twitching on the right side of the body, particularly the upper limb and face. He was given anticonvulsant medication and was symptom-free until 16 September 1975, when he began to write upside down and backward, at which time he was immediately referred to a neurologist, who diagnosed a left parietal malignant astrocytoma. Careful neuropsychological assessment revealed a number of symptoms characteristic of left parietal lesions. (1) Mr. S. had several symptoms of disturbed language function: he was unable to write even his name (agraphia), had serious difficulties in reading (dyslexia), and spoke slowly and deliberately, making many errors in grammar **(dysphasia).** (2) He was unable to combine blocks to form designs and had difficulties learning a sequence of novel movements of the limbs, suggestive of apraxia. (3) He was very poor at mental arithmetic (dyscalculia) and could not correctly solve even simple additions and subtractions. (4) He had an especially low digit span, being able to master the immediate recall of only three digits, whether they were presented orally or visually. (5) He was totally unable to distinguish left from right, responding at chance on all tests of this. (6) He had right hemianopia, probably because his tumor had damaged the geniculostriate connections. As Mr. S.'s tumor progressed, movement of the right side of his body became disturbed, because the tumor placed pressure on the frontal lobe. By the end of October 1975 Mr. S died, neither surgery nor drug therapy being able to stop the growth of the tumor.

The symptoms that Mr. S. exhibited resemble

those of other patients we have seen with left parietal lesions. Curiously, he did not have finger agnosia, one of the Gerstmann symptoms, illustrating the point that even very large lesions do not produce the same effects in every patient. Thus, a parietal syndrome cannot be identified as Gerstmann tried to do.

Symptoms of Right Parietal Lobe Lesions

A perceptual disorder following right parietal lesions was described by John Hughlings-Jackson in 1874. However, not until the 1940s was the effect of right parietal lesions clearly defined by Paterson and Zangwill. A classic paper by McFie and Zangwill, published in 1960, reviewed much of the previous work and described several symptoms of right parietal lesions, which are illustrated in the following patient.

Mr. P., a 67-year-old man, had suffered a right parietal stroke. At the time of our first seeing him (24 h after admission) he had no visual-field defect or paresis. He did, however, have a variety of other symptoms. (1) Mr. P. neglected the left side of his body and of the world. When asked to lift up his arms, he failed to lift his left arm but could do so if one took his arm and asked him to lift it. When asked to draw a clock face, he crowded all the numbers onto the right side of the clock. When asked to read compound words such as ice cream or football, he read "cream" and "ball." When he dressed, he did not attempt to put on the left side of his clothing (a form of dressing apraxia), and when he shaved, he shaved only the right side of his face. He ignored tactile sensation on the left side of his body. Finally, he appeared unaware that anything was wrong with him and was uncertain as to what all the fuss was about (anosagnosia). Collectively, these symptoms are referred to as **contralateral neglect;** we shall return to them shortly. (2) He was impaired at combining blocks to form designs (constructional apraxia) and was generally impaired at drawing freehand with either hand, copying drawings, or cutting out paper figures. When drawing, he often added extra strokes in an effort to make the pictures correct, but the drawings generally lacked accurate spatial relations. Notice, in Figure 17-5 that the attempted drawing of a cube is spatially distorted and contains many superfluous lines, especially on the left side. In fact, it is common for patients showing neglect to fail to complete the left side of the drawing, as illustrated in Figure 17-6*B*. (3) He had a topographical disability, being unable to draw maps of well-known regions from memory. He attempted to draw a map of his neighborhood, but it was badly distorted with respect to directions, the spatial arrangement of landmarks, and distances. In spite of all these disturbances Mr. P. knew where he was and what day it was, and he

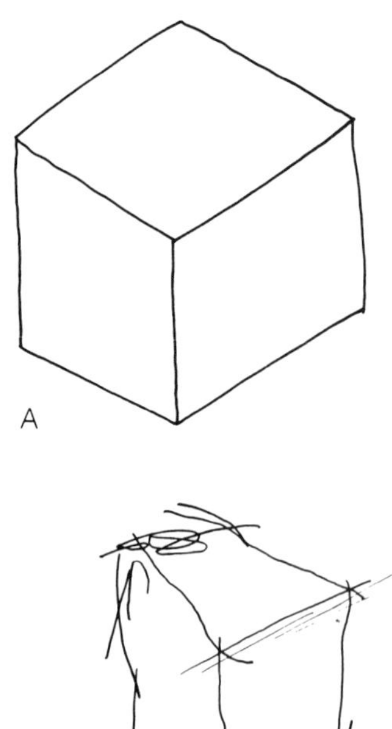

FIGURE 17-5. *A*. The model. *B*. The copy done by a patient with a right parietal stroke. Note the addition of lines to try to make the drawing correct.

FIGURE 17-6. Drawings copied by a patient with contralateral neglect. From F. E. Bloom and A. Lazerson. *Brain, Mind, and Behavior,* 2nd ed. New York: W. H. Freeman and Co., p. 300. Copyright © 1988. Reprinted with permission of W. H. Freeman and Co.)

could recognize his family's faces. He also had good language functions: he could talk, read, and write normally.

The contralateral neglect observed in Mr. P. is one of the most fascinating symptoms of brain dysfunction. Typically there is neglect of visual, auditory, and somesthetic (somatosensory) stimulation on the side of the body and/or space opposite to the lesion, which may be accompanied by denial of the deficit. Recovery passes through two stages. The first, **allesthesia,** is characterized by the person's beginning to respond to stimuli on the neglected side, but doing so as if the stimuli were on the good side. The person responds to and orients to visual, tactile, or auditory stimuli on the left side of the body as if they were on the right. The second stage is called **simultaneous extinction:** the person responds to stimuli on the hitherto neglected side unless both sides are stimulated simultaneously, in which case he or she notices only the stimulation on the side ipsilateral to the lesion.

Neglect presents several obstacles to understanding. For example, where is the lesion located that produces this effect? Figure 17-7 is a composite drawing of the region damaged (as inferred from brain scans) in 13 patients with neglect as described by Heilman and Watson. The area of most overlap among the lesions was the inferior parietal lobule. It should be noted, however, that neglect is occasionally observed following lesions to the frontal lobe and cingulate cortex, as well as to subcortical structures including the superior colliculus and lateral hypothalamus. It is not clear, however, whether the same phenomenon results from these various lesions.

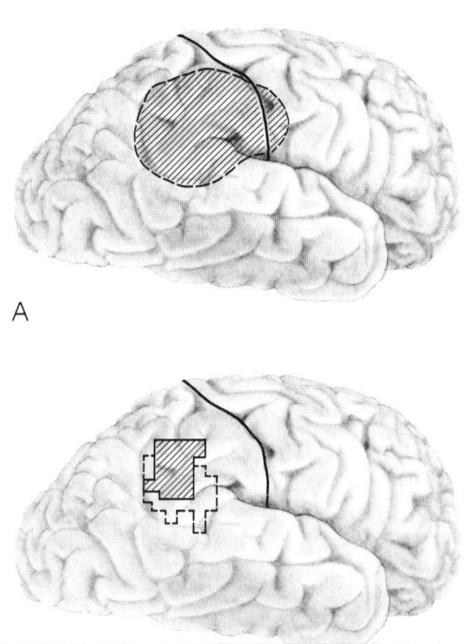

FIGURE 17-7. *A*. Composite drawing of the region damaged (as inferred from brain scans) in 13 patients with contralateral neglect as described by Heilman and Watson. The areas of greatest overlap is the right inferior parietal lobule. *B*. Composite drawing of the region of overlap among lesions producing deficits in Warrington and Taylor's test of recognition of objects seen in unfamiliar views. The shaded region is the one of maximal overlap. Note the similarity between *A* and *B*.

A second problem is why neglect occurs at all. There are two main theories: (1) that neglect is caused by defective sensation or perception, (2) that it is caused by defective attention or orientation. The strongest argument favoring the theory of defective sensation is that a lesion to the parietal lobes, which receive input from all the sensory regions, could disturb the integration of sensation. Denny-Brown and Chambers termed this integration function *morphosynthesis* and its disruption *amorphosynthesis*. A current elaboration of this view hypothesizes that neglect follows right parietal lesion because the integration of the spatial properties of stimuli becomes disturbed. As a result, although stimuli are perceived, their location is uncertain to the nervous system and they are consequently ignored. The neglect is thought to be unilateral because it is assumed that in the absence of right hemisphere function, the left hemisphere is capable of some rudimentary spatial synthesis that prevents neglect of the right side of the world. This rudimentary spatial ability cannot compensate, however, for the many other behavioral deficits resulting from right parietal lesion.

Critchley and later others have suggested that neglect results rather from an inability to attend to input that has in fact been registered. This view has most recently been elaborated by Heilman and Watson. They propose that neglect is manifested by a defect in orienting to stimuli; the defect results from a disruption of a system whose function is to "arouse" the individual when new sensory stimulation is present.

Another common symptom of right parietal lobe lesion has been described by Warrington and her colleagues: patients with right parietal lesions, although capable of recognizing objects shown in familiar views, are badly impaired at recognizing objects shown in unfamiliar ones. For example, a side-view photograph of a bucket is recognized easily; a top-view photograph of the same bucket

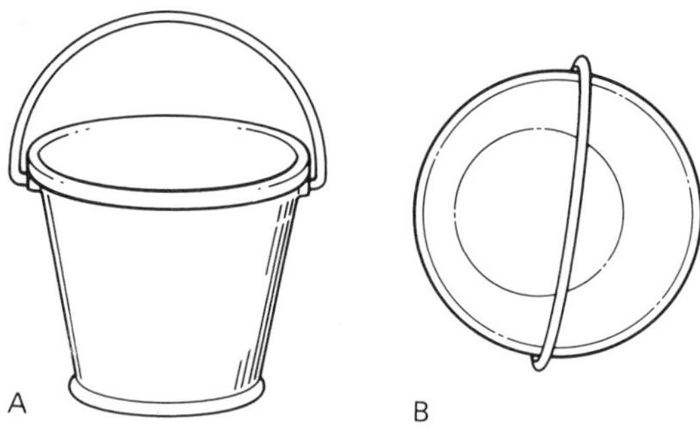

FIGURE 17-8. Drawing of a bucket in familiar *(A)* and unfamiliar *(B)* views. Patients with right parietal lesions have difficulty in recognizing objects in unfamiliar views such as this one.

is recognized only with great difficulty (see Figure 17-8). Warrington concludes that the deficit is not in forming a gestalt, or concept, of "bucket," but rather in perceptual classification—the mechanism for categorizing information as being part of the idea "bucket." Such allocation can be seen as a type of spatial matching in which the common view of an object must be spatially rotated to match the novel view. Warrington and Taylor suggested that the focus for this deficit is roughly the inferior parietal lobule, the same region proposed as the locus of contralateral neglect (Figure 17-7).

Balint's Syndrome

In 1909, Balint described a patient with rather peculiar visual symptoms. The patient showed no obvious signs of mental impairment, displaying no aphasia or apraxia. He had full visual fields and could recognize, use, and name objects, pictures, and colors normally. In spite of this, the patient did have three unusual symptoms. First, although he spontaneously looked straight ahead, when an array of stimuli was placed in front of him, he directed his gaze 35° to 40° to the right and perceived only what was lying in that direction. This symptom included a component of neglect of the left visual field, but in addition there was neglect of part of the right visual field. Second, once the patient's attention was directed toward an object, no other stimulus was noticed. With urging, he could identify other stimuli placed before him, but he would quickly relapse into his previous neglect. Balint concluded that the patient's field of attention was limited to one object at a time, a disorder that made reading very difficult since each letter was perceived separately. Third, the patient had a severe deficit in reaching under visual guidance. Balint described this symptom as **optic ataxia,** a term that is not strictly appropriate, but it has stuck anyway. A disorder of reaching is commonly observed in parietal lobe patients, as illustrated in a case described by Damasio and Benton.

> She consistently misreached for targets located in the nearby space, such as pencils, cigarettes, matches, ashtrays and cutlery. Usually she underreached by 2 to 5 inches, and then explored, by tact, the surface path leading to the target. This exploration, performed in one or two groping attempts, was often successful and led straight to the object. Occasionally, however, the hand would again misreach, this time on the side of the target and beyond it. Another quick tactually guided correction would then place the hand in contact with the object. . . . In striking contrast to the above difficulties was the performance of movements which did not require visual guidance, such as buttoning and unbuttoning of garments, bringing a cigarette to the mouth, or pointing to some part of her body. These movements were smooth, quick and on target. (Damasio and Benton, 1979, p. 171)

Balint's patient turned out to have bilateral softening of the region of areas 39 and 40. **Balint's syndrome** does not seem to occur with unilateral lesions, although it has been reported by others in patients with bilateral lesions. It thus can be considered quite rare. Nevertheless, the deficits in directing gaze and reaching are important in understanding parietal lobe function since, as we shall see, there are cells in areas 5 and 7 of the monkey that fire when the monkey reaches for objects in space.

Summary of the Major Symptoms

Our survey of the literature indicates 15 major reliable symptoms of parietal lobe damage. Table 17-1 summarizes these symptoms, indicates the most probable lesion locus, and provides basic references in which these disorders have been quantified. Details of all these symptoms can be found in Chapters 11, 13, 23, and 24, as well as the present chapter.

Left and Right Parietal Lobes Compared

Although we have discussed the left and right parietal lobe separately and have described functional asymmetry, there is little doubt that lesions to the two hemispheres produce some overlapping symptoms. (See Table 17-2, taken from the classic paper by McFie and Zangwill.) Notice that lesions of either hemisphere are associated with behavioral deficits on four of their seven tests, although particular deficits were more likely to follow damage to one hemisphere. This partial overlap of symptoms is a common feature of lesions of association cortex and implies functional overlap between the highest functions of the hemispheres. The partial

TABLE 17–1. Summary of major symptoms of parietal lobe damage

Symptoms	Most probable lesion site	Basic reference
Disorders of tactile function	Areas 1, 2, 3	Semmes et al., 1960 Corkin et al., 1970
Visual or tactile agnosia	Areas 5, 7	Hécaen and Albert, 1978 Brown, 1972
Apraxia	Areas 7, 40 left	Brown, 1972 Geschwind, 1975 Kimura, 1980
Constructional apraxia	Areas 7, 40 right	Piercy et al., 1960
Disorders of language (alexia, aphasia)	Areas 39, 40 left	Hécaen and Albert, 1978
Acalculia	Areas 39, 40 left	Hécaen, 1969
Impaired cross-modal matching	Areas 39, 40	Butters and Brody, 1968
Contralateral neglect	Areas 7, 40 right	Heilman and Watson, 1977
Poor short-term memory	Areas 39, 40	Warrington and Weiskrantz, 1973
Disorders of body image	Area 7?	Hécaen and Albert, 1978
Right-left confusion	Areas 7, 40 left	Semmes et al., 1960 Benton, 1959
Disorders of spatial ability	Areas 7, 40 right	Semmes et al., 1963 Benton, 1969
Disorders of drawing	Area 40	Warrington et al., 1966
Defects in eye movement	Area 7, 40?	Tyler, 1968
Misreaching	Areas 5, 7	Damasio and Benton, 1979

overlap may be related to the concept of preferred mode of cognitive processing, introduced in Chapter 15. There we noted that many problems can be solved by using either a verbal cognitive mode or a spatial nonverbal cognitive mode, and that genetic, maturational, and environmental factors may predispose people to use different modes. For example, a complex spatial problem, such as reading an upside-down map, can be solved either directly, by "spatial cognition" (the directions to travel are intuited spatially), or by "verbal cognition" (the spatial information is encoded into words and the problem is solved by being "talked" through step by step). There are people who are highly verbal and prefer the verbal mode even when it is less efficient; lesions of the left parietal lobe in these people would be expected to disturb functions that ordinarily are preferentially disrupted by right parietal lesions, as can be seen in Table 17-2. Little direct evidence favors this explanation of functional overlap, but we believe it is a provocative idea that accounts in part for individual differences as well as for the apparent functional overlap revealed by lesion studies.

TABLE 17–2. Effects of left and right parietal lobe lesions compared

	Percentage of subjects with deficit[a]	
	Left (%)	Right (%)
Unilateral neglect	13	67
Dressing disability	13	67
Cube counting	0	86
Paper cutting	0	90
Topographical loss	13	50
Right-left discrimination	63	0
Weigl's sorting test	83	6

[a] Note the small but significant overlap in symptoms of left and right lesions respectively.

Source: Based on data presented by McFie and Zangwill, 1960.

Drawing

Although drawing deficits are known to occur following lesions to either hemisphere, it is generally believed that the deficits in drawing are greater after right than left hemisphere damage, and that it is right parietal damage that has the greatest influence on drawing ability. This conclusion is consistent with the general idea that the right hemisphere plays a dominant role in spatial abilities, but it may not be correct. Rather, it appears that the disturbance in drawing is different after right and left hemisphere lesions, respectively. For example, Kimura and Faust asked a large sample of patients to draw a house and a man. Apraxic or aphasic left-hemisphere patients did very poorly, producing fewer recognizable drawings and fewer lines than did right-hemisphere patients. In contrast, right hemisphere patients tended to omit details from the left side of their drawings and tended to rotate the drawings on the page. Thus, although it is generally believed that drawing is impaired specifically by right parietal lesions, this conclusion may have been premature and based on a restricted, and possibly biased, sample of patients that excluded apraxic and aphasic patients. Drawing is a complex behavior that may require verbal as well as nonverbal (e.g., spatial) processes. For example, if one is asked to draw a bicycle many people will make a mental checklist of items to include (fenders, spokes, chain, etc.). In the absence of language such people would be expected to draw less complete figures. Further, if patients are apraxic, there is likely to be a deficit in making the required movements. Similarly, the parts of a bicycle have a particular spatial organization. If spatial organization is poor, the drawing is likely to be distorted. Figures 17-5*B*, 17-6*B*, and 24-7 provide examples of distorted drawings by patients with right parietal lesions.

Spatial Attention

When we move about the world we are confronted with a vast array of sensory information that cannot possibly all be treated equally by the nervous system. Thus, the brain must select certain information to process. Consider, for example, the sensory overload when we stop to chat with an old friend in a department store. There may be numerous other people around and there will certainly be displays of various items to purchase. Further, there may be competing sounds (others talking, music, cash registers, etc.), as well as novel odors, and so on. Nonetheless, we are able to orient to a small sample of the incoming information and to ignore most of the other input. In fact, we may do this to the exclusion of other, potentially more important, information. This selectivity of the sensory systems is referred to as *selective attention* by cognitive psychologists. Thus, we are said to attend to particular stimuli. Recall in our discussion of the higher level influences on perception (Chapter 11) that we considered a parallel process whereby we selectively interpret ambiguous stimuli according to a preconceived set. Thus, in our concern about muggers in the park at night we interpret stimuli in that context and might ignore a $20 bill on the ground that we would ordinarily notice. In both the department store and mugger examples our sensory input is selectively attended to and it is likely that associational cortex plays some role in this. Recent work by Posner and his colleagues suggests that the parietal cortex may play a significant role in this process, especially for visual-spatial information.

In Posner's experiments, the subjects were asked to press a key as soon as a stimulus appeared. In addition, at the beginning of each trial they were given a visual cue intended to draw their attention to one side of the visual field or the other. On most trials the target was presented in the same field (valid trial), but on some it was in the opposite field (invalid trial). As might be expected, normal subjects were significantly faster on valid than invalid trials. More importantly, however, is Posner's finding that patients with parietal lesions were nearly as good as normal subjects on valid trials but showed a marked impairment on invalid trials requiring the subject to respond to a stimulus presented contralateral to the lesion. In other words, if a stimulus was presented to the left on an invalid trial, patients with right parietal lesions were impaired, but if the stimulus was on the right on an invalid trial, then patients with left parietal lesions were impaired. This result is not simply an example of contralateral neglect, because there is no asymmetry: both left and right parietal patients are impaired on appropriate trials.

Posner has proposed that one function of the parietal cortex is to allow shifts of attention from one stimulus to another, a process that he calls *disengagement*. Parallel experiments by others suggest that right frontal lesions may produce a similar result, although there are slight differences. Finally, we shall see in the next chapter that the temporal cortex may play a role in selecting auditory stimuli as well as certain types of visual stimuli. It is likely that the parietal cortex selects visuospatial information (and possibly auditory-spatial?) and the temporal cortex selects nonspatial information. The frontal lobe may play some greater, more general role in attention.

Clinical Neuropsychological Assessment

As we have seen, restricted lesions of the parietal cortex produce a wide variety of behavioral changes. It is logical to assume that behavioral tests used to evaluate brain damage in neurologically verified cases could be used to predict the locus and extent of damage or dysfunction in new cases. (See Chapter 27 for more detail on the rationale of neuropsychological assessment.) In this section we briefly summarize a number of tests that have proved to be sensitive and valid predictors of brain injury (see Table 17-3). Although these tests do not assess all the symptoms summarized in Table 17-1, they assess a broad range of parietal lobe functions. It would be highly unusual for a person to perform normally on all these tests but show other symptoms of parietal lobe damage.

The two-point discrimination test assesses so-

TABLE 17–3. Standardized clinical neuropsychological tests for parietal lobe damage

Function	Test	Basic reference
Somatosensory	Two-point discrimination	Corkin et al., 1970
Tactile form recognition	Sequin-Goddard Form Board Tactile patterns	Teuber and Weinstein, 1954 Benton et al., 1983
Contralateral neglect	Line bisection	Schenkenberg et al., 1980
Visual perception	Gollin Incomplete Figures Mooney Closure Test	Warrington and Rabin, 1970 Milner, 1980
Spatial relations	Semmes Locomotor Map Right-left differentiation	Semmes et al., 1963 Benton et al., 1983
Language:		
speech comprehension	Token test	de Renzi and Faglioni, 1978
reading comprehension	Token test	
Apraxia	Kimura Box Test	Kimura, 1977

[a] These are standardized tests validated on large samples of patients with known localized brain damage.

matosensory thresholds. Recall that following lesions of the postcentral gyrus, the somatosensory threshold increases in the contralateral side of the body. The test requires the blindfolded subject to report whether he or she felt one or two points touch the skin (usually on the palm of the hand or the face). The distance between the points is at first very large (e.g., 3 cm) and is gradually reduced until the subject can no longer perceive two points. In extreme cases the process is reversed: the distance must be increased to find when the subject first perceives two points.

The Seguin-Goddard Form Board is a test of tactile form recognition. The blindfolded subject manipulates 10 blocks of different shape (e.g., star, triangle, etc.) and attempts to place them in similarly shaped holes on a form board. When the test is completed, the form board and blocks are removed and the subject is asked to draw the board from memory. The precise locus of the lesion producing deficits on this test is controversial, and no claims have been proved. Nevertheless, research on tactile performance in monkeys with parietal lesions (see below) indicates that blindfolded tactile recognition is probably sensitive to lesions of areas 5 and 7, whereas in humans the drawing part—a test of both memory and cross-modal matching—is probably sensitive to lesions in the tertiary zone (areas 37 and 40).

A variety of tests of contralateral neglect have been devised but we favor the one by Schenkenberg and colleagues because it is particularly sensitive. In this test the subject is asked to mark the middle of each of a set of 20 lines, each of which is a different length and is located at a different position of the page, some located left of center, some in the middle, and some right of center. Patients showing neglect typically fail to mark the lines on the left side of the page.

Visual perceptual capacity is easily assessed by either the Mooney Closure Test or the Gollin Incomplete-Figure Test. In both tasks a series of incomplete representations of faces or objects is presented, and the subject must combine the elements to form a gestalt to identify the picture. These tests are especially sensitive to right parietal cortex damage.

The Semmes Body-Placing and Locomotor Map Tests are described in detail in Chapter 19 and so will not be discussed here. In the right-left differentiation test a series of drawings of hands, feet, ears, and so on is presented in different orientations (upside down, rear view, etc.), and the subject's task is to indicate whether the drawing is of the left or right body part. In a verbal variant of this test subjects are read a series of commands (e.g., "Touch your right ear with your left hand"), which are to be carried out, rather than pointing to pictures. Both of these tests are very sensitive to left paietal lobe damage, but caution is advised, because subjects with left frontal lobe damage are also frequently impaired at these tasks.

The token test is an easily administered test of language comprehension. Twenty tokens—four shapes (large and small circles, large and small squares) in each of five colors (white, black, yellow, green, red)—are placed in front of the subject. The test begins with simple tasks (e.g., touching the white circle) and becomes progressively more difficult (e.g., touching the large yellow circle and the large green square). A reading comprehension test can also be given by having the subject read the instructions out loud and then perform according to them.

It is unfortunate that there are no standardized tests of apraxia analogous to the token test for aphasia. However, the Kimura Box Test (see Figure 13-5) is probably the best test currently available, and it may provide the desperately needed analogue. The subject is required to make three consecutive movements of pushing a button with the index finger, pulling a handle with four fingers, and pressing a bar with the thumb. This test is done very poorly by apraxics, and many of them appear unable to perform this very simple series of movements even with extensive practice.

Together, these nine tests provide a simple, standardized, and thorough collection of tests of parietal lobe damage. In addition to these, there is a good series of tests in a "parietal lobe battery" described by Goodglass and Kaplan. We shall discuss the uses of neuropsychological tests in Chapters 27 through 31.

NONHUMAN PARIETAL LOBE FUNCTIONS

In view of the striking parallels in the cytoarchitectonic organization of the posterior parietal cortex of the human and rhesus monkey, it is reasonable to expect evidence of parallel functions in these species, and indeed, this is the case. Little is known about this cortex in other mammals, and it is even difficult to establish convincing homologies with the major areas PE, PG, and PF. We shall therefore restrict our consideration to the study of nonhuman primates. Three types of experiments are relevant to this discussion: (1) those examining the behavioral capacities of different primates, especially on tests of cross-modal matching; (2) those examining the effects of parietal lobe lesions on behavior; and (3) those examining the properties of cells in the parietal cortex.

Nonhuman Primate Cross-Modal Matching and Language Skills

Cross-modal-matching ability has been widely implicated as a necessary correlate of language skills in humans, and it has been suggested that nonhuman primates do not naturally have language because they lack this cognitive function. Because it is assumed that cross-modal matching is performed by the angular and supramarginal gyri and because there are suggestions that nonhuman primates may not possess a homologue of this region, it is of particular interest to know whether they are capable of performing this behavior.

A variety of experimental situations have been devised to test this question. In the simplest of these tests an animal is presented three objects: one (the sample) it can see but not touch, and two others it can touch but not see. One of the hidden objects is identical to the sample. The subject's task is to select this one after handling each of the hidden ones. If the chosen object matches the sample, the animal is given a food reward. By using this procedure Davenport and his colleagues have unequivocally demonstrated cross-modal-matching abilities in chimpanzees, for they not only can match a visually presented object with the tactile equivalent but also can match photographs of an object with its tactile equivalent.

Until recently monkeys were reported to fail or give equivocal results in a matching task, but Jarvis and Ettlinger have shown that various species of monkeys are clearly capable of cross-modal matching and that early failures were an artifact of testing procedures. Furthermore, when they compared the performance of chimpanzees and rhesus monkeys on the same test problems, they found no clear superiority in the performance of the chimps. This result is surprising, for the chimpanzee has the larger parietal association cortex of the two.

The results of these studies imply one of two conditions: either cross-modal matching is not a correlate of language (although perhaps it is a prerequisite for language), or nonhuman primates are capable of some language abilities. Research on several species of apes has indicated that they are indeed capable of acquiring certain language abilities, such as the American Sign Language; thus, the neocortical organization of humans and other great apes may not differ qualitatively. We shall return to this issue in our discussion of language (Chapter 22); we conclude here that there is no compelling behavioral evidence for a significant difference between parietal lobe function in humans and in their nearest primate relatives.

Behavior Following Parietal Lobe Lesions in Nonhumans

The behavioral effects of parietal lobe lesions in monkeys are summarized in Table 17-4. Each of the symptoms listed is also observed in humans although the symptoms are less obvious in monkeys than they are in humans. Unfortunately, there are few studies in which the lesions have been limited to a single cytoarchitectonic area, the lesions usually being placed in the anterior parietal (areas 1, 2, and 3) or posterior parietal (areas 5 and 7) regions.

Tactile Function. Lesions of areas 1, 2, and 3 produce deficits in various tactile-related behaviors. Simple tactile discriminations (e.g., roughness) are disturbed by lesions of primary parietal cortex, whereas most posterior lesions produce a wide variety of symptoms, including deficits in tactile form discrimination, impairment of limb

TABLE 17-4. Summary of the major symptoms of parietal lobe lesions in monkeys

Symptom	Lesion site	Representative reference
Disorders of tactile function	Areas 1, 2, 3, 5, 7	Semmes and Turner, 1977 LaMotte and Mountcastle, 1979 Moffet et al., 1967
Disorders of spatial ability	Areas 5, 7	Sugishita et al., 1978 Mishkin et al., 1982
Unilateral neglect	Areas 5, 7	Denny-Brown and Chambers, 1958 Heilman and Watson, 1977
Defects in eye movements	Areas 5, 7	Latto, 1978 Lynch, 1980
Misreaching	Areas 5, 7	Peele, 1944 Milner et al., 1977

position sense, and deficits in tactile placing and the grasping response. In addition, there is a deficit in discriminating temperature differences of less than 12°C.

Spatial Ability. Monkeys with posterior parietal lesions have an impaired perception of the relations among objects in space, although apparently not of the relation between the monkey's own body and objects in space. A useful task has been devised by Pohl to demonstrate this deficit. Monkeys are presented with two identical plaques, under one of which food is available. The only clue to the correct location is a cylinder, which is located nearer to one plaque than the other. The monkey's task is to learn the relationship between the cylinder and the correct plaque. Monkeys with lesions in area 7 are impaired at this task. Such monkeys are also deficient in finding their home cages when released in the center of an animal room, and they direct manual searches in the dark in the wrong direction. Further, they are poor at learning visually guided routes through mazes. All these symptoms suggest a general spatial disturbance parallel to that observed in humans, which we shall return to in Chapter 24. In addition, the monkeys are impaired at visual guidance of movements in space. Petrides and Iverson studied the performance of monkeys on a behavioral analogue of the route-finding tests (e.g., mazes and maps) used to study special ability in humans. They chose a "bent wire" problem, using metal rods bent to form various routes.

A ring-shaped sweet was threaded on the wire, and the monkey's task was to remove the sweet so that it could be eaten. Monkeys with parietal lesions took significantly longer to remove the sweets; indeed, they completely failed to solve about half of the problems. These data demonstrate a visuospatial deficit analogous to those seen in humans with similar lesions.

Unilateral Neglect. Although unilateral neglect is less conspicuous in monkeys than in humans with parietal lobe lesions, several authors have reported that unilateral parietal lesions in monkeys produce a phenomenon similar to contralateral neglect. For example, Heilman and Watson and their associates have observed that monkeys display extinction to simultaneous visual and somesthetic stimulation and decreased response to threat contralateral to the lesions, occasionally even ignoring food on the side contralateral to the lesion.

Defective Eye Movements. Workers at a number of laboratories have noticed abnormal visual search patterns following posterior parietal lesions in monkeys, and careful study by Lynch and his colleagues has shown several abnormalities in optokinetic **nystagmus,** which is involuntary, rapid movements of the eyeball elicited by stimuli moving through the visual field.

Misreaching. Monkeys with parietal lesions reach with poor accuracy and may appear ataxic as they try to grasp objects with either the fore or hind feet. The reaching deficit is characterized by slowness of movement, abnormal shaping of the hand and fingers during reaching, and an error in the angle of reach of the limb with respect to a target.

We are unaware of any studies of lesions in the posterior parietal cortex of cats, although lesions in primary somatosensory cortex do disrupt tactile discrimination. More research has been done with rats, and we have found deficits in spatial navigation and limb placement from the presumed analogue of posterior parietal lesions in humans.

Microelectrode Studies

In the 1960s, the parietal cortex of the monkey was considered to be a somatosensory area, the anterior zone to be involved in basic somatosensation, and the posterior zone to have some sort of "associate somatic" function. Over the past decade research using microelectrodes to study single units has painted a somewhat different picture, in which the functions of areas 1, 2, and 3, area 5, and several subareas of area 7 can be dissociated. We have described the characteristics of units in areas 1, 2, and 3 in Chapters 9 and 10, and so we shall focus our discussion here on areas 5 and 7.

Area 5. The majority of neurons in area 5 are activated by passive joint rotation or the stimulation of muscles and other deep tissues. More important, however, is the fact that area-5 neurons are most responsive during active movement. Mountcastle and his colleagues found that many cells were only responsive to projections of the arm or manipulations by the hand within the immediate space around the animal to *obtain an object such as food*. This observation was unexpected and fascinating since these same cells were not active during other movements in which the same muscles were used differently, implying that the function of the cells was not simply "somatic." Hyvarinen suggests that area 5 seems to have an important role in somatosensory exploration, reaching for and manipulation of objects. For successful reaching in space, the positions of several joints have to be coordinated; damage to these neurons would impair reaching, and we have seen that this is the case. The neural circuits connecting the posterior parietal cortex with the frontal and limbic cortex (see Chapter 9) may be responsible for the selective activation of area-5 neurons in the presence of goal objects, but this remains to be proved.

Neurons in area 5 have also been shown to be responsive to the expectation of touch, in addition to being touched. This feature is observed when a specific body part (e.g., hand or shoulder) is approached as though contact would be made. These cells discharged in the absence of touch or of any movement by the subject. (Perhaps these cells are activated in us when we say "ouch" just before bumping our knee into a moving cart that we saw but failed to avoid.)

Area 7. Far from being a "somatic association zone," the units in area 7 reveal it to be a truly multimodal region, as we suggested in our theoretical view of the parietal lobe at the beginning of the chapter. Cells in area 7 respond to somatic stimulation, as might be expected in a somatic secondary region, but there are also cells responsive to visual and to auditory stimulation. Further, there are cells in this area that are active during eye movements, cells that may be analogous to those active during visually guided reaching movements.

The details of the characteristics of the cells of area 7 are complex and beyond us here, but some simple generalizations can be made. First, the cells in area 7 have a role in directing movements toward somatosensory, visual, and auditory targets. When the head or limb moves toward a location in space, cells in area 7 are very active, suggesting that they have a major role in coordinating the changes in joint position to direct the movement to the location. It may not be surprising, therefore, that removal of the posterior parietal cortex produces apparent neglect; in the absence of area 7 the brain may detect the stimuli normally but be unable to direct the appropriate movements, resulting in part of the neglect syndrome.

Second, area 7 appears to be functionally differentiated into smaller regions, each of which may have a special role in a particular type of movement. Thus, one zone has cells responsive to both somatic and visual stimuli, a second to somatic and auditory stimuli, and a third to chemical and somatic stimuli. The first zone may be involved in visual and somatic guidance of limb and hand movements, the second in auditory and somatic guidance of the head, and the third in chemical and somatic guidance of the tongue, although this is purely speculative.

The identification of units in the parietal cortex that appear to have a role in the control of movements in space with respect to specific targets is important, for these properties are consistent with two effects of parietal lobe lesions in humans. First, individuals with parietal lesions appear to have a deficit in coordinating segmental movements involving changes in joint position, an effect one might expect if area-7 units were damaged. Second, these individuals have difficulty in manipulating objects in space (constructional apraxia), another effect that might be expected if area-7 units were damaged.

Posner and his associates' work on selective-attention deficits in patients with parietal lesions leads one to expect to find parietal cells whose rate of firing is influenced by attentional factors as in Posner's experiments. Although Moran and Desimone have found such units, curiously they are in V4, which is in the posterior-temporal cortex of the monkey. The work on human lesions has so far been unable to specify the crucial locus for this effect. It is therefore possible that the locus is really posterior-temporal cortex in the human, but this issue has not yet been studied.

REFERENCES

Andersen, R. A. Inferior parietal lobule function in spatial perception and visuomotor integration. *Handbook of Physiology* 5:483–518, 1987.

Balint, R. Seelenlahmung des "Schauens," optische Ataxie, raumliche Störung der Aufmerksamkeit. *Monatsschr. Psychiatr. Neurol.* 25:51–81, 1909.

Benton, A. L. *Right-Left Discrimination and Finger Localization.* New York: Hoeber-Harper, 1959.

Benton, A. L. Disorders of spatial orientation. In P. Vincken and G. Bruyn, eds. *Handbook of Clinical Neurology,* vol. 3. Amsterdam: North-Holland Publishing Co., 1969.

Benton, A. L., K. deS. Hamsher, N. R. Varney, and O. Spreen. *Contributions to Neuropsychological Assessment.* New York: Oxford University Press, 1983.

Bolster, R. B. Cross-modal matching in the monkey *(Macada fasicularis). Neuropsychologia* 16:407–416, 1978.

Brown, J. *Aphasia, Apraxia and Agnosia.* Springfield, IL: Charles C. Thomas, 1972.

Butters, N., and B. A. Brody. The role of the left parietal lobe in the mediation of intra- and cross-modal associations. *Cortex* 4:328–343, 1968.

Corkin, S., B. Milner, and T. Rasmussen. Somatosensory thresholds. *Archives of Neurology* 23:41–58, 1970.

Critchley, M. *The Parietal Lobes.* London: Arnold, 1953.

Damasio, A. R., and A. L. Benton. Impairment of hand movements under visual guidance. *Neurology* 29:170–178, 1979.

Davenport, R. K., C. M. Rogers, and I. S. Russell. Cross-modal perception in apes. *Neuropsychologia* 11:21–28, 1973.

Denny-Brown, D., and R. A. Chambers. The parietal lobes and behavior. *Research Publications of the Association for Research in Mental Disease* 36:35–117, 1958.

Eidelberg, D., and A. M. Galaburda. Inferior parietal lobule: Divergent architectonic asymmetries in the human brain. *Archives of Neurology* 41:843–852, 1984.

Gerstmann, J. Some notes on the Gerstmann syndrome. *Neurology* 7:866–869, 1957.

Geschwind, N. The apraxias: Neural mechanisms of disorders of learned movement. *American Scientist* 63:199–195, 1975.

Goodglass, H., and E. Kaplan. *The Assessment of Aphasia.* Philadelphia: Lea & Febiger, 1972.

Hécaen, H. Aphasic, apraxic and agnosic syndromes in right and left hemisphere lesions. In P. Vincken and G. Bruyn, eds. *Handbook of Clinical Neurology,* vol. 4. Amsterdam: North-Holland Publishing Co., 1969.

Hécaen, H., and M. L. Albert. *Human Neuropsychology.* New York: John Wiley, 1978.

Heilman, K. M., and R. T. Watson. The neglect syndrome — A unilateral defect of the orienting response. In S. Harnad, R. W. Doty, L. Goldstein, J. Jaynes, and G. Krauthamer, eds. *Lateralization in the Nervous System.* New York: Academic Press, 1977.

Hyvarinen, J. *The Parietal Cortex of Monkey and Man.* Berlin: Springer-Verlag, 1982.

Jarvis, M. J., and G. Ettlinger. Cross-modal recognition in chimpanzees and monkeys. *Neuropsychologia* 15:499–506, 1977.

Kimura, D. Acquisition of a motor skill after left hemisphere damage. *Brain* 100:527–542, 1977.

Kimura, D. Neuromotor mechanisms in the evolution of human communication. In H. D. Steklis and M. J. Raleigh, eds. *Neurobiology of Social Communication in Primates: An Evolutionary Perspective.* New York: Academic Press, 1980.

Kimura, D., and R. Faust. Spontaneous drawing in an unselected sample of patients with unilateral cerebral damage. In D. Ottoson, ed. *Duality and Unity of the Brain.* Wenner-Gren Center International Symposium Series, vol. 47. New York: MacMillan, 1987.

LaMotte, R. H., and V. B. Mountcastle. Disorders of somesthesis following lesions of the parietal lobe. *Journal of Neurophysiology* 42:400–419, 1979.

Latto, R. The effects of bilateral frontal eye-field, posterior parietal or superior collicular lesions on visual search in the rhesus monkey. *Brain Research* 146:39–53, 1978.

Luria, A. R. *The Working Brain.* New York: Penguin, 1973.

Lynch, J. C. The functional organization of the posterior parietal association cortex. *Behavioral and Brain Sciences* 3:485–499, 1980.

Lynch, J. C. The role of parieto-occipital association cortex in oculomotor control. *Experimental Brain Research* 41:A32, 1980.

Lynch, J. C., V. B. Mountcastle, W. H. Talbot, and T. C. T. Yin. Parietal lobe mechanisms for directed visual attention. *Journal of Neurophysiology* 40:362–389, 1977.

Mackay, W. A. and D. J. Crammond. Neuronal correlates in posterior parietal lobe of the expectation of events. *Behavioural Brain Research* 24:167–179, 1987.

McFie, J., M. F. Piercy, and O. L. Zangwill. Visual spatial agnosia associated with lesions of the left cerebral hemisphere. *Brain* 73:167–190, 1950.

McFie, J., and O. L. Zangwill. Visual-constructive disabilities associated with lesions of the left cerebral hemisphere. *Brain* 83:243–260, 1960.

Milner, A. D., E. M. Ockleford, and W. Dewar. Visuo-spatial performance following posterior parietal and lateral frontal lesions in stumptail macaques. *Cortex* 13:350–360, 1977.

Milner, B. Complementary functional specializations of the human cerebral hemispheres. In R. Levy-Montalcini, eds. *Neurons, Transmitters, and Behavior.* Vatican City: Pontificiae Academiae Scientiarum Scripta Varia, 1980.

Mishkin, M., M. E. Lewis, and L. G. Ungerleider. Equivalence of parieto-preoccipital subareas for visuospatial ability in monkeys. *Behavioural Brain Research* 6:41–55, 1982.

Moffet, A., G. Ettlinger, H. B. Morton, and M. F. Piercy. Tactile discrimination performance in the monkey: The effect of ablation of various subdivisions of posterior parietal cortex. *Cortex* 3:59–96, 1967.

Moran, J., and R. Desimone. Selective attention gates visual processing in the extrastriate cortex. *Science* 229:782–784, 1985.

Mountcastle, V. B., J. C. Lynch, A. Georgopoulos, H. Sakata, and C. Acuna. Posterior parietal association cortex of the monkey: Command functions for operation within extra-personal space. *Journal of Neurophysiology* 38:871–908, 1975.

Pandya, D. N., and E. H. Yeterian. Architecture and connections of cortical association areas. In A. Peters and E. G. Jones, eds. *Cerebral Cortex: Volume 4, Association and Auditory Cortices.* New York: Plenum, 1985.

Passingham, R. F., and G. Ettlinger. A comparison of cortical functions in man and other primates. *International Review of Neurobiology* 16:233–299, 1974.

Paterson, A., and O. L. Zangwill. Disorders of space perception associated with lesions of the right cerebral hemisphere. *Brain* 67:331–358, 1944.

Peele, T. L. Acute and chronic parietal lobe ablations in monkeys. *Journal of Neurophysiology* 7:269–286, 1944.

Petras, J. M. Connections of the parietal lobe. *Journal of Psychiatric Research* 8:189–201, 1971.

Petrides, M., and S. D. Iverson. Restricted posterior parietal lesions in the rhesus monkey and performance on visuospatial tasks. *Brain Research* 161:63–77, 1979.

Piercy, M., H. Hécaen, and J. de Ajuriaguerra. Constructional apraxia association with unilateral cerebral lesions—Left and right cases compared. *Brain* 83:225–242, 1960.

Pohl, W. Dissociation of spatial discrimination deficits following frontal and parietal lesions in monkeys. *Journal of Comparative and Physiological Psychology* 82:227–239, 1973.

Porter, L. H. An experimental investigation of the parietal lobes and temperature discrimination in monkeys. *Brain Research* 412:54–87, 1987.

Posner, M. I., A. W. Inhoff, F. J. Friedrich, and A. Cohen. Isolating attentional systems: A cognitive-anatomical analysis. *Psychobiology* 15:107–121, 1987.

Posner, M. I., J. A. Walker, J. J. Friedrich, and R. D. Rafal. Effects of parietal lobe injury on covert orienting of visual attention. *Journal of Neuroscience* 4:1863–1874, 1984.

Renzi, E. de, and P. Faglioni. Normative data and screening power of a shortened version of the token test. *Cortex* 14:41–49, 1978.

Schenkenberg, T., D. C. Bradford, and E. T. Ajax. Line bisection and unilateral visual neglect in patients with neurologic impairment. *Neurology* 30:509–517, 1980.

Semmes, J., and B. Turner. Effects of cortical lesions on somatosensory task. *Journal of Investigations in Dermatology* 69:181–189, 1977.

Semmes, J., S. Weinstein, L. Ghent, and H.-L. Teuber. *Somatosensory Changes after Penetrating Brain Wounds in Man.* Cambridge, MA: Harvard University Press, 1960.

Semmes, J., S. Weinstein, L. Ghent, and H.-L. Teuber. Correlates of impaired orientation in personal and extra-personal space. *Brain* 86:747–772, 1963.

Sugishita, M., G. Ettlinger, and R. M. Ridley. Disturbance of cage-finding in the monkey. *Cortex* 14:431–438, 1978.

Teuber, H.-L., and S. Weinstein. Performance on a formboard task after penetrating brain injury. *Journal of Psychology* 38:177–190, 1954.

Traverse, J., and Latto, R. Impairments in route negotiation through a maze after dorsolateral frontal, inferior parietal or premotor lesions in cynomolgus monkeys. *Behavioural Brain Research* 20:203–215, 1986.

Tyler, H. R. Abnormalities of perception with defective eye movements (Balint's syndrome). *Cortex* 4:154–171, 1968.

Warrington, E. K., M. James, and M. Kinsbourne. Drawing disability in relation to laterality of cerebral lesion. *Brain* 89:53–82, 1966.

Warrington, E. K., and P. Rabin. Perceptual matching in patients with cerebral lesions. *Neuropsychologia* 8:475–487, 1970.

Warrington, E. K., and A. M. Taylor. The contribution of the right parietal lobe to object recognition. *Cortex* 9:152–164, 1973.

Warrington, E. K., and L. Weiskrantz. An analysis of short-term and long-term memory defects in man. In J. A. Deutsch, ed. *The Physiological Basis of Memory*. New York: Academic Press, 1973.

THE TEMPORAL LOBES

In the late 19th century three major effects of temporal lobe lesions on behavior were documented: in 1874 Karl Wernicke described a language deficit, in 1899 Bekhterev reported memory impairment, and in 1888 Brown and Schaefer noted a disorder of affect and personality. Only in the past 30 years, however, have the functions of the temporal lobes—especially of the right—been elaborated upon. In this chapter we will review the anatomy of the temporal lobe, present a simple theoretical model of its function, describe the basic symptoms of damage to it in humans, and briefly describe the effects of temporal lobe lesions in nonhumans.

ANATOMY OF THE TEMPORAL LOBES

The temporal lobe comprises all the tissue below the Sylvian fissure anterior to an imaginary line running roughly from the end of that fissure to the boundary of area 37 with area 19, and the boundary of areas 22 and 37 with the parietal association areas 39 and 40 (see Figure 18-1). The region enclosed by these boundaries includes not only neocortex (six layers) on the lateral surface but also phylogenetically older cortex known as **archicortex** and **paleocortex** (three layers) on the medial surface. The neocortical regions include Brodmann's areas 20, 21, 22, 37, 38, 41, and 42. These areas are also sometimes described by the gyri that form them (illustrated in Figure 18-1*A*): Heschl's gyrus (areas 41 and 42), the superior temporal gyrus (roughly area 22), the middle temporal gyrus (roughly areas 21, 37, and 38), and the inferior temporal gyrus (roughly areas 20 and 37). In addition, the sulci of the temporal lobe contain a lot of cortex, as can be seen in Figure 18-2. In particular, the Sylvian fissure (also called the lateral fissure) contains tissue forming the *insula,* which includes gustatory cortex as well as

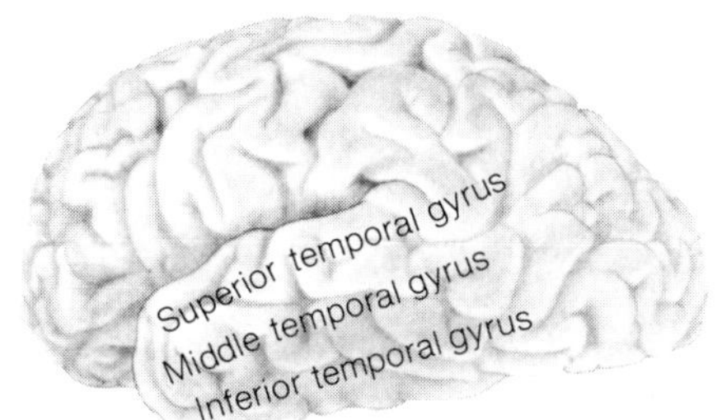

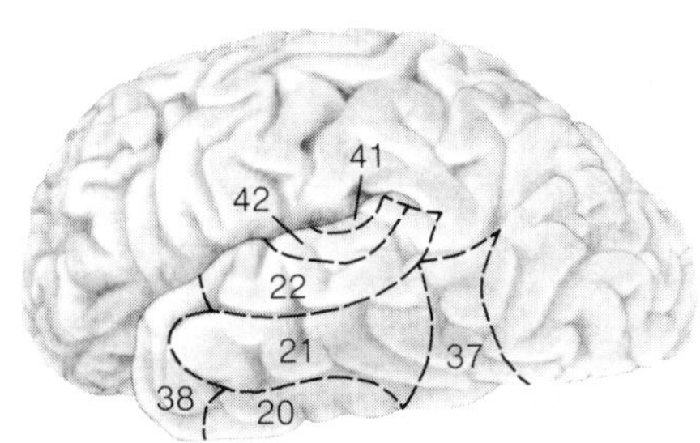

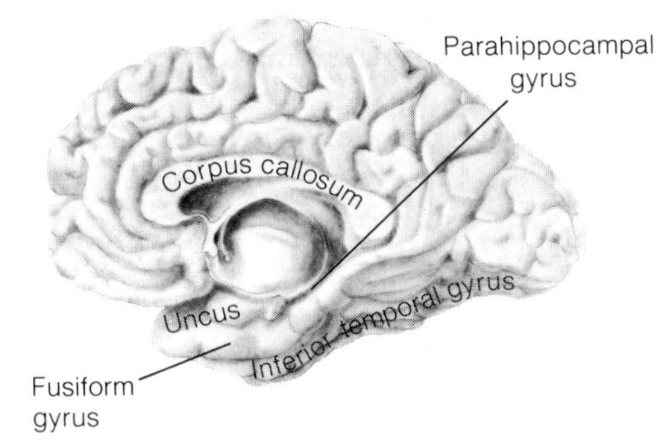

FIGURE 18-1. Gross anatomy of the temporal lobe. *A*. The three major gyri visible on the lateral surface of the temporal lobe. *B*. Brodmann's ctyoarchitectonic zones on the lateral surface. *C*. The gyri visible on a medial view of the temporal lobe.

association cortex. The superior temporal sulcus, which separates the superior and middle temporal gyri, also contains a significant amount of neocortex (see Figure 18-2). The older cortex of the temporal lobe includes both the cortex on the medial surface of the temporal lobe, which forms the fusiform gyrus, parahippocampal gyrus, and uncus, and the hippocampus and amygdala (see Figure 18-1*C* and 18-2*B*), which are subcortical. Thus, the temporal lobe includes auditory, association, and limbic cortex.

Subdivisions and Connections of the Temporal Cortex

Little is known about the subdivisions of the temporal regions in humans, so again we must rely on studies of nonhuman primates in which it has been possible to subdivide areas 21 and 22 into numerous subregions. Figure 18-3 illustrates another feature of temporal lobe anatomy in the monkey, a feature that is probably true of the human brain as well. In the depth of the superior temporal sulcus there is a region of cortex that Pandya calls a multimodal sensory-convergence area. In the monkey this area receives input from auditory, visual, and somatic secondary association cortex, and from other polymodal areas (frontal and parietal) as well as paralimbic cortex.

The temporal lobe is rich in internal connections, afferent projections from the sensory systems, and efferent projections to the parietal and frontal association regions, limbic system and basal ganglia. The left and right temporal lobes are connected via the corpus callosum and anterior commissure, to the neocortex through the former and to the archicortex through the latter.

Studies on the temporal-cortical connections of the monkey have revealed four distinct types of corticocortical connections, which are illustrated in Figure 18-4. The first is a hierarchical procession of connections from the primary and secondary auditory and visual areas, ending in the temporal pole. The second is a series of parallel projections from the visual and auditory association areas into the polymodal regions of the superior temporal sulcus. (There is a projection from area 7 into these regions as well.) The third is a projection from the

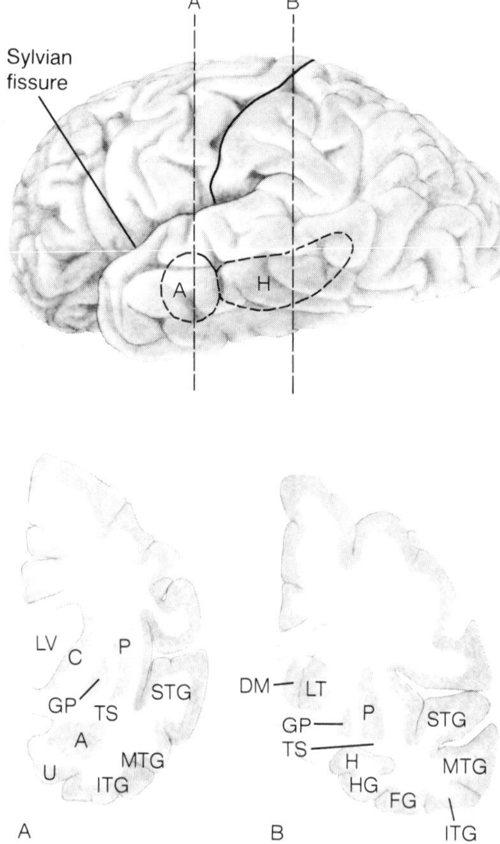

FIGURE 18-2. *Top,* lateral view of the left hemisphere illustrating the relative positions of the amygdala (dashed circle) and hippocampus (dashed oval) buried deep in the temporal lobe. The dashed lines A and B indicate the approximate location in the bottom figure. *Bottom,* Frontal sections through the left hemisphere illustrating the cortical and subcortical regions of the temporal lobe. A, amygdala; C, caudate nucleus; DM, dorsomedial nucleus of the thalamus; FG, fusiform gyrus; GP, globus pallidus; H, hippocampus; HG, hippocampal gyrus; ITG, inferior temporal gyrus; LT, lateral thalamus; LV, lateral ventricle; MTG, middle temporal gyrus; P, putamen; STG, superior temporal gyrus; TS, temporal stem; U, uncus.

auditory and visual association areas into the medial temporal regions. This projection goes first to the entorhinal cortex and then into the hippocampal formation and/or the amygdala. The hippocampal projection is a major one, forming the **perforant pathway.** A disturbance of this projection results in a major dysfunction in hippocampal activity. Finally, the fourth is a series of parallel projections from the association areas to the frontal lobe. These different projection pathways presumably subserve different functions, which will become apparent in the next section. Briefly, the heirarchical sensory pathway probably subserves stimulus recognition; the polymodal pathway probably underlies stimulus categorization; the medial temporal projection is crucial to long-term memory; and, the frontal lobe projection is necessary for various aspects of movement control.

A THEORY OF TEMPORAL LOBE FUNCTION

Being an arbitrarily defined anatomical region, the temporal lobe does not have a unitary function, since it houses primary and secondary auditory cortex, secondary visual cortex, tertiary sensory cortex, and limbic cortex. However, if the primary and secondary auditory cortex are considered separately from the association and limbic cortex, three basic functions of the temporal lobes can be identified: one primarily concerned with auditory sensations and auditory and visual perception, one specialized for long-term storage of sensory input, and one functioning to add affective tone to sensory input.

These three functions are best understood by considering the analysis of sensory stimuli as they enter the nervous system. When a sensory stimulus is received, several processes must occur to allow the motor system to act on the information. First, a stimulus must be identified and a percept must be formed, which requires that information about a given stimulus be integrated from different senses, especially vision, audition, and somesthesis. As we saw in the previous chapter, this integration is the primary function of the tertiary area of the parietal lobe. Note, however, that it is not necessary to code

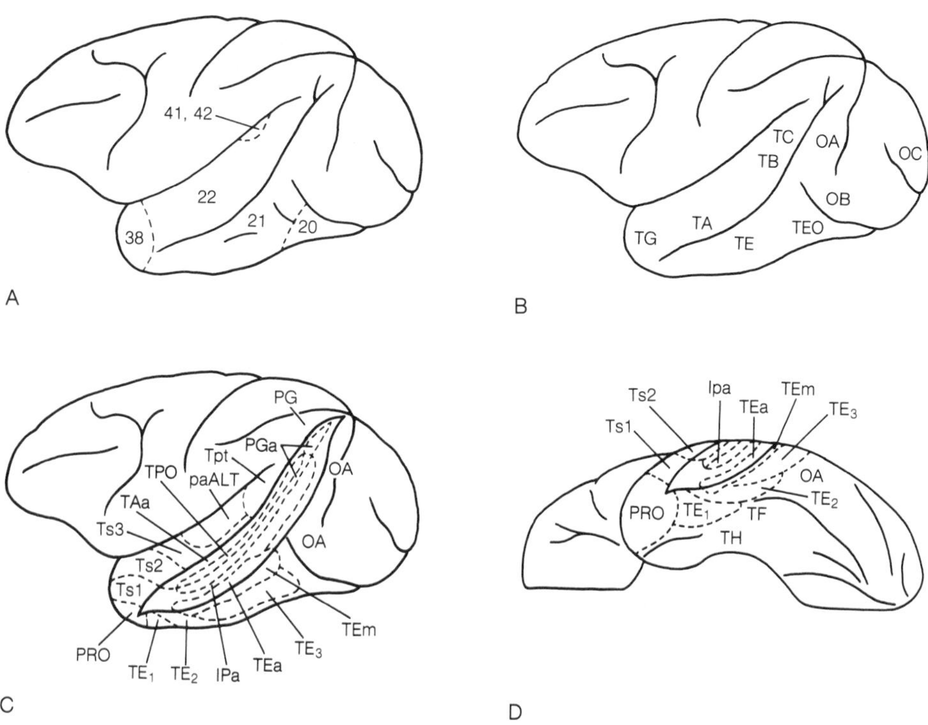

FIGURE 18-3. Cytoarchitectonic regions of the temporal cortex of the rhesus monkey. *A*. Brodmann's areas. *B*. von Bonin and Bailey's areas. *C* and *D*. Lateral and ventral views of Seltzer and Pandya's parcellation showing the multimodal areas in the superior temporal sulcus.

all of the fine details about the stimulus object such as color or fine texture in order to match a key or a pen that is felt with a key or a pencil that is observed. We probably perform this cross-modal matching quite coarsely with little attention to the fine details. Indeed, if after feeling a key and a pen we were shown two keys and two pens, we would no doubt find it nearly impossible to discriminate between the similar stimuli. Second, once we have formed a percept of a stimulus, it needs to be identified and probably categorized or classified with respect to its function. Classification may require a form of directed attention since certain characteristics of stimuli are likely to play a more important role in classification than are others. For example, classifying a fruit as an apple requires that attention be directed away from color and focused upon shape and texture. The process of identification and classification is probably carried out by the temporal association cortex, including especially the superior temporal sulcus. We have seen that the cortex in the sulcus is polymodal, receiving input from all sensory modalities; in addition, it receives input from area 7. The direct sensory inputs provide more fine details about a stimulus, whereas area 7 probably provides the basic percept to build on, including the general shape of objects. Thus, damage to the temporal association cortex leads to deficits in identifying and categorizing stimuli. There is no difficulty in

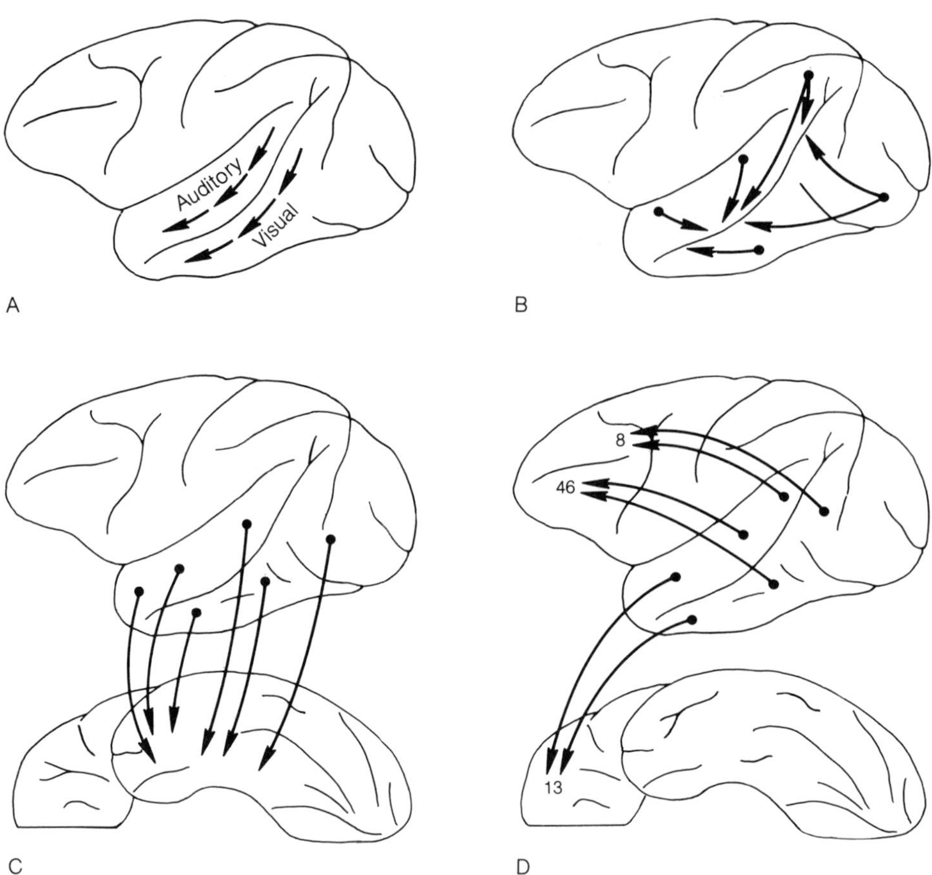

FIGURE 18-4. Summaries of the major intracortical connections of the temporal lobe. *A*. Auditory and visual information progresses from the primary regions toward the temporal pole, en route to the medial temporal regions. *B*. Auditory, visual, and somatic outputs go to the multimodal regions of the superior temporal sulcus. *C*. Auditory and visual information goes to the medial temporal region, including the amygdaloid formation and hippocampal formation. *D*. Auditory and visual information goes to two prefrontal regions, one on the dorsolateral surface and one in the orbital region (area 13).

locating the stimulus or in recognizing that a stimulus is present, however, because we have seen these to be functions of the posterior parietal and primary sensory areas, respectively. It might be predicted that temporal lobe damage would also interfere with cross-modal matching if the stimuli were very similar, although this has not been shown.

The third step in our sensory analysis involves either storing information for future use or in comparing it with material stored previously. Storage requires two components. First, there must be a mechanism that functions to store and to retrieve information; this mechanism appears to be in the temporal lobes, especially the hippocampus. Second, there must be a mechanism for the actual storage of information; there are few clues about the location of this mechanism because brain lesions do not selectively destroy memories. We will return to the problem of where memory is stored in Chapter 21.

The fourth step of sensory-input analysis is assigning connotative or affective properties to stimuli—that is, associating them with motivational or emotional significance. This function is crucial for learning because stimuli become associated with their positive, negative, or neutral consequences, and behavior is modified accordingly. In the absence of this system all stimuli would be treated as equivalent, and there would be a loss of affective response to them. Associating affective properties with particular stimuli is also a function of the temporal lobe, especially the medial temporal cortex and amygdala. Indeed, because of this function, the medial temporal cortex has been called the association cortex of the limbic system. It is also likely that the multimodal cortex of the temporal cortex is also involved in associating affect with stimuli, and it is known that medial temporal lesions have a greater influence on affect if the temporal neocortex, including the multimodal area, is included. To date, most research on temporal lobe function has been done on memory processes and very little on affective processes, partly because studying memory mechanisms is easier than studying affective mechanisms objectively. Indeed, both cognitive psychologists and neuropsychologists barely pay lip service to this latter function, although most would agree it plays an important role in the way we think and behave.

Although possible in principle at least, the anatomical separation of memory and affective functions in the temporal lobe has proved difficult to demonstrate. Visual or auditory input leaving the visual and auditory association regions proceeds to the various regions of the medial temporal lobe. There are no strong empirical grounds for functionally differentiating these medial temporal regions in humans, although it is likely to be the case. The medial temporal cortex then projects primarily to the amygdala and hippocampus, which are relatively specialized for affective and memory functions, respectively. Note, however, that the amygdala and hippocampus are probably not absolutely dissociated, because there is evidence in nonhuman primates that memory defects are more severe when the amygdala is also damaged, and affective changes have been associated with hippocampal lesions in cats (comparable data are not available from studies of primates).

Asymmetry of Temporal Lobe Function

The temporal lobes are sensitive to epileptiform abnormalities. This and the fact that surgical removal of the abnormal temporal lobe is often of benefit in treating epilepsy, has allowed neuropsychologists to carefully study the complementary specialization of the temporal lobes. Comparison of the effects of left and right temporal lobectomy by Milner has revealed that specific memory defects vary according to which side the lesion is on: damage to the left temporal lobe is associated with deficits in verbal memory; damage to the right, with deficits in nonverbal memory. Similarly, left temporal lesions are associated with deficits in processing speech sounds, whereas right temporal lesions are associated with deficits in processing music. Little is known, however, about the relative role of the left and right temporal lobes in affective behavior. Nevertheless, a suggestion of asymmetry comes from unquantified clinical observations that left and right temporal lobe lesions appear to have different effects on personality, and that right, but not left, temporal lesions lead to impairments in interpretation of facial expression.

In reviewing the literature on the results of unilateral temporal lobectomy, one is often struck by the relatively minor effects of removal of such a large zone of the cerebral hemispheres. However, it is incorrect to assume from these studies that removing both temporal lobes would merely add the symptoms of damage to each alone. Bilateral temporal lobe removal produces dramatic effects on both memory and affect that are orders of magnitude greater than those observed following unilateral lesions. (See Chapters 21 and 23 for detailed discussion of the effects of bilateral lesions on memory and affect, respectively.) Thus, although the temporal lobes are relatively specialized in their functions, there is substantial functional overlap: do not be overly impressed by the apparent functional asymmetry.

SYMPTOMS OF TEMPORAL LOBE LESIONS

Eight principal symptoms are associated with disease of the temporal lobes: (1) disturbance of auditory sensation and perception, (2) disturbance of selective attention of auditory and visual input, (3) disorders of visual perception, (4) impaired organization and categorization of verbal material, (5) disturbance of language comprehension, (6) impaired long-term memory, (7) altered personality and affective behavior, and (8) altered sexual behavior. Many disorders of auditory sensation and perception were discussed in Chapter 11; we will, therefore, focus on only two of them here, namely disorders of music and language perception. Table 18-1 summarizes the major symptoms of temporal lobe damage, lists the most probable lesion sites, and cites basic references.

Disturbance of Selection of Visual and Auditory Input

Lesions of the temporal lobes outside the primary and secondary auditory and visual zones produce neither deficits of sensation nor agnosias. Instead, they result in disturbance in focusing attention on specific aspects of sensory input. This is best understood by first considering sensory selection in normal people.

TABLE 18–1. Summary of major symptoms of temporal lobe damage

Symptoms	Most probable lesion site	Basic reference
Disturbance of auditory sensation	Areas 41,42,22	Vignolo, 1969 Hécaen and Albert, 1978
Disturbance of selection of visual and auditory input	Areas 20,21,22 37,38	Sparks et al., 1970 Dorff et al., 1965
Disorders of visual perception	Areas 20,21	Milner, 1968 Meier and French, 1968
Disorders of auditory perception	Areas 41,42,22	Samson and Zatorre, 1988 Swisher and Hirsch, 1972
Impaired organization and categorization of material	Areas 21,38 left	Wilkins and Moscovitch, 1978 Read, 1981
Poor contextual use	Area 21,38	Milner, 1958
Disturbance of language comprehension	Area 22 left	Hécaen and Albert, 1978
Poor long-term memory	Areas 21,38 hippocampus (and possibly amygdala)	Milner, 1970
Changes in personality and affect	Areas 21,38 plus amygdala	Blumer and Benson, 1975 Pincus and Tucker, 1974
Changes in sexual activity	?	Blumer and Walker, 1975

People have a limited capacity to process the wealth of information in their environment and hence must select which inputs to process. This selectivity is generally not conscious, for the nervous system automatically scans input and selectively perceives the environment. (Conscious control can be exerted, of course, as when one searches for a mailbox to post a letter.) Selectivity in auditory perception is best illustrated by the problem of listening to two conversations simultaneously. Because it is impossible to process the two competing inputs concurrently, the auditory system adopts one of two strategies: either one conversation is ignored, or attention shifts back and forth from one conversation to the other. In either case there is a selection of input. Selective perception in the visual system operates similarly. For example, because it is not possible to watch all events of a gymnastics meet simultaneously, attention either is focused entirely on one event or is shifted from one event to another.

Let us now consider the person with temporal lobe damage. We shall see that selection of both auditory and visual input is impaired, which is ordinarily demonstrated only by special testing procedures. Selective attention to auditory input can be tested by using a **dichotic-listening** technique. As we noted in Chapter 15, if a series of pairs of words is presented dichotically, more of the words presented to the right ear will be reported; if tonal sequences are presented dichotically, there will be a left-ear advantage. Exploiting this technique in patients with temporal lobe lesions, Schulhoff and Goodglass have demonstrated that although the expected ear advantages are still present in both cases, left temporal lobe lesions result in an overall drop in the number of words reported, and right temporal lesions result in an overall drop in the number of tonal sequences recognized. One explanation for this effect is that the nervous system has difficulty focusing selectively on the input into one ear and attempts to process all the input concurrently; as a result performance drops significantly. Analogous findings are reported for visual input as well. Dorff and colleagues presented two different visual stimuli simultaneously, one to each visual field. Damage of the left temporal lobe impaired recall of content of the right visual field; however, damage of the right temporal lobe impaired recall of content of *both* visual fields. Again, it may be that the nervous system is now unable to focus on distinctive features of the stimuli to allow efficient perception and storage of the input. In the case of visual input, however, it is noteworthy that right temporal lesions produce bilateral deficits, whereas left temporal lesions produce unilateral ones. This difference implies that the right temporal lobe may have a greater role than the left in selective attention to visual input.

Disorders of Auditory Perception

Music Perception. We briefly discussed music perception in Chapter 11 but have saved a detailed discussion of music until now since it is so closely associated with the functioning of the temporal lobes.

Musical sounds may differ from one another in three aspects: loudness, quality, and pitch. *Loudness* refers to the magnitude of a sensation as judged by a given individual. Loudness, although related to the intensity of a sound as measured in decibels, is in fact a subjective evaluation. In music, loudness is described by such terms as *very loud, soft, very soft,* and so forth. *Quality* refers to the characteristic of a sound by which it can be distinguished from all other sounds of similar pitch and loudness. For example, we can distinguish the sound of a violin from that of a trombone even though they may play the same note at the same loudness. The French word *timbre* is normally used to describe this character of sound. *Pitch* refers to the position of a sound in a musical scale, as judged by the listener. Although it is clearly related to the frequency of the sound, there is more to it.

Consider the note, middle C. This note can be described as a pattern of sound frequencies, as depicted in Figure 18-5. The amplitude of acoustic energy is conveyed by the darkness of the tracing in Figure 18-5. The lowest component of this note is the *fundamental frequency* of the sound pattern, which is 264 Hz, or middle C. The sound frequencies above the fundamental are known as *overtones*, or *partials*. The overtones are generally simple multiples of the fundamental (e.g., 2 × 264, or 528 Hz; 3 × 346, or 792 Hz), as can be seen in Figure 18-5. Those overtones that are multiples of the fundamental are known as *harmonics*. Other sounds are called *transients*.

The classic view, dating back to Helmholtz in the late 1800s, held that pitch perception depended upon the fundamental frequency and that the overtones provided timbre. This now appears to be incorrect. If the fundamental frequency is removed from a note with electronic filters, the overtones are sufficient to determine the pitch of the fundamental frequency—a phenomenon known as *periodicity pitch*. This ability is likely due to the fact that the difference between the frequencies of the various harmonics is equal to the fundamental frequency (e.g., 792 − 528 = 264 = the fundamental). Thus, the auditory system is able to determine this difference and we perceive the fundamental frequency. It appears that it is the right temporal lobe that is making this periodicity pitch discrimination. For example, Zatorre found that patients with right temporal lobectomies, *which included the primary auditory cortex*, were impaired at making pitch discriminations when the fundamental was absent but were normal at making such discriminations when the fundamental was present. Right temporal lesions that spared the primary auditory cortex or left temporal lobectomies did not impair performance. Zatorre suggests that the right temporal lobe has a

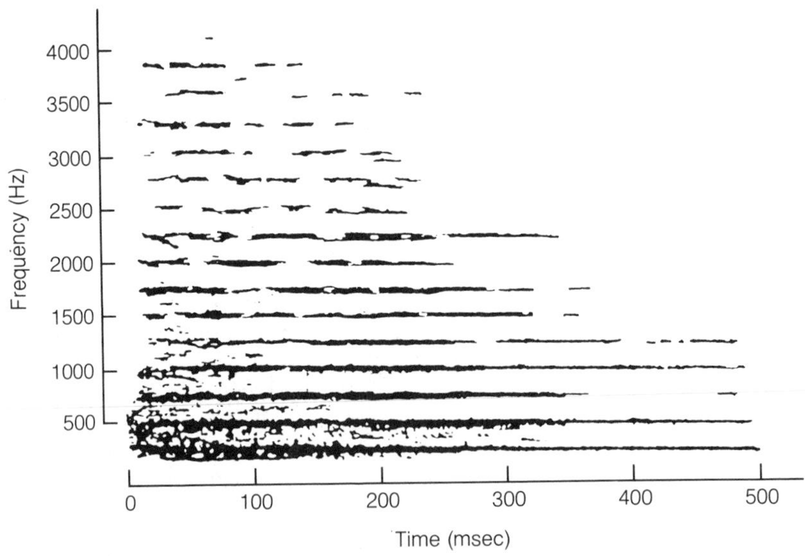

FIGURE 18-5. Spectrographic display of the steady-state portion of a middle C (264 Hz) played on a piano. Bands of acoustical energy are present at the fundamental frequency, as well as at integer multiples of the fundamental (harmonics). For complex tones at this fundamental frequency, the first five harmonics are dominant in the perception of pitch. (After Ritsma, 1967).

special function in extracting pitch from sound, regardless of whether the sound is speech or music. In the case of speech, the pitch will contribute to "tone" of voice, which is known as **prosody.**

There are a variety of other aspects of music that may be specially processed in the right temporal lobe as well. The simplest would be timbre, and indeed, Milner demonstrated that right temporal lesions impair the perception of timbre. In addition, there are more complex aspects, such as musical scales, chords, and progressions, all of which are constructed from single musical notes. Although speculative, it seems likely that we develop a "musical store" much like we develop a "syntactic store" of words. Thus, when we encounter a musical scale or progression, it is recognized as such. The mechanism of such a hypothetical store is unknown, but it may be a function of the right auditory association cortex.

Speech Perception. Speech differs from music in several fundamental ways. First, the sounds of speech largely come from three restricted ranges of frequencies, which are known as *formants.* Figure 18-6*A* illustrates sound spectrograms of different two-formant syllables. The dark bars indicate the frequency bands seen in more detail in Figure 18-6*B*. Figure 18-6*B* shows that the syllables differ in both the onset frequency of the second (higher) formant as well as in the onset time of the consonant. Notice that vowel sounds are in a constant frequency band, but consonants show rapid changes in frequency. Second, the same speech sounds vary from one context in which they are heard to another, yet they are all perceived the same. Thus, the sound spectrogram of the letter "d" in English is different in the words *deep, deck,* and *duke,* yet a listener perceives them to be the same. The auditory system must have a mechanism for categorizing sounds as being the same, and this mechanism must be affected by experience since a major obstacle to learning foreign languages is the difficulty in learning the categories that are treated equivalently. Thus, a word's spectrogram is dependent on the words that preceed and follow it. (There may be a parallel mechanism for musical categorization as well.) Third, speech sounds change very rapidly in relation to each other, and the sequential order of the sounds is critical to understanding. According to Liberman, we can perceive speech at rates of up to 30 segments per second, although normal speech is in the order of 8 to 10 segments per second. Speech perception at the higher rates is truly amazing since it far exceeds the auditory system's ability to transmit all of this information as separate pieces of auditory information. For example, nonspeech noise is perceived as a buzz at a rate of only about 5 segments per second. Clearly, language sounds must be recognized and analyzed in a special way by the brain, much as the echolocation system of the bat is treated specially by the bat brain.

It is likely that the special mechanism for speech perception is in the left temporal lobe, and it may be the timing of the sensory information that is critical. Lackner and Teuber, for example, reported that patients with left temporal lesions perceived two clicks as one at longer intervals than normal. Indeed, in some cases intervals had to be 10 times longer than normal before they were heard as being separate. Similarly, if the task requires an indication of which of two auditory stimuli is presented first, once again left temporal lobe lesions produce a large increase in the necessary interstimulus interval. It is likely that patients with temporal lobe lesions are also impaired at analyzing formant changes, although this has not yet been shown.

Disorders of Visual Perception

Although individuals with temporal lobectomies do not normally have large defects in their visual fields, they do have deficits in visual perception. This was first demonstrated by Milner, who found that her patients with right temporal lobectomies were impaired in the interpretation of cartoon drawings in the McGill Picture-Anomaly Test. For

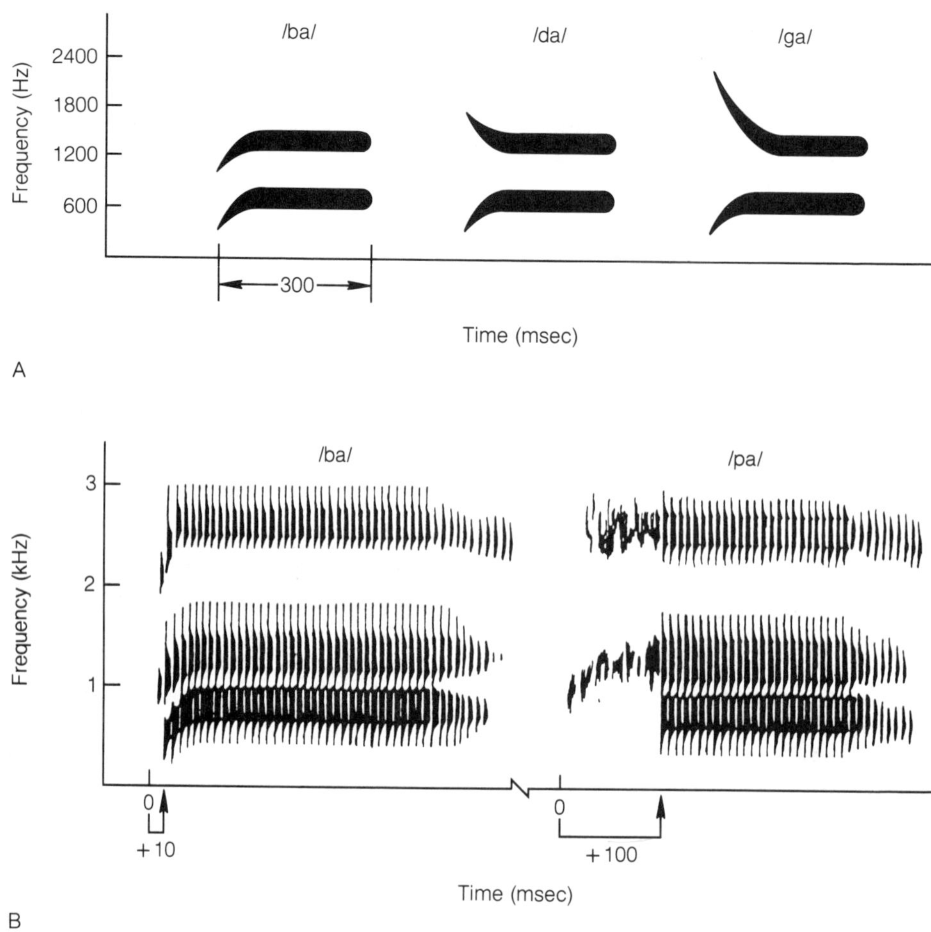

FIGURE 18-6. *A*. Schematic spectograms of three different syllables, each made up of two formants. *B*. Spectograms of syllables differing in voice onset time. (After Springer, 1979).

example, in one item illustrating a monkey in a cage there is an oil painting on the wall of the cage—an obvious oddity or anomaly. But patients with right temporal lesions, although able to accurately describe the contents of the picture, were impaired at recognizing the anomalous character of this and other pictures. Similarly, on a test of visual closure such as the Mooney series or tests requiring the discrimination of complex patterns (see Figure 11-3), patients with temporal lobe damage perform very poorly. Perhaps one of the most interesting visual perceptual deficits is in facial perception and recognition. When Kolb and his associates presented patients with the split-faces test described in Chapter 11 (see Figure 11-7), they found that those with right temporal lobe resections failed to show a bias for that portion of the face falling in the left visual field, suggesting that these patients were perceiving faces abnormally. This conclusion is consistent with reports that patients with right temporal lobe damage are impaired at the recognition and recall of faces or photographs of faces. Furthermore, these patients do not appear able to perceive subtle social signals such as discreet but obvious glances at one's watch, a gesture often intended as a cue to break off a conversation. Presumably the patients fail to perceive the significance of the visual signal.

Categorization of Material

If one is asked to learn a list of words such as "dog, car, bus, apple, rat, lemon, cat, truck, orange," it is a common experience that the words will be categorized into three different classes, namely animals, vehicles, and fruit. If the list is later recalled, the items are likely to be recalled by category, and recall of the categories is likely to be used as an aid in recall. The ability to organize material is especially important for language and memory. For example, it makes possible comprehension of extended sentences, including both the meaning of individual sentences and the information that is inferred from them. Organization of sensory input appears to be a function of the temporal lobes. Studies by Jaccarino-Hiatt and by Wilkins and Moscovitch have shown that patients with left temporal lobectomies are impaired in their ability to do this type of organization, even with single words or pictures of familiar objects. Thus, patients have difficulty in placing words or pictures into discrete categories, even when they are requested to, and they also have difficulty in using categories that most of us use automatically. For example, Milner has found that when such patients are given a category name (e.g., animal) and asked to recall exemplars of the category (e.g., dog, cat, rat), they have difficulty, even though they are fluent in other types of tests. Given that these patients have difficulty in relatively simple types of categorization tasks studied in the laboratory, one can imagine that their difficulty in spontaneous organization may represent a significant deficit in cognition, especially in memory for complex material.

Recently, neurolinguists have proposed that another type of categorization may occur in the left temporal lobe. Semantic categories are heirarchical categories in which a single word might belong to several categories simultaneously. For example, a duck belongs to the categories animal, bird, and waterfowl. Each of these categories represents a refinement of the previous one. Patients with posterior temporal lesions may show dysphasic symptoms in which they can recognize the broader categorization but have difficulty with the more specific one.

Using Contextual Information

The meaning of identical information can vary depending upon the context. For example, a word such as *fall* can refer to a season or to a tumble, depending upon the context. Similarly, context may be a major cue for facial recognition. Most of us have encountered someone completely out of context (e.g., while in Paris we encounter a clerk from our neighbourhood store at home) and been unable to recall who the person is until the information about the context is provided. A more complex example of meaning from context is found in social situations. The interpretation of events, and indeed our role in events, is dependent upon the social context. Thus, stimuli may be interpreted in one way when we are with our parents and in a different way when we are with our peers. This ability to use context as a key to the recognition of stimuli probably depends upon normal temporal lobe function, although data are rather sparse. In one study, Kolb and Taylor showed that temporal lobe patients found it difficult to correctly choose the facial expression appropriate for a faceless cartoon character when the only clue was the context (e.g., surprise party, funeral, argument, etc.). Similarly, we described the deficit of patients with right temporal lobectomies in the McGill Picture-Anomalies Test (see visual perceptual deficits, above). The only clue to the correct choice in the McGill anomalies is the context. Further studies are needed on both visual and auditory stimuli and context.

Language

Since the time of Wernicke, lesions of the left temporal association cortex (primarily area 22) have been associated with disturbed recognition of words, the extreme form being "word deafness": an inability to recognize words as such despite intact hearing of pure tones (a deficit discussed in detail in Chapter 22).

In addition to producing deficits in language comprehension, lesions of the temporal cortex beyond area 22 alter language processes in subtle ways. For example, Jaccarino-Hiatt has shown that nonaphasic patients with left temporal lobectomies have protracted latencies in producing word associations, such as in "table-chair" or "night-day." Furthermore, people with right temporal lobectomies are excessively talkative, suggesting a loss of inhibition of talking. (Excessive talkativeness is, however, a clinical impression not quantitatively documented.) In view of the temporal lobe's role in affect, it would be interesting to know if the affective connotation of language is diminished by temporal lobectomy (we are unaware of any studies of this sort).

Memory

To many neuropsychologists the study of the temporal lobes in synonymous with the study of memory. In fact, in most physiological psychology and neuropsychology texts, index references to the temporal lobes lead one to a discussion of amnesia. The interest in the temporal lobe's function in memory was stimulated in the early 1950s by the discovery that bilateral removal of the medial temporal lobes, including the hippocampus and amygdala, resulted in amnesia for all events after the surgery **(anterograde amnesia).** It is now clear that both the hippocampus and the temporal neocortex are important for memory functions. Milner has demonstrated that disturbances of memory result from damage to area 21; the disturbance increases in direct proportion to the amount of hippocampus damaged. Studies by the same investigator have further indicated a strong asymmetry of temporal lobe memory function (both cortical and hippocampal): lesions of the left temporal lobe result in impaired recall of verbal material, such as short stories, word lists, and so on, whether presented visually or aurally; lesions of the right temporal lobe result in impaired recall of nonverbal material, such as geometric drawings, faces, tunes, and similar material. However, unlike parietal lobe lesions, temporal lobe lesions do not disturb the immediate recall of material such as strings of digits; thus, the temporal and parietal lobes have complementary rather than redundant roles in memory.

The following two case histories demonstrate the role of the left and right temporal lobes in memory. Mr. B., a 38-year-old man, was suffering from an astrocytoma in the left temporal lobe. Prior to the onset he had been a successful executive in an oil company and was noted for efficiency. As his tumor developed he became forgetful, and at the time of hospital admission his efficiency had dropped drastically; he had begun to forget appointments and other important events. Forgetfulness had become such a problem that he had begun to write notes to himself to cover his memory problem, but he often mislaid the notes, leading to even greater embarrassment. On formal tests of memory he had special difficulty in recalling short stories read to him a few minutes earlier. For example, in one test he was read the following story from the Wechsler Memory Scale and asked to repeat it as exactly as possible. "Anna Thompson of South Boston, employed as a scrub woman in an office building, was held up on State Street the night before and robbed of $15. She had four little children, the rent was due and they had not eaten for two days. The officers, touched by the woman's story, made up a purse for her." Mr. B. recalled: "A woman was robbed and went to the police station where they made her a new purse. She had some children too." This is very poor performance for a person of Mr. B.'s intelligence and education. On the other hand, his immediate recall of digits was good; he could repeat strings of seven digits accurately, illustrating the integrity of his left parietal lobe functions. Similarly, his recall of geometric designs was within normal limits, illustrating the asymmetry of memory functions, for his right temporal lobe was still intact.

Ms. C. illustrates the complement of Mr. B.'s syndrome. She was a bright 22-year-old college student who had an indolent tumor of the right temporal lobe. When we first saw her, following surgery, she complained of memory loss. She was within normal limits on formal tests of verbal memory, such as the story of Anna Thompson, but was seriously impaired on formal tests of visual memory, especially geometric drawings. For example, in one test she was shown geometric designs for 10 sec and then asked to draw them from memory. Ten minutes later she was asked to draw them again. She had difficulty with immediate recall (see Figure 18-7), and after 10 min was unable to recall any of the drawings at all.

Affect and Personality

Although the temporal lobe has been known to be associated with disturbance of affect in humans for nearly 100 years, knowledge about the details of this role is still surprisingly fragmentary. Wilder Penfield and others reported that stimulation of the anterior and medial temporal cortex produces feelings of fear, an effect also occasionally obtained from the amygdala.

Temporal lobe epilepsy traditionally has been associated with personality characteristics in which there is an overemphasis on trivia and the petty details of daily life. Pincus and Tucker describe several symptoms of this personality, including pedantic speech, egocentricity, perseveration on discussion of personal problems (sometimes referred to as "sticky," because one is stuck talking to the person), paranoia, preoccupation with religion, and proneness to aggressive outbursts. This constellation of behaviors produces what is described as a *temporal lobe personality,* although very few people combine all these traits. Similar personality traits occur following temporal lobectomy. There appears to be a relative asymmetry in the symptoms, with right temporal lobectomy being more likely to be associated with these personality traits than left temporal lobectomy. This observation has not been quantified, however, and warrants further study. Finally, although temporal lobe epilepsy has long been linked anecdotally to psychosislike episodes, Slater and associates in 1963 first demonstrated a statistical relation between the occurrence of temporal lobe epilepsy and psychosis. Since no such relation has been described between temporal lobectomy and epilepsy, it has been suggested that a chronically abnormal discharging temporal lobe may produce abnormalities in either the biochemistry or the electrophysiology of the brain, leading to psychotic behavior. We return to this issue in Chapter 23.

Sexual Behavior

The role of the temporal lobe in sexual behavior is poorly understood, but it has long been known that bilateral destruction of the entire temporal lobe results in a dramatic increase in sexual behavior that is indiscriminantly directed both heterosexually and homosexually as well as toward inanimate objects. This condition is neither common nor well studied in humans, and it does not occur following unilateral temporal lobe removal. Indeed, although we are unaware that the sexual behavior of people with unilateral temporal lobectomies has been the subject of any formal studies,

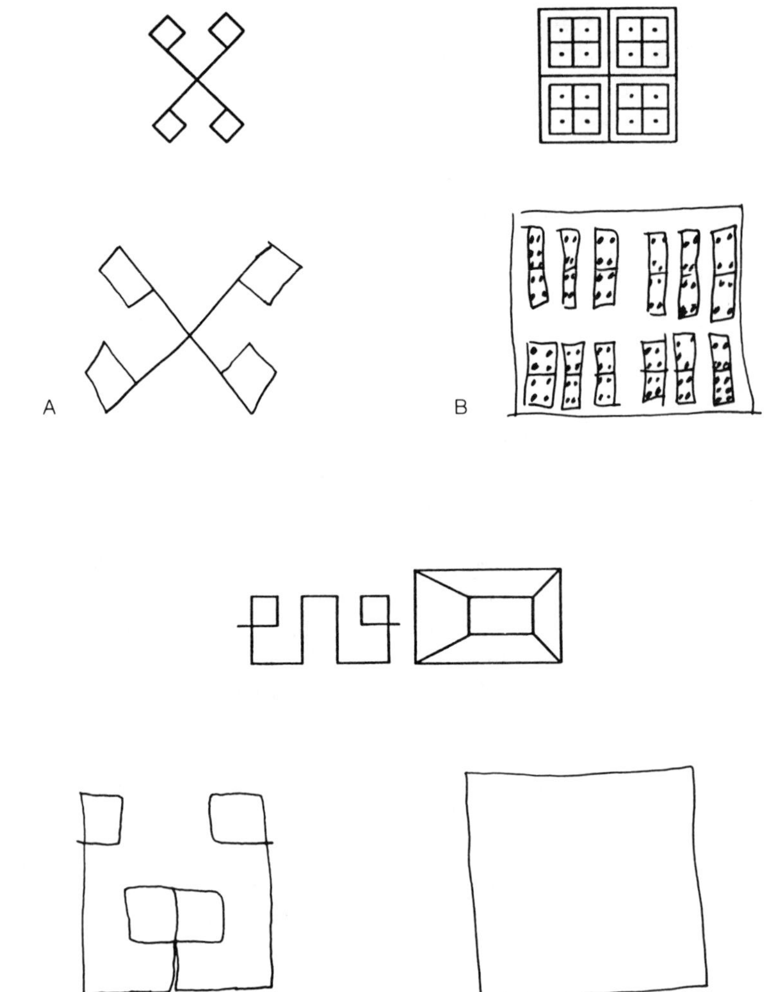

FIGURE 18-7. Illustration of impaired recall of geometric figures in the case of Ms. C. In each set shown *(A, B, C)* the top drawing is the original stimulus and the bottom drawing is Ms. C.'s sketch made immediately after viewing each figure for 10 sec. Note that Ms. C.'s impairment is worse with the more complex figures. Ms. C. was unable to recall even the simplest figure 10 min after viewing it.

we have never heard any complaints of either increased or decreased sexual activity in our experience with these people. Temporal lobe epilepsy is associated with altered sexual behavior, however: Blumer and Walker found 70% of their patient sample to have experienced a change in sexual activity, most commonly a decrease in sexual interest (see Table 18-2). Among these patients it was not unusual for sexual arousal to occur as rarely as once a year. This result must be interpreted cautiously, however, for the data may not reflect the function of the temporal lobes so much as the

TABLE 18-2. Summary of the changes in sexual behavior of 50 temporal lobe epileptics

Symptom	Number of patients showing symptom
Chronic global hyposexuality	29
Postoperative hypersexuality	2[a]
Hypersexuality induced by medication	1
Postictal sexual arousal	4[b]
Ictal sexual arousal	1
Homosexual behavior	2
	35 (70%)

[a] Both patients were preoperatively hyposexual.
[b] One patient also with homosexual behavior, another patient also with hypersexuality induced by medication (Mysoline).
Source: From Blumer and Walker, 1975, p. 207.

effect of chronically abnormal electrical activity on temporal and limbic structures.

Clinical Neuropsychological Assessment of Temporal Lobe Damage

A number of standardized assessment tools have proved to be sensitive and valid predictors of temporal lobe injury (see Table 18-3). Like clinical neuropsychological tests of parietal lobe function, these tests do not assess all the symptoms summarized in Table 18-1, but it would be highly unusual for a person to perform normally on all these tests if there were damage to either temporal lobe.

Auditory and visual processing capacity can be assessed using dichotic listening and the McGill Picture-Anomalies Test, as described earlier in the chapter. The picture-anomalies task is not as sensitive an indicator today as it was when first used in the 1950s, perhaps because television viewing has made the average person more sophisticated in visual perceptual abilities. Nevertheless, a poor score on this test almost invariably denotes right temporal abnormality.

The best test of general verbal memory ability is the revised Wechsler Memory Scale. However, because the Wechsler memory quotient is affected by nonspecific disorders of attention, two subtests —paired associates and logical stories—are often used as a purer measure of verbal memory capacity. The paired-associates subtest requires a subject to learn a series of word pairs (e.g., north-south, cabbage-pen) such that when one word is read (e.g., north, cabbage) its paired-associate word (south, pen) can be recalled. An example of the logical memory test was presented earlier in the chapter, in reference to Mr. B.'s verbal memory defect.

The Rey Complex-Figure Test has proved to be one of the best for evaluating nonverbal memory function of the right temporal lobe (see Figure 11-3*C*). A printed copy of a complex geometric pattern is placed before the subject with the instructions, "Copy the drawing as accurately as you can." Forty-five minutes later the subject is asked to reproduce as much of the figure as he or she can remember. Although the scoring criteria provide

TABLE 18-3. Standardized clinical neuropsychological tests for temporal lobe damage

Function	Test	Basic reference
Auditory processing capacity	Dichotic words and melodies	Sparks et al., 1970
Visual processing capacity	McGill Picture Anomalies	Milner, 1958
Verbal memory	Revised Wechsler Memory Scale; logical stories and paired associates	Milner, 1975
Nonverbal memory	Rey Complex Figure	Taylor, 1969
Language	Token test	de Renzi and Faglioni, 1978

an objective measure of nonverbal memory, the test has the drawback that depressed or poorly motivated subjects may perform poorly, not because there is right temporal lobe damage, but because they refuse to seriously try to recall the figure. There is no easy solution to this problem, since all tests of nonverbal memory are subject to this complication.

Finally, a deficit in language comprehension could be the result of a lesion in any of the language zones of the left hemisphere (that is, in the parietal, temporal, or frontal lobe); there is currently no neuropsychological assessment tool that can localize the area of damage within the left hemisphere. For this reason we once again recommend the token test as the test of choice for language comprehension. Additional tests (described in Chapter 22) may prove useful after the initial screening with the token test.

TEMPORAL LOBE FUNCTIONS IN NONHUMANS

In the 1950s, studies of memory defects in humans with temporal lobe lesions led to the suggestion that the temporal lobes of humans might have functions unlike those of nonhumans, since severe memory defects could not be unequivocally demonstrated in nonhumans. An influential paper by Diamond and Hall in 1969 kindled interest in evolutionary questions regarding the temporal lobe. They proposed that the primate temporal lobe is special, and they questioned whether or not carnivores even have a temporal lobe homologous to that of primates. Since Diamond and Hall's paper, research has indicated that this view is incorrect: both primates and carnivores appear to be good models for temporal lobe function in humans. Without exhaustively surveying research on nonhuman temporal lobe function, we shall demonstrate that the symptoms of temporal lobe lesions in other animals qualitatively resemble those observed in humans.

Anatomy of Nonhuman Temporal Lobes

The cortical extent of the temporal lobes of nonhumans is defined by cytoarchitecture, thalamic projections, and the electrophysiological properties of temporal lobe cells. Analyses if such information suggests an increase in temporal lobe neocortex in primates, especially in comparison with rodents. Indeed, it has been proposed that a major difference between primates and other mammals is the increase in size of both the temporal and the frontal lobes relative to the remaining cerebral cortex. All mammalian species have the equivalent of medial temporal cortex, hippocampus, and amygdala, however.

Effects of Temporal Lobe Lesion in Nonhumans

All the major deficits associated with temporal lobe lesions in humans (with the exception of language deficits) are observed in nonhumans (see Table 18-4). Moreover, many of the effects of temporal lesions are much easier to study in cats and monkeys than in humans. As a result, research on nonhuman animals has greatly clarified understanding of the human temporal lobe.

Auditory Processing

Dewson has demonstrated that unilateral lesion of the superior temporal gyrus (area 22) of the monkey produces deficits in the performance of tasks requiring complex analysis of auditory input. For example, in one experiment monkeys with unilateral lesions confined to area 22 were trained to discriminate between paired sequences of auditory elements, combinations of pure tone (T) and white noise (N). Four sequences were presented: T-T, T-N, N-N, and N-T. The animals' task was to learn to press two bars in a unique sequence for each auditory pair. For example, for T-T the ani-

TABLE 18–4. Summary of symptoms of temporal lobe lesions in monkeys

Symptom	Lesion site	Representative reference
Disorders of auditory processing	Areas 41,42,22	Cowey and Dewson, 1972
Disorders of visual processing	Areas 20,21,38	Ungerleider and Mishkin, 1982
Visual categorization	Area 21	Wilson and DeBauche, 1981
Memory	Hippocampus, amygdala	Mishkin, 1978
		Horel and Pytko, 1982
Sexual behavior	Amygdala, limbic cortex	Kluver and Bucy, 1939

mals were trained to press the left bar twice; for T-N, to press the left bar, then the right. Monkeys with lesions of area 22 were severely impaired at this task. The auditory sensitivity of these animals proved to be normal, but there was a deficit in auditory memory. Lesions of the visual association cortex (areas 20 and 21) had no effect on performance of this task.

Dewson has also demonstrated cerebral asymmetry in auditory processing in monkeys; lesions in area 22 on the left affect auditory discrimination and association to a greater degree than similar lesions on the right do. However, a crucial experiment remains to be done. Wollberg and Newman have shown that area 22 has cells that respond differently to species-typical vocalizations such as hoots or howls. The question is whether lesions of area 22 (especially on the left) would disturb perception of species-typical vocalizations. If so, a symptom analogous to "word deafness" in people might be demonstrated (although this may be pushing the analogy somewhat).

Visual Processing

Converging evidence from studies using monkeys has revealed a sequential pathway for processing visual information that begins in the core visual cortex (area 17) and proceeds through the secondary regions of the temporal cortex, which includes the temporal cortex right to the tip of the temporal pole (areas 20, 21, and 38). Researchers at the National Institute of Mental Health (see Macko et al.) have mapped the visual pathway through the temporal lobe using a type of 2-deoxyglucose tracing procedure, which is a far more accurate analogue of the technique described in Chapter 15 for tracing the visual pathway in humans. The results revealed two distinct visual pathways, one traveling from area 17 through the temporal lobe and eventually to the frontal cortex, and another traveling from area 17 via the parietal cortex to the frontal lobe. It has been suggested that the former route has a special role in object recognition, and the latter has a special role in spatial vision—conjectures that are in basic accord with the observed symptoms.

A number of investigators have been able to functionally distinguish among the posterior temporal cortex (roughly area 20), an area anterior to it (roughly area 21), and the anterior and medial limbic cortex (roughly area 38 plus medial cortex) in monkeys. Lesions of the posterior cortex produce an inability to discriminate and select the essential cues from a visual stimulus and to maintain attention to them. Thus, the animal has difficulty in distinguishing complex visual stimuli from one another, just as the human does with deficits in discriminating complex visual stimuli such as faces from one another. Lesions of area 21 produce a different type of deficit, in which the animal has difficulty in forming visual memories.

The monkeys are able to discriminate among complex visual stimuli but are unable to remember the visual image for more than a few moments, and they are thus impaired at problems requiring such visual memory. Finally, lesions of the anterior zone, including the amygdala, produce deficits in the process of associating visual stimuli with reinforcement connected with them in experiments. To demonstrate this, a monkey is presented with two visual stimuli, such as a square and a cross. A food reward is associated with one of them; if the monkey chooses the correct stimulus, it is reinforced with a peanut or raisin. Once this problem is mastered, the reward properties of the stimuli are reversed, the previously rewarded stimulus now being unrewarded and vice versa. This task therefore requires the animal to associate changing reward properties with the visual stimuli, a requirement that is difficult to meet in the absence of the anterior temporal cortex and/or amygdala.

Finally, neurons of the temporal lobe have been found that are specifically responsive to faces, a result that complements the demonstrations of impaired facial perception and recognition in humans with right temporal lobe removals. Perret and his associates have found many cells in monkeys that respond selectively to both human faces and photographs of monkey faces, despite inversion, rotation, or changes in size or color of the face! It remains to be seen if removal of these cells impairs facial recognition in monkeys, however.

Categorization

Like human patients with temporal lobe damage who have difficulty in organizing and categorizing material, monkeys with lesions of the inferotemporal cortex (roughly area 21) are impaired at categorical perception of visual stimuli. Wilson and DeBauche trained monkeys to discriminate between pairs of stimuli that differed in length, orientation, or texture. For example, a food reward was obtained for choosing a line 10 mm as opposed to 55 mm in length. After successful solution of this problem, the monkeys were given pairs of stimuli in which the correct one was the one closest to the originally correct stimulus. For stimuli differing in length the animals were given lines that were 10, 15, 20, 25, 30, 35, 40, 45, 50, or 55 mm long. Normal animals easily discriminated between lines clearly in a different category (i.e., long and short) but did poorly with lines of similar length within each category. Monkeys with inferotemporal lesions did not show categorical perception. That is, when given a pair such as 15 and 40 mm, they responded with chance accuracy. These results cannot be accounted for by a simple deficit in visual acuity, because monkeys with damage in area 17 did exhibit categorical perception. Wilson and DeBauche conclude that the temporal lobe normally functions to process visual stimuli in such a way as to treat visual inputs as members of classes, a conclusion consistent with the demonstrations of impaired categorization in humans as well as that shown in monkeys with temporal lobe lesions.

Memory

A clear demonstration of a severe memory defect in nonhuman animals analogous to that resulting from bilateral temporal lobe removal in humans has been elusive. As a result, many propose that the functions of the medial temporal lobe in humans reflect an evolutionary shift. Until recently, studies meant to demonstrate analogous memory defects in nonhumans assumed that the critical structure for memory storage is the hippocampus, and it was repeatedly found that bilateral hippocampal lesions in rats, cats, and monkeys failed to produce the human syndrome of anterograde amnesia. A 1978 study by Mishkin sheds light on this apparent discrepancy: memory loss after removal of both the hippocampus and the amygdala in monkeys was much more severe than after removal of either structure alone. Mishkin suggested that both structures have an important role in memory. This hypothesis remains to be studied further, especially in human patients, where the amygdala is virtually always removed along with the hippocampus. It may be that the role of the amygdala has been underestimated in studies of humans. With respect to the memory functions of area 21, we have already noted that lesions in this area in monkeys produce visual memory deficits, again consistent with the result of Milner's human studies. On the other hand, we shall see in our detailed discussion of memory in Chapter 21 that other medial temporal structures (such as the entorhinal cortex), which are also removed in both of Mishkin's studies and in human surgeries, may be crucial for memory functions.

Affect

Bilateral lesions of the amygdala, hippocampus, and lateral temporal cortex are known to produce alterations in affect in both monkeys and cats, but the precise role of each of these structures in affective control is not well understood. The amygdala and anterior temporal neocortex may have similar roles in affective control; Horel and his associates reported that lesions of both regions reduced both attack and escape behavior and made the animals less reluctant to approach novel stimuli. In addition, it is known that monkeys with lesions of either the anterior temporal cortex or the amygdala do not survive in the wild, because they no longer associate with other members of their species. By contrast, animals with more posterior lesions in the temporal lobe are still social creatures, behaving normally in the social group.

Sexual Behavior

Bilateral destruction of the temporal lobes is known to produce profound changes in sexual behavior — chiefly increasing sexual activity — in a variety of mammals. The crucial structure for this effect is the amygdala and its related archicortex and paleocortex. The hippocampus appears to play a minor role, and there is no clear indication of the role of the temporal neocortex in sexual behavior. It would be expected that damage to area 20 produces impaired discrimination of visual sexual objects, but this possibility has not been studied.

Summary

The detailed studies of temporal lobe processes, especially those related to visual processing, beautifully illustrate how studies of brain function in other animals can provide crucial clues to understanding human brain function. It is impossible to do many needed studies in humans because neither surgical nor naturally occurring lesions conform to the anatomical subdivisions of the temporal lobe. a difficulty, however, is that results from studies of the temporal lobe in monkeys appear to be most similar to results from studies of right temporal lobe function in humans. There is not yet any compelling evidence of asymmetrical processing of visual information in monkeys. Perhaps generalizations to left temporal function can be made in the future when we have a better appreciation for the basis of cerebral asymmetry.

REFERENCES

Blumer, D., and D. F. Benson. Personality changes with frontal and temporal lesions. In D. F. Benson and F. Blumer, eds. *Psychiatric Aspects of Neurologic Disease.* New York: Grune & Stratton, 1975.

Blumer, D., and E. A. Walker. The neural basis of sexual behavior. In D. F. Benson and D. Blumer, eds. *Psychiatric Aspects of Neurologic Disease.* New York: Grune & Stratton, 1975.

Campbell, A. Deficits in visual learning produced by posterior temporal lesions in cats. *Journal of Comparative and Physiological Psychology* 92:45–57, 1978.

Chedru, F., V. Bastard, and R. Efron. Auditory micropattern discrimination in brain damaged patients. *Neuropsychologia* 16:141–149, 1978.

Cowey, A., and J. H. Dewson. Effects of unilateral ablation of superior temporal cortex on auditory sequence discrimination in *Macaca mulatta*. *Neuropsychologia* 10:279–289, 1972.

Dewson, J. H. Preliminary evidence of hemispheric asymmetry of auditory function in monkeys. In S. Harnad, R. W. Doty, L. Goldstein, J. Jaynes, and G. Krauthamer, eds. *Lateralization in the Nervous System*. New York: Academic Press, 1977.

Diamond, I. T., and W. C. Hall. Evolution of neocortex. *Science* 164:251–262, 1969.

Dorff, J. E., A. F. Mirsky, and M. Mishkin. Effects of unilateral temporal lobe removals on tachistoscopic recognition in the left and right visual fields. *Neuropsychologia* 3:39–51, 1965.

Geschwind, N. Disconnexion syndromes in animals and man. *Brain* 88:237–294, 585–644, 1965.

Hécaen, H., and M. L. Albert. *Human Neuropsychology*. New York: John Wiley, 1978.

Horel, J. A. The neuroanatomy of amnesia: A critique of the hippocampal memory hypothesis. *Brain* 101:403–445, 1978.

Horel, J. A., E. G. Keating, and L. J. Misantone. Partial Klüver-Bucy syndrome produced by destroying temporal neocortex or amygdala. *Brain Research* 94:349–359, 1975.

Horel, J. A., and D. E. Pytko. Behavioral effect of local cooling in temporal lobe of monkeys. *Journal of Neurophysiology* 47:11–22, 1982.

Iwai, E., and M. Mishkin. Two visual foci in the temporal lobe of monkeys. In N. Yoshii and N. A. Buchwald, eds. *Neurophysiological Basis of Learning and Behavior*. Osaka, Japan: Osaka University Press, 1968.

Jaccarino-Hiatt, G. Impairment of cognitive organization in patients with temporal-lobe lesions. Unpublished Ph.D. thesis, McGill University, 1978.

Jones, B., and M. Mishkin. Limbic lesions and the problem of stimulus-reinforcement associations. *Experimental Neurology* 36:362–377, 1972.

Jones, E. G. The anatomy of extrageniculostriate visual mechanisms. In F. O. Schmitt and F. G. Worden, eds. *The Neurosciences: Third Study Program*. Cambridge, MA: M.I.T. Press, 1974.

Kluver, H., and P. C. Bucy. Preliminary analysis of the temporal lobes in monkeys. *Archives of Neurology and Psychiatry* 42:979–1000, 1939.

Kolb, B., B. Milner, and L. Taylor. Perception of faces by patients with localized cortical excisions. *Canadian Journal of Psychology* 37:8–18, 1983.

Kolb, B., and L. Taylor. Facial expression and the neocortex. *Society for Neuroscience Abstracts* 14:219, 1988.

Lackner, J. R., and H.-L. Teuber. Alterations in auditory fusion thresholds after cerebral injury in man. *Neuropsychologia* 11:409–415, 1973.

Liberman, A. On finding that speech is special. *American Psychologist* 37:148–167, 1982.

Macko, K. A., C. D. Jarvis, C. Kennedy, M. Miyaoka, M. Shinohara, L. Sokoloff, and M. Mishkin. Mapping the primate visual system with [2 —^{14}C] deoxyglucose. *Science* 218:394–397, 1982.

Meier, M. S., and L. A. French. Lateralized deficits in complex visual discrimination and bilateral transfer of reminiscence following unilateral temporal lobectomy. *Neuropsychologia* 3:261–272, 1968.

Milner, B. Psychological defects produced by temporal lobe excision. *Research Publications of the Association for Research in Nervous and Mental Disease* 38:244–257, 1958.

Milner, B. Laterality effects in audition. In V. B. Mountcastle, ed. *Interhemispheric Relations and Cerebral Dominance.* Baltimore, MD: Johns Hopkins University Press, 1962.

Milner, B. Visual recognition and recall after right temporal lobe excision in man. *Neuropsychologia* 6:191–209, 1968.

Milner, B. Memory and the medial temporal regions of the brain. In K. H. Pribram and D. E. Broadbent, eds. *Biological Bases of Memory.* New York: Academic Press, 1970.

Milner, B. Psychological aspects of focal epilepsy and its neurosurgical management. *Advances in Neurology* 8:299–321, 1975.

Mishkin, M. Memory in monkeys severely impaired by combined but not by separate removal of amygdala and hippocampus. *Nature* 273:297–298, 1978.

Nonneman, A. J., and B. Kolb. Lesions of hippocampus or prefrontal cortex alter species typical behavior in the cat. *Behavioral Biology* 12:41–54, 1974.

Penfield, W., and H. H. Jasper. *Epilepsy and the Functional Anatomy of the Human Brain.* Boston: Little, Brown, 1959.

Perret, D. E., P. Smith, D. D. Potter, A. J. Mistlin, A. S. Head, A. D. Milner, and M. A. Jeeves. Neurones responsive to faces in the temporal cortex: Studies of functional organization, sensitivity to identity and relation to perception. *Human Neurobiology* 3:197–208, 1984.

Pincus, J. H., and G. J. Tucker. *Behavioral Neurology.* New York: Oxford University Press, 1974.

Read, D. E. Solving deductive-reasoning problems after unilateral temporal lobectomy. *Brain and Language* 12:116–127, 1981.

Renzi, E. de, and P. Faglioni. Normative data and screening power of a shortened version of the token test. *Cortex* 14:41–49, 1978.

Ritsma, R. Frequencies dominant in the perception of pitch of complex sounds. *Journal of the Acoustical Society of America* 42:191–198, 1967.

Samson, S., and R. J. Zatorre. Discrimination of melodic and harmonic stimuli after unilateral cerebral excisions. *Brain and Cognition* 7:348–360, 1988.

Schulhoff, C., and H. Goodglass. Dichotic listening: Side of brain injury and cerebral dominance. *Neuropsychologia* 7:149–160, 1969.

Seltzer, B., and D. N. Pandya. Afferent cortical connections and architectonics of the superior temporal sulcus and surrounding cortex in rhesus monkey. *Brain Research* 149:1–24, 1978.

Sidtis, J. J. Music, pitch perception, and the mechanisms of cortical hearing. In M. S. Gazzaniga, ed. *Handbook of Cognitive Neuroscience.* New York: Plenum Press, 1984.

Slater, E., A. W. Beard, and E. Glithero. The schizophrenia-like psychosis of epilepsy. *British Journal of Psychiatry* 109:95–150, 1963.

Sparks, R., H. Goodglass, and B. Nickel. Ipsilateral versus contralateral extinction in dichotic listening from hemispheric lesions. *Cortex* 6:249–260, 1970.

Springer, S. P. Speech perception and the biology of language. In M. S. Gazzaniga, ed. *Handbook of Behavioral Neurobiology: Neuropsychology.* New York: Plenum, 1979.

Swisher, L., and I. J. Hirsch. Brain damage and the ordering of two temporally successive stimuli. *Neuropsychologia* 10:137–152, 1972.

Taylor, L. B. Localization of cerebral lesions by psychological testing. *Clinical Neurosurgery* 16:269–287, 1969.

Ungerleider, L. G., and M. Mishkin. Two cortical visual systems. In D. J. Ingle, M. H. Goodale, and R. J. W. Mansfield, eds. *The Analysis of Visual Behavior.* Cambridge, MA: M.I.T. Press, 1982.

Vignolo, L. A. Auditory agnosia: A review and report of recent evidence. In A. L. Benton, ed. *Contributions to Clinical Neuropsychology*. Chicago: Aldine, 1969.

Weiskrantz, L. The interaction between occipital and temporal cortex in vision: An overview. In F. O. Schmitt and F. G. Worden, eds. *The Neurosciences: Third Study Program.* Cambridge, MA: M.I.T. Press, 1974.

Wilkins, A., and M. Moscovitch. Selective impairment of semantic memory after temporal lobectomy. *Neuropsychologia* 16:73–79, 1978.

Wilson, M., and B. A. DeBauche. Inferotemporal cortex and categorical perception of visual stimuli by monkeys. *Neuropsychologia* 19:29–41, 1981.

Wolberg, Z., and J. D. Newman. Auditory cortex of squirrel monkey: Response patterns of single cells to species-specific vocalizations. *Science* 175:212–214, 1972.

Zatorre, R. J. Musical perception and cerebral function: A critical review. *Music Perception* 2:196–221, 1984.

CHAPTER 19

THE FRONTAL LOBES

There is no cerebral structure in which lesions can produce such a wide variety of symptoms, and thus a more bewildering range of interpretations, than the frontal lobes. Some authors have assigned the human frontal lobes the "highest" conceivable functions such as intellectual synthesis and the control of ethical behavior, but other authors demote them, failing to see any special importance in them. In this chapter we first describe the anatomy of the frontal lobes, then present a basic model of frontal lobe function. The effects of frontal lobe damage on human behavior are well documented. We attempt to summarize these effects in an effort to make sense of the extravagant claims about the function of this vast area. We consider the question of whether the frontal lobes are really special in humans, and discuss the idea that the frontal lobes are part of a functional system that includes a number of subcortical structures. First, however, it is necessary to review the anatomy of the frontal lobes.

ANATOMY OF THE FRONTAL LOBES

The frontal lobes of the human brain comprise all the tissue in front of the central sulcus. They are certainly not anatomically homogeneous; however, several areas are functionally and anatomically distinct. These include area 4, or primary motor cortex; area 6, or premotor cortex; supplementary motor cortex (M_{II}); Broca's area; medial cortex (area 32); and prefrontal cortex (see Figure 19-1).

In 1948, Rose and Woolsey noticed that the frontal lobes of all the mammalian species they examined had a region that received projections from the dorsomedial nucleus of the thalamus. They termed this region **prefrontal cortex.** In primates the prefrontal regions are known as the dorsolateral cortex (roughly areas 9, 10, 44, 45, and 46), **orbital frontal cortex** (so called because of its relation to the orbit of the eye, and

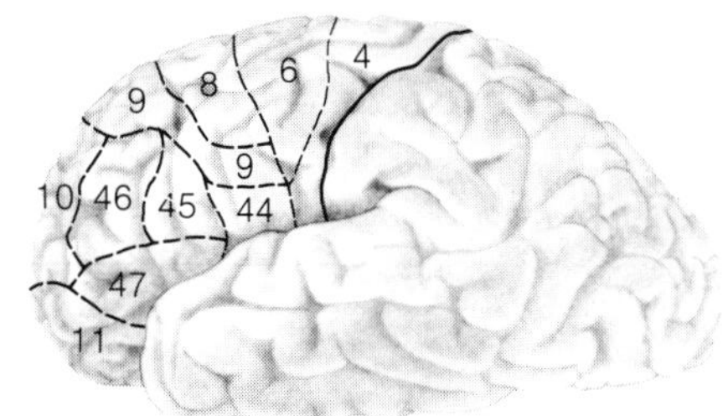

A Lateral View

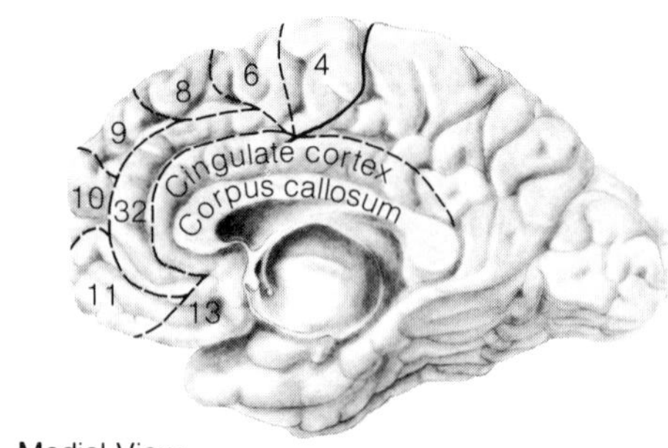

B Medial View

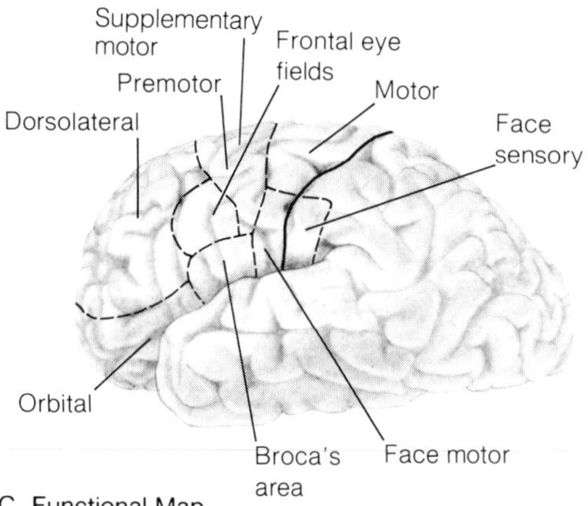

C Functional Map

FIGURE 19-1. *A.* Lateral and *B.* medial views of Brodmann's cytoarchitectonic map of the frontal lobe. *C.* Approximate boundaries of functional zones of the frontal lobe. Note that area 6 contains two functional zones: the premotor cortex on the lateral surface and the supplementary motor cortex on the medial surface.

roughly including areas 11, 13, and 47), and the frontal eye fields (including portions of areas 8 and 9). At one time the prefrontal cortex was called the frontal granular cortex, since the fourth layer of this region has large granular cells that clearly distinguish it from areas 4 and 6, which have no granular fourth layer but have instead a large fifth layer of giant pyramidal cells. This terminology is seldom used today because although all mammalian species have a prefrontal cortex, not all have granular cells and hence do not have a frontal granular cortex.

Subdivisions and Connections of the Frontal Lobe

Brodmann's areas in the frontal lobe are large and probably can be subdivided, as was the case for the parietal and temporal lobes, although this has not yet been done. In particular, the broad expanse of the dorsolateral prefrontal cortex of humans should be divisible both functionally and anatomically. Again, we must turn to the monkey for information on the cytoarchitectonics and connections of the frontal lobe. Figure 19-2 summarizes Walker's subdivisions of the frontal lobe of the monkey. There are two large sulci in the monkey's frontal lobe: the principal and arcuate sulci. Both of these hide significant amounts of tissue, as we saw for the insula and superior temporal sulcus in the temporal lobe. On functional grounds it is likely that the monkey's frontal cortex can be divided into several areas including the dorsolateral cortex (areas 9 and 46), the inferior frontal cortex (areas 11 and 12), the orbital-frontal cortex (areas 13 and 14), medial frontal cortex (area 25, 32), the premotor area, the supplementary motor cortex, and motor cortex. As in the temporal lobe, there are two areas in the frontal lobe that are multimodal and contain cells responsive to combinations of visual, auditory, and somatic stimuli. These areas are in the premotor cortex and area 46, and are illustrated in Figure 9-7*C*.

A good deal of work has been done on the connections of the frontal lobe of the monkey, and they are exceedingly complex. (See Pandya and Yeterian or Goldman-Rakic for detailed reviews.) It is possible, however, to identify several simple principles of frontal lobe connections. First, just as there is a hierarchical system in the sensory cortexes, there is a parallel one in the frontal (motor) cortex. In the latter case the projections are from the prefrontal areas, which are tertiary cortex, to the premotor cortex (area 6) to the motor cortex. Second, there are corticocortical connections that terminate largely in areas 8, 9, and 46. These connections arise from the posterior part of the temporal auditory and visual association regions, area 7, and the medial temporal lobe (Figure 19-3). Further, they are reciprocal, meaning that the frontal lobe returns connections to each of these regions. Third, there is a second set of corticocortical connections that terminate largely in areas 11, 13, and 25, arise from the anterior temporal cortex and medial temporal region, and are reciprocal. The two distinct forms of corticocortical connections are intriguing because they appear to be extensions of the spatial and recognition systems we have followed through the sensory systems. Fourth, there are thalamocortical projections from three thalamic areas including the anterior nuclei, dorsomedial nucleus, and pulvinar. Fifth, the frontal lobe has reciprocal connections with the amygdala, much as the temporal lobe does. Sixth, there is a major connection from the frontal cortex to the caudate nucleus, but this one is not reciprocal. Finally, there are projections from the frontal lobe to other subcortical structures, especially the superior colliculus and hypothalamus, and projections from various brainstem areas to the frontal lobe. Perhaps the most important of these latter connections is that from the dopamine-containing cells of the tegmentum, because it is an abnormality in these projections that is probably responsible for many symptoms of schizophrenia. (We will return to this idea in Chapter 23.)

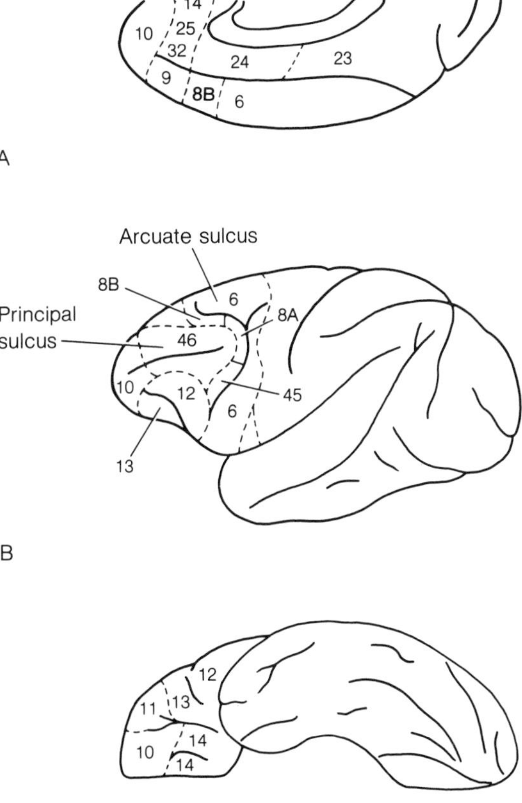

FIGURE 19-2. Medial (*A*), lateral (*B*) and ventral (*C*) views of Walker's cytoarchitectonic map of the frontal lobe of the rhesus monkey.

The complexity and breadth of the frontal lobe connections no doubt contribute to the puzzling array of behavioral changes observed in people with lesions in this region. With respect to understanding the functions of the frontal lobes, the most important connections may well be those with the "motor" structures (such as the basal ganglia), those with the medial temporal structures, and those in the spatial and recognition systems of the parietal and temporal cortex.

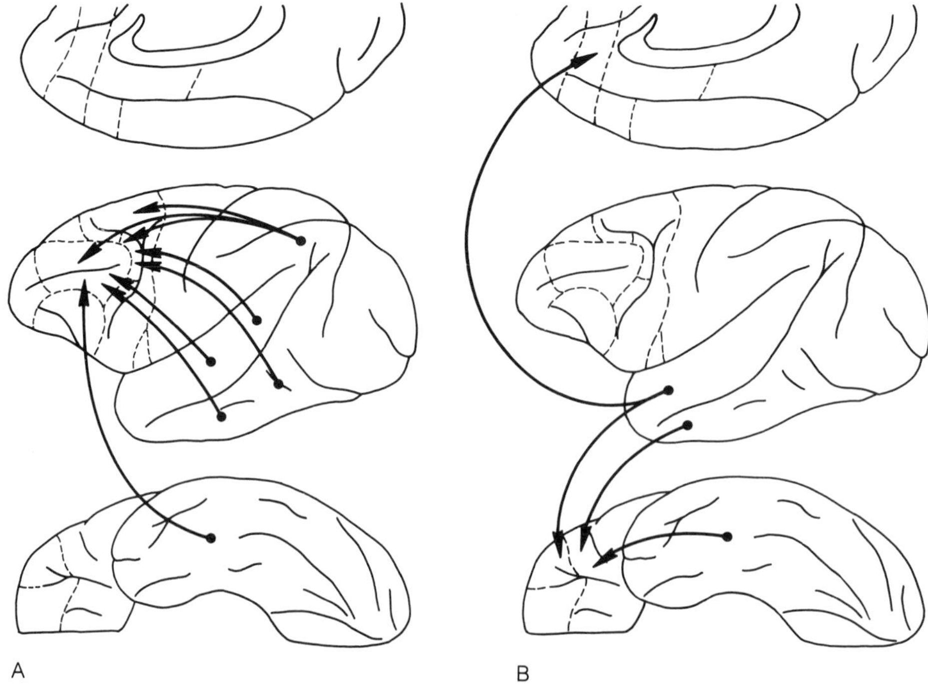

FIGURE 19-3. Schematic illustration of the corticocortical connections to the frontal lobe of the rhesus monkey. *A.* The connections that are probably involved in spatial behavior. *B.* The connections that are probably involved in object recognition.

A THEORY OF FRONTAL LOBE FUNCTION

Background

Historically, claims about the function of the frontal lobes have been extravagant and extreme. From the time of Gall until the 1930s, the frontal lobes were thought by most to be the seat of highest intellect. Functions as varied as "abstract behavior," foresight, intellectual synthesis, ethical behavior, affect, and self-awareness were proposed by a variety of writers.

Hebb's discovery in 1939 brought these prevailing views into question. Administering standard intelligence tests to patients with frontal lobe removals for treatment of epilepsy, Hebb discovered that IQ was not reduced—an astonishing observation in light of the prevailing belief. This test has been repeated by many others with the same results: IQ is not lowered by frontal lobe lesions, and sometimes may actually be raised!

A major reason for the extremes of views regarding frontal lobe functions was that neurologists and neuropsychologists often based their conclusions on single cases. Many of these patients had tumors, and it is now well known that tumor patients frequently do not behave like patients with lesions resulting from other causes. Tumors may produce pressure on widespread parts of the brain, resulting in symptoms unrelated to the region where the tumor actually resides. Furthermore, tumors may include subcortical structures or may result in the production of abnormal electric discharges that themselves may alter the function of widespread areas of brain tissue. An additional problem is that often frontal lobe tumors are larger than tumors elsewhere in the brain. It may be that the large size of the frontal lobes allows a tumor to grow for longer periods without specific motor, sensory, or language problems arising as symptoms.

The advent of frontal lobotomies in psychosurgery provided large numbers of patients with frontal lobe lesions, but studies on these patients did little to reduce extravagant claims of frontal lobe function. Although IQs after frontal lobotomy were lower than those obtained much earlier, they were not, according to a study by Rosvold and Mishkin in 1950, lower than IQs obtained just prior to surgery. In other words, the lower IQ was caused not by the lobotomy per se, but by the psychiatric disease process necessitating the lobotomy—hence the serious flaw in using psychosurgical patients in neuropsychological research. Because no groups of patients with similar psychiatric disease have lesions elsewhere in the brain, the effects of the disease cannot be separated from the effects of the lesion. Furthermore, we now know that severe psychotic disease of the type that might lead to psychosurgery produces serious deficits in neuropsychological test results without surgery.

In 1923, Feuchtwanger did one of the first systematic studies of large numbers of patients with lesions other than tumors or lobotomies. His monograph (cited in Teuber, 1964) should not have been ignored, as it was, by North American neuropsychology, because he anticipated many of the findings of the 1960s and 1970s.

During the 1950s, 1960s, and 1970s, research on the frontal lobes clarified many of the contradictions and inconsistencies of the earlier work. A theoretical model of frontal lobe function is now possible that provides a unified explanation of the various symptoms of frontal lobe damage.

Organization and Function of the Prefrontal Cortex

Before presenting a theory of prefrontal cortex function, the organization of the motor system must be reviewed briefly. The cortical motor system is thought to comprise three levels of function. The first level is composed of neurons whose cell bodies reside in area 4 and whose axons largely synapse directly on spinal motor neurons or cranial nerve motor nuclei. This level is specialized for controlling fine hand, finger, and facial movements. Lesions in this level produce severe chronic deficits in fine-motor control and also reduce speed and strength of limb movements.

The second level of cortical motor function is composed of neurons whose cell bodies lie primarily in areas 4, 6, and 8 of the frontal cortex and in areas 5 and 7 of the parietal cortex. These neurons contribute to three descending systems: one controlling limb movements; another, body movements, and the third, eye movements. All neurons of the limb-control system synapse in the **red nucleus,** although many synapse earlier as well, primarily in the basal ganglia. Similarly, all neurons of the axial system synapse in the brainstem reticular formation, but, again, many of these neurons also synapse en route to the brainstem in the basal ganglia. Cortical lesions in this level of control do not abolish limb or axial movements, since subcortical structures (i.e., red nucleus, basal ganglia, thalamus, etc.) can still operate to produce basic limb and axial movements. Rather, the lesions alter more complex aspects of limb and axial movements, producing more subtle deficits. The effects of lesions in areas 6 and 8, although still poorly understood, appear to impair the smooth transition of separate axial, limb, and hand movements into a fluid series of movements. Lesions in areas 5 and 7 contribute to apraxias, probably because of damage in the visual and tactile guidance of limb and axial movements.

The third level of motor control is composed of the neurons forming the prefrontal cortex. The prefrontal cortex has a nonspecific influence on movement control, and it probably plays little role in actually controlling the components of movement. There have been repeated attempts to develop theories of the precise role of the prefrontal cortex in the control of movement, and although they vary in detail, there is a common theme that the prefrontal cortex is involved in the temporal organization of behavior (e.g., Fuster; Goldman-Rakic). Briefly, it is evident that behavior occurs over time, in three-dimensional space, and in response to the details of sensory information. Complex behavior is made up of a series of smaller units that must be put together in the correct order and at the correct time and place. This is not a simple process. Consider an example. You are asked to sign a document. You look around and finding no pen, you search for one. To do this, you must move your head and eyes and perhaps get up from the desk and walk around, during which you must avoid obstacles while still searching, make the correct movements in space to find the pen, inhibit walking, reach for the pen and form the correct finger posture to pick it up, retract your arm, reinitiate walking back to the desk, and sign the document. To perform an act such as this there must be an overall purpose or plan to the behavior, which, to a naive observer, might seem haphazard at best. The search behavior is made up of many motor acts and requires memory for the things we have just done (we do not want to search in places we have just explored), monitoring of what we are doing, and a "plan" for the movements to follow. In addition, we need to inhibit writing movements until we find the pen and get it to the correct place, and then we need to be able to recall what we were to sign. These components of movement control are collectively referred to as being part of the temporal organization of behavior, and this is the function of the prefrontal cortex. Parenthetically, we have probably all experienced occasions in which the organization of our behavior to some goal has failed. How many times have we started to do something, been distracted by something else, and then been unable to recall what we were doing!

Given that the function of the prefrontal cortex is to provide temporal control of movement, we can make several predictions about some of the components of this system. First, we noted that there must be an ongoing record of what has just been done. This record is independent of the existing sensory information and can be called *temporal memory*. We use temporal memory here to refer to a neural record of recent events. Further, recall that systems for controlling both movement in space and object recognition project to the frontal lobe, although to different places (Figure 19-3). This suggests that there will be temporal memory both for spatial and object information, although they may be localized in different places in the frontal cortex. Second, if the frontal lobe organizes behavior with the aid of temporal memory, then people whose temporal memory is damaged should be dependent upon environmental cues in determining their behavior. That is, behavior will not be under the control of internalized knowledge, but will rather be controlled by external cues. Third, some motor impulses must be inhibited and others excited in order to produce correct behavioral sequences. The absence of the prefrontal cortex might thus release behaviors from inhibition. Fourth, behavior is context-dependent, so a motor score must be flexible enough to allow behavior to vary depending upon the context at any given time. Thus, behavior that is appropriate at one moment may not be appropriate if there are subtle changes in the context. The importance of context-dependent behavior in primate social structure is beautifully illustrated in Jane Goodall's graphic descriptions of the different behavioral patterns exhibited by chimpanzees. The make-up of the social group at any time dictates the behavior of each chimpanzee. Given the presence and position of certain animals, a particular chimp may be bold and relaxed, whereas with a different mixture of animals the chimp is quiet and nervous.

Further, it appears that an error in evaluating the context can have grievous consequences. It may be no accident that the frontal lobe has grown so large in primates who are so highly social.

Asymmetry of Frontal Lobe Function

In view of the asymmetry in parietal and temporal association cortex function, it could be expected that the frontal lobes are organized asymmetrically. This is indeed the case. Furthermore, as expected from the principles of hierarchical organization of the neocortex, this asymmetry is found principally in the prefrontal cortex, the highest level of the motor hierarchy. In keeping with the general asymmetrical organization of the cerebrum, the special role of the left frontal lobe is in controlling movement primarily related to language, and that of the right frontal lobe is in controlling movement primarily related to nonverbal abilities. Like that of the parietal and temporal lobes, the asymmetry of frontal lobe function is relative rather than absolute; studies of patients with frontal lesions indicate that both frontal lobes play a role in nearly all behavior. Milner has emphasized this point, noting that the laterality of function disturbed by frontal lobe lesions is far less striking than that observed from more posterior lesions.

SYMPTOMS OF FRONTAL LOBE LESIONS

The effects of lesions in the lower levels of the motor system were discussed in Chapter 13. Our primary concern here is with the effects of lesions to the prefrontal cortex. However, in our discussion two factors may produce discrepancies between our conclusions and those by others. First, we deal primarily with the effects of *unilateral* frontal lesions. As with the temporal lobe, there is reason to believe that some effects of bifrontal lesions cannot be duplicated by lesions of either hemisphere alone. Table 19-1 summarizes a study comparing the behavioral effects of unilateral and bilateral lesions. People with bifrontal lesions are severely impaired at reporting the time of day and in decoding proverbs — effects seldom seen following unilateral frontal lesions. Although its cause is uncertain, this effect is consistent with the results of much animal work: that is, unilateral frontal lesions have little or no effect on certain tasks, but bifrontal lesions have severe effects.

The second factor in any discrepancy is that we have mainly drawn our conclusions from studies using patients with surgical removals for the relief of epilepsy or the excision of benign tumors and patients with missile wounds of the brain. This choice of patients presents the difficulty that some phenomena may not be observed in them. For example, Denny-Brown and others described the loss of hand and foot grasp reflexes, which appears to result only from very large frontal lesions (possibly bifrontal), such as result from slow-growing tumors or abscesses.

In the past decade the number of specific symptoms of frontal cortex injury has grown steadily. In an effort to organize these symptoms conceptually,

TABLE 19-1. Relative frequency of defective performance on neuropsychological tests

	Percentage of group showing a deficit		
Test	Left (%)	Right (%)	Bilateral (%)
Verbal fluency	70	38	71
Verbal learning	30	13	86
Block construction	10	50	43
Design copying	10	38	43
Time orientation	0	0	57
Proverbs	20	25	71

Source: Adapted from Benton, 1968

TABLE 19–2. Summary of major symptoms of frontal lobe damage

Most probable symptom	Lesion site	Basic reference
Disturbances of motor function		
Loss of fine movements	Area 4	Kuypers, 1981
Loss of strength	4, 6, DL	Leonard et al., 1988
Poor movement programming	Supplementary motor; DL?	Roland et al., 1980 Kolb and Milner, 1981
Poor voluntary eye gaze	Areas 8, 9	Guitton et al., 1982
Poor corollary discharge	Dorsolateral	Teuber, 1964
Broca's aphasia	Area 44	Brown, 1972
Loss of divergent thinking		
Reduced spontaneity	Orbital	Jones-Gotman and Milner, 1977
Poor strategy formation	DL?	Shallice and Evans, 1978
Environmental control of behavior		
Poor response inhibition	Areas 8, 9; 13	Milner, 1964
Risk taking and rule breaking	DL?	Miller, 1985
Impaired associative learning	DL	Petrides, 1982 Drewe, 1975
Poor temporal memory		
Poor recency memory	DL?	Milner, 1974
Poor frequency estimate	DL?	Smith and Milner, 1985
Poor self-order recall	DL?	Petrides and Milner, 1982
Poor delayed response	DL	Freedman and Oscar-Berman, 1986
Impaired spatial orientation	Dorsolateral	Semmes et al., 1963
Impaired social behavior	Orbital; DL	Blumer and Benson, 1975
Altered sexual behavior	Orbital	Walker and Blumer, 1975
Impaired olfactory discrimination	Orbital	Potter and Butters, 1980
Disorders associated with damage to the face area	Face	Taylor, 1979

we have grouped them into about eight major categories (Table 19-2). We do not wish to imply that the brain respects these categories but rather that the categories provide a conceptual framework within which to consider the symptoms.

Disturbances of Motor Function

First, we have grouped together here impairments in a person's ability to make different types of movements.

Fine Movements, Speed, and Strength. Damage to the primary motor cortex is normally associated with a chronic loss of the ability to make fine, independent finger movements, presumably due to a loss of direct corticospinal projections onto motor neurons. In addition, there is a loss of speed and strength in both hand and limb movements in the contralateral limbs. The loss of strength is not merely a symptom of damage to area 4, because lesions restricted to the prefrontal cortex lead to a reduction in hand strength.

Movement Programming. In a classic paper in 1950, Lashley asked how movements are put together in a particular order. How is it, he asked, that a violinist can play an arpeggio so quickly and flawlessly? Clearly, each note is not "thought of" separately. Furthermore, how is it that during a tennis game a player can make very rapid movements, seemingly much too fast to have considered each movement itself? Lashley presumed that this function — serially ordering complex chains of behavior in relation to varying stimuli — must somehow be a function of the neocortex. Although he believed this to be a function of the entire neocortex, it appears more likely to involve only the frontal lobes.

To date, the major support for this role of the frontal lobes comes from two lines of work: studies of the supplementary motor cortex and a single study of movement-copying by patients with frontal excisions. Although removal of the supplementary motor cortex results in a transient disruption of nearly all voluntary movements (including speech if the removal is on the left), there is rapid recovery, and the only permanent disability appears to be in the performance of rapidly alternating movements with the hands or fingers. It has been suggested that the reason relatively minor symptoms result from rather large lesions is that both the left and the right supplementary motor cortexes participate in the control of movement, much as both the left and the right face areas do. This idea is supported by observations that both supplementary areas show an increase in blood flow during *unimanual* tasks in humans; in monkeys, cells in both the left and the right areas show increased activity regardless of which hand is moving. There is also a bilateral projection from each supplementary motor cortex to the basal ganglia.

The lack of information about the effects of lesions of the supplementary motor cortex in humans makes it difficult to infer its functions. Nonetheless, on the basis of lesion, stimulation, and blood-flow studies, Roland and his colleagues have proposed that the supplementary motor areas are "programming areas for motor subroutes." Roland's group suggests that movements composed of sequences of fast, isolated muscular contractions are programmed here to allow them to be run off quickly. Evidence for this idea comes from their observation that human speech — a form of voluntary movement composed of such sequences of fast, isolated muscle contractions — is correlated with a bilateral increase in blood flow to the supplementary motor cortex. Similarly, movements of both the fingers and the limbs are associated with increased blood flow here, implying a general role for the supplementary motor cortex in the programming of movements, possibly both in the initiation of movement and in the execution of established subroutines of especially fast movements.

Further evidence favoring a role for the frontal cortex in movement programming comes from a study by Kolb and Milner. They asked patients with localized unilateral frontal lobectomies, (most of which did not include the supplementary motor cortex) to copy a series of arm or facial movements. Although the patients had some mild impairment in copying the arm movements, it was small compared with the performance of patients with left parietal lobe lesions. In contrast, patients with both left and right frontal lobe damage were very poor at copying a series of facial movements. On analysis of the facial-movement task, the frontal-lobe-lesion groups made more errors of sequence than normal controls or other groups of patients. In other words, patients with frontal lobe lesions had difficulty in ordering the various components of the sequence into a chain of movements. The components were recalled correctly, but in the wrong order. To be sure, these patients made other sorts of errors as well, especially errors of memory in which items were not recalled. This suggests that the difficulty in movement organization might partly be a result of problems with working memory, which we will discuss later in this chapter.

The results of the Kolb and Milner study complement the work of Roland and his associates, implicating the frontal lobe in movement programming. Both lines of work imply that this function is bilaterally represented in the frontal cortex, and it may be that the supplementary motor area has an especially important role in movement programming, although the larger region of the frontal lobe would seem to be involved in the programming of some types of movement.

The observation that the copying of facial but not arm movements was severely disrupted in the patients Kolb and Milner studied implies that the frontal lobe may play a special role in the control of the face, perhaps even including the tongue. We shall see in the next section that patients with frontal lobe damage exhibit relatively little spontaneous facial expression—a result in accord with the possible special role of the frontal lobe in the control of the face.

FIGURE 19-4. Visual search test adapted from Poppelreuter (1917). The subject must locate a duplicate of the shape inside the central box.

Voluntary Gaze. A number of studies using quite different procedures have been reported in which frontal lobe lesions produce alterations in voluntary eye gaze. For example, Teuber presented patients with an array of 48 patterns on a screen. The patterns could be distinguished by either shape or color or both (see Figure 19-4). At a warning signal a duplicate of one of the 48 patterns appeared in the center of the array, and the subject's task was to find the matching pattern and to identify it by pointing to it. Patients with frontal lobe lesions were impaired at finding the duplicate pattern.

Luria recorded patients' eye movements as they examined a picture of a complex scene. The eye-movement patterns of the patients with large frontal lobe lesions were quite different from those of normal control subjects or from patients with more posterior lesions. For example, if a normal control was asked about the age of the people in a picture, his or her eyes fixed on the heads; if asked how they are dressed, the eyes fixed on the clothing. Patients with large frontal lobe lesions tended to glance over the picture more or less at random, and a change in the question about the picture failed to alter the direction or the pattern of eye movements.

In a 1982 study Guitton and his colleagues examined a different type of oculomotor defect in frontal lobe patients. They examined the ability of patients to make voluntary eye movements toward or away from briefly appearing targets presented at random to the right or the left of a fixation point. Normally if a stimulus cue is briefly presented in either visual field, a person will make a quick eye movement, called a *saccade,* toward the stimulus. Patients with frontal lobe lesions had no difficulty at this, and so Guitton and his coworkers added a second feature to the task. Rather than make eye movements toward a target, the patients had to move their eyes to the same place in the opposite visual field. The task therefore required an inhibition of the normal saccade and a voluntary saccade to the similar point opposite. Patients with frontal lesions had two deficits on this variation of the task. First, although normal subjects failed to inhibit a short-latency response toward the cue in about 20% of trials, frontal-lobe-damaged patients had much more difficulty. Second, following the initial saccade in the incorrect direction, normal subjects had no difficulty in making a large corrective saccade toward the opposite field. In contrast, patients with frontal lesions, which included the frontal eye fields, had difficulty in executing the corrective responses when the response had to be generated by the *damaged* hemisphere. In other words, they had difficulty in moving the eyes to the field contralateral to the frontal lesion. Corrective movements could be made normally in the field on the same side as the lesion.

The difficulty that patients with frontal lesions encounter in the visual-search and the saccade tasks indicates the importance of the frontal cortex for certain aspects of oculomotor control. Only the study by Guitton and associates has localized the effect in the frontal eye fields, but it is likely that the most severe deficits in performing search tasks are associated with damage to those fields.

Corollary Discharge. If one pushes on the eyeball, the world appears to move. If one moves one's eyes, the world remains stable. Why? Teuber proposed that for a movement to take place there must be a signal to produce the movement and also a signal that the movement is going to occur. Thus, when one moves the eyes, there is a signal that it will happen and the world stays still. If the eyes are moved mechanically, there is no such signal and the world moves. This signal has been termed **corollary discharge,** or **reafference.**

In 1954, Teuber and Mishkin began to study this process, using a task first designed by Aubert in 1861. If you tilt your head sideways in a lighted room, vertical lines between the ceiling and floor do not tilt; they remain upright. If you tilt your head or body in the dark while looking at a luminous line, the mechanism still works, but not as well. If the task is made more difficult so that you must try to orient a tilted luminous line to the vertical in the dark while your head is also tilted sideways, there will be errors of a few degrees. The task is very difficult. Teuber and Mishkin discovered that if patients with frontal lesions were strapped into a chair that was then tilted, and the task was to set a luminous line to vertical, they were much more severely impaired than patients with more posterior lesions or than controls. This impairment disappeared if the chair was upright, indicating that the problem was not one of orienting the line but of doing so in an abnormal attitude.

Teuber argued that the deficit in the tilted-chair experiment is one of corollary discharge. Stated simply, voluntary movements involve two sets of signals rather than one. They occur simultaneously: the movement command, through the motor system, to effect the movements: and a signal (corollary discharge) from the frontal lobe to the parietal and temporal association cortex that presets the sensory system to anticipate the motor act. Thus, a person's sensory system is able to interpret changes in the external world in light of information about his or her movement. For example, when one is running, the external world remains stable, even though the sense organs are in motion, because there is corollary discharge from the frontal lobe to the parietal-temporal cortex, signaling that the movements are occurring. A frontal lesion can therefore not only disturb the production of a movement but also interfere with the message to the rest of the brain that a movement is taking place. By this indirect means, perception of the world by the posterior association cortex is altered.

Broca's Aphasia. The first symptom of prefrontal cortex damage to be described was the disturbance of language following lesion of the left frontal lobe, by Broca in 1861. After studying additional patients Broca and others proposed that the third frontal convolution of the left hemisphere, area 44, is specialized for producing motor programs for speech — a function Broca described as the "motor image of the word." In this type of aphasia the person has difficulty speaking, doing so only slowly and deliberately. Curiously, although this symptom of frontal lobe damage was the first to be described, it remains the most controversial even to this day. Some question its existence; others, granting that it might really occur, question its nature. We shall return to this problem in our discussion of language in Chapter 22. To date there are no clear indications of what area 44 in the right frontal lobe does. One possibility is that it contributes to the production of tone of voice. It is certain, however, that loss of this zone does not produce aphasia.

Loss of Divergent Thinking

One of the clearest differences between the effects of parietal and temporal lobe lesions and lesions of the frontal lobe is in performance on standard intelligence tests. Posterior lesions produce reliable, and often large, decreases in IQ, but frontal lesions do not. The puzzle is why patients with frontal lobe damage appear to do such "stupid" things. Guilford has noted that traditional intelligence tests appear to measure what can be called *convergent thinking,* in the sense that there is just one correct answer to each question. Thus, definitions of words, questions about events, arithmetic problems, puzzles, block designs, and so forth are all looking for correct answers that are easily scored. There is, however, another type of intelligence, which can be called *divergent thinking.* In this case the number and variety of responses to a single question is emphasized, rather than a particular answer. An example would be a question asking one to list the possible uses of a coat hanger. Zangwill suggested that frontal lobe injury might interfere with this sort of intelligence, rather than the type measured by standard IQ tests. There are several lines of evidence supporting his idea.

Behavioral Spontaneity. It has long been recognized that patients with frontal lobe lesions exhibit what Zangwill referred to as a "certain loss of spontaneity of speech" and a "difficulty in evoking appropriate words or phrases". Subsequent studies by a variety of authors — Milner and, later, Ramier and Hécaen, among others — have been able to quantify this deficit. These researchers gave patients tests similar to Thurstone's Word-Fluency Test: patients were asked to write or to say, first, as many words starting with a given letter as they could think of in 5 min, then as many four-letter words starting with a given letter. Patients with frontal lobe lesions have a low output of words in this test, producing an average of 35 words in total in Milner's sample. Although the principal locus of this defect appears to be in the left orbital-frontal region, lesions in the right orbital-frontal region may also produce a large reduction in verbal fluency. Again we see less asymmetry in the frontal lobes than one might expect. The following case is an example of low spontaneous verbal fluency resulting from a lesion of the right frontal lobe.

Mrs. P., a 63-year-old woman with a B.A. degree, was suffering from a large astrocytoma of the right frontal lobe. Her word fluency is reproduced in Figure 19-5*A*. Four features of frontal lobe damage are illustrated in her test performance. First, her total output of words is remarkably low: only eight words beginning with *s* and six words beginning with *c*. (Control subjects of similar age and education produce a total of about 60 words in the same time period.) Second, we see rule-breaking, which is a common characteristic of such patients on this test. We told her several times that the words starting with *c* could have only four letters. She replied: "Yes, yes, I know, I keep using more each time." Even though she understood the instructions she could not organize her behavior to follow them successfully. Third, her writing is not fluid but rather jerky, much like that seen in a child learning to write, implying that her tumor had invaded area 4 or 6. Finally, Mrs. P. insisted on talking throughout the test — complaining that she simply could not think of any more words — and kept looking around the room for objects starting with the required letter.

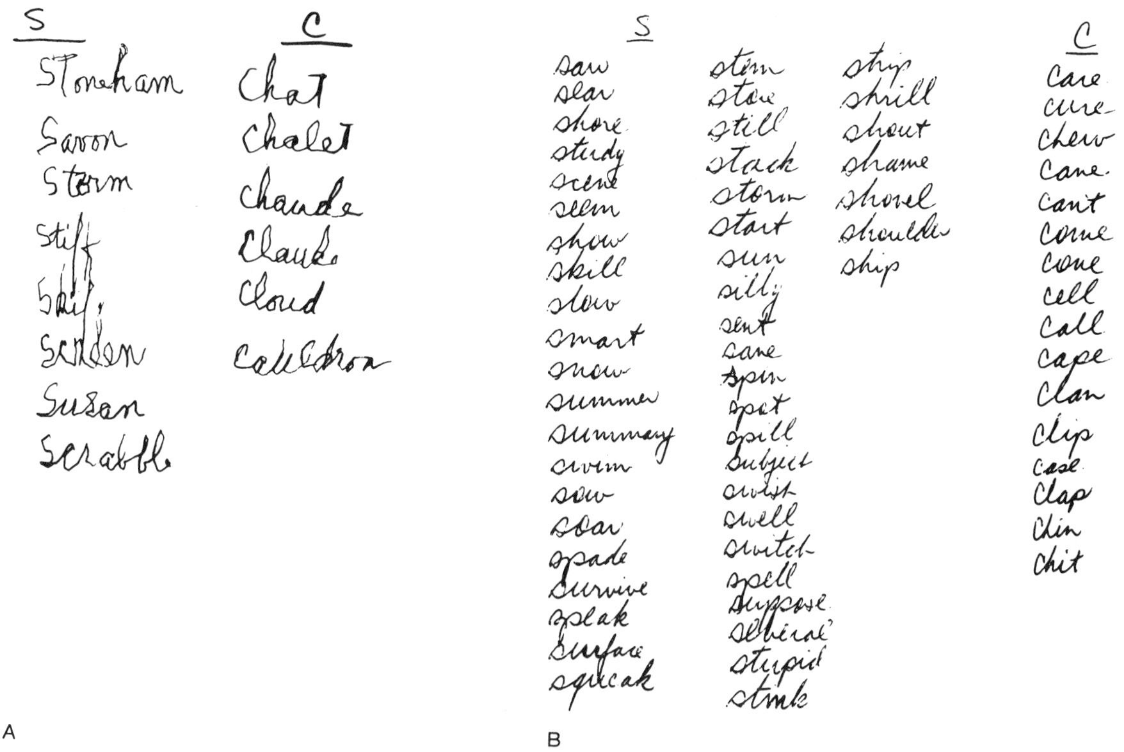

FIGURE 19-5. Word fluency. *A.* Mrs. P's lists. *B.* A normal control subject's lists. Both subjects were given 5 min to write as many English-language words as possible staring with the letter *s* and 4 min to write as many four-letter words as possible staring with the letter *c*. Note Mrs. P's low output and her rule-breaking in the four-letter *c* words. (Mrs. P. was multilingual, although English was her first language.)

Although one locus of low verbal fluency anterior to Broca's area appears to be in the orbital cortex, patients with lesions in the central face area (see Figure 19-1*C*) actually have even lower verbal fluency scores, according to Milner. Although a peculiar result, it appears solid and reliable, and suggests that the face area has some special role in certain aspects of verbal abilities.

A study by Jones-Gotman and Milner raises the question of whether this verbal-fluency deficit might have a nonverbal analogue. The researchers devised an ingenious experiment in which they asked patients to draw as many different drawings, which were not supposed to be representational, as they could in 5 min. The patients were then asked to draw as many different drawings as they could, but this time using only four lines (a circle was counted as a single line). The results showed a beautiful analogue to the verbal fluency results. As can be seen in Figure 19-6, lesions in the right frontal lobe produced a very large drop in the production of different drawings. Normal controls drew about 35 drawings, left frontal lobe patients about 24 drawings, and right frontal lobe patients about 15 drawings. This deficit appears to be related to an impoverished output, high persevera-

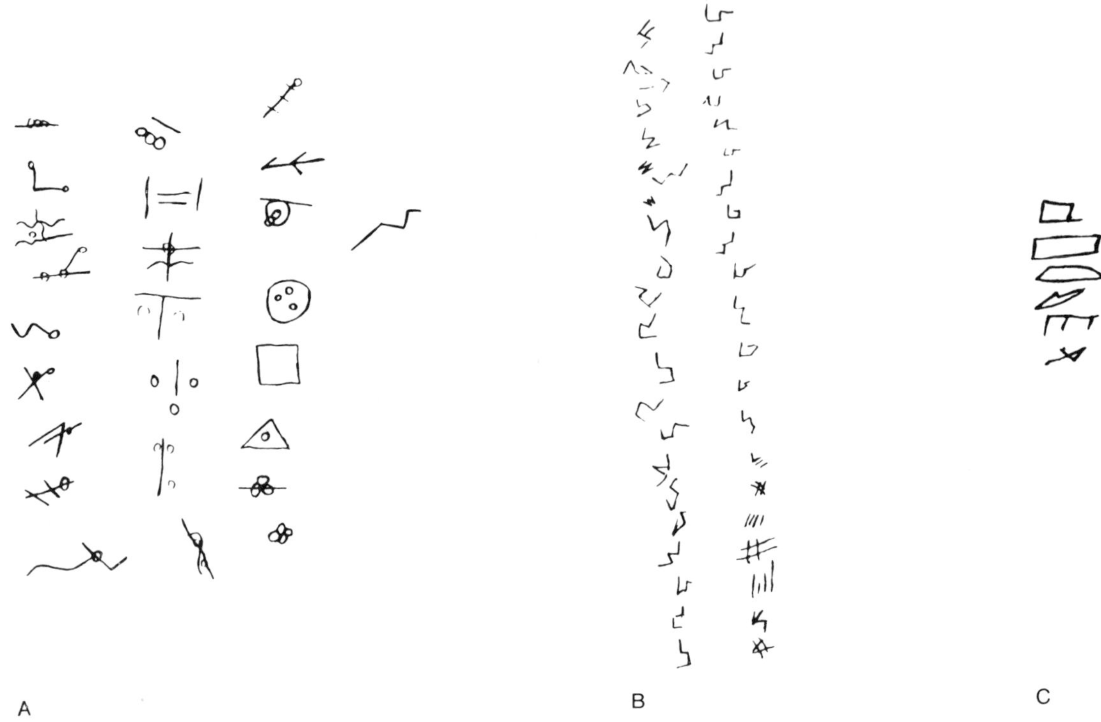

FIGURE 19-6. Design fluency. *A*. A normal subject's drawings, showing perseveration. *B*. A frontal lobe patient's drawings showing perseveration. *C*. A frontal lobe patient's drawings showing lack of spontaneity.

tion, and, in some cases, the drawing of nameable things. As with verbal fluency, lesions in the central face area actually appeared to produce a larger deficit than the more anterior lesions. There is not yet a clear indication whether orbital-frontal lesions affect design fluency more than dorsolateral lesions do. More patients must be studied.

The question arises of whether patients with frontal lobe lesions might actually show a reduced spontaneity of behavior in general. Since these patients have been described as "pseudodepressed" (see below), this might indeed be the case, but we are aware of only two studies that have actually recorded the spontaneous behavior of patients. Kolb and Milner found the following. (1) Patients with frontal lobe removals displayed fewer spontaneous facial movements and expressions than did normal controls or patients with more posterior lesions. (2) There were dramatic differences in the number of words spoken by frontal lobe patients during a neuropsychological interview: patients with left frontal removals rarely spoke, whereas patients with right frontal lesions were excessively talkative. Hence, it would seem worthwhile to study in detail the spontaneous behavior of patients with frontal lesions to determine whether altered spontaneity is a general feature of their behavior. There is some reason to believe this is the case since frontal lobe patients characteristically appear lethargic or lazy: they often have difficulty getting out of bed in the morning, getting dressed, or initiating other daily activities, such as going to work. One patient we saw is a particularly stunning example. He was a prominent lawyer who suffered a midline meningioma in the frontal lobe. The tumor was removed surgically but he was left with bilateral damage to the superior aspect of both frontal lobes. His IQ was still superior (over 140) and his memory for legal matters was unimpaired. Nonetheless he was unable to function in his profession for he could not get up in the morning to go to work, preferring to stay in bed and watch TV. When his wife forced him to get up and go to work, he was disruptive at the office because he could not concentrate on any law-related work. Rather, he was distracted by anything else going on in the office. Curiously, he remained an excellent resource for his colleagues, who nonetheless found his behavior intolerable, consequently preferring to consult him by telephone!

Strategy Formation. Patients with frontal lobe lesions are especially impaired at developing novel cognitive plans or strategies for solving problems. For example, when Shallice and Evans asked subjects questions that required reasoning based upon general knowledge but for which no immediate obvious strategy was available, they found that frontal lobe patients did very poorly and often gave bizarre responses. In a subsequent study, Smith and Milner asked subjects to estimate the average price of a particular object, such as a sewing machine. They suggested that to perform such a task one must develop a strategy that may involve deciding what is a typical sewing machine, judging the range of possible prices, and selecting a representative price for a machine of average quality. They found that patients with frontal lobe lesions, especially right frontal lesions, were very poor at this task. In contrast, patients with temporal lobe damage who showed memory deficits on other tasks, performed like controls on this task. Thus, it seems unlikely that a simple memory explanation will account for the poor performance of the frontal lobe patients.

Environmental Control of Behavior: Impaired Response Inhibition and Inflexible Behavior

Perhaps the most commonly observed trait of frontal lobe patients tested by clinical neuropsychologists is the difficulty they have in using information (feedback) from environmental cues to regulate or change their behavior. This manifests itself in a number of ways.

Response Inhibition. Patients with frontal lobe lesions consistently perseverate on responses in a variety of test situations, particularly those in which there are changing demands. The best example of this phenomenon is observed in the Wisconsin Card-Sorting Test, which has been extensively studied by Milner. Figure 19-7 shows the test material as it appears to the subject. The subject is presented with four stimulus cards, bearing designs that differ in color, form, and number of elements. The subject's task is to sort the cards into piles in front of one or another of the stimulus cards. The only help the subject is given is being told whether the choice is correct or incorrect.

The test works on this principle: the correct solution is first, color; once the subject has figured out this solution, the correct solution then becomes, without warning, form. Thus, the subject must now inhibit classifying the cards on the basis of color and shift to form. Once the subject has succeeded at selecting by form, the correct solution again changes unexpectedly, this time to number of elements. It will later become color again, and so on. Shifting response strategies is particularly difficult for persons with frontal lesions, who may continue responding to the original stimulus (color) for as many as 100 cards until testing is terminated. Throughout this period they may comment that they know that color is no longer correct. They nevertheless continue to sort on the basis of color. For example, one person stated (correctly): "Form is probably the correct solution now so this [sorting to color] will be wrong, and this will be wrong, and wrong again." Such persevera-

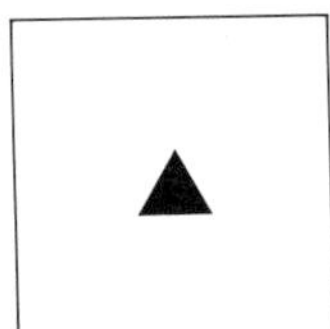

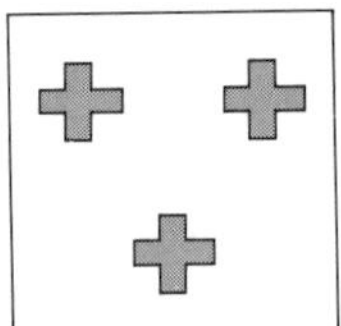
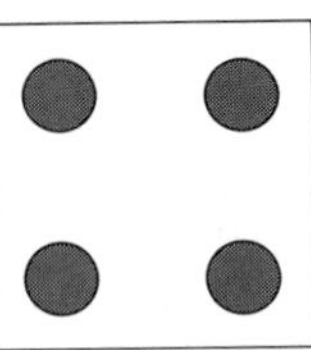

FIGURE 19-7. The Wisconsin Card-Sorting Test, showing test material as presented to the subject. (From B. Milner, Some effects of frontal lobectomy in man. In J. M. Warren and K. Akert, eds., 1964, p. 315. Copyright © 1964 by McGraw-Hill, Inc. Used with permission of McGraw-Hill Book Co.)

tion is common on any task in which a frontal lobe patient is required to shift response strategies, demonstrating that the frontal lobe is necessary for flexibility in behavior. It is important to note that on card-sorting tasks the subjects must not be given any hint that they are to expect a change in the correct solution, because many frontal lobe patients improve dramatically when given this warning. The cue apparently allows enough flexibility in behavior to solve the problem.

It appears from Milner's work that the principal locus of this effect (on card sorting, at least) is roughly around Brodmann's area 9 in the left hemisphere. Lesions elsewhere in the left, and often in the right, frontal lobe will also produce a deficit on this task, although a somewhat attenuated one.

Performance of the Stroop test further demonstrates loss of response inhibition following frontal lobe damage. Subjects are presented with a list of color words (blue, green, red, etc.), each word being printed in colored ink but never in the color denoted by the word (e.g., the word *yellow* is printed in blue, green, or red ink). The subject's task is to name the color in which each word is printed as quickly as possible. Correct response requires an inhibition of reading the color name, an inhibition that is difficult for many control subjects. Perret found that patients with left frontal lesions were unable to inhibit reading the words and thus were impaired at this task.

Risk Taking and Rule Breaking. Frontal lobe patients are distinguished from other patients in their common failure to comply with task instructions. Milner found this to be especially common on tests of stylus-maze learning in which a buzzer indicated an error had occurred and subjects were to stop and start the maze over. Subjects with frontal lobe lesions tended to disregard the signal, thereby continuing the incorrect path and making more errors. This behavior is reminiscent of their inability to modify their responses in the card-sorting task. More recently, Miller gave subjects a task in which words had to be guessed on the basis of partial information. With each additional clue, the subject was assigned a successively lower point value for a correct answer, but points could only be collected if the answer was correct. An incorrect answer forfieted all of the points for an item. Frontal lobe patients took more risks (and made more mistakes) than did other patients, and the risk taking was greatest in those frontal lobe patients who also had temporal lobe damage.

Associative Learning. It has often been claimed that patients with large frontal lobe lesions are unable to regulate their behavior in response to external stimuli. Thus, for example, Luria and Homskaya described patients with massive frontal lobe tumors who could not be trained to respond consistently with the right hand to a red light and with the left hand to a green light, even though the patients could indicate which hand was which and could repeat the instructions. As with many other frontal lobe symptoms, however, there are very few experimental studies of this phenomenon in patients with more restricted cortical injuries, although a 1982 study by Petrides is intriguing. He asked frontal lobe patients to learn arbitrary associations between colors and spatial locations or between colors and hand postures. For example, in the former test, patients were presented with six blue lights and six white index cards placed in a row on a table in front of them. Each light was associated with one and only one of the index cards, and the subjects' task was to learn which card was associated with which light. Damage to either the left or the right hemisphere resulted in poor performance on this task, as well as on an analogous task in which different-colored lights and six hand postures had to be associated in a similar way. Again, the behavioral impairments in the frontal lobe patients could not be attributed to a deficit in memory since temporal lobe patients who performed poorly on other tests of memory performed normally at these tasks.

The deficits observed in associative-learning tasks imply that frontal lobe lesions impair the ability to utilize external cues to guide responses, although the details of this deficit await further study. Nonetheless, it seems likely that a disorder of this sort would render behavior inflexible and disorganized — symptoms we have already seen to be characteristic of frontal lobe patients.

Poor Temporal Memory

It has been argued that the integration of behaviors over time requires a memory for what has just occurred. This memory includes what we referred to earlier as *temporal memory,* which is a memory for what has just happened and where it happened, as well as a memory for the order in which things have happened. The latter form of memory has been referred to as *recency memory*. Although these two forms of memory can be distinguished on conceptual grounds, it is often difficult to distinguish them experimentally since they are clearly related. The distinction is probably not crucial so we shall focus upon the various demonstrations of frontal lobe impairments in some aspect of temporal memory.

The Corsi Experiments: Recency Memory. On the basis of earlier work by others, Philip Corsi designed an ingenious test of recency memory. Subjects were shown a long series of cards, each card bearing two stimulus items, which were either words or pictures. On some cards a question mark appeared between the items, and the subjects' task was to indicate which of the two items had been seen more recently. Successful performance required the subjects to recall the order of presentation of the stimuli. On most test trials the items had both appeared previously, but on some, one item was new. In this case the task became one of simple recognition memory. Patients with frontal lobe lesions performed normally on the recognition trials, but they were impaired in judging the relative recency of two previously seen items. Further, there is relative asymmetry in the frontal lobes in this regard: the right frontal lobe appears more important for memory for nonverbal or pictorial recency; the left frontal lobe appears more important for verbal recency. In contrast, patients with temporal lobe lesions were impaired at the recognition test but not at the recency test. (This latter finding is curious for it seems to be analogous to "blindsight," in that people who fail to recognize items can identify which was observed most recently. Might this suggest that there is a memory location system that is separate from a memory recognition system?)

Frequency Estimation. Smith and Milner approached temporal memory in a different manner. They presented subjects with a series of individual items, some of which were repeated a varying number of times within the series. The task was to estimate the frequency with which each item appeared. The results paralleled Corsi's. Frontal lobe patients performed as well as controls at the lower end of the frequency range (0–3), but the patients with frontal lobe lesions failed to show much sensitivity to frequencies beyond (5–9). The frontal lobe deficits were *material-specific,* meaning that left frontal lobe patients were maximally impaired on a test using words, whereas right frontal lobe patients were most impaired when the items were abstract designs. On these tasks, as with Corsi's tasks, the temporal lobe patients performed better than the frontal lobe patients at the frequency estimations. And again, the frontal lobe patients made no more recognition errors than did the normal control subjects.

Self-Ordering. Many tasks in everyday life require that we generate our own plans to solve them. In a task designed to explore this ability Petrides and Milner presented subjects with stacks of cards on which was displayed an array of 12 stimuli, including words or drawings in parallel versions of the task. The stimuli in the array remained constant, but the position of each stimulus varied randomly from card to card. The subject's task appeared rather simple: Go through the stack and point to only one item on each card, taking care not to point to the same item twice. Thus, the subjects themselves initiated the plan to follow and determined the order of responding. Although the task appears easy to us, frontal lobe patients did not find it so: left frontal lobe lesions were associated with impaired performance of both verbal and nonverbal versions of the task, whereas right frontal lobe lesions were associated only with poor performance on the nonverbal test.

Petrides and Milner suggest that in contrast to the recency tests, the self-ordered tasks require subjects to organize and carry out a sequence of responses. From the moment the subjects begin responding, they must constantly compare the responses they have made with those that still remain to be carried out. Hence, this type of task demands an accurate memory as well as an organized strategy. When questioned about their approach to the task at the end of testing, patients with frontal lesions were less likely than other subjects to report that they had used a particular strategy, and when they had, the strategy often appeared to be ill defined and to have been used inconsistently. The deficit is unlikely to have been one of simple memory, since temporal lobe patients, who would have been expected to have defects of memory, performed normally at this task.

The greater defect following left frontal rather than right frontal lesions may be consistent with the suggestion that the left hemisphere plays a special role in the programming of responses, whether the production of simple sequences of movement such as on the Kimura manual sequence box (Figure 13-5) or on more complex tests such as these.

Delayed Response and Delayed Alternation. In the 1930s, Jacobsen gave impetus to a revolution in research on the frontal lobes when he observed that chimpanzees with frontal lobe lesions are impaired at a task called *delayed response.* In the delayed-response task, the animal is shown where food is located (e.g., under one of two cups) but is prevented from responding for some period, usually a few seconds. After this delay, the animal is allowed to respond, and its accuracy in choosing the correct hiding place for the food is measured. Jacobsen found that although the chimps with frontal lesions recalled that a reward had been placed under one object, they were unable to remember which one, even with quite short delays. The delayed-response test has proved to be one of the most sensitive tests of frontal lobe function because species as diverse as monkeys and rats show an unequivocal deficit. A parallel test, *delayed alternation,* was also devised in which the location of the reward is alternated from one side to the other, with a brief delay between the trials. Oscar-Berman and her colleagues have, over the past number of years, adapted tests from studies of nonhuman subjects to make them suitable for studying human subjects. Their results on the delayed-response and delayed-alternation tests are unequivocal: patients with frontal lobe lesions are impaired at both, and this deficit is not due to a general impairment of memory. Rather, it appears specific to this test of working memory.

Impaired Spatial Orientation

Semmes and her colleagues were the first to demonstrate clearly that patients with frontal lobe lesions have a deficit in spatial orientation. To do this, they devised parallel tests of personal orientation *(egocentric spatial relations)* and of extrapersonal orientation *(allocentric spatial relations),* both diagrammed in Figure 19-8. In the egocentric test the subject's task was to point to the location on his or her body represented by the various numbers shown on the figure (*A*). In the allocentric task the subjects carried a series of maps, one map at a time, into a room where nine dots were painted on the floor in an evenly spaced pattern. The subject's task was to pace out on the floor the route laid out on a given map (*B*).

Because the parietal cortex is known to be involved in spatial relations, Semmes expected the maximal deficits on both of these tasks to result from parietal lesions. But this was not the case. The results showed a double dissociation of egocentric and allocentric spatial relations: that is, the frontal lobe patients were impaired at the egocentric test but not the allocentric, and the parietal lobe patients were badly impaired at the latter test but only slightly at the former. Furthermore, performances on both tests were more severely affected by lesions of the left than of the right hemisphere. Semmes and her coworkers interpreted the impairment following frontal cortical damage as a difficulty with behaviors that depend on the accurate assessment of one's body orientation in space. In contrast, the impairment following parietal cortex damage was interpreted as a difficulty with behaviors involving the spatial relations among external stimuli.

Semmes' results have significantly influenced neuropsychological thinking about spatial orientation and the frontal and parietal lobes, but unfortunately, they may have been misleading. A major difficulty in studying patients with vascular lesions of the left parietotemporal cortex is that they usually are aphasic. Semmes' patients had missile wounds of the brain, and their lesions consequently did not respect the vascular system. This allowed her to study nonaphasic patients. On the other hand, there was considerable variance in her patients' lesions, many of which were well outside areas PF and PG (Figure 17-1*C*), which on anatomical grounds ought to be the focus for spatial disturbances (see Chapter 17). Semmes' hypothesis rests upon her finding that patients with frontal lesions were more impaired at her body-orientation task than were patients with more posterior lesions, but there is reason to believe that this is not the case. Over the years, we have had the opportunity to study a small number of patients with infarcts in the region of areas PG and PF, who were not aphasic at the time we saw them, which in some cases was a long time after their injury. Of six such patients, the performance on the Semmes test had a mean score of about 75% correct, and ranged

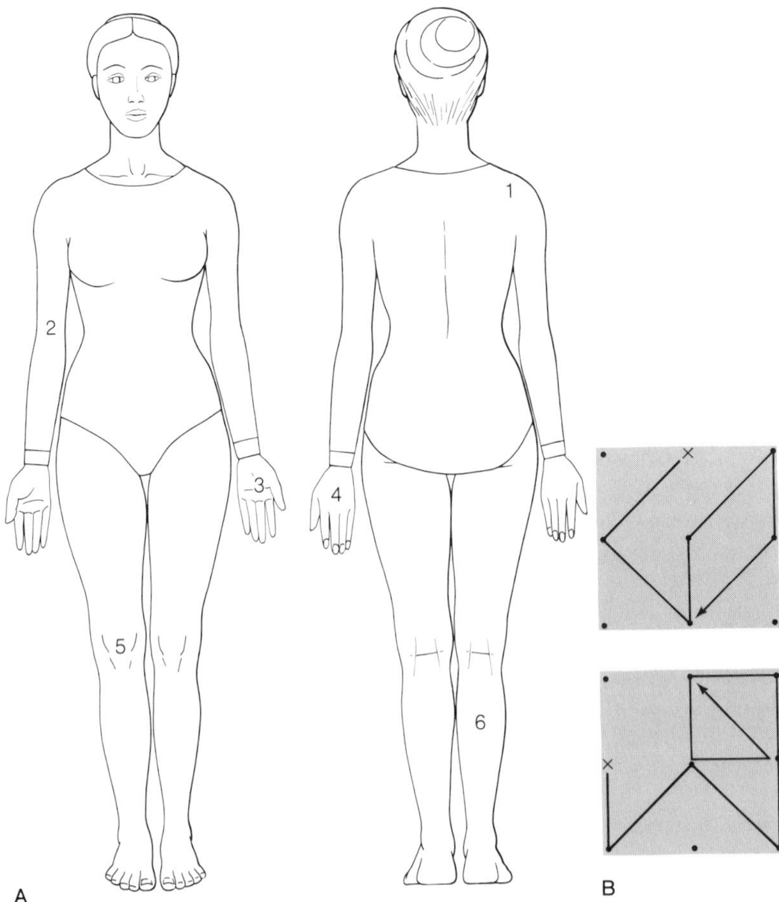

FIGURE 19-8. Sample items from tests by Semmes and her colleagues of personal and extrapersonal orientation. *A*. In the personal-orientation task the subject is required to touch parts of his or her own body as indicated by the numbers on the diagram. *B*. In the extrapersonal-orientation task the subject follows a map painted on the floor to progress from point to point.

from 40 to 80% correct, which is somewhat worse than we find for frontal lobe patients, who average about 85% correct. Control subjects normally score more than 96% correct. Although the variability in the lesions and the small number of cases precludes strong conclusions, we feel confident that patients with posterior parietal lesions perform as poorly on this test as do patients with frontal lobe lesions. Thus, we do not feel that there are strong empirical grounds for proposing that the frontal and parietal cortex play qualitatively different roles in spatial orientation. We will return to this issue in our more extensive discussion of spatial behavior in Chapter 24.

Although patients with right frontal lobe lesions are not severely impaired at the Semmes tests, they are impaired at other tests of spatial orientation. In particular, patients with right frontal lobe lesions have difficulty in successfully solving finger- and stylus-maze tests. For example, in Corkin's study of stylus-maze performance, subjects had to learn to trace a route in a maze, which was out of sight, using a stylus. Each time an incorrect alley was entered a bell rang, providing subjects with feedback about their performance. Although control subjects made an average of about 100 errors in solving this admittedly difficult task, patients with right, but not left, frontal lobe lesions failed to learn the task and were discontinued after about 350 errors. Furthermore, patients with right frontal lobe lesions performed more poorly at this task than did patients with right temporal or parietal lobe lesions, who also were impaired at it.

Although the stylus maze has a spatial component to it, the degree of frontal lobe impairment on this type of test may be related, in part, to the requirements of spatial temporal memory; that is, the solution of the maze requires that the subject remember the information acquired in each previous trial. A deficit in temporal memory would make this more difficult.

Impaired Social and Sexual Behavior

Social and sexual behaviors both require flexible responses that are highly dependent upon contextual cues. It is hardly surprising, therefore, that frontal lobe lesions would interfere with both of these behaviors.

Social Behavior. One of the most obvious and striking effects of frontal lobe damage in humans is a marked change in social behavior and personality. Perhaps the most publicized example of personality change following frontal lobe lesions is that of Phineas Gage, first reported by Harlow in 1868. Gage was a dynamite worker and survived an explosion that blasted an iron tamping bar (3 ft 7 in. long, 1.25 in. wide at its widest point) through the front of his head (see Figure 19-9). After the accident his behavior changed completely. He had been of average intelligence and was "energetic and persistent in executing all his plans of operation." His personality after the injury is described as follows:

> The equilibrium or balance, so to speak, between his intellectual faculties, and animal propensities seems to have been destroyed. He is fitful, irreverent, indulging at times in the grossest profanity, manifesting but little deference for his fellows, impatient of restraint or advice when it conflicts with his desires, at times pertinaciously obstinate, yet capricious and vacilating, devising many plans of operation, which are no sooner arranged than they are abandoned in turn for others appearing more feasible. A child in his intellectual capacity and manifestations, he has the animal passions of a strong man. (Blumer and Benson, 1975, p. 153)

Gage's injury affected primarily the left frontal lobe from the medial orbital region upward to the precentral region.

Although Gage's skull has been examined carefully, the first person with extensive frontal damage to actually undergo close scrutiny at autopsy was a furrier who fell 100 ft from a window. He suffered a compound fracture of the frontal bones and severe injury to the right frontal lobe but, remarkably, was never unconscious and was confused only briefly. Before the fall the man had been good natured and sociable, but afterward he became nasty and cantankerous. Autopsy, about a year after the accident, revealed deep scarring of the orbital part of both frontal lobes, although it was more extensive on the right.

From soon after the turn of the century until about 1950 there were many excellent psychiatric studies of the effect of brain lesions on personality. A consistent finding of this work, (especially Kliest's, cited in Zangwill) was that damage to the orbital regions of the frontal lobe was associated with more dramatic changes in personality than dorsolateral lesions, although the latter also had

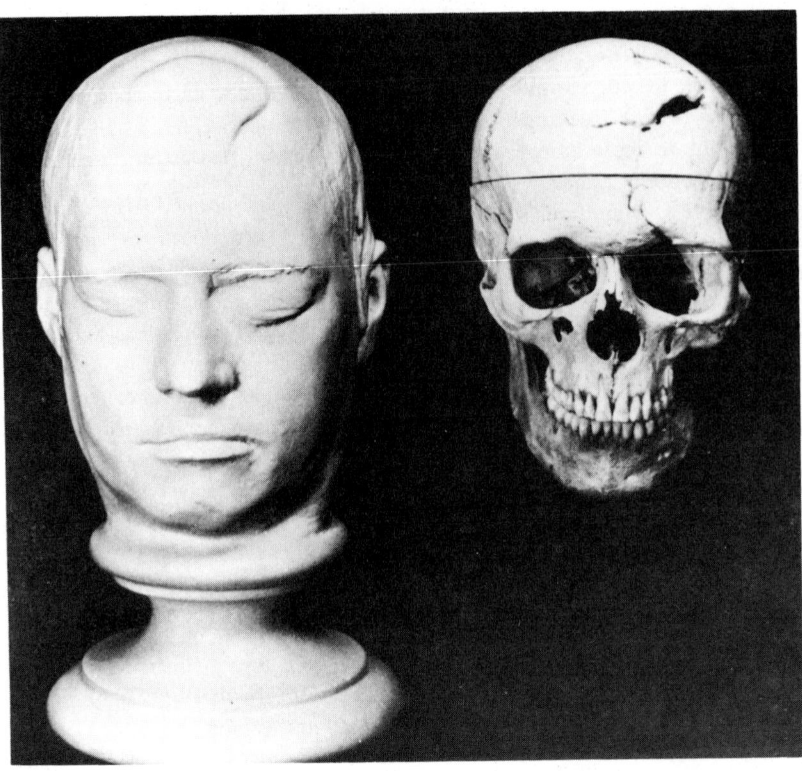

FIGURE 19-9. Bust and skull of Phineas Gage, showing the hole in the frontal bone made by the iron rod blown through his head. (From C. Blakemore, *Mechanics of the Mind.* Cambridge: Cambridge University Press, p. 3. Copyright © 1977. Reprinted with permission of Cambridge University Press.)

significant effects. Although there are abundant clinical descriptions of the effects of frontal lobe lesions on personality, there are few systematic studies. At least two types of personality change have been clinically observed in such patients: Blumer and Benson have termed them as showing **pseudodepression** and exhibiting **pseudopsychopathy.** Patients classified as being pseudodepressed exhibit such symptoms as outward apathy and indifference, loss of initiative, reduced sexual interest, little overt emotion, and little or no verbal output. Patients classified as pseudopsychopathic exhibit immature behavior, lack of tact and restraint, coarse language, promiscuous sexual behavior, increased motor activity, and a general lack of social graces. Incontinence is not uncommon with large traumatic lesions or tumors in the frontal lobes. The following two case histories illustrate the pseudodepressed and pseudopsychopathic frontal personalities, respectively.

At the age of 46, a successful salesman sustained a compound depressed fracture of the left frontal bone in a traffic accident. Treatment included debridement [surgical removal] and amputation of the left frontal pole. Recovery was slow, and 9 months after the injury he was referred for long-term custodial management. By this time, he had recovered motor function with only a minimal limp and slight hyperreflexia on the right side, had normal sensation, no evidence of aphasia, and normal memory and cognitive ability (IQ 118). Nonetheless, he remained under hospital care because of marked changes in personal habits.

Prior to the accident, the patient had been garrulous, enjoyed people, had many friends and talked freely. He was active in community affairs, including Little League, church activities, men's clubs, and so forth. It was stated by one acquaintance that the patient had a true charisma, "whenever he entered a room there was a change in the atmosphere, everything became more animated, happy and friendly."

Following the head injury, he was quiet and remote. He would speak when spoken to and made sensible replies but would then lapse into silence. He made no friends on the ward, spent most of his time sitting alone smoking. He was frequently incontinent of urine, occasionally of stool. He remained unconcerned about either and was frequently found soaking wet, calmly sitting and smoking. If asked, he would matter-of-factly state that he had not been able to get to the bathroom in time but that this didn't bother him. Because of objectionable eating habits he always ate alone on the ward. His sleep pattern was reversed; he stayed up much of the night and slept during the day. He did not resent being awakened or questioned. He could discuss many subjects intelligently, but was never known to initiate either a conversation or a request. He could give detailed accounts of his life prior to the accident, of the hospitals he had been in, the doctors and treatment he had had, but there was an unreality to his conversation. When asked, he would deny illness, state emphatically that he could return to work at any time, and that the only reason he was not working was that he was being held in the hospital by the doctors. At no time did he request a discharge or weekend pass. He was totally unconcerned about his wife and children. Formerly a warm and loving father, he did not seem to care about his family. Eventually, the family ceased visiting because of his indifference and unconcern. (Blumer and Benson, 1975, pp. 156–157)

A 32-year-old white male was admitted for behavioral evaluation. History revealed that he had sustained a gunshot wound in Vietnam 5 years previously. A high-velocity missile had entered the left temple and emerged through the right orbit. Infection necessitated surgical removal of most of the orbital surface of the right frontal lobe. On recovery, he was neither paralyzed nor aphasic but suffered a remarkable change in personality.

Prior to injury he had been quiet, intelligent, proper, and compulsive. He was a West Point graduate and spent the ensuing years as a military officer attaining the rank of captain. Both as a cadet and later as an officer, he was known to be quiet, strict, and rigid. He was considered a good commander, trusted by his men, but never shared camaraderie with his troops or with his peers.

Subsequent to injury, he was outspoken, facetious, brash, and disrespectful. There was no evidence of self-pity, although he frequently made rather morbid jokes about his condition (for example, "dummy's head"). On admission to the hospital, he had just failed at an extremely simple job.

He was not aphasic but misused words in a manner that suggested inability to maintain specific meanings. For instance, when asked whether the injury had affected his thinking his response was, "Yeah — it's affected the way I think — it's affected my senses — the only things I can taste are sugar and salt — I can't detect a pungent odor — ha ha — to tell you the truth it's a blessing this way." When the examiner persisted, "How had it affected the way you think?" his response was "Yes — I'm not as spry on my feet as I was before." He was never incontinent, but did show a messiness in attire. His remarks to the nurses and other female personnel were open and frank but were never blatantly sexual. His premorbid IQ was reported at about 130. Present examination showed a full-scale IQ of 113. (Blumer and Benson, 1974, pp. 155–156)

Blumer and Benson are probably correct in their assertion that all the elements of these syndromes are observable only after bilateral frontal lobe damage. Nevertheless, some elements of these two rather different syndromes can be observed in most, if not all, persons with frontal lobe lesions. Pseudodepression appears most likely to follow lesions of the left frontal lobe; pseudopsychopathic behavior, lesions of the right frontal lobe.

Sexual Behavior. Changes in sexual behavior are among the most difficult symptoms of frontal lobe damage to properly document, largely because of social taboos against investigating people's sex lives. To date, there are no such empirical studies, but there is anecdotal evidence that frontal lesions do alter libido and related behavior. Orbital frontal lesions may introduce abnormal sexual behavior (such as public masturbation) by reducing inhibitions, although the actual frequency of sexual behavior per se is not affected. On the other hand, dorsolateral lesions appear to reduce interest in sexual behavior, although the patients are still capable of the necessary motor acts and can perform sexually if led through the activity "step by step."

Impaired Olfaction

Although olfaction is seldom studied in human subjects, behavioral evidence from studies of nonhuman subjects led Potter and Butters to investigate olfactory detection and discrimination in frontal lobe patients. Their results showed that although olfactory detection was still normal, olfactory discriminatory ability was severely impaired in their patients. The orbital-frontal cortex of other species is known to have significant olfactory input, and cells there are known to respond to specific odors. It is likely that the same is true in humans. Thus, the orbital-frontal cortex may be the core olfactory cortex, a surprising possibility in view of the more strict motor functions that we have described to this point. The importance of olfaction in social and sexual behavior, even in humans, may be significant in understanding the olfactory functions of the frontal cortex, although this is pure speculation at this point. The subject requires a good deal more study.

Symptoms Associated with Damage to the Face Area

Over the years Taylor and his colleagues have accumulated some remarkable data from a small group of patients with localized surgical removals of the precentral and postcentral gyri, containing, respectively, the motor and sensory representations of the face (see Figure 19-1*C*). Unlike removal cortical areas for the hand (see Chapter 11), removal areas for the face is seldom associated with long-lasting somatosensory deficits on the face, even if both the sensory and motor representations are removed completely. This finding is in keeping with the evidence that the face is represented bilaterally in the cortex. There has been no systematic study of the facial motor abilities of patients with removal of both precentral and postcentral gyri, but Kolb and Milner found them able to perform facial-movement sequences normally. Furthermore, although they had difficulty in making individual facial movements in the initial postoperative period, especially on the side of the face contralateral to the lesion, they appeared to have regained normal voluntary facial control a month after surgery, although closer examination might have revealed subtle defects. In addition, their faces were expressive, and they displayed normal spontaneous facial expressions at frequencies well within normal limits.

In the immediate postoperative period patients with left hemisphere facial-area lesions are aphasic, being impaired at both language comprehension and production, as well as being alexic. However, these symptoms subside rapidly, probably having resulted from swelling and trauma associated with the surgical procedure. Within about six months to a year after surgery, only a slight residual expressive dysphasia remains. Yet these same patients are severely impaired at certain other language tests. In particular, they perform very poorly on tests of word fluency and are unable to make effective use of phonetic elements of language.

In addition, these same patients are very poor spellers, occasionally writing words that are unrecognizable. Their low verbal fluency is complemented by a very low design fluency; patients with right facial-area lesions are worse at design fluency than even patients with very large anterior frontal lesions. This lack of spontaneity in verbal and design fluency is remarkable, considering the normal spontaneity of facial expressions noted above.

In summary, unilateral removal of the cortical area representing the face results in no significant chronic loss in sensory or motor control of the face (presumably because of the face's bilateral representation in the cortex) but does result surprisingly in chronic deficits in phonetic discrimination, spelling, verbal fluency, and design fluency. Taylor has preliminary data suggesting that these deficits may result primarily from damage to the precentral motor representation of the face, rather than to the postcentral sensory representation. The origin of these deficits is, however, unexplained to date.

Clinical Neuropsychological Assessment of Frontal Lobe Damage

Considering the number and variety of symptoms associated with frontal lobe damage, surprisingly few standardized neuropsychological tests are useful for assessing frontal lobe function. The available tests (see Table 19-3) are very good, however. As with the parietal and temporal lobe tests discussed in the previous two chapters, it would be highly unusual for a person to perform normally on all these tests if there were damage to either frontal lobe.

The Wisconsin Card-Sorting Test, described earlier (Figure 19-7), is the best available test of dorsolateral frontal cortex function. Briefly, the subject is told to sort the cards into piles in front of one or another of the stimulus cards bearing designs that differ in color, form, and number of elements. The correct solution shifts unbeknownst to the subject once he or she has figured out each solution.

The Semmes Body-Placing Test (Figure 19-8), also described earlier, is a simple, easily administered test of personal spatial orientation. Left frontal lobe patients do more poorly on this test than most other patient groups, the exception being left parietal lobe patients. For this reason the Semmes test should be given in conjunction with a left-right

TABLE 19-3. Standardized clinical neuropsychological tests for frontal lobe damage

Function	Test	Basic reference
Response inhibition	Wisconsin Card Sorting	Milner, 1964
Personal spatial orientation	Semmes Body Placing	Semmes et al., 1963
Verbal fluency	Thurstone Word Fluency	Milner, 1964 Ramier and Hécaen, 1970
Motor	Hand dynamometer Finger tapping Sequencing	Taylor, 1979 Reitan and Davidson, 1974 Kolb and Milner, 1981
Aphasia Language comprehension Spelling Phonetic discrimination	Token test	de Renzi and Faglioni, 1978 Taylor, 1979 Taylor, 1979

differentiation test (see Chapter 17), which often helps to differentiate between patients with lesions of the left frontal lobe and those with left parietal lesions. Although both groups are likely to be impaired at left-right discrimination and perform below control levels, the parietal lobe patients are likely to be reduced to chance performance, whereas the frontal lobe patients are more likely to perform above chance levels.

Recall that the Thurstone Word-Fluency Test (also referred to as the Chicago Word-Fluency Test) requires subjects to say or write as many words as possible beginning with a given letter in 5 min, and then as many four-letter words beginning with a given letter in 4 min. Although subjects with lesions anywhere in the prefrontal cortex are apt to do poorly on this test, subjects with facial-area lesions perform the worst, those with orbital lesions performing only slightly better. Performance is of course poorest when the lesion is in the left hemisphere.

Tests of motor function include tests of strength (hand dynamometer), finger-tapping speed, and movement sequencing. Strength and finger-tapping speed are significantly reduced contralateral to a lesion that is in the vicinity of the precentral or postcentral gyri. Motor sequencing can be assessed by using Kolb and Milner's facial-sequence test, although this test requires considerable practice to administer, and scoring should be from videotaped records. Simpler tests of movement programming such as the Kimura Box Test (Chapter 13) are not suitable because frontal lobe patients are unlikely to perform very poorly unless the lesion extends into the basal ganglia.

As in previous chapters we recommend the token test as a quick screening test for aphasia, to be followed if necessary by more extensive aphasia testing (Chapter 22). Although it is widely believed that damage to Broca's area results in deficits in language production only and not in comprehension, we shall see in Chapter 22 that this is not strictly true. Left frontal lesions in the vicinity of Broca's area produce deficits in comprehension as well as in production. Spelling is seriously impaired by facial-area lesions and can be assessed by any standardized spelling test. Phonetic differentiation, a test described by Stitt and Huntington and used for neurological patients by Taylor, is another means of assessing facial-area function. A series of nonsense words, such as *agma,* is presented and the subject's task is to identify the first consonant sound. This test proves difficult even for controls, but it is most poorly performed by subjects with facial-area damage, especially damage on the left. However, frontal lobe lesions outside the facial area also may impair performance significantly on this test.

In the absence of language deficits it may prove difficult to localize frontal lobe damage in either the left or the right hemisphere with neuropsychological tests, presumably because the two frontal lobes significantly overlap in function. Clinical evaluation of personality as pseudodepressed or pseudopsychopathic (as discussed earlier) may prove useful in localizing the dysfunction to the left or the right hemisphere, respectively, but caution is advised. Unfortunately no standardized quantitative measures of these symptoms are available.

FRONTAL LOBE FUNCTION IN NONHUMANS

An exhaustive survey of the effects of frontal lobe damage in nonhumans being beyond the scope of this book, we shall discuss only the major findings, restricting our discussion largely to monkeys. Before doing so, however, it is of interest that the one obvious difference in the prefrontal cortex of different mammalian species is the size; in animals such as primates and dogs it is large, whereas in animals such as cats and rats it is small. One factor that appears to correlate with the expanse of prefrontal tissue is the complexity of the social interaction between conspecifics (that is, others of the same species). Thus, dogs have a larger expanse of prefrontal cortex than cats, and dogs have a more complex social life than cats. Further, although rats live in social colonies, identification of individual animals in the colony is relatively unimportant, so that contextual cues play an insignificant role in rodent social behavior. It may be, therefore, that a major evolutionary force in the development of the frontal lobe was the development of social groups composed of indentified individuals.

Disturbances of Motor Function

As in the case of humans, damage to the motor cortex of other species leads to a loss of fine movements as well as weakness. Of greater interest are changes in the control of serial order and eye movements (Table 19-4).

Movement Programming. A variety of studies have shown deficits in making complex movements, especially when the animal has supplementary cortex lesions, but there are only a few studies requiring organized movements. Deuel trained monkeys to open a complex latch box. Correct performance of this task required a series of movements, including sliding a bolt along a track, lifting the bolt out, turning a crank 180°, and depressing a knob on the front of a box. To obtain a food reward, the monkeys had to perform these movements correctly and, more importantly, in the correct sequence. Deuel found that small dorsolateral lesions profoundly impaired performance, whereas parietal lobe lesions did not.

Voluntary Gaze. Lesions of the frontal eye fields (area 8) of monkeys impair performance on search tasks analogous to Poppelreuter's search task for humans. More work has been done on the properties of single cells in the frontal eye fields as well as on the effects of stimulating the eye fields. In sum, the results show that this area contains cells responsive to visual stimuli, and cells that discharge before voluntary saccadic movements (i.e., rapid eye movements that function to move the eyes quickly so that particular objects fall on the fovea and thus can be seen in finer detail). Although the frontal eye fields are not necessary for eye movements (animals without a cortex can make rapid eye movements), it seems likely that the frontal eye fields are providing an increased degree of voluntary control, which probably allows increased flexibility in eye movement control so that they are less dependent upon immediate stimuli. That is, saccadic eye movements can probably be made in anticipation of visual events instead of simply in response to them.

Corollary Discharge. There are two sources of evidence that the nonhuman primate frontal lobe plays a role in corollary discharge: studies of frontal eye field cells and experimental use of prisms on the eyes. Bizzi and Schiller, among others, have found that some cells in the frontal eye fields fire simultaneously with movements of the eyes. These cells cannot be causing the eyes to move, for to do so they would have to fire prior to the eye movements (just as to accelerate an automobile you must first depress the gas pedal). Rather, these cells must be monitoring the ongoing movement —a process suspiciously similar to what would be expected from a region involved in corollary discharge.

Further evidence comes from a beautiful experiment by Bossom. In the early 1960s, Held and others performed experiments by fitting prisms to the eyes of animals and humans. As a result, whatever the subject saw was systematically displaced from its true location, all lines appearing subjectively curved and tilted, in keeping with the distortions imposed by the optics of the prism. After the prisms were worn for a few hours the distortions and displacements diminished, and acts such as reaching for objects were performed normally. On abrupt removal of the prisms the distortions were reinstated, requiring readaptation before perception was again normal. An important feature of these experiments was that passively sitting for a few hours did not produce the perceptual change; to induce the adaptation, the individual had to move about in the environment. This requirement implied that adaptation to the prism occurred in the motor system rather than in the sensory systems. With these experiments in mind, Bossom selectively removed frontal, temporal, parietal, or occipital cortex in monkeys to see which lesion, if any, would disrupt prism adaptation. As one would predict from the work of Held, only frontal lesions impaired adaptation to the distorting prisms; parietal, temporal, and occipital lesions did not. Teuber interprets this experiment as showing that corollary discharge is necessary for the adaptation to occur. In other words, the effects of movement must be monitored with respect to sensory input so that the brain can adjust the movements to make them accurate.

Spontaneous Behavior

Behavioral spontaneity in humans was assessed by measuring verbal fluency, design fluency, and spontaneous facial expressions (Table 19-4). It is difficult to find analogies of these behaviors in nonhuman species, although two studies are suggestive. Myers examined the frequency of spontaneous facial expressions and vocalizations in rhesus monkeys. These monkeys have a rich repertory of vocalizations (hoots, howls, etc.) and facial expressions that are as important in social communication as facial expression and certain basic vocalizations (characteristic utterances such as "hmm," crying, laughing, etc.) are among humans. Myers reported that frontal lobe removal resulted in drastically reduced frequencies of facial expressions and vocalizations. Indeed, it was this observation that led Kolb and Milner to study facial expressions in humans with frontal lobe lesions. Unfortunately, because Myers failed to quantify this obser-

TABLE 19-4. Summary of major symptoms of frontal lobe damage in nonhuman primates

Symptom	Lesion site	Basic reference
Disturbances of motor function		
Loss of distal movements	Area 4	Lawrence and Kuypers, 1968
Poor movement programming	DL	Deuel, 1977
Poor voluntary eye gaze	Area 8	Latto, 1978
Poor collorary discharge	DL?	Bossom, 1965
Reduced behavioral spontaneity	Orbital?	Myers, 1972
Environmental control of behavior		
Impaired response inhibition	Orbital	Mishkin, 1964
Poor associative learning	DL	Petrides, 1982
Alterations in mobility	Orbital	Gross and Weiskrantz, 1964
Poor temporal memory		
Poor spatial working memory	Area 46	Funahashi et al., 1986 Passingham, 1985
Poor delayed nonmatching to sample	Medial	Mishkin and Appenzeller, 1987
Poor delayed response	Area 46	Mishkin, 1964
Poor habituation	DL	Butter, 1964
Impaired spatial orientation	DL	Mishkin, 1964
Impaired social and affective behavior	Orbital, DL	Butter and Synder, 1972 Miller, 1976
Impaired olfactory discrimination	Orbital	Tanabe et al., 1975

vation, it is difficult to assess the magnitude of the change in the number of expressions.

MacLean has reported an interesting parallel observation in his studies of squirrel monkeys. These monkeys have a distinctive "cry" that they emit when separated from conspecifics, in addition to a variety of other vocalizations. Removal of midline frontal cortex (roughly areas 24 and 25) abolished separation cries but had no effect on other vocalizations. Removal of the supplementary motor cortex had a transitory effect, much as it does in humans.

Environmental Control

Impaired Response Inhibition and Inflexible Behavior. Impaired response inhibition and inflexible behavior are behavioral deficits analogous to perseveration in card-sorting tasks by humans with frontal lobe damage (Table 19-4). Such behavior is a commonly observed effect of frontal lobe lesions in monkeys and other animals; it can be demonstrated on a wide variety of standard laboratory learning tasks. For example, if an animal is trained to find food under a foodwell located to its left, and the food reward is then shifted to a location under another foodwell to the animal's right, the animal with the frontal lobe lesion persists in looking under the original foodwell. The primary focus for this perseverative response is the orbital-frontal cortex, although this behavior also follows dorsolateral lesions.

Associative Learning. Like humans with frontal lobe lesions, monkeys with such lesions are impaired at learning arbitrary associations between a set of stimuli and a set of responses (Table 19-4). In a monkey analogue of this associative-learning task, which we described earlier, Petrides trained monkeys to make different movements of a lever when presented with different objects. In contrast to his control monkeys, who rapidly acquired the task, monkeys with prefrontal lesions (including area 8 and part of area 6) were unable to learn it, although they were able to master unrelated tasks.

Mobility. Perhaps the oldest established effect of frontal cortex removal in monkeys is an increase in activity, the first report dating back to Robert Ferrier in 1886. Although there are actually few modern studies, the available data appear reliable, showing both rats and monkeys with orbital damage to be excessively active—an effect that is potentiated by food deprivation. Animals with dorsolateral lesions are not normally hyperactive, but they frequently appear hyperreactive to environmental stimuli—a behavioral response that often distracts them while performing neuropsychological tests.

Activity has not been studied systematically in human frontal lobe patients, but in our experience many such patients are hyperactive indeed, and it may present a real challenge to keep them settled in a testing situation. This activity may be indicative of the absence of an internalized control of movement, such that the subjects respond to all the sensory stimuli around them.

Temporal Memory

Perhaps the single most important experimental discovery for understanding the functions of the frontal lobe was Jacobsen's finding that chimpanzees with frontal lobe lesions were impaired at the delayed-response test (see above) (Table 19-4). This single observation led to a new view of the role of the frontal lobes in behavior and began a new field of inquiry. The interpretation of this deficit has been controversial, however, with explanations ranging from deficits in temporal memory (or some related mnemonic process), in attention, in spatial orientation, and in kinesthesis. It is unlikely that the behavioral impairment is due to a single deficit, but as pointed out by others (e.g., Fuster, Goldman-Rakic, Passingham) it is difficult to interpret the deficit without recourse to some sort of memory difficulty. Three additional experiments are especially germane here. First, Passingham presented monkeys with a task in which the animals were required to open each of

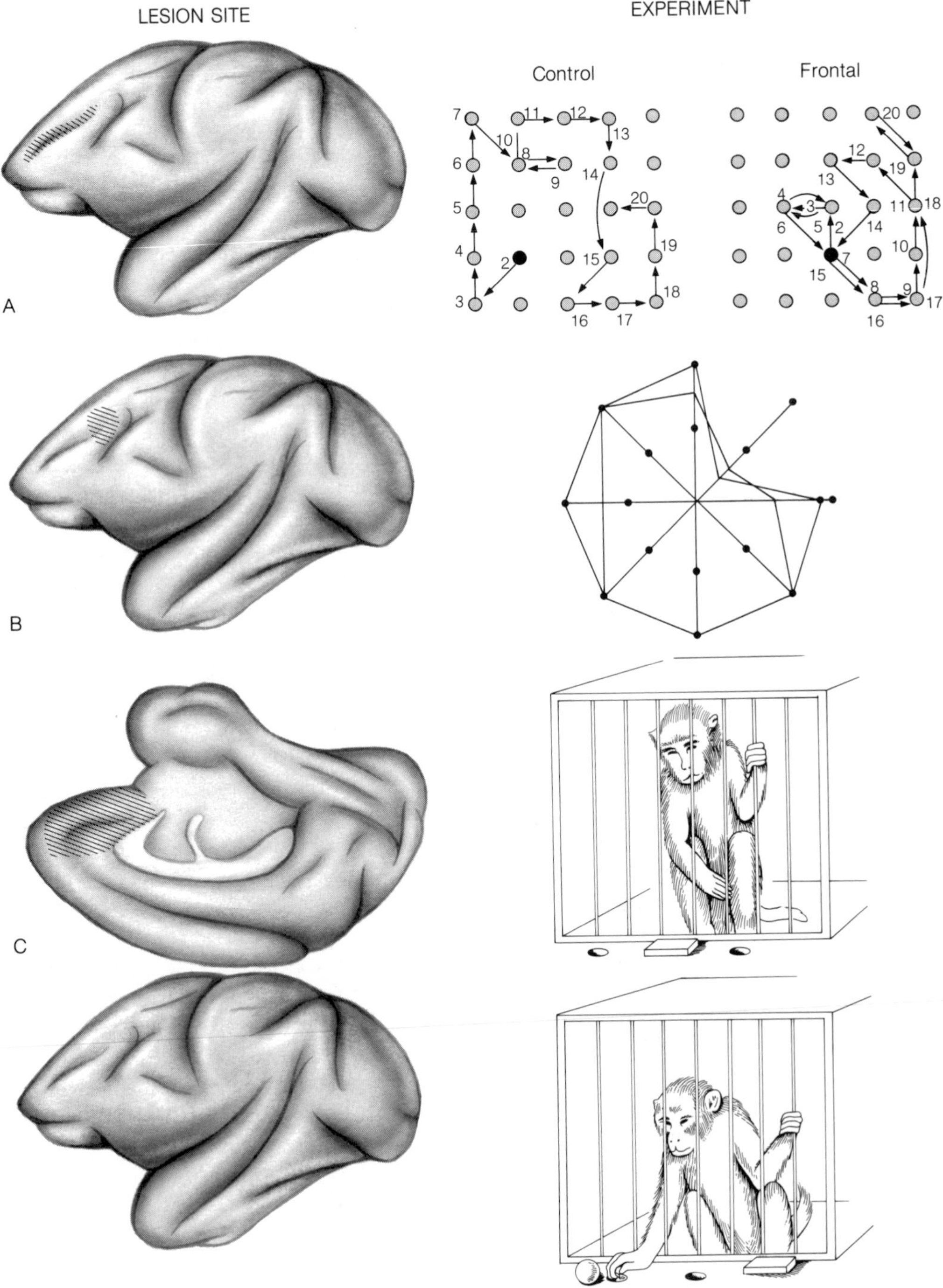
LESION SITE
EXPERIMENT
Control
Frontal
A
B
C

25 doors to obtain a food reward. Food was behind each door only once per day so the animals had to learn not to return to locations where the reward had been obtained already. He found that lesions in area 46 produced marked impairments in this task, much as Petrides and Milner found in their test of self-ordering in humans. Thus, whereas the normal monkeys developed a door-opening strategy that led to few repetitions, the lesioned animals were very inefficient, frequently returning to previously accessed doors (Figure 19-10*A*). In the second experiment, Funahashi, Bruce, and Goldman-Rakic trained monkeys to fixate on a central spot of light while target lights were flashed in different parts of the visual field. The monkeys had to wait for the fixation spot to disappear before moving their eyes to the spot where the target light had been flashed. The researchers found that unilateral lesions in the principal sulcus (part of area 46) impaired the monkey's ability to remember the location of the target in a restricted region of the contralateral visual field, as illustrated in Figure 19-10*B*. They interpret this result as showing that the principal sulcus contains a mechanism for guiding responses on the basis of stored information, which in this case is spatial. The third experiment is one by Mishkin and his colleagues. They trained monkeys in a task known as *delayed nonmatching to sample.* In this test the monkey is confronted with an unfamiliar object, which it displaces to find a reward (Figure 19-10*C*). After a delay the animal sees the same object paired with a new one. The monkey must recognize the object it saw earlier and move the new one instead in order to get a reward. Monkeys with lesions of areas 10 and 32 are impaired at this task. Mishkin interprets this result as showing that this area of frontal cortex participates in the short-term store of this object information.

Taken together, these three experiments point to an unequivocal role of the frontal cortex in some type of short-term memory process, and to the fact that different regions of the prefrontal cortex are involved with the store of different types of information. In view of the anatomical connections (Figure 19-3), it seems likely that area 46 plays a role in providing an internal representation of spatial information, and the medial regions play a similar role with object information. Further support for the role of the sulcus principalis region can be found in the electrophysiological studies showing units in this area that are active during the delay intervals in delayed-response tests, and whose activity ends abruptly when the animal responds. There are neurons in the sulcus principalis that respond selectively to the spatial position of the cues, and one might expect to find similar neurons coding some feature of objects as well.

Habituation is a gradual quantitative response decrement that results from repeated exposure to a stimulus. For example, when one first enters a bakery, the odors are distinctive, but if one works in the same bakery, there is rapid habituation to the odors and they are no longer noticed. A num-

FIGURE 19-10. Schematic illustrations of frontal lesions in monkeys (left side of each figure part). Gray area represents lesion sites in three experiments (right side of each figure) showing a temporal memory deficit. *A*. Passingham's study: the task is to retrieve a food reward from each of 25 boxes, each of which is marked by a circle. Notice that the control animal seldom returns to a previously visited location, whereas the monkey with a sulcus principalis lesion makes numerous errors. *B*. Funahashi et al. study: the task is to fixate at the central point, and then after a brief delay move the eyes to locate a target light flashed at one of the eight endpoints. Correct performance percentage is indicated by the relative positions of the lines along axes drawn through central fixation point. The delay was 3 sec. Note that the monkey performed relatively poorly in one region of the visual field, contralateral to the lesion. Lesions elsewhere in area 46 produced deficits in different regions of the visual field. *C*. Mishkin's study: The monkey is shown an object, which is displaced and food reward obtained. The monkey is then presented with two objects after a short delay; the task is to obtain the reward, which is under the novel object. Monkeys with medial lesions are impaired at this task, which is nonspatial.

ber of studies have suggested that frontal cortex, possibly the dorsolateral region, is involved in normal habituation. Animals with frontal cortex lesions fail to habituate normally, if at all, to novel stimuli or environments, whereas stimulation of the frontal cortex accelerates habituation. Thus, in the absence of frontal cortex the animals' behavior appears stereotyped and repetitive, behavior that may contribute to their increased locomotor activity. Deficits in habituation may also be reducible to changes in short-term memory, although this remains speculation.

Impaired Spatial Orientation

The clear deficits in spatial memory discussed above make it very difficult to determine if there is a spatial-orientation deficit after frontal lesions that is separable from the spatial-memory problems (Table 19-4). Nonetheless, monkeys with frontal lesions are impaired at many tests requiring the use of spatial information, just as people are. It remains to be seen if tests can be devised that will disentangle the spatial-orientation and spatial-memory components to show two independent contributions of the frontal lobe.

Impaired Social Behavior

Several studies show that frontal lobe lesions in monkeys significantly alter social behavior (Table 19-4). In one interesting study Butter and Snyder removed the dominant (so-called alpha) male from each of several groups of monkeys. They removed the frontal lobe from half of these alpha monkeys. When the animals were later returned to their groups, they all resumed the position of dominant male, but within a couple of days all the monkeys without frontal lobes were deposed and fell to the bottom of the group hierarchy.

Analogous studies of wild monkeys have shown similar results: monkeys with frontal lobe lesions fall to the bottom of the group hierarchy and eventually die, because they are helpless alone. It is not known exactly how the social behavior of these animals has changed, but there is little doubt that it is as dramatic as the changes in the social behavior of humans. The social interactions of monkeys are complex and involve a significant amount of context-dependent behavior; the behavior of a monkey will change depending upon the configuration of the proximal social group, and monkeys may lose this ability after frontal lobe lesions. There are likely to be additional components of this behavioral change, however, that relate to the interpretation of species-typical sensory cues, whether they be odors, facial expressions, or sounds.

Impaired Olfaction

There are relatively few studies of olfactory-guided behavior in animals with frontal lesions, but it is known that both rats and monkeys are severely impaired at odor discriminations following orbital-frontal lesions (Table 19-4). In addition, cells have been identified in the orbital gyrus of the monkey that are specific to certain odors. These data add credence to the suggestion that there may be a region in the frontal cortex of mammals that can be considered to be the primary olfactory cortex (see Chapter 10 for details).

OTHER ASPECTS OF FRONTAL LOBE FUNCTION

We have emphasized the results of anatomical and lesion studies in our analysis of frontal lobe function, with passing reference to electrophysiological work. Another way to investigate frontal lobe function is by inference from populations whose frontal lobes might reasonably be believed to be abnormal or at least unlike that of normal adults. This includes both people with diseases affecting the frontal lobe and children whose frontal lobes are not yet mature.

Diseases Affecting the Frontal Lobe

Many of the symptoms of frontal lobe injury are characteristic of people with psychiatric or neurological disorders, including especially schizophrenia (see Chapter 23), Parkinson's disease (see Chapter 13) and Korsakoff's disease (see Chapter 21). In each case there is reason to suppose that the frontal lobes are not functioning normally. Thus, in schizophrenia there is believed to be an abnormality in the mesocortical dopamine projection, which terminates largely in the frontal lobe, a decrease in blood flow to the frontal lobe, and possible frontal lobe atrophy. Schizophrenic patients perform poorly on all tests of frontal lobe function and exhibit abnormalities in control of eye movements, but perform relatively normally on tests of parietal lobe function. Parkinson's disease results from a loss of the dopamine cells of the substantia nigra. Although the primary projection of these cells is the caudate nucleus, there is a direct projection to the prefrontal cortex too and an indirect projection through the dorsomedial nucleus of the thalamus. Parkinson patients are characterized by a lack of facial expression that is similar to that seen in frontal lobe patients and are impaired at the Wisconsin Card-Sorting Test and at delayed response. Finally, patients with Korsakoff's disease suffer from alcohol-induced damage to the **dorsomedial thalamus** and may have a deficiency in catecholamines in the frontal cortex. Korsakoff patients perform poorly on the Wisconsin Card-Sorting Test, as well as on tests of spatial memory such as delayed response. In summary, it seems likely that a disturbance of frontal lobe function contributes significantly to the behavioral symptoms of schizophrenic, Parkinson, and Korsakoff patients.

Frontal Lobe Development

In a study of changes in synaptic density in the prefrontal cortex over a lifespan, Huttenlocher reported that synaptic density increased over the first year of life to a level well above adult levels, and then declined over the next 16 years (Figure 19-11). There was no change over the range between 16 and 72 years in his sample, and a slight decrease in a small sample of 74- to 90-year-old brains. The overproduction of synapses in the infant frontal cortex is typical of other cortical regions, appearing to be a general characteristic of brain development (see Chapter 25 for more details). It has been postulated that cells that fail to make the essential functional synaptic contacts undergo synaptic degeneration, thus eliminating unnecessary redundancy in the brain and improving the efficiency of processing. The slow maturation of the frontal lobe suggests that the temporal organization of behavior may be slow to mature as well, and may not reach maturity until late adolescence. It is difficult to correlate performance on neuropsychological tests with anatomical development because other parts of the brain are developing as well; also, one cannot be certain what role education might play in performance. Nevertheless, we have found that performance on tests like the Wisconsin Card-Sorting Test or tests of design fluency does not reach adult levels until at least 12 years of age, and may be later for tests such as those of design fluency. Further, children do not appear to be socially mature until well into adolescence, and are not recognized as legally competent in most jurisdictions until at least 16 years of age, suggesting that society recognizes the slow development of certain aspects of behavior!

Since one of the most complex aspects of social behavior in primates is its contextual dependence, and given that adults with frontal lobe injuries are particularly poor at this, we asked whether or not children would be able to correctly judge the emotion of people from the context of a situation. To do so, we took advantage of a test we devised to study adult frontal lobe patients. In this test subjects are presented with a series of cartoon situations depicting some emotion-laden situation such as a hold-up, a surprise party, a funeral, and so forth. The face of the key character is left blank and the task is to chose the appropriate expression from a series of facial photographs. Our results showed that although children could match the emotions of people in different photographs as accurately as

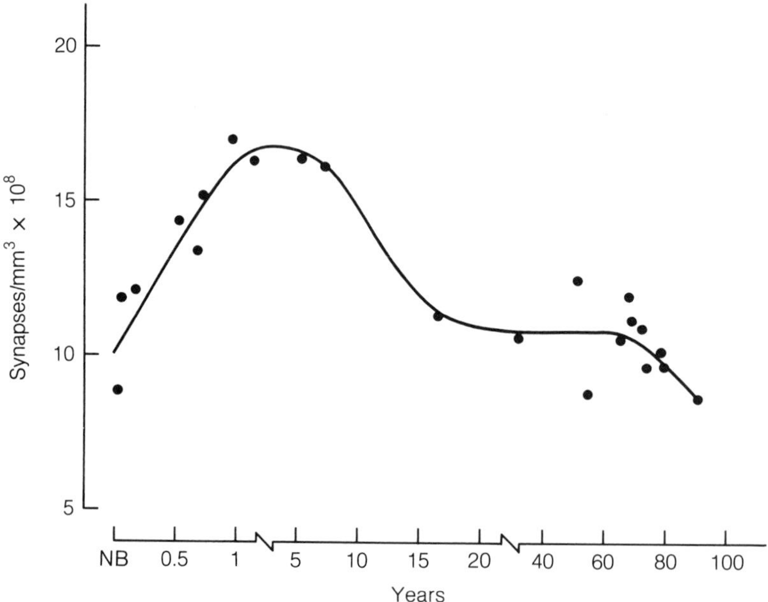

FIGURE 19-11. Synapse counts in layer 3 of the middle frontal gyrus of the human brain as a function of age. The number of synapses increases until 1 year of age and decreases, reaching asymptote at about age 16. There is a further decline in old age, after about age 70. (After Huttenlocher, 1979)

adults by about age 8, they performed as poorly as frontal lobe patients on the contextual test until about age 15. In conclusion, behaviors that would seem to be dependent upon the normal operation of the frontal lobe appear to be slow in developing, as would be predicted from the anatomical studies.

SUMMARY: PARIETAL, TEMPORAL, AND FRONTAL LOBE FUNCTIONS

We began Chapter 17 by asking what cognitive operations are required to account for our behavior. We have seen that damage to the parietal, temporal, and frontal lobes can lead to disturbances of memory, affect, language, spatial orientation, and movement, but that the relative contributions of the three associational zones to these processes is complementary, rather than redundant. Thus, the contribution of the frontal, temporal, and parietal regions to these processes is additive, and probably heirarchical. The fact that behavioral symptoms may be similar after damage to the different regions speaks not to the overlap in functions of the areas but rather to the fact that the same cognitive processes can be disturbed in many ways.

As a general statement it appears that sensory information is divided into spatial and form components and is analyzed by the parietal and temporal regions, respectively. Both spatial and form information then appear to progress to the frontal lobe and medial temporal region, where they must again be reunited. It should be obvious that to study the brain by looking at functional correlates of anatomical regions like the frontal, temporal, or parietal lobe is artificial because we cannot localize memory, spatial behavior, language, affect, or movement in a place in the brain. These inferred cognitive processes are a function of the integrated activity of vast areas of neocortical and subcortical tissue, and are thus subject to disturbance from injury or dysfunction in any of these regions. This is important for we must not be trapped into believing that psychological constructs like spatial behavior or memory will be found in a place in the brain. We shall pursue this line of reasoning further as we look specifically at memory, language, affect, and spatial behavior in Chapters 21–24.

REFERENCES

Benton, A. L. Differential effects of frontal lobe disease. *Neuropsychologia* 6:53–60, 1968.

Bizzi, E., and P. H. Schiller. Single unit activity in the frontal eye fields of unanesthetized monkeys during head and eye movement. *Experimental Brain Research* 10:151–158, 1970.

Blumer, D., and D. F. Benson. Personality changes with frontal and temporal lobe lesions. In D. F. Benson and D. Blumer, eds. *Psychiatric Aspects of Neurologic Disease.* New York: Grune & Stratton, 1975.

Bossom, J. The effect of brain lesions on adaptation in monkeys. *Psychonomic Science* 2:45–46, 1965.

Brown, J. *Aphasia, Apraxia and Agnosia.* Springfield, IL: Charles C. Thomas, 1972.

Bruce, C. J., and M. E. Goldberg. Physiology of the frontal eye fields. *Trends in Neuroscience* 7:436–441, 1984.

Butter, C. M. Habituation of responses to novel stimuli in monkeys with selective frontal lesions. *Science* 144:313–315, 1964.

Butter, C. M., and D. R. Snyder. Alterations in aversive and aggressive behaviors following orbital frontal lesions in rhesus monkeys. *Acta Neurobiologiae Experimentalis* 32:525–565, 1972.

Corkin, S. Tactually guided maze-learning in man: Effects of unilateral cortical excisions and bilateral hippocampal lesions. *Neuropsychologia* 3:339–351, 1965.

Denny-Brown, D. The frontal lobes and their functions. In A. Feilnig, ed. *Modern Trends in Neurology.* New York: Hoeber-Harper, 1961.

Deuel, K. K. Loss of motor habits after cortical lesions. *Neuropsychologia* 15:205–215, 1977.

Drewe, E. A. Go-no-go learning after frontal lobe lesions in humans. *Cortex* 11:8–16, 1975.

Freedman, M., and M. Oscar-Berman. Bilateral frontal lobe disease and selective delayed response deficits in humans. *Behavioral Neuroscience* 100:337–342, 1986.

Freedman, M., and M. Oscar-Berman. Selective delayed response deficits in Parkinson's and Alzheimer's disease. *Archives of Neurology* 43:886–890, 1986.

Funahashi, S., C. J. Bruce, and P. S. Goldman-Rakic. Perimetry of spatial memory representation in primate prefrontal cortex. *Society for Neuroscience Abstracts* 12:554, 1986.

Fuster, J. M. *The Prefrontal Cortex.* New York: Raven Press, 1980.

Fuster, J. M., and R. H. Bauer. Visual short-term memory deficit from hypothermia of frontal cortex. *Brain Research* 81:393–400, 1974.

Goldman-Rakic, P. S. Circuitry of the primate prefrontal cortex and regulation of behavior by representational memory. *Handbook of Physiology*. 373–418, 1987.

Griffin, J. O. Neurophysiological studies into habituation. In G. S. Horn and R. A. Hinde, eds. *Short Term Changes in Neural Activity and Behavior*. New York: Cambridge University Press, 1970.

Gross, C. G., and L. Weiskrantz. Some changes in behavior produced by lateral frontal lesions in the macaque. In J. M. Warren and K. Akert, eds. *The Frontal Granular Cortex and Behavior*. New York: McGraw-Hill, 1964.

Guilford, J. P. *The Nature of Human Intelligence*. New York: McGraw-Hill, 1967.

Guitton, D., H. A. Buchtel, and R. M. Douglas. Disturbances of voluntary saccadic eye-movement mechanisms following discrete unilateral frontal-lobe removals. In G. Lennerstrand, D. S. Lee, and E. L. Keller, eds. *Functional Basis of Ocular Motility Disorders*. Oxford: Pergamon, 1982.

Hebb, D. O. Intelligence in man after large removals of cerebral tissue: Report of four left frontal lobe cases. *Journal of General Psychology* 21:73–87, 1939.

Hécaen, H., and M. L. Albert. Disorders of mental functioning related to frontal lobe pathology. In D. F. Benson and D. Blumer, eds. *Psychiatric Aspects of Neurologic Disease*. New York: Grune & Stratton, 1975.

Held, R. Dissociation of visual function by deprivation and rearrangement. *Psychology Forschung* 31:338–348, 1968.

Huttenlocher, P. R. Synaptic density in human frontal cortex—developmental changes and effects of aging. *Brain Research* 163:195–205, 1979.

Jacobsen, C. F. Studies of cerebral function in primates. *Comparative Psychology Monographs* 13:1–68, 1936.

Jones-Gotman, M., and B. Milner. Design fluency: The invention of nonsense drawings after focal cortical lesions. *Neuropsychologia* 15:653–674, 1977.

Kolb, B. Functions of the frontal cortex of the rat: A comparative review. *Brain Research Reviews* 8:65–98, 1984.

Kolb, B., and B. Milner. Observations on spontaneous facial expression after focal cerebral excisions and after intracarotid injection of sodium Amytal. *Neuropsychologia* 19:514–515, 1981.

Kolb, B., and B. Milner. Performance of complex arm and facial movements after focal brain lesions. *Neuropsychologia* 19:505–514, 1981.

Kolb, B., and L. Taylor. Affective behavior in patients with localized cortical excisions: An analysis of lesion site and side. *Science* 214:89–91, 1981.

Konorski, J., H.-L. Teuber, and B. Zernicki. The frontal granular cortex and behavior. *Acta Neurobiologiae Experimentalis* 32:119–656, 1972.

Kuypers, H. G. J. M. Anatomy of the descending pathways. In V. B. Brooks, ed. *The Nervous System, Handbook of Physiology,* vol 2. Baltimore: Williams and Wilkins, 1981.

Lashley, K. S. The problem of serial order in behavior. In F. A. Beach, D. O. Hebb, C. T. Morgan, and H. W. Nissen, eds. *The Neuropsychology of Lashley*. New York: McGraw-Hill, 1960.

Latto, R. The effects of bilateral frontal eye-field, posterior parietal or superior collicular lesions on visual search in the rhesus monkey. *Brain Research* 146:35–50, 1978.

Lawrence, D. G., and H. G. J. M. Kuypers. The functional organization of the motor system in the monkey. I. The effects of bilateral pyramidal lesions. *Brain* 91:1–14, 1968.

Leonard, G., L. Jones, and B. Milner. Residual impairment in handgrip strength after unilateral frontal-lobe lesions. *Neuropsychologia* 26:555–564, 1988.

Luria, A. R. *The Working Brain.* New York: Penguin, 1973.

Luria, A. R., and E. D. Homskaya. Disturbance in the regulative role of speech with frontal lobe lesions. In J. M. Warren and K. A. Kert, eds. *Frontal Granular Cortex and Behavior.* New York: McGraw-Hill, 1964.

MacLean, P. D. The midline frontolimbic cortex and the evolution of crying and laughter. In E. Perecman, ed. *The Frontal Lobes Revisted.* New York: IBRN Press, 1987.

Markowitsch, H. J., and M. Pritzel. Comparative analysis of prefrontal learning functions in rats, cats and monkeys. *Psychological Bulletin* 84:817–837, 1977.

Miller, L. Cognitive risk taking after frontal or temporal lobectomy. I. The synthesis of fragmented visual information. *Neuropsychologia* 23:359–369, 1985.

Miller, L., and B. Milner. Cognitive risk taking after frontal or temporal lobectomy. II. The synthesis of phonemic and semantic information. *Neuropsychologia* 23:371–379, 1985.

Miller, M. H. Dorsolateral frontal lobe lesions and behavior in the macaque: Dissociation of threat and aggression. *Physiology and Behavior* 17:209–213, 1976.

Milner, B. Some effects of frontal lobectomy in man. In J. M. Warren and K. Akert, eds. *The Frontal Granular Cortex and Behavior.* New York: McGraw-Hill, 1964.

Milner, B. Hemispheric specialization: Scope and limits. In F. O. Schmitt and F. G. Worden, eds. *The Neurosciences: Third Study Program.* Cambridge, MA: M.I.T. Press, 1974.

Milner, B. Some cognitive effects of frontal-lobe lesions in man. *Philosophical Transactions of the Royal Society of London* B298:211–226, 1982.

Milner, B., and M. Petrides. Behavioural effects of frontal-lobe lesions in man. *Trends in Neursciences* 7:403–407, 1984.

Milner, B., M. Petrides, and M. L. Smith. Frontal lobes and the temporal organization of memory. *Human Neurobiology* 4:137–142, 1985.

Mishkin, M. Perseveration of central sets after frontal lesions in monkeys. In J. M. Warren and K. Akert, eds. *The Frontal Granular Cortex and Behavior.* New York: McGraw-Hill, 1964.

Mishkin, M., and T. Appenzeller. The anatomy of memory. *Scientific American* 256:80–89, 1987.

Mishkin, M., and F. J. Manning. Non-spatial memory after selective prefrontal lesions in monkeys. *Brain Research* 143:313–323, 1978.

Myers, R. E. Role of the prefrontal and anterior temporal cortex in social behavior and affect in monkeys. *Acta Neurobiologiae Experimentalis* 32:567–579, 1972.

Orgogozo, J. M., and B. Larsen. Activation of the supplementary motor area during voluntary movement in man suggests it works as a supramotor area. *Science* 206:847–850, 1979.

Pandya, D. N., and E. H. Yeterian. Architecture and connections of cortical association areas. In A. Peters and E. G. Jones, eds. *Cerebral Cortex* 4:3–62, 1985.

Passingham, R. Information about movements in monkeys *(Macaca mulatta). Brain Research* 152:313–328, 1978.

Passingham, R. E. Memory of monkeys *(Macaca mulatta)* with lesions in prefrontal cortex. *Behavioral Neuroscience* 99:3–21, 1985.

Penfield, W., and J. Evans. The frontal lobe in man: A clinical study of maximum removals. *Brain* 58:115–133, 1935.

Perret, E. The left frontal lobe of man and the suppression of habitual responses in verbal categorical behavior. *Neuropsychologia* 12:323–330, 1974.

Petrides, M. Motor conditional associative learning after selective prefrontal lesions in the monkey. *Behavioural Brain Research* 5:407–413, 1982.

Petrides, M., and B. Milner. Deficits on subject ordered tasks after frontal- and temporal-lobe lesions in man. *Neuropsychologia* 20:249–262, 1982.

Poppelreuter, W. *Die psychischen Schädigungen durch Kopfschuss im Kriege 1914/16,* vol. 1. Leipzig: Leopold Voss Verlag, 1917.

Potter, H., and N. Butters. An assessment of olfactory deficits in patients with damage to prefrontal cortex. *Neuropsychologia* 18:621–628, 1980.

Ramier, A.-M., and H. Hécaen. Role respectif des atteintes frontales et de la lateralisation lésionnelle dans les deficits de la "fluence verbale." *Revue de Neurologie* 123:17–22, 1970.

Reitan, R. M., and L. A. Davison. *Clinical Neuropsychology.* New York: John Wiley, 1974.

Renzi, E. de, and P. Faglioni. Normative data and screening power of a shortened version of the token test. *Cortex* 14:41–49, 1978.

Roland, P. E. Metabolic measurements of the working frontal cortex in man. *Trends in Neuroscience* 7:430–435, 1984.

Roland, P. E., B. Larsen, N. A. Lassen, and E. Skinhøj. Supplementary motor area and other cortical areas in organization of voluntary movements in man. *Journal of Neurophysiology* 43:118–136, 1980.

Rose, J. E., and C. N. Woolsey. The orbitofrontal cortex and its connections with the mediodorsal nucleus in rabbit, sheep and cat. *Research Publications of the Association of Nervous and Mental Disease* 27:210–232, 1948.

Rosvold, H. E., and M. Mishkin. Evaluation of the effects of prefrontal lobotomy on intelligence. *Canadian Journal of Psychology* 4:122–126, 1950.

Ruch, T. C., and H. A. Shenkin. The relation of area 13 on the surface of the frontal lobes to hyperactivity and hyperphagia in monkeys. *Journal of Neurophysiology* 6:349–360, 1943.

Semmes, J., S. Weinstein, L. Ghent, and H.-L. Teuber. Impaired orientation in personal and extrapersonal space. *Brain* 86:747–772, 1963.

Shallice, T. Specific impairments of planning. *Philosophical Transactions of the Royal Society, London* B298:199–209, 1982.

Shallice, T., and M. E. Evans. The involvement of the frontal lobes in cognitive estimation. *Cortex* 14:294–303, 1978.

Smith, M. L., and B. Milner. Differential effects of frontal-lobe lesions on cognitive estimation and spatial memory. *Neuropsychologia* 22:697–705, 1984.

Stitt, C., and D. Huntington. Some relationships among articulation, auditory abilities and certain other variables. *Journal of Speech and Hearing Research* 12:576–593, 1969.

Tanabe, T., H. Yarita, M. Iino, Y. Ooshima, and S. F. Takagi. An olfactory projection area in orbitofrontal cortex of the monkey. *Journal of Neurophysiology* 38:1269–1283, 1975.

Taylor, L. Psychological assessment of neurosurgical patients. In T. Rasmussen and R. Marino, eds. *Functional Neurosurgery.* New York: Raven Press, 1979.

Teuber, H.-L. The riddle of frontal lobe function in man. In J. M. Warren and K. Akert, eds. *The Frontal Granular Cortex and Behavior.* New York: McGraw-Hill, 1964.

Teuber, H.-L. Unity and diversity of frontal lobe function. *Acta Neurobiologiae Experimentalis* 32:615–656, 1972.

Teuber, H.-L., and M. Mishkin. Judgment of visual and postural vertical after brain injury. *Journal of Psychology* 38:161–175, 1954.

Tyler, H. R. Disorders of visual scanning with frontal lobe lesions. In S. Locke, ed. *Modern Neurology*. London: J. and A. Churchill, 1969.

Walker, E. A., and D. Blumer. The localization of sex in the brain. In K. J. Zulch, O. Creutzfeldt, and G. C. Galbraith, eds. *Cerebral Localization*. Berlin and New York: Springer-Verlag, 1975.

Warren, J. M., and K. Akert, eds. *The Frontal Granular Cortex and Behavior*. New York: McGraw-Hill, 1964.

Zangwill, O. L. Psychological deficits associated with frontal lobe lesions. *International Journal of Neurology* 5:395–402, 1966.

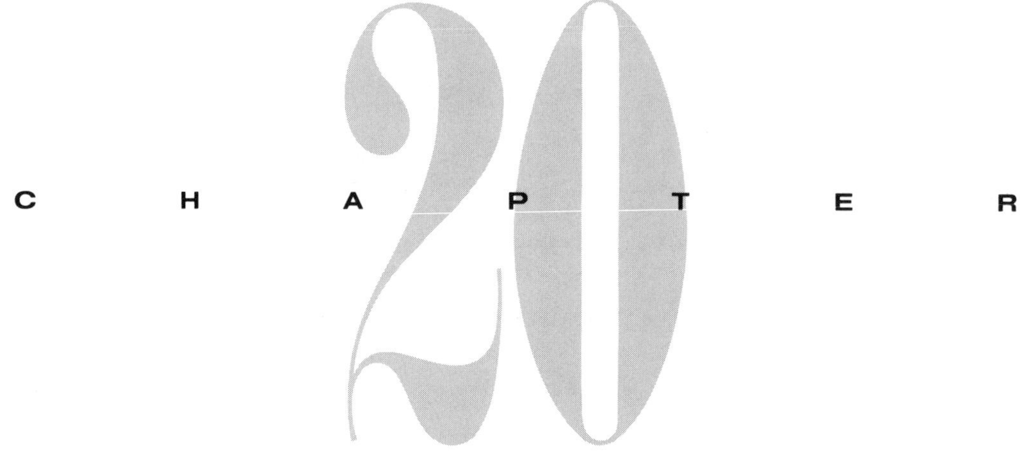

CHAPTER 20

DISCONNECTION SYNDROMES

Disconnection refers to the process of severing the connections between two areas without damaging the areas themselves. The behavioral changes that result can be rather odd and different from what could be expected if the area itself was damaged. Figure 20-1 presents Downer's experiment on a monkey that had received two forms of disconnection. All of the commissures connecting the two halves of the brain were cut. The amygdala on one side was removed. Downer then covered one of the animal's eyes with an occluder and presented objects to it. If the objects were presented to the eye ipsilateral to the hemisphere with the ablated amygdala, the animal appeared "tame," even if the objects were ones that were frightening to monkeys. If the objects were presented to the eye ipsilateral to the intact amygdala, the animals made their usual species-typical responses and appeared "wild." The explanation of the results is as follows. In order to display species-typical behavior to a visual stimulus, the information must be projected from the eye to visual cortex, through the temporal lobes to the amygdala, and from the amygdala to the brainstem and frontal cortex, where autonomic responses, movements, and facial expressions, respectively, are activated. With the commissures between the two halves of the brain disconnected, visual information can only project from an eye to the ipsilateral hemisphere. If that hemisphere contains an intact amygdala, the circuit for activating species-typical behaviors is complete and behavior will be normal. If the hemisphere does not have an intact amygdala, visual information will be disconnected from motor systems and will not be able to elicit species-typical behavior. Had the commissures not been cut, the experiment would not work because information from one hemisphere would be able to cross to the other and each eye would thus have access to the intact amygdala.

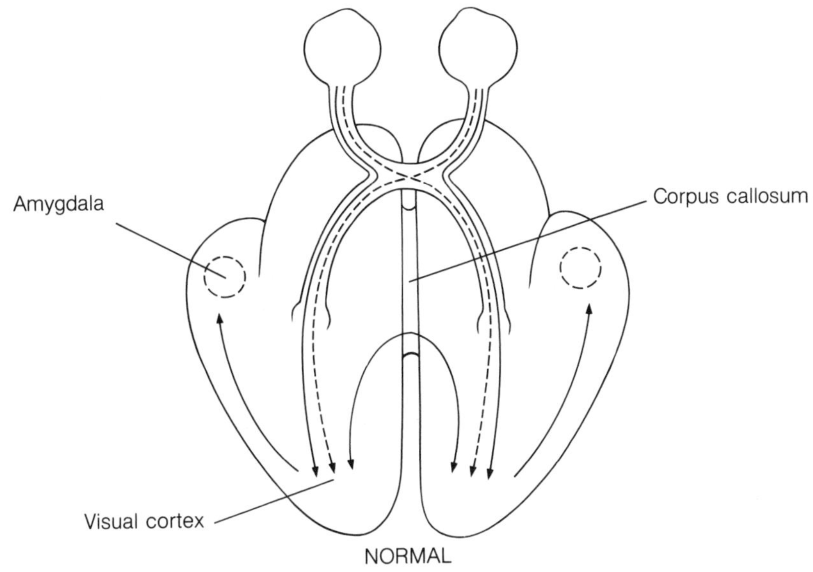

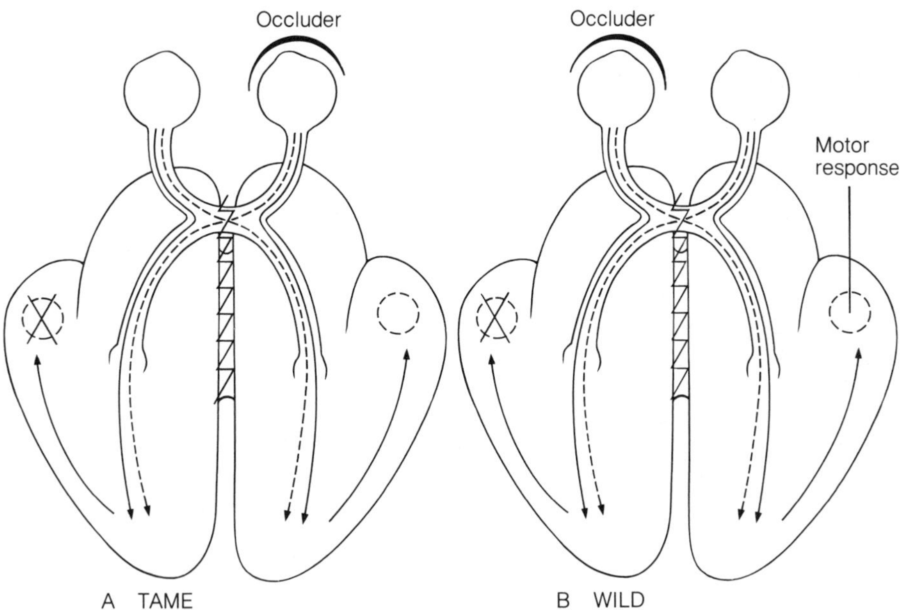

FIGURE 20-1. Downer's experiment. *A.* The commissures between the two halves of the brain are severed, the amygdala on the left is removed, and an occluder covers the right eye. The monkey displays no species-typical behaviors to visual stimuli and is described as "tame." *B.* The left eye is occluded, and in response to visual stimuli the monkey displays species-typical behavior and is classified as "wild."

So far we have emphasized the importance of neocortical and subcortical regions in controlling various aspects of behavior. We have associated particular behavioral deficits with different brain lesions and from these deficits have tried to infer the function of the missing region. In looking at brain function in this way we have postponed discussion of the function of the connections between various regions. In this chapter we consider the function of those various cerebral connections and the effects of cutting them. This process of cutting connections is called *disconnection,* and the ensuing behavioral effects are therefore called *disconnection syndromes.* We begin by reviewing the major connections at the cerebral hemispheres.

ANATOMY OF CEREBRAL CONNECTIONS

There are three major types of fiber connections of the neocortex: association, projection, and commissural fibers (see Chapter 1).

Association Fibers

Two types of association fibers can be distinguished: (1) long fiber bundles that connect distant neocortical areas, and (2) short subcortical U-fibers that connect adjacent neocortical areas. The long fiber bundles include the **uncinate fasciculus,** the superior longitudinal fasciculus, the cingulum, the inferior longitudinal fasciculus, and the inferior frontal-occipital fasciculus.

Projection Fibers

Projection fibers include ascending fibers from lower centers to the neocortex, such as projections from the thalamus, as well as descending fibers from the neocortex to the brainstem and spinal cord.

Commissural Fibers

Commissural fibers primarily function to join the two hemispheres and include principally the corpus callosum, anterior commissure, and hippocampal commissures. The **corpus callosum** (for hard body, from the Latin *callus*) provides the major connection of neocortical areas. In humans it is made up of from 200 million to 800 million fibers, about half of which are unmyelinated and are quite small. Most, but not all areas of the two hemispheres are connected. Figure 20-2 illustrates the patterns of connections between the hemispheres in a rhesus monkey. In rodents almost all cortical areas are connected but the more selective pattern illustrated in this figure is probably representative of humans. Most of area 17, primary visual cortex (V), is devoid of interhemispheric connections, except that portion representing the visual meridian. This has been explained in functional terms: this cortex represents the visual world topographically, and there is no necessity for one half of the representation to be connected to the other. The motor and sensory areas for distal portions of the limbs (mainly the hands and feet) also have no connections. It could be argued that since their essential function is to work independently of each other, connections are not necessary. Among the areas that do receive interhemispheric connections, the density of projections is not homogeneous. Areas of the cortex that represent the midline of the body, such as the central meridian of the visual fields, auditory fields, and trunk of the body on the somatosensory and motor representations have the densest connections. The functional utility of this arrangement is that movements of the body or actions in central space require interhemispheric cooperation. A prominent working hypothesis concerning callosal function is the "zip-

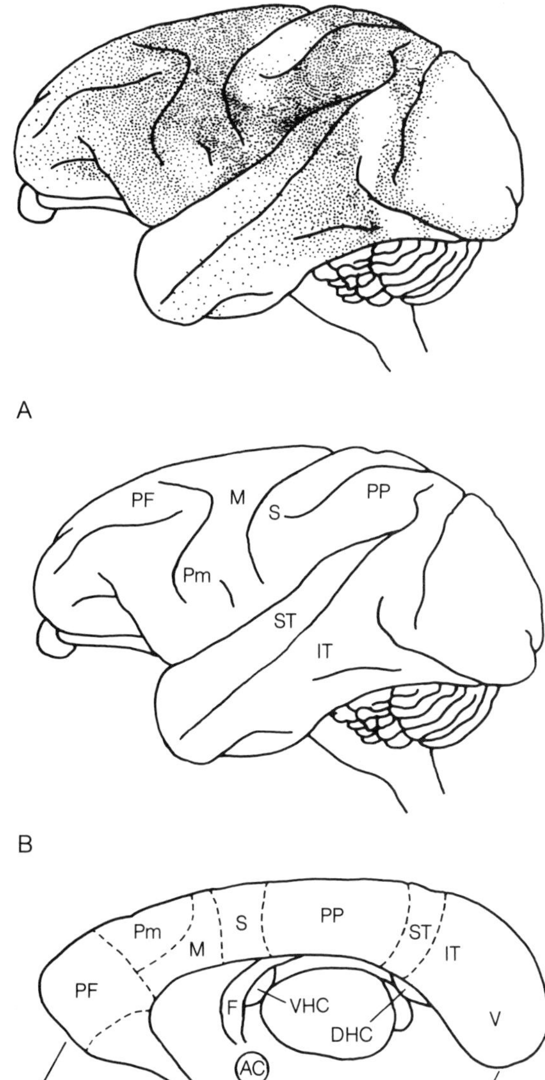

FIGURE 20-2. *A.* The gray areas indicate regions of the cortex of a rhesus monkey that receive projections from the contralateral hemisphere. *B.* Locations (indicated by letters) in which radioactive label was injected (PF, prefrontal cortex; PM, premotor cortex; M, motor cortex; S, sensory cortex, PP, posterior parietal cortex; ST, superior temporal gyrus; IT, inferior temporal gyrus; V, visual cortex (18, 19). *C.* Regions of the corpus callosum showing zones through which label was transported after injections into the cortex (F, fornix; AC, anterior commissure; VHC, ventral hippocampal commisure; DHC dorsal hippocampal commissure). (After Pandya and Seltzer, 1986.)

per'' hypothesis, which suggests that the corpus callosum knits together the representations of the midpoints of the body and space that are divided by the longitudinal fissure.

The connections of the corpus callosum appear to fall into three general classes. (1) Most of the projections are topographic. That is, they go to identical points in the contralateral hemisphere. Presumably these projections knit the two areas together functionally. (2) A second group of projections go to areas to which the homotopic area on the contralateral side projects. Thus, projection zones within a hemisphere also maintain close relations with parallel zones in the contralateral hemisphere. (3) A third group of projections have a quite diffuse terminal distribution. It is possible that these projections alert the appropriate zones of one hemisphere that the other is active. An important aspect of callosal connections is that they go to columns that interlock with hemispheric projections.

The location of fiber projections within the corpus callosum is quite precise. The pattern in the rhesus monkey is illustrated in Figure 20-2*B* and 20-2*C*. The anterior portion of the corpus callosum is called the **genu** (the knee), and it contains the fibers from prefrontal cortex. Fibers through the body of the corpus callosum are respectively, from front to back, from the premotor, motor, somatosensory, and posterior parietal cortex. Fibers in the posterior portion or **splenium** are from superior temporal, inferior temporal, and visual cortex.

The **anterior commissure** is much smaller

than the corpus callosum and functions to connect portions of the anterior temporal lobe, the amygdala, and the paleocortex of the temporal lobe surrounding the amygdala. In humans born with no corpus callosum (a condition called **agenesis of the corpus callosum**), the anterior commissure is greatly enlarged to connect far greater regions of the neocortex.

THE BEHAVIORAL EFFECTS OF DISCONNECTION

Colonnier recounts the interesting story in which Monsieur de la Peyronie in 1741 reviewed all of the literature concerning areas claimed to be the seat of the soul, dismissing each claim in turn. Peyronie then went on to recount some of his own patients cases from which he claimed "whereby it appears that the corpus callosum cannot be either compressed, sphacelated [affected with gangrene] or otherwise injured, but for both reason and all sensations are abolished" (p. 35), from all of which he concluded that the corpus callosum must necessarily be the immediate seat to the soul. Colonnier then notes that by 1941 McCulloch and Garol reviewed the literature and concluded that few impairments could be found after callosum damage except perhaps in complicated symbolic activity.

The clinical effects of disconnection, however, were first seriously considered by Karl Wernicke in 1874 and were very much a part of early neurology. He predicted the existence of an aphasic syndrome (**conduction aphasia**) that would result from severing fiber connections between the anterior and posterior speech zones. Later, in 1892, J. Dejerine was the first to demonstrate a distinctive behavioral deficit resulting from pathology of the corpus callosum. In a series of papers published around 1900 Hugo Liepmann most clearly demonstrated the importance of severed connections as an underlying factor in the effects of cerebral damage. Having carefully analyzed the behavior of a particular patient, Liepmann predicted a series of disconnections of the neocortex that could account for the behaviors. In 1906, after the patient died, Liepmann published the postmortem findings, which supported his hypothesis. He wrote extensively on the principle of disconnection, particularly with respect to the idea that some apraxias might result from disconnection. He reasoned that if a patient were given a verbal command to use the left hand in a particular way, only the verbal left hemisphere would understand the command. To move the left hand a signal would then have to travel from the left hemisphere through the corpus callosum to the right hemispheric region that controls movements of the left hand, as illustrated in Figure 20-3. Interrupting the portion of the corpus callosum that carried the command from the left hemisphere to the right would disconnect the right hemisphere's motor region from the command. Thus, although the subject comprehended the command, the left hand would be unable to obey it (see Figure 20-3*B*). This apraxia would occur in the absence of weakness or incoordination of the left hand, as would occur if there were a lesion in the motor cortex of the right hemisphere, which controls the actual movement of the left hand.

Liepmann's deduction, although brilliant, was ignored for a number of reasons. First, it was published in German and so was not widely read by English-speaking neurologists; Liepmann's papers have only recently been translated into English by Doreen Kimura. Second, except in the extremely unusual case of a patient with a natural lesion of only the corpus callosum, any observed behavioral deficits could be attributed to damage of gray matter itself without reference to connections. Third, a large number of animal studies consistently purported to demonstrate that no significant behavioral effects followed the cutting of the corpus callosum. Not until the late 1950s and

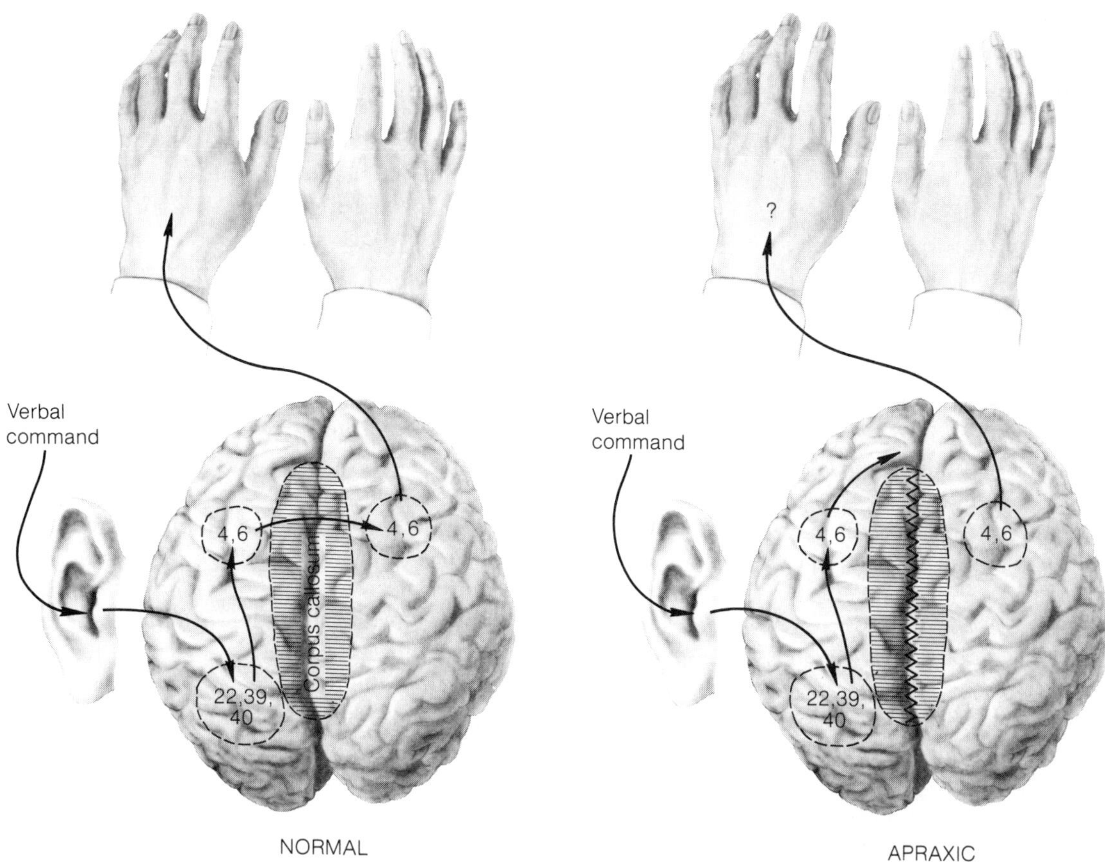

FIGURE 20-3. Liepmann's theory of apraxia resulting from lesions of the corpus callosum. (The jagged line in *B.* indicates section of the callosum.) The verbal command has no way of reaching the motor cortex (area 4) of the right hemisphere to move the left hand. Geschwind proposed that bilateral apraxia could result from a lesion disconnecting the posterior speech zone (areas 22, 39, 40) from the motor cortex of the left hemisphere. In this case the verbal command cannot gain access to either the left or right motor cortex.

1960s did it become clear that the results from the animal studies could be largely attributed to crude behavioral testing.

An important series of papers by Myers and by Sperry in the early 1950s revived interest in the effects of disconnecting neocortical regions. They examined the behavioral effects of severing the corpus callosum of cats. Their work confirmed others' earlier observations that the animals were virtually indistinguishable from their surgically intact counterparts, and indeed appeared normal under most tests and training conditions. Unlike the previous studies, however, their studies revealed that under special training procedures the animals could be shown to have severe deficits. Thus, if the sensory information were allowed separate access to each hemisphere, each could be shown to have its own independent perceptual, learning, and memory processes. Myers' and Sperry's remarkable results were quickly duplicated by dozens of laboratories around the world. The corpus callosum did indeed have an important function. This conclusion has been clearly demonstrated in the subsequent studies by Sperry and his colleagues on the effects of surgical disconnection of the cerebral hemispheres of humans for the treatment of intractable epilepsy (see Chapter 15).

The success of the Myers and Sperry experiments stimulated interest in other connections of the brain. Geschwind began to reassess the clinical effects of naturally occurring neocortical lesions as possibly indicating disconnection of various regions of the cerebral hemispheres. In parallel work, Mishkin began to construct animal models of human disconnection syndromes; by disconnecting related neocortical regions from one another. They have demonstrated the critical interdependence of these regions.

In fact, the anatomical organization of the neocortex allows for relatively easy disconnection. First, the primary sensory areas have no direct connections between each other and so can quite easily be disconnected. Second, even in higher order sensory zones, there are few if any direct connections between sensory systems, so that they can be quite easily disconnected. Third, since the hemispheres are in large part duplicates, and connected by only a few projection systems, they are easy to separate and are sometimes found separated congenitally. In the remainder of this chapter we first discuss the work of Sperry on the "split-brain" patient, who provides an excellent model of disconnection syndromes. Next we reconsider Geschwind's reinterpretation of three classic symptoms of cortical damage (aphasia, apraxia, and agnosia) as disconnection syndromes. Finally, we briefly study Mishkin's animal models of disconnection in the visual and somesthetic systems, the only systems that have been studied in this way to date.

HEMISPHERIC DISCONNECTION

There are three conditions in which the hemispheres become completely separated. First, in humans, the interhemispheric fibers are sometimes cut as a therapy for epilepsy. Second, people are born with congenitally reduced or completely missing interhemispheric connections. Third, in animals, disconnections are performed to trace functional systems, to model human conditions, and to answer basic questions about interhemispheric development.

Epileptic seizures may begin in a restricted region of one hemisphere (most frequently the temporal lobes) and then spread via the fibers of the corpus callosum or anterior commissure to the homologous location in the opposite hemisphere. These seizures can usually be controlled by anticonvulsant medication, but in some cases the medication is of little value, and the seizures may actually become life-threatening because they recur often, sometimes several times in an hour. To relieve this seizure condition, the corpus callosum and anterior commissure can be surgically sectioned to prevent the spread of abnormal electrical activity from one hemisphere to the other. Patients who have received this treatment obtain substantial relief from their epilepsy and frequently show marked improvements in personal well-being, competency, and intelligence. The reason for a congenital lack of interhemispheric connections is not known. Interestingly, albinos of nearly all species and Siamese cats have peculiarities in fiber crossings, mostly a reduced number of uncrossed fibers in the visual system. A number of summaries of research on interhemispheric connections have been published including one by Steele Russel, and colleagues in 1979 and another by Lepore and associates in 1986.

Commissurotomy

Commissurotomy refers to the process of cutting the cerebral commissures as elective surgery for the treatment of epilepsy. The surgeons Philip Vogel and Joe Bogen at the White Memorial Medical Center in Los Angeles reintroduced this technique, and the results of Sperry and his coworkers with their "split-brain" patients are now well known. As a result of the surgery each hemisphere receives fibers that allows it to see only the opposite side of the visual world. Likewise, each hemisphere predominantly receives information from the opposite sides of the body and controls movements on the opposite side of the body. The surgery also isolates speech in those individuals with lateralized speech. Consequently, the dominant hemisphere (usually the left) is able to speak and the nondominant hemisphere is not. Usually about a year or so is required for recovery from the surgical trauma. Within two years the typical patient is able to return to school, household duties, or work. A typical medical examination would not reveal anything unusual in their behavior, and their scores on standard tests are normal. The patients' everyday behavior appears similar to that of normal unified individuals.

Specific tests, however, can show differences in their functioning from that of intact people. Each hemisphere can be shown to have its own sensations, percepts, thoughts, and memories that are not accessible to the other hemisphere. Usual testing procedures involve presenting stimuli to one hemisphere and then testing each hemisphere for what transpired. For example, a person who is asked to touch an object out of view with one hand and then find a similar object with the other hand is unable to correctly match the objects. Odors presented to one nostril cannot be matched with the other, objects seen in one visual field cannot be recognized in the other, and so on. Although the hemispheres function independently, they both do so at a high level. High levels of function even apply to language skills. The nondominant hemisphere although unable to speak, can understand instructions, read written words, match pictures to words, and go from written to spoken words. Language ability is best for nouns and poorer for verbs. The nondominant hemisphere also performs in a superior fashion on a variety of spatial tasks, including copying designs, reading faces, fitting forms into molds, and so on. The nondominant hemisphere also has a concept of self. It can recognize and identify social relations, pictures of the person, pictures of family members, acquaintances, pets and belongings, and historical and social figures. Each hemisphere also has a general awareness of body states like those involved in hunger and fatigue.

Callosal Agenesis and Early Transections

Exceptions to the pattern of results obtained with adult commissurotomy patients are found in individuals who are born without a corpus callosum. These patients are able to perform interhemispheric comparisons of visual and tactile information. The interpretation of these results is that they have enhanced conduction in the remaining commissures (e.g., for vision) and that they develop enhanced abilities to use their few uncrossed projections (tactile). These patients are not without deficits in some features of the tasks, however. There are a number of reports of poor transfer of information if stimuli are complex. Furthermore, nonspecific deficits in task performance have been reported in these patients. Lassonde presented pairs of stimuli to six patients with agenesis of the corpus callosum, asking them if the pairs were the same or different. Letters, numbers, colors, or forms were used. The pairs were presented one on top of the other in one visual field (intrahemispheric task), or one stimulus was presented in one visual field and the other stimulus was presented in the other visual field (interhemispheric task). The acallosal group were as accurate in identifying same-different pairs in either condition. Their reaction times, however, were very slow for both forms of presentation. Lassonde suggests that the callosum participates in hemispheric activation as well as transfer of information. Thus, the acallosal group has alternative ways of obtaining interhemispheric transfer of information but not of activation.

A particularly interesting question, using agenesis patients, has been discussed by Jeeves. This concerns the development of language laterality and other asymmetries. One explanation of why language is lateralized to one hemisphere is that it gets a start there and then that hemisphere actively inhibits its development in the other hemisphere. Of course in individuals with callosal agenesis, the opportunity for such an inhibitory process to work is much reduced. Where do they develop language? The answer seems to be that a significant number of them have language and other functions lateralized similarly to the general population. They also tend to be right-handed, as is the general population. This indicates that the corpus callosum and other commissures are not necessary for the development of asymmetries. This is rather startling when one considers that each hemisphere might have every reason for needing to speak.

There are similarities in the effects of callosal agenesis and the effects of transections made early in life. Lassonde and coworkers compared the performance of five children aged 6 to 16 years on interhemispheric transfer of tactile information and motor learning. The younger children were found to be less affected by the transections than the older children. The researchers suggest that the younger children come to rely on ipsilateral pathways to obtain information and execute movements. That older children are more impaired, suggests that if transections occur early there are possibilities that ipsilateral pathways make new connections, become functionally validated, or simply become more sensitive. There are of course possibilities that the younger children had better represented bilateral speech; however, evidence for greater bilateral speech was not persuasive. There has been some suggestion that the anterior commissure or other commissures could substitute for the corpus callosum, but apparently the somatosensory system does not send projections through other commissures.

SYSTEMS DISCONNECTION

From Liepmann's early theorizing it should be possible to demonstrate conditions such as apraxias in patients with callosal surgery. Sperry, Gazzaniga, and others have extensively studied the effects of hemispheric disconnection on behaviors related to both sensory and motor systems.

Olfaction

Unlike all the other senses, the olfactory system is not crossed. The input from the left nostril goes straight back to the left hemisphere, and the input from the right nostril goes to the right hemisphere. Fibers traveling through the anterior commissure 'join the olfactory regions in each hemisphere, just as fibers traveling through the corpus callosum join the motor cortex of each hemisphere.

If the anterior commissure is severed, odors presented to the right nostril cannot be named, because the left hemisphere, where speech is centered, is disconnected from the information. Similarly, the right hemisphere has the information but has no control of speech. The olfactory function is still intact, however, because the patient can use the left *hand* to pick out an object, such as an orange, that corresponds to the odor smelled. In this case, no connection with speech is necessary, the right hemisphere both containing the olfactory information and controlling the left hand. If requested to use the right hand, the patient would be unable to pick out the object because the left hemisphere, which controls the right hand, is disconnected from the sensory information. Thus, the patient appears normal with one hand and **anosmic** with the other (See Figure 20-4).

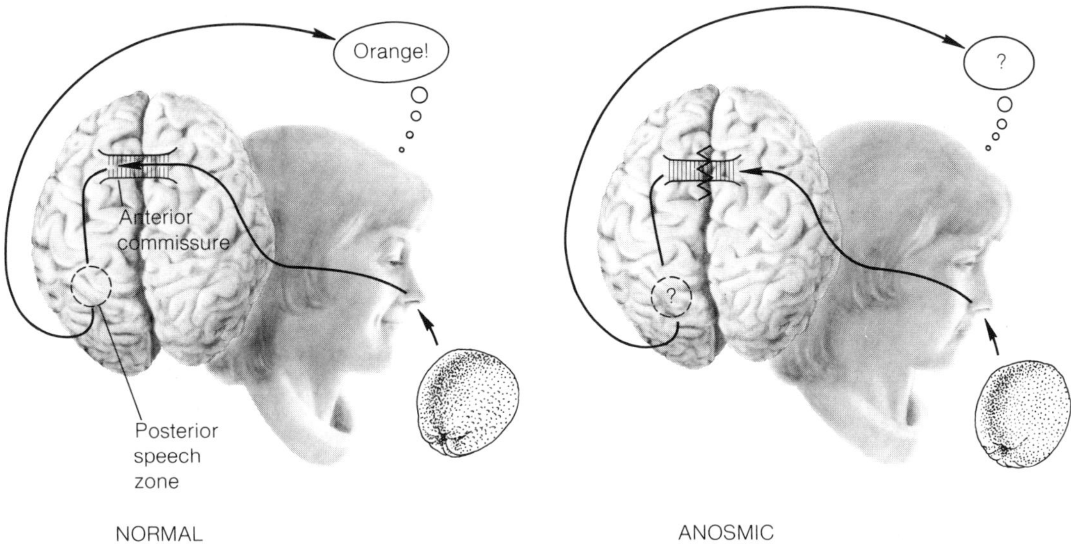

FIGURE 20-4. *A.* In the normal individual olfactory input to the right nostril travels directly back into the right hemisphere and crosses the anterior commissure, thus gaining access to the left (speech) hemisphere. *B.* Anosmia resulting from section of the anterior commissure. (The jagged line indicates the lesion of the anterior commissure.) When the pathway is severed, the left hemisphere has no way of knowing what odor the right hemisphere perceived.

Vision

As described in Chapter 11, the visual system is crossed. Information flashed to one visual field travels selectively to the corresponding region of the visual cortex. Recall, that by using this procedure researchers have demonstrated left and right visual-field superiorities for different types of input. For example, verbal material (such as words) is more accurately perceived when presented to the right visual field, presumably because the input travels to the left, speech, hemisphere. On the other hand, various types of visuospatial input produce a left visual-field superiority, since the right hemisphere appears to have a more important role in analyzing this information. Note, however, that the visual-field superiority observed in normal subjects is *relative*. That is, words presented to the left visual field, and hence right hemisphere, are sometimes perceived, although not as accurately or consistently as when they are presented to the right visual field. The relative effects, of course, occur because either hemisphere potentially has access to input to the opposite hemisphere via the corpus callosum, which joins the visual areas. In the commissurotomy patient there is no longer such access because the connection is severed. Since speech is housed in the left hemisphere of right-handed patients, visual information presented to the left visual field will be disconnected from verbal associations because the input goes to the right, nonlinguistic, hemisphere. Similarly, complex visual material presented to the right visual field will be inadequately processed, because it will not have access to the visuospatial abilities of the right hemisphere. It follows that if material is appropriately presented, it should be possible to demonstrate aphasia, agnosia, alexia, and acopia in a patient who ordinarily exhibits none of these symptoms. This is indeed the case, as we now demonstrate.

Consider the language-related deficits aphasia, alexia, and agnosia. If verbal material were presented to the left visual field, the commissurotomy patient would be unable to read it or to verbally answer questions about it, since the input is disconnected from the speech zones of the left hemisphere. Presentation of the same verbal material to the right visual field presents no difficulties, since the visual input projects to the verbal left hemisphere. Similarly, if an object is presented to the left visual field, the patient would be unable to name it and thus would appear to be either agnosic or aphasic. If presented to the right visual field, this same object would be correctly named, because the left visual cortex "perceives" the object and has access to the speech zones. Thus, we can see that the split-brain patient is aphasic, alexic, and agnosic if verbal material or an object requiring a verbal response is visually presented to the right hemisphere, but this person appears normal if material is presented to the left hemisphere.

A further deficit can be seen if the patient is asked to copy a complex visual figure. As discussed earlier, the right hemisphere is specialized for the perception of complex visual material. Since the right hemisphere controls the left hand we might predict that the left hand would be able to copy the figure but that the right hand, deprived of the expertise of the right hemisphere, would be severely impaired. The left hand draws the figure well, whereas the right hand cannot and is thus acopic.

Somesthesis

Like the visual system, the somatosensory system is completely crossed. Sensations of touch in the left hand travel to the right hemisphere, and those in the right hand travel to the left hemisphere. An object placed in the left hand can be named because the tactile information projects to the right hemisphere, crosses to the left, and subsequently has access to the speech zones. Similarly, if a subject is blindfolded and the right hand molded to form a particular shape, the left hand is able to copy is because the tactile information goes from the right hand to the left hemisphere, then across the corpus callosum to the right hemisphere, and the left hand forms the same shape.

If, however, the two hemispheres are disconnected from each other, the somatosensory functions of the left and right parts of the body become independent. For example, if some object is placed in the left hand of the blindfolded patient, who is then asked to choose the presented object from an array of objects, the left hand can pick out the object, but the right hand cannot. If an object is placed in a blindfolded patient's right hand, the patient can name it, but not if it is placed in the left hand because the sensory input is disconnected from the left (speech) hemisphere.

Disconnection effects can also be demonstrated without the use of objects. For example, if the patient is blindfolded and one hand is shaped in a particular way, the opposite hand is unable to mimic the posture. One hand has no way of "knowing" what the other hand is doing in the absence of input coming from the opposite hemisphere via the corpus callosum. If the patient is not blindfolded, however, he or she can find out what the opposite hand is doing simply by looking at it.

Audition

The auditory system is somewhat more complex than the other systems because it has both crossed and uncrossed connections. Although the left hemisphere appears to receive most of its input from the right ear, it also receives input from the left ear. Words played into the left ear can therefore travel directly to the left hemisphere or can go to the right hemisphere and then to the left via the corpus callosum. In normal subjects dichotic-listening tasks clearly show that the contralateral input is preferred because words presented to the right ear are selectively perceived over words presented to the left ear. Remember, however, that this difference is relative, because some words presented to the left ear are also reported.

The bilateral anatomical arrangement just described appears to reduce the effects of disconnection, but nevertheless one effect has been demonstrated. In the dichotic-listening task, input from the left ear is totally suppressed; the patient reports only those words played to the right ear. That is, digits or words played to the right ear are reported, but no input to the left ear is reported. This is a little surprising, since words played to the left ear, even under these conditions, would have been expected to attain some direct access to the left hemisphere. This direct access does not appear to occur.

Movement

Because the motor system is largely crossed, disconnection of the hemispheres could be predicted to induce several kinds of motor difficulties. First, on any task involving either a verbal command for the left hand to follow or verbal material for the left hand to write, a form of apraxia and agraphia could be expected, because the left hand does not receive instruction from the left hemisphere. That is, the left hand would be unable to obey the command (apraxia) or write (agraphia). These disabilities would not be seen in the right hand because it has access to the speech hemisphere. Similarly, if the right hand were asked to copy a geometric design it might be impaired (acopia) because it is disconnected from the right hemisphere, which ordinarily has a preferred role in the drawing of this type of material. These symptoms of disconnection are in fact observed in commissurotomy patients, although the severity of the deficit declines significantly over time after surgery, possibly because the left hemisphere's ipsilateral control of movement is being used.

A second situation that might be expected to produce severe motor deficits in commissurotomy patients is one in which the two arms must be used in cooperation. Ordinarily, one hand is informed of what the other is doing via the corpus callosum. Preilowski and later Zaidel and Sperry carefully examined the effect of disconnection on this type of bimanual cooperative movement. Patients were severely impaired at alternating tapping movements of the index fingers. Similarly, in a task similar to an Etch-a-Sketch, one requiring that a line inclined at an angle be traced, callosal patients did very poorly. This task requires the use of two cranks, one operated by each hand; one makes the tracing pen move vertically, the other makes the tracing pen move horizontally. A high degree of manual cooperation is required to trace a diagonal line smoothly. If the hemispheres have undergone disconnection, this cooperation is severely retarded since the left and right motor systems are unable to gain information as to what the opposite side is doing, except indirectly, by the patient's watching them.

Dramatic illustrations of conflict between hands can be seen in the following descriptions:

> In one case the patient (W. J.) would repeatedly pick up a newspaper with his right hand and lay it down with his left hand. This would be performed several times until finally the left hand threw the newspaper on the floor. Another patient (R. Y.) was described by a physiotherapist; "He was buttoning his shirt with his right hand and the left hand was coming along just behind it undoing the buttons just as quickly as he could fasten them." However, as in the praxic impairments described earlier, instances of intermanual conflict were generally confined to the first postoperative months and again seemed related to the age of the patient and extent of extra-callosal damage. It is of interest to note that the same patients while inhibiting these episodes of intermanual conflict were able to use their left hand in a purposeful and cooperative manner when "not thinking of what they were doing." For example, they could pour coffee out of a pot held in the right hand into a cup held by its handle with the left hand. The above-

mentioned peculiarities in motor functions were observed only in the complete split-brain patients. (Preilowski, 1975, p. 119)

The Problem of Partial Disconnection

Results from tests of callosal patients raise the question of whether a partial section of the corpus callosum would have as severe effects as a complete disconnection. Recently, surgeons have experimented with partial surgical disconnection of the hemispheres, hoping to attain the same clinical relief from seizures but with fewer neuropsychological side effects. Although the results are still preliminary, partial disconnection, in which the posterior part of the corpus callosum is left intact, appears to combine markedly milder effects than complete commissurotomy with the same therapeutic benefits. For example, Sperry and colleagues have found that patients with partial disconnection are significantly better at motor tasks such as the Etch-a-Sketch. Research on monkeys with partial commissurotomies suggests that the posterior portion of the corpus callosum (splenium) subserves visual transfer (as does the anterior commissure), whereas the region just in front of the splenium affects somatosensory transfer. The functions of the more anterior portions of the corpus callosum are largely unknown, but presumably transfer of motor information may be one function.

Conclusions

The results of studies on surgical disconnection of the hemispheres indicate that many symptoms, including aphasia, alexia, agnosia, agraphia, acopia, and apraxia, can be demonstrated in the *absence of any direct damage* to particular cytoarchitectural or functional neocortical regions. They can also occur for one side of the body and not the other. Symptoms such as aphasia, agnosia, and so forth can be thought of as resulting from *disconnection* of cortical regions rather than as necessarily resulting from damage *to* cortical regions. We shall return to this idea below.

LESION EFFECTS REINTERPRETED AS DISCONNECTION SYNDROMES

In 1965, Geschwind published a theoretically significant monograph, "Disconnexion Syndromes in Animals and Man," that tied together a vast amount of literature and anticipated many of the effects of callosal surgery. Although Geschwind's arguments are complex, his thesis is that certain types of behavioral deficits can be seen as resulting from disconnections between the hemispheres, within a hemisphere, or a combination of both. The value of this monograph is not its review of the data, but rather its forceful reintroduction of the concept first proposed by Dejerine and Liepmann nearly 70 years earlier, that disconnecting neocortical regions can cause a variety of neurological symptoms. To demonstrate the utility of the model, we discuss only the three classic symptoms of left hemisphere damage: apraxia, agnosia, and alexia.

Apraxia

Early in this chapter we noted that if a lesion of the corpus callosum disconnected the left hand from the left hemisphere, that hand would be unable to respond to verbal commands and would be considered apraxic. Suppose, however, that the right hand is unable to respond to verbal commands. Geschwind speculated that this deficit results from a lesion in the left hemisphere that disconnects its motor cortex (which controls the right hand) from the speech zone; thus, the right hand could not respond to verbal commands and would be considered apraxic.

Although Geschwind's model can explain bilateral apraxia in some patients, it must be emphasized that disconnection is not the only cause of apraxia. Because the posterior cortex has direct access to the subcortical neural mechanisms of arm and body movements (see Chapter 12), parietal input need not go through the motor cortex except for control of finger movements. Furthermore, as we noted earlier, patients with sections of the corpus callosum are initially apraxic but show substantial recovery despite a disconnection of the motor cortex of the left and right hemispheres.

Agnosia and Alexia

Geschwind theorized that agnosia and alexia can be produced by disconnecting the posterior speech area from the visual association cortex. They can be produced by a lesion that disconnects the visual association region on the left from the speech zone, as well as a lesion that disconnects the right visual association cortex from the speech zone by damaging the corpus callosum, as illustrated in Figure 20-5. Thus, the patient, although able to talk, is unable to identify words or objects because the visual information is disconnected from the posterior speech zone in the left hemisphere.

EXPERIMENTAL VERIFICATION OF DISCONNECTION EFFECTS

Disconnection can be used experimentally to demonstrate the function of various brain regions. Recall, that we began this chapter with a discussion of Downer's ingenious experiment to demonstrate the effects of temporal lobectomy. Mishkin and others have exploited the disconnections of different brain areas in animals to demonstrate the functional connections in the hierarchical organization of the visual system and, more recently, the soma-

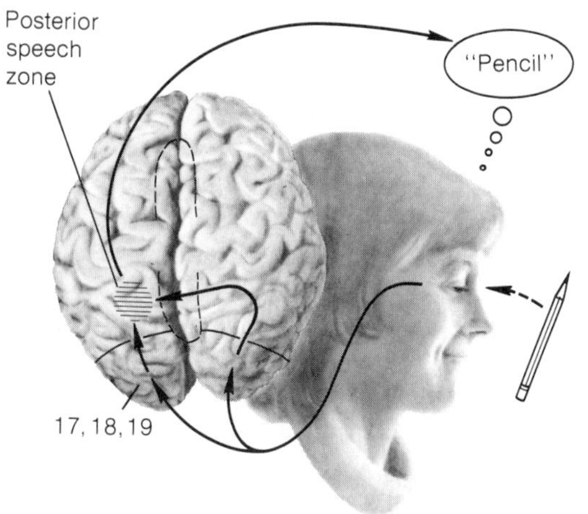

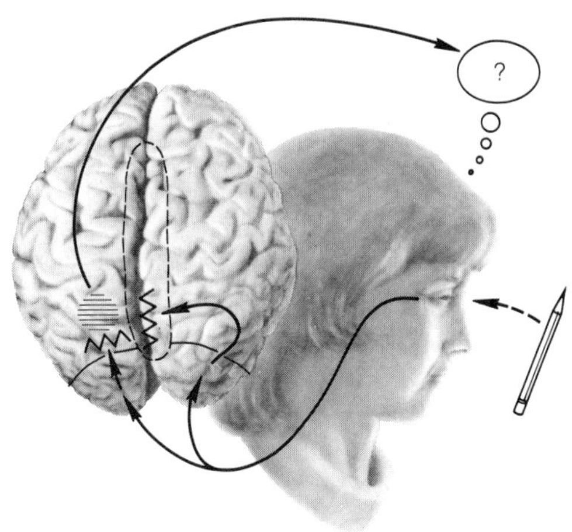

FIGURE 20-5. Geschwind's model of agnosia and alexia resulting from disconnection of the visual cortex from the posterior speech zone. (The jagged lines indicate the lesion of the pathways.) *A*. Normally, the visual input of both hemispheres travels to the posterior speech zone and tertiary sensory cortex, where it is processed to allow speech describing the written word or object. *B*. In the absence of the connection this is no longer possible, and agnosia and alexia result.

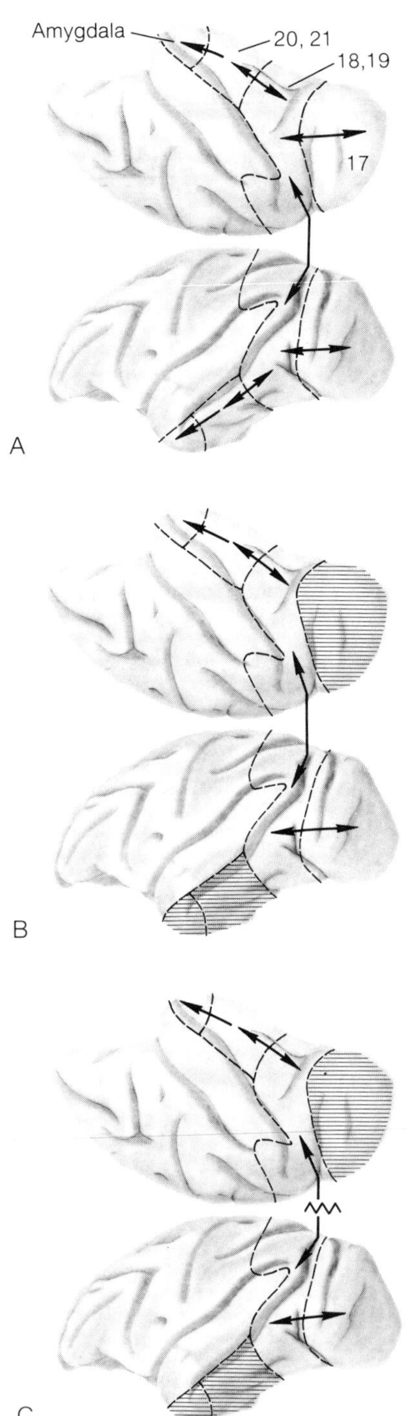

FIGURE 20-6. Disconnection effects in the visual system of monkeys. *A*. The visual system is intact. *B*. The left visual cortex still has access to the visual association cortex of the right hemisphere, and so vision is still possible. *C*. The intact components of the visual system are disconnected, producing major visual deficits. (After Mishkin, 1979.)

tosensory system. This research clearly demonstrates the usefulness of the disconnection approach and has led to significant progress in our understanding of the sensory systems.

The Visual System

Previous discussion of the visual system's hierarchical nature did not consider the connections between the system's various regions. These are summarized in Figure 20-6*A*. In each hemisphere connections run from area 17 to areas 18 and 19 in the same hemisphere. Connections from 18 and 19 Across the corpus callosum to the analogous area on the opposite side, as well as connecting with area 20 on the same side. Area 20 connects to area 21 and the amygdala on the same side, and on the opposite side via the anterior commissure. What would happen to vision if the connections were cut? This question has been addressed in experiments using monkeys as subjects.

Consideration of this question requires that monkeys first be tested to determine their visual capabilities. The easiest method is to teach the animal a visual discrimination such as between a "+" and a "O". Food reinforcement is associated with one stimulus and not with the other. The monkey's task is to identify the correct stimulus and respond to it. Control monkeys learn this problem in 100 to 150 trials or fewer, and so if a monkey that has been operated on fails to learn this problem in 1000 trials, it is assumed that it will not learn it at all; the lesion can thus be inferred to have some important effect on the monkey's ability to discriminate between visual stimuli.

By using tasks of this sort, Mishkin and others

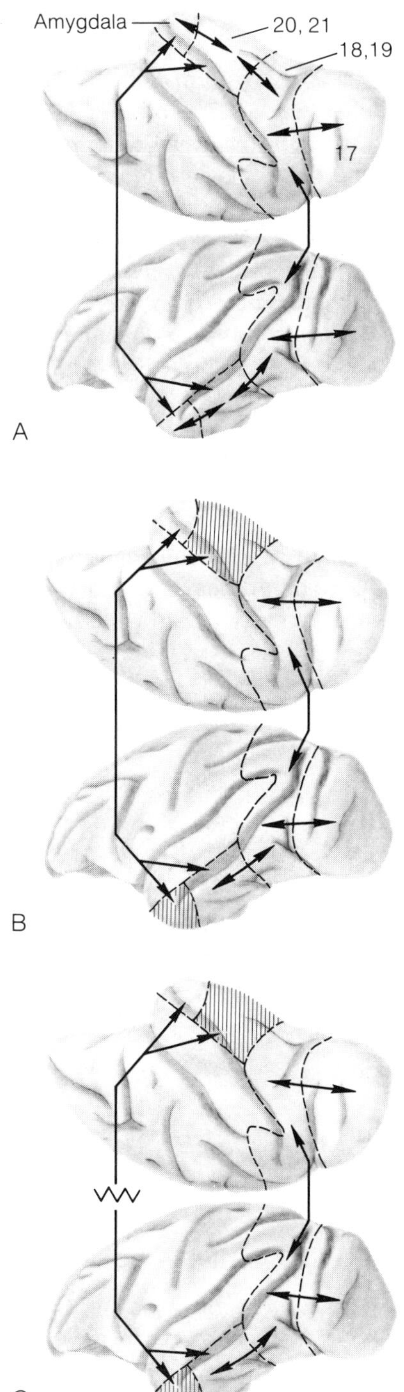

FIGURE 20-7. Disconnection of affect from visual input. *A.* The connections of the normal visual system, including both the callosal and anterior commissural connections. *B.* Even if parts of the system are damaged, it can still function. *C.* If the anterior commissure is severed, visual input is separated from affect, resulting in visual deficits. (After Mishkin, 1979.)

have demonstrated that bilateral lesions in areas 17, 18, and 19, or in 20 and 21, result in an impaired, or abolished, ability to solve visual-discrimination problems. Because unilateral lesions do not have such an effect, what seems to be necessary is one intact trio of areas 17, 18, and 19, and one intact pair of areas 20 and 21. There is, however, one constraint: the remaining regions must be connected. Thus, in Figure 20-6*B* a lesion in area 17 on the right and in 20 and 21 on the left does not disturb performance, since there is still an intact system that can be used. If the connection between the hemispheres is now severed, the neocortical areas are still intact but not connected, and the result is failure on the visual-discrimination problem (Figure 20-6*C*). Clearly, the neocortical regions do not function properly if they are not connected to each other.

Mishkin first studied areas 20 and 21, thinking them to be the final step in the neocortical visual system. More recently he has studied the problem of how visual stimuli might gain what he calls "motivational" or "emotional" significance. Recall that the Klüver-Bucy monkeys with bilateral temporal lobectomies attached no significance to visual stimuli. That is, they would repeatedly taste nasty-tasting objects, or place inedible objects in their mouths. In his 1965 paper Geschwind proposed that this symptom represented a disconnection of the amygdala from the visual system. That is, theoretically at least, although an animal's visual sensory system might be intact, the animal would behave as if it were not because it is disconnected from another system that attaches meaning to visual information. Figure 20-7*A* illustrates the additional connections when the amygdala is included in an extended visual system. Areas 20 and 21 connect with the amygdala on the same side and on the opposite side via the anterior commissure.

To test Geschwind's proposal, Mishkin devised the experiment illustrated in Figure 20-7*B* and *C*. The amygdala was lesioned on the left and the inferior temporal cortex on the right. This arrangement left one complete system of areas 17, 18, 19, 20, 21 and amygdala, and using it the monkey's performance on visual problems was normal, as would be expected. The anterior commissure was then cut, leaving all the necessary pieces of the system intact but disconnecting the intact amygdala from the neocortical portion of the system. Performance on visual problems instantly deteriorated, indicating that there was some interruption of the normal processing of visual material, as would be predicted from Geschwind's model. Other experiments by Mishkin and his colleagues have demonstrated that the orbital-frontal cortex may also play an important role in the system, possibly to guide behavioral responses to biologically relevant visual information.

In another application of the disconnection model to studying the visual system, Nakamura and Mishkin have shown blindness in monkeys after disconnection of the intact visual system from nonvisual regions. Monkeys received unilateral decortications in which the visual areas (in addition to the motor and limbic cortex) were spared. Then the cerebral commissures and contralateral optic tract were severed. Unexpectedly, the animals were blind! None of the animals showed any detectable reaction to visually presented stimuli, whether these were food, fearful objects, threats, or sudden movements. When placed in an unfamiliar environment, they bumped into obstacles and found food objects only by touching them accidentally or tactile exploration. Although some of the monkeys showed some recovery over time, others did not,

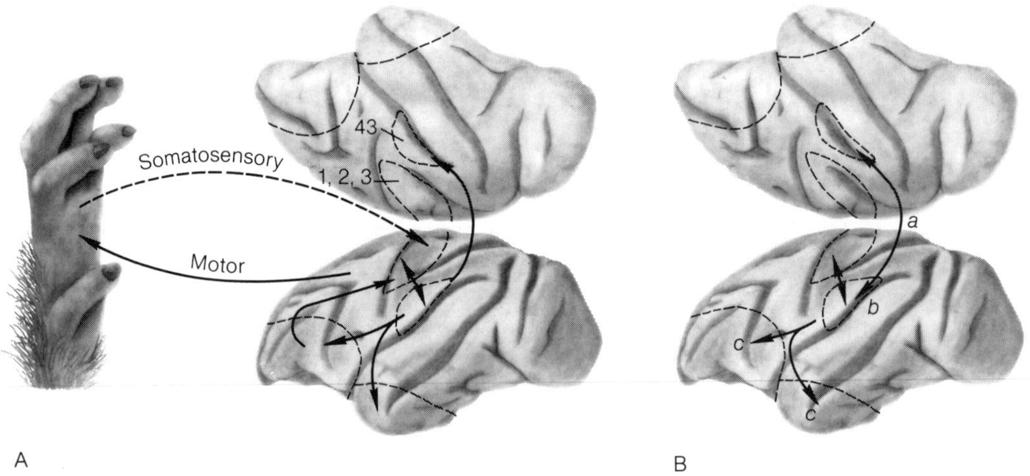

FIGURE 20-8. Mishkin's somatosensory model. *A*. The major intracortical connections of the somatosensory system involved in performing a tactile discrimination. Input travels from the hand to areas 1, 2, and 3, to area 43, and then to the medial temporal and orbital-frontal areas. This input then travels to the motor cortex to produce a response. *B*. A lesion at *a* would render the left hand unable to perform a task learned by the right because the memory is in the left hemisphere. Also, *b* and *c* show that lesions at these points would render the trained right hand unable to perform the task because the primary area is disconnected from the remainder of the system. (After Mishkin, 1979.)

remaining functionally blind even two years after surgery. Further experiments revealed that electrophysiologically the visual cortex was still functioning, yet the animals behaved as though it no longer functioned at all. The results point to an important role of the nonvisual cortex in visual perception and demonstrate the importance of studying connections to, as well as areas of, a functional system.

The Somatosensory System

The logic used in studying the connection of the visual system can be applied to the study of the somatosensory system. Consider the following type of experiment. A monkey is trained to discriminate between two objects by touch alone, using just one hand (the right). Once this problem is learned, the opposite hand, when tested, performs well on the task, either because the information stored in the trained hemisphere is accessible to that hand (see Figure 20-8) or because the information is stored in both hemispheres. The next step is to cut the corpus callosum. Failure of the untrained left hand to solve the problem would indicate that memory of the task is stored in the trained hemisphere. The left hand indeed fails, indicating that the memory of the task is stored in the trained hemisphere. Notice, however, that the trained right hand will still be able to solve the problem. The next question to ask is: Which connections within the trained hemisphere are necessary to continue to perform normally on this task? Mishkin proposes that the connections are something like those diagrammed in Figure 20-8. That is, the primary somatosensory cortex is connected to the secondary somatosensory cortex of both hemispheres. This region in turn is connected to the medial temporal region and/or the orbital-frontal region. If this is true, then the following predictions can be made. First, a lesion at point *a* in Figure 20-8*B* would render the left hand unable to do a task learned by the right hand, because the memory is in the trained hemisphere, as noted above. Second, a lesion of *b* or *c* would render the right, trained hand unable to do the problem, because the primary area is disconnected from the remainder of the system. These predictions remain to be tested directly. Notice that if there were lesions to *b* or *c*, the callosum would not have to be cut, because the memory is not stored in the opposite hemisphere.

CONCLUSIONS

There are a number of issues that have not been touched upon in this chapter that should be briefly mentioned in closing. There are significant species differences in the anatomy and functions of interconnecting hemispheric commissures. Some primitive marsupials do not have a corpus callosum. Some birds, although having interhemispheric commissures, seem to behave as humans might who have no corpus callosum. Sherry has reported that if an occluder is placed over the eye of a food-caching bird, the information it stores in its contralateral hemisphere about where its food is located is not accessible to the other eye. The animals apparently have separate memory stores for each eye. There are also suggestions of a variety of individual differences in callosal size and patterns. De Lacoste-Utamsing and Holloway have suggested that females have a larger corpus callosum than males. Witelson has failed to confirm this report, noting that the intrasex variation is high, but finds that the corpus callosum is larger in left-handers than in right-handers.

We might also suggest that disconnection hypotheses might be applicable to interpretations of various developmental stages of infants. It is well known that myelination of fibers is one of the last events in the maturation of neural systems. Therefore, if certain connections are not matured while others are, features of behavior may very well parallel symptoms observed in disconnection cases. For example, during the course of development, infants will extend their arms to reach for objects in the visual field of the limb. If the object moves across the visual midline, the hand will not follow it but rather the other hand will be extended to grasp for it. A little later in development, the infant will follow the object with a hand even if the object crosses the midline. This sort of behavior could be a result of hemispheric disconnection, attributable to immaturity or lack of myelination of interhemispheric pathways. Similarly, careful consideration of other behaviors displayed by infants could be interpreted in the same way. Mitchel has found that human infants younger than about one year are like split-brain patients in that they are unable to transfer information about objects obtained by touch. In the experiments, infants were conditioned to expect that someone would play "peek-a-boo" on one or the other side of their body, shortly after they were allowed to feel an object of a certain texture in one hand. Then they were allowed to feel the object in the other hand. If intermanual transfer occurred it was expected that they would display the conditioned response, which they did not. Rudy and Stadler-Morris found that rats trained on a spatial-navigation task can learn the task with one hemisphere at 22 days of age but not perform it with the other. By the time they were 25 days of age they did display interocular equivalence. The researches suggest that the 22-day-old rat behaves like a split-brain animal.

Disconnections may be relevant to at least two other lines of inquiry. First, patients with schizophrenia have been reported to have enlargement of the corpus callosum. Observations of this effect have led Beaumont and Dimond to suggest that schizophrenics may show some abnormalities in transfer of information between the hemispheres. Subsequently, a number of reports seem to confirm this suggestion. Schrift and coworkers, although finding evidence for interhemispheric transfer deficits, suggest that these may not be specific to schizophrenia and are difficult to dissociate from focal or hemispheric impairment. Second, people working with patients who have suffered head trauma have often been puzzled by the severe chronic impairments these patients may have in the face of minimal direct brain injury. Gennarelli and his coworkers have suggested that the impairments may be due to diffuse axonal injury. Head trauma often causes twisting and shearing of the two hemispheres, which could result in a traumatic form of disconnection.

Finally, many people have written on the implications of the split-brain cases to support theories of mind and concepts of individuality. We have not touched upon this issue. It is certainly the case that for dualists, who hold that the brain has a corresponding mental representation, there are compelling reasons to consider that there are two brains and two minds in split-brain individuals. For materialists, the philosophical implications are not so weighty. But for everyone, there is a challenge to understand how individuals function in a seemingly integrated way with separated hemispheres.

REFERENCES

Akelaitis, A. J. A study of gnosis, praxis and language following section of the corpus callosum and anterior commissure. *Journal of Neurosurgery* 1:94–102, 1944.

Beaumont, J., and S. Dimond. Brain disconnection and schizophrenia. *British Journal of Psychiatry* 123:661–662, 1973.

Colonnier, M. Notes on the early history of the corpus callosum with an introduction to the morphological papers published in this Festschrift. In F. Lepore, M. Ptito, and H. H. Jasper, eds. *Two Hemispheres—One Brain.* New York: Alan R. Liss, 1986.

De Lacoste-Utamsing, C., and R. L. Holloway. Sexual dimorphism in the human corpus callosum. *Science* 216:1431–1432, 1982.

Downer, J. L. de C. Changes in visual gnostic functions and emotional behavior following unilateral temporal pole damage in the "split-brain" monkey. *Nature* 191:50–51, 1961

Gazzaniga, M. S. *The Bisected Brain.* New York: Appleton-Century-Crofts, 1970.

Gennarelli, T. A., J. H. Adams, and D. I. Graham. Diffuse axonal injury—a new conceptual approach to an old problem. In A. Baethmann, K. G. Go, and A. Unterberg, eds. *Mechanisms of Secondary Brain Damage.* New York: Plenum, 1986.

Geschwind, N. Disconnexion syndromes in animals and man. *Brain* 88:237–294, 585–644, 1965.

Jeeves, M. A. Callosal agenesis: Neuronal and developmental adaptions. In F. Lepore, M. Ptito, and H. H. Jasper, eds. *Two Hemispheres—One Brain.* New York: Alan R. Liss, 1986.

Klüver, H., and P. C. Bucy. Preliminary analysis of functions of the temporal lobes in monkeys. *Archives of Neurology and Psychiatry* 42:979–1000, 1939.

Lassonde, M. The facilitatory influence of the corpus callosum on intrahemispheric processing. In F. Lepore, M. Ptito, and H. H. Jasper, eds. *Two Hemispheres—One Brain.* New York: Alan R. Liss, 1986.

Lassonde, M., H. Sauerwein, G. Geoffroy, and M. Decarie. Effects of early and late transection of the corpus callosum in children. *Brain* 109:953–967, 1986.

Lepore, F., M. Ptito, and H. H. Jasper, eds. *Two hemispheres—One Brain.* New York: Alan R. Liss, 1986.

Mishkin, M. Analogous neural models for tactile and visual learning. *Neuropsychologia* 17:139–152, 1979.

Mitchel, G. F. Self-generated experience and the development of lateralized neurobehavioral organization in infants. *Advances in the Study of Behavior* 17:61–83, 1987.

Myers, R. E. Functions of the corpus callosum in interocular transfer. *Brain* 57:358–363, 1956.

Nakamura, R. K., and M. Mishkin. Blindness in monkeys following non-visual cortical lesions. *Brain Research* 188:572–577, 1980.

Nebes, R. D. Hemispheric specialization in commissurotomized man. *Psychological Bulletin* 81:1–14, 1974.

Pandya, D. N., and B. Seltzer. The topography of commissural fibers. In F. Lepore, M. Ptito, and H. H. Jasper, eds. *Two Hemispheres—One Brain.* New York: Alan R. Liss, 1986.

Preilowski, B. Bilateral motor interaction: Perceptual-motor performance of partial and complete "split-brain" patients. In K. J. Zulch, O. Creutzfeldt, and G. C. Galbraith, eds. *Cerebral Localization.* Berlin and New York: Springer-Verlag, 1975.

Rudy, J. W., and S. Stadler-Morris. Development of interocular equivalence in rats trained on a distal-cue navigation task. *Behavioral Neuroscience* 101:141–143, 1987.

Schrift, M. J., H. Bandla, P. Shah and M. A. Taylor. Interhemispheric transfer in major psychoses. *Journal of Nervous and Mental Disease* 174:203–207, 1986.

Sherry, D. F. Food storage by birds and mammals. *Advances in the Study of Behavior* 15:153–183, 1985.

Sperry, R. W. Lateral specialization in the surgically separated hemispheres. In Schmitt, F. O. and F. G. Worden, eds. *Neurosciences: Third Study Program.* Cambridge, MA: M.I.T. Press, 1974.

Spiegler, B. J., and M. Mishkin. Evidence for the sequential participation of inferior temporal cortex and amygdala in the acquisition of stimulus-reward associations. *Behavioural Brain Research* 3:303–317, 1981.

Steele Russel, I., M. W. Van Hof, and G. Berlucchi, eds. *Structure and Function of Cerebral Commissures.* London: Macmillan and Co., 1979.

Witelson, S. F. Wires of the mind: Anatomical variation in the corpus callosum in relation to hemispheric specialization and integration. In F. Lepore, M. Ptito, and H. H. Jasper, eds. *Two Hemispheres—One Brain.* New York: Alan R. Liss, 1986.

Zaidel, D., and R. W. Sperry. Some long term motor effects of cerebral commissurotomy in man. *Neuropsychologia* 15:193–204, 1977.

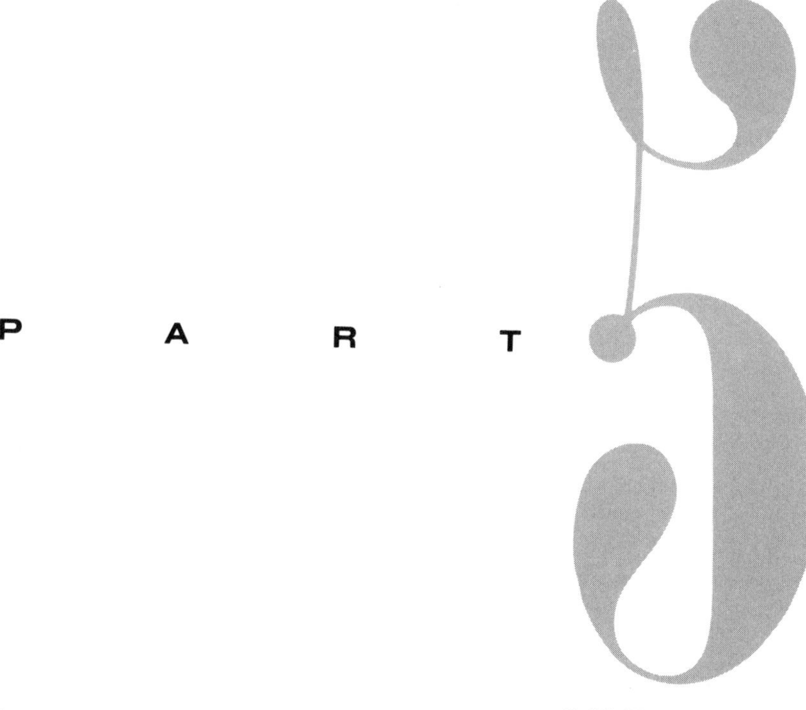

PART 5

HIGHER FUNCTIONS

Just as there has been a long tradition in neurology of studying the lobes of the brain, so has there been a long tradition in psychology of studying memory, language, emotional behavior, and spatial behavior. Chapters 21 through 24 examine brain function from the perspective of the psychologist by focusing on the problems in which psychologists have traditionally had an interest. Of course, some of the things discussed in Part Four will come up again, but the perspective should be sufficiently different and fresh to make the retelling of the tale worthwhile.

MEMORY

Psychologists began studying memory in the mid-19th century; the first monograph, Ebbinghaus's, was published in 1885. Memory, however, has not been the sole province of psychologists. It has been a topic of interest to philosophers from the time of Plato and Aristotle, and more recently it formed an important part of Freud's psychoanalytic theory. The neuropsychological study of memory dates back to about 1915, when Karl Lashley embarked on a lifetime project to identify the neural locations of learned habits. In most of his experiments he either removed portions of the neocortex or made cuts of fiber pathways in hopes of preventing transcortical communication between sensory and motor regions of the cortex. After hundreds of experiments Lashley was still unable to interfere with specific memories. In 1950, he concluded that "it is not possible to demonstrate the isolated localization of a memory trace anywhere in the nervous system. Limited regions may be essential for learning or retention of a particular activity, but . . . the engram is represented throughout the region."

Ironically, only three years later in 1953, a neurosurgeon named William Scoville inadvertently made one of the most influential findings in neuropsychology when he operated on the now famous patient H. M. Bilateral removal of the hippocampus in H. M. made him amnesic for virtually all events following the operation. From Lashley's extensive work no one could have predicted that removal of any structure, let alone a structure that was one believed to be primarily olfactory in function, would result in a person remembering things from the distant but not from the recent past! The surgery had interfered with the process of storing or retrieving new memories but had not touched stored memories themselves. The case of H. M. revolutionized the study of the memory process and shifted the emphasis from a search for the location of memory to an analysis of the process of storing memories. Indeed, Scoville and Milner's description of H. M. is probably the second most influential observation ever made in neuropsychology, with only Broca's surpassing it. Today, few areas in experimental psychology are as active as those relating to the processes involved in human memory.

In this chapter we describe the role of the temporal, frontal, and parietal lobes in memory. Specific attention is paid to the complementary specialization of the left and right hemispheres for the storage of verbal and nonverbal material, respectively. We review the various disorders of memory, neuropsychological theories of memory, and studies of memory processes in nonhumans. But before we consider the facts regarding the pathology of memory, let us examine several theoretical issues.

THE NATURE OF MEMORY

What Is Memory?

Memory is a process that results in a relatively permanent change in behavior. It is never observed and is always inferred. In other words, we cannot identify memories in the brain, but since behavior changes with experience, we logically infer that some process must occur to account for that change. The lesson to be learned from Lashley is that no region in the nervous system can be pointed to as the place *where* we remember. Lesions to a number of brain regions disturb memory, but these regions do not house memory or memories. These regions can be said only to be more involved in the process of remembering than others. It is likely that groups of neurons in different parts of the brain, especially in the cerebral hemispheres, are more or less important for the remembering of different types of information (e.g., verbal, pictorial), but even this specialization is relative rather than absolute. It does not happen, for example, that a person is totally amnesic for verbal material but remembers nonverbal material.

If memories are not stored as discrete things in the brain, how might they be stored? This complex question has no clear answer as yet, but an analogy may help illustrate the kind of process that could be involved. Imagine a hill; water poured onto the soil at its top runs down the hill, eroding small channels in the earth. If more water is poured on the hill, most of it follows the same route of the first water, further deepening the channels. Still more water continues the process. Since the water will always take the same route down the hill, we could say that there is a "memory" for that route. In neurological terms we could conceive of the brain as the hill and the process of memory as the route. Sensory experience enters the brain (top of the hill), flows through the brain (the channels in the hill), and produces behavior (leaves the hill) at the bottom. We can see, therefore, that the memory was not stored in a place, but, rather, was a function of the activity of the entire brain. We do not wish to belabor this analogy, nor for it to be taken literally, but it does demonstrate a simple way by which to conceive of memory as a process of neuronal connectivity rather than as a site to be found in the brain.

What Do We Remember from an Experience?

To consider the pathology of memory we must first examine what is normally remembered. In his classic book *Remembering,* Bartlett made the point that remembering cannot be regarded as the mere revival of previous experience; rather, it is a process of active reconstruction. In his words:

> Remembering is not the re-excitation of innumerable fixed, lifeless and fragmentary traces. It is an imaginative reconstruction, or construction, built out of the relation of our attitude towards a whole active mass of organized past reactions or experience . . . and to a little outstanding detail which commonly appears in image or in language form. It is thus hardly every really exact, even in

> the most rudimentary cases of rote recapitulation. . . . (Bartlett, 1932, pp. 213–214)

> It looks as if what is said to be reproduced is, far more generally than is commonly admitted, really a construction serving to justify whatever impression may have been left by the original. It is this "impression," rarely defined with much exactitude, which most readily persists. So long as the details which can be built up around are such that they would give a "reasonable" setting, most of us are fairly content, and are apt to think that what we build we have literally retained. (Bartlett, 1932, p. 176)

In other words, events are not stored in toto; only certain critical elements are stored from which the event can be reconstructed. The more cues or elements provided contextually, the more exactly the event can be reconstructed and "remembered."

Consider our hill analogy again. If only a trickle or water (minimal sensory input) is poured on the hill, the water will trace only part of the route to the bottom, bypassing many of the small side channels. As more water (i.e., more contextual information) is added, it travels faster down the hill, tracing more and more of the various channels originally followed (i.e., "remembers" the route more precisely).

After a long delay, remembering may correctly identify the essential elements of sensory experience yet incorporate additional elements that, although compatible with the essential sensory experience, are erroneous. It is widely believed that this incorrect embellishment of the critical experience may account for the fallibility of eyewitness evidence in which plausible but erroneous details are "remembered." To return to our hill analogy, if water has not been poured on the hill recently, the channels become less distinct because of environmental processes such as wind erosion and so on. The major channels remain passable, but many of the smaller channels may be lost. When water is again poured on the hill it retraces the major route, but the details of the smaller side channels are lost and new ones, which may or may not coincide with the original, are formed.

Bartlett's proposition that remembering is reconstruction is particularly important in understanding the pathology of memory. An apparent defect in memory could result from a disorder, and not only in the storage of sensory experience but also in the later reconstruction of sensory experience from the critical features. Indeed, in some disorders, such as the amnesia associated with Korsakoff's disease (see below), a deficit in reconstruction may well prove to be a significant component.

Two Types of Memory

In 1890, William James distinguished between what he called *primary* memory, one that endured for a very brief time, and *secondary* memory, "the knowledge of a former state of mind after it has already once dropped from the consciousness" (James, 1890, p. 648). Not until 1958, however, were separate short-term and long-term memories specifically postulated by Broadbent, although a number of authors had hinted at this possibility. Since Scoville and Milner's description of H. M., the concept of two memory systems, short-term and long-term, has become central to neuropsychological theory. Neuropsychological evidence now supports the concept, since patients may suffer one kind of memory loss and not the other.

An experiment by Hebb nicely demonstrates the two kinds of memory behaviorally. College students were asked to repeat strings of digits, such as 83759247. The number of digits that can be recalled is termed the *memory span*. The maximum memory span is about eight. There is little hope of repeating eight digits unless we listen very carefully and then repeat them at once. The memory is brief, and it is striking that even with sustained concentration items in short-term memory fade very quickly and are lost. In Hebb's experiment, nine digits were read aloud to the subjects. Since nine digits are beyond the memory span of most subjects, few correctly recalled the nine. The subjects were then read another set of digits, then a third, and so on, for a total of 24 sets of nine digits. However, unknown to the subjects, every third set repeated the first set. The results showed (see Figure 21-1) that although the short-term memory for nine digits is very brief, the subjects gradually learned the repeating series, as it was evidently stored in long-term memory. Hebb proposed that listening to a set of digits does more than set up a short-term memory. He suggested that some other long-term change must also be beginning and is left behind in the nervous system. Although hearing another string of digits appears to completely wipe out the first set, only the short-term memory is wiped out completely, since long-term memory gradually develops as the repeating set is learned.

Hebb went a step further from the behavioral data and developed a theory of the neurological basis of short-term and long-term memory in his 1949 book. His genius lays in using the associational-learning theory of Clark Hull and his contemporaries in the 1930s and 1940s and in using what was known of nervous system activity to describe the basis of learning and memory. Hebb argued that short-term memory is an active process of limited duration, and that long-term memory involves an actual structural change in the nervous system.

Hebb realized from the earlier anatomical work of Lorenté de No that neurons in the brain are interconnected with many other neurons, and, in turn, each neuron receives input from many synapses on its dendrites and cell body. The resulting neuronal loops (see Figure 21-2) contain neurons whose output signal may be either excitatory or inhibitory. Although the neuronal loops are usually drawn as though they were in the cortex, many of the loops probably run from the cortex to the thalamus or other subcortical structures, such as the hippocampus, and back to the cortex. Because each neuron is believed to both send and receive thousands of outputs and inputs, the number of possible neuronal loops is truly immense.

In Hebb's theory each psychologically important event, whether a sensation, percept, memory, thought, or emotion is conceived to be the flow of activity in a given neuronal loop. Hebb proposed that the synapses in a particular path become functionally connected to form a **cell assembly.** At this point Hebb made the assumption that if two neurons, A and B, are excited together, they become linked functionally. In Hebb's words:

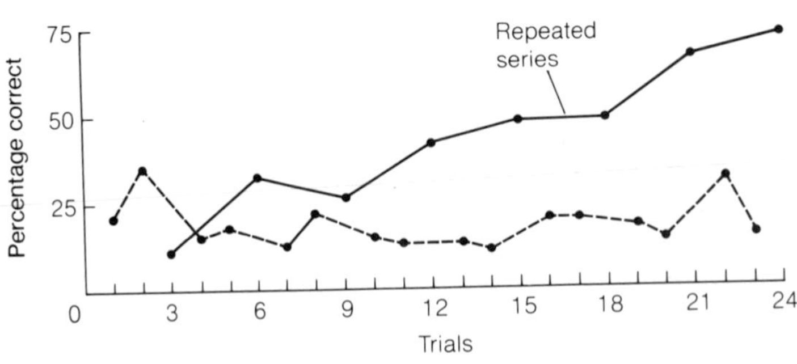

FIGURE 21-1. Performances on the Hebb Recurring-Digits Test. Subjects were asked to read sets of nine digits to recall immediately. Unbeknownst to the subjects, every third set repeated the first set. The subjects gradually learned the repeating series, but they continued to do poorly on the novel series. (After Hebb, 1961.)

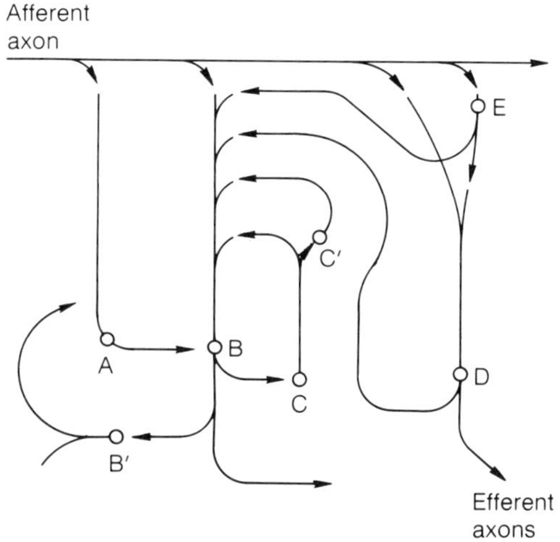

FIGURE 21-2. Simplified diagram of the interconnections of neurons to form neuronal loops. The entering (afferent) axon excites four neurons, A, B, D, and E. Of these, B and D send impulses out of the system (efferent axons) to excite other systems. A-B-B′, B-C, and B-C-C′ form closed loops. (After Hebb, 1972.)

"When an axon of cell A is near enough to excite a cell B and repeatedly or persistently takes part in firing it, some growth process or metabolic change takes place in one or both cells such that A's efficiency, as one of the cells firing B, is increased" (Hebb, 1949, p. 62). In Hebb's view the most probable way in which one cell could become more capable of firing another is that synaptic knobs grew or became more functional, increasing the area of contact between the afferent axon and efferent cell body and dendrites.

In Hebb's view the cell assembly is a system that is initially organized by a particular sensory event but is capable of continuing its activity after the stimulation has ceased. Hebb proposed that to produce functional changes in synaptic transmission, the cell assembly must be repeatedly activated. After the initial sensory input, the assembly would therefore reverberate. Repeated reverberation could then produce the structural changes. Clearly this conception of information storage could explain the phenomena of short- and long-term memory: short-term memory is reverberation of the closed loops of the cell assembly; long-term memory is more structural, a lasting change in synaptic connections.

In Hebb's theory there is yet another factor in long-term memory. For the structural synaptic changes to occur, there must be a period in which the cell assembly is left relatively undisturbed. Hebb referred to this process of structural change as *consolidation,* a period believed to require 15 min to an hour. Its existence was supported by observations that retention failed when brain function was disrupted soon after learning, as, for example, in the amnesia for events just prior to a concussion. The description of H. M.'s case invited a logical extrapolation of Hebb's theory: the hippocampus was assumed to be especially important to the process of consolidation, although just how it is involved could not be specified. New material is not remembered because it is not consolidated; old material is remembered because it was consolidated before the hippocampal damage.

Finally, Hebb assumed that any cell assembly could be excited by others. This idea provided the basis for thought or ideation. The essence of an "idea" is that it occurs in the absence of the original environmental event that it corresponds to.

The beauty of Hebb's theory is that it attempted to explain psychological events by the physiological properties of the nervous system. Now, more than 40 years since Hebb's landmark volume, his theory remains the best attempt to combine the principles of psychological reality and the facts of neuroscience. In a thoughtful review from 1980, Goddard revisited the cell assembly and found that, with a few modifications, it is still a sound metaphor for psychological activity. Goddard bases his argument largely on recent work providing physiological confirmation for Hebb's assertion that there are separate neurological substrates for short-term and long-term memory. On the basis of earlier work by Eccles and others, Bliss and Gardner-Medwin demonstrated unequivocally in 1973 that electrical stimulation of a neuron can produce either brief or long-lasting changes in synaptic transmission, according to the characteristics of the brain stimulation. Brief pulses of current are delivered to an axon over a few seconds and the magnitude of the response is recorded from areas known to receive projections from the stimulated axon. After a stable baseline of response to the stimulation has been established, the stimulation is changed to one of high frequency, driving the system very hard. This high-frequency stimulation is then discontinued and the brief test pulses are resumed. The magnitude of the postsynaptic response can thus be compared with the original baseline and the time course of the decay of changes in response magnitude can be measured as well. Two significant findings emerge from this study. First, response magnitude markedly increases immediately after the high-frequency stimulation (see Figure 21-3). This increase declines over time and returns to baseline, the rate of decline depending on the details of the stimulation. This short-term increase is called *posttetanic potentiation*. Second, the change in response magnitude may not decline to baseline but instead remain elevated, possibly for days or as long as is technically practical to measure it. Various labels have been used for this phenomenon, including **long-term potentiation (LTP), long-term enhancement (LTE),** and *enhancement*. In some cases LTP may be present after two months, and Barnes has shown that LTP is prolonged by occasional repetition of the high-frequency stimulation. The original studies of posttetanic potentiation and LTP were done on the hippocampus, but these phenomena can be demonstrated elsewhere in the brain.

Goddard emphasized the similarity between the phenomena of short-term memory and posttetanic potentiation and between long-term memory and enhancement. He proposed that these physiological events provide a strong basis for Hebb's

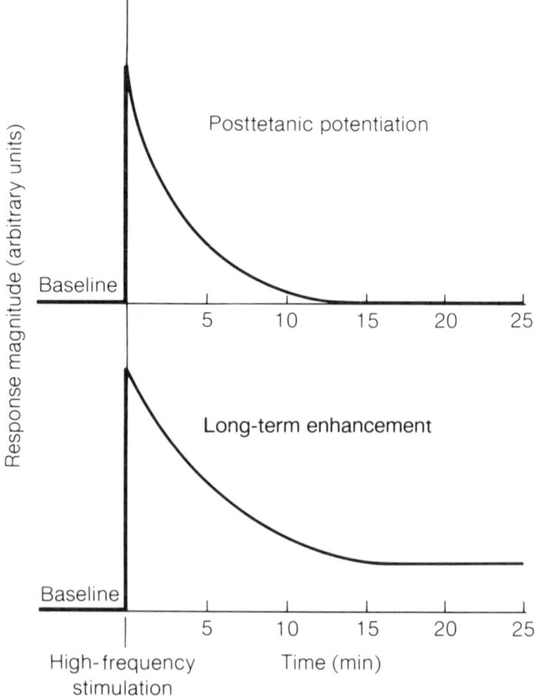

FIGURE 21-3. Time course of change in response magnitude following high-frequency stimulation. In curve *A* the response magnitude returns to baseline, a phenomenon described as posttetanic potentiation. In curve *B* the response strength does not return to baseline activity, indicating long-term potentiation (LTP), which is more properly known as long-term enhancement (LTE). (After Goddard, 1979.)

neuropsychological theory. As attractive as the physiological work is as a model of short-term and long-term memory, it is still a substantial theoretical leap to understanding the effects of lesions on memory, such as the differential effects of temporal lobe and parietal lobe lesions on short-term and long-term memory, respectively. This apparent complication may be resolved in the future as more is learned about the mechanisms of enhancement and posttetanic potentiation. The important point for us now is that there is tentative evidence to support Hebb's theory.

The Nature of Synaptic Change

The demonstration of LTP is important but it still leaves open the question of what change in the brain allows such physiological phenomena, and presumably, memory. Recall that Hebb proposed that there must be changes in the synaptic junction, that make the synapse more "efficient." In recent years this concept has become known as the "Hebb synapse," implying that information is stored by some type of structural modification at the synapse. The nature of the synaptic change in information storage is still uncertain and leads to questions about what changes occur at the synapse. To answer this we must return to the structure of the synapse. Figure 21-4 schematically illustrates a synapse, highlighting the various measures of morphology that have been correlated with learning. Several lines of evidence now have shown that alterations in each of these measures may accompany behavioral change. Thus, in an extensive series of experiments Greenough and his colleagues have shown that when animals are trained in specific tasks or are exposed to specific environments, there are changes in the dendrites of neurons. If there is an increase in the number of dendrites of particular neurons, then it follows that there might be an increase in the number of synapses on these neurons, and Greenough has shown this to be the case. In addition, he and his colleagues have shown that there are qualitative changes in the synapses, presumably including not only new ones but existing ones that have been changed by the experience. These include changes in the size of various synaptic components (Figure 21-4), in vesicle numbers in the size of postsynaptic thickenings, and in the size of the dendritic spines. Importantly, similar changes have been found in neurons exhibiting LTP, thus adding evidence that LTP may be an analogue of normal learning.

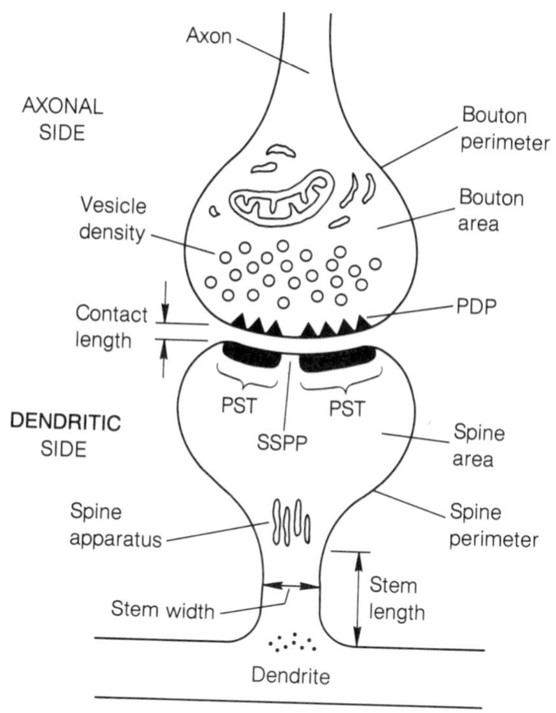

FIGURE 21-4. Measures of synaptic change. PST, postsynaptic thickening; SSPP, subsynaptic plate perforation; PDP, presynaptic dense projection. (After Greenough and Chang, 1985.)

The cause of these changes in the synapse is unknown at present. Various hypotheses have been advanced to suggest that alterations in protein synthesis in neurons might be responsible, possibly because of some sort of change in gene expression in the neurons, which may be expressed through changes in RNA (e.g., see Black et al.). It follows that blocking protein synthesis ought to block both LTP or new learning, and this appears to be so. Another hypothesis is that use of neurons leads to changes in presynaptic calcium permeability, which, in turn, leads to a series of biochemical changes (see Lynch and Baudry for details). At present, although all of these hypotheses remain speculative, it seems highly likely that long-lasting behavioral change stems from a morphological change in neurons.

The Location of Synaptic Change

If a morphological change is the basis of memory, then we must ask which neurons in the brain are modified by experience. It is highly unlikely that every neuron would change with each experience, or, alternatively, that only one neuron would change with each experience. It seems reasonable to suppose that visual experiences would change neurons in the visual system, and auditory and somatosensory experiences would alter those in the respective sensory systems.

At least three problems arise, however. First, a sensory experience could not change every neuron in the relevant system, or all subsequent experiences would be changed. That is, cells in primary visual cortex cannot be allowed to change too much or the information sent to higher areas would be radically different, which would lead to very different sensory experiences and perceptions over time. We know, however, that specific visual environments do change primary visual cortex, which leaves us with a puzzle! Nonetheless, it is logical to suppose that experiences will be more likely to affect higher level sensory areas than lower level ones. Second, if sensory experiences change sensory systems, thus permitting memories of the events, how do we remember ideas or thoughts? Presumably the mechanism is the same but the changes may be "elsewhere," although the location is still a mystery. Third, if experiences result in widespread changes in synapses, how do we find specific memories? It would seem that it memories are widely distributed in large cell assemblies, then it would be a formidable task to locate the memories, especially if they are to be found quickly. Most of us have had the experience of being totally unable to recall some answer for an examination, only to suddenly remember one small fact that appears to allow us access to the entire memory. What mechanism could account for this?

We have assumed here that memories are likely to be stored in the cortex, but they need not be. Decorticated animals can learn many behavioral tasks, and animals with a primitive nervous system (e.g., *Aplysia*), can learn and show evidence of "memory." It is reasonable, therefore, to suppose that memories will be stored in both cortical and subcortical structures. Furthermore, given that many memories are dependent upon sensory processing and that sensory processing is carried out in multiple systems, it is reasonable to assume that memory may be a multiple-component system, with different types of information stored in different places in the brain. This is especially true of short-term memory. Nearly any type of complex information processing requires a capacity for temporary storage, if only because it takes time to transmit the information, and thus one would expect to have specific short-term stores that are independent of one another. Indeed, we have seen that both parietal and frontal lesions produce short-term memory deficits, but of a different nature (see Chapters 17 and 19). There may be separable long-term memory stores as well, but there are likely to be fewer of them, and possibly only one. We will return to these concepts later.

Terminology

The terminology in the study of memory can be confusing. Various terms are used by different authors to describe different forms of memory, and various terms are used to describe lost memory.

Terms for Memory. We have distinguished between short-term and long-term memory, but there are many other terms commonly used to distinguish different forms of memory (Table 21-1). Perhaps the most useful distinction is that between declarative and procedural memory. **Declarative memories** are the facts that are accessible to conscious recollection. That is, they are memories we can recount. The various facts in this book, if remembered, would be declarative memories. **Procedural memories** are skills and "au-

TABLE 21-1. Terms describing two kinds of memory

Fact	Skill
Declarative	Procedural
Memory	Habit
Knowing that	Knowing how
Locale	Taxon
Cognitive mediation	Semantic
Conscious recollection	Skills
Elaboration	Integration
Memory with record	Memory without record
Autobiographical	Perceptual
Representational	Dispositional
Episodic	Semantic
Working	Reference

This table illustrates different types of memory dissociations that have been made by different writers. They share the idea that memory can be subdivided into one or more processes. The different terms in the same columns do not refer to the same things.
Source: After Squire, 1987

tomatic'' operations that are not stored with respect to specific times or places. They are often things we can do, such as motor skills. (For a more detailed discussion of the distinctions between hypothetical types of memory, see Squire's readable book *Memory and the Brain.)*

Memory Loss. Three terms are used to describe loss of memory. **Amnesia** refers to the partial or total loss of memory. A difficulty in recalling events prior to the onset of the amnesia is known as **retrograde amnesia.** An inability to remember events subsequent to the onset of the amnesia is known as **anterograde amnesia.** These amnesias are usually not complete but patchy, some events being remembered and others not.

CANDIDATE BRAIN REGIONS FOR MEMORY

Many of our hunches about the organization of memory have come from the study of pathological memory and its anatomical correlates. Unfortunately, there are few studies in which both the neuropathological and neuroanatomical evidence is adequately assessed, making it difficult to reach firm conclusions. Thus, although there are reports dating back to the turn of the century of amnesic syndromes associated with particular brain pathologies, the neuropsychological investigation is often sketchy at best. More recently, the advent of brain-scanning devices such as the CT scan have allowed thorough psychological investigations to be correlated with estimated pathology from brain scans. Although of considerable interest, such studies are not satisfactory because they do not provide conclusive anatomical evidence. Furthermore, brain diseases do not usually respect anatomical boundaries and there is always variability across cases, so the clinical-pathological correlations must be corroborated with experimental work using nonhuman species. Nonetheless, the clinical literature provides us with a general framework from which to begin.

Brain Lesions and Amnesia

The major diseases that produce brain damage and amnesia include head trauma, vascular disorders (including both strokes and ischemia), infections (e.g., encephalitis), and degenerative processes (e.g., Alzheimer's disease, Korsakoff's disease). Two medical treatments may lead to memory disturbance as well: neurosurgery for the treatment of various disease processes (especially for uncontrollable epilepsy), and electroconvulsive shock (known as ECS or ECT) for depression (see Markowitsch and Pritzel for a detailed review). Patients with these pathologies show about five regions that are consistently said to correlate with some form of memory loss. These include: anterior temporal cortex, the medial temporal region, medial thalamus, mamillary bodies, and basal forebrain. These regions are illustrated in Figure 21-5.

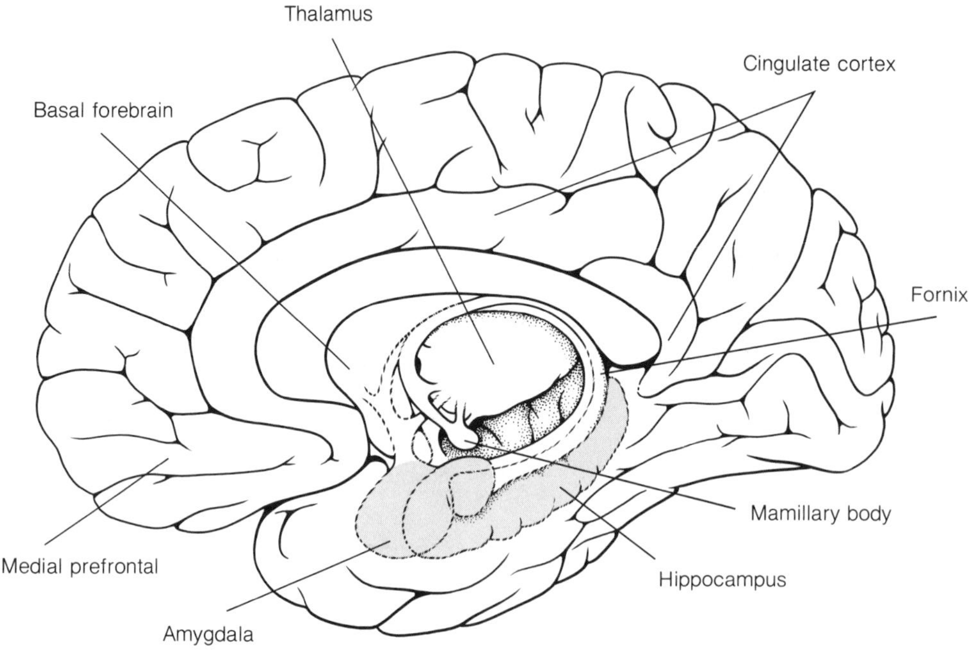

FIGURE 21-5. Sites of brain damage by diseases and other events that can cause memory loss.

Recently, there has been speculation about two other areas, the prefrontal cortex and retrosplenial cingulate cortex, but the association between these regions and amnesia is best seen as hypothetical at this point.

The Temporal Lobe

It has been known since the turn of century that temporal lobe damage was associated with memory loss, although the locus of the damage has been a continuing matter of debate, and there remain several candidate structures including the anterior temporal neocortex, the amygdala, the hippocampus, and the entorhinal cortex. This last cortex, which is Brodmann's area 28, is the major source of hippocampal input and output, as illustrated in Figures 21-6 and 21-7. Thus, damage to the entorhinal cortex would partially destroy afferents to the hippocampus and disrupt its function, and hippocampal damage is consistently associated with significant memory loss. (It is interesting in this context that entorhinal degeneration is one of the first pathological signs of Alzheimer's disease, which is characterized by a significant memory disturbance.) The hippocampal formation is composed of two distinct structures, known as **Ammon's horn** (which is often referred to as the hippocampus) and the dentate gyrus. Ammon's horn can be broken into substructures, known as CA_1, CA_2, and CA_3, on the basis of cytoarchitecture and connectivity. In the 1880s, Sommer observed that the area now known as CA_1 was frequently damaged in epileptics, and this zone is sometimes referred to as "Sommer's sector." It appears that CA_1 is especially vulnerable to ischemic processes, is highly epileptogenic, and is often damaged by high fever in children, leading to the development of childhood epilepsy. Although much of the hippocampal output courses through the entorhinal cortex, there is also a significant output to the mamillary body via a tract known as the fornix, which is illustrated in Figure 21-5. Damage to each of these structures is sometimes associated with amnesic syndromes.

Another region of the medial temporal lobe is the subiculum (Figure 21-6), which lies between the hippocampus and the entorhinal cortex. It sends and receives projections from the hippocampal formation, and although it is not selectively damaged in human disease, experimental lesions placed here in laboratory animals significantly disrupt hippocampal functioning. Finally, the amygdala may have a role in amnesic syndromes. The amygdala lies in front of the hippocampus (see Figure 18-2), and is frequently damaged when the hippocampal area is damaged, as in head trauma, stroke, infection, and temporal lobectomy for the treatment of intractable epilepsy. The amygdala has long been known to have a major role in emotion (see Chapter 23) and to the extent that memories have an affective component, it is reasonable to suppose that the amygdala may play a role in memory, although this role is far from certain.

The Diencephalon

The major structures of the diencephalon are the thalamus and hypothalamus (see Chapter 1). Three substructures of the diencephalon have been associated with amnesia: the dorsal medial (MD) nucleus, the group of anterior nuclei in the thalamus, and the mamillary body of the hypothalamus. Both MD and the mamillary bodies are frequently degenerated in chronic alcoholics who exhibit Korsakoff's syndrome (which we shall discuss in more detail later). The association of damage to both the MD and the mammilary bodies in Korsakoff's syndrome has led to a longstanding debate as to which damage is the more important for the amnesic symptoms in these patients. There are cases of medial thalamic damage of nonalcohol-related origin that show amnesic symptoms, leading to the suggestion that the medial thalamus may be the crucial focus for memory disturbance. In recent years several patients with localized thalamic injuries have been studied thoroughly by neuropsychologists, and their memory syndromes have been carefully documented. A 1979 report by Squire and Moore suggests caution, however. They studied the case of N. A., whose CT scan shows a clear focal lesion in the MD resulting from a miniature fencing foil entering the right nostril and puncturing the base of the brain. Surprisingly, when N.A. was assessed using a PET scan, which measures metabolic activity, his right medial temporal lobe was silent, suggesting that it too was damaged (or disconnected). The lesson here is that brain-behavior correlations from CT scans should be seen as tentative pending a postmortem examination of the brain. N.A.'s lesion may be far more extensive than believed, and certainly not confined to the MD.

As a final note on the diencephalon, there are a series of patients in which bilateral lesions of the medial thalamus have been performed for the relief of pain (see review by Markowitsch and Pritzel). The majority of such patients do not show a lasting memory disturbance after the operation, nor do a smaller group of patients with bilateral lesions of the anterior nuclei. It thus seems likely that the diencephalic damage may either need to extend beyond the medial or anterior nuclei, or to occur in a brain that has other abnormalities, as would be expected in chronic alcoholics.

Basal Forebrain Damage

Two groups of patients have damage to the basal forebrain (Figure 21-5): those with strokes or an-

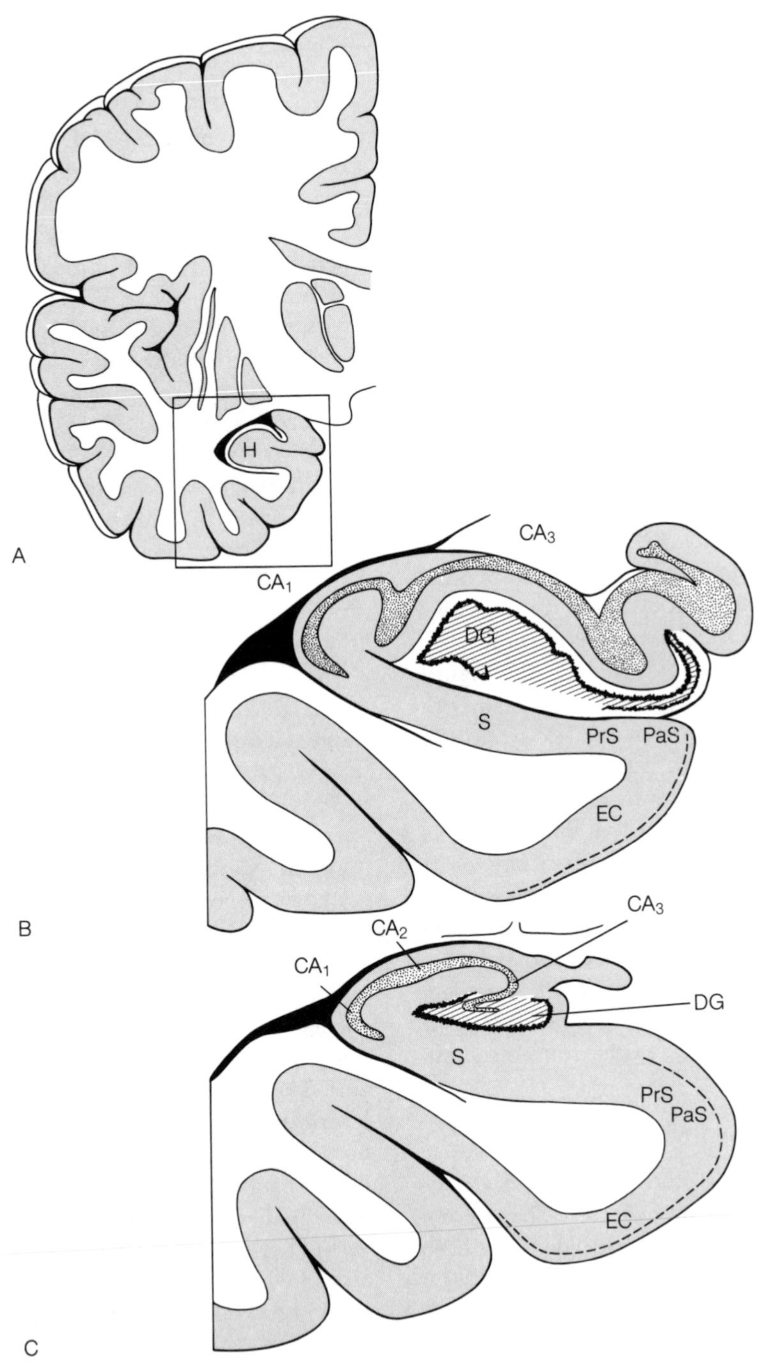

FIGURE 21-6. The hippocampal formation (H) in the human brain. *A*. Frontal section through the right hemisphere. The box indicates the area enlarged in the lower figures. *B*. Section through the anterior hippocampus. *C*. Section through a slightly more posterior section. Abbreviations: DG, dentate gyrus; EC, entorhinal cortex, PaS, parasubiculum; PrS, presubiculum; S, subiculum.

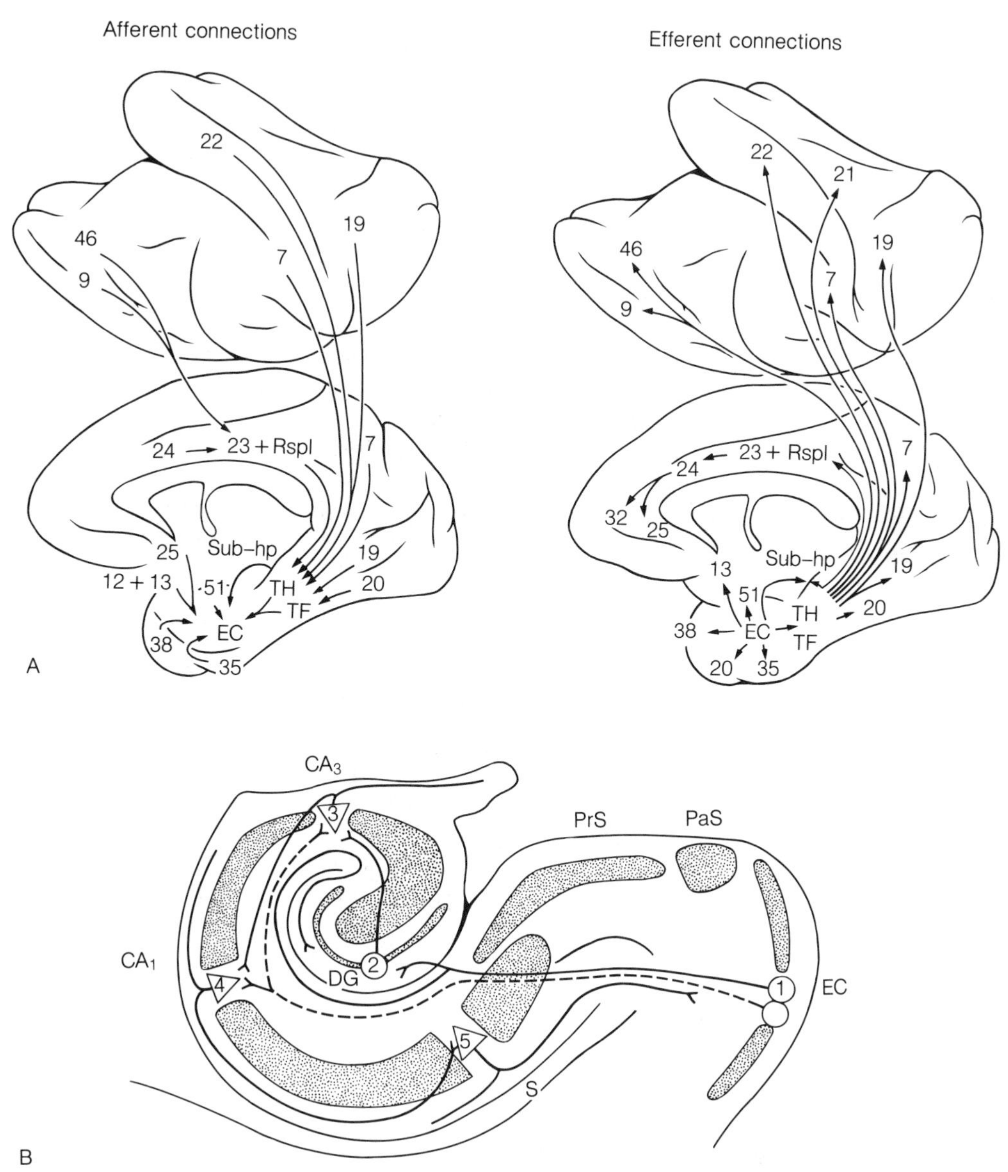

FIGURE 21-7. *A*. The afferent and efferent connections of the entorhinal cortex (EC). Areas EC, TH and TF form the parahippocampal cortex. EC is Brodmann's area 28 and TH and TF are areas described by von Bonin and Bailey and could be called posterior parahippocampal cortex. Rspl, retrosplenial cortex; Sub-hp, subiculum-hippocampus. (After van Hoesen, 1982.) *B*. The major connections of the entorhinal-hippocampal area. The entorhinal input goes to the dentate gyrus (DG), where it synapses. The dentate granule cells synapse on the pyramidal cells of the CA_3, which synapse in turn on the pyramidal cells in CA_1. The axons of the CA_1 cells go to the subiculum (S), and the subicular cells project to the entorhinal cortex (EC). A lesion anywhere in the circuit will disrupt the entire circuit. Notice that there is also an alternative route from EC to CA_1 and CA_3 that bypasses the DG, which may also be important for mnemonic processes. (After Zola-Morgan et al., 1986.)

eurysms of the anterior communicating artery (see Figure 7-1), and those with Alzheimer's disease. The basal forebrain is a loose term used to describe the area that lies in front of and above the optic chiasm, which is the area serviced by branches of the anterior communicating artery. This includes the nucleus accumbens, septal nuclei, anterior hypothalamus, the nucleus of Meynert (which contains the group of cholinergic cells that project to the forebrain), and the prefrontal cortex roughly corresponding to Brodmann's area 13 in the human brain (Figure 19-1). There are now several series of patients in whom the surgical repair of aneurysms of the anterior communicating artery led to an amnesic syndrome, as well as numerous case reports of patients with strokes in this region. It is difficult to localize the cause of the amnesia in these patients, as the damage is variable, and there is not yet an extensive postmortem study of such patients. In contrast to the stroke patients, the patients with Alzheimer's disease have degeneration of the nucleus of Meynert, a finding that led to the cholinergic hypothesis of Alzheimer's dementia (see Chapter 31). Although the correlation between the loss of cholinergic cells and amnesia is firm, we noted earlier that Alzheimer's patients also have widespread cortical degeneration, including loss of entorhinal cortex. They also have degeneration in other neurochemical systems projecting to the neocortex. It is difficult, therefore, to establish that basal forebrain degeneration is responsible for the amnesic syndrome.

Prefrontal Cortex. Direct damage to the frontal lobes does not normally produce amnesia, but amnesic patients often have frontal lobe damage in addition to other pathologies. For example, people with basal forebrain strokes often have damage to the prefrontal cortex (see Figure 21-5), and chronic alcoholics often have atrophy of the frontal cortex, in addition to other pathologies. Schacter reviewed the amnesic syndromes of patients with and without frontal lobe damage and concluded the amnesics with such damage represent a type of amnesic syndrome that is qualitatively different from that exhibited by people with other types of amnesia. In view of the short-term memory difficulties normally observed in frontal lobe patients, their hypothesis is plausible, although it remains speculative at this point.

Retrosplenial Cingulate Cortex. The retrosplenial area lies just behind the back of the corpus callosum, which is known as the splenium. There is but a single report of an amnesic syndrome from damage here (see Valenstein et al.), so its association with amnesia must be considered highly speculative. Nevertheless, there are two reasons to wonder seriously about the possibility of retrosplenial amnesia. First, this area represents a major funnel for information running from the neocortex to the entorhinal cortex. Second, in collaboration with Sutherland, we have found that rats with retroplenial lesions show a striking anterograde and retrograde amnesia in a spatial learning task. We find this result particularly intriguing because the behavioral deficit is as large as that following hippocampal lesions, which was unexpected but consistent with Valenstein and Collegues' human case.

To summarize, there are several areas in which pathology appears to be associated with some form of memory loss. We shall now turn to the nature of the memory loss before returning to the anatomy of memory.

THE TEMPORAL LOBES AND MEMORY

The first suggestion that the temporal lobes might play a critical role in human memory was provided by Bekhterev in 1899. He reported a patient who had shown a severe memory impairment, and he demonstrated on autopsy a bilateral softening in the region of the uncus, hippocampus, and adjoining medial temporal cortex (see Figure 18-2).

In the 1950s, the importance of the hippocampus in human memory was clearly demonstrated in reports describing several patients with bilateral hippocampal damage. Scoville and Milner's patient H. M. is the most thoroughly studied, having been followed for more than 35 years. He was a motor winder by trade and had experienced generalized epileptic seizures that had grown progressively worse in frequency and severity despite very high doses of medication. On 23 August 1953, William Scoville performed a bilateral medial temporal lobe resection in an attempt to stop the seizures. Afterward H. M. experienced a severe anterograde memory impairment that has persisted with little improvement to this day.

The Case of H. M.

H. M.'s IQ is above average (118 on the Wechsler Adult Intelligence Scale), and he performed normally on several different types of perceptual tests such as the Mooney Closure Test (see Chapter 11). H. M.'s memory for events prior to the surgery is good, as is his capacity to recall remote events such as incidents from his school days or jobs he held in his late teens or early twenties, prior to his surgery. Socially, H. M. is quiet and well mannered. He dresses neatly but has to be reminded when to shave. He speaks in a monotone but articulates his words well and has a vocabulary in keeping with his above-average intelligence. His language comprehension is normal and he understands complex verbal material, including jokes.

H. M.'s recall of personal events is interesting and enlightening, as witnessed by the following description. Notice his severe handicap in everyday life and his ability to remember some events but only after prolonged repetition.

H. M. has been cared for all this time by his mother, who usually accompanies him wherever he goes. It so happened, however, that in 1966 the mother was in Hartford Hospital, recovering from a minor operation, just when H. M. was about to leave for Boston. It was his father, therefore, who packed H. M.'s clothes for him and brought him to meet us at Dr. Scoville's office prior to the journey. The father had also taken the patient to visit his mother in hospital that very morning, the third such visit within a week. Yet when we questioned H. M., he seemed not to remember any of these visits, although he expressed a vague idea that something might have happened to his mother. On the journey to Boston, he kept saying that he felt a little uneasy and wondered if something might be wrong with one of his parents, though he could not be sure which one. On being asked who had packed his bag for the trip, he said "Seems like it was my mother. But then that's what I'm not sure about. If there is something wrong with my mother, then it could have been my father." Despite our explaining the situation to him repeatedly during the journey, H. M. was never able to give a clear account of what had happened, and was still feeling "uneasy" when he reached Boston, wondering if something was "wrong" with one of his parents. Gradually, this uneasiness wore off, and although he was told repeatedly that he could telephone home any time he wished, he no longer seemed to know why he should do so. Next day he appeared completely unaware that there had been any question of illness in his family. When asked again who had packed his suitcase, he said "It must have been my mother. She always does these things." It seemed to us instructive how the emotional tone (one of concern and uneasiness), which was associated with the vague knowledge of his mother's illness, appeared to fade away nearly as rapidly as his knowledge of the events provoking it.

During three of the nights at the Clinical Research Center, the patient rang for the night nurse, asking her, with many apologies, if she would tell him where he was and how he came to be there. He clearly realized that he was in a hospital but seemed unable to reconstruct any of the events of the previous day. On another occasion he remarked "Every day is alone in itself, whatever enjoyment I've had, and whatever sorrow I've had." Our own impression is that many events fade for him long before the day is over. He often volunteers stereotyped descriptions of his own state, by saying that it is "like waking from a dream." His experience seems to be that of a person who is just becoming aware of his surroundings without fully comprehending the situation, because he does not remember what went before.

In December, 1967 (eighteen months after the visit to Boston), H. M.'s father died suddenly, and H. M. is said to have become temporarily quite irritable and intractable, rushing out of the house in anger one evening. The cause of the anger was finding that some of his guns were missing. These had been prize possessions of which he often spoke and which he had kept in his room for many years, but an uncle had claimed them as his legacy after the father's death. The patient was upset by what to him was an inexplicable loss, but became calm when they were replaced in his room. Since then, he has been his usual even-tempered self. When questioned about his parents two months later, he seemed to be dimly aware of his father's death. In these and similar respects, he demonstrates some capacity to set up traces of constant features of his immediate environment. In this instance, the continued absence of one of his parents may have served as an unusually effective clue. Until then, H. M.'s entire life had been spent at home with his father and mother.

After his father's death, H. M. was given protected employment in a state rehabilitation centre, where he spends week-days participating in rather monotonous work, programmed for several retarded patients. A typical task is the mounting of cigarette lighters on the cardboard frames for display. It is characteristic that he cannot give us any description of his place of work, the nature of his job, or the route along which he is driven each day, to and from the centre.

In contrast to the inability to describe a job after six months of daily exposure (except for weekends), H. M. is able to draw an accurate floor plan of the bungalow in which he has lived for the past eight years. He also seems to be familiar with the topography of the immediate neighbourhood, at least within two or three blocks of his home, but is lost beyond that. His limitations in this respect are illustrated by the manner in which he attempted to guide us to his house, in June, 1966, when we were driving him back from Boston. After leaving the main highway, we asked him for help in locating his house. He promptly and courteously indicated to us several turns, until we arrived at a street which he said was quite familiar to him. At the same time, he admitted that we were not at the right address. A phone call to his mother revealed that we were on the street where he used to live before his operation. With her directions we made our way to the residential area where H. M. now lives. He did not get his bearings until we were within two short blocks of the house, which he could just glimpse through the trees. (Milner et al., 1968, pp. 216–217)

Formal Tests of H. M.s' Memory

H. M.'s memory has been the subject of literally dozens of papers. The following discussion summarizes some of the major findings on the extent of his amnesia, the central feature of which is a failure in long-term retention for most events in the absence of any general intellectual impairment or perceptual disorder.

Learning and Memory. H. M. is impaired at virtually any kind of learning task in which there is a delay between presentation and recall, particularly if interfering material is presented between trials. For example, when shown photographs of people, he fails to recognize them 2 min later if asked to repeat digits in the interim. He is severely deficient on tests of verbal learning and recall and cannot master sequences of digits beyond his immediate span. H. M. is also impaired at nonverbal tasks such as the delayed recall of a complex geometric design and the recognition of recurrent nonsense patterns.

Maze-Learning Tests. H. M. has been tested on both stylus-and tactile-maze tests. In the former test a wood board has metal bolt heads sticking out as shown in Figure 21-8. The subject must discover and remember the correct route and is told only when he makes errors. H. M. failed to acquire the route even after extensive testing. He did, however, solve a radically shortened version of the maze, although it took him 155 trials. In the tactile-maze test, the subject must learn a similar sort of problem, although in this case he is blindfolded and runs his fingers through alleys, again having to discover the correct route himself. Once again, H. M. failed to learn the complete maze but eventually solved a shortened version of it.

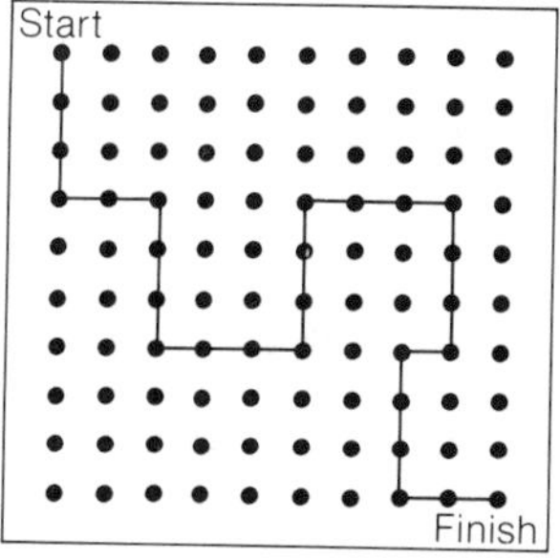

FIGURE 21-8. A visually guided stylus maze. The black circles represent metal bolt heads on a wood base. The task is to discover and remember the correct route, indicated here by the line. Deficits on this task are correlated with the amount of right hippocampus damaged. (After Milner, 1970.)

Classical Conditioning. The question of whether H. M. can be classically conditioned has not been resolved. In 1962, Kimura attempted to condition galvanic skin responses, which were to be elicited by electric shock, to previously neutral stimuli. The experiment had to be abandoned, as it turned out that H. M. showed no GSR response to the shock, even at levels of shock intensity that normal control subjects found disagreeably painful. H. M. apparently noticed the shocks but did not complain. The cause of this unexpected result has not been determined. Although classical conditioning has not been demonstrated in H. M., work by Warrington and Weiskrantz implies that H. M. probably can be classically conditioned. They classically conditioned an eyeblink response in two severe amnesics and demonstrated retention over an interval of 24 h. This significant retention occurred in spite of the subjects' denial that they had ever seen the conditioning apparatus.

Response to Internal States. H. M.'s deficit in GSR implies that he may show a more general deficit in autonomic or other internal signals. For example, it has been noted that he rarely comments on such internal states as hunger, thirst, pain, and fatigue. In order to document these clinical observations, Hebben and colleagues examined his thermal pain perception and his reports of hunger before and after meals. Although H. M.'s somatosensory thresholds appeared normal, he was very poor at discriminating different levels of stimuli found painful by normal subjects and never reported pain after stimuli that others found quite painful. A similar neglect of internal state was seen in his report of hunger. On a scale of 0 to 100 where 0 is "famished" and 100 is "too full to eat another bite," H. M. consistently reported 50, whether he was about to eat or had just eaten. In an attempt to influence his subjective report of satiety, the authors supplied him with as much food as he could eat in one sitting. After he had consumed a complete dinner, his empty tray was removed, and without explanation another full dinner was provided. He apparently did not behave as if anything unusual had happened, and after having eaten the second dinner, except for the salad, he reported simply that he was finished. At that time, however, he rated his satiation at 75! H. M. is clearly impaired at monitoring pain and hunger, although the structural damage responsible for this is uncertain. Hippocampal damage alone is unlikely to produce all the observed effects. Presumably the amygdalectomy plays a significant role, although Anderson's study of the effects of amygdalectomy in humans makes no mention of effects such as those reported for H. M.

Motor Learning. Although H. M. has a severe memory defect on tests of kinesthetic memory, memory for words, and visual location, he is surprisingly competent at motor learning. In one experiment Milner trained H. M. on a mirror-drawing task that required tracing a line between the double outline of a star while seeing the star and his pencil only in a mirror (Figure 21-9). This task is initially difficult even for normal subjects, but they improve with practice. H. M. had a normal learning curve and although he did not remember having performed the task previously, he retained the skill on the following days. Subsequently, Corkin trained H. M. on a variety of manual-tracking and coordination tasks. Although his initial performances tended to be inferior to those of control subjects, he showed nearly normal improvement from session to session.

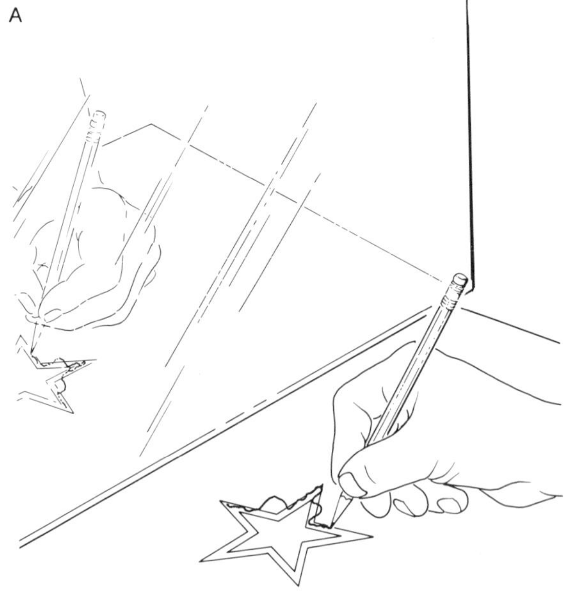

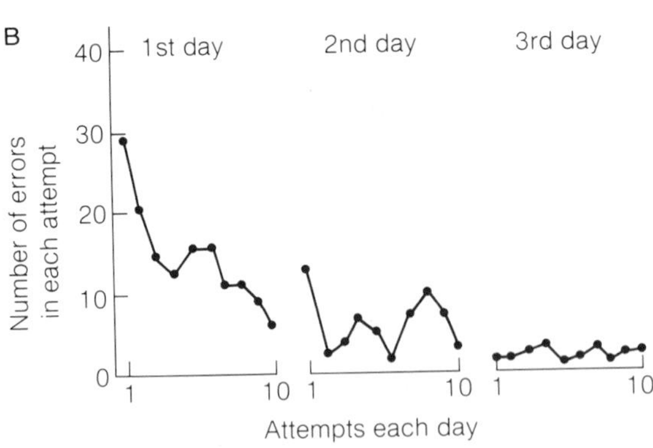

FIGURE 21-9. *A*. In this test the subject's task is to trace between the two outlines of the star while viewing his or her hand in a mirror. The reversing effect of the mirror makes this a difficult task initially. Crossing a line constitutes an error. *B*. H. M. shows clear improvement in motor tasks on the star test, which is a procedural memory. (After Blakemore, 1977.)

In 1981, Cohen and Corkin showed an analogous result on the "Tower of Hanoi puzzle," a well-studied problem involving a number of pegs and a number of blocks of different sizes. To begin the problem, all the blocks are arranged on the "source" peg in size order, with the smallest on the top and the largest on the bottom. The task is to move these blocks one at a time onto a "goal peg," with the largest block again at the bottom and the smallest at the top, while never placing a block onto one smaller than itself. Thus, successful solution requires the use of additional pegs in a specific order. Normal subjects require a decreasing number of moves for solution over successive trials. Despite his inability to remember particular moves and whether they advance or retard solution, H. M.'s performance improved systematically over days, even though his commentary during each trial sounded as though he were solving the puzzle for the first time. In short, H. M. was able to learn the procedures or operations necessary for successful performance of this cognitive skill, despite markedly impaired declarative memory for the task. We shall return to this dissociation in our discussion of amnesia.

The dissociation between the impairment in motor learning and other types of tasks implies that motor skills are stored independently of the hippocampal system. The question of where this might be has not been examined to date, although there is a substantial literature on the acquisition of motor skills by normal subjects. Perhaps psychologists studying motor skills will consider this question in neurological patients.

Other Examples of Bilateral Hippocampectomy

Much has been written and theorized about H. M., but, as we have emphasized throughout the book, studies of single cases are not a legitimate basis for neuropsychological theory. If, for example, H. M. were in some way unusual, as he might very well be, conclusions about the hippocampus and memory drawn from this one subject might be grossly overstated. H. M. is not unusual, however, as we shall see in the evidence described in this section.

Milner has studied two other patients with severe memory defects who also are believed to have bilateral hippocampal damage. They showed many of the same phenomena seen in H. M. One case, P. B., was a civil engineer whose left temporal lobe had been resectioned for relief of seizures. After surgery he had severe anterograde amnesia, which persisted and worsened until he died from unrelated causes 15 years later. At autopsy P. B. was found to have an atrophic right hippocampus opposite the surgically excised left hippocampus. Penfield and Milner proposed that P. B.'s right hippocampus was dead at the time of the operation, resulting in severe amnesia like H. M.'s.

A more recent case of hippocampal damage is especially intriguing. Case R. B. was a male postal worker who, at 52 years of age, had an ischemic episode secondary to a coronary bypass operation. During the next 5 years until his death, R. B. exhibited a marked anterograde amnesia, with only a short retrograde amnesia of unknown duration, possibly a year or two. Upon his death there was a thorough postmortem examination that revealed a bilateral loss of all cells in CA_1, and virtually no other pathology. In particular, the amygdala, MD, and mamillary bodies were intact. R. B.'s performance on formal memory tests was particularly interesting as his IQ was 111 but his memory quotient was only 91. His performance on tests of paired-associate learning and recall of stories or diagrams was very poor indeed, with virtually no recall at all. In contrast, his recall of events preceding his ischemia was slightly better than average. Further, whereas the memory impairment was obvious to his family, there was never any mention of any personality change or of any other cognitive deficit.

R. B is important here for he illustrates one of the few examples in which a patient was carefully studied behaviorally and then, soon after, the patient died of nonneurological causes and a thorough investigation of the brain was carried out. (See Zola-Morgan et al., 1986 for more details of this case.) Furthermore, R. B. illustrates that it is possible to have a severe amnesia with bilateral damage to a remarkably small region of the brain, and that the inclusion of additional medial temporal tissue would not have made his anterograde amnesia much worse. We will return to this point below.

Effects of Unilateral Hippocampal Lesions on Memory

Patients with unilateral lesions of the hippocampus do not suffer from H. M.'s or R. B.'s severe amnesia, but they do have significant memory deficits. The role of the hippocampus in memory can be assessed by correlating the amount of hippocampus removed in a temporal lobectomy with performance on memory tests. That is, since the surgeon removed only as much of the hippocampus as necessary to stop the abnormal epileptiform activity, different patients lose different amounts of hippocampus. The right hand column of Table 21-2 summarizes the results of such an analysis on the right hippocampus. Performance on maze-learning tasks is correlated with damage to the right hippocampus: the larger the removal, the larger the deficit. The same is true of a face-recognition task. On a test of spatial position the subject marks the circle indicated on an exposed 8-in. line, then, after a short delay, attempts to reproduce this position on another 8-in. line. Again, performance is related to the extent of right hippocampus removed. In an ingenious experiment Corsi devised a spatial analogue to Hebb's Recurring-Digits Test. A series of blocks is presented, and the subject learns to tap out a sequence on a block board, illustrated in Figure 21-10. Just as there is a memory span, or maximum number that can be remembered, for digits, normal subjects show a memory span for blocks. Patients and normal control subjects are tested on a series of block sequences that are one more than span. As on the Hebb repeating-digits experiment, one sequence repeats itself every third trial. Normal subjects learn the repeating sequence over several trials, although they are still poor at the novel

TABLE 21-2. Summary of tests that correlate degree of memory defect with amount of unilateral hippocampal removal

Test	Site of lesion: Left hippocampus	Site of lesion: Right hippocampus	Basic reference
Tactile maze learning	—	x	Milner, 1965
Visual maze learning	—	x	Corkin, 1965
Facial recognition	—	x	Milner, 1968
Spatial block span +1	—	x	Corsi, 1972
Spatial position	—	x	Corsi, 1972
Spatial association	—	x	Petrides, 1985
Spatial memory	—	x	Smith and Milner, 1981
Self-ordered design recall	—	x	Petrides and Milner, 1982
Recall of nonsense syllables	x	—	Corsi, 1972; Samuels et al., 1972
Recall of word lists	x	—	Jaccarino-Hiatt, 1978
Digit span +1	x	—	Corsi, 1972
Nonspatial association	x	—	Petrides, 1985
Self-ordered word recall	x	—	Petrides and Milner, 1982
Recall of consonant trigrams	x	—	Milner, 1974

Note: x = significnat impairment; — = normal performance.

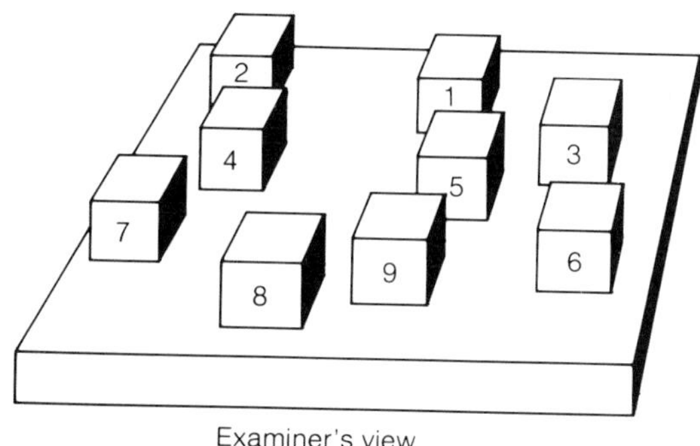

FIGURE 21-10. Sketch of Corsi's Block-Tapping Task. The subject must copy a sequence tapped out by the examiner on the blocks. The block's numbers are visible on the examiner's side but not on the subject's. (After Milner, 1971.)

sequences. Subjects with damage to the right hippocampus do not learn the repeating sequence or do so very slowly (Figure 21-11), whereas subjects with other cortical lesions perform as controls do. This test appears to be the best available noninvasive test or right hippocampal function. More recently, the size of right hippocampal removal has been associated with a deficit in two additional tests of spatial learning and memory—a finding that adds credence to the notion that the right hippocampus may play a role in spatial orientation.

The left-hand column of Table 21-2 summarizes a similar analysis of left hippocampal function. Recall of nonsense syllables (e.g., "p t b") is impaired in direct relation to the amount of hippocampus removed, as is performance on Hebb's Repeating-Digits Test (see Figure 21-11), a nonspatial association test (see Chapter 18), and a test of recall of self-ordered word learning (see Chapter 19).

These results illustrate that both hippocampi are essential for normal memory, and that the left hippocampus can be functionally dissociated from the right. The left is more important in the memory of verbal material, the right in the memory of visual and spatial material.

Stimulation of the Hippocampus During Surgery

If it is assumed that stimulation of the hippocampus disrupts its functioning, then stimulation would be expected to impair memory functions. Chapman and his associates stimulated the hippocampus bilaterally in 2 epileptic patients and unilaterally in 13 others and found that bilateral stimulations produced retrograde amnesia that persisted for a few hours and reached back about two weeks. Immediate memory (digit span) and more remote memories were intact. Unilateral stimulation produced similar but lesser effects on memory.

Although these results appear to support the hypothesized role of the hippocampus in memory, there are problems with this interpretation. In their series at the Montreal Neurological Institute, Theodore Rasmussen and his colleagues stimulated the hippocampus in well over 300 patients

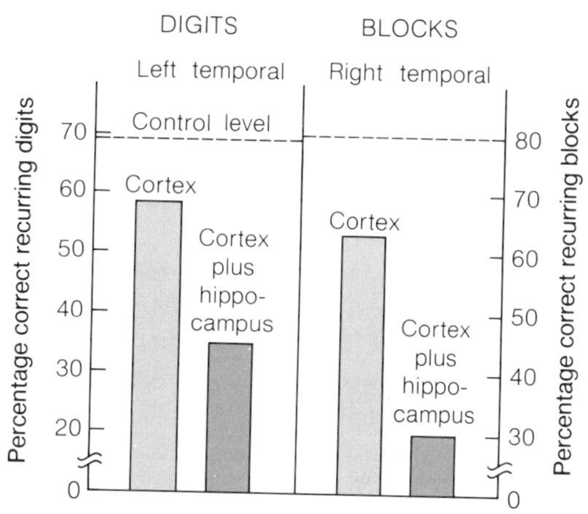

FIGURE 21-11. Summary of double dissociation of left and right hippocampal function. Left temporal lesions, including radical removal of the hippocampus, produced severe deficits on acquisition of the recurring digits. On the other hand right temporal lesions, including radical removal of the hippocampus, produced serious deficits on acquisition of recurring-block sequences. (Redrawn after Milner, 1970; 1971.)

undergoing surgery for temporal lobe epilepsy. Whenever the hippocampal stimulation produced hallucinatory or interpretational responses, there were significant alterations of electrical activity on the temporal cortex. This implies that disturbances of memory from hippocampal stimulation may result from disruption of normal activity elsewhere in the brain. Furthermore, Doty and Overman found that electrical stimulation of the anterior commissure of monkeys prevented acquisition of a visual learning task, but that stimulation elsewhere in the temporal lobe had no effect.

In conclusion, the results of stimulation of the hippocampus are somewhat ambiguous. Stimulation of the temporal lobe does disrupt memory, but the cause and principal locus of this effect have yet to be clearly demonstrated.

Carotid Sodium Amytal Memory Testing

Sodium Amytal testing (see Chapter 15) has shown that if one hippocampus is damaged and the drug is injected into the contralateral hemisphere, there is amnesia for material presented while the drug was active.

Only very simple memory tests can be used during the administration of sodium Amytal, because the drug wears off within a few minutes. Before the drug injection the patient is presented with both verbal and nonverbal items and is told to remember them. For example, the patient is shown two pictures (e.g., hand and cup) and asked to name them and to remember them. He or she is then distracted with mental arithmetic before being asked to recall the names of the pictures. A similar procedure is used for recall of a sentence (e.g., Peter is in the garden). After this baseline testing, sodium Amytal is injected into one hemisphere and testing is repeated, with the difference that the patient is shown two new pictures and given a new sentence to remember. After the drug has worn off, the patient is tested for recall and, failing this, recognition of all the items. Performance on measures of recall are generally very poor in comparison with recognition, which is quite good (over 90%) for both verbal and nonverbal material.

Table 21-3 compares the effects of injection into the hemisphere ipsilateral to and contralateral to a lesion. Injection into the contralateral (normal) hemisphere allows the efficiency of the impaired hemisphere's memory to be tested. Table 21-3 shows that if a patient suffers from temporal lobe epilepsy with a unilateral focus, then, in the absence of the intact hemisphere during the period of anesthesia, the epileptic hemisphere is badly impaired at recognizing the pictures of sentences (59% correct). This is to be compared with 85% recognition when the injection is made into the epileptic hemisphere. Comparison of the two rates indicates that normal memory function requires at least one temporal lobe to be functioning normally. Injection into the side contralateral to the lesion produces an unacceptable memory loss because neither hippocampus is operative. (Remember that 59% correct on a *recognition* test is very poor performance.) Table 21-3 also illustrates that patients with bilateral epileptic foci have significant memory defects when either hemisphere is injected, again implying that one normally functioning temporal lobe is necessary for normal memory. Patients with bilateral epileptic foci are clearly poor risks for surgery, since injection into

TABLE 21-3. Percentage of recognition after injection of sodium Amytal ipsilaterally and contralaterally to lesion

	Site of injection	
	Ipsilateral to lesion (%)	Contralateral to lesion (%)
Unilateral epileptic focus	85	59
Bilateral epileptic focus	50	40

Source: After Jones-Gotman M. Psychological evaluation: Testing hippocampal function. In J. Engle, ed. *Surgical Treatment of the Epilepsies.* New York: Raven Press, 1986

either hemisphere leaves the patient with unacceptable memory defects.

To summarize, there are three principal findings from the sodium Amytal studies. First, if the drug is injected ipsilaterally to the damaged hemisphere, the patient retains over 85% of both the verbal and the nonverbal material. Thus, both temporal lobes are capable of storing both types of memories. This result does not inpugn the previously described studies indicating an asymmetry in memory function, since the memory tests are very simple and do not nearly tax a person's mnemonic abilities. Second, injection of the drug contralateral to the damaged temporal lobe results in substantial memory impairment, retention dropping to 59%. In other words, if the injection is made into the intact hemisphere, the damaged hemisphere is impaired at storing the new material. Third, if injection ipsilateral to a known lesion results in impaired memory, there are strong grounds for predicting that the patient suffers from a bilateral lesion, as in the case of P. B. described above.

Role of the Temporal Neocortex in Memory

Although we have emphasized the role of the medial temporal lobes (hippocampus) in memory, the neocortex of the lateral temporal lobes is also important. Lesions of the anterior temporal lobe sparing the hippocampus result in a variety of memory impairments, although the global amnesia of H. M. is not observed. Milner and her colleagues have double dissociated the effects of damage to the neocortex of the temporal lobe of each hemisphere on several memory tasks. They conclude that lesions of the right temporal lobe result in impaired memory of nonverbal material, whereas lesions of the left temporal lobe result in impaired memory of verbal material. These findings are summarized in Table 21-4, where it can be seen that removal of the right temporal lobe produces deficits on nonverbal tests, including recall of complex geometric figures, paired-associate learning of nonsense figures, and recognition of nonsense figures (see Figure 21-12), of tunes, and of previously seen photographs of faces. No deficits are seen, however, on tests of verbal memory. Removal of the left temporal lobe, on the other hand, produces deficits on verbal tests, such as recall of previously presented stories and of pairs of words, and recognition of words or numbers and of recurring nonsense syllables; such removal has little effect on the nonverbal tests. These studies indicate that although damage to the medial tem-

TABLE 21-4. Summary of the effects of left or right temporal lobectomy on various tests of memory

Test	Site of lesion: Left temporal lobe	Site of lesion: Right temporal lobe	Basic reference
Geometric recall (Rey)	—	x	Taylor, 1969
Paired-associate nonsense figures	—	x	Prisko, 1963
Recognition of nonsense figures	—	x	Kimura, 1963
Recurring nonsense figures	—	x	Kimura, 1963
Recognition of faces	—	x	Warrington and James, 1967
Recognition of unfamiliar melodies	—	x	Zatorre, 1985
Recognition of tunes	—	x	Shankweiler, 1966
Recall of stories	x	—	Milner, 1967
Paired-associate words	x	—	Milner, 1967
Recognition of words, numbers	x	—	Milner, 1967
Recurring nonsense syllables	x	—	Corsi, 1972

Note: x = significant impairment; — = normal performance.

FIGURE 21-12. Example from Kimura's Recurring Nonsense Figures Test. Subjects are shown a series of cards, on each of which is an unfamiliar design. Some designs recur, and it is the subject's task to say whether he or she has seen each design before. Right temporal lesions impair recognition in this task.

poral lobe is associated with severe deficits of memory, so too is damage restricted to just the temporal neocortex associated with memory disturbance.

In a clever experiment, Jones found that patients with left hemisphere lesions could improve their verbal memory by encoding verbal information with the assistance of visual imagery. Thus, memory for a list of paired-associate words improved significantly if the person was told to remember pairs; for example, elephant-bouquet would be remembered by visualizing an elephant holding a bouquet with its trunk. Similarly, patients with right temporal lesions could benefit from the use of verbal encoding. Thus, for example, in the case of "elephant-bouquet" the patient was instructed to verbally encode the pair in a sentence such as "the elephant ate the bouquet." H. M. did not benefit from instructions to use these strategies, indicating that one intact hippocampus is necessary for this type of encoding scheme to be of value.

Summary. Lesions to the temporal lobe produce significant and often tragically severe deficits in long-term memory. These deficits are not modality-specific, because they occur to both visual and auditory material no matter how the material is initially presented or memory is assessed. The deficits are material-specific, however; left temporal lesions specifically impair memory for verbal material and right temporal lesions impair memory of nonverbal material. Although there is no question of memory defects following temporal lobe lesions, there is substantial controversy over what the critical focus for the lesion is to produce the maximal deficit and why there are deficits at all. We address the first question in the next section and save discussion of the last question for our discussion of theories of amnesia.

THE FRONTAL LOBES AND MEMORY

Historically there have been extravagant claims that the frontal lobes are responsible for the highest intellectual functions, but until quite recently there was no evidence that the frontal lobes are involved in memory. In 1963, Prisko devised an experiment based on previous work with experimental animals. It was essentially a "compound-stimulus" task in which two stimuli in the same sensory modality were presented in succession, separated by a short interval. The subject's task was to report whether the second stimulus of the pair was identical to the first. On half the trials the stimuli were the same and on the other half they were different. Thus, the task required the subject to remember the first stimulus of a pair in order to compare it with the second, while suppressing the stimuli that occurred on previous trials. Prisko used pairs of clicks, light flashes, tones, colors, and irregular nonsense patterns as the stimuli. The same stimuli were used repeatedly in different combinations. Patients with unilateral frontal lobe removals showed a marked impairment at matching the clicks, flashes, and colors.

In the Prisko test the subject is required to suppress the memory of previous trials and concentrate only on the first stimulus in the pair. If this behavior is no longer possible after the frontal lesion, then, when a few stimuli constantly recur, the interfering effects of previous trials may seriously impair test performance. That is, because there is difficulty in discriminating the most recent stimulus from others that appeared earlier, the frontal lobe patient's time discriminations become rather blurred. This possibility was tested more directly in an experiment by Corsi, which was discussed previously in Chapter 19.

In Corsi's experiment there were two tasks, one verbal and one nonverbal, and the subjects were required to decide which of two stimuli had been seen more recently. In the verbal task the subjects were asked to read pairs of words presented on a series of cards (e.g., cowboy-railroad). From time to time a card appeared bearing two words with a question mark between them. The subject had to indicate which of the words he or she had read most recently. Sometimes both words had been seen before, but at other times only one had been. In the latter case the task became a simple test of recognition, whereas in the former case it was a test of recency memory. Patients with left temporal removals showed a mild deficit in recognition, as befits their difficulty with verbal memory; the frontal lobe patients performed normally. However, on the recency test both frontal lobe groups (left and right) were impaired, although the left-side group was significantly worse.

The nonverbal task was identical with the verbal, except that the stimuli were photographs of paintings rather than words. Patients with right temporal lobe removals showed mild deficits on recognition, consistent with their visual memory deficit, whereas those with right frontal lobe lesions performed normally. On the recency test the frontal lobe groups were impaired, but now the right-side group was significantly worse. Thus, Corsi's experiments confirm Prisko's results indicating a deficit in the memory of the temporal ordering of events, a conclusion corroborated by Petride's more recent experiments showing deficits in self-ordered tasks in patients with frontal lobe lesions (see Chapter 19). The data from these studies are consistent with the hypothesis that the frontal lobes play some role in the memory processes needed to separate events in time, but Prisko's data also suggest that frontal lobe patients may have another type of memory deficit related to their sensitivity to interference from exposure to new material.

This possibility was tested directly by Moscovitch and Milner. In their experiment patients were read five different lists of 12 words each and were instructed to recall each list immediately after presentation. In the first four lists the words were all drawn from the same taxonomic category, such as sports, followed by a fifth list from a different category, such as professions. Normal subjects show a decline in the number of words correctly recalled from list 1 to 4 (that is, they exhibit **proactive interference**), but they also exhibit an additional phenomenon on list 5: they recall as many words as they did for list 1, thus demonstrating what is referred to as *release from proactive interference*. Frontal lobe patients also showed strong proactive interference, as would be expected from the Prisko experiments, but surprisingly they failed to show release from proactive interference on list 5. These data imply that frontal lobe lesions produce yet another memory defect that is not observed in patients with large temporal lobe lesions, although a similar memory abnormality is observed in certain other types of amnesic disorders such as Korsakoff's syndrome (see below).

Finally, yet another deficit in memory in patients with frontal lobe lesions has been demonstrated in a test of movement copying. In their study of copying of complex arm and facial movements in patients with cortical lesions, Kolb and

Milner found that in addition to errors of sequence, frontal lobe patients made many errors of intrusion and omission; that is, when asked to copy a series of three discrete facial movements, frontal lobe patients left one movement out *(error of omission)* or added a movement seen in a previous sequence *(error of intrusion)*. The errors of intrusion may represent another example of interference effects, but the errors of omission imply a type of short-term memory defect. Specific short-term memory deficits have been suggested previously by Moscovitch to account for the performance of frontal lobe patients on certain memory tests, and we considered this idea in some detail in Chapter 19.

In summary, although frontal lobe lesions are not associated with deficits in standard tests of memory function, they do produce disturbances in certain memory functions. In particular, frontal lobe patients show an increased susceptibility to interference, have a poor memory for temporal order, show poor release from proactive interference, and have difficulty with short-term memory for certain types of material, especially spatial information. It is important to note, however, that the disturbances of memory observed in frontal lobe patients are not observed in patients with medial temporal lobe damage, but they are seen in patients with certain amnesic syndromes. This dissociation is consistent with the idea that some amnesic syndromes may result in part from frontal lobe damage in addition to diencephalic or other damage, rather than from temporal lobe damage, as is often assumed. We shall return to this point shortly.

AMNESIA FROM OTHER NEOCORTICAL DAMAGE

Cortical injuries in the parietal, posterior temporal, and possibly occipital cortex sometimes produce specific long-term memory difficulties. Examples include **color amnesia,** "face amnesia" (prosopagnosia), object **anomia** (inability to recall the names of objects), and **topographical amnesia** (inability to recall the location of an object in the environment). The basis for these deficits is poorly understood, and many appear to require bilateral lesions. It thus seems likely that some sort of disconnection phenomenon (see Chapter 20) is responsible. Topographical amnesia is probably related to posterior parietal injury, but this has been poorly studied, in part because there are few patients with parietal cortex injuries who do not have significant subcortical pathology as well. The parietal cortex is not particularly epileptogenic so there are few surgical cases.

In addition to the various long-term memory deficits from focal cortical lesions, there are many reports of deficits in short-term recall of visual, auditory, or tactile stimuli. This observation is in keeping with the idea that since there are multiple systems for processing sensory input and because the input must be held for processing, there are likely to be multiple places to demonstrate short-term memory deficits. The most likely places are the polymodal sensory areas of the posterior parietal cortex, posterior temporal cortex, and frontal lobe. (We have seen already that frontal lobe lesions produce recency memory deficits.) Warrington and Weiskrantz have presented several cases of specific short-term memory deficits in patients with lesions at the junction of the parietal, temporal, and occipital cortex. One patient, K. F., received a left posterior temporal lesion that resulted in an almost total inability to repeat verbal stimuli such as digits, letters, words, or sentences. In contrast, his long-term recall of paired-associate words or short stories was near normal. In their larger series of cases Warrington and her colleagues found that some patients apparently have defects in short-term recall of visually presented digits or letters but not for the same stimuli presented aurally. These patients have **alexia** but not aphasia. On the other hand, Luria reports patients with just the opposite difficulty: specific deficits for aurally presented but not visually presented verbal items. Luria's patients were aphasic but not alexic.

If the left parietal-temporal region is participating in the short-term storage of verbal material, is it possible that the right parietal lobe is participating in the short-term storage of nonverbal information? Although we are not aware of any published data on this point, the idea seems reasonable. One might expect, for example, that the span on the Corsi Block-Tapping Test would be reduced in patients with right parietal lesions, and preliminary data from Milner show that this may be the case.

Note that the short-term memory deficits reported both by Luria and by Warrington and Weiskrantz occur in the absence of long-term memory defects. In other words, patients may exhibit surprisingly intact recall of verbal material over long delays in spite of markedly reduced short-term recall. This phenomenon implies that short-term and long-term memory are parallel processes and that material is processed separately by both.

AMNESIA FROM DIENCEPHALIC LESIONS

Evidence of diencephalic amnesia comes from two sources: patients with focal lesions of the medial thalamus, and patients with Korsakoff's syndrome. Focal lesions of the medial thalamic area are most commonly produced by vascular accidents, which produce reliable memory problems, but as we noted earlier, there are few cases in which a thorough behavioral and postmortem examination have been done, so the critical lesion remains a mystery. More is known about alcohol-related diencephalic damage, although the anatomical localization remains a problem.

Korsakoff's Syndrome

Long-term alcoholism, especially when accompanied by malnutrition, has long been known to produce defects of memory. In the late 1800s, a Russian physician, S. S. Korsakoff, called attention to a syndrome that he found to accompany chronic alcoholism, the most obvious symptom being a severe loss of memory. He wrote:

> The disorder of memory manifests itself in an extraordinarily peculiar amnesia, in which the memory of recent events, those which just happened, is chiefly disturbed, whereas the remote past is remembered fairly well. . . . This reveals itself primarily in that the patient constantly asks the same questions and repeats the same stories. At first, during conversation with such a patient, it is difficult to note the presence of psychic disorder; the patient gives the impression of a person in complete possession of his faculties; he reasons about everything perfectly well, draws correct deductions from given premises, makes witty remarks, plays chess or a game of cards, in a word, comports himself as a mentally sound person. Only after a long conversation with the patient, one may note that at times he utterly confuses events and that he remembers absolutely nothing of what goes on around him: he does not remember whether he had his dinner, whether he was out of bed. On occasion the patient forgets what happened to him just an instant ago: you came in, conversed with him, and stepped out for one minute; then you come in again and the patient has absolutely no recollection that you had already been with him. Patients of this type may read the same page over and over again, sometimes for hours, because they are absolutely unable to remember what they have read. . . . With all this, the remarkable fact is that, forgetting all events which have just occurred, the patients usually remember quite accurately the past events which occurred long before the illness. What is forgotten usually proves to be everything that happened during the illness and a short time before the beginning of the illness. (Oscar-Berman, 1980, p. 410)

Korsakoff's syndrome has been studied intensely since the seminal paper of Sanders and

Warrington was published in 1971, because Korsakoff patients are far more readily available than individuals with other forms of global amnesia such as H. M. and R. B. Talland has described six major symptoms of Korsakoff's disease.

1. *Anterograde amnesia.* The patients are unable to form new memories. On formal memory tests they are especially bad at learning paired-associate lists.

2. *Retrograde amnesia.* The patients have an extensive impairment of remote memory that covers most of their adult life. This is easily demonstrated by their very poor recognition of famous faces from years past, faces that most normal people as well as N. A. and H. M. recognize accurately.

3. *Confabulation.* Patients make up stories about past events rather than admit memory loss. These stories are often based on past experiences and are therefore often plausible. For example, when asked where he was last night, a man told us that he had been at the Legion with his pals. He had not, but this had been a common practice in the past and so was a plausible story.

4. *Meager content in conversation.* Korsakoff patients have little to say in spontaneous conversation, presumably in part because of their amnesia.

5. *Lack of insight.* Many patients are virtually completely unaware of their memory defect.

6. *Apathy.* Indifference and incapacity persevere in ongoing activities. The patients lose interest in things quickly and generally appear indifferent to change.

These symptoms are all observed in patients who otherwise appear quite normal. They have normal IQs, are alert and attentive, appear motivated, and generally lack other neurological signs of cerebral deficit such as abnormal EEGs.

The symptoms of Korsakoff's syndrome may appear suddenly within the space of a few days. The cause is a thiamine (vitamin B_1) deficiency resulting from prolonged intake of large quantities of alcohol. The syndrome, which is usually progressive, can be arrested by massive doses of vitamin B_1 but cannot be reversed. Prognosis is poor, with only about 20% of patients showing much recovery over a year on a B_1-enriched diet. Many patients demonstrate no recovery even after 10 to 20 years.

Although there has been some controversy over the exact effect that the vitamin deficiency has on the brain, it is currently believed that there is damage in the medial thalamus, and possibly in the mammillary bodies of the hypothalamus, as well as generalized cerebral atrophy. It was widely believed that the severe memory defect results from hypothalamic damage because the mammillary bodies are a recipient of hippocampal efferents through the fornix. Thus, the damage to the diencephalon was seen as a disconnection of the hippocampal circuitry, and this disconnection produced the amnesia. This seems unlikely for several reasons. First, in many cases only the medial thalamus is degenerated and not the mammillary bodies; the reverse is not observed. Second, the major hippocampal efferents depart via the entorhinal cortex and not the fornix. (Actually, the fornical fibers do not originate in the hippocampus but rather in the subiculum.) In addition, there is considerable controversy over whether lesions to the fornix itself even produce amnesia. For example, Woolsey and Nelson report a case in which there was no apparent neuropsychological disturbance (that is, no obvious memory defect) from a malignant tumor that had destroyed the fornix bilaterally. Garcia-Bengochea and colleagues sectioned the fornix bilaterally as a treatment for epilepsy in 14 patients and reported that amnesia did not ensue. There have been two reports of memory loss after fornical section, but because these patients have not come to autopsy it is uncertain just where the lesion is. In summary, the bulk of the evidence suggests that damage to the mammillary bodies or fornix are not sufficient to produce the memory loss.

Diencephalic Contribution to Memory

There are clear differences between the memory loss experienced by diencephalic and temporal lobe patients. For example, although temporal lobe patients show normal release from proactive interference, diencephalic patients do not. Further, individuals with Korsakoff's syndrome have an extensive loss of past memories; temporal lobe patients do not. Moscovitch has suggested that Korsakoff individuals may have two problems: a diencephalic lesion and frontal lobe deterioration — the latter conclusion based on evidence from CT scans that show frontal atrophy in over 80% of Korsakoff amnesics.

OTHER SOURCES OF MEMORY LOSS

Convulsive therapy with Metrazol-induced seizures was introduced by von Meduna in 1933 after the correlation between schizophrenia and epilepsy was observed to be extremely low; von Meduna proposed that they were mutually exclusive. In 1937, Cerletti and Bini replaced Metrazol with electricity to produce **electroconvulsive shock therapy (ECT** or **ECS)**.

The method of ECT is to apply a 70- to 120-volt alternating current for about half a second through temporal electrodes. Treatments are usually given one to three times a week, lasting for 2 to 4 weeks. To protect the body from the physical consequences of the convulsions, tranquilizers, muscle relaxants, and sometimes atropine are given just prior to the shock.

The clearest result of ECT on psychological functioning is its adverse effect on memory — a consequence that has been studied thoroughly. In a 1982 review, Taylor and associates reached several conclusions regarding the nature of the memory loss: (1) Bilateral ECT frequently induces memory changes, even with the standard number of treatments (eight or nine); (2) the effects of ECT on memory appear to be cumulative, greater effects being seen with successive treatments; (3) the majority of cognitive and memory defects appear to be entirely reversible with a return to pretreatment levels of function or better within 6 to 7 months; (4) some subtle but persistent defects may be found some months after ECT, especially in personal or autobiographical material; and (5) the persistent defects tend to be of an irritating rather than a seriously incapacitating nature.

The predominantly anterograde amnesia in ECT patients suggest a similarity between them and temporal lobe patients. Since the hippocampus and amygdala are probably the most epileptogenic structures in the brain, it would not be surprising if the observed amnesia following ECT was a result of disruption of medial temporal structures. The fact that hippocampal seizure activity is known to produce cell death in the hippocampus leads to the question of whether there are permanent structural changes in the hippocampus of ECT patients, but this remains to be studied.

There have been claims that unilateral ECT has significantly less effect on memory than bilateral ECT. The evidence for this is contradictory and not altogether convincing. In a review on ECT Robertson and Inglis conclude that manipulation of electrode placements is the most promising line of research to prevent or reduce memory impairments, but that much basic research remains to be done. It seems reasonable to expect that unilateral ECT on the left might preferentially disturb verbally mediated memory, whereas unilateral ECT on the right might preferentially disturb nonverbal memory. Indeed, there is preliminary evidence that these expectations may be correct. Most of the claims made about the therapeutic powers of ECT remain unproved. In view of unpublished studies by Corkin showing that prolonged repetition of ECT has a very detrimental effect on general neuropsychological functioning, one wonders whether the risk is worth it.

Transient Global Amnesia

In 1958, Fisher and Adams described a previously unrecognized amnesic syndrome: transient global amnesia. The onset is sudden and includes both retrograde and anterograde amnesia, without apparent precipitating cause. Although this syndrome has been subsequently confirmed by many others, little is known of the etiology. It has been linked to concussion, migraine, hypoglycemia, and epilepsy, but the most likely explanation appears to be vascular interruption in the territory of the posterior cerebral artery, from either a transient ischemic attack or an embolism.

Transient global amnesia has usually been assumed to be a one-time event from which there is complete recovery. A recent review by Markowitsch questions these assumptions: the attacks are frequently repeated and there is evidence of permanent memory loss. Indeed, a thorough study by Mazzucchi and colleagues shows that there is a significant chronic memory loss; this is normally overlooked because of the dramatic recovery from global amnesia and because careful memory testing is seldom done on these people.

Traumatic Amnesia

Head injuries commonly produce a form of amnesia, the severity of the injury determining the characteristics of the amnesia. There is typically a transient loss of consciousness followed by a short period of confusion. The period of retrograde amnesia generally shrinks over time, frequently leaving a residual retrograde amnesia of only a few seconds to a minute for events immediately preceding the injury. Further, there is usually an additional period of posttraumatic or anterograde, amnesia.

Duration of the posttraumatic amnesia varies. In one series of patients with severe head injuries Whitty and Zangwill found that 10% had durations of less than 1 week, 30% had durations of 2 to 3 weeks, and the remaining 60% had durations of over 3 weeks. Unfortunately, the authors fail to specify how long the amnesia lasted in the third group. Sometimes certain events, such as the visit of a relative or some unusual occurrence, may be retained as "islands of memory" during this amnesic period. According to Whitty and Zangwill the posttraumatic amnesia commonly ends quite sharply, often after a period of natural sleep.

Infantile Amnesia

One form of amnesia is experienced by everyone and is therefore particularly intriguing: events or things experienced or learned in infancy are forgotten. (We refer readers to the excellent review by Campbell and Spear for more detail.)

The most paradoxical aspect of infantile amnesia is that the early years are generally regarded as being a time of critical importance in a child's development, yet these years are not remembered in adulthood. The evidence suggests that memory of early childhood begins in late preschool or early school years. Although there are some snatches of memory here and there from early childhood, it is difficult to know whether they are true memories or have resulted from repetition of favorite stories by parents.

Infantile amnesia appears to have three plausible explanations. First, the information may still be there but be no longer retrievable. A fascinating experiment done by Yerkes in 1912 is germane to this theory. Yerkes trained worms in a Y-maze, one end of which had a shock grid and the other, moist earth. Once the worms had learned this maze, Yerkes decapitated the creatures and retested the body on the maze over the ensuing days. The body appeared to retain the habit for a while, but appeared to lose the skill as a new head grew. To our knowledge this experiment has not been replicated, but the message of the data is intriguing: as the forebrain develops it either disrupts the memory or blocks its retrieval. Because in human ontogeny the brain clearly develops functionally in a caudorostral sequence, a similar explanation of infantile amnesia is plausible. In other words, as the new areas in the forebrain (i.e., cerebral hemispheres) mature and become functional, they preclude access to the memories laid down earlier.

A second, similar explanation of infantile amnesia suggests that one memory system is used by infants and another develops for adults. Memories are lost because they are not stored in the new, adult system.

A third explanation is that the problem is cellular. As neurons mature, more and more dendritic processes grow. These interfere with the established memories, which are thus lost.

Commissurotomy

Commissurotomy patients, although not amnesic, show a disturbance of memory for both visual and verbal material, and like frontal lobe patients, they make many intrusion and omission errors on tests of movement copying. The cause of the memory deficit is unknown.

ANATOMY OF MEMORY

Having considered the memory losses associated with different brain injuries, we now must ask if we can construct an anatomical circuit that will account for the observed phenomena. As we try to piece together such a mechanism we must first review the facts as they appear from studies of patients. First, bilateral damage to either the hippocampus or the diencephalon produces a global anterograde amnesia. Neocortical damage alone has not been shown to produce such amnesia, although anterior temporal cortex lesions do produce impairments of memory. Unilateral damage does not produce amnesia, even for specific information types, although there may be a relative asymmetry in the effects of lesions.

Second, impairment is found only in tests of declarative memory. That is, amnesics are impaired on tests that measure knowledge of facts and events but are quite capable of normal performance on tests of procedural memory. Thus, H. M. is able to do mirror tracing even though he denies having knowledge of the test or the events surrounding his learning of it. Similarly, Schacter describes an amnesic Alzheimer's patient who denied having played golf before and then proceeded to play a respectable game! Dissociations of this type suggest that there are at least partially separable neural systems for declarative and procedural memory.

There are at least two ways to account for how declarative and procedural memory can be distinguished anatomically. One way is to postulate that in amnesia there is a disconnection between the systems that are necessary for declarative memory and the motor systems that seem modified during procedural memory acquisition. Another sort of explanation is to postulate that memory traces are laid down at least twice. One location would be in the system that executes the behavior. A second location would be in some sort of declarative-related memory store. The first memory trace would permit appropriate task execution, and the second would monitor the execution and would record relevant details of time, place, and success. The idea that there is such a dichotomy in the nervous system has a certain appeal because there is overwhelming evidence that almost every level of the nervous system is capable of some sort of learning and thus of procedural memory, although only certain "high-level" structures appear capable of declarative memory. Squire has made some interesting observations in this regard. He suggests that declarative memory may be a recent event in evolution, dependent upon the evolution of the hippocampus and related cortical structures in mammals (and perhaps an analogous system in birds?). Furthermore, he suggests that declarative memory may develop late in ontogeny, in part because the hippocampus is slow to develop. This would provide an alternative explanation of infantile amnesia.

Third, most amnesics have a period of retrograde as well as anterograde amnesia. Medial temporal lesions produce a period of retrograde amnesia of at least one year, although the precise duration is difficult to measure. Diencephalic lesions produce a longer period of retrograde amnesia, and head trauma and ECT usually produce a shorter period of retrograde amnesia. Nonetheless, on the whole, amnesics show a retrograde amnesia that is of limited duration and an anterograde amnesia that is total. These facts suggest that the neural system damaged in amnesia must be involved in the memory of new facts as well as being involved in memory for a limited period *after* learning. Later, it is either not involved or certainly less involved, in the storage of memories. In order to account for anterograde and retrograde results it has been proposed by several authors that at the time of learning, the medial temporal region establishes some type of functional relationship with memory storage sites. Perhaps the medial temporal region somehow binds together the various sites that have coded the specific data that define an event, which would include time, space, and content. Given that these diffuse data appear to be coded by diffuse regions (i.e., frontal cortex, posterior parietal cortex, polymodal sensory cortex), it would seem that some structure is indeed required for this purpose. The medial temporal region is the only structure in the forebrain that would appear to have the necessary anatomical connections for such a function. It is unclear, however, why this function would continue for a year or longer after an event. It is also not clear what changes in the brain release the medial temporal lobe from its role in memory. Earlier in the chapter we considered the neural changes at the synapse that are correlated with rather simple learning in laboratory preparations. It is probable that similar changes underlie our complex memories and that the medial temporal lobe somehow facilitates or directs these changes, although the mechanism is a matter of conjecture at present.

Theories of the anatomical basis of memory require far better anatomical data than are available from the study of human patients. Recently, the study of nonhuman species, notably monkeys and rats, has supported the general view that the medial-temporal region has a major role in memory. Historically, researchers who made hippocampal lesions in laboratory species were struck more by symptoms such as increased activity, a tendency to perseverate responses, inabilities to chain sequences of movements, than they were by memory loss. Two developments in the late 1970s led to a significant change in emphasis, however. First, O'Keefe and Nadel published an important book in which they argued that the hippocampus functions to construct cognitive maps by which animals locate memories or ideas in the brain, or spatial locations in the world. Their own evidence from lesion and recording work emphasized the study of spatial behavior in rats but the implications of their theory went much further. At about the same time as O'Keefe and Nadel published their book, Olton and his colleagues began to provide evidence that hippocampal lesions in rats produced deficits in a type of short-term memory that they called working memory. This type of deficit was not to be expected from the clinical literature, or from the O'Keefe and Nadel model, a situation that led to the development of a significant literature on spatial learning and memory in the rat. It now appears that neither group was completely correct. Hippocampal damage in rats affects long-term memory of spatial location, but it may also interfere with the manner in which the brain configures coincident sensory inputs, independent of spatial location (see Sutherland and Rudy for details).

Second, in the course of studying the manner in which the inferotemporal cortex processes visual information, Mishkin and his colleagues began to look carefully at the contribution of the anterior temporal cortex and medial temporal regions on visual processing, including visual memory, in monkeys. They found that bilateral lesions that included both the amygdala and hippocampus led to severe deficits on tests of recognition memory. Mishkin's results had an effect much like the

O'Keefe and Nadel and the Olton results. Several groups of researchers began to investigate Mishkin's claim, which has led to significant progress towards developing an anatomical model of memory.

Mishkin's work has especially utilized two behavioral tasks, delayed nonmatching to sample and discrimination learning. In the nonmatching task a monkey is confronted with an unfamiliar object, which it displaces to find a reward (Figure 19-10). After a delay the animal sees the same object paired with a new one. The task is to recognize the original object and to move the new one to gain the reward. In the discrimination-learning test there are 20 pairs of objects, and one object of each pair consistently conceals a reward. The subject is shown each pair daily until it learns to choose the baited object in each pair consistently. A key difference between the tasks is that on the first task the animal sees each pair only once, on the second task it sees the same objects repeatedly over a period of weeks until it learns. An analogy might be learning the face and name of a single person met on only one occasion as opposed to learning the names and faces of 50 classmates to whom one is exposed daily and who one may learn without conscious effort. Mishkin argues that the discrimination-learning task, while appearing to be a more difficult task with greater mnemonic demands, is founded not on individual independent memories, but on "automatic connections" between a stimulus and a response, which he calls a "habit." In contrast, he supposes that in the nonmatching test the solution cannot be done by a habit but rather only by a distinct memory of the stimuli.

Mishkin and his colleagues selectively removed the prime candidate brain areas illustrated in Figure 21-5, finding that combined damage of the amygdala and hippocampus prevented animals from learning the nonmatching test. In contrast, the animals were normal at their acquisition of the object discrimination task. Further work showed similar results, of varying severity, after lesions of the ventral prefrontal cortex, basal forebrain, or a combined lesion of the MD and the mamillary body, as illustrated in Figure 21-13. Mishkin proposed that all of these structures form a circuit of structures that might interact to form a memory, which he refers to as "recognition memory," although it is similar to Squire's declarative memory. Although the details of how this circuit operates are not specified, the model does fit the human clinical data. Two additional pieces of evidence are of interest here. First, he has found that the young monkeys can learn the object-discrimination task long before they can learn the recognition memory task — a result that is consistent with the idea that declarative memory and its neural circuitry develops more slowly than procedural memory and its circuitry. Second, spurred on by the work of O'Keefe and Nadel, and Olton and associates who showed that the hippocampus was important for spatial learning in rodents, Mishkin and Parkinson found that hippocampal lesions interfere with the ability of monkeys to remember the spatial location of objects (see Chapter 24 for more details of these studies).

Mishkin's model has proven useful but more studies have pointed to difficulties in the model. First, Mishkin assumes that the hippocampus and amygdala both play a key role in the formation of memories — a conclusion in accord with the results from H. M. Thus, when the amygdala and hippocampus are individually removed, there is little amnesia; it is only with their joint removal that there is a severe memory disturbance. Unfortunately, the surgical approach used in Mishkin's studies necessarily includes the entorhinal cortex in the joint removal but not in the independent removal of the hippocampus and amygdala. Squire and Zola-Morgan have recently studied monkeys with lesions that include greater or lesser amounts or entorhinal damage. Their results emphasize the unique importance of the hippocampal region: removal of the hippocampus and medial temporal cortex, but sparing the amygdala, produced an amnesic syndrome as severe as the combined hippocampal and amygdala removal. This result is in

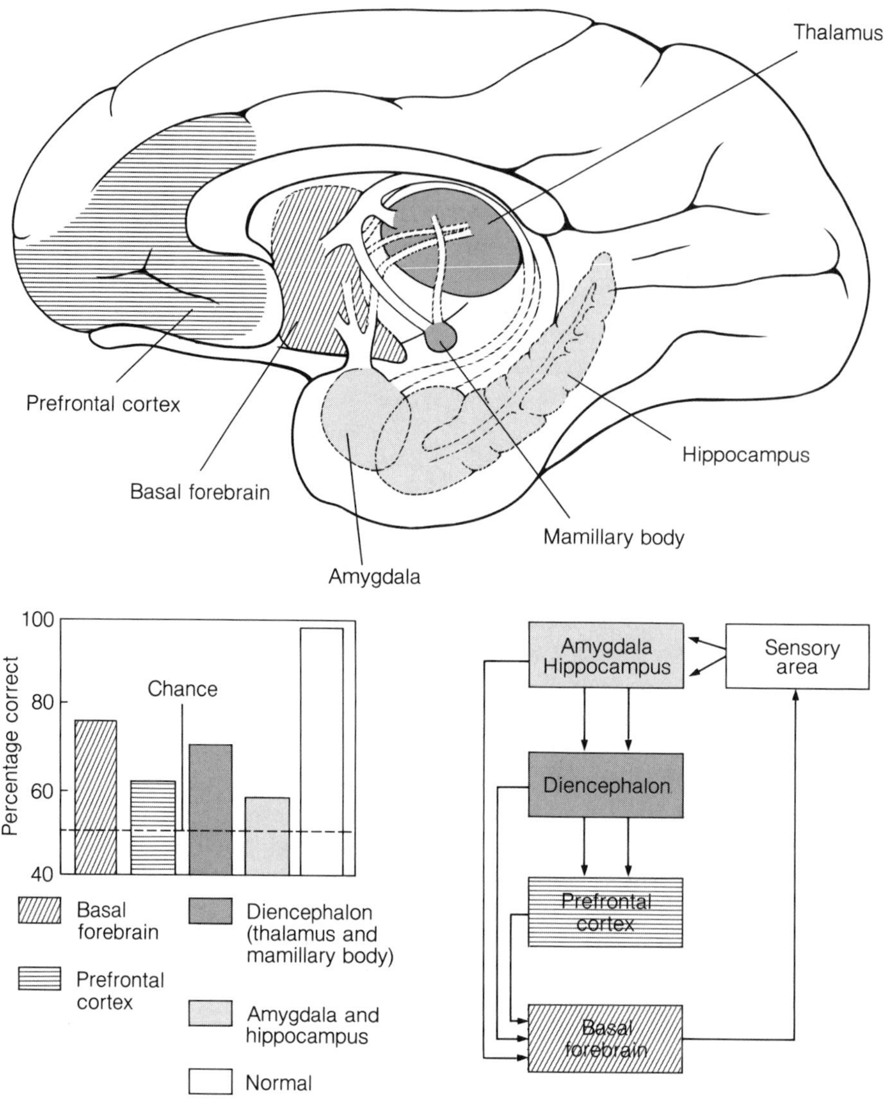

FIGURE 21-13. Summary of Mishkin's results from the delayed nonmatching-to-sample test. Lesions to each of the areas indicated led to greater or lesser deficits in performing the task. Mishkin proposed that the memory trace is laid down in a system in which sensory information enters the forebrain, travels through the heirarchical sensory processing, enters the hippocampus and amygdala, projects to the diencephalon, then to the basal forebrain or the prefrontal cortex both of which projects back to the sensory areas. (After Mishkin and Applenzeller, 1987.)

accord with their patient R. B., who had a severe anterograde amnesia, an interruption in hippocampal processing, and an intact amygdala. A second problem with Mishkin's model is that it is vague on the question of retrograde amnesia, which is an important component of amnesia. A recent experiment by Sutherland and Arnold is germane. They trained rats to find a hidden location in the Morris Water Task (see Chapter 24 for details of this task). They then waited 1, 4, 8, or 12 weeks before producing hippocampal damage in different groups. All groups were retested 2 weeks after the surgery. Their finding was that the longer the period between learning and hippocampal damage, the better the performance. In other words, the neural record of the training must have been changing over the period that the animals were simply living in their cages. This experiment is consistent with the clinical observation of retrograde amnesia in medial temporal amnesics, and suggests that the hippocampus is transiently involved in the memory storage process and that other structures maintain the permanent memories. Thus, a satisfactory anatomical model of memory will need to specify more precisely the role of the hippocampus in memory formation. A final difficulty with Mishkin's model is that it has been based upon the study of performance on a small number of tasks. Having identified the structures that interfere with recognition memories in monkeys, it is now time to begin to use tasks to try to doubly dissociate the various contributions of different regions to memory.

To summarize, there is now mounting evidence from the study of laboratory mammals that supports the view that the hippocampal formation is essential for normal declarative memory. Other structures may play a supporting role too, but their relative roles are as yet unknown. Further, it appears that the neocortex plays a minor role in the formation of memories, although a significant portion of the neural record underlying memories must surely be distributed widely in the cortex.

S.: A CASE OF TOTAL RECALL

We would be remiss if having presented H. M., the man who cannot form new memories, we were to close this chapter without mentioning S., the man who could not forget. So remarkable are the contrasts between the two that the neural capacity lost to H. M. through surgery seems to have been present in S. to excess. Of course, the notion is unlikely to ever be confirmed. Nevertheless, if H. M. has in any way shaped our notion of memory, so, too, should S.

S. was a newspaper reporter who never took notes at briefings as did other reporters, and so came to the attention of his employer. When questioned on the matter, S. repeated verbatim the transcript of the briefing. S. had not considered himself unusual, although he had wondered why other people relied so much on written notes. Nonetheless, at his employer's urging he went to see a psychologist. In this way S. met Luria, with whom he began a 30-year study of his memory. Luria published an account of this investigation, and to this day *The Mind of the Mnemonist* is one of the most readable accounts of unusual memory.

We can document S.'s memory abilities by referring to Table 21-5. S. could look at this table for 2 or 3 min and then repeat it from memory: by columns, by rows, by diagonals, in reverse, in sums, or as a single number. Tested unexpectedly as many as 16 or more years later, S. could repeat the performance without error.

For a good part of his life S. supported himself as a mnemonist, that is, a person who exhibits his memory in performance to audiences. During the course of his work he consigned hundreds of such lists, or lists of names, letters, nonsense syllables, and so forth to memory and was able to recall any of these at some later date.

S.'s ability to commit things to memory hinged on three processes. He could visualize the stimuli mentally, recalling them simply by reading them

TABLE 21-5. Example of tables memorized by S.

6	6	8	0
5	4	3	2
1	6	8	4
7	9	3	5
4	2	3	7
3	8	9	1
1	0	0	2
3	4	5	1
2	7	6	8
1	9	2	6
2	9	6	7
5	5	2	0
x	0	1	x

Note: With only 2 to 3 min study of such a table, S. was able to reproduce it in reverse order, horizontally, or vertically, or to reproduce the diagonals.

from his internal image. He also made multisensory impressions of things. This ability, called **synesthesia,** involves processing any sensory event in all sensory modalities simultaneously. Thus, a word was recorded as a sound, a splash of color, an odor, and a taste, as well as an object with texture and temperature. Finally, S. used the pegboard technique used by many other mnemonists; that is, he used a number of standard images with which he associated new material. In actuality, whereas most mnemonists used this technique as their primary memory device, S. seemed to use it somewhat less, relying more on his internal visual images and his multisensory impressions. Here are some examples of how he saw numbers:

> Even numbers remind me of images. Take the number 1. This is a proud, well-built man; 2 is a high-spirited woman; 3 a gloomy person (why, I don't know); 6 a man with a swollen foot; 7 a man with a mustache; 8 a very stout woman—a sack within a sack. As for the number 87, what I see is a fat woman and a man twirling his mustache. (Luria, 1968, p. 31)

> For me, 2, 4, 6, 5 are not just numbers. They have forms. 1 is a pointed number—which has nothing to do with the way it's written. It's because it's somehow firm and complete. 2 is flatter, rectangular, whitish in color, sometimes almost a gray. 3 is a pointed segment which rotates. 4 is also square and dull; it looks like 2 but has more substance to it, it's thicker. 5 is absolutely complete and takes the form of a cone or a tower—something substantial. 6, the first number after 5, has a whitish hue; 8 somehow has a naive quality, it's milky blue like lime. (Luria, 1968, p. 25)

From Luria's description of S. it seems safe to conclude that there was absolutely no limit to his ability to remember. At least Luria, in the many tests that he gave S., was never able to reach such a limit. What was S.'s ability with respect to short-term memory, long-term memory, and forgetting?

Luria never really tested S. to determine whether he had a short-term memory of the sort that most of us have. That is, once given an item of information did S. forget it a short while later? Luria's report seems to suggest that S. had no short-term memory—everything was put into long-term storage. In fact, S. worried about his inability to forget and attempted to devise strategies for forgetting. He tried to write things down just as most of us do when we do not wish to carry them about as a memory, but the technique did not work.

> Writing something down means I'll know I won't have to remember it . . . so I started doing this with small matters like phone numbers, last names, errands of one sort or another. But I got nowhere, for in my mind I continued to see what I'd written. . . . Then I tried writing all the notes on identical kinds of paper, using the same pencil each time. But it still doesn't work. (Luria, 1968, p. 70)

S. tried other strategies: burning the paper in his mind, or putting things on the blackboard and covering them up or erasing them in his mind. But none of these techniques worked either.

Did S. forget? We have already said that his

long-term memory was amazing, but from Luria's account he did not seem to forget in the same way as the rest of us. When he missed an item, it was not because it was forgotten but because it was hidden from view or hard to see. He was always able to find it. Here is how he accounted for some of the items he had missed in a list:

> I put the image of the *pencil* near a fence . . . the one down the street, you know. But what happened was that the image fused with that of the fence and I walked right on past without noticing it. The same thing happened with the word *egg*. I had put it up against a white wall and it blended in with the background. How could I possibly spot a white egg up against a white wall? (Luria, 1968, p. 36)

S.'s ability to use his imagination was not limited to memorizing things. He could raise his heart rate from 70–72 to 100 beats per minute by imagining that he was exercising and could lower it to 64–66 by imagining that he was relaxing. He could also raise and lower the temperature of his hand by imagining that it was in warm or cold water. He could deal with pain by imagining that he was no longer in his body, and he could stop his sense of time passing by imagining that the hands of a clock no longer moved. He was even able to dark-adapt himself in a lighted room by imagining that he was in a darkened room. This incredible control he had over his autonomic system contrasts with H. M., who was reported to show no changes of galvanic skin response even when receiving mild skin shock.

Did S. pay a price for his memory abilities? Luria clearly takes the position that he did. Luria characterizes S. as a person with little aim in life and seemingly dull and superficial. Luria suggests that S. was not able to reason, to categorize, and to see order in things seen by ordinary people. He also had little ability to deal with metaphors; he visualized and interpreted them literally (e.g., to weigh one's words) and so was puzzled by what was meant by them. He had difficulty in understanding what was meant by simple statements and had greater difficulty understanding the sense of poetry.

In summary we can agree with Luria that S. did have an apparently limitless memory. But whether he payed a penalty for it is another matter. Because Luria's assessments of this question were clinical, not experimental, it is impossible to assess in any objective way the nature and degree of S.'s supposed impairment. (In fact, we also had some difficulty with the meaning of the poetry given to S. to interpret, and in many other situations we saw ourselves responding as S. did.) We conclude from the case of S., then, not that he paid a price, but that he was a person who had no short-term memory but a limitless long-term memory, and so was just the opposite of H. M., who has a short-term memory but no long-term memory. Whatever explanation of memory eventually evolves from the study of the nervous system, it will have to account for each of these extremes.

REFERENCES

Amaral, D. G. Memory: Anatomical organization of candidate brain regions. *Handbook of Physiology: The Nervous System, vol,* 1987.

Anderson, R. Cognitive changes after amygdalectomy. *Neuropsychologia* 16:439–451, 1978.

Barnes, C. A. Spatial learning and memory processes: The search for their neurobiological mechanisms in the rat. *Trends in Neurosciences* 11:163–169, 1988.

Bartlett, F. C. *Remembering.* Cambridge: Cambridge University Press, 1932.

Bekhterev, V. M. Demonstration eines Gehirns mit Zerstörung der vorderen und inneren Theile der Hirnrinde beider Schlafenlappen. *Neurol. Zbl.* 19:990–991, 1900.

Black, I. B., J. E. Adler, C. F. Dreyfus, W. F. Friedman, E. F. LaGamma, and A. H. Roach. Biochemistry of information storage in the nervous system. *Science* 236:1263–1268, 1987.

Blakemore, C. *Mechanics of the Mind.* Cambridge: Cambridge University Press, 1977.

Bliss, T., and A. Gardner-Medwin. Long-lasting potentiation of synaptic transmission in the dentate area of unanesthetized rabbit following stimulation of the perforant path. *Journal of Physiology* 232:357–374, 1973.

Broadbent, D. E. *Perception and Communication.* London: Pergamon, 1958.

Campbell, B. A., and N. E. Spear. Ontogeny of memory. *Psychological Review* 79:215–236, 1972.

Cermak, L. S., ed. *Human Memory and Amnesia.* Hillsdale, NJ: Lawrence Erlbaum Associates, 1982.

Chapman, L. F., R. D. Walter, C. H. Markham, R. W. Rand, and P. H. Crandall. Memory changes induced by stimulation of hippocampus or amygdala in epilepsy patients with implanted electrodes. *Transactions of the American Neurological Association* 92:50–56, 1967.

Cofer, C. N. An historical perspective. In C. N. Cofer, ed. *The Structure of Human Memory.* San Francisco: W. H. Freeman, 1975.

Cohen, N. J., and S. Corkin. The amnesic patient H. M.: Learning and retention of a cognitive skill. *Neuroscience Abstracts* 7:235, 1981.

Corkin, S. Tactually-guided maze-learning in man: Effects on unilateral cortical excisions and bilateral hippocampal lesions. *Neuropsychologia* 3:339–351, 1965.

Corkin, S. Acquisition of motor skill after bilateral medial temporal-lobe excision. *Neuropsychologia* 6:255–265, 1968.

Corsi, P. M. *Human memory and the medial temporal region of the brain.* Unpublished Ph.D. thesis, McGill University, 1972.

Doty, R. W., and W. H. Overman. Mnemonic role of forebrain commissures in macaques. In S. Harnad, R. W. Doty, L. Goldstein, J. Jaynes, and G. Krauthamer, eds. *Lateralization in the Nervous System.* New York: Academic Press, 1977.

Ebbinghaus, H. *Memory.* New York: Teachers College, 1913. (Originally published in 1885). Reprinted by Dover, New York, 1964.

Fisher, C. M., and R. O. Adams. Transient global amnesia. *Transactions of the American Neurological Association* 83:143, 1958.

Gaffan, D. Monkey's recognition memory for complex pictures and the effect of fornix transection. *Quarterly Journal of Experimental Psychology* 29:505–514, 1977.

Garcia-Bengochea, F., O. de La Torre, and O. Esquivel. The section of the fornix in the surgical treatment of certain epilepsies. *Transactions of the American Neurological Association* 79:176–179, 1954.

Goddard, G. V. Component properties of the memory machine: Hebb revisited. In P. W. Jusczyk and R. M. Klein, eds. *The Nature of Thought: Essays in Honor of D. O. Hebb.* Hillsdale, NJ: Lawrence Erlbaum Associates, 1980.

Greenough, W. T., and F. F. Chang. Synaptic structural correlates of information storage in mammalian nervous systems. In C. W. Cotman, ed. *Synaptic Plasticity.* New York: Guilford Press, 1985.

Hebb, D. O. *Organization of Behavior.* New York: John Wiley, 1949.

Hebb, D. O. Distinctive features of learning in the higher animal. In J. F. Delafresnaye, ed. *Brain Mechanisms and Learning.* London: Blackwell, 1961.

Hebb, D. O. *Textbook of Psychology.* Toronto: W. B. Saunders, 1972.

Hebben, N., K. J. Shedlack, H. B. Eichenbaum, and S. Corkin. The amnesic patient H. M.: Diminished ability to interpret and report internal states. *Neuroscience Abstracts* 7:235, 1981.

Hirst, W. The amnesic syndrome: Descriptions and explanations. *Psychological Bulletin* 91:435–460, 1982.

Horel, J. A. The neuroanatomy of amnesia: A critique of the hippocampal memory hypothesis. *Brain* 101:403–445, 1978.

Hyman, B. T., G. W. van Hoesen, L. J. Kromer, and A. R. Damasio. Perforant pathway changes and the memory impairment of Alzheimer's disease. *Annals of Neurology* 20:472–481, 1986.

Jaccarino-Hiatt, G. *Impairment of cognitive organization in patients with temporal-lobe lesions.* Unpublished Ph.D. thesis, McGill University, 1978.

James, W. *The Principles of Psychology.* New York: Henry Holt, 1890.

Jones, M. K. Imagery as a mnemonic aid after left temporal lobectomy: Contrast between material-specific and generalized memory disorders. *Neuropsychologia* 12:21–30, 1974.

Jones-Gotman, M. Memory for designs: The hippocampal contribution. *Neuropsychologia* 24:193–203, 1986.

Jones-Gotman, M. Psychological evaluation: Testing hippocampal function. In J. Engle, ed. *Surgical Treatment of the Epilepsies.* New York: Raven Press, 1986.

Kimura, D. Right temporal-lobe damage: Perception of unfamiliar stimuli after damage. *Archives of Neurology* 8:264–271, 1963.

Kolb, B., and B. Milner. Performance of complex arm and facial movements after focal brain lesions. *Neuropsychologia* 19:491–503, 1981.

Lashley, K. D. In search of the engram. *Symposia of the Society for Experimental Biology* 4:454–482, 1950.

Luria, A. R. *The Mind of a Mnemonist.* New York: Basic Books, 1968.

Lynch, G., and M. Baudry. The biochemistry of memory: A new and specific hypothesis. *Science* 224:1057–1063, 1984.

Mair, W. G. P., E. K. Warrington, and L. Weiskrantz. Memory disorder in Korsakoff's psychosis. *Brain* 102:749–783, 1979.

Markowitsch, H. J. Transient global amnesia. *Neuroscience and Biobehavioral Reviews* 7:35–43, 1983.

Markowitsch, H. J., and M. Pritzel. The neuropathology of amnesia. *Progress in Neurobiology* 25:189–288, 1985.

Mazzucchi, A., G. Moretti, P. Caffara, and M. Parma. Neuropsychological functions in the follow-up of transient global amnesia. *Brain* 103:161–178, 1980.

McNaughton, B. L. Dissociation of short- and long-lasting modification of synaptic efficacy at the terminals of the perforant path. *Society for Neuroscience Abstracts* 3:517, 1977.

Milner, B. Visually-guided maze learning in man: Effects of bilateral hippocampal, bilateral frontal, and unilateral cerebral lesions. *Neuropsychologia* 3:317–338, 1965.

Milner, B. Brain mechanisms suggested by studies of temporal lobes. In F. L. Darley, ed. *Brain Mechanisms Underlying Speech and Language.* New York: Grune & Stratton, 1967.

Milner, B. Visual recognition and recall after right temporal-lobe excision in man. *Neuropsychologia* 6:191–209, 1968.

Milner, B. Memory and the medial temporal regions of the brain. In K. H. Probram and D. E. Broadbent, eds. *Biology of Memory.* New York: Academic Press, 1970.

Milner, B. Interhemispheric differences in the localization of psychological processes in man. *British Medical Bulletin* 27:272–277, 1971.

Milner, B. Disorders of learning and memory after temporal lobe lesions in man. *Clinical Neurosurgery* 19:421–446, 1972.

Milner, B. Hemispheric specialization: Scope and limits. In F. Schmitt and F. Wordon, eds., *The Neurosciences: Third Study Program,* Boston: M.I.T. Press, 1974.

Milner, B. Psychological aspects of focal epilepsy and its neurosurgical management. *Advances in Neurology* 8:299–321, 1975.

Milner, B. Some cognitive effects of frontal-lobe lesions in man. *Philosophical Transactions of the Royal Society of London* B298:211–226, 1982.

Milner, B., S. Corkin, and H.- L. Teuber. Further analysis of the hippocampal amnesic syndrome: 14-year follow up study of H. M. *Neuropsychologia* 6:215–234, 1968.

Milner, B., and B. Kolb. Performance of complex arm and facial movements after cerebral commissurotomy. *Neuropsychologia* 23:791—799, 1985.

Mishkin, M. Memory in monkeys severely impaired by combined but not by separate removal of amygdala and hippocampus. *Nature* 273:297–298, 1978.

Mishkin, M., and T. Appenzeller. The anatomy of memory. *Scientific American* 256(6):80–89, 1987.

Mishkin, M., B. Malamut, and J. Bachevalier. Memories and habits: Two neural systems. In G. Lynch, J. L. McGaugh, and N. M. Weinberger, eds. *Neurobiology of Learning and Memory.* New York: Guilford Press, 1984.

Moscovitch, M. Multiple dissociations of funtion in amnesia. In L. S. Cermak, ed. *Human Memory and Amnesia.* Hillsdale, NJ: Lawrence Erlbaum Associates, 1982.

Müller, G. E., and A. Pilzecker. Experimentelle Beiträge zur Lehre vom Gedächtnis. *Zeitschrift für Psychologie* 1:1–288, 1900.

O'Keefe, J., and L. Nadel. *The Hippocampus as a Cognitive Map.* Oxford: Oxford University Press, 1978.

Olton, D. S., J. T. Becker, and G. E. Handelmann. Hippocampus, space and memory. *Behavioral and Brain Sciences* 2:313–366, 1979.

Olton, D. S., and B. C. Papas. Spatial memory and hippocampal function. *Neuropsychologia* 17:669–682, 1979.

Oscar-Berman, M. Neuropsychological consequences of long-term chronic alcoholism. *American Scientist* 68:410–419, 1980.

Parkinson, J. K., E. A. Murray, and M. Mishkin. A selective mnemonic role for the hippocampus in monkeys: Memory for the location of objects. *Journal of Neuroscience* 8:4159–4167, 1988.

Penfield, W., and G. Mathieson. An autopsy and a discussion of the role of the hippocampus in experiential recall. *Archives of Neurology* 31:145–154, 1974.

Penfield, W., and B. Milner. Memory deficit produced by bilateral lesions in the hippocampal zone. *Archives of Neurology and Psychiatry* 79:475–497, 1958.

Petrides, M. Deficits on conditional associative-learning tasks after frontal- and temporal-lobe lesions in man. *Neuropsychologia* 23:601–614, 1985.

Petrides, M., and B. Milner. Deficits on subject-ordered tasks after frontal- and temporal-lobe lesions in man. *Neuropsychologia* 20:249–262, 1982.

Prisko, L. *Short-term memory in focal cerebral damage.* Unpublished Ph.D. thesis, McGill University, 1963.

Rasmussen, T., and B. Milner. Clinical and surgical studies of cerebral speech areas in man. In K. J. Zulch, O. Creutzfeldt, and G. C. Galbraith, eds. *Cerebral Localization.* Berlin and New York: Springer-Verlag, 1975.

Renzi, J. E., de. Memory disorders following focal neocortical damage. *Philosophical Transactions of the Royal Society, London* B298:73–83, 1982.

Robertson, A. D., and J. Inglis. The effects of electroconvulsive therapy on human learning and memory. *Canadian Psychological Review* 18:285–307, 1977.

Sainsbury, R. S., and G. W. Jason. Fimbria-fornix lesions and sexual-social behavior in the guinea pig. *Physiology and Behavior* 17:963–967, 1976.

Samuels, I., N. Butters, and P. Fedio. Short-term memory disorders following temporal-lobe removals in humans. *Cortex* 8:283–298, 1972.

Sanders, H. I., and E. K. Warrington. Memory for remote events in amnesic patients. *Brain* 94:661–668, 1971.

Schacter, D. L. Memory, amnesia, and frontal lobe dysfunction. *Psychobiology* 15:21–36, 1987.

Schacter, D. L., and H. F. Crovitz. Memory function after closed head injury: A review of the quantitative research. *Cortex* 13:150–176, 1977.

Scoville, W. B., and B. Milner. Loss of recent memory after bilateral hippocampal lesions. *Journal of Neurology, Neurosurgery and Psychiatry* 20:11–21, 1957.

Serafetinides, E. A., R. D. Walter, and D. G. Cherlow. Amnestic confusional phenomena, hippocampal stimulation, and laterality factors. In K. H. Pribram and R. Isaacson, eds. *The Hippocampus*, vol. II. New York: Plenum, 1975.

Shankweiler, D. *Defects in recognition and reproduction of familiar tunes after unilateral temporal lobectomy.* Paper presented at the 37th Annual Meeting of the Eastern Psychological Association, New York, 1966.

Smith, M. L., and B. Milner. The role of the right hippocampus in the recall of spatial location. *Neuropsychologia* 19:781–793, 1981.

Squire, L. R. A stable impairment in remote memory following electroconvulsive therapy. *Neuropsychologia* 13:51–58, 1975.

Squire, L. R. The neuropsychology of human memory. *Annual Review of Neuroscience* 5:241–273, 1982.

Squire, L. R. *Memory and the Brain.* New York: Oxford University Press, 1987.

Squire L. R. Memory: Neural organization and behavior. *Handbook of Physiology: The Nervous System,* vol 5, 1987.

Squire, L. R., and S. Zola-Morgan. Memory: Brain systems and behavior. *Trends in Neurosciences* 11:170–175, 1988.

Squire, L. R., and R. Y. Moore. Dorsal thalamic lesion in a noted case of human memory dysfunction. *Annals of Neurology* 6:503–506, 1979.

Sutherland, R. J., and K. Arnold. Temporally graded loss of memory after hippocampal damage. *Neuroscience* 22:S175, 1987.

Sutherland, R. J., I. Q. Whishaw, and B. Kolb. Contributions of cingulate cortex to two forms of spatial learning and memory. *Journal of Neuroscience* 8:1863–1872, 1988.

Sutherland, R. J., and J. W. Rudy. Configural association theory: The role of the hippocampal formation in learning, memory, and amnesia. *Psychobiology* 17:129–144, 1989.

Talland, G. A. *The Pathology of Memory*. New York: Academic Press, 1969.

Taylor, J. R., R. Tomphins, R. Demers, and D. Anderson. Electroconvulsive therapy and memory dysfunction? Is there evidence for prolonged defects? *Biological Psychiatry* 17:1169–1193, 1982.

Taylor, L. Localization of cerebral lesions by psychological testing. *Clinical Neurosurgery* 16:269–287, 1969.

Teuber, H. L., B. Milner, and H. G. Vaughan. Persistent anterograde amnesia after stab wound of the basal brain. *Neuropsychologia* 6:267–282, 1968.

Von Cramen, D. Y., N. Hebel, and U. Schuri. A contribution of the anatomical basis of thalamic amnesia. *Brain* 108:993–1008, 1985.

Van Hoesen, G. W., The parahippocampal gyrus. New observations regarding its cortical connections in the monkey. *Trends in Neurosciences* 5:345–350, 1982.

Valenstein, E., D. Bowers, M. Verfaellie, K. M. Heilman, A. Day, and R. T. Watson. Retrosplenial amnesia. *Brain* 110:1631–1646, 1987.

Warrington, E., and M. James. An experimental investigation of facial recognition in patients with unilateral cerebral lesions. *Cortex* 3:317–326, 1967.

Warrington, E. K., and L. Weiskrantz. Further analysis of the prior learning effect in amnesic patients. *Neuropsychologia* 16:169–177, 1978.

Warrington, E. K., and L. Weiskrantz. An analysis of short-term and long-term memory defects in man. In J. A. Deutsch, ed. *The Physiological Basis of Memory*. New York: Academic Press, 1973.

Weiskrantz, L. Neuroanatomy of memory and amnesia: A case for multiple memory systems. *Human Neurobiology* 6:93–105, 1987.

Weiskrantz, L., and E. K. Warrington. The problem of the amnesic syndrome in man and animals. In K. H. Pribram and R. Isaacson, eds. *The Hippocampus*, vol. II. New York: Plenum, 1975.

Whitty, C. W. M., and O. L. Zangwill. Traumatic amnesia. In C. W. M. Whitty and O. L. Zangwill, eds. *Amnesia*. London: Butterworth, 1966.

Woolsey, R. M., and J. S. Nelson. A symptomatic destruction of the fornix in man. *Archives of Neurology* 32:566–568, 1975.

Yerkes, R. M. The intelligence of earthworms. *Journal of Animal Behavior* 2:332–352, 1912.

Zaidel, D., and R. W. Sperry. Memory impairment after commissurotomy in man. *Brain* 97:263–272, 1974.

Zangwill, O. L. Remembering revisited. *Quarterly Journal of Experimental Psychology* 24:123–138, 1972.

Zola-Morgan, S., L. Squire, and D. G. Amalral. Human amnesia and the medial temporal region: Enduring memory impairment following a bilateral lesion limited to field CA_1 of the hippocampus. *The Journal of Neuroscience* 6:2950–2967, 1986.

Zola-Morgan, S., L. R. Squire, and D. G. Amaral. Amnesia following medial temporal lobe damage in monkeys: The importance of the hippocampus and adjacent cortical regions. *Society for Neuroscience Abstracts* 14:1043, 1988.

Zola-Morgan, S., L. Squire, and M. Mishkin. The neuroanatomy of amnesia: Amygdala-hippocampus versus temporal stem. *Science* 218:1337–1339, 1982.

Zatorre, R. Discrimination and recognition of tonal melodies after unilateral cerebral excisions. *Neuropsychologia* 23:31–41, 1985

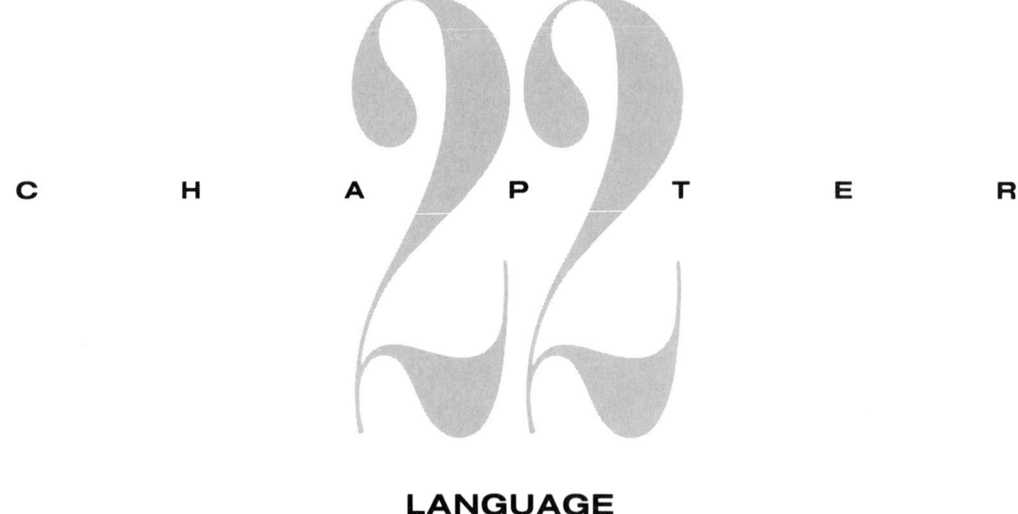

CHAPTER 22

LANGUAGE

In this chapter we briefly review the history of thought regarding the neurological basis of language, examine the cortical and subcortical speech zones as mapped by stimulation and lesion studies, consider disorders of and theoretical models for language, and, finally, examine the phylogenetic origins of language.

HISTORICAL VIEWS

In the early 1800s, Gall, in his phrenology, was the first to propose a relation between localized regions of the brain and specific behaviors. Bouillard agreed with Gall and attempted to provide clinical proof that the organ of language resided in the anterior lobes of the brain. Indeed, in 1825 Bouillard even proposed asymmetry of brain function, suggesting that the hemisphere had a special role in complex movement such as fencing, writing, and speech. This proposal was supported by Dax in 1836, when he described a series of cases demonstrating that disorders of language were consistently associated with lesions of the left hemisphere. Although the hypothesis that speech is localized in the frontal lobe of the left hemisphere was revived in 1861 by Auburtin, it was Broca who provided the anatomical proof of the theory, and it is an irony of science that the anterior speech zone became known as Broca's area. The primary disturbance resulting from damage to Broca's area appeared to be a defect in the motor component of speech production. In 1875, Wernicke demonstrated that a lesion in the temporal-parietal cortex produced a form of language disturbance that differed from that described by Broca. This region became known as Wernicke's area. Wernicke proposed that Broca's area was the center of language production, whereas Wernicke's area was the center of language understanding. Wernicke's proposals led to a flurry of "brain diagrams" in the late 1800s, each purporting to describe how lesions to Broca's and Wernicke's area, as well as to associated regions and their interconnections, could produce specific disturbances in language functions.

Although the localizationists held the dominant view at the turn of the century, there were dissenting voices, most notably those of Hughlings-Jackson, Freud, Marie, and Head. Hughlings-Jackson contended that language is a dynamic process that derives from the integrated function of the whole brain, and although he conceded a special role for the left hemisphere in language, he believed that the right hemisphere and subcortical structures must also play a significant role in language function. He argued that the more complex a task is, the greater the number of regions and structures in the brain that must be involved. For example, the ability to write one's name involves a much smaller, more localized brain region than the ability to write a book. Thus, a person might be unable to write a book after damage to virtually any region of the association cortex, but the ability to write one's name would be impaired only by a restricted lesion in the temporal-parietal cortex. By the 1920s, the pendulum had swung in favor of a holistic view of language function, especially after the publication of Head's elegant and influential attack on localizationists in 1926. Not until the 1950s and 1960s did the localizationist view of language function regain credibility, through Geschwind's theoretical writings.

Today it is reasonable to say that the primary language functions of the brain are housed in broadly defined language zones in the left hemisphere, including Broca's and Wernicke's areas, as well as in other zones of association cortex within the left hemisphere, especially the tertiary zone of the left temporal cortex. Lesser, and poorly understood, roles are played by the association cortex of the right hemisphere and by subcortical structures, including especially the basal ganglia and posterior thalamus.

SPEECH ZONES MAPPED BY STIMULATION AND ABLATION

The zones of the neocortex involved in language, and particularly in speech, have been identified by careful investigations of the effects both of cortical stimulation during surgery and of the effects of surgery on behavior. Accumulating results from hundreds of patients has made it possible to construct statistically defined regions of the neocortex concerned with language processes.

Electrical Stimulation

The investigations undertaken by Penfield and his associates on patients undergoing surgical treatment of epilepsy were the first to clearly identify the extent of the neocortical speech zones. Subsequent work by others has confirmed Penfield's findings and has clarified and extended them by the use of more quantitative behavioral recording techniques. The major findings are as follows:

1. Stimulation of a number of cortical areas (Figure 22-1) with a low-voltage electric current interferes with speech. These areas include the classical areas of Broca and Wernicke in the left hemisphere, as well as the sensory and motor representations of the face in both hemispheres and in a region known as the supplementary motor area, or M_{II}, of both hemispheres.

2. Penfield and Roberts conclude that stimulation produces two effects on speech:
a. Positive effects, meaning vocalization, which is not speech but rather a sustained or interrupted vowel cry, such as "Oh . . . " Vocalization can be elicited by stimulation of either the face area or the supplementary motor region of either hemisphere.
b. Negative effects, meaning the inability to vocalize or to use words properly. These include a

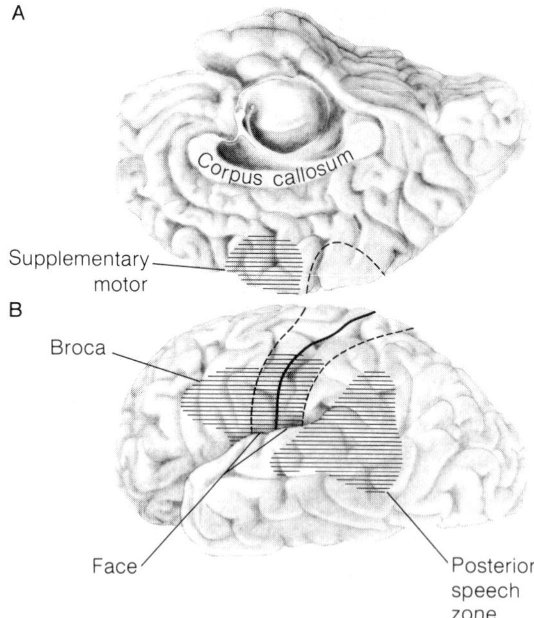

FIGURE 22-1. Shaded areas indicate the zones in which electric stimulation may interfere with speech. Note that the posterior areas are much larger than the classical Wernicke's area. Speech is also disrupted by stimulation in the face or supplementary motor areas of the right hemisphere. *A*. Medial view of the left hemisphere. *B*. Lateral view of the left hemisphere.

variety of aphasialike errors: (i) Total arrest of speech or an inability to vocalize spontaneously; this occurs from stimulation throughout the shaded zones in Figure 22-1. (ii) Hesitation and slurring of speech: hesitation occurs from stimulation throughout the zones of Figure 22-1; slurring occurs primarily from stimulation of the face area in either hemisphere. (iii) Distortion and repetition of words and syllables; distortion differs from slurring in that the distorted sound is an unintelligible noise rather than a word. These effects occur primarily from stimulation of the classical speech zones, although occasionally from the face area as well. (iv) Confusion of numbers while counting; for example, a patient may jump from "six" to "nineteen" to "four" and so on. Confusion in counting results from stimulation of Broca's or Wernicke's area. (v) Inability to name despite retained ability to speak. "An example is 'That is a . . . I know. That is a. . . . 'When the current was removed, the patient named the picture correctly. Another example is, 'Oh, I know what it is. That is what you put in your shoes.' After withdrawal of the stimulating electrodes, the patient immediately said 'foot'" (Penfield and Roberts, 1959, p. 123). Naming difficulties arise from stimulation throughout the anterior (Broca's) and posterior (Wernicke's) speech zones. (vi) Misnaming; may occur when the subject uses words related in sound such as "camel" for "comb," uses synonyms such as "cutters" for "scissors," or perseverates by using the same name twice. For example, a picture of a bird may be named correctly but the next picture, a table, is also called a bird. Misnaming, like naming difficulties, occurs during stimulation of both the anterior and the posterior speech zones.

3. Ojemann and Mateer report that during stimulation in the region of Broca's area, patients are unable to make voluntary facial movements similar to those illustrated in Figure 13-6. Curiously, stimulation of these same points may also disrupt phonemic discrimination as measured by the phonetic differentiation test described in Chapter 19. These authors also describe defects in short-term memory resulting from stimulation in roughly the zone identified from lesion studies (Chapter 21).

4. Most reports agree that the extent of the cortical language zones as marked by stimulation varies considerably among subjects, although there is little indication of what this variation may reflect. Ojemann has found that, on the whole, the language area is larger in males than females. In view of the superior verbal skills of females, this result implies, paradoxically, that the size of the language area may be inversely related to ability. Such a hypothesis is supported by his observation

that in multilinguals the poorer language is disrupted over a larger area than the better one. The possibility that improved efficiency requires less neural activity is intriguing and warrants further study. One parallel result by Richard Haier has found an inverse correlation between abstract reasoning and cerebral metabolic activity. One is tempted to conclude that "smart brains work better, not harder." In this regard, it would seem worthwhile to correlate the size of the speech zones with performance on a variety of verbal tests.

5. Ojemann makes two additional observations. First, he notes that stimulation at particular points has very discrete effects. Stimulation of one cortical site will alter a language function, such as naming, on every trial, and it will only alter one of several language functions tested. Second, in view of the high variability between persons in the extent of language representation, Ojemann suggests that the biological substrate for human language meets conditions that are likely to lead to rapid evolution. That is, there is high variance in a trait that is almost certainly subject to selection by the environment.

Several important conclusions can be drawn from these results. First, the data do not support strict localizationist models of language, since stimulation of the anterior and posterior speech zones has remarkably similar effects on speech functions. Second, stimulation of the neocortex considerably beyond the classical areas of Broca and Wernicke disturbs speech functions. The area involved is remarkably similar to the speech zones defined more recently by regional blood-flow studies (see Chapter 15). Compare, for example, Figures 15-11 and 22-1. Third, stimulation of the speech zones affects more than just talking, for there are deficits in voluntary motor control of facial musculature as well as of short-term memory and reading. Fourth, removal of the cortex surrounding the posterior speech zone, mapped in Figure 22-1, does not produce lasting aphasia, even though fibers connecting the visual areas to the speech regions may be disrupted. Thus, it seems clear that these connections are not essential in the coordination of these two areas. Fifth, it has proved difficult to classify the transient aphasia following surgery, because each patient appears to be unique. There is also little evidence for a distinctive type of aphasia associated specifically with damage to either the anterior or posterior speech zones. In other words, there is no evidence for pure motor or sensory aphasias as postulated by Wernicke. Sixth, chronic speech and language deficits occur only if lesions are made within the classical speech zones (see Figure 22-2). Although stimulation of the face areas and supplementary motor zones arrests speech, removal of these zones has no chronic effect on speech. Recall, however, that

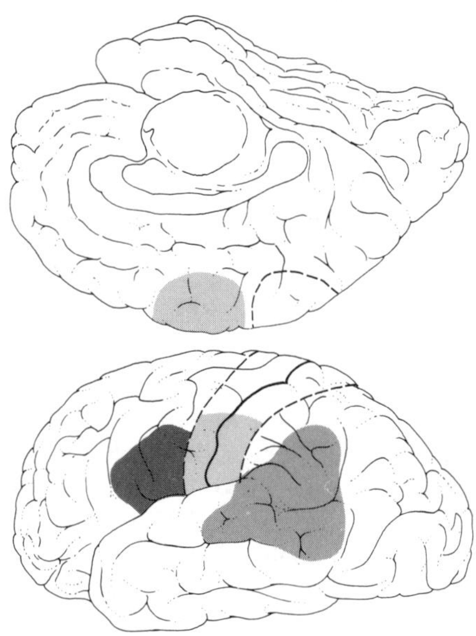

FIGURE 22-2. Summary of the effects of lesions on speech. Damage to the two darker areas produces chronic aphasia, damage to the lighter areas produces transient aphasia, and damage outside these areas does not produce aphasia.

face-area lesions do chronically impair other language functions (see Chapter 19).

One issue arising from the study of lesion patients is the relative importance of the anterior and posterior speech zones. Recall that in 1906, Marie published his celebrated paper claiming that Broca's area plays no special role in language. His conclusion was based on the study of cases in which there appeared to be destruction of Broca's area without aphasia and of cases in which there was Broca's aphasia without damage to Broca's area. Marie undoubtedly overstated his case, but his point was well taken and led to a controversy that persists to this day. We are inclined to agree with Zangwill's suggestion that although Broca's area undoubtedly plays a significant role in the normal control of articulate speech, damage to the area does not have the severe consequences on language that lesions in the posterior speech zone have. Furthermore, the severity of aphasia is far more variable following lesions to Broca's area than to Wernicke's area. Some patients with lesions in Broca's area may have only mild articulatory disorders, whereas others have severe disturbances of both expression and comprehension. Jefferson was probably correct in his suggestion that this variability reflects the extent of subcortical damage in addition to the damage to Broca's area itself.

Subcortical Components in Language

At the same time that Broca was describing a cortical center for speech control, Hughlings-Jackson proposed that subcortical structures are critical to language. In 1866, he wrote: "I think it will be found that the nearer the disease is to the corpus striatum, the more likely is the defect of articulation to be the striking thing, and the farther off, the more likely it is to be one of mistakes of words." Although he was the first to propose that aphasias result from subcortical damage, this proposition was not seriously considered until 1959, when Penfield and Roberts proposed that the thalamus, especially the **pulvinar,** functions to coordinate the activity of the cortical speech zones. In recent years evidence from stimulation and lesion studies has supported Hughlings-Jackson's proposal, although the importance and the precise role of the thalamus is still under debate.

In the course of surgical treatment of **dyskinesia,** electrodes are placed in the thalamus and an electric current applied in order to precisely define the electrode's position. For example, movements evoked by stimulation would indicate placement in motor thalamus, whereas somatosensory changes such as tingling sensations in the skin would indicate placement in the somatosensory thalamus. When the electrode is properly placed, a stronger current is passed, producing a lesion intended to relieve the dyskinesia. Careful study of language functions during these procedures, especially by Ojemann and by Cooper and their respective colleagues, has indicated that the pulvinar and the lateral posterior-lateral central complex of the left thalamus have a role in language not shared by other subcortical structures (see Figure 1-14). Stimulation of the left ventrolateral and pulvinar nuclei of the thalamus produces speech arrest, difficulties in naming, **perseveration,** and reduced speed of talking. Stimulation has also been reported to produce positive effects on memory, because it improves later retrieval of words heard during stimulation. As a result it has been proposed that the thalamus has some role in activating or arousing the cortex.

Lesions of the ventrolateral thalamus and/or pulvinar on the left have been associated with a variety of disturbances of speech and language processes. Symptoms include postoperative dysphasia, which is usually transitory; increased verbal-response latency; decreases in voice volume; alterations in speaking rate and slurring or hesitation in speech; and impaired performance on tests of verbal IQ and memory.

To summarize, there is evidence that the left posterior thalamus, including the pulvinar, lateral posterior, and lateral ventral regions, has a significant role in language. The nature of this role is still uncertain.

SPEECH ZONES MAPPED BY REGIONAL BLOOD FLOW

Studies of cerebral blood flow have shown that normal speech involves activation of the anterior and posterior language areas, as illustrated in Figure 15-11. Recent advances in PET scanning have allowed more sophisticated analysis of blood flow during different levels of linguistic processing. For example, Petersen and his coworkers asked subjects to perform three different tasks. In the first, words were passively presented either visually or auditorily. The task was to process the word but to do nothing (a sensory task). In the second task, the subject was to repeat the word (an output task). In the final one (an association task), the subject generated a use for the target word (for example, if "cake" was presented, to say "eat"). The authors monitored blood flow with PET and analyzed their data using a subtraction technique. Thus, in the sensory task they looked for changes from baseline blood flow by taking the difference in activity in the two states. In the output task they subtracted the sensory activity, and in the association task, they subtracted the output activity.

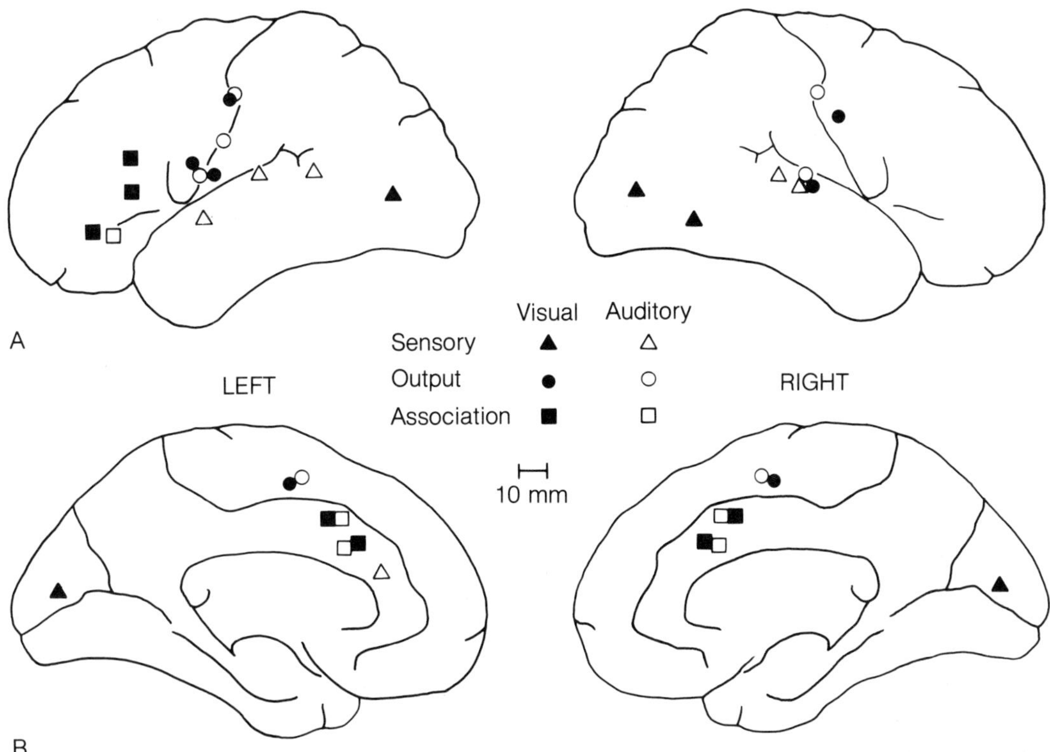

FIGURE 22-3. Schematic lateral (*A*) and medial (*B*) surface views of the left and right hemispheres with superimposed cortical activation foci. The key to the activation conditions is in the figure. Note that for passive presentations of words there is no overlap between visual (filled triangle) and auditory (open triangle) sensory tasks. There is considerable overlap, however, between the output and the association data for each modality. (After Petersen et al., 1988.)

Their results (Figure 22-3) lead to several different conclusions.

First, in the passive task there is increased blood flow bilaterally in the primary and secondary visual areas for the visual stimulus, and in the primary and secondary auditory areas for the auditory stimulus. Second, there is absolutely no overlap in the visual and auditory activation during the passive task, implying that the processing of the word forms in the two modalities is completely independent. Third, there is activation of the motor and sensory face areas bilaterally during the output task, as well as bilateral activation of the supplementary speech area. Fourth, for the association task there is activation of the frontal lobe, especially the left inferior region, corresponding roughly to Brodmann's area 47. Finally, there is bilateral activation of the anterior cingulate area during the association task, although it is unclear why this would be so, although lesions of this area sometimes produce mutism.

In summary, studies of this sort are confirming the role of the classical anterior and posterior speech zones in language, but show that other regions are involved as well. Furthermore, they show that the posterior speech zone may be devoted largely to the analysis of auditory input, since there was no increase in blood flow in this region for visual stimuli.

DISORDERS OF LANGUAGE

Before the neurology of language is given a theoretical description, the disorders of language must first be considered, since theoretical formulations of language function must be able to account for the disorders observed. We first describe the types of deficits observed in language and then consider the classification of aphasias.

Language Deficits and Neurological Damage

Normal language depends on a complex interaction among sensory integration and symbolic association, motor skills, learned syntactic patterns, and verbal memory. **Aphasia** refers to a disorder of language apparent in speech, writing (*agraphia*), or reading (*alexia*) produced by injury to brain areas specialized for these functions. Thus, disturbances of language due to severe intellectual impairment, loss of sensory input (especially vision and hearing), or paralysis or incoordination of the musculature of the mouth (**anarthria**) or hand (for writing) are not considered to be aphasic disturbances. These disorders may accompany aphasia, and they complicate the study of it.

Goodglass and Kaplan have broken language disturbances down into nine basic types, which we have subgrouped into disorders of comprehension and of production of language.

Disorders of Comprehension. Disorders of comprehension can be either auditory or visual, each related to the method of presentation of verbal material.

Auditory Comprehension. Comprehension of auditory input may be disturbed even though the primary auditory cortex per se is not damaged. For example, a person may act as though a word was not heard at all (so-called word deafness) or as though only fragments of the word were heard. The commoner defect lies not in failing to recognize that a word was spoken but rather in failing to attach meaning to the word (much as if it were spoken in a foreign language unknown to the hearer). In some cases auditory comprehension is particularly impaired when words are presented in isolation rather than in the context of a sentence. In some aphasics comprehension of individual words is intact, but certain grammatical constructions are not discriminated properly. For example, the phrases "the lost man's wallet" and "the man's lost wallet" involve the same words but have totally different meanings.

Visual Comprehension. Because comprehension of written material (i.e., reading) is based on prior mastery of auditory language, it is not surprising that deficits in reading (alexia) accompany deficits in auditory comprehension. A disturbance of reading is commonly associated with impaired comprehension of auditory material, but these two symptoms may occur independently of each other. As with auditory defects, defects in visual comprehension may involve a deficit in recognizing individual letters or words as being letters or words, or a deficit in attaching meaning to the symbols written on a page.

Disorders of Production. There are at least eight disorders of production, which range from an inability to form words, to an inability to place words together to form a spoken or written sentence.

Articulation. Speaking requires the ability to make the sounds of vowels and consonants, which will then be placed in different combinations to form words and sentences. People with severe deficits in articulation are unable to produce simple sounds, even by imitation. Noises may actually be produced, but frequently each attempt to form a word produces the same nonsense syllable. In milder forms the person may be able to articulate many sounds, especially vowel sounds, but usually will have extreme difficulty in making difficult sounds such as consonant blends. For example, one man that we saw would say "huah" for "ch" and "buh" for "bl." Deficits in articulation may result from any of three different causes. First, there may be a defect in the peripheral speech mechanisms of the larynx, pharynx, and tongue. This disorder is not an aphasia but is termed **dysarthria.** Second, there may be a defect in choosing the desired sound from all those available in a person's repertory. Third, there may be a deficit in the motor system that prevents the desired sound from being properly pronounced.

Word Finding. Words are formed by combining sounds; to do this correctly it is necessary to choose the appropriate words from the large available repertory. Virtually all aphasics suffer from some restriction in the repertory of words available, and even when words are produced, it takes longer than normal to do so. If this difficulty in finding words occurs in the absence of other aphasic symptoms, the disorder is called **anomia.** Difficulty in finding words often results in the person's deliberately choosing a word that approximates the intended idea when the intended word cannot be found. For example, one woman we saw substituted words such as *cow* for *milk* and *cigar* for *pipe*.

Paraphasia. Goodglass and Kaplan define **paraphasia** as the production of unintended syllables, words, or phrases during the effort to speak. Paraphasia differs from difficulties in articulation in that sounds are correctly articulated, but they are the wrong sounds, and either distort the intended word (e.g., *pike* instead of *pipe*) or produce a completely unintended word (e.g., *my mother* instead of *my wife*).

Loss of Grammar and Syntax. Words must be placed together to produce proper grammar and syntax. Some individuals are totally unable to place words together into grammatically correct sequences and so restrict their sentences to short utterances of two or three words. Choosing correct verb tense may be especially difficult, in which case nearly all verbs are in the present tense, usually of a simple form such as "He go." It is curious that many of these aphasics are able to produce long strings of memorized sequences such as in counting numbers or reciting days of the week and months of the year; some individuals can even recite previously learned poetry or prayers or repeat sentences they have just heard. The preservation of these abilities, however, in the face of an inability to produce spontaneous sentences, demonstrates that some associative ability is missing or seriously impaired.

Repetition. Although many aphasics can repeat aurally presented material, others cannot, even though other language functions may appear fairly intact. Disorders of repetition may result either from deficits in comprehension or articulation—in which case there are associated aphasic symptoms—or from a selective dissociation between auditory-input and speech-output systems. In the case of selective dissociation, the disorder of repetition may be the only significant language disturbance and may go unnoticed except through special testing.

Verbal Fluency. Verbal fluency is the ability to produce words in uninterrupted strings. Low verbal fluency may be associated with word-finding difficulty or may occur in the absence of any other language disturbances. Recall that frontal lesions, even on the right, may reduce word output even though no other deficits in language use or production are known.

Writing. Writing, one of the most complex of language abilities, may be disturbed in a wide variety of ways. First, it may result from disturbance in movement of the limb to produce letters and words—although this disorder would not be a disturbance of language per se. At a more complex level, writing may be impossible (agraphia) because of an inability to recall the form of letters or the correct movements necessary to produce them. Many of the deficits observed in oral language may also occur in written language, as in **paragraphia,** which is the writing of the incorrect word or a perseveration in writing the same word repeatedly.

Prosody. **Prosody** (from the Greek for song) refers to the tone or accent of language. Normally the term is used to refer to the loudness of voice, the relative duration of different phonemes, and the vocal pitch. The closest physical correlates are intensity, time pattern, and vocal frequency, respectively. Monrad-Krohn described three classes of prosodic abnormality: *hyperprosody,* an excessive or exaggerated prosody, sometimes characterizing mania and only occasionally observed in aphasics; *dysprosody,* a distorted prosody in which listeners perceive a foreign accent (usually Welsh or German in native English speakers); and *aprosody,* an attenuation or lack of normal prosody, such as is often observed in people with Parkinson's disease.

Classification of Aphasias

Since the time of Wernicke people have attempted to describe different types of aphasia by identifying clusters of symptoms associated with particular brain lesions. This has proved to be a difficult task, partly because so few cases are thoroughly studied, and partly because so few well-studied cases ever come to autopsy. Thus, there is constant debate over which lesions produce which cluster of aphasic symptoms. Although many researchers have considered different types of aphasias to be totally independent of one another, there is no convincing empirical proof of this claim. As Brown puts it:

> All disorders of speech understanding, even those with the most limited pathology, are likely to have an expressive element, while some defect in speech comprehension should be a constant feature of the motor aphasias. The importance of this finding has certainly not received proper attention in the literature. One need only point to the fact that there is not one careful study of speech comprehension in restricted cases of Broca's aphasia, nor a comparable study, of the much rarer word-deafness, of the true state of expressive speech. (Brown, 1972, p. 14)

In spite of considerable disagreement over the number of types of aphasias, there are classification systems that are widely used. An example of one is given in Table 22-1. Broadly defined, aphasias are classified into three general categories: **fluent aphasias,** in which there is fluent speech but difficulties either in auditory verbal comprehension and/or the repetition of words, phrases, or sentences spoken by others; **nonfluent aphasias,** in which there are difficulties in articulating but relatively good auditory verbal comprehension; and *"pure" aphasias,* in which there are selective impairments of reading, writing, or recognition of words. Within each of these broad categories of aphasia, numerous subtypes are often distinguished, including Wernicke's aphasia, transcortical aphasia, conduction aphasia, anomic aphasia, and Broca's aphasia.

Wernicke's Aphasia. Wernicke's, or **sensory, aphasia** is the inability to comprehend words or to arrange sounds into coherent speech. Luria has proposed that this type of aphasia has three characteristics. First, to hear and make out the sounds of speech, one must be able to qualify sounds — that is, to include sounds in the system

TABLE 22-1. Definition of aphasic syndromes

Syndrome	Type of speech production	Type of language errors
Fluent		
Wernicke (sensory)	Fluent speech, without articulatory disorders	Neologism and/or anomias, or paraphasias, poor comprehension; poor repetition
Transcortical (isolation syndrome)	Fluent speech, without articulatory disorders; good repetition	Verbal paraphasias and anomias; poor comprehension
Conduction	Fluent, sometimes halting speech, but without articulatory disorders	Phonemic, paraphasias and neologisms; phonemic groping; poor repetition; fairly good comprehension
Anomic	Fluent speech, without articulatory disorders	Anomia and occasional paraphasias
Nonfluent		
Broca, severe	Laborious articulation	Speechlessness with recurring utterances or syndrome of phonetic disintegration; poor repetition
Broca, mild	Slight but obvious articulatory disorders	Phonemic paraphasias with anomia; agrammatism; dysprosody
Transcortical motor	Marked tendency to reduction and inertia, without articulatory disorders; good repetition	Uncompleted sentences and anomias; naming better than spontaneous speech
Global	Laborious articulation	Speechlessness with recurring utterances; poor comprehension; poor repetition
"Pure"		
Alexia without agraphia	Normal	Poor reading
Agraphia	Normal	Poor writing
Word deafness	Normal	Poor comprehension; poor repetition

Source: After Mazzocchi and Vignolo, 1979

of phonemes that are the basic units of speech in a given language. An example will illustrate. In the Japanese language the sounds "l" and "r" are not distinguished; a Japanese hearing English cannot distinguish these sounds because the necessary template is not in the brain. Thus, although this distinction is perfectly clear to English-speaking persons, it is not to native Japanese. This is precisely the problem that a person with Wernicke's aphasia has in his or her own language: the inability to isolate the significant phonemic characteristics and to classify sounds into known phonemic systems. The second characteristic of Wernicke's aphasia is that there is a defect in speech. The affected person can speak, and may speak a great deal, but he or she confuses phonetic characteristics, producing what is often called **word salad.** The third characteristic is an impairment in writing. A person who cannot discern phonemic characteristics cannot be expected to write, because he or she does not know the **graphemes** (pictorial or written representation of a phoneme) that combine to form a word.

Transcortical Aphasia. **Transcortical aphasia** (also sometimes called **isolation syndrome**), is a curious type of aphasia in which individuals can repeat and understand words and name objects but cannot speak spontaneously, or they are also unable to comprehend words although they can still repeat them. This type of aphasia is presumed to be caused by loss of the secondary sensory cortex (association cortex). Comprehension could be poor because words fail to arouse associations. Production of meaningful speech could be poor because even though the production of words is normal, words are not associated with other cognitive activity in the brain.

Conduction Aphasia. **Conduction aphasia** is a paradoxical deficit: people with this disorder can speak easily, name objects, and understand speech, but cannot repeat words. The simplest explanation for this problem is that there is a disconnection between the "perceptual word image" in the parietal-temporal cortex and the "motor image of the word" in the frontal cortex. There has, however, never been any clear proof that cutting the connections actually causes this syndrome, and there is considerable debate over whether this symptom really occurs in the absence of other symptoms, especially impaired short-term memory.

Anomic Aphasia. People with **anomic aphasia** (sometimes called **amnesic aphasia**) comprehend speech, produce meaningful speech, and can repeat speech but have great difficulty in finding the names of objects. For example, we saw a patient who when shown a picture of a ship anchor simply could not think of the name and finally said, "I know what it does. . . . You use it to anchor a ship." Although he had actually used the word as a verb he was unable to use it as a noun. This symptom is most likely to result from a lesion in the angular gyrus, but virtually all aphasics have naming difficulties. Luria and Hutton emphasize that this type of aphasia cannot be explained simply; it appears likely that the same symptom may result from any one of three causes. First, to name an object one must identify its distinguishing characteristics. A person having difficulties in isolating these characteristics will not name it properly. Second, to name an object, having isolated its characteristics, one must also develop the auditory form of the word. Thus, a person who does not retain the word's auditory structure will be unable to produce it. Finally, to produce the word, one must select the appropriate word from those expressing ideas closely associated with it. For example, when asked to name a butterfly, a person may have difficulty in choosing the correct word from associated words such as moth, fly, or insect. In failing to do so the person may utter the word *moth* or even *bird.* Clearly this problem is quite different from the inability to identify distinguishing characteristics. It is possible that each of these three naming problems represents a separate neurological deficit, but this possibility is rather difficult to prove.

Broca's Aphasia. In **Broca's aphasia** a person has difficulty in speaking, although continues to understand speech. Broca's aphasia is also known as *motor, expressive,* or *nonfluent aphasia.* This aphasia features a pattern of speech in which a person speaks in a very slow, deliberate manner with very simple grammatical structure. Thus, all

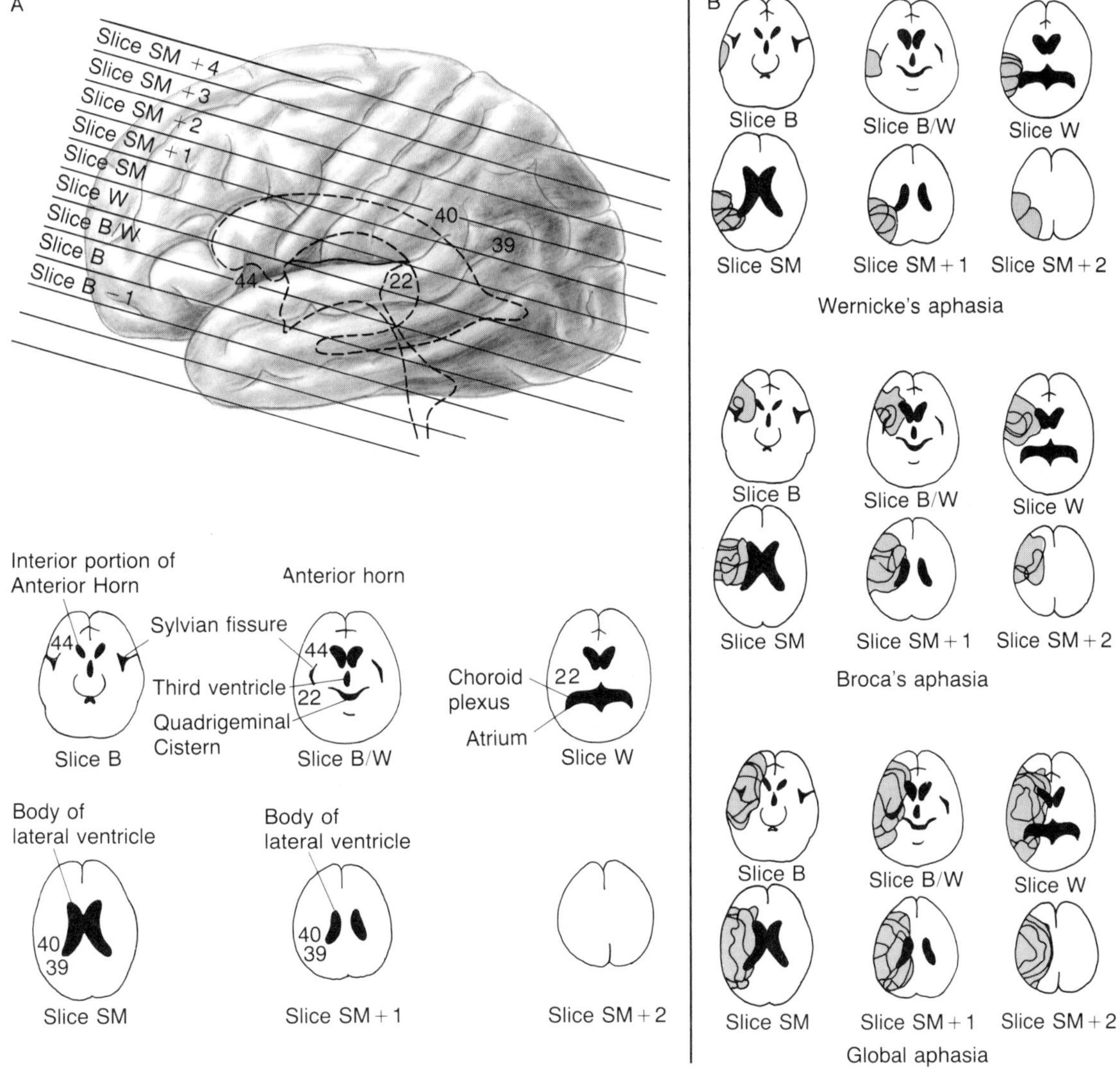

FIGURE 22-4. *A.* Lateral (top) and cross-sectional (bottom) views of the relation of major language areas to the shape of the ventricles on CT-scan slices. *B.* Cross-sectional composite CT-scan lesion sites for four Wernicke's, three Broca's, and five global aphasics. (After Naeser et al., 1981.)

the forms of a verb are likely to be reduced to the infinitive or the participle. Nouns are most apt to be expressed only in the singular, and conjunctions, adjectives, adverbs, and articles are very uncommon. Only the key words necessary for communication are used.

There is still no adequate explanation for Broca's aphasia. Broca assumed that the problem was an impairment of the "motor image of the word," but it is uncertain what this supposition implies about brain function. Certainly, however, the deficit is not one of making sounds, but rather one of switching from one sound to another.

Localization of Lesions in Aphasia

Distinct variation in the language disorders of different aphasics is readily apparent clinically and has been recorded for over a century. It is logical to presume that the individual symptomatology is related to the precise pathology, but this is difficult to prove. The possibility of defining the site and extent of lesions in vivo has been greatly increased by the introduction of new scanning procedures, specially the CT scan.

The first systematic attempt to correlate pathology with brain scan data was published by Benson in 1967. He correlated the locus of pathology as inferred from radioisotope brain scans (see Chapter 6) and found that patients classified as nonfluent aphasics (whom he characterized as having low verbal output, dysprosody, dysarthria, and obvious articulatory disorders) had lesions located anterior to the central fissure; fluent aphasics (whom he classified as having paraphasia, with "press of speech and a distinct lack of substantive words") had a posterior lesion. Benson thus felt that an anterior or a posterior localization could be reliably diagnosed in a majority of aphasics based solely on their verbal output. Although Benson's study was an important step in localizing lesions in aphasia, radioisotope scans are rather gross measures. The advent of the CT scan provided not only a means of producing an anterior-posterior distinction but

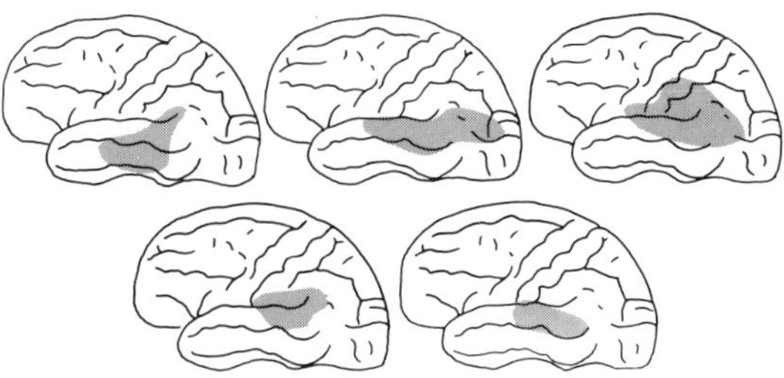

A Wernicke's aphasia

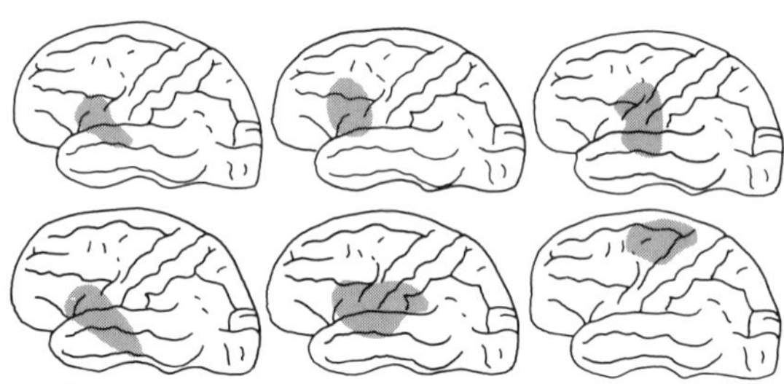

B Broca's aphasia

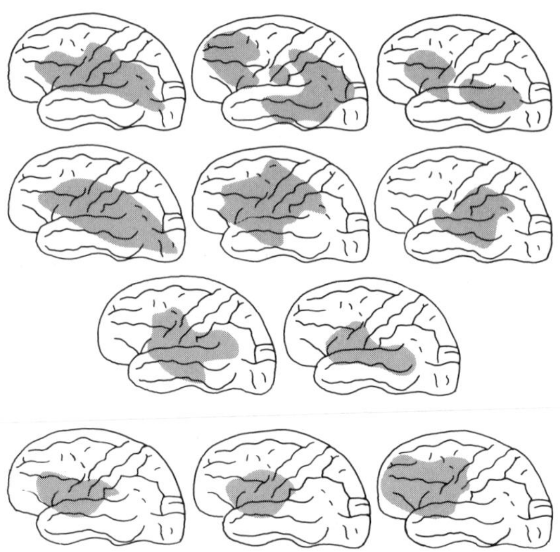

C Global aphasia

FIGURE 22-5. Maps of lesions in individual cases of Wernicke's (*A*), Broca's (*B*), and global aphasia (*C*). The lower row of global aphasics shows examples that spare Wernicke's area. (After Mazzocchi and Vignolo, 1979.)

also of measuring the dorsoventral extent of a lesion. Two groups have been particularly successful in using CT scans in the study of aphasia. The first, Naeser and her colleagues, have described the relation between CT scans and aphasia using the procedure illustrated in Figure 22-4. Basically, the locus of pathology is determined from the scan and the relation between the pathology and the cortical language areas inferred from the known relations between the ventricles and the cortical areas. The second, Mazzocchi and Vignolo, have attempted to control intersubject differences in the orientation of the CT scan by using a slightly different method. In essence, this consists of determining the angle of the CT sections, tracing the contours of the lesion on each CT section, and transferring them onto a standard lateral diagram of the hemisphere, as illustrated in Figure 22-5. The results of these two procedures are in general agreement with Benson's conclusions: Wernicke's aphasia (a fluent aphasia) is correlated with damage in the posterior speech zone and Broca's aphasia (a nonfluent aphasia) is correlated with damage to the anterior speech zone. In addition, both groups have shown that global aphasia results from larger lesions in the left hemisphere, usually including both the anterior and the posterior speech zones, and that other types of aphasia (e.g., conduction aphasia) may have similar anatomical correlates.

NEUROLOGICAL MODELS OF LANGUAGE

Geschwind's reformulation and clarification of Wernicke's localization model has proved conceptually useful, and forms a basis for most current positions on the neurology of language function.

The Wernicke-Geschwind Model

The Wernicke-Geschwind model is built on the assumption that the neural basis of speech and language involves the following structures: Broca's area, Wernicke's area, the arcuate fasciculus (which connects Broca's area with Wernicke's area), the precentral and postcentral face area, the angular gyrus, and the auditory and visual cortex (see Figure 22-6). Broca's area is assumed to house programs for the complex coordination of muscles for speech; Wernicke's area, the mechanism for transforming auditory input into meaningful units, or words; the arcuate fasciculus joins the anterior and posterior speech zones; the face area directs the movements of the face, tongue, etc.; and the angular gyrus (area 39) combines sensory input to house "visual patterns" of letters, words, and so on, and acts in some way to convert a visual stimulus into the appropriate auditory form. Geschwind has neatly summarized how these parts of the cortex function in the production of language.

> When a word is heard, the output from the primary auditory area of the cortex is received by Wernicke's area. If the word is to be spoken, the pattern is transmitted from Wernicke's area to Broca's area, where the articulatory form is aroused and passed on to the motor area that controls the movement of the muscles of speech. If the spoken word is to be spelled, the auditory pattern is passed to the angular gyrus, where it elicits the visual pattern. When a word is read, the output from the primary visual areas passes to the angular gyrus, which in turn arouses the corresponding auditory form of the word in Wernicke's area. It should be noted that in most people comprehension of a written word involves arousal of the auditory form in Wernicke's area. Wernicke argued that this was the result of the way most people learn written language. He thought, however, that in people who were born deaf, but had learned to read, Wernicke's area would not be in the circuit.
>
> According to this model, if Wernicke's area is damaged, the person would have difficulty comprehending both spoken and written language. He should be unable to speak, repeat, and write

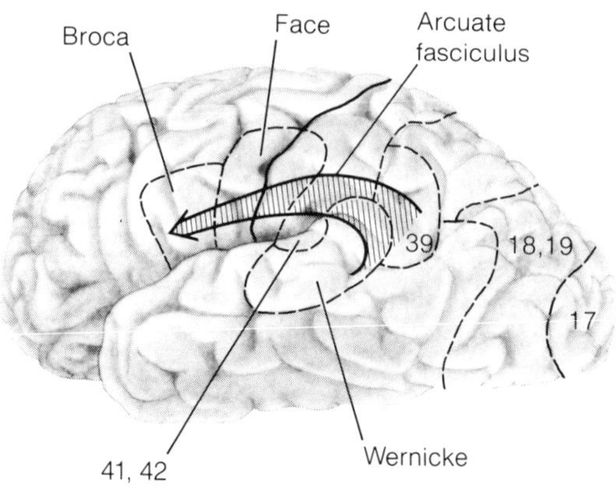

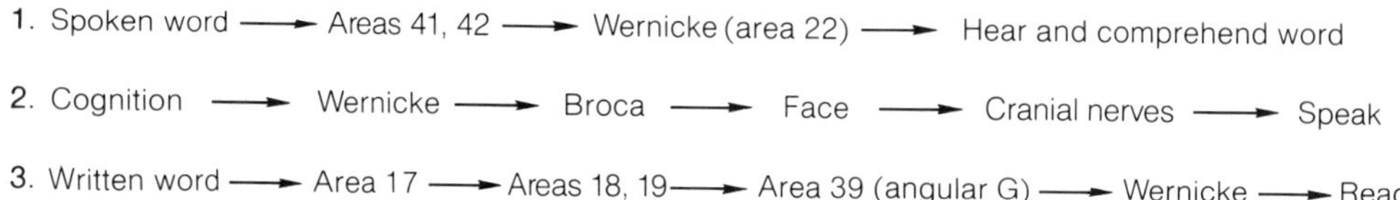

FIGURE 22-6. Geschwind's model of the neurology of language, showing the regions of the cortex involved. Items 1 to 3 illustrate how the model explains different language functions.

> correctly. The fact that in such cases speech is fluent and well articulated suggests that Broca's area is intact but receiving inadequate information. If the damage were in Broca's area, the effect of the lesion would be to disrupt articulation. Speech would be slow and labored but comprehension should remain intact. (Geschwind, 1972, p. 344)

Further, damage to the arcuate fasciculus would not be expected to disturb either the comprehension or the production of speech, but rather should make it difficult to repeat speech, because the auditory recognition and speech production regions would be disconnected.

Two other abilities can be considered in this model: reading and writing. In theory, these abilities require the integrity of the angular gyrus to act as a way station between the visual and auditory regions (see Figure 22-6). To be meaningful, visual input must be translated into auditory form in this region. Similarly, before a word can be written, the auditory input must be translated into visual form. Thus, people with lesions of the angular gyrus would be expected to be unable to read or write. Although these people can speak and can comprehend speech, they cannot recognize a word spelled aloud, nor can they spell a word aloud.

Problems with the Wernicke-Geschwind Model

However popular and useful the Wernicke-Geschwind model of language function has been, its rigid localizationist bias leaves it open to a number of criticisms.

As we described earlier, stimulation of speech zones does not always interrupt speech, and when speech is interrupted, the interruption is of the same type in both the anterior and posterior speech zones. Indeed, Ojemann has recently found that stimulation-induced naming errors are more likely to occur from stimulation of the anterior speech zone than of the posterior zone! Furthermore, Ojemann and Mateer report that stimulation of the same sites disrupted both the production of sequential oral-facial movements and the ability to discriminate phonemes such as "la" and "ba." The apparent functional homogeneity within widespread regions of the speech zones is difficult to reconcile with a strict localizationist view of language function. Different effects would be expected from different portions of the speech circuitry.

Studies of lesion patients do not support a distinction between disorders of language production and understanding, since both expressive and receptive speech disorders are present in all aphasic patients with naturally occurring lesions, and surgical destruction of portions of the language zones seldom results in permanent aphasia.

The model does not include subcortical components of language—regions that play a significant, even if poorly understood, role in language.

The studies of Penfield and Roberts and of Rasmussen and Milner indicate that the corticocortical connections from the visual and auditory regions to the speech zones, and the arcuate fasciculus joining the speech zones themselves, can apparently be surgically removed without incurring aphasia. This observation contradicts Geschwind's case studies, which show that accidental lesions of the cortex surrounding Wernicke's area produce aphasia. The discrepancy is explained by the considerable difference between the lesions in the patients studied by Geschwind and those done surgically. For example, the surgical lesions are shallower, bleed less, and are precise and restricted to the cortex; natural lesions almost certainly include subcortical damage, and remaining cortex may function abnormally.

In summary, although the Wernicke-Geschwind model of localization of language function is conceptually useful, it presents several serious difficulties. Curiously, it still seems to be widely accepted in clinical neurology.

Multiple-Route Models

One of the basic principles of cortical function is that sensory information is processed in multiple channels. This appears to be true not only for basic sensory and perceptual functions, but also for memory functions, as we saw in Chapter 22. It is reasonable to suppose, therefore, that language-related sensory input would also be processed in multiple channels. Cognitive psychologists have proposed various models of parallel processing of sensory input relating to language, but there is little neurological evidence relevant to these hypotheses. Recall, however, that Petersen and his colleagues found that passive visual and auditory presentation of words led to increased blood flow in independent cortical areas (Figure 22-3), and that there was no activation in the region of Wernicke's area in any of their visual tasks. Thus, visual input appears to have access to output systems without processing in Wernicke's area, which is quite inconsistent with the Wernicke-Geschwind model. Curiously, the blood-flow studies also show that it is the frontal rather than the posterior cortex that is involved in associative aspects of language. Apparently, there is direct access of the visual and auditory systems to the language-related associative processes of the frontal lobe. (These processes are called *semantic associational* processes by cognitive psychologists.) Future studies will have to combine cognitive and neurobiological approaches in the study of language processing to help us identify the nature of the multiple routes that may be involved in language processing.

ASSESSMENT OF APHASIA

Since World War II there has been widespread interest in establishing a standard systematic pro-

TABLE 22-2. Summary of the major tests of aphasia

Test	Basic reference
Aphasia test batteries	
Boston Diagnostic Aphasia Test	Goodglass and Kaplan, 1972
Functional communicative profile	Sarno, 1969
Neurosensory center comprehensive examination for aphasia	Spreen and Benton, 1969
Porch Index of Communicative Ability	Porch, 1967
Minnesota Test for Differential Diagnosis of Aphasia	Schuell, 1965
Wepman-Jones Language Modalities Test for Aphasia	Wepman and Jones, 1961
Aphasia screening tests	
Halstead-Wepman Aphasia Screening Test	Halstead and Wepman, 1959
Token test	de Renzi and Vignolo, 1962

cedure for assessing aphasia, for use both in providing standardized clinical descriptions of patients and in facilitating comparison of patient populations in neuropsychological research. In the past 25 years a number of manuals on aphasia testing have appeared. Table 22-2 summarizes the most widely used. The first group of tests are considered to be test batteries, because they provide a large number of subtests designed to systematically explore the language capabilities of the subject. They typically include tests of (1) auditory and visual comprehension; (2) oral and written expression including tests of repetition, reading, naming, and fluency; and (3) conversational speech. Because these test batteries have the disadvantages of being lengthy and requiring special training to administer, some brief aphasia screening tests have been devised. The two most popular, the Halstead-Wepman and the token test, are frequently used as part of standard neuropsychological test batteries (see Chapter 27) because they are short and easy to administer and to score. These tests do not replace the detailed examination of the aphasia test batteries, but they can be used to identify language disorders. If a fine description of the linguistic deficits is desired, the more comprehensive aphasia batteries must be given.

Problems with Assessment Batteries

Although models and test batteries of aphasia may be useful for evaluating and classifying the status of a patient, they are not a substitute for an experimental analysis of language disorders. In an evaluation of current interpretations of aphasic language disorders, Marshall has pointed out some of the inadequacies of batteries and has argued that there is still the need for the development of a psychobiology of language disorders. Whereas the batteries attempt to classify patients into a number of groups, a psychobiological approach would concentrate on individual differences and peculiarities and from these attempt to reconstruct the processes through which the brain produces language. On the practical side Marshall notes that only about 60% of patients will fit into a schema such as the Wernicke-Geschwind classification. Others have noted a similar lack of success in classifying patients according to other methods. For example, most patients with a language impairment show a deficit in naming that can be elicited by having them look at pictures or objects. Scores on standard tests often tell little about the impairment. A number of patients may be able to name a violin, but one might know only that it is a musical instrument, another might know that it is a stringed instrument, and still another might know that it is similar to a cello and not a trumpet. Furthermore, some patients may have selective naming deficits such that they are unable to name objects that are inside houses (bathrooms). Some may not be able to name buildings, people, colors, and so forth. Obviously, individuals which differ in this way are inappropriately classified as simply anomic. Furthermore the differences that they do display can reveal some important insights into the neural organization of language. At the present time there are no good guidelines for developing a science of the neural basis of language, but such a science could have some of the elements of the reading analyses developed by Coltheart and others (See Figures 22-7 and 22-8).

Sex Differences in Aphasia

We have noted in our discussion of cerebral asymmetry (Chapter 16) that there are sex differences in the impairments of language that follow brain injury. This possibility was ignored in early studies on language function, in test batteries, and in neural-modeling work on language function. Clearly, however, any adequate model, battery, or theory of language function must consider such differences, if they exist. As we noted, McGlone has argued that the female brain is more symmetrical than the male brain, with language represented bilaterally. Consequently, damage to either hemisphere produces a mild language impairment in females, but damage to the left hemisphere produces severe aphasia in males. A clear prediction of McGlone's results is that the incidence and severity of aphasia in females should be less than it is in males. We have noted, however, that a number of studies have not obtained this result.

Kimura, using the same patient population used by McGlone, divided the patients with left hemisphere lesions not only by sex but also by lesion location. About two-thirds of the patients had vascular problems, primarily strokes, and the remainder had tumors or seizures, and all had only unilateral damage. Aphasia was less common after left hemisphere damage in females than in males. A surprising result was obtained when the patients

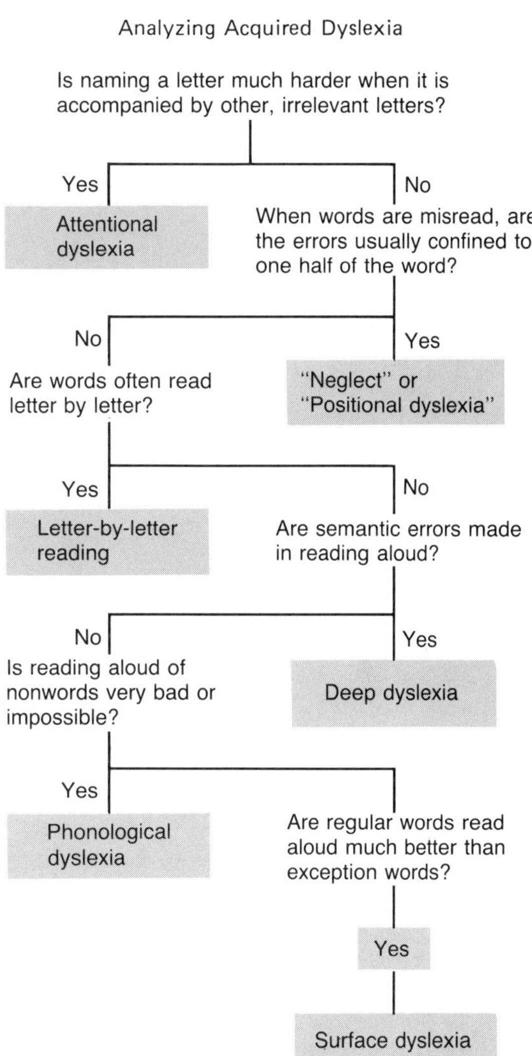

FIGURE 22-7. Flow chart for the analysis of dyslexia (After Coltheart, 1981.)

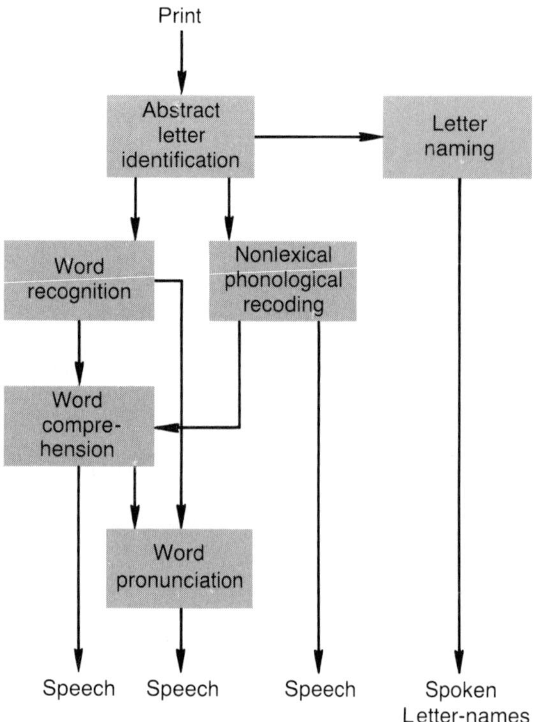

FIGURE 22-8. Examples of subsystems used in reading. Note that speech from print can follow a number of different routes and can be independent of comprehension or pronunciation. (After Coltheart, 1981.)

were grouped by lesion site: restricted to either the anterior or the posterior cortex, with the lateral fissure used as the dividing line. For women, aphasia was much more common after anterior lesions than after posterior lesions, but for men aphasia was slightly more common after posterior lesions, and the distribution of aphasic cases was more equal across the two regions. These results are illustrated in Figure 22-9. A further analysis revealed that in males aphasia might result from damage to anterior, central, temporal, parietal, or (rarely) occipital lesions. In females, it was very much dependent on the anterior region, with a small incidence of aphasia also in the temporal region.

These are surprising results, but Kimura found a similar pattern of results on other tests. The patients were given a manual praxic task requiring them to copy a series of unfamiliar arm movements. Impairments or apraxia in females were restricted to patients with damage in the anterior cortex, whereas in males manual apraxia occurred with lesions throughout the left hemisphere with the highest incidence following lesions in the parietal cortex.

These results can account for the lower incidence in aphasia observed in females. Since aphasia mainly follows anterior lesions in females but both anterior and posterior lesions in males, fewer aphasic females would be expected. It is much more difficult to account for the sex differences in speech location, however. From a speculative point of view, if females are less lateralized for language function, the right posterior cortex may be able to compensate for left posterior cortex damage via large interhemispheric connections. On the other hand, it may be the case that the posterior cortex of females has a somewhat different role, perhaps mediating perceptual speed or incidental information, than that for males. As Kimura notes, these possibilities require future study. In conclusion, there is little doubt that Kimura's results pose a problem for the Wernicke-Geschwind model of language organization and for any model of cortical organization of function. Future research will hopefully clarify some problems with interpreting the results. It is not known, for example, whether subcortical pathology in the sexes would be different. Possibly, vascular organization in men and women is such that strokes in any portion of the left cortex are accompanied by consistent subcortical damage with the same damage only following anterior strokes in females. Thus, the differential impairments would relate not so much to cortical pathology as to subcortical pathology.

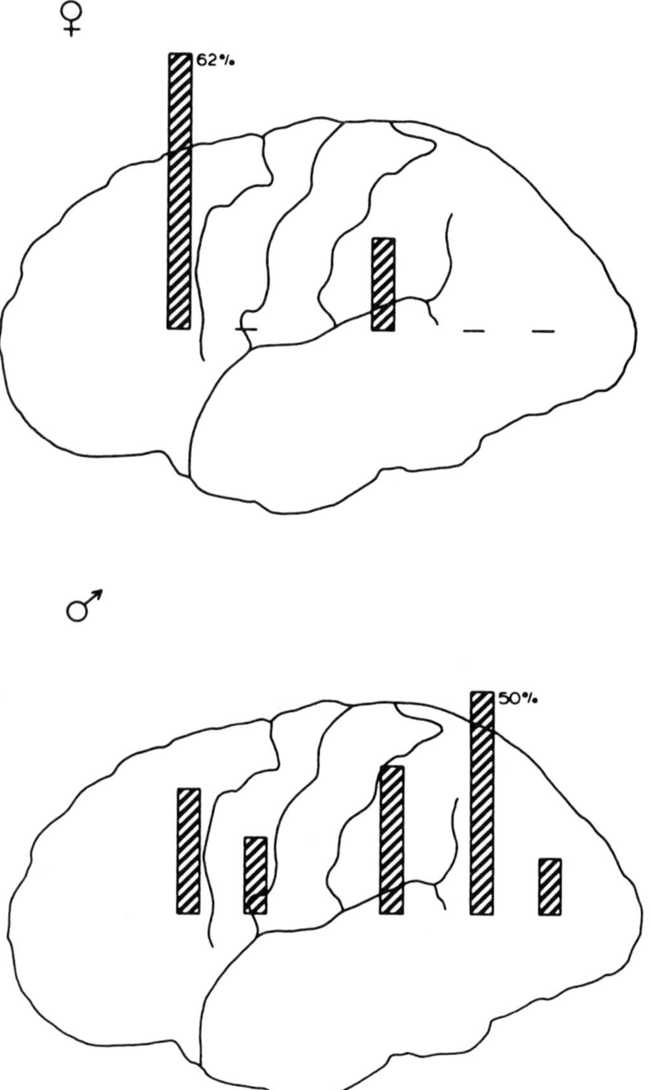

FIGURE 22-9. Incidence of aphasia after anterior, central, temporal, parietal, and occipital lesions, in females (*A*) and males (*B*). (From D. Kimura; copyright 1987, Canadian Psychological Association, reprinted with permission.)

ASSESSMENT OF DYSLEXIA

The assessment of reading disorders is becoming a special branch of the study of language. This results from the fact that it is possible to be more objective in the analysis of reading than for writing and speaking, because there is a large pedagogical science of reading, and because in addition to the **acquired dyslexias** (impairments in reading that follow brain damage), **developmental dyslexias** (failure to learn to read during development) are common and require diagnosis and remediation.

Coltheart has argued that the most objective approach to the study of reading is model-building. A model (the models are much like algorithms) is constructed and then reading-disabled individuals are tested in order to both define the impairment and to test the utility of the model. The model-building approach differs from classical neurological approaches, in which dyslexia is defined in terms of whether it occurs in conjunction with other disorders, such as dysgraphia or dysphasia and in which the primary intent is to correlate the impairment with the locus of brain damage. The model-building approach can be traced to Hinshelwood's analysis, first published in 1900. Hinshelwood recognized that there are different types of reading disorders, including (1) the inability to name letters (letter blindness), (2) the inability to read words (word blindness), and the inability to read sentences (sentence blindness). The Hinshelwood taxonomy and its subsequent elaboration has led to the current hypothesis that reading is composed of a number of independent abilities, which may have an independent anatomical basis. Figure 22-7 gives in flowchart form some different types of impairments in reading that have been encountered. In addition to naming the impairment, questions are asked in order to identify the type of impairment. The following are brief descriptions of these impairments.

1. *Attentional dyslexia.* When one letter is present, naming is normal. When other letters are present, naming is difficult. Even if the letter is specially colored, underlined, has an arrow pointing to it, and is pointed to by the tester, it may be named incorrectly. The same phenomenon may occur when one, as opposed to more than one, word is present.

2. *Neglect.* Persons may misread the first half of a word (e.g., "whether" as "smother"), or they may misread the last part of a word (e.g., "strong" as "stroke"). This syndrome has received little investigation.

3. *Letter-by-letter reading.* Affected individuals read words only by spelling them out to themselves (aloud or silently). When the spelling is done silently, it can be detected by the increase in time taken to read long words. Frequently, the person can write but then has difficulty in reading what was written.

4. *Deep dyslexia.* The key symptoms in this disorder are semantic errors: persons with **deep dyslexia** read semantically related words in place of the word they are trying to read (e.g., *tulip* as *crocus* and *merry* as *Christmas*). Nouns are the easiest for them to read, followed by adjectives and then verbs. Function words present the greatest difficulty. Those who suffer from deep dyslexia also find it easier to read concrete rather than abstract words and are completely unable to read nonsense words. They are also generally impaired at writing and in their short-term verbal memory (digit span).

5. *Phonological dyslexia.* The one symptom of **phonological dyslexia** is an inability to read nonwords aloud; otherwise reading may be nearly flawless.

6. *Surface dyslexia.* The **surface dyslexic** is unable to recognize words directly but can understand them by using letter-to-sound relations; that

is, the word can be understood if it is sounded out. This reading procedure works well as long as the words are regular ones (*home, dome*), but not if the word are irregular (*come* will be read as *comb*). Spelling is also impaired but is phonetically correct. Surface dyslexia will not occur in languages that are totally phonetic (such as Italian). Surface dyslexia is a common symptom of children who have difficulty in learning to read.

The explanation of reading that comes from the model-building approach is that reading is composed of a number of independent skills or subsystems, one or another of which may not be functioning in an impaired reader. Marshall cleverly demonstrates this idea with the following example of two lines of poetry that can be read either for sense or for sound:

Kuh! Sie Kuh! Sie kann der . . .
Wer Du ja Wanduhr?

The sound reader will read this as "Goosey, Goosey Gander,/Where do you wander?" Someone reading for the sense of the German will read it as "Cow! You Cow!/Who do you think you are, you and your clock on the wall?" The central idea to be obtained from this example is that in normal readers sense and sound are computed in parallel, whereas in the dyslexic, one or the other process may be absent. The deep-dyslexic patient is unable to process for sound and so attempts to read for sense. The surface dyslexic is able to process for sound but not for sense. A model of how parallel systems may be organized and interact is illustrated in Figure 22-8. Note that there are two quite separate ways of obtaining speech from print, and a still different way of producing letter names.

The important features of the model-building approach are that it does not demand that anatomical-functional relations be used, it can be equally applied to other disorders of speech, and it may eventually give an alternative perspective of how the anatomical organization of language must be arranged.

RIGHT HEMISPHERE CONTRIBUTIONS TO LANGUAGE

Although there is little doubt that the left hemisphere of right-handed people is the predominant hemisphere in language, there is growing evidence that the right hemisphere does have some language abilities. The best evidence has come from studies of split-brain patients in whom the linguistic abilities of the right hemisphere has been systematically studied using various techniques for lateralizing input to one hemisphere. These studies have shown that the right hemisphere has little or no speech but surprisingly good auditory comprehension of language, including both nouns and verbs. There also appears to be some reading but little writing ability in the right hemisphere. Thus, although the right hemisphere appears able to recognize words (semantic processing), it has virtually no understanding of grammatical rules and structures (syntactic processing). Complementary evidence favoring a limited role of the right hemisphere in language comes from studies of people who have had the left hemisphere removed, a procedure known as **hemispherectomy.** If the left hemisphere is lost early in development, the right hemisphere is able to acquire considerable language abilities (see Chapter 25 for details), although it is by no means normal. Left hemidecortication in adulthood is far more debilitating, however, and in all such cases there are severe deficits in speech. Nonetheless, these people do have surprisingly good auditory comprehension. Reading is limited, however, and writing is usually absent. In general, it appears that left hemidecorticated people have language abilities that are reminescent of

TABLE 22-3. Language activities of the two hemispheres

Function	Left hemisphere	Right hemisphere
Gestural language	+	+
Prosodic language		
Rhythm	++	
Inflection	+	+
Timbre	+	++
Melody		++
Semantic language		
Word recognition	+	+
Verbal meaning	++	+
Concepts	+	+
Visual meaning	+	++
Syntactic language		
Sequencing	++	
Relationships	++	
Grammar	++	

Source: Modified from Benson, 1986.

that of the right hemisphere of commissurotomy patients.

In summary, it appears that although the right hemisphere cannot speak, it is capable of considerable language comprehension, especially of auditory material. A final source of evidence comes from the effects of right hemisphere lesions on language functions. Aphasia is rare after right hemisphere lesions (this aphasia is known as **crossed aphasia**), even after right hemispherectomy, but there is growing evidence of subtle linguistic impairments associated with right hemisphere injuries. These include changes in vocabulary selection, responses to complex statements with unusual syntactic construction, and the comprehension of metaphors. In addition right orbital-frontal lesions reduce verbal fluency. Further, there is a deficit in the comprehension of tone of voice, and possibly in the production of similar emotional tone (prosody).

In reviewing the role of the right hemisphere in language, both Benson and Zaidel have concluded that the only strictly left hemisphere function in language concerns the syntactic elements of language (Table 22-3). This includes several factors: production, timing, and sequencing of the movements required for speaking, as well as the understanding of the rules of grammar. The relative roles of the two hemispheres in other aspects of language comprehension still need to be clearly specified.

ORIGINS OF SPEECH AND LANGUAGE

Origins of Language

Speculations about human language origins are centuries old, but recently there has been some progress in providing evidence for some of the more plausible theories. (A beautiful little paper by Hewes summarizes the history of theories of the phylogenesis of speech. It is recommended for anyone interested in the problem.) An obvious explanation of speech is that it slowly evolved from various kinds of vocalizations. Hewes has reviewed many of the variants of this theory, including the "pooh-pooh" theory (speech evolved from noises associated with strong emotion), the "bow-wow" theory (speech evolved from noises first made to imitate natural sounds), the "yo-he-ho" theory (speech evolved from sounds made to resonate with natural sounds), and the "sing-song" theory (speech evolved from noises made while playing or dancing). These examples by no means exhaust the list of imaginative theories of speech origin. A major difficulty with these kinds of theories is that it is very hard to collect evidence to support them. Nevertheless, Steklis and Raleigh argue strongly for the vocalization evolutionary theory. The evidence they put forth includes the following: the theory is parsimonious, involving as it does a direct rather than an indirect, explanation; many nonhuman primates use nonemotional types of vocalizations in a rudimentary communicative style; and the evolution of new types of skilled movements would have provided a neural basis for the refined movements of the vocal system prerequisite for speech.

In addition to this theory, there are two other major theories that deserve consideration, if not for their explanatory power, then at least because they are supported by a substantial amount of research. One theory postulates that language in its present form is of recent origin. The second theory postulates that language is very old and only gradually evolved into its present form from its original gestural base. In a sense, these two theories are compatible, in that language may have evolved in a gestural form and then been rapidly transformed into a vocal form.

Speech as a Recently Evolved Ability

Let us consider the evidence that language (as we use it) has a relatively recent origin. Swadish developed a list of 100 basic lexical concepts that he expected to be found in every language. These included such words a I, two, woman, sun, green. He then calculated the rate at which these words would have changed as new dialects of language were formed. His estimates suggest that the rate of change was 14% every 1000 years. When he compared the lists of words spoken in different parts of the world, his estimates suggested that between 10,000 and 100,000 years ago everyone spoke the same language. According to Swadish's logic, language would have its origins at about this time because diversification would have begun almost as soon as language developed. Of course, hominids have been around for 4 million years, so how can one rule out the possibility that they were speaking much earlier than 100,000 years ago?

Lieberman has studied the properties of the vocal tract that enable modern humans to make the sounds that are used for language. Modern humans have a low larynx and a large throat, and these features make them unique. Modern apes and newborn humans have neither of these characteristics and cannot produce all the sounds used in human speech. On the basis of skull reconstructions, Lieberman suggests that Neanderthal man was also unable to make the sounds necessary for modern speech. Specifically, he would not have been able to produce the vowels "a," "i," and "u."

The change in the position of the larynx in modern humans is not only important for language but signifies a considerable change in respiratory and feeding patterns in modern humans. Figure 22-10 illustrates the location of the larynx in human infants, in a chimpanzee, and in an adult human. Arrows indicate the flow of air during respiration and the flow of fluid during drinking. Note that the human infant can drink and breath at the same time, since the high location of the larynx allows milk to flow around the larynx and into the esophagus. The chimp, similarly, is able to swallow and breath at the same time. The low larynx in the adult human, however, demands that respiration stop to prevent choking during drinking.

If Lieberman's hypothesis about the relation between speech and the structure of the vocal tract is correct, then it can be concluded that modern speech did not exist before about 100,000 years ago, before the appearance of Cro-Magnon man.

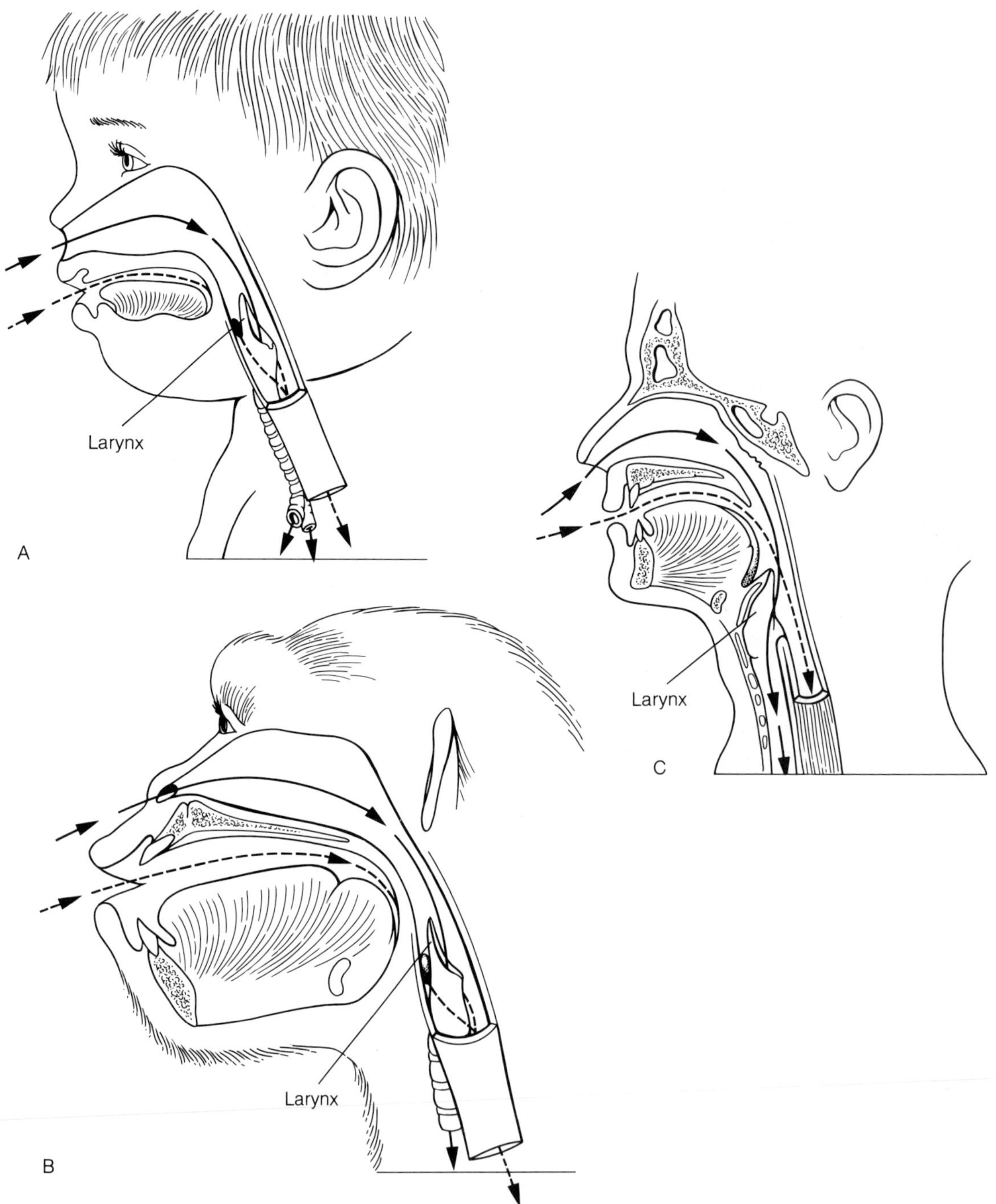

FIGURE 22-10. Cross-sectional views of the vocal tract in *A.* human baby, *B.* adult chimpanzee, *C.* adult human. Note the high position of the larynx in the human baby and the adult chimp, which permits them to ingest food or fluids without concomitantly arresting respiration. In adult humans the low location of the larynx permits speech production but requires that respiration be arrested during swallowing. (After Laitman, 1986.)

Another line of evidence for recent speech goes like this. The ability to write and the ability to speak seem to have a lot in common. Most notably, they both require very fine movements and many movement transitions. Therefore, it is possible that speech and writing appeared at about the same time. Alexander Marshack has found that the first symbols that humans made date back to about 30,000 years ago. Accordingly, this would be evidence that speech appeared at about this time. What seems to link these three separate lines of evidence, making the recency hypothesis plausible, is that the first appearance of modern humans, *Homo sapiens sapiens,* can be dated to about 40,000 to 100,000 years ago. Possibly the evolution of modern humans was quite sudden and one of their adaptive strategies was language. In opposition to the notion of recently acquired speech, Holloway argues from paleontological evidence (e.g., the size of Broca's area as revealed by endocasts) that rudimentary language was probably displayed by *Australopithecus* roughly 2.5 to 3.5 million years ago.

Speech as a Gestural Language

The origins of the gestural theory of language can be dated to the 15th century. This theory suggests that primitive gestures and other body movements gradually evolved into modern language. It is assumed that effective hunting and farming and the maintenance of social groups required some kind of communication system, and that this need was the impetus for the evolution of language. Until recently there was no evidence that supported the gestural theory, but now at least two lines of research can cite evidence in its favor. The evidence from the first line of research is that gestural language and vocal language depend on the same neural systems. The evidence from the second line is that nonhuman primates are able to use gestures or symbols for at least rudimentary communication. The first evidence is important because if the neural systems were different, it would weaken the argument that one type of language evolved into the other. The second is important because it shows that a similar, although much smaller, brain is capable of language, thus making it unnecessary to evolve an entirely new neural system for speech.

It has long been thought that an experiment showing that gestural languages and vocal language depend on the same brain structure would support the idea that gestural language evolved into vocal language. As early as 1878, Hughlings-Jackson suggested that a natural experiment, the loss of language in people using sign language, would provide the appropriate evidence, and he even observed a case that seemed to indicate sign language was disrupted by a left hemisphere lesion, as is vocal language. A definitive review of similar cases by Kimura confirms that lesions disrupting vocal speech also disrupt signing. Of a total of 11 patients with signing disorders following brain lesions, 9 right-handers had disorders following a left hemisphere lesion. One left-handed patient had a signing disorder following a left hemisphere lesion, and one had a signing disorder following a right hemisphere lesion. These proportions are identical to those found for vocal patients who become aphasic. These results strongly favor the idea that the language systems that control vocal speech also control signing. They offer little support for any alternative view (e.g., that signing, being more spatial in nature than vocal speech, is controlled by the right hemisphere).

On the basis of other evidence, Kimura favors the idea that gesture and speech depend on the same neural systems. She examined the ability of stroke patients to perform sequences of face or arm movements that required transitions of posture from one movement to the next (i.e., the type of movements required for sign language). Lesions in the language zone that produced aphasia, particularly in the left parietal cortex, also disrupted the ability to make postural transitions. Tasks that required repetitive movements such as tapping or turning a screw were not disrupted.

In summary, it seems that there is a similarity between lesions that produce vocal language disturbances and those that disrupt the movements required for gestural language. But at this point one must ask if emotional sounds and facial expressions were also precursors of language or whether there may have been something special about certain kinds of gestures. The evidence seems not to support the idea that emotional sounds or expressions evolved into language. First, emotional expressions in apes cannot be conditioned for use as signs with the ease with which gestures can be conditioned. Second, the neural mechanisms controlling emotional expressions in both apes and man are different from those controlling language. Myers has shown that frontal lesions disrupt emotional expression in monkeys, and Kolb and Milner have found that frontal, but not parietal, lesions disrupt emotional expressions in humans (Chapter 23).

If it is true that gestures had evolved into vocal language by the time *Homo sapiens sapiens* appeared, it is possible to make at least one testable prediction. It is very likely that the first gestures were genetically rather than culturally transmitted. These gestures should still be genetically transmitted and so should still be found in all groups of humans. A subset of this group of gestures should also be used by man's close relatives, the apes. The begging gesture, hand outstretched, of chimpanzee and human is likely an example of these gestures.

A question that can be raised with respect to gestural theories is why there is a shift to vocalizing. Hewes proposes that this derives from facial expressions, which themselves derive from gesturing. Two reasons are given for the increased use of the face: (1) as the individual increases the use of tools the hands are full and cannot be used for gesturing; (2) as language becomes more complicated there are clearly upper limits to the number of possible facial and manual expressions. A relevant observation that supports the gestural proposal is that hand gestures still accompany language. Indeed, in the absence of a common language people elaborate hand and facial gestures to communicate.

Myers has proposed a slightly different version of the gestural theory. He argues that the development of language is a logical consequence of the increasing development of the control of facial musculature. Prosimians (lemurs) are unable to produce facial expressions, rhesus monkeys and other monkeys are able to produce a limited range of facial expressions, and chimpanzees have a complex repertory of facial movements, but only humans have developed the movements for speech and the necessary changes in the vocal tract. Myers proposes that Broca's area creates a qualitatively different type of vocal output. This idea is not entirely inconsistent with Kimura's notion described above. In fact, Kimura notes that the same movement transitions required for arm gestures are necessary for vocal speech, for example, in the transition from "be-ba-be" or "de-da-de." She argues, however, that these transitions are produced by the left parietal cortex rather than by Broca's area.

Evidence for Languagelike Processes in Apes

Although no nonhuman primates have a verbal language analogous to that of humans's, one approach to the study of human language is to attempt to trace the phylogenetic origins of speech. Some recent demonstrations of languagelike processes in apes have generated interest in this approach, and the results have important implications for understanding human brain function—and may also have practical applications. For example, are there alternative forms of communication that can be substituted for the lost speech of the aphasic? In this section we shall consider the evidence for languagelike processes in apes, the theories of the phylogenetic development of language, and the applications to humans of research on the phylogenetic origins of language in nonhumans.

Several people have tried to teach chimpanzees to talk. The most persistent attempts were undertaken by Hayes and Nissen and by the Kelloggs, who raised chimps in their homes with the idea that they might learn to talk if raised with humans from birth. They did not. Viki, the Hayes' chimp, after extensive training learned to make noises for about four words, none of them properly formed. For example, the word *cup* sounded like *krup* when Viki "said" it. These early studies were dismal failures in view of the obvious neurological similarity between apes and humans. Then in the 1960s, two totally new approaches appeared virtually simultaneously. Both were based on the premise that auditory communication must be bypassed and something visual used. The Gardners pioneered the use of American Sign Language (Ameslan); the Premacks used plastic symbols. It is interesting that Yerkes, in 1925, first proposed the idea of teaching sign language to chimps. The notion was apparently not considered a worthwhile endeavor!

The Gardners began by bringing Washoe, a year-old chimp, into their home. The aim was to teach Washoe the hand movements, or signs, that refer to various objects or actions (known as exemplars) that are found in Ameslan. These signing gestures, analogous to words in spoken language, have specific movements that begin and end in a prescribed manner in relation to the signer's body (see Figure 22-11). The Gardners molded Washoe's hands to form the desired shapes in the presence of the exemplar of the sign, reinforcing her for correct movements. In addition, rather than using verbal language, the Gardners used Ameslan to communicate with each other in Washoe's presence. Thus, Washoe was raised in an environment filled with signs. Washoe learned, and learned well. She was able to correctly sign for objects and to ask for objects with high accuracy. Most of her errors were in the same class. For example, she might use the sign for cat when identifying a dog.

Washoe also picked up signs by observing the signing of others. One example was the sign for *smoke*. Apparently several of the workers on the project smoked, and, using Ameslan, they would request, in front of Washoe, smokes (cigarettes) from fellow workers. Washoe was fascinated by smoking, and soon added the sign to her vocabulary. Another example was the sign for toothbrush. This sign is made by moving an extended forefinger back and forth in front of the teeth. Washoe learned this sign on her own as well. Washoe's signing did not include nouns only but also pronouns and action verbs. For example, she could sign statements such as "You go me," meaning "Come with me."

Two questions arise, however: whether chimpanzees generalize the use of specific signs, and whether they can make up their own signs. In one experiment to test these questions, a chimp had been taught five food-related signs: food, fruit, drink, candy, and banana. The test was to show her new fruits and vegetables and to ask her what they were. The result was fascinating, as a couple of examples will illustrate. When a radish was shown, the chimp (who had previously eaten radishes) signed "candy-drink" or "drink-fruit." The sign "fruit" was used 85% of the time to label fruit, but only 15% of the time for vegetables, whereas "smell" was used 65% of the time to label citrus fruits, presumably because chimps eat the outer skin, which is rather aromatic when bitten into.

Another experiment addressed the question of abstraction. Could the chimps learn verbal commands, and could they generalize back and forth from signs to words? To test this idea, a chimp was trained on English words such as *spoon*. Having learned that the verbal word *spoon* referred to an object, he was then taught the Ameslan sign for spoon, but not in the presence of the object, rather in relation to the auditory representation, the spoken word *spoon*. Would the chimp, if asked what the object was, be able to make the "jump" and sign for the object? The answer was yes.

A large number of chimps have now been studied, and although there are clear differences among

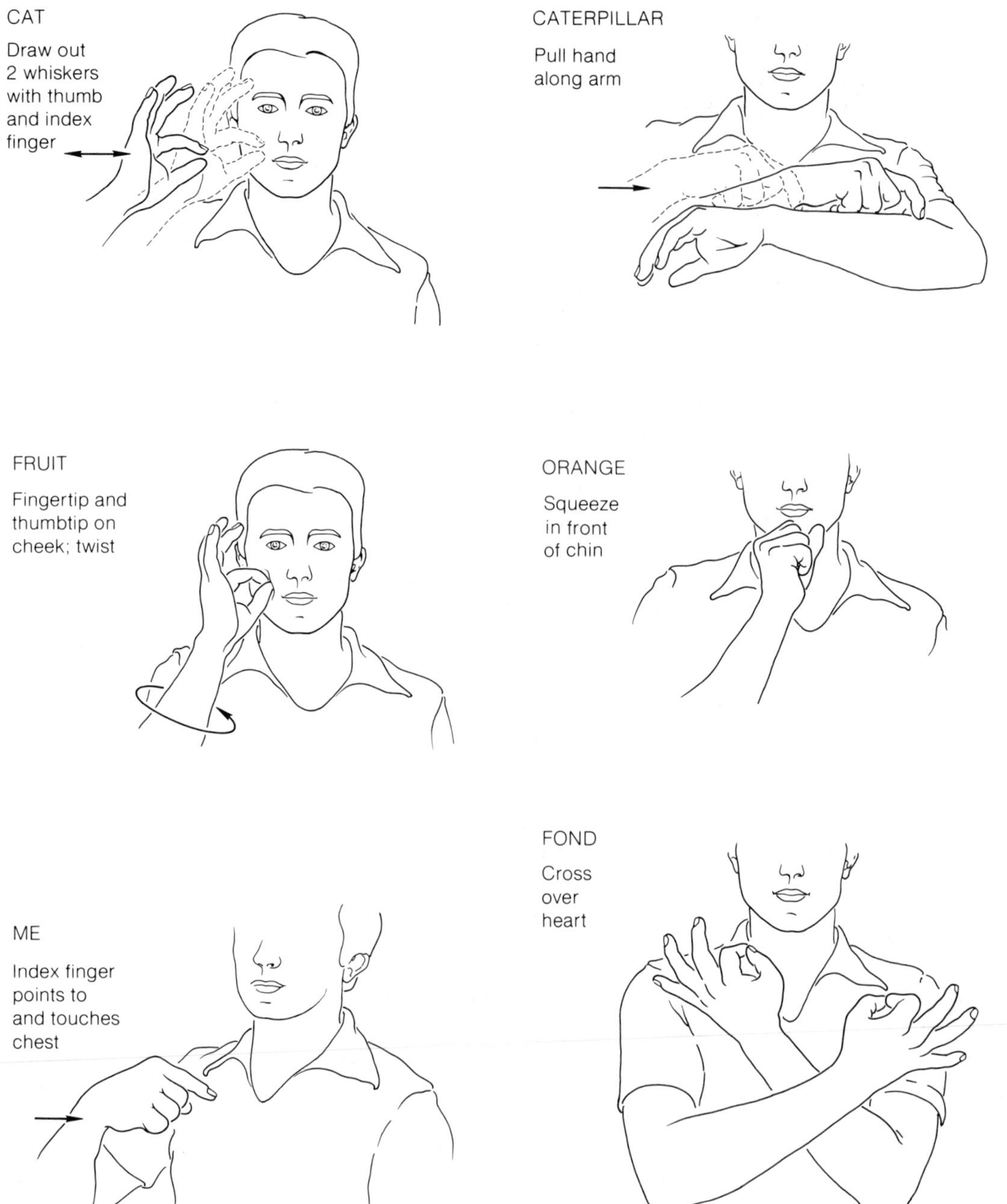
CAT
Draw out
2 whiskers
with thumb
and index
finger
CATERPILLAR
Pull hand
along arm
FRUIT
Fingertip and
thumbtip on
cheek; twist
ORANGE
Squeeze
in front
of chin
ME
Index finger
points to
and touches
chest
FOND
Cross
over
heart

FIGURE 22-11. Examples from American Sign Language. The Gardners and others taught such symbols to the chimpanzees in their studies. (After Gustason et al., 1975.)

the individual animals, all have mastered a large number of signs. Attempts to teach Ameslan to other species of great apes have proved very successful; Patterson has found gorillas to have an even better predisposition to acquire sign language than chimpanzees.

Premack approached the study of language abilities of chimpanzees in a different way. He taught his chimpanzee, Sarah, to read and write with variously shaped and colored pieces of plastic, each representing a word (see Figure 22-12). Premack first taught Sarah that different symbols represented different nouns, just as Washoe had been taught in sign language. Thus, for example, Sarah learned that a pink square was the symbol for banana. Sarah was then taught verbs so that she could write and read such combinations as "give apple" or "wash apple." Her comprehension could easily be tested by writing messages to her (hanging up symbols) and then observing her response. This was followed by much more complicated tutoring in which Sarah successfully mastered the interrogative (Where is my banana?), the negative, and finally the conditional (if, then). It is readily apparent that Sarah had mastered a fairly complicated communication system analogous to simple human language.

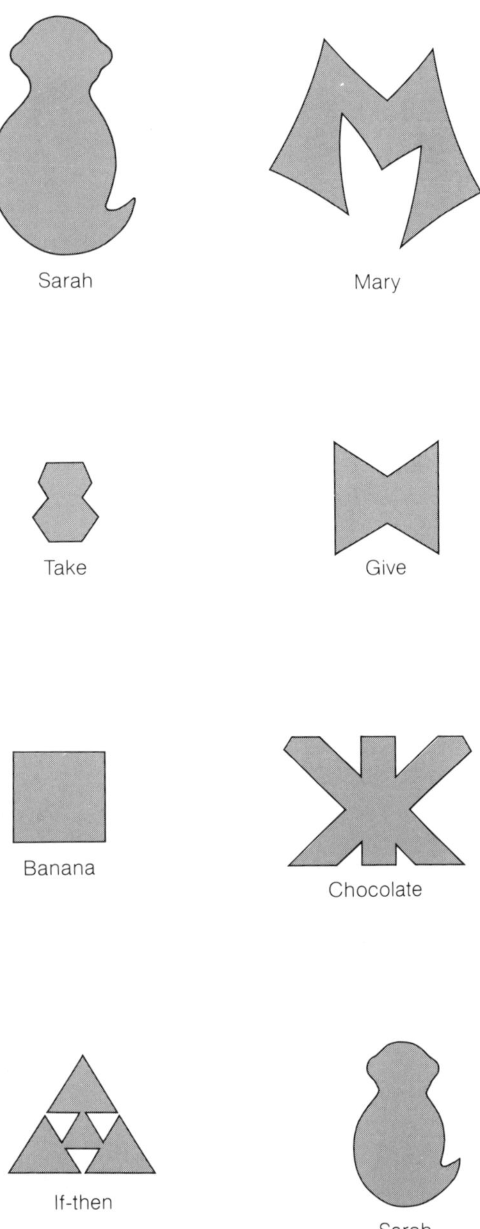

FIGURE 22-12. An example of a "conversation," using plastic symbols, with Premack's chimpanzee, Sarah. Note that the message is written from top to bottom. (After Premack and Premack, 1972. Copyright © 1972 by *Scientific American,* Inc. All rights reserved.)

A more recent project has demonstrated even more complex language learning in the chimpanzee. After carefully studying the results of the Gardners' and Premacks' projects, Rumbaugh and Gill from the Yerkes Regional Primate Center launched Project Lana. This project involved teaching their chimp, Lana, to communicate by means of a keyboard programmed by a computer. The keyboard was composed of nine stimulus elements and nine primary colors, which could be combined together in nearly 1800 combinations (lexigrams), as illustrated in Figure 22-13, to form a language now known as Yerkish. This project differs from the previous ones in being a collaborative effort of a psychologist, linguist, and computer specialist.

Lana had to learn simply to type out her mes-

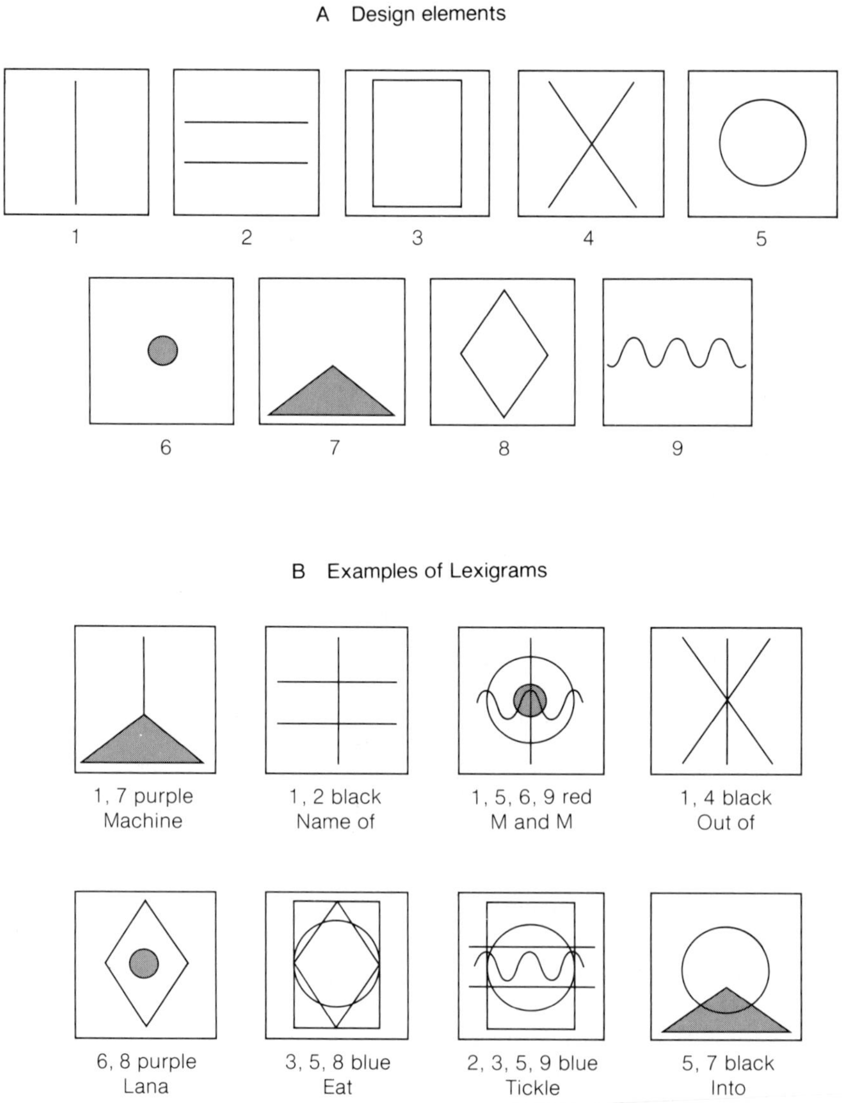

A Design elements

1 2 3 4 5

6 7 8 9

B Examples of Lexigrams

1, 7 purple
Machine

1, 2 black
Name of

1, 5, 6, 9 red
M and M

1, 4 black
Out of

6, 8 purple
Lana

3, 5, 8 blue
Eat

2, 3, 5, 9 blue
Tickle

5, 7 black
Into

FIGURE 22-13. *A*. The nine basic design elements in Yerkish that are combined together to form lexigrams. *B*. Examples of lexigrams. (From von Glaserfeld, 1977. Copyright © 1977. Reprinted with permission.)

sages on the keyboard. She was first trained to press keys for various single incentives; the requirements then became increasingly complex as she mastered the various types of statements, such as the indicative (Tim move into room), the interrogative (Tim move into room?), the imperative (Please Tim move into room), and the negative (Don't Tim move into room). Lana is now capable of strings of six lexigrams and makes few errors, most being "typing errors" or errors caused by distraction.

One of the initial goals of Project Lana was to engage in conversation with a chimpanzee. This has been accomplished by having the experimenter type messages on the board and then allowing Lana to respond. She actually learned to initiate conversation on her own, and engaged in conversations such as that illustrated in Table 22-4.

Further studies by Rumbaugh's group have demonstrated that chimpanzees are capable of symbolic communication with one another: two chimpanzees in adjoining rooms were able to use Yerkish to ask each other for specific foods. Further study showed they could even communicate reliably with regard to sharing tools for obtaining foods. When forced to rely on nonsymbolic means of communication, such as facial expression or body posture, their joint accuracy declined from 95 to 10%. This latter result implies that the chimpanzees comprehend the symbolic and communicative functions of the symbols that they use and are not using subtle nonsymbolic cues to communicate.

Lenneberg and others have argued that human mathematical abilities are derived from the same foundation as language. Thus, whether chimpanzees possess the ability to acquire and use mathematical skills is an important question. Rumbaugh and his colleagues on Project Lana have begun to consider this problem. Lana has learned the concept of "more" and "less" and can accurately determine whether a group of four washers is more or less than a group of five washers, when surface area, mass, and spatial arrangement of the washers are varied randomly. The question now under study is whether Lana can learn names of precise numbers and the ordinal relations involved among the numbers 1 through 10.

TABLE 22-4. A conversation with Lana

Lana:	Milk name-of-this.
Tim:	Yes.
Lana:	Milk this. ? Tim give Lana coffee.
Tim:	No. (Although at times he has honored this request, this time he elected not to, for milk, not coffee, was the incentive appropriate to her state of heightened food motivation.)
Lana:	? Tim move milk coffee. (This was the first suggestion that she was going to ask Tim to move something from one point to another in space. She had not received specific training to ask that this be done.)
Tim:	(No response.)
Lana:	? Tim move behind room.
Tim:	Yes. (Thereupon Tim set down the pitcher of milk and moved behind the room to the general area of the vending devices where the milk would ordinarily be loaded into the machine. Lana's response was to hoot with apparent agitation; she also displayed piloerection [fur standing on end—an indication of agitation] and a furrowed brow. In a few seconds, Tim returned to the anteroom, picked up the milk, and stood once again in Lana's full view.)
Lana:	Milk of this coffee. ? Tim give milk name-of. ? Time move milk behind. . . . (The sentence was not completed; however, Tim interpreted it to mean that Lana did not know how to finish what promised to be a novel question and one that was quite appropriate to the context.)
Tim:	? Behind what.
Lana:	? Tim move milk behind room. (With this statement Lana had asked for the first time that a person move something other than his own body from one point to another in space.)
Tim:	Yes. (He then loaded the vending device with milk, and Lana began to work for it by requesting it repeatedly.)

Source: From Rumbaugh and Gill, 1977, p. 175.

A Word of Caution

As provocative as the language studies in apes have proved to be, there have been criticisms. Terrace and his colleagues have questioned the relevance of the ape language studies to the study of human language. As Terrace notes, although apes can learn vocabularies of visual symbols, the important question is not whether the apes have a good memory for symbols but whether the apes can spontaneously combine such symbols by using a systematic grammar to create new meanings. Terrace notes that although pigeons and other animals can learn complex chains of responses to obtain a food reward, these responses are not related one to another as words in a sentence are. For example, a pigeon can be trained to peck on four keys of different colors in a particular sequence regardless of the physical position of the colors; nevertheless, colors do not combine to form a grammatical sentence. Likewise, although an ape may produce sequences of symbols that a human observer sees as grammatically related, it does not follow that the ape was aware of the inferred relations. If, for example, in response to the question "What that?" Washoe signed "Water bird" in the presence of a swan, Washoe's response clearly appears creative and meaningful.

> Nevertheless, there is no basis for concluding that Washoe was characterizing the swan as a "bird that inhabits water." Washoe had a long history of being asked "what that?" in the presence of objects such as birds and bodies of water. In this instance, Washoe may have simply been answering the question, "what that?" by identifying correctly a body of water and a bird, in that order. Before concluding that Washoe was relating the sign "water" to the sign "bird," one must know whether she regularly placed an adjective (water) before, or after, a noun (bird). That cannot be decided on the basis of a single anecdote, no matter how compelling that anecdote may seem to an English-speaking observer. (Terrace et al., 1979, pp. 895–896)

To support their argument Terrace and his colleagues analyzed more than 19,000 multisign utterances of an infant chimpanzee (Nim) as well as reanalyzing film of Washoe and other chimps. They claimed to have found no evidence for what appeared to be grammatical construction; most of the apes' utterances were prompted by their teachers' prior utterances and could thus be explained by nonlinguistic processes. Indeed, the authors were struck both by the absence of creativity in the apes' utterances and by the dependence of their utterances on the prior utterances of their teachers. This is quite unlike the advanced multiword sequences produced by young children.

The Gardners, in turn, have questioned the Skinnerian stimulus-response methodology used by Terrace. They argue that chimps and humans are aware of the consequences of their actions and use language to influence subsequent events. In view of Terrace's criticisms, therefore, and given that the machine languages (e.g., Yerkish) are more objective and easier to quantify and to analyze than Ameslan, the machine language approach may help resolve these differences.

Other Approaches to Primate Language

The studies on the gestural capabilities of great apes are impressive; they have, however, tended to obscure at least two important relevant investigations into language origins. First, only recently has attention been given to the large range of sounds that apes use in communication. Goodall's studies on the chimpanzees of Gombe indicate that our closest relatives have as many as 32 separate vocalizations. These are summarized in Figure 22-14. Goodall notes that the chimps seem to understand these calls much better than do humans, but she also notes that her field assistants, who were most familiar with the chimps, favored an even greater number of divisions than the 32 noted in Figure 22-14. If these calls are used in combination, the complexity of vocalization is further increased. These results must be accepted as significant when it is considered that intensive training of domestic chimps produce vocabularies of between 50 and 200 words. Since humans combine only about 2 to 3 dozen sounds together to produce speech, chimp language does not seem so distant from ours as we might think. Although the sign language studies with chimps have made an impression in the pop-

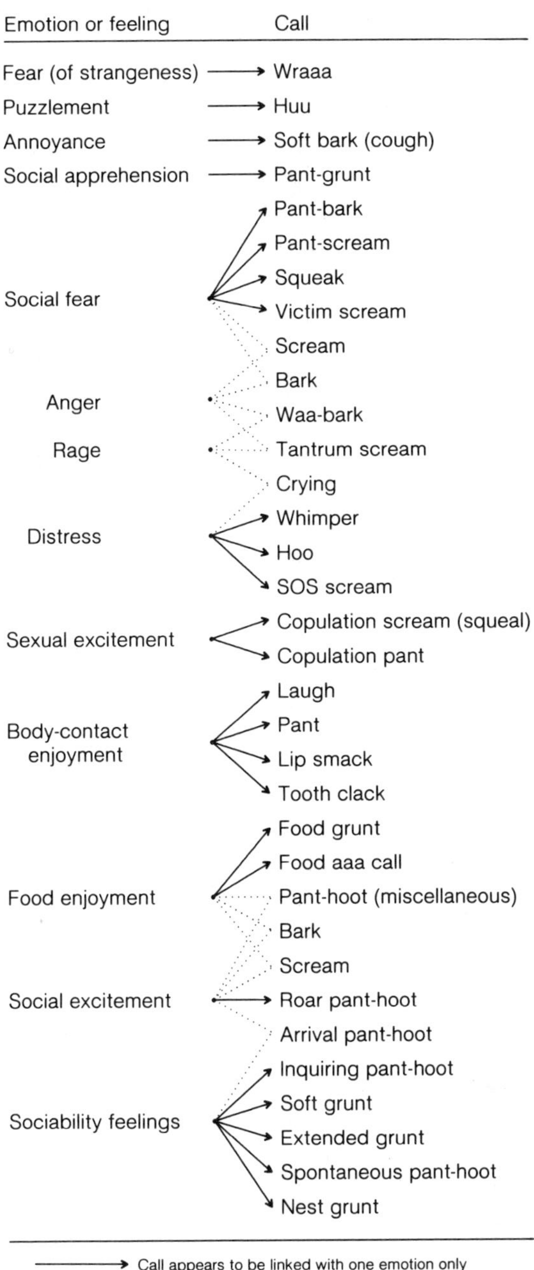

FIGURE 22-14. Chimpanzee calls and the emotion or feeling with which they are most closely associated. (From Goodall, 1986. Reprinted with permission.)

ular press, continued naturalistic ape studies that consider the range of sounds, their context, and combinations along with accompanying facial and body gestures may in the end give us our best insight into the origins of language.

A second area of neglect in the investigation of ape language concerns comprehension. It may well be the case that sophisticated levels of comprehension preceded more complex overt language. Herman has discussed this question in some detail. He notes, for example, that human infants' comprehension precedes and exceeds speech production. In addition, Herman notes that studies with bottle-nosed dolphins and California sea lions demonstrate that they have substantial comprehension capacities for language. The dolphins, especially, were often able to understand new sentences that demanded the understanding and processing of both semantic and syntactic information in the artificial languages that were used. Thus, it may be the case that chimps in natural habitats have sophisticated levels of comprehension that would not be apparent if only the spectral analysis of the sounds they make are analyzed. At least the inference to be drawn from many of Goodall's observations of their behavior do suggest that the animals' levels of comprehension have been underestimated.

A final point is germane to this discussion. To what extent do animals understand the calls they make? It seems to us that if an animal does understand the calls that it makes and can use them voluntarily, then even if it has few calls, it has taken its first and most important step on the way to language. Again, observations of wild chimps do suggest that they are aware of the significance of their vocalizations and are able to modify them as situations change.

Applications of the Chimpanzee Studies

A major implication of the work with chimpanzees is that communication does not require talking or even the ability to talk. Thus, a person with severe aphasia could potentially be taught some other form of language. In view of the reports that strokes produce impairment in Ameslan signing in deaf patients, either the Premack symbols or the Project Lana Yerkish would seem more appropriate for this purpose. Glass and his coworkers have used Premack symbols with encouraging results. Interestingly, noun symbols were learned readily, but verbs sometimes took weeks to learn. This difference is reminiscent of the observation that the right hemisphere of the split-brain patient is unable to process natural-language verbs.

It is relevant in this context to note that a symbol language was devised and published by Bliss in 1942. This language, known as Bliss Symbols or semantographics, is essentially similar to a simplified Chinese, being the clear, pictorial representation of real things as we see them. Each symbol looks like the object it represents; abstractions and intangibles are represented by geometric objects associated with them. The language is composed of 100 symbol elements that are recombined to form different words, as illustrated in Figure 22-15.

The simplicity of this system is apparent. The language has now been tried with nonvocal children with very favorable results. For example, Harris-Vanderbeiden and her colleagues imple-

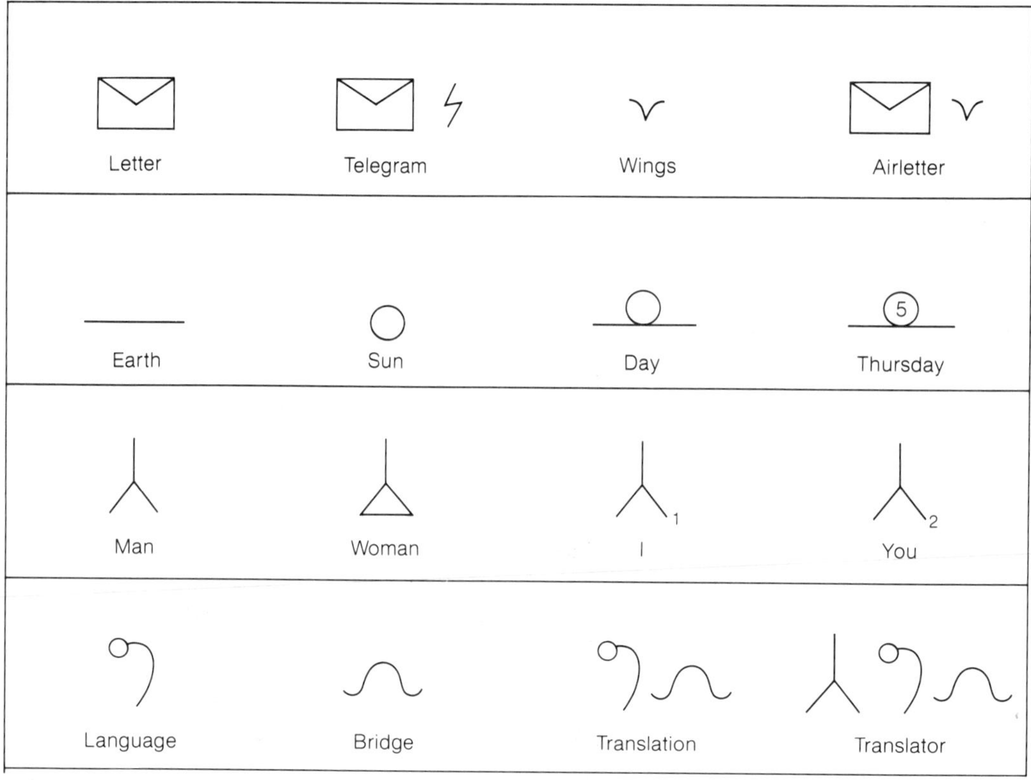

FIGURE 22-15. Examples of the Bliss language system. The symbols are pictorial and build on one another logically. This system has proved useful for teaching nonvocal children, and it holds promise for use with aphasic adults.

mented a modified Bliss system for children with cerebral palsy. With about 20 h of training these children had all mastered at least some symbols that could be used for communication. One child who had an IQ of about 56 learned about 75 symbols, which she could use for both respondent and expressive communication.

To our knowledge this system has not yet been applied to aphasic patients, but it appears very promising. It is considerably more complex than the chimpanzee symbol systems used to date, and its pictorial component might make it a better choice for aphasic persons than Yerkish.

REFERENCES

Benson, D. F. Fluency in aphasia. *Cortex* 3:373–394, 1967.

Benson, D. F. Aphasia and lateralization of language. *Cortex* 22:71–86, 1986.

Bliss, C. W. *Semantography*. Sydney, Australia: Semantography Publications, 1942.

Brown, J. *Aphasia, Apraxia and Agnosia*. Springfield, IL: Charles C. Thomas, 1972.

Brown, J. The neural organization of language: Aphasia and lateralization. *Brain and Language* 3:482–494, 1976.

Caplan, D., and J. C. Marshall. Generative grammar and aphasic disorders: A theory of language representation in the human brain. *Foundations of Language* 12:583–596, 1972.

Chomsky, N. On the biological basis of language capabilities. In R. W. Rieber, ed. *Neuropsychology of Language*. New York: Plenum, 1976.

Coltheart, M. Acquired dyslexias and normal reading. In R. N. Malatesha and H. A. Whitaker, eds. *Dyslexia: A Global Issue*. The Hague: Martinus Nijhoff, 1984.

Coltheart, M. Disorders of reading and their implications for models of normal reading. *Visible Language* XV:245–286, 1981.

Cooper, I. S., I. Amin, R. Chandra, and J. M. Waltz. A surgical investigation of the clinical physiology of the LP-pulvinar complex in man. *Journal of Neurological Science* 18:89–100, 1973.

Gardner, B. T., and R. A. Gardner. Two-way communication with an infant chimpanzee. In A. M. Schrier and F. Stolinitz, eds. *Behavior of Nonhuman Primates,* vol. 4. New York: Academic Press, 1971.

Gardner, B. T., and R. A. Gardner. Feedforward versus feedbackward: An ethological alternative to the law of effect. *Behavioral and Brain Sciences* 11:429–493, 1988.

Geschwind, N. Language and the brain. *Scientific American* 226:76–83, 1972.

Glaserfeld, E. von. The Yerkish language and its automatic parser. In D. M. Rumbaugh, ed. *Language Learning by a Chimpanzee*. New York: Academic Press, 1977.

Glass, A. U., M. S. Gazzaniga, and D. Premack. Artificial language training in global aphasics. *Neuropsychologia* 11:95–103, 1973.

Goodall, J. *The Chimpanzees of Gombe*. Cambridge, MA: Harvard University Press, 1986.

Goodglass, H., and E. Kaplan. *The Assessment of Aphasia and Related Disorders*. Philadelphia: Lea and Febiger, 1972.

Green, E. Psycholinguistic approaches to aphasia. *Linguistics* 53:30–50, 1969.

Gustason, G., D. Pfetzing, and E. Zawoklow. *Signing Exact English*. Silver Spring, MD: Modern Signs Press, 1975.

Halstead, W. C., and J. M. Wepman. The Halstead-Wepman aphasia screening test. *Journal of Speech and Hearing Disorders* 14:9–15, 1959.

Harris-Vanderbeiden, D., W. R. Brown, P. MacKenzie, S. Reinen, and C. Scheibel. Symbol communication for the mentally handicapped. *Mental Retardation* 13:34–37, 1975.

Hayes, K. J., and C. H. Nissen. Higher mental functions of a home reared chimpanzee. In A. M. Schrier and F. Stolinitz, eds. *Behavior of Nonhuman Primates,* vol. 4. New York: Academic Press, 1971.

Herman, L. M. Receptive competencies of language-trained animals. *Advances in the Study of Behavior* 17:1–55, 1981.

Hewes, G. W. Language origin theories. In D. M. Rumbaugh, ed. *Language Learning by a Chimpanzee.* New York: Academic Press, 1977.

Holloway, R. L. Human paleontological evidence relevant to language behavior. *Human Neurobiology* 2:105–114, 1983.

Hughlings-Jackson, J. Notes on the physiology and pathology of learning. In J. Taylor, ed. *Selected Writings of John Hughlings-Jackson.* London: Hodder, 1932.

Jefferson, G. Localization of function in the cerebral cortex. *British Medical Bulletin* 5:333–340, 1949.

Kellogg, W., and L. Kellogg. *The Ape and the Child.* New York: McGraw-Hill, 1933.

Kimura, D. Neuromotor mechanisms in the evolution of human communication. In H. D. Steklis and M. J. Raleigh, eds. *Neurobiology of Social Communication in Primates: An Evolutionary Perspective.* New York: Academic Press, 1979.

Kimura, D. Neural mechanisms in manual signing. *Sign Language Studies* 33:291–312, 1981.

Kimura, D. Are men's and women's brains really different? *Canadian Psychology* 28:133–147, 1987.

Laitman, J. T. L'origine du language articule. *La Recerche* 181:1164–1173, 1986.

Larsen, B., E. Skinhøj, and N. A. Lassen. Variations in regional cortical blood flow in the right and left hemispheres during automatic speech. *Brain* 101:193–209, 1978.

Lenneberg, E. H. *Biological Foundations of Language.* New York: John Wiley, 1967.

Lieberman, P. *On the Origins of Language: An Introduction to the Evolution of Human Speech.* New York: Macmillan, 1975.

Luria, A. R., and J. T. Hutton. A modern assessment of basic forms of aphasia. *Brain and Language* 4:129–151, 1977.

Marshall, J. C. Biological constraints on orthographic representation. *Philosophical Transactions of the Royal Society of London* 298:165–172, 1982.

Marshall, J. C. The description and interpretation of aphasic language disorder. *Neuropsychologia* 24:5–24, 1986.

Mateer, C. Asymmetric effects of thalamic stimulation on rate of speech. *Neuropsychologia* 16:497–499, 1978.

Mazzocchi, F., and L. A. Vignolo. Localization of lesions in aphasia: Clinical-CT scan correlations in stroke patients. *Cortex* 15:627–654, 1979.

McGlone, J. Sex differences in human brain asymmetry: A critical survey. *Behavioral and Brain Sciences* 5:215–264, 1980.

Menzel, E. W. Communication about the environment in a group of young chimpanzees. *Folia Primatologia* 15:220–232, 1971.

Miller, G. A. *Language and Speech.* San Francisco: W. H. Freeman, 1981.

Monrad-Krohn, H. The third element of speech; prosody and its disorders. In L. Halpern, ed. *Problems of Dynamic Neurology.* Jerusalem: Hebrew University Press, 1963.

Myers, R. E. Comparative neurology of vocalization and speech: Proof of a dichotomy. *Annals of the New York Academy of Sciences* 280:745–760, 1976.

Naeser, M. A., R. W. Hayward, S. A. Laughlin, and L. M. Zatz. Quantitative CT scan studies in aphasia. I. Infarct size and CT numbers. *Brain and Language* 12:140–164, 1981.

Newcombe, F., and Marshall, J. C. On psycholinguistic classifications of the acquired dyslexias. *Bulletin of the Orton Society* 31:29–46, 1981.

Ojemann, G. A., ed. The thalamus and language. *Brain and Language* 2:1–120, 1975.

Ojemann, G. A. Models of the brain organization for higher integrative functions derived with electrical stimulation techniques. *Human Neurobiology* 1:243–250, 1982.

Ojemann, G. A., and O. D. Creutzfeldt. Language in humans and animals: Contribution of brain stimulation and recording. *Handbook of Physiology: The Nervous System,* vol. 5. Bethesda, MD: American Physiological Society, 1987.

Ojemann, G. A., and C. Mateer. Cortical and subcortical organization of human communication: Evidence from stimulation studies. In H. D. Steklis and M. J. Raleigh, eds. *Neurobiology of Social Communication in Primates: An Evolutionary Perspective.* New York: Academic Press, 1979.

Ojemann, G. A., and C. Mateer. Human language cortex: Localization of memory, syntax, and sequential motor-phoneme identification systems. *Science* 205:1401–1403, 1979.

Patterson, F. G. The gestures of a gorilla: Language acquisition in another pongid. *Brain and Language* 5:72–97, 1978.

Penfield, W., and L. Roberts. *Speech and Brain Mechanisms.* Princeton, NJ: Princeton University Press, 1959.

Petersen, S. E., P. T. Fox, M. I. Posner, M. Mintun, and M. E. Raichle. Positron emission tomographic studies of the cortical anatomy of single-word processing. *Nature* 331:585–589, 1988.

Porch, B. E. *Index of Communicative Ability.* Palo Alto, CA: Consulting Psychologists Press, 1967.

Premack, A. J., and D. Premack. Teaching language to an ape. *Scientific American* 227:92–99, 1972.

Premack, D. *Intelligence in Ape and Man.* Toronto: Wiley, 1976.

Rasmussen, T., and B. Milner. Clinical and surgical studies of the cerebral speech areas in man. In K. J. Zulch, O. Creutzfeldt, and G. C. Galbraith, eds. *Cerebral Localization.* Berlin and New York: Springer-Verlag, 1975.

Renzi, E. de, and L. A. Vignolo. The token test: A sensitive test to detect disturbances in aphasics. *Brain* 85:665–678, 1962.

Ricklan, M., and I. S. Cooper. Psychometric studies of verbal functions following thalamic lesions in humans. *Brain and Language* 2:45–64, 1975.

Rumbaugh, D. M., and T. V. Gill. Lana's acquisition of language skills. In D. M. Rumbaugh, ed. *Language Learning by a Chimpanzee.* New York: Academic Press, 1977.

Sarno, M. T. *The Functional Communication Profile: Manual of Directions.* New York: Institute of Rehabilitation Medicine, New York University Medical Center, 1969.

Savage-Rumbaugh, E. S., D. M. Rumbaugh, and S. Boysen. Symbolic communication between two chimpanzees. *Science* 201:641–644, 1978.

Schuell, H. *Differential Diagnosis of Aphasia with the Minnesota Test.* Minneapolis: University of Minnesota Press, 1965.

Searleman, A. A review of right hemisphere linguistic capabilities. *Psychological Bulletin* 84:503–528, 1977.

Spreen, O., and A. L. Benton. *Neurosensory Center Comprehensive Examination for Aphasia.* Victoria, Canada: University of Victoria, 1969.

Steklis, H. D., and M. J. Raleigh. Requisites for language: Interspecific and evolutionary aspects. In H. D. Steklis and M. J. Raleigh, eds. *Neurobiology of Social Communication in Primates: An Evolutionary Perspective.* New York: Academic Press, 1979.

Swadish, M. *The Origin and Diversification of Language.* J. Sherzer, ed. Chicago: Aldine-Atherton, 1971.

Terrace, H. S., L. A. Petitto, R. J. Sanders, and T. G. Beyer. Can an ape create a sentence? *Science* 206:891–902, 1979.

Wepman, J. M., and L. V. Jones. *Studies in Aphasia: An Approach to Testing.* Chicago: University of Chicago Education-Industry Service, 1961.

Whitaker, H. A. *On the Representation of Language in the Human Brain.* Edmonton, Canada: Linguistic Research, Inc., 1971.

Zaidel, E. Language in the right hemisphere. In D. F. Benson, and E. Zaidel, eds. *The Dual Brain.* New York: Guilford Press, 1985.

Zangwill, O. L. Excision of Broca's area without persistent aphasia. In K. J. Zulch, O. Creutzfeldt, and G. C. Galbraith, eds. *Cerebral Localization.* Berlin and New York: Springer-Verlag, 1975.

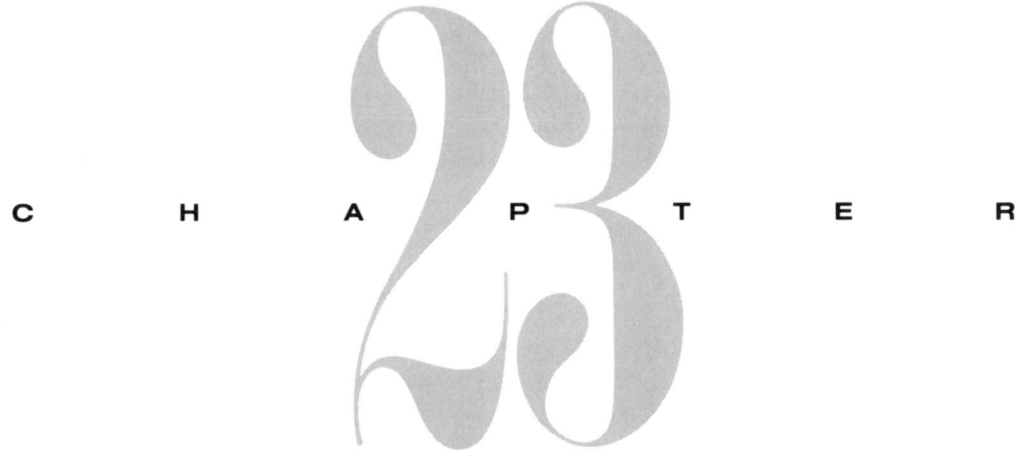

CHAPTER 23

EMOTIONAL PROCESSES

Virtually any alteration of central nervous system activity can change an individual's personality; impairments of movement, perception, language, or memory affect how an individual behaves and is perceived by others. Nevertheless, the scientific study of changes in personality, emotion, and social behavior following brain injury lags far behind the study of cognitive functions, in large part due to the difficulties in defining, recording, and evaluating these behaviors. Over the past decade a view has emerged that there is both a lateralization of control of certain emotional processes, the right hemisphere being dominant, and a localization of control to the frontal and medial temporal regions. Further, it has been proposed that certain major psychiatric disturbances such as schizophrenia and depression may result from abnormalities in the normal cerebral control of emotional behavior.

In this chapter we shall summarize current thinking and research on the neurological control of emotional processes in the normal and abnormal brain. We begin by reviewing the development of thought regarding the neurology of emotional behavior before considering what emotion is, what the candidate structures that play a major role in emotional behavior might be, and then the more recent experimental investigations of this question. Finally, we shall consider the biological bases of schizophrenia and depression and conclude with a brief consideration of psychosurgery.

HISTORICAL VIEWS

Interest in the biology of emotions dates back to Darwin's book, *The Expression of Emotions in Man and Animals,* published in 1872. In this work Darwin attempted to explain the origin and development of the principal expressive behaviors in humans and other animals. Darwin believed that human emotional expression could only be understood in the context of the expressions of other animals for, he suggested, our emotional behavior is determined by our evolution. Although Darwin's book was a best seller in its time, its influence was short-lived and temporarily forgotten. Psychologists began to speculate about emotions at the turn of the century, but with little knowledge about the neural basis of emotional behavior. By the late 1920s, physiologists began to examine the relationship between autonomic, endocrine, and **neurohumoral** factors and inferred emotional states, with particular emphasis upon measuring indices like heart rate, blood pressure, and skin temperature (see reviews by Dunbar or Brady). Philip Bard made one of the first major discoveries while working in Walter Cannon's laboratory in the late 1920s. It had been known from Franz Goltz's studies in the 1890s that decorticated dogs could show strong "rage" responses to seemingly trivial stimuli; the dogs acted as though a seriously threatening stimulus confronted them. Working with cats, Bard showed that this response was dependent upon the diencephalon, which includes the thalamus and hypothalamus. He found that if the diencephalon was intact, animals would show strong "emotional" responses, but if the animals were decerebrate (see Figure 8-1), leaving the diencephalon disconnected from the midbrain, they did not. Later studies by many authors (especially Eckhard Hess in the 1940s and John Flynn in the 1960s) showed that stimulation of different regions of the hypothalamus could elicit different types of "affective responses" such as behavior associated with attack on another cat (**piloerection,** hissing, baring of teeth) or attack of a prey animal (crouching, whiskers and ears forward, pouncing), including eating the animal. The lesion and stimulation studies on the diencephalon were important because they led to the idea that the thalamus and hypothalamus contained the neural circuits for the expression of emotional behaviors, including both the overt behaviors and the autonomic responses such as changes in blood pressure, heart rate, respiration, and so on. The role of the cortex was perceived as being largely one of inhibiting the thalamus and hypothalamus. Conversely, the thalamus played a role in activating the cortex during autonomic arousal, which presumably would help to direct the emotion to the appropriate stimulus.

A second major idea in the history of the neurology of emotions came in 1937 when Papez proposed that the structure of the "limbic lobe" forms the anatomical basis of emotions. Papez reasoned that the limbic structures acting on the hypothalamus produce emotional states. Although for Papez the neocortex played no part in producing emotional behavior, he believed the cortex to be necessary to transforming events produced by limbic structures into what we experience as "emotions." The Papez theory had the appeal of combining behavioral phenomena having no known neurological substrates with anatomical structures having no known function.

The idea of an emotional brain gained instant approval because of the predominance of Freudian thinking in the 1930s. That an ancient, deep part of the central nervous system controls emotions and instincts unconsciously, with the neocortex producing consciousness, was a concept with natural appeal for a Freudian-based psychology.

A third major finding came in 1939, when Klüver and Bucy announced the rediscovery of an extraordinary behavioral syndrome that had first been noted by Brown and Schaefer in 1888. The syndrome, resulting from bilateral anterior temporal lobectomy in monkeys, included (1) tameness and a loss of fear; (2) indiscriminate dietary behavior, the monkeys being willing to eat many types of previously rejected foods; (3) greatly increased autoerotic, homosexual, and heterosexual activity, with inappropriate object choice (e.g, sexual mounting of chairs); (4) **hypermetamorphosis,** or a tendency to attend to and react to every visual stimulus; (5) a tendency to examine all objects by mouth; and (6) visual agnosia. One aspect of this extraordinary behavior was that animals who normally showed strong aversion to stimuli such as snakes or to "threat" stares from humans or other animals now showed no fear of these stimuli whatsoever. Similar behavior has been seen in other species as well. For example, we once observed a cat with bilateral "medial temporal" lesions wander into a room housing monkeys. It showed not the slightest concern that the monkeys were screeching at it and throwing things in its general direction. Normal cats would never venture into such a room and would piloerect if they merely looked into a monkey colony.

The **Klüver-Bucy syndrome** has subsequently been observed in people with a variety of neurological diseases. For example, Marlowe and colleagues reported a patient with Klüver-Bucy symptoms resulting from meningoencephalitis (inflammation of the brain and the meninges).

> As regards his visual functions, the patient seemed unable to recognize a wide variety of common objects. He examined each object placed before him as though seeing it for the first time, explored it repetitively and seemed unaware of its significance. As a result, he exhibited difficulty in the spontaneous employment of tools and other mechanical devices, but could initiate utilization of such objects by imitating the gestures of others, and could care for at least some daily needs in this way. Thus, when handed his razor, he would regard it in a bewildered fashion, but would accompany another patient to the bathroom and imitate all movements of his escort, even the most idiosyncratic, with precision; he could in this way succeed in shaving. Other ordinary tasks could be performed on the same imitative basis. Difficulties in recognition, it should be added, extended to people as well as to objects; he failed, for example, to recognize his parents during innumerable hospital visits. However, his ability to match simple pictures, geometric designs, letters of the alphabet and objects was demonstrably preserved when the tasks were taught non-verbally. Visual orientation was defective, the patient losing his way around the hospital when unattended, and visual distractibility was prominent; he seemed unable to distinguish between relevant and irrelevant objects and actions.
>
> Behavioral patterns were distinctly abnormal. He exhibited a flat affect, and, although originally restless, ultimately became remarkably placid. He appeared indifferent to people or situations. He spent much time gazing at the television, but never learned to turn it on; when the set was off, he tended to watch reflections of others in the room on the glass screen. On occasion he became facetious, smiling inappropriately and mimicking the gestures and actions of others. Once initiating an imitative series, he would perseverate copying all movements made by another for extended periods of time. In addition, he commonly generated a series of idiosyncratic, stereotyped gestures employing primarily his two little fingers which he would raise and touch end-to-end in repetitive fashion.
>
> He engaged in oral exploration of all objects within his grasp, appearing unable to gain information via tactile or visual means alone. All objects that he could lift were placed in his mouth and sucked or chewed. He was commonly observed to place his fingers in his mouth and suck them. He did not attempt to pick up objects directly with his mouth, using his hands for that purpose, but was observed to engage in much olfactory behavior. When dining he would eat with his fingers until reprimanded and a fork placed in his hand; he was thereafter able to imitate use of a fork, but failed to remaster the task of eating with utensils spontaneously. He would eat one food item on his plate completely before turning to the next. Hyperbulimia [excessive, insatiable appetite] was prominent; he ingested virtually everything within reach, including the plastic wrapper from bread, cleaning pastes, ink, dog food, and feces. Although his tastes were clearly indiscriminate, he seemed to prefer liquids or soft solids.
>
> The patient's sexual behavior was a particular

> source of concern while in hospital. Although vigorously heterosexual prior to his illness, he was observed in hospital to make advances toward other male patients by stroking their legs and inviting fellatio by gesture; at times he attempted to kiss them. Although on a sexually mixed floor during a portion of his recovery, he never made advances toward women, and, in fact, his apparent reversal of sexual polarity prompted his fiancee to sever their relationship. (Marlowe, Mancall, and Thomas, 1975, pp. 55–56)

The appearance of the Klüver-Bucy syndrome apparently requires that the amygdala and inferior temporal cortex be removed bilaterally. H. M., the amnesic patient described in Chapter 21, does not exhibit the syndrome in spite of bilateral removal of the medial temporal structures. Furthermore, monkeys with bilateral amygdalectomies do not show the Klüver-Bucy syndrome unless the temporal cortex is added. Finally, there is a single case of a man with a bilateral temporal lobectomy identical to the Klüver-Bucy removal, and he showed all of the Klüver-Bucy symptoms, with the exception of orality. Instead of placing novel objects in his mouth he repeatedly inspected them visually.

At about the time of Klüver and Bucy's discovery a less dramatic, but in many ways more important, discovery was made. Jacobson studied the behavior of chimpanzees in a variety of learning tasks following frontal lobe removals. In 1935, he reported his findings on the effects of the lesions at the Second International Neurology Congress in London. He casually noted that one particularly neurotic chimp appeared more relaxed following the surgery, leading a Portuguese neurologist, Egas Moniz, to propose that similar lesions in people might relieve various behavioral problems. Thus was born psychosurgery and the frontal lobotomy! Unbelievably, not until the late 1960s was any systematic research done on the effects of frontal lobe lesions on the affective behavior of nonhuman animals. Hence, frontal lobotomies in humans were performed without an empirical basis. Experiments by several laboratories have now clearly shown that frontal lobe lesions in rats, cats, and monkeys all have severe effects on social and affective behavior.

THE NATURE OF EMOTION

Think of any significant "emotional experience" that has happened to you. Perhaps you have had a serious fight with a close friend, or have received some unexpected, wonderful news. Such experiences cannot be described as unitary events because emotional experiences differ in multiple ways from one another and from other cognitions. Thus, an emotional experience may include all sorts of "thoughts" or plans about who said or did what, or what will be done in the future. Further, one's heart may be pounding, the throat dry, the underarms moist, the limbs trembling, or the face flushed. There may be strong "feelings" (e.g., anger, happiness) that cannot be verbalized. And, there may be significant changes in facial expression, tone of voice, body posture, or even tears of sadness or joy. Having identified (introspectively) some of the components of an emotional experience, we might then ask "What is emotion?" As we have posed it (and set up the reader for it!), this obviously is not a simple question.

Emotion is not a thing but is an inferred state that has many components, each of which may, in principle, be quantified. Historically, theories of emotion have recognized this and most theorists agree that the concept of emotion includes at least three principal components. First, there are physiological components that include central and autonomic system activity and the resulting changes in visceral activity, as well as neurohormonal activity. Hence, among others, there are changes in heart rate, blood pressure, distribution of blood flow, perspiration, changes in the digestive system, and the release of various hormones that may effect the brain or the autonomic system. Although a topic of some debate, it seems likely that at least some emotional states (e.g., happiness versus sadness) can be differentiated by their associated physiological changes. Second, there are distinctive overt behaviors that are associated with emotional states. Examples would be facial expression, tone of voice, or posture. These behaviors are especially important to others because they convey information that can undoubtedly be different from what we verbalize. The perception of a person who says she is fine but is sobbing uncontrollably is different from the perception of the same person if smiling. Third, there are cognitive processes that are inferred from self report. These processes include both subjective feelings (e.g., love, hate) as well as other cognitions such as "plans, memories, or ideas." The theoretical distinction between the different components of an emotional experience is significant because there appears to be little correlation among the three when they are all measured in the same subjects.

It is evident that the study of the neural basis of emotion presents the psychologist with a major challenge; there is simply no uniform definition of what emotion is, nor is there a standardized way to quantify it. Two investigators interested in emotion might focus upon facial expression as a measure of emotion by filming people surreptitiously. One investigator might analyze the film by studying the asymmetry in the facial musculature of individuals during smiling, and reach inferences about the role of the cerebral hemispheres controlling smiling. A second investigator might record the incidence of smiling in brain-damaged patients and reach conclusions about the role of different neural areas in smiling behavior. Each of these is a legitimate line of inquiry, but it is not unreasonable to ask whether either of these studies is really investigating "emotion." (We leave the readers to reach their own conclusions.) The message we wish to leave is that studies purporting to study the neural basis of emotion must be viewed critically with an eye to the question of how the authors are defining, and measuring, emotion.

CANDIDATE STRUCTURES IN EMOTIONAL BEHAVIOR

Multiple Systems

One of the consistent principles of neural organization is that there are multiple systems controlling virtually every behavior. Sensory information enters the cortex through multiple channels that have distinctly different roles in sensory analysis. Once in the cortex, information travels through multiple parallel systems subserving different functions. Recall that visual information follows a ventral route through the temporal lobe and a dorsal route through the parietal lobe. The former route appears to play a role in object recognition, and the latter route plays a role in spatial location. Similarly, we have seen that the frontal, temporal, and parietal lobes have distinct roles in processes usually referred to as short-term memory. In keeping with this general principle of brain organization, it is likely that there are multiple systems, both cortical and subcortical, that contribute to the experience of an emotion. For example, there must be systems that process significant social stimuli, which are presumably species-specific, including olfactory stimuli (called **pheromones**), tactile stimuli (especially to sensitive body zones), visual stimuli (facial expressions), and auditory stimuli (**phonemes,** crying, screaming, etc.) Although it could be argued that these stimuli are processed by the same systems that analyze other sensory inputs, there is good reason to believe that there may be separate systems. Olfaction provides a good example.

Many mammals have a specialized receptor organ, known as Jacobson's organ, which is specialized to analyze species-typical odors. When animals such as cats encounter certain odors (especially urine from other cats) they close their nostrils and appear to stare off into space with an odd "look" on their face, a behavior that is known as *flehmen.* Actually, the cats are forcing the air through the mouth and into a special duct (which allows the air access to Jacobson's organ) that is connected to the accessory olfactory system. Virtually the only odors that produce this behavior in cats are certain ones from other cats, including urine and ear wax but not feces. (Curiously, we have found that human urine is sometimes also effective.) This system is thus specialized for species-typical odors and is not used otherwise. One interesting property of this system is that it shows habituation (repeated exposure to the same urine reduces the likelihood of flehmen), and cats appear able to remember the odors of familiar cats. Thus, they do not show flehmen to their own urine, or to that of cats they live with. Urine from novel cats will produce prolonged episodes of flehmen, and urine from familiar, but not coresident, cats will produce shorter episodes. Although there is little evidence of such specialized systems for other senses, there is still evidence of special processing. There are cells in the temporal lobe of monkeys that are specially tuned for species-typical calls; these cells are relatively insensitive to other sounds. Recall too that there are temporal cortical cells that are specialized for faces.

In addition to possible specialized sensory processing of emotionally relevant sensory information, it is possible that there are "higher level" systems that process other aspects of this information. Perhaps there is a unique system for cross-modal matching of prosody and facial expression. In addition to multiple systems that may encode specific species-typical information, there may be a general cortical system that is involved in identifying "affective" attributes of stimuli. An interesting experiment by Gazzaniga and LeDoux illustrates such a system. They presented split-brain subjects with visual information to one or the other visual field. The subjects' task was to describe the stimulus verbally and to give it a rating on a 5-point scale from "dislike very much" to "like very much." The results were striking. As expected, only the items in the right visual field (and therefore sent to the left, speaking, hemisphere) were described accurately. In contrast, however, the rating was identical for stimuli in each visual field. Clearly, the pathways processing the affective significance of the stimuli are distinct from the pathway processing their objective properties. This distinction is reminiscent of the difference between knowing "what" and "where" a stimulus is, as illustrated by blindsight (see Chapter 11). There may be a third system that processes "subjective feeling" about a stimulus independent of where or what it is. We have all had the subjective experience of immediately recognizing something like an odor or sound, even though we cannot identify what the stimulus is. We may say that we have a "feeling" or "intuition" about the stimulus. This affective system may be important for memory and, since it probably involves the amygdala, may at least partly account for the role of the amygdala in memory.

The analysis of multiple channels in the sensory systems has identified different properties of sensory experiences that appear to form separate processing modules. Color, orientation, motion, and depth all appear to be independent properties of visual stimuli. The application of the concept of multiple neural systems to emotion has the distinct disadvantage that we have not identified the different sensory modules that appear to be processed differently. Nonetheless, it seems likely that autonomic stimuli form a distinct module, and the neural circuitry involved is well known. The dimensions of other components remains to be determined. It seems likely, however, that there will be separate modules for different aspects of overt behavior (facial expression, prosody) and perhaps for cognitive processes as well.

Studies of Nonhuman Primates: Prefrontal and Paralimbic Lesions

Although it is commonplace to hear spouses or relatives complain of "personality change" in brain-damaged individuals, the parameters of these changes have been poorly specified in human subjects. Even the behavioral changes in people like Phineas Gage (Chapter 19) are described in general terms, which seldom are defined objectively. Nonetheless, the study of nonhuman subjects, particularly nonhuman primates, has made it possible to identify various brain regions that undoubtedly have a significant role in emotional processes. During the past 20 years studies have been conducted on several species of Old- and New-World monkeys with lesions of the frontal cortex, paralimbic cortex, or amygdala — the structures that now appear to be the most important forebrain areas involved in emotional behavior. The results of such studies show six consistent changes in emotional behavior after frontal lesions, which are summarized in Table 23-1.

First, there is an overwhelming consensus that there is a reduction in social interaction following frontal lesions, especially following orbital-frontal lesions. Following orbital-frontal lesions monkeys become socially withdrawn and fail even to reestablish close preoperative relationships with family members. The animals sit alone, seldom if ever engage in social grooming or contact other monkeys, and in a free-ranging natural environment they become solitary, leaving the troop altogether. Anterior temporal lesions produce a milder version of this syndrome, reducing social grooming and social interaction with conspecifics. Lesions elsewhere in the cortex have no obvious effect.

Second, there is a loss of social dominance following orbital-frontal lesions: monkeys that were previously dominant in a group do not maintain their dominance after their operations, although the fall may take weeks to complete. The rate of fall from dominance probably depends upon the aggressiveness of other monkeys in the group.

Third, monkeys with orbital-frontal lesions show inappropriate social interaction. For example, females with such lesions may challenge and threaten unfamiliar male monkeys, whereas normal females typically exhibit gestures of submission in response to dominance gestures displayed by unfamiliar males. (Male monkeys are much larger than females.) Such monkeys may also approach without hesitation any animal, irrespective of the latter animal's social dominance. This behavior frequently results in retaliatory aggression from the dominant, intact animals. Similarly, when approached by dominant animals, frontal monkeys may simply ignore them or run away, rather than performing normal submissive gestures such as allowing mounting. Curiously, frontal monkeys show an increased aversion to threat by people, possibly reflecting a decrease in aggressive behavior.

Fourth, monkeys with large frontal lesions show a change in social preference. When normal monkeys are released into a large enclosure that has

TABLE 23-1. Summary of changes in social behavior of monkeys with frontal cortical lesions

Symptoms	Basic reference
Reduced social interaction	Franzen and Myers, 1973; Deets et al., 1970; Bowden et al., 1971; Raleigh and Steklis, 1981; Myers and Swett, 1970; Myers, Swett, and Miller, 1973
Loss of social dominance	Snyder, 1971
Inappropriate social interaction	Brody and Rosvold, 1952; Butter and Snyder, 1972; Deets et al., 1970
Altered social preference	Suomi et al., 1970
Reduced facial expression and/or body gestures	Franzen and Myers, 1973; Myers, 1972
Reduced vocalization	Aitkin, 1981; Franzen and Myers, 1973; Myers, 1972

conspecifics behind a glass barrier, they will generally sit next to an animal that is only visible through the glass. Although normal animals prefer to sit beside intact monkeys of the opposite sex, frontal monkeys prefer to sit with frontal monkeys of the same sex, presumably because they are less threatening.

Fifth, frontal and anterior temporal monkeys largely lose the use of their facial expressions, posturings, and gesturings in social situations — the effects being larger after frontal than after temporal lesions. Thus, monkeys with frontal lesions show a drastic drop in the frequency and variability of facial expressions and are described as "poker-faced." The one exception to this is in the frequency of submissive or agitated expressions such as the "grimace" expression. This loss of facial expression is not a simple loss of muscle control of the face because the animals do produce expressions. They just fail to produce them often. Lesions of the cingulate or visual association cortex seem to have no effect.

Finally, lesions of the frontal or anterior limbic cortex reduce spontaneous social vocalizations. Indeed, following anterior cingulate lesions, rhesus monkeys effectively make no normal vocalizations at all. Curiously, the nonvocal social behavior of these animals is normal.

In summary, lesions of the orbital-frontal cortex of monkeys produce marked changes in social behavior. In particular they become less socially responsive and fail to produce or to respond to species-typical stimuli. Damage to the paralimbic cortex produces milder effects, the animals showing a reduction in social interaction. Importantly, in spite of the significant changes in the sensory processing abilities of animals with visual association lesions, there appear to be very few obvious changes in the affective behavior of these animals.

The changes in emotional processes in monkeys with frontal lesions are especially intriguing because they suggest that similar changes might be found in humans with frontal lobe injuries. In particular, since monkeys fail to make appropriate vocal and gestural behaviors and fail to respond normally to those made by conspecifics, one might predict that humans with frontal lobe injuries would show similar abnormalities. Furthermore, it might be predicted that disorders such as schizophrenia, which are characterized by significant changes in social interactions, might also involve frontal dysfunction.

Premorbid Emotional Processes

It is often stated that the personality of human brain-injured patients is at least partly dependent upon their premorbid, or preinjury, state. People who are depressive before their injury are more likely to be depressive afterwards; people who are cheerful are more likely to remain so. There has been no systematic study of this phenomenon, but in our experience there is far more intersubject variability in the emotional behavior of brain-damaged people than there is in most tests of cognitive function. A study by Peters and Ploog on the social behavior of squirrel monkeys with frontal lesions is relevant here. Although these authors found many of the changes in social behavior previously observed by others, they also noted that some monkeys seemed less changed by their lesions. Two dominant monkeys received similar orbitofrontal lesions, but whereas one completely lost his dominant position, the second remained dominant but did not exert the dominance strongly. In another social group the second monkey might have been challenged and lost this position. Differences in the premorbid behavior of the lesioned monkeys, as well as in the group structure, appear to have contributed to the change in social behavior. In contrast, when frontal monkeys are given neuropsychological learning tests such as delayed-response tests, it is typical that all animals show a much more similar behavioral change. This is important because it is probably true of humans as well: the effects of brain damage on processes like language or memory are more consistent than the effects on emotion. Or, stated differently, the premorbid personality of human patients with cortical injuries is likely to influence the extent of postinjury changes in emotional processes. This has been completely neglected in research to date and adds a major complication as we try to draw generalizations about emotional processes.

Studies of Nonhuman Primates: Amygdalectomy

In their original studies Klüver and Bucy observed grossly abnormal emotional behavior after removal of the amygdala and the adjacent paralimbic cortex and temporal neocortex. Subsequent work showed that destruction of the amygdala alone produced much of the syndrome, as monkeys whose amygdalas had been removed show a reduced aversion to biologically relevant stimuli that normal monkeys found threatening. In general, there is a loss of fear of humans and a general taming in such monkeys. In one study of free-ranging monkeys, Dicks and his colleagues showed that four of six animals with amygdalectomies failed to rejoin their original groups when freed and all died within a short time. The two remaining animals were younger and they did rejoin their group but rarely initiated social activity. Studies of single unit activity in the amygdala have shown cells that respond to species-typical aversive visual stimuli, a result that is consistent with the loss of response to such stimuli after lesions.

The close anatomical connections between the orbital-prefrontal cortex and the amygdala, and the emotional changes following lesions to either region, suggest that they belong to some neural circuit regulating emotional behavior. Disconnecting the amygdala from its visual input via the temporal lobe also produces alterations in emotional behavior, which suggests that the amygdala may form part of a system for processing socially relevant visual information. Such a system would function in parallel to the object-recognition system of the anterior temporal cortex and hippocampus, and the spatial system of the posterior parietal cortex. This third system may be part of the "subjective system" that we postulated earlier.

Asymmetry and Emotion

In the 1930s, clinicians were reporting detailed observations of patients with large unilateral lesions, noting an apparent asymmetry in the effects of left and right hemisphere lesions. The best known descriptions are those of Goldstein, who suggested that left hemisphere lesions produce "catastrophic" reactions characterized by fearfulness and depression, whereas right hemisphere lesions produce "indifference". The first systematic study of these contrasting behavioral effects was done by Gainotti in 1969, who showed that catastrophic reactions occurred in 62% of his left hemisphere sample, compared with only 10% for his right hemisphere cases. In contrast, indifference was commoner in the right hemisphere patients, occurring in 38%, as compared with only 11% of the left hemisphere cases. Significantly, however, Gainotti reported that catastrophic reactions were associated with aphasia, and indifference reactions with neglect.

Although it is tempting to assume that the emotional reactions observed in stroke patients reflect complementary functioning of the two hemispheres in emotional processes, our experience with patients undergoing cortical resections suggests that the situation is more complex. In general, right hemisphere excisions appear to release talking, left hemisphere lesions to reduce it. (Remember that none of these patients are aphasic, nor do they exhibit persistent neglect.) These effects are especially obvious following frontal lobe lesions. The content of the speech released by right hemisphere lesions has not been carefully studied, but it is our impression that it is significantly affected by the lesion site. Patients with right frontal lesions characteristically make poor jokes and puns and tell pointless stories, often liberally embellished with profanity. Further, the right frontal lobe patient is usually intensely amused by the stories he or she is telling and will persist even if others are ambivalent to them. On the other hand, lesions of the right temporal and/or parietal lobe produce a totally different type of speech in individuals that is characterized by excessive concern for their personal lives. They often go to great lengths to rationalize their personal shortcomings, and they are generally unaware that others may be bored with their talking. Many of these patients also exhibit symptoms of paranoia, often being convinced that friends or family either are not supportive or are against them. They are excessively suspicious of neuropsychological assessments, insisting either that the assessments are unnecessary or that they would rather do them when they are "feeling better."

It is obvious that a simple left-right distinction of catastrophic indifference is far too simple; both the site and the side of the lesion are important in understanding the changes in emotional behavior. This ought not to surprise us, however, since the same is true of cognitive behaviors. In order to understand the organization of emotional processes, we must therefore attempt to separate the components of the behaviors as we have done for the study of cognitive processes. As a first step, we shall consider the production of affective behavior separately from the interpretation of affective stimuli.

PRODUCTION OF EMOTIONAL BEHAVIOR

Mood is inferred largely from facial expression, tone of voice, and frequency of talking, and so these are sensible behaviors to study first in an analysis of emotional behavior in brain-damaged people. Another way to study emotional behavior is to assess mood and related behaviors using various rating scales — both self-administered scales and those administered by others. Finally, behavior can be studied by anesthetizing one hemisphere briefly using sodium Amytal.

Ratings of Mood

Robinson and his colleagues administered self-report inventories to people with left or right hemisphere strokes. In a series of studies they found that left frontal lesions produce depressive symptoms, but right frontal lesions do not. In addition, they sometimes found right posterior strokes to produce depressive symptoms as well. Robinson has suggested that the reason for the affective change is related to a disruption in catecholamine projections to the remaining hemisphere, which is a reasonable proposal in view of the likely role of catecholamines in affective disorders (see below). Robinson's studies have stimulated considerable interest, and although they have not always been replicated, the general conclusion seems to be that although left frontal lesions produce depressive symptoms soon after stroke, the symptoms decline over time and there may be little evidence of depression after a few months. Curiously, a recent study of chronic brain injuries in Vietnam war veterans has found that left orbitofrontal patients have a more cavalier attitude towards interpersonal problems than do other patients. In contrast, right orbitofrontal lesions made this population more "edgy" and "anxious."

Facial Expression and Spontaneous Talking

Facial expression is one of the most salient cues to emotion in humans, and in recent years there has been a good deal of study about its production in normal people. (See the 1986 volume edited by Bruyer for details.) Overall, studies of neurological patients have found a reduction in the frequency and intensity of facial expressions relative to more posterior lesions. There is also a suggestion that large right hemisphere lesions may have greater effects on facial expression than similarly sized left hemisphere lesions, although this does not appear to be true in patients with restricted frontal or temporal lobectomies (Figure 23-1). In a series of studies, Kolb and his colleagues have found that

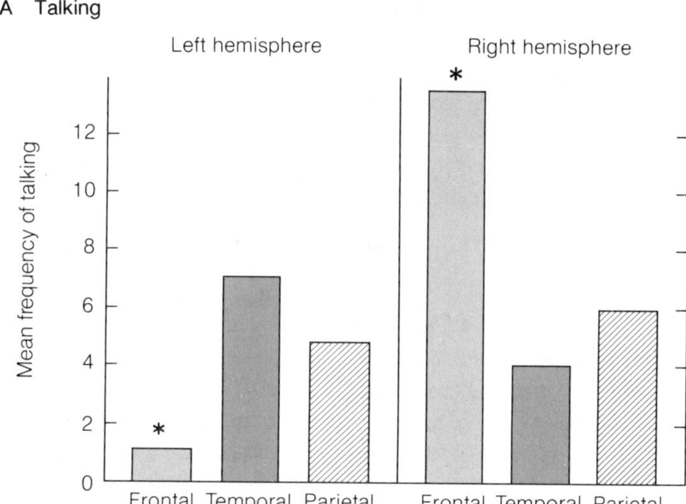

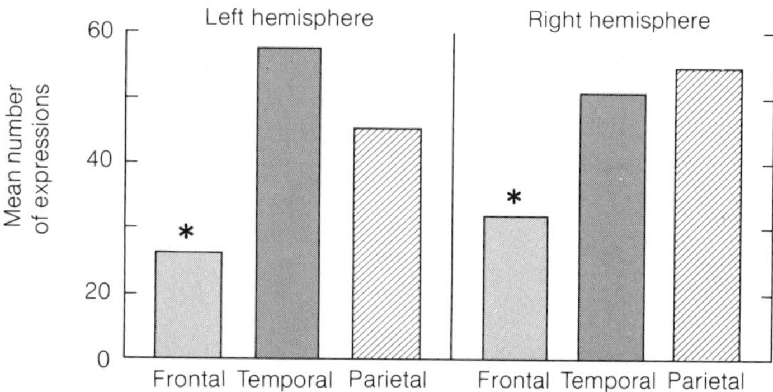

FIGURE 23-1. *A.* Relative frequencies of spontaneous talking and *B.* facial expressions during routine neuropsychological testing. Note that frontal lobe lesions significantly reduce the number of facial expressions. The level of spontaneous talking is significantly reduced for left frontal lesions and increased for right frontal lesions. Stars indicate a significant difference from other groups with same-side lesions. (After Kolb and Milner, 1981; Kolb and Taylor, 1981.)

whether facial expressions are measured in terms of frequency, quantitative scoring of facial movements elements, or subjective rating by judges, both left and right frontal lobe patients show a reduction in facial expression relative to temporal lobe groups. Furthermore, this result occurs whether the expressions are spontaneous or posed. Similarly, the same patients are impaired at copying a series of facial movement sequences, whereas patients with more posterior lesions are unimpaired. However, the side of the lesion clearly affects spontaneous talking in frontal lobe patients.

Right frontal lesions appear to markedly increase talking, whereas left frontal lesions decrease it (Figure 23-1). There can be little doubt that such changes in facial expression and talking would be perceived to produce marked changes in personality by friends and relatives of frontal lobe patients, regardless of whether the lesion were in the left or right hemisphere.

Tone, or Prosody

Spoken language carries two types of information: that derived directly from the content, and that inferred from the tone of voice. There is little doubt that the former is a function of the left hemisphere, and there is now good reason to suspect that the latter is a function of the right. For example, when Tucker and colleagues asked patients to express particular affective states such as anger, happiness, and sadness when they read emotionally neutral sentences, patients with right hemisphere lesions produced the sentences with relatively flat affect compared with patients with left hemisphere lesions. This absence of tone in speech has been termed **aprosodia** and can be measured on a wide-band spectogram, as was done by Kent and Rosenek.

Abnormalities in tone of voice in right hemisphere patients has led Ross to propose that there may be a set of aprosodias analogous to aphasias in left hemisphere speech (see Table 23-2). *Motor aprosodia,* an inability to produce affective components of language, is proposed to result from damage in the region of Broca's area in the right hemisphere. *Sensory aprosodia,* a deficit in the interpretation of the emotional components of language, is presumed to result from damage to the region in the right hemisphere analogous to Wernicke's area. Ross's proposal may have merit and deserves serious consideration, but at present it is without much scientific support. Furthermore, like aphasias, which are virtually never purely of one type, aprosodias are certainly not as pure as Ross has suggested.

Temporal Lobe Personality

One way in which to quantify social or affective behavior is to have patients and their friends complete rating scales of various behavioral traits such as "anger," "sadness," and "religiosity." In their study of the behavior of temporal lobe patients Bear and Fedio asked them and their friends to do just this, with the scales related to the traits sum-

TABLE 23-2. Ross's proposed classification of aprosodias

Type of Aprosodia	Spontaneous prosody and gesturing	Prosodic repetition	Prosodic comprehension	Comprehension of emotional gesturing
Motor	Poor	Poor	Good	Good
Sensory	Good	Poor	Poor	Poor
Global	Poor	Poor	Poor	Poor
Conduction	Good	Poor	Good	Good
Transcortical motor	Poor	Good	Good	Good
Transcortical sensory	Good	Good	Poor	Poor
Mixed transcortical	Poor	Good	Poor	Poor
Anomic (alexia with agraphia)	Good	Good	Good	Poor

TABLE 23-3. Summary of characteristics attributed to temporal lobe epileptics

Emotionality	Deepening of all emotions, sustained intense manic-depressive disease
Elation, euphoria	Grandiosity, exhilarated mood; diagnosis of manic-depressive disease
Sadness	Discouragement, fearfulness, self-depreciation; diagnosis of depression, suicide attempt
Anger	Increased temper, irritability
Aggression	Overt hostility, rape attacks, violent crimes, murder
Altered sexual interest	Loss of libido, hyposexualism; fetishism, transvestism, exhibitionism, hypersexual episodes
Guilt	Tendency to self-scrutiny and self-recrimination
Hypermoralism	Attention to rules with inability to distinguish significant from minor infraction, desire to punish offenders
Obsessionalism	Ritualism; orderliness; compulsive attention to detail
Circumstantiality	Loquaciousness, pedantry; being overly detailed or peripheral
Viscosity	Stickiness; tendency to repetition
Sense of personal destiny	Events given highly charged, personalized significance, divine guidance ascribed to many features of patient's life
Hypergraphia	Keeping extensive diaries, detailed notes; writing autobiography or novel
Religiosity	Holding deep religious beliefs, often idiosyncratic multiple conversions, mystical states
Philosophical interest	Nascent metaphysical or moral speculations, cosmological theories
Dependence, passivity	Cosmic helplessness, "at hands of fate"; protestations of helplessness
Humorlessness, sobriety	Overgeneralized ponderous concern; humor lacking or idiosyncratic
Paranoia	Suspicious, overinterpretative of motives and events; diagnosis of paranoid schizophrenia

Source: After Bear and Fedio, 1977.

marized in Table 23-3. Each of these traits had previously been attributed to temporal lobe epileptics, who presumably have temporal lobe lesions producing their epileptic condition. The epileptic patients self-reported a distinctive profile of humorless sobriety, dependence, and obsessionalism; raters differentiated the temporal lobe patients on the basis of nearly every trait listed in Table 23-3 but rated them most strongly on the traits described as "circumstantiality," "philosophical interests," and "anger" (see descriptions in Table 23-3). Furthermore, right and left temporal lobe patients could be distinguished: the right temporal patients were described as more obsessional and the left temporal ones are more concerned with "personal destiny". In a 1983 study Fedio and Martin examined temporal lobectomy patients on the same scale, finding that surgical removal of the epileptogenic tissue produced a decrease in the characteristic personality traits, presumably because the abnormal temporal lobe tissue that produced the seizures also interfered with normal function. Nonetheless, these patients still differed from normal control subjects: the left temporal lobectomy cases rated themselves more harshly, reported hypergraphic tendencies, and professed a reflective style of thinking that centered on themes of religiosity and personal destiny. Right temporal lobectomy patients rated themselves less adversely but claimed to have developed more feelings of anger, sadness, and aggression. These ratings are in general accord with our clinical experience and quantify the clinical impressions of a temporal lobe personality observed by many others. The source of this personality change is still unknown.

Affect Under Sodium Amytal

From the studies detailed above it is reasonable to expect that patients under the effects of carotid sodium Amytal would exhibit changes in personality related to the side of drug injection. For example, from Gainotti's results a depressive-catastrophic reaction could be predicted to follow injection into the speaking hemisphere, and an indifference reaction to follow injection into the nonspeaking hemisphere. Study results are, however, contradictory. The most widely cited results are those collected by Terzian and by Rossi and Rosandini. They report that injections into the left hemisphere indeed provoke a catastrophic reaction as the drug wears off. The patient "despairs and expresses a sense of guilt, of nothingness, of indignity, and worries about his own future or that of his relatives, without referring to the language disturbances overcome and to the hemiplegia just resolved and ignored." As the drug wore off after injection into the right hemisphere, a "euphorical" reaction was reported, as the patient "appears without apprehension, smiles and laughs and both with mimicry and words expresses considerable liveliness and sense of well-being." These results are provocative, but unfortunately a number of groups have been unable to confirm them. For example, in one report on 104 patients Milner noted only rare depression, and there was no systematic asymmetry in the euphoria. Furthermore, Kolb and Milner found no asymmetry in either the frequency or the quality (e.g., happy or sad) of facial expressions following injection into the left and right hemispheres, respectively.

The difference between the results of the Italian investigators and Milner's group is unlikely to be resolved in the near future. There is one relevant methodological difference: in the two Milner studies each patient could be used as his or her own control, because both hemispheres were injected, although on different days. In the Terzian and the Rossi and Rosandini studies most patients were injected in only one hemisphere. Another possible difference is that the injection volume is somewhat larger in the Milner studies, presumably leading to a greater anesthetic effect. In any event, until such results are replicated by others, they should be interpreted with caution.

Psychiatric Disturbance

Although the majority of brain-damaged people do not exhibit psychotic behaviors, symptoms such as hallucinations, mania, or delusions of persecution are occassionally reported. Curiously, such symptoms are virtually always associated with right hemisphere lesions, although it may be that such symptoms are masked by aphasia after left hemisphere lesions. In any event, the cause of the psychotic symptoms in brain-damaged patients is obscure.

Summary

As summarized in Table 23-4, emotional or social behavior is markedly altered by cerebral lesions. Taken together, the studies lead to several conclusions. First, lesions of the left hemisphere have different effects on emotional behavior from lesions of the right. Second, occurrences of aphasia and unilateral neglect are significant factors in predicting occurrences of depressive-catastrophic and indifference reactions, respectively; these reactions are uncommon in the absence of aphasia and neglect. Third, the frontal lobes appear to have a special role in producing facial expression; like nonhuman primates with frontal lesions, humans with frontal injuries show sharp reductions in facial expression. Fourth, the frontal lobes are asymmetrical in their role in spontaneous talking: left frontal lesions appear to inhibit spontaneous talking, whereas right frontal lobe lesions appear to release it. Fifth, temporal lobe damage is associated with a constellation of behavioral symptoms, many of which are related to damage to just the left or the

TABLE 23-4. Summary of experiments on production of emotional behavior in neurological patients

Behavior	Characteristics	Basic reference
Clinical behavior of patients with natural lesions	Catastrophic reactions from left hemisphere lesions; indifference from right hemisphere lesions	Gainotti, 1969; 1972; Goldstein, 1939
Facial expression	Reduced by frontal lesions Reduced by right hemisphere lesions Asymmetry altered	Kolb and Milner, 1982; Buck and Duffy, 1980; Borod et al., 1986; Bruyer, 1981
Spontaneous speech	Decreased by left frontal lesions; increased by right frontal lesions	Kolb and Taylor, 1981
Tone, or prosody, of speech	Right hemisphere lesions impair mimicry of emotional states	Tucker et al., 1977; Shapiro and Danly, 1985
Temporal lobe traits	Temporal lobe personality	Bear and Fedio, 1977; Waxman and Geschwind, 1974; Sachdev and Waxman, 1981; Fedio and Martin, 1983
Sodium Amytal	Catastrophic reactions to left injection; indifference reactions to right injection	Terzian, 1964; Rossi and Rosandini, 1967
	No evidence of asymmetrical effects	Rovetta, 1960; Milner, 1967; Kolb and Milner, 1981

right hemisphere. Sixth, transient changes in mood are more likely to be associated with left frontal lesions, whereas psychotic symptoms, which are relatively uncommon after brain damage, nearly always follow right hemisphere injuries. Finally, the occurrence, in persons without known brain damage, of many traits of personality or emotional behavior that are characteristic of brain-damaged groups leads us to speculate that differences in cerebral organization, whether genetically or environmentally derived, form the basis of different human personalities. For example, one could hypothesize that people who are hypercritical may have relatively smaller, or less active, temporal lobes or that people without much facial expression have smaller, or less active frontal lobes. Since we have noted previously that people vary widely in their performance on neuropsychological tests of cognitive behavior, it would be interesting to explore the relation between the performance on measures of cognitive and emotional behavior in the *same normal subjects*. Concordance of measures on the two types of tests would be provocative indeed.

INTERPRETATION OF AFFECTIVE STIMULI BY NEUROLOGICAL PATIENTS

Emotional behavior might appear to be abnormal not only because a person is unable to produce the appropriate behavior but also because he or she misinterprets the social or emotional signals coming from others. The interpretation of affective stimuli by neurological patients has been studied in a number of ways, each of which is considered separately (see Table 23-5).

Judgment of Mood

Heilman and his colleagues asked patients to judge the mood of a speaker after listening to him read a sentence in which he successively feigned anger,

TABLE 23-5. Summary of experiments on interpretation of emotionally relevant stimuli in neurological patients

Experiment	Characteristics	Basic reference
Judgment of mood in others	Right hemisphere lesions impair comprehension	Heilman et al., 1975
	Right temporal lesions impair perception of intonation	Tompkins and Mateer, 1985
Judgment of propositional affect	Left hemisphere lesions impair comprehension	Kolb and Taylor, 1981
Comprehension of verbal humor	Left hemisphere lesions impair comprehension of captioned	Gardner et al., 1975
	cartoons; right hemisphere lesions alter understanding of jokes	Brownell et al., 1983; Bihrle et al., 1986
Comprehension of nonverbal humor	Right hemisphere lesions impair comprehension	Gardner et al., 1975
Matching pictures of emotional facial expressions	Right hemisphere lesions impair performance	DeKosky et al., 1980; Kolb and Taylor, 1981; Cicone et al., 1980; Bowers et al., 1987

joy, or some other emotion. Patients with right hemisphere lesions (largely temporal-parietal) were more impaired at the task than patients with analogous left hemisphere lesions. This impairment at perceiving emotional tone in language is referred to by Ross as a sensory aprosodia, and he predicts that it results from temporal-parietal lesions on the right, just as Heilman and his coworkers report. It is likely, however, that patients with right temporal lobectomies, who, it should be recalled, are impaired at musical perception, will be quite impaired at the judgment of emotional tone whether or not the analogue of Wernicke's area is removed. A preliminary study by Tompkins and Mateer suggests this may be true, but more study is required.

Comprehension of Humor

The ability to be humorous and appreciate humor is one of our most intriguing behaviors and certainly contributes to our personality. Little is known about the neurological basis of humor competence, except for three interesting studies by Gardner and his associates. In the first they examined the comprehension and appreciation of humorous material following left or right hemisphere lesions. They asked patients to choose the funniest of four cartoons, which were either with or without captions). The results showed that all of the patients were impaired at the task, but there was an asymmetry in the pattern of errors. Patients with left hemisphere lesions did well on the cartoons *without* captions, whereas patients with right hemisphere lesions did well on the cartoons *with* captions. Further, the behavior of the two patient groups differed. Those with left hemisphere lesions behaved "normally" those with right hemisphere lesions tended to exhibit one of two extreme reactions: either they laughed at nearly every item, even when their understanding was doubtful, or, more commonly, they displayed little reaction to any item, even when their understanding seemed adequate. Thus, although both left and right hemisphere damage impaired the appreciation of humor, the right hemisphere lesions appear to have had a more fundamental effect on the patient's behavior.

In a second study, Brownwell and colleagues assessed the appreciation of jokes by patients with right hemisphere damage. They hypothesized that the appreciation of jokes presupposes two elements: sensitivity to the surprise element entailed in the punch line of the joke, and appreciation of the coherence that results when the punch line has been integrated with the body of the joke. In other words, the surprise element must be appreciated as being related to the content of the prelude; if it is not, the humor is lost. In order to study the verbal humor of their patients, they presented subjects with a short story leading up to a punch line, followed by four alternative endings. One ending was a surprise that followed the story, one was a surprise that was a nonsequitur with the story, and the other two contained no surprise but were statements that followed the coherence of the story. Consider the following example, "The neighborhood borrower approached Mr. Smith on Sunday afternoon and inquired: 'Say Smith, are you using your lawnmower this afternoon?' 'Yes, I am,' Smith replied warily. The neighborhood borrower then answered: 'Fine, then you won't be needing your golf clubs, I'll just borrow them.'"

In the Brownwell study the subjects did not receive the last sentence but were given four choices. (1) Correct ending: "Fine, then you won't be needing your golf clubs, I'll borrow them." (2) Nonsequitur ending: "You know, the grass is greener on the other side." (3) Neutral ending: "Do you think I could use it when you're done?" (4) Sad ending: "Gee, if only I had enough money, I could buy my own."

Patients with right hemisphere damage did poorly at this test because although they reliably chose surprise endings, they were as likely to choose a nonsequitur as the correct ending. The patients recognized that a joke must end in a surprise, and they recognized which endings were surprising, but they could not establish an interpretation of the story that tied the ending coherently to the body of the joke.

Taken together, the Gardner studies imply that right hemisphere patients in particular have an atypical sense of humor, a result concordant with clinical descriptions of these patients as having inappropriate responses to jokes, stories, or conversations. There is no hint concerning where this deficit is most likely to arise, although on the basis of clinical reports, the frontal lobe would seem the obvious place to look.

Judgment of Facial Expression

There has been considerable interest in the perception of facial expression in normal subjects over the past decade, in large part due to the seminal work of Ekman and his colleagues. It is now recognized that people are capable of discriminating between six different classes of facial expression (happy, sad, angry, surprised, afraid, and disgusted), and that this ability transcends cultural or linguistic barriers. Thus, people from New Guinea recognize the same categories of facial expressions as do people from France. In order to study the ability of patients with cerebral lesions to appreciate different facial expressions, Kolb and Taylor did a series of experiments in which subjects were asked to match different photographs of faces on the basis of emotion inferred from the facial expression. Patients with right hemisphere lesions were especially poor at matching facial expressions, a result consistent with the inferred role of the right hemisphere in the processing of faces. Curiously, patients with left frontal lesions did poorly at the test relative to the other left hemisphere groups. In a follow-up study, Kolb and Taylor gave a similar test to a much larger sample of patients and found a significant impairment in left frontal lobe subjects, as well as in right frontal and temporal subjects (Figure 23-2). This result suggests that although the right hemisphere may be dominant for the processing of faces and facial expression, the left hemisphere may also play a role. One possibil-

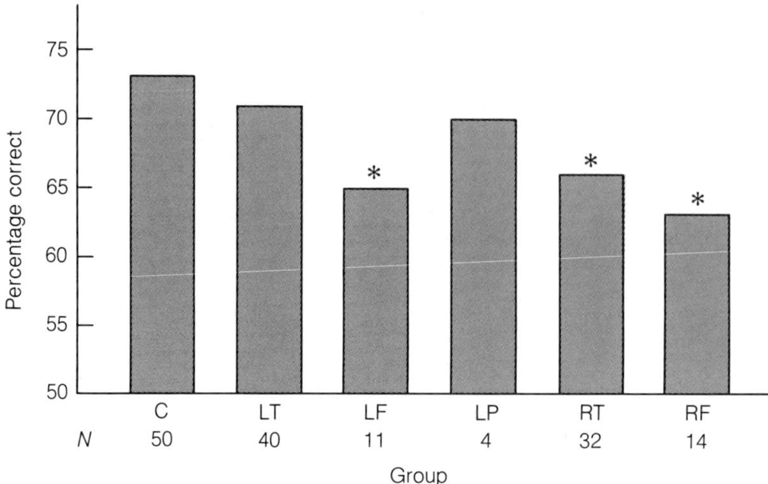

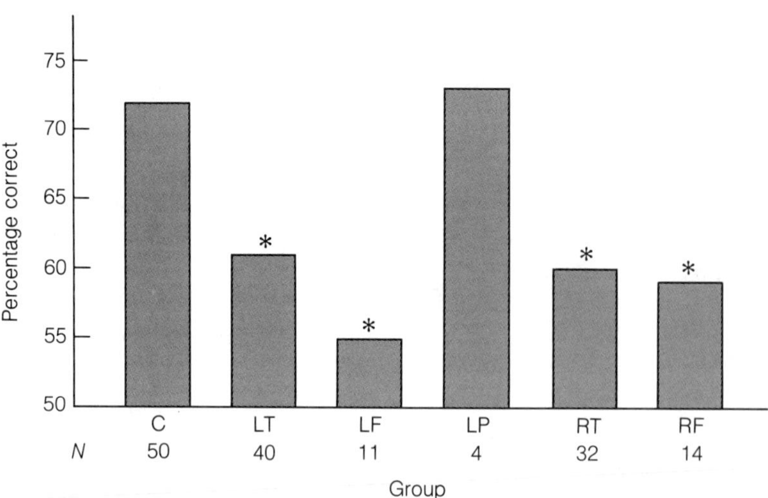

FIGURE 23-2. *A.* Performance of control subjects and surgical excision patients on a test of matching facial expressions and *B.* (LF) matching facial expressions to cartoon situations. Note that both left (LF) and right frontal (RF) lobe lesions impair performance on both perceptual tests. Temporal lobe lesions have asymmetrical effects: left temporals (LT) are impaired only on the interpretative test, whereas the right temporals (RT) are impaired at both tests. *C.* control subjects, LP: left parietal. Stars indicate significant difference from other groups with same-side lesions. (Kolb and Taylor, 1988.)

ity is that the left hemisphere assigns verbal tags to expressions, which presumably aids in recognition.

Judgments of Emotional Situations

Like the appreciation of facial expression, the comprehension of emotional situations is central to understanding emotion in others. Cicone and associates asked patients to match a target scene, such as a man being robbed, with one of four other scenes that displayed the same emotion, although in a different situation. Thus, given a choice of a man winning a lottery, a woman chopping, a man in quicksand, and a child eating ice cream, the match to a man being robbed would be the man in quicksand, because both pictures represent frightening situations. Right hemisphere patients were more impaired than left hemisphere patients on a purely visual form (drawings of scenes) and were as impaired on a verbal version (spoken or written form). These authors conclude that the difficulty in understanding emotional situations is general among right hemisphere patients, but secondary to language impairment in left hemisphere patients. This may be true, but the degree of impairment in verbal tasks is almost certainly related to the size of the lesion in the right hemisphere patients. Kolb and Taylor found that their patients with small right hemisphere excisions were not impaired at judging emotion from verbal descriptions of emotional situations, but patients with equivalent left-side lesions were. For example, the patients were asked to pair the correct emotion with a propositional statement such as "This man is at a funeral"; left, but not right, hemisphere patients were less accurate than controls.

Recently, Kolb and Taylor showed subjects cartoon drawings like those illustrated in Figure 23-3 and asked subjects to chose one of six photographs as being appropriate for the missing face. In this situation both left and right frontal or temporal lobe patients were impaired, whereas a small group of left parietal patients performed normally. This result was unexpected and is consistent with the hypothesis that both the left and right frontal and temporal lobes are involved in judgments of emotional situations.

Much more study of the judgment of emotional situations is needed, but as a general conclusion it appears that right hemisphere lesions have a greater effect on this ability than do those on the left—a result consistent with the inappropriateness of much behavior in patients with right hemisphere lesions, especially lesions that include the frontal lobe. Nonetheless, left hemisphere lesions certainly affect the judgment of emotional situations, although not necessarily for the same reasons.

Summary

The research on the interpretation of emotion is subject to many criticisms, in part because of the difficulty in designing the experiments. In addition, the research can be criticized on the grounds that the sample sizes in most studies are small and the lesions are highly variable. Aphasia in left hemisphere patients makes the study of these people difficult, and some studies simply compare right hemisphere patients with controls. Very few studies include patients with left frontal lobe damage, and the few that do are significant in that they consistently report changes in the interpretation of affective stimuli. In view of these difficulties, our conclusions must therefore be cautious. First, we can conclude that the interpretation of emotionally significant stimuli is impaired by cerebral lesions, just as these same lesions impair the production of emotional behavior. Second, although damage to either hemisphere appears to influence the interpretation of stimuli, damage to the right hemisphere appears to have greater effects, even on the interpretation of certain types of verbal stimuli. Third, the frontal lobes may have a larger effect on the interpretation of emotional stimuli than do other cortical lesions, but this is based on few

FIGURE 23-3. Examples of cartoon situations in which patients were asked either to produce the appropriate expression or to choose the appropriate expression from several choices for the blank face. (Kolb and Taylor, 1988.)

studies. A major challenge for future studies is to demonstrate focal effects of right hemisphere lesions on the interpretation of emotional stimuli. It is likely that frontal and posterior regions have a different interpretive role, but there is no evidence as yet to indicate what this difference might be.

LATERALITY STUDIES

In recent years, attention in laterality studies has turned to the lateralization of affective processes. The basic logic applied in these studies has been to present material to one hemisphere, using dichotic or tachistoscopic techniques (see Chapter 15), in order to demonstrate a difference in the performance of the two hemispheres. If one hemisphere were superior to the other at recognizing tone of voice or facial expression, for example, it could be inferred that the superior hemisphere had some dominant role in this function. We shall review these studies briefly, dividing them by whether they investigate the production of affective behavior or the perception of emotional stimuli.

Production of Affective Behavior

Few studies have examined the neuropsychology by which affective behaviors are produced in normal subjects. Those that have centered on the study of eye movements and facial expression. One study, by Schwartz and colleagues involved observing the direction of horizontal eye movements made during emotional and nonemotional tasks. Emotionally loaded statements, such as "Picture and describe the last situation in which you cried," produced significantly more gaze shifts to the left than to the right. In contrast, nonemotional questions such as "What is the primary difference between the meanings of the words *recognize* and *remember*?" produced more gaze shifts to the right than to the left. By use of the hypothesized relation between gaze shift and lateralization, these results were interpreted as demonstrating a special role for the right hemisphere in regulating emotional processes. These data are provocative, but they are not a very direct measure of affective behavior.

A series of studies by Campbell has demonstrated that facial expressions are not always symmetrical, but rather tend to occur predominantly on the left side of the face. The asymmetries may range from the hardly noticeable—such as the flicker of a smile on the left side of Mona Lisa's face (on the right of the painting, of course)—to the pronounced—such as a raised eyebrow, wink, or lopsided smile on the left side of the face. In one study, Moscovitch and Olds surreptitiously recorded the laterality of facial expressions of people in restaurants, finding a left-side preponderance of facial expression. They confirmed this observation by carefully analyzing video recordings of people recounting sad and humorous stories, again finding a left-side bias in facial expressions. Asymmetrical production of facial expression can be interpreted as showing that the right hemisphere is specialized in that function, a conclusion consistent with its presumed specialization in the perception of facial expressions. It is tempting to speculate that right hemisphere specialization in producing and interpreting facial expression is analogous to the left hemisphere specialization in producing and interpreting language, but this has yet to be proved. In our discussion of the Teuber-Yin theory of facial perception (Chapter 1), we noted that the apparent specialization of the right hemisphere in the perception of faces could easily be interpreted as a specialization for the perception of complex visual stimuli, of which faces are an example.

Perception of Relevant Stimuli

To date, in studies of perception of normal subjects of emotionally loaded stimuli, only the visual and auditory modalities have been examined. For both modalities the stimulus usually is presented to one hemisphere selectively, either alone or in competition with information simultaneously presented to the opposite hemisphere. Two procedures have been used for the visual presentation. In one, faces with different expressions (e.g., sad and happy) are presented tachistoscopically to the left or right visual field, and the subject is asked to identify the facial expression. The results show the left visual field to be superior at correct identification. This superiority can be interpreted as demonstrating a right hemisphere specialization for the perception of facial expression, an important aspect of nonverbal communication. The second procedure involves an ingenious technique devised by Dimond. By the use of special contact lenses Dimond and his colleagues were able to selectively project several types of films to the left or right hemisphere. Subjects rated each film on a scale of 1 to 9 on the four emotional dimensions of humorous, pleasant, horrific, or unpleasant. Films presented to the right hemisphere were judged more unpleasant and horrific and produced greater autonomic nervous system activation (as measured by heart rate) than when these same films were presented to the left hemisphere of other subjects. Dimond and his colleagues concluded that the two hemispheres hold an essentially different emotional view of the world. Curiously, if the films were shown to both hemispheres simultaneously, the ratings closely resembled those of the right visual field (the left hemisphere), suggesting that left hemisphere perception is dominant. It could be predicted that a left hemisphere lesion might result in a more negative view of the films, although this has not been studied.

Studies of asymmetries in the auditory perception of emotions have generally employed a dichotic-listening technique, which generally shows a left-ear superiority for emotional material such as laughing or crying. One of the most compelling experiments was conducted by Ley and Bryden. They employed a number of short sentences spoken in happy, sad, angry, and neutral voices. These sentences were dichotically paired with neutral sentences of similar semantic content. Subjects were instructed to attend to one ear and to report the emotional tone of the target sentence and indicate its content by checking off items on a multiple-choice recognition sheet. Virtually every subject showed a left-ear advantage for identifying the emotional tone of the voice and at the same time a right-ear advantage for identifying the content. This result is analogous to that of Dimond and colleagues, who found that the two hemispheres deal with visual material in a different way.

Summary

Laterality studies generally confirm the conclusions from studies of neurological patients: the right hemisphere has a predominant role in emotional behavior. In particular, studies in both normal and neurological subjects suggest a right hemisphere superiority for recognizing emotional aspects of stimuli. Nevertheless, this conclusion is not universally accepted, although the data appear to favor it. For example, in a thoughtful review Tucker concluded that the right hemisphere has a special role in mediating negative emotions, whereas the left hemisphere is more implicated in positive emotions. There is little reason to believe that the brain is arranged in this manner, however, and it seems more parsimonious to us to view the right hemisphere as being more involved than the left in all aspects of emotional behavior. The nature of this role is a matter for debate and will become an increasingly important focus for research over the coming decade.

NEUROBIOLOGY OF SCHIZOPHRENIA AND DEPRESSION

We have considered the effects of cerebral damage on emotional processes, emphasizing the role of both the right hemisphere and the frontal and medial temporal structures in emotional behavior. Accumulating evidence from the fields of neuropsychology, neurochemistry, psychiatry, and neurology indicates that the loss of specific neurotransmitter systems may also produce abnormalities in emotional behavior, abnormalities that are quite different from those resulting from cortical injury. Recall, for example, that a loss of the dopamine projections to the striatum is responsible for the symptoms of Parkinson's disease. Could analogous losses of other specific transmitter pathways be the cause of two of the most debilitating diseases of emotional behavior — schizophrenia and depression? Although there is little doubt that environmental factors play a significant role in the etiology of both of these disorders, there is now good reason to believe that environmental factors may interact with abnormalities of transmitter systems in the brain and with other as yet unknown variables to produce both depression and schizophrenia. We first review the transmitter pathways, before considering their role in emotional behavior.

Amine Pathways

Three **biogenic amines,** which are **putative transmitters** in the brain, are believed to be important in emotional behavior: dopamine, norepinephrine, and serotonin. Each of these substances is manufactured in a restricted region of the brainstem and sent via long axons to various places, especially to one in the forebrain (see Figure 23-4).

Dopaminergic Projections. There are two principal dopaminergic projection systems to the forebrain: the nigrostriatal and the mesocortical. The nigrostriatal system arises from cell bodies in the substantia nigra, whose axons project primarily to the caudate nucleus and putamen. It is the loss of these projections that is responsible for Parkinson's disease. The mesocortical system begins with cell bodies in the tegmentum, in a region just above the substantia nigra known as the *ventral tegmental area of Tsai*. Axons of these neurons project to the limbic system, including certain regions of the frontal lobe. It is an abnormality of these cells that is believed to occur in schizophrenia.

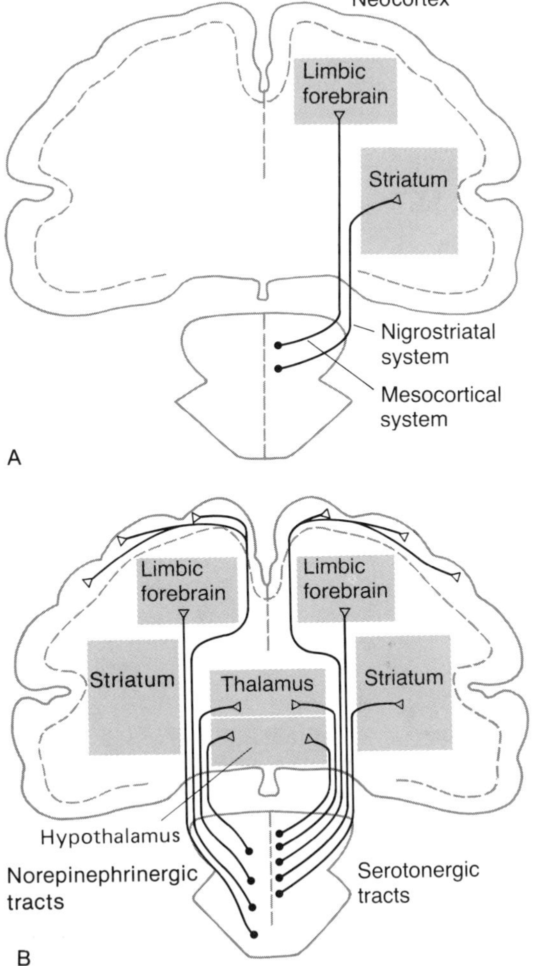

FIGURE 23-4. Schematic drawings of central biogenic aminergic tracts. *A*. Dopaminergic tracts. *B*. Norepinephrinergic and serotoninergic tracts. (After Sachar, 1981.)

Norepinephrine. Norepinephrinergic innervation of the brain arises from cell bodies at the level of the **pons** in and around a nucleus known as the *locus ceruleus*. Fibers from this region form six major norepinephrinergic tracts projecting to the hypothalamus, thalamus, limbic system, neocortex, cerebellum, and spinal cord (see Figure 23-4). An abnormality in norepinephrine may be responsible for some symptoms of depression.

Serotonin. Serotonin-containing neurons are found in nine clusters of cells lying in the midline region of the pons and upper brainstem known as the *raphé regions*. These neurons project widely throughout the brain, as illustrated in Figure 23-4, innervating all those structures also receiving projections from dopamine or norepinephrine neurons. Like norepinephrine, serotonin has a putative role in depression.

The Dopamine Theory of Schizophrenia

From research on drug action, on autopsied brains, on the metabolites of psychotic patients, and on the observed side effects of movement-disorder treatments one conclusion is supported: There is evidence favoring the hypotheses that there is an abnormality in the mesocortical dopamine system of schizophrenics. Perhaps the strongest evidence favoring a role for dopamine in **schizophrenia** comes from studies of the action of antipsychotic drugs. Antipsychotic drugs, or **neuroleptic drugs,** are known to act on the dopamine synapse, and dopamine agonists, which enhance the action of dopamine (cocaine, amphetamine, and L-dopa), can induce psychotic symptoms that are almost indistinguishable from classic paranoid schizophrenia. Further, if a schizophrenic takes heavy doses of amphetamine, the schizophrenic symptoms are heightened.

Since there is no evidence of cell loss as in Parkinson's or **Alzheimer's disease,** we must ask what type of abnormality in the dopamine system is responsible for schizophrenic symptoms. There are five possibilities: (1) too much dopamine is released by the dopaminergic neurons; (2) too little dopamine is released and the receptors are hypersensitive, a condition known as **denervation supersensitivity;** (3) dopaminergic receptors are hypersensitive to the normal amount of dopamine released; (4) some other system, which is antagonistic to dopamine, is underactive; or (5) there is a malfunction of a feedback pathway that controls some component of the dopamine system. Studies of postmortem schizophrenic brains have demonstrated that schizophrenics have up to twice as many dopamine receptors as normal controls—lending credence to the second or third suggestion. We must be cautious however, since most of the evidence favoring any dopaminergic abnormality in schizophrenia is still circumstantial.

If the mesocortical dopamine system is involved in schizophrenia, then we might expect that those regions of the cortex receiving dopaminergic projections (medial temporal and prefrontal) would show other abnormalities. This is indeed the case. Studies of regional blood flow and glucose-uptake have both shown evidence that the frontotemporal regions are functionally abnormal. In particular, there is a common, but not unanimous, finding of hypofrontal glucose-uptake, implying a reduced frontal lobe activity. Further, Risberg has studied regional blood flow in a person before and after amphetamine intoxication and found the major change to be a large increase in frontal blood flow. Amphetamine is a dopaminergic agonist and would be expected to increase activity in areas with heavy dopaminergic terminations like the frontal cortex. Finally, in our studies of the neuropsychological test performance of patients with schizophrenia, we have found evidence of bilateral frontal and temporal lobe dysfunction in the presence of normal parietal lobe function. We return to neuropsychological studies of schizophrenic patients in Chapter 30.

The dopamine theory of schizophrenia is far from proved and has important weaknesses. One is that although neuroleptic drugs block dopamine receptors rapidly, the core symptoms of schizophrenia disappear gradually over several weeks. Could this be due to actions of the drugs on other systems, actions that take weeks to become effective? Further, CT scans of schizophrenic patients reveal an enlarged ventricle, implying that schizophrenics may suffer from brain atrophy. Sachar wonders if this implies that in some forms of schizophrenia the psychotic episodes are secondary to a primary lesion of the brain that has not yet been recognized. Thus, the dopamine hypothesis, even if correct for the psychotic phase, may be inadequate to account for the entire illness, and the search continues for the primary brain disturbance. In view of the evidence of frontal-temporal dysfunction in schizophrenia, the place to look would seem to be in these regions.

Structural Abnormalities in Schizophrenic Brains

Numerous studies have looked at the gross morphology of the brains of schizophrenics, both in autopsied tissue, as well as in MRI and CT scans. Although the results are variable, most agree that schizophrenics have brains that are lighter than normal, and in which the ventricles are enlarged. There have also been suggestions that schizophrenics have smaller frontal lobes, or at least a reduction in the number of neurons in the prefrontal cortex, and thinner parahippocampal gyri. One of the most interesting findings is that of Kovelman and Scheibel, who found pronounced abnormalities in the orientation of cells in the hippocampi of deceased schizophrenics: rather than finding a consistent parallel orientation characteristic of normal brains, the schizophrenics had a more haphazard organization (Figure 23-5). There are two important aspects of this result. First, whereas the brains of schizophrenic patients showed this pathology, it was not true of other pathologies involving the hippocampus, including chronic alcoholism, Alzheimer's disease, temporal lobe epilepsy, and Huntington's chorea. Second, it seems unlikely that the disorientation the researchers observed can develop at any time except during embryogenesis. This is consistent with the long-held view that schizophrenia is a developmental disorder.

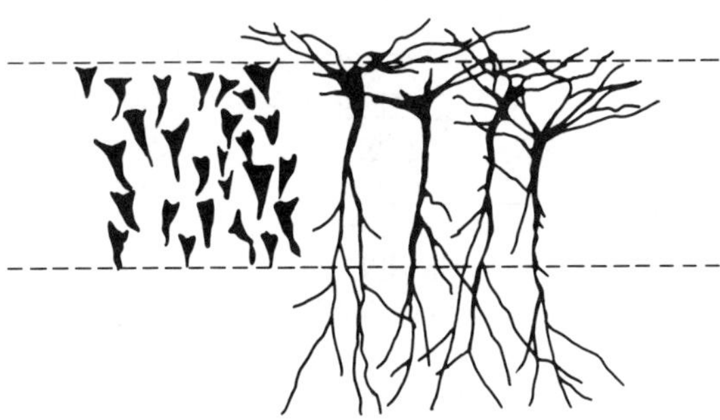

A Organized (normal)

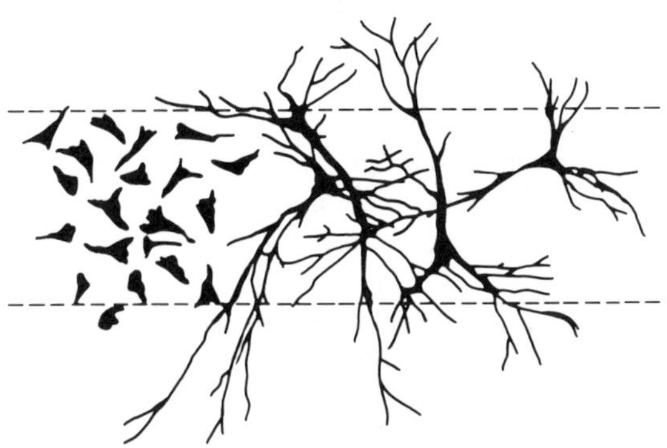

B Disorganized (schizophrenic)

FIGURE 23-5. Examples of pyramidal cell orientation from the hippocampus of *(A)* normal (organized) and *(B)* schizophrenic (disorganized) brains. (After Kovelman and Scheibel, 1984.)

Two Types of Schizophrenia?

The limitations in the effectiveness of neuroleptic drugs in treating schizophrenia, and the evidence of structural abnormalities in the schizophrenic brain led Crow to propose that there may be two distinct pathological syndromes in schizophrenia. The first type (Type I, equivalent to acute schizophrenia) is characterized by positive symptoms including delusions, hallucinations, and thought disorder. The second type (Type II, equivalent to chronic schizophrenia) is characterized by negative symptoms including flattened affect and poverty of speech. Crow proposed that Type I would be associated with dopaminergic abnormality and would be more responsive to neuroleptic medication, whereas Type II would be related to structural changes in the brain. Since chronic amphetamine use has long been known to produce positive schizophrenic symptoms, Crow's hypothesis would explain why amphetamine could produce psychosis in the absence of the structural abnormalities found in many schizophrenic brains. Crow's hypothesis has led to considerable interest, although it is by no means proven.

Neurobiological Hypotheses of Depression

The existence of genetic elements in a large proportion of depressive disorders implies an associated biological abnormality, but no such abnormality has ever been conclusively identified in the brain or body fluids of any depressed person. Evidence favoring a biological abnormality derives largely from studies of the influence of antidepressant drugs on depressive symptoms and neurotransmitters, and from studies of **neuroendocrine** function in depressed individuals.

Neurotransmitters. The most prevalent idea is that depression involves a functional deficiency in monoamines: depression is hypothesized to result from a deficiency of serotonin or norepinephrine or both, and antidepressants work by increasing the availability of these amines. Like the dopamine theory of schizophrenia, the data in support of a monoamine theory of depression are largely circumstantial, and there is the difficulty that antidepressant drugs are very slow to work, even though their action on the monoamine synapse is believed to be rapid. Nevertheless, most authors believe that brain norepinephrinergic and serotoninergic pathways are strongly implicated in the chemical pathology of depressive disorders. The role is not a simple one, however, and cannot be viewed as merely a case of "too little or too much."

Neuroendocrine Function. Both norepinephrine and serotonin modulate the secretion of hormones by the hypothalamus. There are many clinical signs of hypothalamic disturbance in depression, the best established abnormality being an oversecretion of the hormone hydrocortisone (cortisol). Normally, the secretion of hydrocortisone fluctuates, peaking at about 8:00 A.M. and virtually ceasing in the evening. In contrast, about 50% of depressed patients secrete excessive amounts of hydrocortisone (about two times the normal level), especially in the evening. Carroll and his colleagues have shown that whereas normal people or patients with other psychiatric diagnoses show a suppression of hydrocortisone secretion when given dexamethasone, about 40% of depressed people show no suppression at all. The dexamethasone-suppression test (DST) is becoming a standard clinical test for depression and is proving particularly useful because the absence of suppression is a good predictor of positive outcome from antidepressant therapy.

Rhythms and Depression. Physiological functions are known to be *homeostatic,* meaning that behaviors and other physiological processes are switched on and off as they are required. One example of such an organization is **circadian rhythm,** which is a switching on and off of functions over a 24-h cycle. Many bodily functions fluctuate by circadian rhythms, including sleep and waking, temperature, and activity. Jet lag provides an example of what happens when these rhythms become disrupted because it may lead to physical debilitation including irritability, weight loss, and elements of depression. Over the past decade the view has developed that affective disorders may result from a disruption of circadian rhythms. There are now several variations on the details of this idea, but the general concept is that there is some sort of impairment in the efficiency in which sleep and other rhythms are locked together in time, much as in jet lag. The disruption may be caused by either an environmental or physiological event that results in different physiological functions not being switched on as required. The dexamethasone-suppression test is thus seen simply as a measure of one abnormality.

The attraction of this theory is that it is consistent with the growing evidence that there are multiple chemical and physiological abnormalities in depression, especially in endocrine systems that normally cycle. The circadian-rhythm hypothesis suggests that antidepressant medication would have an action on sleep-waking cycles, and they do. One puzzling aspect of antidepressant medication has been the slow latency of a clinical response. Given that various rhythms are likely to respond differently to various antidepressant agents, the slow and unpredictable clinical response might be expected. Furthermore, if there are continuing environmental stimuli that are effective in disrupting the rhythms, one would expect relapse, which is observed. The circadian-rhythm hypothesis is certain to lead to considerable research over the coming years, but it is already having a significant clinical influence, as many psychiatric facilities are opening up units to monitor EEG and other rhythmic activity in depressed patients. (For an excellently readable account of the circadian-rhythm hypothesis, see Healy.)

Cortical Function in Depression. We have seen that there are abnormalities both in monoamine levels and in neuroendocrine function in depressed persons, but we still must consider what effects these abnormalities might have on neocortical function. First, since serotonin is a vasodilator, its absence would be predicted to reduce blood flow because of relative vasoconstriction. It does: both blood-flow and PET studies have shown a bilateral reduction of cerebral activity in depressed persons. Second, diffuse reduction of cerebral activity might be expected to produce a variety of neuropsychological symptoms related to poor cerebral processing throughout the cortex. The extent of the deficit would be revealed by the difficulty of the test, rather than by the specific function assessed. This appears to be the case. Third, since serotonin is thought to play a key role in the sleep-waking cycle, it might be expected that EEG studies would reveal cortical abnormalities in this cycle. They do: Kupfer and Thase have found that slow-wave sleep is abnormal and that the onset of paradoxical sleep (rapid eye movement sleep, or dreaming) is more rapid in depressed people. The researchers believe this measure to be as sensitive as the DST as a clinical test for depression. Further, they believe that the prognosis of effectiveness of any particular antidepressant agent is likely to appear in the EEG before it does so clinically. Finally, it might be predicted that some depressed people would exhibit only regional reduction in cortical activity because of some local disruption of neurotransmitter levels, and thus that there might be different types of depressions characterized by different patterns of cerebral dysfunction. This hypothesis is difficult to test, but studies by Flor-Henry and by Ross and Rush have proposed unique and testable models of this sort, although neither enjoys much empirical support to date.

Summary

Although our understanding of the biological bases of schizophrenia and depression is only at a very elementary level, the available data imply that both disorders have biological correlates that are of particular interest to neuropsychologists. In particular, evidence of frontal-temporal dysfunction in schizophrenia is consistent with neuropsychological theories that these regions are especially important in the control of emotional processes. Although symptoms of schizophrenia can be expected to differ from those resulting from the effects of cortical lesions, it seems reasonable to study schizophrenic patients using the same methods found to be useful with lesion patients. With this in mind, Pittman, Kolb and their colleagues have found reductions in facial expression and spontaneous talking in schizophrenic patients, and Kolb and Taylor have found abnormalities in the interpretation of facial expression in schizophrenic subjects as well. For example, schizophrenic subjects perform as poorly as left frontal lobe patients at the interpretation of the cartoons illustrated in Figure 23-3. (Curiously, they are normal at the matching of facial expressions, much like left temporal lobe subjects.) By studying the effects of both removal (brain lesions) and disruption (schizophrenia) of frontal and temporal zones, it may be possible to better understand the neurological bases of emotional behavior, an understanding that would be of enormous practical benefit in treating people with biologically based disorders of emotional processing.

PSYCHOSURGERY

The debate over the use of surgery to treat emotional disorders has become a contentious issue over the past decade, especially in the United States. We do not wish to enter the debate but rather will describe psychosurgery and its uses. For an excellent discussion of the psychosurgery issue, we recommend the 1980 text by Valenstein, *The Psychosurgery Debate.*

What Is Psychosurgery?

Psychosurgery is defined by Valenstein as destruction of some region in the brain in order to alleviate severe and otherwise intractable psychiatric disorders. In order to distinguish current psychosurgical techniques from earlier and cruder "lobotomy" operations, the term *psychiatric surgery* has been suggested as a substitute by some, although the term refers to the same procedures. Brain surgery intended to repair damage in order to alleviate symptoms resulting from known neurological disease is not considered psychosurgery, even if the patient has severe behavioral and emotional symptoms. Brain surgery to alleviate intractable pain is normally considered to be psychosurgery since the brain operations are performed on normal brain tissue and because serious emotional disturbances often accompany chronic pain.

The belief that mental aberrations are related to disturbances of brain function goes back to primitive peoples. The practice of opening the skull *(trepanning)* for magical-medical purposes was apparently performed extensively over the world dating back at least to about 2000 B.C. Modern psychosurgery is normally traced to the Portuguese neurologist Egas Moniz, who started the prefrontal procedures in 1935. On the basis of studies of a small sample of monkeys and chimpanzees by Jacobsen, Moniz reasoned that destruction of the frontal lobe of psychiatrically ill people might be beneficial. Although he initially used alcohol injected into the frontal lobes to induce a frontal lesion, he soon switched to a technique in which nerve fibers were cut with a special knife called *leukotome* (from the Greek *leuko,* meaning white nerve fibers; *tome,* meaning a cutting instrument). The procedure involved drilling holes over the frontal lobes and inserting a leukotome into the white matter to sever the frontal connections. Later modifications in the procedure were made in the United States by Freeman and Watts, including the Freeman-Watts procedure of drilling the holes in the temples and the lateral transorbital procedure of Freeman in which the leukotome was inserted through the bony orbit above the eyeball. It is impossible to estimate accurately how many psychosurgical procedures were performed worldwide, although Valenstein feels that the best estimate for the United States is about 35,000 between 1936 and 1978.

The introduction of antipsychotic drugs in the mid-1950s led to a sharp reduction in the number of psychosurgical operations, but there still were a significant number of psychiatric patients who were not helped by the drugs. There has thus been a continuing interest in surgical intervention to change behavior, but since the 1960s there has been a change in the nature of the psychosurgical procedures employed, in part because of advances in the neurosciences. There are currently about 12 different targets of psychosurgical operations, which are summarized in Figure 23-6. These procedures generally produce smaller lesions than the original lobotomy-type procedures.

Who Receives Psychosurgery?

According to Valenstein, there is general agreement among psychiatrists and neurosurgeons who recommend or practice psychosurgery about who are the most appropriate patients for these operations. The major group of patients are described as "suffering from very intense and persistent emotional responses." This is taken to include patients suffering from depression, obsessive-compulsive disorders, anxiety, and phobias. Further, there is a group for patients in which psychosurgery is performed for pain symptoms, the pain usually being described as "intense, persistent, crippling, and intractable." Normally, all these disturbances are claimed to be of long duration and resistant to other treatments such as drugs, ECT, and psychotherapy.

It is difficult to estimate the amount of psycho-

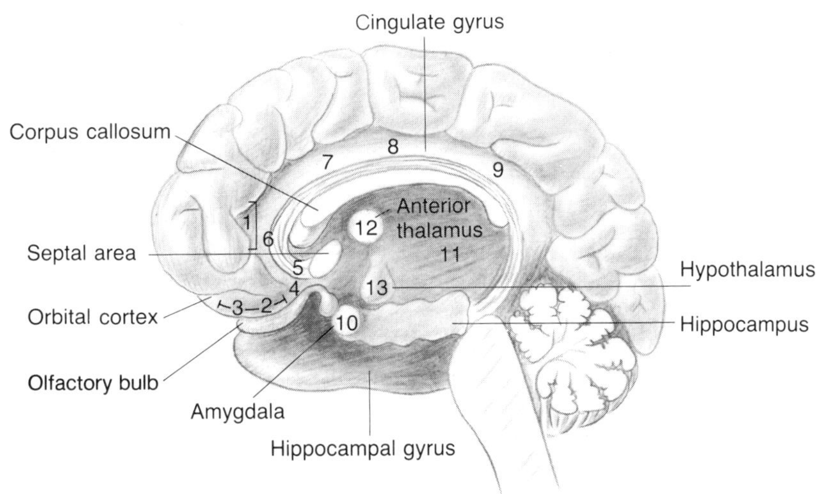

FIGURE 23-6. Approximate targets of psychosurgical operations currently in use. *Frontal lobe procedures.* (1) bimedial leukotomy; (2) yttrium lesions in subcortical white matter; (3) orbital undercutting; (4) bifrontal stereotaxic subcaudate tractotomy; (5) anterior capsulotomy (destruction of fibers of internal capsule); (6) mesoloviotomy (similar to rostral cingulotomy, but lesion invades the genu—"knee"—of the corpus collosum). *Cingulotomies:* (7) anterior cingulotomy; (8) midcingulotomy; (9) posterior cingulotomy. *Amygdalectomy:* (10) amygdalectomy or amygdalotomy. *Thalamotomies:* (11) thalamotomy of the dorsomedial, centromedian, or parafascicular nuclei; (12) anterior thalamotomy. *Hypothalamotomy:* (13) section of the posterior, ventromedial, or lateral hypothalamus. (After Valenstein, 1980.)

surgery currently performed. Valenstein estimates that 141 neurosurgeons in the United States performed approximately 400 operations per year between 1971 and 1973, a figure that has declined steadily since then. In England, approximately 200 to 250 psychosurgical procedures have been performed per year between 1970 and 1977—a figure about twice as high as in the United States. Less psychosurgery seems to be performed in Canada, however, the rate being about one-half that in the United States.

Comment

The effectiveness of psychosurgery as a treatment for psychiatric disorders is not easily discernible. The United States has formed a commission (the National Commission for the Protection of Human Subjects of Biomedical and Behavioral Research) with the mandate of studying psychosurgery and making recommendations to the government regarding its further practice in the country. The differences of opinion are large and the necessary scientific data are few—making any decision regarding psychosurgery very difficult indeed. For the neuropsychologist, an important question must be the issue of the cognitive price to be paid for surgical destruction of normally functioning brain tissue. We have seen throughout this text that virtually any cortical damage is associated with cognitive loss, often of an unexpected nature. There are now two extensive neuropsychological studies (see Corkin, and Mirsky and Orzack) that have shown there are surprisingly few deficits in cognitive functioning after cingulotomy, but we are unaware of any similar studies of patients undergoing other types of psychosurgical procedure. Thus, although there may be claims that psychosurgery is effective as a treatment of various disturbances, the cognitive price paid by the patients remains unstudied. As we have noted before, absence of evidence does not constitute evidence of absence. At present, we believe that with the possible exception of psychosurgery for the relief of chronic pain, there is little justification for the use of psychosurgical procedures until more is known about them. As we shall discuss in relation to recovery of function from brain lesions (Chapter 25), the processes following brain lesions are extremely complex and poorly understood. Changes may continue for years after brain damage (e.g., calcification), and so follow-up studies must do careful analyses of patients over the course of years. We are inclined to believe that for many patients psychosurgical procedures may be equivalent to using a sledgehammer for a hangnail. It may be a "cure," but the cost may not be worth it.

The psychosurgery question has broader implications. These have been spelled out in detail by Valenstein and are worth considering because they apply to many treatment strategies involving mental and psychiatric health. Central among the important questions is when is it permissible to institute or experiment with a new treatment. Psychosurgical treatment was instituted and promoted as a treatment without adequate background animal research. Treatment and patient selection were not subject to screening by any ethical committees. Follow-up studies, when done, were usually superficial and lacked scientific rigor. Nevertheless, in the view of the treatment-founding experimenters, competitive therapies and the general prognosis for patients was sufficiently dismal to warrant the use of psychosurgery. This dilemma is still with us, but now it additionally applies to the chronic administration of drugs, the use of electroconvulsive shock therapy, and the developing use of brain grafts for the treatment of degenerative brain disorders.

IS THERE AN ANATOMY OF EMOTION?

Having considered the changes in emotional behavior that follow brain damage and that are found in different diseases of the brain, we must ask whether it is yet possible to construct an anatomical circuit that will account for the observed phenomena. We began the chapter by considering the question "what is an emotion?". We noted that most theorists have concluded that emotion includes an autonomic component, an overt behavioral component, and a cognitive component. Neuropsychological studies of emotion in humans have ignored the autonomic component, looked only superficially at the overt component, and focused upon certain aspects of the cognitive component. The evidence from studies of the behavior of brain-damaged subjects shows that both left and right frontal and temporal lobe injuries alter behavior, but in dissociable ways. In contrast to studies of memory or language, there is an asymmetry in the brain's control of affect, but it is not simply a verbal-nonverbal distinction. Studies of cognitive aspects of emotion have pointed to a dominant role of the right hemisphere in the processing of faces and facial expression, as well as in the processing of prosody. There has been little study of the subjective aspect of emotions in cognitive studies, however. Studies of schizophrenic and depressed patients have shown a relationship between overt behavior and some cognitive measures and suggested neurochemical and structural changes, but it is difficult to combine these results with those from brain-damaged patients, except that symptoms resemble those seen in frontal or temporal lobe patients.

In summary, it does not seem possible to provide a theory of the anatomical circuit of emotions at present. Although it is likely that the right hemisphere plays a different role from that of the left in certain emotional processes, especially cognitive processes, the nature of this difference is unclear. The left-right distinction is certainly not as distinct as it is for language, and it would be a naive mistake to suggest that the right hemisphere is emotional and the left verbal. Furthermore, one of the principles of cortical organization is that functions are localized. Thus, even if the right hemisphere plays a special role in some emotional processes, we must specify the anatomical focus and the precise nature of this function. This will require not only better behavioral-pathological correlations on large samples of subjects, but it will require a better identification of the components of the components of emotional processing that are being affected. This is a tall order and represents a significant challenge for future studies.

REFERENCES

Aitken, P.G. Cortical control of conditioned and spontaneous vocal behavior in rhesus monkeys. *Brain and Language* 13:171–184, 1981.

Andreasen, N., H. A. Nasrallah, V. Dunn, S. C. Olson, W. M. Grove, J. C. Ehrhardt, J. A. Coffman, and J. H. W. Crossett. Structural abnormalities in the frontal system in schizophrenia. *Archives of General Psychiatry* 43:136–144, 1986.

Bear, D. M., and P. Fedio. Quantitative analysis of interictal behavior in temporal lobe epilepsy. *Archives of Neurology* 34:454–467, 1977.

Benes, F. M., J. Davidson, and E. D. Bird. Quantitative cytoarchitectural studies of the cerebral cortex of schizophrenics. *Archives of General Psychiatry* 43:31–35, 1986.

Benson, D. F., and D. Blumer, eds. *Psychiatric Aspects of Neurological Disease.* New York: Grune & Stratton, 1975.

Bihrle, A. M., H. H. Brownell, J. A. Powelson, and H. Gardner. Comprehension of humorous and nonhumorous materials by left and right brain-damaged patients. *Brain and Cognition* 5:399–411, 1986.

Blumer, D. Temporal lobe epilepsy and its psychiatric significance. In D. F. Blumer and D. Benson, eds. *Psychiatric Aspects of Neurological Disease.* New York: Grune & Stratton, 1975.

Borod, J. C., E. Koff, M. Perlman Lorch, and M. Nicholas. The expression and perception of facial emotion in brain-damaged patients. *Neuropsychologia* 24:169–180, 1986.

Bowden, D. M., P. S. Goldman, H. E. Rosvold, and R. L. Greenstreet. Free behavior of rhesus monkeys following lesions of the dorsolateral and orbital prefrontal cortex in infancy. *Experimental Brain Research* 12:265–274, 1971.

Bowers, D., H. B. Coslett, R. M. Bauer, L. J. Speedie, and K. M. Heilman. Comprehension of emotional prosody following unilateral hemispheric lesions: Processing defect versus distraction defect. *Neuropsychologia* 25:317–328, 1987.

Brady, J. V. Emotional behavior. *Handbook of Physiology* Vol. III:1529–1552, 1960.

Brody, E. B., and H. E. Rosvold. Influence of prefrontal lobotomy on social interaction in a monkey group. *Psychosomatic Medicine* 14:405–415, 1952.

Brown, R., N. Colter, J. A. Corsellis, T. J. Crow, C. D. Frith, R. Jagoe, E. C. Johnstone. Postmortem evidence of structural brain changes in schizophrenia. *Archives of General Psychiatry* 43:35–42, 1986.

Brown, S., and E. A. Schaefer. An investigation into the functions of the occipital and temporal lobe of the monkey's brain. *Philosophical Transactions of the Royal Society, part B* 179:303–327, 1888.

Brown, W. A., R. Johnston, and D. Mayfield. The 24-hour dexamethasone suppression test in a clinical setting: Relationship to diagnosis, symptoms, and response to treatment. *American Journal of Psychiatry* 136:543–547, 1979.

Brownell, H. H., D. Michel, J. Powelson, and H. Gardner. Surprise but not coherence: Sensitivity to verbal humor in right-hemisphere patients. *Brain and Language* 18:20–27, 1983.

Bruyer, R. Asymmetry of facial expression in brain damaged subjects. *Neuropsychologia* 19:615–623, 1981.

Bruyer, R., ed. *The Neuropsychology of Face Perception and Facial Expression.* Hillsdale, NJ: Lawrence Erlbaum Associates, 1986.

Bryden, M. P. *Laterality: Functional Asymmetry in the Intact Brain.* New York: Academic Press, 1982.

Buchtel, H., F. Campari, C. de Risio, and R. Rota. Hemispheric differences in discriminative action time to facial expressions. *Italian Journal of Psychology* 5:159–169, 1978.

Buch, R., and R. J. Duffy. Nonverbal communication of affect in brain-damaged patients. *Cortex* 16:351–362, 1980.

Butter, C. M., and D. R. Snyder. Alterations in aversive and aggressive behaviors following orbital frontal lesions in rhesus monkeys. *Acta Neurobiologiae Experimentalis* 32:525–565, 1972.

Campbell, R. Asymmetries in interpreting and expressing a posed facial expression. *Cortex* 14:327–342, 1978.

Campbell, R. The lateralisation of emotion: A critical review. *International Journal of Psychology* 17:211–229, 1982.

Carlsson, A. Does dopamine have a role in schizophrenia? *Biological Psychiatry* 13:3–21, 1978.

Carmon, A., and I. Nachshon. Ear asymmetry in perception of emotional nonverbal stimuli. *Acta Psychologia* 37:351–357, 1973.

Carroll, B. J., G. C. Curtis, and J. Mendels. Neuroendocrine regulation in depression. II. Discrimination of depressed from non-depressed patients. *Archives of General Psychiatry* 33:1051–1058, 1976.

Chaurasia, B. D., and H. K. Goswami. Functional asymmetry in the face. *Acta Anatomica* 91:154–160, 1975.

Chorover, S. L. The psychosurgery evaluation studies and their impact on the commission's report. In E. Valenstein, ed. *The Psychosurgery Debate.* San Francisco: W. H. Freeman, 1980.

Cicone, M., W. Wapner, and H. Gardner. Sensitivity to emotional expression and situations in organic patients. *Cortex* 16:145–158, 1980.

Corkin, S. A prospective study of cingulotomy. In E. Valenstein, ed. *The Psychosurgery Debate.* San Francisco: W. H. Freeman, 1980.

Crow, T. J. Neurohumoral and structural changes in schizophrenia: Two dimensions of pathology. *Progress in Brain Research* 55:407–417, 1982.

Crow, T. J., and E. C. Johnstone. Schizophrenia: Nature of the disease process and its biological correlates. *Handbook of Physiology,* vol 5. Bethesda, MD: American Physiological Society, 1987.

Danly, M., and B. Shapiro. Speech prosody in Broca's aphasia. *Brain and Language* 16:171–190, 1982.

Davis, K. L., and P. Berger. Pharmacological investigations of the cholinergic imbalance hypotheses of movement disorders and psychosis. *Biological Psychiatry* 13:23–49, 1978.

Deets, A. C., H. F. Harlow, S. D. Singh, and A. J. Blomquist. Effects of bilateral lesions on the frontal granular cortex of the social behavior of rhesus monkeys. *Journal of Comparative and Physiological Psychology* 72:452–461, 1970.

DeKosky, S. T., K. M. Heilman, D. Bowers, and E. Valenstein. Recognition and discrimination of emotional faces and pictures. *Brain and Language* 9:206–214, 1980.

Dicks, D., R. E. Myers, and A. Kling. Uncus and amygdala lesions: Effects on social behavior in the free-ranging monkey. *Science* 165:69–17, 1969.

Dimond, S. J., and L. Farrington. Emotional response to films shown to the right or left hemisphere of the brain measured by heart rate. *Acta Psychologia* 41:255–260, 1977.

Dimond, S. J., L. Farrington, and P. Johnson. Differing emotional response from right and left hemispheres. *Nature* 261:690–692, 1976.

Dunbar, H. F. *Emotions and Bodily Changes,* 4th ed. New York: Columbia, 1954.

Ekman, P., W. V. Friesen, and P. Ellsworth. *Emotion in the Human Face.* New York: Pergamon, 1972.

Farley, I. J., K. S. Price, E. McCullough, W. Deck, W. Hordynsku, and O. Hornykiewicz. Norepinephrine levels in chronic paranoid schizophrenia: Above-normal levels in limbic forebrain. *Science* 200:456–458, 1978.

Fedio, P., and A. Martin. Ideative-emotive behavioral characteristics of patients following left or right temporal lobectomy. *Epilepsia* 254:S117–S130, 1983.

Flor-Henry, P. On certain aspects of the localization of the cerebral systems in regulating and determining emotion. *Biological Psychiatry* 14:677–698, 1979.

Flor-Henry, P., and Z. J. Koles. EEG studies in depression, mania and normals: Evidence for partial shifts of laterality in the affective psychoses. *Advances in Biological Psychiatry* 4:21–43, 1980.

Franzen, E. A., and R. E. Myers. Neural control of social behavior: Prefrontal and anterior temporal cortex. *Neuropsychologia* 11:141–157, 1973.

Gainotti, G. Réactions "catastrophiques" et manifèstations d'indifférence au cours des atteintes cérébrales. *Neuropsychologia* 7:195–204, 1969.

Gainotti, G. Emotional behavior and hemispheric side of the lesion. *Cortex* 8:41–55, 1972.

Gardner, H., P. K. Ling, L. Flamm, and J. Silverman. Comprehension and appreciation of humorous material following brain damage. *Brain* 98:399–412, 1975.

Gazzaniga, M., and J. E. Le Doux. *The Integrated Mind.* New York: Plenum, 1978.

Goldstein, K. *The Organism: A Holistic Approach to Biology, Derived from Pathological Data in Man.* New York: American Book, 1939.

Grafman, J., S. C. Vance, H. Weingartner, A. M. Salazar, and D. Amin. The effects of lateralized frontal lesions on mood regulation. *Brain* 109:1127–1148, 1986.

Haggard, M. P., and A. M. Parkinson. Stimulus and task factors as determinants of ear advantages. *Quarterly Journal of Experimental Psychology* 23:168–177, 1971.

Haug, J. O. Pneumoencephalographic studies in mental disease. *Acta Psychiatrica Neurologia Scandinavia* (suppl. 165) 38:1–104, 1962.

Healy, D. Rhythm and blues. Neurochemical, neuropharmacological and neuropsychological implications of a hypothesis of circadian rhythm dysfunction in the affective disorders. *Psychopharmacology* 93:271–285, 1987.

Hécaen, H., J. de Ajuriaguerra, and J. Massonet. Les troubles visuo-constructifs par lesion parieto-occipitale droite. *Encephalé* 40:122–179, 1951.

Heilman, K., M. R. Scholes, and R. T. Watson. Auditory affective agnosia. *Journal of Neurology, Neurosurgery and Psychiatry* 38:69–72, 1975.

Horel, J. A., E. G. Keating, and L. J. Misantone. Partial Klüver-Bucy syndrome produced by destroying temporal neocortex or amygdala. *Brain Research* 94:347–359, 1975.

Kent, R. D., and J. C. Rosenbek. Prosodic disturbance and neurological lesion. *Brain and Language* 15:259–291, 1982.

King, F. L., and D. Kimura. Left-ear superiority in dichotic perception of vocal nonverbal sounds. *Canadian Journal of Psychology* 26:111–116, 1972.

Klüver, H., and P. C. Bucy. Preliminary analysis of the temporal lobes in monkeys. *Archives of Neurology and Psychiatry* 42:979–1000, 1939.

Kolb, B., and B. Milner. Observations on spontaneous facial expression after focal cerebral excisions and after intracarotid injection of sodium Amytal. *Neuropsychologia* 19:505–514, 1981.

Kolb, B., and L. Taylor. Affective behavior in patients with localized cortical excisions: Role of lesion site and side. *Science* 214:89–91, 1981.

Kolb, B., and L. Taylor. Facial expression and the neocortex. *Society for Neuroscience Abstracts* 14:219, 1988.

Kolb, B., and I. Q. Whishaw. Performance of schizophrenic patients on tests sensitive to left or right frontal, temporal, or parietal function in neurological patients. *Journal of Nervous and Mental Disease* 171:435–443, 1983.

Kovelman, J. A., and A. B. Scheibel. A neurohistologic correlate of schizophrenia. *Biological Psychiatry* 19:1601–1621, 1984.

Kupfer, D. J. Toward a unified view of affective disorders. In M. Zales, ed. *Affective and Schizophrenic Disorders.* New York: Brunner/Mazel, 1983.

Kupfer, D. J., and M. E. Thase. The use of the sleep laboratory in the diagnosis of affective disorders. *Psychiatric Clinics of North America* 6:3–25, 1983.

LeDoux, J. E. Cognition and emotion. In M. S. Gazzaniga, ed. *Handbook of Cognitive Neuroscience.* New York, Plenum, 1984.

Ley, R. G., and M. P. Bryden. Hemispheric differences in processing emotions and faces. *Brain and Language* 7:127–138, 1979.

Ley, R. G., and M. P. Bryden. A dissociation of right and left hemispheric effects for recognizing emotional tone and verbal content. *Brain and Cognition* 1:3–9, 1982.

MacLean, P. D. The midline frontolimbic cortex and the evolution of crying and laughter. In E. Perecman, ed. *The Frontal Lobes Revisited.* New York: IBRN Press, 1987.

Malamud, N. Organic brain disease mistaken for psychiatric disorder. In D. R. Benson and D. Blumer, eds. *Psychiatric Aspects of Neurological Disease.* New York: Grune & Stratton, 1975.

Marlowe, W. B., E. L. Mancall, and J. J. Thomas. Complete Klüver-Bucy syndrome in man. *Cordex* 11:53–59, 1975.

Mathew, R. J., J. S. Meyer, D. J. Francis, K. M. Semchuk, K. Mortel, and J. L. Claghorn. Cerebral blood flow in depression. *American Journal of Psychiatry* 137:1449–1450, 1980.

McHugh, P. R., and M. F. Folstein. Psychiatric syndromes of Huntington's chorea. In D. F. Benson and D. Blumer, eds., *Psychiatric Aspects of Neurological Disease.* New York: Grune & Stratton, 1975.

Milner, B. Brain mechanisms suggested by studies of the temporal lobes. In C. H. Millikan and F. L. Darley, eds., *Brain Mechanisms Underlying Speech and Language.* New York: Grune & Stratton, 1967.

Mirsky, A. F., and M. H. Orzack. Two retrospective studies of psychosurgery. In E. Valenstein, ed. *The Psychosurgery Debate.* San Francisco: W. H. Freeman, 1980.

Moscovitch, M., and J. Olds. Asymmetries in spontaneous facial expressions and their possible relation to hemispheric specialization. *Neuropsychologia* 20:71–82, 1982.

Myers, R. E. Role of the prefrontal and anterior temporal cortex in social behavior and affect in monkeys. *Acta Neurobiologiae Experimentalis* 32:567–579, 1972.

Myers, R. E., and C. Swett. Social behavior deficits of free-ranging monkeys after anterior-temporal cortex removal: A preliminary report. *Brain Research* 18:551–556, 1970.

Myers, R. E., C. Swett, and M. Miller. Loss of social group affinities following prefrontal lesions in free-ranging macaques. *Brain Research* 64:257–269, 1973.

Papez, J. W. A proposed mechanism of emotion. *Archives of Neurology and Psychiatry* 38:725–744, 1937.

Peters, M., and D. Ploog. Frontal lobe lesions and social behavior in the squirrel monkey *(Saimiri)*: A pilot study. *Acta Biologica Medica (Germany)* 35:1317–1326, 1976.

Pitman, R. K., B. Kolb, S. P. Orr, and M. M. Singh. Ethnological study of facial behavior in nonparanoid and paranoid schizophrenic patients. *American Journal of Psychiatry* 144:99–102, 1987.

Price, B. H., and M. Mesulam. Psychiatric manifestations of right hemisphere infarctions. *Journal of Nervous and Mental Disease* 173:610–614, 1984.

Raleigh, M. J., and H. D. Steklis. Effects of orbitofrontal and temporal neocortical lesions on the affiliative behavior of vervet monkeys *(Ceropithecus aethiops sabaeus). Experimental Neurology* 73:378–389, 1981.

Risberg, J. Regional cerebral blood flow measurements by 133 Xe-inhalation: Methodology and applications in neuropsychology and psychiatry. Brain and Language 9:9–34, 1980.

Robinson, R. G., K. Kubos, L. B. Starr, K. Rao, and T. R. Price. Mood disorders in stroke patients. *Brain* 107:81–93, 1984.

Robinson, R. G., and B. Szetela. Mood change following left hemispheric brain injury. *Annals of Neurology* 9:447–453, 1981.

Ross, E. D. The aprosodias: Functional-anatomical organization of the affective components of language in the right hemisphere. *Archives of Neurology* 38:561–569, 1981.

Ross, E. D., and A. J. Rush. Diagnosis and neuroanatomical correlates of depression in brain-damaged patients. *Archives of General Psychiatry* 38:1344–1354, 1981.

Rossi, G. F., and G. Rosandini. Experimental analysis of cerebral dominance in man. In C. H. Millikan and F. L. Darley, eds. *Brain Mechanisms Underlying Speech and Language.* New York: Grune & Stratton, 1967.

Rovetta, P. Discussion of paper "Amytal intracarotides per lo studio della dominanza emisferica." *Rivista di Neurologia* 30:460–470, 1960.

Sachar, E. J. Psychobiology of schizophrenia. In E. R. Kandel and J. H. Schwartz, eds. *Principles of Neural Science.* New York: Elsevier North-Holland, 1981.

Sachdev, H. S., and S. G. Waxman. Frequency of hypergraphia in temporal lobe epilepsy: An index of interictal behaviour syndrome. *Journal of Neurology, Neurosurgery, and Psychiatry* 44:358–360, 1981.

Sackeim, H. A., M. S. Greenberg, A. L. Weiman, R. C. Gur, J. P. Hungerbuhler, and N. Geschwind. Hemispheric asymmetry in the expression of positive and negative emotions. *Archives of Neurology* 39:210–218, 1982.

Sackheim, H., R. S. Gur, and M. Saucy. Emotions are expressed more intensely on the left side of the face. *Science* 202:434–436, 1978.

Safer, M., and H. Leventhal. Ear differences in evaluating emotional tones of voice and verbal content. *Journal of Experimental Psychology: Human Perception and Performance* 3:75–82, 1977.

Schwartz, G. E., R. J. Davidson, and F. Maer. Right hemisphere lateralization for emotion in the human brain. Interactions with cognition. *Science* 190:186–288, 1975.

Shapiro, B. E., and Danly, M. The role of the right hemisphere in the control of speech prosody in propositional and effective contexts. *Brain and Language* 25:19–36, 1985.

Silberman, E. K., and H. Weingartner. Hemispheric lateralization of functions related to emotion. *Brain and Cognition* 5:322–353, 1986.

Snyder, D. R. Social and emotional behavior in monkeys following orbital frontal ablations. Unpublished Ph.D. Thesis, University of Michigan, 1971.

Snyder, S. H. *Biological Aspects of Mental Disorder.* New York: Academic Press, 1980.

Suomi, S. J., H. F. Harlow, and J. K. Lewis. Effect of bilateral frontal lobectomy on social preferences of rhesus monkeys. *Journal of Comparative and Physiological Psychology* 70:448–453, 1970.

Terzian, H. Behavioral and EEG effects of intracarotid sodium Amytal injection. *Acta Neurochirurgica* 12:230–239, 1964.

Thorne, B. M. Brain lesions and affective behavior in primates. A selected review. *Journal of General Psychology* 86:153–162, 1972.

Tompkins, C. A., and C. A. Mateer. Right hemisphere appreciation of intonational and linguistic indications of affect. *Brain and Language* 24:185–203, 1985.

Tucker, D. M. Lateral brain function, emotion, and conceptualization. *Psychological Bulletin* 89:19–46, 1981.

Tucker, D. M., R. T. Watson, and K. M. Heilman. Discrimination and evocation of affectively intoned speech in patients with right parietal disease. *Neurology* 27:947–950, 1977.

Valenstein, E. S., ed. *The Psychosurgery Debate.* San Francisco: W. H. Freeman, 1980.

Valenstein, E. S. *Great and Desperate Cures.* New York: Basic Books, 1986.

Van Pragag, H. M. Significance of biochemical parameters in the diagnosis, treatment and prevention of depressive disorders. *Biological Psychiatry* 12:101–131, 1977.

Watson, S. J., P. A. Berger, H. Akil, M. J. Mills, and J. D. Barchas. Effects of naloxone on schizophrenia: Reduction in hallucinations in a subpopulation of subjects. *Science* 201:73–76, 1978.

Waxman, S. G., and N. Geschwind. Hypergraphia in temporal lobe epilepsy. *Neurology* 24:629–636, 1974.

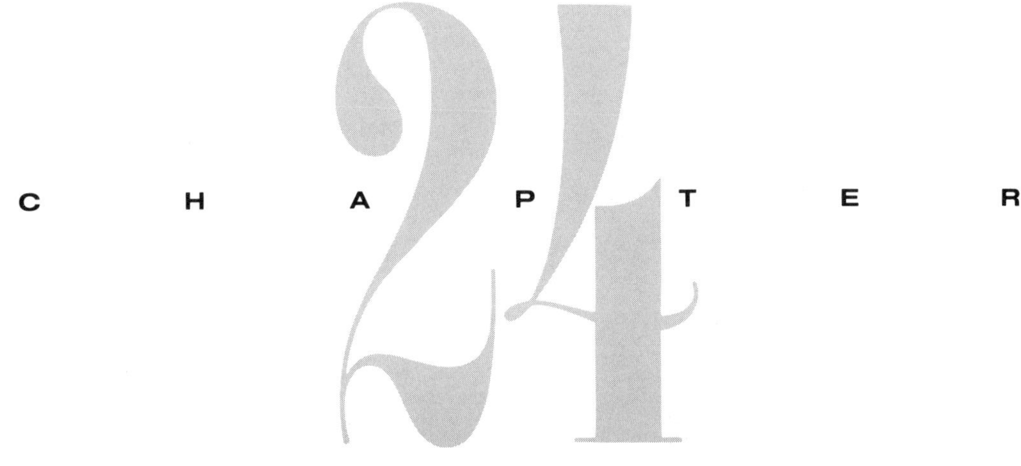

CHAPTER 24

SPATIAL BEHAVIOR

There is the well-known story of the rambler who, making his way to Down, became lost. Meeting a farmer he asks if the farmer knows where Down is.

"Yes, it's over yonder," says the farmer.

"And how do I get there?" asks the rambler.

"You can't get there from here," says the farmer.

An attempt to deliver a comprehensive account of space may leave us in much the same position as the rambler. The concept of "space" has many interpretations that are not equivalent. Our body occupies space, it moves through space, it interacts with things in space, and it can mentally rotate and manipulate representations of space. Other objects also occupy space and maintain relations in space with one another and with us. Philosophers have asked whether objects exist without space, or conversely, whether space exists without objects. They also ask whether space is a feature of the universe or merely a creation of our brain? How do the concepts of space develop as humans grow from infancy? Small animals' (e.g., dogs, cats, and children) representations of space must be very different from that of airline pilots. What further complicates the issue is that many of the elements that can be subsumed under the concept "space" fit equally well in other domains, for example, as sensory abilities, memory or attention processes, or motor behaviors. It is this diversity that no doubt led Ratcliff to comment at the end of a 1982 review, "This has been a selective and highly speculative review and its conclusions are certainly incomplete and quite probably wrong." (p. 325) In this chapter we will suggest that there are a number of spatial systems, each with a separate neural representation. For more detailed summaries of information on spatial behavior, see the excellent and comprehensive texts by de Renzi (1982), by O'Keefe and Nadel, and by Potegal.

BACKGROUND

In modern accounts of cerebral organization it is assumed that spatial processing is a special function of the right hemisphere, but it is only since about 1960 that this view has gained widespread acceptance. John Hughlings-Jackson was the first to propose that the right hemisphere might have some special perceptual function to complement the language functions of the left hemisphere. In his famous 1874 paper, "On the Nature of the Duality of the Brain," he predicted that a person with damage restricted to the posterior part of the right hemisphere would have a distinctive syndrome.

> The patient would have difficulty in recognizing things; he would have difficulty in relating what had occurred, not from lack of words, but from a prior inability to revive images of persons, objects and places, of which the words are symbols. . . . He could not put before himself ideal images of places one after another; could not re-see where he had been, and could not therefore tell of it in words. (Taylor, 1932, p. 144)

Hughlings-Jackson was proposing a spatial-perceptual function for the right hemisphere, although he admitted that the evidence for his position was not strong, remarking that, "as will be seen, my facts are very few." (ibid., p. 145) A series of papers by a number of investigators between 1876 and 1905 described various cases with spatial-perceptual difficulties, confirming Jackson's view that such disorders exist. Although most of these cases appeared to have bilateral damage, rather than right posterior damage, a view nonetheless persisted at the turn of the century that the right hemisphere might have a special role in the mediation of spatial thinking.

World War I led to further advances in the understanding of spatial disturbances accompanying brain injury, but the possibility that there was an association between spatial deficits and right hemisphere damage was largely ignored. By 1950, a large number of "spatial deficits" had been described (see Table 24-1), but the main point that had escaped notice was the asymmetrical representation of spatial function in the two hemispheres, perhaps because most of the published reports were single-case studies, which could be easily discounted. It was the systematic studies of Zangwill

TABLE 24-1. Summary of types of "spatial" deficits described in the clinical literature

Behavior	Basic reference
Impaired eye movements to points in space	Balint, 1909; Tyler, 1968
Poor localization of visual, auditory, or tactile stimuli in space	Head, 1920; Shankweiler, 1951; Holmes, 1919
Misreaching for objects	Brain, 1941
Neglect for left hemispace	Brain, 1941; Oxbury et al., 1974
Right-left confusion	Benton, 1959
Constructional apraxia	Benton, 1979
Amnesia for routes and locations	Paterson and Zangwill, 1944
Impaired performance on mazes	Corkin, 1965; Milner, 1965
Defective locomotion in space	Semmes et al., 1963
Poor drawing	McFie and Zangwill, 1960
Impaired performance at tests of mental spatial transformations (geometry, mazes, mental rotation, etc.)	DeRenzi, 1982
Inability to determine visual or tactile line orientation	Benton et al., 1978; DeRenzi, et al., 1971
Defective shape discrimination	DeRenzi and Scotti, 1969

and of Hécaen, and their coworkers in the 1950s that forced a reexamination of the role of the right hemisphere in spatial performance. There now is little doubt that the right hemisphere has a selective role in spatial behavior, but certain disorders of spatial processing are observed in people with damage to the left hemisphere or with bilateral damage.

THE ORGANIZATION OF SPATIAL BEHAVIOR

Position, Cue, and Place Responses

One way of dividing spatial activities is in terms of the sensory-motor responses that people and animals make when they move around their environments. O'Keefe and Nadel have classified these behaviors into three types: position, cue, and place responses.

Position Responses. These are movements made with the body or self used as a reference. They include such acts as turning to the left or right, moving a limb or body part. They require no external cues for their performance. A common example of a position response would include always turning left when entering a given door, automatically putting objects such as keys on a hook or table, and characteristic expression, gesture, or utterances. Once the movements are acquired, they are performed almost automatically and without conscious monitoring. Position responses are also referred to as *egocentric* in the sense that they are made with respect to the person's own body.

Cue Responses. These movements are directed by a particular cue. They include such acts as walking toward or away from an object, following an odor or sound, and reaching to pick up a visible object. No other cues are necessary for the response, and generally changes in **stimulus gradient** (the sound gets louder when approached) are sufficient to direct a movement. Salmon that select appropriate rivers and swim to their spawning ground are thought to do so using olfactory cue responses. Moths that fly to light are thought to be making visual cue responses. When we move toward an object such as a tree, house, or mountain we are making cue responses.

Place Responses. These movements take a person to a particular location or object, which may even be hidden from view. Usually the relational properties of surrounding cues, no one of which is necessary, guide movement. The cues need to be far enough away that they change relationship with each other (from the point of view of the traveler) sufficiently slowly that the viewer can orient using them. A common example of use of a place response would be that made by an individual who parks a car in an empty parking lot only to come back and find the parking lot full and the car hidden. The person might nevertheless walk to the car quite accurately by remembering where the car was in relation to the size of the lot and surrounding buildings. An interesting feature of place responses is that they seem to be acquired effortlessly and latently (without conscious effort). For example, a person may notice a screwdriver on a counter without thinking much about it. Sometime later when it is needed the previous experience will be recalled and the object retrieved.

These different "strategies" are used routinely in everyday life, and they may be used concurrently or sequentially. In order to study their use, researchers design tasks that force the use of one or another strategy so that it can be studied in isolation. Figure 24-1 illustrates a number of tasks used to study the spatial navigation strategies of the rat. Part *D* of the figure illustrates a typical research room with a rich array of visual cues including cupboards, pictures, windows, and so forth. The various "mazes" illustrated in *A, B,* and *C* can replace the swimming pool that is in the room. The mazes are, *A:* the Olton Eight-Arm Maze, *B:* the

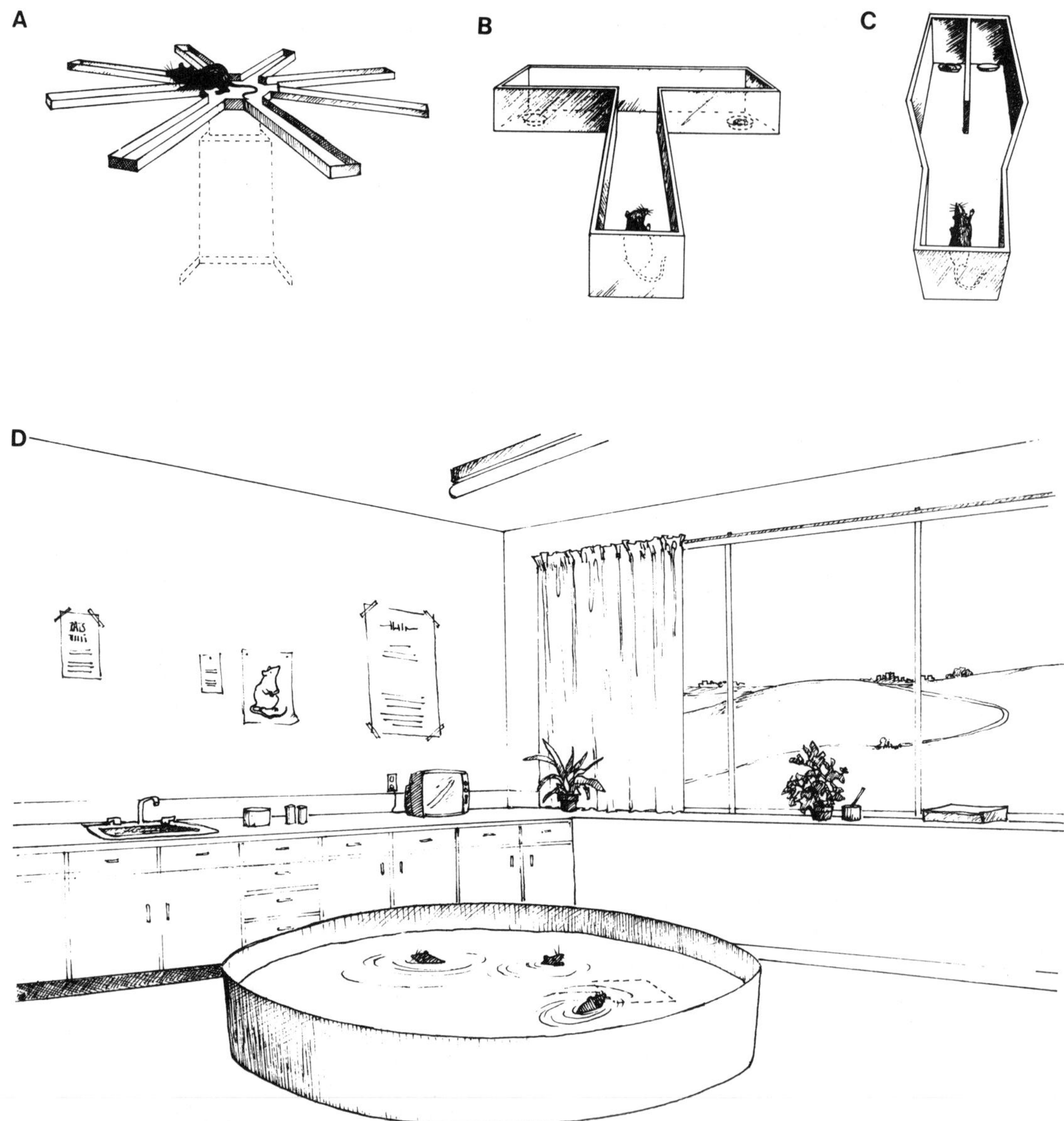

FIGURE 24-1. Tasks used to study spatial behavior in rodents. *A.* Olton's Radial-Arm Maze. *B.* T-maze. *C.* Grice Box. *D.* Morris Water Task. The radial-arm maze was designed as a test of foraging behavior in animals by Olton. The rat must learn which alleys contain food and which alleys have been visited on a given day. The Grice Box is a test of left-right differentiation. The food is placed in one alley until the animal has learned its location, then the position of the food is reserved to the other alley. The Morris Water Task requires the animal to learn the location of a submerged, hidden platform. The only cue to the position of the platform is its spatial relation to cues about the room. All of the mazes are usually used in open rooms in which the animals can use the many surrounding cues as aids to orientation.

T-maze, *C:* the Grice Box, and *D:* the Morris Swimming Pool. (Rats are excellent swimmers and because of their small size, which leaves them at risk of losing normal body temperature if they stay in water for long, are highly motivated to escape from water). Position response can be elicited in all of the mazes. For example position responses may be used by a rat if it is required always to turn right to find food in the dryland mazes or to turn right to find a hidden platform located to the right of a start point in the swimming pool. Cue responses can be studied by marking the correct arm of the mazes with a distinctive cue or by placing a visible platform in the swimming pool. Place responses can be elicited by having the target, food, or the hidden platform in a location that can only be identified in relation to surrounding room cues. For example, food could always be located on the ends of a set of four arms on the eight-arm maze. To perform correctly, an animal must enter only those arms. In the swimming pool, the rat is released from different points in the pool and can only swim directly to the hidden platform if it can identify its location in relation to surrounding room cues. Once rats are trained on a task, probes can be used to find out how they make their responses. For example, if a rat is given food in the right arm in the T-maze, the strategy it uses to get there can be probed by turning the maze 180°. If the rat turns right, it must have solved the original problem using a position response. If it turns left, it must be using a place response because it is no longer turning right in relation to its own body but is locating the food using its relation to surrounding room cues. Note that the food remains in the same place in the room even though the maze is moved. Many more imaginative tests can be used with these mazes. Surrounding cues can be moved or removed, animals can be trained in one location and moved to another, and animals can be subjected to a variety of experimental treatments, tested at different ages, and so on. Interestingly, earlier in this century it was thought that animals like rats learned mazes by making position responses. Tolman, however, suggested that rats and humans probably create spatial maps of their environment and solved maze tasks using place responses. Recent work with the Olton and Morris Mazes has demonstrated that rats can learn place response in a single trial (as quickly as humans) and remember it for days. Sherry has demonstrated that food-storing birds can remember thousands of locations in which they have previously stored food. Further testament to the power of place ability comes from everyday experiences of students. We can often remember the location in a book that we read a passage even though our retention of the content of the passage may be negligible.

Similar test arrangements have been devised to study spatial abilities in primates and people, except the procedures have been tailored to each species' abilities. As an example, in Acredolo's Test, children are brought into a small, nondistinctive room that has a door at one end, a window at the other end, and a table along one wall. They are walked to a corner of the table and blindfolded. While blindfolded, they are walked in a circuitous route back to the door or to the window, the blindfold is removed and they are asked to return to the point at which they had been blindfolded. Unknown to the children, sometimes the table has been moved. If a child uses a place response, he or she returns to the correct place, even though the table has been moved from that location. If a child uses a cue response, she or he walks directly to the table. If a child uses a position response, he or she turns in the direction he or she had originally turned when first entering the room. Two general types of tests are used for primates, free-ranging search tests and the WGTA (Wisconsin General Test Apparatus) Test. The most widely used tests are performed in the WGTA. The primate sits in a cage and a screen is raised in front of the cage allowing the animal to see a table on which objects are located. Usually, a peanut is hidden under one object. The correct object may be the one on the animals right (position task), it may always be the only novel object (cue task), or it may always be the object that is found in the same location on two consecutive trials (place task), and so on.

Body, Grasping, and Distal Space

Spatial behavior can be further divided by considering the space around an individual as being composed of three functionally different subspaces (Figure 24-2), each of which may have a distinct neural representation. First, there is the body surface, on which stimuli can be localized. An inability to localize points on the body or neglect of the body would represent a disorder of *body space.* Second, there is the space immediately around the individual, which Grusser has termed the *grasping space.* Abnormalities of reaching or of eye movements to objects would be an example of a disorder of this subspace. Finally, beyond the grasping space is a region that can be called *distal space.* Distal space includes not only the world around an individual but *time space* (past and present) and *order space* (the sequence in which events are ordered or happen). The different strategies described above (position, cue, and place responses) may be used for operations in each kind of space.

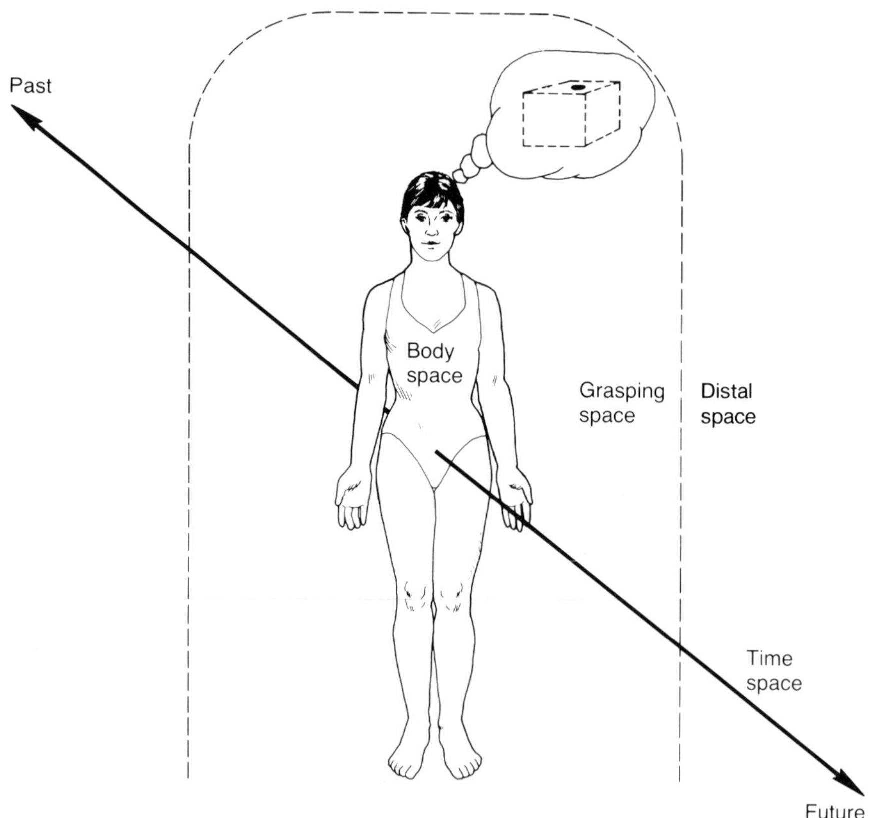

FIGURE 24-2. A conceptual model of the compartments of space.

Dividing space provides a useful vehicle for understanding how the brain represents it. In particular, it forces us to think of space not as a thing, but rather as something that can be broken down into constituent parts, just as language and memory are not things, but are shorthand descriptions for large classes of behavior. Furthermore, these subspaces are the areas in which people and other animals operate, and so we can be reasonably assured that each subspace has some type of neural representation. What we do not know is how separable each representation is.

The Evolution and Development of Spatial Behavior

In various portions of this book we have argued that the body and brain evolved in a series of steps. In this evolution animals first navigated with whole-body movements, then with coordinated limb movements, and finally they became capable of making discrete limb movements. Was there a parallel evolution of spatial navigation strategies? The question has not been studied extensively, but it is widely believed that position responses and cue responses evolved quite early, whereas place responses evolved and became more versatile as the neocortex developed. Furthermore, as limb movements developed, the guidance strategies became elaborated, not just for guiding locomotion but also for directing limb movements. Developmentally, there is evidence that strategies develop in this order: position response, cue response, and place response. Certainly, studies on baby rats show that they are capable of cue responses before 22 days of age (the age of weaning) and are able to make place responses only after this age. Acredolo, using the room and table test described above, has reported that 3-year-old children tend to use position responses, turning in the direction previously turned, older children used a cue response and go to the table, and the oldest children, 7-year-olds, use a place response in going to the correct location in the room. This development of spatial navigation strategies has an analogue in Piaget's developmental stages: egocentric (position), concrete (cue), and formal (place), which develop roughly over the same age range.

Sensory Control of Spatial Behavior

A disproportionate number of the studies on spatial behavior, especially place behavior, involve vision processes, and this is understandable. Body and vestibular cues (for balance) are generally not very useful for guiding us around the world. They are very useful for indicating body posture and movement of body parts. This has led Potegal to suggest that these senses are more importantly related to position responses (or egocentric responses). Olfaction and audition also have properties that limit their use in navigation. Both are excellent stimuli for guiding responses (e.g., a salmon swimming up a river to spawn or a hunter tracking an animal by its cries) but it is less likely that they would be used for place responses. On the other hand, visual cues are exquisitely suited for place responses. A boatman traveling by night from the mouth of the Seal River across Hudson's Bay to Churchill, Ontario can accurately reach port simply by keeping the north star to the left and 45° to the rear. According to Pick and Rieser, Pulawat Islanders can travel thousands of miles in open boats using a conceptual navigation strategy. A hypothetical island is placed over the horizon off to the side of the route between their starting point and destination. They then mark off their journey using the relations between this point, themselves, stars, and other cues. That humans and many other animals use visual information for making complex navigation decisions with such ease almost compels us to expect that vision has a special role in spatial navigation.

Real Space and Cognitive Space

To this point we have described space in terms of the actions we make within it. It is usual in experimental literature to postulate that space really has the features that it appears to have. Consequently it is referred to as **Euclidian space,** but we could just as well refer to it as **real space.** But there must be an internal representation of space. For example, we can mentally draw a map of a route from one point to another, or imagine looking at an object from the side opposite our actual vantage point without actually moving. It seems obvious that real space must have cognitive representations in the brain and this representation can be referred to as **cognitive space.** We should not expect that cognitive space should have the rich detail of real space, both because such detail would be impossible to store and also because we have ready access to the details of places simply by going to them. Cognitive representations of space are dependent on experience and change with experience. For this reason children are unable to form complex cognition representations, especially of distal space. As they mature, they are able to produce more accurate representations. But these representations are fragile, even in normal people. One of us recalls returning to the farm where he grew up only to find that the big farm house had shrunk to a cottage and the huge lawns that he had to mow were little more than small patches of grass. The other of us had a representation of the eastern part of North America as of a series of cities from Chicago to Montreal, separated by short distances. The territory west of Chicago was, however, vast, and cities were far apart. This cartography led him to attempt to drive from Ontario to Nova Scotia in an afternoon.

The important point about cognitive representations of space is that each of our subspaces can be represented cognitively. Thus, we can have a mental image of body parts even when they are absent as in phantom limbs, and of things and places in space whether they are visible or not. Within the realm of cognitive space, we can include the dimension of time. Time is obviously cognitive—we do not actually observe it—but the concept of time is conceptually different from a mental map of places, although places can exist within different dimensions of time. Little is known about the neurological representation of time, but we do know that people with frontal lobe damage often have a blithe disregard for time and have difficulty in temporally organizing their behavior. We do not know, however, how people make neural representations of long-range plans that extend their commitment for years into the future or how they create neural constructs of their past that enable them to place themselves within a culture constrained by ancient traditions and histories.

There have been some attempts to describe the properties of cognitive space. One of its properties includes mental rotation. Corballis has revived much of the literature and the tests used to evaluate mental rotation. **Mental rotation** is the ability to adopt novel perspectives, to see the other side of things, to see ourselves, and so on. Factor analysis of spatial abilities suggests that they can be subdivided into two categories: visualization and orientation. **Visualization** is the ability to manipulate or rotate two- and three-dimensional pictorially presented stimulus objects. **Orientation** is the ability to remain unconfused by the changing orientation in which spatial configuration may be presented. The neural mechanisms that represent cognitive space, however, do place constraints on how real space is represented. For example, horizontal and vertical lines separated by 90° are readily differentiated, whereas oblique lines separated by the same angle are not. In fact some animals and some patients with brain damage may be unable to differentiate obliques at all.

Some researchers have suggested that cognitive space is organized analogously to real space and that animals and people have "cognitive maps" representing the real world. O'Keefe and Nadel have argued that the hippocampus is the neural substrate for cognitive maps, but others have argued that such representations are in the neocortex. At present the map-in-the-head idea is speculative at best. Nevertheless, the concept raises some interesting questions. O'Keefe and Nadel have argued that information may be stored in neural systems in much the same way that objects are found in the world. That is, for language, words of one kind may be in one location, and words of another kind might be in another location. Finding an appropriate word may be like looking for an object in the real world. If we need the name of a bird we search in restricted parts of neural space for bird names, pushing incorrect bird names and even the names of other flying creatures out of the way as we go. Such an idea provides an explanation for curious slips of the tongue, such as when thinking of the name of one person we accidentally and inappropriately blurt out the name of another. It might also account for the curious symptoms of deep dyslexics (Chapter 29), who when given a word like *bird* to read say *butterfly*. We may also store other kinds of information in spatiallike coordinate systems. People find graphs and figures to be good ways of representing large amounts of information. Look at the map of the world in Figure 24-3. The different patterns represent distributions of brain size of peoples of the world. The map summarizes an enormous number of calculations in a simple way, at the same time showing us that there is a very good relationship between brain size and climate. (The explanation seems to be that round heads conserve heat and narrow heads dissipate it. Incidentally, round heads also have a larger internal volume than narrow heads.)

Summary

In this section we have suggested that movements involving space can be divided into position, cue, and place responses. There is a gradation in sensory control such that each response is more dependent upon the kinesthetic-vestibular, olfactory-auditory, and visual systems, respectively. We have also suggested that in terms of evolution and development the behaviors emerge in this sequence —position, cue, and place. Finally, we have pointed out that real space seems to have a cognitive representation in the brain. The details of this

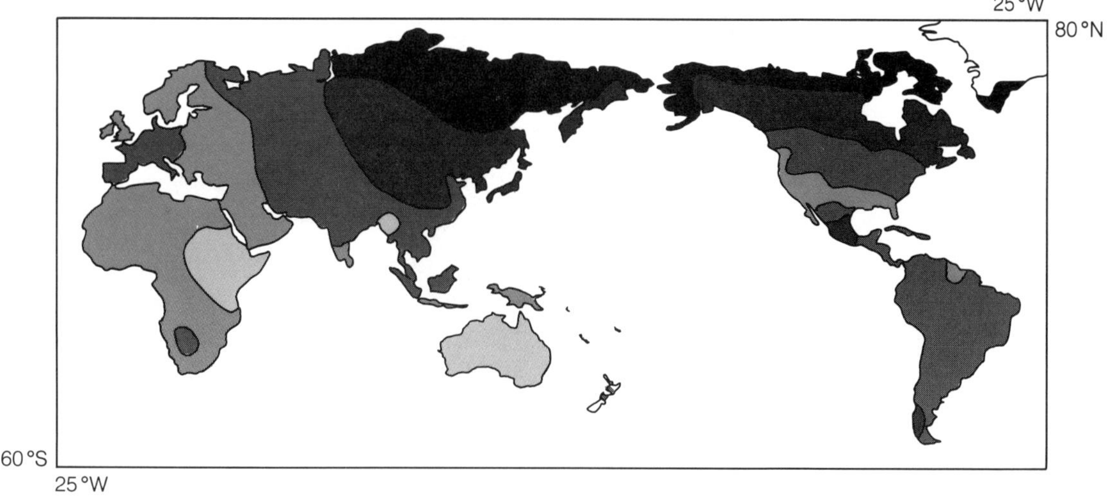

FIGURE 24-3. Map of cranial capacity of people originating in different parts of the world. Darker shading indicates larger cranial capacity. (After Beales, K. L., et al., 1984.)

representation are not as rich as those of real space but by way of compensation, we can manipulate our cognitive representations to alter our points of view.

NEURAL REPRESENTATION OF SPACE

Our own work with rats has shown that after complete neocortex removal, they perform position and cue responses well, but they cannot perform place responses. Thus, although the cortex may be involved in the former responses, it is clear that it has a special importance for place responses. Mishkin and his coworkers in a series of experiments carried out over the last 20 years have suggested that there are at least two neural systems that process the information involved in representing objects in visual space: the posterior parietal cortex and the inferior temporal cortex. Both receive information over pathways that begin in visual cortex. A dorsal pathway projects to posterior parietal cortex. A ventral pathway projects to inferior temporal cortex. These pathways and their targets are shown in Figure 24-4. Experimental work shows that the dorsal system locates objects

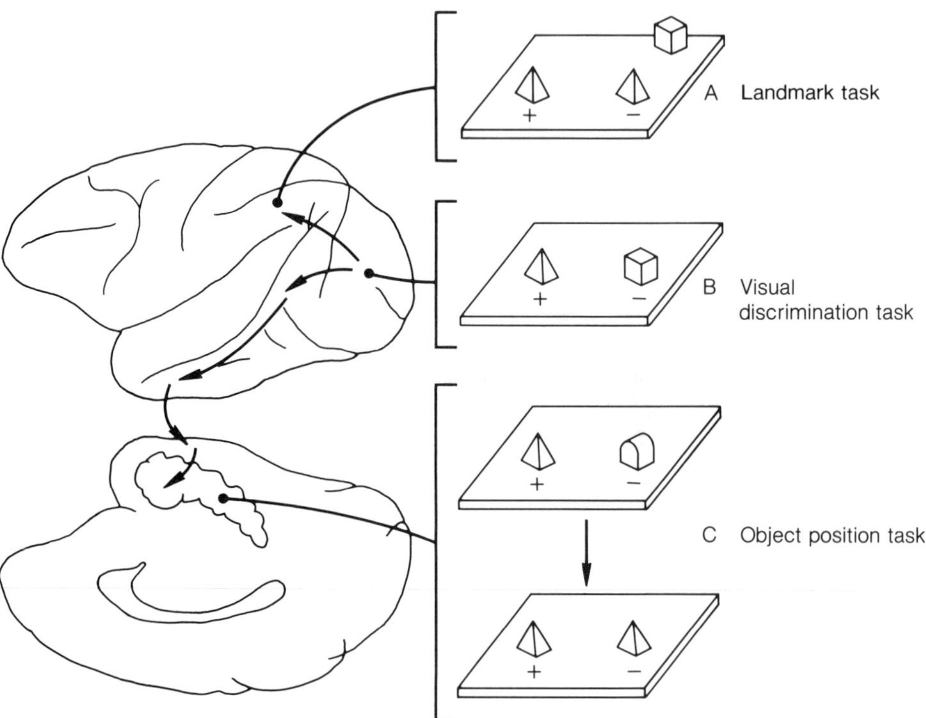

FIGURE 24-4. Three tests of learning that show two fundamental processes: one for spatial location, a second for object discrimination, and a third for recall of the two. *A*. Anatomical pathway of the spatial location system. *B*. Anatomical pathway of the object identification system. *C*. Convergence of spatial location and object identification systems in the hippocampus.

in space but does not identify them, and conversely the ventral pathway identifies objects but does not indicate their location. Both posterior parietal cortex and inferior temporal cortex send projections to frontal cortex where they instruct movements, including eye movements, reaching movements, and locomotion (Figure 19-3). Posterior parietal cortex and inferior temporal cortex also project to the hippocampus (Figure 21-7), and, as we will suggest below, the hippocampus combines information from the two systems to form spatial concepts.

It might seem a little peculiar that the location of an object and its identity are neurally separated. How do we then know that "the pen is on the far left corner of the desk?" Presumably the spatial representation of the object at a location is made where the two systems converge in the hippocampus. The separation of the pathways, however, may also be functional. There is no necessary relation between objects and space: one location in space could be occupied by different objects at different times and any object could conceivably occupy many different spaces. There may also be many occasions when spatial location is important but the identity of the object occupying it is not, or vice versa. By analogy, a large map (representing visual space) and a box of model cars indicating taxicabs (representing objects) can provide a simple illustration of how the system works. Both map and cars exist quite independently but when a car is placed on the map, the two make a meaningful spatial representation; that is, Harry's taxi is at the corner of 4th and Main.

Functions of Posterior Parietal and Inferior Temporal Cortex

How has the function of posterior parietal and inferior temporal cortex been demonstrated? Pohl demonstrated the function of the dorsal pathway using a task that is now referred to as a **landmark task.** Monkeys were presented with two covered foodwells. A cube stood near the wells, closer to one well than to the other in a position that varied from trial to trial (Figure 24-4*A*). The monkeys were rewarded with a peanut for uncovering the well nearer the cube. Monkeys with parietal cortex lesions had a great deal of difficulty performing the task. The same animals had no difficulty learning other kinds of visual discriminations. The function of the ventral pathway was revealed by Mishkin and his coworkers using a **delayed nonmatching-to-sample task.** A monkey is confronted with a distinctive object, under which it finds a peanut. Next the animal is confronted with two objects, one of them the object seen earlier and the other an unfamiliar object. The food is now concealed under the new object (Figure 24-4*B*). The monkey is therefore rewarded for recognizing and avoiding the familiar object and choosing the new one. Each trial makes use of a totally new pair of objects. The difficulty of the problem can be increased by lengthening the delay between the initial display and the subsequent choice. Damage to the inferior temporal cortex disrupts the animal's ability to perform this task.

Function of the Frontal Cortex

A number of experiments indicate that the frontal cortex is important for spatial discriminations. The most dramatic demonstration comes from experiments by Nakamura and his coworkers. They spared all of the visual areas of the posterior cortex while removing all cortex anterior to it in monkeys. The monkeys failed to show any signs of vision, but recordings of single cell activity in the visual areas revealed that the cells were functioning normally. Thus, removal of frontal cortex renders animals chronically blind even though the visual system is functioning. A number of studies have demonstrated that more selective impairments follow more restricted lesions in visual cortex. Haaxma and Kuypers have demonstrated that if the finger area of motor cortex is disconnected from visual centers, a monkey is no longer able to pick up food using the pincer grasp. Goldman-Rakic has demonstrated that if selective lesions are made in the dorsolateral prefrontal cortex, monkeys have impairments in directing their eyes to visual targets (Figure 19-10). Mishkin and his coworkers have demonstrated that lesions to medial frontal cortex disrupt nonmatching-to-sample tasks in the monkey, presumably because this area of frontal cortex is a target of inferior temporal cortex.

Function of the Hippocampus

Monkeys with lesions restricted to the hippocampus perform the landmark task and the nonmatching-to-sample task well, if the delay time between stimulus presentation and response is short. If the task is changed so that place becomes the relevant variable, they fail completely. This is the way the **place task** was presented by Parkinson. The monkey is presented with three foodwells, two of which were marked by distinctive objects. The monkey is allowed to take a peanut from the foodwell under each object. On the next trial one of the objects plus a second identical object are placed over the foodwells in such a way that one of the objects remains in the location it had occupied on the previous trial and its pair is on one of the other two foodwells. The monkey is supposed to choose the object that remains at the same location across the two trials. Note that in order to be correct, the monkey must know both the object and its location. Monkeys with hippocampal removals completely fail this task, independent of delays.

There is a substantial body of evidence that animals and people with hippocampal damage have a great deal of difficulty on place tasks, for example, finding hidden objects or finding their way around in space (see O'Keefe and Nadel). If experience with a place or environment occurs before hippocampal damage, then the impairment is much milder or absent. It may be possible to account for these findings in the following way. Locating a given object in space requires information from the posterior parietal location system and also from the inferior temporal object-recognition system. If the relationship between object and place is made by the hippocampus, then in its absence, forming spatial concepts should be difficult or impossible. This seems to be the case. If it is postulated that the hippocampus, once having formed a spatial concept, sends the information back to the neocortex for permanent storage, then the retention of old spatial information in the face of an inability to deal with new spatial information is explained.

We must point out that in suggesting this model we have speculated with some findings and have made quite a few assumptions. We have also been very selective in our choice of experimental literature. There is a lot of supporting research that we have not covered (see Table 24-2). For example, the idea that the hippocampus is involved in spatial abilities derived from single cell and ablation studies on the rat, and only later was the idea applied to monkey and human research. We have also only discussed visual space. There is evidence that shows that the other sensory systems have an organization that parallels that of the visual system. Finally, this model is based largely on only a few experimental problems administered to laboratory animals. The results must still stand the scrutiny of other kinds of tests given in more natural environments. Nevertheless, in the following sections we will refer back to this neural model as a way of explaining a number of clinical findings.

Summary

In this section we have presented a model of spatial representation. The model postulates that the posterior parietal cortex sets up a coordinate system representing space and locates objects in that space, although it does not identify the objects. In addition, the parietal cortex is responsible for directing movement to stimuli in space (see Chapter 17). The inferior temporal cortex identifies objects but not their spatial location. Both of these areas receive projections from the primary sensory cortex,

TABLE 24-2. Visual-spatial deficits in monkeys and rats with neocortical lesions

Lesion	Task	Basic reference
Parietal		
Monkeys	Landmark	Pohl, 1973; A. D. Milner et al., 1977; Ungerlieder and Brody, 1977; Brody and Pribram, 1978; Ungerleider and Mishkin, 1982
	Stylus maze	A. D. Milner et al. 1977
	Patterned string	Ungerleider and Brody, 1977
	Home-cage finding	Sugishita et al., 1978
	Route following	Petrides and Iverson, 1979
Rats	Lashley and Hebb-Williams mazes	Boyd and Thomas, 1977; Thompson, 1979; McDaniel and Thomas, 1978
	Radial arm maze	Kolb et al., 1983
Frontal		
Monkeys	Delayed-response type	Mishkin and Pribram, 1955, 1956; Goldman and Rosvold, 1970; Goldman et al., 1971
	Personal orientation	Brody and Pribram, 1978
	Extrapersonal orientation	Brody and Pribram, 1978
Rats	Delayed-response type	Kolb et al., 1974; Wikmark et al., 1973
	Radial arm maze	Kolb et al., 1983
	Spatial-reversal type	Divac, 1971; Nonneman et al., 1974
	Morris water task	Kolb et al., 1983; Sutherland and Rudy, 1982

for example, the visual cortex. Both areas send a variety of projections to other brain areas including frontal cortex and the hippocampus. It is postulated that the frontal cortex is responsible for directing movements to targets in space on the basis of stored information (see Chapter 19). The hippocampus is involved in combining information from the spatial coordinate system and from the object system in order to form spatial representations that include both location and identity of an object. Finally, it is suggested that the hippocampus sends new learned spatial representations to a long-term memory system in the neocortex.

SPATIAL DISORDERS

Balint's Syndrome and Related Disorders

Disorders of visual-spatial exploration were described first by Badal in 1889, but it was Balint and later Holmes who first analyzed defective visual exploration in detail. There now appear to be about eight different defects of visual exploration, which usually result from bilateral lesions of the posterior cortex and do not occur all at once (see Table 24-3). Perhaps the most dramatic symptoms are those first described by Balint. Balint's patient had bilateral damage to occipital and parietal cortex that included parts of the dorsal temporal lobes. The patient also had a zone of unilateral damage to dorsal parietal and motor cortex (Figure 24-5). This patient came to Balint's atten-

TABLE 24-3. Deficits in visual-spatial exploration

Displaced visual attention
Inability to perceive more than one stimulus
Defective visual control of movement (optic ataxia)
Inability to follow a moving target
Defective accommodation and convergence
Inability in maintaining fixation
Inability to voluntarily direct gaze to targets (gaze apraxia)
Abnormal visual search

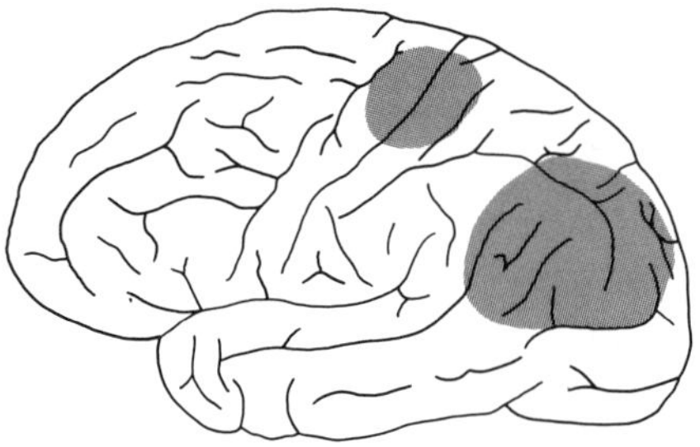 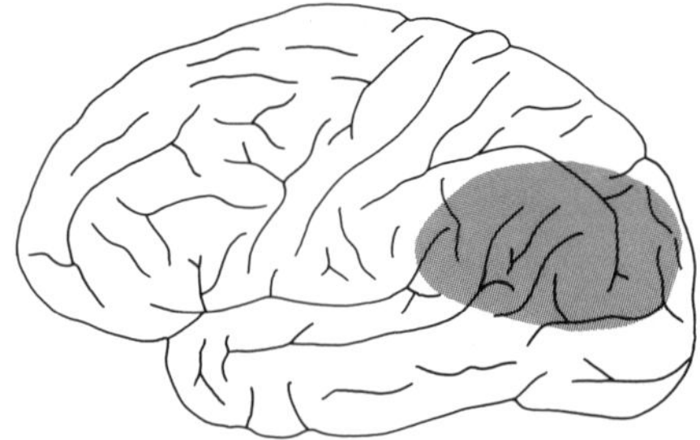

FIGURE 24-5. Balint's schematic drawing of the areas of softening in his patient's brain. (After de Renzi, 1982.)

tion after suffering a stroke and the patient's condition remained unchanged for 6 years. The patient had complete visual fields, was reported to be capable of eye movements, and recognized and named colors, objects, and pictures. When stimuli were presented, the patient directed his gaze 35° to 40° to the right and only saw what was in that direction. Only after prompting would the patient look to the right and notice objects there. Once the patient's attention was directed to an object, nothing else was noticed. This occurred for objects of all sizes from a pin to a human figure. The patient would not look over a picture or scene. The impairment resulted in a defect in reading because the patient focused on a single letter and only with difficulty would work backward through a word to decode it. The patient was impaired in reaching. If requested to grasp an object or to point to a target, he groped and only hit by chance. Misreaching even extended to lighting a cigar, which he attempted to light in the middle. The patient was also unable to estimate distance and could not tell which of two objects were closer.

There are some differences in symptoms in six Holmes' patients, who had penetrating missile wounds of the brain. Most notably, Holmes' patients were impaired in a number of aspects of eye movement. They had difficulty looking at a stimulus whether it was visually or verbally presented, had trouble maintaining visual fixation, in following a moving target, in converging to an approaching object, and in blinking in response to a visual threat. These patients also failed to appreciate spatial features of a stimulus at which they were looking and which they were able to recognize. They had trouble localizing objects in space, estimating distance, discriminating length and size, and in evaluating depth and thickness. As a result they ran into objects when walking, had difficulty in reading, and in counting scattered objects. The patients also sometimes failed to notice objects placed before them, and like Balint's patients they were unable to notice anything else once their attention had been attracted by a stimulus.

Subsequent to these early reports, there have been a large number of accounts of patients with similar symptoms. Symptoms of patients vary, however, depending upon how an injury was acquired, whether it was bilateral, and where it was located. Figure 24-6 illustrates misjudgment by a patient studied by Allison and his colleagues who had bilateral posterior cortical lesions resulting in small lower temporal-quadrant field defects accompanied by dramatic deficits in the visual control of reaching and other movements (so-called **optic ataxia**) as well as by deficits in eye movements.

> A manifestation of visual disorientation noted by the nursing staff five months after operation was

FIGURE 24-6. A patient with Balint's syndrome demonstrates a visual-spatial deficit in his attempt to pour fluid into a glass (After Allison et al., 1969.)

> when he attempted to light a cigarette. He took it out of the packet and put it in his mouth, then clumsily took a match out of the matchbox and lit it, afterwards directing the flame towards his lower lip, missing the cigarette. . . . He could not pour fluid from a bottle into a glass but spilled it on the tablecloth (Figure 24-6). He was unable to shake hands without first groping for the preferred hand. It could be demonstrated that visual memory was intact and did not contribute to his errors. When an object (e.g., a matchbox) was held up either above his head, to the right or to the left and he was asked to note its position, close his eyes for a moment and then point in the general direction in which he had seen the object, he did this correctly. Therefore, it appeared that his ability to remember the position of an object in space was not impaired. (Allison et al., 1969, 324–326)

In order to dissociate the many deficits that people like this suffer, various investigations have centered on two aspects of visual function, namely *visual localization* and *depth perception.* Consider the following representative studies. To demonstrate a disorder of spatial localization independent from a disorder of reaching or pointing, Hannay and coworkers projected one or two dots on a screen for 300 ms. Two seconds later an array of numbers, each of which identified a point where a dot may have been, was projected, and the task was to indicate the position of the dot. Patients with right hemisphere lesions were impaired at this task in comparison with those with left hemisphere lesions and normal controls. This deficit is not simply a manifestation of neglect, since errors were equally distributed in the left and right visual fields. It is apparent that an inability to localize points in space would make it difficult indeed to direct movements, resulting in an apparent "spatial" deficit.

An important cue to spatial location of objects is depth. To discover its importance, try catching a ball with one eye closed. The discovery of a profound impairment in depth perception has been claimed dating back to Balint, but a significant problem of interpretation arises when the inference of impaired depth is based on misreaching, since an impairment might result from many different deficits. Nonetheless, there is now good evidence that depth perception can be markedly abnormal in the presence of good acuity. A study by Carmon and Bechtoldt provides a compelling example. Their patients were presented with random dot stereograms developed previously by Julesz to study cues necessary to perceive depth. Subjects look into eyepieces and are shown an apparently random array of dots. When viewed with one eye alone, the array has no contour or depth, the pattern looking rather like a complex crossword puzzle with black and white boxes. However, when each eye independently views a stereogram, a striking figure-ground contour suddenly appears because of slight disparities between the stereograms shown to the two eyes. Most normal subjects and patients with left hemisphere damage easily perceive the contours, but patients with right hemisphere damage are very poor at this test, illustrating a defect in depth perception. This result has been replicated by others, supporting the idea that the mechanism involved in at least some aspect of the perception of depth is more strongly represented in the right hemisphere.

Many of the deficits displayed by these patients appear to be related to parietal cortex damage, most likely within the secondary and tertiary areas. Given Mishkin's studies outlined above, the parietal spatial system, which projects to frontal cortex, may be involved. Its function is to provide a coordinate system of visual space and locate objects in this space. In the absence of this system a patient will still see an object but will not be able to accurately direct eye or hand movements to it. Furthermore, various investigators have identified neurons in the posterior parietal cortex of monkeys that respond to stimuli within grasping space. It is likely that these are cells that can project to the motor system in order to guide the limbs during voluntary movements toward targets in various spatial locations. Finally, there are neurons that appear to have a role in directing head or eye movements toward stimuli in grasping space, again providing evidence that the parietal cortex has a special role in directing movements to visual targets.

Object-Location Memory

It is difficult to distinguish impairments in detection of objects from impairments in memory. Some features of object-detection impairments, however, do suggest a memory impairment. Goldman-Rakic has reported a series of studies using rhesus monkeys that had small lesions placed in the frontal cortex, along the principal sulcus. The monkeys were trained to fixate on a spot of light in the center of a TV monitor. A dot of light was flashed briefly in their visual field. The monkeys were required to wait for the fixation spot to disappear before directing their gaze to the visual target. With unilateral lesions, the monkeys were unable to direct their gaze to the target with even short delays. If there was no delay, they were able to make the response. By varying the location of the lesion, it was possible to produce selective deficits in different parts of the visual field. These experiments demonstrate that the principal sulcus contains a mechanism for guiding responses on the basis of stored information in the absence of external cues and furthermore demonstrates that the memory for the location of objects may be mapped in visuospatial coordinates. There is a parallel to these eye-movements results in experiments that require monkeys to reach to a target. If a monkey is given a delayed-response task in which location of the object is the relevant task variable, impairments are obtained after short delays following lesions to the principal sulcus. Other discrimination tasks that do not require memory for spatial location are not impaired by these lesions.

Passingham has also reported impairments in memory in rhesus monkeys with principal sulcus lesions in a more naturalistic task. In his experiment the monkeys were trained to retrieve peanuts from behind 25 different doors in the shortest number of trials, without returning to a door for a second time. This task taxed the monkey's spatial memory for doors it had opened. The monkeys with lesions were severely impaired at this task. A somewhat analogous deficit has been reported by Petrides and Milner in people with frontal lobe damage. Patients were presented with a set of pages containing the same array of visual stimuli; however, the position of the stimuli varied from page to page. They were required to point to one of the stimuli on each page but were asked not to point to the same place twice. Thus, the patients were required to remember the selections they had previously made. The frontal lobe patients displayed impairments at this task.

As we have discussed, the frontal cortex has important connections with the basal ganglia so that it might be expected that spatial memory impairments of a similar kind could follow basal ganglial lesions. Ingle and Hoff have reported an interesting finding with frogs, indicating that just such an impairment can be obtained. A visible barrier was placed beside a frog and then removed. After a delay, a large dark object loomed toward the frog, causing it to leap away. Normal frogs avoided leaping into the location of the barrier's previous location or leaped in such a way that they landed behind it, indicating that they remembered where it had been. Frogs with basal ganglial lesions behaved as if they failed to remember a barrier's previous location, although they avoided it quite well when it was present.

Topographical Disorientation

There are many clinical reports of patients with a gross disability in finding their way about their surroundings, even in environments with which they were familiar before the onset of their disease. Many of these reports are difficult to interpret because the patients also experienced other spatial deficits such as left-right confusion, contralateral neglect, deficits of sensory-spatial analysis, and visual-field defects. Nevertheless, **topographical disorientation** has been observed in patients in whom it has been claimed that other spatial deficits were minimal. The first report of a topographical memory disorder was that of Hughlings-Jackson's (1876) patient with a glioma in her right temporal lobe. This patient had difficulty finding her way in a park near her home. In 1890, Foerster provided a more extensive report. His patient was a 44-year-old postal clerk who developed a right hemianopia, followed a few days later by a left hemianopia, leaving him with a small area of central vision. The patient's most striking disability was in remembering where objects were located and building up a picture of a route. He was unable when blindfolded to learn to point to furniture in his room or to remember the location of a toilet a few steps from his room. His impairment was retrograde. He was unable to describe or draw the spatial arrangement of his office or home or of well-known places in the city. He was also unable to draw maps of areas of the world or city, yet he could express some geographical ideas verbally.

DeRenzi summarizes a case thoroughly studied by Meyer at the turn of the century that is considered a landmark description of topographical disorientation:

> Whenever he left his room in the hospital, he had trouble in finding the way back, because at any chosen point of the route he did not know whether to go right, left, downstairs or upstairs (on one occasion, he walked from the main floor down to the basement, instead of going up to the first floor, where his bed was located). When he eventually arrived in front of his own room, he did not recognize it unless he chanced to see some distinguishing feature, such as the black beard of his roommate, or a particular object on the bedside table. . . .
>
> When taken to sections of the city he knew before his illness and required to lead the way, he tried hard to find familiar landmarks, such as a signboard, the name of a street, the tramcar numbers, etc., but this information, though effectively indicating to him he was near his home, failed to provide clues for choosing the right direction. . . .
>
> Required to provide verbal information concerning routes or places well known before the disease, he performed fairly well as long as he could rely on purely verbal knowledge. Thus he was able to give the names of the intermediate stations on the railway line he used daily, or the location of the main building of the city. Yet, he met with considerable difficulty when the way had to be retraced from spatial memory; for instance, when required to tell how he would walk between two sites chosen at random in the city, he could only say the initial street and then he became confused. . . .
>
> He grossly mislocated cities and states on a map of his country as well as of Europe, a task with which he was familiar, since he had been a post-office clerk. (deRenzi, 1982, p. 213)

This patient, as well as some others described in the literature, did not have double hemianopia (that is bilateral damage), indicating that such extensive visual impairments are not necessary for the amnesia. Subsequent studies have described a number of variations in the symptoms of topographical disorientation. Some patients are unable to name buildings or landmarks which had been familiar. Others retain this ability. Some patients are able to describe routes and draw maps but are disoriented because they cannot identify familiar buildings or landmarks. Other patients can navigate routes but are unable to describe or draw maps of them. Some patients are able to navigate in familiar places but become disoriented in new places, and others can eventually learn to navigate in new places by painstakingly memorizing buildings and landmarks and the routes that they should choose between them.

It would be helpful to be able to sort out these complex clusters of symptoms by identifying subcomponents with different anatomical loci. In order to make some sense out of these apparently complex observations, Paterson and Zangwill have suggested that topographical disorders can be subdivided into two different impairments: topographical agnosia and topographical amnesia. **Topographical agnosia** was defined as a failure to identify the individual features of places or buildings while retaining the ability to identify and recognize classes of objects such as hills, buildings, or churches. **Topographical amnesia** refers to an inability to remember topographical relationships between landmarks that can be identified individually. But we should also distinguish between the anterograde and the retrograde features of the disorder. People who retain the ability to orient in environments that were familiar before their injury but who cannot orient in novel environments are obviously different from patients who lose all topographical ability. Finally, it is necessary to identify patients that have true topographical disorders but compensate by using other strategies.

The most useful anatomical distinction that can presently be used to subdivide topographical disorders, is that between the contribution of the hippocampus and posterior neocortex. As we argued above, identifying the spatial locations of objects requires knowledge of both the object and its location. Since these different features of spatial analysis are performed by different cortical systems, the information must be brought together. The structure thought to be involved in encoding the relationship is the hippocampus. Accordingly patients with only hippocampal damage should show symptoms of topographical disorientation. According to Milner and her colleagues, the well-studied patient H. M. does show complete inability to navigate in novel environments or even to learn to navigate in them. He is able, however, to find his way around in environments with which he was familiar before his surgery. For a time it was thought that H. M.'s severe memory problems occurred because he had combined lesions of the amygdala and hippocampus. More recently, however, studies with rats, primates, and humans have confirmed the central and important role of the hippocampus. In fact, studies of all of these species have shown that if damage is restricted to a small portion of the hippocampus, CA_1 through which information leaves it, there is severe anterograde amnesia. Squire, for example, has described the patient R. B. as having complete anterograde amnesia after suffering complete CA_1 loss after an ischemic episode. Thus, it seems safe to conclude that complete anterograde topographical disorders can be associated with hippocampal damage. Patients would be familiar with their old environments, including the buildings and other landmarks in them. They would also have no severe associated agnosias or impairments of vision.

A growing body of anatomical evidence shows that the major projections of the hippocampus go back to the neocortex via the temporal lobe. Further, it is thought that over time spatial relations formed in the hippocampus are sent to the neocortex for permanent storage via these pathways. It is very likely, therefore, that patients with posterior neocortical damage should show topographical disorders that are retrograde; that is, they would include loss of spatial relations learned before brain injury occurred. We have pointed out above that most patients described as having topographical disorders do have posterior neocortical damage. Furthermore, some of these patients have severe visual-field restriction, showing that the lesions invade primary visual cortical areas. This damage would sever the pathways that mediate object discrimination and consequently produce severe anterograde topographical deficits as well.

Topographical Memory

To this point, our discussion of topographical disorders has been narrow, as we have discussed it within the confines of spatial abilities. Some aspects of topographical disorders, particularly symptoms that involve the hippocampus, may fall within the broader category of memory. Hippocampal damage produces amnesia that is global, and spatial amnesia forms only a part of the deficit syndrome. This opens up a number of speculative options. First, there may be a number of separate cognitive abilities that require the hippocampus in order to perform complex associations, and spatial functions may be but one of its responsibilities. Second, the complex demands of spatial abilities and their overriding importance for survival may have been the evolutionary impetus that led to the development of the hippocampus. This phylogenetically prepared hippocampus may then have been used for other mnemonic functions. Third, the hippocampus may have no particular relation to any cognitive function but may be a general memory-forming and storing system. At present there is no evidence that is helpful for deciding among these options.

In a recent theoretical paper, Sutherland and Rudy have presented a model of how the hippocampus may work, which incidentally seems to favor the general-function view. They suggest that the hippocampus is involved in only a certain class of memories. They call these memories *configurations,* which they define as relationships between events that have a certain kind of conditional form. Here's an example of a configuration: A rat is taught to press a bar when a light comes on ($L^+ =$ food reward for pressing after the light comes on) or when a tone comes on (T^+) but not when the light and tone come on together ($LT^- =$ no food) forming the configurational discrimination L^+T^+/LT^-. They argue that a configurational discrimination is fundamentally different from what they call simple associations, such as "light on-push bar." The special feature of a configuration is that the meaning of one stimulus can only be understood in relation to some other stimulus. For example, learning that a certain visible object is at a certain location is a simple association. Learning that a particular object provides reward only if it occurs in a certain relation to some other cue is a configurational association. Thus, Sutherland and Rudy argue that the hippocampus is not required for learning the identity of an object nor is it required for knowing the location of an object, but it is required for knowing either that an object occurs at a location at a given time, that it bears some unique relation to that place dependent upon the observer's location, or that it has a unique relation to some other object. According to this explanation, topographical relations are configurations and thus are dependent upon hippocampal function. They argue that the strength of their theory is that it not only explains why hippocampal-damaged people and animals get lost but also why they cannot perform operant or classical discriminations that have a configurational form.

Spatial Thought

The terms *spatial thought* and *conceptual spatial performance* have been used to describe the processes needed to solve problems that require mental rotation or manipulation of stimuli in order to reach some solution to a problem. For example, when asked to describe what would be seen from a pilot's perspective in an airplane, an observer on the ground must mentally assume the perspective of the pilot looking down, rather than the observer's actual perspective of looking up. Similarly, when asked to solve tests such as the folding or unfolding of patterns, one must mentally manipulate the patterns to arrive at the correct solution. It would seem likely that the neural systems necessary for object location and object identity would be necessary for these types of manipulations.

CONTRALATERAL NEGLECT AND THE SPECIAL ROLE OF THE RIGHT HEMISPHERE

In the human clinical reports on spatial disorders it is often noted that right hemisphere damage results in more frequent and more obvious spatial deficits than left hemisphere damage (Figure 24-7). This view is supported by: (1) neuropsychological studies on normal populations, (2) the phenomenon of contralateral neglect that follows right hemisphere damage in humans, and (3) studies on human patients who have undergone elective surgery involving unilateral hippocampal removal. We will discuss only the last two phenomena here, because the first was discussed in the chapters on cerebral asymmetry (Chapters 15 through 16).

Perhaps one of the most interesting and puzzling findings in the clinical literature is the profound contralateral neglect that is reported to follow some instances of right parietal cortex damage. We discussed the symptoms and stages of recovery in detail in the chapter dealing with the parietal cortex (Chapter 17). Here is a brief recap. Following right parietal cortex lesions, patients ignore the contralateral half of the world and the contralateral half of their body in all sensory modalities. They behave as if nothing in the contralateral half of their world exists. When asked to draw a picture, bisect a line, or read, they perform as if the left half of the object, line, or word does not exist. There are a number of puzzling features to the phenomenon. First, it is not simply the case that each hemisphere constructs a representation of the contralateral field. Comparable left hemisphere damage does not produce a comparable effect. Also, if the right hemisphere does play a special role in spatial abilities, one would expect that spatial deficits should

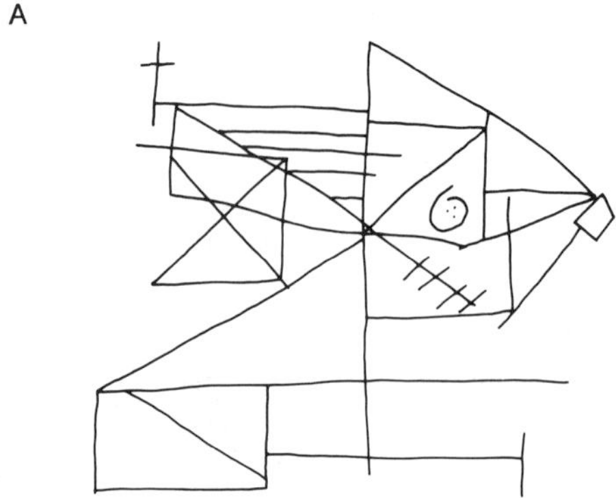

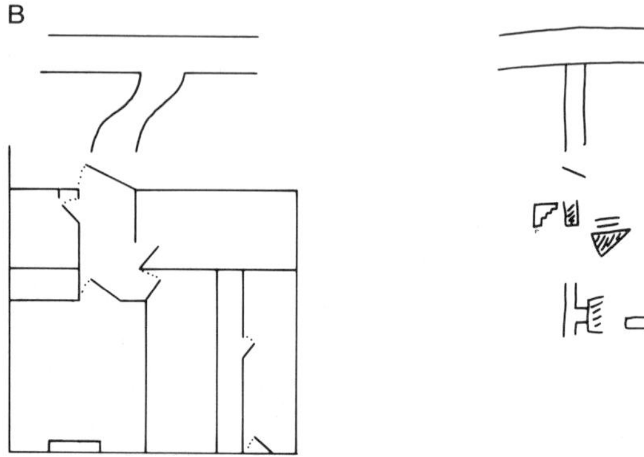

FIGURE 24-7. *A.* A copy of the Rey figure by a patient with a right parietofrontal missle wound (After Ratcliff, 1982). *B.* Drawing of the floor plan of the house of a patient with a right frontoparietal tumor: by a psychologist (left) and by the patient (right). (Redrawn from McFie et al., 1950.)

be bilateral and that is obviously not the case. De Renzi has reviewed the many explanations that attempt to account for this finding, including hypotheses that relate to attention, eye movements, and hemispheric competition. His most compelling explanation is that the right hemisphere is in some way involved in constructing central representations of space.

Experiments supporting this view come from two clever studies by Bisiach and his associates. Patients were asked to give a verbal description of a place that was previously ascertained to be familiar to them — the cathedral square in Milan. The subjects were first requested to imagine themselves facing the front of the cathedral from the opposite side of the square and to describe the scene. Then they were requested to imagine the vantage point to be the central entrance of the cathedral, facing their former position. Patients with contralateral neglect failed to describe details of the left side of the square regardless of their vantage point. In other words, when they switched from the first to the second vantage point, they then described the side of the square they had previously neglected. Their neglect is clearly not one of memory, nor is it attributable to field defects or other primary sensory loss. Neglect in this test is likely due to a loss of a cerebral representation or "image" of a part of the external world, the lost part varying with the frame of reference of the observer of the image.

In a second experiment Bisiach's patients were given two tasks. In both they were required to view objects and to judge whether their two sides were the same or different from the central portion. In a static viewing condition they were allowed to see the entire design for 2-sec. As expected, the patients ignored the left side of the designs. In the second viewing condition, the design was passed behind a slit in front of the patient over a 2-sec period. The subject was able to see the entire design in the same viewing location as it passed by. Again, the patients made errors and the errors were attributable to left-sided neglect. Since the characteristics of neglect described in these two experiments cannot be easily attributed to perceptual errors or biases it seems more likely that they stem from processes of reconstructing central representations of the world.

Smith and Milner's studies of patients who had received elective surgery removing the hippocampus as a treatment for epilepsy show a selective involvement of the right hippocampus in spatial memory. In the task, 16 small toys were used as stimulus objects and they were spread out over a table. The subject was told that this was a test of ability to estimate prices, and that an estimate of the average price of a real object represented by the toy would be required. The subject was told to point at the toy, name it, and think of a price. After 10-sec the price was asked for; the subject then moved on to the next toy. The subject then moved away from the table and was asked to recall the objects that had been seen. Following the test of object recall, a sheet of brown paper, the same size as the original table, was placed before the subject and he or she was asked to place the toys at their original location. The recall tests were then repeated 24-h later. The object array is illustrated in Figure 24-8*A*. Scores were given for the recall of the object's names; in addition the displacement distances were measured between the object's original location and the patient's immediate placement, and between the original location and the patient's delayed placement. On the measure of name recall, both right and left hippocampal-damaged patients were moderately impaired, with the left hippocampal patients having lower scores than the right hippocampal patients. The results of the spatial component for the experiment are shown in Figure 24-8*B*. The scores for the left temporal and control groups were comparable, but the scores of the right hippocampal group were extremely poor on both immediate and delayed recall tests.

Summary

There are two general kinds of spatial disorder that occur after brain damage. One is characterized by

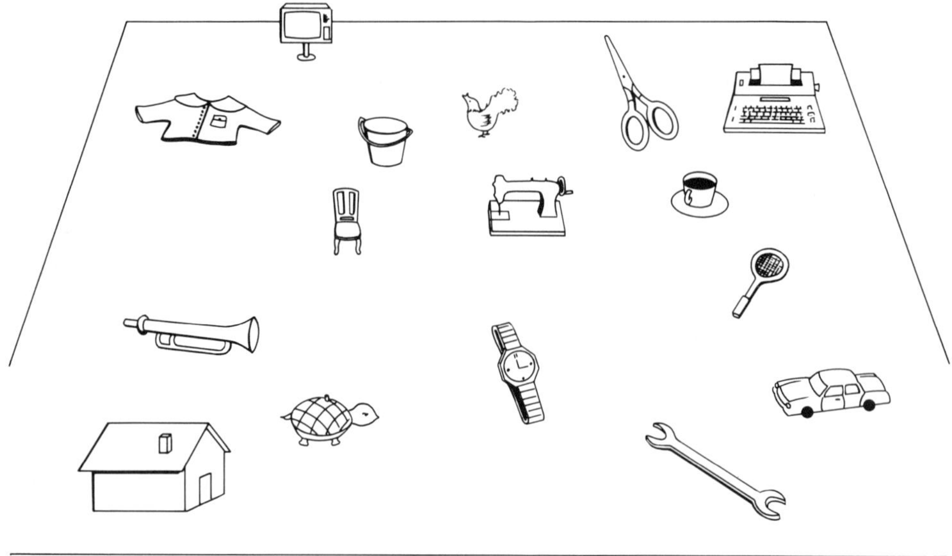

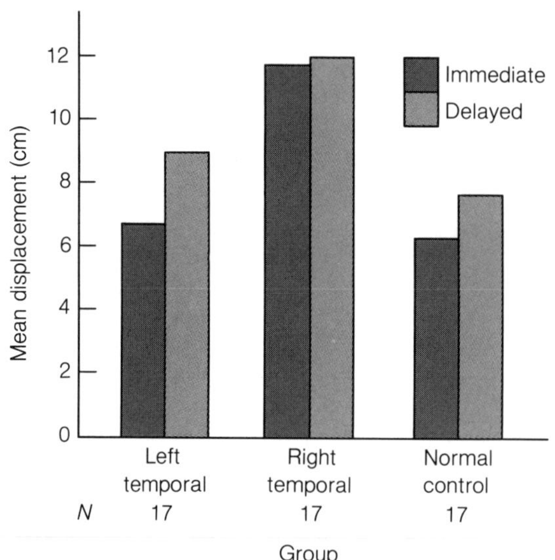

FIGURE 24-8. Test of spatial memory for objects *(A)* with the typical arrangement of the toys on the 16 fixed locations. *B*. Graph of the performance by left temporal and right temporal patients and controls on the recall of absolute location. (After Smith and Milner, 1981.)

impairments in directing eye and limb movements, and the second is characterized by impairments in topographical orientation. Possibly the first group of impairments is related to a pathway that projects from primary sensory cortexes to posterior parietal cortex, and from there to the frontal cortex and to the hippocampus. Possibly the second group of impairments are related to damage to a pathway from primary sensory cortexes that project to the inferior temporal cortex, and from there to the hippocampus and frontal cortex. The hippocampus has a special role in combining information from the two systems to form spatial representations. Finally, the right hemisphere is described as having a special role in forming spatial images and in forming spatial memories in humans.

INDIVIDUAL DIFFERENCES

Sex Differences

There is agreement that there are differences in spatial abilities between the sexes. Adult males usually perform better on spatial tests than adult females. The male advantage in spatial ability is generally contrasted with a female advantage in language skills, fine-motor movements, and perceptual speed. The female advantage is conceded to be quite small in statistical terms, about 0.2 standard deviations, but the male advantage is thought to be large, about 0.5 standard deviations. Interest in spatial abilities first came to the attention of researchers in the early part of this century in studies designed to predict mechanical aptitude. As interest developed in spatial abilities, studies eventually began to include mixed age and sex groups from which the generalization that adult males performed better than adult females gradually emerged. When Maccoby and Jacklin reviewed this literature in 1974, the idea that this sex difference emerged in adolescence and was due to environmental influences became a dominant view. Subsequently, many studies have demonstrated sex differences in much younger children. Part of the difficulty in resolving age and sex differences in spatial abilities relates to the large number of tests that have been used and the diversity of the populations tested. In a review, however, Newcombe has interpreted the evidence as suggesting that small sex differences are present in childhood and increase slightly with age.

Another issue related to spatial differences comes from evidence that females and males differ in their abilities on such skills as chess, mathematics, music, and art. Mathematical aptitude has received the closest scrutiny. A large number of studies have shown that males outperform females on tests of quantitative ability. Studies in the United States, including the Scholastic Aptitude Test and the Johns Hopkins University mathematical talent search, suggest that these differences become apparent in participants in adolescence and become more evident at the high end of the performance scale. Among top scorers on the college board's aptitude tests, males outnumber females by about 17 : 1. It is worth noting, however, that by this point there are only a small number of individuals in the sample. Halpern has discussed the results of these sorts of studies in some detail. First, it is the case that females have not been encouraged to play chess, or become composers or mathematicians, and this will contribute to their small numbers in these occupations. More interestingly, however, it has been suggested that it is not so much the occupations themselves that are the relevant factors but the spatial demands that are embedded in them. The suggestion is that males have a slight advantage over females in spatial abilities and this will lead them to be somewhat more successful in these endeavors than females.

Our primary interest is in explaining brain function and for this reason sex-related spatial differences are of interest. Just the same, we should issue some common-sense cautions. First, findings of sex difference do not mean that the cognitive abilities of the sexes are vastly different. Females and males use the same cognitive processes effectively. Second, the range of abilities in female and male groups is larger than that between sex groups. Consequently, females and males will be found at all levels of the ability scale. Third, if females are given practice on spatial tasks, their performance improves toward male levels. Thus, there is no reason to believe that occupational choices will be primarily a result of spatial differences. Fourth, under most test conditions and for most test groups, environmental contributions or influences cannot easily be factored out. Taken together, these constraints suggest that the social, cultural, and economic consequences of the differences for the daily lives of individuals are not large enough to create much excitement. Even in occupations such as engineering and architecture, which are traditionally thought to be heavily dependent on spatial factors, women can be as successful or more successful than men. The Soviet Union is usually given as an example of a country in which there are more women in these occupations than men.

Nevertheless, the existence of gender differences, however small, are of real interest to students of brain function. On the practical side, they must be considered when tests for brain function are developed, normed, and administered. They must also be considered a relevant factor in interpreting the consequences of brain damage. More important than these considerations, however, they provide an important key to understanding brain organization and function. There are a limited number of explanations for the differences (ignoring environmental influences), and isolation of the relevant factors is therefore a real possibility. The differences may be genetic, in which case they are sex-linked and probably determined by a recessive gene on the X chromosome. Alternatively, they may be hormonally produced and emerged as a result of the action of hormones on neural organization and function.

Genetic Contributions

We have discussed the issue of genetic contribution to sex-related spatial differences in the chapters on cerebral asymmetry (Chapters 15 and 16). The usual explanation for a genetic basis goes something like this. During the formative period of the evolution of modern humans, a differentiation of roles in food gathering was adaptive. A primary occupation for males was hunting, an occupation requiring an ability to find one's way about in space. Hunting also required the ability to throw spears and aim arrows, both of which are putative spatial skills. Males endowed with way-finding and throwing abilities would be more successful than those who were not and would consequently be selected. It is quite irrelevant that those skills are no longer needed today, males will tend to get them anyway.

McGee has reviewed a large body of literature that suggests that spatial skills are heritable. A number of studies have suggested that spatial abilities may be enhanced by an X-linked, recessive gene. Traits that are thought to be carried by a single gene on the X chromosome are said to be sex-linked. If the gene is recessive, more males than females will be affected. Under this arrangement, according to the usual estimates, about 50% of males and about 25% of females will carry the gene and have enhanced spatial abilities. As a result about one-fourth of females will score above the male median on tests of spatial abilities, a finding obtained in most studies. The recessive-gene hypothesis has been put to a number of tests, but it has not emerged unscathed. According to the hypothesis, certain correlations should emerge in the offspring of different families, but these correlations have not been obtained. A more difficult problem concerns the tests used to obtain scores for correlations. Studies using different tests have obtained different correlations, raising the possibility that there may be different kinds of spatial abilities. These difficulties suggest either that alternative inheritance models should be considered or that sex-related differences have other explanations.

Hormonal Influences

Three lines of evidence suggest that hormones influence sex differences in spatial abilities: (1) developmental studies, (2) studies of persons with chromosomal-hormonal abnormalities, and (3) studies investigating the relationship between androgenicity and spatial abilities.

We have noted above that sex differences are found more reliably in adults than in prepubescent children. This suggests that sex-related cognitive differences may be related to the hormonal changes that occur during puberty. That some differences are obtained earlier could also be accounted for by sex-related hormonal influences that occur prenatally or in the early postnatal period. This hypothesis seems to be supported by studies on patients with **Turner's syndrome.** About half of all females with Turner's syndrome have a single X chromosome rather than the normal XX pair. Their intelligence and verbal abilities are normal and distributed throughout the population range, but their spatial abilities are impaired. They get extremely low scores on tests of mental rotation, block design of the Wechsler Adult Scale, the spatial subtest of the Primary Mental Abilities Test, the Road-and-Map Test of Direction Sense, and tests of imaginary movements and direct rotation. The results are counterintuitive and at variance with the recessive-gene hypothesis, which would predict that they ought to be similar to males, who also have one X chromosome. Since females with Turner's syndrome produce no gonadal hormones, the suggestion is that gonadal hormones influence spatial abilities. Studies examining this hypothesis now suggest that levels of androgens (masculinizing hormones) or a balance between estrogen and androgens might determine spatial abilities. Some workers have pushed this relation to the point that they argue that the more androgens that females receive, the better their spatial abilities. For males, who are already receiving a high level of androgens, more might be too much and spatial and other abilities might be impaired. Consequently, females receiving large amounts of androgen and males receiving moderate amounts would be expected to have enhanced spatial skills. The mechanisms that hormones are thought to influence in order to modulate spatial abilities are in the brain. Presumably they are the same neural systems, discussed above, that are responsible for spatial abilities in general. The nature of their influence is presently not known. Early in life, hormones may influence neural connections, neural growth, and cell death, thus sculpting quite a different spatial-neural system for individuals with enhanced spatial abilities. On the other hand, hormones can selectively modulate neural function in these systems via yet unknown mechanisms.

Handedness

Traditionally, there are three general lines of evidence that lead to an interest in the spatial abilities of left-handed people. It is often noted that left-handedness might confer a special spatial advantage. Some famous artists such as da Vinci and Michelangelo were left-handed, left-handedness is common in tennis players and baseball pitchers, and there are some reports that left-handers are disproportionately represented in faculties of engineering and architecture. A quite different picture emerges from studies of learning disabilities. It is thought that if an individual suffers left hemisphere brain damage in infancy, language and handedness will move to the right hemisphere. This logic underlies part of the explanation for the disproportionate number of left-handed individuals found in groups with learning disabilities. A third line of research concerns sex differences. It is thought that the conventional female brain is more bilaterally organized for language, and the conventionally organized male brain is more bilaterally organized for spatial abilities. From this it has been suggested that left-handers should be different. At the very least, if the representation of language is moved into the right hemisphere, spatial abilities will be "crowded" with the risk that they will be less well represented.

Levy is a recently recognized proponent of the "crowding" position. She has predicted that in some left-handers, spatial abilities will be crowded out of the right hemisphere and this will be reflected in poorer spatial scores on spatial tests. In a study on graduate students at the California Institute of Technology, she did find evidence to support her position. There was no verbal IQ difference in left- and right-handers, but left-handers had lower performance IQ scores than right-handers. This finding suggests that direct tests of spatial abilities would also find lower scores in left-handed populations. Harshman and colleagues have reviewed the subsequent research that attempted to test this hypothesis. Some studies find that left-handers perform more poorly on spatial tests, and some find that they do not.

In an extensive study on cognitive abilities and brain organization, Harshman and colleagues have reported results that suggest that relations to handedness may be more complex than initially thought. Harshman's group administered a large battery of tests to three large populations. In some of the populations a sex-by-handedness interaction was obtained. Overall, males performed better on spatial tests than females, as was expected. In some of the populations, left-handedness in males was associated with lower spatial scores, but was associated with higher spatial scores in females. In an attempt to find out why this effect only occurred in certain populations, Harshman's group examined the effect of other variables and uncovered a three-way interaction of sex, handedness, and reasoning ability. Among what he defined as a high-reasoning group, left-handed males had lowered spatial scores and left-handed females had higher spatial scores than right-handed comparison groups. Among low-reasoning groups the relationship was reserved: left-handed males had high spatial scores and left-handed females had low spatial scores in relation to their comparison group. In retrospective analysis of previous studies, Harshman and his coworkers suggest that contradictory results obtained in previous work could be accounted for by differences in the groups sampled. That is, if a sample group was a university population, high spatial scores might be expected from left-handed females and low spatial scores might be expected from left-handed males (e.g., Levy's C.I.T. study). If a sample population was more heterogeneous, the opposite pattern of results might be obtained.

There is no obvious simple interpretation of Harshman's results. If masculinity, handedness, and spatial ability can all be attributed to the influence of androgens, moderate androgen influence might account for high spatial abilities in males, and excessively high levels might account for poorer spatial abilities. High levels of androgens could also account for left-handedness and high spatial abilities in females. This, however, provides no satisfactory explanation for scores on reasoning ability, unless this factor is unrelated to sex. There is also a related problem. Sex is relatively easy to define. There is also some consensus concerning what tests measure spatial abilities, although the issue is by no means clear-cut. The introduction of the term *reasoning ability* may pose some problems, however. Even in Harshman's own groups, different tests were used to estimate reasoning ability in his different samples. Furthermore, the Raven Progressive Matrices were used to divide the sample into reasoning groups in one of these populations. There are people in some circles who might argue that the matrices are a test of spatial abilities. Apart from the difficulties in Harshman's study, the finding of interactions does raise some interesting methodological possibilities. If there are different populations of males and of females, who in addition have differences in spatial abilities, they would provide a control for putative environmental influences on spatial abilities. That is, one would expect that environmental influences on right- and left-handed males would be quite similar, so that if there is a population of left-handed males with low spatial abilities this could not be attributed to environment.

Neuropsychological Spatial Tests

There are a surprising number of tests that have been used to measure spatial abilities. Our problem in understanding them can be simplified by considering factor-analysis results of the kinds reported by McGee. **Factor analysis** is a mathematical procedure used to find what is common within a heterogeneous group of elements. When the procedure has been applied to spatial tests, two separate spatial factors, or abilities, have been identified. Examples of the kinds of tests that would be used to measure each spatial ability are illustrated in Figure 24-9. The two factors are visualization and orientation, and the following are their main features.

Visualization. Visualization tests involve the ability to mentally manipulate, rotate, twist, or invert two- or three-dimensional stimulus objects. The underlying ability seems to involve a process of recognition, retention, and recall of a configuration in which there is movement among the internal parts of the configuration. The ability includes the recognition, retention, and recall of an object manipulated in three-dimensional space; or the folding or unfolding of flat patterns (see Figure 24-9*A*). McGee has suggested that visualization is important to two areas of mental functioning: imagery and mathematical ability, especially for the study and understanding of geometry and algebra.

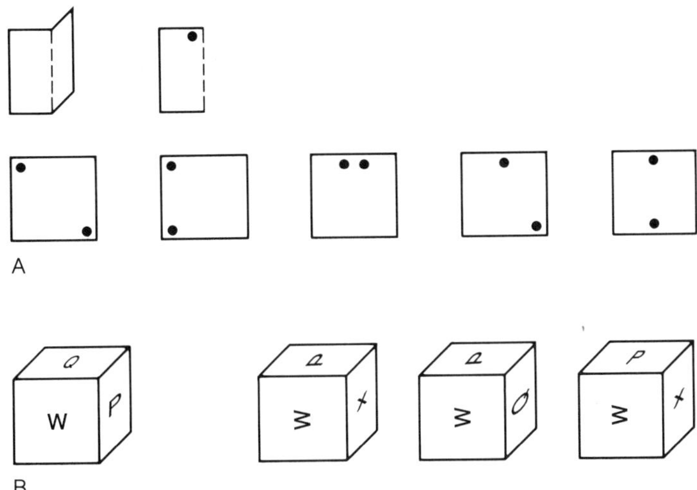

FIGURE 24-9. Sample test items similar to those used to measure visualization and orientation spatial abilities. *A*. Visualization. Imagine folding and unfolding a piece of paper. *A*. Represents a square piece of paper being folded. After being folded, a hole is punched through all of the thicknesses. Which figure is correct when the paper is unfolded? *B*. Orientation. Compare the three cubes on the right with the one on the left. No letter appears on more than one face of a given cube. Which of the three cubes on the right could be a different view of the cube on the left? (After Halpern, 1986.)

Orientation. Orientation tests involve the comprehension of the arrangement of elements within a visual stimulus pattern and the aptitude to remain unconfused by the changing orientation in which a spatial configuration may be presented (see Figure 24-8*B*). McGee suggests that orientation ability is related to field independence — the ability to orient an object accurately while ignoring the background that encloses it.

What strikes us as interesting about the factor-analysis results is that visualization and orientation may be related differentially to the anatomically dissociated spatial systems described above. Recall that the posterior parietal system is involved in constructing a set of spatial coordinates within which to locate objects, the inferior temporal system is involved in object identification, and the hippocampus is involved in locating identified objects and determining the relations between objects. The properties of the visualization tests suggest that what is required is that a spatial framework be constructed and locations be identified within that framework. This seems to be a posterior parietal function. For example, in the test illustrated in Figure 24-9*A*, all of the information needed to solve the task is contained in the test figure. Once the problem is solved, the other items are simply used to indicate the answer. The spot that is on the field also has no specific identity. On the other hand, the orientation tests require calculating the relationship between objects, and this seems to be a hippocampal function. Note that on the tests in Figure 24-9*B*, not only is visual field important, the identity of the objects on the visual field is important. The problem is also best solved by comparing the test problem with each of the possible answers.

If spatial abilities are in fact limited to two factors, a number of specific predictions can be made about the effects of brain damage on performance of spatial tests. All spatial tests containing unfamiliar test items should be impaired by posterior parietal and frontal eye-field damage, because this cortical system sets up the spatial coordinates within which objects are located. Inferior temporal damage or hippocampal damage should disrupt performance only on orientation tests, since they require both object identification and a spatial-coordinate system. The utility of this prediction can be evaluated by considering the literature on spatial test performance by brain-damaged populations. Our perusal of this literature suggests that this prediction will be fulfilled.

Nevertheless, there are three problems. First, the kinds of tests used for factor-analysis studies (see McGee for a summary) are not identical with those used for neuropsychological analyses. As a result, many of the tests used in the factor-analysis studies have not been given to brain-damaged patients, and many of the tests given to neurological patients cannot be easily categorized as visualization or orientation tests with respect to weightings determined by factor analysis. Second, many tests that are devised for studies of brain-damaged patients have theoretical origins that have very little to do with either anatomical logic or factor-analysis findings. Consequently, it is not obvious what aspects of spatial abilities they evaluate. Furthermore, many tests are not obviously tests of one ability or the other. Depending upon how they are administered, the form they are presented in, and their construction, they probably have mixed attributes. Third, many students of spatial functions have an avowed interest in lobe differences and hemisphere differences. On the surface, most spatial tests will not respect these boundaries. They will have purely spatial solutions (and therefore be more sensitive to right hemisphere function), purely verbal solutions (and therefore be more sensitive to left hemisphere functions), or various mixtures (with obvious consequences). But more importantly, they will likely make demands upon systems that include more than one lobe or hemisphere, which might leave the impression that they are nonspecific, which as we have seen would not be the case.

Summary and Commentary

In this section we have pointed out that there are striking individual differences in spatial abilities. Generally, females do not perform as well as males on a wide range of spatial tests. Sex differences are apparent in young children on some tests but differences become more evident in adolescence. Sex differences can be accounted for in two ways. The differences may be due to a recessive gene on the X chromosome or may be produced by the influence of sex hormones on brain maturation or function. Factor analysis suggests that there are in fact two different spatial abilities: visualization and orientation. These abilities may be related to anatomical systems described in earlier sections. Although spatial deficits have been found in brain-damaged people on a wide range of spatial tests, anatomical systems, factor-analysis results, and neuropsychological testing have not been combined to produce a unified picture of spatial abilities.

We have noted in reading the literature on spatial abilities and sex differences that disproportionate attention is given to paper-and-pencil tests and tests that are designed to be analogies of real-world situation. This has led to a rather narrow focus on spatial issues. For example, the suggestion is advanced that males as hunters have more need of certain spatial skills than females, who would be more involved in food-gathering functions. We wonder if this is a real distinction. It is easy to imagine that the spatial demands of knowing where animals are, knowing how to get to them, and finding one's way back again are much the same as knowing where plants are, knowing how to get to them, and finding one's way back. It is also not obvious to us that the spatial skills involved in making arrowheads or axes are very different from those involved in making baskets, weaving cloth, or preparing food. There is also another set of considerations that is relevant. We usually imagine spatial ability to be something we use in wayfinding or object localization. The matter may be more complicated. Jane Goodall, in describing the social behavior of chimpanzees, notes that it is very important for them to monitor moment-to-moment the actions of other animals in their group. The presence or absence of individual B can make a world of difference to individual A's momentary well-being. Whether C is sitting beside E and not beside D can also have enormous relevance. These are social problems, but they are also spatial problems. Thus, it may very well be the case that the origins of some aspects of spatial abilities have origins that are not obviously spatial in nature.

REFERENCES

Acredolo, L. P. Frames of reference used by children for orientation in unfamiliar spaces. In G. Moore and R. Gooledge, eds. *Environmental Knowing*. Stoudsberg, PA: Dowden, Hutchinson, and Ross, 1976.

Allison, R. S., L. J. Hurwitz, J. G. White, and T. J. Wilmot. A follow-up study of a patient with Balint's syndrome. *Neuropsychologia* 7:319–333, 1969.

Archibald, Y. M. Time as a variable in the performance of hemisphere-damaged patients on the Elithorn Perceptual Maze Test. *Cortex* 14:22–31, 1978.

Bálint, R. Seelenlähmung des Schauens, optische Ataxie, räumlielie Störung der Aufmerksamkeit, *Mschr. Psychiatry and Neurology* 25:51–81, 1909.

Becker, J. T., J. A. Walker, and D. S. Olton. Neuroanatomical bases of spatial memory.*Brain Research* 200:307–321, 1980.

Beales, K. L., C. L. Smith, and S. M. Dodd. Brain size, cranial morphology, climate, and time machines. *Current Anthropology* 25:301–330, 1984.

Benton, A. L. *Right-Left Discrimination and Finger Localization.* New York: Hoeber-Harper, 1959.

Benton, A. L. Disorders of spatial orientation. In P. J. Vinkey, and G. W. Bruyn, eds. *Handbook of Clinical Neurology* vol. 3. Amsterdam: Elsevier North-Holland, 1969.

Benton, A. L. Visuoperceptive, visuospatial, and visuoconstructive disorders. In K. M. Heilman and E. Valenstein, eds. *Clinical Neuropsychology.* New York: Oxford University Press, 1979.

Benton, A. L. Spatial thinking in neurological patients: Historical aspects. In M. Potegal, ed. *Spatial Abilities: Development and Physiological Foundations.* New York: Academic Press, 1982.

Benton, A. L., A. Elithorn, M. L. Fogel, and M. Kerr. A perceptual maze test sensitive to brain damage. *Journal of Neurology, Neurosurgery, and Psychiatry* 26:540–544, 1963.

Benton, A. L., K. deS. Hamsher, N. R. Varney, and O. Spreen. *Contributions to Neuropsychological Assessment.* New York: Oxford University Press, 1983.

Benton, A. L., and H. Hécaen. Stereoscopic vision in patients with unilateral cerebral damage. *Neurology* 20:1084–1088, 1970.

Benton, A. L., N. R. Varney, and K. deS. Hamsher. Visuospatial judgment: A clinical test. *Archives of Neurology* 35:364–367, 1978.

Bisiach, E., E. Capitani, C. Luzzatti, and D. Perani. Brain and conscious representation of outside reality. *Neuropsychologia* 19:543–552, 1981.

Bisiach, E., and C. Luzzatti. Unilateral neglect of representational space. *Cortex* 14:129–133, 1978.

Boyd, M. G., and R. K. Thomas. Posterior association cortex lesions in rats: Mazes, pattern discrimination, and reversal learning. *Physiological Psychology* 5:455–461, 1977.

Brain, W. R. Visual disorientation with special reference to lesions of the right cerebral hemisphere. *Brain* 64:244–272, 1941.

Brody, B. A., and K. H. Pribram. The role of frontal and parietal cortex in cognitive processing. *Brain* 101:607–633, 1978.

Butters, N., M. Barton, and B. A. Brody. Role of the parietal lobe in the mediation of cross modal associations and reversible operations in space. *Cortex* 6:174–190, 1970.

Butters, N., C. Soeldner, and P. Fedio. Comparison of parietal and frontal lobe spatial deficits in man: Extrapersonal vs. personal (egocentric) space. *Perceptual and Motor Skills* 34:27–34, 1972.

Carmon, A., and H. P. Bechtoldt. Dominance of the right cerebral hemisphere for stereopsis. *Neuropsychologia* 7:29–39, 1969.

Coltheart, M., K. Patterson, and J. C. Marshall, eds. *Deep Dyslexia.* London: Routledge, 1980.

Corballis, M. C. Mental rotation: Anatomy of a paradigm. In M. Potegal, ed. *Spatial Abilities* New York: Academic Press, 1982.

Corkin, S. Tactually-guided maze-learning in man: Effects of unilateral cortical excisions and bilateral hippocampal lesions. *Neuropsychologia* 3:339–351, 1965.

Corkin, S. The role of different cerebral structures in somaesthetic perception. In E. C. Carterette and M. P. Friedman, eds. *Handbook of Perception* vol. 6. New York: Academic Press, 1978.

Cowie, R. J., J. R. Krebs, and D. F. Sherry. Food storing by marsh tits. *Animal Behavior* 29:1252–1259, 1981.

Divac, I. Frontal lobe system and spatial reversal in the rat. *Neuropsychologia* 9:209–217, 1971.

Goldman, P. S., and H. E. Rosvold. Localization of function within the dorsolateral prefrontal cortex of the rhesus monkey. *Experimental Neurology* 27:291–304, 1970.

Goldman, P. S., H. E. Rosvold, B. Vest, and T. W. Galkin. Analysis of delayed-alternation deficit produced by dorsolateral prefrontal lesions in the rhesus monkeys. *Journal of Comparative and Physiological Psychology* 77:212–220, 1971.

Goldman-Rakic, P. S. Circuitry of primate prefrontal cortex and regulation of behavior by representational memory. In V. B. Mountcastle, F. Plum and S. R. Geiger, eds. *Handbook of Physiology,* vol. 5, Bethesda, MD: American Physiological Society, 1987.

Grusser, O. J. The multimodal structure of the extrapersonal space. In A. Hein and M. Jeannerod, eds. *Spatially Oriented Behavior.* New York: Springer-Verlag, 1987.

Haaxma, R., and H. G. J. M. Kuypers. Intrahemispheric cortical connections and visual guidance of hand and finger movements in the rhesus monkey. *Brain* 98:239–260, 1975.

Halpern, D. F. *Sex Differences in Cognitive Abilities.* Hillsdale, NJ: Lawrence Erlbaum, 1986.

Hannay, H. J., N. R. Varney, and A. L. Benton. Visual localization in patients with unilateral brain disease. *Journal of Neurology,Neurosurgery and Psychiatry* 39:307–313, 1976.

Harshman, R. A., E. Hampson, and S. A. Berenbaum. Individual differences in cognitive abilities and brain organization, Part I: Sex and handedness differences in ability. *Canadian Journal of Psychology* 37:144–192, 1983.

Head, H. *Studies in Neurology.* London: Oxford University Press, 1920.

Hécaen, H., J. de Ajuriaguerra, and J. Massonet. Les troubles visuoconstructifs par lésions parieto-occipitales droites. Rôle des perturbations vestibulaires. *Encephâle* 1:122–179, 1951.

Hécaen, H., C. Tzortzis, and M. C. Masure. Troubles de l'orientaiton spatiale dans une pereuve de recherce d'itineraire lors des lésions corticales unilaterales. *Perception* 1:325–330, 1972.

Hécaen, H., C. Tzortzis, and P. Rondot. Loss of topographical memory with learning deficits. *Cortex* 16:525–542, 1980.

Holmes, G. Disturbances of visual space perception. *British Medical Journal* 2:230–233, 1919.

Holmes, G., and G. Horax. Disturbances of spatial orientation and visual attention, with loss of stereoscopic vision. *Archives of Neurology and Psychiatry* 1:385–407, 1919.

Ingle, D., and K.v S. Hoff. Neural mechanisms of short-term memory in frogs. *Society for Neuroscience Abstracts* 14:692, 1988.

Jackson, J. H. On the nature of duality of the brain. *Brain* 38:80–103, 1915.

Klingon, G. H., and D. C. Bontecou. Localization in auditory space. *Neurology* 16:879–886, 1966.

Kolb, B., A. J. Nonneman, and R. K. Singh. Double dissociation of spatial impairments and perseveration following selective prefrontal lesions in rats. *Journal of Comparative and Physiological Psychology* 87:772–780, 1974.

Kolb, B., R. J. Sutherland, and I. Q. Whishaw. A comparison of the contributions of the frontal and parietal association cortex to spatial localization in rats. *Behavioral Neuroscience* 97:13–27, 1983.

Levy, J. Possible basis for the evolution of lateral specialization of the human brain. *Nature* 224:614–615, 1969.

Maccoby, E. E., and C. N. Jacklin. *The Psychology of Sex Differences.* Stanford CA: Stanford University Press, 1974.

McDaniel, W. F., and R. K. Thomas. Temporal and parietal association cortex lesions and spatial and black-white reversal learning in the rat. *Physiological Psychology* 6:300–305, 1978.

McFie, J., M. F. Piercy, and O. L. Zangwill. Visual-spatial agnosia associated with lesions of the right cerebral hemisphere. *Brain* 73:167–190, 1950.

McFie, J., and O. L. Zangwill. Visual-constructive disabilities associated with lesions of the left hemisphere. *Brain* 83:243–260, 1960.

McGee, M. G. Human spatial abilities: Psychometric studies and environmental, genetic, hormonal, and neurological influences. *Psychological Bulletin* 86:889–918, 1979.

Milner, A. D., E. M. Ockleford, and W. Dewar. Visuo-spatial performance following posterior parietal and lateral frontal lesions in stumptail macaques. *Cortex* 13:350–360, 1977.

Milner, B. Visually-guided maze learning in man: Effects of bilateral hippocampal, bilateral frontal, and unilateral cerebral lesions. *Neuropsychologia* 3:317–338, 1965.

Milner, B. Interhemispheric differences in the localization of psychological processes in man. *British Medical Bulletin* 27:272–277, 1971.

Milner, B., S. Corkin and H.-L. Teuber. Further analysis of the hippocampal amnesic syndrome: 14-year follow-up study of H. M. *Neuropsychologia* 6:215–234, 1968.

Mishkin, M., and T. Appenzeller. The anatomy of memory. *Scientific American* 256:80–89, 1987.

Mishkin, M., M. E. Lewis, and L. G. Ungerleider. Equivalence of parieto-preoccipital subareas for visuospatial ability in monkeys. *Behavioural Brain Research* 6:41–55, 1982.

Mishkin, M., and K. H. Pribram. Analysis of the effects of frontal lesions in monkeys: I. Variations of delayed alternation. *Journal of Comparative and Physiological Psychology* 48:492–495, 1955.

Mishkin, M., and K. H. Pribram. Analysis of the effects of frontal lesions in monkeys: II. Variations of delayed response. *Journal of Comparative and Physiological Psychology* 49:36–40,1956.

Mishkin, M., and L. G. Ungerleider. Contribution of striate inputs to the visuospatial functions of parieto-preoccipital cortex in monkeys. *Behavioural Brain Research* 6:57–77, 1982.

Morris, R. G. M. Spatial localization does not require the presence of local cues. *Learning and Motivation* 12:239–260, 1981.

Morris, R. G. M., P. Garrud, J. Rawlings, and J. O'Keefe. Place navigation impaired in rats with hippocampal lesions. *Nature* 297:681–683, 1982.

Nakamura, R. K., S. J. Schein, and R. Desimone. Visual responses from cells in striate cortex of monkeys rendered chronically 'blind' by lesions of nonvisual cortex. *Experimental Brain Research* 63:185–190, 1986.

Neff, W. D. Localization and lateralization of sound in space. In A. V. S. De Reuck and J. Knights, eds. *Hearing Mechanisms in Vertebrates.* Ciba Foundation Symposium. London: Churchill, 1969.

Newcombe, N. Sex-related differences in spatial ability: Problems and gaps in current approaches. In M. Potegal, ed. *Spatial Abilities.* New York: Academic Press, 1982.

Nonneman, A. J., J. Voigt, and B. E. Kolb. Comparisons of behavioral effects of hippocampal and prefrontal cortex lesions in the rat. *Journal of Comparative and Physiological Psychology* 87:249–260, 1974.

O'Keefe, J., and L. Nadel. *The Hippocampus as a Cognitive Map.* New York: Clarendon Press, 1978.

Olton, D. S. The function of septo-hippocampal connections in spatially organized behaviour. In *Functions of the Septo-Hippocampal System,* Ciba Foundation Symposium 58. New York: Elsevier North-Holland, 1978.

Olton, D. S., J. T. Becker, and G. E. Handelmann. Hippocampus, space and memory. *Behavioral and Brain Sciences* 2:313–366, 1979.

Oxbury, J. M., D. C. Campbell, and S. M. Oxbury. Unilateral spatial neglect and impairments of spatial analysis and visual perception. *Brain* 97:551–564, 1974.

Parkinson, J. K., E. A. Murray, and M. Mishkin. A selective memonic role for the hippocampus in monkeys: Memory for the location of objects. *The Journal of Neuroscience* 8:4159–4167, 1988.

Passingham, R. E. Memory of monkeys *(Maccaca mulatta)* with lesions in prefrontal cortex. *Behavioral Neuroscience* 99:3–21, 1985.

Paterson, A., and O. L. Zangwill. Disorders of visual space perception associated with lesions of the right cerebral hemisphere. *Brain* 67:331–358, 1944.

Petrides, M., and S. K. Iversen. Restricted posterior parietal lesions in the rhesus monkey and performance on visuospatial tasks. *Brain Research* 161:63–77, 1979.

Petrides, M., and B. Milner. Deficits on subject-ordered tasks after frontal-and temporal-lobe lesions in man. *Neuropsychologia* 20:249–292, 1982.

Pick, H. L., and J. J. Rieser. Children's cognitive mapping. In *Spatial Abilities,* M. Potegal, ed. New York: Academic Press, 1982.

Pohl, W. Dissociation of spatial discrimination deficits following frontal and parietal lesions in monkeys. *Journal of Comparative and Physiological Psychology* 82:227–239, 1973.

Potegal, M., ed. *Spatial Abilities.* New York: Academic Press, 1982.

Ratcliff, G. Spatial thought, mental rotation and the right cerebral hemisphere. *Neuropsychologia* 17:49–54, 1979.

Ratcliff, G. Disturbances of spatial orientation associated with cerebral lesions. In M. Potegal, ed. *Spatial Abilities: Development and Physiological Foundations.* New York: Academic Press, 1982.

Ratcliff, G., and G. A. B. Davies-Jones. Defective visual localization in focal brain wounds. *Brain* 95:49–60, 1972.

Ratcliff, G., and F. Newcombe. Spatial orientation in man: Effects of left, right, and bilateral posterior cerebral lesions. *Journal of Neurology, Neurosurgery, and Psychiatry* 36:448–454, 1973.

Ratcliff, G., R. M. Ridley, and G. Ettlinger. Spatial disorientation in the monkey. *Cortex* 13:62–65, 1977.

Renzi, E. de, *Disorders of Space Exploration and Cognition.* New York: John Wiley, 1982.

Renzi, E. de, P. Faglioni, and P. Previdi. Spatial memory and hemispheric locus of lesion. *Cortex* 13:424–433, 1977.

Renzi, E. de, P. Faglioni, and G. Scotti. Tactiles, spatial impairment and unilateral cerebral damage. *Journal of Nervous and Mental Disorders* 146:468–475, 1968.

Renzi, E. de, P. Faglioni, and G. Scotti. Judgment of spatial orientation in patients with focal brain damage. *Journal of Neurology, Neurosurgery, and Psychiatry* 34:489–495, 1971.

Renzi, E. de, and G. Scotti. The influence of spatial disorders in impairing tactual discrimination of shapes. *Cortex* 5:53–62, 1969.

Semmes, J. A non-tactual factor in astereognosis. *Neuropsychologia* 3:295–315, 1965.

Semmes, J., S. Weinstein, L. Ghent, and H.-L. Teuber. Correlates of impaired orientation in personal and extra-personal space. *Brain* 86:742–772, 1963.

Shankweiler, D. Performance of brain damaged patients on two tests of sound localization. *Journal of Comparative and Physiological Psychology* 54:375–381, 1951.

Sherry, D. F. Food storage by birds and mammals. *Advances in the Study of Behavior* 15:153–188, 1985.

Smith, M. L., and B. Milner. The role of the right hippocampus in the recall of spatial location. *Neuropsychologia* 19:781–793, 1981.

Squire, L. R. Mechanisms of memory. *Science* 232:1612–1619, 1986.

Sugishita, M., G. Ettlinger, and R. M. Ridley. Disturbance of cage finding in the monkey. *Cortex* 14:431–438, 1978.

Sutherland, R. J., and J. W. Rudy. Configural association theory: The role of the hippocampal formation in learning, memory and amnesia. *Psychobiology* 16:157–163, 1988.

Taylor, J. *The Selected Writings of John Hughlings-Jackson.* London: Hodder, 1932.

Thomas, R. K., and V. K. Weir. The effects of lesions in the frontal or posterior association cortex of rats on maze III. *Physiological Psychology* 3:210–214, 1975.

Thompson, R. Hippocampal and cortical function in a maze devoid of left and right turns. *Physiology and Behavior* 23:601–603, 1979.

Tolman, E. C. Cognitive maps in rats and men. *Psychological Review* 55:189–208, 1948.

Tyler, H. R. Abnormalities of perception and defective eye movements (Balint's syndrome). *Cortex* 4:154–171, 1968.

Ungerleider, L. G., and B. A. Brody. Extrapersonal spatial orientation: The role of posterior parietal, anterior frontal, and inferotemporal cortex. *Experimental Neurology* 56:265–280, 1977.

Ungerleider, L. G., and M. Mishkin. Two cortical visual systems. In D. Ingle, M. A. Goodale, and R. J. W. Mansfield, eds. *Analysis of Visual Behavior.* Cambridge, MA: M.I.T. Press, 1982.

Whishaw, I. Q. The decorticate rat. In B. Kolb and R. Tees, eds. *The Cortex of the Rat.* Cambridge, MA: M.I.T. Press, 1989.

Wikmark, R. G. E., I. Divac, and R. Weiss. Retention of spatial delayed alternation in rats with lesions in the frontal lobes. *Brain, Behavior and Evolution* 8:329–339, 1973.

Zangwill, O. L. *Cerebral Dominance and Its Relation to Psychological Function.* Edinburgh: Oliver & Boyd, 1960.

PART 6

DEVELOPMENT AND RECOVERY

There are two tremendously powerful ways of studying how the brain works: its growth and the behavior that flows from that growth can be correlated, or its recovery from damage and the reconstitution of behavior that follows can be correlated. This section deals with these processes. Chapter 25 examines the emergence of behavior from the developing brain, and Chapter 26 examines the emergence of behavior after brain damage. The two processes have much in common. It is noteworthy that in development there is a hierarchical emergence of behavior that has as some of its other characteristics a rostral-caudal organization (maturation occurs in the head first and the back last) and a proximal-distal organization (maturation proceeds from the trunk to the limbs). Many of the same principles seem to apply for recovery, in that lower functions recover more rapidly than higher functions, and recovery often has a rostral-caudal and proximal-distal progression.

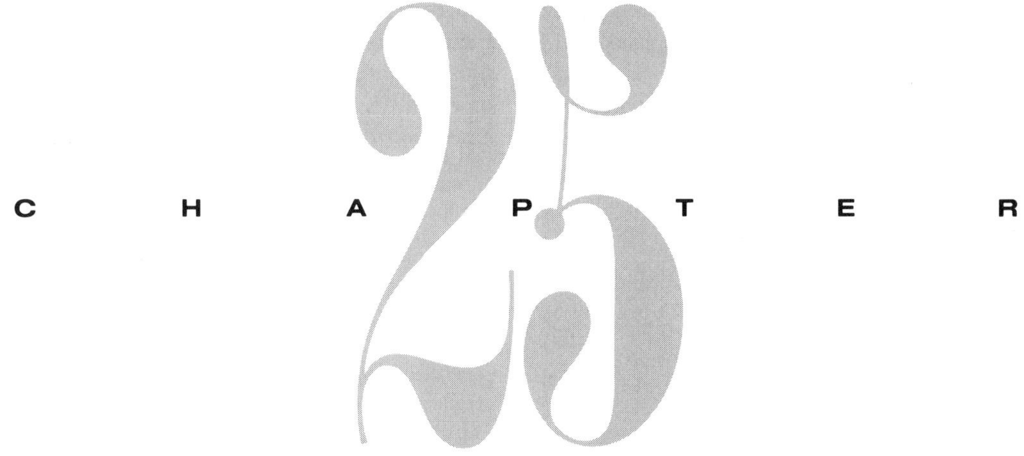

CHAPTER 25

DEVELOPMENT OF FUNCTION

Some people are attracted to developmental neuropsychology because they believe that children are neurologically simpler than adults and therefore easier to study. Others believe that analysis of the behavior and development of children will give important clues about the relative contributions of heredity and environment to the development of particular behaviors. Still others are compelled by practical necessity: they must develop programs for children who have special problems in school. The growth of developmental neuropsychology as a field of inquiry has raised further questions. Why does the brain in early life appear to be so flexible in compensating for injury and for variations in the environment? Is there an optimal environment in which development should occur? Is there an optimal method of instruction that should be used in education? How can one brain be so much more efficient than another that appears so similar under superficial examination? Thus, the object of developmental neuropsychology is to better understand nervous system function in early life, and to see whether such an understanding can contribute answers to questions such as those we have just raised.

METHODOLOGY

Behavioral changes related to neural function can be examined in three ways. The first is to look at nervous system maturation and correlate it with the development of specific behaviors. The second, the converse, is to look at behavior and then make inferences about neural maturation. The third is to relate brain malfunction or damage to behavioral disorders or cognitive deficits. Although each of these procedures is widely used, each is associated with methodological difficulties that deserve comment.

Initially, the first method, relating neural development to the emergence of specific behaviors, might seem ideal. The development of both the nervous system and behavior is orderly and similar in sequence from person to person, suggesting that correlations may be made easily (see Figure 25-1). This approach, however, has not been as useful as expected, for a number of reasons. To begin with, the nervous system develops in a relatively unremitting way, whereas behavioral changes depend on education and learning. Thus, a behavior may emerge in one environment but not in another.

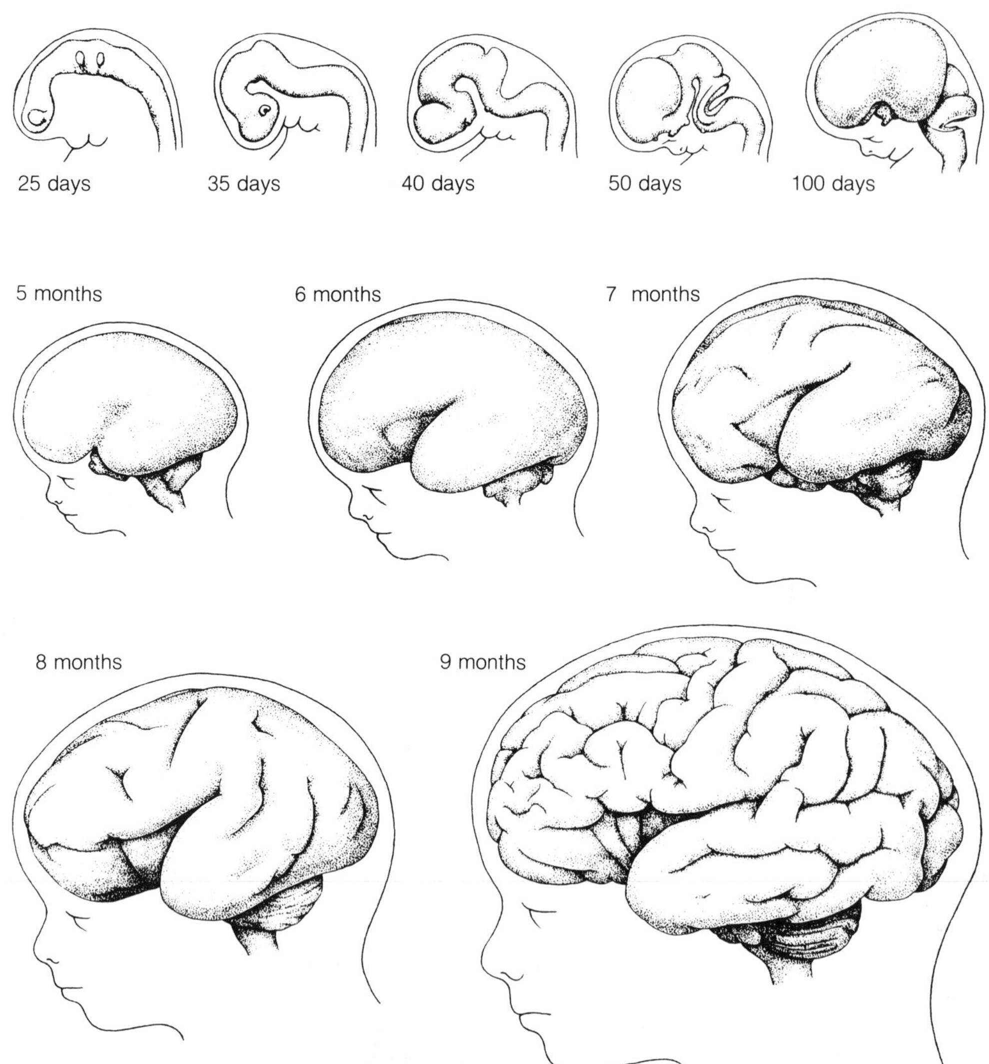

FIGURE 25-1. Prenatal development of the human brain showing a series of embryonic and fetal stages. (Adapted from W. M. Cowan. The development of the brain. *Scientific American* 241:112–133, 1979.)

Next, because age-related changes in the human nervous system are directly observable only in extraordinary circumstances, a relevant neural substrate may be difficult to identify. For example, hundreds of studies on animals have attempted, with little success, to determine some anatomical or biochemical substrate of memory. This general failure bodes ill for such correlations in humans, because in theory it is easier to correlate a neural-behavioral change in animals. Finally, behaviors deemed important may also be irrelevant. For example, there is a tendency to emphasize school behaviors as the most important for study; although these are certainly important, it must be remembered that the human brain did not evolve in a schoollike environment. The basic functions and abilities of the brain may be revealed by the study of much more fundamental processes. Reading requires spatial skills and sequencing ability. How reading skills develop may be better understood by analyzing these more basic abilities than by studying reading per se. Because developmental research focused on nervous system changes is difficult to conduct, most of it is done with animal models. Nevertheless, the principles obtained from this research should be applicable to humans.

The second approach, the analysis of nervous system function by inference from sequential changes in behavior, is not widely used. This is partly because the psychologists most interested in human development have not been primarily interested in brain function. Also, hypotheses about brain function are hard to verify because the human nervous system cannot be manipulated during development. Nevertheless, this approach is important because it is the only way models of the function of the normal human nervous system can be obtained.

The third approach, relating brain malfunction to behavioral disorders, is widely used in adult neuropsychology, but it has drawbacks when applied to developmental problems. First, much evidence suggests that the function of an immature brain may not be comparable to that of an adult brain. Freud's work, and subsequently Piaget's, suggest first that the immature brain might be incapable of certain adult functions, and second that there is no *one* immature brain. That is, the brain may be changing in such a way that principles applicable at one age are inappropriate for another age. This discontinuity may be one reason why estimates of intelligence obtained from very young children correlate poorly with their adult intelligence. Another obstacle to directly applying adult neuropsychology to developing brains is the plasticity or adaptability of the immature brain. Brain damage occurring in infancy may often go unnoticed because an undamaged portion of the brain adopts the function of the damaged zone. For example, if the speech zones of an infant's left hemisphere are damaged, speech may develop on the right. Such does not occur in an adult. Nevertheless, this approach remains important and provides major clues about the organization of the developing brain.

We point out these pitfalls in developmental neuropsychology not to deter study of developmental problems, but to caution that the neuropsychology of children may not be identical to that of adults. It is true that when adult standards are used, infants may look surprisingly like adults in a number of ways. But this similarity could be an artifact of researcher expectation: if the infant's brain is expected to be like the adult's, and if it is therefore studied only with tests initially designed for the study of adults, then phenomena peculiar to infants and children may be ignored.

A NEURAL PERSPECTIVE ON DEVELOPMENT

Cellular Basis of Brain Development

The process of brain growth and differentiation consists of a series of biological changes occurring at a particular age and in a relatively fixed sequence. These include (1) the migration of cells, (2) the formation and growth of axons, (3) the formation of dendrites, (4) the formation of synaptic connections, and (5) myelination. This program of development has two extraordinary features. First, subcomponents of the nervous system are formed from cells whose destination and function are predetermined before they migrate from the wall of the ventricles. Second, development is marked by an initial abundance of cells, branches, and connections, with an important part of subsequent maturation consisting of cell death or pruning back of the initial surfeit. Since the discovery of this second aspect of development, the common image of brain development as one of building a nervous system by the successive addition of parts has been replaced by the image of sculpting a nervous system from a larger unformed neural edifice.

Because of either deficits in the genetic program, intrauterine trauma, the influence of toxic agents, or other factors, peculiarities or errors in development can occur that may contribute to obvious and severe deformities such as those listed in Table 25-1. Less pronounced deficits may become manifest in such things as learning disabilities or may contribute only to subtle differences in individuality. In the following sections each of these normal biological processes is briefly described along with abnormalities that occur when a process is not properly completed.

Cell Migration. Nerve cells form by division in the inner, or ventricular, lining of the brain. Here a cell gives rise to two daughter cells which either migrate or undergo further division. The division of germinal cells may be complete by the middle of gestation, whereas migration of cells to targets may continue for a number of months and may even continue postnatally. The precise timing of the development and migration of cells to different cytoarchitectonic regions varies by area. Furthermore, adjacent germinal areas on the ventricular wall may, at the same time, produce cells destined for quite distinct layers in different cortical areas. By the fifth embryonic month, cortical layers V and VI are visible, and subsequent layers develop and continue to mature up to about 8 months postnatally. The mechanisms that control migration and determine the destination of migrating cells is not well understood. It is known that spe-

TABLE 25-1. Types of abnormal development

Type	Symptom
Anencephaly	Absence of cerebral hemispheres, diencephalon, and midbrain
Holoprosencephaly	Cortex forms as a single undifferentiated hemisphere.
Lissencephaly	The brain fails to form sulci and gyri and corresponds to a 12-week embryo.
Micropolygyria	Gyri are more numerous, smaller, and more poorly developed than normal.
Macrogyria	Gyri are broader and less numerous than normal.
Microencephaly	Development of the brain is rudimentary and the person has low-grade intelligence.
Porencephaly	Symmetrical cavities in the cortex, where cortex and white matter should be
Heterotopia	Displaced islands of gray matter appear in the ventricular walls or white matter, caused by aborted cell migration
Agenesis of the corpus callosum	Complete or partial absence of the corpus callosum
Cerebellar agenesis	Portions of the cerebellum, basal ganglia, or spinal cord are absent or malformed.

cialized filaments provide a pathway for migrating cells to follow.

Once a group of cells has arrived at the surface, differentiation (formation of axons, dendrites, etc.) begins. Subsequently, a new group of cells migrates from the inner lining through the layers already present to form a new outer layer. Thus, a structure such as the cortex matures from its inner to its outer surface.

Migration can stop prematurely, leaving a group of cells that should normally appear as an outer layer scattered instead among inner layers of cells. Caviness and Sidman have made a major study of disturbed cell migration in the cortex of a genetic mutant mouse called the reeler mouse. In this animal the first-generated cells lie near the surface and the last-generated lie deepest, creating a cortex that is inverted from that of a normal mouse. Despite their aberrant position, the cells receive and give off appropriate connections, but the mice have an abnormal, reeling movement. Cases of failure or incomplete cell migration in humans have also been described.

Axonal Growth. Axons begin sprouting from neurons as they migrate to their targets. Sprouting axons grow in a given direction either because the cell body is oriented in a particular way or because of other, unknown factors. The growing end of the axon, called the growth cone, was first recognized and described by Ramón y Cajal in the 1890s. He wrote:

> I had the good fortune to behold for the first time that fantastic ending of the growing axon. In my sections of the three-day chick embryo, this ending appeared as a concentration of protoplasm of conical form, endowed with ameboid movements. It could be compared with a living battering ram, soft and flexible, which advances, pushing aside mechanically the obstacles which it finds in its way, until it reaches the area of its peripheral distribution. This curious terminal club, I christened the growth cone. (Ramón y Cajal, 1937)

In general, the axon grows at a rate of 7 to 170 μm per hour. Axon branching occurs at the growth cone. It is possible that the growth cone forms synapses and retains the capacity to renew growth, which may thus underlie the formation of new synapses during the course of learning.

A major unanswered question in developmental neurobiology concerns the forces that initiate and guide axonal growth. Axons have specific targets that they must reach if the neuron is to survive and become functional. Some axons grow because they are towed from their cell bodies by a structure that is growing away from the region, such as when the muscles grow away from the spinal cord early in development. Other axons traverse enormous distances and are able to overcome obstacles such as being moved to another location, having their cell bodies rotated, or having their targets moved. Although the forces that guide this homing are not understood, there are several possibilities: axons may follow an electrical or chemical gradient or a particular physical substrate, or they may send out many branches, or shoots, and when one reaches an appropriate target the others follow. It is also possible that several such mechanisms may be operating simultaneously or sequentially.

The formation of appropriate neural pathways may be disrupted in any of a number of ways. Axons may be unable to reach their target if their way is blocked, as may happen following scaring from head trauma during the early months of life. Their development may also be disrupted by anoxia, ingestion of toxic materials, malnutrition, or some other disturbance. Several reports of anomalous fiber systems in mutant strains of mice also suggest that abnormalities could have a genetic basis. There have been cases in which the corpus callosum is of abnormal size or is absent, and cases in which the fiber pathways in the hippocampal system are abnormal. In a number of albino animal species, and possibly also in human albinos, the ipsilateral optic pathway is reduced in size and area of distribution. Since the brain processes information sequentially, similar disruption of transcortical or interhemispheric connections during development could be related to the cognitive difficulties that some humans have. In fact, it has been suggested that some learning disorders might originate in delayed, incomplete, or inappropriate formulation of the cortical fiber system.

Axonal development might also be disrupted if the axons' target is damaged, in which case the axonal system may degenerate or may occupy an inappropriate target. Should the latter event occur the behavior supported by the invaded area may also be disrupted. In a well-documented study of abnormal fiber growth Schneider has shown that if the optic tectum in the hamster is removed on one side at birth, the fibers that should normally project to it project instead to the opposite side. This aberrant pathway is functional, but in a curious way. If a visual stimulus is presented to the eye contralateral to the damaged tectum, the hamster turns in the direction opposite to that of the stimulus. The message has traveled from the eye to the wrong tectum, a tectum that would ordinarily receive input from the opposite side of the world. The abnormalities of posture and movement seen in some sorts of **athetosis** and **dystonia** in children may occur because fiber systems supporting posture and movement invade the wrong target, causing an intended movement to be disrupted by an inappropriate movement. Should this be the case, it is not surprising that lesions in the thalamus, which might sever such an abnormal connection, can result in improved posture and movement.

Axons also appear to be capable of overcoming obstacles to reach their targets. For example, if the spinal cord is partially sectioned, pyramidal tract axons that should pass through the damaged portion of the cord may cross over to the undamaged side of the cord and then complete their journey to their appropriate target by recrossing the cord. Axons may also fill in for other axons. If the pyramidal cells of one hemisphere of the cortex are destroyed in early life, the axons of pyramidal cells from the other hemisphere will occupy the targets of the missing cells.

Dendritic Growth. In contrast to the development of axons, dendrite growth usually starts after the cell reaches its final position in the cortex and proceeds at a relatively slow rate. The growth of dendrites parallels that of axons, growth and division also occurring at a growth cone. Generally, the growth of dendrites is timed to intercept the axons that are to innervate them. Although dendritic development begins prenatally in the human, it continues for a long time postnatally. Before birth there are few dendritic spines on dendrites but after birth they begin to develop and densely cover the maturing dendrites. During development, cells undergo stages in which they have an overabundance of branches and spines which they subsequently lose. The loss of dendrites and spines is sometimes referred to as *pruning*. The remaining branches may undergo extensive growth and branching (Figure 25-2).

In studies of abnormalities in dendrites it is difficult to determine whether a disorder is specifically dendritic or is secondary to inappropriate cell location, abnormal innervation, ingestion of a neurotoxin, or some other cause. Reduced afferent innervation is known to lead to a reduction in the number of dendritic spines. Studies of the cerebral cortex in various types of mental retardation indicate a number of dendritic abnormalities. Dendrites may be thinner, with fewer than the normal numbers of spines; the dendrites may be short stalks with small spines; or there may be simply a reduction in spine number. What causes these changes is not known, but the histology gives the general impression that they are a carry-over from the embryonic condition.

Synaptic Formation

It was thought initially that synaptic formation might be orderly and parallel the various developmental patterns of cell migration and maturation.

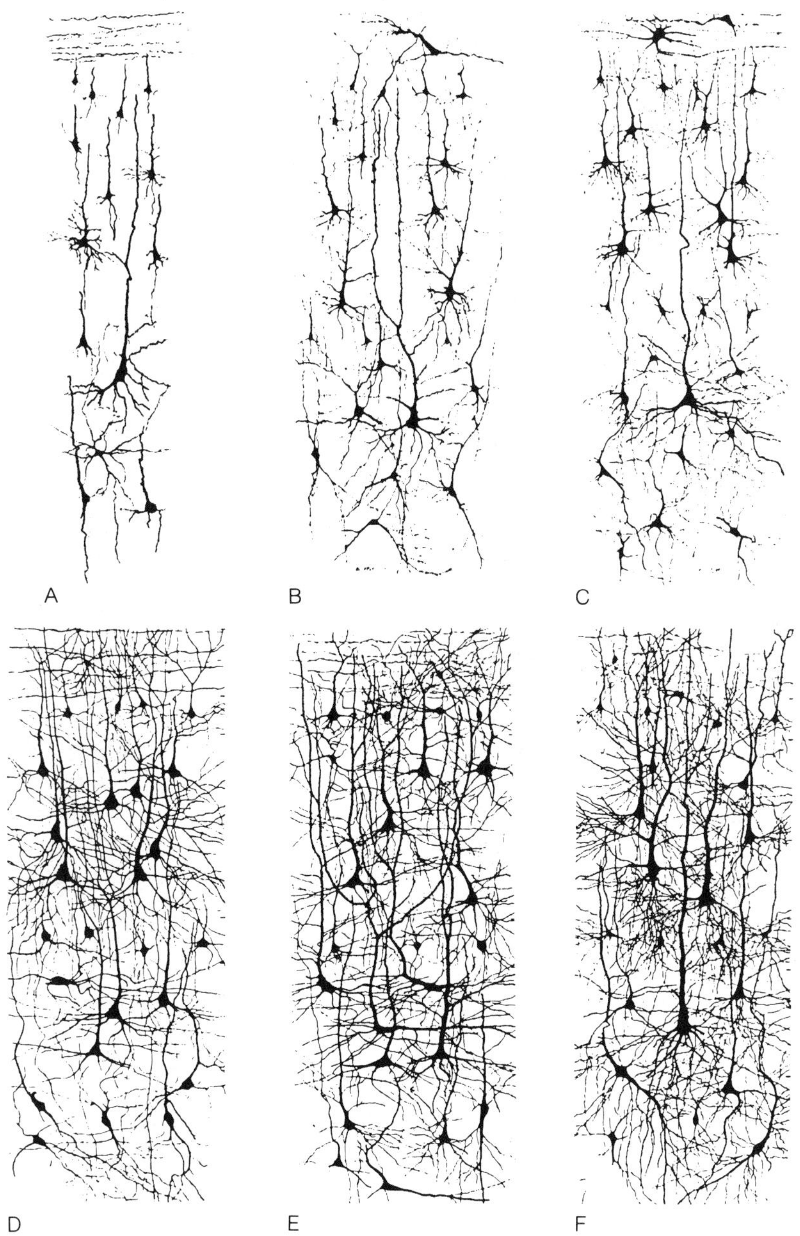

FIGURE 25-2. Postnatal development of human cerebral cortex around Broca's area taken from camera-lucida drawing of Golgi-cox preparations. *A.* Newborn: reflex sucking, rooting, swallowing, infantile grasping, blinks to light. *B.* One month: Extends and turns neck when prone, looks at mother, follows objects, smiles when played with. *C.* Three months: infantile grasp and sucking modified at will, looks at moving objects, watches hands. *D.* Six months: Grasps objects with both hands, supports weight on hands when prone, stands briefly, laughs, primitive "ga-goo" sounds, smiles at self in mirror. *E.* Fifteen months: smiles at self in mirror, grasps objects between thumb and forefinger (pincer grasp), walks, understands and says words. *F.* Twenty-four months: walks up and down stairs, partial self-dressing, uses simple sentences, points to body parts, says no (terrible two's). (From E. Lenneberg. *Biological Foundations of Language.* New York: John Wiley, © 1967.)

Surprisingly, Rakic and his coworkers have found that synaptic formation occurs concurrently in all cortical layers and in all cortical areas. Synapses in the rhesus monkey were found to start developing in the last two months before birth and to continue for several months after birth. Thereafter, there was a rapid decline during the second part of the first year of life and a slower decline during the rest of life. In humans, synaptic density is thought to increase until about 2 years of age, after which about 50% of synapses are lost by age 16. The process of loss of synapses is sometimes referred to as *shedding*. These results suggest that if experience alters synapses during development, it does so by influencing survival, rather than by regulating their initial formation.

It is clear from many studies that a given brain region sends axons to only a limited number of other regions, and that synapses are made only in a specific part of certain cells in that region. The locations of synapses are determined in part by genetic instruction, in part by the orientation of the cell when the axons arrive, in part by the timing of axon arrival (axons apparently compete for available space), and in part by the use they are given once a connection is made. In addition, the pharmacology of the synapse is flexible. For example, it has been found that individual neurons can become either norepinephrinergic or cholinergic depending on their environment. Malfunctions in any of these features of synaptic formation may cause abnormal brain development.

Myelination. Myelination is the process by which the support cells of the nervous system begin to surround axons and provide them with insulation. Although nerves can become functional before myelination, it is assumed that they reach adult functional levels as myelination is completed. Thus, myelination provides an index of the maturity of structures from which axons project and to which they project.

If myelination is used as an index of maturation, then the anatomical developmental work of Flechsig indicates that the neocortex begins a sequential development at a relatively early age. The primary sensory areas and motor areas show some myelination just before term. The secondary cortical areas become myelinated within the next four postnatal months, and by the fourth month the tertiary areas of the cortex are becoming myelinated. Although myelination begins during the early postnatal period, it continues to increase beyond 15 years of age and may increase in density as late as age 60. Any disruption in this ongoing process can potentially cause neural, and hence behavioral, abnormalities.

Postnatal Brain Development. After birth, the brain does not grow uniformly but rather tends to increase its mass during irregular periods commonly called *growth spurts*. In his analysis of brain-body weight ratios, Epstein found consistent spurts in brain growth at 3–10 months to 1.5 years, and 2–4, 6–8, 10–12, and 14–16 years. The increment during the first spurt was about 30% by weight, and increments during subsequent spurts were about 5 to 10% by weight. Paradoxically, the increase takes place in the face of losses in neurons, dendrites, and synapses and is likely due to an increase in growth of the processes of the cells that remain. It might be thought that cognitive changes accompany the periods of brain growth, and that is the case. Significantly, the first four brain-growth stages coincide with the classically given ages of onset of the four main stages of intelligence development described by Piaget.

ENVIRONMENTAL INFLUENCES ON DEVELOPMENT

The environment in which development occurs can profoundly influence behavior, as has been suggested by anecdotal reports about how deprivation has produced impoverished behavior in children. For example, Singh and Zingg report that children raised by wolves behave like wolves and are difficult to socialize; on the other hand, Skeels reports that children removed from substandard orphanages (and placed in a mental institution) develop normal intelligence by adulthood, but those that are not removed remain retarded. The children in the mental institution apparently received attention from the patients that was not given to those that remained in the orphanage. These reports are seemingly confirmed by Harlow in formal studies on the effects of early deprivation on the maturation of monkeys. How do the conditions of early environment affect nervous system development? There are several possibilities, each of which has received some support in recent experimental work. (1) The nervous system develops independently, but requires stimulation for maintained function. (2) The nervous system develops independently in part, but requires stimulation for continued maturation beyond some point. Inappropriate stimulation may change the system's properties. (3) The properties of the nervous system are not innate, but develop only with appropriate stimulation. Experimental work has been advanced most by studies using the visual system as a model and such work has provided support for each of these possibilities. In all cases the importance of stimulation is emphasized. The term **functional validation** is sometimes used to express the idea that to become fully functional a neural system requires stimulation at some point.

Environmental Influences on Brain Size

The simplest measure of the effects of environment on the nervous system is brain size. Environmental influences on animal brain size have been investigated; domestic animals have certain cortical areas that are up to 10 to 20% smaller than those of animals of the same species and strain raised in the wild. These differences are apparently related to factors that occur early in life, since animals born in the wild and later domesticated have brains the same size as animals raised in the wild. The part of the brain that seems to be most affected by a domestic upbringing is the occipital cortex, which is reduced in size by as much as 35% in some animals. This reduction may be related to smaller eye and retina size.

An extensive experimental literature now exists on the effects of environmental manipulation on brain size and anatomy. Exposure to an enriched environment increases brain size, most noticeably in the neocortex, with the greatest increase occurring in the occipital neocortex. Related to increased size are increases in the density of glial cells, in the number of higher order dendritic spines on neurons, in the number of synaptic spines, and in the size of synapses. These changes are most pronounced if enriched experience is given in early life; similar less pronounced effects can be obtained with more prolonged exposure given in later life. In addition to these anatomical changes, enriched animals can perform better than their impoverished counterparts on a number of tests of learning and memory. However, given that the enriched environment of the laboratory experiment may be less than or only equivalent to that of a wild habitat, these findings mean that exposure to an impoverished laboratory retards the development of the nervous system and reduces performance on a number of tests.

Environmental Influences on Function: Examples from the Visual System

Clinical studies have shown that disturbances of the optics of the eye (e.g., cataracts and astigmatism) during early life cause long-lasting impairments of vision even after the optical defects are corrected. These impairments, called **amblyopia** — dimness of vision without obvious impairment of the eye — are presumed to be caused by changes in the central nervous system. Behavioral studies have shown that amblyopia can be produced in animals; its case has been extensively analyzed in studies using cats and monkeys. This area of research now provides one of the most penetrating insights into factors affecting development and deserves careful study.

Hubel and Wiesel and others have described the response patterns of normal cells in area 17 of the visual cortex. They recorded the activity of cells in anesthetized animals while visual stimuli were presented on a screen placed in the animal's visual field. The cells respond to a number of properties of a visual stimulus, including its orientation and direction; they also respond according to which eye it is presented and are affected by binocular disparity (the different view each eye has of the stimulus). Using a profile of the activity of cells in a normal cat's area 17, Hubel and Wiesel addressed the question of the function of area 17 in kittens whose eyes had not yet opened. In 8-day-old kittens they found that although the cells are sluggish and become fatigued quickly, they show the properties of the adult cat's cells to the first presentation of visual stimulation. The results of this and similar studies suggest that the visual system has normal response capacity before being stimulated by light. What, then, of the environment's contribution?

To assess the contributions of the environment, two conditions of visual deprivation have been used: **binocular deprivation** and **monocular deprivation.** In the first, animals are deprived by being reared in the dark or by their eyelids being sutured before they open. This deprivation produces no change in the retina and only mild changes in the lateral geniculate nucleus — the major relay of the visual cortex. By contrast, cells in the visual cortex undergo disturbances of protein synthesis and have fewer and shorter dendrites, fewer spines, and 70% fewer synapses than normal. Analysis of the properties of these cells shows that after a number of months of early deprivation there are severe abnormalities, which disappear to some extent with normal visual experience. Deprivation in later life does not produce the same initial period of abnormality. Thus, visual stimulation in early life is important for continued development of visual cells, but the visual system retains some ability to compensate.

The second deprivation condition, monocular deprivation, surprisingly has a severer effect than binocular deprivation. If one eyelid is sutured during early life, the eye appears to be essentially blind for a period of weeks after opening, although its function does improve somewhat with time. Cell-recording studies show either that stimulation in the deprived eye cannot activate cells in the cortex or that in those few cases in which it can, the cells are highly abnormal. The experiments also show that the earlier deprivation occurs, the shorter the deprivation period required and the severer the effects. These results confirm that deprivation can retard development, and that early deprivation is the most influential. The experiments also suggest that factors other than deprivation alone must be operative to produce the severe effects found.

Apparently competition also contributes to the severity of deficits in the deprived eye. Kratz and coworkers found that if the normal eye of an animal was removed after the other eye had been deprived for 5 months, the deprived eye gave comparatively normal responses in 31% of the cells, compared with only 6% when the normal eye was present. This finding is confirmed by a number of more indirect experiments. These results imply that the deprived portion of the visual system has the capacity to function but is inhibited from doing so by the good portion of the visual system. If inhibition of function is removed, the deprived portion of the visual system begins to function.

Can the visual system be changed by manipulation less drastic than complete sensory deprivation? Hirsch and Spinelli fitted kittens with lenses that brought a set of horizontal stripes into focus on one retina and a set of vertical stripes into focus on the other. After later removal of the lenses, they found that cells responded only if the stimulus was oriented close to the horizontal when viewed with the eye that had seen horizontal during the exposure period, and only to a stimulus oriented close to the vertical when viewed with the eye that had seen vertical stripes. These findings have been confirmed for kittens raised in an environment of stripes or of spots or in an environment organized to be devoid of movement. In fact, work by Blakemore and Mitchell indicates that one hour of exposure on day 28 after birth is sufficient to bias a cortical unit to respond to a particular pattern.

In summary, this work suggests that the visual system is genetically programmed to make normal connections and normal responses, but can lose much of this capacity if it is not exercised during the early months of life. When part of the system is deprived, in addition to loss of capacity caused by the deprivation, the system is inhibited by the remaining functional areas, and the defect is potentiated. Removal of inhibition can permit some degree of recovery. Finally, if the environment is so arranged that the system is exposed to stimuli of one type, the cells in the system are biased to respond to stimuli of that type.

Although these conclusions come from experiments performed on a relatively low level of the visual system, the results can be generalized to other sensory systems and cortical areas. For example, our inability to perceive certain sounds in languages unfamiliar to us may result partly from disuse, inhibition, or the development of an incompatibility set within the auditory cortex. These experiments suggest speculative questions about the function of the brain. Under normal circumstances, how much do used portions of the brain tend to inhibit unused portions of the brain? Does the development of language in one hemisphere inhibit its development in the other? These questions will be asked in future experiments undertaken to analyze the secondary and tertiary areas of the cortex.

A BEHAVIORAL PERSPECTIVE ON DEVELOPMENT

Asymmetry

Just as asymmetrical function of the adult brain has been a focal point for neurological study, so has the development of asymmetry been a focal point for development studies. Most of the research with children has been designed to demonstrate lateralization of function, emphasizing the question of the age at which asymmetry first appears. The central theoretical issue in this research revolves around the hypotheses of maturation of asymmetry as opposed to invariance of asymmetry. According to the **maturation hypothesis** asymmetry develops with aging, is not necessarily hemisphere-specific, and may be influenced in important ways by environmental events. According to the **invariance hypothesis** functions are asymmetrically located in the hemispheres because they depend on certain anatomical circuitry of the brain, and this in turn is presumably genetically determined. If and when a particular behavior becomes lateralized may still depend on both the age the behavior develops and the form in which it is acquired. Because of the complexities of the questions that are asked, the results of many studies on asymmetry are equivocal. Some of the difficulties in interpretation have been reviewed by Bryden. Let handedness serve as an example. Hand preference for writing cannot, obviously, be determined in infants. Therefore, an assumption has to be made that hand strength or some other measure will serve as an indication of handedness. Even if a good correlation is obtained between a measure such as hand strength and the hand subsequently used for writing, such a relation would be expected by chance alone, since most people are right-handed. Even if perfect correlations were subsequently obtained, environmental influences must still be accounted for; after all, children copy their parents. Then, a neural substrate has to be found. This is likely to be difficult. For speech it is thought that the large left temporal planum is the substrate, yet it is larger on the left in only about 60 to 70% of people, whereas speech is lateralized to the left in a much higher proportion of people. At the present time the invariance hypothesis is strongly favored. It is thought that each hemisphere has a special potential for acquiring various functions, and that this relation between hemisphere and function would only be changed if brain damage were incurred. Even then, however, the way in which a hemisphere acquires a functional capacity may be hemisphere-specific. As will be pointed out in the following sections, under certain circumstances both hemispheres may learn to speak, but each will be constrained in its use of language in specific ways. Table 25-2 gives examples of the earliest ages and side of lateralization of a number of representative functions. Undeniably, lateralization is found even in the very immature brain, and it is this that provides compelling support for the invariance hypothesis.

Asymmetry in the Auditory System

Asymmetry in the auditory system has been demonstrated in infants only a few weeks old. Entus combined the dichotic-listening technique with a test known by the awesome name of the ***nonnutritive high-amplitude sucking paradigm.*** In the study the infant was given the opportunity to suck on a nipple and then to learn that if it increased its sucking rate it would receive an auditory stimulus through one or the other side of a pair of earphones. Entus presented phonemes such as "ma" and "ba," or the note A (440 Hz) played on different instruments, such as the piano or viola. Entus found that the infants changed their sucking rate in such a way that they received more phonemes through the right earphone than the left, and more musical notes through the left earphone than the right. This evidence suggested that there was a lateralized brain preference — left for phonemes, right for notes — as early as 22 days. In support of this conclusion a variety of evoked-potential and electroencephalographic studies suggest that very young infants have similarly lateralized preferences for phonemes and tones. In

TABLE 25-2. Studies showing age of asymmetry for different behaviors

System	Age	Dominance	Basic reference
Auditory			
Speech syllables	Preterm	Right ear	Molfese and Molfese, 1980
Music	22–140 days	Left ear	Entus, 1977
Phonemes	22–140 days	Right ear	Entus, 1977
Words	4 years	Right ear	Kimura, 1963
Environmental sounds	5–8 years	Left ear	Knox and Kimura, 1970
Visual			
Rhythmic visual stimuli	Newborn	Right	Crowell et al., 1973
Face recognition	7–9 years	Left field	Marcel and Rajan, 1975
	6–13 years	Left field	Witelson, 1973
	9–10 years	None	Diamond and Carey, 1977
Somatosensory			
Dichaptic recognition	All ages	Left	Witelson, 1977
Motor			
Stepping	<3 months	Right	Peters and Petrie, 1979
Head turning	Neonates	Right	Turkewitz, 1977
Grasp duration	1–4 months	Right	Caplan and Kinesbourne, 1976
Finger tapping	3–5 years	Right	Ingram, 1975
Strength	3–5 years	Right	Ingram, 1975
Gesturing	3–5 years	Right	Ingram, 1975
Head orientation	Neonates	Right	Michel, 1981

addition, many studies using the standard dichotic-listening technique have found an adultlike asymmetry in children 3 years of age and older.

Asymmetry in the Visual System. There have been many attempts to use the tachistoscopic method of visual presentation to demonstrate perceptual asymmetries in the visual system of children. In a thorough review, Witelson concluded that not one tachistoscopic study of left hemisphere specialization in children is free of methodological difficulty or provides unequivocal results. Tachistoscopic studies of right hemisphere specialization have been more convincing and have indicated right hemisphere effects in children as young as 6 years of age. From their use of a strobe-light test Crowell and colleagues even suggest a right hemisphere effect in newborns. Using findings that repetitive strobe-light flashes produce bilateral photic driving in adults (i.e., particular EEG waves occurring in both hemispheres at the same frequency as the flash), he tested newborn babies for the same phenomenon. Newborns showed photic driving only in the right hemisphere (or in some cases not at all); Crowell interpreted this result as evidence of right hemisphere specialization for the perception of rhythmic visual stimuli.

Asymmetry in Motor Control. The study of the development of hand preference is intriguing in view of the relation between handedness and cerebral control of language. Thus, the emergence of hand preference (presumably for the right hand) is commonly inferred to be indicative of left hemisphere specialization. Although this inference is somewhat tenuous at best, it is nevertheless worthy of consideration. After hundreds of studies on this subject, considerable disagreement remains about results and their interpretation alike. The major problem is deciding how to measure hand preference. If frequency of reaching is taken as the measure, there appears to be a *left*-hand preference at about 4 to 5 months, followed by a switch to a *right*-hand preference at about 6 to 9 months, which increases from then until 8 to 9 years. Measures of grasp duration, however, favor the right hand as early as 1 month of age. In general, although hand preference is evident in most tests by 1 year, the data at early ages are far from clear.

Observations favoring left hemisphere specialization for motor control by age 3 or earlier include increased right-hand gesturing during speech (as seen also in adults) and reduced speed for finger tapping with the right hand, but not the left, when in competition with talking—a finding similar to those of analogous experiments with adults.

A study by Ingram is intriguing: she found both left- and right-hand effects in the same children, according to the task tested. At age 3 the right hand was stronger, the right fingers tapped faster, and the right hand showed increased gesturing during speech. Thus, the right hand showed an adult response pattern. The left hand copied hand postures of the deaf alphabet and finger spacing of a hand position significantly better. The left-hand tasks may be interpreted as measuring spatial control of hand and finger movements, thus indicating that the right hemisphere is specialized for certain aspects of spatial motor control as early as age 3. Curiously, this result is not obtained with adults.

Does Asymmetry Develop?. According to many studies of the development of asymmetry, the differences become greater with age. Can this be taken as evidence that lateralization of function continues to develop? Apparently not, because the methodological and theoretical problems of such an inference have often been pointed out. Lateralization scores are usually used to indicate relative differences of function of the two hemispheres, not degree of difference or specialization. Therefore, to use difference scores across different ages to indicate development of lateralization would be inappropriate. The emergence of such differences may indicate the development of cognitive ability, not of its lateralization.

What Determines the Development of Asymmetry?. According to an old doctrine called *Muller's law of specific nerve energy,* an area of the brain performs its given function because it receives fibers from a given sensory system. For example, we see with the visual cortex because that region receives fibers from the eye. This doctrine's explanatory usefulness is open to dispute, however. And if the law is not an entirely adequate explanation of why we see with a particular area of the cortex (we could, for example, hear with color and see with sounds), what is the explanation for why we speak with one hemisphere? What is its special property that it can assume that function? What property allows the other hemisphere to support nonlanguage abilities? One explanation is that the anatomy of particular areas is well developed, making it easier for one hemisphere to adopt a given function than for the other. Thus, language becomes a left hemisphere function because the left temporal cortex is genetically programmed to be well developed and process auditory sounds more easily than the right; likewise, because the right hemisphere is well developed in other areas, it adopts other functions. We believe this the most likely explanation, although other theories have been proposed favoring either greater activity of the reticular activating system on one side than on the other, or environmental factors. Our explanation is at least consistent with the principles obtained from experiments on the cat's visual system. Lateralization is innate, but requires functional validation, as we shall see below.

Environmental Influences on Asymmetry. Although the evidence so far recounted suggests an inborn predisposition toward lateralization of cerebral function, there is convincing evidence that environmental factors play a significant role. Recall that although the cat's visual system appears functionally and anatomically mature when the eyes open, visual deprivation, especially of just one eye, seriously affects the system. Similarly, it is reasonable to suppose that the environment could enhance or retard the development of other cerebral functions such as language. Two lines of evidence support this proposition: (1) the absence of normal cerebral lateralization in illiterate or deaf adults, and (2) anomalous hemispheric development following social isolation and experiential deprivation.

Asymmetry in Illiterate and Deaf People. Studies by Cameron and colleagues and by Wechsler have reported that aphasia is equally probable following either left or right hemisphere damage in illiterate persons. Furthermore, Tzavaras and coworkers, using a dichotic-listening task, have reported that illiterate subjects showed a greater right-ear effect for language stimuli than literate subjects. These are provocative findings, for they imply that experience with language—particularly complex language skills such as reading and writing—somehow influences cerebral asymmetry.

An analogous finding is that literate, congenitally deaf persons have abnormal patterns of cerebral organization, as indicated by two different lines of work. First, according to Neville, two different laboratories have independently reported that congenitally deaf persons fail to show the usual right visual-field superiority in tasks of linguistic processing. This failure could be interpreted as evidence that if experience with auditory language is absent, lateralization of some aspect or aspects of nonauditory language functions is abolished. Second, Neville reported that during perception of life drawings, visual evoked potentials were significantly larger on the *right* in children with normal hearing, and significantly larger on the *left* in deaf children who used American Sign Language to communicate. Curiously, there was no asymmetry at all in children who could not sign but merely used pantomime to communicate. From the signers' left hemisphere effect for line drawings Neville inferred that the deaf signers acquired their sign language much as normal children acquire verbal language: with their left hemispheres. However, since sign language has a visuospatial component, certain visuospatial functions may have developed in the left hemisphere, producing an unexpected left hemisphere effect. The lack of asymmetry in nonsigners could mean that the absence of language experience somehow abolished certain aspects of cerebral asymmetry or, alternatively, that the expression of cerebral asymmetry depends on language experience. If the nonsigners learn Ameslan, and do so before puberty (the reasons are discussed below), they might develop an asymmetrical evoked-potential pattern similar to those of children who already sign.

Although congenital deafness may alter certain aspects of cerebral organization, Kimura, in reviewing 11 cases of signing disorders following brain damage, finds the similarity with speakers is remarkable. Her results are summarized in Table 25-3. Note that of the nine right-handed signers with left hemisphere lesions, all had a signing disorder. In two left-handers, one had a disorder with a left hemisphere lesion and one had a disorder with a right hemisphere lesion. These values are just those that would be expected in a population of vocal communicators. Sign comprehension and writing comprehension were affected in much the same way as was signing, but reading was undisturbed. Kimura postulates that reading was spared because it is not syllabically based (see the discussion below on patients with hemidecortications) but is achieved rather by visual-to-visual matching. The instructive feature of Kimura's review is that it shows that the development of a language based on signs has the same anatomical basis as do regular vocal languages. This strongly supports the idea that language has a preferential base and that this base is anatomically determined.

TABLE 25-3. Manual signing disorders in left- and right-handed patients

	Disorder with left hemisphere lesion	Disorder with right hemisphere lesion
Right-handers	9	0
Left-handers	1	1

Source: Adapted from Kimura, 1981.

Genie: The Effect of Social Isolation and Experiential Deprivation on Language. It is well known that deprivation retards development. An important question is whether deprivation retards or prevents the development of cerebral lateralization and, further, whether a child so deprived can "catch up," wholly or partly. Genie is a child whose isolation resulted from a deliberate attempt to keep her from normal social and experiential stimuli.

> Genie was found when she was 13 years, 9 months, at which time she was an unsocialized, primitive human being, emotionally disturbed, unlearned, and without language. She had been taken into protective custody by the police, and, on November 4, 1970, was admitted into the Children's Hospital of Los Angeles for evaluation with a tentative diagnosis of severe malnutrition. She remained in the Rehabilitation Center of the hospital until August 13, 1971. At that time she entered a foster home where she has been living ever since as a member of the family.
>
> When admitted to the hospital, Genie was painfully thin, had a distended abdomen, and appeared to be six or seven years younger than her age. She was 54.5 inches tall and weighed 62.25 pounds. She was unable to stand erect, could not chew solid or even semi-solid foods, had great difficulty in swallowing, was incontinent of feces and urine, and was mute.
>
> The tragic and bizarre story which was uncovered revealed that for most of her life Genie suffered physical and social restriction, nutritional neglect, and extreme experiential deprivation. There is evidence that from about the age of 20 months until shortly before admission to the hospital Genie had been isolated in a small closed room, tied into a potty chair where she remained

> most or all hours of the day, sometimes overnight. A cloth harness, constructed to keep her from handling her feces was her only apparel of wear. When not strapped into the chair she was kept in a covered infant crib, also confined from the waist down. The door to the room was kept closed, and the windows were curtained. She was hurriedly fed (only cereal and baby food) and minimally cared for by her mother, who was almost blind during most of the years of Genie's isolation. There was no radio or TV in the house and the father's intolerance of noise of any kind kept any acoustic stimuli, which she received behind the closed door, to a minimum. (The first child born to this family died from pneumonia when three months old after being put in the garage because of noisy crying.) Genie was physically punished by the father if she made any sounds. According to the mother, the father and older brother never spoke to Genie although they barked like dogs at her. The mother was forbidden to spend more than a few minutes with Genie during feeding. (Fromkin et al., 1974, pp. 84–85)

At Genie's birth (by Caesarean section) she was 7 lb, 7.5 oz and according to the pediatrician's records was within normal weight limits at 11 months. There is no suggestion of retardation, her only serious physical anomaly being a dislocated hip.

It is unknown whether Genie ever began to speak words prior to her isolation, but when she was discovered she did not speak at all. Her only sound was a "throaty whimper." Even when angry, although she would scratch at her face, blow her nose violently into her clothes, and urinate, she would not vocalize, possibly because she had been whipped by her father when she did. Genie's inability to talk may have been due to similar emotional factors or may have had a physiological basis. Comprehensive tests of language comprehension were first administered about 11 months after Genie's discovery. By this time Genie was able to understand and produce individual words and names, although her comprehension was far beyond her ability to use words. One source of her problems in using words for talking was probably a physical difficulty in learning the necessary neuromuscular controls over her vocal organs. After all, while other children were learning this control she was learning to repress all sounds. As a result, Genie's speech is in a monotone and very low volume, although it has shown marked improvement with time.

In spite of her physical problems with speech Genie is clearly learning language. Hers is similar to development in normal children in that her speech is governed by rules: her basic sentence elements are in a fixed order, and syntactic and semantic relations are expressed systematically. Her speech does, however, differ from that of normal children. For example, although her vocabulary is much larger than that of children with equivalent syntactic abilities, she clearly has more difficulty than normal children in learning rules of grammar. She uses no question words, no demonstratives, no particles, and no rejoinders. She produces negative sentences by the addition of the negative element to the beginning of the sentence rather than reorganizing the sentence as children at her stage in language development would do (e.g., "No can go").

Genie's cognitive development was quite rapid. In May 1973 her Stanford-Binet mental age was 5–8. Because this value far exceeds her linguistic abilities, Genie's right hemisphere functions may be far superior to her left hemisphere functions.

Results of her dichotic listening are provocatively unusual for a right-handed person: although both ears show normal hearing, there is a strong left-ear, hence right hemisphere, effect for both verbal and nonverbal (environmental) sounds. In fact, the right ear is nearly totally suppressed, a phenomenon also characteristic of split-brain patients for the left ear. In short, the dichotic-listening results imply that Genie's right hemisphere is processing both verbal and nonverbal acoustic stimuli, as would be the case in people with a left hemispherectomy in childhood. The possibility that Genie is using her right hemisphere for language suggests that her capacity for language acquisition is limited, as it is in left hemispherectomy patients (see below). This conclusion is supported by her retarded development of syntactic skills despite possession of a large vocabulary.

To date, Genie has not been assessed for neuropsychological functions such as are measured by visuospatial or praxic tests. In view of the Liepmann-Kimura theory that the left hemisphere controls movement, it would be interesting to determine whether Genie has difficulty in performing sequential motor movements.

Genie's dichotic results suggest a curious puzzle: Why has deprivation of auditory and verbal experience caused a shift in speech lateralization? (Speculations of this type are risky at best, since there is no "average brain," and all inferences about brain function are based on group averages. Thus, any hypothesis about an individual must be treated as pure conjecture and heavily spiced with skepticism. After all, it is possible that Genie's speech would have developed in the right hemisphere even if she were raised normally.) Given this caution, we will consider different hypotheses to explain why Genie's right hemisphere has speech along with nonspeech functions.

At least three explanations for Genie's abnormal lateralization are plausible. The first hypothesis is that disuse of the left hemisphere (functional validation) may simply have resulted in degeneration. Thus, it would be interesting to have a CT scan of Genie's brain to see if there are any gross morphological changes. The second hypothesis is that in the absence of auditory stimulation the left hemisphere is now actively inhibited by the right hemisphere or by some other structure. This possibility is congruent with the studies done on monocular deprivation in cats. Recall that after monocular deprivation in kittens, the experienced eye actively inhibited input from the deprived eye. This inhibition could only be released by inhibiting the active cells pharmacologically. By analogy, Genie's left hemisphere could have been actively inhibited from assuming its function when the chance arose. Since Genie was not deprived of visuospatial experience, the right hemisphere would not have been inhibited from assuming its normal functions. The third hypothesis is that Genie's left hemisphere is now performing some other functions. In the absence of a thorough neuropsychological assessment, it is difficult to theorize just what the new functions might be. One possibility is that the left hemisphere was able to assume its preferred role in motor control, and in the absence of competition from speech functions the left hemisphere has an even greater control of motor functions than normal. This idea actually suggests increased cerebral lateralization for at least one function in Genie, but it remains to be tested. It is unfortunate that tests of praxic functions were not administered repeatedly throughout the period of language development.

BRAIN INJURY AND DEVELOPMENT

Although it was known in 1861 that damage to the left frontal cortex could abolish speech, by 1868 Cotard had observed that children with left frontal lesions developed normal adult language functions. This was the origin of the idea that brain injury has milder and more short-lived effects if it is sustained in childhood. In the 1930s, Margret Kennard put the idea to scientific study. She compared the effects of unilateral motor cortex lesions on infant and adult monkeys. The impairments in the infant monkeys were milder than those in the adults. The generalization that **sparing** of function follows infant lesions became known as the **Kennard principle.** For a time the idea received wide acceptance and a good deal of experimental support, but then gradually, particularly in recent years, it first became evident that earlier may not always be better, and then it became apparent that earlier may actually be worse. Of course, exactly which effect is obtained depends on the behavior under examination, the extent of brain damage, and the actual age of injury. With respect to cognitive function in humans, it is clear that speech survives early brain damage, but some elements of syntax and some nonlanguage functions may not survive, and general intellectual ability may in fact decline. In this section we shall examine some of the evidence that supports these conclusions.

Effect of Age

A number of studies have suggested that age is an important variable when considering the effects of early lesions. In general the studies suggest that there are three critical age divisions; before 1 year of age, 1 to 5 years and over 5 years. Lesions incurred before age 1 tend to produce disproportionate impairments compared with those that occur later. Lesions incurred between 1 and 5 years do allow reorganization of brain function, including sparing of language functions. Lesions later than age 5 permit little or no sparing of function. These results are revealed in studies on language and studies on general intelligence. For example, Kornhuber and coworkers found that IQ is more severely reduced in children under 5 years of age than in children older than 5. Furthermore, the lesion size was related to IQ in the older group, but was not related to IQ in the younger group, in which even small lesions produced disproportionate impairments. In a comparison of the effects of lesions incurred before and after age 1, Riva and Cazzaniga found that earlier lesions reduce IQ more than the later lesions.

Effect of Brain Damage on Language

It is now well known that language deficits resulting from cerebral injury in childhood are usually short-lived, and that recovery is nearly complete. Furthermore, transient language disorders following right hemisphere damage are commoner in children than in adults, the incidence running at about 8% and 2%, respectively (see Table 25-4). The Basser study, which gave a value of 35% with aphasia, is thought to be inaccurate, since many of the subjects may have had bilateral lesions.

Alajouanine and Lhermitte studied 32 cases of childhood aphasia, finding writing deficits in all

TABLE 25-4. Summary of studies of aphasia resulting from unilateral lesions

Study	Age range of subjects	Number of cases	Percentage with right hemisphere lesions
Childhood lesions			
Guttman, 1942	2–14	15	7
Alajouanine and Lhermitte, 1965	6–15	32	0
McCarthy, 1963	After language acquisition	114	4
Basser, 1962	Before 5	20	35
Hécaen, 1976	3½–15	17	11
TOTAL	2–15	198	8
Adult lesions			
Russell and Espir, 1961	—	205	3
Hécaen, 1976	—	232	0.43
TOTAL	—	437	1.6

Source: Adapted from Krashen, 1973 and Hécaen, 1976.

TABLE 25-5. Frequency of different symptoms in 15 cases caused by left hemisphere lesions in childhood

Symptom	Number of cases	Percentage	Evolution of symptoms
Mutism	9	60	From 5 days to 30 months
Articulatory disorders	12	80	Persistent in 4 cases
Auditory verbal comprehension disorders	6	40	Persistent in 1 case
Naming disorders	7	46	Persistent in 3 cases
Paraphasia	1	7	Disappearance
Reading disorders	9	60	Persistent in 3 cases
Writing disorders	13	86	Persistent in 7 cases
Facial apraxia	2		Transient
Acalculia	11		(Not reported)

Source: Adapted from Hécaen, 1976.

and reading deficits in about half of the children, in addition to difficulty in speaking. Six months after the injury they observed total recovery of spontaneous language in about one-third, although significant improvement was noted in all the others. When reexamined at one year or more after the injury, 24 of the 32 children had normal or almost normal language, although 14 still had some degree of dysgraphia; 22 of the children were eventually able to return to school.

Similarly, Hécaen followed postinjury recovery of aphasia and related symptoms in 15 children with left hemisphere unilateral lesions, as summarized in Table 25-5. Besides disorders of speech, nearly all the children had disorders of writing and calculation as well. Of these 15 children, 5 showed complete recovery within 6 weeks to 2 years. Most of the remaining children showed considerable improvement, the only remaining deficit often being a mild difficulty in writing, a finding similar to that of Alajouanine and Lhermitte.

Woods and Teuber have studied about 50 patients with prenatal or early postnatal brain damage to either the left or the right hemisphere. Using normal siblings as controls, they came to the following conclusions:

1. Language survives after early left-side injury.

2. Much of this survival seems attributable to occupancy of a potential language zone in the right hemisphere.

3. This shift of language location is not without a price, because some kinds of visuospatial orientation are impaired.

4. Early lesions of the right hemisphere produce deficits similar to those produced by similar lesions in adulthood.

In other words, if a child sustains a lesion of the left hemisphere that produces right hemiplegia, language functions are remarkably more intact than after a comparable lesion in an adult, presumably because some, or all, of the language abilities have moved to the right hemisphere. Presumably, language *crowds* into the right hemisphere at the expense of visuospatial functions. On the other hand, a lesion of the right hemisphere, which produces left hemiplegia, does not produce impairments in language ability.

A summary of this pattern of results obtained

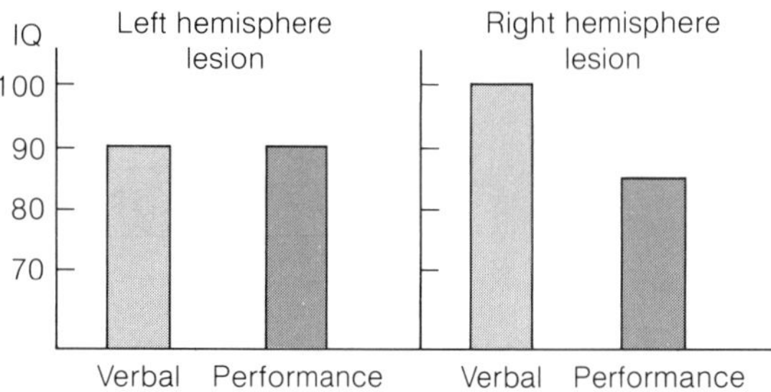

FIGURE 25-3. IQs on subtests of the Wechsler Intelligence Test for Adults, who while infants had suffered a lesion of the left or the right hemisphere, as determined by the occurrence of hemiparesis. Note that both verbal and performance scores are depressed by left hemisphere lesions, whereas only performance scores are depressed by right hemisphere lesions. The results suggest that if language moves to the right hemisphere, that hemisphere's functions are sacrificed to accommodate this shift. The results suggest that right hemisphere functions do not shift sufficiently to interfere with language (After Teuber, 1975.)

from verbal and performance scores of the Wechsler Intelligence scales is summarized in Figure 25-3. Left hemisphere lesions depress both verbal and performance scores. Right hemisphere lesions depress only performance scores. In a subsequent study, Woods examined the effects of lesions incurred earlier than age 1. The main finding was that right hemisphere lesions impaired *both* verbal and performance IQ. Riva and Cazzaniga confirm these results and also note that lesions occurring before 1 year of age produce more severe overall impairments than those occurring after age 1.

It is worth noting that not all aspects of language function are spared after early lesions. Woods has found that on a speech-shadowing task, which requires a person to repeat passages of speech as they are read, adult right and left hemisphere lesions produce equal impairments. Virtually identical impairments follow early childhood lesions, even though speech is significantly spared by the early left hemisphere lesions.

Reorganization of Language

If we accept the evidence that early brain damage spares language and that sparing may occur because the control of language is transferred to the opposite hemisphere, it is possible to address a set of three different questions. These concern the actual language functions that are transferred, the type of brain damage that causes them to be transferred, and the age range during which transfer can take place. The first two questions have been addressed experimentally by Rasmussen and Milner, but the third is as yet incompletely answered.

Using the carotid sodium Amytal and dichotic-listening tests, Rasmussen and Milner localized language in a large number of patients who had received left hemisphere injury early in life but had returned to the hospital later in life because of complications. They found that the patients divided into three groups, as shown in Table 25-6: in one group speech was in the left hemisphere, in the second speech was represented bilaterally, and in the third speech was in the right hemisphere. The patients who had speech in the left hemisphere were found to have damage that did not invade the anterior speech zone (Broca's area) or the posterior speech zone (Wernicke's area). Examples of brain damage that did not produce a shift in language lateralization are shown in Figure 25-4*A*. Both

TABLE 25-6. Changes in hemispheric speech representation following early brain damage

		Percentage with speech representation		
	Handedness	Left	Bilateral	Right
No early damage	Right	96	0	4
	Left or mixed	70	15	15
Early damage	Right	81	7	12
	Left or mixed	28	19	53

Source: Adapted from Rasmussen and Milner, 1975, pp. 248–249.

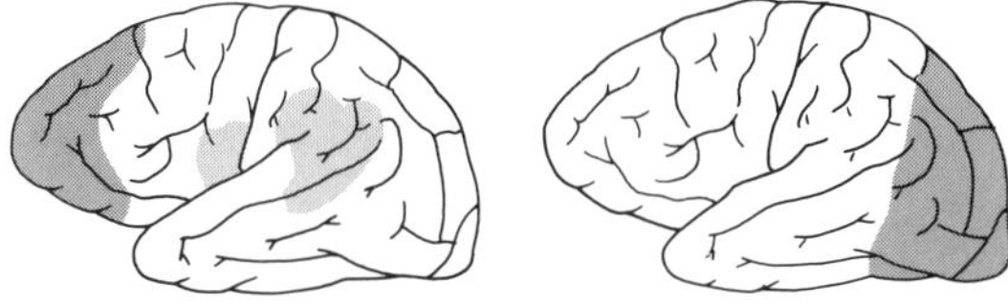

A No shift in language

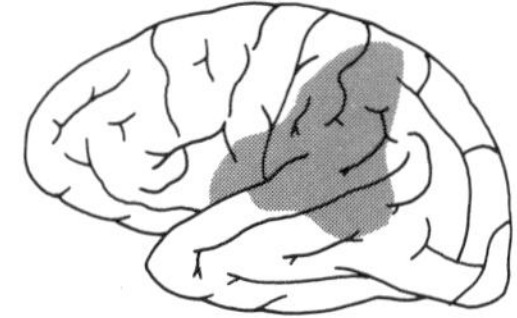

B Complete shift of language

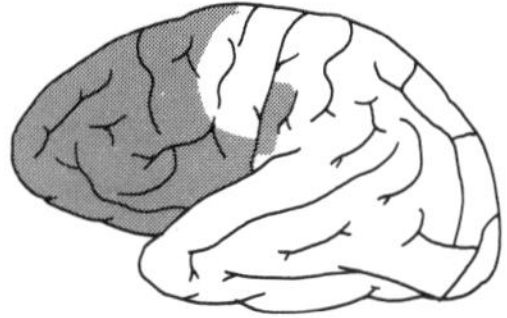

C Shift of anterior speech functions

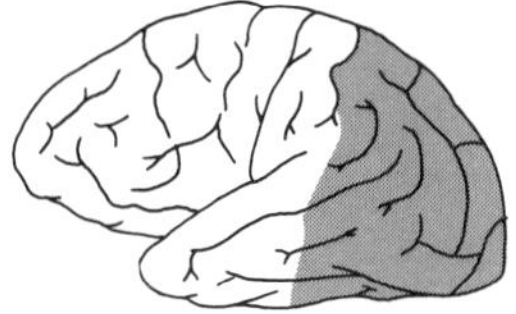

D Shift of posterior speech functions

FIGURE 25-4. Relations between early brain damage and hemisphere changes in language organization. *A*. Anterior and posterior lesions after which language remained in the left hemisphere. The lightly shaded portion of the first figure shows location of language zones. *B*. An anterior–posterior lesion that causes all language to move to the right hemisphere. *C*. An anterior lesion that causes the anterior speech zone to shift to the right hemisphere. *D*. A posterior lesion that caused the posterior speech zone to shift to the right hemisphere. (After Rasmussen and Milner, 1977.)

exemplar lesions are large yet the dichotic-listening test showed a right-ear advantage, and in the sodium Amytal tests the patients were mute on both naming (giving the names of objects, e.g., What is —experimenter holds up object) and repetition (e.g., Name the days of the week in order) tasks after left hemisphere injection. The light shading in the left-hand portion of Figure 25-4*A* shows the locations of the anterior and posterior speech zones.

An example of a lesion in a patient that produced a complete shift of language to the right hemisphere is illustrated in Figure 25-4*B*. This patient showed a left-ear advantage on the dichotic-listening test and was mute for naming and repetition after right hemisphere sodium Amytal injection. Note that the lesion invaded both the anterior and posterior speech zones. That the lesion did invade both speech zones was typical for patients who developed right hemisphere speech after early left hemisphere lesions.

Examples of the lesions in patients who had bilateral speech are shown in Figure 25-4*C* and 25-4*D*. The patient in Figure 25-4*C* had a large left frontal lobe lesion at 6 years of age that included the anterior language zone. At age 18 the patient was right-handed and had a right-ear advantage for digits and a left-ear advantage for melodies. On the sodium Amytal tests, a left hemisphere injection produced a disturbance in series repetition (counting, reciting the days of the week forward or backward, or oral spelling), but naming was less disturbed. A right hemisphere injection produced a disturbance in both series repetition and naming. Since it is assumed that the right-ear advantage for digits is an indication of left hemisphere speech and that the absence of series repetition after left hemisphere sodium Amytal injection is an indication of intact speech in the left posterior speech zone, it can be concluded that the lesion did not cause a complete shift of speech from the posterior left speech zone. Since naming was disturbed after a right hemisphere injection of sodium Amytal, it is assumed that left hemisphere speech functions of the anterior zone had shifted to the right hemisphere.

The patient in Figure 25-4*D* had a large posterior lesion that was incurred at 2.5 years of age. Testing at age 16 showed that she was left-handed and had a left-ear advantage for both digits and melodies. Sodium Amytal tests showed that naming was disturbed by both left and right injections, whereas series repetition was done well after the left but not the right hemisphere was injected. In this case it is thought that the large posterior lesion incurred early in life had caused speech functions of the posterior zone to shift to the right, while the anterior speech zone still retained some speech function.

The Invariance and Maturation Hypotheses

Explanations for recovery of language from early brain damage take two forms. The *invariance hypothesis* argues that the left hemisphere is specialized for language at birth and that the right hemisphere must acquire language abilities after the left hemisphere is damaged. The *maturation hypothesis* argues that both hemispheres are initially involved in language but gradually the left hemisphere becomes more specialized for language control. Lenneberg refined the maturation hypothesis by proposing that lateralization of function develops rapidly between the ages of 2 or 3 to 5, and then proceeds more slowly until puberty, by which time it is complete. Lenneberg reasoned that if cerebral damage occurred in the potentially dominant hemisphere, recovery would be complete and rapid, because language would simply develop in the undamaged hemisphere. Furthermore, damage to either hemisphere would produce a transient language disturbance because language was still under the control of both hemispheres. Between the ages of 3 and 10 cerebral damage may produce aphasia, but recovery occurs over time because the intact cerebral hemisphere is still able to take over. Damage after age 10 would produce language disorders resembling those observed in adults, because the intact hemisphere becomes increasingly specialized and less able to adapt. By about age 14 the ability to reorganize is lost, and prognosis for recovery is poor. Lenneberg defined the time span from about age 2 to 14 as the critical period for the development of language, and, more broadly, for cerebral lateralization, Krashen has subsequently revised Lenneberg's upper age limit of 14 down to age 5. Support for the maturation hypothesis comes, obviously, from the fact that children recover from aphasia, but also from the purported finding that **crossed aphasia** (i.e., aphasia from right hemisphere lesions) is commoner in children than adults.

The results that we have described to this point, particularly those of Rasmussen and Milner, support the invariance hypothesis. Their findings show that language has a strong affinity for the left hemisphere and will not abandon it unless an entire center is destroyed, and even then it might shift only partly to the other hemisphere. This affinity is thought to be based on the special innate anatomical organization of the left hemisphere—remember that the left planum temporale is larger than the right one. In the examination of their series of patients with early left hemisphere lesions, Rasmussen and Milner also noted that childhood injuries to the left hemisphere occurring after 5 years of age rarely changed speech patterns. They argued that recovery that occurs after about age 6 occurs not through transfer to the other hemisphere but by intrahemispheric reorganization, possibly with intact surrounding zones acquiring some control over speech. Further evidence for the invariance hypothesis comes from the study of Woods and Teuber. As is illustrated in Figure 25-3, left, but not right, hemisphere lesions cause a decline in both verbal and performance IQ scores, a result that argues against the idea that the right hemisphere has equal potential for language. Finally, the evidence that crossed aphasia is commoner in children than adults derives mainly from Basser's study, and Woods and Teuber have convincingly argued that these data are severely contaminated with bilateral effects.

Given that the invariance hypothesis is correct, there is evidence to suggest that functional validation must still occur; that is, practice with language is necessary to establish left hemisphere preeminence. Woods has reported that if left hemisphere lesions occur before the first birthday, both verbal and performance IQ are severely depressed. If left hemisphere lesions occur after 1 year of age neither verbal or performance IQ are affected. Right hemisphere lesions at any age lower only performance IQ. It seems likely that the results of the lesions before age 1 might be due to a disruption of verbal functions that had been insufficiently validated, or perhaps disrupted by the invasion of performance functions. We must note, however, that this suggestion is speculative, that IQ is at best an imprecise measure of language, and that a more systematic study of these patients using linguistic tests is called for.

Effects of Hemidecortication

If a person has life-threatening seizures resulting from severe infantile cerebral injury, the neocortex of an entire hemisphere may be surgically removed to control the seizures. Although most such surgery is performed during the patient's early adolescence, it is sometimes done in the first year of life, before speech has developed. These latter cases are particularly germane to the question of how cerebral lateralization develops. If the hemispheres vary functionally at birth, then left and right hemispherectomies would be expected to produce different effects on cognitive abilities. If they are not, then no cognitive differences would result from left or right hemidecortications.

Can One Hemisphere Take over the Functions of the Other? The general results of recent studies of linguistic and visuospatial abilities in patients with unilateral hemidecortications support the conclusion that both hemispheres are functionally specialized, although both hemispheres appear capable of assuming some functions usually performed by the missing hemisphere. Table 25-7 summarizes these data. Notice that the left hemidecortication produces no severe aphasia or obvious language deficits. Yet the right hemisphere cannot completely compensate for the left hemisphere, for the patients have deficits in using complex language. Note that right hemidecortication produces no severe deficits in visuospatial abilities. Yet the left hemisphere cannot completely compensate for the right hemisphere, evidenced by the patients' difficulty in performing complex visuospatial tasks.

In an analysis of language abilities, Dennis and Whitaker found that unlike right hemisphere removals, left hemisphere removals produced deficits in understanding auditory language when the meaning was conveyed by complex syntactic structure, particularly if the sentence contained an error (e.g., "The tall guard wasn't shot by the armed robber"), and produced difficulty in determining sentence implication, integrating semantic and syntactic information to replace missing pronouns, and forming judgments of word interrelations in

TABLE 25-7. Summary of effects of hemidecortication on verbal and visuospatial abilities

	Left hemidecorticate	Right hemidecorticate
Intelligence	Low normal	Low normal
Language tests		
Simple	Normal	Normal
Complex (e.g., syntax)	Poor	Normal
Visuospatial tests		
Simple	Normal	Normal
Complex	Normal	Poor

Source: Based on data from Kohn and Dennis, 1974 and Dennis and Whitaker, 1976.

sentences. In an analysis of word comprehension, Dennis has found that both hemispheres understand the meaning of words and both hemispheres can spontaneously produce lists of names of things. When searching for words using different cues, the left hemisphere has an advantage over the right. Both hemispheres can name an object from its picture or from its description but the left hemisphere can identify it on the basis of "rhymes with," whereas the right hemisphere is deficient in using this type of cue. In an analysis of reading skills, Dennis and her coworkers found that both hemispheres had almost equal ability in higher order reading comprehension; however, the left hemisphere was superior to the right in reading and spelling unfamiliar words, and in using sentence structure to achieve fluent reading. The left hemisphere also read prose passages with greater decoding accuracy, more fluency, and fewer errors that violated the semantic and syntactic structure of the sentence. The superiority of the left hemisphere seems to be its ability to manipulate and exploit language rules. The right hemisphere is not without its strengths in language. Performance was better with the right hemisphere in a task that required learning an association between nonsense words and symbols. In summarizing the studies on language Dennis suggests that if written language is thought of as a combination of meaning structure (morphology), sound structure (phonology), and picture structure (logography), then the isolated left hemisphere will show superior performance with morphology and phonology and inferior performance with logographic cues, whereas the isolated right hemisphere will show superior performance with logographic cues and inferior performance with morphological and phonological cues.

An almost analogous pattern of results is observed on tests of visuospatial function. Kohn and Dennis found that although patients with right hemisphere removals performed normally on simple tests of visuospatial function such as drawing, they were significantly impaired on complex tests such as maze problems or map-reading tests.

To summarize, each hemisphere can assume some of the opposite hemisphere's functions if the opposite hemisphere is removed during development, but neither hemisphere is totally capable of mediating all of the missing opposite's functions. Thus, although the developing brain gives evidence of considerable plasticity, there is convincing evidence against equipotentiality: both appear to have a processing capacity that probably has an innate structural basis. Furthermore, there seems to be a price for assuming new responsibilities. With few exceptions patients undergoing hemidecortication are of below-average, or at best only average, intelligence, and they are frequently less than normally proficient at tests of the intact hemisphere's function.

A Note of Dissent. Although the experiments of Dennis and her coworkers seem internally consistent and consonant with other lines of research on the organization of language (see Chapters 22 and 29), Bishop has questioned the methodological adequacy of the demonstrations. She points out that in the 1974 study of Kohn and Dennis two of five left decorticate patients understood reversible passive sentences, and one may have been too young to perform the task. Furthermore, Bishop argues that if subjects with comparable IQs are tested on the Kohn and Dennis task and then used as a control group, neither left nor right hemidecorticates differ from the control group. Likewise, she argues that the performance of the three subjects in the 1976 Dennis and Whitaker study also have performance scores that fall within the range of control values. In presenting these methodological criticisms, Bishop does not dispute the left-for-language hypothesis, but rather suggests that the evidence that supports it is weak. Bishop's criticisms are telling and point out the difficulties involved in drawing conclusions from studies with small numbers of subjects and in obtaining appropriate control groups to compare with people who have brain damage. At the same time we must also note that Zaidel (see Chapter 29) comes to similar conclusions about the superiority of the left hemisphere for language in hemidecorticate and split-brain patients, and so we must conclude that the left-for-language hypothesis maintains a relatively strong position, despite methodological questions about some of the studies that are presented in its support.

A THEORY OF COGNITIVE DEVELOPMENT

Three general theoretical positions can be postulated to account for the ontogeny of cerebral specialization. We have called these (1) the maturation hypothesis, (2) the invariance (left-for-language) hypothesis, and (3) the parallel-development hypothesis. According to the maturation hypothesis either hemisphere can be specialized for either language or nonlanguage functions, and the occurrence of specialization is entirely a matter of chance. According to the invariance hypothesis the left hemisphere is special and is organized genetically to develop language skills; the right hemisphere is postulated to be a dumping ground for whatever is left over. According to the **parallel-development hypothesis,** both hemispheres, by virtue of their construction, play special roles, one hemisphere being destined to specialize in language and the other in nonlanguage functions. Although there are fairly good arguments for each hypothesis, in our view a parallel-development theory that initially permits some flexibility, or equipotentiality, most usefully encompasses most of the available data. The cognitive functions of each hemisphere can be conceived as being hierarchical. Simple, or lower level, functions are represented at the base of the hierarchy, corresponding to functions in primary, sensory, motor, language, or visuospatial areas. More complex, or higher level, functions are represented further up the hierarchy, the most complex being at the top; these functions are the most lateralized. At birth the two hemispheres functionally overlap because each is processing low-level behaviors. By age 5 the newly developing higher order cognitive processes have very little overlap, and each hemisphere thus becomes increasingly specialized. By puberty each hemisphere has developed its own unique functions (Figure 25-5).

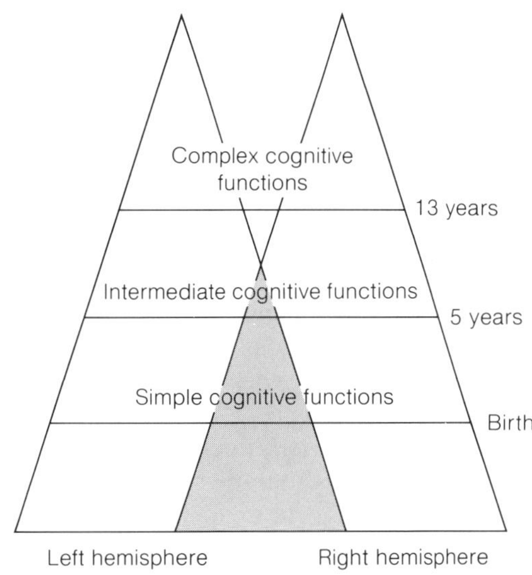

FIGURE 25-5. A model of the development of cognitive function in the left and right hemispheres of normal people. At the bottom of the pyramids cognitive functions are relatively simple (e.g., for language, simple functions could include babbling and the use of simple nouns), and the functions of the two hemispheres overlap considerably. At the top of the pyramids, representing very complex functions, the functions of the two hemispheres do not overlap at all (e.g., for language, complex functions could include the use of adult language structure). It is important to note that the hemispheres are not themselves becoming more lateralized with respect to a given function; rather, they are developing new functions that are more specialized. Since both hemispheres show functional overlap in the early years of life, each can adopt the functions of the other if brain damage has occurred at an early age.

Note that the cerebral hemispheres are not becoming more lateralized in development; rather, as Witelson has pointed out, the developing cognitive functions are built on the lower functions, which are innately located in one hemisphere or the other.

All models of cerebral development must answer the question of how functions become restricted to one hemisphere, rather than becoming bilateral. The parallel-development hypothesis answers that question. In a series of papers, Moscovitch emphasizes the possibility that one hemisphere actively inhibits the other (recall our earlier discussion of the effects of monocular deprivation in cats), thus preventing the contralateral hemisphere from developing similar functions. This active inhibition presumably develops at about age 5, as the corpus callosum becomes functional. Moscovitch proposes that this inhibitory process not only prevents the subsequent development of language processes in the right hemisphere, and vice versa, but also inhibits expression of the language processes already in the right hemisphere. Support for this idea comes from the observation that the right hemisphere of commissurotomy patients appears to have greater language abilities than expected from the study of normal patients, presumably because the right hemisphere is no longer subject to inhibition by the left. Furthermore, Netley reports that people born with no corpus callosum demonstrate little or no functional asymmetry as inferred from dichotic listening, suggesting that the absence of interhemispheric connection results in attenuated hemispheric differentiation. This phenomenon follows directly from the Moscovitch proposal.

EXPERIMENTAL APPROACHES TO EARLY RECOVERY

It is becoming increasingly clear that the mechanisms mediating recovery of function from injury sustained in infancy are behaviorally and anatomically quite different from the mechanisms that mediate recovery after lesions inflicted in adults. The best illustration of the role of age comes from a series of studies on the function of the dorsolateral and orbitofrontal areas of the prefrontal cortex.

The dorsolateral cortex receives projections from the parvocellular subdivision of the dorsomedial nucleus of the thalamus (Figure 25-6). In fact, the distribution of this projection defines this cortical zone. Many studies of the function of this area show that if it is damaged in adult monkeys, rats, or other animals, they show profound impairments of spatial delayed responses or spatial delayed alternation. In these tasks the animal must make a choice between two spatially located objects, and each trial is separated by a delay. For example, a monkey must remember that a peanut is located in one of two cups, but each trial is separated by a short delay during which it cannot see the cup. Generally, lesioned animals do not perform above chance on this task, and the deficit is not attributable to interference with performance by sensory or motor difficulties, surgical shock, or lack of opportunity to learn. That is, even though they seemingly "know" what to do, they make errors. On a host of other tasks, such as visual discriminations, these monkeys show no deficits. In addition to showing this behavioral deficit, histological analysis shows that the projecting fibers from the dorsomedial nucleus die after lesioning, and the cell bodies of these fibers degenerate.

Akert and colleagues and subsequently others have removed the dorsolateral cortex of monkeys within the first two months of life and studied the monkeys on spatial reversals over the next year of life. During this time the monkeys show no impairment when compared with age-matched control animals. Nevertheless, degeneration of cells in the thalamus are found. These early studies seemed to suggest that other brain structures, most likely the basal ganglia, could assume this function. However, this simple interpretation was complicated by Goldman's 1971 finding that if the monkeys were tested for as long as two years, they gradually developed the adult deficit or, as it has been phrased, "they grew into the deficit." These results are instructive, first because they show that a subcortical structure can control the behavior in a seemingly normal way for a period of time, and second, because they show that the function is "given up" with maturation.

Goldman and Galkin studied the behavior and anatomy of monkeys that had been removed from the womb before term, subjected to surgery, and then replaced. These animals show no deficits as infants or when mature and also show no cellular degeneration in the dorsomedial thalamus. Earlier, Kolb and Nonneman had obtained identical results with the rat, which does not require preterm surgery because it is more immature at birth than the monkey. The studies of Goldman and Galkin and of Kolb and Nonneman imply that if cortical damage occurs sufficiently early in life, the brain is able to reorganize in some way to achieve complete compensation. One type of evidence for reorganization is that the monkeys have gyri and sulci not

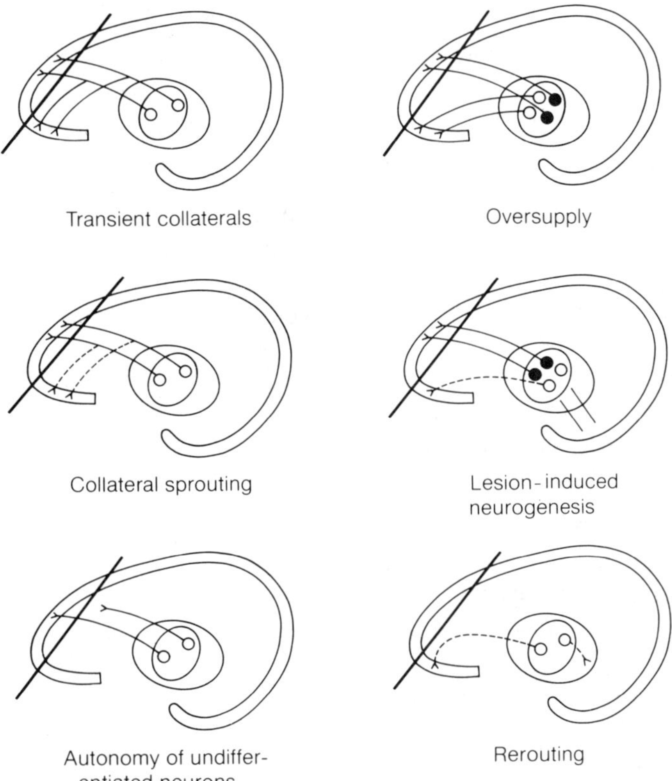

FIGURE 25-6. Diagram of possible alternative explanations of the preservation of neurons in the dorsomedial nucleus of the thalamus after surgical resection of the dorsolateral frontal cortex in the monkey prior to birth. Black circles indicate degenerated neurons; open circles, preserved neurons. (From Goldman and Galkin, 1978. Reprinted with permission.)

observed in normal monkeys. Other evidence is that cells of the dorsomedial nucleus remain intact, permitting the hypothesis that the new connections that they make most likely sustain behaviors of delayed alternation. Goldman and Galkin have suggested a number of types of reorganization that might account for the survival of these cells (Figure 25-6).

1. *Transient collaterals.* The fibers that enter the dorsolateral cortex from the dorsomedial thalamus may initially have collaterals going elsewhere, which under normal conditions degenerate, but which in instances of dorsolateral cortex damage survive.

2. *Oversupply.* There is an oversupply of neurons in the dorsomedial nucleus, but normally only those that innervate the dorsolateral cortex survive.

3. *Collateral sprouting.* The immature neurons do not die, because in early life they can sprout collaterals to new cortical areas and so replace their severed axons.

4. *Lesion-induced neurogenesis.* Although the original neurons are killed by the lesion, new cell bodies form and replace them.

5. *Autonomy of undifferentiated neurons.* Although normal neurons die if their target is destroyed, undifferentiated neurons can survive to make new connections.

6. *Rerouting.* If axons from the thalamus have not yet entered the neocortex, they are able to seek out and innervate alternative targets.

Many of the studies on animals with prefrontal cortex damage have assessed behavior using one test, or at most only a few tests. Kolb and Whishaw have adapted the neuropsychological procedures developed for humans and applied them to investigations in the rat. Rats that had received neonatal or adult frontal cortex damage were tested on a "test battery" that evaluated many different aspects of the animals' learned and unlearned behavior. They found that learned behaviors (e.g., spatial reversals) were spared by the neonatal lesions, but species-typical behaviors (e.g., nest building, food hoarding) were abolished. They interpreted the results to mean that what rats are preprogrammed to do cannot survive lesions at any age, whereas things that are heavily dependent on learning are somehow spared by the early lesions. A second interesting finding was that the brains of the rats with neonatal lesions are reduced in size by 25%, whereas the brains of the rats that were operated on as adults shrunk by less than 12%. This size reduction, which in humans would be the equivalent of about 200 g, was not due to a larger lesion size but was produced by shrinkage of the entire neocortex. Subsequent analysis of this cortical shrinkage suggests that it is true of human brains as well (see Figure 25-7). Besides providing a possible explanation of the small brain size reported in a subset of retarded children, the results from the rat studies seem applicable to humans in another way. After frontal cortex damage in infancy, humans seem to show the same sparing of learned behaviors despite the loss of what could be called human-typical behaviors. The case history of the patient J. P. best illustrates this point.

At the age of 20, J. P. was referred for psychiatric examination because of his repeated difficulties with the law. A pneumoencephalogram plus follow-up exploratory surgery showed that J. P. had what seemed to be a congenital absence of both frontal lobes.

J. P.'s behavior had always been peculiar. In his preschool years he was noted for his wandering, which carried him miles from home, and for his Chesterfielding, or valetlike manners. He had school difficulties from the beginning. On one occasion his first-grade teacher had just written a letter to his parents complimenting them on having such a well-mannered child, when she looked up and found him exposing himself and masturbating before the class. He got by in school because

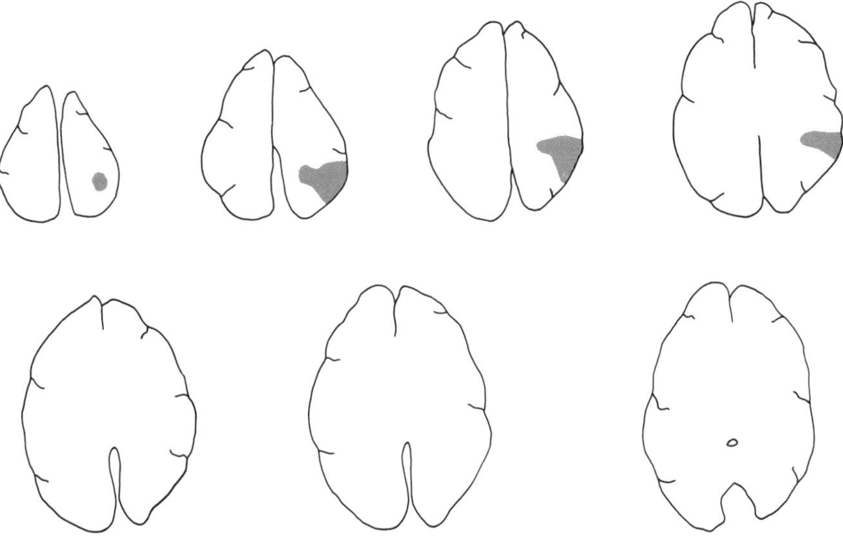

FIGURE 25-7. Summary of the CT scan from S. S., who had a birth-related injury to the right posterior cortex. Note that the right hemisphere is smaller at every plane. (After, Kolb, B. and Whishaw, I. Q., 1989.)

of his abilities in language, but he failed the third and fourth grades and did not finish high school, even after being sent to a variety of special schools. Throughout his life he was known for his wanderings and his love of taking cars and driving them hundreds of miles from home using the navigational criteria of "I steer by the compass and never make turns." In later life he was tested by Ralph Reitan, Brenda Milner, and others. His IQ was strictly average, but he failed all tests of frontal lobe function, including the category test and the Wisconsin Card-Sorting Test. Halstead, after testing J. P., thought he resembled a Univac machine, so stereotyped were his responses. Everyone who met J. P. was struck by how dissociated he seemed from the world. He had no friends in life and had made no sexual contacts or other social attachments. He once took a girl out to dinner, but ran off with her purse when she went to the washroom. In school he was hated by all the boys. He was once described as a "stranger in the world without knowing it." Ackerly summarized his impressions of him in the following way: "What seemed to command our attention and sympathy was his 'aloneness'—detachment not from the immediate physical environment of things and people, but from anything beyond that—anything that gave meaning to life, love, friendship, comradeship. He is indeed a veritable stranger in this world with no other world to flee to for comfort." Throughout his life he was never able to hold a job for more than a few weeks. Ackerly seems to have pinpointed the dichotomy of J. P.'s existence by describing him not as a case of mental deficiency but as a case of social deficiency.

SUMMARY

The pattern of nervous system development is specified genetically, from the very earliest stages of development. Nevertheless, neural development is marked by an initial superabundance of cellular elements and connections, the loss of which appears to be related to behavioral maturation. It is becoming increasingly clear that damage to the developing nervous system can produce behavioral changes that are different from those that follow adult lesions. During infancy there may also be periods of differential sensitivity. In humans, the most striking result is that language is spared following left hemisphere lesions. Still, age-related effects do occur. Damage before age 1 is associated with sparing of language function but also is accompanied by widespread deficits in other abilities. Damage after 1 year of age but before 5 is more selectively associated with the sparing of language. After 5 years of age even sparing of language does not occur. Processes that mediate these changes can be effectively studied using animal models. More specifically, animal studies have revealed a number of paradigms in which the neural consequences of early damage are different from those of adult damage. In some cases early lesions result in widespread cortical shrinkage, whereas in other cases certain populations of cells are spared following infant, but not adult, damage.

REFERENCES

Ackerly, S. S. A case of paranatal bilateral frontal lobe defect observed for thirty years. In J. M. Warren and K. Akert, eds. *The Frontal Granular Cortex and Behavior.* New York: McGraw-Hill, 1964.

Akert, K., O. S. Orth, H. Harlow, and K. A. Schultz. Learned behavior of rhesus monkeys following neonatal bilateral prefrontal lobotomy. *Science* 132:1944–1945, 1960.

Alajouanine, T., and F. Lhermitte. Acquired aphasia in children. *Brain* 88:653–662, 1965.

Basser, L. Hemiplegia of early onset and the faculty of speech with special reference to the effects of hemispherectomy. *Brain* 85:427–460, 1962.

Bishop, D. V. M. Linguistic impairment after hemidecortication for infantile hemiplegia? A reappraisal. *Quarterly Journal of Experimental Psychology* 35A:199–207, 1963.

Blakemore, C., and D. E. Mitchell. Environmental modification of the visual cortex and the neural basis of learning and memory. *Nature* 241:467–468, 1973.

Bryden, M. P. *Laterality: Functional Asymmetry in the Intact Brain.* New York: Academic Press, 1982.

Cameron, R. F., R. D. Currier, and A. F. Haerer. Aphasia and literacy. *British Journal of Disorders of Communication* 6:161–163, 1971.

Caplan, P. J., and M. Kinesbourne. Baby drops the rattle: Asymmetry of duration of grasp by infants. *Child Development* 47:532–534, 1976.

Caviness, V. S., Jr., and R. L. Sidman. Time of origin of corresponding cell classes in the cerebral cortex of normal and reeler mutant mice: An autoradiographic analysis. *Journal of Comparative Neurology* 148:141–152, 1973.

Crowell, D. H., R. H. Jones, L. E. Kapuniai, and J. K. Nakagawa. Unilateral cortical activity in newborn humans: An early index of cerebral dominance? *Science* 180:205–208, 1973.

Curtiss, S. *Genie: A Psycholinguistic Study of a Modern-Day "Wild Child."* New York: Academic Press, 1978.

Dennis, M. Capacity and strategy for syntactic comprehension after left or right hemidecortication. *Brain and Language* 10:287–317, 1980.

Dennis, M. Language acquisition in a single hemisphere: Semantic organization. In D. Caplan, ed. *Biological Studies of Mental Processes.* Cambridge, MA: M.I.T. Press, 1980.

Dennis, M., M. Lovett, and C. A. Wiegel-Crump. Written language acquisition after left or right hemidecortication in infancy. *Brain and Language* 12:54–91, 1981.

Dennis, M., and H. A. Whitaker. Language acquisition following hemidecortication: Linguistic superiority of the left over the right hemisphere. *Brain and Language* 3:404–433, 1976.

Diamond, R., and S. Carey. Developmental changes in the representation of faces. *Journal of Experimental Child Psychology* 23:1–22, 1977.

Entus, A. K. Hemispheric asymmetry in processing of dichotically presented speech and non-speech stimuli by infants. In S. J. Segalowitz and F. A. Gruber, eds. *Language Development and Neurological Theory.* New York: Academic Press, 1977.

Epstein, H. T. Growth spurts during brain development: Implications for educational policy and practice. In J. S. Chard and A. F. Mirsky, eds. *Education and the Brain.* Chicago: University of Chicago Press, 1978.

Flechsig, P. *Anatomie des menschlichen Gehirns und Rückenmarks.* Leipzig:Georg Thieme, 1920.

Freud, S. *The Standard Edition of the Complete Psychological Works of Sigmund Freud.* J. Strachey, tr. and ed., in collaboration with A. Freud. London: Hogarth, 1954.

Fromkin, V. A., S. Krashen, S. Curtiss, D. Rigler, and M. Rigler. The development of language in Genie: A case of language acquisition beyond the "critical period." *Brain and Language* 1:81–107, 1974.

Goldman, P. S. Functional development of the prefrontal cortex in early life and the problem of neuronal plasticity. *Experimental Neurology* 32:366–387, 1971.

Goldman, P. S., and T. W. Galkin. Prenatal removal of frontal association cortex in the fetal rhesus monkey: Anatomical and functional consequences in postnatal life. *Brain Research* 152:451–485, 1978.

Guttman, E. Aphasia in children. *Brain* 65:205–219, 1942.

Harlow, H. F. *Learning to Love.* San Francisco: The Albion Publishing Co., 1971.

Hécaen, H. Acquired aphasia in children and the ontogenesis of hemispheric functional specialization. *Brain and Language* 3:114–134, 1976.

Hirsch, H. V. B., and D. N. Spinelli. Modification of the distribution of receptive field orientation in cats by selective visual exposure during development. *Experimental Brain Research* 13:509–527, 1971.

Hubel, D. H., and T. N. Wiesel. Receptive fields of cells in striate cortex of very young, visually inexperienced kittens. *Journal of Neurophysiology* 26:994–1002, 1963.

Ingram, D. Motor asymmetries in young children. *Neuropsychologia* 13:95–102, 1975.

Kimura, D. Speech lateralization in young children as determined by an auditory test. *Journal of Comparative and Physiological Psychology* 56:899–902, 1963.

Kimura, D. Neural mechanisms in manual signing. *Sign Language Studies* 33:291–312, 1981.

Kimura, D., R. Battison, and B. Lubert. Impairment of nonlinguistic hand movements in a deaf aphasic. *Brain and Language* 3:566–571, 1976.

Knox, C., and D. Kimura. Cerebral processing of non-verbal sounds in boys and girls. *Neuropsychologia* 8:227–237, 1970.

Kohn, B., and M. Dennis. Selective impairments of visuo-spatial abilities in infantile hemiplegics after right hemidecortication. *Neuropsychologia* 12:505–512, 1974.

Kolb, B., and A. J. Nonneman. Sparing of function in rats with early prefrontal cortex lesions. *Brain Research* 151:135–148, 1978.

Kolb, B., and I. Q. Whishaw. Neonatal frontal lesions in the rat: Sparing of learned but not species typical behavior in the presence of reduced brain weight and cortical thickness. *Journal of Comparative and Physiological Psychology* 95:863–879, 1981.

Kolb, B., and I. Q. Whishaw. Plasticity in the neocortex: Mechanisms underlying recovery from early brain damage. *Progress in Neurobiology* 32:235–276, 1989.

Kornhuber, H. H., Bechinger, D., Jung, H., and Sauer, E. A quantitative relationship between the extent of localized cerebral lesions and the intellectual and behavioural deficiency in children. *European Archives of Psychiatry and Neurological Sciences* 235:129–133, 1985.

Krashen, S. D. Lateralization, language learning and the critical period: Some new evidence. *Language Learning* 23:63–74, 1973.

Kratz, K. E., P. D. Spear, and D. C. Smith. Postcritical-period reversal of effects of monocular deprivation on striate cells in the cat. *Journal of Neurophysiology* 39:501–511, 1976.

Lenneberg, E. *Biological Foundations of Language.* New York: John Wiley, 1967.

Lomas, J., and A. Kertesz. Patterns of spontaneous recovery in aphasic groups: A study of adult stroke patients. *Brain and Language* 5:388–401, 1978.

Marcel, T., and P. Rajan. Lateral specialization for recognition of words and faces in good and poor readers. *Neuropsychologia* 13:489–497, 1975.

Michel, G. F. Right handedness: A consequence of infant supine head-orientation preference? *Science* 212:685–687, 1981.

Milner, B. Psychological aspects of focal epilepsy and its neurological management. *Advances in Neurology* 8:299–321, 1975.

Molfese, D. L., and V. J. Molfese. Cortical responses of preterm infants to phonetic and nonphonetic speech stimuli. *Developmental Psychology* 16:574–581, 1980.

Moscovitch, M. The development of lateralization of language functions and its relation to cognitive and linguistic development: A review and some theoretical speculations. In S. J. Segalowitz and F. A. Gruber, eds. *Language Development and Neurological Theory.* New York: Academic Press, 1977.

Netley, C. Dichotic listening of callosal agenesis and Turner's syndrome patients. In S. J. Segalowitz and F. A. Gruber, eds. *Language Development and Neurological Theory.* New York: Academic Press, 1977.

Neville, H. Electroencephalographic testing of cerebral specialization in normal and congenitally deaf children: A preliminary report. In S. J. Segalowitz and F. A. Gruber, eds. *Language Development and Neurological Theory.* New York: Academic Press, 1977.

O'Shea, L., M. Saari, B. A. Pappas, R. Ings, and K. Stauge. Neonatal 6-hydroxydopamine attenuates the neural and behavioral effects of enriched rearing in the rat. *Society for Neuroscience: Abstracts* 9:558, 1983.

Peters, M., and B. F. Petrie. Functional asymmetries in the stepping reflex of human neonates. *Canadian Journal of Psychology* 33:198–200, 1979.

Piaget, J. *Biology and Knowledge.* Chicago: The University of Chicago Press, 1971.

Rakic, P., J.-P. Bourgeois, M. F. Eckenhoff, N. Zecevic, and P. S. Goldman-Rakic. Concurrent overproduction of synapses in diverse regions of the primate cerebral cortex. *Science* 232:232–235, 1986.

Ramón y Cajal, S. *Recollections of My Life. Memoirs of the American Philosophical Society,* vol. 8, 1937.

Rasmussen, T., and B. Milner. Clinical and surgical studies of the cerebral speech areas in man. In K. J. Zulch, O. Creutzfeldt, and G. C. Galbraith, eds. *Cerebral Localization.* Berlin and New York: Springer-Verlag, 1975.

Rasmussen, T., and B. Milner. The role of early left-brain injury in determining lateralization of cerebral speech functions. *Annals of the New York Academy of Sciences* 299:355–369, 1977.

Riva, D., and L. Cazzaniga. Late effects of unilateral brain lesions sustained before and after age one. *Neuropsychologia* 24:423–428, 1986.

Russell, R., and M. Espir. *Traumatic Aphasia.* Oxford: Oxford University Press, 1961.

Schneider, G. E. Early lesions of superior colliculus: Factors affecting the formation of abnormal retinal projections. *Brain Behavior and Evolution* 8:73–109, 1973.

Segalowitz, S. J., and F. A. Gruber, eds. *Language Development and Neurological Theory.* New York: Academic Press, 1977.

Sidman, R. L. Development of interneuronal connections in brains of mutant mice. In F. P. Carlson, ed. *Physiological and Biochemical Aspects of Nervous Integration.* Englewood Cliffs, N.J.: Prentice-Hall, 1968.

Singh, J. A. L., and R. M. Zingg. *Wolf Children and Feral Man.* New York: Harper, 1940.

Skeels, H. M. Adult Status of children with contrasting early life experiences. *Monographs of the Society for Research in Child Development* 31:1–65, 1966.

Teuber, H.-L. Recovery of function after brain injury in man. In *Outcomes of Severe Damage to the Nervous System,* Ciba Foundation Symposium 34. Amsterdam: Elsevier-North Holland, 1975.

Turkowitz, G. The development of lateral differentiation in the human infant. In S. J. Dimond and D. A. Blizard, eds. Evolution and lateralization of the brain. *Annals of the New York Academy of Science* 299:213–221, 1977.

Tzavaras, A., G. Kaprinis, and A. Gatzoyas. Literacy and hemispheric specialization for language: Digit dichotic listening in illiterates. *Neuropsychologia* 19:565–570, 1981.

Wechsler, A. F. Crossed aphasia in an illiterate dextral. *Brain and Language* 3:164–172, 1976.

Witelson, S. F. Early hemisphere specialization and interhemispheric plasticity: An empirical and theoretical review. In S. J. Segalowitz and F. A. Gruber, eds. *Language Development and Neurological Theory.* New York: Academic Press, 1977.

Woods, B. T. The restricted effects of right-hemisphere lesions after age one; Wechsler test data. *Neuropsychologia* 18:65–70, 1980.

Woods, B. T. Impaired speech shadowing after early lesions of either hemisphere. *Neuropsychologia* 25:519–525, 1987.

Woods, B. T., and H.-L. Teuber. Early onset of complementary specialization of cerebral hemispheres in man. *Transactions of the American Neurological Association* 98:113–117, 1973.

Witelson, S. F., and W. Pallie. Left hemisphere specialization for language in the newborn. *Brain* 96:641–646, 1973.

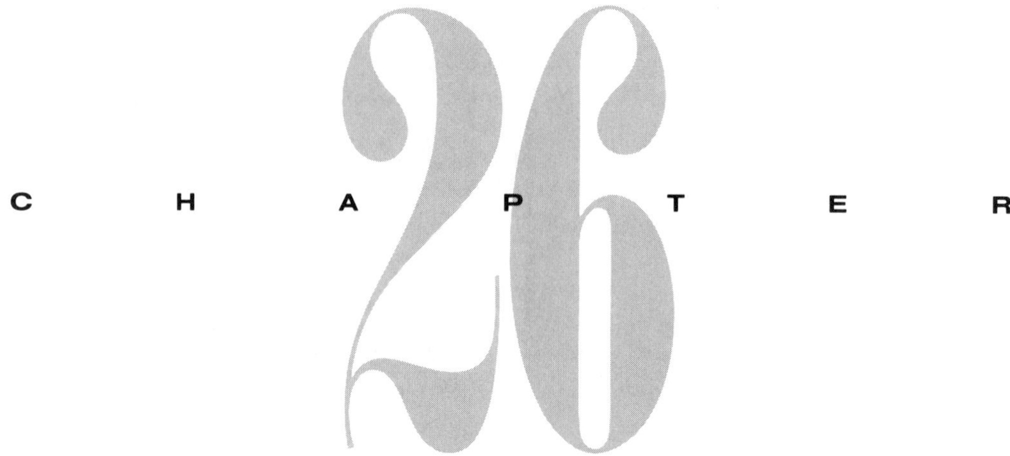

CHAPTER 26

RECOVERY OF FUNCTION

> On the afternoon of June 16, 1783, Dr. Samuel Johnson, the famed English lexicographer, sat for his portrait in the studio of Miss Frances Reynolds, the sadly untalented sister of Sir Joshua Reynolds. Despite his 73 years and marked obesity, Johnson afterwards walked the considerable distance from the studio to his home. He went to sleep at his usual hour in the evening and awoke according to his account around 3 a.m. on June 17. To his surprise and horror, he found that he could not speak. He immediately tested his mental faculties by successfully composing a prayer in Latin verse. Next he tried to loosen his powers of speech by drinking some wine, violating his recently acquired habits of temperance. The wine only put him back to sleep. Upon reawakening after sunrise, Johnson still could not speak. He found, however, that he could understand others and that he could write. His penmanship and composition were somewhat defective. . . . Johnson proceeded to summon his physicians, Drs. Brocklesby and Heberden, who came and examined him. They prescribed blisters on each side of the throat up to the ear, one on the head, and one on the back, along with salts of hartshorn (ammonium carbonate). Heberden, who was one of London's leading doctors, predicted a speedy recovery. His confidence proved quite justified: the therapeutic regimen was so efficacious that Johnson's speech began returning within a day or two. Recovery proceeded smoothly over the next month, and even the mild disorders in writing lessened. Johnson finally was left with a slight but stable dysarthria until he succumbed to other causes later in the next year. (Rosner, 1974, p. 1)

The case of Dr. Johnson has been described and discussed a number of times by different neuroscientists because he was a famous and interesting person and because his transitory illness is not fully explained and invites speculation. (The reader may try to diagnosis and then compare the result with that published by Critchley.) Obviously, his aphasia provides an example of almost complete loss of a rather specific function (he could still write) and seemingly rapid and almost complete recovery. The story also contains a testimony to the knowledge and insight of his doctors because their prediction with regard to outcome was correct. There are, however, many questions the critical reader may wish to ask. How much weight should self-testimony be accorded? Did he in fact have a stroke or any other brain disorder? We can believe that he might discover, when alone in the middle of the night, that he could not speak because he was known to have the habit of talking to himself. But, since he was an eccentric, we might also believe that the stroke was faked for one or another purpose. Given that his disorder was real, what was it and where was it? Some neurologists have thought that the lesion was very small or was only a transitory blood clot. Others, such as Critchley, have speculated that because he could not speak but could think, compose Latin verse, and write might be evidence that he had bilateral speech. This latter idea may be negated in view of Murray's hypothesis that Johnson had Tourette's syndrome, which is thought to involve a dysfunction of the right hemisphere. Even given that Johnson had had a stroke and that all the testimony concerning it was correct, it might still be asked whether his is a representative case of recovery.

Luria describes a case with more severe loss of function and less complete recovery in his book *The Man with a Shattered World.* The book describes the condition of a former soldier, Lyova Saletsky, who received a fractured skull and accompanying brain damage from a bullet wound in the battle of Smolensk. The damage was centered in the posterior left hemisphere intersections of the occipital, temporal, and parietal cortex. Luria first saw Saletsky 3 months after the injury and then at 3-week intervals for the next 26 years. During this time Saletsky painfully and slowly "relearned" the art of reading and writing. (It may have been a matter of relearning to use his remaining skill rather than relearning the skill per se.) In doing so he compiled a diary, in which he gives a moving account of his initial deficits, recovery, and residual problems. The following is an example of what Saletsky had to say about his condition.

> I remember nothing, absolutely nothing! Just separate bits of information that I sense have to do with one field or another. But that's all! I have no real knowledge of any subject. My past has just been wiped out!
>
> Before my injury I understood everything people said and had no trouble learning any of the sciences. Afterwards I forgot everything I learned about science. All my education was gone.
>
> I know that I went to elementary school, graduated with honors from the middle school, completed three years of courses at the Tula Polytechnic Institute, did advanced work in chemistry, and before the war, finished all these requirements ahead of time. I remember that I was on the western front, was wounded in the head in 1943 when we tried to break through the Germans' defense in Smolensk, and that I've never been able to put my life together again. But I can't remember what I did or studied, the sciences I learned, subjects I took. I've forgotten everything. Although I studied German for six years, I can't remember a word of it, can't even recognize a single letter. I also remember that I studied English for three straight years at the Institute. But I don't know a word of that either now. I've forgotten these languages so completely I might just as well never have learned them. Words like *trigonometry, solid geometry, chemistry, algebra,* etc., come to mind, but I have no idea what they mean.
>
> All I remember from my years in the secondary school are some words (like signboards, names of subjects): *physics, chemistry, astronomy, trigonometry, German, English, agriculture, music,* etc., which don't mean anything to me now. I just sense that somehow they're familiar.

When I hear words like *verb, pronoun, adverb,* they also seem familiar, though I can't understand them. Naturally, I knew these words before I was wounded, even though I can't understand them now. For example, I'll hear a word like *stop!* I know this word has to do with grammar — that it's a verb. But that's all I know. A minute later, I'm likely even to forget the word *verb* — it just disappears. I still can't remember or understand grammar or geometry because my memory's gone, part of my brain removed.

Sometimes I'll pick up a textbook on geometry, physics, or grammar but get disgusted and toss it aside, since I can't make any sense out of textbooks, even those from the middle school. What's more, my head aches so badly from trying to understand them, that one look is enough to make me nervous and irritable. An unbearable kind of fatigue and loathing for it all comes over me. (Luria, 1972, pp. 140–142)

To these two celebrated examples we could add many more, who like Johnson showed dramatic spontaneous recovery, or who like Saletsky showed amazing strength and perseverance in compensating for their disability. But unlike Johnson, many people show little or no recovery, as Kertesz has described to be the case for global aphasia caused by cerebrovascular accidents. Many other people show much less resilience than Saletsky. Here are two examples of patients we have known. H.P. was an extremely intelligent teacher who after a left hemisphere stroke, which occurred in middle age, suffered from what might best be described as Broca's aphasia. Despite showing almost daily signs of excellent recovery and frequent good humor and insight, he committed suicide within months of his stroke. Knowing H. P., we cannot help feeling that this was his reasoned solution to an infirmity that he could not accept. Nevertheless, feelings of depression are common after brain damage, and his act may have been pathological rather than reasoned and free. D. S. was an equally intelligent middle-aged man who worked in the theater industry but whose real pleasure was his hobby of carpentry. After a right hemisphere stroke he no longer showed an interest in theater, cinema, or even watching TV, and he no longer displayed any interest or skill in carpentry. His family did not understand this change and was unable to give him any support. He remains in a passive and dependent condition and gives no indication of trying to improve his lot. Finally, there are cases in which recovery simply does not occur, as is illustrated by the Quinlan's story of their daughter, Karen Ann.

Twenty-one years after her birth at St. Clare's hospital, Karen Ann Quinlan was returned to the same hospital in a deep coma from which she never roused. After attending a birthday party the night of 14 April, 1975 and consuming a few gin and tonics, she slipped into unconsciousness. No one ever determined exactly why. She had been on a crash diet to slim down to a size 7 bikini and had not eaten all day. It would later be found that she also had taken a mild "therapeutic" amount of a tranquilizer, and aspirin. Whatever the cause, Karen Ann fell quickly into a coma and for a period of time — no one every knew exactly how long — she stopped breathing. The resulting oxygen starvation caused the cognitive area of her brain to die. In the hospital, Karen Ann was fed by tubes inserted in her nostrils and her breathing was supported by a respirator. Her weight dropped from 120 pounds to 90, 80, and finally to 70. Her body gradually contracted to the fetal position and became rigid. By the end of July, Karen Ann's family, on the advise of their physicians, Morse and Javed, gave their permission to remove the respirator that was assumed to be keeping their daughter alive. However, the attorney for the hospital, Theodore Einhorn, informed the Quinlans that as Karen Ann was over 21 they were not her legal guardians and that they would have to be appointed by a judge as legal guardians before their request would be followed. The subsequent legal cases, in which the family was represented by Paul Armstrong, a Legal Aid Society attorney, attracted international interest. The central issue of the case was whether Joseph Quinlan could be named her legal guardian for the purpose of authorizing the discontinuance of all extraordinary means of sustaining her life, since no recovery was expected and since medical science could not help her. The case was lost in the initial trial but was eventually won before the Supreme Court of New Jersey. This was a landmark decision because it was the first right-to-die ruling ever made in legal history. Karen Ann was subsequently removed from the respirator and moved to a nursing home. There she remained unchanged until she died more than ten years later.

The previous examples point to the variability in prospects for recovery from brain damage. What we know today tells us that recovery depends on the type, location, and extent of brain damage, the person (including unique organizational features of his or her brain), and also on the person's attitude and the attitude and support of physicians, therapists, and family. Knowledge of how each of these variables apply to any one person is a central challenge in therapy.

In the United States, and the statistics are probably representative worldwide, there are approximately 300,000 reported cases of stroke each year. They account for almost half of the hospitalizations for neurological disability and about 10% of all deaths. In addition, there are more than 400,000 cases of head injury admitted to hospitals each year and of these three-quarters will show evidence of brain damage. Of approximately 300,000 people who become permanently disabled each year, most are neurological cases.

For many kinds of brain damage the outcome is uncertain as illustrated in Figure 26-1. The figure summarizes the consequences of a closed-head injury to 1285 patients that was of sufficient severity to produce 6 h of coma, during which no eye-opening occurred, no recognizable words were uttered, and no commands were followed. What is interesting is the enormous variation in the prospects for recovery. Over 40% of the patients die,

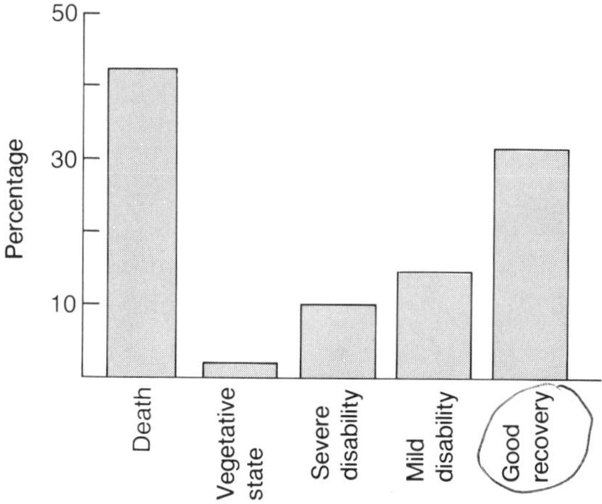

FIGURE 26-1. Recovery prospects from a closed-head injury that produces six hours of coma. (After Levin et al., 1982.)

but among those who survive, the majority make a reasonably good recovery. It is important to note, however, that among those who make a good recovery less than 50% can return to work and many of these may not regain complete job competency. As Finger and Stein point out, many people have an expectation that recovery will not occur and they consequently do not encourage rehabilitation. Others may be overly optimistic. In the following section we describe the processes of recovery, the cellular processes that take place after brain damage, present evidence about how each may result in behavioral change, and offer information about the prospects for recovery of function. Finally, we present results from some new experimental approaches that are directed toward restoring function.

EXAMPLES OF THE PROCESS OF FUNCTIONAL RECOVERY

Recovery is seldom a sudden restitution of function, but rather is usually a slow change that follows a relatively predictable sequence. Examination of the stages of the sequence and their associated behaviors often reveals an apparent reemergence of lower level functions in succession. More normal behavior is manifest only in the last stage of the sequence. In Hughlings-Jackson's terms the lesion or trauma produces a complete deevolution of the behavior followed by reevolution. Teitelbaum and his coworkers have pointed out tellingly, that recovery often parallels the sequential development of the behavior in infants. Several examples of such events are worth considering.

Recovery from Spinal Cord Section

Kuhn has given a detailed description of the effects of complete spinal cord transection in humans. He notes considerable variability in the extent to which spinal reflexes recover after cord section. Some people show virtually no recovery, and their muscles atrophy; others recover sufficiently that their legs will support their weight, and they show no muscle atrophy. For those who show pronounced recovery of spinal reflexes, Kuhn describes four major stages or steps in the process of recovery. Estimates about the extent of recovery can be made from the rapidity with which a patient enters each stage. It is noteworthy that the development of spinal cord function in infants appears to parallel these recovery stages.

1. *Spinal shock.* Spinal shock is a state of profound depression of all reflexes below the level of section. Shock varies in severity from person to person and in duration, lasting from 1 to 6 weeks. Some reflexes, such as penile erection in males, may not be depressed at all. As stated above, for some few individuals there is no evidence of recovery beyond this stage.

2. *Minimal reflex activity.* In this stage slight flexion or extension of the foot, some toe twitches, and extension of the large toe occur. Anal and bladder reflexes for waste secretion may also be present.

3. *Flexor activity.* The first major reflexes to return are flexor reflexes, consisting of such movements as dorsiflexion of the big toe and fanning of the toe, dorsiflexion of the foot, and flexion of the leg and thigh. Stimuli found most effective in eliciting limb flexion were tactile, particularly effective were unpleasant stimuli, and the zones with the lowest thresholds were the foot area and the genital area.

4. *Extensor activity.* Extensor movements generally become apparent as early as 6 months after injury and continue to develop for years. They consist of extension and stiffening of one or both legs; in some patients there is only a slight tightening of limbs, whereas in others the limbs assume pillarlike rigidity. In some people in the latter group this activity is sufficient to permit prolonged standing in warm water without support.

The most effective stimuli for eliciting extension are proprioceptive, such as stretching the flexors of the thigh muscles at the thigh (as occurs during shifting from a sitting to a lying position) or squeezing the thigh muscles. Tactile stimulation becomes effective in eliciting extensor responses somewhat later, and the lowest thresholds are on the thigh or the back of the knee and spread distally to include the foot surface.

It can be seen from this description that recovery from spinal cord section can be quite extensive. However, these people can make no voluntary movements and receive no sensation from below the area of the lesion.

Recovery from Hypothalamic Lesions

In 1951, Anand and Brobeck observed that lesions of the lateral hypothalamus of rats and cats produced **aphagia** (inability to eat or chew), which ultimately led to death. Teitelbaum and Stellar reported 3 years later that if the animals are artificially fed for a period of time, they recover the ability to eat. Analyzing this recovery process, Teitelbaum and Epstein found that feeding behavior recovered in an orderly sequence: first the animals ate only small amounts of wet food and maintained themselves on this diet, later they began to eat dry food, and eventually maintained themselves on dry food and water. Many workers have observed this sequence of recovery in many species of animals that have received hypothalamic and other types of brain lesions that affect feeding. Interestingly, this sequence of recovery bears close resemblance to the development of eating in young animals; feeding begins with suckling, progresses to ingestions of dry food and eventually to maintenance on dry food and water. Teitelbaum and others have thus argued that the process of recovery is analogous to the process of **encephalization: ontogenetic development of behavior in the individual as successively higher levels of function mature.**

In addition to their deficits in feeding, animals with lateral hypothalamic lesions display another behavioral abnormality that has been called **sensory neglect.** This phenomenon was first described by Marshall and associates, using a variety of simple but ingenious tests. Using Von Frey hairs (hairs of different thickness), cotton swabs, and pins to test tactile responsiveness; pieces of chocolate, shaving lotion, and ammonia to test olfactory responsiveness; and various visual stimuli, they found that on the first day following the lesion the rats would only respond to stimuli if they were presented to the tip of the nose. Gradually, as recovery proceeded, the area of the body to which the animal would orient increased, spreading from the tip of the nose to the front paws, to the rear paws, and finally to the back. There was a very close relation between the recovery of feeding and the recovery of sensory responsiveness to the snout, and between the recovery of responsiveness to the body and the recovery of locomotion (see below).

The same technique of analyzing sequential behavioral changes has been extended to behaviors other than feeding. Numerous studies with many species of animals have suggested that large lesions of the posterior portions of the hypothalamus produce **somnolence** that leads eventually to death. In 1969, McGinty found that with care rats with such lesions would recover from the somnolence and eventually sleep less than normal rats. Analyzing the processes of recovery Robinson and Whishaw argued that the somnolence was due more to a loss of voluntary movement than to disruption of a sleep center. Sleep abated as movement recovered, and the residual impairment was an inability to initiate and maintain voluntary movement. More recently, Golani and colleagues have supported this suggestion. To analyze the details of the recovery of movement, they used a version of the Eshkol Wachman system of movement notation—originally developed for ballet choreography and analysis.

Figure 26-2 gives examples of sequential recovery of movement. Golani and his coworkers found that exploratory movements in the rat recover along several relatively independent dimensions that appear successively. During recovery the animal develops antigravity support, which allows it to stand and support its weight. The animal develops longitudinal movements that allow it to extend forward. It then develops scans of the head in a forward and lateral direction, which progressively increase in amplitude over days until it can turn completely around as well as walk forward. Interestingly, each time the animal initiates walking it does so with the sequence of movements illustrated during recovery. These authors argue that the isolation of relatively independent dimensions of movement during recovery suggests the existence of corresponding neural systems. The development of movement in infant rats follows a similar sequence to that seen in recovery. Many of these components can also be observed in the features of movements displayed each time a normal animal begins to move.

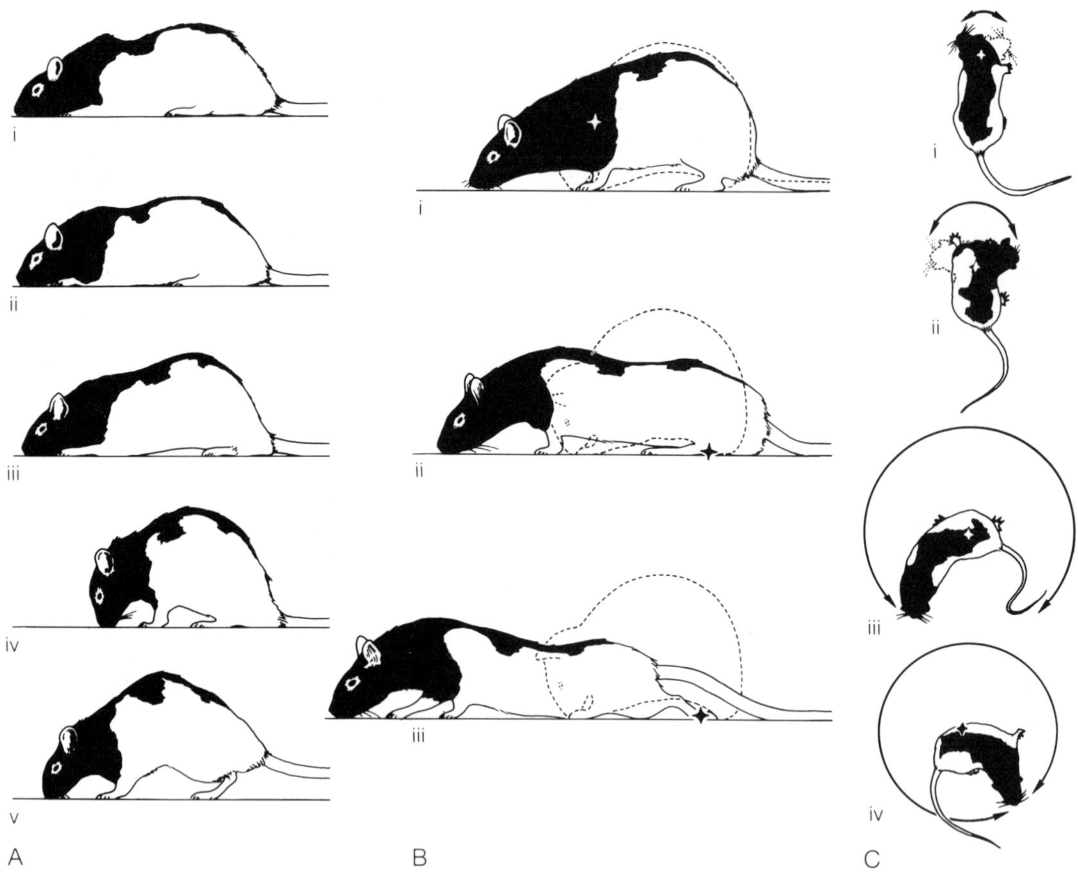

FIGURE 26-2. Recovery of (*A*) posture, (*B*) forward scanning, and (*C*) turning in a rat that had been given large posterior lateral hypothalamic lesions. Broken-line and solid-line drawings indicate the extreme positions that the rat assumes during each phase. Recovery occurs over time, in the sequence indicated by the Roman numerals. In each sequence recovery begins with the head and proceeds caudally. (After I. Golani et al., 1979. Reprinted with permission.)

It is now recognized that lateral hypothalamic lesions damage many ascending and descending fiber systems between the brainstem and forebrain (including dopaminergic, norepinephrinergic, cholinergic, serotoninergic nonspecific systems, and ascending somatosensory fibers and descending motor tracts). In a sense the animal model is an analogue for many kinds of damage that occur in the brainstem and which also affect some of these systems. Thus, for example, coma produced by brainstem damage could be analogous to somnolence, induced by hypothalamic damage and recovery could be expected to parallel that in animals and be affected by treatments that have proved helpful in accelerating recovery in animals.

In the examples given above the first effect of the lesion is manifest as an almost complete absence of eating or of certain kinds of movements. Both abilities recover, but do so in stages that appear to parallel behavioral development in infant animals. This parallelism suggests that recovery represents a sequential emergence of higher levels of function. Finally, if hypothalamic damage is not excessive, the animals recover a level of function that approximates normal. Many studies on animals with lesions indicate that if the initial lesions are small, the animals begin to recover at more advanced stages, but they nevertheless follow the same sequence. If the lesions are particularly large, recovery may be arrested short of completion.

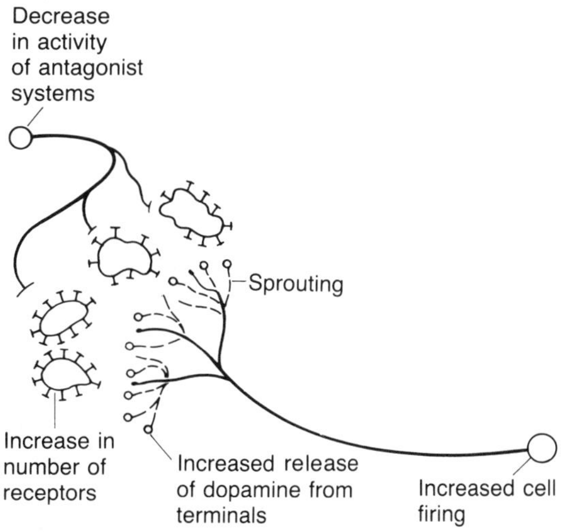

Recovery from Dopamine Depletions

Because it has been possible to develop clear descriptions of behavioral changes that follow lateral hypothalamic lesions, this experimental preparation has become a favorite model for the study of recovery of function. A major recent thrust of research on recovery has been to investigate the biochemical changes that underlie recovery. Stricker and Zigmond have made a detailed study of the role that dopamine plays in this syndrome. The hypothalamic lesions do cut dopamine-containing fibers that are projecting to the basal ganglia, and the concomitant decrease in dopamine seems closely correlated with some of the symptoms of the lesions. A further refinement of the analysis of dopamine contributions comes from studies in which dopamine is selectively depleted with the neurotoxin 6-hydroxydopamine. Following depletion, many of the symptoms peculiar to the lateral hypothalamic syndrome are induced. Animals are akinetic (inactive), do not eat or drink, and have difficulty orienting to sensory stimulation. If the depletions are no greater than about 96%, substantial behavioral recovery appears to occur. How can a system that had been depleted to this extent mediate recovery and then sustain seemingly normal behavior? The many changes postulated to underlie this recovery are illustrated in Figure 26-3 and include (1) increased firing in the remaining dopamine cells, (2) sprouting of the remaining dopamine cells so that they can fill in for cells that have been destroyed, (3) an increase in the number of dopamine receptors, permitting a more potent action of the remaining dopamine, (4) a decrease in the activity of cells that are normally antagonistic to dopamine, and (5) an increased release of dopamine from the remaining terminals. The range of changes that occur after the lesions is quite surprising, but they are also a testimony to the remarkable capacity of the brain to restore **homeostasis,** that is, its normal biochemical balance. Of course, dopamine decreases are not the only changes that follow hypothalamic lesions, but the research on dopamine changes provides a good model for studying changes in other neurochemical systems.

FIGURE 26-3. Hypothetical changes in dopamine and allied systems that might underlie recovery that takes place after the system has been damaged.

Recovery from Motor Cortex Damage

Twitchell has given a very detailed description of recovery from hemiplegia in humans produced by thrombosis, embolism, or stroke of the middle cerebral artery. The recovery sequence closely parallels the development of reaching and the grasp response described by Twitchell in infants. Immediately following arterial occlusion there was onset of hemiplegia marked by complete flaccidity of the muscles and loss of all reflexes and voluntary movements. Recovery occurred over a period of days or weeks and followed a relatively orderly sequence in each patient. Some patients recovered relatively normal use of their limbs; for others, recovery was arrested at one or another stage. Complete recovery of use of the arms, when it occurred, appeared between 23 and 40 days after the lesion. Recovery occurred in the following sequence: (1) return of tendon and stretch reflexes, (2) development of rigidity, (3) grasping that was facilitated by, or occurred as part of, proprioception (that is, as part of postural reflexes of turning, righting, etc.), (4) development of voluntary grasping (this involved recovery of movement in the sequence of shoulder, elbow, wrist, and hand, first in the flexor musculature, then in the extensor musculature), (5) facilitation of grasping by tactile stimulation of the hand, and, finally, (6) grasping that occurred predominantly under voluntary control. Voluntary grasping continued to improve until independent movements of the fingers were well developed. About 30% of patients reached the last stage of recovery; the others showed arrested recovery at one of the preceding stages.

In these patients, loss of function was initially profound, and in many cases it resulted in complete suppression of all reflexes, including spinal reflexes, so that the muscles were left completely flaccid. The sequential recovery can be thought of as involving first the return of spinal-tendon and stretch reflexes, then rigidity and proprioceptive facilitation from the midbrain, then tactile facilitation from the forebrain, and finally the return of voluntary control. The actual degree of recovery was no doubt determined by the extent of cortical damage. Some patients who never went through the latter sages probably had the most severe cortical damage.

Recovery from Aphasia

Kertesz has recently reviewed the prospects of recovery from aphasia with examples of his own case histories. An example of recovery from each of his different patient subgroups is shown in Figure 26-4. All of the patients received the Western Aphasia Battery, which assesses spontaneous speech content, fluency, comprehension, and repetition, from which an aphasia quotient was derived. Kertesz makes the following generalizations from this work. (1) Posttraumatic (head-injury) patients showed the most rapid, and often almost complete, recovery, whereas recovery in stroke patients was less pronounced and in some groups may be almost absent. (2) Initial deficits in anomic patients were the least severe and initial deficits in global aphasics were the most severe, with intermediate severity occurring for other groups. The

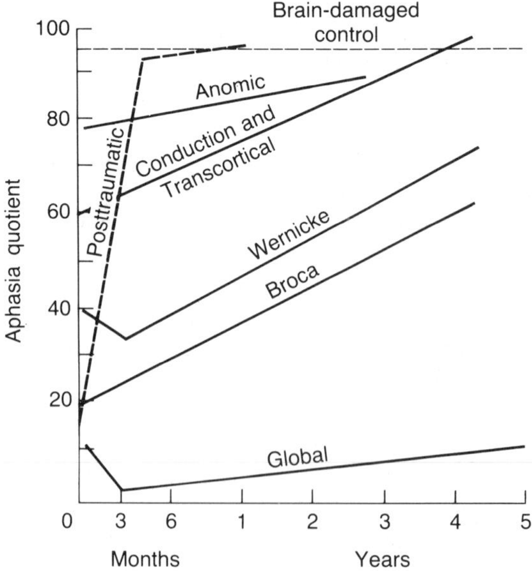

FIGURE 26-4. Initial deficits and recovery in stroke patients with different language disorders (solid lines) and a post-trauma patient (dashed line). Each line is a representative patient. (After Kertesz, 1979.)

actual rate of recovery, given initial impairments, was often quite similar in all groups. (3) There was a tendency, when recovery occurred, that the patient progressed to one of the other stages, but recovery usually stopped with anomic aphasia. (4) Most recovery occurred in the first 3 months (not illustrated in Figure 26-4), with some recovery occurring in the next 6 months and less occurring in the following 6 months. Thereafter, little or no recovery occurred. (5) There was some evidence that younger patients showed better recovery, and the effects of intelligence, occupation, and sex in these patients were slight if present. (6) The language components most resistant to brain damage were naming, oral imitation, comprehension of nouns, and yes-no responses — functions that may be partly mediated by the right hemisphere. Kertesz's analysis of aphasia is not based on the linguistic properties of language, but unquestionably such analysis is necessary. It may also be worthwhile to introduce a word of caution with respect to the sequences of recovery. Basso and colleagues note that patients who are fluent (Wernicke's) do not turn into nonfluent (Broca's) aphasics. This is understandable because the lesion locations for each type are thought to be distinct.

Recovery from Amnesia

There are many reports of the loss of memory and its subsequent recovery following brain lesions or concussions. There is some difference in opinion on the sequence of events during recovery. Barbizet reports a case that illustrates one point of view, or possibly one type of syndrome of recovery. A 40-year-old man suffered a head trauma and was in a coma for 7 weeks. Five months after the trauma he was completely amnesic for the 2 preceding years and had gross memory disturbances for events back to early childhood. Eight months after trauma the period of complete amnesia had shrunk to 1 year, and the period of partial amnesia extended back to the age of 4. Sixteen months after trauma his amnesia was limited to the 2-week period before trauma. Thus, his recovery represented a progressive shrinkage of the amnesia, from past to present.

Whitty and Zangwill report a somewhat different pattern of recovery following less severe head injury. They report that, as a rule, retrograde amnesias are very short, usually of a few seconds' duration. If they are longer, the shrinkage of amnesia may not be strictly chronological. Sometimes more recent events are recalled first and then serve as a magnet for piecing together a continuous memory.

Despite the difference of opinion (a not uncommon event in areas of memory research, and one that may be attributable to differences in type of damage, location, etc.), both of the above reports present a period of complete amnesia, a period of recovery either of time or events, and a period of residual deficit. The nature of the deficit and the processes of recovery seem reminiscent of those we have just described for other types of deficits; that is, a sequential recovery from **diaschisis** with some residual deficit. The parallel between the recovery of memory and the recovery from aphagia, paralysis, and so forth suggests that recovery from all types of brain trauma involves some common processes.

Descriptions of recovery as a sequential development have obvious practical and theoretical utility. From a practical perspective good sequential descriptions allow any patient to be monitored for rate and degree of recovery. If recovery is arrested before completion, residual abilities can be understood within the context of the recovery stage reached. Theoretically, stages of recovery provide insights into the brain's organization and provide background information for enhancing recovery or for overcoming residual deficits.

Summary

Recovery follows some kinds of brain damage. It may involve recovery in the remaining portions of an incompletely damaged neural system or recovery from the suppression of function within a system. An interesting feature of recovery is that it can be gradual and orderly and proceed in what appears to be stages. In some ways these stages seem to parallel the well-known rostral-caudal and proximal-distal ontological development of the body and of behavior. The recapitulation of development as seen in recovery from spinal shock or motor cortex damage in humans or feeding and walking in the rat is remarkable but can also be used as a diagnostic indication of how recovery is proceeding. It is not clear that cognitive functions show the same orderly sequence of recovery, but speech sometimes recovers in a sequence of global-to-anomic aphasia and memory sometimes returns in a past-present sequence. More knowledge about how cognitive functions recover may depend on progress in analyzing their normal structure.

CELLULAR EVENTS ASSOCIATED WITH BRAIN DAMAGE

Brain damage produces a number of short, intermediate, and long-term changes in brain tissue in addition to the actual loss of tissue caused by the initial insult. Precisely what changes occur will depend on the type of brain damage, and so, for simplicity, the following descriptions derive from the changes that follow brain lesions. Terms associated with these processes are defined in Table 26-1.

Changes at the Site of Damage

A lesion made either by a puncture wound or ablation leaves a vacuole, or cavity, of variable size. Due to degeneration of surrounding tissue, accumulation of fluid, and shrinkage of surrounding tissue, the cavity may expand in size for about a week and then begin to contract. With time it may completely disappear and thus may not be visible on CAT scans. The shrinkage of the cavity may cause distortions of surrounding tissue such that the ventricles expand to compensate for the loss in tissue volume. Ventricular expansion may be visible on CAT scans and provide a clue that damage has been incurred. Within about an hour after damage, dead tissue surrounds the cavity, and surrounding this area of **necrosis** is an area of tissue consisting of injured, dead, and normal cells. Within 24 h **phagocytes** (astrocytes and microglia) infiltrate the area to remove debris. By 3 to 7 days new capillaries proliferate in the area. These processes may continue for several months until the debris is removed and only the glial cells remain. Inspection of stained tissue may show many small, dark glial cells filling the area, a process called **gliosis,** and among these the astrocytes form a scar in the area. The scar may hamper or block any functional regeneration of remaining neural cells.

Changes Distal to the Site of Damage

Damage in one area not only kills local cells but may cut the fibers of cells located at a distance and also produce changes in cells that previously innervated the region or were innervated by it. These changes may involve the breakdown or death of the tissue, a process called *degeneration.* There are a number of kinds of degeneration, which seem to involve different processes. The location of and the terms for some of these processes are illustrated in Figure 26-5.

When a nerve is severed, the portion distal to the cut always degenerates. This fact was first noted by Waller in the early 1850s and is so certain that its occurrence is thought to constitute the only law of neuroanatomy. Such degeneration is called **Wallerian,** or **anterograde, degeneration.** The process of Wallerian degeneration in the central nervous system is different in part from what occurs in the peripheral nervous system. Centrally, the axons degenerate, as does the myelin that wraps around them, and there is little or no regen-

TABLE 26-1. Degenerative events following brain damage

Term	Definition
Anterograde degeneration	Also called orthograde or Wallerian degeneration. The certain degeneration of an axon after it has been cut from the cell body.
Astrocyte activity	Astrocytes invade areas of damage to remove debris and through attachments made by their many processes seal or scar the area.
Calcification	Accumulation of large deposits of calcium at some locations where neural degeneration takes place. Deposits can be seen on brain scans.
Chromatolyses	Literally, color dissolution. After injury, fatigue, or exhaustion, cell Nissl substance breaks down. Loss of Nissl and affinity for stain makes the cell colorless to microscopic examination.
Gliosis	Replacement of cell bodies by glial cells in areas undergoing degeneration.
Necrosis	Localized death of individual cells or groups of cells.
Phagocytosis	Removal of dead cells by mitochondria and astrocytes.
Retrograde degeneration	The death of the remaining axon, cell body, and dendrites after the axon is cut. The process may be reversible before it is complete.
Terminal degeneration	The shrinkage and degeneration of terminals after the axon is cut from the cell body.
Transneuronal degeneration	The death of neurons that innervate or are innervated by a damaged or destroyed neuron.

eration. The damage can be visualized in the following way. Normal myelin can be stained dark blue by certain stains (e.g., the Weigert method). In the absence of myelin, portions of the brain where the axons had been take up no stain and so leave a negative image of the route that had been taken by the axon. In the peripheral nervous system the process is different in that some regeneration occurs. The **Schwann cells** that form the myelin do not all die, and they subsequently multiply and form a bridge that regenerating fibers can cross to reinnervate their target. Reinnervation may not occur in the central nervous system because the **oligodendrocytes** that form its myelin do not proliferate, and also because scar tissue may block regrowth. The end feet of cut axons also change, becoming dense and small. This reaction occurs within a day or two, and the material may be visible for months if certain stains (e.g., Fink-Heimer) are used. The degeneration of the end feet is called **terminal degeneration** and, as is noted elsewhere, it is employed as a useful sign of the destination of different neural systems.

The proximal portions of the axon and the cell body may not always degenerate, but if they do, the process is called **retrograde degeneration.** In the cell body the Nissl substance disappears, the nucleus is displaced to the periphery of the cell, and the cell may swell to double its normal size. For some neurons (e.g., motor neurons) retrograde degeneration is reversible, whereas in others (e.g., thalamic neurons) it is not. In the former case the cells return to normal size, but in the latter they shrink and are removed by phagocytosis. Retrograde degeneration can be detected because the absence of Nissl substance makes the cell colorless, a process called **chromatolysis,** and this can be detected by the negative image the cells leave

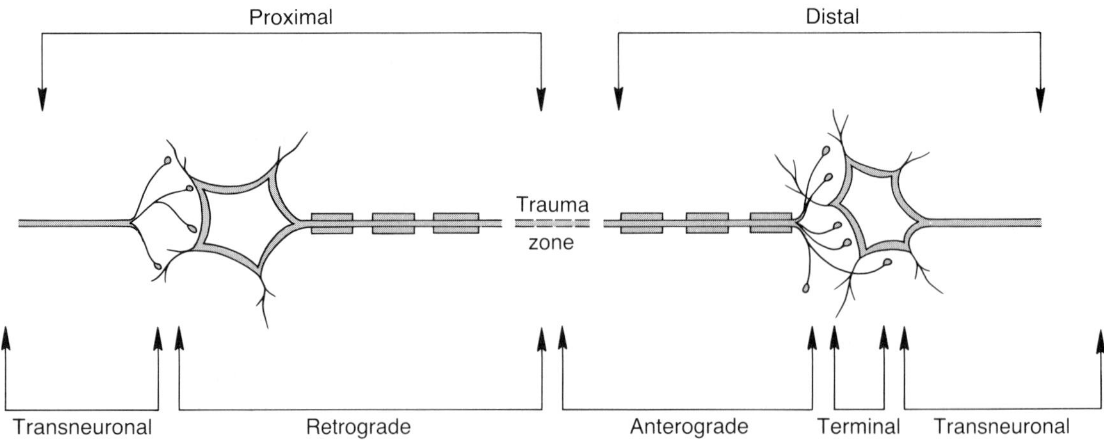

FIGURE 26-5. The spatial terminology for cell and fiber degeneration. (After Beresford, 1965.)

because they have lost their affinity for Nissl stains.

Cells that innervate or are innervated by a degenerating neuron may also die, a process called **transneuronal degeneration.** This process was first observed in the visual system. When the optic nerve is cut, cells of the lateral geniculate body completely degenerate. It is thought that the cells degenerate either because they require an optimal level of stimulation from the optic nerve to survive or because some necessary trophic (nutritional) substance is supplied by the optic nerve's end feet. (A similar type of process appears to occur in muscles, because when their nerves are cut they shrink and waste away.) Transneuronal degeneration may occur across more than one synapse; for example, cells in the visual cortex may also begin to die after the lateral geniculate body degenerates. Transneuronal degeneration may also occur in the opposite direction, in the cells of innervation. The former process is referred to as anterograde and the latter as retrograde transneuronal degeneration. Transneuronal degeneration may also be associated with accumulating deposits of calcium, a process called **calcification.** For example, in response to neocortex damage, calcification may occur in degenerating thalamic neurons (also a site of retrograde degeneration) and in the basal ganglia (a possible site of secondary transneuronal degeneration). These deposits can be so pronounced that they are easily seen in histological material or with CAT scans. The reasons for calcification and the way that it occurs are not known, but its presence in CAT scans can be taken as an indication of certain kinds of cortical or subcortical damage.

The occurrence of these different degenerative processes provides evidence relevant to a number of issues that the reader might wish to consider. First, the fact that degenerative changes occur in so many places and in so many ways makes it impossible to state that even the most refined lesion can be localized. For example, a small ablation in the frontal cortex may be easily visualized and may appear to be localized; but retrograde degeneration and calcification will occur in the thalamus; secondary transneuronal degeneration and calcification will appear in the basal ganglia; and Wallerian and terminal degeneration will appear throughout the neocortex, brainstem, and spinal cord. Clearly, brain damage cannot be strictly localized. Second, it is important to note that degeneration has been a key not only to understanding brain damage but also to understanding how the different parts of the brain are connected with one another. Schoenfeld and Hamilton have argued that a thorough analysis of these changes should be a part of the proper assessment of all types of brain damage. Third, many of these degenerative changes are known to continue for years, but as yet we have no idea how they are associated with changes in behavior. Fourth, degeneration may be different if brain damage occurs in infancy (see Chapter 25).

PHYSIOLOGICAL EVENTS ASSOCIATED WITH BRAIN DAMAGE

One of the earliest theories of recovery of function was formulated by Munk in 1881. He suggested that regions of the brain that were not otherwise occupied could assume functions previously mediated by the injured area. The area substituting for the damaged one would ordinarily not have become involved in mediating the function in question. However, there is little evidence that any portions of the brain are standing by unused until required. Subsequent proposals variously suggested that recovery occurs through regrowth, compensation by surrounding areas, removal of inhibition from surrounding areas, and so forth. Munk's and some subsequent proposals failed to recognize that the initial deficits may not have been entirely due to focal damage.

Von Monakow recognized another factor. In 1911, he formulated the concept that he called *diaschisis* (from the Greek, meaning to split in two or to split apart): after a brain injury not only is neural tissue and its function lost, but several neural areas related to the damaged areas are also depressed and their function is consequently absent for a time. In von Monakow's words:

> What characterizes all kinds of shock is a temporary cessation of function which affects a wide expanse of physiologically built up functions, and a restitution which goes on in well defined phases, sometimes shorter, sometimes longer, sometimes even retrospectively in the shape of fragments of functions in retrograde amnesias. The diaschisis proper has its point of attack beyond the limits of anatomically disturbed tissue in those parts of the grey substance which are connected with the focus by fibers. (von Monakow, 1911/1960, p. 241)

The term *diaschisis* has been described by some as peculiar at best and horrible at worst, because what neural changes are to be encompassed within its meaning have never been precisely specified. Von Monakow meant that some aspects of recovery could be attributed to reemergence of function of the depressed zones rather than to plasticity, rewiring, sprouting of remaining fibers, or other neural changes that might be occurring at the same time. In the absence of any proper neural correlate for diaschisis some people have equated the term with shock. Certainly, shock is easier to pronounce and spell than diaschisis, although it implies an overall suspension of function rather than a splitting of function. Rather than debate the merits of the terms, we shall describe some examples of neural and other changes that contribute to some of the immediate deficits that follow brain damage.

Shock

In 1841, Marshall Hall recognized that damage to the spinal cord resulted in a temporary loss of spinal reflexes, a phenomenon that became known as *spinal shock*. Sherrington in the early 1900s demonstrated that the shock was caused by depriving the spinal cord of its connections from the brain. Cutting the cord or transecting it with the local anesthetic procaine produced shock, but recutting it after reflexes had recovered did not reinstate shock. The duration of shock seems related to the amount of input that the spinal cord receives, as can be inferred from two sets of data. Shock lasts for days in humans, a number of hours in cats, and is almost absent in frogs, suggesting a relation between the number of descending fibers (or perhaps some special properties of the fibers) and shock duration. Shock also has a shorter duration if only some of the input to the spinal cord is interrupted or if it is interrupted in a number of stages. The details of how removal of input produces shock are not fully understood. It is hypothesized that spinal cells have an optimal resting excitation that is maintained in part by the release of neural transmitter substances from descending fibers. When this tonic influence is lost, the cells are depressed and return to normal resting excitability only gradually. Support for this idea comes from work by Grillner in cats. He found that pharmacological agents that stimulated spinal cord norepinephrine receptors could arrest spinal shock. The understanding of spinal shock has played an important role in the therapy of people who have received spinal injury. Before World War I it was believed that reflexes were permanently abolished. In 1917, Head and Riddoch showed that if infections were controlled, patients could be maintained indefinitely and that reflexes began to return within 2 to 3 weeks. By analogy, the principle of spinal shock can be generalized to other parts of the brain with the assumption that cells everywhere will show temporary depression when their input is removed. Indeed, as noted above, some die when deafferentated.

Edema

Edema, or swelling of tissue following trauma, occurs in the area surrounding the lesion but may, through pressure and other mechanisms, affect distant areas. In general, interstitial (between cell) tissue is like a collapsed balloon with respect to fluid, and in the brain it contains less fluid than other tissue. Due to either increased capillary pressure, changes in constituency of capillary fluid, or increased porosity of the capillaries, fluid flows into or accumulates in the interstitial space, causing it to balloon. The ensuing pressure probably depresses neuronal function. Edema, as well as many other posttraumatic symptoms, can be lessened by cortisone. (It has been suggested that excessive use of cortisone so effectively suppresses symptoms that patients may walk directly to the morgue. Clearly, it is difficult to balance the ameliorative effects of symptom suppression against the body's own restorative functions.) Some posttraumatic deficits may be caused by edema. The drop in IQ that occurs after cortical surgery for the treatment of epilepsy, as reported by Milner, is shown in Figure 26-6. Immediately after surgery, irrespective of the lesion location (temporal, frontal, parietal), IQ drops and then returns to preoperative levels within a year. The initial drop may be due in part to edema, because it is lessened by treatment with cortisone.

Blood Flow

The rate of blood flow through the arteries of the brain can be used as a measure of its metabolic activity. It is thought that blood flow is controlled by CO_2 released by tissue metabolic activity; accordingly, if activity is high, then CO_2-release will be high, which will in turn increase blood flow. Blood flow can be measured by placing special detectors on the skull, which measure the flow of a radioactive inert gas that has been injected into the carotid artery. The more blood that flows, the higher the radioactivity count. Using this technique with brain-damaged patients, Skinhøj was able to show an immediate reduction in blood flow after injury had occurred, and Meyer and his coworkers were able to detect a reduction in blood flow for as long as a month after injury, even in the intact hemisphere. It is thought that when tissue is damaged, its metabolic activity drops, causing a decrease in the release of CO_2 and a concomitant reduction in blood flow. Presumably, distant neural areas show decreased activity because they lose contacts with the damaged area and reflect this by decreased metabolic activity, decreased CO_2

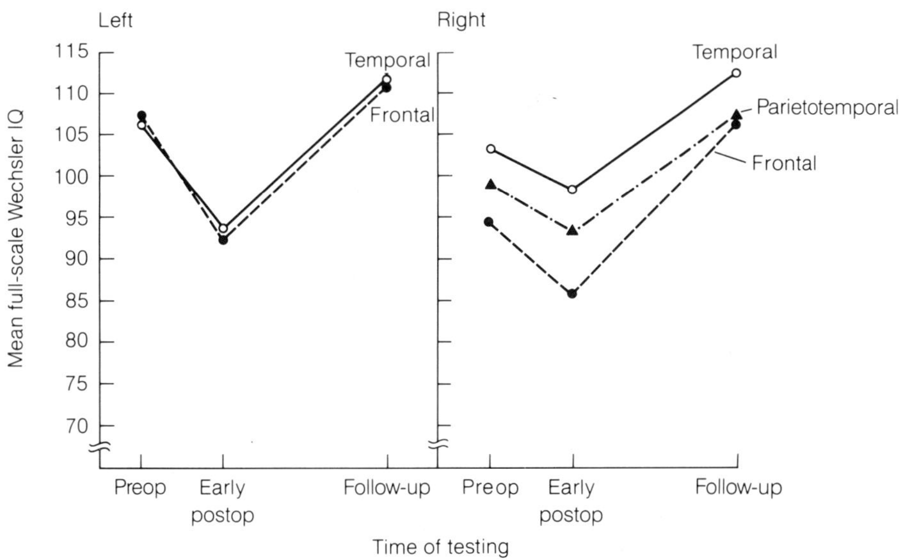

FIGURE 26-6. Mean preoperative, early postoperative, and long-term follow-up Wechsler IQ rating for 51 patients (38 male, 13 female) classed according to side and site of the cortical excisions carried out to relieve epilepsy. Number of cases: left temporal (open circle), 19; left frontal (filled circle), 6; right temporal (open circle), 13; right frontal (filled circle), 6; right parietotemporal (filled triangle), 7. (From B. Milner. Psychological aspects of focal epilepsy and its neurosurgical management. In D. Purpura, J. P. Penry, and R. D. Walker, eds. *Advances in Neurology,* vol. 8. New York: Raven Press, Copyright © 1975. Reprinted with permission.)

release, and reduced blood flow. Clearly, these events conspire to reduce overall brain activity, which will in turn be reflected in a lowering of behavioral function.

Neurotransmitter Release

The levels of many brain neurotransmitters are known to change after brain damage, but these neurotransmitters have not been exhaustively examined nor have their changes been correlated with behavioral changes. Here we will give only one example of the types of correlations that are being attempted. In an animal model of human stroke, Robinson and his coworkers have cut the middle cerebral artery on one side of the rat brain and measured brain catecholamines (norepinephrine and dopamine) in various locations. They found reduced levels of these transmitters in many brain areas 5 days later, with recovery, and even overcompensation, occurring 3 weeks later. Robinson, influenced by the catecholamine hypothesis of mental illness, proposes that both the physical and the behavioral apathy that follows strokes may be caused in part by the decline in catecholamine levels. Obviously, this is an intuitively appealing hypothesis. We may note, however, that this hypothesis depends on the correctness of this explanation of mental illness, and it does not exclude other possible behavioral-transmitter relations. Hassler and his coworkers are now reporting many complex changes in the concentrations of transmitters and other chemicals after brain damage.

Glucose Uptake

The Sokoloff technique of deoxyglucose labeling has been used by Pappius to evaluate changes in the brain after trauma. The technique involves injecting [^{14}C]-deoxyglucose into the circulatory system. The deoxyglucose has many of the same biochemical properties of glucose, and it is mistaken for glucose by energy-requiring active brain cells and so crosses the blood-brain barrier to enter brain cells as an energy source. Unlike glucose, its metabolism is relatively incomplete, and because it is unable to pass back out of the cells, it accumulates in them for a time. If the brain is removed and cut about an hour after injection and placed on a film negative, the film will receive the most intense exposure from the [^{14}C] in areas that had high glucose utilization. Pappius, realizing that brain metabolism and function are closely coupled, damaged the neocortex of rats and then measured glucose uptake over a number of days. In the neocortex ipsilateral to the lesion glucose utilization fell by over 60% 3 days after the injury and did not return to normal until 5 days after it. Metabolism also fell by nearly 25% in the undamaged hemisphere. When rats were treated with steroids before, or just after, brain damage, the decline in metabolic activity was only about 20% in the damaged hemisphere and about 10% in the undamaged hemisphere. Pappius was able to show that the decline in metabolic activity was not due entirely to edema and so must be caused by some as yet unknown process. These results provide another explanation for the behavioral depression that follows brain damage.

Changes in Electrical Activity

Changes in the electrical activity of neurons may, of course, reflect any or all of the physiological events mentioned above. Nevertheless, electrical activity does change following brain damage, and it can be used as an index of posttraumatic function. Glassman has observed transient suppression of sensory-evoked potentials and reduction in fast EEG activity near areas of damage in the cat neocortex, and such changes also occur in humans. It is also well known that brainstem damage produces many changes in forebrain EEG activity, at least in part because the damage cuts ascending fibers of systems that are responsible for producing forebrain EEG activity. In an illustrative study Kolb and Whishaw made lesions in a large number of brainstem locations and observed that forebrain EEG activity that depends on noncholinergic systems could be transiently abolished by certain types of brain damage. In many cases recovery in these noncholinergic systems was very gradual, lasting for 2 or more weeks. In a study of single-cell activity Barnes and colleagues observed that motor neurons in the spinal cord became transiently hyperpolarized (more difficult to fire) after the spinal cord was transiently disconnected with a cold block. Although this explains loss of reflex activity, it does not explain whether hyperpolarization is due to withdrawal of excitation from the brain or to the imposition of inhibition from residual circuitry.

Autoneurotoxicity

It has been known for a long time that brain damage, strokes, or ischemic attacks (arterial constriction) that cut off blood flow to parts of the brain also produced damage in those parts of the brain. Recent studies now show that tissue death is not immediate but delayed, sometimes for hours or days, and that some parts of the brain (i.e., the CA_1 cells of the hippocampus) are particularly sensitive to oxygen deprivation. These observations suggested that something other than oxygen loss might produce the damage. One causative agent for this delayed cell death has now been identified. It is thought that the excitatory neurotransmitter, glutamate, is released by oxygen deprivation and it then overexcites cells causing them to die. In a sense the cells release a neurotoxin that kills them. This idea has been experimentally supported by findings that indicate that substances that excite glutamate receptors are potent neurotoxins. The identification of a causative agent in cell death combined with the fact that cell death is not immediate suggests that there is a possibility of preventing cell death. This may be done in two ways, either blocking the release of glutamate or by blocking glutamate receptors. Very vigorous experimental research is being conducted in an effort to achieve one of these two objectives in a clinically acceptable way. This endeavour is aided by an energetic attempt by pharmaceutical companies to develop drugs that will selectively block glutamate receptors involved in this type of cell death.

Summary

These examples of brain changes following trauma illustrate that there is not one physiological event that can be unequivocally related to the depression of function that follows brain damage or to subsequent recovery when it occurs. Changes include shock in areas remote to the damage, edema or swelling of traumatized tissue, reductions in blood flow, changes in neurotransmitter release, reductions in glucose use, and autoneurotoxicity. These many changes complicate easy explanations for behavioral changes that follow brain damage and make it difficult to identify appropriate remedial procedures.

POSSIBLE MECHANISMS RESPONSIBLE FOR RECOVERY

So far we have considered mechanisms thought to produce shock and recovery from shock, but a substantial portion of overall recovery is thought to involve reorganization of remaining undamaged tissue, or else reorganization of tissue around the area of the lesion. Flourens first propounded the latter idea, but Lashley brought it to prominence in the first half of this century.

Lashley believed that recovery of function was not only expected but was relatively easy to explain since the brain worked on the principles of mass action (the entire cortex participates in each function) and equipotentiality (each area of the cortex is equally able to assume control of any given behavior). Although Lashley's original position was extreme, he moderated it, applying the notions of mass action and equipotentiality only to functional areas. The following experiment illustrates the type of evidence that Lashley brought forth in support of his position. He electrically stimulated the area of the precentral gyrus of rhesus monkeys on four separate occasions over a period of 18 days. On each test he obtained relatively constant responses from each site stimulated, and on different tests he found that areas such as those representing the arms and legs remained relatively fixed. However, within any one area, stimulation of the same point on different tests resulted in widely different movements, and at different times the same movement was obtained from separate and shifting areas. These results suggested to Lashley that "within the segmental areas the various parts of the cortex may be equipotential for the production of all of the movements within that area." (Lashley, 1929, p. 154)

Subsequent work has given Lashley's conclusion little support, because use of more refined techniques to perform the same experiments did not confirm his results. Doty and his coworkers repeatedly stimulated the motor cortex of dogs and found that the movements obtained from a given site are amazingly constant over long periods. Craggs and Rushton implanted an array of electrodes into the cortex of a baboon and found remarkable stability of response with repeated stimulation. In Lashley's experiments the surgical procedures were repeated on each test, whereas in Doty's and in Craggs and Rushton's the animals were chronically implanted so that after initial surgery the electrodes were fixed and no further surgical trauma occurred. It seems likely that Lashley's results can be attributed in part to trauma (tissue edema, etc.), and in part to slight differences in the placement of his electrodes. Certainly it is now accepted that Doty's findings on what is called the *stability of points* negate the belief that recovery occurs because of equipotentiality alone.

Strictly speaking, *equipotentiality* means that every subarea of a region is involved in mediating a given function. Although as shown above there is little evidence to support such a strict view, there is evidence that under certain circumstances equipotentiality, if more flexibly defined, is realized. In this view an area may play no role in the control of a particular behavior until a lesion occurs, at which point reorganization takes place, giving other areas, particularly adjacent ones, some part of the damaged area's function. The experiments of Glees and Cole support just such a hypothesis. They identified the thumb area of the monkey's neocortex with electrical stimulation, removed the area, and then remapped the surrounding tissue after a period of recovery. During recovery the animals began to use the thumb, and when the cortex was remapped, the areas surrounding the lesion were found to produce thumb movements.

A modified equipotentiality interpretation may explain the recovery in the following case reported by Bucy and coworkers. They studied a man with a **pyramidal tract** sectioned in the lower brainstem as a treatment for involuntary movements. During the first 24 h after surgery he had complete flaccid hemiplegia, followed by slight return of voluntary movement in his extremities. By the 10th day he was able to stand alone and walk with assistance. By the 24th day he could walk unaided. Within 7 months maximum recovery seemed to have been reached, and he could move his feet, hands, fingers, and toes with only slight impairment. At autopsy, $2\frac{1}{2}$ years later, about 17% of his pyramidal tract fibers were found to be intact. The recovery in his ability to move his toes and fingers seems attributable to that remaining 17%, doing the job previously done by the entire tract. This suggests that the system displays substantial equipotentiality. Lawrence and Kuyper's experiments with pyramidal tract lesions in rhesus monkeys might be interpreted as supporting this conclusion. They found that a few remaining pyramidal tract fibers could support relatively independent finger movements, apparently irrespective of the location of the fibers. If all the fibers were removed, there was no recovery of finger movement.

If it is accepted that functional areas have the ability to compensate for damage, how does this occur? Several neural mechanisms have been suggested as important in mediating such recovery, including (1) regeneration, (2) sprouting, (3) denervation supersensitivity, and (4) disinhibition or release of potential compensatory zones from inhibition. Associated with these mechanisms are several possible ways of facilitating the process of recovery. In attempts to account for recovery, a number of terms have become popular; some of the commonest of these are defined in Table 26-2.

Regeneration

Regeneration is a process by which neurons damaged by trauma regrow connections to the area they previously innervated. Regeneration is a well-known and common occurrence in the peripheral nervous system, where both sensory and motor neurons send forth new fibers to reinnervate their previous targets (Figure 26-7). It is believed that Schwann cells multiply and provide a tube or tunnel that guides the regenerating fibers to their appropriate destination.

The stimulus to search for and promote regeneration in the mammalian brain comes in large part from studies on amphibians. They display almost complete regeneration of nervous system elements after brain damage. Studies by Sperry and others have shown that regenerating axons can circumvent scarring and form topographically correct connections that reestablish normal behavior. Given that this occurs in amphibians, it is thought that the same regeneration could be promoted in the mammalian brain if only the mechanisms of regeneration in the amphibian brain were understood.

TABLE 26-2. Compensatory mechanisms that may follow brain damage

Term	Definition
Behavioral compensation	Use of a new or different behavioral strategy to compensate for a behavior lost due to brain damage, e.g., notetaking to compensate for loss of memory.
Collateral sprouting	The growth of collaterals of axons to replace lost axons or to innervate targets that have lost other afferents.
Denervation supersensitivity	The proliferation of receptors on a nerve or muscle when innervation is interrupted that results in an increase in response when residual afferents are stimulated or when chemical agonists are applied.
Disinhibition	Removal of inhibitory actions of a system usually by destroying it or blocking its action pharmacologically.
Nerve growth factor	A protein that may be secreted by glial cells that promotes growth in damaged neurons and facilitates regeneration and reinnervation by cut axons.
Regeneration	Process by which damaged neurons, axons, or terminals regrow and establish their previous connections.
Rerouting	Process by which axons or their collaterals seek out new targets when their normal destination has been removed.
Silent synapses	A hypothetical synapse that is thought to be present but whose function is not behaviorally evident until the function of some other part of the system is disrupted.
Sparing	A concept that refers to a process that allows certain behaviors or aspects of behavior to survive brain damage.
Sprouting	Growth of nerve fibers to innervate new targets, particularly if they have been vacated by other terminals.
Substitution	The idea that an unoccupied or underused area of the brain will assume functions of a damaged area (not in vogue today).
Transient collaterals	Collaterals that at some time during development innervated targets that they subsequently abandon as development proceeds.
Vicaration	A version of substitution theory that suggests that the functions of damaged areas can be assumed by adjacent areas. The term is unlikely to catch on.

There have been a number of attempts to devise ways of facilitating regeneration. One is the use of a substance called **nerve-growth factor (NGF)**, a high-molecular-weight protein that is either produced or taken up from glia by nerve terminals and then transported to the cell body to play some role in maintaining normal growth or the health of a cell. There have been a number of attempts to determine whether injection of NGF into lesioned areas promotes functional regeneration as yet there has been no conclusive evidence that it does so.

Two approaches have been formulated for developing ways of helping regenerating fibers to bridge areas of scarring. One is to build artificial tubes or bridges across the area of scarring; the second is to place relatively undifferentiated neural tissue in the lesion to provide a medium through which regenerating fibers can grow. Kromer and colleagues have reported some success with this technique. They sectioned the cholinergic pathway, which innervates the septum from the hippocampus, transplanted embryonic brain tissue into the gap, and found that regenerating cholinergic fibers grew through the bridge to reinnervate the hippocampus in what appeared to be a normal fashion. A particularly interesting feature of these

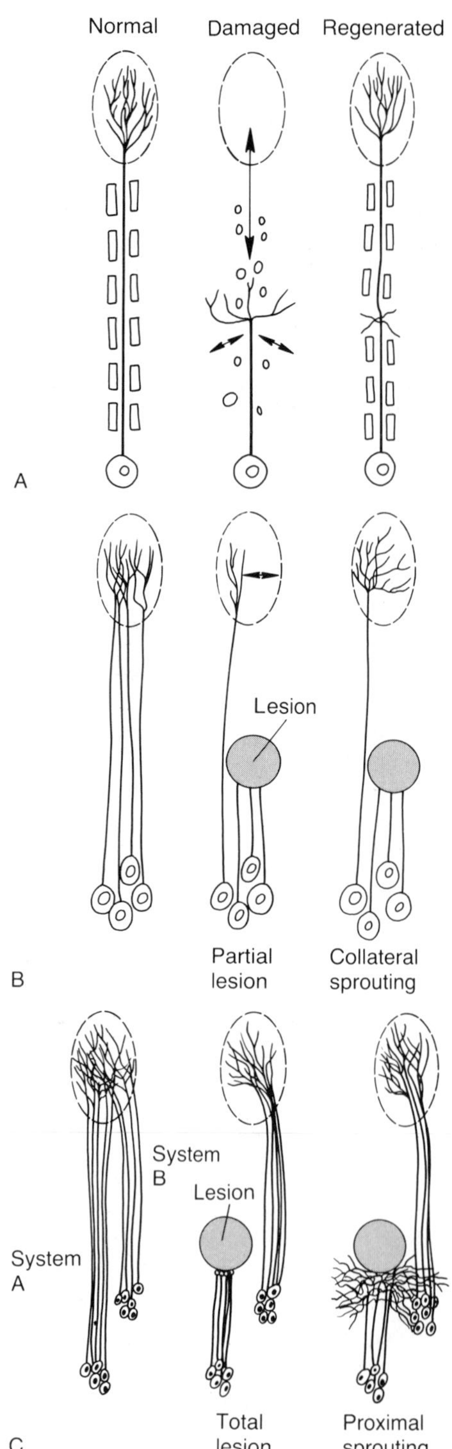

FIGURE 26-7. Three models of axonal sprouting by which damaged central axons might reestablish functional connections. *A.* True regeneration of severed axons involving regrowth of the axon back to its target site. Present in the peripheral human nervous system and in invertebrates and in the central nervous system of rats under favorable conditions. *B.* Collateral sprouting in intact neurons. Known to occur and be functional in the brain catecholamine and serotonin fibers. *C.* Reinnervation of systems that have been disconnected, as yet a hypothetical explanation of recovery. (After Björklund, 1985.)

results is that the embryonic tissue, in addition to providing a bridge, stimulates the damaged system to regenerate. These experiments appear to provide one of the most promising avenues for developing ways of stimulating functional regeneration.

Sprouting

Some early studies on the effect of sectioning some of the afferent fibers to muscles suggested that the remaining fibers sprouted branches that occupied the sites left vacant by the lesioned axons. Convincing evidence now shows that similar **sprouting** takes place in the brain after lesions (Figure 26-7*B*). Lynch and his coworkers and others have examined the rate at which sprouting occurs and have addressed the question of whether the newly formed connections are functional. Using the rat's hippocampus as their model, they cut one of the inputs to the granule cells of the hippocampus. They then addressed the question of function by recording evoked potentials from the denervated area. In addition, they examined the anatomical basis of regrowth by staining the hippocampus with chemicals that highlight the synaptic terminals of interest so that synaptic distribution could be assessed with the electron microscope. Their results show the following. (1) Remaining fibers send sprouts to reinnervate vacated portions of the granule cells. (2) Other fiber systems from adjacent portions of the cell sprout and reinnervate the unoccupied area. (3) Even fibers not connected with the cells grow and occupy a deserted space. The process of sprouting appears to be quite rapid and may be complete in 7 to 10 days. Evoked potentials indicate that the new connections are electrophysiologically functional. Whether they are behaviorally functional is open to inquiry.

Another form of sprouting is shown in Figure 26-7*C*. In this case the path of one of two interconnecting systems has been severed and so the remaining system has sent connections to mesh with the proximal portions of the severed axons. It is not known if such hypothetical connections are functional.

Denervation Supersensitivity

The idea of **denervation supersensitivity** arose from the work of Cannon and Rosenblueth in 1949. They found that when the afferent fibers to a muscle were cut, the muscle became hyperresponsive to the application of its neurotransmitter. Hypersensitivity is presumed to occur because receptors proliferate on the muscle cell in areas where they were not previously located. As a result a given amount of drug produces a greater effect because there are more receptors available to be stimulated. Similar receptor proliferation is thought to occur in the brain.

Denervation supersensitivity appears to be a particularly pronounced occurrence after certain biochemical lesions of the nervous system. For example, it has been found that when the dopamine terminals of the brain are destroyed with a neurotoxin, animals previously unaffected by injections of L-dopa (which is converted into dopamine in the brain) become profoundly activated by the drug. It is suggested that this effect occurs because the removal of dopamine synapses produces a proliferation of dopamine receptors, which then give an enormous response to stimulation from what ordinarily might be considered a small amount of dopamine.

A question remains about denervation supersensitivity: Is it a mechanism with some adaptive or compensatory value? There is a certain appeal in the idea that supersensitivity may compensate for reductions in neurotransmitter supply (caused by lesions, poisons, or aging), but as yet there is no evidence to suggest that this happens.

Disinhibition of Potential Compensatory Zones

In 1971, Wall and Egger mapped the thalamic and neocortical regions in which stimulation of a rat's forelimb or hindlimb resulted in an evoked potential. After then cutting the pathway from the lower spinal cord to the brain to sever the connections with the hindlimb, they again stimulated the forelimb or hindlimb. As expected, there was no response in the hindlimb regions, but the forelimb region was normal. After 3 days, however, there was a remarkable change. The region that had previously exhibited evoked potentials on stimulation of the hindlimb now showed these potentials on stimulation of the forelimb. The response looked normal, as if it had always been wired up to the forelimb. Why?

Most available evidence indicates that sprouting could not account for the effect and that there must be preexisting *silent synapses* (connections that are present but not functioning). Evoked potentials elicited over pathways formed by sprouting generally take between 7 and 10 days to occur. It seems likely, therefore, that fibers from the forelimb were always connected to the hindlimb area but were kept under some form of inhibition and thus were not functional. Once fibers from the hindlimb area were severed the competing input was lost and the area became functionally a forelimb area. These findings seem to suggest that an area that could *potentially* become involved in a response is larger than mapping studies usually suggest. The results also suggest that the areas may not become involved in a response unless competing or inhibitory systems are abolished; that is, unless **disinhibition** occurs. A good example of the applicability of this idea was mentioned previously. If one eye of a kitten is occluded, the cells that it should normally drive are taken over by the nonoccluded eye. In fact, the animal appears completely blind to stimulation of the previously occluded eye. However, Kratz and associate have found that if the good eye is removed, the previously blind eye becomes functional to a rather surprising extent. The blindness of the previously occluded eye seems to be due to inhibition from the good eye. Duffy and colleagues found that drugs that block inhibiting synapses (bicuculline) were also able to restore vision to the blind eye. In fact, in a rather ingenious experiment Sherman and coworkers destroyed a small part of one retina and occluded the other eye. When the occluder was removed, the animal was blind in all parts of the occluded eye except that part corresponding to the damaged portion of the retina of the nonoccluded eye. Apparently areas of the cortex that would normally receive input from the damaged part of the retina require input to inhibit the function of the corresponding area of the other eye.

These findings suggest that in various parts of the brain there is considerable overlap in innervation, but that specificity is maintained though inhibition. Removal of inhibition allows some takeover by the previously inhibited area. How general is this effect? The answer is not known, but Geschwind has raised the question of whether the recovery of language is mediated by such a mechanism. He suggests that language may be learned in both hemispheres, but that its use in the subordinate hemisphere is inhibited in some way. Damage in the dominant hemisphere disinhibits the subordinate hemisphere, and recovery can be attributed to this release. Although there is not much firm evidence to support this suggestion, it illustrates an imaginative use of the concept of disinhibition.

CHRONIC EFFECTS OF BRAIN DAMAGE IN ADULTS

The use of such words as **plasticity** and the emphasis placed on recovery of function in a great deal of basic research give the impression that the brain has an unlimited potential for recovery and reorganization after injury. Although there is a paucity of information on long-term recovery, on the basis of the available evidence the following generalizations can be made. (1) Recovery is likely in complex behaviors that comprised many components through processes that are referred to as *behavioral compensation*. (2) Recovery is most pronounced after incomplete lesions, such as those common after trauma from concussions or penetrating head wounds. (3) Recovery is unlikely for specific functions controlled by localized brain areas if all of the area is removed. Even in making these generalizations, we must emphasize that the available evidence indicates that there are always residual and permanent deficits after brain damage, and that extensive recovery is the exception, not the rule.

Behavioral Compensation

The ability to be employed and self-supporting is unquestionably dependent on many behavioral abilities and configurations of those abilities. Brain damage may affect some of those behaviors more than others, but there are numerous possibilities for compensation. Studies by Dresser and his coworkers show that when gainful employment is used as a measure of recovery, as was done for veterans injured in the Korean War, recovery was pronounced. Approximately 80% were employed. This measure gives the highest rate of recovery of any we have found in the literature and strongly suggests that some factor such as behavioral compensation is operating. This is not to minimize in any way the seriousness of the problem that 20% were not employed. Nor does it speak to the quality of employment. Oddy and Humphrey suggest that work is not a sensitive index of recovery. Forty-eight of the 54 closed-head injury patients were back at work within 2 years, but many were restricted in their work activity and believed that they had not regained their full working capacity.

Other aspects of their social life also suffered—they had not resumed all leisure-time activities and social contacts. Interestingly, of all aspects of social relations, those with siblings suffered most. Oddy and Humphrey emphasize that therapy should not be directed only toward return to work but also toward leisure activities and social relations.

One way of examining what the chronic effects of brain damage are and how individuals cope is to study self-reports of people who have been brain damaged. Generally, very little attention is given to these reports, but they provide a valuable insight into questions of recovery. Fredrick Linge, a clinical psychologist we know, has described the changes that he has undergone after suffering brain damage in an automobile accident. He was in a coma for the first week after the accident and was not expected to achieve significant recovery. Nevertheless, he was able to return to a relatively demanding clinical practice about a year after his accident. But he was changed by the brain damage and had to make changes in his life-style and work routine to cope. He describes his adjustments in the following way:

> In learning to live with my brain damage, I have found through trial and error that certain things help greatly and others hinder my coping. In order to learn and retain information best, I try to eliminate as many distractions as possible and concentrate all my mental energy on the task at hand. A structured, routine, well-organized and serene atmosphere at home, and, as far as possible, at work, is vital to me. In the past I enjoyed a rather chaotic life style, but I now find that I want "a place for everything and everything in its place." When remembering is difficult, order and habit make the minutiae of daily living much easier.

In learning to live what is essentially a new life-style he recognizes changes that seemed for the worst but also some that seemed for the better. On one hand he states:

> I cannot cope with anger as well as I was able to do before my accident. Rage, related to my losses, does not lie just under the surface waiting to explode as it did earlier in my recovery. Yet, like any other person living in the real world, situations arise which make me justifiably angry. Before my accident, it took a lot to make me angry, and I am still, today, slow to anger. The difference is that now, once I become angry, I find it impossible to "put the brakes on" and I attribute this directly to my brain damage. It is extremely frightening to me to find myself in this state, and I still have not worked out a truly satisfactory solution, except insofar as I try to avoid anger-provoking situations or try to deal with them before they become too provoking.

On the other hand, he states:

> My one-track mind seems to help me to take each day as it comes without excessive worry and to enjoy the simple things of life in a way that I never did before. As well, I seem to be a more effective therapist, since I stick to the basic issues at hand and have more empathy with others than I did previously. (Linge, 1980, pp. 6–7)

The self-report by Linge shows that studies on recovery cannot be limited to measures such as reemployment or even renewed social contacts. These measures may, in many cases, indicate that recovery is complete, but they do not detail how the individual himself has changed, or how he has changed other aspects of the world, in order to cope. It is noteworthy that Linge was a professional psychologist who lived in a social milieu in which people were willing to help him reestablish himself. Many people who do not have, or who have not established, a similar position will have a much more difficult time "recovering." This is an important point for understanding the chronic effects of brain damage. Linge makes our point well by stating that not only must the brain-damaged person change the external environment, he or she must change the internal environment as well. We can go still further and state that studies on recovery of function are incomplete if they do not examine both these aspects of the brain-damaged person.

Recovery from Traumatic Lesions

As noted above, Kertesz has reported that greater recovery from aphasia is possible after traumatic injuries than after cerebrovascular accidents (Figure 26-4). This is probably because strokes damage large areas of the brain, both cortically and subcortically, and in doing so remove entire functional areas, whereas damage from traumatic injuries may be more diffuse and spare some parts of many areas. For example, a small residual part of a system may mediate substantial recovery, as was the case for the patient from the study by Bucy and colleagues who recovered nearly normal motor abilities with 17% of the pyramidal tract. Studies on war veterans have also shown that there are good prospects for recovery from penetrating head injuries.

In Teuber's analysis the deficits of war veterans on tests given 1 week after injury were compared with those given 20 years later. These patients are excellent subjects for study because they received standard tests after induction into the Army and were relatively young at the time of injury, the immediate aftermath of the injury is documented, and the kind and extent of recovery can be documented through prolonged follow-up by veterans' services. A summary of the results is given in Figure 26-8. They reveal that about 40% show some recovery from motor defects, 30% showed some recovery from somatosensory defects, 40% showed some recovery from visual defects, and 20% showed some recovery from initial dysphasia. These findings are probably quite reliable if we can generalize from the visual-field tests; according to

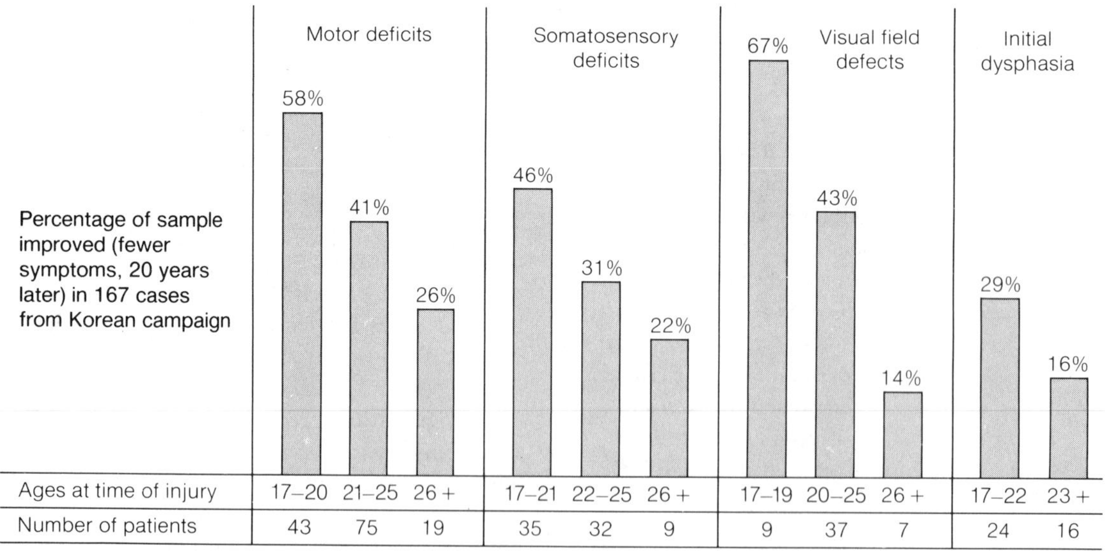

FIGURE 26-8. Estimated improvement from initial examination (with no more than 1 week of injury) and follow-up examination (20 years later) for some body regions (extremities, sides of face) for which symptoms were recorded (reflex changes, paralysis, weakness) for the motor system; the somatosensory system; the visual field; and in symptoms interpreted as dysphasia. Note the advantage for groups of lower age at the time of wounding. (After Teuber, 1975.)

Teuber, the Harms procedure of determining field defects allows for an extremely accurate assessment and is highly reliable in the hands of different testers at different times. Two comments can be made about Teuber's analysis. First, it must be noted that more than half of the patient population showed no recovery at all, and the failure of more than 75% of patients to show recovery from dysphasia is not encouraging. The latter figure is supported by Luria's report that 66% of his dysphasic patients show no recovery. Second, the analysis is not quantitative and there is no estimate of the degree of recovery. A study on a larger population of war veterans, those from Vietnam, has been made by Mohr and his coworkers. In general, their results are consistent with those of Teuber in that a great deal of recovery of function is to be expected from penetrating brain injury. In fact, Mohr reports more extensive recovery from aphasia (34%) than does Teuber, and Mohr reports that the recovery continued for years after injury. An addendum to these studies may be made. Zihl and von Cramon report that practice in localizing lights led to an increase in the visual field in partially blind patients, an increase that would not have occurred without practice. It is not known what effect specific therapy may have had on the patients reported in the veteran studies.

Recovery from Surgical Lesions

Throughout this book we have emphasized that localized brain damage can produce specific impairments. The studies on patients with atrophic lesions have been used to provide a data base from which tests are obtained and the tests are then used for diagnostic purposes. Quite clearly, if recovery is at all pronounced, the diagnostic utility of the tests will be lessened; that is, a given test would not be useful if it did not reveal brain damage after a certain recovery period had passed. With this idea in mind it seems pertinent to ask: How reliable are the tests with respect to recovery time from surgery? Fortunately, an answer to the question can be obtained because the tests have been given to patients within days of surgery and up to as long as 20 years after surgery. Unfortunately, the effects of recovery seem so frequently to have been absent that the breakdown of data at different test-retest intervals is not reported. Table 26-3 summarizes the results from some studies in which tests were given a few days before surgery, within 20 days after surgery, and one to 20 years after surgery. The results show that after dorsolateral frontal lesions there is no recovery in card sorting, after right temporal lesions there is no recovery in recall of the Rey figure, and after cerebral lesions there is no recovery in finger position sense or arm-movement copying. The finding of no recovery is also reported in some other studies. Jones-Gottman and Milner tested patient groups within 2 weeks of surgery and 1 or more years later on tests of spontaneous drawing. The subjects were told to invent as many unnameable drawings as they could within 5 min. Although all patient groups showed some reduction in performance relative to control groups, patients with right frontal lesions were the most impaired, and there were no differences in performance in patients tested shortly after surgery and those tested more than a year after it. There also seems to be little or no recovery in memory after bilateral hippocampal removal. In a 14-year follow-up, Milner and her colleagues report that the amnesic patient H. M. had a presurgical IQ of 104; it was 112 at the 2-year follow-up; and 118 at the 9-year follow-up. Yet despite this improvement in intelligence score, his anterograde amnesia remained essentially unchanged.

In the case of H. M. the improvement in IQ was probably due to a lessening of epileptic seizures. In some studies on patients with atrophic lesions a degree of recovery has been noted on some tests. In 1975, Milner reported that patients with left temporal lesions have preoperative verbal memory scores of 12, early postoperative scores of 4.4, and 5- to 20-year follow-up scores of 8. This improvement is significant. There are a number of possible explanations for why recovery should have oc-

TABLE 26-3. Presurgical, postsurgical, and follow-up performance on neuropsychological tests by patients with cortical lesions

Test	Lesion	Preop	Postop	Followup	Control	Reference
Card-sorting categories	Frontal	3.3	1.4	1.3	4.6	Milner, 1963
Card-sorting errors	Frontal	54.9	73.2	78.2	37.7	Milner, 1963
Rey-figure copy score	Right temporal	31.2	30.6	29.8	34.9	Taylor, 1969
Rey-figure recall score	Right temporal	15.4	15.3	13.8	24.2	Taylor, 1969
Finger position sense	Central					
Incidence of deficit (%)						
Ipsilateral		24	14	6	—	Taylor, 1969
Contralateral		36	43	65	—	
Arm-movement copying	Left parietal		73	75.8	90.2	Kolb and Milner, 1981

curred on this test. First, the score is a composite of logical memory (recall of stories) and paired-associate learning. It is not clear which component of the test recovered. Blakemore and Falconer studied paired-associate learning in 86 temporal lobectomy patients for up to 10 years after surgery. They found the deficit lasted for 2 to 3 years, but thereafter there was progressive recovery, provided the patients were young. Hence, recovery could have been due to improvement in one facet of the task. Second, Jones has shown that if left temporal lobe patients are taught to use imagery (i.e., for the associate word pair "bouquet-elephant," they imagine an elephant with a bouquet of flowers in its trunk), they show substantial improvement in memory. Hence, recovery may have been due to the development of alternative memory strategies. Third, temporal cortex must have rather special properties that allow rapid memory storage. This property probably also makes it especially prone to epilepsy. It is possible, this postulate accepted, that if any of this area remains, it retains a special capacity for plasticity that is not as evident in other brain areas. Considered together, although recovery occurs on this test, it is not clear that recovery is due to recovery of verbal memory per se. In summary, we feel that the results from some of the studies reported here are very important to the question of recovery of function. The implications of the results are that if the test is specific for certain brain areas and if the lesions remove the entire area, recovery will not occur. What makes this position particularly persuasive for us is that the surgical patients had tumors or epilepsy at the site of the lesions, which could have encouraged the function to move elsewhere. Yet there is little or no evidence in the test results to suggest that any such transfer took place.

VARIABLES AFFECTING RECOVERY

There are many variables other than just lesion size that affect the rate of recovery from brain damage. These are not discussed fully in many papers because measurements are so difficult to make, patient groups are often small to begin with, which precludes dividing them into subcategories, or simply because a particular researcher may not think they are important. These variables include age, sex, handedness, intelligence, and personality. Each of these variables will not be discussed here in full, but overall it is thought that if a person is to incur brain damage, recovery will be best if the person is young, intelligent, optimistic, left-handed, and female. Youth is one of the easier variables to measure. Teuber found that on a number of tests, recovery by soldiers from natural lesions in the 17–20 age group is greater than that for the 21–25 age group, which in turn is greater than that for the age group 26 and over (Figure 26-8). Perhaps 40 is the upper limit, because Milner reports that patients over 40 who have removals near the posterior temporal speech zone in the left hemisphere show less recovery than younger patients. It is noteworthy that age does not always appear as a significant factor in studies of recovery, as noted by Kertesz. It should also be remembered that age is a contributing factor to many kinds of brain damage; that is, strokes and other kinds of brain abnormality are common in older people and these are also just the people who may be showing declines in motor and cognitive function due to the normal processes of aging. Thus, recovery may tend to be obscured by aging.

A number of experimental models have been developed to examine the effects of age on recovery of function. Gall and colleagues damaged one of the afferents to the granule cells of the hippocampus and then examined sprouting by the remaining hippocampal afferents. They found that in infant rats, sprouting was extensive and invaded the entire dendritic field of the granule cells, in 21-day-old rats sprouting was attenuated, but in adult rats sprouting was virtually absent. If one assumes, therefore, that something like sprouting underlies some aspects of recovery of function, then this provides a convincing model for a neural basis for enhanced recovery in younger individuals. Contrasted to this approach, it should be noted that other researchers find that function can often be disrupted more profoundly in animals that are injured in infancy than if injury occurs in adulthood. Some of this evidence was reviewed in Chapter 25. Some anatomical evidence to support such effects can also be mentioned. Figure 26-9*A* shows the brain weight of rats that received small frontal cortex lesions in adulthood, at 10, 5 and 1 day of age. Note that the infant lesions produce a greater reduction in brain weight than the adult lesions and also that the weight reduction was quite profound for the 1-day-old group. This difference was not due to lesion size or to differences in tissue removed. The 1-day-old and 5-day-old rats also showed many behavioral abnormalities when adult. They were retarded in acquiring various tasks that adult brain-damaged animals could perform quite well. Curiously, the rats with removals at 10 days of age performed as well as control rats on many tasks and clearly fared better than adult subjects. These behavioral changes had an anatomical correlate: there was an enhanced dendritic growth in the cortex of 10-day-old rats with lesions and dendritic stunting in the 1-day-old group. It seems to us that future research will have to carefully examine how such changes can promote recovery of function as contrasted with those that might actually have a negative effect on recovery. At present, it seems sufficient to note that whatever changes do take place, the experimental evidence seems quite convincing that they are more likely to take place at particular times during development.

Handedness and sex, both for much the same reason, may influence the outcome of brain damage. Recall that a number of theories argue that there is less lateralization, or some other organizational differences, in the female brain. Likewise, familial left-handers are thought to be less lateralized in function than right-handers. For both groups it is thought that damage in a particular location can be ameliorated to some extent by the remaining functional portions of the system that are located in the undamaged hemisphere. There is, however, an inherent logical weakness in this view. If part of a functional area is located elsewhere and remains undamaged, then the lesions are really not complete and behavioral comparisons of recovery will be confounded. A similar sort of confounding may well be applicable to considerations of the factor of intelligence. Although the ultimate recovery of a very intelligent individual may be excellent in relation to the recovery of others, their actual residual deficit may be equal simply because they would normally function at a higher level. The question of personality is still more difficult to evaluate. It is widely thought that

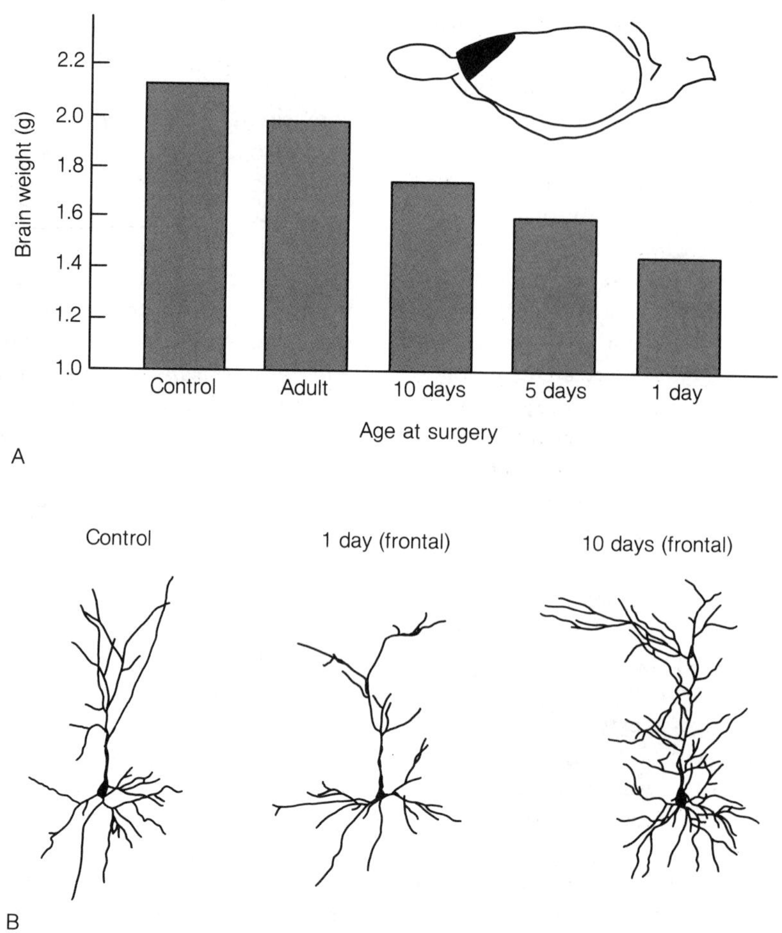

FIGURE 26-9. *A.* Brain weights of control rats and rats that received frontal lesions (see insert) as adults or at 10, 5, and 1 day of age. *B.* Drawings of cortical pyramidal cells from parietal cortex. Note the increased arbor after a lesion at 10 days and the decreased arbor after a lesion at 1 day (After Kolb and Whishaw, 1989.)

optimistic, extroverted, or easygoing people have a better prognosis. Yet personality is notoriously difficult to measure, and brain damage may change personality.

Just as the study of animals has provided animal models of how age influences brain changes after damage, similar studies provide evidence that sex effects can be examined in experimental animal paradigms. Loy and Milner have examined axonal sprouting of norepinephrine fibers into the hippocampus after damage was inflicted on certain hippocampal afferents. They found that sprouting was more vigorous in younger animals than in older animals and that at both ages sprouting was more extensive in female animals. The reason for the sex difference is not obvious, but there are two possible explanations. It is possible that female sex hormones promote sprouting in female rats or alternatively that male sex hormones create a biochemical climate that inhibits sprouting in male animals. As a way of balancing the advantage that this experiment appears to accord female rats, Yu reports just the opposite sex-related effect in a different experimental paradigm. Yu cut the hypoglossal nerve in male and female rats and then measured the rate at which it grew back to innervate the tongue. The regeneration rate was faster in the male rats, and furthermore, the administration of testosterone to either sex accelerated regeneration. These seemingly contradictory findings should not seem surprising, since sex-related brain research is still in its formative stages, but the results do illustrate the importance of considering sex a relevant variable in the study of recovery of function.

Summary

Adults who receive brain damage show better recovery if the damage is caused by head injury than if it is caused by cerebrovascular accident. This is because trauma frequently spares more tissue than strokes. The more extensive the damage, the poorer are the prospects for recovery. When the measure of recovery is a complex skill, comprising many components, recovery may be extensive because there are many strategies available for obtaining the same end. When a specific skill is tested, no recovery occurs if the entire neural area sustaining that skill is destroyed.

THERAPEUTIC APPROACHES TO BRAIN DAMAGE

There are three major experimental therapeutic approaches to brain damage. (1) Rehabilitation procedures consist of a variety of behavioral and psychological therapies. (2) Pharmacological therapies can be used to promote recovery in the immediate postsurgery period. (3) Transplantation techniques can be used to restore normal brain functioning. Therapeutic procedures are widely used with mixed results, and pharmacological and transplantation techniques are only in the animal experimental stage.

Rehabilitation

The objective of rehabilitation is to return a patient to a level of function that approximates his or her previous normal level. From the practical point of view, knowing what goes on in the brain is not essential for this endeavor. What is more important is knowing what procedures may be useful to restore function. Bach-y-Rita has reviewed some of the important points that relate to this objective. (1) Stimulation in the early postoperative period is thought to be useful. This can include talking to people even though they are in a coma, interacting with them, or playing music with an activating rhythm. (2) If there are impairments in the use of a body part, forced use is helpful. This may include tying or having a person sit on a good arm to force the use of the impaired one. (3) Practice should be extensive and far in excess of what would be required for an unimpaired individual. This is because increments may only be small and because substitution behaviors (behaviors different from those normally used) may have to be developed to accomplish a given goal. (4) Tasks on which training is given should be relevant to real life needs and should include tasks needed for daily living. In some hospitals patients are fed by nurses and cared for in other ways and they are taken in wheel chairs to physiotherapy. Much of the therapy that they required could be done at the bedside. (5) Nonprofessionals, particularly family members, should be included in therapy. Usually therapy and training are labor intensive, time-consuming, and costly if only professionals are used. (6) Motivation should be considered an important component of therapy since the long work periods, sometimes accompanied by only small gains, can be frustrating. (7) Training should be continued even after plateaus are reached. Very often therapy may cease once progress in recovery is slowed. Continued work, however, even if it produces small increments, may eventually mean the difference between dependency and self-sufficiency. (8) Finally, tasks should be broken down into simpler components since attention span or motor abilities may be limited initially.

Therapy for brain damage often involves innovation and the development of techniques that are relevant to individual patients. We were once asked to recommend a therapy for a depressed motor cycle racer who had suffered extensive brain damage after crashing a hang glider. We half-seriously suggested a tricycle, which his caregivers then constructed for him. He underwent a dramatic improvement in attitude and was soon racing the tricycle around the hospital grounds and taking trips to town. The exercise and attitude change helped him tackle other tasks to help his recovery. Substitution systems may be useful for some patients. For example, visual information could be recorded from a video camera and presented in a tactile form on the skin as a partial substitute for vision. Various machines, especially computers, can be used to perform specific tasks. A number of therapy programs have included using trained animals to perform certain routine tasks. Biofeedback techniques are useful for the reeducation of certain motor skills.

Pharmacological Therapies

There has been a long-standing interest in the use of pharmacological therapies for ameliorating the effects of brain damage. This extensive research has been reviewed by Feeney and Sutton. Much of the thrust for the research comes from observations that amphetamine treatment can restore certain functions in brain-damaged animals. For example, cats with motor cortex damage that results in the permanent loss of visual and tactile placing responses were reported to have the responses restored by amphetamine treatment.

A model demonstration of how postsurgical pharmacological therapy can aid recovery has been made by Feeney. Rats were trained to walk on a narrow beam and then subjected to unilateral neocortex damage in the hindlimb region of the sensorimotor cortex. After damage, the number of times the rats failed to correctly place their contralteral (to the lesion) rear paw when walking on the beam was measured. Relatively normal walking was usually restored by about 30 days after injury. If the rats were treated with amphetamine (a catecholamine stimulant that produces locomotion in rats), they recovered within about 7 days. If they were treated with haloperidol (a dopaminergic antagonist that blocks movement) or restrained, recovery was profoundly slowed. The administration of these drugs in the absence of actual experience of walking on the beam was without effect. The results suggest the rate of recovery can be promoted if pharmacological treatments and experience are combined shortly after brain damage. A vigorous search for the mechanisms underlying the therapeutic effects of amphetamine is currently underway since the procedures are likely to be useful for the treatment of human brain-damaged patients. This research consists of studying the underlying transmitter systems that may be involved in recovery, including norepinephrine, dopamine, serotonin, and acetylcholine, and the study of the role in gangliosides (glycosphingolipids found in membranes that are active in cells' membrane functions) and nerve growth factors.

Brain Tissue Transplants

The idea and the techniques of transplanting neural tissue in mammals go back to the first decade of this century, and a summary of most of the research can be found in Björklund and Stenevi. Yet until a few years ago the idea that neural transplantation had any practical possibilities was viewed as rather remote. This view has now radically changed. A model procedure for tissue transplantation techniques is illustrated in Figure

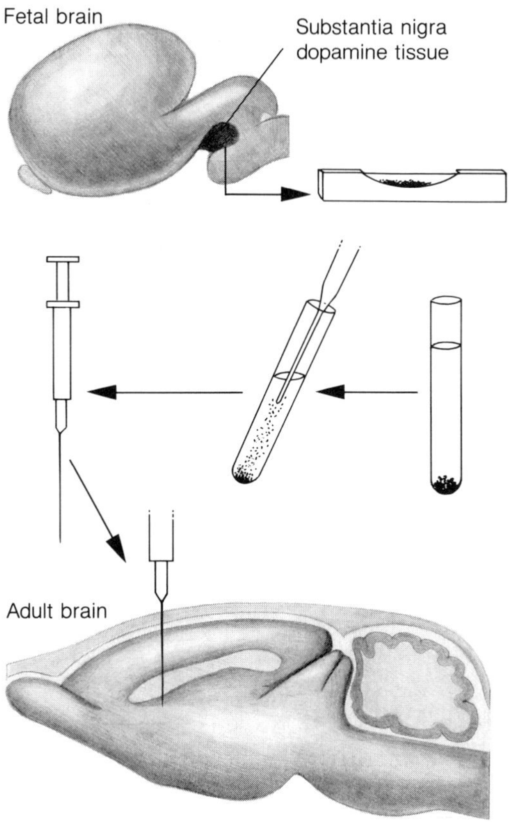

FIGURE 26-10. Principal steps in the grafting procedure, as described in the text (After A. Björklund, U. Stenevi, R. H. Schmidt, S. B. Dunnett, and F. H. Gage. Introduction and general methods of preparation. *Acta Physiologica Scandinavica* 522:1–8, 1983.)

26-10. Fetal tissue, containing undeveloped embryonic cells, is dissected from a fetal brain. The tissue is transferred to a dish containing saline. It is then treated in a test tube to disocciate the fetal brain cells from glia, blood vessels, and other tissue. It is then transferred to a syringe and injected into an appropriate location in the brain of a recipient adult animal. All aspects of the procedure can be varied in different ways. Tissue may come from different brain sites, donors of different ages, and different species donors. The separation procedures may in future include techniques that extract only the cells of interest or may involve cloning of cells for transplant. The injection procedures may in future involve injections of other substances (such as nerve growth factor) that enhance incorporation of the graft into the host brain.

The brain appears sheltered from the normal rejection processes that hamper transplant success in the rest of the body. As a result, successful grafts can be made not only within the body but between individuals and across species. The following are the prerequisites for successful grafts. First, Seiger and Olson have found that fetal grafts survive best. Tissue taken from prenatal rats survives well, tissue from rats a few days or weeks old survives poorly, and tissue from adult rats fails to survive at all. Second, the grafts need to receive a blood supply quickly. To accomplish this many experiments are done in which grafts are made in the anterior chamber of the eye or near the vessel-rich pia mater of the ventricles. Stenevi and his coworkers found that when neonatal **norepinephrinergic neurons** were transplanted to this site, about 500 of a total of 1500 neurons were present 6 months later. When implanted into the brain after brain damage, some time must pass to allow blood vessel proliferation before a transplant can be made. The transplants seem to show a high degree of normal differentiation and organization. They also make connections with the host tissue. An example from the hippocampus will demonstrate this point. The circuitry of the hippocampus is well known from anatomical and electrophysiological studies. One of its inputs is from the anteriorly located septum. Cholinergic cells in this region make highly specific connections with certain portions of the dendrites of hippocampal neurons. If this pathway is cut, the cholinergic terminals will disappear from the hippocampus. If a transplant of septal cells is placed in the location of the cut, its fibers will grow into the hippocampus and in 1 to 3 months will reoccupy the dendritic zones previously occupied by septal cells. The accuracy of the terminal occupation on the cells can be confirmed histochemically. An AChE (acetylcholinesterase) stain produces a large black band coloring a specific area of the dendrites of hippocampal cells. After the transplant has taken, the AChE-stained zone reappears in its appropriate location. A particularly positive feature of the grafts is that when placed almost anywhere, they send axons to make appropriate connections. As a result the graft works when placed in the zone of damage, in the ventricle, or at other sites convenient for the technological manipulations of the experimenter. The embryonic cells seem to have a homing instinct as well as a passport no longer available to adult cells and so they can travel through the nervous system at will. A word of caution! The transplants may not only go to their appropriate locations but may be promiscuous and make other contacts. This aspect of their behavior has not been adequately controlled.

The newly formed connections made by grafts are behaviorally functional. Dunnett and coworkers trained rats to alternate their responses to two arms of a T-maze for a reward. This is easy and presumably fun for the normal rat, but not for rats with transected septal axons. They persistently run to the same side in the maze. After brain grafts with septal cells, correct alternation performance is gradually restored to almost 89% of normal levels as the graft makes its new connections. The application of the technology of brain grafts is obvious. After brain damage, degenerating tissue is simply replaced. An almost immediate application is to Parkinson's and Alzheimer's disease, both of which seem to be caused by the loss of a specific group of cells. Recall that in the case of Parkinson's disease, cells of the substantia nigra degenerate and consequently the brain is depleted of the transmitter substance dopamine, which the cells supply to their terminals. The loss of dopamine produces the constellation of symptoms that constitute the disease. Figure 26-11*A* gives a box diagram of the presumed role of dopamine as a behavioral modu-

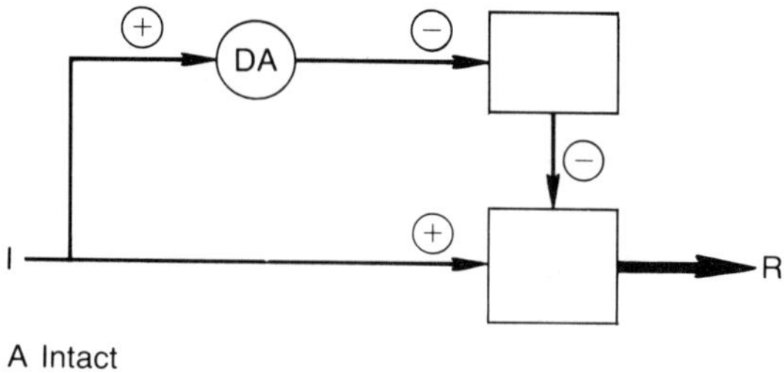

A Intact

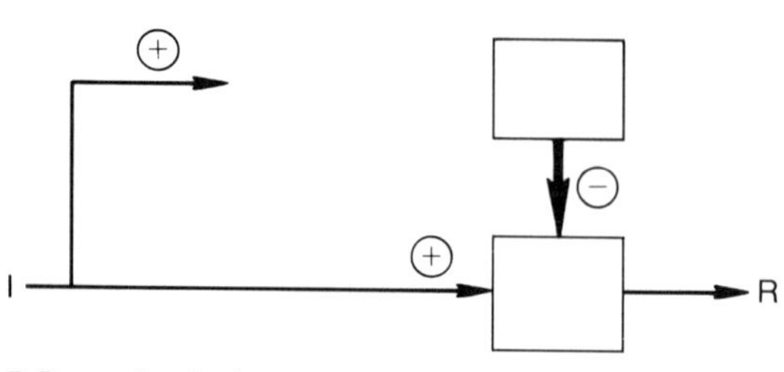

B Dopamine lesion

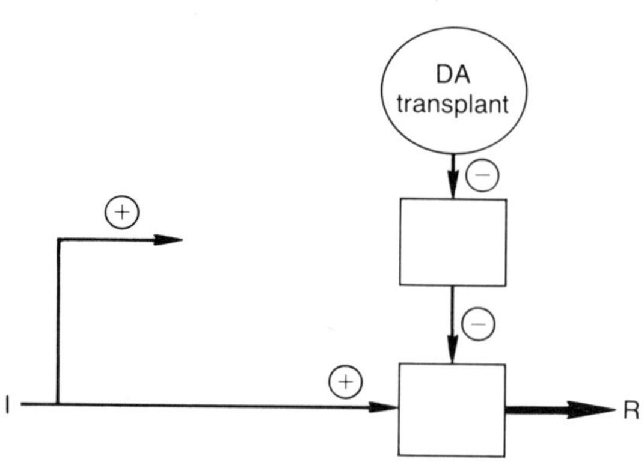

C Dopamine transplant

FIGURE 26-11. Proposed mode of action of the dopamine (DA)-producing brain grafts in the promotion of behavioral recovery. *A*. The behavioral response (R) evoked by an activating sensory input (I) is modulated through an inhibitory control mechanism of which the DA pool forms an important part. *B*. The response can no longer occur in the absence of dopamine. *C*. The sensory response pathway is reopened by the dopamine transplant.

lator in the normal brain. Figure 26-11*B* shows the parkinsonian condition (or the rat analogue in which dopamine is reduced experimentally). A putative remedy for the disease is to place a brain graft of embryonic cells into the brain as is shown in Figure 26-11*C*. Does it work? Perlow and coworkers destroyed the dopamine system on one side of the brain of rats and replaced it with a graft of fetal dopamine cells. The dopamine cell transplant reduced parkinsonian symptoms (abnormal turning induced by apomorphine) by about 50%. Both Björklund and Dunnett and their respective coworkers have obtained some therapeutic effects, some absence of change, and some deleterious effects with grafts into rats with dopamine-system damage. When dopamine is depleted from one side of the striatum, rats rotate toward the side of the lesion when given amphetamine, they fail to orient in the opposite direction to sensory stimulation, and they are unable to use the limb contralateral to the lesion for reaching. Dopamine grafts restore normal responses to amphetamine, restore orienting, but they fail to restore use of the limb for reaching. An impairment also emerges, the rats have greater difficulty learning to turn in a circle in the direction contralateral to their good hemisphere. When dopamine is depleted bilaterally, the rats are akinetic, fail to eat and drink normally, and fail to orient to sensory stimulation bilaterally. Bilateral grafts of neonatal dopamine cells improve locomotion and orienting but do not restore normal feeding and drinking abilities.

The application of this technology to humans is already in the experimental stage. A number of clinical trials have begun in which dopamine-producing cells have been implanted into the brains of parkinson patients. As yet it is too early to get a good idea about how the tests will turn out. Some of the groups making the implants have not been involved in the experimental animal tests and some have not done adequate preoperative evaluations of the patients. The supply of dopamine cells is not an obstacle to progress since cells seem transplantable across species and since dopamine cells from other parts of the body, such as the adrenal cortex, seem effective. In addition, trials with animals are in progress in which small beads of polyester are implanted in the brain. The beads hold dopamine which can be released slowly over weeks or months. The approach can be also used with Alzheimer's disease, which is now thought to result from a loss of cholinergic cells that project to the neocortex, in much the same way that cholinergic septal cells project to the hippocampus, and which are important for the maintenance of memory.

REFERENCES

Anand, B. K., and J. R. Brobeck. Hypothalamic control of food intake. *Yale Journal of Biology and Medicine* 24:123–140, 1951.

Bach-y-Rita, P., ed. *Recovery of Function: Theoretical Considerations for Brain Injury Rehabilitation.* Bern, Switzerland: Hyuber Publishers, 1980.

Barbizet, J. *Human Memory and Its Pathology.* San Francisco: W. H. Freeman, 1970.

Barnes, C. D., R. T. Joynt, and B. A. Schottelius. Motor neuron resting potentials in spinal shock. *American Journal of Physiology* 203:1113–1116, 1962.

Basso, A., E. Capitani, and E. Zanobio. Pattern of recovery of oral and written expression and comprehension in aphasic patients. *Behavioral Brain Research* 6:115–128, 1982.

Beresford, W. A. A discussion of retrograde changes in nerve fibers. *Progress in Brain Research* 14:33–57, 1965.

Björklund, A., and U. Stenevi, eds. *Neural Grafting in the Mammalian Central Nervous System. Fernstrom Foundation Series,* vol. 5. New York: Elsevier, 1985.

Blakemore, C. B., and M. A. Falconer. Long-term effects of anterior temporal lobectomy on certain cognitive functions. *Journal of Neurology, Neurosurgery and Psychiatry* 30:364–367, 1967.

Bucy, P. C., J. E. Keplinger, and E. B. Siqueira. Destruction of the "pyramidal tract" in man. *Journal of Neurosurgery* 21:385–398, 1964.

Cannon, W. B., and A. Rosenblueth. *The Supersensitivity of Denervated Structures.* New York: Macmillan, 1949.

Craggs, M. D., and D. N. Rushton. The stability of the electrical stimulation map of the motor cortex of the anesthetized baboon. *Brain* 99:575–600, 1976.

Critchely, M. Dr. Samuel Johnson's aphasia, *Medical History* 6:27–44, 1962.

Doty, R. W. Conditioned reflexes formed and evoked by brain stimulation. In D. E. Sheer, ed. *Electrical Stimulation of the Brain.* Austin: University of Texas Press, 1961.

Dresser, A. C., A. M. Meirowsky, G. H. Weiss, M. L. McNeel, A. G. Simon, and W. F. Caveness. Gainful employment following head injury. *Archives of Neurology* 29:111–116, 1973.

Duffy, F. H., S. R. Snodgrass, J. L. Burchfield, and J. L. Conway. Bicuculline reversal of deprivation amblyopia in the cat. *Nature* 260:256–257, 1976.

Dunnett, S. B., W. C. Low, S. D. Iversen, U. Stenevi, and A. Björklund. Septal transplants restore maze learning in rats with fornix-fimbria lesions. *Brain Research* 251:335–348, 1982.

Eshkol, N., and A. Wachmann. *Movement Notation.* London: Weidenfeld and Nicolson, 1958.

Feeney, D. M., and R. L. Sutton. Pharmacotherapy for recovery of function after brain injury. *CRC Critical Reviews in Neurobiology* 3:135–197, 1987.

Finger, S., and D. G. Stein. *Brain Damage and Recovery.* New York: Academic Press, 1982.

Flourens, P. Investigations of the properties and the functions of the various parts which compose the cerebral mass. In G. von Bonin, ed. *The Cerebral Cortex.* Springfield, IL: Charles C. Thomas, 1960.

Gall, C., R. McWilliams, and G. Lynch. Accelerated rates of synaptogenesis by "sprouting" afferents in the immature hippocampal formation. *Journal of Comparative Neurology* 193:1047–1061, 1980.

Geschwind, N. Late changes in the nervous system. An overview, In D. G. Stein, J. J. Rosen, and N. Butters, eds. *Plasticity and Recovery of Function in the Central Nervous System.* New York: Academic Press, 1974.

Glassman, R. B. Recovery following sensorimotor cortical damage: Evoked potentials, brain stimulation and motor control. *Experimental Neurology* 33:16–29, 1971.

Glees, P., and J. Cole. Recovery of skilled motor function after small repeated lesions of motor cortex in macaque. *Journal of Neurophysiology* 13:137–148, 1950.

Golani, I., D. L. Wolgin, and P. Teitelbaum. A proposed natural geometry of recovery from akinesia in the lateral hypothalamic rat. *Brain Research* 164:237–267, 1979.

Grillner, S. Locomotion in the spinal cat. In R. B. Stein, K. G. Pearson, R. S. Smith, and J. B. Redford, eds. *Control of Posture and Locomotion.* New York: Plenum, 1973.

Guillery, R. W. Binocular competition in the control of geniculate cell growth. *Journal of Comparative Neurology* 144:117–130, 1972.

Hall, M. *On the Diseases and Derangements of the Nervous System.* London: Bailliere, 1841.

Hassler, R., P. Haug, C. Nitsch, J. S. Kim, and K. Paik. Effect of motor and premotor cortex ablation on concentrations of amino acids, monoamines, and acetylcholine and on the ultrastructure in rat striatum. A confirmation of glutamate as the specific corticostriatal transmitter. *Journal of Neurochemistry* 38:1087–1098, 1982.

Head, H., and G. Riddoch. The automatic bladder, excessive sweating and some other reflex conditions in gross injuries of the spinal cord. *Brain* 15:188–263, 1917.

Hughlings-Jackson, J. *Selected Writings of John Hughlings-Jackson.* J. Taylor, ed. London: Hodder, 1932.

Jones, M. K. Imagery as a mnemonic aid after left temporal lobectomy: Contrast between material-specific and generalized memory disorder. *Neuropsychologia* 12:21–30, 1974.

Jones-Gottman, M., and B. Milner. Design fluency: The invention of nonsense drawings after focal cortical lesions. *Neuropsychologia* 15:653–674, 1977.

Kertesz, A. *Aphasia and Associated Disorders.* New York: Grune & Stratton, 1979.

Kolb, B., and B. Milner. Performance of complex arm and facial movements after focal brain lesions. *Neuropsychologia* 19:491–503, 1981.

Kolb, B., and I. Q. Whishaw. Effects of brain lesions and atropine on hippocampal and neocortical electroencephalograms in the rat. *Experimental Neurology* 56:1–22, 1977.

Kolb, B., and I. Q. Whishaw. Plasticity in the neocortex: Mechanisms underlying recovery from early brain damage. *Progress in Neurobiology* 32:235–276, 1989.

Kratz, K. E., P. D. Spear, and C. D. Smith. Postcritical-period reversal of effects of monocular deprivation on striate cortex cells in the cat. *Journal of Neurophysiology* 39:501–511, 1976.

Kromer, L. F., A. Björklund, and U. Stenevi. Innervation of embryonic hippocampal implants by regenerating axons of cholinergic neurons in the adult rat. *Brain Research* 210:153–171, 1980.

Kuhn, R. A. Functional capacity of the isolated human spinal cord. *Brain* 73:1–51, 1950.

Lashley, K. S. Temporal variation in the function of the gyrus precentralis in primates. *American Journal of Physiology* 65:585–602, 1923.

Lashley, K. S. *Brain Mechanisms and Intelligence.* Chicago: The University of Chicago Press, 1929.

Lawrence, D. G., and H. G. J. M. Kuypers. The functional organization of the motor system in the monkey: I. The effects of bilateral pyramidal lesions. *Brain* 81:1–14, 1968.

Levin, H. S., A. L. Benton, and R. G. Grossman. *Neurobehavioral Consequences of Closed Head Injury.* New York: Oxford, 1982.

Linge, F. What does it feel like to be brain-damaged? *Canada's Mental Health* 28:4–7, 1980.

Loy, R., and T. A. Milner. Sexual dimorphism in extent of axonal sprouting in rat hippocampus. *Science* 208:1281–1284, 1980.

Luria, A. R. *The Man with a Shattered World.* Lynn Solotoroff, trans. New York: Basic Books, Jonathan Cape, Ltd., 1972.

Lynch, G. S., S. Deadwyler, and C. W. Cotman. Post lesion axonal growth produces permanent functional connections. *Science* 180:1364–1366, 1973.

Lynch, G., G. Rose, C. Gall, and C. W. Cotman. In M. Statini, ed. *Golgi Centennial Symposium Proceedings.* New York: Raven Press, 1975.

Markowitsch, H. J., and M. Pritzel. Von Monakow's diaschisis concept: Comments on West et al. (1976). *Behavioral Biology* 22:411–412, 1978.

Marshall, J. F., B. H. Turner, and P. Teitelbaum. Sensory neglect produced by lateral hypothalamic damage. *Science* 174:523–525, 1971.

McGinty, D. J. Somnolence, recovery and hypersomnia following ventromedial diencephalic lesions in the rat. *Electroencephalography and Clinical Neurophysiology* 26:70–79, 1969.

Meyer, J. S., M. Shinohara, T. Kauda, Y. Fukuuchi, A. D. Ericsson, and N. N. Kole. Diaschisis resulting from acute unilateral cerebral infarction. *Archives of Neurology* 23:241–247, 1970.

Milner, B. Effect of different brain lesions on card sorting. *Archives of Neurology* 9:90–100, 1963.

Milner, B. Psychological aspects of focal epilepsy and its neurosurgical management. *Advances in Neurology* 8:299–321, 1975.

Milner, B., S. Corkin, and H. -L. Teuber. Further analysis of the hippocampal amnesic syndrome: 14-year follow-up study of H. M. *Neuropsychologia* 6:215–234, 1968.

Mohr, J. P., G. H. Weiss, W. F. Caveness, J. D. Dillon, J. P. Kistler, A. M. Meirowsky, and B. L. Rish. Language and motor disorders after penetrating head injury in Viet Nam. *Neurology* 30:1273–1279, 1980.

Monakow, C. V. von Lokalization der Hirnfunktionen. *Journal für Psychologie and Neurologie* 17:185–200, 1911. (Reprinted in G. von Bonin. *The Cerebral Cortex*. Springfield, IL: Charles C. Thomas, 1960)

Munk, H. *Über die Funktionen der Grosshirnrinde. Gesammelte Mitteilungen aus den Jahren.* 1877–1880. Berlin: August Hershwald, 1881.

Murray, T. J. Dr. Samuel Johnson's abnormal movements. In A. J. Friedhoff and T. N. Chase, eds. *Advances in Neurology* vol. 35. New York: Raven Press, 1982.

Oddy, M., and M. Humphrey. Social recovery during the year following severe head injury. *Journal of Neurology, Neurosurgery, and Psychiatry* 43:798–802, 1980.

Pappius, H. M. Local cerebral glucose utilization in thermally traumatized rat brain. *Annals of Neurology* 9:484–491, 1981.

Pappius, H. M. Dexamethasone and local cerebral glucose utilization in freeze-traumatized rat brain. *Annals of Neurology* 12:157–162, 1982.

Perlow, M. J., W. J. Freed, B. J. Hoffer, A. Sager, L. Olson, and R. J. Wyatt. Brain grafts reduce motor abnormalities produced by destruction of nigrostriatal dopamine system. *Science* 204:643–647, 1979.

Quinlan, J., and J. Quinlan. *Karen Ann: The Quinlans Tell Their Story*. Toronto: Doubleday, 1977.

Robinson, R. G., F. E. Bloom, and E. L. F. Battenberg. A fluorescent histochemical study of changes in noradrenergic neurons following experimental cerebral infarction in the rat. *Brain Research* 132:259–272, 1977.

Robinson, T. E., and I. Q. Whishaw. Effects of posterior hypothalamic lesions on voluntary behavior and hippocampal electroencephalograms in the rat. *Journal of Comparative and Physiological Psychology* 86:768–786, 1974.

Rosner, B. B. Recovery of function and localization of function in historical perspective. In D. G. Stein, J. J. Rosen, and N. Butters, eds. *Plasticity and Recovery of Function in the Central Nervous System*. New York: Academic Press, 1974.

Schoenfeld, T. A., and L. W. Hamilton. Secondary brain changes following lesions: A new paradigm for lesion experimentation. *Physiology and Behavior* 18:951–967, 1977.

Seiger, A., and L. Olson. Quantification of fiber growth in transplanted monoamine neurons. *Cell Tissue Research* 179:285–316, 1977.

Sherman, S. M., R. W. Guillery, J. H. Gaas, and K. J. Sanderson. Behavioral electrophysiological and morphological studies of binocular competition in development of geniculocortical pathways of cats. *Journal of Comparative Neurology* 158:1–18, 1974.

Sherrington, C. S. *The Integrative Action of the Nervous System,* 2nd ed. New Haven: Yale University Press, 1947.

Skinhøj, E. Bilateral depression of CSF in unilateral cerebral diseases. *Acta Neurologica Scandinavica,* suppl. 14, 41:161–163, 1965.

Sokoloff, L. The deoxyglucose method: Theory and practice. *European Neurology* 20:137–145, 1981.

Sperry, R. W. Mechanisms of neural maturation. In S. S. Stevens, ed. *Handbook of Experimental Psychology.* New York: John Wiley, 1965.

Stenevi, U., A. Björklund, and N. -A. Svendgaard. Transplantation of central and peripheral monoamine neurons to the adult rat brain: Techniques and conditions for survival. *Brain Research* 114:1–20, 1976.

Stricker, E. M., and M. J. Zigmond. Recovery of function after damage to central catecholamine-containing neurons: A neurochemical model for the lateral hypothalamic syndrome. In J. M. Sprague and A. N. Epstein, eds. *Progress in Psychobiology and Physiological Psychology,* vol. 6. New York: Academic Press, 1976.

Taylor, L. B. Localization of cerebral lesions by psychological testing. *Clinical Neurosurgery* 16:269–287, 1969.

Taylor, L. B. Psychological assessment of neurosurgical patients. In T. Rasmussen and R. Marino, eds. *Functional Neurosurgery.* New York: Raven Press, 1979.

Teitelbaum, P., and A. N. Epstein. The lateral hypothalamic syndrome: Recovery of feeding and drinking after lateral hypothalamic lesions. *Psychological Review* 69:74–90, 1962.

Teitelbaum, P., and E. Stellar. Recovery from the failure to eat produced by hypothalamic lesions. *Science* 120:893–895, 1954.

Teuber, H. -L. Recovery of function after brain injury in man. In *Outcome of Severe Damage to the Nervous System,* Ciba Foundation Symposium 34. Amsterdam: Elsevier North-Holland, 1975.

Twitchell, T. E. The restoration of motor function following hemiplegia in man. *Brain* 74:443–480, 1951.

Twitchell, T. E. The automatic grasping response of infants. *Neuropsychologia* 3:247–259, 1965.

Wall, P. D., and M. D. Egger. Formation of new connections in adult rat brains after partial deafferentation. *Nature* 232:542–545, 1971.

Waller, A. V. Experiments on the section of the glossopharyngial and hypoglossal nerves of the frog, and observations of the alterations produced thereby in the structure of their primitive fibers. *Philosophical Transactions* 140:423–429, 1850.

West, J. R. The concept of diaschisis: A reply to Markowitsch and Pritzel. *Behavioral Biology* 22:413–416, 1978.

West, J. R., S. A. Deadwyler, C. W. Cotman, and G. S. Lynch. An experimental test of diaschisis. *Behavioral Biology* 18:419–425, 1976.

Whishaw, I. Q., and B. Kolb. Behavioral and anatomical studies of rats with complete or partial decortication in infancy. In C. R. Almli and S. Finger, eds. *The Behavioral Biology of Early Brain Damage*. New York: Academic Press, 1984.

Whitty, C. W. M., and O. L. Zangwill. Traumatic amnesia. In C. W. M. Whitty and O. L. Zangwill, eds. *Amnesia*. London: Butterworths, 1966.

Yu, W. H. A. Sex differences in the regeneration of the hypoglossal nerve in rats. *Brain Research* 238:404–406, 1982.

Zihl, J., and D. von Cramon. Restitution of visual field in patients with damage to the geniculostriate visual pathway. *Human Neurobiology* 8:5–8, 1982.

PART 7

APPLIED HUMAN NEUROPSYCHOLOGY

This last part of the book describes the application of the fundamental principles of human neuropsychology to both neuropsychological assessment and the understanding of a variety of socioeducational problems. Chapters 27 and 28 describe the principles and applications of neuropsychological assessment. In no other area is the application of neuropsychological testing used more than in the field of education. Chapter 29 describes the application of neuropsychology in the study of learning disabilities. There has been a gradual movement to apply neuropsychological testing procedures to psychiatric populations, and so Chapter 30 describes some of the concepts that are emerging from this research. Chapter 31 considers the application of neuropsychology to head trauma and degenerative disorders, principally Alzheimer's disease. Finally, for the use of those who are interested in the details of testing and scoring, we have included norms that we have compiled from studies that have used the tests described in this book.

The true potential of neuropsychology lies not only in its contribution to the understanding of brain function but also — and this will be its real test — in the applicability of the basic knowledge to human problems. We have a moral and ethical responsibility to apply the basic knowledge wisely, and with the utmost care and caution. Neuroscientists in other areas will be watching with a very critical eye. Perhaps the major difficulty in successful application of neuropsychological principles is the problem of individual differences. Up to this point in the book we have emphasized the consistent relation between brain function and behavior. In practice, however, brain-behavior relations vary considerably from person to person. Such variability can be attributed to a number of factors. For example, individuals in the general population vary widely in their ability at any particular skill, and this variance influences the effects of brain injury or dysfunction. An architect with injury to the right hemisphere may suffer deficits in visuospatial analysis that make it impossible for him or her to return to work as an architect — even though he or she is still better at visuospatial ability than the average person! Further, personality variables influence a person's response to brain injury and affect the degree of recovery following it. Although other disciplines in applied neurology, must also contend with variation, it is less of a burden for them because they deal largely with physical signs and symptoms that vary less than the cognitive processes measured by neuropsychologists. It is for this reason that neuropsychological principles must be applied carefully and conservatively to avoid serious errors that would be harmful both to individual patients and (less importantly) to the reputation of a field with so much potential. Thus, those who would be called neuropsychologists must have a solid grounding in the fundamentals of neuroscience, and in neuropsychology in particular. Throughout this book we have emphasized the importance of a basic understanding of how the nervous system operates, to its minute particulars, whether it be a neuron or a synapse. Failure to learn basic lessons before applying neuropsychological principles will only ensure, mediocrity at best and incompetence at worst. At the same time, competent neuropsychologists must not be *overly* cautious, because if the competent fail to apply the basic knowledge, the incompetent will surely fill the field.

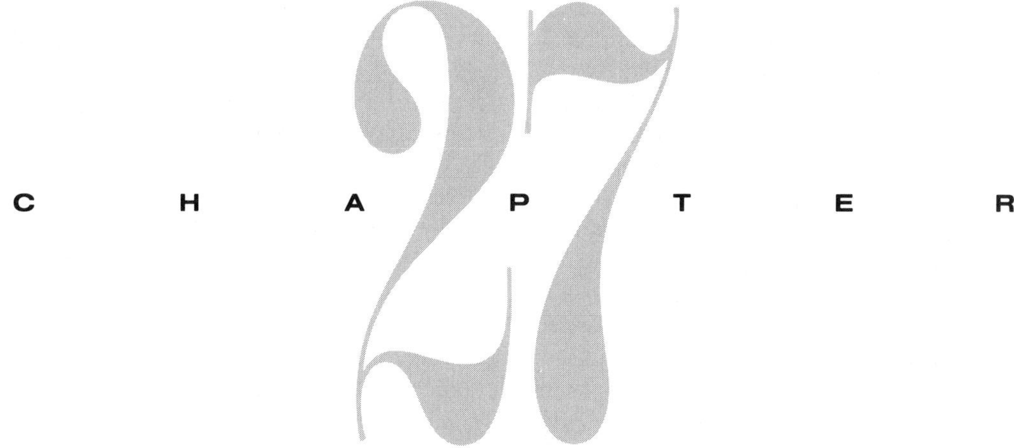

NEUROPSYCHOLOGICAL ASSESSMENT

After World War II many neuropsychological laboratories were established in Europe and North America. These have been principally responsible for the development of neuropsychological assessment as a tool in clinical neurology. We make no attempt to thoroughly review all the tests used in neurological assessment (we recommend Lezak's book for further discussion of the range of available tests). Rather, we review: (1) the rationale and goals of neuropsychological assessment, (2) the types of disorders for which it is most useful, (3) the characteristics of useful neuropsychological tests, (4) currently used formal test batteries, and (5) examples of an informal composite battery.

RATIONALE OF ASSESSMENT

Factors Affecting Performance on Neuropsychological Tests

Throughout Chapters 8 to 24 we have seen that circumscribed lesions in different cortical regions may produce discrete behavioral changes. In Chapters 17, 18, and 19 we argued that it would thus seem reasonable to work backward from this knowledge to localize unknown brain damage. That is, given a particular behavioral change, one should be able to predict the site or sites of the disturbance most likely causing the change. There are, however, several problems in working backward in such a manner. First, research patients are often chosen for specific reasons. For example, whereas patients with rapidly expanding tumors would not be chosen for research because their results are so difficult to interpret, neurosurgical patients are ideal research subjects because the extent of their damage is known. Differences in etiology of the neurological disorder might therefore be expected to make assessment difficult.

The second problem is related to the size of the lesion and the sensitivity of the tests. If a large region of the brain is dysfunctioning, then the assessment test need not be particularly sensitive to demonstrate the dysfunction. On the other hand, if the lesion is small, the behavioral effect may be rather specific (as we have seen). For example, a lesion in the right somatosensory representation of the face may produce very subtle sensory changes, and unless specific tests of nonverbal fluency are used (see Chapter 19), the cognitive changes may go unnoticed, even with dozens of tests.

The third problem, a related one, is assessment time. Since neuropsychological tests must be sensitive to changes in a vast number of behaviors and skills, many different tests must be administered for a diagnosis to be made. Thus, existing one-shot tests of organic impairment, **organicity,** or brain dysfunction are invalid when used alone. Although it is true that many people with brain damage do poorly on some of these tests, it is also true that many people with known brain damage do well on them. And even among those people who are impaired at them, there is no localization of the neurological problem. In addition, there is the continual problem of false positives. Individuals may be impaired at *particular* tests for many reasons, only one of which may be brain damage or dysfunction. An adequate assessment requires time, often 6 or more hours, which clearly requires more than one sitting with the subject.

The fourth problem is that various factors may interact with brain pathology to make interpretation of test results difficult. Tests are seldom developed for subjects who are older than 60 or who are culturally disadvantaged. Test scores therefore cannot be interpreted with strict cutoff criteria — that is, performance below a particular level cannot always be taken as indicating brain damage. Further, intelligence alters the investigators' expectations of performance on different tests: someone with an IQ of 130 may be relatively impaired on a test of verbal memory but, compared with someone with an IQ of 90, may appear normal. Thus, unlike standard psychometric assessment, neuropsychological assessment must be flexible. This clearly makes interpretation difficult and requires extensive training in fundamental neuropsychology and neurology as well as in neuropsychological assessment. Finally, we have seen in several earlier discussions that there are significant sex-related differences on test performance. The reason for the differences is not relevant clinically, rather one must simply be aware of their presence.

The fifth problem is that test performance is often biased by demographics. Educational and cultural factors influence test results so it is necessary to collect norms appropriate to the population being assessed. For example, in one three-city study of the effects of head trauma it was found that normal subjects in one city performed as poorly as brain-damaged subjects in another. There were significant demographic differences that influenced the test performance and thus had to be factored out in the study.

A final problem is that current neuropsychological assessment procedures cannot easily discriminate between people with extensive brain damage and people with gross cerebral *dysfunction* such as occurs in schizophrenia. Although schizophrenic individuals would not appear to have focalized lesions, they do certainly appear to have grossly dysfunctioning brains.

Goals of Neuropsychological Assessment

The goal of assessment in general clinical psychology is the diagnosis of the disorder for the purpose of effecting behavioral change. For example, intelligence and achievement tests may be given to schoolchildren as a means of trying to identify particular problem areas as an aid in teaching. Similarly, personality tests are used with an eye toward defining and curing a behavioral disorder.

The goals in clinical neuropsychology are different in some respects. First, the assessment aims to diagnose the presence of cortical damage or dysfunction and to localize it where possible. In doing so, there is an attempt to provide and accurate and unbiased estimate of a person's cognitive capacity. Second, assessment is used to facilitate patient care as well as rehabilitation. Serial assessments can provide information concerning the rate of recovery and the potential for resuming a previous lifestyle. Third, neuropsychological assessment can identify the presence of mild disturbances in cases in which other diagnostic studies have produced equivocal results. Examples might be the effects of head trauma or the early symptoms of a degenerative disease. Fourth, a related goal is to identify unusual brain organization that may occur in left-handers or in people with childhood brain injury. This information is particularly valuable to the surgeon, who would not wish to inadvertently remove primary speech zones during surgery, and such information is likely to be obtained only from behavioral measures. In such disorders as focal epilepsy the primary evidence corroborating abnormal EEG may be behavioral, because radiological procedures often fail to pinpoint the abnormal brain tissue giving rise to the seizures. In addition, because some recovery of function may be expected following brain injury, this recovery must be documented not only with rehabilitation in mind but also to determine the effectiveness of any medical treatment, particularly for neoplasms or vascular abnormalities. Further, the patient and the family must understand the patient's possible residual deficits so that realistic life goals and rehabilitation programs can be planned.

Application of Neuropsychological Assessment to Specific Disorders

Neuropsychological assessment is most useful for people with cerebral vascular disorders, acute traumatic lesions, neoplasms, and epilepsy; it is of limited value for people with infections of the brain, progressive brain disease such as multiple sclerosis, or dementias — none of which are usually localized. Once a person behaves as if demented, test results have little validity and provide little useful information.

The importance of comprehensive neuropsychological assessments for people with cerebral vascular disorders or traumatic lesions cannot be overemphasized: in such people a partial assessment is often worse than none at all. For example, standardized intelligence tests may produce results that misleadingly suggest dementia, because IQ tests emphasize verbal skills and ignore other skills necessary for day-to-day living. On the other hand, just the opposite may also be true: people with normal or near normal IQs may fail to perform normally on other tests of specific mental functions critically important in normal daily activities. An inadequate assessment may fail to diagnose these deficits, leading to invalid conclusions about an individual's neuropsychological functioning.

In the case of cerebral tumors, neuropsychological studies may provide baselines for assessing initial and later effects of surgery, irradiation, or chemotherapy. In the absence of radiological evidence such studies may also promote proper clinical neurological assessment by providing evidence of brain dysfunction resulting from disease processes.

Neuropsychological assessment has a most important diagnostic role in the preoperative localization of lesions in focal epilepsy. It is not uncommon for focal epileptics to demonstrate no positive signs in radiological or other neurological tests while showing clearly localized behavioral deficits. Further, particularly in the case of temporal lobe epilepsy where there may be risk to memory, neuropsychological assessment may be invaluable in identifying hippocampal damage in the hemisphere contralateral to the major focus.

Finally, neuropsychological assessment is beginning to be used to evaluate undesirable side effects of various pharmacological treatments, particularly in the treatment of movement disorders such as Parkinson's disease. Because the effects of various pharmacological treatments for both psychiatric and neurological disorders are as yet poorly understood, side effects from high or chronic doses of various drugs are common. Neuropsychological assessment can provide an objective measure of unwanted deficits in cognitive functioning.

Although neuropsychological assessment has many roles and goals in the diagnosis and treatment of neurological disease, we must emphasize a serious concern. Hebb once wrote, "a half-baked psychologist is worse than none at all." It is also true that "a half-baked neuropsychologist is worse than none at all." Neuropsychological assessment is complex and requires extensive training to properly evaluate the results. Experience in interpreting personality or intelligence tests is not sufficient background to begin neuropsychological assessment.

Intelligence Testing in Neuropsychological Assessment

Most neuropsychological assessments begin with either the Wechsler Adult Intelligence Scale (WAIS) or its revision, the WAIS-R. These two versions are necessary for repeated testing, and they correlate highly with each other. The Wechsler scales have proved invaluable in providing a base level of cognitive functioning. These scales present a distinct advantage: they provide separate scores for verbal and for performance subtests, as well as an overall IQ.

The verbal scale consists of six subtests. (1) Information: questions such as "Where is Egypt?" "Who wrote *Hamlet*?" (2) Comprehension: questions requiring some reflection before answering, such as "Why are child-labor laws needed?" (3) Arithmetic: questions such as "How many hours will it take a man to walk 24 miles at the rate of 3 miles an hour?" (4) Similarities: questions such as "In what way are these two pairs of items alike— an orange and a banana, an egg and a seed? (5) Digit span: tests the number of digits that can be repeated in correct sequence, forward and backward. (6) Vocabulary: asks for the meaning of words ranging from easy (e.g., winter) to difficult (e.g., travesty).

The performance scale consists of five subtests: (1) Digit symbol: nine symbols (e.g., +) are paried with digits 1–9 in a key above the response sheet. The task is to pencil in as many of the symbols corresponding to each of 90 digits as possible in 90 sec. This requires rapid eye movement and short-term visual store. (2) Picture completion: the subject indicates what is missing in each of a series of pictures. (3) Block design: red and white blocks must be used to form a design presented on a card. (4) Picture arrangement: several cards with cartoonlike drawings are presented in mixed-up order, and the subject is required to order them so that they tell a coherent story. (5) Object assembly: pieces of simple jigsaw puzzles are given to the subject who must assemble them as quickly as possible.

Although the distinction between the verbal and performance subtests is serendipitous, the subtests have proved useful as a rough measure of left and right hemisphere function, respectively. The IQs obtained on the verbal and performance sections both have a mean of 100 and a standard deviation of 15. A difference of more than 10 points between the verbal and performance scores is usually taken to be a clinically significant difference, although statistically this interpretation is somewhat liberal. A number of studies have shown that well-defined left hemisphere lesions produce a relatively low verbal IQ, whereas well-defined right hemisphere lesions produce a relatively low performance IQ. Diffuse damage, on the other hand, tends to produce a low performance IQ, leading to the erroneous belief that the verbal-performance IQ difference is not diagnostically useful. Although a reduced performance IQ is not definitive, it is rare to obtain a relatively low verbal IQ, and its appearance should not be ignored.

A recent evaluation of the WAIS subscales and IQ values was performed by Warrington and her colleagues who did a retrospective study of 656 unselected patients with unilateral brain damage. Table 27-1 summarizes their results, showing that lesions of the left hemisphere depressed verbal IQs, whereas lesions of the right hemisphere depressed performance IQs, the exception in both cases being that of occipital lesions. Importantly, however, the verbal-performance discrepancy score was less

TABLE 27-1. Mean WAIS verbal and performance IQs for different patient groups

Group	Left hemisphere lesion			Right hemisphere lesion		
	(*n*)	VIQ	PIQ	(*n*)	VIQ	PIQ
Frontal	40	94.2	99.8	38	107.01	101.3
Temporal	58	97.0	102.1	50	108.0	98.5
Parietal	49	98.0	100.9	33	108.2	87.9
Occipital	16	109.8	95.6	5	104.4	108.8
Frontal-temporal	47	93.6	97.4	27	105.0	98.0
Frontal-parietal	48	96.1	103.2	34	105.9	97.7
Temporal-parietal	48	85.3	97.5	31	109.5	92.8
Parietal-occibital	24	86.7	88.9	22	102.3	81.0
Frontal-temporal-parietal	17	87.0	97.4	19	105.1	89.8
Frontal-temporal-parietal occipital	23	98.0	107.0	19	111.1	96.8

Source: After Warrington et al., 1986.

than 10 in 53% of left hemisphere cases and 43% of right hemisphere cases. A small number of cases had discrepancy scores of greater than 10 in the opposite direction: 6% with left hemisphere lesions and 3% with right hemisphere lesions, respectively. (It is curious in Warrington's study that the patients with left parietal or temporal-parietal lesions did not show a large IQ drop, considering that one would expect them to be dysphasic. Since language skills were not mentioned in the Warrington study, it is possible that her analysis excluded aphasic subjects. In our experience dysphasic patients have very depressed verbal IQs, as would be expected.)

Warrington also analyzed seven subtests on the WAIS including arithmetic, similarities, digit span, vocabulary, picture completion, block design, and picture arrangement. Overall, the four verbal tests were performed significantly more poorly by left hemisphere frontal, temporal, or parietal patients. There were no differences between these left hemisphere groups on these tests, however. The performance tests were less predictive of lesion side as only the right parietal patients were significantly poorer on block design and picture arrangement.

One difficulty in postinjury intelligence testing is that there must be a premorbid estimate of intellectual level. A relatively low IQ cannot be ascribed to a brain injury unless there is some idea of what the IQ was before the injury. This estimate is usually informal and based upon the person's education, occupation, and socioeconomic background. Wilson and colleagues describe a statistical procedure for estimating premorbid IQ.

Memory Testing in Neuropsychological Assessment

Most neuropsychological assessments begin with some general measure of memory function, usually the Wechsler Memory Scale (WMS), or its recent revision, the WMS-R. The WMS yields a memory quotient (MQ) that generally approximates the WAIS verbal IQ. The WMS-R is composed of nine subtests, with a second (delayed) presentation of four of them. The subtests include: (1) information and orientation (e.g., name, date, place, etc.); (2) mental control (alphabet, counting backwards, counting by three's); (3) figural memory (recall of abstract patterns); (4) logical memory (recall of short stories); (5) visual paired associates (learn the association between abstract drawings and arbitrary colors); (6) verbal paired associates (learn the association between two words); (7) digit span (repeat digits forwards or backwards); and (8) visual memory span (repeat a series of taps on squares, much as in the Corsi blocks, Figure 21-10). Recall of the stories, figures, and two paired-associate tests is retested 30 min after initial presentation. Five measures are derived from the subtests, including general memory, attention/concentration, verbal memory, visual memory, and delayed recall. The mean and standard deviation of each scale is 100 and 15, respectively.

The WMS has been criticized for its composite MQ and the WMS-R is a marked improvement. Nonetheless, because the WMS-R has been available only since 1987, there have not been any systematic studies of the usefulness of the different memory indexes.

TEST BATTERIES

It is evident that to be thorough a useful neuropsychological assessment requires a series of different tests. Hence, neuropsychological batteries have been developed that are given routinely as a group. Basically, there are two types of test batteries: those that constitute a formal battery of commercially available tests, and those that are informal composite batteries assembled for use with particular populations. The choice of one type over another depends largely on the nature of the clinical question being addressed and on the nature of the population being assessed. On the whole, the ready-made batteries are not as good as the less formal composite batteries, although they have the important advantage of being much easier to obtain. We shall consider three well-known formal batteries (Halstead-Reitan, Luria's Neuropsychological Investigation, and the Luria-Nebraska Neuropsychological Battery) and provide an example of a composite test battery. First, however, we shall consider the characteristics of useful batteries.

Characteristics of Useful Neuropsychological Batteries

At least five important criteria characterize useful neuropsychological tests.

Thoroughness. To be useful a group of tests must test a wide variety of functions. They must identify the hemisphere containing speech; measure general intelligence and memory; measure sensory, perceptual, and motor functions; assess language functions; and, finally, examine frontal lobe function.

Laterality of speech is most easily determined by a verbal dichotic-listening test, and general intelligence is most frequently measured by one of the Wechsler scales. Memory testing requires consideration of both verbal and nonverbal aspects as well as short-term and long-term memory. The Wechsler Memory Scale, widely used as a general test of memory, is primarily verbal and must be supplemented with visual tests.

Visual and auditory sensory functions are usually thoroughly examined by neurologists, but somatosensory function is not — largely because it is tedious and time-consuming to do so. If there is any evidence of a lesion to the central regions, somatosensory tests are invaluable. Motor functions such as reflexes, balance, gait, and the like are usually thoroughly examined by neurologists, but praxic functions frequently are not, again because of time limitations. Tests for apraxia are, however, easy to administer and score and should be included if practical.

Language functions can be assessed by tests of the subjects's speech and also by the many tests of aphasia, reading, writing, and arithmetic abilities. Tests of language functions should not be limited to a simple conversation, for subtle defects may often be overlooked.

Finally, a thorough assessment protocol will include tests of left and right frontal lobe function.

Ease and Cost. Tests should be easy to administer and score. Much of the testing often must be done by psychometrists, and the results interpreted by the neuropsychologist. Thus, it is essential that tests be given in a standard format and scored objectively so that the neuropsychologists can be assured of consistent results from tests being administered by more than one psychometrist. The tests should also be inexpensive. Cost constraints are not a good reason to administer a partial assessment protocol.

Time. Tests should not take excessively long to administer. Because subjects are often weak and easily tired, it is desirable to complete testing as quickly as possible without compromising thoroughness.

Adaptability. Often subjects are not very mobile, possibly being restricted to wheelchairs or even bedridden. It is therefore essential that the tests be portable and adaptable to varying constraints determined by the health of the subject.

Flexibility. Research is continually improving tests and devising newer, better ones. It is important that tests be substituted or improved in the light of new data. Test batteries that employ complex formulas or cutoff scores are thus less desirable because they necessarily lose their flexibility.

Halstead-Reitan Battery

The most widely known battery is the Halstead-Reitan battery, presumably because it is the most readily available. Essentially it is based on a series of tests originally devised by Halstead in the late 1940s. It began as a battery of seven tests selected for their power to discriminate between patients with frontal lobe lesions and other patient groups or normal controls. The current version of the battery consists of about 10 basic tests, 8 of which are listed below and several others of which are given mention.

Wechsler Intelligence Scale. Either the WAIS, WAIS-R, or the Wechsler-Bellevue Intelligence Scale, Form I, is administered.

Category Test. A category test is primarily a test of abstracting ability. A variety of stimulus figures varying in size, shape, number, intensity, color, and location are projected on a screen for the subject's viewing. These figures can be grouped by abstract principles, and it is the subject's task to determine the principle. This test is sensitive to left or right frontal lobe damage.

Critical Flicker-Fusion Test. The rate at which flashing lights appear steady or fused into a constant light, is assessed by using a light-flashing stroboscope. This test is often not included in the battery.

Tactile-Performance Test. The Seguin-Goddard Form Board Test described in our discussion of parietal lobe tests in Chapter 16 is a tactile-performance test. Blindfolded subjects are asked to place blocks of wood of various shapes (square, star, half-moon, etc.) into holes of similar shape in the form board; later they are asked, without having seen the board, to draw it from memory. Although Halstead and Reitan believed this was a frontal lobe test, many authors, including ourselves, have found that frontal lobe patients are not impaired at this task, but right parietal patients are. Indeed, it is difficult to understand why this test would ever have been considered a test of frontal lobe pathology.

Rhythm Test. The rhythm test, a subtest of the Seashore Test of Musical Talent, requires the subject to discriminate between like and unlike pairs of musical beats. Subjects with right temporal lobe removals are impaired at this task.

Speech-Sounds Perception Test. The speech-sounds perception test is an auditory acuity test in which the subject listens to a tape recording of 60 spoken nonsense words, all of which have an "ee" vowel sound in the middle with different beginning and ending consonant sounds. The subject selects the word heard from a series of alternatives. This is a test of left hemisphere function, presumably taxing mainly either the left posterior temporal-parietal cortex around Wernicke's area or possibly the left face area.

Finger-Oscillation Test. On the finger-oscillation test the subject's finger-tapping speed is measured on a key resembling a Morse code key. Halstead found a slight slowing of tapping speed in patients with cortical lesions, and Reitan has claimed this test to be one of the most sensitive in the battery. This conclusion is not universally accepted and we have found the test to be unreliable in lateralizing pathology, especially if the lesion is in the temporal or occipital cortex.

Time-Sense Test. A time-sense test measures the subject's visual-motor reaction time and ability to estimate elapsed time. The task is to watch a clock hand rotate around a clock face and then to estimate sweep time from memory. The memory component of this test has not proved useful and is not generally used.

Auxiliary Tests. Other tests included in the original battery but not always administered include the trail-making test, aphasia screening test, and the Minnesota Multiphasic Personality Inventory (MMPI). The trail-making test requires subjects to draw lines to connect either consecutive numbers or letters scattered randomly on a page and in a second part to alternate between the two sequences (i.e., A-1-B-2-C-3 . . .); the aphasia screening test is an altered version of the Wepman Aphasia Test; and the MMPI is a widely used self-report questionnaire alleged to diagnose psychiatric abnormalities.

To ascertain the presence of brain damage, a summary value is obtained, known as the Halstead Impairment Index. This index is determined by counting the number of tests on which the results fall in the range characteristic of the performance of brain-damaged subjects.

Although the Halstead-Reitan battery is widely used and has been an important pioneer effort in neuropsychological assessment, it is subject to a number of serious criticisms. The tests are not theoretically based, but rather are largely derived from 27 tests that Halstead originally chose in hopes of finding tests to identify subjects with frontal lesions. Thus, the 10 tests that are used are really clinically based and are difficult to interpret theoretically. Furthermore, the norms for the tests are not well founded, being based on a small sample. Memory functions are poorly and naively assessed, even though more is probably known about memory and its assessment than about any other cerebral function. In addition, the tests are not sensitive enough; many subjects with small focalized lesions would show no significant abnormalities on the battery. The test is sensitive to the effects of aging on behavior and cannot therefore reliably discriminate between subjects 45 years of age or older and brain-damaged subjects. An additional problem is that the battery, and particularly the category test, is not really portable and is thus difficult to administer to bedridden subjects. The most serious problem, however, is that the battery, although containing a large number of tests, does not meet our criteria for thoroughness (as discussed in the previous section). There is no measure of somatosensory function, praxic function, or gnostic function. Furthermore, there is evidence that the tests used are highly correlated, and therefore redundant, and that some of the individual tests (e.g., the trail-making test) may actually be better predictors of brain damage than the impairment index. A final problem, by no means unique to the Halstead-Reitan battery, is its inability to distinguish between psychotic and brain-damaged subjects. For example, Watson and coworkers found that Reitan-trained examiners were unable to differentiate, at better than a chance level, patients with known brain damage from patients diagnosed as schizophrenic. This inability is a chronic problem of all neuropsychological batteries, no doubt reflecting the gross frontal and temporal lobe dysfunction in schizophrenia discussed in previous chapters.

Because of the limitations of the original Halstead-Reitan battery, there have been numerous attempts to modify it for specific populations (see Lezak for examples). Many clinicians have added their own tests, especially tests of memory, to supplement the basic battery. What is needed, however, is a thorough revision of the battery with updated and extended norms and validation studies on subjects with verified lesions, incorporating many of the improvements that have been made by different groups.

Luria's Neuropsychological Investigation

Luria's test battery is not widely known in the Western world, having been first published in English as a battery by Christensen in 1975. Based on about 35 years of research by Luria and his colleagues in the Soviet Union, it is probably the most thorough battery available, as the summary of the tests in Table 27-2 shows. Because the nonpsychometric nature of Luria's battery makes it difficult to describe all of the tests briefly, we have presented an example of one test and its interpretation in Tables 27-3 and 27-4.

TABLE 27-2. Summary of Luria's neuropsychological investigation

Determination of cerebral dominance

Investigation of motor functions
- Motor functions of the hands
- Oral praxis
- Speech regulation of the motor act

Investigation of acousticomotor organization
- Perception and reproduction of pitch relations
- Perception and reproduction of rhythmic structures

Investigation of the higher cutaneous and kinesthetic functions
- Cutaneous sensation
- Muscle and joint sensation
- Stereognosis

Investigation of the higher visual functions
- Visual perception of objects and pictures
- Spatial orientation
- Intellectual operations in space

Investigation of impressive speech
- Phonemic hearing
- Word comprehension
- Understanding of simple sentences
- Understanding of logical grammatical structures

Investigation of the higher visual functions
- Articulation of speech sounds
- Reflected (repetitive) speech
- The nominative function of speech
- Narrative speech

Investigation of writing and reading
- Phonetic analysis and synthesis of words
- Writing
- Reading

Investigation of arithmetical skill
- Comprehension of number structure
- Arithmetical operations

Investigation of memory processes
- The learning process
- Retention and retrieval
- Logical memorizing

Investigation of intellectual processes
- Understanding of thematic pictures and texts
- Concept formation
- Discursive intellectual activity

Source: Adapted from Christensen, 1975.

The principal advantages of Luria's battery are the following. (1) It is based on theoretical principles of neuropsychological functioning, making the interpretation a logical conclusion of the theory. (2) It is thorough, inexpensive, easy to administer, flexible, and brief, taking only about 1 hour to administer. (3) It measures the actual behavior of the subject rather than inferred cognitive processes, thus making interpretation more straightforward. There are, however, also disadvantages of the Luria procedure. (1) The scoring is subjective and is based on clinical experience. It is

TABLE 27-3. Example of Luria's assessment tests: Test 1, Investigation of higher visual functions

Procedure	Materials
Investigation of objects and pictures	Objects and pictures
The patient is asked to examine carefully objects or clearly drawn pictures of objects (with no time limit) and to name them.	
If speech is disturbed, nonverbal communication can be used.	
The patient is asked to examine and name complicated or indistinct pictures of objects.	
The patient is asked to examine and name pictures of objects that are scribbled over or superimposed one on another (Poppelreuter's test).	
The patient is asked to identify a figure in a complex design (Gottschaldt).	
The patient is asked to complete a structure from which a portion is missing by choosing from a series of offered insets the one that matches the particular structure (example from Raven's test). No time limit is imposed.	
The presentation of these tests may be varied. The figure may be presented for only a short period of time, or the pictures may be presented in the wrong position.	
In simplified forms the patient is asked to trace the outline of the figure with his finger, or he may be given leading questions, or the examiner may point to any one of the essential signs.	

Source: From Christensen, 1975, p. 69.

TABLE 27-4. Interpretative guideline for Luria's test of objects and pictures

Behavior	Lesion
Perception of objects and pictures	
The patient perceives only one sign—the most conspicuous or prominent—but fails to correlate it with the other signs or to integrate the necessary group of signs; he draws premature conclusions regarding the meaning of the pictures, guessing at it from a single fragment that he has perceived. E.g., he may identify the pair of spectacles . . . as "a bicycle" because he cannot synthesize two circles and a series of lines into the required image. In less marked cases these difficulties are only brought to light during the examination of the most complex visual structures. The patient hardly ever expresses confident opinions regarding the meaning of pictures; he is constantly in doubt or he complains of his poor eyesight.	Lesions in occipitoparietal divisions of the cortex. *Optic agnosia*
The patient can perceive a picture and evaluate it properly, but he can only perceive one picture or one element at a time.	*Simultaneous agnosia*
The patient loses sight of the whole picture if he examines its details. His examination of the objects is accompanied by ataxia of gaze.	
The patient looks at the picture passively; he does not change the direction of his gaze and he does not seem to attempt to "seek out" the identifying signs; usually he reaches a confident conclusion about what the picture represents; he shows no doubt and there is no attempt at correction.	Lesion of the frontal lobes
The patient evaluates the picture in the position it is shown to him; he does not turn it over and he makes no attempt to invert it mentally. Complex visual stimuli give him the impression of chaos. . . . He may also persevere in the same perception, i.e., the different pictures begin to be interpreted in the same way.	
The patient neglects the left side.	Lesion of the right hemisphere

Source: From Christensen, 1975, pp. 72–73.

unlikely that a novice to neuropsychology or neurology could easily master the interpretation without extensive training. On the other hand, experienced neuropsychologists or neurologists ought to find the battery easy to learn. (2) Because the manual that accompanies the battery offers no validation studies, it must be taken on faith that the tests really measure what Luria claims they do. This criticism is the most serious, because most Western neuropsychologists are likely to continue to use psychometric assessment tools reporting validation studies.

The Luria-Nebraska Neuropsychological Battery

This recently devised test battery is an attempt to standardize the Luria test procedures, but it should not be considered as a substitute for Luria's Neuropsychological Investigation. Golden has selected items from Christensen's manual on the basis of whether they discriminated between normal subjects and neurologically impaired subjects to produce a standardized administration and scoring procedure for the Christensen tests. A score is thus obtained for most of the measures summarized in Table 27-2. Although the idea of standardizing the test items is sound, in so doing a very different test battery than that used by Luria has been produced.

> It is not the items, per se, but the manner in which Luria made use of them as a means of testing hypotheses concerning various abilities, deficits or functions which is his method and his unique contribution to neuropsychological assessment. Consequently, the incorporation of items drawn from Luria's work into a standardized test should not be interpreted to mean that the test is an operationalization or standardization of Luria's method. (Spiers, 1981, p. 339).

Golden and his colleagues have been very energetic over the past few years and have published an impressive number of papers on their battery. Nevertheless, the battery has not been widely accepted by neuropsychologists.

> A considerable gap separates the evaluations of this battery made by Golden and his colleagues from those by neuropsychologists who are not affiliated with them. Golden and his group, without exception, offer data supporting their claims that this battery is a diagnostically efficient instrument. Other neuropsychologists have concluded that the battery is unreliable. (Lezak, 1983, p. 570).

Our reading of the literature leads us to concur with Lezak. The usefulness and validity of this battery is far from proved. Neuropsychologists would be better advised to use Christensen's version of Luria's procedures or one of the composite batteries described below than to use the Luria-Nebraska.

Informal Composite Batteries

In the course of studying the consequences of brain injury, psychologists have devised many tests with which to demonstrate double dissociation of different cortical regions. Many of these tests are inappropriate for clinical application, but some are particularly well suited for use in the diagnosis of brain injury. By using tests of this sort it is possible to assemble informal test batteries that can be easily changed with additions or subtractions to suit the assessment problems of individual subjects. Examples of this form of informal composite battery are described by Benton and colleagues; Lezak; McKenna and Warrington; Milberg and colleagues; Newcombe; Smith; and Taylor. We will describe two of these informal batteries as examples, namely the Boston Process Approach and a group of tests based largely on work at the Montreal Neurological Institute.

The Boston Process Approach had its origins in Edith Kaplan's study of the dissolution of function in patients with brain damage. Over the years, she and her colleagues (especially Harold Goodglass)

TABLE 27-5. A representative sample of the tests used in the Boston Process Approach to neuropsychological assessment

Intellectual and conceptual functions
WAIS-R
Raven's Standard Progressive Matrices
Shipley Institute of Living Scale
Wisconsin Card-Sorting Test
Proverbs test
Memory functions
WMS
Rey Auditory Verbal Learning Test
Rey Complex Figure
Benton Visual-Recognition Test
Consonant trigrams test
Cowboy Story-Reading Memory Test
Corsi Blocks
Language functions
Narrative writing sample
Tests of verbal fluency
Visuoperceptual functions
Cow-and-circle experimental test
Automobile puzzle
Parietal lobe battery
Hooper Visual Organization Test
Academic skills
Wide-range achievement test
Self-Control and motor functions
Porteus Maze Test
Stroop Color-Word Interference Test
Luria Three-Step Motor Program
Finger tapping

have combined tests that have proven to be valid in the clinical discrimination of patients with and without brain damage, with tests that purport to measure specific cognitive functions. The current version of the battery is summarized in Table 27-5. Strict cutoff scores are not used in this battery but rather the qualitative nature of how patients solve the various tests, and the pattern of test performances, are looked at. This type of analysis provides a more precise delineation of functions than a strict quantitative approach, which is characteristic of the Halstead-Reitan or Luria-Nebraska batteries. Thus, the *relative* strengths and weaknesses of each patient is assessed. Details and examples of this process in neuropsychological assessment is given in the reference by Milberg and colleagues.

Because of our affiliation with the Montreal Neurological Institute, we have chosen to use the tests derived from nearly 40 years of research on neurosurgical patients by Brenda Milner, Laughlin

TABLE 27-6. An example of an informal composite battery

Determination of speech lateralization
Handedness questionnaire
Dichotic digits or words
General intelligence
WAIS-R
Peabody Picture Vocabulary Test-Revised
General academic skills
Wide-range achievement test
Visuoperceptual
McGill Picture Anomolies
Mooney Faces
Rey Complex Figure — copy
Line bisection
Memory
WMS-R
Corsi Block Span
Facial memory test
Spatial
Right-left differentiation
Semmes Body-Placing Test
Somatosensory
Passive movement
Point localization
Two-point discrimination
Simultaneous extinction
Language
Object naming
Chapman-Cook Speed of Reading
Spelling
Token test
Hippocampal function
Corsi Recurring Blocks
Frontal lobe
Wisconsin Card-Sorting Test
Chicago Word-Fluency Test
Motor function
Hand dynamometer
Finger tapping
Kimura Box Test
Complex arm- and facial-movement copying

Taylor, and their colleagues. In addition, we have borrowed tests from others, particularly Doreen Kimura and H.-L. Teuber and his associates. We describe these tests briefly here and provide a more extensive description, including normative data, in Chapter 32.

The tests in this battery are based primarily on research with patients with surgical excisions for indolent tumors or epilepsy. Although not all of the tests were developed in Montreal, all have been extensively researched on neurosurgical patients before and after surgery, as well as later in follow-up, sometimes pursued over periods of 20 years after surgery.

Table 27-6 summarizes the tests in the battery, most of which have been discussed in other contexts earlier in the book (see Chapters 17–19); each test will therefore be discussed only briefly. First, general intelligence and speech lateralization are assessed using standard techniques, namely Wechsler scales and dichotic digits or words. Visuoperceptual abilities are assessed by a series of pictures making up the McGill Picture-Anomalies Test: looking at a series of pictures, each containing something strange or unusual, the subject must point to the oddity in the picture. The Mooney Faces Test requires the subject, examining an incomplete sketch of a face, to perceive the face, and then indicate the sex and age of the person. Finally, the Rey Complex Figure is copied as accurately as possible. The Mooney Faces and the Rey Figure tests are particularly sensitive to right parietal lobe damage, whereas the McGill Picture-Anomalies Test is most sensitive to right temporal lobe damage.

Memory is assessed by a number of tests, beginning with the revised WMS, with special emphasis upon the delayed-recall tests. In addition, the widely used Rey Complex Figure (see Figure 11-3*C*) is recalled after a delay of 30 min. The verbal-memory tests are sensitive to left temporal lobe damage, the nonverbal tests to right temporal lobe damage.

Among the spatial tests are a right-left differentiation test and the Semmes Body-Placing Test. Somatosensory tests include tests of sensitivity of the hands, face, and feet to light touch and passive movement. Language functions are assessed by standard tests of naming, reading, spelling, and language comprehension, the only unusual test being that of phonetic discrimination, described in Chapter 19. Tests of hippocampal, frontal lobe, and motor function have all been discussed previously, in Chapters 17 through 19.

The principal advantage of using the Montreal tests is that the hundreds of research cases on which they are based have surgically induced lesions that were carefully photographed and sketched by the surgeons so that test performance could be accurately correlated with lesion location and extent. Since the patients were tested both before and after surgery, as well as in follow-up, those tests that were not reliable indicators of localized brain injury have been eliminated. Furthermore, although the original research patients were usually epileptic, subsequent studies have shown the tests to be even more sensitive to other disorders such as strokes and tumors, and they can be used to discriminate between individuals with different types of disorders, as described in the following chapters.

REFERENCES

Benton, A. L., D. deS. Hamsher, N. R. Varney, and O. Spreen. *Contributions to Neuropsychological Assessment: A Clinical Manual.* New York: Oxford University Press, 1983.

Christensen, A.-L. *Luria's Neuropsychological Investigation.* New York: Spectrum Publications, 1975.

Golden, C. J. A standardized version of Luria's neuropsychological tests. In S. Filskov and T. J. Boll, eds. *Handbook of Clinical Neuropsychology*. New York: Wiley-Interscience, 1981.

Kimura, D., and J. McGlone. *Neuropsychology Test Procedures*. Manual used at the University Hospital, London, Ontario, Canada, 1983.

Levin, H. S., and A. L. Benton. Neuropsychologic assessment. In A. B. Baker and R. J. Joynt, eds. *Clinical Neurology*. vol 1. New York: Harper & Row, 1986.

Lezak, M. D. *Neuropsychological Assessment,* 2nd ed. New York: Oxford University Press, 1983.

McFie, J. *Assessment of Organic Intellectual Impairment*. New York: John Wiley, 1975.

McKenna, P., and E. K. Warrington. The analytical approach to neuropsychological assessment. In I. Grant and K. M. Adams, eds. *Assessment of Neuropsychiatric Disorders*. New York: Oxford University Press, 1986.

Milberg, W. P., N. Hebben, and E. Kaplan. The Boston process approach to neuropsychological assessment. In I. Grant and K. M. Adams, eds. *Assessment of Neuropsychiatric Disorders*. New York: Oxford University Press, 1986.

Newcombe, F. *Missile Wounds of the Brain*. London: Oxford University Press, 1969.

Reitan, R. M., and L. A. Davison. *Clinical Neuropsychology: Current Status and Application*. New York: John Wiley, 1974.

Smith, A. Principles underlying human brain functions in neuropsychological sequelae of different neuropathological processes. In S. B. Filskov and T. J. Boll, eds. *Handbook of Clinical Neuropsychology*. New York: Wiley-Interscience, 1981.

Spiers, P. A. Have they come to praise Luria or to bury him: The Luria-Nebraska controversy. *Journal of Consulting and Clinical Psychology* 49:331–341, 1981.

Taylor, L. B. Psychological assessment of neurosurgical patients. In T. Rasmussen and R. Marino, eds. *Functional Neurosurgery*. New York: Raven Press, 1979.

Warrington, E. K., M. James, and C. Maciejewski. The WAIS as a lateralizing and localizing diagnostic instrument: A study of 656 patients with unilateral cerebral excisions. *Neuropsychologia* 24:223–239, 1986.

Watson, C. G., R. W. Thomas, D. Anderson, and J. Felling. Differentiation of organics from schizophrenics by use of the Reitan-Halstead organic test battery. *Journal of Consulting and Clinical Psychology* 32:679–684, 1968.

Wilson, R. S., G. Rosenbaum, and G. Brown. The problem of premorbid intelligence in neuropsychological assessment. *Journal of Clinical Neuropsychology* 1:49–56, 1979.

APPLICATIONS OF NEUROPSYCHOLOGICAL ASSESSMENT

Having surveyed the basic principles of neuropsychological theory and assessment, we now provide examples of the application of the tests and theory to clinical problems by presenting case histories to illustrate the use of neuropsychological tests in neuropsychological assessment. In this chapter we describe the test results and case histories of 12 patients: 4 neurosurgical cases, 4 neurological cases, and 4 miscellaneous cases. These cases will provide a feel for the clinical application of neuropsychological tests and will provide an introduction to the next two chapters, in which we consider the use of these tests to study disorders that do not have known neurological correlates: learning disabilities and mental disorders.

NEUROSURGICAL CASES

To illustrate the application of neuropsychological tests to neurosurgical cases we have borrowed four cases from Laughlin Taylor at the Montreal Neurological Hospital. We also refer the reader to Chapter 15, where we contrasted two other such patients.

Case 1

This 33-year-old man had a history of seizures beginning 4 years before his admission to the hospital. His neurological examination on admission was negative, but he was having increasingly frequent seizures, which were characterized by head and eyes turning to the right: a pattern that suggests supplementary motor cortex involvement. Radiological and EEG studies suggested a left frontal lobe lesion, a suggestion that was confirmed at operation when a poorly differentiated astrocytoma was removed, as illustrated in Figure 28-1*A*. The only difficulty the patient experienced before surgery was in doing the Wisconsin Card-

A Case 1

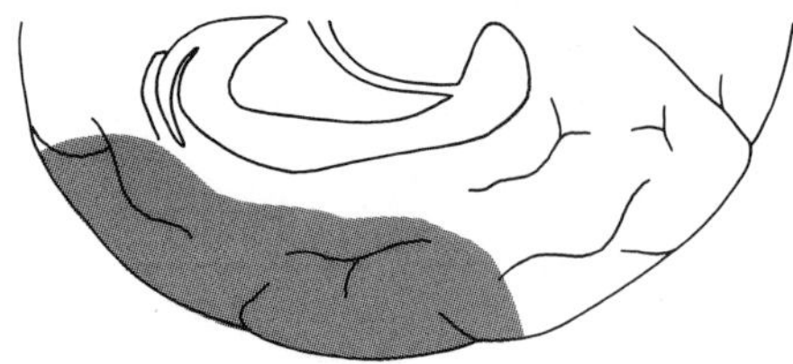

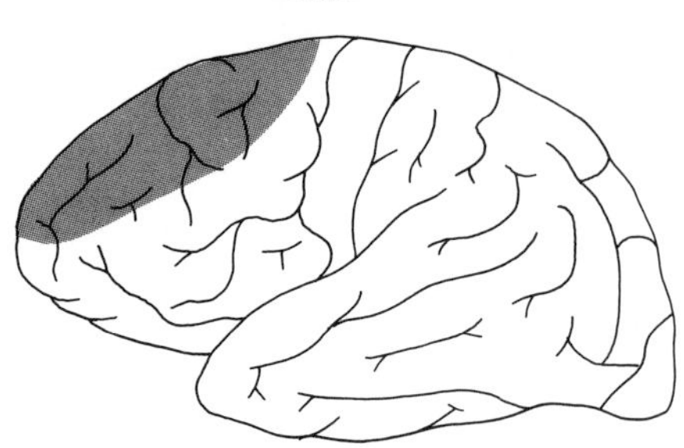

	Preop.		Postop.	
Full scale IQ	115		102	
verbal IQ	111		103	
performance IQ	117		99	
Memory quotient	118		108	
Verbal recall	20		14	
Nonverbal recall	10.5		10	
Card sorting	1 cat.[a]		1 cat.[a]	
Finger position sense	Left	Right	Left	Right
	60/60	60/60	60/60	60/60
Drawings: copy	36/36		35/36	
recall	21/36		24/36	

[a] Significantly low score.

B Case 2

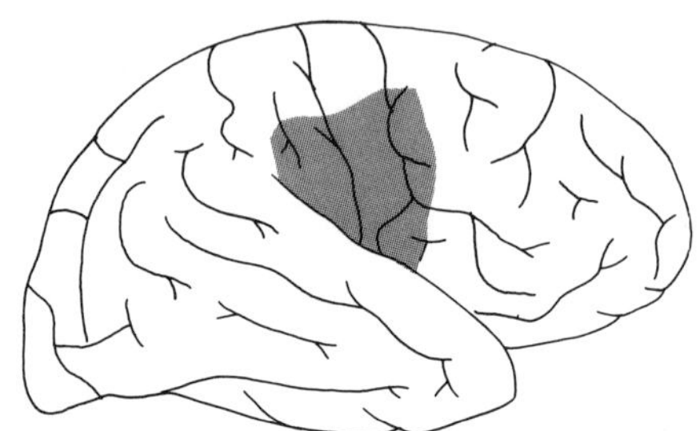

	Preop.		Postop.	
Full scale IQ	97		97	
verbal IQ	100		106	
performance IQ	94		88[a]	
Memory quotient	94		92	
Verbal recall	13.5		14.0	
Nonverbal recall	3.5[a]		7.0	
Card sorting	0 cat.[a]		1 cat.[a]	
Finger position sense	Left	Right	Left	Right
	55/60[a]	59/60	54/60[a]	60/60
Drawings: copy	28/36[a]		26.5/36[a]	
recall	4/36[a]		9.5/36[a]	

[a] Significantly low score.

C Cases 3 and 4

Left hemisphere

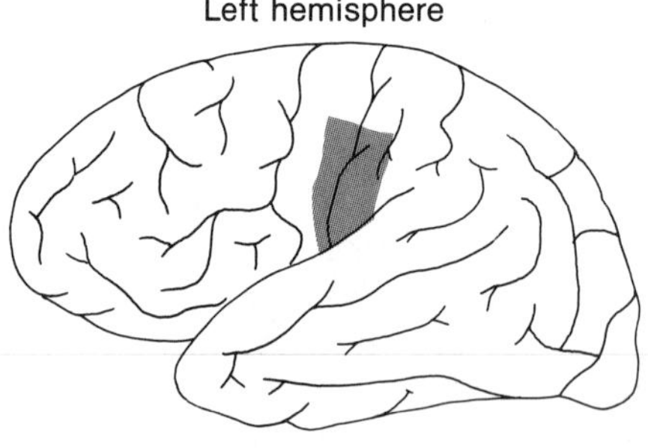

Right hemisphere

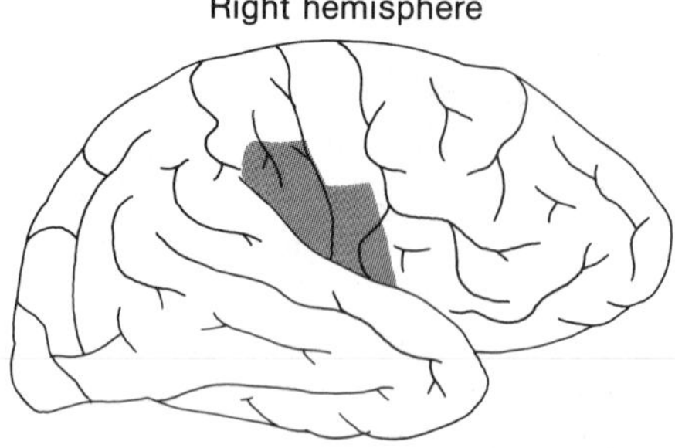

	Preop.	Postop.		Preop.	Postop.
Two-point	Left	1.1 cm	0.7 cm	1.2 cm	5.0 cm[a]
Discrimination on face	Right	1.4 cm[a]	2.2 cm[a]	0.6 cm	12 cm
Phoneme discrimination	75/108	58/108[a]		82/108	87/108
Spelling	14/35[a]	10/35[a]		30/35	30/35
Word fluency	38	20[a]		47	39

[a] Significantly low score.

Sorting Test, where numerous perserverative errors were made and only one category was correctly sorted. Two weeks after surgery all the intelligence ratings, memory quotient, and delayed verbal-recall scores decreased, but these scores remained in essentially the same ratio to one another. Other tests were essentially unchanged, the only significantly low score again being on the sorting test. If this patient was like other patients with similar lesions, it is likely that on follow-up a year after surgery his intelligence ratings and memory scores would have returned to the preoperative level, although his card sorting would be unlikely to show any improvement. Furthermore, he would almost certainly have had a chronic deficit in copying sequences of movements of the face, although he was not given this test.

Case 2

This 26-year-old man had a history of 8 years of seizures dating back to an episode of meningitis in which he was thought to have an intracerebral abscess. Subsequently he developed seizures beginning in the left side of his face and hand, and he was referred as a candidate for surgery since his seizures were uncontrolled by medication. Before surgery, the patient scored within normal limits on tests of intelligence and general memory, although he did have difficulty with delayed recall of verbal material. He had slight defects of finger-position sense on the left hand, which together with some weakness in the left arm and leg pointed to damage in the right central area. In addition, he had difficulty in copying and recalling the Rey Complex Figure and was unable to sort cards in the Wisconsin Test, results suggesting that his lesion might extend into frontal and temporal areas as well.

The right face area and a region extending into the right frontal lobe were removed at surgery. After this removal there remained some residual epileptiform abnormality in both the frontal lobe and the superior temporal gyrus. Postoperative testing showed improvement both in verbal IQ and in long-term verbal memory, but the patient had persistent difficulties on the card-sorting test, with finger-position sense on the left hand, and on the copy and recall of the Rey Figure. There was also a decline in performance IQ. The difficulty with finger position is to be expected with the removal in this man, but the continuing difficulties with card sorting and the Rey Figure imply that dysfunctioning areas remain in his right hemisphere, as reflected by the residual spiking in the frontal and temporal regions.

Cases 3 and 4

These two cases are presented together to emphasize the contrasting effects of their left and right hemisphere removals, respectively. Both patients had long-standing epilepsy of unknown origins. The left hemisphere patient, a 13-year-old boy, had a total removal of the precentral and postcentral face area, whereas the right hemisphere patient, a 23-year-old man, had a similar removal on the left and additional removal of some parietal cortex, as illustrated in Figure 28-1*C*.

Before surgery, both patients had average intelligence and memory ratings, which were unaffected by the surgery. The left hemisphere patient performed normally on all preoperative tests, however. Following surgery, the left hemisphere patient continued to have a sensory loss on the right side of his face and impaired spelling, but in addition he now had difficulty with phoneme discrimination and word fluency. These symptoms are typical of patients with left face-area lesions, as described in Chapter 19. In contrast, the patient with a similar removal of the right face area had a large sensory loss on the left side of his face, but

Figure 28-1. Psychological test results before and after operation for four cases. (After Taylor, 1969; 1979.)

showed no other significant deficits. Curiously, when we tested these patients at the copying of sequences of facial movements, they showed no impairment whatsoever, although there was a slight contralateral weakness in moving the face. This result suggests that the sensory and motor control of the face are organized rather differently from one another.

Summary of Neurosurgical Cases

These four cases, in conjunction with those in Chapter 15, provide us with several lessons. First, neuropsychological tests can measure specific functions of the brain; they are not measures of general brain damage. Second, neuropsychological tests can discriminate and doubly dissociate quite small areas of damage in neurosurgical cases. This implies that these tests would be extremely sensitive to more global pathology such as strokes or tumors, and indeed they are. In addition, however, the sensitivity of the tests suggests that they may be useful in identifying poorly developed functions in other populations such as learning-disabled children. We return to this point in Chapter 29. Third, the test results indicate that neuropsychological tests can reflect the absence of brain tissue or the presence of damaged or disturbed tissue. Fourth, it should be apparent that intelligence tests by themselves are not reliable measures of brain damage. Although the temporal lobe patients described in Chapter 15 did exhibit large decreases in IQ, similar drops were not seen in the four cases described here, even though three of them did have other cognitive deficits. Finally, it is obvious that a broad range of tests must be used, including careful measurement of somatosensory functions, if an accurate picture of cerebral functioning is to be obtained.

NEUROLOGICAL CASES

Few neuropsychologists have the good fortune to study or assess neurosurgical patients with focal lesions. More commonly, patients are referred by neurologists or other physicians after a stroke or some other naturally occurring disease. Assessment in these cases if far more difficult, but as we shall see in the following examples, composite test batteries can still be very useful in describing the functional state of the remaining brain.

Case 5

This 28-year-old right-handed woman had undergone emergency surgery following the bursting of an aneurysm in the right temporal lobe. Surgical reports indicated that portions of the right temporal and parietal cortex were damaged, and she had a left quadrantic hemianopsia, indicating that the lesion extended posteriorly into the visual cortex. She was referred to us 2 years after the accident, at which time she was in good health and attending a university, but she was having social problems as well as difficulty with mathematics. The results of her neuropsychological assessment are summarized in Table 28-1, where it can be seen that she experienced several deficits consistent with right posterior damage. Her performance IQ was 10 points lower than her verbal IQ, she had difficulty obtaining closure on the Mooney Faces Test, and her recall of visual material was well below the level expected for a woman of her age and intelligence. In contrast, she performed within expected limits on tests of left hemisphere and frontal lobe function.

Case 6

A 22-year-old woman was referred to us by a clinical psychologist to assess the possibility of "organic" dysfunction. She had on several occasions engaged in bizarre behaviors such as undressing in public and urinating on other people and on one occasion had attacked her roommate. Following these episodes she was confused and amnesic about her behavior during the "attack" as well as about the period just prior to the outburst. Her neuropsychological test results indicated that her left tem-

TABLE 28-1. Examples of neuropsychological assessments of neurological patients

Test	Normal control	Case 5 Right temporal aneurysm	Case 6 Left temporal epilepsy	Case 7 Left hemisphere stroke	Case 8 Traffic accident
Speech lateralization dichotic words:					
left ear	25	18	2[a]	F	16
right ear	46	50	15	F	25
handedness	R	R	R	R	R
General intelligence					
full-scale IQ	107	113	104	F	115
verbal IQ	109	117	95[a]	F	127
performance IQ	105	107[a]	111	108	96[a]
Visuoperceptual					
Mooney Faces (abbreviated)	18/19	12/19[a]	16/19	16/19	17/19
Rey Complex Figures—copy	32/36	24/36[a]	31/36	30/36	34/36
Memory					
Wechsler Memory quotient	107	115	87[a]	F	100[a]
Rey Complex Figures—recall	22/36	11/36[a]	18/36[a]	17/36[a]	13/36[a]
delayed recall of stories and paired-associates	13	17	7[a]	—	23
delayed recall of drawings	12	6[a]	10	9	2[a]
Spatial					
right-left differentiation	52/60	48/60	43/60	51/60	35/60[a]
Semmes Body Placing	32/35	30/35	30/35	—	35/35
Language					
reading	12	12	7[a]	F	20
object-naming	23/36	20/26	14/26[a]	F	—
Frontal lobe					
Wisconsin Card-Sorting Test	6.0 cat.	5.8 cat.	4.0 cat.	3.0 cat.	2.4 cat[a]
Chicago Word Fluency	62	50	38	F	52
Motor function					
complex arm	92%	94%	89%	72%[a]	82%[a]
face	88%	90%	89%	20%[a]	30%[a]

[a]Abnormally poor score.
F = could not be assessed because of dysphasia.

poral lobe was abnormal, because her verbal memory as well as reading and object-naming were impaired, and she had a very low recall of dichotic words (see Table 28-1). Our diagnosis of temporal lobe epilepsy with a left-side focus was partially confirmed by a neurologist when EEG studies showed left hemisphere abnormality. As frequently occurs in epilepsy, a CT scan failed to reveal any unusual features, and there is nothing in the woman's history to account for the epilepsy. The seizures are completely controlled with Dilantin, but her neuropsychological deficits remain.

Case 7

This 60-year-old woman suffered a stroke that, from her CT scan, appeared to be localized in the face area and Broca's area on the left. She was referred to us a year after the stroke because of her poor progress with the speech pathologist in regaining her speech. In view of her marked dysphasia we first administered a token test, only to find that although this woman appeared to understand many of the things spoken to her, she was severely dysphasic, thereby obtaining a very poor score on the token test. In view of this result, we gave her only a modified battery, designed to answer the referral question of what could be expected if she were to continue speech therapy. Her test results, which are summarized in Table 28-1, showed that she was of average intelligence when measured with a nonverbal test, and she performed normally on all nonverbal tests of memory and perception that we administered. In contrast, she had real difficulty in copying movements, even though she had no **hemiparesis.** Indeed, she was totally unable to copy sequences of facial movements, although she could manage individual facial movements, with some difficulty. These results led us to conclude that this woman was aphasic and had a facial apraxia, leading us to be pessimistic about her chances for further recovery of speech functions.

Case 8

This is the case of a 37-year-old man who had been in a traffic accident some 15 years earlier. He was in a coma for 6 weeks and suffered secondary injury from brain infection. At the time of his accident, he was a student in a graduate program in journalism, having previously obtained a B.A. with honors in English literature. When we first met him, he had severe motor problems, needing canes to walk, and was both apraxic and ataxic. He had great difficulty in pronouncing words, especially when hurried or stressed, but careful language testing on the token test revealed no aphasic symptoms; his language problems were entirely anarthric. Since the time of his accident this man had lived at home with his parents and had not learned the social skills necessary to cope with his handicap. In short, he was being treated as though he was retarded and was being completely looked after by his family. Indeed, the patient himself believed he was retarded and he was very reluctant to attempt rehabilitation programs. At the urging of his family we gave him a thorough assessment to evaluate his potential. His results were surprising, even to us. As summarized in Table 28-1, his IQ was superior (WAIS verbal IQ of 127), and although he had deficits on some tests, especially those involving motor skills, his performance on most tests was average or above average. Despite his obvious motor handicaps, this man clearly was not retarded. One significant cognitive loss, however, was his nonverbal memory, which was very poor. Armed with our test results we were able to show him and his family that he could look after himself and should seek occupational therapy through a government agency for the handicapped.

Summary of Neurological Cases

Most neurological referrals are not intended to diagnose brain damage; as this has already been done by the neurologist; modern radiological technology can identify most brain pathology (with the exception of some epilepsies as well as the effects of mild head trauma. See Chapter 31). CT scans and similar devices do not describe the particular behavioral symptoms that an individual may experience, however, and this is where careful neuropsychological assessment can be very helpful both in understanding the disorder and in planning rehabilitation. Again, we must emphasize that a thorough battery of tests is necessary for these functions, to identify both the weaknesses and the strengths of each individual.

EXAMPLES OF OTHER DISORDERS

Neuropsychologists are often asked to assess people without known neurological disease. In many of these cases there is a need to identify the cognitive deficits and strengths that different people have in order to plan rehabilitative programs or to identify the correct institutional placements. It is foolish for the psychologist to try to identify brain pathology in these people since it is almost certainly not focal and cannot be verified by other means. Nevertheless, the study of individuals with certain disorders may provide insight into the nature of the causes of the disease, a point we return to in the next two chapters.

Case 9

This 31-year-old man was diagnosed independently by two psychiatrists as being schizophrenic. When assessed by us, he had been on a small dose of chlorpromazine for 2 days and appeared rather lucid, having no delusions or hallucinations during the testing. His test results, however, showed serious neuropsychological abnormalities, especially in tests of frontal and temporal lobe function (see Table 28-2). We have found a similar pattern of abnormality in other diagnosed schizophrenics; we shall return to this in Chapter 30.

Case 10

Although Tourette's syndrome is relatively rare, diagnosis of this disease has become commoner in recent years, possibly because the symptoms are becoming better known. We have seen about 80 such cases from all across North America and present here one that is representative. This was a 9-year-old boy who was displaying frequent facial and body tics, as well as some involuntary vocalizations. Although he was reported to have had a difficult birth, his developmental milestones were

TABLE 28-2. Examples of neuropsychological assessments of nonneurological patients

	Case 9	Case 10	Case 11	Case 12
Test	Schizophrenic	Gilles de la Tourette	Learning disabled	Dementia
General intelligence				
full-scale IQ	98	100	94	86
verbal IQ	100	103	87[a]	89
performance IQ	95	95	104	87
Visuoperceptual				
Mooney Faces	15/19	20/26	26/26	11/26[a]
Rey Figure—copy	35/36	18/26[a]	15/36[a]	0[a]
Memory				
Wechsler Memory quotient	90[a]	81[a]	92	66[a]
Rey Figure—recall	1/36[a]	6/36[a]	7/36[a]	0[a]
delayed recall of stories and paired-associates	8[a]	18	19	0[a]
delayed recall of drawings	9	6[a]	8	0[a]
Spatial				
right-left differentiation	44/60	42/60	27/60[a]	30/60[a]
Semmes Body Placing	16/35[a]	29/35	22/35[a]	25/35[a]
Frontal lobe				
Wisconsin Card-Sorting Test	2.5 cat.[a]	6.0 cat.	5.0 cat.	0 cat.[a]
Chicago Word Fluency	30[a]	22[b]	30[b]	4[a]

[a]Abnormally poor score.
[b]Within acceptable range for this age.

normal and there was no evidence of neurological disease. He was, however, having difficulty in school and his tics were making his social adjustment difficult. His intelligence rating was strictly average, although his performance IQ was 8 points lower than his verbal IQ. His long- and short-term verbal memory were within normal limits but his visual memory was very poor; his copy and recall of the Rey Figure were typical of a child 4 years younger. Perhaps surprisingly, however, this boy did not perform poorly on other tests, particularly those normally performed poorly by children with learning disabilities. We have found that this boy's pattern of test results is typical of both children and adults diagnosed as having Tourette's syndrome, although the cause of the tics and the cognitive deficits remains unknown. In view of the very poor visual memory skills in these people, it is important for them to plan occupations not requiring heavy demands on visual memory.

Case 11

This 10-year-old boy was referred to us by a local school psychologist because of his slow progress and difficultly with peer relations. He had no history of neurological disease and had experienced normal developmental milestones. His intelligence rating was average, although his performance score showed an advantage of 17 points. His digit span was especially poor: he was unable to recall more than five digits even with repeated testing. His memory rating was also within the average range, although he had difficulty with the immediate recall of short stories, a result consistent with his poor immediate recall of digits. Further, he had difficulty with both the copying and the recall of the Rey Figure, scoring well below the expected range for his age. Like most learning-disabled children, this boy also had real difficulty in differentiating left from right, scoring at a chance level. Performance on most other tests was, however, within normal limits, a pattern we find to be typical of children with learning difficulties.

Case 12

This 40-year-old man had been admitted to a nursing home, apparently suffering from some type of presenile dementia. His neurological exam was negative, but when we first saw him, he was incontinent and generally unresponsive. This latter symptom made testing very difficult, although with urging he did complete most tests given to him. Intelligence testing revealed a low-average IQ, a result that contrasted with his apparent dementia. Memory testing revealed significant dysfunction, however, as he was completely unable to recall even very simple drawings. He was unable to copy the Rey Figure and performed very poorly on every other test given to him, a result consistent with his dementia. In this case neuropsychological testing only confirmed the obvious, and led us to be rather pessimistic regarding the man's future.

Summary

We have chosen a variety of cases in this last section to illustrate the range in test patterns that can be expected from individuals without obvious neurological disorders. The use of tests with these individuals must be very judicious and is best directed toward the planning of remedial programs. Nevertheless, neuropsychological testing of these cases may offer some insight into the nature of the disorders, as we shall see in the next chapter.

The technology of neuropsychology can be applied to virtually any problem in which psychologists use traditional assessment techniques. This range includes general counseling, vocational guidance, assessment of juvenile delinquents for the courts, assessment related to legal matters such as suits arising from injuries in traffic accidents, and placement of retarded people in occupational-training programs. Neuropsychology does not offer a panacea for any of these problems, but it can add an important tool to the arsenal used in general psychological assessment.

A Word of Caution

We have emphasized the usefulness of neuropsychological information for a variety of applied settings, but we would be remiss if we failed to caution against overuse or abuse of this information. As useful as neuropsychological data can be for general counseling, we are not proposing that neuropsychological techniques be applied to every person who sees a neurologist, psychologist, psychiatrist, or counselor. First, it would be a waste of resources, since the vast majority of clinical problems presented to mental health and counseling services are related to problems in coping with everyday life and are largely unrelated to neurological functioning, at least at our current state of knowledge.

Second, there is a real risk of labeling people as brain damaged because of their failure to perform normally on particular tests. There are numerous reasons for poor performance on psychological tests, only one of which is actual brain damage. In the absence of physical symptoms or a sudden change in behavior it would be an error to assume the cause of poor performance to be brain damage. Furthermore, there is a tendency to assume that identifying a person as brain-damaged solves the clinical problem, and to stop there. This is of course a false assumption, since the goal of the clinician is treatment as well as assessment. Labeling a person as brain-damaged does little in the way of treatment and may actually deter treatment if the label is interpreted as meaning that nothing can be done. Indeed, we have found that the decision to administer and to use neuropsychological information requires a healthy dose of common sense in addition to technical savvy.

REFERENCES

Taylor, L. B. Localisation of cerebral lesions by psychological testing. *Clinical Neurosurgery* 16:269–287, 1969.

Taylor, L. B. Psychological assessment of neurosurgical patients. In T. Rasmussen and R. Marino, eds. *Functional Neurosurgery*. New York: Raven Press, 1979.

CHAPTER 29

LEARNING DISABILITIES

Once upon a time, the animals decided they must do something heroic to meet the problems of a "new world." So they organized a school. They adopted an activity curriculum consisting of running, climbing, swimming, and flying. To make it easier to administer the curriculum, all the animals took all the subjects. The duck was excellent in swimming, in fact better than his instructor. But he made only passing grades in flying and was very poor in running. Since he was slow in running, he had to drop swimming and stay after school to practice running. This was kept up until his web feet were badly worn and he was only average in swimming. But average was quite acceptable, so nobody worried about that—except the duck. The rabbit started at the top of his class in running, but had a nervous breakdown because of so much make-up work in swimming. The squirrel was excellent in climbing but he developed frustrations in flying class because his teacher made him start from the ground up instead of from the treetop down. He developed "charlie horses" from overexertion and he got a C in climbing and a D in running. The eagle was a problem child and was severely disciplined. In climbing classes he beat all the others to the top of the tree, but insisted on using his own way to get there. At the end of the year an abnormal eel that could swim exceedingly well, and also run, climb, and fly a little, had the highest marks and was class valedictorian. The prairie dogs stayed out of school and fought the tax levy because the administration would not add digging and burrowing to the curriculum. They apprenticed their child to a badger and later joined the groundhogs and gophers to start a free school. (Author unknown, but told by Sam Rabinovich)

This fable expresses one view of the challenge for neuropsychology in education. Are learning problems a manifestation of disabilities or individual variation? Large numbers of children enter schools in which they are required to master a core curriculum. Some of them are completely unable to meet any demands of the school system they enter, some learn but only with great difficulty, some have to repeat one or more grades, some graduate but fail to master certain subject areas, and some even graduate without mastering basic knowledge in any area. For those who fail, the educational experience often leaving emotional and attitudinal scars that are carried throughout life. Of course, the difficulties that individuals encounter in school can have any of a number of causes. A child may be disturbed by an unhappy home life, be bored or dislike school, dislike a teacher, have no aptitude for school, have low "intelligence," or have a physical handicap, including brain damage. Some school systems may be equipped to assess these kinds of problems and deal with them objectively. Most have no resources for either assessment or remediation. Whether or not a school system is equipped to deal with the learning problems of an individual, neuropsychology now receives enough publicity that the question of whether a child has a brain or cognitive problem that precludes effective learning will probably rise.

Although neuropsychological assessment can often produce a useful answer to this question, there are general issues that require consideration. If someone has a problem in school, is it because they are not sufficiently intelligent? If they have a problem in a school subject, could it not be that they have a unique brain with propensities for some subjects but not others? Let us consider these issues.

Traditionally, many people have held the view that intelligence is an entity that is normally distributed throughout the population: some people are very intelligent, most are average, and some are retarded. Gould has traced the history of this idea, and he and others have criticized the view that there is an entity "intelligence" that can be measured with tests. Nevertheless, the application of this view in education quite naturally leads to the conclusion that school performance should be normally distributed; that is, some children should do well and others should fail. Fulfillment of this expectation produces no strong desire to label certain children as learning-disabled or to search for new strategies of instruction for those who progress is not excellent. Opposed to this view is the idea that an otherwise normal individual can have a severe disability in learning certain things.

HISTORICAL BACKGROUND

The term *learning disability* is an umbrella label used to refer to a wide variety of school-related problems. The key feature of the term, and one that accounts for its popularity, is the implication that the disability is much like a physical handicap, and were it absent, the individual would be completely normal. A number of formal definitions of learning disabilities have been proposed. They usually include assumptions to the effect that the individual has adequate intelligence, opportunity to learn, adequate instruction, and an adequate home environment, yet still does not succeed. These definitional features are illustrated by the definition of dyslexia devised by the World Federation of Neurology: "A disorder manifested by difficulty in learning to read despite conventional instruction, adequate intelligence, and sociocultural opportunity. It is dependent upon fundamental cognitive disabilities which are frequently of constitutional origin." This is a typical medical diagnostic definition. It assumes a single underlying sort of medical disorder that can be identified and treated. Virtually every phase of this and similar definitions has been disputed. For example, why should it be called a disorder? What is meant by conventional instruction? What is meant by adequate intelligence, and so forth? To appreciate the difficulties with definitions, some of the history of ideas about learning disabilities is helpful.

Aphasiological Origins

Much of the early history of learning disabilities had as its central concern one disability: **dyslexia,** an inability to read properly. The history of dyslexia has been recounted by Critchley, who points out that ideas about dyslexia emerged within an "aphasiological context," supporting the idea that it was due to brain damage occurring in language areas at an early age. In the study of adult-acquired reading disorders, Kussmaul in 1877 is thought to have been the first person to specifically isolate "word blindness"—an inability to read that was caused by brain damage and that persisted in the presence of intact sight and speech. In 1892, Dejerine placed the responsibility for dyslexia on a lesion in the posterior portions of the left hemisphere. The word *dyslexia* was coined by Berlin in 1887. When James Hinshelwood (1895), a Glasgow eye surgeon, and Pringle Morgan (1896), a Seaford general practitioner, first observed students who were incapable of learning to read, they assumed that their reading failed to developed because their prerequisite brain areas were absent or abnormal. It seemed logical to conclude that **developmental dyslexia** (congenital dyslexia) was similar in form to **acquired dyslexia** (dyslexia due to brain damage after reading had been achieved). Developmental deficits in other spheres, such as math, also would be due to some underlying brain problem.

Strephosymbolia

Largely due to the work of Samuel T. Orton in the 1920s and 1930s the aphasiology view was gradually replaced with the belief that it was delayed function, not anatomical absence, that caused the disorder. Orton, the director of a medical clinic in Iowa, noted that dyslexia was correlated with left-handedness and tendencies toward letter and word reversals or inversions when learning to read or write. He termed such dyslexia *strephosymbolia* (form the Greek, meaning twisted symbols). Orton thought that the nondominant hemisphere, which he postulated had a reversed image of things, was excessively dominant or not sufficiently controlled. He also suggested that if the instructor was clever or persevered, education could establish normal dominance and thus normal reading. His concept and term were largely ignored until revived in the 1960s with the growing interest in neuropsychology.

Environment

When sociologists and educational psychologists became interested in learning disabilities, they thought environmental explanations, rather than neurological explanations, could account for dyslexia. This was perhaps motivated by the belief or hope that environmental causes could be reversed more easily than neurological ones. This notion led to a variety of attempts to improve learning through early enrichment programs.

Learning Disabilities

The term *learning disability* had its origins in an address given in 1963 by Samuel A. Kirk. Kirk argued for better descriptions of children's school problems, but he excluded children with sensory handicaps and mental retardation from the children he called learning-disabled. His definition and address were influential because members of his audience got together and formed the "Association for Children with Learning Disabilities," and this society in turn popularized the label. Gaddes has pointed out that it is unfortunate that many subsequent definitions have stressed the exclusion of other disabilities, because this has led to the erroneous belief that learning disabilities can only be present in children with at least average intelligence. He correctly points out that low intelligence and a learning disability may both have the same cause.

The search for labels has resulted in a proliferation of terms that ostensibly attempt to dissociate the learning-disabled from the retarded and brain

TABLE 29-1. "Do-it-Yourself Terminology Generator"

Secondary	Nervous	Deficit
Minimal	Brain	Dysfunction
Mild	Cerebral	Damage
Minor	Neurological	Disorder
Chronic	Neurologic	Desynchronization
Diffuse	CNS	Handicap
Specific	Language	Disability
Primary	Reading	Retardation
Developmental	Perceptual	Deficiency
Disorganized	Impulsive	Impairment
Organic	Visual-motor	Pathology
Clumsy	Behavior	Syndrome
Functional	Psychoneurologic	Complex

Directions: Select any word from first column, add any word from second and third columns. If you don't like the result, try again. It will mean about the same thing.

Source: From Fry, 1968. Reprinted with permission of Edward Fry and the International Reading Association

damaged. In a light vein, Fry published a "Do-It-Yourself Terminology Generator," shown in Table 29-1, to emphasize the proliferation of terms in the field and the inaccuracies in description. From this list about 2000 terms can be fabricated that have been or could be used to describe the syndromes observed.

The Brain Again

Recent developments in neuropsychology are now reviving the popularity of the hypotheses that the brain is causal in many learning disabilities. Ideas of localization and lateralization of function provide the theoretical background for the idea that there will be a lot of variation in the abilities of different individuals. A person may be a good musician but a poor artist, a good writer but a poor mathematician, a good historian but a poor scientist, and so on. A person may also do poorly in every academic sphere but still have talents to be a success in life. If the idea of individual abilities based on individual differences in brain function is accepted, focus is removed from the emphasis on general intelligence and directed toward special skills.

THE INCIDENCE OF LEARNING DISABILITIES

Rutter and Yule have made the assumption that if reading ability were distributed as a normal curve, they would expect to find 2.28% of the school-age population to be retarded in both reading and intelligence. An examination of a large population of children from a number of different studies showed specific reading retardation in 3.5% of 10-year-olds on the Isle of Wight, 4.5% of Isle of Wight 14-year-olds, and over 6% of London 10-year-olds. The number in excess of 2.28% were individuals who were retarded in reading but not in intelligence. On the basis of these data Rutter and Yule argue that there is a "hump" at the lower end of the reading distribution produced by a population of poor readers who do have adequate intelligence but are impaired at reading. They called this group **specifically reading retarded** as compared with **reading-backward.** Rutter and Yule also called attention to some additional differences between those who are specifically reading retarded and those who are backward. Among the reading-backward the sex ratio was equal, but among the specifically reading retarded 76% were boys. In the backward group, 11% had a known brain disorder, but none of the specifically-reading-retarded group had such a condition. The backward group also had a higher incidence of motor, praxic, speech, and other developmental abnormalities. When the developmental progress of the two groups was compared in reading and arithmetic, the specifically-reading-retarded group made less progress in reading and spelling than the backward group, but they made more progress in arithmetic. Rutter and Yule go to some length to point out that specific reading retardation is not the same as dyslexia, as that term is traditionally defined; nevertheless, their central point was that a learning disability that does not involve general retardation exists.

Gaddes tried to determine the proportion of children with learning disabilities as reported in various prevalence studies from both North America and Europe. He found that most estimates of the need for special training for learning disabilities range from between 10 and 15% of the school-age population, although only about 2% actually receive special education.

A problem in collecting prevalence estimates is that a learning disability is an emerging problem. When children enter the first grade, few are as yet learning-disabled. One popular method of defining a learning disability is to use a 2-year cutoff criterion; that is, if an individual is 2 years behind as determined by a standard test, then that individual is learning-disabled. When this criterion is used, then less than 1% of 6-year-olds are disabled, 2% of 7-year-olds are disabled, and so on until at age 19, 25% would be disabled. This emerging incidence occurs because the learning-disabled are falling behind at a rate that is proportional to their degree of impairment. Even these kinds of calculations may be difficult to apply in certain regions. For example, the wide range achievement test (WRAT) is frequently used to determine grade equivalent performance. When Snart and colleagues gave the test to children in Stettler, an Alberta, Canada town with a population of about 5000, they found that the average child performed 2 years ahead of the expected grad norms. That is, a child 2 years behind in that school system would actually be classified as normal by WRAT criteria. Although Siegel disputes the interpretation of the Stettler study, the point is still worth considering. Not all school populations should be expected to be equal.

Another way of collecting estimates could be to ask teachers how many children in their classes are receiving special help and, therefore, could be learning-disabled. Unfortunately, many schools cannot provide such information because they have no resources for special education and so do not use that kind of classification. Myklebust and Johnson suggest that reading (or any other academic skill) can be assessed by deriving a learning quotient based on the child's performance, age, and grade level. Regardless of what measure is used, it may well be necessary to derive norms for performance in any area before fully objective definitions of what constitutes a learning disability for that area can be obtained.

TYPES OF LEARNING DISABILITIES

We would like to provide the reader with a simple classification of learning disabilities along with some estimate of their incidence. All we can say, however, is that the classification and incidence reflect rather well the emphasis placed on appropriate conduct and certain academic specialties in school systems. Good behavior, reading, arithmetic, and spelling are areas of emphasis in all schools, and the classification of learning disability reflects this emphasis. Although art, music, and physical education are taught in most schools, referrals for failure in these areas are extremely uncommon. Were art, and not reading, the core subject in the early years of school, we suspect that current catalogs of types of disabilities would be quite different. These comments are not made entirely tongue in cheek. If one purpose of neuropsychological assessment is to evaluate cognitive function, a restricted emphasis will unquestionably lead to a restricted view about what constitutes the distribution of cognitive function.

There are a number of classifications of learning disabilities, but those in neuropsychology emphasize disorders of reading. In summarizing syndromes presented to a clinic specializing in learning disabilities over a 2-year period, Denckla reports that of 484 children aged 6 to 16, 76% were classified as primarily dyslexic, with or without some associated problems, and 18% were classified as hyperactive. Thus, reading and behavior problems were the commonest reasons for referral. The American Psychiatric Association's *Diagnostic and Statistical Manual of Mental Disorders* (DSM-III) provides a number of classifications of disorders arising in childhood. Excluding mental retardation and mental disorders, the DSM III describes disorders in reading, arithmetic, and motor activity along with some mixed classifications. The U.S. Department of Health, Education, and Welfare identifies 10 characteristics most often cited by various authors as being associated with a learning disability: (1) **hyperactivity;** (2) perceptual-motor impairments; (3) emotional lability (instability); (4) general coordination deficits; (5) disorders of attention (short attention span, distractibility, perseveration); (6) impulsivity; (7) disorders of memory and thinking; (8) specific learning disabilities, including especially those of reading (dyslexia), arithmetic, writing, and spelling; (9) disorders of speech and hearing; and (10) equivocal neurological signs and irregular EEG. It must be noted that not all learning-disabled children exhibit all the symptoms. Critchley points out that for every learning-disabled child with coordination problems, there is a child with better than normal coordination. This as yet insufficiently studied variability underscores the points that not all learning disabilities are the same and that there are presumably multiple causes.

Some authors categorize the learning disabilities into four symptom complexes, which are not mutually exclusive: (1) dyslexia-dysgraphia, (2) motor-perceptual, (3) language delay, and (4) hyperactivity. For the purposes of this chapter we shall concentrate our attention on dyslexia, since it provides a good model for the study of learning disabilities in general and is usually a central school problem of learning-disabled individuals.

CAUSES OF LEARNING DISABILITIES

Five major factors are most frequently cited as possible causes of learning disabilities: (1) structural damage, (2) brain dysfunction, (3) abnormal cerebral lateralization, (4) maturational lag, and (5) environmental deprivation. Although no data unequivocally and totally support any one of these theories, there is reason to believe that all these factors may contribute to disabilities.

Structural Damage

Since the symptoms of brain damage in adulthood resemble childhood learning disabilities (e.g., dyslexia), the cause of learning disabilities may be similar structural damage, perhaps resulting from birth trauma, encephalitis, anoxia, early childhood accidents, and so on — in general, causes similar to those that produce cerebral palsy (Table 12-2). Although no doubt a cause for a small minority of children, structural damage is not likely to be the cause of learning disability in most children, since many neurological symptoms associated with brain damage in adults are not typically observed in children. For example, children with developmental dyslexia do not have hemianopsias or scotomas, which are symptoms that would certainly occur in a large percentage of dyslexic adults. Furthermore, to date EEG and CT studies have not demonstrated structural damage: abnormal EEGs similar to those correlated with known brain damage are not consistently correlated with learning disabilities.

Since clear evidence of brain damage is absent in many children who have learning disorders, Gaddes suggests that they be classified as a group separate from those with brain damage and those with minimal brain damage. He suggests the brain damage classification be reserved for those who have what are called "hard signs," such as brain tumor, bleeding, penetrating injury, and hemiplegia. He suggests that children with minimal brain damage are those who have what are called "soft neurological signs": developmental delay, language retardation, motor clumsiness, perceptual deficits, right-left problems, hyperactivity, poor body image, and poor hand-eye coordination. Children with learning disabilities would be those with none of these signs, but with a specific difficulty in one or more school subjects. Some people may find these distinctions problematical. For educators there is little advantage to the distinction since any group may have a learning disability that requires their special attention. Children with learning disabilities may also have some of the "soft signs" such as left-right confusion but still show no evidence of structural damage. Nevertheless, the classification is worth mentioning because it does direct attention to a conventional view: that is, many learning disabilities do not seem to be accompanied by obvious structural damage.

The idea that structural damage is involved in learning disabilities cannot be dismissed until anatomical studies have been made, at autopsy, on the brains of learning-disabled individuals. At present only a few studies have been reported. Drake examined the brain of a 12-year-old boy who died of cerebral hemorrhage. In school he had been impaired in arithmetic, writing, and reading, but he had normal intelligence. Autopsy showed that there were atypical gyral patterns in the parietal lobes, an atrophied corpus callosum, and neurons in the underlying white matter that should have migrated to the cortex.

Galaburda's group have examined the brain of a 20-year-old man who had previously had a reading disability despite average intelligence. Visual inspection of the brain showed it to be normal, but microscopic examination showed several left hemisphere abnormalities. *Polymicrogyria* (numerous small convolutions) and other architectural abnormalities were found in the left frontal and parietal cortex. The location of abnormal brain regions are shown in Figure 29-1. Subcortical abnormalities occurred in the medial geniculate nucleus and the lateral posterior nucleus of the thalamus of the same individual. This, they suggest, would explain why the intact right hemisphere of this individual had not developed the ability to mediate normal reading. Since this original report, this group has reported similar findings in three additional cases.

Another structural abnormality that may be a cause of reading disabilities may be **arteriovenous malformations.** These consist of aggregates of blood vessels in a rather restricted area of the brain. The results of at least three studies suggest that they are congenital in origin, more common in males than females, often found in the posterior speech regions, and are associated with reading disabilities (See Geschwind and Galaburda).

Although these studies are intriguing, they do not make a convincing case of themselves. First, the number of subjects is small. Second, at least two of the autopsy cases had been epileptic and had displayed other problems at one time, so that neither was a case of a "pure" learning disability. Still, this line of research should provide valuable information in the future. The Orton Dyslexia Society has designated the Galaburda laboratory as a "brain bank" for anatomical research on dyslexia.

Brain Dysfunction

It is not necessary to have direct brain damage to have neurological deficits. As we noted earlier, for example, there is little doubt that schizophrenia results from abnormal brain function, but brain lesions do not produce schizophrenia. Rather, some abnormal physiological or biochemical process is most likely responsible. A similar logic has been applied to the study of learning disabilities: such disabilities may result, not from direct damage, but from malfunction of some portion of the cerebral cortex. Tentative support for this view comes from electrophysiological recording studies associating specific high-frequency EEG abnormalities with various types of learning disabilities. These studies are controversial, however. In a review Hughes concludes that EEG and AEP (average evoked potential) studies of children with learning disabilities are encouraging enough to justify further investigation of these techniques as diagnostic tools, but to date no firm conclusions have been reached.

One view of the brain dysfunction hypothesis holds that the dysfunction results from defective

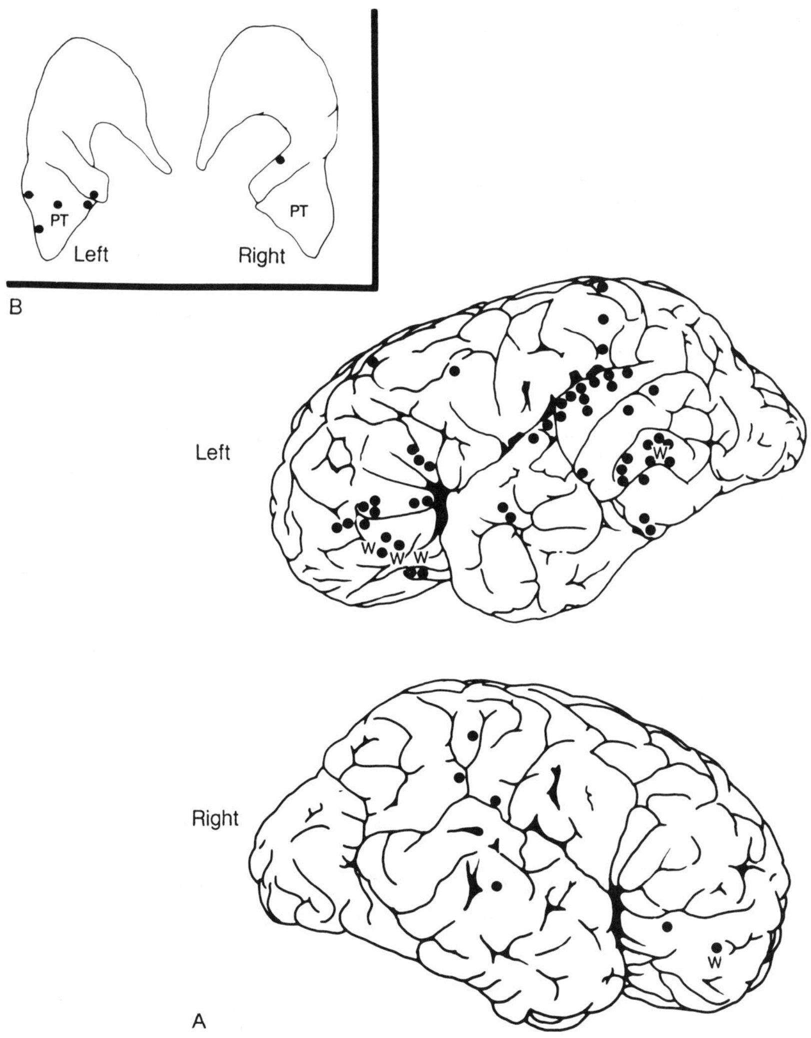

Figure 29-1. *A.* Drawings of the two hemispheres showing with filled circles the location of areas of cell abnormalities in the brain of an individual that was diagnosed as reading-disabled. The inset (*B*) shows a horizontal section of the planum temporale (PT) including Heschl's gyrus (H), to illustrate its (abnormal) symmetrical pattern. The filled circles on the sections indicate areas of cortical anomalies and indicated that the involvement is asymmetrical. W indicates brain warts. (From Geschwind, N. and A. M. Galaburda, 1985, MIT Press.)

"arousal mechanisms." Since the neocortex is normally activated by subcortical structures, it is argued that if the subcortical input were missing or abnormal, then a particular cortical region would dysfunction. This conclusion has been inferred from two principal sources. First, Douglas has found that learning-disabled children have difficulty on continuous-performance tests requiring them to react to particular stimuli while ignoring others. Similarly, reaction-time studies show these children to have slower mean reaction times to signals. On tests of visual searching — in which the child is asked to search among several alternatives to find a picture identical to a standard picture — the learning-disabled children choose impulsively and quickly, making many more errors than normal children, who perform more slowly. Douglas concludes that the deficits on these types of tasks result from some form of inadequate cerebral activation. It could be predicted that learning disabilities, of some types at least, should improve with drugs that increase cerebral activation. This is indeed the case: both amphetamine and caffeine, cerebral stimulants, improve performance on the tests used by Douglas, and they are frequently used effectively in the treatment of hyperactive children.

An alternative dysfunction theory proposes that brain malfunction results from abnormal metabolism, due either to diet or to abnormal metabolic processes. Recent work has shown that if diet is modified — especially if foods containing sugar are reduced — learning disabilities are significantly mitigated. This finding supports the idea that inadequate diet may contribute to learning disabilities by causing abnormal brain function. One difficulty in treating learning disabilities with proper nutrition is that people's needs for various minerals, vitamins, and other nutrients vary widely. It may be that some children require certain nutrients in amounts far exceeding the usual. For example, vitamin D-resistant rickets is a disorder requiring amounts of vitamin D that would be lethal to most people. Although it is conceivable that extremely large amounts of some vitamin or mineral are required in children with learning disorders, the missing factor would be extremely difficult to identify. One study is intriguing in this respect. Analyzing specimens of hair from normal and learning-disabled children, Pihl and Parkes found significant differences between the groups in the levels of sodium, cadmium, cobalt, lead, manganese, chromium, and lithium. When levels of these elements were measured in the hair, it was possible to accurately pick 98% of all the children diagnosed as learning-disabled from a second sample of children. Although Pihl and Parkes could not identify the cause of the abnormal levels of trace elements, their success in diagnosing additional children leads us to seriously consider biochemical factors as causal in learning disabilities.

Abnormal Cerebral Lateralization

A variety of theories rest on Orton's premise that learning disabilities result from reduced or abnormal cerebral lateralization. This premise is based on the assumption that, since language is lateralized in the left hemisphere of most adults, such lateralization must be advantageous, and its absence would be deleterious to the acquisition of language skills. Normal lateralization could be absent for a number of reasons. Orton's explanation of learning disabilities would seem to be easy to evaluate experimentally. For example, if children were divided into two groups (normal and learning-disabled) and then tested for dichotic and visual-field asymmetries, the disabled group should not show asymmetries. In the past 20 years dozens of studies have examined dichotic and visual-field asymmetries in this way, but the data are far from unequivocal. Satz concludes:

> One might ask what light the preceding review of laterality studies sheds, if any, on the problem of cerebral dominance and reading disability. The answer should be — not much. The reason for this somewhat discouraging view lies in the numerous methodological and conceptual problems that continue to plague research efforts in this area. (Satz, 1976, p. 288)

Witelson argues that there may be an association between developmental dyslexia and two neurological abnormalities: a lack of right hemisphere specialization for spatial processing, and a dysfunction in left hemisphere processing of linguistic functions. That is, being located in both hemispheres, spatial functions result in an interference with the left hemisphere's processing of linguistic functions. The person approaches linguistic functions in a visual-holistic manner rather than a phonetic-analytic manner, which would be expected to produce deficits in language but superiority in spatial skills.

Because of current popular interest in hemispheric asymmetry, the belief that impaired cerebral lateralization is the source of problems in learning-disabled children has become attractive. Kinsbourne and Hiscock have been outspoken critics of this theory. Their principal criticism centers on the assumption that reduced lateralization of language should be detrimental to language development and school performance. As discussed in Chapter 16, anomalous language lateralization in left-handers is not consistently correlated with cognitive deficit, nor is left-handedness consistently correlated with learning disability.

The Geschwind-Galaburda Hypothesis

The Geschwind-Galaburda hypothesis is an attempt to account for observed variation in individual brains, individual differences in various abilities, the high incidence of learning disabilities and of exceptional abilities in males, as well as an apparent association of autoimmune disorders in exceptional groups. The hypothesis is that testosterone is released by the male embryo to produce male physical characteristics and also changes brain organization to produce the neural basis of male behavioral characteristics. As a by-product of performing its job it also produces some brain changes that underlie exemplary abilities; it also produces some casualties. An additional aspect of the hypothesis is that among males in general and among males with exceptional abilities there is a high incidence of **autoimmune disorders** (migraines, allergies, asthma, thyroid disorders, ulcerative colitis, etc.). The hypothesis is that testosterone also affects the development of the immune system with the consequence that there is increased susceptibility to autoimmune disorders.

The beginning of this hypothesis lay in Geschwind's observation that the planum temporale (an area thought to represent speech in the left hemisphere) is asymmetrical, being larger on the left and smaller on the right in most right-handers. This asymmetry was proposed to represent the underlying neural asymmetry that gave rise to the left hemisphere's dominant role in language. Since males are thought to show greater deviance from this asymmetrical pattern, the possibility that testosterone played a role was suggested. During embryonic development the male fetal gonads produce high levels of testosterone, levels that are comparable to that of adult males. Levels fall just before birth, and rise and fall again just after birth, to rise yet once more at puberty. It was proposed that the embryonic surges of testosterone delayed the development of the left hemisphere, allowing the right hemisphere both space and time for greater development. Thus, males in general would have some comparatively better developed areas in the right hemisphere which would presumably endow them with superior spatial skills. If the testosterone-induced asymmetry produced some particularly large right hemisphere areas, these could result in special abilities, such as precocious mathematical reasoning. It was also possible, however, that testosterone could result in malformed brain areas, thus producing casualties that include learning disabilities. The developmental abnormalities, of which a putative example is shown in Figure 29-1, would be an example of an anatomical casualty.

The appeal of the Geschwind-Galaburda hypothesis is that it can account for the general observation that females tend to do better at language-related tasks than males, and males tend to do better at spatial tasks than females. It can also account for the high incidence of precocity and the high incidence of learning disabilities among males. The proposed shift in cerebral dominance can also provide an explanation for the high incidence of left-handedness among the precocious and among the learning-disabled. Finally, since the effects of testosterone on the brain will in some ways be paralleled by its effects on the immune system, it accounts for the high incidence of autoimmune disease in the precocious and learning-disabled male populations. In addition, the theory is modifiable to allow deviations in hormonal functions to produce incidences of learning disabilities, precociousness, left-handedness and autoimmune disorders in females. An additional appeal of the hypothesis is that it is testable and allows for the development of animal models.

Despite its superficial attractiveness, the hypothesis has not yet received much in the way of experimental tests or support. Galaburda and coworkers have made a detailed reexamination of the planum temporale asymmetries reported in Geschwind and Levitsky's original study. The key finding was that when there was no asymmetry in the planum temporale, it was not because the area on both sides was small but because both sides were large. When the asymmetry was reversed the size of the areas was also completely reversed. Simply slowing down the development of the left hemisphere would be unlikely to account for this result. Thus, a new hypothesis was favored. It was suggested that in early development both sides are equal and large but as development progressed one or the other side could be reduced in size through the loss of neurons. Testosterone, presumably, would play a deciding role in how this sculpting was to proceed. This new mechanism, however, does not provide the same attractive explanation for the anomalous cell growth observed in the learning-disabled brains (Figure 29-1). Consequently, we feel that this imaginative hypothesis should be accepted as a challenge for future research but not as an adequate current explanation for special abilities or for learning disabilities.

Maturational Lag

The **maturational-lag hypothesis** postulates that cognitive functions involved in language, reading, and other complex behaviors are organized hierarchically, and that the levels in the hierarchy develop sequentially during ontogeny. Should one level of the hierarchy be slow to develop, the entire hierarchy is retarded in development, since higher functions depend on the integrity of lower ones. The delayed maturation of cortical functions could result from a variety of factors: two examples are delayed myelination of a particular region, and slow development of the connections of association regions, which delays the hookup of sensory and motor regions with associative cortex. Although some studies suggest that various functions in learning-disabled children are slow in maturing, the type of study needed here is a careful longitudinal analysis of children tested on a large number of perceptual, motor, and cognitive skills for a period of 10 to 15 years. When learning-disabled children have been reexamined in adulthood, they have been found to still have their characteristic impairments. For example, Frauenheim studied 40 adults who were diagnosed as dyslexic in childhood and found that on test performance and on self-report evaluations they were essentially unchanged from the time of diagnosis. This result does not support the maturational-lag hypothesis.

Environmental Deprivation

The work of Rosensweig and associates has shown that environmental factors can alter the neocortical development of rats. Rats raised in enriched environments have a thicker cortex with increased numbers of dendritic spines than rats raised in impoverished environments. This work implies, then, that the environment in which children are raised may affect behavior indirectly by altering brain development. The notion has considerable appeal and has led to the development of programs such as Operation Headstart. To date there is no unequivocal experimental evidence that environmental factors, short of impoverishment such as that suffered by Genie (Chapter 25), can produce learning disabilities. However, Money has argued in a "feisty" review that institutional confinement, neglect, and child abuse can cause retarded intellectual development and even retardation in physical growth. Accordingly, he states that environmental deprivation should rank high on the list of causes of learning disabilities and should be actively investigated.

A subtle variant of the deprivation hypothesis is called the **birth date effect.** This hypothesis comes from the Barnsley and colleagues' studies on the birth dates of North American hockey players. In senior hockey leagues there is a negative relationship between birth month and number of players. Over 30% of players have birth dates in the first quarter of the year (16% in January), while fewer than 15% have birth dates in the last quarter of the year (5% in December). Furthermore, a disproportionate number of the superstars have first-quarter birth dates. This birth discrepancy is not present in beginning leagues but emerges progressively as players are promoted through the leagues. The explanation of the discrepancy appears straightforward. Players enter the most junior league according to age, a child must be 8 years old between January 1 and December 31 of the year they enter Mite hockey. Equal numbers of children born in each month enter. But, children born in December enter hockey a year earlier than children born in January, who in effect have had to wait a year. The younger smaller children are at a developmental disadvantage from the outset. Throughout their playing career they receive less playing time and reinforcement and thus are more likely to become frustrated, develop a lower expectation of themselves as hockey players, and are more likely to drop out.

Research on the effects of relative age on educational achievement produce similar results. Beattie has reported that children entering school at a younger age achieve significantly less than their older classmates. Both Diamond and Maddux have found that children entering Grade 1 at an early age were more likely than their older classmates to be classified as learning-disabled later on in their school career. Furthermore, Maddux and coworkers have found that among children who are classified as gifted, a larger proportion entered school late than entered school early. This effect may last into later grades and even into university. The rather simple birth date effect stands in sharp contrast to the brain hypotheses and is cause for sober reflection by neuropsychologists when in the process of making a diagnosis.

Do Learning Disabilities Have a Genetic Basis?

Any consideration of the possibility that learning disorders have a genetic basis must recognize some of the obstacles to the demonstration. First, as discussed above, learning disabilities may have many environmental causes, which must be excluded from genetic causes. Since it is not clear in individual cases what a putative cause might be, such exclusions are typically difficult to make. Second, learning disabilities take many forms. At present, criteria for categorizing types of learning disabilities are poorly developed. Third, the incidence of learning disabilities is related to the quality of schooling. Average length of schooling and the demands made by schools on students have undergone rapid change in the past two generations. Thus, it is difficult to compare the reading abilities of many children with those of their parents. Fourth, learning-disabled individuals are typically of average intelligence, as are their parents, and as we shall see, people of strictly average intelligence (that is, full-scale IQs around 100) generally find school difficult. Fifth, the ability to read is itself probably inherited, making it difficult to sort out the contribution made by inherited reading skill as compared with a supposed inherited causal factor underlying a disability.

Despite the difficulties in doing this kind of research, the possibility of genetic causes has been repeatedly raised. As early as 1905, Thomas noted the familial nature of "word blindness," and since then many authors have made reference to the high incidence of learning disabilities within certain families. Two other types of evidence also support the genetic hypothesis. For dyslexia the ratio of about four males to one female is commonly reported (see Critchley for a summary of studies between 1927 and 1968). If only environmental factors were responsible, a more equal sex ratio would be expected. Twin studies also find a higher incidence of dyslexia in identical rather than in fraternal twins. Despite the familial nature of learning disabilities, however, attempts by Defries and Decker and others have not been successful in relating this incidence to any genetic model. Therefore, it is simply not certain that disabilities are inherited.

DYSLEXIA

Reading is a complex business that requires a number of abilities. These include letter-identification skills, phonological skills (converting letters into sounds using certain rules), grapheme skills (the visual gestalt of a word used to access a previously learned sound), sequencing skills in which a number of sounds are analyzed and combined in sequence, and short-term memory skills to retain pieces of information as they are sequentially extracted from written material. Acquired information is also important. Knowledge of words in the form of a **lexicon** (a dictionarylike memory store), containing their meanings, knowledge of the way in which they can be combined, and information about the ideas with which they can be associated are importantly related to reading. Thus, reading is a multiprocess and multistage behavior. As such it is possible, in theory if not in fact, for it to be disrupted in many different ways.

It is generally accepted that reading can be accomplished in one of two ways. Consider the following example, which illustrates the two ways. Imagine that you are reading a novel about a man named Fzylx from Worcester. Let us assume that you have never encountered either the man's name or his hometown before. When you read the names, you would presumably attempt to pronounce the various letters to arrive at a satisfactory pronunciation of the words. Suppose that the next day you overhear two people discussing a novel about a man named Felix from Wooster. At first, you might be struck by the similarity between the plot of your book and theirs, until you realize that they are not actually talking about Fzylx from Worcester! What has happened? When you read Fzylx and Worcester, you encountered two common problems in reading English. First, you had to read a name that is not English and so you have no rules by which to read it. You may feel comfortable with your pronunciation, since it allows you to read it, but you may be wrong. Second, you encounter an irregular word; that is, a word that is not pronounced the way it is spelled. The only way to pronounce this type of word correctly is to memorize it. This type of reading is called **graphemic reading** (sometimes called lexical reading). It can be used for regular words as well, but it must be used for irregular words or words that are not found in English. Incidentally, it is also the way Arabic numerals must be read (e.g., 4) and the way international symbolic road and direction signs must be read. The other way to read is to do what you tried to do with Fzylx and Worcester. You simply convert a letter or group of letters into sounds (phonemes) that will provide the clue to the meaning of the words. Stated differently, the sounds that you get by analyzing letter groups will lead you to the correct pronunciation and you will be able to access your memory, or lexicon, for the meaning and connection of the word. This is known as **phonological reading.**

Bradley and Bryant have suggested that the phonological procedure is used by beginning readers, but that as reading skill is attained the graphemic procedure becomes more important. They suggest that the transition occurs between 6 and 10 years of age. Thus, normal reading initially involves phonological skills and then later becomes dependent on graphemic skills. This may be why many people find it hard to find typographical errors when they proofread. Rather than reading phonologically, they read graphemically and with practice at graphemic reading only part of the word need be read before attention is shifted to the next word. If the spelling error is not within the portion of the word "read," it will not be noticed. As we shall see below, it has been suggested that whereas phonological reading must be a function of the left hemisphere, graphemic reading may be a function of the right hemisphere.

Given that there are two reading processes, two or three different kinds of impairments, which could occur at different ages, should be observed. A child who is incompetent in the phonological procedure will have difficulty in the early stages of reading. A child who is competent in the phonological procedure but who is incompetent in graphemic reading will have difficulty later on. Frith has demonstrated just such types of age-related disabilities among poor readers. It may also follow that a child who is impaired at the first type will be hampered in making the transition to the second type as well. We should note here that by no means would these types of impairments exhaust the types of poor readers. People with a poor short-term auditory memory may not correctly derive the sense of written material they read because they forget the meaning of phrases as they proceed. This type of disability may be particularly obvious at still older ages, once reading material becomes more complex. People with poor long-term memory may not understand the sense of words despite good decoding skills simply because they do not have much information about the meaning of the words. This type of individual would be like English-speaking people who are reading Italian. They would be able to read the words because they know phonetic rules, but they would not understand what they read because they would not know what the words meant. In fact, people who are demented are often just like this. They can read but they understand nothing.

There are three approaches to the analysis of the problems of the dyslexic individual. One is to identify the reading problem without regard to its underlying causes. Such an approach may also give some information about underlying causes, but this is by no means certain. A second approach is to describe and analyze the dyslexic in a variety of different ways, cataloging various symptoms, in order to come to conclusions about underlying causes. A third way is to use neuropsychological assessment procedures, derived from research on adult brain-damaged patients, to evaluate brain and cognitive function in the disabled reader and relate that information to the reading disorder. All three approaches have generated interesting insights into the dyslexic individual, although it would be correct to say that the amount and complexity of the information they have generated is astonishing. As a testament to the cornucopia of theories and findings it might be enlightening to catalog some theories of dyslexia and then to discuss a selected few later on.

Malatesha and Dougan have reviewed studies that provide various subclassifications of dyslexia. They found that 7 studies describe two subtypes, 21 studies describe three subtypes, and 3 studies describe four subtypes. To add to this complexity, most subtypes in most of the different studies are derived in quite different ways, using different assessment techniques and different classification criteria. Some studies emphasize visual and auditory processing differences, some emphasize hemisphere specialization, some emphasize memory difference, some emphasize deficits in certain aspects of reading, whereas others are based on postulated types of brain damage or dysfunction, and so on. It appears to us that the problem of classification and subclassification will remain complex. As we shall describe below, there is a great deal of variation in test performance even in individuals who are reported to have the same type of learning disability. It would seem, therefore, that assessment providing a number of different evaluation criteria combined with counseling directed toward the special problems of each individual will remain the most effective approach for both research and remediation.

Language Analysis

Based on the analysis of reading, writing, and spelling patterns, Boder has proposed that there are three subtypes of dyslexia: dysphonetic, dyseidetic, and dysphonetic-dyseidetic. As we shall discuss, these groups correspond quite closely to those described above that include individuals having a disability in phonological processing, graphemic processing, or a combined deficit of both types.

1. *Dysphonetic*. The **dysphonetic** subgroup is the largest (>60%). These types of reading-disabled individuals are thought to have a disability in developing phonic- and word-analysis skills; that is, they are unable to decode written words or to write them using phonic or sound principles. They recognize the words on the basis of visual patterns and confuse words with similar visual patterns (e.g., diesel and dress) or meanings (e.g., planet and moon).

2. *Dyseidetic*. **Dyseidetic** individuals have deficits in recognizing words by their visual configurations, but they are able to use phonic skills to read them or render a relatively correct spelling. They have difficulty in developing a sight vocabulary. Their misreadings involve phonic renditions (talc for talk) as do their misspellings (laf for laugh).

3. *Dysphonetic-Dyseidetic*. This group consists of individuals who combine both types of deficits and are unable to develop either a sight or a phonic vocabulary. They are essentially alexic.

The three groups are discerned by using a diagnostic screening test that assesses their ability to discriminate between known and unknown words. The Boder classification is similar to a number of other classifications, particularly that of Johnson and Myklebust, who also divide dyslexics into subgroups with primary impairments in visual processing (recognizing words by sight) and auditory processing (recognizing words by sound). The approach is also similar to that devised by Coltheart and others, which is described in Chapter 22 and illustrated in Figures 22-7 and 22-8. The models were initially designed to analyze acquired dyslexia, they can be applied equally well to developmental dyslexia.

The reading tests described to this point depend on the fact that some education in reading has taken place. Bradley and Bryant have developed an interesting approach that is initially reading-independent. They have tested children's ability in sound categorization before they started to read. The tests involve giving the child three or four words and asking him or her to pick out the word that does not share a phoneme in common with the others. For example, in the series "hill, pig, and pin," *hill* would be the correct choice; in the series "cot, pot, and hat," *hat* would be the correct choice, and in the series "pin, bun, and gun," *pin* would be the correct choice. They found that when the same children were older and had started to learn to read, those who were initially poor at sound categorization were those who became backward in reading and spelling. They argue that the initial insensitivity to rhyme and alliteration is causal to subsequent reading impairment, because if the children who were initially impaired were given special training on rhyme and alliteration, their reading was far less impaired after training in reading began. According to Bradley and Bryant, at least one cause of reading deficiency would be a basic deficiency in phonological awareness.

It is possible that children who are at risk for learning disabilities could be detected still earlier. Frith has suggested that articulation in babies' babbling may give clues about those who are at risk. Tees and Werker have reported that young infants can detect differences between all known speech sounds, but as they acquire language their detection abilities become restricted to only those sounds used in their own language, which they are exposed to daily. It is possible, according to Tees and Werker, that the acquisition of language-related discrimination may be retarded or poorly developed in those who are at risk for learning disabilities. Should these possibilities prove cor-

TABLE 29-2. Deficits associated with dyslexia

Deficit	Reference
Asymmetry	Gordon, 1980; Orton, 1925, 1937; Silver and Hagen, 1982
Attention	Douglas, 1976
Auditory and visual	Myklebust and Johnson, 1962; Wepman, 1960, 1961
Cerebellar-vestibular	Ayres, 1978; Frank and Levinson, 1976; Levinson, 1980
Development	Critchely, 1964; Staz et al., 1971; Satz and Sparrow, 1970
Dichotic listening	Bryden, 1970; Zurif and Carlson, 1970
Dyschrometria (time-telling)	Myklebust and Johnson, 1962
EEG	Ahn et al., 1980; Duffy et al., 1980; Maccario et al., 1982
Eye movements	Pavlidis, 1981; Pirozzolo and Rayner, 1977; Zangwill and Blakemore, 1972
Intersensory integration	Birch, 1962; Birch and Belmont, 1965
Memory	Myklebust and Johnson, 1962; Lyle, 1968
Motor	Orton, 1937; McFie, 1952
Naming or fluency	Denckla, 1972; Denckla and Rudel, 1976; Eakin and Douglas, 1971; Perfetti and Hogaboam, 1975; Spring, 1976
Orientation (left-right, etc.)	Benton, 1959; Myklebust and Johnson, 1962
Rhythmic movements	Bradley and Bryant, 1983; Klicpera et al., 1981
Serial ordering	Bakker, 1972; Corkin, 1974
Spatial frequency	Lovegrove et al., 1980
Spatial-general	Witelson, 1974
Speech-motor sequencing	Frith, 1981
Temporal sequencing	Johnson and Mykelbust, 1967
Topographic (map-reading)	Myklebust and Johnson, 1962
Verbal	Jorm, 1979; Vellutino, 1977
Visuomoter (letter reversals, etc.)	Orton, 1925, 1937
Visual processing	Lyle and Goyen, 1975
WAIS (verbal-performance)	Reed, 1967; Huelsman, 1970
WAIS (subtests)	Graham and Kamano, 1958; Hunter and Johnson, 1971; Rugel, 1974; Lyle and Goyen, 1969

rect, remediation in the use of phonic skills, such as that suggested by Bradley and Bryant, could be begun as early as the first year of life.

Analysis of Correlated Deficits

On the surface it might be hoped that reading deficits would display themselves in a straightforward manner. This seems not to be the case, because it has long been known that dyslexic individuals have a wide variety of different symptoms that occur in clusters and that vary considerably between individuals. We cannot discuss each of the many peculiar symptoms here, but for the reader's information they are listed in Table 29-2 along with some relevant references. Note, we do not pretend that this list is complete. We suggest that these symptoms should not be thought of as necessarily uninformative, unrelated, or irrelevant. On the basis of the simplest postulate, they might all be produced by a common underlying deficit. We need only turn to the description of the symptoms of Parkinson's disease, which although many and complex are produced by the absence of only a few types of brain cells containing the neurotransmitter dopamine, for reassurance that complex symptoms do not invariably indicate complex underlying causes. Dyslexia may be associated with many kinds of symptoms because language has a superordinate role in the control of behavior, because there is an intimate relation between the control of language and the control of movement, and because development of dyslexia itself may produce secondary symptoms. Just the same, attempts have been made to see if the various symptoms are causally related to dyslexia. Rutter and Yule suggest that clumsiness and incoordination; difficulties in the perception of spatial relations; directional confusion; right-left confusion; disordered temporal orientation; difficulties in naming colors and recognizing the meaning of pictures; inadequate, inconsistent, or mixed cerebral dominance; bizarre spelling; and a family history of reading difficulties do seem related to dyslexia, but it is not clear that the relation is causal. On the other hand, they conclude that low intelligence and mixed-handedness are definitely not important as causal factors. Vellutino has specifically asked which of the capacities of visual perception and visual memory, intersensory integration, temporal order and recall, and verbal processing are of central importance to reading. On the basis of a review of the available research and logical argument, he finds that only a deficit in verbal processing is causally related to dyslexia. He suggests that many of the other deficits occur because tests require verbal processing for their solution. When the verbal component of the test is removed, there is improvement or even normalcy. There have also been suggestions that eye movement deficits are causal to dyslexia. Pirozzolo and Hansch have reviewed this literature and argue that it is unlikely that eye movement problems cause dyslexia, but they do admit that for some dyslexics eye-movement abnormalities may be part of the underlying pathology that complicates dyslexia.

In summary, the consensus about correlated deficits is that they are not causal to dyslexia. Some may themselves be symptoms of the underlying pathology, some may compound the disability, and some may produce other kinds of learning disabilities, but dyslexia seems to be due to some abnormality in language-related brain systems. Vellutino concludes that the normal reader should be seen as a verbal gymnast who can use a variety of devices for reading, whereas the impaired reader does not have this repertoire.

NEUROPSYCHOLOGICAL EVALUATION

When the neuropsychological approach is adopted, it generally contains the following assumptions. (1) A disability may exist in only one or a few spheres of endeavor. (2) A specific disability or skill can be detected using a neuropsychological testing procedure. (3) If one method or strategy of instruction is unsuccessful, another might be more successful. (4) It should be possible to predict a strategy for remediation of a learning disability from the neuropsychological test results. Although none of these assumptions has yet received anything like adequate scientific support, at least one reason that neuropsychology is becoming a popular approach is that the assumptions do hold out more hope for helping learning-disabled children than does the view that they are simply not intelligent enough to succeed. Even if neuropsychology offers no help in remediation, however, it may still be useful for purposes of counseling. The case of Ms. P. illustrates this point. For Ms. P. it was not a cure for her problems, or a substitute for other types of therapy, but it did provide her with information about her problems that she had been unable to obtain elsewhere.

Ms. P., a 19-year-old woman, was referred to us by a friend of hers. She was working as a nurse's aide and had found her work so enjoyable that she was considering entering a nursing program. However, she had not completed high school and generally had a poor academic record. She came to us for guidance as to whether or not she could handle the nursing program. In discussing her academic record we learned that Ms. P. had particular difficulty with language skills, and her reading was so poor that she was unable to pass the written exam for a driver's license. In view of Ms. P's real interest in further education in nursing we decided to administer reading tests plus a complete neuropsychological battery to see if the requisite cognitive abilities were present. The results showed an overall IQ on the WAIS of 85, but there was a 32-point spread between her verbal IQ of 74 and her performance IQ of 106—a difference so large as to suggest that her left hemisphere was functioning very poorly at best. Her performance on specific tests of left hemisphere function confirmed this hypothesis, because her verbal memory, verbal fluency, spelling, reading, and arithmetic skills were extremely poor. On the other hand, her spatial skills were good, as were her nonverbal memory and her performance on tests such as the Wisconsin Card-Sorting and Semmes Body-Placing Tests. In short, her language skills were those of a 6-year-old although she had attended school for 11 years. This verbal ability contrasted with her other abilities, which were normal for a person of her age.

In view of the test results we explained to Ms. P. our belief that it was unlikely that she could handle a nursing program because of her deficient language skills. We believed also that she was unlikely to develop these skills, especially since—as we inadvertently discovered—none of her five brothers and sisters could read either! We explained to Ms. P. that she was by no means retarded, but that just as some people had poor musical ability, she had poor verbal ability. (Further, we were able to arrange an aural administration of the driver's tests, which she passed.) Finally, we explained Ms. P.'s problem to her husband, a well-educated man with a master's degree. In the short time they had been married he had become totally frustrated with her inability to balance the bank account, read recipes, and so forth and was beginning to believe his wife was either "crazy or retarded." They now had an understanding of their problem, and hopefully would be able to work out domestic routines to minimize its impact. Unfortunately, we subsequently learned that the marriage did not last.

Neuropsychological assessment should offer insight into the abilities of individual learning-disabled children because it assesses performance on a wide range of tests sensitive to all areas of brain function. Usually children are not dyslexic or dyscalculic alone but have a number of associated symptoms. Teachers and parents are usually unaware of the associated deficits, and once the deficits are explained, it is often easier for both to understand the nature of the handicaps. The tests should also be able to distinguish between children who have central reading impairments and those who have problems caused by emotional or environmental causes. Consideration of individual test results should also give some suggestions for strategies for special instruction. Details about the application of various neuropsychological assessment procedures can be obtained from reviews such as those by Denckla; Gaddes; and Rourke. Perhaps the most obvious question that should be asked about such an application is whether tests derived from studies on adult brain-damaged populations are applicable to children. Our own studies on dyslexic children suggest that they are applicable, provided that some care in interpretation is taken.

There have been many studies on the IQ test results of learning-disabled children. Rugel has summarized the results from studies that included a total of 1521 reading-disabled children and 554 control children. We have produced a graphic representation of these results in Figure 29-2. The dyslexic group displays low subscale scores on four tests: arithmetic, coding, information, and digit span. This profile, typical in many studies, is referred to as the "ACID" profile. Dyslexic children typically have a mean full-scale IQ that averages about 7 points lower than that of control children, but their mean IQ is roughly 100. Whishaw and Kolb have found that children over 8 show the ACID profile, whereas those younger than 8 may often not show a deficit in the information or arithmetic subscales. This suggests that these deficits in older children and adults are secondary to the underlying impairment that produces dyslexia. Performance on both tests will depend on acquisition of school-related skills, so that it seems reasonable that if school performance is deficient, deficits will emerge as the children fall behind. Deficits in coding and digit span may be more directly related to the underlying impairment that produces dyslexia. We should point out that some studies do

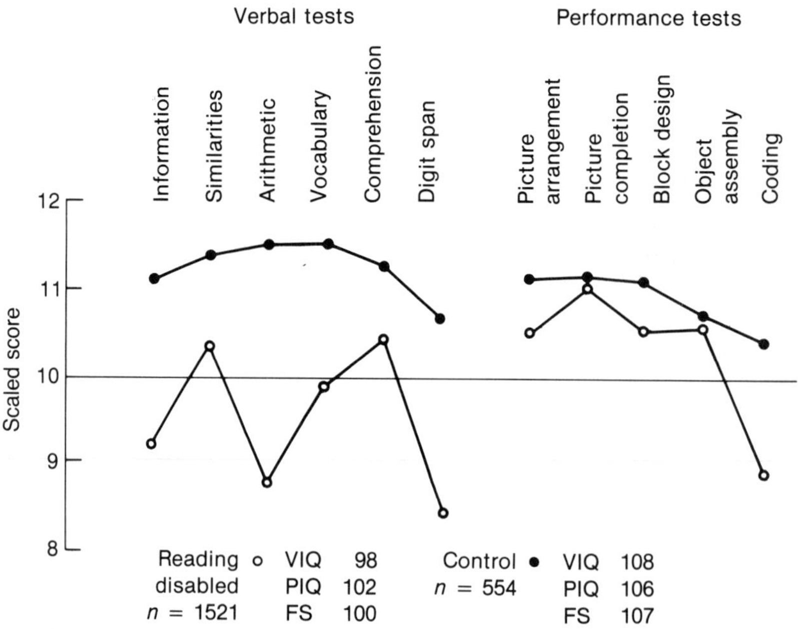

Figure 29-2. Intelligence test profiles of developmentally dyslexic and control subjects. Note the low scores on arithmetic, coding, information, and digit span referred to as the ACID profile. (VIQ, verbal IQ: PIQ, performance IQ; FS, full-scale IQ) (From Rugel, 1974; after Whishaw and Kolb, 1984.)

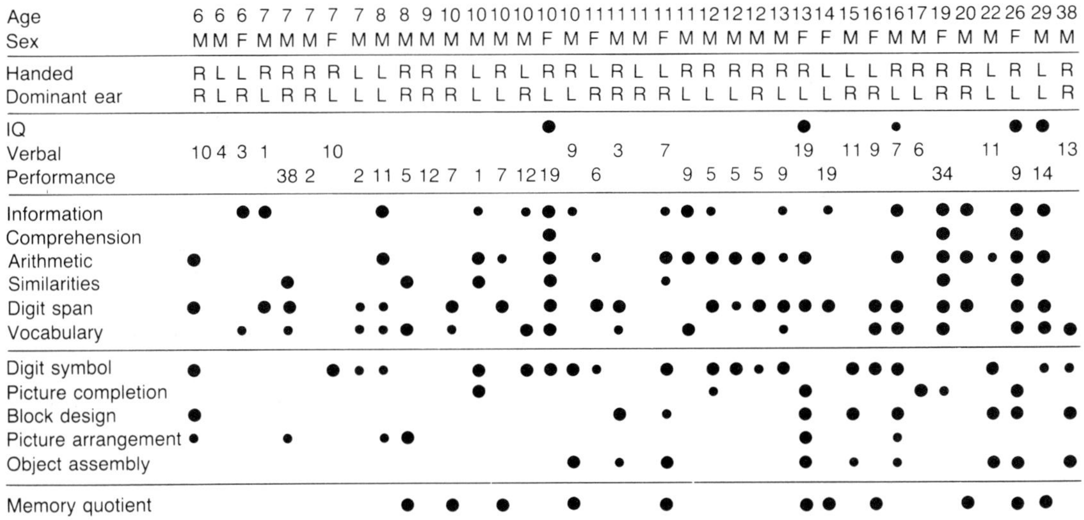

Age 6 6 6 7 7 7 7 7 7 8 8 9 10 10 10 10 10 10 10 11 11 11 11 11 11 12 12 12 12 13 13 14 15 16 16 16 17 19 20 22 26 29 38
Sex M M F M M M F M M M M M M M M F M F M M F M M M M M F F M F M M F M M F M M
Handed R L L R R R R L L R R R L R L R R L R L L R R R R R R L L L R R R R L R L R
Dominant ear R L R L R R L L L R R R L L R L L R R R R L L L R L L L R R L L R R L L L R
IQ
Verbal 10 4 3 1 10 9 3 7 19 11 9 7 6 11 13
Performance 38 2 2 11 5 12 7 1 7 12 19 6 9 5 5 5 9 19 34 9 14
Information
Comprehension
Arithmetic
Similarities
Digit span
Vocabulary
Digit symbol
Picture completion
Block design
Picture arrangement
Object assembly
Memory quotient

Figure 29-3. Scatter in WISC performance and age, sex, and handedness for developmentally dyslexic subjects. Large dots show scores one standard deviation below the population norm; small dots, scores three-quarters of a standard deviation below the population norm. Note the scatter on the subtest scores. (After Whishaw and Kolb, 1984.)

not find emerging deficits on these tests; the different results may be related to the dyslexic population studied or the age groups included in the study. Lyle and Goyen did not find emerging deficits in information and arithmetic, but the impairments they did find were not pronounced and the groups included in the study were quite young. We feel that the age-related trends are important if the Wechsler Intelligence Scale for Children (WISC) test pattern is used for diagnosis. First, it explains commonly observed IQ decreases that are found when children are tested before 8 years of age and again when they are older. Second, it suggests that the values of the WISC patterns are less useful for the diagnosis of very young children.

Although the IQ of dyslexic children is average, typically very high scores are not found. In a group of 30 children and adults we found only 2 individuals with full-scale IQs as high as 114. This makes it difficult to find adequate control groups with which to compare dyslexic children. Whishaw and Kolb used two control groups, one consisting of children who were referred for testing because they had poor grades and the other consisting of children who were selected from classes because their school performance was strictly average; that is, they had no failing grades and no grades that were above average. The poor-grades group had a mean IQ of 110 and the average-grade groups had a mean IQ of 120. This result may be idiosyncratic to the study area, but it does have implications for counseling. In most Canadian school systems an average IQ of about 110 seems prerequisite for high school graduation and an average IQ of about 115 seems prerequisite for university entrance. Thus, in addition to their specific disability, the dyslexic groups will be at a disadvantage compared with their classmates regarding their potential for school success — a point that should be considered when advising parents and schools about remedial instruction and future prospects.

Many researchers have commented that there

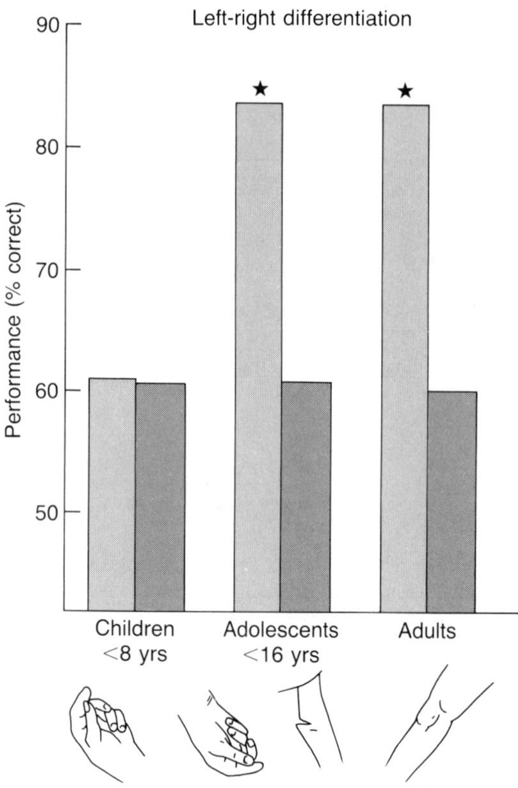

Figure 29-4. Performance on the left-right discrimination test by control (light bars) and dyslexic (dark bars) subjects. Stars signify significant group differences (After Whishaw and Kolb, 1984.)

are large verbal-performance IQ differences in dyslexic individuals, and it has been suggested that two different types of dyslexics can be identified on the basis of these scores. In addition, Denckla has pointed to the "scatter" of the IQ subscores. Figure 29-3 illustrates both of these features in a population of dyslexics ranging in age from 6 to 38. The figure also gives information about handedness, dominant ear on a dichotic-listening test, and Wechsler Memory Quotient. Although verbal-performance differences and scatter of subtest results are a feature of this group, Whishaw and Kolb were unsuccessful in organizing these results into meaningful subgroups. Nevertheless, for the experienced counselor the pattern displayed by any individual may be meaningful.

In comparing the dyslexic group to the control groups on other tests of our composite test battery, it was found that the tests did discriminate between the two groups, but their effectiveness was dependent in part on the individual's age. This age-dependent effect was clear in three different tests. In the test of left-right differentiation (Figure 29-4) neither control nor dyslexic children were able to score above chance if they were younger than 8. After the age of 8 the control children performed well, but the dyslexic groups continued to perform at chance. Another kind of emerging difference was found on tests of word fluency, in which variations did not occur at younger than 8 years but became increasingly large in older age groups (Figure 29-5). This result seems to suggest that control children show increasingly improved fluency performance, but the dyslexic group remains almost static. A third pattern was obtained on the Semmes Body-Placing Task. Here, significant group differences only emerged in adults, and then they seemed to depend on the fact that adult control subjects displayed virtually perfect performance on the tests. The results of these various tests suggest to us that although the tests can be applied to children with some success, a great deal of caution in interpretation is required for the younger children, and retesting at different ages is worthwhile.

The overall performance of dyslexic subjects on tests of our composite test-battery is illustrated in Figure 29-6. This summary shows performance on tests sensitive to left and right hemisphere function and to the function of different lobes. The measures represent standard deviations below performance of the control group. It is noteworthy that some deficits appear on all tests except the Wisconsin Card-Sorting Test and the Mooney Faces Test — tests thought to be sensitive to frontal lobe and right parietal function, respectively.

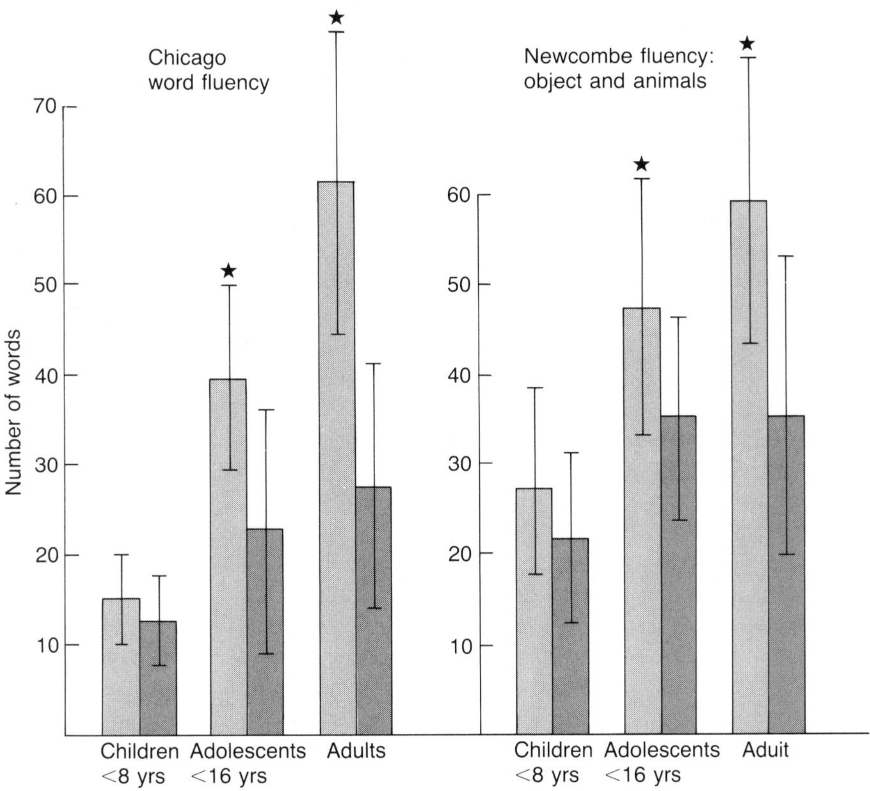

Figure 29-5. Performance (mean and standard deviations) on Chicago Word-Fluency and Newcombe Objects-and-Animals Fluency Tests by control (light bars) and dyslexic (dark bars) subjects. Stars signify significant group differences. (After Whishaw and Kolb, 1984.)

The largest overall deficits occurred on tests of left-right discrimination, paired-associate learning, verbal IQ, memory quotient, word fluency, and performance IQ. The common feature of these tests is that they are sensitive to the function of the parietal lobes, particularly the left parietal lobe.

THE NEURAL BASIS OF DYSLEXIA

There are a number of hypotheses about what neural abnormalities cause dyslexia. One view, articulated most emphatically by Jorm, is that dyslexia is caused by a genetically based dysfunction of the left inferior parietal lobule. This argument is based on the assumption that the major problem encountered by dyslexics is that of accessing the meaning of written words via phonological recoding. Jorm's hypothesis is not inconsistent with some long-standing views of dyslexia, but support for it as an exclusive hypothesis would require that other kinds of damage in the left hemisphere could not produce dyslexia and also that dyslexia could not be caused by damage to the right hemisphere. Of course, unequivocal answers about what other

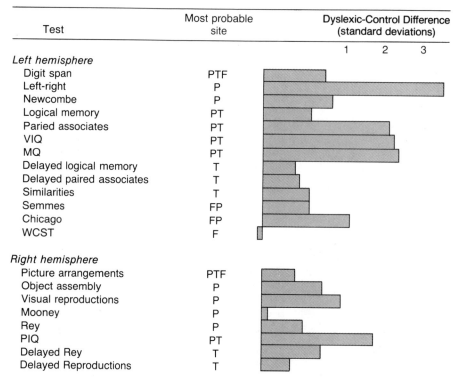

Summary of Relative Performance

Test	Most probable site
Left hemisphere	
Digit span	PTF
Left-right	P
Newcombe	P
Logical memory	PT
Paried associates	PT
VIQ	PT
MQ	PT
Delayed logical memory	T
Delayed paired associates	T
Similarities	T
Semmes	FP
Chicago	FP
WCST	F
Right hemisphere	
Picture arrangements	PTF
Object assembly	P
Visual reproductions	P
Mooney	P
Rey	P
PIQ	PT
Delayed Rey	T
Delayed Reproductions	T

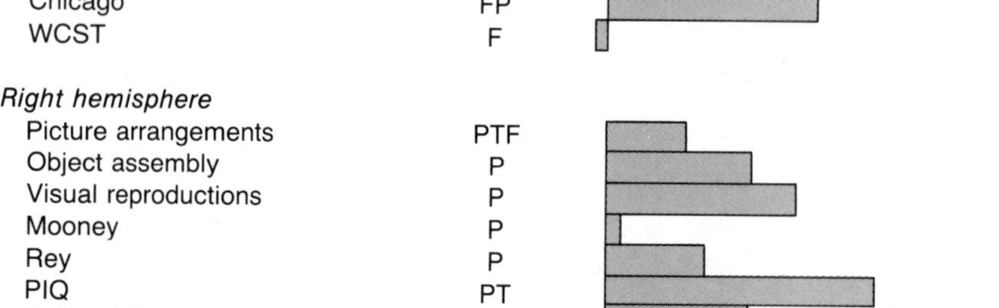

Figure 29-6. Summary of performance of developmentally dyslexic and control groups. Left, theoretical relation between tests and hemisphere; middle, theoretical relation between tests and lobes; right, deficit (standard deviations) in dyslexic group as contrasted with a control group. (After Whishaw and Kolb, 1984.)

areas of the brain might contribute to dyslexia cannot be given, but other possibilities cannot be excluded. It is worth noting here that the traditional view holds that language function resides almost exclusively in the left hemisphere. Therefore, it is usual to assign language disabilities to abnormalities in the left hemisphere and to assign residual language capacities that survive brain damage to the remaining portions of the left hemisphere. There is, however, some evidence that the right hemisphere does have significant language abilities and that language capacities surviving left hemisphere damage may be the product of the right hemisphere. If both of these possibilities are realities, then they open other avenues for understanding dyslexia. First, if the right hemisphere does have language abilities, damage to it could cause a reading impairment resulting in a form of dyslexia. Second, if the right hemisphere has language abilities, the reading that survives left hemisphere damage may be the product of the right hemisphere and not the product of residual parts of the left hemisphere. Since these options provide some interesting possibilities for understanding some of the symptoms of dyslexia, we shall briefly review some of the evidence supporting the hypothesis for right hemisphere language.

Coltheart, in reviewing evidence for right hemisphere language, suggests that if the right hemisphere is questioned in a subtle way, evidence that it has language abilities is found. If it is simply asked to read or speak, it displays no language abilities at all. He and his colleagues have examined the reading abilities of patients who had received extensive damage to both the posterior and anterior speech zones of the left hemisphere. These patients display a fascinating reading syndrome called **deep dyslexia.** When asked to read words, they make semantic errors (e.g., *play* for *act, close* for *shut),* visual errors (e.g., *queue* for *quiz, duel* for *deuce),* and derivation errors (e.g., *wisdom* for *wise, born* for *birth),* and they are completely unable to derive phonology from print or to effectively read low-imagery words or function words. As an example of a disability with function words, a patient could read *fly* when it appeared in the sentence, "The fly buzzed in my ear," but could not read it when it appeared in the sentence, "The bird will fly away." Coltheart suggests that these errors in reading are not produced by residual portions of the left hemisphere because all the symptoms appear together as a group in all the patients, irrespective of the location of the left hemisphere brain damage. He suggests then that the patients are reading with their right hemisphere and the errors that they make reveal something about the way the right hemisphere deals with language. The errors suggest that the right hemisphere reads using graphemic procedures, hence the visual errors; its comprehension is limited to concrete words, hence the derivational errors; and its analytical capacities are largely associational, hence the categorically correct semantic errors.

Support for Coltheart's view comes from at least one other study on focally brain-damaged patients, but one in which the patients had damage that was largely restricted to Broca's area. Langmore and Canter suggest that the spelling errors of the Broca's area patients are attributable to the graphemic-spelling strategy of the right hemisphere.

One other line of research also suggests that the right hemisphere has a certain form of language ability. Zaidel has made an extensive study of patients with corpus callosum sections. These patients have two intact hemispheres but the language abilities of each hemisphere can be examined separately by presenting words or other stimuli to each hemisphere selectively. Zaidel's experiments are comprehensive and cannot be reported here in detail, but they demonstrate that the right hemisphere is largely mute, has no short-term verbal memory, and cannot read phrases, but can read simple concrete words using grapheme cues. The left hemisphere, in contrast, can perform graphemic-to-phonetic conversions, perform grammatical analysis, read phrases, and has short-term verbal memory, but it seems least specialized for semantic analysis. Zaidel suggests that these findings are applicable to understanding the underlying problems of learning-disabled children. Specifically, analysis of the disabilities of dyslexic children should reveal groups who function either with the right hemisphere or the left hemisphere, resembling the callosal-sectioned patients in some of their reading disabilities.

If we accept the evidence from these three lines of research, it seems logical to conclude that both hemispheres in normal individuals may be involved in reading. The left hemisphere does phonological and grammatical analysis, whereas the right hemisphere is involved in graphemic analysis and the extraction of certain kinds of semantic information. Interestingly, Pirozzolo and Rayner, using a tachistoscopic study, have even suggested that the visual system segregates these two types of information as reading progresses. They suggest that during normal reading, foveal vision (from the center of the retina) is used by the left hemisphere for phonetic decoding, while peripheral vision is used by the right hemisphere for graphemic decoding. The dual-process notion also suggests to us that damage to either the right or the left hemisphere could produce dyslexia, but that its characteristics after each type of damage might be different. It is possible, however, that things could be even more complex than this because any hypothetical damage is thought to occur early in life, thus permitting the brain to make various adjustments as maturation proceeds. Also, dyslexic individuals have a variety of associated symptoms, which often differ from one individual to another. In the following sections we shall speculate on three neural models that might be relevant to explanations of dyslexia. All three models include the assumption that verbal language will be preserved irrespective of the type of damage to either cortex because speech acquisition takes place very early in life. Reading may not receive a similar priority for sparing, since its acquisition occurs relatively late in life.

In Chapter 25 we described the language abilities of people who had received surgical removal of the left or right hemisphere when they were very young. The studies of Dennis show that although either hemisphere can learn to speak, there are language deficits that suggest there are constraints on the skills that each hemisphere is able to acquire. Stated simply, the isolated left hemisphere shows superior performance in dealing with the meaning of words and their sound structure, whereas the right hemisphere shows superior performance when dealing with the visual structure of words. If one takes an extreme position and assumes that dyslexic individuals have unilateral impairments as severe as those of patients who have undergone hemispherectomies, it can be postulated that there are two types of dyslexics. One group would have language completely lateralized on the left, and this group would be impaired at graphemic reading. They would be able to read regular words and show no impairments in the early stages of reading, but they would show impaired sight reading when older and would not be able to read or spell irregular words. They would also be impaired in decoding numbers and other symbols that cannot be translated into phonetic form. The second group would have language completely lateralized to the right. They would be impaired at phonological reading and would have trouble converting letters into sounds using phonetic rules. They would be impaired in initial attempts to acquire phonological reading but would eventually be able to recognize words and symbols, such as numbers, by sight. Interestingly, these two groups would correspond to Boder's dyseidetic and dysphonetic types of dyslexics.

Of course, this extreme hypothesis does not correspond to what is known about dyslexia. Dyslexic individuals do have two intact hemispheres, but if they have subtle damage to either the left or the right hemisphere, something like the impairments given in this description might be true. It is likely, however, that their speech organization is more complex. In Chapter 25 we described the organization of language in people who received cortical damage prior to age 5. Recall that Rasmussen and Milner found that these people could be divided into three groups: in the first, speech was in the right hemisphere, in the second, speech was in the left hemisphere, and in the third, speech was represented bilaterally. The last group could be further subdivided depending on which of the two speech zones was shifted to the opposite hemisphere. Using this model it could be postulated that there are more than two kinds of dyslexia. Two types, a left or a right hemisphere type, might be similar to those described above. Other types would include individuals in whom the left posterior zone was shifted to the right, who would be poor at phonetic reading (assuming the phonetic analysis is a function of the posterior cortex); and individuals in whom the anterior zone had shifted to the right, who would be poor at phonetic spelling (assuming that language production is a function of the anterior cortex).

There is still a third possibility, one that might be the most plausible, although it also does not exclude either model described above. These might be individuals in whom speech is "normally" lateralized but who have weaknesses in, rather than the complete loss of, one or another speech zone. For these individuals the brain areas involved in reading would be those that are used by normal readers, but there would be a range of abnormalities from subtle to severe depending on the extent of the anatomical abnormality. Their deficits would not be absolute, but proportional to the demands made on reading abilities.

We can represent these various possibilities in the form of a table (Table 29-3). For the purposes of example, we have assumed that phonetic reading is performed by the left posterior hemisphere and phonetic spelling is done by the left anterior hemisphere, whereas graphemic reading is done by the right posterior hemisphere and graphemic spelling is done by the right anterior hemisphere. Using this example, it can be seen that there are a variety of deficits that can occur depending on the site of any anatomical abnormality. Some other symptoms of dyslexia might also be generated using this model. If one assumes, for example, that handedness is specified in most people by the function of the left posterior cortex, then it can be seen that for some types of dyslexia there might be alterations in handedness. In fact, depending on what kind of function one might like to attribute to any particular brain region, hypotheses for most types of learning disabilities, including their associated symptoms, could be derived from this type of model. We emphasize, however, that we do not present this model as dogma, but simply as an example of how the characteristics of various learning disabilities might be understood.

TABLE 29-3. Model of reading and spelling abilities associated with different types of neural organization

Neural structure present	Reading-spelling performance
Left hemisphere only	Phonetic reading and spelling
Right hemisphere only	Grapheme reading and spelling
Broca left; Wernicke right	Phonetic spelling — grapheme reading
Wernicke left; Broca right	Phonetic reading — grapheme spelling
Weak left or right Broca	Poor phonetic or grapheme spelling
Weak left or right Wernicke	Poor phonetic or grapheme reading

ADULT OUTCOME OF LEARNING DISABILITIES

There are a variety of views about the outcome of children with learning disabilities. The most optimistic study is reported by Critchley, in which 20 dyslexic boys attended a private school and received special instruction according to the Orton-Gillingham-Stillman method. This group eventually produced two medical doctors, one college professor, one lawyer, two research scientists, six owners or managers of businesses, one school principal, three teachers, one actor, one factory foreman, and one skilled laborer. There are some reports in the popular press of similar, though perhaps not such absolute, success of various private schools for learning-disabled individuals. The majority of these studies do not report such optimistic outcomes and the most thorough of them gives frankly pessimistic results about academic outcome. Spreen has examined the progress of 203 learning-disabled individuals over a 10-year period. The sample included a group that was diagnosed as learning-disabled with no neurological impairments, a group diagnosed as minimally brain damaged, and a group that had definite brain damage. The learning-disabled group were compared with 52 control individuals. The following conclusions derive from the assessments, personal interviews, parental interviews, and other observations made of these groups.

1. Typically the control group fared better than the learning-disabled group, who fared better than the minimally brain-damaged group, who fared better than the definitely brain-damaged group in all areas of assessment. Spreen argues that this has important implications since educators may not think that the presence or absence of neurological impairments is relevant to the outcome of school

programs. It was also found that all three handicapped groups were inferior to the control group in all areas of study including art and physical education. They also had a poorer attitude toward school.

2. Individuals in all but the control group suffered through a miserable and usually short school career and then suffered a miserable social life full of disappointments and failures. They also had a relatively poor chance for advanced training and skilled employment. They did not, however, have a higher incidence of juvenile delinquency or psychiatric problems.

3. Interviews with subjects and their parents gave similar factual information about their situation. Parents, however, tended to report more serious effects on the well-being, happiness, and social interaction of their children than were reported by the children. The children also had less clear memories of their childhood than the control children. As the subjects aged they developed firmer plans for their future and made better occupational adjustments, but they also gave increasingly poorer impressions of their school experiences. The eventual social adjustment in females was poorer than in males.

In all, although learning-disabled individuals eventually managed to make personal adjustments and find jobs, their dislike of and dissatisfaction with school remained. The major evidence from this and other follow-up studies also suggests that the effects of remedial educational programs were not particularly significant, except perhaps for those individuals with very high IQ scores. Reports of extravagant success seem to derive largely from private schools that select only high-IQ students from relatively affluent homes.

We should perhaps end this section by asking whether there is a challenge for neuropsychology in the area of learning disabilities or whether all available avenues of remediation have been fairly tried. We think that there is a challenge. First, we think that the impairments of each individual child have to be adequately assessed in order to assess the cognitive deficits that are likely to be particular to each child. Second, once specific problem areas have been identified, specialized teaching programs can be devised to circumvent the neuropsychological handicaps. Third, we feel there may be little point in trying to teach children those things that it seems clear they are not going to learn. It may be that education should be more explicitly directed to the acquisition of skills that may be subsequently used to gain employment. Fourth, we feel that counseling should be an important part of the educational process both for the learning-disabled individual and for parents. Counseling should be directed not only toward helping them overcome their own negative attitudes toward the educational system but also toward helping them come to understand their own unique handicaps, including some strategies that they can use to circumvent some of their handicaps. Fifth, we feel that there should be continued research into alternative education strategies that are consistent with neuropsychological findings. Erickson and colleagues have demonstrated that digit span in a subject of average intelligence could be increased from 7 to 79 with 230 h of training. Could similar training of learning-disabled children, who have poor short-term verbal memory, improve this memory to permit them to deal more effectively with certain aspects of school course work?

HYPERLEXIA

Hyperlexia is a term describing unusual reading ability in otherwise cognitively impaired individuals. Hyperlexia is marked by a precocious development of reading abilities between the ages of 3 and 5 years. Very often the children teach themselves to read. Their precocious reading ability is often accompanied by exceptional memory abilities, such as remembering words, TV shows, names of streets, the weather, or birthdays. Reading may not be completely fluid as there are often articulatory defects and prosodic abnormalities involving intonation and rate of speech. Generally, comprehension of what is read is impaired and the subjects show emotional withdrawal, occasional **echolalia** and symptoms of **autism.** As shown by Cobrinik, tests of intelligence often show IQ's below 50 with sparing on only a few subtests—usually digit span and occasionally block design and similarities.

The causes of hyperlexia and its associated cognitive abnormalities, or of other precocious abilities displayed by otherwise cognitively impaired individuals, is not known. It has been variously suggested that these children have islands of a normal functioning brain in an otherwise impaired brain, that through some developmental abnormality they are overdeveloped in some brain areas and underdeveloped in others or that they are using otherwise adequate brains in a functionally unusual manner.

Whatever the cause of hyperlexia, it does provide an interesting comparison with dyslexia. At the very least it demonstrates that the acquisition of reading ability and its maintenance does not require a complement of cognitive processes that include understanding and reasoning as displayed by normal readers. This supports the Vellutino hypothesis that there is a neural substrate that can be dedicated to the process of reading. In the absence of a normal substrate reading is difficult to acquire, but in its presence reading can be acquired in the absence of other cognitive functions.

The Savant Syndrome

Related to hyperlexia is the **savant syndrome,** and hyperlexics may be special cases of savants. The savant syndrome, or idiot-savant syndrome, was first described by Down in 1887 and was recently reviewed by Treffert. Since Down's description there have been several hundred cases reported in the literature. They are remarkably similar in that they have a narrow range of special abilities and the triad of symptoms of retardation, blindness, and musical genius is common among them. The term *idiot savant* was coined by combining the once acceptable classification of mental retardation—*idiot*—with *savant,* or knowledgeable person. Despite its perjorative connotation the term has endured. Savants are marked by mental handicaps resulting from a developmental disability or mental illness combined with a talent that stands in contrast to their other functions (talented savants) or in contrast to the abilities of the general population (prodigious savants). It is estimated to occur in males about six times more frequently than in females. The skill can appear quite suddenly and disappear equally quickly. Skills that are frequently displayed by savants include calendar calculations (some can tell the day of a person's birthday over thousand year periods), mathematical ability, musical ability including the ability to play new pieces of music on hearing them once, sculpting, drawing, and peculiar feats of memory, including memory of the weather for every day of life, retention of the names and dates of all visits received, and the date of every burial and the names of those in attendance in a parish over a 35-year time. At present there are no adequate theories to explain these abilities although new studies with imaging devices do indicate that these individuals frequently have brain damage, which explains their retardation but not their special abilities.

HYPERACTIVITY

Hyperactivity is distinguished from other types of learning disabilities because the hyperactive child is a behavioral problem in school and all aspects of school performance are usually disrupted. Hyperactive children may have specific learning disabilities in addition to hyperactivity, and these may contribute to hyperactivity. A number of diagnostic labels have been given to hyperactive children, and accordingly they have been classed as being minimally brain dysfunctional, hyperkinetic, or having hyperkinetic impulsive disorder. DSM-III gives the following characteristics of the disorder:

1. Excessive general hyperactivity or motor restlessness for the child's age. In preschool and early school years, there may be incessant haphazard, impulsive running, climbing, or crawling. During middle childhood or adolescence, marked inability to sit still, up and down activity, and fidgeting are characteristic. The activity differs from the norms for the age both in quality and quantity.

2. Difficulty in sustaining attention, such as inability to complete tasks initiated or a disorganized approach to tasks. The child frequently "forgets" demands made or tasks assigned and shows poor attention in unstructured situations or when demands are made for independent, unsupervised performance.

3. Impulsive behavior.

4. Duration of at least one year.

It is thought that in infancy hyperactive children characteristically have poor and irregular sleep, colic, and feeding problems. It is thought that they are not cuddly and do not like to be held still for long. Later they are described as bypassing walking in favor of running, and as being driven to handle and play with everything. By the time they reach kindergarten they are demanding, do not listen, and do not play well with other children. Other people, outside the home, may begin to reject the child because of its behavior. By the time the child enters school, its activity, low tolerance for frustration, poor concentration, and poor self-esteem lead to a referral for assessment. By adolescence the individual is a school failure, and 25 to 50% may begin to experience problems with the law. Their behavior remains restless, they withdraw from school, and they fail in developing social relations and in maintaining steady employment.

Hyperactivity is extremely common and is described by Weiss and Hechtman as the commonest behavioral disturbance among children. Estimates of its incidence vary because of problems with definition and differences in tolerance shown by different societies. The ratio of boys to girls is described as being as high as 5 : 1 to 9 : 1. In Rutter's Isle of Wight study an incidence of 1 in 1000 was reported, but in North America, where the tolerance for hyperactive behavior seems lower, estimates of incidence as high as 6 in 100 have been reported. It does seem that parents' and teachers' estimates of what constitutes normal behavior may be unrealistic, for Weiss and Hechtman note that in surveys of parents and teachers as many as 50% of children are reported as hyperactive. Interestingly, Gaddes has commented that as yet no measures of activity have been made from hyperactive children to quantify their "activity" objectively.

The cause of hyperactivity is simply not known. Brain damage, encephalitis, genetics, dopamine decreases, food allergies, high lead concentrations, and various home and school environments have been suggested as causes. It is unlikely that there is a single cause, and hence comprehensive, multidisciplinary assessment is recommended.

Recommended therapy includes counseling for the child and parent and careful structuring of the home and school environments. Beginning in the 1960s and continuing to the present, treatment with amphetaminelike stimulants, such as Ritalin, has been popular. The effectiveness of Ritalin or other drug treatment as a long-term solution is doubted. When Ritalin is effective, it may be because, as a stimulant, it allows the individual to concentrate on the tasks at hand. The drug may also have a general sedative effect on children.

The prognosis for hyperactive children has been reported by Weiss and Hechtman as being relatively poor. Their life-style continues to be impulsive and is often marked by geographical moves, accidents, and problems with the law. In later life their major problems may be with poor self-esteem and social skills, but they are not regarded as hyperactive by their employers, and they do not become mentally disturbed or adult criminals.

REFERENCES

Ahn, H., L. Princhep, E. R. John, H. Baird, M. Trepeten, and H. Kaye. Developmental equations reflect brain dysfunctions. *Science* 210:1259–1262, 1980.

Ayres, A. J. Learning disabilities and the vestibular system. *Journal of Learning Disabilities* 11:11–29, 1978.

Bakker, D. J. *Temporal Order in Disturbed Reading: Developmental and Neuropsychological Aspects in Normal and Reading-Retarded Children.* Rotterdam: Rotterdam University Press, 1972.

Barnsley, R. H., Thompson, A. H. and Barnsley, P. E. Hockey success and birthdate: The relative age effect. *Canadian Association of Health, Physical Education, and Recreation* Novembre-Decembre:23–27, 1985.

Benton, A. *Right-Left Discrimination and Finger Localization.* New York: Hoeber-Harper, 1959.

Birch, H. G. Dyslexia and maturation of visual function. In J. Money, ed. *Reading Disability: Progress and Research Needs in Dyslexia.* Baltimore: Johns Hopkins Press, 1962.

Birch, H. G., and L. Belmont. Auditory-visual integration, intelligence, and reading ability in school children. *Perceptual and Motor Skills* 20:295–305, 1965.

Boder, E. Developmental dyslexia: A diagnostic screening procedure based on three characteristic patterns of reading and spelling. *Learning Disorders* 4:298–342, 1971.

Bradley, L., and P. E. Bryant. Categorizing sounds and learning to read—A causal connection. *Nature* 301:419–421, 1983.

Bruck, M. The suitability of early French immersion programs for the language disabled child. *Canadian Journal of Education* 34:50–73, 1978.

Bryden, M. P. Laterality effects in dichotic listening: Relations with handedness and reading disability in children. *Neuropsychologia* 8:443–450, 1970.

Cobrinik, L. Unusual reading ability in severely disturbed children. *Journal of Autism and Childhood Schizophrenia* 4:163–175, 1974.

Coltheart, M. Deep dyslexia: A right hemisphere hypothesis. In M. Coltheart, K. E. Patterson and J. Marshall, eds. *Deep Dyslexia.* London: Routledge, 1980.

Corkin, S. Serial ordering deficits in inferior readers. *Neuropsychologia* 12:347–354, 1974.

Critchley, M. *Developmental Dyslexia.* Springfield, IL: Charles C. Thomas, 1964.

Defries, J. C., and S. N. Decker. Genetic aspects of reading disability: A family study. In R. N. Malatesha and P. G. Aaron, eds. *Reading Disorders: Varieties and Treatments.* New York: Academic Press, 1982.

Denckla, M. B. Color-naming defects in dyslexic boys. *Cortex* 8:164–176, 1972.

Denckla, M. B. Critical review of "Electroencephalographic and neurophysiological studies in dyslexia." In A. L. Benton and D. Pearl, eds. *Dyslexia: An Appraisal of Current Knowledge.* New York: Oxford University Press, 1978.

Denckla, M. B., and R. Rudel. Naming of object-drawings by dyslexic and other learning disabled children. *Brain and Language* 13:1–15, 1976.

Dennis, M. Capacity and strategy for syntactic comprehension after left or right hemidecortication. *Brain and Language* 10:287–317, 1980.

Diamond, G. H. The birthdate effect—A maturational effect? *Journal of Learning Disabilities* 16:161–164, 1983.

Douglas, V. I. Perceptual and cognitive factors as determinants of learning disabilities: A review chapter with special emphasis on attentional factors. In R. M. Knights and D. J. Bakker, eds. *The Neuropsychology of Learning Disorders.* Baltimore: University Park Press, 1976.

Drake, W. Clinical and pathological findings in a child with a developmental learning disability. *Journal of Learning Disabilities* 1:468–475, 1968.

Duffy, F. H., M. B. Denckla, P. H. Bartels, and G. Sandini. Dyslexia: Regional differences in brain electrical activity by topographic mapping. *Annals of Neurology* 7:412–420, 1980.

Eakin, S., and V. I. Douglas. "Automatization" and oral reading problems in children. *Journal of Learning Disabilities* 4:31–38, 1971.

Erickson, K. A., W. G. Chase, and S. Faloon. Acquisition of a memory skill. *Science* 208:1181–1182, 1980.

Frank, J., and H. H. Levinson. Dysmetric dyslexia and dyspraxia. *Academic Therapy* 11:133–143, 1976.

Frauenheim, J. G. Academic achievement characteristics of adult males who were diagnosed as dyslexic in childhood. *Journal of Learning Disabilities* 11:476–483, 1978.

Frith, U. Experimental approaches to developmental dyslexia. *Psychological Research* 43:97–109, 1981.

Fry, E. A do-it-yourself terminology generator. *Journal of Reading* 11:428–430, 1968.

Gaddes, W. H. Prevalence estimates and the need for definition of learning disabilities. In R. M. Knights and D. J. Bakker, eds. *The Neuropsychology of Learning Disorders.* Baltimore: University Park Press, 1976.

Gaddes, W. H. *Learning Disabilities and Brain Function.* New York: Springer-Verlag, 1980.

Galaburda, A. M., J. Corsiglia, G. D. Rosen, and G. F. Sherman. Planum temporale asymmetry, reappraisal since Geschwind and Levitsky. Neuropsychologia 25:853–868, 1987.

Geschwind, N., and A. M. Galaburda. *Cerebral Lateralization.* Cambridge, MA: The M.I.T. Press, 1985.

Gordon, H. W. Cognitive asymmetry in dyslexic families. *Neuropsychologia* 18:645–656, 1980.

Gould, S. J. *The Mismeasure of Man.* New York: Norton, 1981.

Graham, E. E., and D. Kamano. Reading failure as a factor in the WAIS subtest patterns of youthful offenders. *Journal of Clinical Psychology* 14:302–305, 1958.

Huelsman, C. B. The WISC syndrome for disabled readers. *Perceptual and Motor Skills* 30:535–550, 1970.

Hughes, J. R. Electroencephalographic and neurophysiological studies in dyslexia. In A. L. Benton and D. Pearl, eds. *Dyslexia: An Appraisal of Current Knowledge.* New York: Oxford University Press, 1978.

Hunter, E. J., and L. C. Johnson. Developmental and psychological differences between readers and nonreaders. *Journal of Learning Disabilities* 4:572–577, 1971.

Johnson, D. J., and H. R. Myklebust. *Learning Disabilities.* New York: Grune & Stratton, 1967.

Jorm, A. F. The cognitive and neurological basis of developmental dyslexia: A theoretical framework and review. *Cognition* 7:19–33, 1979.

Kinsbourne, M., and M. Hiscock. Does cerebral dominance develop? In S. J. Segalowitz and F. A. Gruber, eds. *Language Development and Neurological Theory.* New York: Academic Press, 1977.

Klicpera, C., P. H. Wolff, and C. Drake. Bimanual co-ordination in adolescent boys with reading retardation. *Developmental Medicine and Child Neurology* 23:617–625, 1981.

Langmore, S. E., and G. J. Canter. Written spelling deficit of Broca's aphasics. *Brain and Language* 18:293–314, 1983.

Levinson, H. N. *Dyslexia.* New York: Springer-Verlag, 1980.

Lovegrove, W. J., M. Heddle, and W. Slaghuis. Reading disability: Spatial frequency specific deficits in visual information store. *Neuropsychologia* 18:111–115, 1980.

Lyle, J. G. Performance of retarded readers on the memory-for-designs test. *Perceptual and Motor Skills* 26:851–854, 1968.

Lyle, J. G., and J. D. Goyen. Performance of retarded readers on the WISC and educational tests. *Journal of Abnormal Psychology* 74:105–112, 1969.

Lyle, J. G., and J. D. Goyen. Effect of speed of exposure and difficulty of discrimination on visual recognition of retarded readers. *Journal of Abnormal Psychology* 84:673–676, 1975.

Maccario, M., S. J. Hefferen, S. J. Keblusek, and K. A. Lipinski. Developmental dysphasia and electroencephalographic abnormalities. *Developmental Medicine and Child Neurology* 24: 141–155, 1982.

Maddux, C. D. First-grade entry age in a sample of children labeled learning disabled. *Learning Disability Quarterly* 3:79–83, 1980.

Maddux, C. D., D. Stacy, and M. Scott. School entry age in a group of gifted children. *Gifted Child Quarterly* 25:180–184, 1981.

Malatesha, R. N., and D. R. Dougan. Clinical subtypes of developmental dyslexia: Resolution to an irresolute problem. In R. N. Malatesha and P. G. Aaron, eds. *Reading Disorders.* New York: Academic Press, 1982.

McFie, J. Cerebral dominance in cases of reading disability. *Journal of Neurology and Psychiatry* 15:194–199, 1952.

Money, J. Child abuse: Growth failure, IQ deficit, and learning disability. *Journal of Learning Disabilities* 15:579–582, 1982.

Myklebust, H. R., and D. Johnson. Dyslexia in children. *Exceptional Children* 29:14–25, 1962.

Orton, S. T. Word-blindness in school children. *Archives of Neurology and Psychiatry* 14:581–615, 1925.

Orton, S. T. *Reading, Writing and Speech Problems in Children.* New York: Norton, 1937.

Pavlidis, G. Th. Do eye movements hold the key to dyslexia? *Neuropsychologia* 19:57–64, 1981.

Perfetti, C. A., and T. Hogaboam. The relationship between single word decoding and reading comprehension skill. *Journal of Educational Psychology* 67:461–469, 1975.

Pihl, R. O., and M. Parkes. Hair element content in learning disabled children. *Science* 198:204–206, 1977.

Pirozzolo, F. J., and E. C. Hansch. The neurobiology of developmental reading disorders. In R. N. Malatesha and P. G. Aaron, eds. *Reading Disorders: Varieties and Treatments.* New York: Academic Press, 1982.

Pirozzolo, F. J., and K. Rayner. Hemispheric specialization in reading and word recognition. *Brain and Language* 4:248–261, 1977.

Reed, J. C. Reading achievement as related to differences between WISC verbal and performance I.Q.'s. *Child Development* 38:835–840, 1967.

Rosensweig, M. R., D. Krech, E. L. Bennett, and M. C. Diamond. Effects of environmental complexity and training on brain chemistry and anatomy: A replication and extension. *Journal of Comparative and Physiological Psychology* 55:427–429, 1962.

Rourke, B. P. Neuropsychological assessment of children with learning disabilities. In S. B. Filskov and T. J. Boll, eds. *Handbook of Clinical Neuropsychology*. New York: John Wiley, 1981.

Rugel, R. P. WISC subtest scores of disabled readers: A review with respect to Bannatyne's categorization. *Journal of Learning Disability* 17:48–55, 1974.

Rutter, M., and W. Yule. The concept of specific reading retardation. *Journal of Child Psychology and Psychiatry* 16:181–197, 1975.

Satz, P. Cerebral dominance and reading disability: An old problem revisited. In R. M. Knights and D. J. Bakker, eds. *The Neuropsychology of Learning Disorders*. Baltimore: University Park Press, 1976.

Satz, P., and S. S. Sparrow. Specific developmental dyslexia: A theoretical formulation. In D. Bakker and P. Satz, eds. *Specific Reading Disability: Advances in Theory and Method*. Rotterdam: Rotterdam University Press, 1970.

Satz, P., D. Rarden, and J. Ross. An evaluation of a theory of specific developmental dyslexia. *Child Development* 42:1009–1021, 1971.

Siegel, L. S. On the adequacy of the wide range achievement test (WRAT): A reply to Snart, Dennis, and Brailsford. *Canadian Psychology* 25:73–74, 1984.

Silver, A. A., and R. A. Hagen. A unifying concept for the neuropsychological organization of children with reading disability. *Developmental and Behavioral Pediatrics* 3:127–132, 1982.

Snart, F., S. Dennis, and A. Brailsford. Concerns regarding the wide range achievement test. *Canadian Psychology* 24:99–104, 1983.

Spreen, O. Neuropsychology of learning disorders: Post-conference review. In R. M. Knights and D. J. Bakker, eds. *The Neuropsychology of Learning Disorders*. Baltimore: University Park Press, 1976.

Spring, C. Encoding speed and memory span in dyslexic children. *The Journal of Special Education* 10:35–40, 1976.

Tees, R. C., and J. Werker. *The development of speech perception: Evidence of functional decline in neonatal ability*. Paper given at Winter Conference on Brain Research, Keystone, Colorado, January, 1981.

Treffert, D. A. The idiot savant: A review of the syndrome. *American Journal of Psychiatry* 145:563–572, 1988.

U. S. Department of Health, Education and Welfare. Minimal brain dysfunction in children. *National Institute of Neurological Diseases Monograph* 3:1–18, 1966.

Vellutino, F. R. Alternative conceptualizations of dyslexia: Evidence in support of a verbal-deficit hypothesis. *Howard Educational Review* 47:334–353, 1977.

Vellutino, F. R. Toward an understanding of dyslexia: Psychological factors in specific reading disability. In A. L. Benton and D. Pearl, eds. *Dyslexia: An Appraisal of Current Knowledge*. New York: Oxford University Press, 1978.

Weiss, G., and L. Hechtman. The hyperactive child syndrome. *Science* 205:1348–1354, 1979.

Wepman, J. M. Auditory discrimination, speech and reading. *The Reading Teacher* 9:325–333, 1960.

Wepman, J. M. The interrelationships of hearing, speech and reading. *The Reading Teacher* 14:245–247, 1961.

Whishaw, I. Q., and B. Kolb. Neuropsychological assessment of children and adults with developmental dyslexia. In R. N. Malatesha and H. A. Whitaker, eds. *Dyslexia: A Global Issue.* The Hague: Martinus Nijhoff, 1984.

Witelson, S. F. Hemispheric specialization for linguistic and nonlinguistic tactual perception using a dichotomous stimulation technique. *Cortex* 11:3–17, 1974.

Witelson, S. F. Early hemisphere specialization and interhemispheric plasticity, an empirical and theoretical review. In S. J. Segalowitz and F. A. Gruber, eds. *Language Development and Neurological Theory.* New York: Academic Press, 1977.

Zaidel, E. The split and half brains as models of congenital language disability. In C. L. Ludlow and M. E. Doran-Quine, eds. *The Neuropsychological Basis of Language Disorders in Children.* Besthesda: National Institute of Neurological and Communicative Disorders and Stroke (22). 1978.

Zangwill, O. L., and C. Blakemore. Dyslexia: Reversal of eye-movements during reading. *Neuropsychologia* 10:371–373, 1972.

Zurif, E. B., and G. Carlson. Dyslexia in relation to cerebral dominance and temporal analysis. *Neuropsychologia* 8:351–361, 1970.

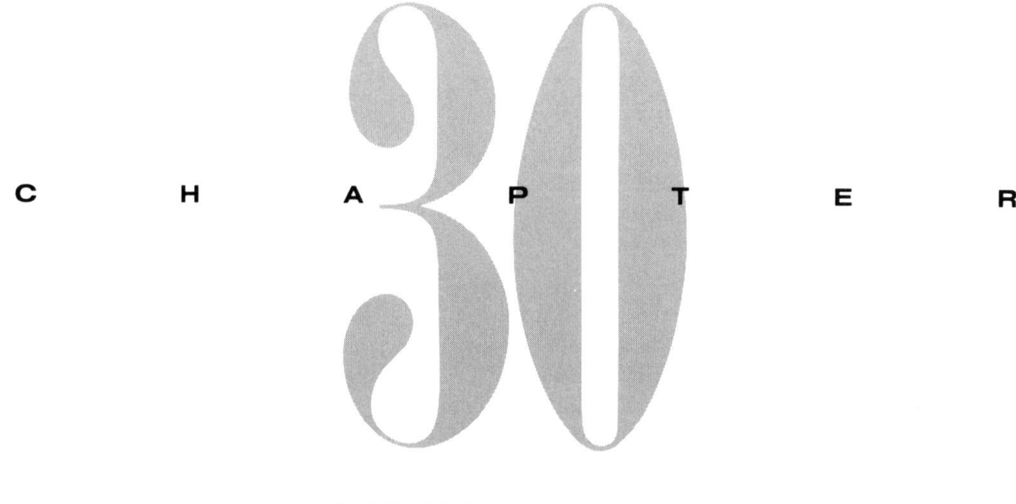

CHAPTER 30

PSYCHIATRIC AND MOTOR DISORDERS

Advances in neuropsychological assessment have led to an increase in the use of neuropsychological tests in psychiatric settings. Psychiatric diagnosis is always difficult at best, and neuropsychological evaluations may provide objective information to aid in classifying patients for treatment as well as in evaluating prognosis. It may also help in understanding the problems that patients have. There is, however, a lot of misunderstanding about the nature and potential of neuropsychological tests. Perhaps because of the attempts to use one-shot tests of "organicity," such as the Bender-Gestalt or MMPI, clinical psychologists are frequently asked to help determine whether patients' behavioral disturbances are "functional" or "organic" in nature. In other words, the psychologist is being asked for an opinion on whether the abnormal behavior in a patient can be ascribed to brain dysfunction or to some other "mental" disorder. This question is clearly inappropriate. As we have seen, especially in Chapters 15 through 26, the question to ask is not whether or not someone's brain is functioning normally. Normal brain function is hardly a yes-or-no issue. Clinically, it may be more reasonable to ask whether a patient is experiencing neuropsychological deficits that could account for the observed behavioral symptoms, and whether the test profile is suggestive of a particular diagnosis. Of course, the second question assumes that different disorders are associated with particular patterns of test results. This is the major topic of this chapter. We shall ask whether some of the commoner "psychiatric" and "motor" disorders are associated with consistent neuropsychological profiles and whether these profiles appear robust enough to help in diagnosis. Because the literature is so large we have been selective in our discussion and have tried to restrict ourselves to those studies that are comprehensive or particularly incisive (e.g., Table 30-1).

TABLE 30-1. Representative neuropsychological studies of psychiatric and motor disorders

Disease	Basic reference
Schizophrenia	Flor-Henry and Yeudall, 1979 Kolb and Whishaw, 1983
Affective disorders	Flor-Henry and Yeudall, 1979
Tourette's syndrome	Shapiro et al., 1974 Sutherland et al., 1982
Parkinson's disease	Pirozzolo et al., 1982 Bowen et al., 1972
Huntington's disease	Fedio et al., 1979 Wexler, 1979

SCHIZOPHRENIA

Speculation concerning a biological cause of **schizophrenia** has led to repeated attempts to identify structural abnormalities in the brains of schizophrenics (Chapter 23). Although the results have often proved equivocal, it does appear as though there is some abnormality in the mesocortical dopaminergic system. Further, there is good evidence that neither the frontal nor the temporal lobes are functioning normally in schizophrenia. In view of this, we should expect to find significant impairment in the performance of neuropsychological tests by schizophrenics, and we do.

Heaton and Crowley reviewed 132 studies published between 1960 and 1978 that considered the accuracy of neuropsychological tests in discriminating patients with various psychiatric diagnoses from patients with known brain damage. Overall, Heaton and Crowley conclude that, with the exception of chronic schizophrenia, the majority (75%) of psychiatric patients could be correctly classified. Hence, there appears to be a consensus that schizophrenics do poorly on neuropsychological tests. The crucial question, however is *how* they do poorly.

Over the past decade a view has emerged suggesting that schizophrenics may do especially poorly on tests of left hemisphere function. Flor-Henry has emphasized left temporal lobe dysfunction as a characteristic of schizophrenic patients, although he does not exclude the possibility of poor performance on frontal lobe tests as well. Similarly, other researchers such as Piran and colleagues have been struck with an apparent shift in handedness and eye dominance to the left in schizophrenics, again suggesting left hemisphere pathology. It does seem puzzling, however, that neuropsychological impairments would be restricted just to tests sensitive to left hemisphere function since the biological evidence would lead one to anticipate a bilateral impairment. More recent evidence suggests that this may indeed be the case. There is good evidence that if schizophrenics are tested on a broad range of tests known to be sensitive to both left and right hemisphere function, they perform poorly on tests believed to measure both left and right frontal or temporal lobe function. For example, we studied the performance of schizophrenic patients on a composite battery similar to the one summarized in Chapter 27 but included additional tests of frontal lobe function, including the copying of complex facial movements and the Gotman-Milner Design Fluency Test. The results showed that schizophrenics were significantly impaired, relative to age-matched controls, on every test sensitive to frontal and temporal lobe function but performed with normal limits on tests sensitive to parietal lobe function (See Table 30-1).

Overall, it appears that schizophrenics do perform poorly on neuropsychological measures and that they may have a reliable pattern of test results: they perform poorly on tests of long-term verbal and nonverbal memory, as well as on tests sensitive to left or right frontal lobe function. Performance on tests of visual discrimination, spatial orientation, and short-term verbal and nonverbal memory appears to be less affected, and most schizophrenics appear to perform these tests normally. We must caution, however, that people who have been chronically institutionalized as schizophrenics may not perform normally on *any* tests, rendering the assessment of them futile at best. (For a detailed account of the effects of antipsychotic medication on test performance see Heaton and Crowley.) Furthermore, there is little evidence that any neuropsychological assessment procedure represents a test profile specific to schizophrenia. One reason may be that there is more than one form of schizophrenia, which results in more than one form of neuropsychological test profile. This remains to be shown.

AFFECTIVE DISORDERS

In our discussion of biological correlates of affective disorders in Chapter 23 we considered possible neurochemical abnormalities in affective disorders but, unlike the data for schizophrenia, we were unable to provide much more than circumstantial evidence in support of any such proposed abnormality. There is a similar dearth of information about the neuropsychological test preformance of people with affective disorders. Heaton and his colleagues summarize only six studies on affective patients, and all of these used only one or two measures. Flor-Henry and others have suggested that affective patients do especially poorly on tests sensitive to right hemisphere function, but their neuropsychological evidence is not yet compelling. Recently, many writers have commented on the similarity between the "symptoms" of aging and those of depression, especially the poor performance of both types of people on tests of nonverbal memory. The reasons for an aging-depression similarity is unknown and may simply reflect a failure to process sensory information, although probably for different reasons in the two conditions. We must conclude that to date there does not appear to be a reliable pattern of neuropsychological tests results for people with different affective disorders.

TOURETTE'S SYNDROME

Although **Tourette's syndrome** is less common than schizophrenia or affective disorders, it has attracted a lot of interest, in large part because of the interesting symptoms and because of the activity of the Tourette's Syndrome Association. Scattered reports of specific biological disturbances associated with Tourette's syndrome have appeared in the literature, but pathological studies are virtually nonexistent, and even the clinical boundaries of the syndrome are in dispute (see Chapter 13 for a detailed discussion of common symptoms). Most of the inferences about the biological nature of Tourette's syndrome have been derived from the studies of the therapeutic effects of drugs such as haloperidol, the current drug of choice in treating this disease. Neuropsychological studies thus have much to offer both in the diagnosis of Tourette's syndrome and in the study of the neurological basis of the disorder.

The extensive volume on Tourette's syndrome, which was edited by Friedhoff and Chase, contains virtually all of the neuropsychological studies on Tourette patients. Although standard neuropsychological test batteries (e.g., the Halstead-Reitan) do not identify consistent abnormalities in Tourette patients, there nevertheless may be a distinctive and reliable pattern of test results. Sutherland and his colleagues gave a composite test battery to a large sample of children and adults with Tourette's syndrome and found a consistent pattern of results. The patients were especially bad at drawing and remembering complex geometric figures, although they also performed poorly on the Chicago Word-Fluency Test and recall of the Wechsler logical stories. The poor performance of these patients on the Rey Figure was particularly striking since even patients with superior verbal IQs, such as the adult Tourette patient illustrated in Figure 30-1, performed very poorly, even when compared with control children or schizophrenic patients. These results, as well as similar findings by Shapiro, suggest that Tourette patients may have a right frontotemporal dysfunction, but owing to the limited number of studies published to date, this conclusion must be considered tentative.

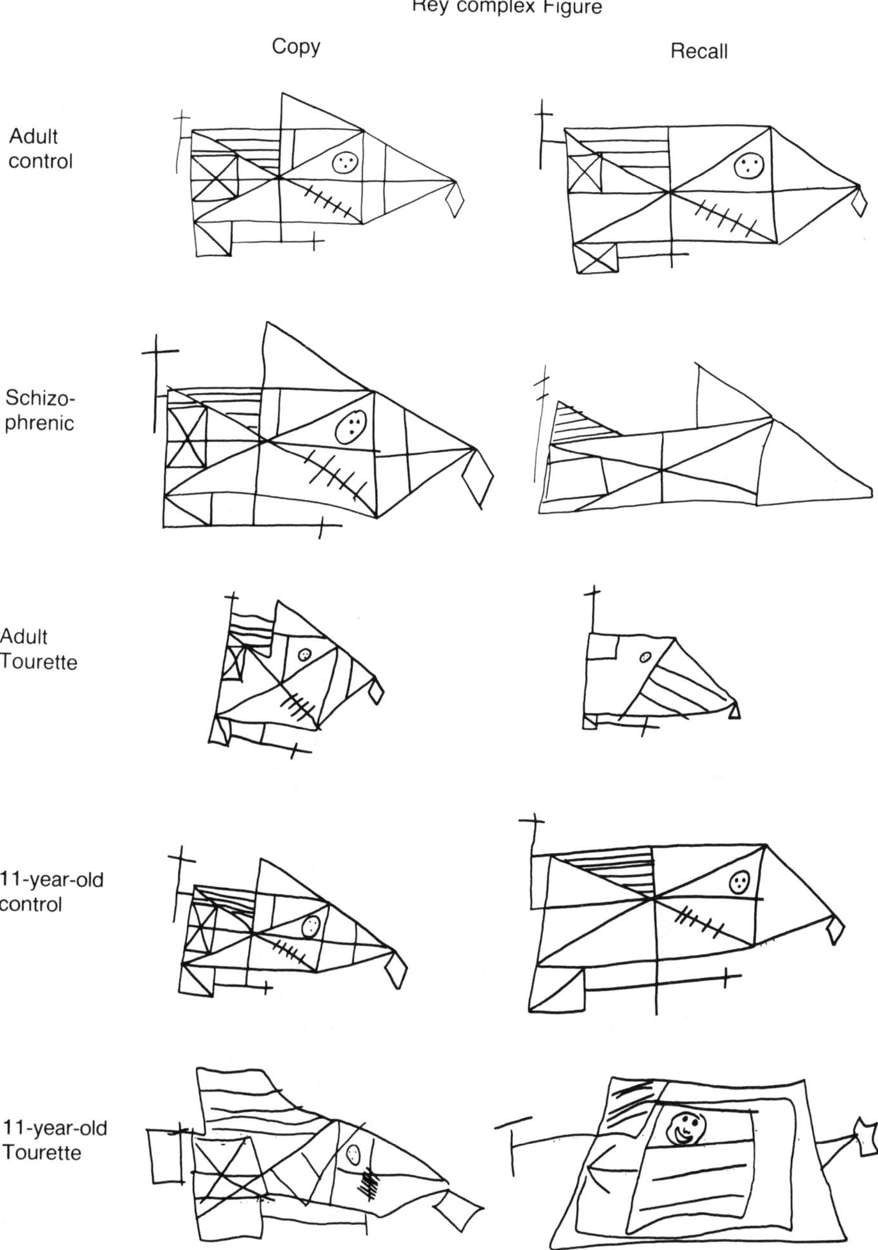

FIGURE 30-1. Representative performance by a normal adult control, a schizophrenic, an adult Tourette patient, a normal child, and a child Tourette patient on the Rey Complex Figure: copying and recall. The Tourette patients are impaired at both the copying and the recall; the schizophrenic patient is impaired only at the recall. (After Sutherland et al., 1982.)

PARKINSON'S DISEASE

The pathology of **Parkinson's disease** is probably the best studied of all the pathologies of degenerative diseases (see Chapter 13), but the extent of neocortical abnormality remains controversial. Parkinson patients who are clearly demented at death have been known for some time to show structural cortical changes similar to those of **Alzheimer's disease,** but it has more recently been suggested that Alzheimer-like neocortical abnormalities may be a characteristic of all Parkinson patients. For example, Hakim and Mathieson found that of 34 Parkinson patients' brains they examined, only 1 did not have clear evidence of Alzheimer-like abnormalities. Further, of the 34 patients, only 19 were claimed to have shown any clinical evidence of dementia, although no psychological tests were done on their sample.

Neuropsychological investigations in other populations have confirmed the possibility of a general cognitive deterioration in Parkinson patients. For example, in their extensive study Pirozzolo and coworkers found Parkinson patients to be significantly impaired relative to age-matched controls on several subtests of the WAIS (information, digit span, digit symbol, and block design) and on measures of verbal memory (logical stories, paired associates). In addition, Parkinson patients are impaired at the Wisconsin Card-Sorting Test. In contrast, however, there is no evidence of aphasia, agnosia, or apraxia in Parkinson patients.

In addition to symptoms of generalized dementia in Parkinson patients there is evidence of an independent deficit in visuospatial abilities. For example, Boller and his colleagues have found Parkinson patients to be impaired at a wide array of visuospatial tests, independent of intellectual impairment. Studies of laboratory animals with damage to the nigrostriatal system (largely the striatum) have also led to a suggestion of deficits in spatial abilities, although the reasons remain unclear.

HUNTINGTON'S CHOREA

Huntington's chorea is another degenerative disorder (Chapter 13) that has recently become of particular interest to neuropsychologists, primarily because it may be possible to identify cognitive markers for the disease before the motor symptoms first appear. This is especially important for genetic counseling since there are currently few ways to diagnose the disease until the degenerative motor symptoms appear. Neuropsychological studies have thus tended to compare known Huntington patients to control subjects as well as to people who could be considered "at risk" for Huntington's since they had at least one parent with the disease. Extensive studies by Fedio and colleagues and by Wexler have shown that it may in fact be possible to identify those people "at-risk" who will later develop Huntington's disease. These authors have found that patients known to have Huntington's disease are impaired at a broad range of memory (e.g., Wechsler Memory Scale, recall of the Rey Figure), perceptual (e.g., copy of the Rey Figure, tachistoscopic, and dichaptic recognition), and various frontal lobe tests (e.g., Chicago Word-Fluency, stylus maze). People in the at-risk groups appeared to perform poorly only at the frontal lobe tests, suggesting that these tests might be useful as predictors of the disease. The effectiveness of these tests as predictors will be seen in the coming years as the subjects from these studies do, or do not, begin to display other symptoms. There is a large-scale study currently being conducted in Canada in which people at-risk are having genetic tests (which are now able to identify those individuals who will develop Huntington's symptoms) as well as neuropsychological assessments. Notwithstanding the moral challenges in such a study, this study is likely to provide valuable clues about the neuropsychological changes that are (or are not) present in the early stages of Huntington's chorea.

CONCLUSIONS

Neuropsychological tests are likely to be used increasingly in the assessment of people with both "motor" and "psychiatric" disorders. There is evidence that people with some diseases may show distinctive patterns of test results (e.g., Tourette's, Huntington's), and those with other diseases may not (e.g., schizophrenia, Parkinson's). Skillful use of neuropsychological tests results for people with the disorders discussed here, as well as for people with other less well studied diseases, may prove invaluable in the future, both in differential diagnosis and patient management. We must emphasize, however, that these tests are not properly used merely as measures of organicity. When carefully chosen and used, the results of neuropsychological tests present a reliable measure of the cognitive capacities of people; we have a reasonable degree of confidence that the profiles of neuropsychological deficits in different diseases reflect the anatomically and physiologically unique neurological dysfunction underlying these different disorders. Nonetheless, the tests that are most commonly used to study psychiatric patients were not developed for this use, and must be used and interpreted with great care. The reader is directed to a comprehensive volume by Grant and Adams for a complete discussion of the neuropsychological assessment of patients with psychiatric disorders.

REFERENCES

Boller, F., D. Passafiume, M. C. Keefe, K. Rogers, L. Morrow, and Y. Kim. Visuospatial impairment in Parkinson's disease: Role of perceptual and motor factors. *Archives of Neurology* 41:485–490, 1984.

Bowen, F. P., M. M. Hoehn, and M. D. Yahr. Parkinsonism: Alterations in spatial orientation as determined by a route walking test. *Neuropsychologia* 10:335–361, 1972.

Fedio, P., C. S. Cox, A. Neophytides, G. Canal-Frederick, and T. N. Chase. Neuropsychological profile of Huntington's disease: Patients and those at risk. *Advances in Neurology* 23:239–256, 1979.

Flor-Henry, P. Lateralized temporal-limbic dysfunction and psychopathology. *Annals of the New York Academy of Science* 280:777–795, 1976.

Flor-Henry, P., and L. T. Yeudall. Neuropsychological investigation of schizophrenia and manic-depressive psychosis. In J. Gruzelier and P. Flor-Henry, eds. *Hemisphere Asymmetries of Function in Psychopathology.* Amsterdam: Elsevier North-Holland, 1979.

Friedhoff, A. J., and T. N. Chase, eds. *Gilles de la Tourette Syndrome. Advances in Neurology,* vol. 35. New York: Raven Press, 1982.

Grant, I., and K. M. Adams, eds. *Neuropsychological Assessment of Neuropsychiatric Disorders.* New York: Oxford University Press, 1986.

Gruzelier, J., and P. Flor-Henry, eds. *Hemisphere Asymmetries of Function in Psychopathology.* Amsterdam: Elsevier North-Holland, 1979.

Hakim, A. M., and G. Mathieson. Dementia in Parkinson's disease: A neuropathologic study. *Neurology* 29:1209–1214, 1979.

Heaton, R. K., L. E. Badde, and K. L. Johnson. Neuropsychological test results associated with psychiatric disorders in adults. *Psychological Bulletin* 85:141–162, 1978.

Heaton, R. K., and T. J. Crowley. Effects of psychiatric disorders and their somatic treatments on neuropsychological test results. In S. B. Gilskov and G. J. Boll, eds. *Handbook of Clinical Neuropsychology*. New York: John Wiley, 1981.

Incagnoli, T., and R. Kane. Neuropsychological functioning in Tourette's syndrome. *Advances in Neurology* 35:305–310, 1982.

Joschko, M., and B. Rourke. Neuropsychological dimensions of Tourette's syndrome: Test-retest stability and implications for intervention. *Advances in Neurology* 35:297–304, 1982.

Kolb, B., and I. Q. Whishaw. Performance of schizophrenic patients on tests sensitive to left or right frontal, temporal, or parietal function in neurological patients. *Journal of Nervous and Mental Disease* 171:435–443, 1983.

Piran, N., E. D. Bigler, and D. Cohen Motoric laterality and eye dominance suggest unique pattern of cerebral organization in schizophrenia. *Archives of General Psychiatry* 39:1010, 1982.

Pirozzolo, F. J., E. C. Hansch, J. A. Mortimer, D. D. Webster, and M. A. Kuskowski. Dementia in Parkinson's disease: A neuropsychological analysis. *Brain and Cognition* 1:71–83, 1982.

Shapiro, E., E. K. Shapiro, and J. Clarkin. Clinical psychological testing in Tourette's syndrome. *Journal of Personality Assessment* 38:464–478, 1974.

Sutherland, R. J., B. Kolb, W. M. Schoel, I. Q. Whishaw, and D. Davies. Neuropsychological assessment of children and adults with Tourette's syndrome: A comparison with learning disabilities and schizophrenia. *Advances in Neurology* 35:311–322, 1982.

Wexler, N. S. Perceptual-motor, cognitive, and emotional characteristics of person at risk for Huntington's disease. *Advances in Neurology* 23:257–272, 1979.

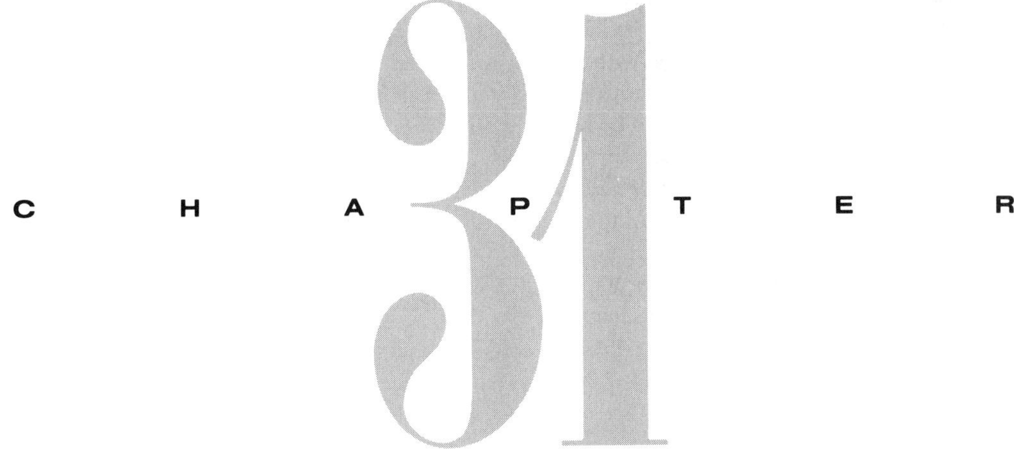

HEAD TRAUMA AND DEGENERATIVE DISEASES

Improvements in the standard of living and in medical treatments have led to increased life expectancies in Western countries. One effect of this increased lifespan is that people with head injuries are more likely to survive and to live to old age and, as the mean age of the population increases there is an increasing number of people suffering degenerative diseases of the nervous system, many of which lead to dementia. The growing recognition that behavioral disorders are a major contribution to disability from head trauma and degenerative diseases has led to an increasing involvement of neuropsychologists with these disorders. In this chapter we consider a selected number of such disorders including head trauma, Alzheimer's disease, and chronic alcohol abuse. We group these disorders together because they present similar diagnostic problems for clinical neuroscience, including neuropsychology.

HEAD TRAUMA

Epidemiology

Because there has been no agreement on what constitutes an injury sufficient to affect the brain, it has proven difficult to obtain reliable estimates of the frequency of closed-head injuries. Nonetheless, with the development of sophisticated neuroradiological procedures such as MRI and PET, it is becoming evident that brain injury from head trauma is a major public health problem in industrialized countries. For example, in one telephone survey in Sweden, cerebral concussion producing even brief unconsciousness was reported by 5% of those interviewed. In addition, it is estimated that an equal number of people are likely to have had a **concussion** without obvious unconsciousness, although they would have been confused about the events surrounding the blow to the head. In the United States, the National Institute of Neurological and Communicative Disorders and Stroke estimates that more than 400,000 people with new head injuries are admitted to U.S. hospitals each year. Estimates of the number of people who have mild head injuries, without hospitalization, vary widely but are probably in the order of *at least* an additional 100,000 per year. An additional 100,000 people die from trauma and are not included in most statistics. Overall, it appears that the frequency of closed-head injuries in industrialized countries ranges from about 300 to 450 per 100,000 population *per year*. Projected over one's lifespan, the chances of such an injury are high indeed. Thus, it has been estimated that a child's chances of having a significant closed-head injury are 1 in 30 *before they are old enough to drive!* The single most important factors in the incidence of closed-head injury are age and sex. Thus, children and elderly people are more likely to suffer injuries from falls than are others, and males between 15 and 30 are very likely to have brain injuries, especially from automobile and motorcycle accidents (see Figure 31-1), a statistic that is reflected in automobile insurance rates.

Pathology of Closed-Head Injury

The pathological effects of closed-head injury are summarized in Table 31-1. In Chapter 7 we discussed the coup and countercoup injuries (Figure 7-5), which are major causes of primary injury to the brain. In addition, there are numerous second-

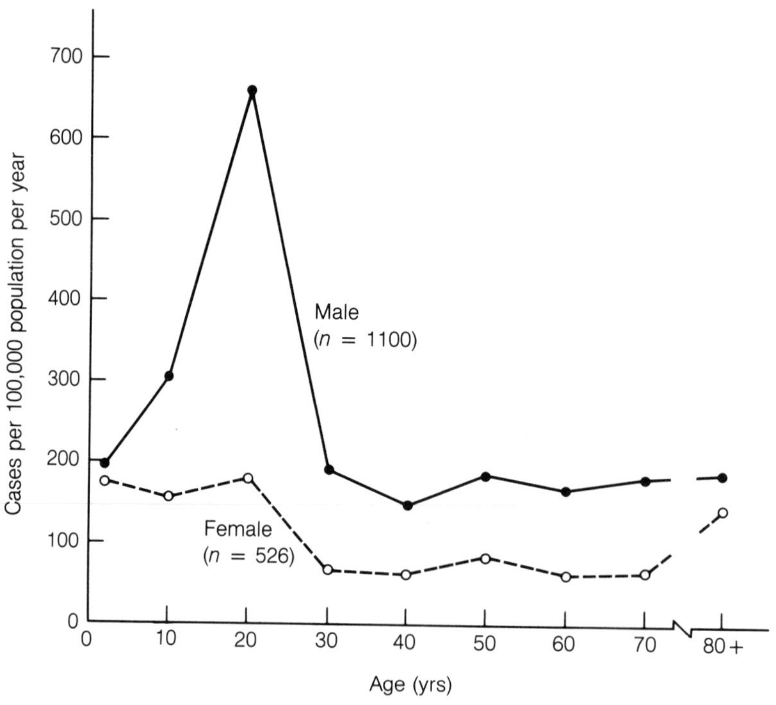

FIGURE 31-1. Incidence rates of head trauma in Olmsted County, Minnesota, 1965–1974. (After Annegers et al., 1980).

TABLE 31-1. Primary and secondary brain injury after closed-head trauma

Primary (immediate on impact) brain injury
Macroscopic lesions
Contusions underlying the site of impact (coup)
Contrecoup contusion frequently in the undersurfaces of the frontal lobes and the tips of the temporal lobes.
Laceration of the brain from depressed skull fracture
Microscopic lesions
Widespread shearing or stretching of nerve fibers
Secondary mechanisms of brain injury
Intracranial hemorrhage
Edema in white matter adjacent to focal mass lesions
Diffuse brain swelling—hyperemia
Ischemic brain damage
Raised intracranial pressure
Brain shift and herniation
Secondary insult from extracerebral events
Effects of multiple/systemic injury
Hypoxia
Fat embolism
Delayed effects
Degeneration of white matter
Disturbed flow of cerebrospinal fluid—hydrocephalus

Source: After Levin et al., 1982.

ary effects, of which the most important may be ischemia, edema, and damage to white matter, especially the corpus callosum. We have seen previously that certain regions of the brain such as the hippocampus are especially sensitive to ischemia, so it would not be surprising to see medial temporal lobe degeneration after head trauma. Edema is common from trauma anywhere in the body but it is particularly problematic inside the skull because it leads to increased cranial pressure, which itself can damage the brain. Postmortem examination of brains from patients with severe head injuries show dilation of the ventricles and a diffuse loss of myelin. Oppenheimer studied the brains of patients who sustained "mild concussion" and concluded that permanent damage in the form of microscopic lesions can be inflicted on the brain from what usually are regarded as "trivial head injuries." Although some of these lesions may be visible in CT scans (in the order of 5% of cases with mild head injuries), recent studies with MRI suggest that the majority of cases with "mild head injury" may have lesions. For example, Wilberger and his colleagues reported that in a series of 24 patients without any evident lesion on repeated CT scans, all demonstrated lesions on MRI scans. Similarly, a parallel study by Levin and his colleagues reported that of 16 consecutive admissions with "minor or moderate" closed-head injury, 1 had an abnormal CT scan, and 14 had abnormal MRI scans. In summary, the conclusion appears inescapable that even mild head trauma may be associated with some pathology.

Finally, it appears that people who sustain head injuries are more likely to sustain subsequent head injuries and there is a strong suggestion in the literature that the effects of even very mild head injuries may be cumulative. Boxers provide an excellent example because it is well established that they sustain significant brain injuries leading to a condition called *traumatic encephalopathy* (known more commonly as the "punch drunk syndrome") even though the period(s) of unconsciousness by individual boxers may have been few and of short duration. Mohamad Ali is a good case in point, as he now shows marked neurological symptoms resembling Parkinson's disease yet he was never "knocked out" and took some pride in claiming he was never hurt.

Behavioral Assessment of the Severity of Brain Injury

Although neuroradiological measures can provide objective indicators of neural status after closed-head injury, behavior is the most important measure of the integrity of the nervous system. In the immediate postinjury period there are two common measures of behavior: coma and amnesia. In fact, before the development of CT scans and MRI scans, the depth and duration of coma were the most useful indicators of brain injury. Since clinical judgment on the depth of coma was largely subjective and unreliable, the Glasgow Coma Scale

TABLE 31-2. The Glasgow Coma Scale

Response	Points	Index of wakefulness
		Eye opening
None	1	Not attributable to ocular swelling
To pain	2	Pain stimulus is applied to chest or limbs
To speech	3	Nonspecific response to speech or shout, does not imply the patient obeys command to open eyes
Spontaneous	4	Eyes are open, but this does not imply intact awareness
		Motor response
No response	1	Flaccid
Extension	2	"Decerebrate." Adduction, internal rotation of shoulder, and pronation of the forearm
Abnormal flexion	3	"Decorticate." Abnormal flexion, adduction of the shoulder
Withdrawal	4	Normal flexor response; withdraws from pain stimulus with abduction of the shoulder
Localizes pain	5	Pain stimulus applied to supraocular region or fingertip causes limb to move so as to attempt to remove it
Obeys commands	6	Follows simple commands
		Verbal response
No response	1	(Self-explanatory)
Incomprehensible	2	Moaning and groaning, but no recognizable words
Inappropriate	3	Intelligible speech (e.g., shouting or swearing), but no sustained or coherent conversation
Confused	4	Patient responds to questions in a conversational manner, but the responses indicate varying degrees of disorientation and confusion
Oriented	5	Normal orientation to time, place, and person

Note: The summed Glasgow Coma Scale is equal to E + M + V (3–15).
Source: After Teasdale, B., and B. Jennett, 1974

(Table 31-2) was designed to provide an objective indicator of the degree of unconsciousness. In this scale three indices of wakefulness are evaluated including eye opening, motor response, and verbal response. By giving the Glasgow Scale serially it has proven possible to identify objectively the recovery from unconsciousness. A score of 8 or less is often used as a criterion for severe closed-head injury, and one of 9–12 for moderate injury. One difficulty with the scale as a measure of the severity of brain injury is that up to 50% of hospital admissions have scores of 13–15, thus indicating no coma, but these people may have significant sequelae of the head injury. Measurement of posttraumatic amnesia (PTA), which was first suggested by Russell in the 1930s, is an alternative measure of severity of injury. The definition of PTA varies because it may include the period of coma or it may be restricted to the period of anterograde amnesia. In any event, there is good evidence that the duration of PTA is correlated (imperfectly) with later memory disturbance, as illustrated in Figure 31-2. A commonly used scale is as follows: PTA < 10 min = very mild injury; PTA 10–60 min = mild injury; PTA 1–24 h = moderate injury; PTA 1–7 days = severe injury; PTA > 7 days = very severe injury. One problem with using PTA, however, is that there is no consistent method of measuring it in different studies. Thus, it is measured by retrospective questioning of people, by measures of disorientation, or by neuropsychological assessment, each of which yields a different estimate of severity of injury. Two useful procedures have

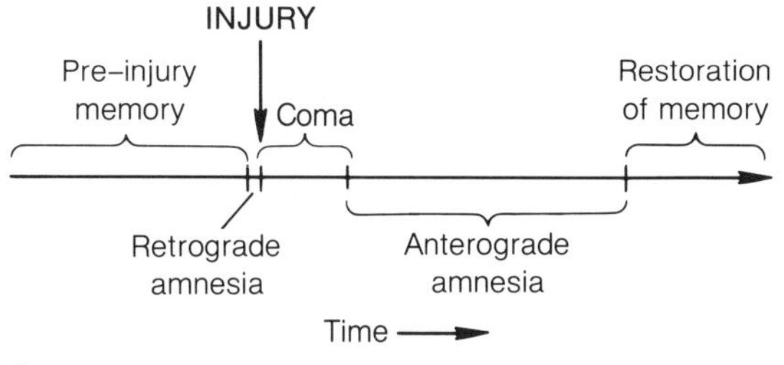

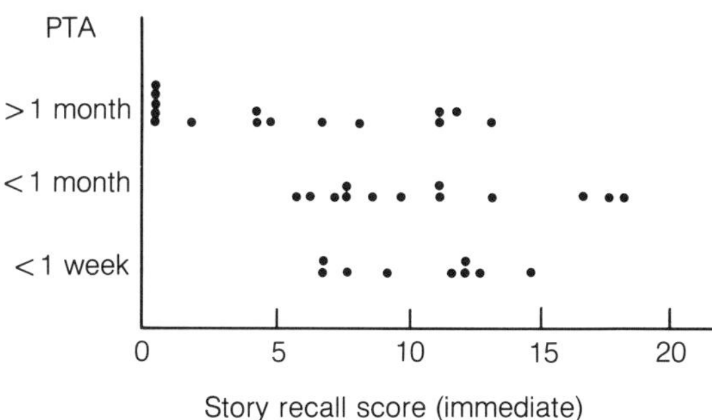

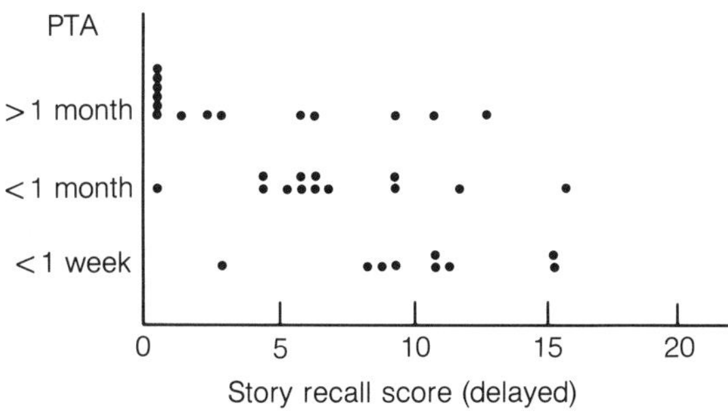

FIGURE 31-2. *A*. Schematic sequence of acute alterations in memory after closed-head injury. The period of coma and anterograde amnesia are often called the period of posttraumatic amnesia (PTA), although PTA may sometimes be equivalent to the anterograde amnesia. (After Levin et al., 1982.) *B*. Histogram showing the distribution of individual scores of story recall by patients in three groups distinguished by the period of PTA. Scores represent recall of the second of two stories. (After Newcombe, 1987.)

been proposed recently, one in the United States by Levin and his colleagues and another by Fortuny and colleagues in England, and if they become widely used it should be easier to compare patients in different studies.

Recovery from Closed-Head Injury

Although it is commonly stated that recovery from head trauma may continue for 2 to 3 years, there is little doubt that the bulk of the cognitive recovery occurs in the first 6 to 9 months. In general, recovery of memory functions appears to be somewhat slower than general intelligence and, in general, the final level of memory performance is lower than for other cognitive functions. There is probably a relationship between severity of injury (as inferred from coma or PTA) and general cognitive recovery, but this is highly variable. Levin and his colleagues have suggested that people with brainstem damage, as inferred from oculomotor disturbance, have a poorer cognitive outcome, and this is probably true of people with initial dysphasias or hemiparesis as well. Although the prognosis for significant recovery of cognitive functions is good, there can be less optimism regarding the recovery of social interactions or personality, which often show significant change. Numerous studies support the conclusion that the quality of life, in terms of social life, perceived stress levels, and leisure activities, is significantly poorer following closed-head injury, and that this condition is chronic. For example, Klonoff and her colleagues administered various self-report inventories to patients 2 to 4 years after their injuries. More than 50% of the cases reported physical problems including limb weakness, pain and stiffness, which indicates that people often have multiple problems in addition to the brain injury. More importantly, they complained about their social contacts and leisure activities. Furthermore, relatives of patients report great strain, which appears to increase over time. A study by Brooks and colleagues found that the relatives (spouses and parents) of 74% of patients complained of personality change 5 years after injury and more than 50% complained of mood changes, temper, irritability, and threats of violence. Unfortunately, there have been few attempts to develop measurement tools to measure changes in psychosocial adjustment in brain-injured people, so we must rely largely on descriptions and self reports, which provide little insight into the causes of these problems.

Chronic Neuropsychological Consequences of Head Trauma

It is difficult to make generalizations about the neuropsychological consequences of head trauma. The most obvious, and reliable, complaint is of impaired memory, but there are likely to be impaired performance on some subtests of the WAIS-R, difficulties with tests that are speeded or require intense concentration, as well as ideosyncratic problems on specific tests. Although seldom assessed, there is also likely to be a deficit in tests of interhemispheric transfer. One major difficulty in summarizing the effects of closed-head injuries is that people may suffer diffuse damage, which may manifest itself as low average performance on a variety of tests, or focal damage, which may lead to deficits on tests sensitive to specific cognitive functions. In addition, the blow to the head and the subsequent neural changes (Table 31-1) are unique for each patient, so the nature and severity of the brain damage will not be precisely the same in any two patients. Consider the following two cases, which are typical.

U. B. was a 44-year-old female with 2 years of college education who was in an automobile accident in which the left side of her head hit the dashboard. She was unconscious for less than 30 min, and when we saw her 4 months after the accident she had an anterograde amnesia for about 2 h before the accident and a PTA of about 1 month, although there were islands of memory throughout the PTA period, the first being within 24 h of the accident. She had paralysis of the left side of her face, and in her left fingers and toes for a couple of days after the injury, and still complains of an inability to taste. Although she was not dysphasic, she claimed to have been unable to read after the accident and her reading was still slow when we saw her. Her CT scan did not reveal a lesion, although there was some right temporal lobe edema. When we saw her she complained of poor memory and concentration, and had not returned to her job. Her full-scale IQ on the WAIS-R was 102, placing her in the average range (Table 31-3). Her performance IQ was 14 points lower than her verbal IQ, however, because she had difficulty with the digit symbol, block-design, and

TABLE 31-3. Test performance of U. B.

Test	Score
WAIS-R	
Full-scale IQ	102
Verbal IQ	109
Performance IQ	95[a]
WMS-R	
Verbal memory	92[a]
Visual memory	100
General memory	93[a]
Attention/Concentration	96
Delayed recall	114
Dichotic words	
Right ear	16/30[a]
Left ear	18/30
Total	34/60[a]
Mooney Closure	23/26
Rey Copy	36/36
Rey Recall	24/36
Kimura Recurring Figures	23
Left/Right differentiation	47/60
Semmes Body-Placing	34/35
Wisconsin Card-Sorting	6 cat
Chicago Word-Fluency	27[a]
Copy face-movement sequences	86/90

[a]Significant impairment.

object-assembly subtests, all of which are timed and require sustained concentration. On the WMS-R her general memory index was 93, which was well below her verbal IQ of 109. Curiously, she performed rather well on tests of visual memory. Her performance on most other tests was within normal limits, with the exception of her performance on the word fluency, design fluency, and the dichotic-listening tests in which she reported about half as many words as expected for her IQ and age. These results suggest damage to the right orbital-frontal area, although this is difficult to reconcile with her left-sided weakness and paralysis, which suggests a more dorsolateral injury. Further, although she showed a classic right temporal lobe personality (see Chapter 23), her performance on nonverbal memory tasks was good. Finally, it is difficult to understand why a right frontal lobe lesion would produce dyslexia.

The second case is one described by Newcombe. An 8-year-old girl sustained a left temporal-parietal skull fracture in a car crash that killed her parents. She was initially dysphasic, with a right hemiparesis, both of which conditions eventually resolved. Although the girl appeared to be happy and stable after her traumatic accident, she was doing very poorly in school and was 2 years behind in reading. It was therefore logical to ascribe her difficulties to the serious head injury. In particular, her WISC-R verbal IQ was only 92, and her performance IQ was 95, with considerable variation in subscale performance (range of 2 to 15). Further investigation revealed that her father, who was a skilled craftsman, was dyslexic, and her 12-year-old sister was also a poor reader, scoring 3 years behind her peers on tests of reading comprehension. Of particular importance, her sister's verbal IQ was 90, whereas her performance IQ was 120. Thus, the claim that the injured girl's reading problem was attributable to her accident is controversial, to say the least! Nevertheless, it is reasonable to speculate that her performance IQ might have been reduced by the accident.

These two cases illustrate some of the difficulties facing neuropsychologists who deal with people with closed-head injuries. In particular, there may be acute neurological signs that are not consistent with later behavioral change, and conversely, there may be behavioral complaints that are not consistent with neurological evidence. In addition, it is difficult to know what the premorbid state of the person was, so it is difficult to determine what behavioral changes have occurred. Nonetheless, both cases show a reduced performance IQ relative to the verbal IQ, which is typical of closed-head injuries.

Although an objective assessment of the cognitive abilities of people with closed-head injuries is an important neuropsychological task, there is an additional question that must be answered, namely the prognosis for recovery. Unfortunately, clinical neuropsychological assessment relies on standardized and relatively complex tasks that may or may not correlate with real-life problems. Thus, as Newcombe has emphasized, standard neuropsychological tests can be performed successfully by patients who nevertheless report post-traumatic problems in following academic discourse, telephone conversations, or fast speech. In contrast to patients with localizable lesions of the brain, mild head trauma victims appear to have deficits in general processing; deficits that are not measured by current neuropsychological assessment batteries. It is likely that people who have suffered head trauma experience deficits in the function of tertiary areas, but in contrast to people with lesions in one area, people with diffuse damage to several tertiary areas may have rather different symptoms. Neuropsychology will have to develop new tests to quantitatively measure these handicaps, with emphasis upon complex cognitive processing.

The difficulty that current neuropsychological assessment procedures have in providing an objective and quantitative picture of the functioning of people with closed-head injuries is not unique.

Other disorders with diffuse damage, such as dementing diseases, present similar problems.

Psychiatric Aspects of Closed-Head Injury

Disabilities in coping and in social interaction are commonplace after head injury, but they are difficult to characterize objectively or to quantify. Typically, patients are described as having either a *frontal syndrome,* which seems to imply a lack of foresight and concern, irresponsibility, and a loss of insight, or a *temporal lobe syndrome,* which seems to imply irritability and hostility. (In view of the complexity of the effects of frontal and temporal lobe lesions as described in Chapters 18 and 19, this use of such terms is neither recommended nor encouraged!) In addition, there appear to be two types of psychiatric syndromes known as a postconcussional syndrome and posttraumatic psychosis.

The **postconcussional syndrome** is defined by Levin and coworkers as a constellation of somatic and psychological symptoms including headache, dizziness, fatigue, diminished concentration, memory deficit, irritability, anxiety, insomnia, hypochondriacal concern, hypersensitivity to noise, and photophobia. Most concussion victims suffer some of these symptoms immediately after the injury and it appears that more than 50% of people with mild head trauma still suffer at least one of these symptoms 6 weeks after the injury. These symptoms are more likely to be prolonged in people who have been described as "neurotic" or "anxious" prior to the injury. Further, the presence of such symptoms in the absence of any physical symptoms is often associated with social difficulties with close relatives who may become frustrated with the complaints.

Posttraumatic psychosis is a broad term that may refer to depressive or manic reactions, or to other forms of psychotic behavior. The psychotic reactions, including hallucinations or disordered thought, may result from temporal lobe seizures or from neurochemical abnormalities, either of which could result from the head trauma. *Posttraumatic depression* has not been well studied but it may be an appropriate reaction to serious neurological injury, especially if there are obvious deficits such as sensory loss, dysphasia, or weakness. Furthermore, there are likely to be feelings of helplessness in people who awake in neurological units and who have a retrograde amnesia for the events surrounding their admission to hospital. And again, neurochemical changes resulting from the injury could lead to depression as well.

Most postconcussional and psychotic reactions appear to subside over time, but the preinjury personality and other social factors almost certainly interact with the length and severity of the symptoms.

Summary

Closed-head injury can produce both a focal lesion and diffuse damage. These injuries lead to specific deficits that can be measured by neuropsychological tests as well as more "global" deficits in information processing and social behavior, neither of which have proven amenable to quantification by standardized tests. The large number of people that suffer head trauma and the relative insensitivity of neuropsychological evaluation to the specific problems of these people make these patients a major challenge for clinical neuropsychology.

ALZHEIMER'S DISEASE

Historical Background

That people can become depressed, suffer from lapses in memory, become senile and demented in old age is well known. Furthermore, beginning with earliest writings, reference to "fatuity" and "dotage" regularly appear in the literature associated with aging. Historically, social attitudes toward aging and age-related changes have been quite variable, with some societies respecting people of old age and looking to them for guidance and wisdom and other societies displaying disinterest or even contempt for the aged. Explanations for age-related changes have been equally variable, with occasional writers suggesting that some of the debilitating age-related changes represented the process of disease and others suggesting that they were a routine part of the aging process. An additional important feature in influencing views toward aging has been the structure of societies. Attitudes vary between societies that are well established and those in flux, and they vary between societies with disproportionately young and disproportionately old populations.

Population structures like those now developing in North America and Europe have never been experienced previously. Since 1900, the percentage of older people has been steadily increasing. In 1900, about 4% of the population had attained 65 years of age. By 1980, about 10% of the population was over 65. It is fully expected that this trend will continue in developed nations and begin to emerge in developing nations. With the rise in the number of older people, there are parallel increases in the numbers of people with cognitive impairments related to an aging brain. This becomes a significant social and medical problem considering the stress imposed on families and medical support systems.

It is obviously not the case that every person who becomes old also becomes depressed, forgetful, or demented. Some people live to very old age and at the same time enjoy active, healthy, productive lives. Other people may show symptoms of senility at an age at which they would be considered young. Prevalence studies have found that in the population of 65 and older, the incidence of severe dementia is between 1 and 6% and the incidence of mild dementia is between 3 and 20%. This range is wide and the values imprecise because it is difficult to obtain reliable estimates. Attitudes toward aging, methods of reporting conditions in the aged, and whether a family looks after a disabled person or sends him or her to an institution, as well as the criteria used by researchers, all influence the data obtained from prevalence studies. The prevalence of dementia also varies with aging, with older age groups having higher incidences of dementia. Between ages 65 and 70, approximately 3 to 5% may be demented. This value rises to about 5 to 7% between 70 and 75, to 7 to 9% between 75 and 80, and to about 25% by age 85 and over. Interestingly, people living into their 90's or 100's have a reduced incidence of dementia, presumably because the demented subgroups have died at an earlier age. Although the incidence of dementia increases in populations 65 and older, younger cases do occur, even among people in the 30- to 40-year-old range. At present there is relatively little known about prevalence based on other characteristics, including sex, social class, or country of domicile.

There are of course many causes of the dementia of old age and some of the more prevalent causes are listed in Table 31-4. It is estimated, however, that over 65% of the people suffering from various degrees of dementia have Alzheimer's disease. Compared with the incidence of other degenerative neurological disorders, Alzheimer's disease is more frequent than Parkinson's disease. It has been estimated that about one half million people were afflicted with each disease in the United States in 1976. By the 1980s the number of dementia cases had grown to more than 1 million and by 1985 one estimate had put the number to between 1.5 and 2 million people. Comparatively speaking, about one-quarter million had multiple sclerosis, 10,000 had Huntington's disease, and 5000 had amyotrophic lateral sclerosis (Lou Gehrig's disease). A still more instructive aspect of these numbers concerns the care required for the dementia patients. About half of these people are under institutional care, where they make up more than 60% of the population of nursing homes and various chronic care hospitals.

Definition of Alzheimer's Disease

By the 1800s, it was recognized that there were age-related brain changes. It was noted that the

TABLE 31-4. A short list of possible causes of dementia

Alzheimer's disease
Down's syndrome
Multiinfarct dementia
Toxic substances (drugs, alcohol)
Metabolic deficiency (e.g., vitamin B_{12})
Endocrine (e.g., hypothyroidism)
Infectious (e.g., neurosyphilis)
Inflammatory (e.g., vasculitis)
Posttraumatic and postanoxic
Genetic (e.g., Huntington's disease)
Degenerative (e.g., Parkinson's disease)
Cerebral tumors
Subdural hematoma
Hydrocephalus

Source: After Van Crevel, 1986.

cortex of the brain underwent ventricular dilation and atrophy and the association between atrophy and senile dementia was noted by a number of people. The modern definition of Alzheimer's disease stems from a case study published by the German physician Alois Alzheimer in 1906. The patient was a 51-year-old woman for whom Alzheimer described a set of clinical and neuropathological findings. This description of symptoms and pathology became known as Alzheimer's disease. Until quite recently, Alzheimer's disease was considered a presenile dementia (to characterize the youth of the patient), but by the 1970s it became clear that the symptoms and pathology were similar in both young and old patients. Currently, the designation of Alzheimer's disease disregards age and considers only the clinical symptoms and neuropathology, although the term is sometimes modified as presenile or senile type. In 1983, Reisberg edited a standard reference on Alzheimer's disease, and in 1986 Swaab and coworkers edited a comprehensive experimental report on the disease.

The clinical definition of Alzheimer's disease according to the DSM-III includes the following three criteria. It takes into account that there can be other forms of dementia and that these can have different causes and courses: (1) dementia, (2) insidious onset with uniformly progressive deteriorating course, and (3) exclusion of all other specific causes of dementia by the history, physical examination, laboratory tests, psychometric, and other special studies.

There are now a large number of known neuropathological correlates of Alzheimer's but the three primary indicators of the disease are described below. In noting the relation between these signs and the symptoms of the disease, it must be pointed out that the direct causes of each are not known.

1. *Neuritic plaques (NPs).* **Neuritic plaques,** also known as senile plaques, are found chiefly in the cerebral cortex. Increased concentration of these elements in the cortex have been correlated with the magnitude of cognitive deterioration. The plaques consist of a central core of homogeneous protein material known as *amyloid,* surrounded by degenerative cellular fragments. These include axonal and dendritic processes and other components of cells. These plaques are generally considered to be nonspecific phenomena in that they can be found in diminished numbers in non-Alzheimer's patients, in dementias cased by other known events, and in patients with Down's syndrome.

2. *Paired helical filaments (PHFs).* **Paired helical filaments** are also known as neurofibrillary tangles and are found in both the cerebral cortex and in the hippocampus, with the posterior half of the hippocampus more severely affected than the anterior half. Light-microscope examination has shown that the filaments have a double helical configuration. They have been described mainly in human tissue and have also been observed in patients with Down's syndrome, patients with Parkinson's disease, and in patients with other forms of dementias.

3. *Granulovacuolar bodies.* The **granulovacuolar bodies** consist of an outer membrane with a small dense granule in its center. These are more

common in Alzheimer's patients than in the general aged population.

Other Anatomical Correlates

Increased attention to Alzheimer's disease is leading to the identification of an enormous number of associated brain changes. The notion that it is a disease primarily related to the loss of acetylcholine neurons that project from the basal forebrain (just anterior to the hypothalamus) to the neocortex, and which secondarily causes the anatomical changes described above, has gained recent currency. As the following descriptions will show, this is a simplistic view. There are widespread changes in the neocortex and limbic cortex and there are associated changes in a number of neurotransmitter systems, none of which alone can be simply correlated with the clinical symptoms. Interestingly, most of the brainstem, cerebellum, and spinal cord are relatively spared.

Neocortical Changes. The changes in the neocortex are not uniform. Although the cortex becomes shrunken or atrophied, losing as much as one third of its volume as the disease progresses, some areas are relatively spared. Figure 31-3 shows a lateral and medial view of the human brain on which stippling indicates areas of degeneration. The darker the stippling, the more severe the degeneration. As is clearly shown in this figure, the primary sensory and motor areas of the cortex, especially visual cortex, and sensorimotor cortex are spared. The frontal lobes are less affected than posterior cortex but areas of most extensive change are parietal tertiary areas, inferior temporal cortex, and limbic cortex.

Limbic Cortex Changes. The limbic system undergoes the most severe degenerative changes in Alzheimer's disease, and of the limbic structures the entorhinal cortex is affected earliest and most severely. A number of sources agree that it is the entorhinal cortex that shows clearest evidence of cell loss. This has important implications for understanding some of the symptoms of the disease. Entorhinal cortex is the major relay through which information from the neocortex gets to the hippocampus and through which information from the hippocampus is sent back to the neocortex (see Chapter 21). Consequently, loss of this cortex is equivalent to loss of the hippocampal formation. Since memory loss is an early and enduring symptom of the disease, it is most likely due to the degenerative changes that take place in this area of the cortex.

Cell Changes. Although many studies describe loss of cells in the cortex of Alzheimer's patients, there is dispute. There seems to be a substantial reduction in large cells, but these cells may shrink rather than disappear. The more widespread cause of cortical atrophy, however, appears to be loss of dendritic arborization. Figure 31-4 illustrates cells drawn by Scheibel, showing a normal adult pattern, and an early, advanced, and terminal pattern of pyramidal cells obtained from patients who had Alzheimer's disease. The earliest changes appear to be a loss of spines on dendrites, followed by a loss of small dendrites and then loss of larger dendrites. In advanced stages the triangular pattern of the cell gives way to a pear shape and irregular swellings appear on the dendritic shaft. According to Scheibel, this pattern of changes appears to reverse the maturational pattern of the cells. The cause of these changes is presently unknown. It is worth noting, however, that the changes are not simply typical of aging. There is evidence that normal old people show increases in dendritic arborization, rather than the Alzheimer's pattern illustrated here.

Neurotransmitter Changes. A great deal of publicity has been given to findings that acetylcholine levels are reduced in Alzheimer's disease and this has led to the idea that changes in this transmitter are causal in the memory declines shown by patients. Two points are relevant here,

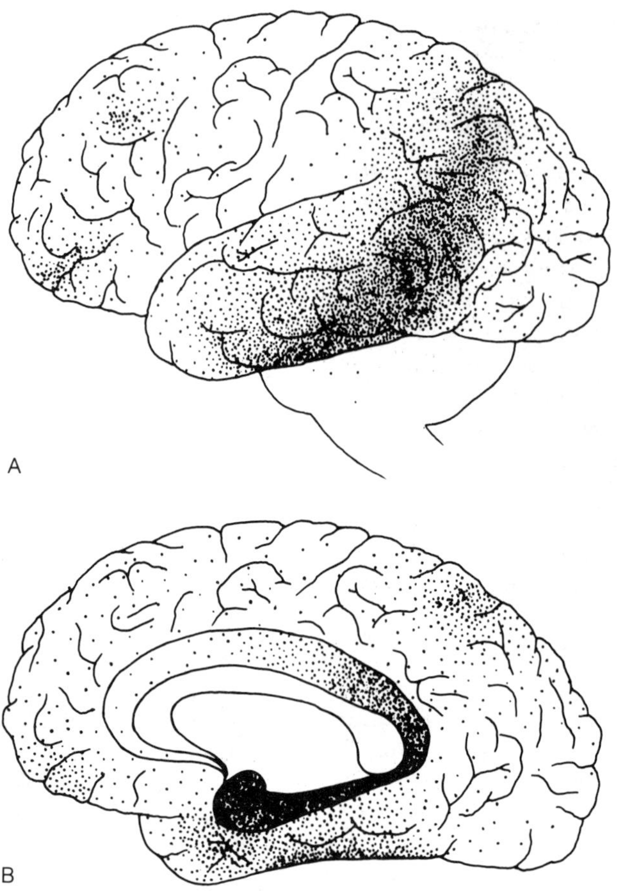

FIGURE 31-3. Schematic representation of distribution and severity of degeneration on *(A)* lateral and *(B)* medial aspect of the brain in an average Alzheimer case. The darker the area, the more pronounced the degeneration. White areas are spared, with only basic change discernible. (After Brun, 1983.)

however. First, there are marked reductions in many transmitter systems. Second, the reductions in any one system are uneven from patient to patient. There are problems in estimating transmitter system levels through the course of the disease. The brain is not accessible for samples so that estimates are usually taken from urine or blood samples and these measures are usually by-products of neurotransmitter metabolism. The other source of tissue is that obtained at autopsy and so samples here represent terminal levels of biochemical activity. There are now a number of published studies on transmitter levels. The most representative of these from Carlsson shows reductions of about 50% in dopamine, 25% in norepinephrine, 50% in acetylcholine, and about 50% in serotonin. The most interesting feature of the changes is not the absolute decreases in any individual patient but the pattern of decreases. Although aged-matched controls also show reductions in transmitter levels, when the pattern of reductions in all three transmitter substances is plotted, the Alzheimer patients show greater reductions in two or more transmitters and in this way they distinguish themselves from the control groups. This observation of combined neurotransmitter reductions, especially of acetylcholine and serotonin may be extremely relevant to cognitive declines. Using the rat, Vanderwolf and his coworkers have demonstrated that one of the two activated EEG patterns of the neocortex requires acetylcholine; the other requires serotonin. If both are absent, rats display chronic sleeplike EEG activity even though they walk around. If they are asked to perform in learning tests, they show a complete absence of learning and memory, behaving essentially as if they had no neocortex at all. If Alzheimer's patients undergo the same EEG changes and end up with a "sleeping" neocortex their severe cognitive impairments would be understandable.

Putative Causes of Alzheimer's Disease

At present there is no known cause of Alzheimer's disease. Consequently, research is being directed toward a large number of potential causes. We should note here, though, that most of the research thrust is quite new. Only a few years ago there was very little research on aging and no funding agencies directing their interests toward diseases that complicate the aging process. That is gradually changing and a large number of research projects are being directed toward aging in general and Alzheimer's disease in particular. These new re-

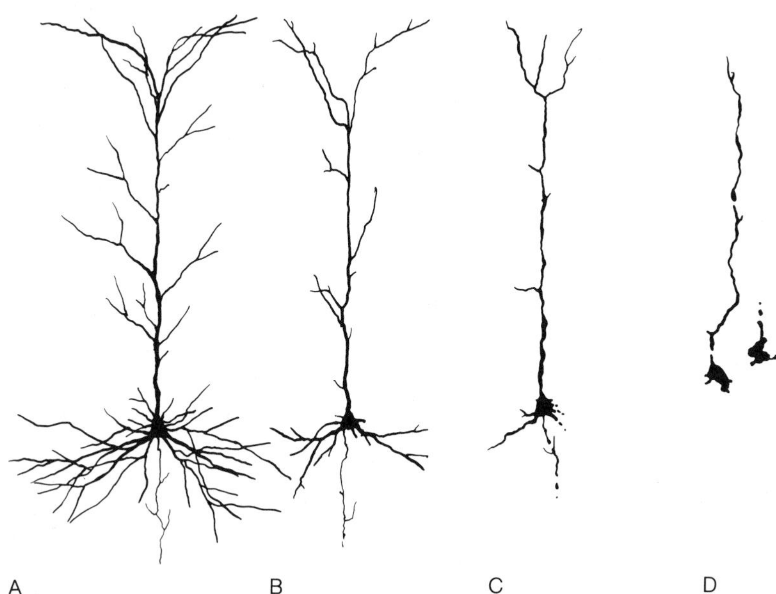

FIGURE 31-4. Sequence of changes in a cortical pyramidal cell during development of Alzheimer's dementia. *(A)* normal adult pattern; *(B)* early stages of disease marked by patchy spine loss and thinning out of the dendritic tree, especially horizontally oriented branches; *(C)* advanced stage with almost complete loss of basilar dendrites; and *(D)* terminal stage. Drawn from Golgi-stained sections of human prefrontal cortex. (After Scheibel, 1983.)

search fronts are currently being directed toward the following putative causes.

Genetics. There is an increased frequency of Alzheimer's disease in families that have had a member with Alzheimer's disease. If a sibling has had the disease, the risk is 3.8% and if a parent has had the disease the risk is 10%. Researchers are also interested in the relations between Down's syndrome and Alzheimer's disease since the neural changes that lead to dementia in Down's syndrome are very similar to those in Alzheimer's disease. There is also increased risk of Alzheimer's disease in families that have had a Down's syndrome member. Consequently, it is thought that a gene or a group of genes, possibly some close to the Down's syndrome gene, could be identified as promoting or causing Alzheimer's disease.

Trace Metals. Early studies with animals have identified neurofibrillary degeneration, similar to that in Alzheimer's disease, after the animals were given aluminum salts. Research that followed up this hint found increases of 10 to 30 times the normal concentration of aluminum in Alzheimer patient's brains. At present it is not known why aluminum accumulates or whether taking action to reduce accumulation could be helpful.

Immune Reactions. It is thought, in some quarters, that in old age the immune system loses its ability to recognize the individual's own body. As a result it develops antibrain antibodies that then cause neuronal degeneration.

Slow Viruses. The idea for the existence of slow viruses came from studies on a Papua New Guinea tribe that ate the brains of deceased members. Years later individuals would become ataxic with a disease called *kuru,* die and apparently pass on a virus to others, which in turn took years to display symptoms. Likewise, a disease called **Creutzfeldt-Jakob's disease** also appears to be caused by slow viruses and it can be passed on to other humans and animals. In both diseases the brain changes have some similarity to those of Alzheimer's disease. There has been a suggestion that material from human patients has caused Alzheimer's in chimpanzees. Attempts to replicate the experiment, to locate viruses, or to identify their source have so far been unsuccessful.

Blood Flow. Originally, most Alzheimer's disease was attributed to poor circulation. More recently, studies have confirmed that there is a profound reduction in the amount of blood delivered to the brain and the amount of glucose extracted from the blood. This has become readily apparent from PET studies. In normal people, blood flow to the brain declines by over 20% between the ages of 30 and 60, but the brain compensates by more efficient oxygen uptake. In Alzheimer's there is an enhanced decline but no compensatory mechanisms. The greatest decreases in blood flow are found in those areas of the brain in which the most degenerative change is seen. Of course, what is not known here is whether the decline in blood flow and glucose use are causal or secondary to degenerative brain changes. At least one pharmacological attempt to treat Alzheimer's involves stimulating brain blood flow.

Abnormal Proteins. The three main pathological changes associated with Alzheimer's disease—plaques, neurofibrillary tangles, and granulovacuolar bodies—reflect an accumulation of protein that is not seen in normal brains. This has led to the suggestion that unusual proteins are being produced and are accumulating, thus disrupting normal protein production and use.

Clinical Symptoms and Progress

The most insidious feature of Alzheimer's disease is its slow onset and steady progress that gradually robs a patient first of recent memory, then of more remote memory, and finally of the abilities to recognize family members and to function independently. A detailed description of the stages of the disease and clinical symptoms has been given by Reisberg and is reproduced in Table 31-5. As pointed out by Reisberg, the disease progress is gradual, and patients spend several months to years in each of the stages. Reisberg also describes levels of impairments in five measures of cognitive function (concentration, recent and past memory, orientation, social functioning, and self-care) that are descriptive parallels of the stages shown in Table 31-5.

Studies on the prognosis of the disease suggest that patients rated as being in the forgetfulness stage may remain there and show no further deterioration. Therefore the symptom of forgetfulness has doubtful prognostic value. For patients classified in the later stages on the scale, 2-year follow-ups generally find further deterioration. Therefore,

TABLE 31-5. Scale of behavioral change in Alzheimer's disease

Degree of cognitive decline	Symptoms
None	No subjective complaints of memory deficit. No memory deficit evident on clinical interview.
Very mild	Complains of memory deficit, most frequently in following areas: (a) forgetting where one has placed familiar objects; (b) forgetting names one formerly knew well. No objective evidence of memory deficit on clinical interview. No objective deficits in employment or social situations. Appropriate concern with respect to symptomatology.
Mild	Earliest clear-cut deficits. Manifestations in more than one of the following areas: (a) patient may have gotten lost when traveling to an unfamiliar location; (b) coworkers become aware of patient's relatively poor performance; (d) patient may read a passage or a book and retain relatively little material; (e) patient may demonstrate decreased facility in remembering names upon introduction to new people; (f) patient may have lost or misplaced an object of value; (g) concentration deficit may be evident on clinical testing. Objective evidence of memory deficit obtained only with formal tests. Decreased performance in demanding employment and social settings. Denial begins to occur and mild to moderate anxiety is displayed.
Moderate	Clear-cut deficit on clinical interview in: (a) decreased knowledge of current and recent events; (b) memory of personal history; (c) concentration deficit on serial subtractions; (d) decreased ability to travel, handle finances, etc. Inability to perform complex tasks. Denial is dominant defense mechanism. Flattening of affect and withdrawal from challenging situations.
Moderately severe	Cannot function without some assistance. Unable to recall a major relevant aspect of current life: e.g., address or telephone number, names of close family members, name of schools from which they graduated. Frequent disorientation to date, day, season, and place. An educated person may have difficulty counting backward by 4's from 40 and 2's from 20.
Severe	May occasionally forget the name of spouse. Will be largely unaware of all recent events and experiences in their lives. Retain some knowledge of their past lives but this is sketchy. May have difficulty counting back or forward to and from 10. Will require some assistance with activities of daily living, e.g., may become incontinent, will require travel assistance but occasionally will display ability to travel to familiar locations. Diurnal rhythm frequently disturbed. Can recall their own name and distinguish familiar from unfamiliar persons in their environment. Personality and emotional changes occur. These may include delusional behavior, obsessive symptoms, anxiety, or loss of purposeful behavior.
Very severe	All verbal abilities are lost. Frequently there is no speech at all — only grunting; incontinent of urine; requires assistance in toileting and feeding. Loses basic psychomotor skill, e.g., ability to walk. The brain appears to no longer be able to tell the body what to do.

Source: After Reisburg, 1983.

rating in the later stages clearly has prognostic value. In the final stages of the disease, patients become susceptible to other disorders, infections, or pneumonia.

Neuropsychological Assessment

Neuropsychological evaluation of Alzheimer's disease patients serves a number of functions. First, assessment can serve to establish the presence and severity of the deficits. One of the difficulties with evaluating whether cognitive changes are related to Alzheimer's disease is that in the early stages of the disease, symptoms may simply resemble benign changes associated with aging. If tests can reveal certain patterns in cognitive and behavioral change that are specific to Alzheimer's disease, then both diagnosis and treatment can be aided. Test patterns that are definitive in diagnosis have not been developed. Spinnler and Della Sala have given an overview of test performance they have obtained, which when used with other methods of evaluation such as CT scans, PET scans, and EEG evaluation gives diagnostic accuracy to about 80%. Others, such as Bowles and coworkers, have attempted to evaluate strategies used by Alzheimer patients as compared with other populations. They found, for example, that on tests of naming, the errors made by Alzheimer patients are more related to failure of concept identification than were the errors of an aged control group. It must be remembered, of course, that diagnosis is presumptive and must await confirmation at autopsy. An additional function for tests with diagnostic objectives is to determine whether there are different types of Alzheimer's disease. Interest has focused specifically on comparisons of the presenile type, which occurs in quite young individuals, and the senile type that occurs in older patients. Other areas of interest concern familial forms, in which a member of the family has had the disease, and nonfamilial forms. Finally, the issue of sex differences in patterns of deficits and progress of the disease is also a topic of interest. To date, opinions are divided on whether neuropsychological evaluations can give definitive answers. For example, Loring and Largen have reported greater impairments on some tasks in presenile than in senile patients, but Grady and coworkers have not confirmed this report. This may be because of some inherent problems in studying the two populations, such as the more rapid development of the presenile form. Finally, interest has been directed toward the study of individual differences in the patterns of impairments of Alzheimer patients. Martin and coworkers, although noting that global impairments appear in Alzheimer patients, nevertheless remark on the wide individual differences seen in patients. Consequently, they argue against general averaging of the deficits within populations.

Second, assessment can attempt to distinguish Alzheimer's disease from other dementia-causing conditions. The difficulty in diagnosis is that symptoms displayed by Alzheimer patients can be confused with those displayed by depressive patients, by patients who have suffered one or a number of small strokes, by patients with Huntington's disease, or by patients with other dementia-causing diseases. Fuld has used IQ subtest scales to distinguish Alzheimer's disease impairment patterns from patterns of impairments produced by cerebrovascular disease. Alzheimer patients are marked by the striking deficits they show on digit symbol and block design, with successively milder impairments on object assembly, similarities and digit span, and information and vocabulary. Other Alzheimer's-sensitive tests include backward digits, telling the time on clocks without numbers, and object naming. Of course, diagnosis can be aided by considering a patient's history. Additionally, Alzheimer patients will be expected to have deficits on tests of both left and right hemisphere function, and the impairments will not be marked by sudden onset.

Third, assessment can serve to monitor the progress of the disease. This has special utility in treatment. It can be expected that many forms of treatment will be developed for experimental use, and assessment will require objective tests that can allow repeated evaluation.

Fourth, assessment can be directed to basic research questions concerning brain function. The pattern of brain damage that occurs with Alzheimer's disease is distinctive, and so it has been recognized that examination of the way cognitive functions are fragmented by the disease will reveal insight into the neural structure of cognitive function. In an examination of the encoding of memory, Becker and coworkers have reported that Alzheimer patients encode less than control subjects during learning, but they forget what they have learned at the same rate as control subjects. Martin and coworkers confirm the more specific encoding deficit. In an examination of reading patterns, Cummings and coworkers have found that reading aloud remains relatively preserved, but memory for what is read is severely impaired. In an examination of naming impairments, Huff and coworkers have observed that Alzheimer patients have difficulties in producing the names of objects and in distinguishing among objects within a category. They conclude that the anomia deficit is characterized by a loss of information about specific objects and their names, rather than by simply a problem of retrieval. Murdoch and coworkers have examined the language impairments connected with Alzheimer's and compared them to impairments in other populations. They note that the language impairments are most notable on tasks requiring cognitive processing. Finally, others, such as Wilson and coworkers, have undertaken studies involving comparisons of different cognitive functions. They note, for example, that the pattern of deficits on language tasks are much more affected than facial-recognition tasks, presumably because of the more demanding cognitive processing required in the former. Presumably, these lines of inquiry will become more fruitful as brain metabolism studies are combined with specific forms of cognitive analysis.

CHRONIC ALCOHOL ABUSE

Excessive alcohol consumption can lead to disorders such as Korsakoff's syndrome (see Chapter 21), or alcoholic dementia, which is associated with reliable and profound cognitive deficits. Most cases of excessive alcohol intake do not result in such syndromes, however, but are instead associated with a variety of relatively milder cognitive impairments, some of which can be detected with neuropsychological tests. Although there are patterns to the cognitive losses reported across studies, there is significant disagreement in the literature over the cause, nature, and severity of these deficits. The inconsistency in cognitive changes associated with alcohol abuse is perplexing, inasmuch as various neuroradiological measures (pneumoencephalogram, CT scan) have led to general agreement that chronic alcohol abuse leads to enlargement of the ventricles and widening of the cerebral sulci. (Wider sulci imply that there is cortical atrophy.) In addition, quantitative Golgi studies have shown a loss of dendritic branches and dendritic spines similar to those observed in dementing diseases (see Figure 31-4), especially in the hippocampus and dentate gyrus.

The variability across behavioral studies reflects not only the general difficulty in characterizing the behavioral effects of subtle changes in the nervous system, as we saw for head trauma and Alzheimer's disease, but also the influence of demographic and alcoholism-related factors that interact to influence test performance. These factors include (1) heterogeneous subject populations with wide variation in variables such as age, sex, occupation, and education; (2) duration of abusive drinking and subsequent sobriety prior to assessment; and (3) medical complications related to alcohol consumption, such as nutritional deficiency, liver dysfunction, head trauma, and abuse of other drugs. Thus, there is now a view emerging that the neuropsychological consequences of prolonged excessive alcohol consumption result from an interaction of factors, one of which is brain damage resulting directly from the toxic effects of ethanol.

Neuropsychological Correlates of Chronic Alcohol Abuse

In contrast to Alzheimer and head trauma patients, chronic alcoholics are not impaired on standard intelligence tests; alcoholics perform in the average range and seldom show a verbal-performance difference. On the other hand, studies repeatedly show poor performance on block design, and sometimes on object assembly, both of which are timed and require sustained concentration. Curiously, these tests are also affected by head trauma, possibly for similar reasons. Alcoholics tend to complain that their memories are impaired, but most abstinant alcoholics perform within normal limits on standard memory tests, such as the Wechsler Memory Scale. There are subtle memory deficits, however, that can be demonstrated on tests requiring subjects to process unfamiliar, especially nonverbal, information. Paired-associate learning and recall of the Rey Figure provide examples. (See Ryan and Butters, 1986 for a review.) Perhaps it is most surprising that alcoholics do not have more severe memory problems since amnesia is the most salient symptom of Korsakoff's syndrome. Furthermore, in view of the evidence of dendritic loss in the hippocampus of alcoholics one might expect to find poor performance on tests sensitive to hippocampal function, and there is a single study suggesting this. Hence, when we administered the Corsi Span + 1 tests (see Chapter 21) to alcoholic patients, we found that although their block and digit spans were normal, they failed to learn the repeating sequence in the Span + 1 Test—a result similar to that of patients with hippocampal damage (see Figure 31-5).

There have been dozens of studies looking at the performance of alcoholics on tests like the Halstead Category Test and the Wisconsin Card-Sort-

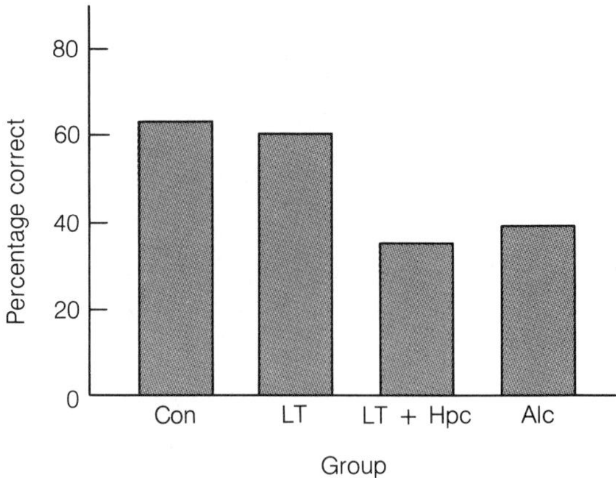

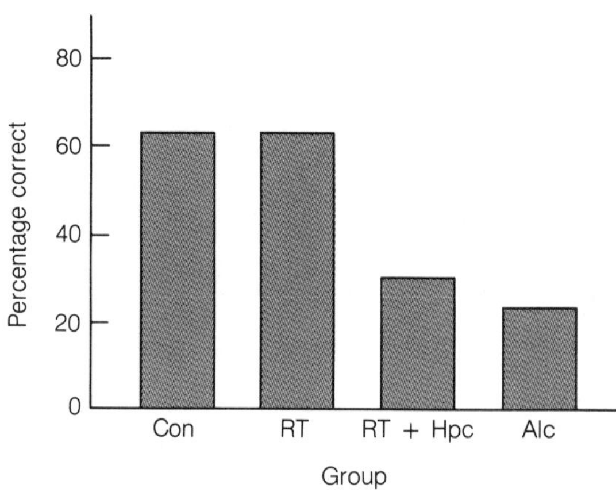

FIGURE 31-5. Mean percentage correct for the control and alcoholic subjects in the current experiment compared with the data from temporal lobe patients previously published by B. Milner. The temporal lobe patients had either the temporal cortex alone or the temporal cortex plus the hippocampus removed. The alcoholic patients performed as poorly as the patients with the hippocampus removed. Con = control; LT = left temporal; RT = right temporal; LT + Hpc = left temporal plus hippocampal damage; RT + Hpc = right temporal plus hippocampal damage; Alc = alcoholic. (After Wilson et al., 1987.)

ing Test, and although deficits are not always found, it appears that older alcoholics with a long history of drinking have considerable difficulty with these tests. Ryan and Butters suggest that chronic alcoholics fail to use hypothesis-testing strategies in a normal manner, which leads to deficits on most tests of problem solving. These types of deficits in alcoholics have led to the suggestion that they are most impaired at tests of frontal-lobe function, but the empirical support for this proposition is inconsistent at best. Still, in view of the evidence of diencephalic amnesia (Chapter 21), the pathology of which includes some of the primary afferents to the frontal lobe, this hypothesis would seem worthy of further investigation.

There have been suggestions that alcoholics are especially poor at tests of visuospatial function, leading to the proposal that the right hemisphere is more affected by alcohol. Although there is evidence that alcoholics are poor at visuospatial tasks, it seems likely that it is because the tests are likely to rely on skills that are less well practiced than verbal tasks, so the threshold for an impairment, which is usually small anyway, is lower for the nonverbal tasks. Furthermore, performance of many tasks (such as the Kimura Recurring-Figures Test) that are sensitive to right hemisphere lesions is unaffected in alcoholics, and there is no convincing evidence that cerebral atrophy is greater in the right hemisphere.

In conclusion, although chronic alcoholic abuse does not produce a characteristic pattern of neuropsychological deficits, there is no evidence that alcohol abuse leads instead to a diffuse cerebral dysfunction. Performance on intelligence tests is within normal limits, as is the performance on the majority of standard neuropsychological tests. Nevertheless, many alcoholics have difficulty with tasks requiring novel problem solving and have subtle memory deficits. A problem with neuropsychological studies of alcoholics is that although the tests used are sensitive to focal cortical lesions, they are not designed to measure subcortical functions. Furthermore, we have no guarantee that evidence of cognitive deficits in alcoholics can be taken as evidence of specific pathology. It is possible that people with deficits on tests such as the Rey Figure or the Corsi Span + 1 are prone to become alcoholic. Notwithstanding these constraints, we believe that the possibility of relatively specific deficits resulting from chronic ethanol abuse warrants serious consideration.

REFERENCES

Annegers, J. F., J. D. Grabow, R. V. Groover, E. R. Laws, L. R. Elveback, and L. T. Kurland. Seizures after head trauma: A population study. *Neurology* 30:683–689, 1980.

Becker, J. T., F. Boller, J. Saxton, and K. L. McGonigle-Gibson. Normal rates of forgetting of verbal and non-verbal material in Alzheimer's disease. *Cortex* 23:59–72, 1987.

Bond, M. R. Neurobehavioral sequelae of closed head injury. In I. Grant and K. M. Adams, eds. *Neuropsychological Assessment of Neuropsychiatric Disorders.* New York: Oxford University Press, 1986.

Bowles, N. L., L. K. Obler, and M. L. Albert. Naming errors in healthy aging and dementia of the Alzheimer type. *Cortex* 23:519–524, 1987.

Brooks, N., L. Campsie, C. Symington, A. Beattie, and W. McKinlay. The five year outcome of severe blunt head injury: A relative's view. *Journal of Neurology, Neurosurgery, and Psychiatry* 49:764–770, 1986.

Brun, A. An overview of light and electron microscopic changes. In B. Reisberg, ed. *Alzheimer's Disease.* New York: The Free Press, 1983.

Carlsson, A. Changes in neurotransmitter systems in the aging brain and in Alzheimer's disease. In B. Reisberg, ed. *Alzheimer's Disease.* New York: The Free Press, 1983.

Cullum, C. M., and E. D. Bigler. Ventricle size, cortical atrophy and the relationship with neuropsychological status in closed head injury: A quantitative analysis. *Journal of Clinical and Experimental Neuropsychology* 8:437–452, 1986.

Cummings, J. L., J. P. Houlihan, and M. A. Hill. The pattern of reading deterioration in dementia of the Alzheimer type: Observations and implications. *Brain and Language* 29:315–323, 1986.

Fortuny, L. A., M. Briggs, F. Newcombe, G. Ratcliffe, and C. Thomas. Measurement of the duration of post-traumatic amnesia. *Journal of Neurology, Neurosurgery and Psychiatry* 43:377–379, 1980.

Fuld, P. A. Psychometric differentiation of the dementias: An overview. In B. Reisberg, ed. *Alzheimer's Disease.* New York: The Free Press, 1983.

Grady, C. L., J. B. Haxby, B. Horwitz, G. Berg, and S. I. Rapoport. Neuropsychological and cerebral metabolic function in early vs. late onset dementia of the Alzheimer type. *Neuropsychologia* 25:807–815, 1987.

Grant, I., and W. Alves. Psychiatric and psychosocial disturbances in head injury. In H. L. Levin, J. Grafman, and H. M. Eisenberg, eds. *Neurobehavioral Recovery from Head Injury.* New York: Oxford University Press, 1987.

Huff, F. J., S. Corkin, and J. H. Growdon. Semantic impairment and anomia in Alzheimer's disease. *Brain and Language* 28:235–249, 1986.

Klonoff, P. S., W. G. Snow, and L. D. Costa. Quality of life in patients 2 to 4 years after closed head injury. *Neurosurgery* 19:735–743, 1986.

Levin, H. S., A. L. Benton, and R. G. Grossman. *Neurobehavioral Consequences of Closed Head Injury.* New York: Oxford University Press, 1982.

Levin, H. S., H. E. Gary, W. M. High, S. Mattis, R. M. Ruff, H. M. Eisenberg, L. F. Marshall, and K. Tabaddor. Minor head injury and the postconcussional syndrome: Methodological issues in outcome studies. In H. S. Levin, J. Grafman, and H. M. Eisenberg, eds. *Neurobehavioral Recovery from Head Injury.* New York: Oxford University Press, 1987.

Loring, D. W., and J. W. Largen. Neuropsychological patterns of presenile and senile dementia of the Alzheimer type. *Neuropsychologia* 23:351–357, 1985.

Martin, A., P. Brouwers, C. Cox, and P. Fedio. On the nature of the verbal memory deficit in Alzheimer's disease. *Brain and Language* 25:323–341, 1985.

Martin, A., C. Cox, P. Brouthers, and P. Fedio. A note on different patterns of impaired and preserved cognitive abilities and their relation to episodic memory deficits in Alzheimer's patients. *Brain and Language* 25:181–198, 1985.

Murdoch, B. E., H. J. Chenery, V. Wilks, and R. S. Boyle. Language disorders in dementia of the Alzheimer type. *Brain and Language* 31:122–137, 1987.

Newcombe, F. Psychometric and behavioral evidence: Scope, limitations, and ecological validity. In H. S. Levin, J. Grafman, and H. M. Eisenberg, eds. *Neurobehavioral Recovery from Head Injury.* New York: Oxford University Press, 1987.

Oppenheimer, D. R. Microscopic lesions in the brain following head injury. *Journal of Neurology, Neurosurgery and Psychiatry* 31:299–306, 1968.

Oscar-Berman, M., and R. J. Ellis. Cognitive deficits related to memory impairments in alcoholism. In M. Galanter, ed. *Recent Developments in Alcoholism* vol 5. New York: Plenum Press, 1987.

Reisberg, B., ed. *Alzheimer's Disease.* New York: The Free Press, 1983.

Reisberg, B. Clinical presentation, diagnosis, and symptomatology of age-associated cognitive decline and Alzheimer's disease. In B. Reisberg, ed. *Alzheimer's Disease.* New York: The Free Press, 1983.

Russell, W. R. Cerebral involvement in head injury. *Brain* 35:549–603, 1932.

Ryan, C., and N. Butters, Cognitive deficits in alcoholics. In B. Kissin and H. Begleiter, eds. *The Pathogenesis of Alcoholism.* New York: Plenum Press, 1983.

Ryan, C. and N. Butters, The neuropsychology of alcoholism. In D. Wedding, A. MacNiell-Horton, Jr., and J. Webster, eds. *The Neuropsychological Handbook: Behavioral and Clinical Perspectives.* New York: Springer-Verlag, 1986.

Scheibel, A. B. Dendritic changes. In B. Reisberg, ed. *Alzheimer's Disease.* New York: The Free Press, 1983.

Spinnler, H., and S. Della Sala. The role of clinical neuropsychology in the neurological diagnosis of Alzheimer's disease. *Journal of Neurology* 235:258–271, 1988.

Swaab, D. F., E. Fliers, M. Mirmiran, W. A. van Gool, and F. van Haaren. Aging of the brain and Alzheimer's disease. *Progress in Brain Research* 70:299–311, 1986.

Tarter, R. E., and C. M. Ryan. Neuropsychology of alcoholism: Etiology, phenomenology, process, and outcome. In M. Galanter, ed. *Recent Developments in Alcoholism,* Vol 1. New York: Plenum Press, 1983.

Teasdale, G., and B. Jennett. The Glasgow coma scale. *Lancet* 2:81–84, 1974.

Van Crevel, H. Clinical approach to dementia. In D. F. Swaab, E. Fliers, M. Mirmiran, W. A. van Gool, and F. van Haaren, eds. *Progress in Brain Research* 70:3–13, 1986.

Vanderwolf, C. H. Near-total loss of "learning" and "memory" as a result of combined cholinergic and serotonergic blockade in the rat. *Behavioral Brain Research* 23:43–57, 1987.

Wilberger, J. E., Z. Deeb, and W. Rothfus. Magnetic resonance imaging in cases of severe head injury. *Neurosurgery* 20:571–576, 1987.

Wilkinson, D. A. Examination of alcoholics by computed tomographic (CT) scans: A critical review. *Alcoholism: Clinical and Experimental Research* 6:31–45, 1982.

Wilson, B., B. Kolb, L. Odland, and I. Q. Whishaw. Alcohol, sex, age, and the hippocampus. *Psychobiology* 15:300–307, 1987.

Wilson, R. S., A. W. Kaszniak, L. D. Bacon, J. H. Fox, and M. P. Kelly. Facial recognition memory in dementia. *Cortex* 18:329–336, 1985.

C H A P T E R 32

NEUROPSYCHOLOGICAL TEST PROCEDURES AND NORMS

A major disadvantage of using an informally composed test battery in making a neuropsychological assessment is that the tests are seldom given as a group to a single population of normal controls. Thus, the testing conditions for control and patient populations may be rather different, especially if taking one test affects performance on others or if demographic factors interact with test performance. Furthermore, the neurological patients must often be compared across studies and the data are seldom compiled. Finally, there is rarely any information regarding the test performance of people other than neurological patients, making it difficult to evaluate neurological patients compared with those who suffer from disorders such as schizophrenia or alcoholism in addition to their neurological complaint.

In this final chapter we provide such information for a group of tests that we have found to be very useful clinically over the past 10 years (see Table 27-4). These tests are largely drawn from tests devised and validated by others, especially at the Montreal Neurological Institute, and should not be construed to form a formal battery. Rather, they should be seen as a collection of tests that may be especially applicable to some types of patient populations or certain research questions. Cutoff scores cannot be used with these tests; rather the neuropsychologist must consider an idiosyncratic pattern of test results in light of the basic information in earlier chapters of this text when evaluating a patient. Many of the tests can be constructed from the descriptions or references provided. Some are available commercially from DK Consultants (Department of Psychology, University Hospital, London, Canada) and related tests, which accompany Benton and colleagues' manual, are available from Oxford University Press, New York.

In this chapter we briefly review the tests and then summarize norms for normal controls of different ages, summarize published data from neurological patients, and provide our original data from patients diagnosed as schizophrenic, alcoholic, learning-disabled, or having Tourette's syndrome. In addition, we summarize the performance of a sample of left-handed university students.

THE TESTS

General Intelligence

We normally administer the Wechsler scale appropriate for the age of the patient. In the event that a Wechsler scale has been administered recently by another psychologist, the Peabody Picture Vocabulary Test can be given as a quick validation of the Wechsler score; in our experience the Peabody score is usually about 5 points higher than the verbal IQ on the WAIS, and even slightly more than on the WAIS-R. As we mentioned earlier, intelligence ratings serve primarily as a valuable reference for the validity and interpretation of other test data, especially memory scores, and do not in themselves offer a great deal of help in localizing brain injuries.

Speech Lateralization

The best noninvasive test of speech lateralization is dichotic listening. The original Kimura tapes (available from DK Consultants) are as good as any for this purpose, although for very bright subjects there may be a ceiling effect (that is, since the test is too easy for them they may obtain a perfect score even after brain injury.) It must be remembered that dichotic listening is not a foolproof measure of speech lateralization; it is merely a means of inferring the likely locus of speech, and scores may be influenced by many methodological factors (see Chapter 15).

Visuoperceptual Tests

Three useful tests of visual perceptual skills are the copying of the Rey Figure, the Mooney Closure Test (for a similar test see Kimura and McGlone), and a test of drawing (see Table 32-1). The complex figure test was devised by Rey to investigate both perceptual organization and visual memory in brain-damaged subjects (see Figure 11-3*C*). The Rey Figure has been extensively used and studied and has been found to be a very sensitive measure both of perceptual-motor skill and of visual memory. Osterrieth standardized Rey's procedure, Visser prepared a manual for it, and a summary of the scoring criteria are found in Lezak. A recent study by Binder is informative, as he showed how stroke patients tend to lose the overall configuration of the design: right hemisphere patients tend to leave out units of the test, and left hemisphere patients tend to fragment the test, rather than drawing it as a unit. Taylor finds that frontal lobe patients, especially right frontal lobe patients, tend to be sloppy in their production of the copy, although the test is neither distorted nor fragmented. Thus, although the copy of the Rey Figure is often perceived to be a test of right posterior function, it is more complex, and interpretation of the score must consider both the actual score and the configuration of the design. Table 32-2 provides means and standard deviations for copying and recall of the Rey Figure for a randomly selected sample of school-aged subjects collected from the Lethbridge (Alberta, Canada) public and private school systems.

The Mooney Faces Test (see Figure 11-3*D*) has also been extensively researched and found to be selectively sensitive to right posterior lesions. In our experience normal subjects are almost never impaired at this test, nor are many pathological groups such as schizophrenics, and so the presence of a deficit on this test must be taken seriously.

Like many psychologists, we use a drawing test because it allows subjects to relax with a more familiar task and because it is sensitive to many kinds of disorders. We use a draw-a-bicycle task since bicycles are well known to everyone and because they are very complex. The orientation of the bicycle (left or right) is taken by some to be clini-

TABLE 32-1. Summary of published means for neurological patients

	Patient group						
	Frontal		Temporal		Parietal		
Test	Left	Right	Left	Right	Left	Right	Basic reference
Visuoperceptual							
Mooney Faces	38/44	39/44	38/44	35/44		31/44[a]	Milner, 1980
Rey Copy			33/36	30/36			Taylor, 1969
Memory							
Delayed verbal recall	18.1	15	9.6[a]	16.5	15	17	Milner, 1967
Digit span	6.1	6.3	5.5[a]	6.5	5.6[a]	6.8	Newcombe, 1969
Recurring figures			21/40	9/40	23/40	24/40	Milner, 1967
Rey Recall			22/36	14/36[a]			Taylor, 1969
Spatial							
Semmes Figures	24.35	30/35[a]	32/35	32/35	27/35[a]	33/35	Teuber, 1964
Right-left	75%	83%	72%	78%	50%	76%	See text
Language							
Newcombe Fluency I	27	30	22[a]	28	23[a]	27	Newcombe, 1969
Newcombe Fluency II	16	18	15	19	16	17	Newcombe, 1969
Newcombe Fluency III	13	15	11[a]	14	13	14	Newcombe, 1969
Chapman-Cook Reading			11[a]	17			Milner, 1967
Frontal lobe							
Wisconsin Card:							
Categories[b]	3.3[a]	3.3[a]	5.3	5.3	4.5	4.5	Milner, 1964
Perseverative errors[b]	40[a]	40[a]	9	9	22	22	Milner, 1964
Chicago Fluency	35[a]	57	58	58	44[a]		Milner, 1964, 1967

[a]Differs significantly from control.
[b]Data from left and right hemisphere lesions are not separated in the published reports.

cally significant, but we have not found it so. One difficulty with using drawing tests is that there are seldom any objective criteria for their scoring. We have devised a scoring protocol for bicycles and have normed this test using hundreds of subjects (see Tables 32-3 and 32-4). In addition to our scoring criteria, we look for relative inattention to one side of the page or drawing and at the size of the drawing, because it is claimed that left hemisphere lesions decrease drawing size and right hemisphere lesions increase it.

Memory

Milner's extensive studies linking certain memory functions with the temporal lobes have provided several tests useful for assessing memory functions. Although the Wechsler Memory Scale is not a sensitive test of memory, it is a useful starting point, and its revised version is a significant improvement. If the original form is given, we administer a delayed recall of the drawings, stories, and paired associates with a delay of about 20 min. (The revised form includes this delayed recall.) Although it is unusual for patients to have difficulty with the simple Wechsler drawings, poor recall must be considered significant. Milner has found the delayed recall of the stories and paired associates to be especially sensitive to left temporal lobe damage, as summarized in Table 32-1, where "delayed verbal recall" refers to the sum of the two stories and a single attempt at recall of the paired associates.

Long-term recall of visual material is assessed using both a delayed (30 min) recall of the Rey Figure and the Kimura Recurring-Figures Test, which is available from DK Consultants. In the former test, the subjects are asked to reproduce as exactly as they can the complex geometric figure

TABLE 32-2. Rey-Copying and Recall scores (mean and standard deviation) for school subjects aged 6 to 18

			Rey Copy		Rey Recall	
Age	Sex	(*n*)	Mean	S.D.	Mean	S.D.
6	♀	(111)	16.96	7.86	10.79	5.80
	♂	(81)	16.25	8.16	10.18	5.81
	Total	(192)	16.66	7.97	10.53	5.80
7	♀	(184)	21.03	7.76	13.18	5.86
	♂	(169)	21.57	7.59	13.99	6.69
	Total	(353)	21.29	7.67	13.57	6.28
8	♀	(155)	23.74	7.97	16.36	6.45
	♂	(192)	23.57	8.04	16.32	7.03
	Total	(347)	23.64	8.00	16.34	6.77
9	♀	(154)	26.61	6.87	18.29	6.27
	♂	(175)	26.33	7.01	19.07	6.06
	Total	(329)	26.46	6.94	18.71	6.16
10	♀	(146)	27.95	7.13	19.83	6.53
	♂	(155)	26.50	7.95	19.64	6.89
	Total	(301)	27.20	7.58	19.73	6.71
11	♀	(126)	29.29	6.75	22.88	6.33
	♂	(154)	28.06	7.73	22.35	6.92
	Total	(280)	28.61	7.31	22.59	6.65
12	♀	(119)	30.54	7.29	23.25	6.16
	♂	(106)	29.84	5.95	23.15	6.65
	Total	(225)	30.21	6.69	23.20	6.38
13	♀	(106)	32.80	4.15	24.47	6.38
	♂	(131)	32.50	4.52	24.69	6.25
	Total	(237)	32.63	4.35	24.59	6.29
14	♀	(89)	33.46	3.20	26.28	5.56
	♂	(91)	33.60	3.19	26.21	5.27
	Total	(180)	33.53	3.18	26.24	5.40
15	♀	(48)	33.62	3.10	26.39	6.63
	♂	(68)	33.60	2.92	25.73	6.18
	Total	(116)	33.60	2.98	26.00	6.35
16	♀	(30)	34.63	1.13	26.43	5.64
	♂	(40)	34.49	1.65	27.29	5.33
	Total	(70)	34.55	1.45	26.92	5.44
17	♀	(38)	34.86	1.51	25.63	6.34
	♂	(39)	34.73	2.12	27.31	5.56
	Total	(77)	34.79	1.83	26.49	5.97
18	♀	(19)	34.37	3.58	26.05	5.93
	♂	(14)	33.79	3.66	27.46	3.15
	Total	(33)	34.12	3.57	26.65	4.93

TABLE 32-3. Scoring procedure for draw-a-bicycle test

Part	Representation	Score
Wheels	2 circles	2 (1 for each wheel)
	2 tires	1
	Spokes	2 (any spokes; 1 for each wheel)
Frame	Front wheel	1
	Back wheel	1
	Middle "V"	1
	Seat	1
	Handlebars	1
Drive	Rear wheel sprocket	1
	Front sprocket	1
	Chain	1
	2 pedals	1
	2 pedal supports	1
Function	Can coast	1
	Can be driven	1
	Parts in the right place	1
	Parts in proportion	1
——	Well drawn	1
	Total possible score	20

Note: In our sample 49.6% of females and 46.6% of males pointed the bicycle to the left.

that they drew 30 min earlier. Patients with right temporal lobe lesions are especially poor at this, although frontal lobe patients may embellish their drawings and should be encouraged to draw only what they actually recall. The same scoring criteria are used for the recall as for the copying. In the recurring-figures test, subjects are shown a series of nonsense drawings (see Figure 20-12), which they are to remember. They are then shown a much larger series and asked to pick out the ones they saw previously. Again, right temporal lobe patients are especially poor at this test.

In addition to measures of long-term memory it is useful to assess short-term verbal and nonverbal memory. Digit span is the commonest way to assess verbal short-term memory, and the Corsi Block Test is a very useful analogue for nonverbal short-term memory. In the Corsi test the visual span is determined using the block board illustrated in Figure 21-10. (The blocks are about 1 in. square.) The subject's task is to copy the sequence demonstrated by the examiner, as described in Chapter 21 for the Span + 1 test. Although there are no published data for this test, Brenda Milner and her associates find that right parietal lobe patients have reduced block spans, just as left parietal lobe patients have reduced digit spans. We have found the mean for digit span to be 6.9 (S.D. = 0.6), and for block span in the same control subjects to be 5.7 (S.D. = 0.7). As a rule of thumb, one can expect the block span to be one fewer than the digit span.

Spatial Orientation

Two tests of spatial orientation were drawn from the extensive studies of Semmes and her colleagues. In the right-left differentiation test the subject is shown a series of pictures of body parts (hands, arms, eyes, ears, legs) and clothing (lapels, shoes) and asked to determine if each is of the left or right. Most people find this test difficult, scoring only about 80% correct. Patients with left parietal lesions respond strictly at chance, however. Although data for neurological patients are not published for this test, we have computed scores for those patients studied by Kolb and Milner and have summarized them in Table 32-1. Other excellent tests of right-left discrimination are found in Benton's manual.

In the Semmes Body-Placing Test (see Figure 19-8) the subject is shown five drawings similar to those in Figure 19-8 and the task is to point to the location of each of the numbers on the subject's own body. Patients with frontal lobe lesions are poor at this task, largely because they point inaccurately. Patients with left parietal lobe lesions confuse left and right in the test, a deficit that also leads to impaired performance (see Table 32-1). This test can be constructed by using the model in Figure 19-8 and placing numbers on the following locations: (1) front view: right cheek, right palm, left shoulder; rear view: left shoulder, left hand; (2) front view: left forehead, right forearm, right shin; rear view: left shoulder, right elbow, left hand; (3) front view: left shoulder, right wrist, left thumb, right knee; rear view: right shoulder, left forearm, middle finger; (4) front view: left ear, right thumb, left forearm, right knee; rear view: left ear, left shoulder, left middle finger, right calf;

TABLE 32-4. Draw-a-bicycle test (mean and standard deviation)

Age	Sex	(*n*)	Mean	S.D.	Age	Sex	(*n*)	Mean	S.D.
2–4	♀	(16)	3.0	1.7	13	♀	(115)	9.8	2.8
	♂	(15)	3.7	2.5		♂	(119)	12.8	3.6
	Total	(31)	3.2	2.1		Total	(234)	11.3	3.6
5	♀	(22)	4.6	2.4	14	♀	(129)	10.8	3.3
	♂	(15)	6.2	3.8		♂	(120)	12.6	3.5
	Total	(37)	5.3	2.9		Total	(249)	11.6	3.5
6	♀	(20)	6.5	2.3	15	♀	(197)	10.6	2.8
	♂	(19)	6.4	2.7		♂	(188)	13.6	3.4
	Total	(39)	6.5	2.5		Total	(385)	12.0	3.4
7	♀	(24)	6.1	2.1	16	♀	(182)	10.7	3.9
	♂	(29)	8.0	2.8		♂	(207)	13.5	3.6
	Total	(53)	7.1	2.7		Total	(389)	12.2	3.6
8	♀	(22)	7.5	2.0	17	♀	(174)	10.9	3.0
	♂	(16)	9.3	2.4		♂	(187)	13.5	3.8
	Total	(38)	8.3	2.3		Total	(361)	12.2	3.7
9	♀	(24)	8.2	1.9	18	♀	(119)	12.1	3.4
	♂	(16)	10.1	2.9		♂	(98)	14.2	3.9
	Total	(40)	9.0	2.3		Total	(217)	13.1	3.8
10	♀	(27)	9.6	2.3	19	♀	(46)	12.6	3.7
	♂	(27)	11.4	4.0		♂	(35)	14.2	4.0
	Total	(54)	10.5	3.3		Total	(81)	13.3	3.9
11	♀	(17)	9.1	1.7	20–29	♀	(116)	11.4	3.9
	♂	(25)	11.8	3.8		♂	(133)	14.1	4.0
	Total	(42)	10.8	3.3		Total	(249)	12.8	4.1
12	♀	(47)	10.6	3.4	30–50	♀	(43)	11.1	3.9
	♂	(60)	12.0	3.4		♂	(16)	11.1	3.9
	Total	(107)	11.4	3.5		Total	(59)	11.0	3.9

(5) front view: left eye, right wrist, right little finger, left ring finger, right shin; rear view: left thumb, left middle finger, right first finger, right knee.

Somatosensory Testing

Three tests are especially useful for identifying somatosensory defects: two-point discrimination, point localization, and position sense. Detailed procedures for these tests can be found in Corkin and colleagues' 1970 article. Briefly, in the two-point discrimination test the subject's ability to tell if the palm has been touched with one or two probes is determined. The point localization test determines how close two touches need to be for the subject to perceive them to be in exactly the same place. This test can be administered either to the palm, the foot, or the face. Finally, the position sense test is a measure of the sensitivity of the digits to induced movement up or down.

Lesions that invade the core somatosensory cortex of the precentral gyrus severely disturb somatosensation on the contralateral hand, as summarized in Table 32-5. Although these tests may be tedious to administer, patients with central lesions may only show a deficit on careful somatosensory testing, as illustrated by Case 4 described in Chapter 27.

Language

We normally use three language tests: the token test, the Newcombe Fluency Test, and the Chapman-Cook Speed-of-Reading Test. As we have mentioned earlier, the token test is an aphasia screening test that we give only to those subjects in whom language comprehension difficulties are suspected. De Renzi and Vignolo present clear instructions and norms for this test, which can be purchased from University Park Press, 233 East Redwood St., Baltimore, Maryland 21202.

The Newcombe Fluency Tests require the patient to produce orally the names of as many objects (Test 1), animals (Test II), or animal-color-animal-color alternations (Test III) as possible in 1 min each. Although a simple test for most people, left hemisphere patients consistently score below the level of control or right hemisphere patients, the greatest deficit appearing in patients with left posterior temporal or parietal lobe lesions. Finally, we often administer a reading test such as the wide range achievement test (WRAT) or the

TABLE 32-5. Summary of Corkin et al. somatosensory data

	2-point	Point localization	Position sense
Control data			
Right hand	7.6 ± 2.0 mm	3.28 ± 2.62 mm	58/60+
Left hand	8.0 ± 1.9 mm	3.04 ± 2.48 mm	58/60+
Patient data[a]			
Parietal[b]			
Ipsilateral hand	0%	26%	6%
Contralateral hand	78%	81%	78%
Frontal or temporal:			
Ipsilateral hand	3%	0%	0%
Contralateral hand	0%	5%	5%

[a]Numbers indicate the percentage of patients whose score deviated from the control value by more than 2.54 × control standard deviation.

[b]Only those parietal lobe patients whose lesions had invaded the precentral gyrus are included.

TABLE 32-6. Chicago Word-Fluency norms

	Total			Female			Male		
Age (yrs)	n	$\bar{x}$	S.D.	n	$\bar{x}$	S.D.	n	$\bar{x}$	S.D.
6	80	9.28	4.47	40	9.85	4.58	40	8.70	4.33
7	133	15.87	8.22	72	17.22	8.20	61	14.26	8.00
8	197	21.52	9.29	85	23.72	10.34	112	19.85	8.05
9	208	25.93	10.18	90	28.41	9.93	118	24.03	10.01
10	189	29.98	11.92	86	33.16	11.83	103	27.32	11.39
11	146	37.08	11.98	75	39.03	10.57	71	35.01	13.07
12	140	40.58	13.00	84	44.52	12.98	56	34.61	10.61
13	167	45.07	14.10	76	51.37	13.65	91	39.81	12.26
14	175	48.46	14.72	85	52.64	14.30	90	44.52	14.08
15	120	47.35	15.22	51	51.57	13.28	69	44.23	15.88
16	69	48.28	13.69	28	53.43	10.54	41	44.76	14.56
17	79	49.65	17.51	37	53.65	17.63	42	46.12	16.83
18	30	61.47	15.29	18	64.22	14.98	12	57.33	15.42

Note: The test requires the subject to write as many words as possible beginning with the letter "s" in 5 min and as many four-letter words as possible beginning with the letter "c" in 4 min. Results are totals for both sets of responses.

Chapman-Cook Speed-of-Reading Test. Both of these tests are available from most suppliers of psychometric instruments.

Frontal Lobe Tests

The frontal lobes are the most difficult regions to assess using psychological tests because it is difficult to find tests appropriate for routine clinical use that dissociate the left and right frontal lobes. The best test of frontal lobe function available is the Wisconsin Card-Sorting Test, which can be purchased from Psychological Assessment Resources, Inc., P.O. Box 98, Odessa, Florida 33556 (see Figure 19-7). According to Milner, patients with left dorsolateral-frontal lesions (around area 9) are the most impaired at this task, although patients with right dorsolateral lesions are also impaired. Damage to the orbitofrontal cortex may be without effect. Another useful test is the Chicago Word-Fluency Test (Table 32-6), which, in contrast to the card-sorting test, is most sensitive to orbitofrontal damage and less affected by dorsolateral lesions. Again, both left and right hemisphere lesions impair performance on this test, although somewhat more so on the left.

Miscellaneous Tests

Depending on the referral question, we routinely add other tests to our assessment, especially the Kimura Manual Sequence Box, the copying of arm and facial movements, a handedness questionnaire, and a measure of hand strength. All these tests are described in detail in Kimura and McGlone, and any test materials necessary can be purchased from DK Consultants.

SUBJECT POPULATIONS

Perhaps the most frustrating impediment to the use of a composite collection of tests taken from research reports is that data for normal control subjects are often not provided, the main comparison being the relative performance of two or more groups of neurological patients. We have therefore undertaken to establish norms for normal control subjects on the tests that we use routinely. Further, since many neurological referrals are confounded by psychiatric diagnoses as well, we have compiled data on people with diagnoses of chronic alcoholism and schizophrenia and availed ourselves of the opportunity to study people with Tourette's syndrome. Finally, since we have used our tests to assess the cognitive development of children making slow progress in school, we have collected data from a sample of school-age children.

Normal Subjects

We administered the entire collection of tests to 107 adult control subjects, which we have broken down by age and sex in Table 32-7. We recruited "average" people by contacting various local community organizations and self-help groups to solicit volunteers. Children were obtained from local school systems by searching for "average" students or by testing entire classrooms of students. The left-handed subjects were entirely composed of a freshman university population since we were interested in seeing if this admittedly select group would be impaired relative to right-handers at any of the tests. They were not! The designation of familial and nonfamilial left-hander was made by asking the students if they had any close relatives (parents, grandparents, aunts, uncles, or siblings)

TABLE 32-7. Summary of control data

	Age group (*n*)				
Test	5–9 yrs (6)	10–15 yrs (14)	16–30 yrs (67)	31–44 yrs (26)	45–60 yrs (14)
Intelligence					
Verbal IQ	116.0 ± 9.6	118.0 ± 13.4	116.0 ± 10.0	114.0 ± 9.4	120.0 ± 10.6
Performance IQ	123.0 ± 10.1	118.0 ± 12.4	116.0 ± 9.9	114.0 ± 12.7	121.0 ± 13.2
Full-scale IQ	122.0 ± 5.1	120.0 ± 13.2	117.0 ± 8.5	115.0 ± 10.5	123.0 ± 11.4
Visuoperceptual					
Mooney Faces	22.6 ± 1.2	22.7 ± 2.2	22.4 ± 2.0	23.2 ± 2.2	19.9 ± 5.1
Rey Copy	16.4 ± 9.8	32.6 ± 3.5	35.1 ± 1.5	33.2 ± 6.1	34.5 ± 2.1
Memory					
MQ	95.0 ± 6.7	112.0 ± 13.8	108.0 ± 12.0	114.0 ± 15.1	123.0 ± 16.1
Delayed stories	20.3 ± 6.9	13.8 ± 5.4	12.8 ± 6.9	14.7 ± 4.7	13.5 ± 4.1
Delayed associates	8.0 ± 1.7	9.5 ± 1.2	7.7 ± 3.5	8.4 ± 3.2	7.4 ± 3.4
Digit span	12.2 ± 3.5	11.6 ± 2.5	11.0 ± 2.6	10.8 ± 2.8	9.3 ± 2.5
Recurring figures	—	—	24.7 ± 7.8	21.7 ± 10.9	21.6 ± 7.1
Rey Recall	11.6 ± 7.1	22.9 ± 6.8	22.7 ± 7.0	19.5 ± 6.7	18.3 ± 6.7
Spatial					
Semmes Figures	20.5 ± 6.5	30.2 ± 6.1	31.1 ± 2.8	33.7 ± 1.7	34.2 ± 1.2
Right-left	60.0 ± 1.1	80.0 ± 10.5	84.0 ± 5.7	84.0 ± 6.2	79.0 ± 6.3
Language					
Newcombe I	29.0 ± 10.9	27.3 ± 14.0	28.9 ± 7.7	25.4 ± 7.1	27.8 ± 5.2
II	9.2 ± 2.7	13.2 ± 3.8	22.5 ± 4.4	20.9 ± 3.8	19.5 ± 3.6
III	—	—	17.0 ± 6.9	16.2 ± 3.6	16.2 ± 3.3
Frontal lobe					
Wisconsin Card	2.6 ± 2.1[a]	4.9 ± 2.2[a]	5.8 ± 4.7	5.3 ± 1.6	6.0 ± 0.0
Chicago Fluency	16.3 ± 4.9	39.7 ± 12.8	64.0 ± 15.9	66.6 ± 17.6	58.7 ± 25.6

Note: Numbers represent means and standard deviations.
[a]Only one deck of cards was used.

TABLE 32-8. Summary of data by handedness and gender

	Age group (n)				
	29.2 yrs (107)	19.3–1.86 yrs (34)	20.8–4.3 yrs (22)	29.7 yrs (30)	29 yrs (77)
Test	Right	Left familial	Left nonfamilial	Male	Female
Intelligence					
Verbal IQ	116.0 ± 10.0	120.0 ± 9.7	116.0 ± 9.1	116.0 ± 11.2	116.0 ± 9.5
Performance IQ	116.0 ± 11.0	116.0 ± 11.9	119.0 ± 9.2	112.0 ± 9.5	117.0 ± 11.1
Full-scale IQ	117.0 ± 9.0	120.0 ± 10.0	119.0 ± 8.8	115.0 ± 10.0	117.0 ± 9.0
Visuoperceptual					
Mooney Faces	22.0 ± 3.0	21.5 ± 1.1	21.9 ± 1.3	21.9 ± 4.1	22.3 ± 2.4
Rey Copy	34.5 ± 3.4	35.3 ± 1.4	35.2 ± 1.2	34.9 ± 1.4	34.4 ± 3.9
Memory					
MQ	112.0 ± 15.0	113.0 ± 15.3	109.0 ± 11.9	107.0 ± 12.8	114.0 ± 14.8
Delayed stories	19.4 ± 0.5	18.8 ± 6.5	14.9 ± 6.4	12.1 ± 5.6	14.0 ± 6.2
Delayed associates	17.3 ± 2.8	9.4 ± 1.8	9.2 ± 1.7	7.2 ± 3.5	8.1 ± 3.4
Digit span	10.7 ± 2.7	12.1 ± 2.6	11.2 ± 2.2	10.3 ± 3.0	10.9 ± 2.5
Recurring figures	23.0 ± 7.9	—	—	19.3 ± 7.3	24.2 ± 8.7
Rey Recall	21.7 ± 7.0	25.1 ± 6.2	26 ± 6.3	19.9 ± 5.9	21.7 ± 7.4
Spatial					
Semmes Figures	33.0 ± 2.1	32.6 ± 3.1	32.8 ± 2.6	33.5 ± 2.5	33.4 ± 2.4
Right-left	84.0 ± 6.0	83.0 ± 6.9	87.0 ± 2.3	84.0 ± 5.1	83.0 ± 6.3
Language					
Newcombe I	28.0 ± 7.4	28.0 ± 6.3	24.4 ± 7.4	26.5 ± 7.2	28.4 ± 7.4
II	22.0 ± 4.3	22.5 ± 6.9	20.0 ± 4.6	22.0 ± 5.3	21.5 ± 3.9
III	16.7 ± 5.6	16.2 ± 3.8	16.0 ± 2.3	16.5 ± 4.0	16.8 ± 6.1
Frontal lobe					
Wisconsin Card	5.6 ± 1.0	4.8 ± 1.2[a]	4.4 ± 0.9[a]	5.6 ± 1.1	5.7 ± 1.1
Chicago Fluency	64.0 ± 18	69.0 ± 18.9	60.0 ± 13.3	60.0 ± 2.0	65.0 ± 16.6

Note: Numbers represent means and standard deviations.
[a]Only one deck of cards was used.

who were also left-handed. All subjects were Caucasian.

Schizophrenic Subjects

Two psychiatrists independently diagnosed these subjects as schizophrenic using the DSM-III criteria. None of the patients had any history of prior neurological illness or substance abuse, and none had clinically obvious side effects from their neuroleptic medication at the time of testing. All of the patients had been on a neuroleptic for at least 24 h before testing began. They had a mean age of 29 years, a mean of 12 years of education, and an average of 3.6 prior admissions with the same diagnosis at discharge.

Alcoholic Subjects

The alcoholic subjects were recruited from a local Alcoholics Anonymous group and a government alcohol treatment center. They were all self-proclaimed alcoholics and reported an abusive drinking history of from 5 to 20 years and had suffered physical (hospitalization) or psychosocial consequences (marital breakdown, loss of employment, conflict with the law, etc.) as a result of their excessive drinking. They were between 19 and 55 years of age and had 8 to 14 years of education. All of the alcoholic subjects had been abstinent for more than 4 months.

Learning-Disabled Subjects

These children were referred by the local school systems as having severe difficulties in school, especially in reading, in spite of intelligence ratings within the average range. Children with obvious emotional problems were not included in the sample.

Subjects with Gilles de la Tourette's Syndrome

Although Tourette's syndrome is a relatively rare disorder, we had an opportunity to study a large group of these patients. We include them in our patient population here because they provide an example of how neuropsychological tests may provide insight into the nature of disorders of unknown etiology and because they have a unique pattern of test results. These subjects were obtained from a local health unit, the Canadian

TABLE 32-9. Summary of all cross correlations

Test	Verbal IQ	Performance IQ	Full IQ	Wechsler MQ	Stories	Paired associates	Delayed stories	Delayed associates	Wechsler figures	Delayed figures	Rey Recall	Kimura Figures	Digit span	Left-right	Newcombe I	II	III	Rey Copy	Mooney Faces	Block span	Card sorting	Chicago	Semmes
Verbal IQ																							
Performance IQ	*																						
Full-scale IQ	*	*																					
Wechsler MQ	*	*	*																				
Stories	*		*	*																			
Paired associates	*	*	*	*	*																		
Delayed stories				*	*	*																	
Delayed associates																							
Wechsler figures																							
Delayed figures				*																			
Rey Recall									*														
Kimura Figures		*							*														
Digit span	*		*	*																			
Left-right																							
Newcombe I																							
II															*								
III																*							
Rey Copy											*												
Mooney Closure																							
Block span																							
Card sorting																							
Chicago Fluency	*		*	*	*	*						*											
Semmes Placing																							*

[a]Indicates correlations over +.3 ($p < .01$).

TABLE 32-10. Summary of data by patient group

Test	Age group (n)					
	Tourette's		Schizophrenic	Alcoholic	Learning disabled	
	10–14 yrs (14)	15+ yrs (12)	28.5 yrs (30)	40 yrs (23)	5–9 yrs (17)	10–15 yrs (31)
Intelligence						
Verbal IQ	108	113	105[a]	114	102	101
Performance IQ	101	105	95[a]	112	102	100
Full-scale IQ	106	110	98[a]	114	102	102
Visuoperceptual						
Mooney Faces	22.6	23	20	21	19.5	22
Rey Copy	28	31	32.5	32.9	18[a]	29.1
Memory						
MQ	102	100	89[a]	110	85	98
Delayed stories	13	11.8	6.7[a]	14.1	14.6	12.6
Delayed P.A.L.	9.1	8.8	8.4[a]	9.3	7.6	9.2
Digit span	11.8	12.4	11.0	10.3	7.7	8.8
Recurring figures	—	—	—	—	—	—
Rey Recall	17.2[a]	20.1[a]	10.8[a]	16.75[a]	7.8[a]	18.1[a]
Spatial						
Semmes Figures	30	32	30	33.3	18.7	27
Right-left	75	80	77	80	63[a]	69[a]
Language						
Newcombe I	27	34	25	25	15	24
II	17	22	20	20	13	17
III	13	16	14	15	6	13
Frontal lobe						
Wisconsin Card	4.5	5	2.9[a]	3.9	3.7	5.1
Chicago Fluency	34[a]	46[a]	36[a]	55.5	19	32

[a]Differs significantly from control scores.

Tourette Society, and the American Tourette Syndrome Association. Some of these subjects were receiving no medication at the time of testing; the others were receiving pimozide, haloperidol, clonidine, or Cogentin.

TEST SCORES

We will not extensively discuss the test results, as most of these data have been discussed in the previous two chapters. Rather, we have summarized the data into tables, which can be used for comparison purposes.

Normal Controls

Test results for normal controls are divided arbitrarily into three age groups: 16 to 29 years, 30 to 44 years, and 45 to 60 years (see Table 32-7). A further analysis was made to determine if there might be differences related to gender, and these data are summarized in Table 32-8, along with the scores for left-handers. There was very little difference in the performance of people as they aged, although memory scores did appear to deteriorate somewhat. There were no obvious gender differences or differences related to handedness. We return to these factors below.

In order to determine the relation between the different tests, all the adult control subjects were pooled and each test was correlated with every other test. Correlations coefficients exceeding .3 ($p < .01$) were considered significant and are summarized in Table 32-9. Perhaps the most interesting correlations are those between intelligence and memory scores and between intelligence and Chicago Fluency scores. In view of these correlations it is obviously difficult to consider using cutoff scores for patient groups since the cutoff must slide with IQ. Finally, age correlates positively with Wechsler Memory Quotient (MQ). This result implies that the age correction on the MQ is too liberal, a factor that should be considered in assessing memory in older patients. (The Revised Wechsler Scale has a new set of age-corrected norms, which hopefully will correct the age-related problems of the original scale.)

TABLE 32-11. Summary of significant correlations between age, sex, alcoholism, and neuropsychological measures

Variable	Alcohol	Sex	Age
Demographics			
Age	—	—	—
Sex	—	—	—
Education	+.37	—	—
Years drinking	−.79	—	—
Months sober	−.50	—	—
Wechsler Adult Intelligence Scale			
Block design	+.36	—	−.34
Digit symbol	—	—	−.35
Temporal lobe			
Wechsler raw score (Memory)	—	—	−.26
Memory passages	—	—	—
Delayed memory passages	—	—	—
Paired associates	—	+.26	−.36
Delayed paired associates	+.37	—	−.31
Drawings	—	—	−.29
Delayed drawings	—	—	−.37
Rey Recall	+.52	—	−.37
Dichotic total words	—	—	−.28
Parietal lobe			
Rey Copy	+.44	—	−.26
Newcombe Fluency	—	—	—
Left/Right	—	—	—
Mooney Closure	—	—	−.33
Frontal lobe			
Wisconsin Card Sorting	—	—	—
Chicago Word-Fluency	+.27	—	—
Semmes Body-Placing	—	—	—

$p < .01$ or better. Subscales or factors not shown were not significant.

The test scores for children have been summarized in Table 32-7 by dividing the children into two age groups. Comparison of the adults' and children's scores reveals that children find many of the tests more difficult than adults, a difference that is no doubt related to the level of cognitive development in children. A different set of simpler logical stories was used for the young children, since in our experience they had difficulty in understanding Wechsler stories.

Patient Groups

Each of the patient groups displays a different pattern of test results (see Table 32-10). Schizophrenic patients are impaired at every test of frontal and temporal lobe function but perform normally on tests believed to measure parietal lobe function. Those diagnosed as having Tourette's syndrome had an unusual pattern of test results suggestive of right orbitofrontal dysfunction, although there is no known neurological correlate of this. Learning-disabled children perform especially poorly at tests sensitive to left parietal and temporal lobe function, although some children have a severe disability at drawing the Rey Figure as well. Finally, alcoholics are surprisingly normal at most of our tests, a significant impairment appearing only at long-term recall of the Rey Figure.

Sex and Age

In the course of analyzing the performance of alcoholic subjects, we separated out sex and age as factors and ran a correlation matrix on the population. We found that there were virtually no sex-related correlations, the only statistically significant one being on paired-associate learning — on which females did better than males. There were many measures that correlated with age, however, as can be seen in Table 32-11.

CONCLUDING COMMENTS

The tests that we have described in this chapter represent only a small fraction of the tests used in neuropsychological assessment, but they have been used extensively for neurological patients (see Taylor), for those undergoing psychiatric surgery (see Corkin et al., 1977) and stereotaxic surgery for Parkinson's disease, and for the assessment of children with learning disorders. We have found them to be useful and reliable measures both for routine clinical assessments and as a starting point for various research projects. There are, of course, many aspects of cerebral function that these tests do not measure, and other specific tests may be necessary for particular assessment questions and patient populations. Nevertheless, the data we have summarized in this chapter should be useful complements to the manuals by Benton and colleagues and by Kimura and McGlone, and to the excellent assessment text by Lezak. We caution, however, that none of these sources can be used validly without a thorough understanding of the basic material of this text.

The usefulness of any scientific endeavor is eventually measured by its technological applicability to the betterment of humankind. We believe that in the decades to come neuropsychology will indeed be applied to a plethora of human problems. It is up to those in the field to apply it wisely.

REFERENCES

Benton, A. L. Psychological testing. In A. B. Baker and L. H. Baker, eds. *Clinical Neurology,* vol. 1. Philadelphia: Harper & Row, 1982.

Benton, A. L., K. deS. Hamsher, N. R. Varney, and O. Spreen. *Contributions to Neuropsychological Assessment.* New York: Oxford University Press, 1983.

Binder, L. M. Constructional strategies on complex figure drawings after unilateral brain damage. *Journal of Clinical Neuropsychology* 4:51–58, 1982.

Corkin, S., B. Milner, and T. Rasmussen. Somatosensory thresholds: Contrasting effects of postcentral-gyrus and posterior parietal-lobe excisions. *Archives of Neurology* 23:41–58, 1970.

Corkin, S., H.-L. Teuber, and T. E. Twitchell. A study of cingulatomy in man: A summary. In W. H. Sweet, ed. *Neurosurgical Treatment in Psychiatry, Pain and Epilepsy.* Baltimore: University Park Press, 1977.

Kimura, D., and J. McGlone. *Neuropsychology Test Procedures.* University of Western Ontario, London, Ontario, 1983.

Kolb, B., and B. Milner. Performance of complex arm and facial movements after focal brain lesions. *Neuropsychologia* 4:491–503, 1981.

Kolb, B., and I. Q. Whishaw. Performance of schizophrenic patients on tests sensitive to left or right frontal, temporal, or parietal function in neurological patients. *Journal of Nervous and Mental Disease* 171:435–443, 1983.

Lezak, M. D. *Neuropsychological Assessment,* 2nd ed. New York: Oxford University Press, 1983.

Milner, B. Some effects of frontal lobectomy in man. In J. M. Warren and K. Akert, eds. *Frontal Granular Cortex and Behavior.* New York: McGraw-Hill, 1964.

Milner, B. Brain mechanisms suggested by studies of temporal lobes. In F. L. Darley, ed. *Brain Mechanisms Underlying Speech and Language.* New York: Grune & Stratton, 1967.

Milner, B. Complementary functional specializations of the human cerebral hemispheres. In R. Levi-Montalcini, ed. *Nerve Cells, Transmitters and Behavior.* Vatican City: Pont. Acad. Scientiarum, 1980.

Newcombe, F. *Missile Wounds of the Brain.* London: Oxford University Press, 1969.

Renzi, E. de., and L. A. Vignolo. The token test: A sensitive test to detect disturbances in aphasics. *Brain* 85:665–678, 1962.

Semmes, J., S. Weinstein, L. Ghent, and H.-L. Teuber. Correlates of impaired orientation in personal and extrapersonal space. *Brain* 86:747–772, 1963.

Sutherland, R. J., B. Kolb, W. M. Schoel, I. Q. Whishaw, and D. Davies. Neuropsychological assessment of children and adults with Tourette's syndrome: A comparison with learning disabilities and schizophrenia. In A. J. Friedhoff and T. N. Chase, eds. *Gilles de la Tourette Syndrome.* New York: Raven Press, 1982.

Taylor, L. B. Localization of cerebral lesions by psychological testing. *Clinical Neurosurgery* 16:269–287, 1969.

Taylor, L. B. Psychological assessment of neurosurgical patients. In T. Rasmussen and R. Marino, eds. *Functional Neurosurgery.* New York: Raven Press, 1979.

Teuber, H.-L. The riddle of frontal lobe function in man. In J. M. Warren and K. Akert, eds. *Frontal Granular Cortex and Behavior.* New York: McGraw-Hill, 1964.

Visser, R. S. H. *Manual of the Complex Figure Test.* Amsterdam: Swets and Zeitlinger, 1973.

Whishaw, I. Q., and B. Kolb. Neuropsychological assessment of children and adults with developmental dyslexia. In R. N. Malalesha and H. A. Whitaker, eds. *Dyslexia: A Global Issue.* Boston: Martinus Nijhoff, 1984.

Wilson, B., B. Kolb, L. Odland, and I. Q. Whishaw. Alcohol, sex, age, and the hippocampus. *Psychobiology* 15:300–307, 1987.

APPENDIX

AN ATLAS OF THE HUMAN BRAIN

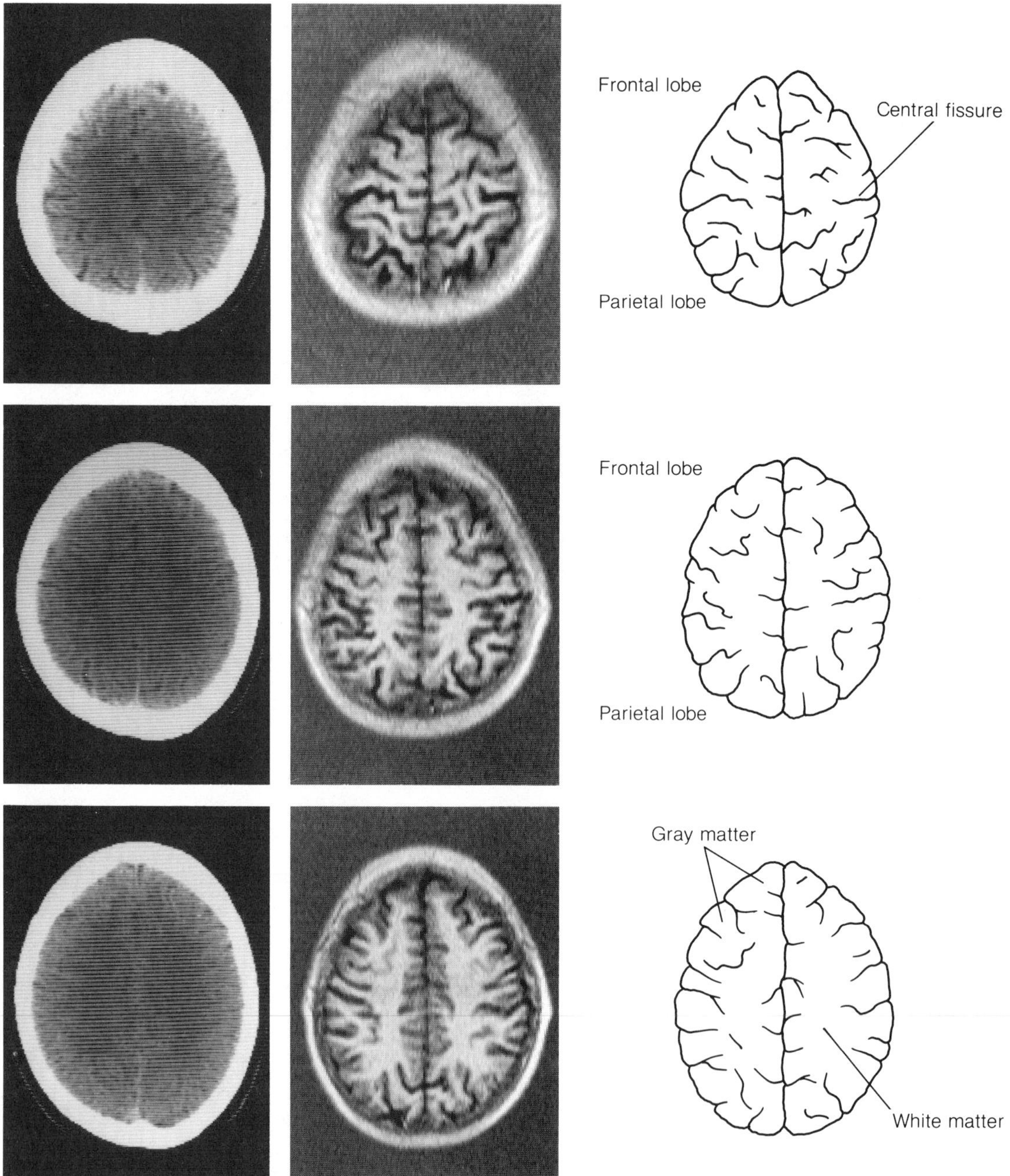

FIGURE A-1. A series of CT scans, MRI scans, and drawings illustrating nine horizontal cuts through the brain. (Scans provided by Brenda Kosaka and David Li, The University of British Columbia Health Sciences Centre.)

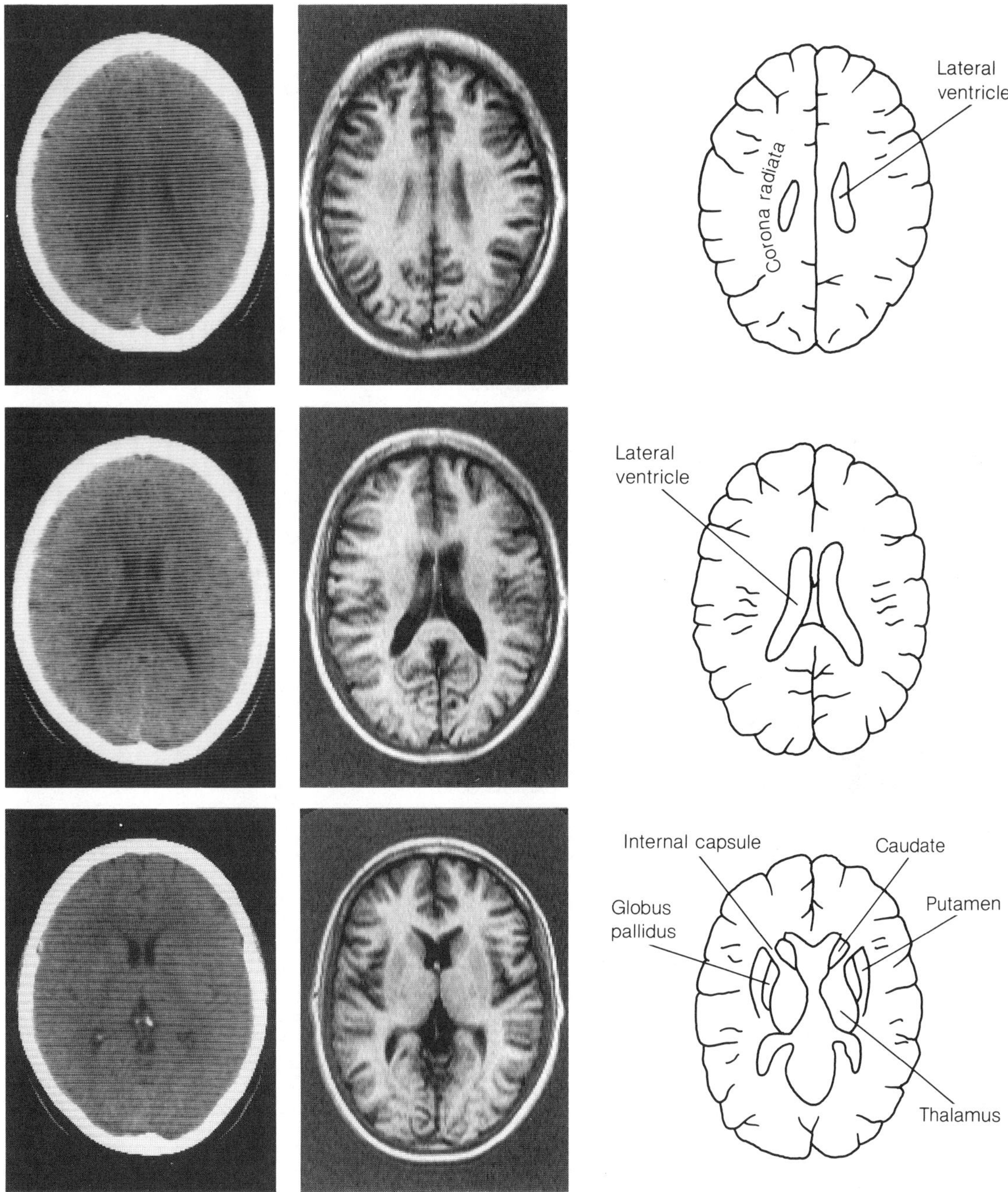

FIGURE A-1 *(continued)*

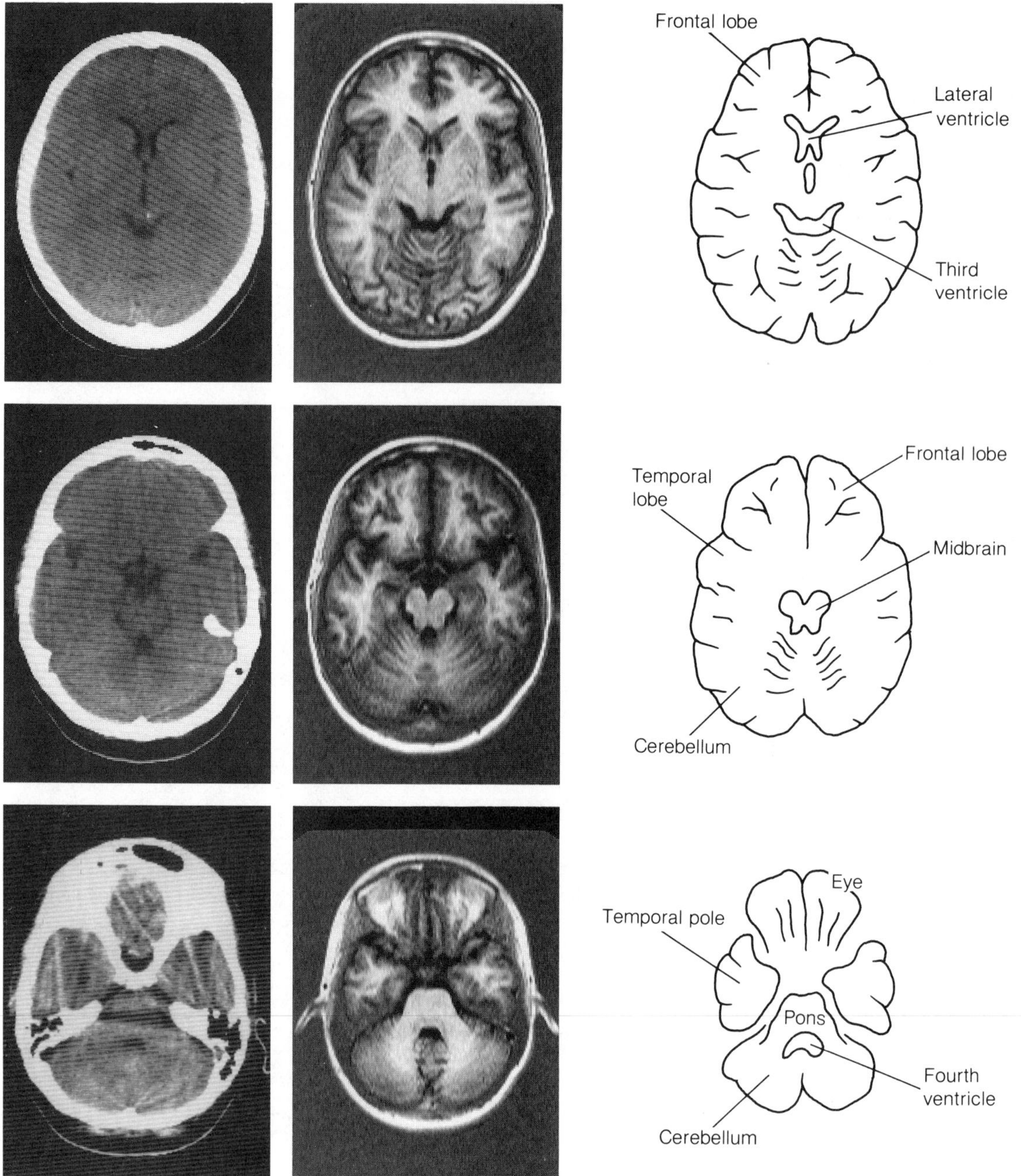

FIGURE A-1 *(continued)*

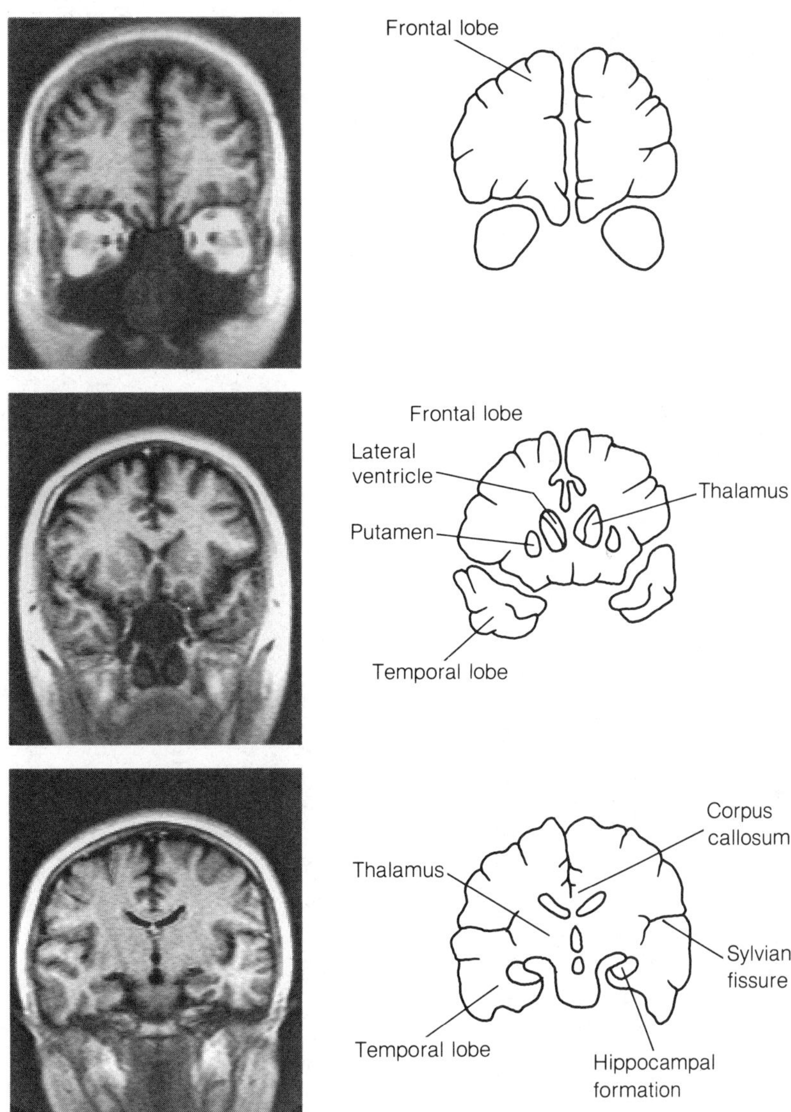

FIGURE A-2. A series of MRI scans and drawings illustrating six coronal cuts through the brain. (Scans provided by Brenda Kosaka and David Li, The University of British Columbia Health Sciences Centre.)

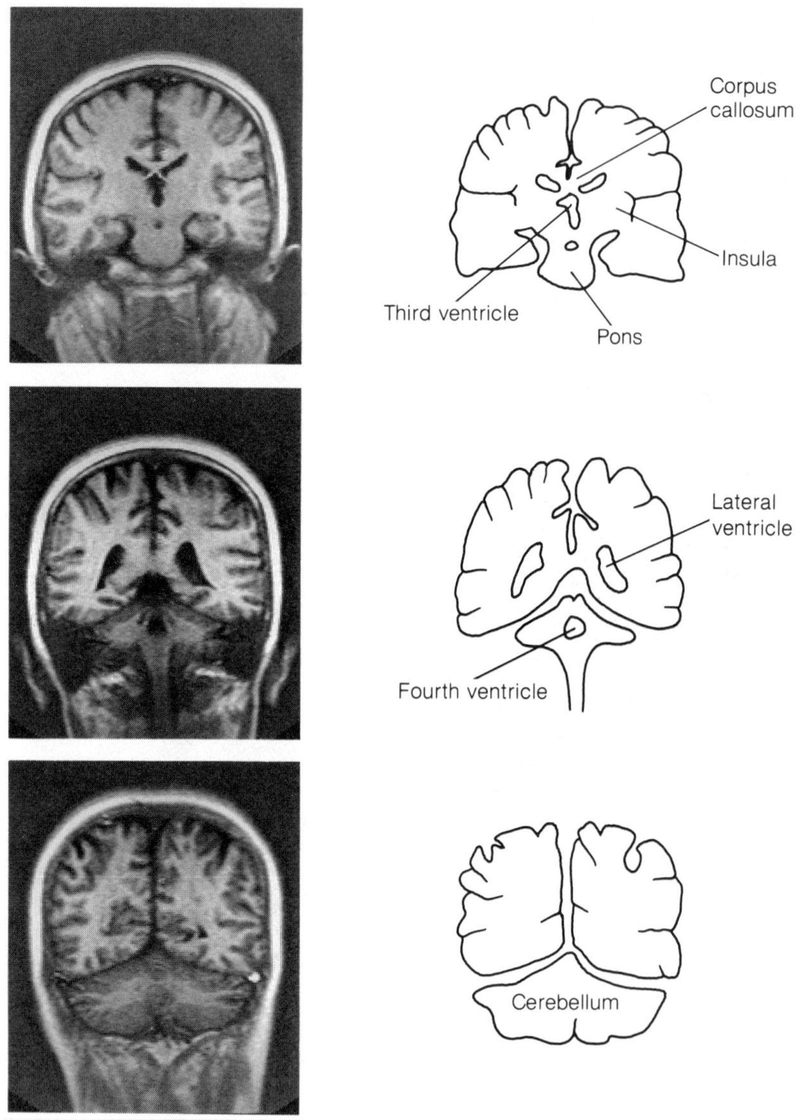

FIGURE A-2 *(continued)*

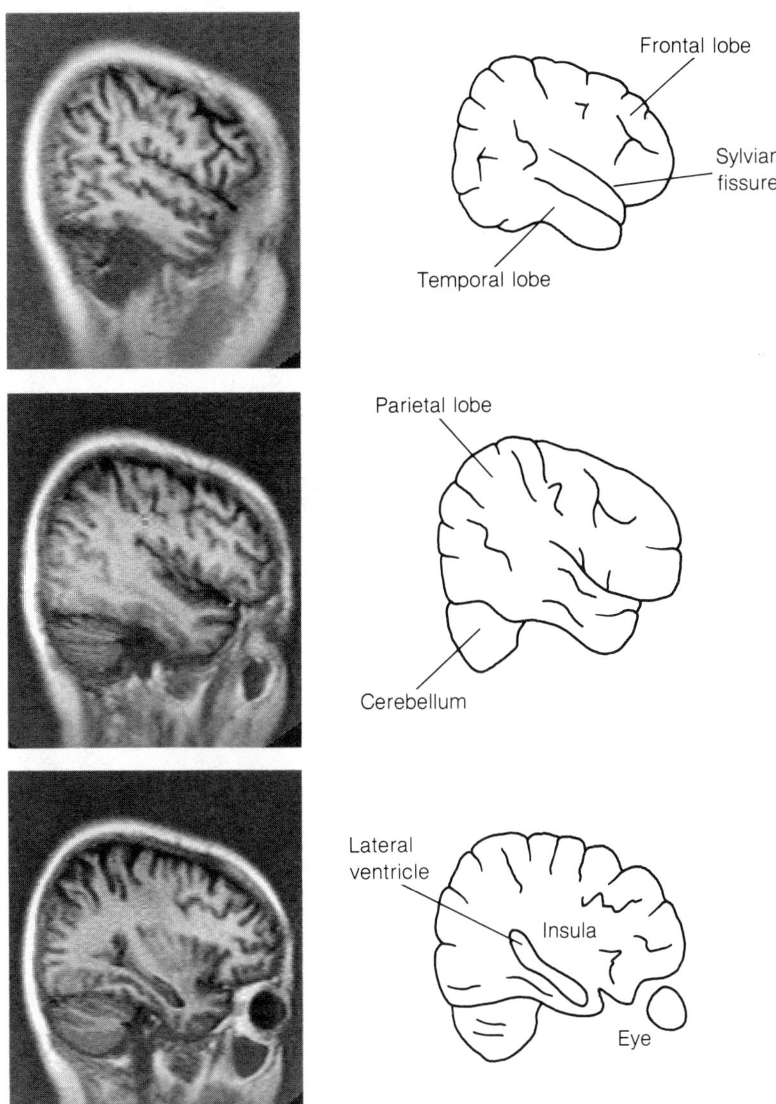

FIGURE A-3. A series of MRI scans and drawings illustrating six sagittal cuts through the brain. (Scans provided by Brenda Kosaka and David Li, The University of British Columbia Health Sciences Centre.)

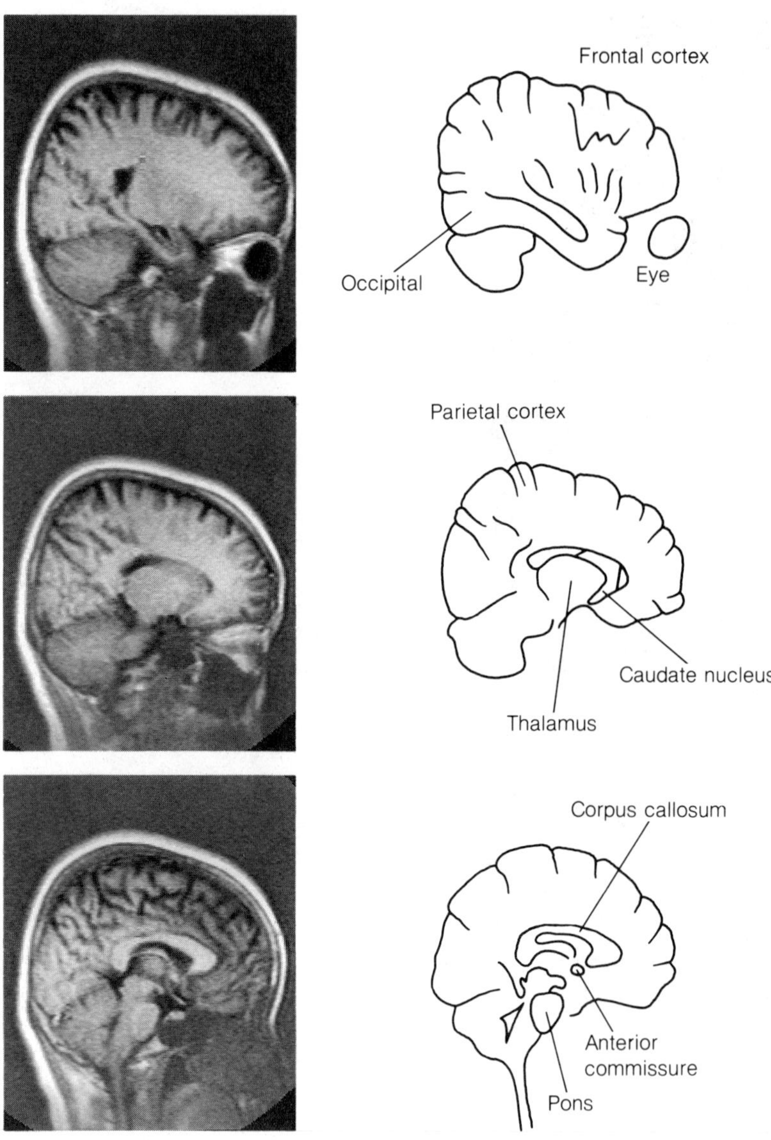

FIGURE A-3 *(continued)*

GLOSSARY

Ablation. Intentional destruction or removal of portions of the brain or spinal cord; brain lesion.

Absence attack. Temporary loss of consciousness in some forms of epilepsy.

Acalculia. Inability to perform mathematical operations

Accessory cells. Cells that, originating from germinal cells (spongioblasts), contribute to the support, nourishment, conduction, and repair of neurons; occasionally the origins of tumors. The accessory cells are the astrocytes; oligodendrocytes; and ependymal, microglial, and Schwann cells.

Achromatopsia. Inability to distinguish different hues despite normally pigmented cells in the retina. Sometimes called *cortical color blindness.*

Acopia. Inability to copy a geometric design.

Acquired dyslexia. When an individual who can read suffers brain damage and can no longer read, the dyslexia is referred to as *acquired,* to distinguish it from developmental dyslexia, which is a failure to learn to read.

Action potential. The brief electrical impulse by which information is conducted along an axon. It results from brief changes in the membrane's permeability to potassium and sodium ions.

Adenosine triphosphate (ATP). Adenosine triphosphate, a molecule important to cellular energy metabolism. The conversion of ATP to ADP (adenine diphosphate) liberates energy. ATP can also be converted to cyclic AMP, which serves as an intermediate messenger in the production of postsynaptic potentials by some neurotransmitters, and in the mediation of the effects of polypeptide hormones.

Afferent. Conducting toward the central nervous system or toward its higher centers.

Afferent paresis. Loss of kinesthetic feedback resulting from lesions to the postcentral gyrus (areas 1, 2, 3), producing clumsy movements.

Afterdischarge. Abnormal discharges from neurons that occur following an epileptic seizure or brain stimulation.

Agenesis of the corpus callosum. A condition in which the corpus callosum fails to develop.

Agnosia. Partial or complete inability to recognize sensory stimuli, unexplainable by a defect in elementary sensation or by a reduced level of alertness.

Agraphia. Decline or loss of the ability to write.

Akathesia. A condition of motor restlessness, ranging from a feeling of inner disquiet to an inability to sit or lie quietly.

Akinesia. Absence or poverty of movement.

Akinetic seizures. Seizures producing temporary paralysis of muscles, characterized by a sudden collapse without warning. Commonest in children.

Alexia. Inability to read.

Allesthesia. The sensation of touch experienced at a point remote from the place touched.

Alpha rhythm. A regular (approximately 10 Hz) wave pattern in the EEG, found in most subjects when they are relaxed with eyes closed.

Alzheimer's disease. A degenerative brain disorder that first appears as a progressive memory loss and later develops into a generalized dementia. The origin of the disease is unknown but cholinergic cells in the basal forebrain and cells in the entorhinal cortex appear to degenerate first.

Amativeness. Inclination to love. Localized by the phrenologists in the nape of the neck.

Amblyopia. Dimness of vision without obvious impairment of the eye itself.

Ammon's horn. Part of the hippocampus.

Amnesia. Partial or total loss of memory.

Amnesic aphasia. An aphasic syndrome characterized by the inability to name objects and the production of unintended syllables, words, or phrases during speaking.

Amines. A class of compounds, some of which are neurotransmitters, which have a component that is formed from ammonia by replacement of one or more hydrogen atoms and thus has an NH attached.

Amino acids. A class of biologically active compounds containing an NH_2 chemical group.

Amusia. Inability to produce (motor) or to comprehend (sensory) musical sounds.

Amygdala. A set of nuclei in the base of the temporal lobe; part of the limbic system.

Anarthria. Incoordination of the musculature of the mouth, resulting in speechlessness.

Anastomosis. The connection between parallel blood vessels that allows them to communicate their blood flows.

Aneurysm. Vascular dilations resulting from localized defects in vascular elasticity; a sac is formed by the dilation of the walls of an artery or of a vein and is filled with blood.

Angiography. Radiographic imaging of blood vessels filled with a contrast medium.

Angioma. Collections of abnormal blood vessels, including capillary, venous, and arteriovenous malformations, resulting in abnormal blood flow.

Angular gyrus. Gyrus in the parietal lobe corresponding roughly to Brodmann's area 39; important in language functions.

Anomia. Difficulty in finding words, especially those naming objects.

Anomic aphasia. An inability to name objects.

Anopia. Loss of vision.

Anosmia. Absence of the sense of smell.

Anosodiaphoria. Indifference to illness.

Anosognosia. Loss of ability to recognize or to acknowledge an illness or bodily defect; usually associated with right parietal lesions.

Anterior commissure. Fiber tract that joins the temporal lobes.

Anterograde amnesia. Inability to remember events subsequent to some disturbance of the brain such as head injury, electroconvulsive shock, or certain degenerative diseases.

Anterograde degeneration. When a nerve cell is damaged, it completely or partly degenerates. Degeneration of the parts of the cell that lie distal to the trauma, with the cell body used as reference, is called *anterograde degeneration*. For example, when an axon is cut, anterograde degeneration occurs in the section from the cut to the synaptic terminals.

Anterograde transport. Transport by a neuron, usually along axons, of substances in a direction that is away from the cell body.

Aphagia. Inability to eat or chew.

Aphasia. Defect or loss of power of expression by speech, writing, or signs, or of comprehending spoken or written language due to injury or disease of the brain.

Apraxia. Inability to carry out purposeful movements in the absence of paralysis or paresis.

Aprosodia. A condition in which there is a loss of production or comprehension of the meaning of different tones of voice.

Arachnoid. A thin sheet of delicate collagenous connective tissue that follows the contours of the brain.

Archicortex. Portion of cerebral cortex that develops in association with olfactory cortex and is phylogenetically older than the neopallium and lacks its layered structure. Also called *archipallium, allocortex,* and *olfactory cortex.* Corresponds to the dentate gyrus and hippocampal gyrus in mature mammals.

Arcuate fasciculus. A long bundle of fibers joining Wernicke's and Broca's areas.

Argyll-Robertson pupil. Constriction of the pupil of the eye to accommodation, but not to light. Used to diagnose damage to the midbrain relays of the third cranial nerve (oculomotor).

Arteriovenous (A-V) malformation. Abnormality of both the arterial and venal blood flow. It often appears as a mass of vessels that are intertwined and lie on the surface of the cortex.

Asomatognosia. Loss of knowledge or sensory awareness of one's own body and bodily condition. May occur on one or both sides of the body. Most commonly results from damage to the right parietal lobe.

Association cortex. All cortex that is not specialized motor or sensory cortex. (The term survives from an earlier belief that inputs from the different senses meet and become associated.)

Astereognosis. Inability, with no defect of elementary tactile sensation, to recognize familiar objects by touch.

Astrocyte. A type of glial cell. *See also* accessory cells.

Astrocytoma. A slow-growing brain tumor resulting from the growth of astrocytes.

Asymbolia. Inability to employ a conventional sign to stand for another object or event.

Asymbolia for pain. An inability to understand the meaning of pain.

Ataxia. Failure of muscular coordination; any of various irregularities of muscular action.

Athetosis. A motor disorder marked by involuntary movements of slow writhing movements, especially in the hands.

Attentional dyslexia. A disorder in which naming a letter is more difficult when it is accompanied by a second letter.

Auditory agnosia. Impaired capacity to identify nonverbal acoustic stimuli.

Aura. A subjective sensation, perceptual experience, or motor phenomenon that precedes and marks the onset of an epileptic seizure or migraine.

Autism. The condition in which a person is dominated by self-centered thought or behaviors that are not subject to change by external stimulation. In children the condition is often called *infantile autism* and is characterized by a failure to relate normally to people or external stimulation. These children generally have severe language disorders and exhibit repetitive behaviors such as rocking.

Autoimmune disease. An immune reaction that is directed against one's own body.

Automatic behaviors. Stereotyped units of behavior linked in a fixed sequence, e.g., grooming and chewing. Also called *reflexive, consummatory,* and *respondent* behaviors.

Autoradiography. When radiolabeled substances are injected into the bloodstream they are incorporated into cells and transported along the cells' processes. If the tissue is exposed to a photographic film it "takes its own picture" and reveals the route taken by the radiolabeled substance.

Autotopagnosia. Inability to localize and name the parts of one's own body; e.g., finger agnosia (*see* agnosia).

Average evoked potential (AEP). The computerized average of a number of evoked potentials from sensory input.

Axon. A thin neuronal process that transmits action potentials away from the cell body to other neurons (or to muscles or glands).

Axon hillock. The site of origin of a nerve impulse.

Balint's syndrome. An agnosic syndrome composed of three deficits: (1) paralysis of eye fixation with inability to look voluntarily into the peripheral visual field, (2) optic ataxia, and (3) disturbance of visual attention such that there is neglect of the peripheral field. Results from large bilateral parietal lesions.

Basal ganglia. A group of large nuclei in the forebrain, including the caudate nucleus, putamen, globus pallidus, claustrum, and amygdala.

Bell-Magendie Law. The law, named after its cofounders, states that the dorsal roots of the spinal cord are sensory and the ventral roots of the spinal cord are motor.

Beta rhythm. Irregular EEG activity of 13–30 Hz generally associated with an alert state.

Bilateral. Occurring on or applying to both sides of the body.

Binocular deprivation. Removal of visual stimulation from both eyes by raising an animal in the dark, bandaging the eyes, or some similar technique.

Biochemical techniques. Refers to the use of measures of biologically relevant chemicals in tissue. It includes various types of assay procedures for determining the presence or concentration of different compounds.

Biogenic amines. Refers to a group of neurotransmitters including norepinephrine, dopamine, and serotonin.

Birthdate effect. The time of the year that a person is born can influence their success when entrance into leagues or schools is determined by birthdate because some entrants will be older and some younger than average producing differential advantages due to age.

Bitemporal hemianopsia. Loss of vision in both temporal fields due to damage to the medial region of the optic chiasm.

Blood-brain barrier. A functional barrier produced by the glial cells and cells in the walls of the capillaries in the brain. This mechanism prevents the passage of many substances into the brain.

Brain abscess. A localized collection of pus in the brain formed from tissues that have disintegrated as a result of infection.

Brain hypothesis. The idea that the brain produces behavior, as opposed to some other body organ such as the heart.

Brain scan. *See* radioisotope scan.

Brainstem. In this book text it includes the hypothalamus, midbrain, and hindbrain. Some authorities also include the thalamus and basal ganglia.

Broca's aphasia. An expressive or nonfluent aphasia; cliefly a defect of speech; results from a lesion to Broca's area.

Broca's area. A region of the left frontal lobe (frontal operculum) believed to be involved in the production of language. Damage results in Broca's aphasia.

Brodmann's map. A map of the cerebral cortex devised by Brodmann; it is based on cytoarchitectonic structure and labels anatomical areas by number. (It conforms remarkably closely to functional areas based on lesion and recording studies.)

Brown-Sequard syndrome. A condition of unilateral paralysis and loss of joint sensation and contralateral loss of pain and temperature sensation caused by damage to one half of the spinal cord.

Calcification. The accumulation of calcium in various brain regions after brain damage.

Catecholamine. A class of neurotransmitters that includes epinephrine, norepinephrine, and dopamine.

Caudate nucleus. A nucleus of the basal ganglia.

Cell assembly. A hypothetical collection of neurons that become functionally connected; proposed by Hebb to be the basis of ideation, perception, and memory.

Cell body. *See* soma.

Central sulcus. A fissure running from the dorsal border of the hemisphere near its midpoint, obliquely downward and forward until it nearly meets the lateral fissure, dividing the frontal and parietal lobes. Also called *fissure of Rolando.*

Cerebellum. A major structure of the hindbrain specialized for motor coordination.

Cerebral arteriosclerosis. Condition marked by loss of elasticity and by thickening and hardening of the arteries. Eventually results in dementia.

Cerebral compression. A contraction of the brain substance due to an injury that has caused hemorrhage and the development of a hematoma.

Cerebral contusion. A vascular injury resulting in bruising and edema and hemorrhage of capillaries.

Cerebral cortex. The layer of gray matter on the surface of the cerebral hemispheres composed of neurons and their synaptic connections that form four to six sublayers.

Cerebral hemorrhage. Bleeding into the brain.

Cerebral hypoxia. Deficiency in the amount of oxygen getting into the brain in the bloodstream.

Cerebral ischemia. Deficiency in the amount of blood getting to the brain. This may be restricted to limited regions. It may be due to an obstruction or constriction of cerebral arteries.

Cerebral laceration. A contusion severe enough to physically breach the brain substance.

Cerebral palsy. A group of disorders that results from brain damage acquired prenatally.

Cerebral trauma. An injury to the brain, usually resulting from a blow to the head.

Cerebral vascular accident. *See* stroke.

Cerebral vascular insufficiency. Deficiency in the amount of blood getting to the brain.

Cerebrospinal fluid (CSF). A clear, colorless solution of sodium chloride and other salts that fills the ventricles inside the brain and circulates around the brain beneath the arachnoid layer in the subarachnoid space.

Choroid plexus. A tissue that lines the cerebral ventricles and produces cerebrospinal fluid.

Chromatolysis. The loss of protein in a damaged cells resulting in loss of its ability to absorb stain; literally the breakdown of its ability to be colored.

Chromosome. Strands of DNA combined with protein in the nucleus of each cell that contain the genetic code determining the structure and function of the individual.

Cingulate cortex. A strip of limbic cortex lying just above the corpus callosum along the medial walls of the cerebral hemispheres.

Cingulate sulcus. A cortical sulcus that is located on the medial wall of the cerebral hemisphere just above the corpus callosum.

Class-common behaviors. Those behaviors and behavioral capacities common to all members of a phylogenetic class.

Cognition. A general term used to refer to the processes involved in thinking.

Cognitive set. The tendency to approach a problem with a particular bias in thought. For example, when searching for a mail box one will have a cognitive set for mail boxes but not for cats.

Cognitive space. Space or time about which a person has knowledge.

Color agnosia. Inability to associate particular colors with objects, or objects with colors.

Color amnesia. An inability to remember the color of common objects.

Color anomia. Inability to name colors; generally associated with other aphasic symptoms. Also called *color aphasia.*

Commissure. A bundle of fibers connecting corresponding points on the two sides of the central nervous system.

Commissurotomy. Surgical disconnection of the two hemispheres by cutting the corpus callosum.

Complete partial seizure. A focal seizure that most commonly originates in the temporal lobe and is characterized by subjective feelings, automatisms, and motor symptoms. Sometimes referred to as a *temporal lobe seizure.*

Computerized tomography (CT) scan. An x-ray procedure in which a computer draws a map from the measured densities of the brain; superior to a conventional x rays since it provides a three-dimensional representation of the brain. Also called by the trade name *EMI-Scan.*

Computerized transaxial tomography. A technique by which a series of brain x rays are used to construct a three dimensional representation of the brain. *See also* computerized tomography (CT) scan.

Concussion. A condition of widespread paralysis of the functions of the brain that occurs immediately after a blow on the head.

Conduction aphasia. A type of fluent aphasia in which, despite alleged normal comprehension of spoken language, words are repeated incorrectly.

Constructional apraxia. The inability to perform well-rehearsed and familiar sequences of movements involved in making or preparing something. The deficit is not attributable to an inability to move or to perform the individual acts required for the task.

Contralateral. Residing in the side of the body opposite the reference points.

Contralateral neglect. Neglect of part of the body or space contralateral to the lesion.

Contrast X ray. Radiographic procedure using the injection of radiopaque dye or air into the ventricles, or of dye into the arteries, for purposes of diagnosis.

Corollary discharge. Transmission by one area of the brain to another, informing the latter area of the former's actions. Commonly used more specifically for a signal from the motor system to the sensory systems that a particular movement is being produced.

Corpus callosum. Fiber system connecting the homotopic areas of the two hemispheres. Split-brain patients are those whose corpus callosum has been severed.

Cortex. An external layer. In this text it is synonymous with "neocortex." *See also* neocortex.

Cranial nerves. A set of 12 pairs of nerves conveying sensory and motor signals to and from the head.

Creutzfeldt-Jakob's disease. A form of senile dementia in which there is generalized cortical atrophy. The cause is unknown, but a slow acting virus is suspected.

Crossed aphasia. The aphasia that results from damage to the right hemisphere.

Cytoarchitectonic maps. Maps of the cortex based on the organization, structure, and distribution of the cells.

Deafferentation. The process of removing the afferent input to a structure or region of the nervous system.

Decerebrate rigidity. Excessive tone in all muscles, producing extension of the limbs and dorsoflexion of the head because antigravity musculature overpowers other muscles; caused by brainstem or cerebellar lesions.

Decerebration. The process whereby the cerebral hemispheres come to be disconnected from the brainstem and, therefore, are deprived of sensory input and the ability to affect behavior.

Declarative memory. The type of memory that is illustrated by the ability of an individual to recount the details of events, including time, place, and circumstances, as compared with the ability to perform some act or behavior. Quite literally it refers to the ability to recount what one knows. The ability is lost in many types of amnesia.

Decortication. Removal of the cortex of the brain.

Decussation. Crossing of pathways from one side of the brain to the other.

Deep dyslexia. A reading impairment that follows large lesions to the hemisphere dominant for speech. It is characterized by a peculiar constellation of errors that suggests the reading is being performed by the nondominant hemisphere.

Delayed nonmatching-to-sample task. A behavioral test in which the subject is presented with a sample stimulus and then after some delay the subject is presented with the same stimulus and another, novel stimulus. The subject's task is to choose the novel stimulus to obtain reward.

Delusions. Beliefs opposed to reality but firmly held despite evidence of their falsity; characteristic of some types of psychotic disorders.

Dendrites. Treelike processes at the receiving end of the neuron.

Denervation supersensitivity. A condition of increased susceptibility to drugs, resulting from proliferation of receptors after denervation (removal of terminations) of an area.

Deoxyribonucleic acid (DNA). A long, complex macromolecule consisting of two interconnected helical strands. Strands of DNA, along with their associated proteins, constitute the chromosomes, which contain the genetic information of the animal.

Depolarization. Inward transfer of positive ions erasing a difference of potential between the inside and the outside of the neuron.

Dermatome. The area of skin supplied with afferent nerve fibers by a single spinal dorsal root.

2-Deoxyglucose (2-DG). A sugar that interferes with the metabolism of glucose. A radioactive marker (such as C-14) can be attached to the 2-DG. When this compound is taken up by the blood it is transported to the brain and will stay in the brain regions that have been most active, which provides a method to measure metabolic activity.

Desynchronization. A change in EEG activity from a high-amplitude slow pattern to low-amplitude fast pattern.

Developmental dyslexia. The inability to learn adequate reading skills even when opportunity and appropriate instruction are given.

Diaschisis. A special kind of shock following brain damage in which areas connected to the damaged area show a transitory arrest of function.

Dichaptic test. A procedure for simultaneously presenting different objects to each hand to determine which hand is most effective at identifying the object.

Dichotic listening. A procedure of simultaneously presenting a different auditory input to each ear through stereophonic earphones.

Diencephalon. A region of the brain that includes the hypothalamus, thalamus, and epithalamus.

Diplopia. Perception of two images of a single object; double vision.

Disconnection. Severing, by damage or by surgery, of the fibers that connect two areas of the brain such that the two areas can no longer communicate; also, the condition that results.

Disinhibition. Removal of inhibition from a system.

Dissolution. According to an unproved theory, the condition whereby disease or damage in the highest levels of the brain would produce not loss of function but rather a repertory of simpler behaviors as seen in animals who have not evolved that particular brain structure.

Distal. Being away from, or distant to, some point.

Dorsal root. The fibers that carry sensory information enter the dorsal (posterior in humans) portion of the spinal cord; those that enter each segment of the cord are collected together in a nerve, called a *dorsal root.*

Dorsal root ganglion. The cell bodies of the sensory fibers are located adjacent to the portion of the spinal cord into which their axons enter. The protuberance produced by their aggregation is called the *dorsal root ganglion.*

Dorsomedial thalamus. A thalamic nucleus providing a major afferent input to the prefrontal cortex; degenerates in Korsakoff's disease, leading to a severe amnesic syndrome.

Double dissociation. An experimental technique whereby two areas of neocortex are functionally dissociated by two behavioral tests, each test being affected by a lesion to one zone and not the other.

Dura mater. A tough, double layer of collagenous fiber enclosing the brain in a kind of loose sack.

Dysarthria. Difficulty in speech production caused by incoordination of the speech apparatus.

Dyscalculia. Difficulty in performing arithmetical operations.

Dyseidetic. Individuals who have difficulty recognizing words by their visual configurations.

Dyskinesia. Any disturbance of movement.

Dyslexia. A difficulty in reading.

Dysphasia. Impairment of speech caused by damage to the central nervous system.

Dysphonetic. Individuals who are unable to decode words or recognize them using phonic or sound principles.

Dystonia. An abnormality of muscle tone, usually excessive muscle tone.

Echolalia. Condition in which a person repeats words or noises that they hear.

Efferent. Conducting away from higher centers in the central nervous system and toward muscle or gland.

Electroconvulsive shock therapy (ECT or ECS). The application of a massive electric shock across the brain as a treatment for affective disorders.

Electroencephalography or electroencephalogram (EEG). Electrical potentials recorded by placing electrodes on the scalp or in the brain.

Electromyography or electromyogram (EMG). Recording of electrical activity of the muscles as well as the electrical response of the peripheral nerves.

Electron microscope. A microscope that creates images of very small objects by bouncing electrons off the object and creating a picture via the objects' resistance to electrons.

Embolism. The sudden blocking of an artery or a vein by a blood clot, bubble of air, deposit of fat, or small mass of cells deposited by the blood current.

Encephalitis. Inflammation of the central nervous system as a result of infection.

Encephalization. The process by which higher structures such as the cerebral cortex have taken over the functions of the lower centers; may imply either a phylogenetic or an ontogenetic shift of function.

Encephalization quotient (EQ). The ratio of the actual brain size to the expected brain size for a typical mammal of that body size.

Encephalomalacia. Softening of the brain, resulting from vascular disorders caused by inadequate blood flow.

Encephalopathy. Chemical, physical, allergic, or toxic inflammation of the central nervous system.

Encorticalization. The process by which the cerebral cortex has taken over the functions of the lower centers; may imply either a phylogenetic or an ontogenetic shift of function.

Endoplasmic reticulum (ER). An extensive internal membrane system in the cytoplasm.

Ribosomes attach to part of ER to form the rough ER.

Entorhinal cortex. The cortex found on the medial surface of the temporal lobe that provides a major route for neocortical input to the hippocampal formation. The entorhinal cortex often shows degeneration in Alzheimer's disease.

Ependymal cells. Glial cells forming the lining of the ventricles; some produce cerebrospinal fluid.

Epilepsy. A condition characterized by recurrent seizures of various types associated with a disturbance of consciousness.

Epithalamus. A collection of nuclei forming the phylogenetically most primitive region of the thalamus; includes the habenulae, pineal body, and stria medullaris.

Equipotentiality. The hypothesis that each part of a given area of brain is able to encode or produce the behavior normally controlled by the entire area.

Ergotamine. A drug used in the treatment of migraine and tension headaches that acts by constricting cerebral arteries.

Ethology. The study of the natural behavior of animals.

Euclidean space. Real space, with three dimensions, according the the laws of Euclid.

Evoked potential (EP). A short train of large, slow waves recorded from the scalp, reflecting dendritic activity.

Excitatory neurotransmitter. Transmitter substances that decrease a cell's membrane potential and increase the likelihood that it will fire.

Excitory postsynaptic potential (EPSP). A small change in the membrane potential of a cell that leads to depolarization and increased likelihood that the cell will fire.

Extinction. A term used in learning theory referring to the fact that the probability that a behavior will occur decreases if reinforcement is withheld.

Face amnesia. An inability to remember faces.

Factor analysis. A statistical procedure that is designed to determine if the variability in scores can be related to one or more factors that are reliably influencing performance.

Fasciculation. A small local contraction of muscles, visible through the skin, representing a spontaneous discharge of a number of fibers innervated by a single motor nerve filament.

Festination. Tendency to engage in behavior at faster and faster speeds; usually refers to walking, but can include other behaviors such as talking and thinking.

Fissure. A cleft, produced by folds of the neocortex, that extends to the ventricles.

Fluent aphasia. Refers to a speech disorder in which a person articulates words in a language-like fashion, but what is said actually makes little sense. Also called *Wernicke's aphasia;* it usually results from damage to the left posterior cortex. *See also* Wernicke's aphasia.

Focal seizures. Seizures that begin locally and then spread; for example, from one finger to the whole body.

Forebrain. In this text, the term for the cerebral hemispheres, basal ganglia, thalamus, amygdala, hippocampus, and septum.

Frontal lobes. All the neocortex forward of the central sulcus.

Frontal operculum. The upper region of the inferior frontal gyrus.

Functional maps. Maps of the cortex constructed by stimulating areas of the brain electrically and noting elicited behavior, or by recording electrical activity during certain behaviors. Such maps relate specific behaviors to brain areas.

Functional validation. According to theory, the need of a neural system for sensory stimulation if it is to become fully functional.

Generalized seizures. Bilaterally symmetrical seizures without a local onset.

Geniculostriate system. A system consisting of projections from the retina of the eye to the lateral geniculate nucleus of the thalamus, then to areas 17, 18, 19, and then to 20, and 21; involved in perception of form, color, and pattern.

Genu. The bulbous part of the anterior portion of the corpus callosum.

Gerstmann syndrome. A collection of symptoms due to left parietal lesion, alleged to include finger agnosia, right-left confusion, acalculia, and agraphia. A source of some controversy.

Glial cells. Supportive cells of the central nervous system.

Glial sheath. Glial cells, such as oligodendroglia and Schwann cells, that wrap themselves around the axons of neurons, thus forming a sheath.

Glioblastoma. A highly malignant, rapidly growing brain tumor; commonest in adults over 35 years of age; results from the sudden growth of spongioblasts.

Glioma. Any brain tumor that arises from glial cells.

Gliosis. Glial cells migrate to and proliferate in areas of neural tissue where damage has occurred. Their presence serves as a sign of tissue damage.

Globus pallidus. Literally, means "pale globe or sphere". Part of the basal ganglia that receives projections from the caudate nucleus and sends projections to the ventral lateral nucleus of the thalamus.

Glycoprotein. A class of proteins consisting of a compound of protein with a carbohydrate group.

Golgi apparatus. A complex of parallel membranes in the cytoplasm that wraps the product of a secretory cell or a protein manufactured by a nerve cell.

Graded potential. An electrical potential in a neuron or receptor cell that changes with the intensity of the stimulus. Also known as a *generator potential.*

Grand mal attack. Seizure characterized by loss of consciousness and stereotyped, generalized convulsions.

Granulovacuolar bodies. Abnormal structures in the brain that are characterized by granules (small beadlike masses of tissue) and vacuoles (small cavities in the protoplasm of cells).

Grapheme. Refers to the pictorial qualities of a written word that permits it to be understood without being sounded out; a group of letters that conveys a meaning.

Graphemic reading. The meaning of a word is derived from the picture that it makes as a whole rather than by sounding out the syllables.

Graphesthesia. The ability to identify numbers or letters traced on the skin with a blunt object.

Gray matter. Any brain area composed predominantly of cell bodies.

Gyrus. A convolution of the cortex of the cerebral hemispheres.

Habituation. Gradual quantitative decrease of a response after repeated exposure to a stimulus.

Hallucinations. Perceptions for which there are no appropriate external stimuli; characteristic of some types of psychotic disorders.

Hebephrenic schizophrenia. A form of schizophrenia characterized by silly behavior and mannerisms, giggling, and shallow affect.

Hematoma. A local swelling or tumor filled with effused blood.

Heme group. A nonprotein, insoluble, iron protoporphyrin constituent of hemoglobin, a constituent of blood.

Hemiballism. A motor disorder characterized by sudden involuntary movements of a single limb.

Hemiparesis. Muscular weakness affecting one side of the body.

Hemiplegia. Paralysis of one side of the body.

Hemispherectomy. Removal of a cerebral hemisphere.

Hindbrain. A region of the brain that consists primarily of the cerebellum, medulla, pons, and fourth ventricle.

Hippocampus. Primitive cortical structure lying in the anterior medial region of the temporal lobe.

Histochemical techniques. A number of techniques that rely on chemical reactions in cells to mark features of a cell of microscopic visualization.

Histofluorescent technique. Literally, cell flourescence, a technique whereby a flourescent compound is used to label cells.

Homeostasis. The maintenance of a chemically and physically constant internal environment.

Hominid. General term referring to primates that walk upright, including all forms of humans, living and extinct.

Homonomous hemianopsia. Total loss of vision due to complete cuts of the optic tract, lateral geniculae body, or area 17.

Horseradish perioxidase (HRP). A compound that, when introduced to a cell, is then distributed to all of its parts, thus allowing the cell to be visualized.

Huntington's chorea. A hereditary disease characterized by chorea (ceaseless, involuntary, jerky movements) and progressive dementia, ending in death.

Hydrocephalus. A condition characterized by abnormal accumulation of fluid in the cranium, accompanied by enlargement of the head, prominence of the forehead, atrophy of the brain, mental deterioration, and convulsions.

6-Hydroxydopamine (6-OHDA). A chemical selectively taken up by axons and terminals of norepinephrinergic or dopaminergic neurons that acts as a poison, damaging or killing them.

Hyperactivity. More activity than normally expected.

Hyperkinesia. A condition in which there is an increase in movements of a part or all of the body.

Hyperlexia. A condition in which a person is given to excessive reading, or is a precocious reader, often without understanding the meaning of what is read.

Hypermetamorphosis. A tendency to attend and react to every visual stimulus, leading to mental distraction and confusion.

Hyperpolarization. The process by which a nerve membrane becomes more resistant to the passage of sodium ions and consequently more difficult to excite with adequate stimulation. During hyperpolarization the electrical charge on the inside of the membrane relative to the outside becomes more negative.

Hypothalamus. Collection of nuclei located below the thalamus; involved in nearly all behavior including movement, feeding, sexual activity, sleeping, emotional expression, temperature regulation, and endocrine regulation.

Ideational apraxia. A vague term used to describe a disorder of gestural behavior in which the overall conception of how a movement is carried out is lost. This disorder emerges when a person is required to manipulate objects.

Ideomotor apraxia. Describes an inability to use and understand nonverbal communication such as gesture and pantomime.

Idiopathic seizures. Seizure disorders that appear to arise spontaneously and in the absence of other diseases of the central nervous system.

Illusions. False or misinterpreted sensory impressions of real sensory images.

Immunohistochemical staining. An antibody-based label, which, when applied to tissue postmortem, will reveal the presence of some specific molecule or close relatives.

Infarct. An area of dead or dying tissue resulting from an obstruction of the blood vessels normally supplying the region.

Inferior colliculus. The nucleus of the tectum of the midbrain that receives auditory projections and is involved in whole-body orientation to auditory stimuli.

Inhibitory neurotransmitter. A neurotransmitter that increases the membrane polarity of a cell, making it less likely to produce an action potential fire.

Inhibitory postsynaptic potential (IPSP). A small localized change that increases a membrane's potential, making it less likely that an action potential will occur.

Interneuron. Any neuron lying between a sensory neuron and a motor neuron.

Invariance hypothesis. A hypothesis that suggests that the structure of each cerebral hemisphere will ensure that it will develop a set of specialized functions, i.e., the left hemisphere is specialized at birth for language.

Ipsilateral. Located on the same side of the body as the point of reference.

Isolation syndrome. *See* transcortical aphasia.

Jacksonian seizures. A focal seizure that has consistent sensory or motor symptoms such as a twitching in the face or hand.

Kennard principle. Early brain damage produces less severe behavioral effects than brain damage incurred later in life. The term was coined after Kennard reported this phenomenon in a series of papers based on the study of neonatally brain-damaged monkeys.

Kindling. Production of epilepsy by repeated stimulation; for example, by an electrode in the brain.

Kinesthesis. The perception of movement or position of the limbs and body; commonly used to refer to the perception of changes in angle of joints.

Klüver-Bucy syndrome. A group of symptoms resulting from degeneration of the dorsomedial thalamic nucleus; produced by chronic alcoholism.

Korsakoff's syndrome (or Korsakoff-Wernicke disease). A metabolic disorder of the central nervous system due to a lack of vitamin B_1 (thiamin); often associated with chronic alcoholism.

Landmark test. A behavioral test in which the subject must learn the association between a specific cue (the landmark) and the location of reward.

Lateral fissure. A deep cleft on the basal surface of the brain that extends laterally, posteriorly, and upward, thus separating the temporal and parietal lobes. Also called *Sylvian fissure.*

Laterality. Side of the brain that controls a given function; hence studies of laterality are devoted to determining which side of the brain controls various functions.

Lateralization. The process whereby functions come to be located primarily on one side of the brain.

Lateral system. One of the two major motor groups of tracts in the motor system. The lateral system includes the lateral corticospinal tract, which originates in the neocortex, and the rubrospinal tract, which originates in the red nucleus in the brainstem.

Lesion. Any damage to the nervous system.

Letter-by-letter reading. The meaning of a text is determined by extracting information from each letter, one letter at a time.

Lexicon. A dictionary, or memory store, in the brain that contains words and their meanings.

Light microscope. A microscope that relies of shining light through tissue in order to visualize that tissue through an eyepiece.

Limb-kinetic apraxia. A form of apraxia in which the person is unable to make voluntary movements of the limbs in response to verbal commands. Presumed to result from a disconnection of the motor program from language.

Limbic system. An elaboration of the structures of the limbic lobe to form a hypothetical functional system originally believed to be important in controlling affective behavior. The neural systems that line the inside wall of the neocrotex.

Lipofuscin granules. Dark-pigmented substance that accumulates in brain cells as they age.

Localization of function. Hypothetically, the control of each kind of behavior by a different specific brain area.

Long-term enhancement (LTE). A long-lasting change in the postsynaptic response of a cell that results from previous experience with a high-frequency stimulation. Also known as *enhancement* and *long-term potentiation (LTP).*

Long-term potentiation (LTP). *See* long-term enhancement (LTE).

Lysomes. One of the small bodies containing digestive enzymes seen with the electron microscope in many types of cells.

Macular sparing. A condition in which the central region of the visual field is not lost even though temporal or nasal fields are.

Magnetic resonance imaging (MRI). *See* nuclear magnetic resonance.

Magnetoencephalogram (MEG). Magnetic potentials recorded from detectors placed outside the skull.

Mass action hypothesis. The hypothesis that the entire neocortex participates in every behavior.

Massa intermedia. Mass of gray matter that connects the left and right thalami across the midline.

Maturational-lag hypothesis. Explanations of a disability that suggest that a system is not yet mature or is maturing slowly.

Maturation hypothesis. Argues that both hemispheres are initially involved in language but gradually the left hemisphere becomes more specialized for language control.

Medial longitudinal fissure. Fissure that separates the two hemispheres.

Medulla oblongata. The portion of the hindbrain immediately rostral to the spinal cord.

Medulloblastoma. Highly malignant brain tumor found almost exclusively in the cerebella of children; results from the growth of germinal cells that infiltrate the cerebellum.

Meninges. The three layers of protective tissue — the dura mater, arachnoid, and pia mater — that encase the brain and spinal cord.

Meningioma. An encapsulated brain tumor growing from the meninges.

Meningitis. Inflammation of the meninges.

Mental rotation. Ability to make a mental image of an object and imagine it in a new location relative to its background.

Mesencephalon. Middle brain; term for the middle one of the three primary embryonic vesicles, which subsequently comprises the tectum and tegmentum.

Metastasis. A transfer of a disease from one part of the body to another. This is a common characteristic of malignant tumors.

Metastatic tumor. A tumor that occurs through the transfer of tumor cells from elsewhere in the body.

Microfilaments. Small tubelike processes in cells, the function of which is uncertain, but they may be involved in controlling the shape, movement, or fluidity of the cytoplasm or substances within the cell.

Microtubules. Fiberlike substances in the soma and processes of nerve cells that are involved in transporting substances from the soma to the distal elements of the cell or from distal portions of the cell to the soma.

Midbrain. The short segment between the forebrain and hindbrain including the tectum and tegmentum.

Migraine. A type of headache characterized by an aching, throbbing pain, frequently unilateral. It may be preceded by a visual aura presumed to result from ischemia of the occipital cortex induced by vasoconstriction of cerebral arteries.

Migraine stroke. A condition in which a cerebral vessel constricts, cutting off the blood supply to a cortical region. If the constriction is severe enough and lasts more than a few minutes, then neuronal death may occur, leading to an infarct.

Mitochondria. A complex organelle within the

cell that through a number of processes produces most of the cell's energy.

Monoamine. Refers to a group of neurotransmitters, including norepinephrine and dopamine, that has an amine (NH_2).

Monoclonial antibody. An antibody that is cloned or derived from a single cell.

Monocular blindness. Blindness in one eye caused by destruction of its retina or optic nerve.

Monocular deprivation. Deprivation of visual experience to one eye by closure or bandaging.

Morphological reconstruction. Reconstruction of the body of an animal, often from only skeletal remains.

Motoneurone. Sherrington's term for the unit formed by motor neurons and the muscle fiber to which their axon terminations are connected.

Motor aphasia. An aphasic disorder in which the person is unable to make the correct movements of the mouth and tongue to form words; a form of nonfluent aphasia. It contrasts with sensory aphasia in which speech is fluent but without content.

Motor neuron. A neuron that has its cell body in the spinal cord and that projects to muscles.

Motor program. A hypothetical neural circuit so arranged that it produces a certain type of movement, for example, walking.

Multiple sclerosis (MS). A disease of unknown cause in which there are patches of demyelination in the central nervous system. This may lead to motor weakness or incoordination, speech disturbance, and sometimes to other cognitive symptoms.

Myasthenia gravis. A condition of fatigue and weakness of the muscular system without sensory disturbance or atrophy. It results from a reduction in acetylcholine available at the synapse.

Mycotic infection. Invasion of the nervous system by a fungus.

Myelin. The lipid substance forming an insulating sheath around certain nerve fibers; formed by oligodendroglia in the central nervous system and by Schwann cells in the peripheral nervous system.

Myelin stains. Stains that stain glial cells, particularly those that wrap themselves around axons.

Myelination. Formation of myelin on axons. Sometimes used as an index of maturation.

Myoclonic spasms. Massive seizures consisting of sudden flexions or extensions of the body and often beginning with a cry.

Narcolepsy. Condition in which a person is overcome by uncontrollable, recurrent, brief episodes of sleep.

Nasal hemianopsia. Loss of vision of one nasal field due to damage to the lateral region of the optic chiasm.

Natural selection. A proposition in the theory of evolution that animals with certain adaptive characteristics will survive in certain environments and pass on their genetic characteristics to their offspring, while less fortunate animals, lacking those characteristics, die off.

Necrosis. Cell death or death of tissue, usually as individual cells, groups of cells, or in small, localized areas.

Neglect dyslexia. Misreading errors that are usually confined to a single half of a word.

Neocortex. Newest layer of the brain, forming the outer layer or "new bark;" has four to six layers of cells. In this text it is synonymous with "cortex." *See also* cortex.

Neotony. The fact that newly evolved species often resemble the young of their ancestors.

Nerve growth factor (NGF). A protein that plays some role in maintaining the growth of a cell.

Nerve impulse. Movement or propagation of an action potential along the length of an axon; begins at a point close to the cell body and travels away from it.

Neuritic plaques. Areas of incomplete necrosis that are often seen in the cortex of people with senile dementias such as Alzheimer's disease.

Neuroblast. Any embryonic cell that develops into a neuron.

Neuroendocrine. Pertaining to the interaction of the neural and endocrine (hormonal) systems.

Neurofibril. Any of numerous fibrils making up part of the internal structure of a neuron; may be active in transporting precursor chemicals for the synthesis of neurotransmitters.

Neurohumoral. A general word used to refer to the action of hormones upon the brain.

Neuroleptic drug. A drug that has an antipsychotic action principally affecting psychomotor activity and is generally without hypnotic effects.

Neurologist. A physician specializing in the treatment of disorders of the nervous system.

Neuron. The basic unit of the nervous system; the nerve cell; its function is to transmit and store information; includes the cell body (soma), many processes called dendrites, and an axon.

Neuron hypothesis. Idea that the functional units of the brain are neurons.

Neuropsychology. The study of the relation between brain function and behavior.

Neurotoxin. Any substance that is poisonous or destructive to nerve tissue; for example, 6-hydroxydopamine, placed in the ventricles of the brain, will selectively destroy the norepinephrine and dopamine systems.

Neurotransmitter. A chemical released from a synapse in response to an action potential and acting on postsynaptic receptors to change the resting potential of the receiving cell; chemically transmits information from one neuron to another.

Neurotropic viruses. Those viruses having a strong affinity for cells of the central nervous system, as opposed to pantropic viruses, which attack any body tissue.

Nissl stains. Cells that are selectively taken up by the protein (Nissl substance) in the cell body.

Node of Ranvier. A space separating the Schwann cells that form the covering or myelin on a nerve axon; because the nerve impulse jumps from one node to the next its propagation is accelerated.

Nonfluent aphasia. An inability or impairment of speech that follows brain damage, particularly to the frontal part of the hemisphere dominant for speech, and which is characterized by difficulty in articulating words.

Norepinephrinergic neurons. Neurons that contain norepinephrine in their synapses or use norepinephrine as their neurotransmitter.

Nuclear magnetic resonance (NMR). An imaging procedure in which a computer draws a map from the measured changes in the magnetic resonance of atoms in the brain. Also known as *magnetic resonance imaging (MRI).*

Nucleolus. An organelle within the nucleus of a cell that produces ribosomes.

Nucleus. A spherical structure in the soma of cells that contains DNA and that is essential to cell function; also, a group of cells forming a cluster that can be identified histologically.

Nystagmus. Constant, tiny eye movements that occur involuntarily and have a variety of causes.

Occipital horns. Most posterior projections of the lateral ventricles that protrude into the occipital lobe.

Occipital lobes. A general area of the cortex lying in the back part of the head.

Olfaction. The sense of small or the act of smelling.

Oligodendrocytes. Specialized support, or glial cells in the brain that form a covering of myelin on nerve cells to speed the nerve impulse. Also called *oligodendroglia.*

Optic ataxia. A deficit in the visual control of reaching and other movements as well as a deficit in eye movements.

Optic chiasm. The point at which the optic nerve from one eye partially crosses to join the other, forming a junction at the base of the brain.

Orbital-frontal cortex. Cortex that lies adjacent to the cavity containing the eye but that, anatomically defined, receives projections from the dorsomedial nucleus of the thalamus.

Organic brain syndrome. A general term for behavioral disorders that result from brain malfunction attributable to known or unknown causes.

Organicity. A general term used to refer to abnormal behavior that is assumed to have a biological (organic) basis. The term is of limited value in neuropsychology.

Orientation. Direction.

Paired helical filaments. Two spiral filaments made of chains of amino acids.

Paleocortex. The portion of the cerebral cortex forming the pyriform cortex and parahippocampal gyrus. Also called the *paleopallium.*

Pantropic viruses. Those viruses that attack any body tissue. *See also* neurotropic viruses.

Papilledema. Swelling of the optic disk; caused by increased pressure from cerebrospinal fluid. Used as a diagnostic indicator of tumors or other swellings in the brain.

Paragraphia. The writing of incorrect words or perserveration in writing the same word.

Paralimbic cortex. Area of three-layered cortex that is adjacent to the classically defined limbic cortex and has a direct connection with the limbic cortex, for example, cingulate cortex.

Parallel-development hypothesis. Both hemispheres, by virtue of their anatomy, play special roles, one for language and one for space.

Paraphasia. The production of unintended syllables, words, or phrases during speech.

Paraplegia. Paralysis of the legs due to spinal cord damage.

Paresis. A general term for loss of physical and mental ability due to brain disease, particularly from syphilitic infection; a term for slight or incomplete paralysis.

Parietal lobes. A general region of the brain lying beneath the parietal bone.

Parieto-occipital sulcus. A sulcus in occipital cortex.

Parkinson's disease. A disease of the motor system that is correlated with a loss of dopamine in the brain and is characterized by tremors, rigidity, and reduction in voluntary movement.

Peptides. Part of protein, a class of molecules that yield two or more amino acids.

Perception. A cognition resulting from the activity of cells in the various sensory regions of the neocortex beyond the primary sensory cortex.

Perforant pathway. A large anatomical pathway connecting the entorhinal cortex and subiculum with the hippocampal formation.

Peripheral nerves. Those nerves that lie outside the spinal cord and the brain.

Perseveration. Tendency to repeatedly emit the same verbal or motor response to varied stimuli.

Petit mal attack. Seizure characterized by a loss of awareness during which there is no motor activity except blinking or turning of the head, rolling of the eyes; of brief duration (10 sec typically).

Phagocytes. Cells that engulf microorganisms, other cells, and foreign particles as part of the lymphatic system's defenses.

Pheromone. A substance produced by one individual that is perceived (as a odor) by a second individual of the same species, and that leads to a specific behavioral reaction in the second individual. Pheromones act as chemical signals between animals of the same species.

Phoneme. A unit of sound that forms a word or part of a word.

Phonological. Refers to sound, as in theories of reading that emphasize the role of sound in decoding the meaning of words.

Phonological reading. Reading that relies on sounding out the parts of words.

Phrenology. The long-discredited study of the relation between the skull's surface features and mental faculties.

Pia mater. A moderately tough connective tissue that clings to the surface of the brain.

Piloerection. Erection of the hair.

Pineal body. An unsymmetrical structure in the epithalamus, thought by Descartes to be the seat of the soul, but now thought to be involved in circadian rhythms.

Pituitary gland. A collection neurons at the base of the hypothalamus.

Place task. A task in which an animal must find a place that it cannot see by using the relationship between two or more other surroundings cues.

Planum temporale. The cortical area just posterior to the auditory cortex (Heschl's gyrus) within the Sylvian fissure.

Plasticity. According to theory, the ability of the brain to change in various ways to compensate for loss of function due to damage.

Pneumoencephalography. An X-ray technique in which the cerebrospinal fluid is replaced with air introduced through a lumbar puncture.

Poliomyelitis. An acute viral disease characterized by involvement of the nervous system and possibly paralysis. There may be atrophy of the affected muscles, leading to a permanent deformity.

Polyribosomes. Structures formed by the combination of mRNA and ribosomes that serve as the actual sites for protein synthesis.

Pons. A portion of the hindbrain; composed mostly of motor fiber tracts going to such areas as the cerebellum and spinal tract.

Positron emission tomography (PET). An imaging technique in which a subject is given a radioactively labeled compound such as glucose, which is metabolized by the brain, and the radioactivity is later recorded by a special detector.

Postconcussional syndrome. A constellation of somatic and psychological symptoms including headache, dizziness, fatigue, diminished concentration, memory deficit, irritability, anxiety, insomnia, hypochondriacal concern, hypersensitivity to noise, and photophobia, all of which are typical after a suffering a brief period of disturbed consciousness, usually after a blow to the head.

Postsynaptic membrane. The membrane lying adjacent to a synaptic connection across the synaptic space from the terminal.

Post-traumatic psychosis. A psychotic reaction that occurs after head trauma.

Praxis. An action, movement, or series of movements.

Precentral gyrus. The gyrus lying in front of the central sulcus.

Preferred cognitive mode. Use of one type of thought process in preference to another, for example, visuospatial instead of verbal; sometimes attributed to the assumed superior function of one hemisphere over the other.

Prefrontal cortex. Cortex lying in front of primary and secondary motor cortex; thus, tertiary or association cortex in the frontal lobe.

Presynaptic membrane. The terminal membrane adjacent to the subsynaptic space.

Primary projection area. An area of the brain that first receives a connection from another system.

Primary sensory area. *See* primary zones.

Primary zones. Areas of the cortex that first receive projections from sensory systems or that projects most directly to muscles. Also known as *primary sensory areas.*

Proactive interference. Proactive interference is said to occur when something already experienced interferes with the learning of new information.

Procedural memory. Memory for certain ways of doing things or for certain movements. This memory system is thought to be independent from memory used to "tell about" the ability (i.e., discursive memory).

Projection maps. Maps of the cortex made by tracing axons from the sensory systems into the brain and by tracing axons from the neocortex to the motor systems of the brainstem and spinal cord.

Prosencephalon. Front brain; term for the most anterior part of the embryonic brain, which subsequently evolves into the telencephalon and diencephalon.

Prosody. The variation in stress, pitch, and rhythm of speech by which different shades of meaning are conveyed.

Prosopagnosia. Inability, not explained by defective visual acuity or reduced consciousness or alertness, to recognize familiar faces. Very rare in pure form, and thought to be secondary to right parietal lesions.

Proximal. Being close to something.

Pseudodepression. A condition of personality following frontal lobe lesion in which apathy, indifference, and loss of initiative are apparent symptoms but are not accompanied by a sense of depression in the patient.

Pseudopsychopathy. A condition of personality following frontal lobe lesion in which immature behavior, lack of tact and restraint, and other behaviors symptomatic of psychopathology are apparent but are not accompanied by the equivalent mental or emotional components of psychopathology.

Psychoactive drug. Any chemical substance that alters mood or behavior by altering the functions of the brain.

Psychometrics. The science of measuring human abilities.

Psychosis. A major mental disorder of organic or emotional origin in which the individual's ability to think, respond emotionally, remember, communicate, interpret reality, and behave appropriately is sufficiently impaired so that the ordinary demands of life cannot be met. The term is applicable to conditions having a wide range of severity and duration (e.g., schizophrenia, depression).

Psychosurgery. Surgical intervention to severe fibers connecting one part of the brain with another or to remove or destroy brain tissue with the intent of modifying or altering disturbances of behavior, thought content, or mood for which no organic pathological cause can be demonstrated by established tests and techniques (e.g., lobotomy).

Ptosis. Drooping of the upper eyelid from paralysis of the third nerve (oculomotor).

Pulvinar. Thalamic nucleus that receives projections from the visual cortex and superior colliculus and sends connections to secondary and tertiary temporal and parietal cortex.

Putamen. A nucleus of the basal ganglial complex.

Putative transmitters. Chemicals strongly suspected of being neurotransmitters but not conclusively proved to be so.

Pyramidal cells. Cells that have a pyramidal-shaped cell body. They usually send information from one region of the cortex to some other brain area.

Pyramidal tract. The pathway from the pyramidal cells of the fifth and sixth layers of the neocortex to the spinal cord.

Pyramidalis area. Brodmann's area 4.

Pyriform cortex. Old cortex; subserves olfactory functions.

Quadrantic anopsia. Blindness in one quadrant of the visual field due to some damage to the optic tract, lateral geniculate body, or area 17.

Quasi-evolutionary sequences. A hypothetical ancestral lineage of a contemporary species that is composed of the currently living species that most closely resemble the ancestors. A quasi-evolutionary sequence for humans would include hedgehogs, tree shrews, bushbabies, rhesus monkeys, and chimpanzees.

Radioisotope scan. Scanning of the cranial surface with a Geiger counter after an intraveneous injection of a radioisotope has been given, to detect tumors, vascular disturbances, atrophy, and so forth.

Reading backward. Individuals who are unable to read irrespective of the cause.

Reafference. Confirmation by one part of the nervous system of the activity in another. *See also* corollary discharge

Real space. The space that one sees around oneself, three dimentional space.

Receptive field. The area from which a stimulus can activate a sensory receptor.

Receptors. Proteins on a cell membrane to which other molecules can attach.

Reciprocal inhibition. Activation of one muscle group with inhibition of its antagonists.

Red nucleus. A nucleus in the anterior portion of the tegmentum that is the source of a major motor projection.

Regeneration. A process by which neurons damaged by trauma regrow connections to the area that they previously innervated.

Resting potential. Normal voltage across a nerve cell membrane; varies between 60 and 90 mV in the cells of different animals.

Reticular formation. A mixture of nerve cells and fibers in the lower and ventral portion of the brainstem, extending from the spinal cord to the thalamus and giving rise to important ascending and descending systems. Also known as the *reticular activating system.*

Reticular matter. An area of the nervous system composed of intermixed cell bodies and axons; has a mottled gray and white, or netlike, appearance.

Retrograde amnesia. Inability to remember events that occurred prior to the onset of amnesia.

Retrograde degeneration. Degeneration of a nerve cell that occurs between the site of damage and the cell body and includes the cell body and all of its remaining processes.

Retrograde transport. The transport of material by neurons from their axons back to the cell body. Labels or dyes can be placed at the temination of an axon and they will be picked up by the axonal arborization and transported to the cell body; this makes it possible to trace pathways.

Rhinencephalon. Alternative term for the limbic system, literally means "smell brain."

Rhombencephalon. The hindmost posterior embryonic part of the brain, which divides into the metencephalon and myelencephalon.

Ribonucleic acid (RNA). A complex macromolecule composed of a sequence of nucleotide bases attached to a sugar-phosphate backbone. Messenger RNA (mRNA) delivers genetic information from a portion of a chromosome to a ribosome (ribosomal or rRNA), where the appropriate molecules of transfer RNA (tRNA) assemble the appropriate amino acids to produce the polypeptide coded for by the active portion of the chromosome.

Righting reflex. A reflex whereby an animal placed in an inverted posture returns to upright; survives low decerebration, hence a reflex.

Roentgenography. Photography using X rays.

Saccule. One of two vestibular receptors of the middle ear; stimulated when the head is oriented normally; maintains head and body in an upright position.

Saltatory conduction. Propagation of a nerve impulse on a myelinated axon; characterized by its leaping from one node of Ranvier to another.

Savant syndrome. A syndrome characterized by various degree of retardation along with some special, sometimes supranormal, skill.

Scanning electron microscope (SEM). Special kind of electron microscope that can produce three dimensional images of an object.

Schizophrenia. A type of psychosis characterized by disordered cognitive functioning and poor social adjustment (literally splitting of thought and emotive processes); probably due to brain malfunction.

Schwann cells. Glial cells that form myelin in the peripheral nervous system.

Scotoma. Small blind spot in the visual field caused by small lesions or epileptic focus or migraines of the occipital lobe.

Secondary projection area. An area of the cortex that receives projections from or sends projections to a primary projection area.

Sensation. The result of activity of receptors and their associated afferent pathways to the corresponding primary sensory neocortical areas.

Sensory aphasia. *See* Wernicke's aphasia.

Sensory neglect. A condition in which an individual does not respond to sensory stimulation.

Septum. A nucleus in the limbic system that when lesioned in rats produces sham rage and abolishes the theta EEG waveform.

Serial lesion effect. A term used to describe the observation that slowly acquired lesions, or lesions that occur in stages, tend to have less severe symptoms after equivalent size lesions that are acquired at one time.

Sexual selection. A process of evolution in which the processes involved in determining who mates with whom also determines the characteristics of the offspring that will be produced.

Simultaneous extinction. Second stage of recovery from contralateral neglect; characterized by response to stimuli on the neglected side as if there were a simultaneous stimulation on the contralateral side.

Single-photon emission computed tomography (SPECT). An imaging technique in which a subject is given a radioactively labeled compound such as glucose, which is metabolized by the brain; the radioactivity is later recorded by a special detector. Similar to PET, but less accurate, it has the advantage of not requiring a cyclotron to produce the isotopes.

Soma. Cell body.

Somatic muscles. Muscles of the body that are attached to the skeleton.

Somatosensory zone. Any region of the brain responsible for analyzing sensations of fine touch and pressure and possibly of pain and temperature.

Somnolence. Sleepiness; excessive drowsiness.

Sparing. The saving of some brain functions from disruption after the occurrence of a lesion early in life (usually before that function has developed).

Spatial summation. Tendency of two adjacent events to add; hence two adjacent postsynaptic potentials add or subtract.

Specifically reading retarded. Individuals who have adequate intelligence to read but cannot read.

Spinal cord. The part of the nervous system enclosed in the vertebral column.

Spinal reflex. Response obtained when only the spinal cord is functioning.

Splenium. Generally, a bandlike structure, but the term is used to refer to the posterior rounded end of the corpus callosum.

Spongioblasts. Immature cells that develop into glial cells.

Spreading depression. A condition in which a wave of depolarization spreads across the cortical surface, leading to a period in which the tissue is functionally blocked.

Sprouting. The phenomenon following partial damage whereby remaining portions of a neuron or other neurons sprout terminations to connect to the previously innervated area.

Stellate cell. Nerve cells that are characterized by having a star-shaped cell body. They serve largely as association cells whose processes remain within the region of the brain in which the cell body is.

Stereognosis. The recognition of objects through the sense of touch.

Stimulation. The act of applying a stimulus or an irritant to something; the occurrence of such a stimulus or an irritant.

Stimulus. An irritant or event that causes a change in action of some brain area.

Stimulus gradient. A gradient along which the salience of a cue increases or decreases, i.e., odors get stronger as the source is approached.

Storage granules. Vesicles in the terminal that are presumed to store neurotransmitters.

Stretch reflex. The contraction of a muscle to resist stretching; mediated through a muscle spindle, a special sensory receptor system in the muscle.

Stroke. The sudden appearance of neurological symptoms as a result of severe interruption of blood flow.

St. Vitus' dance. *See* Syndenham's chorea.

Subarachnoid space. The space between the arachnoid layer and the piameter of the meninges.

Substantia nigra. A nucleus area in the midbrain containing the cell bodies of axons containing dopamine. In freshly prepared human tissue the region appears black, hence the name (Latin, meaning black substance).

Sulcus. A small cleft produced by folding of the cortex.

Superior colliculus. Nucleus of the tectum in the midbrain that receives visual projections and is involved in whole-body reflexes to visual stimuli.

Supplementary motor cortex. A relatively small region of the cortex that lies outside the primary motor cortex but that when stimulated will also produce movements.

Surface dyslexia. An inability to read words on the basis of their pictographic or graphemic representations while retaining the ability to read using phonological, or sounding-out, procedures.

Sylvian fissure. *See* lateral fissure.

Synapse. The point of contact between two cells. Classically, this refers to the junction between an axonal terminal and another cell, but other types of contacts are also found.

Synaptic cleft. Space between the end foot of a neuron and the cell to which it connects.

Synaptic knob. Also called *bouton termineau, end foot, synapsis, synapse, terminal knob. See* synapse.

Synaptic vesicles. Small vesicles visible in electron-microscopic pictures of terminals; believed to contain neurotransmitter.

Syndenham's chorea. An acute childhood disorder characterized by involuntary movements that gradually become severe, including virtually all movements, including speech. Also known as *St. Vitus' dance.*

Synethesia. The ability to perceive a stimulus of one sense as a sensation of a different sense, as when sound produces a sensation of color.

Symptomatic seizures. Seizures that have specific symptoms that may aid in localizing the seizure origin.

Tachistoscope. A mechanical apparatus consisting or a projector, viewer, and screen by which visual stimuli can be presented to selective portions of the visual field.

Tactile. Pertaining to the sense of touch.

Tardive dyskinesia. Slow, abnormal limb or body part movements.

Tectopulvinar system. Portion of the visual system that functions to locate visual stimuli. Includes superior colliculus, posterior thalamus, and areas 20 and 21.

Tectum. The area of the midbrain above the cerebral aqueduct (the roof); consists of the superior and inferior colliculi, which mediate whole-body response to visual and auditory stimuli, respectively.

Tegmentum. The area of the midbrain below the cerebral aqueduct (the floor); contains sensory and motor tracts and a number of nuclei.

Telencephalon. Term for the endbrain; includes the cortex, basal ganglia, limbic system, and olfactory bulbs.

Temporal lobes. Lobes found laterally on the head, below the lateral sulci adjacent to the temporal bones.

Temporal summation. Tendency of two events related in time to add; hence two temporally related postsynaptic potentials add or subtract.

Terminal degeneration. Degeneration of the terminals of neurons. It can be detected by selective tissue staining.

Tertiary projection area. An area of the cortex that receives projections from or sends projections to a secondary projection area. *See also* association cortex.

Thalamus. A group of nuclei of the diencephalon.

Thermoregulation. The ability to regulate body temperature.

Theta rhythm. A brain rhythm with a frequency of 4 to 7 Hz.

Threshold. The point at which a stimulus produces a response.

Thrombosis. A plug or clot in a blood vessel, formed by the coagulation of blood.

Topographic maps. Maps of the neocortex showing various features, projections, cell distributions, and soon.

Topographical agnosia. An inability to recognize one's location in space, such as a failure to recognize one's own neighborhood.

Topographical amnesia. An inability to remember the location of things or places.

Topographical disorientation. Confusion regarding one's location in space.

Tourette's syndrome. Disease characterized by involuntary movements of body parts and involuntary words and sounds.

Tract. A large collection of axons coursing together within the central nervous system.

Transcortical aphasia. Aphasia in which people can repeat and understand words and name objects but cannot speak spontaneously, or can repeat words but cannot comprehend them.

Transient ischemia. A short-lived condition of inadequate supply of blood to a brain area.

Transneuronal degeneration. The degeneration of cells that synapse with or are synapsed onto by a damaged cell, for example, section of optic tracts results in the degeneration of lateral geniculate body cells.

Tumor. A mass of new tissue that persists and grows independently; a neoplasm; it surrounds tissue and has no physiological use.

Turner's syndrome. A genetic condition in which a female has only a single X chromosome. Women with Turner's syndrome have severe spatial deficits.

Uncinate fasciculus. A fiber tract connecting temporal and frontal cortex; a hooked or curved tract.

Unilateral visual neglect. Neglect of all sensory events of one or more modalities of stimulation when the stimulation is restricted to one half of the world as defined by the central axis of the body.

Unit activity. The electrical potential of a single cell.

Utricle. The largest of the subdivisions of the labyrinth. It is the major organ of the vestibular system, which provides information about the position of the head.

Ventral root. The tract of fibers leaving the spinal cord, hence motor; on the ventral portion of the spinal cord of animals or on the anterior portion of humans.

Ventricles. The cavities of the brain that contain cerebrospinal fluid.

Ventriculography. An X-ray technique whereby, the contours of the ventricles are highlighted using an opaque medium introduced into the ventricle through a cannula inserted through the skull.

Ventromedial system. One of the two major groups of tracts in the motor system. The ventromedial system is made up of the vestibulospinal tract, reticulospinal tract, and the tectospinal tract, which originate in the brainstem, and the ventral corticospinal tract, which originates in the neocortex.

Vestibular system. A sensory system with receptors in the middle ear that respond to body position and movement.

Visual agnosia. Inability to combine visual impressions into complete patterns — therefore an inability to recognize objects; inability to perceive objects and to draw or copy them. *See also* agnosia.

Visualization. Ability to form a mental image of an object.

Voluntary movement. Any movement that takes an animal from one place to another; can be elicited by lower-level sensory input or executed through lower and postural support and reflex systems. Also called *appetitive, instrumental, purposive,* and *operant* movement.

Wallerian degeneration. *See* anterograde degeneration.

Wernicke's aphasia. Inability to comprehend speech or to produce meaningful speech; follows lesions to posterior cortex.

Wernicke's area. The posterior portion of the superior temporal gyrus, roughly equivalent to area 22.

White matter. Those areas of the nervous system rich in axons covered with glial cells.

Wilson's disease. A genetic disease characterized by the failure to metabolize copper, which is concentrated in the brain.

Word salad. A term used to refer to fluent aphasia in which a person produces intelligible words that appear to be strung together randomly.

INDEX OF NAMES

INDEX OF TOPICS